The Concise Princeton Encyclopedia of **American Political History**

The Concise Princeton Encyclopedia of

ADVISORS

Richard R. John

Ira I. Katznelson

Jack N. Rakove

Julian E. Zelizer

American Political History

DISCARD

EDITOR

Michael Kazin
Georgetown University

ASSOCIATE EDITORS

Rebecca Edwards
Vassar College

Adam Rothman
Georgetown University

PRINCETON UNIVERSITY PRESS

Princeton and Oxford

Copyright © 2011 by Princeton University Press

Published by Princeton University Press, 41 William Street,
Princeton, New Jersey 08540

In the United Kingdom: Princeton University Press,
6 Oxford Street, Woodstock, Oxfordshire OX20 1TW
press.princeton.edu

Library of Congress Cataloging-in-Publication Data

The concise Princeton encyclopedia of American political
history / advisors Richard R. John . . . [et al.] ; editor
Michael Kazin.
        p. cm.
    Includes bibliographical references and index.
    ISBN 978-0-691-15207-3 (pbk. : alk. paper) 1. United
States—Politics and government—Encyclopedias. 2. Politi-
cal science—United States—History—Encyclopedias. I.
Kazin, Michael, 1948- II. Title.

 E183.C74 2011
 320.03—dc22   2011009777

British Library Cataloging-in-Publication Data is available

This book has been composed in Adobe Garamond
and Myriad
Printed on acid-free paper.

Printed in the United States of America
10 9 8 7 6 5 4 3 2 1

Contents

Preface

What is political history? The answer may seem obvious. In everyday language, "politics" in a democratic nation like the United States is the subject of who gets elected to office and what they do with the powers granted to them by voters, laws, and constitutions. It is an endless contest of speech making, lawmaking, fund-raising, and negotiating in which ambitious actors spend their lives struggling to come out on top.

This definition may seem like common sense, but it does not capture what most political historians actually do. Many authors who engage in the serious study of past politics try to understand the larger forces that propel changes in governments, laws, and campaigns. The most influential historians, in particular, have always framed the narrative of legislative give-and-take and winning and losing office within a context of grand historical themes and developments. In the 1890s, Frederick Jackson Turner argued that the frontier experience shaped American democracy. For him, regional identities and cultures drove political development. Early in the twentieth century, Charles and Mary Beard contended that the clash of economic interests was at the root of every turning point in U.S. history—from the drafting of the Constitution to the Civil War. At mid-century, Richard Hofstadter used the psychological concept of "status anxiety" to explain the fervor of both Populist and Progressive reformers. In recent decades, leading scholars have sought to illuminate evolving tensions within the body politic by focusing on intersecting differences of religion and cultural taste, race and ethnicity, gender and class.

The Concise Princeton Encyclopedia of American Political History also assumes an expansive definition of politics: the meaning and uses of power in the public sphere and the competition to gain that power. The word *politics* derives from the Greek word for "citizen," and the rights, powers, and obligations of citizens and their governments have been at the core of the subject since the days of Aristotle, Plato, and Herodotus.

Another tradition has been with us since the building of the Acropolis: history is a constant debate. In this spirit, our contributors offer interpretations of their topics, not merely a factual record or a summary of views held by others. Each article ends with a bibliography meant to guide the reader to some of the most significant works on that topic.

The study of politics in the United States has featured several interpretive approaches since the first serious histories of the subject were published in the middle of the nineteenth century. First, at a time when universities were just beginning to train historians, such self-taught, eloquent writers as George Bancroft and Henry Adams wrote multivolume narratives of presidents and diplomats. Their prose was often vivid, and their judgments had a stern, moralizing flavor.

By the early twentieth century, such grand personal works were being supplanted by a rigorously empirical approach. This was a style of history pioneered by disciples of the German academic scholar Leopold von Ranke, who declared that the past should be studied "as it really was." Rankean scholars wrote careful monographs which piled fact upon fact about such subjects as the decisions that led to independence and the making of new state constitutions. They believed a "scientific" approach could produce a political history with the opinions of the historian left out.

At the same time, however, a new group known as the "progressive" historians was garnering controversy and a large readership outside academia as well as among scholars. Such leading progressives as Turner, the Beards, and Vernon Parrington described a long-standing division between, on the one hand, the makers of elite, urban culture and big business and, on the other hand, small farmers and self-taught, self-made men from rural areas and the frontier. These historians were sympathetic toward the reform movements of their day—from the Populists in the 1890s to the New Dealers of the 1930s—which portrayed themselves as fighting for "the people."

By the 1940s, a reaction to the progressive scholars was gathering force. Such historians as David Potter, Daniel Boorstin, and the political scientist Louis Hartz joined Hofstadter in arguing that politics in the United States had long been characterized more by a consensus of values than by a conflict over economic interests. Such "counterprogressive" scholars argued that most Americans had always embraced liberal capitalism and rejected any politicians and movements that aimed to do more than tinker with the existing system.

This sober, often ironic sensibility was challenged head-on in the late 1960s by historians—most of them young—who were inspired by contemporary movements for African American freedom, feminism, and against the war in Vietnam. These "New Left" scholars revived the progressive emphasis on sharp, ongoing conflict but located its wellsprings among workers, racial and ethnic minorities, and women—groups that had previously received little attention from political historians. Influential scholars like Eric Foner, Gerda Lerner, Nathan Huggins, Eugene Genovese, and Alan Brinkley embedded their narratives of power in a rich context of class relations, racial identities, and cultural assumptions. Arguing that ordinary people were as much agents of change as were national politicians and government officials helped to democratize understanding of the past, even as it deemphasized such durable institutions as the courts, Congress, and the major political parties.

More recently, an increasing number of scholars have turned away from focusing on American politics in isolation from similar developments occurring elsewhere in the world. Their "transnational" perspective challenges patriotic vanities by chipping away at the notion that the United States ever stood apart from ideas and social movements that shook other lands and peoples. Thomas Bender interprets the North's victory in the Civil War as producing a newly potent national state much like those emerging at the same time in Japan, Italy, Argentina, and Germany. Similarly, Daniel Rodgers describes how American reformers in the early twentieth century tried to apply policy ideas they had picked up on visits with fellow progressives and moderate socialists in Europe.

Whatever the individual approach, nearly every contemporary historian implicitly applies a broad definition of politics to her or his work. Historians are interested not only in such traditional topics as presidents, bureaucratic institutions, and constitutions but also in popular ideology and consciousness, social movements, war, education, crime, sexuality, and the reciprocal influence of mass culture on political thinking and behavior. At the same time, scholars in fields outside of history—especially in political science and law—have demonstrated a growing interest in the American past. Meanwhile, best-seller lists routinely include one or more skillful narratives about past presidents, diplomacy, and the politics of war. This is an exciting time to be a political historian in the United States.

The Concise Princeton Encyclopedia of American Political History is an abridged version of *The Princeton Encyclopedia of American Political History*, a two-volume work published in 2010. The *Concise* edition collects 150 articles (drawn from 187 in the original encyclopedia) in a single, portable volume. Although shorter and more streamlined than the parent work, the *Concise* preserves the editors' broad definition of American political history, with essays on traditional topics as well as those that exemplify the creative changes that mark the discipline.

Periods

Which issues, parties, institutions, events, and leaders were dominant in different spans of time? In chronological order, these essays include the era of a new republic (1789–1827), the Jacksonian era (1828–45), sectional conflict and secession (1845–65), Reconstruction (1865–77), the Gilded Age (1870s–90s), progressivism and the Progressive Era (1890s–1920), the conservative interregnum (1920–32), the New Deal Era (1933–52), the era of consensus (1952–64), the era of confrontation and decline (1964–80), and the conservative ascendancy (1980–2004). The essays provide an overview of pivotal elections, political developments, policies, and policy makers, and the rise and fall of major party coalitions.

Institutions

This category includes the presidency, the House of Representatives, the Senate, and the Supreme Court; as well as the cabinet departments; the Electoral College; local, state, and territorial governments; and civil service. But it also includes such nongovernmental institutions as party nominating conventions, think tanks, interest groups, and public opinion polls, as well as such topics as citizenship, whose legal and political history is critical to understanding the politics of ethnicity, immigration, and gender.

Movements

Mass movements have had a major impact on political change in the United States. This category includes both long-lived movements that still exist—such as labor and pacifism—and ones of great historical significance that now exist only in memory, such as abolitionism and Prohibition.

Major Political Parties

This category includes lengthy articles on the Democrats and Republicans in different periods as well as shorter essays about defunct major parties, such as the Federalists and Whigs. The essays discuss the impact of key elections, leaders, events, and social changes on the fortunes and evolution of these organizations whose competition has done much to structure the political order from the 1850s to the present.

Ideas and Philosophies

This category includes such hotly contested and undeniably significant concepts as conservatism, liberalism, republicanism, radicalism, Americanism, feminism, and democracy. It also includes articles about how religion has influenced politics and vice versa.

War and Foreign Policy

The rest of the world has been a major influence on the development of the American polity and on a variety of related subjects—from the growth of the military, to the Fourteenth Amendment, to the rise of the African American freedom movement in the 1940s and 1950s. The essays about the nation's wars discuss the effect of military operations on domestic debate and policy as well as the role of military leaders and battles in shaping electoral outcomes.

Founding Documents

This category includes the Articles of Confederation as well as the Declaration of Independence, the Constitution, and the initial amendments to it, the Bill of Rights. Articles in this category discuss the genesis of these documents as well as debates about their meaning and application over the next two centuries and beyond.

Regions

In wide-ranging essays, authors focus on the major issues, dominant institutions, and pivotal actors in the politics of New England, the Middle Atlantic, the South since the end of Reconstruction, the Midwest, the Great Plains, the Rocky Mountains, the Pacific Coast, and Alaska and Hawai'i. These contributions examine how the expansionist, regionally diverse character of U.S. history has shaped its political evolution.

Issues

This category includes subjects and actors whose significance has been perennial in U.S. history, as in the political history of every modern nation: the economy (banking policy, agrarian politics, consumers, taxation, transportation), cities and suburbs, class and crime. These are the "issues" that—since the beginning of the republic—politicians, movements, and voters have debated, and that have spurred major pieces of legislation and court rulings.

The best political histories teach readers a good deal that is new to them but do so in clear, direct, evocative prose. This work is intended to help readers at all levels of knowledge to understand patterns and connections in U.S. history, from its colonial origins to the present day, and to serve as a first step to further research. All our contributors combine expertise with an ability to write for a broad audience.

We hope you find this concise encyclopedia both instructive and a pleasure to read.

Recommended Reading

For excellent surveys of historical scholarship about U.S. politics, see Richard J. Jensen, "Historiography of American Political History," in *Encyclopedia of American Political History*, edited by Jack P. Greene (1984), 1–25; Meg Jacobs and Julian E. Zelizer, "The Democratic Experiment: New Directions in American Political History," in *The Democratic Experiment: New Directions in American Political History*, edited by Meg Jacobs, William J. Novak, and Julian E. Zelizer (2003), 1–19; Sean Wilentz, "American Political Histories," *OAH Magazine of History* (April 2007), 23–27. For excellent essays on significant individuals, see *American National Biography* (2002). The latter is also available online (with a subscription). A bracing history of the historical profession in the United States is Peter Novick's *That Noble Dream* (1989).

Michael Kazin
Editor in Chief

Alphabetical List of Entries

Alphabetical List of Entries

Topical List of Entries

Topical List of Entries

Contributors

Sean Adams, *History Department, University of Florida*
energy and politics

Patrick Allitt, *Department of History, Emory University*
religion and politics since 1945

John Ashworth, *School of American and Canadian Studies, University of Nottingham*
Democratic Party, 1828–60

Dean Baker, *Center for Economic Policy and Research, Washington, D.C.*
economy and politics since 1970

Paula Baker, *Department of History, Ohio State University*
campaign law and finance to 1900; campaign law and finance since 1900

James M. Banner Jr., *National History Center*
Federalist Party

Lois Banner, *Department of History, University of Southern California*
feminism

Kyle Barbieri, *Hillsborough Community College and Polk Community College, Florida*
Republican Party, 1968–2008 (coauthor)

David H. Bennett, *Department of History, Maxwell School, Syracuse University*
nativism

Edward D. Berkowitz, *Elliott School of International Affairs, George Washington University*
Social Security

Stuart M. Blumin, *Department of History, Cornell University*
antiparty sentiment

Matthew Bowman, *Department of History, Georgetown University*
Electoral College; party nominating conventions

Amy Bridges, *Department of Political Science, University of California–San Diego*
cities and politics

Stephen Brooks, *Department of Political Science, University of Windsor*
foreign observers of U.S. politics

W. Elliot Brownlee, *Department of History, University of California–Santa Barbara*
taxation since 1913

Frank M. Bryan, *Department of Political Science, University of Vermont*
New England

Richard Buel Jr., *Department of History (emeritus), Wesleyan University*
War of 1812

Paul Buhle, *Departments of History and American Civilization, Brown University*
anarchism

Charles W. Calhoun, *Department of History, East Carolina University*
Republican Party to 1896

Christopher Capozzola, *Department of History, Massachusetts Institute of Technology*
World War I

Daniel Carpenter, *Department of Government, Harvard University*
regulation

Robert W. Cherny, *Department of History, San Francisco State University*
the Great Plains; the Pacific Coast

Elisabeth S. Clemens, *Department of Sociology, University of Chicago*
interest groups

Edward Countryman, *Department of History, Southern Methodist University*
colonial legacy

Matthew J. Countryman, *Department of History, University of Michigan*
race and politics since 1933

Joe Creech, *Lilly Fellows Program and Christ College, Honors College of Valparaiso University*
religion and politics, 1865–1945

Joseph Crespino, *Department of History, Emory University*
South since 1877, the

Donald T. Critchlow, *Department of History, Saint Louis University*
conservatism (coauthor)

Elliott Currie, *Department of Criminology, Law, and Society, University of California–Irvine*
crime

John Patrick Diggins, *deceased, Graduate Center, City University of New York*
liberal consensus and American exceptionalism

John Dinan, *Department of Political Science, Wake Forest University*
state constitutions

Ellen Carol DuBois, *Department of History, University of California–Los Angeles*
woman suffrage

Max M. Edling, *Department of History, Uppsala University*
Constitution, federal

Rebecca Edwards, *Department of History, Vassar College*
gender and sexuality

Robin L. Einhorn, *Department of History, University of California–Berkeley*
taxation to 1913

Richard E. Ellis, *Department of History, University at Buffalo, State University of New York*
Democratic Party, 1800–28

Nicole Etcheson, *Department of History, Ball State University*
Midwest, the

Michael W. Flamm, *Department of History, Ohio Wesleyan University*
conservative ascendancy, 1980–2008

Contributors

Maureen A. Flanagan, *Department of History, Michigan State University*
progressivism and the Progressive Era, 1890s–1920

Anne L. Foster, *Department of History, Indiana State University*
Spanish-American War and Filipino Insurrection

Steve Fraser, *New York University*
business and politics

Michael A. Genovese, *Department of Political Science, Loyola Marymount University*
presidency to 1860

Michael Gerhardt, *School of Law, University of North Carolina–Chapel Hill*
impeachment

Steven M. Gillon, *Department of History, University of Oklahoma*
Democratic Party, 1932–68

Marcia Tremmel Goldstein, *Department of History, University of Colorado*
Rocky Mountain region (coauthor)

Lewis L. Gould, *Department of History (emeritus), University of Texas–Austin*
Gilded Age, 1870s–90s; Republican Party; Republican Party, 1896–1932

Amy S. Greenberg, *Department of History, Pennsylvania State University*
Mexican-American War

Richard F. Hamm, *Department of History, University at Albany, State University of New York*
Prohibition and temperance

Stanley Harrold, *Department of Social Sciences, South Carolina State University*
abolitionism

D. G. Hart, *Intercollegiate Studies Institute*
religion and politics to 1865

David C. Hendrickson, *Department of Political Science, Colorado College*
Articles of Confederation

Williamjames Hull Hoffer, *Department of History, Seton Hall University*
Supreme Court

Susan Hoffmann, *Department of Political Science, University of Western Michigan*
banking policy

David A. Horowitz, *Department of History, Portland State University*
anti-statism

Jane Armstrong Hudiburg, *Annapolis, Maryland*
Senate

Andrew Hunt, *Department of History, University of Waterloo*
pacifism

Sarah E. Igo, *Department of History, University of Pennsylvania*
public opinion polls

Maurice Isserman, *Department of History, Hamilton College*
communism; era of confrontation and decline, 1964–80; New Deal Era, 1932–52

Meg Jacobs, *Department of History, Massachusetts Institute of Technology*
consumers and politics

Dennis W. Johnson, *Graduate School of Political Management, George Washington University*
campaign consultants

Robert D. Johnston, *Department of History, University of Illinois–Chicago*
class and politics since 1877

Stephen Kantrowitz, *Department of History, University of Wisconsin–Madison*
Reconstruction Era, 1865–77

Michael B. Katz, *Department of History, University of Pennsylvania*
welfare

Michael Kazin, *Department of History, Georgetown University*
Americanism; Democratic Party, 1800–2008; populism

Alexander Keyssar, *John F. Kennedy School of Government, Harvard University*
voting

Michael J. Klarman, *Harvard Law School*
segregation and Jim Crow

Jennifer Klein, *Department of History, Yale University*
economy and politics, 1945–70

James T. Kloppenberg, *Department of History, Harvard University*
liberalism

Gary J. Kornblith, *Department of History, Oberlin College*
class and politics to 1877

J. Morgan Kousser, *Division of the Humanities and Social Sciences, California Institute of Technology*
race and politics, 1860–1933

Alan M. Kraut, *Department of History, American University*
health and illness

David E. Kyvig, *Department of History, Northern Illinois University*
amendment process

Matthew D. Lassiter, *Department of History, University of Michigan*
suburbs and politics

Steven F. Lawson, *Department of History, Rutgers University*
civil rights

Allan J. Lichtman, *Department of History, American University*
elections and electoral eras; presidency, 1860–1932; presidency, 1932–2008

Patricia Nelson Limerick, *Center of the American West, University of Colorado*
Rocky Mountain region (coauthor)

James Livingston, *Department of History, Rutgers University*
economy and politics, 1860–1920

John Majewski, *Department of History, University of California–Santa Barbara*
economy and politics to 1860

Chandra Manning, *Department of History, Georgetown University*
    Civil War and Reconstruction; sectional conflict and secession, 1845–65

Joseph A. McCartin, *Department of History, Georgetown University*
    labor movement and politics

Stuart McConnell, *History, Pitzer College*
    veterans

Lisa McGirr, *Department of History, Harvard University*
    conservative interregnum, 1920–32

Alan McPherson, *School of International and Area Studies, University of Oklahoma*
    foreign policy and domestic politics, 1865–1933

Yanek Mieczkowski, *Division of Social Sciences, Dowling College*
    Republican Party, 1932–68

James A. Morone, *Department of Political Science, Brown University*
    political culture

Kevin P. Murphy, *Department of History, University of Minnesota*
    homosexuality

James Oakes, *Graduate Center, City University of New York*
    race and politics to 1860

Peter S. Onuf, *Department of History, University of Virginia*
    federalism

Jeffrey L. Pasley, *Department of History, University of Missouri*
    era of a new republic, 1789–1827

William Pencak, *Department of History and Religious Studies, Pennsylvania State University*
    Middle Atlantic, the

Michael Perman, *Department of History, University of Illinois–Chicago*
    Democratic Party, 1860–96

Christopher Phelps, *School of American and Canadian Studies, University of Nottingham*
    radicalism

Sarah T. Phillips, *Department of History, Columbia University*
    economy and politics, 1920–45

Kim Phillips-Fein, *Gallatin School, New York University*
    era of consensus, 1952–64

Dan Plesch, *Center for International Studies and Diplomacy, University of London*
    United Nations

Charles L. Ponce de Leon, *Department of History, California State University–Long Beach*
    press and politics

Kevin Powers, *Department of History, Georgetown University*
    cabinet departments

Richard Gid Powers, *College of Staten Island, and Graduate Center, City University of New York*
    anticommunism

Jack N. Rakove, *Department of History, Stanford University*
    Bill of Rights

Eric Rauchway, *Department of History, University of California–Davis*
    globalization

William J. Reese, *Departments of Educational Policy Studies and History, University of Wisconsin–Madison*
    education and politics

Brian Holden Reid, *Department of War Studies, King's College, London*
    armed forces, politics in the

Joanne Reitano, *Social Science Department, La Guardia Community College, City University of New York*
    tariffs and politics

Leo P. Ribuffo, *Elliott School of International Affairs, George Washington University*
    Democratic Party, 1968–2008

Andrew Rich, *Franklin and Eleanor Roosevelt Institute*
    think tanks

Adam Rome, *Department of History, Pennsylvania State University*
    environmental issues and politics

Doug Rossinow, *History Department, Metropolitan State University*
    New Left

Adam Rothman, *Department of History, Georgetown University*
    slavery

Andrew J. Rotter, *Department of History, Colgate University*
    Vietnam and Indochina wars

Mark Rozell, *School of Public Policy, George Mason University*
    Republican Party, 1968–2008 (coauthor)

Anne Sarah Rubin, *History Department, University of Maryland–Baltimore County*
    Confederacy

Leonard J. Sadosky, *Department of History, Iowa State University*
    Declaration of Independence; foreign policy and domestic politics to 1865

Nick Salvatore, *Industrial and Labor Relations School and Program in American Studies, Cornell University*
    socialism

Elizabeth Sanders, *Department of Government, Cornell University*
    agrarian politics

David Sarasohn, *The Oregonian*
    Democratic Party, 1896–1932

Gregory Schneider, *Department of Social Sciences, Emporia State University*
    conservatism (coauthor)

Robert Schulzinger, *Department of History, University of Colorado–Boulder*
    Korean War and cold war

Carlos A. Schwantes, *Department of History, University of Missouri–St. Louis*
    transportation and politics

William G. Shade, *Department of History (emeritus), Lehigh University*
    Whig Party

Contributors

Robert E. Shalhope, *Department of History, University of Oklahoma*
    republicanism

Michael Sherry, *Department of History, Northwestern University*
    war and politics

John Shy, *Department of History, University of Michigan*
    war for independence

Stephen Skowronek, *Department of Political Science, Yale University*
    presidency, the

Bartholomew H. Sparrow, *Department of Government, University of Texas–Austin*
    territorial government

Jeremi Suri, *Department of History, University of Wisconsin–Madison*
    transnational influences on American politics

Jon C. Teaford, *Department of History, Purdue University*
    local government; state government

Daniel J. Tichenor, *Department of Political Science, University of Oregon*
    immigration policy

Anand Toprani, *Department of History, Georgetown University*
    Iraq wars of 1991 and 2003

Gil Troy, *Department of History, McGill University*
    campaigning

Cyrus Veeser, *Department of History, Bentley College*
    Caribbean, Central America, and Mexico, interventions in, 1903–34

Penny M. Von Eschen, *Department of History, University of Michigan*
    foreign policy and domestic politics since 1933

Samuel Walker, *School of Criminology and Criminal Justice, University of Nebraska–Omaha*
    civil liberties

Harry L. Watson, *Department of History and Center for the Study of the American South, University of North Carolina–Chapel Hill*
    Jacksonian era, 1828–45

Robert Westbrook, *Department of History, University of Rochester*
    democracy

Richard D. White Jr., *Public Administration Institute, Louisiana State University*
    civil service

John S. Whitehead, *Department of History, University of Alaska, Fairbanks*
    Alaska and Hawai'i

Allan M. Winkler, *Department of History, Miami University*
    World War II

Julian E. Zelizer, *Department of History, Princeton University*
    House of Representatives

Aristide R. Zolberg, *Department of Political Science, New School for Social Research*
    citizenship

abolitionism

A major reform movement during the eighteenth and nineteenth centuries, abolitionism sought to end slavery and free millions of black people held as slaves. Also known as the antislavery movement, abolitionism in the United States was part of an international effort against slavery and the slave trade in the Atlantic World. Its historical roots lay in black resistance to slavery, changing interpretations of Christian morality, eighteenth-century ideas concerning universal human rights, and economic change. Some of slavery's opponents advocated gradual abolition and others immediate abolition. By the 1830s the term *abolitionism* applied only to the latter.

Early Development

Race-based slavery, whereby people of European descent relied on the forced labor of Africans and their descendants, began on a large scale during the sixteenth century as a result of European colonization in the Americas. By the middle of the seventeenth century, slavery had reached the portion of Great Britain's North American colonies that later became the United States. In the American form of slavery, the enslaved lost customary rights, served for life, and passed their unfree condition on to their children. From the start, those subjected to slavery sought freedom through self-purchase, court action, escape, or, more rarely, rebellion. There were major slave revolts in New York City in 1712 and Stono, South Carolina, in 1739.

The first white abolitionists in America were members of the Society of Friends (Quakers), who—like their coreligionists in Britain—held slavery to be sinful and physically dangerous to slave and master alike. During the 1740s and 1750s, Quaker abolitionists John Woolman of New Jersey and Anthony Benezet of Pennsylvania urged other American members of the society to end their involvement in the slave trade and gradually free their slaves. With the American Revolution (1775–83), abolitionism spread beyond African Americans and Quakers. Natural rights doctrines rooted in the European Enlightenment and endorsed by the Declaration of Independence, black service in Patriot armies, black petitions for emancipation, evangelical Christianity, and the activities of the earliest white abolition societies encouraged the American North to lead the world in political abolitionism. Starting with Vermont in 1777 and Massachusetts in 1783, all the states north of Delaware had by 1804 either ended slavery within their jurisdiction or provided for its gradual abolition. Meanwhile, Congress in 1787 included a clause in the Northwest Ordinance banning slavery in the Northwest Territory. During the 1780s, states in the Upper South eased restrictions on masters who wished to free individual slaves, and small, Quaker-dominated, gradual abolition societies spread into Delaware, Maryland, and Virginia.

Revolutionary-era abolitionism peaked during the 1780s. Thereafter, several developments stopped and then reversed the southward advance of antislavery sentiment. The invention of the cotton gin in 1793 and resulting expansion of cotton cultivation into the Old Southwest reinvigorated slavery. The brutal Haitian slave revolt that began in 1791 and culminated in the creation of an independent black republic in 1804 led white Southerners—who feared they could not control free African Americans—to believe that slavery had to be strengthened rather than abolished. An aborted revolt conspiracy led by the slave Gabriel near Richmond, Virginia, in 1800 bolstered this belief. As a direct result of increased white defensiveness, antislavery societies in the Upper South disbanded or declined. Meanwhile, in the North, a new scientific racism encouraged white residents to interpret social status in racial terms, restrict black access to schools, churches, and jobs, and regard enslavement as suitable for black Southerners.

White gradual abolitionists came to accept a contention that emancipation must be linked with expatriation of former slaves to avoid the formation of a dangerous and uncontrollable free black class. The American Colonization Society (ACS), organized by prominent slaveholders in 1816, claimed its objective was to encourage gradual abolition by sending *free* African Americans to Africa. It became the leading American antislavery organization of the 1820s and established Liberia as a black colony in West Africa. For a time black leaders, facing increasing oppression in the United States, agreed with this strategy. Best represented by black sea captain Paul Cuffe, they cooperated with the ACS during the 1810s, hoping that a homeland beyond America's borders would undermine slavery there and throughout the Atlantic World. Yet, by the 1820s, most free African Americans believed the ACS's real goal was to strengthen slavery by removing its most dedicated opponents—themselves.

Immediate Abolitionism

Three factors led to the emergence, during the late 1820s and early 1830s, of a more radical form of abolitionism dedicated to immediate emancipation and equal rights for African Americans in the United States. First, black abolitionists convinced a small minority of white Northerners that the ACS was a proslavery fraud. Second, signs of black unrest inspired urgency among white abolitionists who wished to avoid a race war in the South. In 1822 a free black man named Denmark Vesey organized a major slave conspiracy in Charleston, South Carolina. Seven years later in Boston, black abolitionist David Walker published his revolutionary *Appeal to the Colored Citizens of the World*. Slave preacher Nat Turner in 1831 led a slave revolt in Southampton County, Virginia, which left nearly 60 white residents dead. Third, the convergence of northern economic modernization with a massive religious revival known as the Second Great Awakening encouraged increasing numbers of white people to regard slavery as a barbaric, outmoded, and sinful practice. They believed it had to be ended if the country were to prosper and avoid God's wrath.

All these factors influenced the extraordinary career of William Lloyd Garrison, a white New Englander who began publishing his weekly newspaper, *The Liberator*, in Boston in 1831. Late in 1833 Garrison brought together in Philadelphia a diverse group—including a few black men and a few white women—to form the American Anti-Slavery Society (AASS). Rejecting all violent means, the AASS pledged to rely on "moral suasion" to achieve immediate, uncompensated emancipation and equal rights for African Americans in the United States. White men dominated the organization's leadership, but thousands of black men and thousands of women of both races lent active support. A few African Americans, including former slaves Frederick Douglass, Henry Highland Garnet, and Sojourner Truth, emerged as leaders in this biracial abolitionist movement. As they became antislavery activists, such white women as Susan B. Anthony and Elizabeth Cady Stanton grew conscious of their own inequality and initiated the women's rights movement.

Although members of the AASS comprised a tiny, despised minority, the organization spread rapidly across the North. In 1835 and 1836 its members sent thousands of antislavery petitions to Congress and stacks of abolitionist propaganda into the South. Their efforts, combined with Turner's revolt and the 1833 initiation of gradual abolition in the British West Indies, produced another fierce proslavery reaction. Abolitionists could not safely venture into the South. In the North, mobs beat abolitionist speakers and destroyed abolitionist meeting places, schools, and printing presses. They also attacked black communities.

A More Aggressive Abolitionism

Antiabolitionism and the failure of peaceful agitation to weaken slavery split the immediatist movement in 1840. Garrison and his associates, centered in New England, became social perfectionists, feminists, and anarchists. They denounced violence, unrighteous government, and organized religion. They refused to vote and embraced dissolution of the Union as the only way to save the North from

the sin of slavery and force the South to abolish it. Known as Garrisonians, they retained control of the AASS and, until the Civil War, concentrated on agitation in the North.

The great majority of abolitionists (black and white) insisted, however, that church and government action could end slavery. They became more willing to use violent means, rejected radical assertions of women's rights, and formed aggressive organizations. The American and Foreign Anti-Slavery Society (1840–55), led by New York City businessman Lewis Tappan, concentrated on converting churches to immediatism and continued to send antislavery propaganda into the South. The Liberty Party (1840–48) employed a variety of political strategies. The more radical Liberty abolitionists, centered in upstate New York and led by Gerrit Smith, maintained that slavery was always illegal, that immediatists had an obligation to go south to help slaves escape, and that Congress could abolish slavery in the southern states. The more conservative—and by far more numerous—Liberty faction depended on two Cincinnati residents, Gamaliel Bailey and Salmon P. Chase, for intellectual and political leadership. It accepted the legality of slavery in the southern states, rejected abolitionist aid to help slaves escape in the South and sought to build a mass political party on a platform calling not for abolition but removing U.S. government support for slavery.

Meanwhile, black abolitionists led in forming local vigilance associations designed to protect fugitive slaves, and most of them supported the AFASS and the Liberty Party. In 1846 they joined church-oriented white abolitionists in the American Missionary Association, an outgrowth of the AFASS that sent antislavery missionaries into the South. Douglass, who in 1847 began publishing the *North Star* in Rochester, New York, remained loyal to Garrison until 1851, when he joined the radical wing of the Liberty Party.

In 1848 members of the Liberty Party's conservative wing helped organize the Free Soil Party, dedicated to preventing the spread of slavery into American territories. By then they had essentially ceased to be immediatists. In 1854, when Congress opened Kansas Territory to slavery, they worked with antislavery Whigs and Democrats to form the Republican Party, which nominated its first presidential candidate in 1856. The Republican Party formally aimed only at ending slavery within the national domain. Many of its leaders claimed to represent the interests of white Northerners against the domination of slaveholders. But members of the party's "Old Liberty Guard" and such former Free Soilers as Charles Sumner of Massachusetts and Joshua R. Giddings of Ohio held Republicans to a higher standard. As Radical Republicans, they pressed for abolition and equal rights for African Americans.

After 1848 the more radical members of the Liberty Party—known as radical political abolitionists—maintained their tiny organization. They excelled in Underground Railroad efforts and resistance in the North to the Fugitive Slave Law of 1850. More than any other abolitionist faction, the radical political abolitionists supported John Brown's raid at Harpers Ferry in 1859. Brown and his biracial band had hoped to spark a slave revolt but were easily captured by Virginia militia and U.S. troops. Brown's actions, nevertheless, angered and frightened white Southerners; after his capture and prior to his execution that December, his elegant appeals for racial justice aroused sympathy among many Northerners.

Abolitionism during the
Civil War and Reconstruction

Brown's raid and the victory of Republican candidate Abraham Lincoln in the presidential election of 1860 precipitated the secession movement among white Southerners, which led to the Civil War in 1861. As the war began, Lincoln, who advocated the "ultimate extinction" of human bondage, believed former slaves should be colonized outside the United States and promised not to interfere with slavery in the South. He feared that to go further would alienate southern Unionists and weaken northern support for the war. Abolitionists, nevertheless, almost universally supported the war because they believed it would end slavery. Garrison and his associates dropped their opposition to forceful means, and church-oriented and radical political abolitionists rejoined the AASS. As the organization's influence grew, Garrison's friend Wendell Phillips emerged as the North's most popular orator. Phillips, Frederick Douglass, Sojourner Truth, and other prominent abolitionists joined Radical Republicans in lobbying Lincoln in favor of making emancipation and racial justice Union war aims. Abolitionists—especially black abolitionists—led in urging the president to enlist black troops.

When, in January 1863, Lincoln issued the Emancipation Proclamation, declaring slaves in areas under Confederate control to be free, abolitionists worried that—by resting emancipation on military necessity rather than racial justice—he had laid an unsound basis for black freedom. But they recognized the proclamation's significance, particularly its endorsement of enlisting black troops. Young white abolitionist men became officers in the otherwise segregated black regiments. Abolitionists advocated voting rights, education, and landownership for African Americans as compensation for generations of unrequited labor. These, they maintained, were essential to black economic and political advancement. In this regard abolitionists were similar to Radical Republicans, but they were much more insistent on involving African Americans in rebuilding the Union. They reacted negatively to Lincoln's December 1863 Reconstruction plan that would leave former masters in control of the status of their former slaves. As a result, in 1864 a few abolitionists joined a small group of Radical Republicans in opposing Lincoln's renomination for the presidency. However, Garrison, Douglass, and most leaders of the AASS believed they could influence Lincoln and continued to support him.

During the summer of 1861, abolitionist organizations had begun sending missionaries and teachers into war zones to minister to the physical, spiritual, and educational needs of the former slaves. Women predominated, in part because younger abolitionist men had enrolled in Union armies. The most ambitious effort occurred in the South Carolina Sea Islands centered on Port Royal, which Union forces captured in 1861. There, and at locations in Virginia, Kentucky, and Louisiana, abolitionists attempted to transform an oppressed people into independent proprietors and wage laborers. Their efforts encouraged the formation of black churches, schools, and other institutions but had serious shortcomings. Northerners did not understand southern black culture, tended toward unworkable bureaucratic policies, and put too much faith in wage labor as a solution to entrenched conditions. When the former slaves did not progress under these conditions, most abolitionists blamed the victims.

Nevertheless, with the end of the Civil War in May 1865 and the ratification that December of the Thirteenth Amendment, making slavery illegal throughout the United States, Garrison declared that abolitionism had succeeded. He ceased publication of the *Liberator* and urged the AASS to disband. He believed the Republican Party could henceforth protect black rights and interests. A majority of immediatists, including Douglass, Phillips, and Smith, were not so sure and kept the AASS in existence until 1870. Black abolitionists became especially active in lobbying on behalf of the rights of the former slaves and against the regressive policies of Andrew Johnson, Lincoln's successor as president. In 1866 and 1867 most abolitionists opposed ratification of the Fourteenth Amendment, contending that it did not insufficiently protect the right of black men to vote. Thereafter, they supported the stronger guarantees the Fifteenth Amendment provided for adult black male suffrage, although a minority of feminist abolitionists—led by Stanton—objected that enfranchisement of white women should take precedence.

When the Fifteenth Amendment gained ratification in 1870, the AASS declared that abolitionism had achieved its ultimate objective and disbanded. The organization was too optimistic. During the 1870s and 1880s, southern states—having rejoined the Union—curtailed black rights and the white North acquiesced. The abolitionists bear some responsibility for this tragic outcome. Nevertheless, they played a crucial role in ending slavery, in creating black institutions in the postwar South, and in placing protections for minority rights in the Constitution.

See also slavery.

FURTHER READING. James D. Essig, *The Bonds of Wickedness: American Evangelicals against Slavery 1770–1808*, 1982; Lawrence J. Friedman, *Gregarious Saints: Self and Community in American Abolitionism, 1830–1870*, 1982; Stanley Harrold, *American Abolitionists*, 2001; Idem, *The Rise of Aggressive Abolitionism: Addresses to the Slaves*, 2004; James Oliver Horton and Lois E. Horton, *In Hope of Liberty: Culture, Community, and Protest among Northern Free Blacks 1700–1860*, 1997; Julie Roy Jeffrey, *The Great Silent Army of Abolitionism: Ordinary Women in the Antislavery Movement*, 1998; Matthew Mason, *Slavery and Politics in the Early American Republic*, 2006; James M. McPherson, *The Struggle for Equality: Abolitionists and the Negro in the Civil War and Reconstruction*, 1964, reprint, 1992; Richard H. Sewell, *Ballots for Freedom: Antislavery Politics in the United States 1837–1860*, 1976; James Brewer Stewart, *Holy Warriors: The Abolitionists and American Slavery*, 2nd ed., 1997.

STANLEY HARROLD

agrarian politics

Agrarian politics describes the strategies, tactics, and values of the farmer-based political movements that played a prominent reform role in American political history. Its purest manifestation came in the Populist movement of the 1880s and 1890s, but its language, goals, and methods persisted, in a more subdued way, in the New Deal Era and beyond.

Agrarian politics played an important role in the evolution of American democracy and the construction of public institutions to regulate business without diminishing its productive energies. Indeed, the regulatory goal of agrarian politics after the Civil War provided the confidence that consumers, service users, and investors needed to buy, sell, and ship in a market economy. Agrarian politics—egalitarian, rights-based, inclusive, electoral, and targeted at the legislature where the most numerous classes presumably have their best shot—produced important structural reforms of national institutions, at least those not won by war: the Bill of Rights, direct election of senators, antimonopoly laws, an income tax, regulation of big business (starting with railroads), a monetary system controlled by public officials and not based on gold, the right of workers to organize and bargain collectively (and of agricultural cooperatives to similarly operate without being charged as "conspiracies in restraint of trade" under the Sherman Act), and the lowering of tariffs (the most prevalent and burdensome taxes) on goods consumed and used by ordinary people, to name just a few.

The term *agrarian* is virtually synonymous with *republican*, denoting a mode of politics and political thought nurtured by British and French Enlightenment philosophy that flowered in eighteenth-century North America. It was no doubt encouraged by the immigration of dissenters and the mode of settlement in what became (in 1789) the United States—a nation of independent landowners who belonged to diverse religious communities, themselves permeated by democratic demand, in contrast to the hierarchical denominations prevalent in the Old World.

Agrarianism's central tenets were galvanized by the struggle for independence from Great Britain. Its foremost philosopher was Thomas Jefferson, the apostle of sturdy yeoman farmer democracy (or, more accurately, *self-government*), whose creed came together in the cauldron of revolution and who provided the revolutionary language of that struggle. Agrarianism's principal antagonist was Alexander Hamilton, the foremost intellectual advocate of economic industrialism, commercialism, and political elitism.

In Jefferson's philosophy, the hand of government should be as light as possible, keeping opportunities open without favoritism, exploitation, or needless constraints on human affairs; and that hand's guidance should be in the legislature, the popular branch of the people's elected representatives. If its public officials became unresponsive to the sufferings of their constituents, the spectacle of a passionate people rising up in arms against its government (as in Shays's Rebellion in 1787) was not for Jefferson the nightmare it was for Hamilton.

Popular mobilization *against* bad, and *for* better, government, with wide participation by citizens and guaranteed commitment not to infringe on the personal rights on which good government depended—these were the tenets of Jeffersonian republicanism that shaped the rhetoric and action of agrarian politics. Individual rights, but a strong role for collective action; decentralized power, but enough governmental authority to protect the people from private exploitation—these became the central tensions of agrarian republicanism. This may sound like the rosiest statement of an American creed. But while an American creed without Alexander Hamilton, business politics, and a powerful presidency is possible to imagine, an American political history without Jeffersonian republicanism is not.

Yet agrarian reformers had to struggle for decades to achieve their political goals; their successes were episodic, concentrated in reform periods like the Populist and Progressive eras, and the New Deal. Their opponents had far greater material resources and the deference of many elected officials (as well as the federal courts, historically skeptical of regulation and redistribution).

The first national manifestation of agrarian politics came in the battle over the Constitution itself. Given the elite composition and Hamiltonian persuasion of many delegates at Philadelphia, the small farmers of the interior and less-developed regions who had constituted the left flank of the Revolution would not accept this ominous concentration of power in a national government without the guarantees of the Bill of Rights, and only its promise got the new Constitution ratified.

In the next decades came the spread of yeoman settlement at the expense of the native population, to whom few of the agrarian democrats would grant equal citizenship rights. For white Americans, the Jacksonian era brought a broadening of suffrage to all adult white males, the moving of presidential nominations to a large meeting of partisan delegates from local jurisdictions (the party-nominating convention), the war with a national bank seen as serving only elite interests, and the democratizing of government service in the partisan spoils system later reviled by the well educated (who saw their own placement in those jobs as a matter of natural right and governmental efficiency). Though the new national government had been conceived without partisanship (and in fear of it), it was the fundamental agrarian republican vehicle of popular government.

Bureaucracy would inevitably expand, but the notion of autonomous and expert bureaucratic governance never achieved legitimacy in an agrarian republic where universal suffrage preceded any significant growth of executive power. Nor has it today, despite the dramatic expansion of the executive branch in the New Deal, cold war, and Great Society eras. Agrarian politics cherishes collective action at the grass roots, and hails laws that tax the rich and restrain the powerful, but prefers to accomplish those goals with minimal bureaucratic discretion. Agrarian movements press for clear and specific laws, powerful in their precision and automatic sanctions, leaving little to presidential or bureaucratic imagination. "Thou shalt not, on penalty of a hefty fine and jail term, do the following" is the favored preamble of an agrarian statute.

The practice of slavery was the shame of one region in the agrarian heartland, and of elites elsewhere who tolerated it—including Jefferson himself. Racism was a system of elite social control in the South, and was not implicit in agrarian republicanism. To the contrary, the disfranchising and segregation laws developed in the South at the end of the nineteenth century were a response to the threat that agrarian populism would succeed and confront the Democratic Party elite with a biracial, class-based reform coalition.

Beginning in the late 1860s, a sequence of agrarian movements—the Grange, antimonopoly and greenback movements; the Farmers' Alliance; the Agricultural Wheel, an important farm organization that began in Arkansas and ultimately merged with the Farmers' Alliance; the Populist Party; and the Farmers' Union—had put democratic demands on the agenda of national politics. In demanding expansion of government powers, they abandoned the Jeffersonian-Jacksonian antipathy to big government and affirmed the faith that an aroused populace with universal (male) suffrage could seize and purify the state, turning it away from elite privilege and toward the common good. Agrarian radicals won few legislative victories in the Gilded Age—the Sherman Act, the Interstate Commerce Act, and the first postwar attempt at an income tax were greatly weakened or, in the latter case, struck down by the Supreme Court—though the agrarians did accomplish a considerable radicalization of the Democratic Party in 1896.

The defeat of the Populist Party in the South, and the contraction of the electorate that followed it, sapped the promise of agrarian reform, however. Thereafter, agrarians relied on an alliance of white farmers and workers within a Democratic Party tainted with racism and less committed to reform than their forebears in the Populist and Greenback-Labor parties had been.

While the agrarians could not elect their most popular leader, William Jennings Bryan, to the presidency, the Democratic Party he presided over lost most of its elite wing and strengthened its farmer and labor base after 1896. Dissident agrarian Republicans in the Midwest and the mountain states joined the mostly southern Democratic agrarians to accomplish the key economic and political reforms of the Progressive Era, and to oppose President Woodrow Wilson's war preparedness program in 1915–16.

Critically expanded with the influx of millions of urban lower-middle-class voters, the agrarian-labor coalition put through many reforms of the New Deal: the Agricultural Adjustment Act, the Tennessee Valley Act, the Silver Purchase Act, the Glass Steagall (banking regulation) Act, the Securities Act, the National Labor Relations Act, the Public Utility Holding Company Act, the Farm Security Act, and the Huey Long–inspired Income Tax Act of 1935.

After World War II, agrarianism waned with the industrialization of the South and the West, and the rise of the civil rights struggle. In the southern heartland of agrarian politics, race had always been an enormous hurdle to class politics. It was, nevertheless, still possible to identify the occasional agrarian political style among southern Democrats. Texas representative Wright Patman fought the banks and the Federal Reserve over credit, interest rates, and the supply of money until he lost his House Banking Committee chair to a more urbane and conservative Democrat in the 1970s. In the early 1980s and as late as the early 1990s, congressional representatives of farm states and districts battled those same antagonists in one of the most serious threats to Federal Reserve Board autonomy that the agency had ever experienced. Former Texas commissioner of agriculture Jim Hightower was a radical agrarian critic of the administrations of Ronald Reagan, George H. W. Bush, and George W. Bush.

Yet agrarian politics was born in a yeoman agricultural society and the thick web of community self-help activities and movement-readiness of that past America. Whether it could continue in a thoroughly urban era was always open to question. The city, for Jefferson and his followers, was a place where citizens lost their independence, dignity, and virtue, in a polity dominated by the wealthy and a politics naturally inclined toward Hamiltonianism. Early agrarians saw the city as a place of weaker cultural strictures that people confused with freedom.

The greenback-populist transformation of the Jeffersonian creed in the late 1870s and 1880s acknowledged that most Americans had lost their independence to the powerful forces of the emerging industrial and commercial marketplace. It would take a much more powerful government to level the playing field, and so the Jeffersonian animus against government was abandoned as a matter of practical necessity. Vulnerable workers (who had lost their artisanal autonomy decades before the farmers had to confront the railroad and the commodity market) could sometimes be recruited to farmer-labor politics, as demonstrated fitfully in the greenback and populist movements and the Progressive Era, and more successfully in the New Deal.

The Republican Party's "Reagan Revolution" of 1980 revived the Gilded Age assault on government, using populist language without the populist class base or policy impetus. But the Democratic Party also did its part to bury agrarianism by adopting a new form of cultural liberalism. Agrarians were radical on economics and conservative on morals, which President Franklin Roosevelt had recognized when he led the repeal of Prohibition and pushed that hotly contested social issue back to the states and localities. Supreme Court decisions in the 1960s and 1970s that outlawed prayer in public schools and public functions and nationalized abortion rights took away that structural dodge, and thus contributed to the defeat of the agrarian impulse in American politics. The agrarians who remained would have to choose between their moral and religious passions and their agrarian economics. Each of the two major political parties offered half, but only half, and the agrarian soul was clearly torn.

Of course, fewer and fewer rural and small town people existed in the early twenty-first century. Despite some protection in the Senate, the steady dwindling of farm and ranch populations and the towns and businesses they once supported had weakened rural political clout. The results of earlier political successes and the rise of agribusiness also made farmers much more conservative than they once were.

Nevertheless, cultural norms were imbedded and perpetuated in memory and in institutions, and the legacy of agrarian politics may be, to some extent, self-perpetuating. However, one imagines that it would take a serious economic downturn, and perhaps a revolt against a Hamiltonian presidency, to induce a genuine revival of agrarian republican politics.

See also populism.

FURTHER READING. Joyce Appleby and Terrence Ball, eds., *Thomas Jefferson: Political Writings*, 1999; Lawrence Goodwyn, *Democratic Promise: The Populist Movement in America*, 1976; Otis L. Graham, Jr., *An Encore for Reform:*

The Old Progressives and the New Deal, 1967; Matthew Hild, *Greenbackers, Knights of Labor, and Populists*, 2007; Michael Kazin, *A Godly Hero: The Life of William Jennings Bryan*, 2006; Robert McMath, *Populist Vanguard*, 1975; Bruce Palmer, *Man over Money: The Southern Populist Critique of American Capitalism*, 1980; Elizabeth Sanders, *Roots of Reform: Farmers, Workers, and the American State, 1877–1917*, 1999; T. Harry Williams, *Huey Long*, 1981.

ELIZABETH SANDERS

Alaska and Hawai'i

Alaska and Hawai'i, the forty-ninth and fiftieth states, may be considered a political region when viewed from the mainland United States. The two share a number of historical and political characteristics that are decidedly different from those of the contiguous 48 states. They were both part of an American expansion into the Pacific in the nineteenth century, and each experienced a prolonged territorial period in the twentieth century. Alaska and Hawai'i saw direct military action in World War II and joined forces in a 15-year period after the war to achieve statehood. In the early twenty-first century, both still discuss the relative success that they hoped statehood would bring but which still seems unfulfilled. Each state contains a mix of indigenous and settler populations with a greater political prominence of native minorities than on the mainland. These similar experiences differentiate Alaska and Hawai'i from the mainland more than unite them in a common region. Each sees itself as a political area separate from the contiguous states.

In the first half of the nineteenth century, Alaska—then known as Russian America—was a European colony, governed by the commercial Russian-American Company. Hawai'i was an independent kingdom. American entry into the China trade in the 1790s brought American ships into ports in both Russian America and Hawai'i. American commercial contact increased with the expansion of the Pacific whaling industry. American missionaries, many of whom became permanent settlers, arrived in Hawai'i in the 1820s. With the admission of California as a state in 1850, U.S. commercial presence in the Pacific swelled. Overtures for the annexation or purchase of Russian America and Hawai'i were widespread.

The outbreak of the Civil War turned mainland attention away from the Pacific. The end of the war reignited dreams of Pacific expansion. Secretary of State William Seward negotiated the purchase of Alaska for $7.2 million in less than a month in early 1867 from a Russian government ready to divest its North American holdings. A predicted rush of settlement to the north did not occur. Uncertain of what Alaska's political form should be, the United States left the northern region in a nebulous condition as a customs and military district, not as an American territory with any form of elected government. Alaska's population remained low until gold discoveries in the late 1880s revived interest in the north.

Though overtures of annexation were made to Hawai'i after the war, the monarchy sought to distance itself from the United States and kindle relations with Britain. The island kingdom, however, drew closer to the United States in trade relations when a reciprocity treaty, first signed in 1875 and renewed in 1887, allowed raw sugar grown in the islands to enter the United States duty free. The ensuing boom in sugar production created the need for an ever increasing labor supply. The plantations recruited substantial numbers of Chinese, Japanese, Portuguese, and later Filipino workers. By the mid-1890s, the newly arrived workers outnumbered native Hawaiians and the smaller Caucasian commercial community of Americans and Europeans (locally called *haoles*) in an overall population of 100,000.

In the late 1880s and early 1890s, tensions increased between the *haoles*, many of whom were now third-generation settlers, and the monarchy. In 1893 the *haoles*, with the aid of a U.S. Marine contingent in Honolulu, staged a revolution against Queen Lili'uokalani. The revolutionaries asked for U.S. annexation but were initially turned down because James Henderson Blount, an investigator sent by President Grover Cleveland, concluded that Hawaiian natives did not support the revolution. The revolutionaries then created the independent Republic of Hawai'i. Finally, in 1898, under the euphoria of U.S. victory in the Spanish-American War, Congress agreed to annex Hawai'i. The subject of the Hawaiian Revolution and the annexation remains controversial more than a century later. Was the annexation spearheaded by local settlers who manipulated Congress to annex Hawai'i, or was the annexation an act of mainland imperialists who found a group of willing settlers to help execute their plan? Nearly all modern interpretations agree that native Hawaiians did not support the overthrow of their kingdom. Hawai'i became an American territory in 1900. It differed from previous territories in the western United States in that the native population had full voting rights and representation in the territorial legislature.

The Twentieth-Century Territorial Period

During the first four decades of the twentieth century, Alaska and Hawai'i followed quite different paths of political and economic development. Hawai'i functioned much like earlier American territories. It had an elected legislature and an appointed governor, who was selected from island residents. As an American territory, it came under federal anti-Asian immigration legislation. Chinese immigration ended immediately, while Japanese immigration was halted for men in 1907-8 and women in 1924. Asian immigrants were forbidden naturalization by federal precedent. Their children born in Hawai'i were American citizens under the Fourteenth Amendment. Thus, in

the early decades of territorial life, resident Asians were not a part of Hawai'i's political process. In the late 1920s and early 1930s, local-born Asians came of voting age and entered the territorial legislature. By 1940 the Hawai'i territorial legislature was one of the most racially diverse in the nation, containing Hawaiian, Causcasian, Chinese American, Japanese American, and African American members.

In the pre–World War II period, sugar continued to be the economic mainstay of the islands. The companies dominating the industry, known locally as the Big Five, were owned predominantly by island residents. Local companies successfully bought out both Californian and German interests between 1900 and 1920. Hawai'i's economy was characterized by hierarchically managed plantations, but Hawai'i differed from other Pacific plantation cultures in that the territory maintained a tax-supported public school system for children of all races.

Hawai'i's economy and population were also influenced by the growth of military installations built between 1900 and 1940. The federal government saw Hawai'i as the centerpiece for its Pacific military presence. By 1940, the naval installation at Pearl Harbor as well as army installations at Schofield Barracks and Hickam Field gave the islands a military population of approximately 25,000 to 30,000, out of a total population of 423,000.

While territorial Hawai'i grew economically and in population, Alaska followed a different path of development. Gold strikes at Juneau in southeastern Alaska in the 1880s brought a modest increase in population. The Klondike gold strike of 1896–98, though technically in Canada, brought a rush of mainland settlers into Alaska, where gold was then discovered at Nome in 1899 and Fairbanks in 1902. Alaska's population, which stood at 32,000 (mostly indigenous natives) in 1890, doubled to 63,000 in 1900. Such a population increase, which remained stable over the next decade, led to the creation of a full territorial government with a small elected legislature in 1912. Hopes for economic expansion increased with the growth of the canned salmon industry and further discoveries of gold and copper. During World War I, Alaska canned salmon became a staple for American soldiers in Europe, and Alaska copper became a main source of supply for war munitions.

The economy of Alaska was absentee controlled. The canned salmon industry was owned by firms in San Francisco and Seattle, and the metals industry was controlled by outsiders, including the New York–based Guggenheim/Morgan conglomerate known as the Alaska Syndicate. Local residents increasingly resented the grip of the "outside interests," whom they accused of controlling the small, 24-member territorial legislature.

Unlike Hawai'i, where the federal government built a substantial military infrastructure, Alaska was left relatively unfortified until 1940, when Congress made appropriations to increase airfields and troop levels as a guard against both a Japanese naval or air attack and an "over the pole" aerial attack from German-occupied Norway. In 1940 Alaska, with a population of 72,000, was still an underdeveloped territory. It had seemingly little in common with its more prosperous Pacific neighbor 2,500 miles directly south.

World War II and the Statehood Movement

But American entry into World War II in late 1941 brought the two territories closer together. The bombing of Pearl Harbor in December 1941, followed by the bombing of Dutch Harbor in the Aleutians in June 1942 and the ensuing battles of Attu and Kiska in 1943, united Alaska and Hawai'i in the American consciousness as centers of the Pacific campaign. Hundreds of thousands of military personnel and civilian workers from the mainland flooded both territories. Hawai'i's population doubled to 860,000 by 1944; Alaska's more than tripled to 230,000 at the same time. Though the military infrastructure of Hawai'i was solidly in place by 1941, the military buildup of Alaska, which had begun only in 1940, increased dramatically and helped the cities of Fairbanks and Anchorage to emerge from their earlier status as small towns, if not villages. The most dramatic infrastructure improvement was the building of the 1,500-mile Alaska Highway in only nine months from March to November 1942.

Each territory had a different political experience during the war. Hawai'i was placed under martial law a few hours after the Pearl Harbor attack and remained so until 1944. Though about 1,000 Japanese and Japanese Americans in Hawai'i were arrested and interned for supposedly subversive activities, the massive relocation and internment of that population, which occurred so dramatically in the western United States, did not occur in Hawai'i, largely through the cooperation of the business community and Army commander Delos C. Emmons. The tricky question of the service of Japanese Americans in the military was resolved through initiatives in Hawai'i and Washington to create the 100th Infantry Battalion and the 442nd Regimental Combat Team. Both groups were highly decorated by the end of the war.

Alaska escaped the imposition of martial law, though Japanese Americans in the territory were interned, and Aleuts were relocated to southeastern Alaska. The political development of the northern territory was heavily shaped during the war by the extended governorship of Ernest Gruening, an easterner and New Deal civil servant, who served from 1939 to 1953. Gruening created territorial reserve guard units to include Alaska natives (Indians and Eskimos) in the war effort and then encouraged natives to run for political office. One native, William Paul, had served in the territorial legislature from 1925 to 1929, and in 1944 the election of two natives, Frank Peratrovich and Andrew Hope, started a tradition of native representation unbroken to the present day. In 1945 Gruening championed the passage of the Alaska Equal Rights Act, which ended racial discrimination against natives in public accommodations.

The end of World War II in 1945 spelled changes and common causes for Alaska and Hawai'i. Though there was an initial demobilization of military forces in 1946, national decisions for a permanent cold war military presence in both territories were made by 1947. In both territories, 1946 also marked the emergence of statehood movements. World War II convinced residents of both territories to shed their second-class status and gave them hope that Congress would grant statehood.

A plebiscite in Hawai'i in 1940 endorsed statehood, but Congress delayed hearings until 1946. Initial signs pointed to quick congressional action, but delay ensued when Senator Hugh Butler of Nebraska feared that the islands' largest labor union, the International Longshoremen's and Warehouse Union, was under Communist influence. Meanwhile, Alaska held a plebiscite in 1946 that endorsed statehood. Congressional statehood hearings soon began in the northern territory. While concerns over Communist influence delayed action on Hawai'i, fears that Alaska did not have a sustainable economy, except for its military defense role, stymied the northern region. During the early 1950s, Congress was narrowly split between Republicans and Democrats. Each party feared that the admission of one state might tip the balance, as Hawai'i was considered Republican and Alaska Democratic.

To attract national attention in the 1950s, each territory sought to convince Congress of its fitness for statehood. Both states wrote and ratified new constitutions. Alaska had been politically underdeveloped, so it eliminated counties in the proposed new state and established one unified state court system. Both states increased the size of their legislatures, and Hawai'i lowered the voting age from 21 to 20 and Alaska to 19. While waiting for statehood, Japanese Americans increased their representation in the Hawai'i territorial legislature. In 1952 Congress passed the McCarran-Walter Act, which ended the prohibition of naturalization for Japanese and Korean immigrants. (The prohibition of Chinese naturalization had been ended during World War II.) Thus, all of Hawai'i's residents now could become citizens and vote.

In the late 1950s, the congressional delegates from Alaska and Hawai'i (Bob Bartlett and John Burns) co-coordinated their statehood initiatives to ensure congressional passage for both. In 1958 Congress finally voted to admit Alaska as the forty-ninth state. Alaska's statehood bill was significant because it made a grant of 103 million acres (out of 365 million acres in the territory) directly to the state to help spur economic development. In 1959 Congress voted to admit Hawai'i as the fiftieth state. Residents then ratified statehood in local plebiscites with substantial majorities, 8 to 1 in Alaska and 17 to 1 in Hawai'i. Both states officially joined the union in 1959.

In the 50 years since statehood, Alaska and Hawai'i have retained certain common characteristics but have rarely worked together on any particular issue such as they did for statehood. Both continue to be major bastions of America's Pacific military presence. Internally, each state has pursued different objectives. Alaska's quest for economic sustainability was advanced by oil discoveries in the late 1960s on portions of the lands (Prudhoe Bay) granted to the state in 1959. Other land issues have also been in the forefront. Native land claims, acknowledged but held in limbo by the federal government since 1867, were finally settled in 1971 with the passage of the Alaska Native Claims Settlement Act (ANCSA), which apportioned some 44 million acres of land and $962 million in cash to 13 native corporations. A final settlement of most of the remaining federal lands was made in 1980 with the passage of the Alaska National Interest Lands Conservation Act (ANILCA), which placed 131 million acres of wilderness lands in the National Park Service and National Wildlife Refuge System.

In Hawai'i issues of economic development were not so pressing, but the new state grew substantially, with tourism replacing agriculture as a mainstay of the economy. Asian Americans continued to advance politically in the state, and Hawai'i elected both Chinese and Japanese Americans to Congress for the first time. On the other hand, many native Hawaiians perceived that their influence in the islands, politically and culturally, declined in the years since statehood. As a result, there was a Hawaiian Movement in the last decades of the twentieth century to revive traditional Hawaiian culture and, in some cases, to call for political independence. Debates over the proper disposition of native lands, held originally by the monarch but transferred to the United States after annexation, have yet to be resolved.

As a political region in the twenty-first century, Alaska and Hawai'i are more different from the mainland than they are alike. Native issues have been a common concern, but the natives of the two states have not made a common cause. Both states are in the mid-Pacific, distant from the mainland, but 2,500 miles from each other. Still, the common memory of their wartime heritage and joint battle to join the union as the last two states should keep them united in the American mind for some time to come.

See also territorial government.

FURTHER READING. Tom Coffman, *Nation Within: The Story of America's Annexation of the Nation of Hawai'i*, 1998; Lawrence Fuchs, *Hawaii Pono: A Social History*, 1961; Stephen Haycox, *Alaska: An American Colony*, 2002; Haunani-Kay Trask, *From a Native Daughter: Colonialism and Sovereignty in Hawai'i*, 1993; John S. Whitehead, *Completing the Union: Alaska, Hawai'i, and the Battle for Statehood*, 2004.

JOHN S. WHITEHEAD

amendment process

The creation of a mechanism to formally alter the terms of the U.S. Constitution provided a means of bridging the gulf between the conflicting goals of stability and adaptability in the basic principles, structure, and functions of American national government. From the time that effective legal instruments to define and limit governmental powers began to appear, a question persisted as to how such arrangements could be altered short of a revolution or coup d'etat so that a government would perform those tasks, and only those tasks, that political society desired of it. The British solved the problem through sweeping parliamentary declarations at moments of crisis to refine the original instrument of articulated and confined royal power, the Magna Carta of 1215. The 1628 Petition of Rights, the 1689 Bill of Rights, and the 1701 Act of Settlement further confined the ruler and led to a multipart and not entirely consistent framework for government. This collection of legislative acts came to be referred to often, if somewhat inaccurately, as an unwritten constitution.

Operating under royal charters or other instruments laying out quite specifically the terms for their rule, the British North American colonies functioned as subordinates of the mother country but with more coherent written frameworks of government. In their quest for independence in the 1770s, the rebellious colonies demonstrated their commitment to the concept of constitutionalism and their resistance to British-imposed changes in fundamental arrangements that lacked popular sanction.

Creating an Amendable Constitution

The initial U.S. state and federal constitutions put into effect after the Declaration of Independence usually contained specific provisions for their own amendment. The federal Articles of Confederation were no exception, stipulating that a majority of the Congress could initiate changes in constitutional arrangements, but these would only take effect if the legislatures of every state endorsed the provision for reform. As the first U.S. government began to function in the midst of ongoing war with Britain, various deficiencies in the Articles of Confederation became apparent, especially in matters of finance. Efforts to amend the articles failed repeatedly, however, when they failed to win the unanimous support of the states.

The need to devise satisfactory amendments for the articles propelled the convening of a convention of the states in Philadelphia in 1787. The framers' decision to construct an entirely new basic instrument for their federation, submit it for the approval of the Confederation Congress, and stipulate that it would go into operation if ratified by conventions in at least 9 of the 13 states was a radical approach to the process of amending the Articles of Confederation.

If the states initially embraced the new instrument, they would subsequently be bound to accept altered arrangements lacking their unanimous consent. The founders thus set a bold standard that amendment could fundamentally reconfigure a government, not merely make modest revisions in its terms.

Discussion of a proper constitutional amending process continued throughout the Philadelphia convention, intertwined with considerations of federal versus state authority, large state versus small state power, and majority preference versus a higher consensus for fundamental commitments. Contemplation of an amending process was entangled with discussion of how the Constitution itself could be legitimately ratified. The convention reached a Lockean conclusion that the sovereign people had the right to constitute a new government when previous arrangements proved wanting and when their representatives specifically chosen for the purpose agreed to the new Constitution. Moreover, once approved, the new fundamental instrument could then be amended if such a proposal came from two-thirds of each house of Congress, or, in the absence of congressional action, if two-thirds of the states summoned another constitutional convention. In any case, amendments proposed by either means would take effect only if ratified by three-fourths of the states through conventions of popularly elected delegates or decisions of states' legislatures—whichever method the Congress chose. These multiple avenues to amendment were incorporated into the new Constitution's Article V and submitted with the rest of the document to the Confederation Congress. Swift approval there, however, was not an indicator of certain ratification by state conventions, which proved to be a greater test.

The frame of government that 55 men produced in Philadelphia between May and September 1787 met a mixed reception, not only from the convention's members, a few of whom refused to sign it, but also from the politically alert public. The principal objection to the proposed Constitution was its lack of rights guaranteeing individual protections against abusive conduct by the new government. Faced with stiff and potentially fatal resistance to ratification in, first, the Massachusetts conventions and, subsequently, in Maryland, Virginia, New York, and elsewhere, the Constitution's proponents narrowly carried the day by calling attention to the availability of the amending process and agreeing to submit proposals for a Bill of Rights. The reassurance provided by the existence of Article V was crucial to the ratification of the Constitution by the requisite number of states.

Fulfilling the pledge to provide a Bill of Rights through constitutional amendment became the highest priority of James Madison, one of the Constitution's most influential framers and one of its leading protectors in the first House of Representatives. Insistent that the pledge to enact a Bill of Rights not be neglected in the face of other pressing needs in establishing a functioning government, Madison refined a long list of proposals from the various state ratifying conventions. His efforts in the House and those of colleagues in the Senate achieved adoption of a package of 12 amendments during the first session of Congress in 1789. Two years later, 10 of the 12 measures, subsequently referred to as the Bill of Rights, were ratified by enough state legislatures to put them into effect. Anti-Federalist criticism of the Constitution was undercut by this effective first employment of the amending process, and thereafter confidence in the new national government grew steadily.

Reshaping American Government in the Nineteenth Century

As the Constitution began to function, flaws in the document soon became evident. The Eleventh and Twelfth Amendments were easily adopted in 1798 and 1804 to remedy problems involving suits of state governments by citizens of other states and the lack of clarity in the Electoral College's process for selecting presidents and vice presidents, a matter that became clear during the election of 1800. Thereafter, given the cumbersome nature of the amending process and its requirement of supermajority consensus, a preference soon emerged for resolving most constitutional disputes through judicial review. Prior to 1860, Congress approved only one more amendment, a measure forbidding grants of foreign titles to American citizens, and it failed to win ratification. As the sectional crisis came to a head following the election of Abraham Lincoln, Congress made a desperate effort to avert conflict by approving an amendment to preserve slavery in states where it existed. This first effort at a Thirteenth Amendment came too late to avert southern secession and gained ratification by only two northern states.

The Civil War led to a fundamental reformulation of the Constitution through three amendments. All were designed by the Congress to confirm the Union victory. Southern state acceptance was required as the price of regaining full participation in national affairs. The Thirteenth Amendment, adopted in 1865, not only abolished slavery but also demonstrated that the amending process could reverse, not merely modify, previous constitutional arrangements. The Fourteenth Amendment (1868) bestowed the privileges and immunities of citizenship as a birthright, regardless of race or previous condition of servitude, and also promised equal protection and due process of law to all citizens. In essence, this amendment asserted the dominant authority of the national government over the states in the federal relationship. The Fifteenth Amendment (1870) took the further step of guaranteeing adult male citizens suffrage regardless of race. Although southern grumbling about coerced ratification of the Reconstruction Amendments would persist, the process of making these amendments met the Article V standard and represented a choice made by the South to accept its loss on the battlefield and take the necessary steps to regain its place in national government.

Accelerated Amending in the Twentieth Century

The amending process would not be employed again for more than 40 years, stirring new doubts that it could function in ordinary circumstances. However, the Supreme Court's 1895 rejection of an income tax and the Senate's repeated refusal to accept the principle of popular election (instead of state legislative selection) of its members led to public demands for fundamental reform. The House and a majority of state legislatures embraced both proposals, and the Senate finally capitulated, fearing that if it did not, states would employ the alternative Article V process of demanding a constitutional convention that would be beyond congressional control. The adoption and ratification of the Sixteenth (income tax) and Seventeenth (direct election of senators) Amendments were completed in 1913, encouraging a belief that amendment was possible and stimulating successful campaigns for nine amendments in little more than a half century.

In 1913 long-standing temperance and women's rights campaigns turned their attention to quests for amendments to prohibit alcoholic beverages and grant woman suffrage. Mobilizing public pressure on Congress and benefiting from the crisis of World War I, both crusades achieved success by the end of the decade. Congressmen who did not favor Prohibition but hoped to make the issue go away agreed to vote for the amendment if a provision was added requiring ratification within seven years, something they thought unlikely. This first effort to frustrate amendment by placing a time limit on the Article V process failed miserably. The Eighteenth Amendment was ratified in 1919, 13 months after Congress proposed it. The Nineteenth Amendment encountered more resistance, but ratification of woman suffrage was completed shortly before the 1920 election.

Both amendments proved disappointing, however; the Eighteenth because many Americans did not wish to abandon drinking alcohol and the Nineteenth because suffrage neither changed the partisan balance nor brought full equality for women. Within a few years, a campaign was underway to repeal national Prohibition, based in part on the belief that it was undermining respect for the Constitution. Perceiving that state legislators had succumbed to pressure from temperance advocates rather than that they reflected majority will, the anti-Prohibition movement insisted that a repeal amendment be sent for ratification to popularly elected state conventions. After the 1932 election seemed to show that the electorate wanted repeal by favoring wet Democrats over dry Republicans, the convention ratification process, unused since the endorsement of the original Constitution, functioned smoothly and quickly, bringing Prohibition to an end in December 1933 with

the Twenty-First Amendment. That a constitutional provision could be repealed a mere 14 years after its implementation revealed an unanticipated flexibility in the amendment process. Whereas the Civil War amendments had demonstrated that original constitutional provisions could be overturned, the repeal of national Prohibition made it clear that amendments could be toppled if public and legislative opinion changed direction substantially.

The amending process was used repeatedly during the twentieth century to make technical changes in the Constitution that seemed far less consequential than alcohol control, income taxation, or suffrage expansion, but subtly reshaped the functioning of government. The Twentieth Amendment of 1933 reset the calendar to initiate presidential and congressional terms more promptly after a national election. It ended lengthy postelection periods, during which discredited lame ducks continued to exercise power and serve rejected interests. The Twenty-Second Amendment of 1951, limiting a president to two terms, represented a reaction of Republicans and conservative southern Democrats to the four electoral victories of Franklin D. Roosevelt. The measure had the unexpected consequence of politically weakening second-term presidents unable to run again. The Twenty-Third Amendment (1961), granting the District of Columbia three electoral votes, and the Twenty-Fourth (1964), eliminating the poll tax, were small steps toward civic participation for African Americans, symbolic victories for proponents of major civil rights reform, but so modest that even congressional opponents did not strenuously object. The Twenty-Fifth Amendment (1967), establishing procedures to deal with presidential disability and fill vice presidential vacancies, was expected to be rarely needed. Within a decade, however, it was used twice in a single term as both Spiro Agnew and Richard Nixon resigned: their replacements, Gerald Ford and Nelson Rockefeller, were presidential selections, confirmed by Congress rather than the choice of voters. The Twenty-Sixth Amendment (1971), lowering the suffrage age from 21 to 18, was, like the preceding technical amendments, quickly ratified once adopted by Congress.

The steepest hurdle in the amending process appeared to be obtaining congressional approval, with more than 10,000 proposed amendments failing that test in the Constitution's first two centuries. Some came close but failed to win congressional approval, such as measures requiring a national referendum on a declaration of war; limiting executive agreements with foreign nations; overturning Supreme Court rulings requiring equal-sized legislative districts, forbidding school prayer, protecting flag burning as symbolic free speech; and requiring an annually balanced federal budget. A few measures obtained the required two-thirds congressional approval but fell short of ratification by three-fourths of the states. The child labor amendment of the 1920s languished in state legislatures at first, then appeared unnecessary after adoption and judicial acceptance of the New Deal's Fair Labor Standards Act. The equal rights amendment (ERA) and District of Columbia amendment, adopted in the 1970s with ratification time limits, likewise succumbed, the ERA falling only three states short of the necessary 38.

The importance of state ratification in the overall system was underscored in 1992, as the process was completed for an amendment approved by Congress in 1789 as a part of the original package of 12 that had no time limit on ratification. After 203 years, words drafted by James Madison were added to the Constitution in a Twenty-seventh Amendment that prohibited a Congress from raising its own salary. Despite doubts regarding the amendment's viability after such a long time, as well as unhappiness with its limitation on congressional prerogatives, Congress chose not to challenge the stark language of Article V as to the bounds of the amending process.

A Difficult but Manageable Method for Constitutional Change

As its repeated use over more than two centuries has shown, the Constitution's Article V amending process provides a workable mechanism for altering the basic terms of government when a supermajority consensus to do so can be achieved. The failure to bring the process to a successful conclusion often reflects a general unwillingness to tamper with the framers' design, widely regarded as a work of genius. At times, an inability to achieve the required federal and state supermajority consensus in the face of sectional, ideological, and partisan divisions has also been involved. Yet the successful operation of the amending process provides fundamental confirmation of a living, evolving Constitution, one whose unamended features gain reendorsement whenever its other terms are altered, and thus one whose legitimacy no longer rests simply on the original intent of the framers.

See also Articles of Confederation; Bill of Rights; Constitution, federal.

FURTHER READING. Bruce Ackerman, *We the People*, 2 vols., 1991–98; Richard B. Bernstein, with Jerome Agel, *Amending America: If We Love the Constitution So Much, Why Do We Keep Trying to Change It?* 1993; Alan P. Grimes, *Democracy and the Amendments to the Constitution*, 1978; Michael Kammen, *A Machine That Would Go of Itself: The Constitution in American Culture*, 1986; David E. Kyvig, *Explicit and Authentic Acts: Amending the U.S. Constitution, 1776–1995*, 1996; Idem, *Repealing National Prohibition*, 1979; Idem, ed., *Unintended Consequences of Constitutional Amendment*, 2000; Sanford Levinson, ed., *Our Undemocratic Constitution: Where the Constitution Goes Wrong (and How We the People Can Correct It)*, 2006; Idem, *Responding to Imperfection: The Theory and Practice of Constitutional Amendment*, 1998; Clement E. Vose, *Constitutional Change: Amendment Politics and Supreme Court Litigation since 1900*, 1972.

DAVID E. KYVIG

Americanism

Americanism has two different meanings: it signifies both what is distinctive about the United States (and the colonies and territories that formed it) *and* loyalty to that nation, rooted in a defense of its political ideals. Those canonic ideals—self-government, equal opportunity, freedom of speech and association, a belief in progress—were first proclaimed during the era of the Revolution and early republic and have developed more expansive meanings since then. Thanks to a powerful civil rights movement, *social* equality, for example, fully entered the canon only in the decades after World War II. But the bundle of ideals associated with Americanism has proved remarkably supple over time, which helps to account for its enduring appeal to people in other lands as well as at home.

Its shifting content is not the only thing that distinguishes Americanism from the patriotisms generated by other powerful nation-states. Love of any country requires attachment to its supposed virtues, past and present. Affection for "Holy Russia"—its fields and forests and Orthodox Church—long predated the Soviet Union and easily survived it. Traditional Japanese patriots revere the uniqueness of their national tongue and of Shinto, a pantheistic faith linked closely with an unbroken imperial house. Americanism, by contrast, has been rooted less in a shared culture than in shared political ideals.

Like Americans, French patriots may pay homage to the Enlightenment-born ideals of their revolution—liberty, equality, fraternity—but French patriotism includes a stronger cultural component than does America's national creed. Americans have always fought more over how to define and apply the national ideals than about the merits of their language or cuisine. As the historian Richard Hofstader wrote, "It has been our fate as a nation not to have ideologies but to be one." The resulting battles to define Americanism have alternately divided the nation and unified it, producing both internal strife and solidarity against foreign enemies. These two tendencies have often crested together during wartime. Americanism's propensity to generate both conflict and cohesion continues in the early twenty-first century, when the United States has no rival on the world stage but when "Americanism" is fought about nearly everywhere.

From the Puritans to the Pledge of Allegiance

The concept itself is nearly as old as the first European settlements to endure on the land mass of North America. John Winthrop was thinking about his church, not a nation, when in 1630 he told those fellow Puritans who sailed with him to a New World that "we must consider that we shall be as a city upon a hill, the eyes of all people are upon us." But Winthrop's notion that America ought to be a model for Christendom and beyond soon transcended the intra-Protestant dispute that had led to the founding of the Massachusetts Bay Colony. In 1763 another New Englander, John Adams, wrote that America's settlement was "the Opening of a grand scene and design in Providence." Adams believed his young land was destined to break the grip of feudal laws and customs, thus showing how individuals could free themselves from an irrational, often tyrannical past. During and just after the war for independence, such thinking was commonplace in sermons, pamphlets, and even in the diaries of ordinary men and women. The new nation had the potential to be more than what Tom Paine called "an asylum for mankind." It had a mission to liberate the world.

For many Americans, that messianic ambition was fused with religious meaning. The Second Great Awakening of the early nineteenth century spawned thousands of new Protestant churches and made the passion of evangelicalism the common discourse of most inhabitants, whether free or slave. Since that spiritual upsurge, the idea that anyone, regardless of learning or social background, can "come to Christ" has dovetailed with the belief in equal rights emblazoned in the Declaration of Independence. This synthesis of evangelical Protestantism and republicanism was found in no other nation—at least not with such passionate conviction and for such a long period of time.

Over the past two centuries, Americanism has been put to a variety of uses, benign and belligerent, democratic and demagogic. During the first decades of the nineteenth century, the quasi-religious ideal took luxuriant, imperial form. It inspired the notion of Manifest Destiny, which legitimized the conquest of lands occupied by Native American tribes as well as by Mexicans in the Southwest. It was omnipresent among both Jacksonian Democrats, who defined it as the gospel of rough hewn, self-made men in conflict with "the rich, the proud, [and] the privileged," and their Whig opponents, whose "American System" called for higher tariffs and a national bank. It also animated, in the 1850s, the attempt by the new American Party (the Know-Nothings) to drive Irish immigrants from political power wherever the "papists" had established a foothold.

At the same time, the national faith was provoking an equally prophetic critique. In the forefront were abolitionists, both black and white, who scored the hypocrisy of a slave-holding republic. In 1829 David Walker demanded that white citizens "compare your own language" in the Declaration of Independence "with your cruelties and murders inflicted . . . on our fathers and on us—men who have never given your fathers or you the least provocation! ! ! ! ! !" In the 1850s, William Lloyd Garrison called the Constitution "a covenant with hell," and Frederick Douglass asked, "What to the slave is the Fourth of July?"

Yet few radicals rejected the ideals themselves. At the end of his famous Independence Day speech in 1852, Douglass predicted the abolition of slavery in his lifetime. He drew his optimism from "the great principles" of that same Declaration of Independence "and the genius of American institutions" as well as from an enlightened spirit he believed was swelling on both sides of the Atlantic. Such figures initiated a vital countertradition. Since the antebellum era, dissidents have routinely cited the gap between America's utopian promise and its disappointing reality.

The Civil War brought two contending versions of Americanism into a bloody conflict, the terms of which were not finally settled until Reconstruction had run its course in the mid-1870s. In many ways, the war's "new birth of freedom" renewed the national faith. Yet no sooner had Reconstruction begun to wane, than anxiety grew about the weakness of Americanism in the fast-growing, culturally fragmented land. On the eve of the war, Carl Schurz, a German-born reformer and foe of slavery, had confidently predicted, "True Americanism, tolerance and equal rights will peacefully overcome all that is not reconcilable. . . ." By the 1870s it seemed that jagged splits along lines of region, race, religion, class, and immigrant status could tear the industrializing society apart.

For national leaders, it thus became essential to Americanize the population if Americanism were to prosper. Never before had patriots made so self-conscious an attempt "to make a religion out of citizenship," as the political theorist Michael Walzer puts it. The massive Grand Army of the Republic created the ritual of Memorial Day to associate love of country with selfless loyalty in battle. Veterans, ministers, and teachers urged that the flag be displayed in every public building and many private ones.

In 1892 Francis Bellamy, a devout Christian attracted to socialism, wrote a short pledge to the Stars and Stripes that he hoped would bind American children to a shared set of beliefs. An admirer of the French Revolution, Bellamy mused about including "equality and fraternity" in the pledge but decided that would be too controversial in a society riven by differences of race and ideology. So he restricted himself to a single line: "one nation indivisible, with liberty and justice for all." His Pledge of Allegiance was quickly adopted by schools throughout the land (Congress added "under God" in 1954).

As that example suggests, a reassertion of Americanism was not always intended to produce political conformity at the turn of the twentieth century. Dissenters could appropriate the national faith as readily as conservatives. Three years after the pledge was drafted, Eugene Debs, the railroad unionist who would soon become leader of the Socialist Party, emerged from jail to greet a throng of his supporters. "Manifestly the spirit of '76 still survives," he declared, "The fires of liberty and noble aspirations are not yet extinguished."

The Armoring of Americanism

Yet as the United States grappled with a flood of new immigrants and became an imperial power, the most aggressive promoters of Americanism were eager to prop up the established order. These figures weren't necessarily conservative, as we now define the term. But Theodore Roosevelt's praise of the melting pot and of martial virtues stemmed from his fear that immigrants who retained even a shred of loyalty to their native countries weakened America's resolve in a dangerous world.

Inevitably, such fears intensified during World War I. All but ignoring the First Amendment, the federal government jailed radicals who opposed the war and looked the other way when vigilantes forced German Americans to prostrate themselves before the flag. The new American Legion crafted a "100 per cent Americanism" that stressed only the self-protective, coercive aspects of the creed. In the 1920s, this defensive style of Americanism merged with the desire for cultural homogeneity to produce a spate of restrictive immigration laws. Throughout this period, racists had little difficulty rationalizing racial segregation as an essential component of the "American way of life."

The armoring of Americanism in the early twentieth century produced some unexpected consequences. Wartime service in uniform or in defense industries allowed immigrants to legitimize their struggles for justice by draping them in the mantle of Americanism. Those struggles were further validated during World War I as federal officials enticed ethnic workers with the promise of "industrial democracy" and the idea that, in America, "The People ARE the Government." Even the immigration restrictions of the 1920s, by weakening ties between immigrants and their countries of origin, fostered an Americanization from below that set the stage for a new regime of cultural pluralism.

Patriots Left and Right in the Twentieth Century

During the 1930s and World War II, New Deal liberals managed to daub Americanism with a tolerant, populist hue. The federal government hired artists to paint historical murals in post offices that highlighted the exploits of farmers and workers. It also published guides to every big city and region that documented the riches of local histories and cultures. In the new National Archives building next to the Capital Mall, the founding documents of the United States were displayed as if they were the relics of secular saints. Meanwhile, such film-makers-turned-wartime-propagandists as Frank Capra depicted America as one big friendly house for ordinary people of all religions and races (even if, in most of their productions, the minorities politely kept to their own rooms).

Yet the Left's attempt to marry class-consciousness to nationalism did not fare as well. During the Great Depression, CIO organizers described their nascent unions as expressions of "working-class Americanism," while pro-Soviet radicals portrayed communism as "Twentieth-Century Americanism." But

domestic opponents ridiculed these leftist twists on a common theme, and they all but vanished during the cold war. The new global conflict recast Americanism as the antithesis of communism and identified the national creed as the last best hope of a world threatened by totalitarianism and yearning for freedom.

The subsequent hunt for "un-American activities" brought to a close the long period during which no single political faction controlled the meaning of the national canon. The civil rights struggle of the late 1950s and early 1960s did reinvigorate the dissident tradition, for a time. But by the late 1960s, Americanism had become virtually the exclusive property of the cultural and political right.

The politics of the Vietnam War played a critical role in this change. In a decisive break with tradition, leading activists in the protest movements of the era took issue not just with government policies but also with the ideals from which those policies were supposedly drawn. Young radicals did not seek to draw attention to the distance between America's promise and its reality as much as to debunk the national creed itself as inherently reactionary and destructive.

That cynical view held firm among dissenters through the remainder of the twentieth century and beyond, despite a sprinkling of anti-war posters declaring that "peace is patriotic." In 2001 Noam Chomsky, one of the most popular writers on the left, dismissed patriotism as the governing elite's way of telling its subjects, "You shut up and be obedient, and I'll relentlessly advance my own interests."

Meanwhile, conservatives redoubled their efforts to claim Americanism as their cause. They successfully yoked such rituals as saluting the flag, honoring the Founding Fathers, and singing patriotic songs to their larger purposes. But their success occurred largely by default.

How Exceptional a Nation?

The conflict of words and symbols drew new attention to an ongoing debate about the degree to which, in the context of world history, America has been an "exceptional" nation. From Alexis de Tocqueville to Louis Hartz, leading interpreters, whether admirers or critics, focused on what seemed distinctive about the character and ideology of Americans and viewed the development of the nation as unique. The list of exceptional qualities is a lengthy one. It includes the primacy of individual identity over communal ties, belief in almost unlimited social mobility, absence of an established state church and the consequent flourishing of both diverse denominations and grassroots piety, and a potent tradition of antiauthoritarian and anticentralist politics. One should also add the remarkable self-confidence of most Americans, particularly white ones, that they live in a nation blessed by God that has a right, even a duty, to help other nations become more like the United States. Over the decades, the exceptionalist argument was repeated so often—by scholars, journalists, and politicians—that it hardened into cliché.

Perhaps some exceptionalisms, some nationalist ideologies, are more equal than others. For over 200 years, the idea of America—as new Jerusalem or new Rome or something in between—has had a uniquely potent meaning for a broad variety of people outside the United States: from French aristocrats like Tocqueville to European Communists like Antonio Gramsci to Islamic terrorists like Mohammed Atta to teenagers all over the world. Recently, non-American scholars have joined U.S. historians in concentrating on the fragmented, disputatious nature of American society and the influence of those factors on the development of nationalist ideology. But there remains a persistent inclination by academics as well as ordinary citizens in other lands to view America as a whole—to examine how "it" uses and abuses its ideology both within the nation's borders and outside them.

What makes *Americanism* exceptional is thus its confluence with the realities of historical development itself. Ultimately, Americanism demands understanding on its own terms because of the unrivaled power for good or ill that the United States wields in the world. As the historian David Hollinger wrote in 2002, the United States is "the most successful nationalist project in all of modern history. . . . Its significance is measured by its sheer longevity, its influence in the world arena, and its absorption of a variety of peoples through immigration, conquest, and enslavement and emancipation."

The success of the American nation has, in turn, bestowed tremendous power on the notion of Americanism, with all its contradictions and silences. It allows Mormons from Utah and Pentecostalists from Missouri to go into the world, converting people to a faith marked by the material success of its adherents as much as by the appeal of their doctrines and ceremonies. It has also given dissident groups in the United States the ability to inspire analogous movements in other parts of the globe. The U.S. movement for black freedom helped galvanize the anti-apartheid struggle in South Africa, and the radical feminist movement (although indebted to texts by non-Americans like Juliet Mitchell and Simone de Beauvoir) to spark like-minded insurgencies on every continent. The same is true of the gay and lesbian rights movement, spawned in the United States at the end of the 1960s.

The recent rise of anti-Americanism notwithstanding, one cannot neglect the worldwide appeal of Americanist ideology in the laudable desire to internationalize the study and teaching of U.S. history. The very perception that such a distinct set of "values" exists was greatly boosted, particularly from World War II on, by the unmatched power and allure of the American nation itself. Of course, no "civilizing mission" proceeds by discourse alone. Yet without a well-developed, internally persuasive ideology,

no national mission, whether civilizing or barbarous, ever gains much sway.

See also conservatism; liberalism; republicanism.

FURTHER READING. Gary Gerstle, *American Crucible: Race and Nation in the Twentieth Century*, 2001; Louis Hartz, *The Liberal Tradition in America: An Interpretation of American Political Thought since the Revolution*, 1955; Eric Hobsbawm, *Nations and Nationalism since 1780: Programme, Myth, Reality*, 1990; David Hollinger, *Postethnic America: Beyond Multiculturalism*, 1995; Anatol Lieven, *America Right or Wrong: An Anatomy of American Nationalism*, 2004; Cecilia Elizabeth O'Leary, *To Die For: The Paradox of American Patriotism*, 1999; Ernest Tuveson, *Redeemer Nation: The Idea of America's Millennial Role*, 1968; Michael Walzer, *What It Means to Be an American*, 1992.

MICHAEL KAZIN

anarchism

Often described as having exhausted its historical mission—or at least its political significance—anarchism has come back repeatedly in U.S. political history. With the collapse of the Soviet model in 1989 and growing public distaste for its corporate capitalist alternative in the decades since, the anarchist dream found newer generations of disciples, newer projects in ecology, and decentralized political-economic models.

Anarchism first grew to considerable numbers in the United States among the German immigrant community of the 1870s–80s. Its visionaries opposed all forms of class society, all political and economic hierarchies, capitalists and state authorities alike. Their influence reached a high point in Chicago in the mid-1880s, with newspapers, schools, athletic societies, and militia, all crushed by authorities in the aftermath of an 1886 bombing incident in the city's Haymarket Square on May Day. Repression spread rapidly across German American communities, the labor movement's radical cutting edge was demobilized, and an anarchist era ended. Individual immigrant anarchists, notably Johann Most, retained a following and helped bring about a new generation of mostly Jewish immigrant anarchists, notably Alexander Berkman and Emma Goldman. A more individualistic and cultural-minded Yankee anarchist trend also formed around issues like women's rights and birth control. An attempt to form utopian colonies of cooperative labor, inspired by Edward Bellamy's 1888 novel *Looking Backward*, brought a fresh wave of perfectionists into a type of anarchist politics little appreciated by immigrant radicals fixed on ideas of class struggle.

In 1901 the assassination of President William McKinley by the anarchist-influenced Leon Czolgosz seemed to end the movement's prospects in another wave of repression, but the founding of the Industrial Workers of the World (IWW) four years later revived it gloriously. Drawing heavily from European immigrant traditions, the "Wobblies" made anarcho-syndicalist ideas of workers' councils substituting for political and economic government seem poetic as well as genuinely American. The Lawrence, Massachusetts, textile strike of 1912 united more than a dozen nationalities under Wobbly banners, and songster Joe Hill wrote famous and hilarious ballads before being executed by authorities in Utah in 1915. The IWW did not officially oppose U.S. entry into the World War I, but its unwillingness to support the war brought horrendous attacks upon the Wobblies, including long prison sentences for their leaders. The Communist movement that grew out of the war drew upon anarchist traditions but also swallowed or crushed anarchist movements everywhere: Bolshevism seemed to be a philosophy of action, rather than patient education of workers, and a global movement uniting the world's oppressed, including the colonized peoples, but one linked to decisive state force.

A largely cultural movement with anarchist sympathies remained. Before their exile to Europe, avant-garde Dadaists breathed anarchist sentiment into nascent modern art during the late 1910s. Meanwhile, small cooperative colonies with nude swimming and free thought survived in some places; likewise free-spirited schools for children, pacifist and non-English language (mainly Yiddish) publications held on. The defense of Italian American anarchists Nicola Sacco and Bartolomeo Vanzetti, executed by the state of Massachusetts in 1927, became a cause for embattled immigrant radicals at large, with a strong sense of martyrdom that passed from anarchist to Communist sensibilities.

Not until the later 1940s did anarchists have a larger public influence, mostly but not entirely cultural in form. In the wake of the Holocaust, the horror of atomic warfare and the saber rattling of the world's two surviving superpowers, a new generation of anarchist sympathizers began to gather on both coasts. Dwight Macdonald's *Politics* magazine (1944–49)—the most important anarchist publication after the aging Yiddish *Fraye Arbeter Shtimme* (Free Workers' Voice)—sparkled, then faltered and disappeared. In the San Francisco Bay area, KPFA, first station of what would become the Pacifica radio network, offered thousands of listeners anarchist-flavored politics and avant-garde culture.

The religious anarchist-pacifist Catholic Worker group, established during the 1930s and barely tolerated by Church authorities, joined with a post-Marxist Ban the Bomb sentiment in resisting nuclear weapons testing and the staging of government drills in preparation of war. Allen Ginsberg, Lawrence Ferlinghetti, and others loosely called "Beats" added a decisive cultural flavoring to these antiwar, antigovernment sentiments. These latter savants presaged the movements of the 1960s and imprinted upon them a sense of radicalism far exceeding old notions of a future rational, worker-run economy. *Liberation* magazine, absorbing an eclectic opposition to the state and a generous spirit, was the paper bridge to the New Left.

The Students for a Democratic Society (SDS), ideologically uncertain until its sudden takeover by factions of Marxist-Leninists in 1969, discovered an identity for itself as "student syndicalism," an IWW-like belief in student autonomy, self-direction, and resistance to the corporate control of campus. Able to synthesize antidraft sentiment, youth revolt, and insistence on wider democracy than older generations would accept, SDS was hugely popular for a few years among millions of young people. Not since the immigrant brigades of the 1880s had so many rebels shaped by roughly anarchist doctrines exerted themselves so successfully against state-imposed rules (such as Selective Service and drug laws) and social norms (premarital sex, heterosexuality, unmarried cohabitation, and most of all, women's passivity). Nothing was quite so anarchist or short-lived as Hippiedom, and nothing so quickly rendered avant-gardism into popular culture.

But, once again, by 1980, this time through absorption and political reversion, anarchism seemed dead and beyond revival. When the first strains of the globalized economy began to reveal the depths of ecological devastation and the deteriorating condition of populations in the global South, Wobbly-like themes of a global people's movement against capitalist globalization returned to anarchist doctrines. State socialism having failed, decentralization became fashionable among rebellious sections of the young. And so, a new Students for a Democratic Society suddenly came back to life in 2006. No ideology could be described as dominant in the new SDS, but some form of anarchism was the overwhelming favorite of emerging activists.

Two other, apparently dissimilar phenomena had been hidden within the political culture of the late twentieth century and early twenty-first. During the 1980s, Liberation Theology, a vision and practice of egalitarian, anti-imperial, and anticorporate religiosity, encouraged and embraced the landless and their supporters on several continents. It owed so little to any centralized authority that, in effect, it embraced anarchist principles. Its influence was mainly among younger activist clergy and idealists of a dwindling liberal Christian community in the United States. Meanwhile, a DIY, "do it yourself," impulse flourished among young people in the former factory districts of large cities, where cheap rents or "squats" offered space to artists and musicians seeking their own versions of community. With each technological shift, the possibilities of self-created art by masses of youngsters inspired the restless and creative-minded.

How much did such diverse impulses owe to historic anarchism? It is a difficult question to answer. It seems that the belief in a self-created community against the power of the state and its economic partners lived on more in spirit than in doctrine. But it could not die.

See also communism; labor movement and politics; New Left.

FURTHER READING. Paul Avrich, *Anarchist Voices: An Oral History of Anarchism in America*, 1994; Paul Buhle and Nicole Schulman, eds., *Wobblies: A Graphic History*, 2005; David DeLeon, *The American as Anarchist: Reflections on Indigenous Radicalism*, 1996; Bruce Nelson, *Beyond the Martyrs: A Social History of Chicago Anarchism, 1870–1900*, 1988; Alice Wechsler, *Emma Goldman in America*, 1984.

PAUL BUHLE

anticommunism

Under close analysis, political movements sometimes turn out to be coalitions of antagonistic groups brought together for a time by a common antipathy that overcomes their enmity toward each other. Such was the case with American anticommunism, an activist movement distinct from the passive anticommunism sentiment that was the common reaction of almost all Americans to communism, to the extent that they thought about it. This coalition included Jews, Protestants, and Catholics in an age of religious and ethnic tensions. It included white racist anti-Communists and black anti-Communists during the Jim Crow era. There were socialist, liberal, and conservative anti-Communists; there were ex-Communist anti-Communists and former fellow traveler anti-Communists. There were soberly realistic experts on communism and the Soviet Union, and there were conspiracy theorists in thrall to paranoid fantasies that saw all American reform as a "red web" with Moscow at the center. It should come as no surprise, then, that American anti-Communists expended at least as much energy fighting one another as they did the common enemy.

Some historians have seen American anticommunism as simply the twentieth-century manifestation of nineteenth-century nativism and antiradicalism. Nativists and antiradicals, the countersubversive anti-Communists, *were* among the first to mobilize opposition to the Russian Revolution and its American supporters, and remained a noisy and generally disruptive presence throughout the history of anticommunism. But while anticommunism's opponents often succeeded in making the countersubversive part stand for the anti-Communist whole, that was not the whole story.

The Bolshevik Revolution of November 1917 produced three political reactions in the United States: liberal internationalists (whose views were summarized in Woodrow Wilson's Fourteen Points of 1918 with his vision of a world organization of liberal democratic nation-states); the progressive left, which agreed with Lenin that world revolution and

an international workers' state were the only solution to militarism, imperialism, and the injustices of capitalism; and, finally, anti-Communists, who believed that communism was such a threat to American values that it could not merely be contained, as the liberal internationalists advocated, but had to be actively opposed by exposing the activities of American Communists and their supporters. Liberal internationalists, who ran American foreign policy for the rest of the century, generally regarded both the progressive left and their anti-Communist opponents as dangerous extremists and pests who made it difficult to pursue a rational foreign policy. For their part, anti-Communists saw themselves as a protest movement on the defensive against a power structure of liberal internationalists who failed to understand the Communist threat.

The Beginning

The history of anticommunism passed through five stages from its beginnings in 1917 until communism's collapse as an international movement at the end of the 1980s. The first period began with the Bolshevik takeover in Russia that touched off a series of Communist revolutions in Europe. When these were followed by a general strike in Seattle in February 1919 and a wave of political bombings that spring, many Americans and much of the press feared that America was also on the brink of a revolution. The government formed an antiradical division of the Justice Department, led by the young J. Edgar Hoover, who led a roundup of alien anarchists and Communists in December 1918 and January 1919, intended as a prelude to an attack on the entire American radical movement.

A disorganized movement of more responsible and knowledgeable anti-Communists, motivated by communism's threat to their own group interests, included Jewish anti-Communists like Louis Marshall of the American Jewish Committee, who tried to protect American Jews from the Jewish-Bolshevik stereotype, and socialists like Abraham Cahan, editor of the *Jewish Forward*, who was dismayed by the fate of Jewish socialists in Russia. Among Catholic anti-Communists Father Edmund A. Walsh of Georgetown University (founder of its Foreign Service School) saw communism primarily as an enemy of the Roman Catholic Church, while Patrick Scanlan of the *Brooklyn Tablet* saw anticommunism as a way to advance Catholics at the expense of the Church's rivals.

There were black anti-Communists, like George Schuyler, Harlem editor of the *Pittsburgh Courier*, who targeted black Communists for denunciation and satire. There were disillusioned ex-Communists and ex-fellow travelers. After Stalin's repression of his rivals in the late 1920s, ex-Communists such as Ben Gitlow, Jay Lovestone, Isaac Don Levine, Bertram Wolfe, and Eugene Lyons, and ex-front members such as J. B. Matthews (whose *Memoirs of a Fellow*

Traveler became classic reading for right-wing anti-Communists) became anti-Communist activists. Labor anti-Communists like Samuel Gompers and David Dubinsky worried about Communist attempts to subvert the unions. But there were also countersubversive anti-Communists concocting fanciful red web smears, among them Attorney General Harry Daugherty, Blair Coan, Richard Whitney, Nesta Webster, Ralph Easley, and Hamilton Fish, who held the first congressional investigations of communism in 1930 and 1931.

Anti-Fascism Versus Anti-Communism

The second chapter in the history of anticommunism began in 1933, when Hitler came to power in Germany. Anti-Communists now had to choose which of the two evils, Nazism or communism, was the more immediate threat. Some, notably right-wing countersubversives and many Catholics, saw Hitler as the lesser of two evils, even an ally. In the 1930s, charismatic radio preacher Father Charles Coughlin used his newspaper *Social Justice* and his nationwide broadcasts to give voice to an anti-Semitic Catholic anticommunism, although he was opposed by anti-Communist liberal Catholics who were themselves terrified at losing the allegiance of the working class and who fought Communists in the labor unions. Once again the irresponsibility of countersubversives discredited all anti-Communists. Martin Dies of the House Un-American Activities Committee, whose staff director was J. B. Matthews, convulsed the country by "exposing" the actress Shirley Temple for lending her name to a front group. Dies also gave lunatic countersubversives like Elizabeth Dilling (who wrote *The Red Network* and *The Roosevelt Red Record*) a respectful hearing.

Left anti-Communists came to regard the Hitler-Stalin pact as a litmus test separating true anti-Nazis from supine Communists following the Moscow party line. Sidney Hook led the drive against the fronts and helped found the anti-Communist American Committee for Cultural Freedom in 1939. He also organized the Dewey Commission of Inquiry into the Truth of the Moscow Trials. Anti-Communist union leader John L. Lewis took his mine workers out of the Congress of Industrial Organizations (CIO), charging it was Communist dominated, while Matthew Woll, David Dubinsky, and George Meany fought Communists within the CIO and hired Jay Lovestone as the CIO's liaison with anti-Communist unions in Europe.

During this 1939–41 period, anti-Communists were subjected to what historian Leo Ribuffo called the "brown scare," in which the entire movement was blamed for the Nazi sympathies of a few. A serious body of writing emerged that exposed the reality of Communist subversion and espionage, such as Eugene Lyons's *The Red Decade*, 1941; Walter Krivitsky's *In Stalin's Secret Service*, 1939 (edited by Isaac Don Levine); and Jan Valtin's *Out of the Night*, 1939.

Former Soviet espionage agent Whittaker Chambers took his revelations about Soviet spy networks to the State Department in 1939, but they were ignored until after the war, when Chambers became an icon of countersubversive anticommunism.

Perceived opposition to or half-hearted support for the war effort weakened anticommunism during World War II. The government staged a show sedition trial of notorious right-wing anti-Communists in 1944 to expose their Nazi sympathies, as alleged in John Roy Carlson's *Undercover*. Catholic anti-Communists also resented Franklin D. Roosevelt's war policy and judged the success of the war by the outcome in Poland and Lithuania, where pro-Soviet governments reigned. By the end of the war, anticommunism stood discredited for skepticism about the good intentions of Stalin and American Communists, who were, respectively, America's most important ally and the war's most vigorous supporters.

The Domestic Cold War

The third stage of anti-Communist history began with the end of World War II and the Russian occupation of Eastern Europe. The American Catholic community was galvanized by the Communist takeover of Catholic Poland, Hungary, Romania, and the rest of Eastern Europe. Bishops led protest parades in cities across the country and commissioned a study of the influence of Communists in the government, which they saw as blocking aid to the captive nations. Father John Cronin, a labor priest from Baltimore, wrote the report with the assistance of the FBI, and the Chamber of Commerce gave it national circulation during the 1946 congressional elections.

President Harry Truman, a liberal internationalist, was deeply suspicious of domestic anticommunism, likening it to witch-hunting, and actually commissioned a report to support this conclusion. This perspective led Truman to agree with a reporter's characterization of the Communists-in-government issue as a red herring. That all but ceded the security issue to countersubversive Republicans and to J. Edgar Hoover's FBI, paving the way for the emergence of Senator Joseph R. McCarthy as the new face of the anti-Communist movement.

The great spy cases of the late 1940s seemed at last to prove that a vast Communist conspiracy reached to the highest levels of the government and penetrated secret defense installations. Hoover's FBI rode a wave of popularity from its success in the spy and Smith Act cases that imprisoned the leadership of the American Communist Party. To create public support for the internment of Communists and their sympathizers in the event of hostilities with the Soviet Union, Hoover launched a mass media campaign to indoctrinate the public in anti-Communist ideology.

Liberal anti-Communists mobilized to fight Communist influence in culture and politics. With the help of the CIA, they organized the Congress for

Cultural Freedom, founded by Arthur Koestler and Sidney Hook, to combat the Soviet peace offensive against the Marshall Plan and the Truman Doctrine, and sponsored anti-Communist intellectual journals like *Preuves* and *Encounter*. Anti-Communist liberals like Eleanor Roosevelt, Hubert Humphrey, Walter Reuther, Arthur Schlesinger Jr., and David Dubinsky launched the Americans for Democratic Action to combat communism in the Democratic Party and opposed Henry Wallace's progressive campaign for president in 1948.

McCarthyism and the Collapse of the Anti-Communist Consensus

The fourth stage of anti-Communist history began with the rise of Senator McCarthy in 1950, bringing to an end this uneasy coalition of conservative, left, and liberal anti-Communists, and leaving the movement nearly totally discredited and with little influence in American politics. McCarthy's indiscriminate smearing of liberals during his notorious Senate hearings conjured up images of anticommunism as the new face of American fascism, and his incredible Senate speech accusing George Marshall of being a Communist traitor raised questions about his sanity. His reign between 1950 and 1954 demolished whatever fragile consensus had bound together liberal, socialist, and conservative anti-Communists in the early cold war years.

Their support for McCarthy pushed conservative and countersubversive anti-Communists outside the respectable mainstream of American politics. Liberal and left anti-Communists were wary of anything that might associate them with such pariahs. That reluctance was reinforced with the emergence of Robert Welch's John Birch Society, built around its leader's theory that Dwight D. Eisenhower himself was a "conscious, deliberate agent of the Soviet conspiracy." A vigorous liberal counterattack against Welch succeeded in branding all ideological anticommunism as "extremist," the kiss of death in American politics. The Kennedy administration used the extremist issue against right-wing anti-Communists, as did Lyndon Johnson in his 1964 campaign against Barry Goldwater, another anti-Communist icon. The Kennedy administration ended anti-Communist indoctrination programs in the armed forces, claiming they fueled dangerous extremism. By this time it was inadvisable for anti-Communists to bring up the subject of communism as an ideological justification for the cold war without being (self-)caricatured as belonging to the lunatic anti-Communist right.

Meanwhile, developments in the Roman Catholic Church were carrying the mass of American Catholics out of the anti-Communist movement. Anticommunism had been a vehicle to social respectability for American Catholics because it allowed them to demonstrate their patriotism. McCarthy's disgrace had been a serious setback, but with the election of Kennedy, American Catholics felt they could dispense with the tainted crutch of anticommunism. Pope John XXIII opened the Church to a dialogue with the left, and the Kennedy administration's equation of anticommunism with extremism provided more motivation for Catholics to discard the movement, to the dismay of true believers like William F. Buckley Jr.

One of the paradoxes of the Vietnam War was that it was an essentially anti-Communist conflict in which there was little discussion of the anti-Communist ideological basis for the war, leaving by default the liberal internationalist domino theory as its justification. Nevertheless, the disastrous course of the war, the publication of the *Pentagon Papers*, the Watergate scandal, and the Church Committee investigations of government security agencies in 1975 resulted in anticommunism being blamed not only for Vietnam but, by implication, for a misguided cold war foreign policy. By the end of the 1970s, the United States had a president, Jimmy Carter, who decried the nation's alleged "inordinate fear of communism." Anticommunism had achieved the dubious status of national scapegoat for much of what had gone wrong at home and abroad, a point driven home by a library of revisionist histories about the cold war and McCarthyism.

Rebirth and Redemption?

Now began the fifth and final chapter in the story of American anticommunism: its improbable and vigorous rebirth during the Ronald Reagan administration. By 1976 anticommunism was, in the opinion of Norman Podhoretz, the editor of *Commentary* (sponsored by the anti-Communist American Jewish Committee), a taboo term in American political discourse. Meanwhile, Soviet dissidents like Andrei Sakharov and Alexander Solzhenitsyn scolded Americans for abandoning anticommunism. Podhoretz revived the discussion of communism and helped organize the Committee on the Present Danger (along with Paul Nitze and Eugene Rostow), populated with surviving members of the Jewish, Socialist, and labor union anti-Communist movements along with big business conservatives, retired military officers, and old-time architects of cold war foreign policy.

The Committee launched a withering attack on Carter's arms negotiations strategy and furnished the Reagan campaign with its foreign policy expertise. Almost all its members were appointed to powerful positions in the Reagan administration.

Reagan was arguably the nation's first and only truly anti-Communist president, a product of labor union anticommunism of the late 1940s and early 1950s. He appointed the anti-Communist William F. Casey as director of central intelligence. Casey convinced Reagan that the time was ripe to roll back communism, and the administration began funneling arms, money, and moral support to anti-Communist insurgencies and dissidents around the world. Reagan's Evil Empire speech of 1983 unabashedly made the anti-Communist critique of the Soviet Union the moral basis for American foreign policy, and he used Catholic and AFL-CIO anti-Communists to aid the Polish Solidarity movement that opened the first fatal crack in the iron curtain.

With the collapse of the Soviet Union in 1991, American anticommunism had achieved its main goal. Outside of the movement itself, it got little credit. Because it is identified with the most intolerant elements of American politics, its worthwhile contributions have been generally ignored, though commentators from Russian and Eastern Europe have been more generous in giving American anticommunism some share of the credit for communism's demise. But the American anti-Communist remains, and probably will remain, a prophet without honor in his own country and in his own house.

See also communism, nativism.

FURTHER READING. M. J. Heale, *American Anticommunism: Combating the Enemy Within, 1830–1970*, 1990; Richard Gid Powers, *Not without Honor: The History of American Anticommunism*, 1995; Ellen Schrecker, *Many Are the Crimes: McCarthyism in America*, 1998.

RICHARD GID POWERS

antiparty sentiment

Hostility toward the political party has been an important dimension of American culture from the earliest days of the republic. During the first three or four decades following the adoption of the Constitution, antiparty sentiment derived primarily from the central tenets of classical republican theory, as this ancient body of thought was developed and reshaped by British political philosophers during the seventeenth and eighteenth centuries. Particularly important were two related concepts: that effective and just government flows from the decisions of virtuous leaders pursuing the public good rather than their own or others' private interests; and that the political influence of those interests and interest groups that do emerge within society must be transitory and contained, so that no single interest acquires enduring power over all others and over the republic as a whole. The notion of party was antithetical to these concepts and was universally condemned by the Founding Fathers (who used the terms *party* and *faction* interchangeably), even before anything resembling an institutionalized political party appeared on the American landscape.

To be sure, some of the most prominent spokesmen for the republican creed—Thomas Jefferson, James Madison, Alexander Hamilton, John Adams, and even George Washington, whose Farewell Address of 1796 remains the classic American warning against the dangers of party—quickly behaved in accordance with the first system of enduring alignments that could be identified as partisan. But the Federalists and Republicans of the early republic did not develop the elaborate institutional structures of later political parties, and their leaders perpetuated antiparty principles, in public discourse at least, by claiming that they and their allies worked for the common good while their opponents threatened good government by representing a specific constellation of interests. As the historian Richard Hofstadter has pointed out, neither party accepted the legitimacy of the other, while in power or as a formal opposition. Both sought to eradicate the other, and when the Republicans succeeded in doing this in the aftermath of the War of 1812, they were able to interpret their success as the fulfillment of classic republican principles.

The factionalism that soon bedeviled the triumphant Republicans gave way during the 1830s and 1840s to a fully institutionalized and enduring two-party system, and to a new set of ideas that legitimated the party as necessary to the functioning of a viable democracy. In this era of mass voter mobilization by Democrats and Whigs (the latter replaced by Republicans before the Civil War), well-organized parties linked themselves not only to new theories of power and legitimate opposition but also to popular ideas and symbols intended to establish each party as truly national and fully American, and therefore less worrisome as ongoing representatives of specific programs and interests. Antiparty sentiment, in this new environment, was deliberately weakened; yet, it survived not merely as an old-fashioned idea but discovered a new foundation in the very success of political parties as institutions.

As the parties grew, they developed professional roles and a set of cultural and behavioral codes that emphasized institutional loyalty and reward. Perhaps more than party platforms supporting or opposing one or another interest-based program, professionalism and patronage undermined each party's republican character. Increasingly, Americans defined partisan activists as "politicians," driven by the quest for power and for private reward in the form of government jobs or contracts rather than by service to the public good, even when that good was loftily declared in the party's specific program. And in the pursuit of power and its spoils, politicians debased the electoral process with vulgar campaign practices and widespread bribery and intimidation at the polls. The corruption that followed from self-interest was now to many Americans—including regular voters and avid partisans—the concrete property of the party system.

Even before this system was fully formed, antiparty sentiment helped fuel a number of dissenting movements, including several that put themselves forward as alternative political parties, freer from the corruption inherent in routine partisan activity. The Know-Nothings of the 1850s, for example, attracted some of their adherents by portraying themselves in this way. Such dissent could emerge, too, from within the parties, as it did in the decades following the Civil War, when groups of mostly well-to-do Republicans, and somewhat later their counterparts in the Democratic Party, urged civil service reform, educational campaigns, voter registration, secret balloting, and other changes to a party system increasingly perceived as disreputable.

These reforms may have succeeded in elevating the reputation of the political system, but they did not prevent a general weakening of partisan identity during the course of the twentieth century. Traditional antiparty themes such as political careerism, corruption, and the pursuit of interests opposed to the general good continued and still remain persuasive in political discourse. They have manifested themselves in a long trend toward independent voter registration (by the end of the twentieth century, independents were as numerous as either Democrats or Republicans among registered voters), toward the elevation of nonpartisanship as apolitical ideal, and toward more personalized political campaigns, stressing the qualities of the candidate rather than his or her party affiliation and in many cases portraying the candidate as a political outsider transcending mere partisanship. Even third-party movements have been more frequently organized around highly visible and often charismatic leaders, from Theodore Roosevelt and Robert La Follette to Ross Perot and Ralph Nader.

Parties remain central to the American political process. But they continue to function within a culture long suspicious about partisan methods and motives and newly inclined to reduce the role of parties in the shaping of public affairs.

See also republicanism.

FURTHER READING. Glenn C. Altschuler and Stuart M. Blumin, *Rude Republic: Americans and Their Politics in the Nineteenth Century*, 2000; Ronald P. Formisano, *The Transformation of Political Culture: Massachusetts Parties, 1790s–1840s*, 1983; Richard Hofstadter, *The Idea of a Party System: The Rise of Legitimate Opposition in the United States, 1780–1840*, 1969; Richard L. McCormick, ed., *Political Parties and the Modern State*, 1984; Joel H. Silbey, *The American Political Nation, 1838–1893*, 1991; Mark Voss-Hubbard, *Beyond Party: Cultures of Antipartisanship in Northern Politics before the Civil War*, 2002; Michael Wallace, "Changing Concepts of Party in the United States: New York, 1815–1828," *American Historical Review* 74 (December 1968), 453–91.

STUART M. BLUMIN

anti-statism

Although conservative Austrian economist Friedrich A. Hayek first employed the term *statism* in 1944 as part of a critique of modern governance, hostility to centralized political power has profound roots in the American experience. Borrowing notions from liberal theorists John Locke and Adam Smith, American Revolution leaders contrasted natural property rights with the privileges of political and market power. A concurrent republican ideology endorsed liberation from government coercion and freedom from the tyrannies of bureaucracy and standing armies. By the 1830s, the followers of President Andrew Jackson had codified such sentiment into a campaign against government-licensed monopolies like the Second Bank of the United States. Free market advocates of nineteenth-century producer democracy continued to celebrate the perceived advantages of a government whose laissez-faire policies left corporations and individual enterprisers freed from state interference. Not surprisingly, Congress and the federal courts viewed regulation of business and the workplace as violations of constitutional rights of property.

As a complex industrial order convinced Progressive-era reformers like educator John Dewey and economist Richard T. Ely to advocate government use of scientific expertise to serve the general welfare, small business and independent farming interests increasingly took exception. In Wisconsin, the Democratic Party contested rule by reform-minded Republicans in 1912 and 1914 with charges that "tax-eating commissions" and remote bureaucrats had imposed paternalistic rule on ordinary people. A similar cry characterized the protests of Idaho Republican Senator William E. Borah in the 1920s. "The remorseless urge of centralization" and "the insatiable maw of bureaucracy," complained Borah, deprived "more and more the people of all voice, all rights touching home and hearthstone, of family and neighbor."

Suspicion of government rule accelerated in the later stages of President Franklin D. Roosevelt's New Deal. Employing a "brain trust" of academic advisers and planning consultants to fashion a consumer-oriented revival of the economy, Roosevelt came under fire for a lack of political accountability to constituencies beyond his electoral coalition. As producer interests attacked the administration's judicial and executive reorganization plans, deficit spending, ties to organized labor, and sponsorship of social experimentation, critics began to picture Washington, D.C., as a hotbed of "strangers" to the American way. During World War II, when domestic agencies like the Office of Price Administration (OPA) and the National Resources Planning Board (NRPB) sought systemic solutions to wartime inflation and prospects of postwar unemployment, congressional critics of government concentration closed down New Deal agencies and welcomed a spate of polemics about the dangers of excessive bureaucracy.

Hayek's anti-statist treatise, *The Road to Serfdom*, was one of five such works published in 1944. The unitary economic power of the managerial state was a threat to human freedom and personal liberty, insisted the author, because it sought to control productive output and distribution. Behind government collectivism, Hayek saw the shadowy hand of technical specialists who used their expertise to advance an agenda that furthered their own role in the administrative machinery. By focusing on the political intelligentsia's ties to state power, Hayek anticipated Milovan Djilas's descriptions of the New Class. A former official in Communist Yugoslavia imprisoned for dissenting views, Djilas contended that socialized economies allowed managers and officials to serve their own class interests by administering collectivized property.

Speculation over the policy-making influence of New Class intellectuals prompted a number of social scientists in the United States to apply such a model at home. Sociologist Alvin W. Gouldner's *The Future of Intellectuals and the Rise of the New Class* (1979) suggested that knowledge elites were often responsible for policies involving state regulation of production and the provision of social welfare services. Beginning in the late 1960s, a more critical portrait emerged from a group of neoconservatives including economist Milton Friedman, sociologist Daniel P. Moynihan, social commentator Michael Novak, and editor Norman Podhoretz. These critics condemned a powerful cabal of collectivist bureaucrats and planners who consolidated a hold on power by providing social services to the poor and administering an antibusiness regulatory structure.

As federal involvement in civil rights placed Washington, D.C., in a controversial light in the South and elsewhere in the 1950s and 1960s, antigovernment discourse broadened. The first politician to exploit such hostility was Alabama governor George C. Wallace. Running in several Democratic presidential primaries outside the South in 1964, Wallace abandoned rhetoric about white supremacy and focused on the social engineering of a federal government that ruled by executive or judicial edict. Arizona's Republican Senator Barry Goldwater made a similar case in the general election campaign. Centralized planning, bureaucracy, and regimentation, charged Goldwater, had produced a government of "easy morals and uneasy ethics." Although Republican Richard Nixon occasionally embraced conservative critiques of big government and the liberal establishment, Ronald Reagan proved to be the twentieth century's most successful inheritor of the anti-statist mantle. Campaigning for Goldwater in 1964, Reagan warned that "government can't control the economy without controlling the people." Two years later the popular Republican sailed into the California governor's chair by directing conservative critiques of state power to exposure of the seemingly wasteful welfare programs of President Lyndon B. Johnson's Great Society. Similar approaches energized Reagan's election to the White House in 1980. Promising to "take the government off the backs of the people," the populist conservative heralded "an era of national renewal" freed from federal bureaucracy and excessive taxation. Accordingly, Reagan cut taxes, reduced corporate regulation, trimmed welfare spending, and limited federal civil rights enforcement.

Following the election of President George H. W. Bush in 1988, Republican strategists boasted of a "new paradigm" that rejected rule by experts and bureaucrats. By the early twenty-first century, however, increasing concerns about health care, social security, pension viability, and federal responses to the threats of terrorism and natural disasters profoundly complicated the conversation about state power. After more than two centuries of heated debate over the proper place of government in a democratic society, Americans seem as uncertain as ever over the legitimate role of knowledge professionals, human service practitioners, and administrative specialists who have ruled in their name.

See also conservatism.

FURTHER READING. Alan Brinkley, *The End of Reform: New Deal Liberalism in Recession and War*, 1995; Thomas Byrne Edsall, with Mary D. Edsall, *Chain Reaction: The Impact of Race, Rights, and Taxes on American Politics*, 1991; Friedrich A. Hayek, *The Road to Serfdom*, 1944; David A. Horowitz, *America's Political Class under Fire: The Twentieth Century's Great Culture War*, 2003.

DAVID A. HOROWITZ

armed forces, politics in the

In considering the connection between politics and the American armed forces, three features are most noteworthy: first, the political attitudes and relations that develop within the services; second, the political connections that develop with civilians, notably political leaders, outside the services; and third, the role of the armed forces as a political lobby—not just in terms of their role in promoting debates over national security but in relation to their place and function in society. Such an approach was pioneered in Samuel P. Huntington's book *The Soldier and the State* (1957). Soldiers in particular have played a significant part in American politics even before independence. The glamor and heroism implicit in military service have proved alluring. Electoral competition at every level could be promoted if the candidate had been in earshot of what George Washington described as the "charming sound" of bullets. The American republic shared one important feature with the Roman republic of antiquity: both witnessed a large degree of interpenetration between military and political institutions, with politicians eager to become military men, and vice versa. But American military heroes, unlike their Roman counterparts, have not sought to overthrow the U.S. Constitution and set up a dictatorship. They have preferred advancement within strict constitutional boundaries and have rarely sought to overstep them.

The Legacy of the Revolution

The emphasis on political supervision of military affairs before 1783 reflects the revolutionary character of the revolt against the British crown. Ironically, discontent with British rule and agitation for self-government and then independence in the former colonies underlined the degree to which they had inherited British military attitudes. Occupation by small numbers of British troops provoked a latent suspicion of and hostility toward regular, standing armies and a disinclination to pay for them. Americans came to believe that standing armies were a source of tyranny, a threat to the values of popular freedom eventually expressed as liberal democracy. Here lay a source of perpetual distrust that runs throughout American history. Civilians suspected soldiers of harboring antidemocratic tendencies, and soldiers believed that civilians were prepared to indulge their prejudices to the degree that they might endanger American security itself.

In 1775 George Washington's commission as commander in chief and those of all his senior generals were issued by a Continental Congress responding to the interests of the various states and the level of commitment of each to the Revolution. "Political generals"—leaders who could exert influence over important areas of the home front—could be found in all American wars. But whether these were professional politicians or not, they unleashed disenchantment with the system of promotion and, in turn, stirred up political agitation against the leaders who had appointed them. Throughout the Revolution, Washington shrewdly ensured that civilians always remained in control. In his official relations with the Continental Congress and the state governments, Washington chose to overlook lethargy, ignorance, and inexperience—although he inveighed against these in private—and treated them with deference, conscious of the precedents he was establishing. Civilians have been attacked in all American wars for failure to understand how to wage war and treat military men. In 1783 such discontent threatened to get out of control during the Newburgh Conspiracy, an attempt by Continental Army soldiers to secure back pay by threatening a military coup. Washington acted energetically to thwart any military intervention in politics and ensure that legitimate grievances over back pay were brought before Congress in a respectful manner.

The image of Cincinnatus, the successful Roman general who laid aside his command to return meekly to agricultural pursuits, lacking either ambition or a thirst for power, remained a potent element of the American military tradition for 150 years. It continued to exert influence after the rise of military professionalism, stimulated by the 1802 founding of the United States Military Academy at West Point. The professional ethos came to embrace discipline, duty, physical fitness, and manly virtue. Soldiers believed themselves expert; they evinced a sense of superiority in relation to civilians; they felt a more powerful patriotism, were singular and devoted, moderate and rational by comparison with their selfish, grasping,

and often unscrupulous political masters. From such attitudes grew the myth that soldiers avoided political entanglements. Winfield Scott boasted that he never voted; George B. McClellan admitted to doing so only once, in 1860; so, too, did Ulysses S. Grant, in 1856. Yet all these men sought the presidency. Only Grant was successful, serving two terms and desirous of a third. McClellan served as governor of New Jersey (1878–81). Many other military officers engaged in politics. In 1858 P. G. T. Beauregard ran for mayor of New Orleans, and the later General Montgomery C. Meigs thought nothing of building up congressional alliances to aid him in a dispute with the secretary of war, John B. Floyd.

Civilian Control and the Two Party System

The presumption of political "innocence" among regular officers arose partly from resentment at the failure of American leadership from the War of 1812 onward to distinguish between high political and military rank. During the Mexican-American War (1846–48), the tensions between President James K. Polk and his generals Winfield Scott and Zachary Taylor resulted not from a clash of values but from the Democratic president's justified fear that Scott and Taylor, as Whigs, would exploit any military success in subsequent runs for the presidency. Polk briefly considered placing Democrat senator Thomas Hart Benton as a lieutenant general over both of them before abandoning the idea. However, throughout the nineteenth century the nonregular soldier appeared to fit the Cincinnatus model more closely. In Andrew Jackson's first inaugural address on March 4, 1829, he declared that "the bulwark of our defence is the national militia." High rank in volunteer service proved a path to the presidency not just for Jackson, but also for William Henry Harrison, Franklin Pierce, Rutherford B. Hayes, James A. Garfield, Benjamin Harrison, and William McKinley.

In 1861 many Americans blamed the outbreak of the Civil War on selfish partisanship that had inflamed passions. Abraham Lincoln thus treated the enlistment of northern Democrats in support of the war effort as a high priority. He offered many of them senior commissions, including Benjamin F. Butler, Daniel E. Sickles, John A. Logan, and John A. McClernand. James G. Blaine, later a Republican presidential candidate and secretary of state, contended in his *Twenty Years of Congress* (1884–86) that the war could not have been won without them. War Democrats also included Secretary of War Edwin M. Stanton and Judge Advocate General Joseph Holt. Indeed, disappointed Republicans calculated that 80 out of 110 brigadier generals' commissions and 80 percent of all generals' commissions had gone to the Democratic Party opposition. In 1861–62, the three most important commands were held by Democrats: George B. McClellan, who presided as general in chief; Henry W. Halleck, who in July 1862 succeeded him; and Don Carlos Buell.

All these generals were West Point graduates. Professional soldiers tend to be conservative in politics, and before 1861 West Point had been criticized for nurturing an "aristocratic" elitism among regular officers. For years afterward Republicans accused it of having sheltered a treasonous "slave power" conspiracy, as over 26 percent of West Point graduates resigned and sought commissions in the armies of the Confederacy. The leading Democratic generals were spokesmen for military professionalism, and thus made claims for their superior knowledge of military science. They argued that they should be able to make decisions free of "political" harassment. McClellan, who admired the code of the southern gentleman, and Buell, who had southern relatives through marriage, gained a reputation for being slow, overly cautious, and incapable of making the most of their opportunities. Their Republican critics on the Congressional Joint Committee on the Conduct of the War equated their reluctance to engage southern armies in "vigorous" operations to their conservative political views. Such critics as Senator Benjamin F. Wade of Ohio, ridiculed McClellan's use of military jargon—especially "lines of retreat"—as an excuse for moral cowardice. One War Democrat, Senator Andrew Johnson of Tennessee, joined in such denunciation because he saw McClellan as a rival for the 1864 Democratic nomination, which he eventually won after leaving the service.

Few of the antebellum regulars among the senior officers of the Union Army were opposed to slavery. In 1861 outright abolitionists, like David Hunter, were a beleaguered minority. After McClellan's removal in November 1862, the influence of Democrats waned. A growing number, like Henry W. Halleck, Ambrose E. Burnside, and Joseph Hooker, came to embrace the Emancipation Proclamation. In 1863 an aggrieved Abner Doubleday still complained that proslavery "cliques" ran the army and that "anti-McClellan men" were held back. Nonetheless, under the Grant-Sherman regime of 1864–65 most of the significant commands were held by West Pointers, though Grant evinced a skill at handling "political generals" like Butler. The soldiers in the ranks—especially in the East—who had previously adored McClellan did not vote for him in the presidential election of 1864. Lincoln and the Republican Party won 77.5 percent of the soldiers' vote.

After the Civil War, the powerful support offered to the Republican Party by the veterans' organization, the Grand Army of the Republic, foreshadowed the political sway of such twentieth-century successors as the American Legion.

The partisanship of 1861–65 had also bequeathed a bitter legacy. The sense that the regular army was "apart" from American society probably dates from the 1840s, but it came to assume greater symbolic importance after 1877. Such disillusionment had less impact in the U.S. Navy, which expanded rapidly after the 1880s. Democratic societies, in any case, have felt less antipathy toward navies, as they represented a lesser direct threat to liberty.

Resentment of the army's marginal role at the conclusion of the Indian Wars diminished respect in the ranks for the Constitution and popular democracy. Brevet Major General Emory Upton became the mouthpiece for such views. Upton argued that volunteers were invariably ineffective and that civilian control remained the central reason for American military failures. Henceforth, he argued, all decision making should be the monopoly of military professionals.

The U.S. triumphs in both world wars revealed these claims to be misguided. The role of military men in policy making worked smoothly, especially from 1941–45. Harmony prevailed because to work effectively civilian control requires trust, not sulky acquiescence. The chief of staff during World War II, George C. Marshall, spoke out candidly when he disagreed with President Franklin D. Roosevelt, but he never made any disagreements public. The basic system continued to work well after 1945 despite interservice squabbling over budgets. Most differences could be subsumed in pursuit of the common goal of winning the cold war. But the dramatic dismissal of General Douglas MacArthur in 1951 for colluding with a Republican congressman while criticizing President Harry S. Truman's policy in the Korean War (1950–53) was a portent of the tensions that would develop after 1989 with the collapse of the cold war consensus.

MacArthur's dismissal led to a revival in interest in civil-military relations, especially after the publication of Arthur M. Schlesinger Jr. and Richard H. Rovere's book on the controversy, *The General and the President and the Future of American Foreign Policy* (1952). Yet MacArthur's political record before the Korean War, in which he acted prudently and democratically as supreme commander of the Allied Powers (1945–51) in postwar Japan, belies the fear that he hankered for the military's dominance in politics.

The postwar détente smiled favorably on younger candidates for political office who fought in "the good war." All the victorious presidential candidates from 1960–92, with the exception of Ronald Reagan, had respectable service records in the U.S. Navy: John F. Kennedy, Lyndon B. Johnson, Richard Nixon, Gerald Ford, Jimmy Carter, and George H. W. Bush. Service records or the lack of them would continue to be controversial in President Bill Clinton's relations with the U.S. Army, especially, and would resurface in the 2004 presidential election in the exchanges over the relative merits of the incumbent president, George W. Bush, who did not serve in Vietnam, in comparison with that of the Democratic Party candidate, Senator John Kerry, a decorated Vietnam War veteran.

Given the importance of military service to candidates, it was hardly unexpected that the Second World War's higher commanders—mostly generals—would pursue political careers. Former Army Chief of Staff Marshall served as secretary of state (1947–49), setting a precedent whereby, after 1945, retired military men were often preferred candidates for this office, and as secretary of defense (1950–51) in the Truman administration. Dwight D. Eisenhower served two terms as president (1953–61); at the beginning of his political career, Eisenhower appeared ideologically ambiguous, and could have gained either the Democratic or Republican nomination. His instincts proved to be more conservative, however. He was committed to fiscal conservatism and "small government," suspicious of the civil rights movement, and hostile to high defense expenditures. Eisenhower's policies were subject to scathing criticism by some generals, most notably Maxwell D. Taylor in his *The Uncertain Trumpet* (1959). In 1961 John F. Kennedy summoned Taylor from retirement to become chairman of the Joint Chiefs of Staff.

Civil Military Relations since Vietnam

Compared with the MacArthur controversy during the Korean War, a civil-military consensus held up to the strain of conducting the Vietnam War reasonably well—until it was clear the conflict could not be won. By December 1969, however, the notion became popular that the errors of the war were due, as *Time* magazine explained in a feature exploring the army's "stab-in-the-back complex," to civilian leaders forcing military men to fight with "one hand tied behind their back." Another popular scapegoat was the media, which was accused of corroding support for the war by mischievous reporting, although most news agencies (both print and television) had been consistent supporters of the war. By the 1980s, however, the military had changed its tack and drew very different lessons that advised less, rather than more, force.

The reaction of all three services to the humiliation of defeat in Vietnam ushered in a new period of civil-military tensions. An initial solution was expressed in the Powell Doctrine, which resolved that the United States should never again intervene militarily unless victory was virtually guaranteed, and should always plan an "exit strategy"—a euphemism for retreat. Its author, General Colin Powell, then chairman of the Joint Chiefs of Staff, seemed to demand a right of veto over policy which echoed McClellan's practice and Upton's complaints.

At the same time, the armed services had given ground to technically minded civilian think tanks and the private sector. Many tasks were contracted out to private firms and such business techniques as management models and systems analysis were increasingly employed. Under Robert S. McNamara, secretary of defense from 1961–67, the value of military experience had been subordinated to earlier, similar, techniques, advanced by "whiz kids" equipped with slide rules. But, from the 1990s onward, civilianization represented a major assault on the military ethos; in short, the military could be treated as "just another profession." Other armed forces with comparable traditions, like the British, faced similar threats.

The Future of Civil Control

The armed forces reacted to such challenges with a politically alert response that exploited unprecedented levels of public support evident since the Gulf War of 1991. Senior officers did not hesitate to express partisan political opinions. The habit of endorsing presidential candidates began with Admiral William J. Crowe for Clinton in 1992. Powell and General Norman Schwarzkopf, former commander in chief of the U.S. Central Command and overall commander in the Gulf War of 1990–91, supported Robert Dole in 1996; the majority of the senior military supported George W. Bush in 2000 (and Powell served as his first secretary of state). In December 2007, more than 100 retired admirals and generals (with 54 of them at four-star rank) endorsed Senator John McCain for the Republican nomination.

It is therefore ironic that the most bitter recent political tussle between the armed forces and a presidential administration should be with that of the party that the military supported at the polls. Opposition to Secretary of Defense Donald H. Rumsfeld escalated as the 2003 invasion of Iraq touched off a long war. In April 2006, a group of retired senior officers launched a scathing attack on Rumsfeld, violating the principle laid down by George Marshall that disputes should never be made public until the administration concerned has left office.

Such events pose serious questions for the future of civilian control. The military risks being seen as just another political lobby that invites purges of its senior ranks. In 2007–8, criticism of the role of General David Petraeus as the "front man" of the Bush administration's policy in Iraq hinted that the neutrality of the armed forces, and especially the U.S. Army, had become suspect. Scholars have detected a rise in the "militarization" of American society, and fear that the army again stands apart from the mainstream of American society. Officers frequently voice hostility to what they see as a hedonistic society that contrasts unfavorably with their own ethos. This shift to increased politicization, Richard H. Kohn has argued, can only be arrested when civilians especially regard the armed forces with renewed knowledge and sympathy. Such knowledge cannot be assumed to exist among the members of any one political party. Donald Rumsfeld provoked more hostility than any other secretary of defense for 40 years. Servicemen and women must also reflect on the price paid for forfeiting political neutrality.

See also war and politics.

FURTHER READING. James G. Blaine, *Twenty Years of Congress*, 2 vols., 1884–86; Marcus Cunliffe, *Soldiers and Civilians: The Martial Spirit in America, 1775–1865*, 1968; Peter D. Feaver and Richard H. Kohn, eds., *Soldiers and Civilians: The Civil Military Gap and American National Security*, 2001; Don Higginbotham, *George Washington and the American Military Tradition*, 1985; Samuel P. Huntington, *The Soldier and the State: The Theory and Politics* of Civil-Military Relations, 1957; Richard H. Kohn, "The Danger of Militarization in an Endless 'War' on Terrorism," Journal of Military History 73 (January 2009), 177–208; Idem, "The Erosion of Civil Control of the Military in the United States Today," Naval War College Review 55 (Summer 2002), 9–59; Idem, "Using the Military at Home: Yesterday, Today and Tomorrow," Chicago Journal of International Law 4 (Spring 2003), 165–92; Anne C. Loveland, American Evangelicals and the U.S. Military, 1942–1993, 1996; Brian Holden Reid and Joseph G. Dawson III, eds., "The Vistas of American Military History, 1800–1898," special issue, American Nineteenth Century History 7 (June 2006), 139–321; Richard Rovere and Arthur M. Schlesinger Jr., General MacArthur and President Truman: The Struggle for Control of American Foreign Policy, 1952, reprint, 1992; Maxwell D. Taylor, The Uncertain Trumpet, 1959; Emory Upton, The Military Policy of the United States, 1904, reprint, 1968; Russell F. Weigley, "The American Military and the Principle of Civilian Control from McClellan to Powell," Journal of Military History 57 (October 1993), 27–58; Idem, "The Soldier, the Statesman and the Military Historian," Journal of Military History 63 (October 1999), 807–22.

BRIAN HOLDEN REID

Articles of Confederation

The Articles of Confederation and Perpetual Union, drafted in 1776, formed the first written constitution of the United States, in which the 13 newly independent states entered "into a firm league of friendship with each other, for their common defense, the security of their liberties, and their mutual and general welfare, binding themselves to assist each other, against all force offered to, or attacks made upon them, or any of them, on account of religion, sovereignty, trade, or any other pretense whatever." Known to history as the unfortunate predecessor of the federal Constitution of 1787, the articles have generally had a bad reputation, for on the eve of the 1787 convention the Congress they created had virtually ceased to function. In the estimation of Federalist critics, the articles provided for a system of federal government that was "radically vicious and unsound," requiring not amendment but "an entire change in its leading features and characters."

Despite these failures, which even the friends of state sovereignty were often willing to concede, the Articles of Confederation are nevertheless highly significant. Until the Civil War, and even in some measure thereafter, the articles were frequently invoked to justify contending interpretations of the nature of the union and the powers allocated to state and national governments by the 1787 Constitution. Many aspects of the articles found their way into that constitution—the change, as James Madison insisted, consisted "much less in the addition of new powers to the Union, than in the invigoration of its original powers." In the drafting of the Articles

of Confederation, Americans confronted for the first time the great promise—and problems—entailed by the construction of their federal union. The idea that 13 independent sovereignties could elaborate an effective system of cooperation on a virgin continent was inspiring, and augured a new ordering of state relations utterly unlike the European system, with its war-prone and clashing sovereignties.

The drafting of the articles and the subsequent experience of union, however, also showed how difficult it would be to actually establish such a system. From the beginning the union was surrounded, and nearly submerged, by contentious disputes among its states and sections. It was widely believed in Great Britain that no such system of cooperation among the American states could possibly succeed. In 1776, as David Ramsay of South Carolina recalled two years later, "Our enemies seemed confident of the impossibility of our union; our friends doubted it; and all indifferent persons, who judged of things present, by what has heretofore happened, considered the expectation thereof as romantic."

Origin and Purpose

The committee of the Continental Congress charged with drafting articles of confederation first met in May 1776, pursuant to the critical decisions in the first two weeks of May pointing toward a declaration of independence, the pursuit of foreign recognition and assistance, the establishment of new state governments, and the making of the union. Delegates to Congress, conscious that they would be setting vital precedents, had divided on which of these momentous acts should come first, if come they must, but they finally decided in the rush toward independence to do all four things together and at once.

Our understanding of the articles is hobbled by the absence of anything approaching a full record of the debates in either the drafting committee or the Congress. Unlike 1787, when James Madison resolved to take detailed notes of the proceedings, only fragmentary records remain of these debates, though we are assured they were voluminous.

The committee charged with devising terms of confederation issued its report on July 12, 1776, based on a draft in the hand of John Dickinson. Historians differ on the question of how much the initial conception of confederation changed over the next year, as debate over the terms continued in confidential sessions of the Congress. Some argue that the change was substantial, with a decided shift away from national control toward state sovereignty; others insist that the basic character of confederation changed very little between the first and final drafts. Though the finished product lost the provision granting Congress the authority to cut off the extravagant claims of the states with land claims beyond the Appalachians, the initial and final draft each provided for a league of states rather than a centralized government. Neither proposed that Congress be vested with the all-important power of taxation. Each established the dependence of the federal government on the state governments for the requisition of troops and revenues, and each made clear that the rights not surrendered by compact to the federal authority were retained by the states.

The promise of confederation was most eloquently conveyed by John Witherspoon, delegate from New Jersey. Witherspoon saw the union as the working out, under the novel conditions and circumstances of North America, of the "peace plan" tradition in European thought, and he expressed the hope that "a well planned confederacy among the states of America" might "hand down the blessings of peace and public order to many generations." Europe had progressed from its former "disunited and hostile situation" to the "enlarged system called the balance of power." It lay with America to take a step beyond the balance of power "to a state of more perfect and lasting union."

The paradigm shift that Witherspoon described—from balance of power to federal union—conveys a world of meaning and experience intensely relevant to his generation. But it was one thing to state in words this grand and glorious vision, quite another to bring it to fruition. As Witherspoon and others recognized in 1776, and which would be repeatedly echoed thereafter, Americans had a serious security problem, one represented by the likely interaction of the ambitions of foreign powers and internal divisions among the American states. In the absence of lasting confederacy, Witherspoon warned, the peace to follow the achievement of independence would raise the certain prospect "of a more lasting war, a more unnatural, more bloody, and much more hopeless war, among the colonies themselves." Given the profound regional differentiation of the colonies, that grim prospect was a much pondered outcome, and it profoundly conditioned attitudes toward the union.

"The colonies," as John Adams recalled in 1818, "had grown up under constitutions so different, there was so great a variety of religions, they were composed of so many different nations, their customs, manners, and habits had so little resemblance, and their intercourse had been so rare, and their knowledge of each other so imperfect, that to unite them in the same principles in theory and the same system of action, was certainly a very difficult enterprise." The most serious division was between the New England and the southern states. Neither region wished for a separate national identity; but forming a durable union out of these heterogeneous materials often seemed, from 1776 to 1787, to be a virtually hopeless enterprise.

Provisions

The articles, as finally submitted to the states, allowed one vote for each of the 13 states. The compact also allocated burdens according to the value of all land within each state. Both provisions provoked intense disagreement, though, together in the same document they formed something of a compromise. The one-state one-vote provision was disadvantageous to the southern states, led by Virginia, and the provision for dividing the burdens of the war fell most severely on New England. It would allow the southerners, wrote one New Englander, "by their negroes being left at home, [to] till their lands and git Bread & Riches, while some other States may be greatly distressed." The formula assessing burdens according to land value had been resorted to in preference to the more obvious criterion of population because the delegates were unable to reach agreement over how to count slaves, the discussion of which had disclosed the fundamentally incompatible perspectives of North and South.

A key provision, adopted at the urging of Thomas Burke of North Carolina, held, "Each state retains its sovereignty, freedom, and independence, and every power, jurisdiction, and right, which is not by this Confederation expressly delegated to the United States, in Congress assembled." By the same token, the United States did enjoy authority over those matters imparted to it by the confederation. Despite the absence of a clause empowering Congress to use force against recalcitrant states, some Americans believed that such a power was implicit in the confederation. Thomas Jefferson, a later apostle of nullification, noted in 1786, "When any one state in the American Union refuses obedience to the Confederation by which they have bound themselves, the rest have a natural right to compel them to obedience."

The articles provided that 9 out of 13 states were necessary in order to reach decisions on important matters, a provision adopted in order to ensure "a due Balance" among the states and sections. Without the agreement of nine states, Congress could not "engage in a war, nor grant letters of marque or reprisal in time of peace, nor enter into any treaties or alliances, nor coin money, nor regulate the value thereof, nor ascertain the sums and expenses necessary for the defense and welfare of the United States, or any of them, nor emit bills, nor borrow money on the credit of the United States, nor appropriate money, nor agree upon the number of vessels of war, to be built or purchased, or the number of land or sea forces to be raised, nor appoint a commander in chief of the army or navy."

Perhaps the most unusual feature of the Articles of Confederation is the resemblance it had to the "constitution of the British empire," as the Americans had come to understand it. That mixture of executive, judicial, and "federative" powers that, in the American theory, had belonged to king and council, were basically given to "the United States in Congress assembled"; those powers that belonged to the legislatures of the provincial colonies passed to the newly founded states. In the traditional theory of the British constitution, the king enjoyed the powers of war and peace and of leagues and alliances that John Locke had identified with the "federative power." This authority went to the Continental Congress under the articles, which excluded the states from everything touching on foreign relations. By the same token, the arrangement the Americans made among themselves displayed the same dependence on the provincial legislatures that, in their view, had characterized the imperial constitution. While Congress was to propose, the states were to dispose. Unlike the Congress established by the 1787 Constitution, which was undoubtedly a legislative body, the Congress of the Confederation is best thought of as a "plural Executive" or "deliberating Executive assembly" that would be the agent rather than the master of the states.

Controversy and Crisis

When independence was declared, the expectation among many congressmen was that Articles of Confederation would be rapidly drafted and ratified. In fact, it took 16 months, until November 1777, for the articles to be submitted to the states for approval, and it was not until 1781 that consent was received from all 13 states (with the last hold-out, Maryland, succumbing to pressure from the French minister to the United States).

This sequence of events created an anomalous constitutional situation for the American states and, both at the time and subsequently, aroused much disagreement over what it meant. In effect, the American states had agreed to get hitched in 1776 but experienced grave difficulties and delays in reaching agreement on the terms. What was their constitutional relationship during this time of declared mutual love but not yet fully licit union? Until March 1781, the Articles of Confederation were not binding on the American states, but the states were nevertheless bound together by the sacred promises of the Declaration of Independence, which Jefferson would later call "the fundamental act of union of these states." Nationalists in later years argued that Congress from 1776 to 1781 actually enjoyed its authority from a revolutionary grant given to it by the American people; states' righters countered that no such people were recognized in the formal terms of union and that Congress before 1781 could scarcely be thought to have more authority than it enjoyed after ratification.

Another great debate in which the Articles of Confederation and Perpetual Union figured was just how permanent the union really was. In arguing that the union preceded the states, nationalists sought to counter any assumption that the states might enjoy a right to nullify federal laws within their jurisdiction or to secede from the union. The union, in their view, was perpetual. This perspective, however, was complicated by the fact that when the Federal Convention proposed revised terms of union, it violated the amendment procedures of the Articles of Confederation. Instead of requiring unanimous consent, as the articles had done, the federal Constitution would enter into operation and allow for amendments with the consent of three-fourths of the states. This was either a flagrant violation of constitutional propriety or a stark admission that the old union had ceased to exist. It was on the latter ground that the Federalists rested their case for the Constitution, but that, in turn, implied that the union was not perpetual and could be changed or dissolved by the acts of the states.

These now somewhat obscure controversies were once of commanding interest to Americans, and indeed formed part of the preliminaries to the Civil War. Whatever conclusion might be reached as to the validity of the contending cases in theory, little disagreement exists that, in practice, the Articles of Confederation institutionalized a huge gap between what Congress was responsible for doing and what it could actually accomplish. In the artful summary of one historian, Congress "could ask for money but not compel payment; it could enter into treaties but not enforce their stipulations; it could provide for raising of armies but not fill the ranks; it could borrow money but take no proper measures for repayment; it could advise and recommend but not command." It was the paralysis in government produced by that gap that provided the chief impetus on the road to the Philadelphia convention. Despite these acknowledged deficiencies, the 1783 Treaty of Paris securing American independence was achieved under the government provided by the articles; so, too, was the 1787 Northwest Ordinance establishing the terms under which western territories would be settled and admitted into the union.

A Distant Mirror

The 1787 federal Constitution had many imitators in foreign lands, but it is the "weak" and "defective" version of American federal union that most resembles international organization in the twentieth century. The boast sometimes heard in American history that America's federal union would be the model and beginning of the federation of the world proved only half right: modern international organizations (such as the United Nations, the North Atlantic Treaty Organization, and the European Union) are saddled with allocations of power and authority that mimic the articles in their bold aims and weak structures, leaving these associations always in danger of either disintegration or ineffectiveness. In the 1990s, the American political philosopher Benjamin Barber held that the Articles of Confederation had surprising relevance in dealing with the world of globalization, with its contending forces of profound interdependence and fanatical tribalism. The dilemma of modern governance—of nation-states that are too large for the small things in life and too small for the big things—shows that the generic problem the Articles of Confederation were intended to address remains very much with us. Repelled by visions of both international anarchy and a universal state, the contemporary world seems fated to experience all over again the trials and tribulations of states that bind themselves in "firm leagues of friendship" while reserving to themselves the maximum degree of autonomous action.

See also Bill of Rights; Constitution, federal.

FURTHER READING. Benjamin R. Barber, *Jihad vs. McWorld*, 1995; Murray Forsyth, *Unions of States: The Theory and Practice of Confederation*, 1981; H. James Henderson, *Party Politics in the Continental Congress*, 1974; David C. Hendrickson, *Peace Pact: The Lost World of the American Founding*, 2003; Jerrilyn Greene Marston, *King and Congress: The Transfer of Political Legitimacy, 1774–76*, 1987; Richard B. Morris, *The Forging of the Union, 1781–1789*, 1987; Paul C. Nagel, *One Nation Indivisible: The Union in American Thought, 1776–1861*, 1964; Peter S. Onuf, "Anarchy and the Crisis of the Union," in *To Form a More Perfect Union*, edited by Herman Belz, Ronald Hoffman, and Peter J. Albert, 272–302, 1992; Idem, "The First Federal Constitution: The Articles of Confederation," in *The Framing and Ratification of the Constitution*, edited by Leonard W. Levy and Dennis J. Mahoney, 82–97, 1987; Jack N. Rakove, *The Beginnings of National Politics: An Interpretive History of the Continental Congress*, 1979.

DAVID C. HENDRICKSON

B

banking policy

Banking policy has been debated in the United States since Alexander Hamilton and Thomas Jefferson squared off in George Washington's cabinet over the first Bank of the United States. Banks are depository financial institutions: people and firms deposit money in these intermediaries, which, in turn, lend it to other people and firms. Banking policy aims to ensure safety for depositors and borrowers and the financial soundness of banks. But there is more at stake than the banking industry. Banks allocate capital among the competing claims of individuals and firms, industries and regions, pursuing social goals and economic development. Further, the banking process is closely related to the nature and availability of the money supply, thus banking policy has long been entangled with monetary policy.

The big issues at stake are pragmatic and political. What arrangements will *work well* to provide and allocate money and credit? What implications do alternative arrangements have for the *distribution of power*: When do banks have too much economic power or political influence? U.S. banking policy debates have been about the *structure* of banking organizations—banks and regulatory agencies—as well as about rules that constrain their *practices*. Some of the organizations launched or redesigned in those debates are gone, but most remain. In the twenty-first century, banking firms include commercial banks and savings banks, savings and loan associations (S&Ls), and credit unions. Three federal agencies regulate commercial banks: the Office of the Comptroller of the Currency in the Treasury Department attends to national banks; the Federal Reserve System has responsibility for state banks that are its members; and the Federal Deposit Insurance Corporation (FDIC) oversees nonmember state banks. Federal S&Ls are supervised by the Office of Thrift Supervision, also in Treasury, while credit unions are overseen by the independent National Credit Union Administration. Public agencies in the states supervise and regulate depository intermediaries chartered under state laws. The Deposit Insurance Fund in the FDIC insures deposits in banks and S&Ls, while credit unions have a separate deposit insurance fund. Two rediscount institutions—Federal Reserve Banks and Federal Home Loan Banks—lend to depository intermediaries of all types. How did we get here?

First Bank of the United States

The first Bank of the United States was chartered by Congress in 1791. Alexander Hamilton, secretary of the treasury, proposed the bank to provide credit for economic development and a reliable circulating medium and to assist the government as fiscal agent. At the time, and until establishment of the Federal Reserve System more than a century later, what should comprise the circulating medium remained at issue. Provisions in the new Constitution had ended issuance of paper money by the states. The national government had taken up the practice during the Revolution, but Hamilton wanted to stop it, arguing that the temptation to run the printing presses excessively would be irresistible in an emergency. Bank notes, on the other hand, issued in the process of commercial lending, would not be inflationary. In laying out the bank's design, Hamilton identified dimensions of bank structure and practice that policy makers have manipulated in pursuit of workable institutions throughout U.S. history: capitalization, ownership, governance, and permissible assets and liabilities.

Thomas Jefferson, then secretary of state, led the opposition. Jefferson championed an agrarian economy, and so rejected the importance of aggregating capital for the development of manufacturing and commerce. Neither did he see merit in increasing circulating medium with bank notes. As a "hard money" (gold and silver, also called specie) advocate, Jefferson viewed paper money as inflationary regardless of whether it was issued by a bank or a government. But in a letter to George Washington disputing the bank's constitutionality, he rested the weight of his objection on its evils as a corporation. Jefferson opposed corporations as artificially contrived entities for the private accumulation of wealth. The economic inequality they engendered would threaten political equality. Jefferson indicted the first Bank of the United States as a corporation, and because the new Constitution did not explicitly grant Congress the power to charter corporations, charged that it was unconstitutional. Nonetheless, Washington signed the statute establishing the Bank.

The Bank of the United States operated from 1791–1811, augmenting capital and the money supply and serving as the government's fiscal agent, as planned. But in response to the unanticipated increase in the number of state-chartered banks, from four to over one hundred, it developed the additional function of de facto state bank regulator. As its charter approached expiration, President James Madison supported renewal, but a majority of Jefferson's Republican Party defeated it in Congress in 1811.

Second Bank of the United States

Over the next five years, the number of state banks doubled; they issued paper notes used as currency and drove inflation. As specie disappeared from circulation and efforts to sell Treasury notes to fund the

War of 1812 largely failed, the government accepted state bank notes but found it difficult to use them across the states to pay soldiers and buy supplies. In a pragmatic consensus, Congress chartered a second Bank of the United States in 1816 to provide for a "uniform currency," which meant adequate but not inflationary levels of currency and credit available throughout the United States. John Calhoun developed the positive argument for the bank's constitutionality on which centralized monetary policy rests into the twenty-first century: the Constitution gives Congress authority to "coin money" and "regulate the value thereof." Bank paper had become money, and though the founders had not foreseen this, they had intended to provide authority to regulate whatever served as money.

The second Bank of the United States performed poorly at first. It fed the boom that followed the War of 1812 and then contributed to the financial panic of 1818–19. But under Nicholas Biddle, who became bank president in 1823, it was widely viewed by contemporary policy makers as effective. Andrew Jackson nevertheless vetoed the bill renewing its charter in 1832. He argued that the corporate charter provided a monopoly on banking with the government's deposits and that the bank's economic power resulted in political influence. Efforts to override the veto failed and the second Bank was wound down as its charter expired in 1836.

State Banks
In 1833 Jackson directed Treasury Secretary Roger Taney to transfer government deposits from the Bank of the United States to selected state banks. Some chroniclers have interpreted this as favoritism for "pet banks" or an example of Jackson's support for states' rights. But Jackson opposed incorporated banking in the states as well as at the national level. He believed that the mechanisms involved in using bank notes as money inherently robbed common people. Jackson's solution was to return to hard money. Accordingly, his administration used government deposits in state banks as leverage to prohibit bank issuance of small notes and to require payment in specie on demand.

By the eve of Jackson's bank veto, state legislatures had chartered some 400 banks. Like Congress, they used banks to aggregate capital and provide commercial credit, a circulating medium, serve as the state's fiscal agent, and regulate other banks. Pragmatic legislators also used banks to finance public improvements and state operations, and to ensure credit for agriculture. They initially responded to Jackson's bank veto by chartering more banks and enlarging existing banks. But following the Panic of 1837, a partisan rift opened. A majority of Democrats moved to Jacksonian opposition to all incorporated banking. Whigs insisted that banks were needed, at a minimum, to provide capital for economic development. The issue in the state banking debates changed from how to design banks to whether to charter them at all.

The institutional outcome of these debates was the "free bank." This model emerged in New York as a compromise among Jacksonian opponents of all incorporated banking, free enterprisers who objected to requiring legislative authority to bank, and supporters of regulated banking. To address charges of monopoly, New York's free banking law was a general law, permitting anyone to bank who met its requirements. To protect noteholders, a new bond-backed currency was devised. A bank deposited bonds of public jurisdictions with the state's comptroller. If the bank refused to pay hard money on demand for its notes, the comptroller was to sell the bonds and redeem the notes.

National Banks
With the Civil War, banking policy returned to the agenda in Washington. Treasury Secretary Salmon P. Chase sold bonds, mostly to banks, to finance the war, and insisted that they pay in specie. By late 1861, major banks had no more specie and the government was confronted—as in the War of 1812—with the need for a uniform currency acceptable across state lines. Chase requested and Congress passed the National Currency Act of 1863, repealed and replaced by the National Bank Act of 1864. The statute aimed in the short run to finance the war but ultimately to achieve a national currency without raising Jacksonian specters of private power run amok in a single national bank or a currency wildly over-issued by many state banks. Modeled on the states' free banking laws, the National Bank Act provided for privately owned banks that would issue bond-backed currency. Minimum capitalization of these banks depended upon size of place, but all were very small compared to the first and second banks of the United States. The statute established the Office of the Comptroller of the Currency in the Treasury Department to regulate national banks and issue the currency.

Banks chartered under the National Bank Act became significant actors in the U.S. economy, but the approach did not result in the unified national banking system that was expected. To motivate state banks to convert to national charters, Congress placed a prohibitive tax on their notes. But as state banks learned to make loans in the form of deposit credit, legislatures returned to chartering banks to meet needs not well served by national banks, notably credit for agriculture, real estate, and local business. The distinctive U.S. dual banking system emerged. The National Bank Act did not result in one currency either. State bank notes disappeared, but since national banks were not operational quickly enough to meet the government's need for Civil War cash, the Treasury issued notes, dubbed "greenbacks." Greenbacks circulated with national bank notes, short-term U.S. bonds, gold and gold certificates, silver and silver certificates.

Institutional arrangements framed by the National Bank Act served the expanding economy poorly in the decades following the Civil War. Farmers' interests were ravaged as commodity prices declined in a long deflationary trend. In the populist critique that developed, the problem was the return to the gold standard, which arbitrarily limited the money supply, in tandem with bank control of credit allocation. The National Bank Act's pyramiding reserve arrangements (country banks held reserves in city banks, which in turn held reserves in larger "reserve city" banks) were charged with channeling every community's money to big banks in the East—the "money trust"—which loaned it to stock market speculators. In a reversal of the Jacksonian anti-inflation stance, farmers called for expanding the money supply through means subject to government—not bank—control, including greenbacks and remonetizing silver. In the realigning election of 1896, Democratic presidential candidate William Jennings Bryan championed free coinage of silver against supporters of the gold standard. The Democratic Party became home to farmers in the West and South, while erstwhile Democrats who favored the gold standard moved into the Republican fold to form a party system that stood until the New Deal.

Business and banking interests also indicted the National Bank Act's currency and reserve provisions. In their critique, these arrangements provided no leverage for countering the debilitating business cycles and financial panics that plagued the economy. The bond-backed currency was inelastic. It should be replaced with currency backed by bank assets and issued in the process of extending short-term commercial credit; the supply was expected to expand and contract automatically in keeping with productive needs (the "real bills" doctrine). Reserve provisions, which required that each bank *keep* reserves, should be changed to facilitate *using* reserves.

Federal Reserve System
More than 40 years after the National Bank Act, the Panic of 1907 and the severe contraction that followed finally provoked the Federal Reserve Act of 1913. This statute reflected compromises of ideology and interest as policy makers tried to design arrangements that would work. Old Guard Republicans and eastern bankers proposed a privately owned central reserve bank with monetary policy discretion. Conservative Democrats and small business agreed with private ownership but feared Wall Street control; they called for decentralized reserve banks and believed that self-regulating asset currency made monetary policy discretion unnecessary. Bryan Democrats insisted on government control of any reserve system and government-guaranteed currency. Determined to achieve banking reform, President Woodrow Wilson brokered compromises. The Federal Reserve Act established 12 regional Federal Reserve Banks owned by commercial bankers, a Federal Reserve Board (the

Fed) comprising presidential appointees to regulate reserve banks, and new Federal Reserve notes backed by the assets of the bank that issued them and guaranteed by the government. National banks were required to join the Federal Reserve System; state banks were permitted to join.

The Federal Reserve System did not prevent the Great Depression or widespread bank runs. Indeed, easy money policy in 1927 and 1928, deployed under leadership of the Federal Reserve Bank of New York, was a factor in the speculative boom in the stock market that ended with the crash of October 1929. Once retrenchment was under way, an indecisive Federal Reserve Board permitted the money supply to contract along with the economy, intensifying the downward spiral into Depression. The Banking Act of 1935, introduced at the insistence of President Franklin Roosevelt's Fed chairman Marriner Eccles, responded to these mistakes by strengthening the Federal Reserve Board and subordinating the Federal Reserve Banks. The statute empowered the Board to wield the known instruments of discretionary monetary policy. Bank reserve requirements, previously fixed in the Federal Reserve Act, could be adjusted by the Fed within a statutory range. The discount rate, which had been the purview of the separate Federal Reserve Banks, became subject to Board approval. Open market operations, unknown when the Federal Reserve Act was passed in 1913, had been "discovered" in practice by the Federal Reserve Banks. Resolving a tug of war between the reserve banks (banker control) and the Federal Reserve Board (public control), the legislation vested authority to use this tool in a newly constituted Federal Open Market Committee, effectively controlled by the Board.

Depression-Era Changes to Depository Institutions
In the Banking Act of 1933 (the Glass-Steagall Act), Congress took aim at banking practices which had contributed, along with the Fed's easy money policy, to the stock market crash. As the stock market boom gained steam, large banks had financed the underwriting of securities (stocks and bonds), thus reaping fees; made loans to insiders for speculation in securities; *and* peddled securities to the public. To address this conflict of interest, the statute erected the "Glass-Steagall wall" that prohibited commercial bank involvement with investment banking (securities dealers). To restore public confidence in bank safety, it required deposit insurance for commercial banks. Funded with premiums paid by banks and backed by a government guarantee, the Federal Deposit Insurance Corporation (FDIC) is a public corporation that pays depositors if a bank cannot.

Depression-era legislation also put home ownership finance on a firmer footing. Savings and loan associations (S&Ls) were community-based depository intermediaries, chartered under state laws, devised to provide fixed-rate, fully amortizing loans for home ownership. The bipartisan Federal Home Loan Bank

Act of 1932 established 12 regional Federal Home Loan Banks to make loans to S&Ls so that S&Ls could meet depositors' withdrawal pressure and borrowers' credit demand. Legislation in 1933 created a federal charter, and a 1934 statute provided for S&L deposit insurance.

Credit unions moved onto the national policy agenda during the Depression as well. Underpinned by a populist philosophy, credit unions are cooperatives, mutually owned by depositors. The Federal Credit Union Act of 1934 authorized a federal charter, which made it easier to organize credit unions in states with nonexistent or unwieldy enabling laws. In 1970, federal legislation gave them deposit insurance and an independent regulator.

Deregulation

These Depression-era banking arrangements stood for decades but were increasingly challenged by macroeconomic dynamics, financial market innovations, and shifting ideology. Inflationary spikes in the 1960s and stagflation in the 1970s led to "disintermediation": bank and S&L depositors transferred money to new money market instruments in pursuit of higher interest, while big borrowers went elsewhere for loans. Advocacy for deregulation gained ground among elites. The rationale was that easing asset and liability constraints would facilitate soundness in individual depository institutions, and that unleashing competition in the industry would improve macroeconomic efficiency. In 1971, President Richard Nixon's Commission on Financial Structure and Regulation (the Hunt Commission), laid out a comprehensive deregulatory reform agenda which was largely implemented over the next two decades.

The bipartisan Depository Institutions Deregulation and Monetary Control Act of 1980 phased out interest rate ceilings on deposits and substantially eliminated states' usury ceilings, permitted S&Ls and credit unions to offer checking accounts, and expanded banks' asset powers. At the same time, to increase monetary policy leverage, the statute extended the reach of the Fed. All depository institutions became subject to the Fed's reserve requirements and gained borrowing privileges. In 1982 the Garn-St. Germain Act moved further in the direction of expanding depository institutions' asset and liability options.

Whether due to too much deregulation or too little, in the 1980s much of the S&L industry collapsed, and its insurance fund went bankrupt. Commercial banks got into trouble too: several large banks failed and the bank insurance fund dipped into the red. The Financial Institutions Reform, Recovery and Enforcement Act of 1989 resolved the S&L crisis. It replaced S&ls' original deposit insurer with a new fund located in the FDIC, and S&ls' independent regulator with a new agency located in the Treasury Department. These changes moved toward the Hunt Commission objective of consolidating S&L and commercial bank regulation. In 1991 the Federal Deposit Insurance Corporation Improvement Act recapitalized the bank insurance fund and established new risk-based deposit insurance premiums: banks could compete aggressively but would need to pay a commensurate price for deposit insurance. In 2006, the S&L and commercial bank deposit insurance funds were merged into a single Deposit Insurance Fund.

In addition to easing asset and liability constraints and standardizing regulation across classes of depository institutions, the deregulatory agenda called for easing barriers to entry into banking. State and federal bank regulators progressively undermined restrictions on interstate banking and branching rooted in the Jeffersonian-Jacksonian-populist fear of concentrated wealth. The Riegle-Neal Interstate Banking and Branching Efficiency Act of 1994 eliminated what was left of these restrictions. In 1999, Congress ticked off the last major item on the deregulatory agenda: ease barriers to entry across the lines between banking and other financial services. The Financial Institutions Modernization Act (Gramm-Leach-Bliley Act) demolished the Glass-Steagall wall between commercial banking and the securities industry and removed the prohibition, dating from 1956, on banks dealing in insurance.

Under the "modernized" regulatory framework, bank size increased dramatically, and organizations of nationwide and regional scope combined banking with securities underwriting and brokerage and insurance. These organizations would be tested in terms of the same fundamental issues that Hamilton and Jefferson debated: Do they *work well* to achieve the goals of banking policy? Are they *too powerful* in the economy or in democratic politics?

In the financial crisis of 2008, deregulated U.S. banking failed its first significant test. At the root of the crisis were the large volume of subprime residential mortgages originated after 2000 and resulting waves of defaults and foreclosures. These loans were extended with inadequate attention to borrowers' ability to repay and had features, like variable interest rates, which had been mostly eliminated by Depression-era regulatory moves but reappeared with deregulation. The loans were assembled into pools on the basis of which mortgage-backed securities were issued. Three large banks heavily involved in subprime mortgage lending failed in 2008. Most subprime mortgages, however, were originated not by banks but by mortgage brokers and mortgage bankers, their way paved by banking deregulation. Similarly, securitization was mostly provided not by commercial banks and S&Ls, but by Wall Street investment banks. Even so, commercial banks were major *buyers* of the mortgage-backed securities built on low-quality mortgages—and this is the link between inadequately regulated mortgage lending, even outside of banks, to the failure of banking in 2008. As commercial banks realized that they could not assess one another's safety and soundness due to exposure to mortgage-backed securities, interbank lending, and therefore lending to business customers in the real economy, ground to a halt. The open question in banking policy is whether policy makers had learned, this time, that unregulated financial capitalism will—sooner or later—undermine the real economy.

See also business and politics; economy and politics.

FURTHER READING. Thomas F. Cargill and Gillian G. Garcia, *Financial Reform in the 1980s*, 1985; Robert A. Degen, *The American Monetary System: A Concise Survey of Its Evolution since 1896*, 1987; Susan Hoffmann, *Politics and Banking: Ideas, Public Policy, and the Creation of Financial Institutions*, 2001; Donald F. Kettl, *Leadership at the Fed*, 1986; Robert Kuttner, *The Squandering of America: How the Failure of Our Politics Undermines Our Prosperity*, 2007; Robert E. Litan, with Jonathan Rauch, *American Finance for the 21st Century*, 1998; James Livingston, *Origins of the Federal Reserve System: Money, Class, and Corporate Capitalism, 1890–1913*, 1986; John M. McFaul, *The Politics of Jacksonian Finance*, 1972; J. Carroll Moody and Gilbert C. Fite, *The Credit Union Movement: Origins and Development, 1850–1980*, 2nd ed., 1984; Irwin Unger, *The Greenback Era: A Social and Political History of American Finance, 1865–1879*, 1964; Lawrence J. White, *The S&L Debacle: Public Policy Lessons for Bank and Thrift Regulation*, 1991; Jean Alexander Wilburn, *Biddle's Bank*, 1967.

SUSAN HOFFMANN

Bill of Rights

On September 25, 1789, the first Congress sent a packet of 12 constitutional amendments to the states. Two years later, ten of these amendments became part of the Constitution after Virginia's ratification provided their necessary approval by three-fourths of the states. Over time, these amendments came to be known collectively as the Bill of Rights, and their adoption is generally portrayed as a critical concluding act in the story of constitutional reform that began with the Federal Convention of 1787. Since the early twentieth century, the interpretation of the rights enumerated in the first eight amendments, along with the equal protection and due process clauses of the Fourteenth Amendment (ratified in 1868), has emerged as the richest and most controversial realm of modern constitutional jurisprudence.

At the time of their adoption, however, the amendments were as much an anticlimax to the great constitutional debate of the late 1780s as its culmination. The major changes that the anti-Federalist critics of the Constitution sought in 1787–88 involved the structure of the new federal government and the division of power between the Union and the states. The limited scope of the amendments that James Madison introduced in the House of Representatives on June 8, 1789, hardly satisfied the anti-Federalists'

deeper concerns. Nor did most of the Federalist supporters of the Constitution who dominated the new Congress agree that amendments were necessary. It took a fair amount of hectoring from Madison even to get his congressional colleagues to consider the subject of amendments. Once Congress sent the amendments out for ratification, it took the states much longer to approve the ten articles that were adopted than it had to act on the original Constitution.

Once ratified, the amendments were largely forgotten. The Bill of Rights imposed restrictions only on the national government, not the states. Well into the nineteenth century, most of the governance that affected the daily lives of Americans occurred at the level of the states and local communities, where the federal guarantees did not apply. As the scope of federal activity gradually expanded after the Civil War, the national Bill of Rights slowly began to develop its own constitutional jurisprudence. But the critical evolution came later, after the Supreme Court, developing what is known as the Incorporation Doctrine, construed Section I of the Fourteenth Amendment to apply the protections enumerated in the federal Bill of Rights against state and local governments. In the 1960s and 1970s, a slew of decisions extended this doctrine almost comprehensively.

The Tradition of Declarations of Rights

The belief that bills of rights were an essential safeguard of liberty occupied a prominent and venerable place in Anglo-American constitutional thinking during the seventeenth and eighteenth centuries. The classic example was Magna Carta, the famous agreement between the protesting barons of England and the domineering King John. Its negotiation in 1215 was thought to mark the moment when an English nation began to recover the ancient liberties it had lost in 1066, when William the Conqueror sailed from Normandy to impose the yoke of feudal rule on a free people. To this way of thinking, a bill of rights was a compact negotiated between a ruler and his subjects. It was not so much the source of the rights they claimed as proof and confirmation that they already possessed the liberties and privileges in question.

There were other helpful examples of such documents of more recent vintage. In 1628, at an early point in the great constitutional controversies between the Stuart monarchy and its opponents, Parliament had presented King Charles I with a Petition of Right meant to affirm fundamental rights dating to Magna Carta and beyond. In 1689 the new monarchs William and Mary accepted a Declaration of Rights framed by the so-called Convention Parliament as an implicit condition of their accession to the throne after the flight of Mary's father, James II. Once legally reenacted by Parliament later that year, it became formally known as the Bill of Rights. Closer to home, many individual colonies had their own declarations of rights, often reiterating the customary rights and liberties that they and their English countrymen claimed but also including other statements of special importance to particular provinces.

There is no simple way to categorize the statements these documents could contain. In contemporary usage, a declaration of rights could combine broad principles of governance and general affirmations of natural rights to life, liberty, and property with the specific protections of common law procedures of trial and adjudication. Equally important, constitutional thinking before the revolutionary era did not regard statements of rights as legally binding commands that formally limited the power of government. Instead they identified principles and procedures that rulers *ought* to respect and follow. But the leading principle of Anglo-American constitutionalism after 1689 was the idea of legislative supremacy, which meant that the Crown, the executive branch of government, could no longer be allowed to assert the power to make law unilaterally, as a mere expression of royal will. The best way to protect the rights and liberties of a people was to empower and enable their duly elected representatives to act as lawmakers. A second security lay in the power of juries to prevent royal judges from deciding cases on their own authority. The right to vote for representatives and to serve on juries offered the best political safeguards a free people could enjoy.

The Revolutionary Controversy

In the mid-eighteenth century, these views were commonly held in both Britain and its American colonies. The great imperial controversy that began with the parliamentary Stamp Act of 1765 and ended with Americans declaring independence a decade later exposed the limited utility of bills of rights as instruments for checking power. The controversy pivoted on the British claim that the legislative supremacy of Parliament trumped the colonists' belief that they could be taxed and governed only by the acts of their elected representatives. Appealing to their colonial charters and statements of rights was only one of many ways in which the colonists tried to prove they were exempt from the jurisdiction of Parliament. There were occasional suggestions that the dispute might be resolved by negotiating an American bill of rights to clarify the respective powers of empire and colonies. But the colonists could not overcome the dominant principle of British authority: that Parliament was the supreme source of law within the empire. If the colonists were loyal subjects of that empire, they must ultimately acknowledge its sovereignty over them.

The Americans would not acknowledge such sovereignty, and war came in April 1775, followed by the decision for independence 15 months later. During this final crisis, legal government effectively collapsed in most of the colonies, replaced by a network of extra-legal committees, conventions, and congresses. By early 1776, many Americans recognized that independence was inevitable, and individual colonies began petitioning the Continental Congress for permission to create new legal governments to replace both the revolutionary committees and the old colonial institutions. That would require writing constitutions to establish institutions grounded on republican rather than monarchical principles.

In the process, eight states adopted declarations of rights to accompany the new constitutions they were drafting. In three states (Pennsylvania and North Carolina in 1776, Massachusetts in 1780), these declarations became integral parts of the new constitutions. In others, they remained independent documents of uncertain authority. Some states, like New York, while not adopting distinct declarations, did include articles specifying particular rights in the constitutional text.

Whatever form these statements took, they were not initially regarded as firm commands that the new governments were fully obliged to obey. Their original purpose was more political than legal. In a literal-minded way, Americans in 1776 saw themselves emerging from the condition known as a "dissolution of government," a situation well described by John Locke a century earlier. In that condition, a people exercising their natural right to form a compact of government were entitled and indeed expected to state the principles on which they were acting. By stating their rights, a people could remind themselves, their descendants, and their rulers of the basic purposes of the government they were forming. Hopefully, the rulers would not overstep the just boundaries of their power. But if they did, the existence of such declarations would enable a people to judge their ruler's behavior and oppose or resist the encroachments of the power of the state upon the liberty of society.

In adopting these constitutions and declarations, the revolutionaries did not immediately abandon the assumptions of legislative supremacy they had inherited from the Anglo-American constitutional tradition. Historically, the major threat to rights was perceived to lie in the unchecked power of the Crown and the great purpose of identifying and protecting rights was to secure the people as a whole, conceived as a collective entity outside of government, from its arbitrary will. The idea that a legislative assembly composed of the people's own representatives could also threaten their rights was not easy to conceive. These early statements of American constitutionalism sometimes included articles affirming the principle of separation of powers, as laid down by the Baron de Montesquieu in his influential treatise *The Spirit of the Laws*. A republican people had a right not to be subjected to a government in which the three forms of power (legislative, executive, and judicial) were concentrated in the same hands. But that did not make all three departments of power equal in authority. The legislature was the dominant branch, and its dominant role included protecting the rights of the people.

Developments after 1776

That inherited understanding was severely tested in the first decade after independence was declared. The war forced the legislatures to unprecedented levels of activity. The measures they adopted to keep the military struggle going intruded on people's lives and liberties in novel and costly ways, through economic dislocations that affected the property rights that Anglo-American thinking had long deemed almost sacred. Inevitably, these laws had a differential impact on various sectors of society, driving criticism of the elected legislatures that faced unpleasant choices in distributing the burden of waging a prolonged and difficult war. As Americans grew more critical of the performance of these governments, it also became possible to think of a bill of rights as a potential restriction on the authority of the people's own representatives.

A second, closely related development at the state level of governance also had a profound impact on American ideas. Calling a written charter of government a constitution did not by itself make such documents into supreme fundamental law. The constitutions drafted in 1776 were not only written in haste but also promulgated by the provincial conventions that drafted them, and not submitted to the people for ratification. In this sense, they did not embody a form of law higher than ordinary legislation, but were merely statutes, admittedly of exceptional importance, but still potentially subject to revision by later sessions of the legislature. They were not, in other words, constitutions in the exalted sense of the term: supreme law that would set benchmarks against which ordinary acts of government could be measured.

The movement to find a way to distinguish constitutions as supreme law began in Massachusetts and led to an important procedural breakthrough. Two conditions had to be satisfied, several Massachusetts towns argued, for a constitution to become fully constitutional. First, it had to be drafted by a special body elected for that purpose alone. Second, it then had to be ratified by the sovereign voice of the people, assembled in their town meetings. This doctrine took hold with the adoption of the Massachusetts Constitution of 1780, and marked a milestone in American constitutional theory and practice. Thomas Jefferson, among others, elaborated on this idea in his *Notes on the State of Virginia*, first published in France in 1784.

These developments raised provocative questions about the value and authority of bills of rights. How could a declaration or bill of rights operate as an effective restraint on the people's own representatives? If constitutions were regarded as fundamental law, unalterable by ordinary acts of government, could the authority of bills of rights also be enhanced by following the precedent of the three states that integrated their statements of rights into the text of the constitution proper? If that happened, declarations of rights could operate less as statements of principle and more as legal commands, leaving open the possibility of their enforcement by the independent judiciaries the new constitutions had also created.

James Madison's Reformulation of the Problem of Rights

When Jefferson sent copies of his *Notes on Virginia* back home, he also asked James Madison whether the work would be appropriate for an American audience. One of Jefferson's concerns was that his adverse comments on the Virginia constitution would be taken amiss. After reading the work closely, Madison agreed with Jefferson's charge that the constitution had no greater authority than a statute. Madison also took the leading role in persuading the Virginia legislature to enact the Bill for Religious Freedom that Jefferson drafted in the late 1770s. Among other things, that bill affirmed that freedom of conscience—the right to believe whatever one wished about religious matters—was a fundamental natural right that no state could legitimately abridge. But the concluding paragraph of the bill also restated the constitutional dilemma that Jefferson had addressed in *Notes on Virginia*. A right recognized only by statute could also be repealed by statute, because one legislature had no power to bind its successors.

Jefferson and Madison had first met in 1776, while serving on the committee on religion in the lower house of the new Virginia legislature. Both were products of the eighteenth-century Enlightenment that regarded the previous centuries of religious persecution and warfare as a blight on European and Christian civilization. Their shared commitment to the principles of freedom of conscience and separation of church and state formed one basis of their deep personal friendship. But to Madison, even more than Jefferson, the idea of protecting an individual right to believe whatever one wished in matters of religion contributed to a broader rethinking of the problem of protecting rights in a republican society.

The basis for this rethinking came from Madison's experience in the Virginia legislature (1784–86). Notwithstanding his success in securing passage of the Bill for Religious Freedom, his three terms of legislative service convinced him that representative assemblies could not be relied upon to act as guardians of the people's rights. Too many recent acts seemed designed to promote one set of interests over another, without giving due attention to the rights of the losing minority. This was especially the case when matters of property were at stake. Madison was responding to the enormous upsurge in economic legislation that the war had made necessary, and which still plagued Americans in the mid-1780s as they wrestled with the public debt the war had created and other economic problems that accompanied the return of peace.

For Madison, as for most Anglo-American thinkers of the age, the protection of property was a fundamental purpose of society, as John Locke had made clear a century earlier in his *Second Treatise of Government*. But Madison combined his original commitment to freedom of conscience with his new appreciation of the problem of economic legislation to recast the problem of protecting rights in republican terms. The traditional problem under monarchical governments had been to protect the people against the arbitrary power of the Crown. But in a republic, where executive power seemed weak and derivative, the greater danger would come from a far more powerful legislature. Moreover, the real force driving the adoption of unjust laws would come not from the ambitions of the legislators but from the people themselves—or rather, from majorities among the people that would use legislative power to act unjustly toward disfavored minorities. Coming as he did from the upper stratum of Virginia's ruling class of landed slave owners, Madison was thinking of the interests of his own class. But his insight remained a profound one. In a republican government, unlike a monarchy, one could not naively assume that the people would unite to protect their collective rights against the concentrated power of the state. Historically, bills of rights had been seen as instruments negotiated between the people's representatives and their monarchical rulers. What use would they be when representatives and rulers were one, and when the people were the very source of the problem?

One other critical conclusion followed from this analysis. If the people themselves could threaten private rights, at which level of government would they pose the greater danger: national or state? Here Madison first formulated his famous argument about the problem of the "factious majority"—that is, a majority of citizens claiming democratic authority to rule but acting in ways inimical to either the "public good" or "private rights." The smaller the society, Madison reasoned, the easier it would be for such mischievous majorities to form. It followed that such majorities could coalesce more easily within the limited confines of the states than would be the case in the "extended republic" of an expansive and expanding federal union. National government should prove less "factious" than state government, and rights more secure at the national level than within the smaller compass of the states or localities. Moreover, Madison also understood that the states would remain the real locus of daily governance. If, then, one hoped to make rights more secure, a way had to be found to enable the national government to check or correct the unjust misuse of power at the state level. As he prepared for the Federal Convention that would meet at Philadelphia in May 1787, Madison reached the radical conclusion that the best way to protect rights would be to give the national legislature a negative on state laws, akin to the detested veto the British crown had enjoyed over colonial legislation.

The Convention's Great Oversight
In somewhat diluted form, Madison's proposal for a negative on state laws was part of the Virginia Plan

that formed the basic agenda for the deliberations at Philadelphia. By mid-July, that proposal was dead, and with it, Madison's hope that the adoption of a federal constitution would provide a means for dealing with the problem of protecting rights within the individual states. Ten days after the convention rejected the negative, it adjourned to allow a Committee of Detail to convert the resolutions adopted thus far into a working draft of a constitution. In its own deliberations, that committee briefly considered prefacing the constitution with some statement of principles akin to the state declarations. But as one of its members, Edmund Randolph, noted, the situation of 1787 was not the same as that of 1776. "We are not working on the natural rights of men not yet gathered into societies," Randolph observed, "but upon those rights, modified by society, and *interwoven with* what we call the rights of states."

The convention did include a few clauses protecting specific rights in the completed draft of the Constitution: the right to trial by jury in criminal cases; a prohibition on the suspension of habeas corpus except "in Cases of Rebellion or Invasion"; the guarantee that "Citizens of each State shall be entitled to privileges and Immunities of Citizens in the several States." A prohibition on religious tests for office-holding would open the right to participate in government to all, but the fundamental right to vote was left a matter of state, not federal, law. Similarly, a prohibition on state laws impairing the obligation of contracts was consistent with Madison's desire to prevent the states from enacting legislation inimical to vested rights of property (since such laws would advantage debtors over creditors).

Important as these individual provisions were, they did not amount to a comprehensive statement of fundamental rights. On September 12, five days before the convention adjourned, Elbridge Gerry and George Mason (the author of the Virginia Declarations of Rights of 1776) moved to correct that omission by proposing the adoption of a general bill of rights. By that point, most delegates knew that the two men would refuse to sign the completed Constitution. After cursory debate, their motion was rejected. The delegates apparently did not believe that the absence of a bill of rights would impair the prospects for ratification.

The convention's Federalist supporters (as they soon became known) quickly realized this was a major political miscalculation. Anti-Federalists almost immediately made the absence of a declaration of rights a rallying point against the Constitution. This was hardly their sole objection, nor even the most important. But the convention's failure to protect rights seemed to confirm the charge that the Constitution was in reality designed to consolidate all effective power in one supreme national government, leaving the states to wither away and the people's liberties at the mercy of distant institutions they could not control.

An early speech by James Wilson, a framer and leading Pennsylvania Federalist, inadvertently reinforced the opponents' concerns. Speaking outside the statehouse where the Constitution was written, Wilson argued that it would actually have been dangerous to provide explicit protection for such cherished rights as freedom of press or conscience. Properly understood, the Constitution vested only specific, explicitly designated powers in the new government. Providing for the protection of rights whose exercise the Constitution did not in fact threaten, Wilson argued, would imply that such a power had indeed been granted.

This was a lawyer's argument, and politically it proved counterproductive. By Wilson's logic, there was no need for the Constitution to protect the Great Writ of habeas corpus either; yet it did. By being too clever by half, Wilson only reinforced anti-Federalist suspicions that the Constitution was a lawyer's document that skillful politicians could exploit to run roughshod over the people's liberty.

With Wilson's October 6 speech serving as a lightning rod, the omission of a bill of rights became a staple theme of anti-Federalist rhetoric. Drawing on the provisions found in the state declarations, they argued that the Constitution should be amended to provide explicit protection for an array of rights, ranging from freedom of conscience and press to the "liberty to fowl and hunt in seasonable times, on the lands they hold" and "to fish in all navigable waters." Most Federalists remained unpersuaded. The convention might have miscalculated, but that did not mean that a constitution lacking such articles was truly defective.

In arguing for the adoption of rights-protecting amendments, anti-Federalists straddled a line between the traditional ideas of 1776 and the new constitutional norms that had emerged since. On the one hand, they did not fully imagine that a bill of rights, if adopted, would create a set of commands or rules that citizens could enforce at law, for example, by asking a court to provide a specific remedy when a right was infringed. Bills of rights were still regarded as *political* documents, a device for enabling the people to act in their political capacity to check abuses by government. This was a very traditional understanding. But many anti-Federalists also embraced the new way of thinking about written constitutions that had developed since 1776. By arguing that rights would remain insecure unless they were explicitly included in the constitutional text, they abandoned the older view that rights derived their authority from multiple sources, such as nature or custom. A right that was not incorporated in the text of a constitution might cease to be either a constitutional or a fundamental right.

The decisive fact making the adoption of a bill of rights more likely, however, was not the force of anti-Federalist reasoning. It was, rather, that narrow divisions in several key states—most notably Virginia

and New York, the tenth and eleventh to ratify—inclined Federalists to agree to *recommend* the consideration of an array of amendments to the first Congress to meet under the Constitution. This concession was the price of ratification. To portray it as a firm bargain, as many histories have done, probably goes too far. It was more an expectation than a deal, and since Federalists successfully insisted that the states should ratify the Constitution without conditions or contingencies, they got the better of the deal.

Madison Again

Madison left the federal convention believing that its rejection of his proposed negative on state laws would leave the protection of individual and minority rights in the same vulnerable position as before. Though his disappointment eased over time, he shared the general Federalist misgivings about the utility of bills of rights. "Experience proves the inefficacy of a bill of rights on those occasions when its controul is most needed," Madison wrote Jefferson in October 1788. "Repeated violations of these parchment barriers have been committed by overbearing majorities in every State." Those majorities that concerned him were more popular than legislative, for in Madison's analysis, the problem of how best to protect rights required that one first identify where "the real power in a Government lies." In a republic, that power resided with "the majority of the Community," and he simply doubted that such popular majorities would allow a mere declaration of rights to deter them from pursuing their violations of "private rights."

This analysis of rights was, again, political rather than legal. But political considerations of a different kind were driving Madison to accept the idea of adding rights-protecting amendments to the Constitution. He had taken that position in the Virginia ratification convention in June, and he soon repeated it publicly during a tough race for election to the House of Representatives. Yet even then, Madison thought that the chief value of a declaration of rights would lie in its effect on public opinion. As the rights declared gradually acquired "the character of fundamental maxims of free Government" and were "incorporated with the national sentiment," they would work to "counteract the impulses of interest and passion" that would still drive most citizens. It took a suggestion from Jefferson, writing from France, to prod Madison to concede that such articles might also enable the independent judiciary the Constitution would create to act as a "legal check" against abuses of power.

Consistent with his public statements, Madison assumed the burden of convincing the new Congress to take up the subject of amendments. This proved an uphill struggle. Federalists had gained easy control of both houses in the first federal elections, and few of them believed they were obligated to take up the question of amendments. For their part, anti-Federalists knew they would be unable to secure the structural changes to the Constitution they desired most, and without those, a mere statement of rights did not seem so important. Thus it fell to Madison to push what he privately called "the nauseous project of amendments."

In preparing for this task, Madison reviewed all the amendments that the various state ratification conventions had proposed. From this list of over 200 proposals, he culled the 19 clauses he introduced in the House of Representatives on June 8, 1789. Two of his proposals related to congressional salaries and the rule for apportioning House seats among the states. The rest were concerned with identifying constitutional rights. They would not appear as separate, supplemental articles but rather be inserted at those points in the Constitution where they seemed most salient.

In drafting these clauses, Madison avoided the principle-propounding language of 1776. He did include one set of articles that would have added a second preamble to the Constitution, this one affirming the fundamental right of a sovereign people to form and reform governments designed to secure "the enjoyment of life and liberty, with the right of acquiring and using property; and generally of pursuing and obtaining happiness and safety." The House eliminated this familiar language. The Senate subsequently rejected another article that Madison called "the most valuable amendment on the whole list": a proposal to prohibit the states from violating "the equal right of conscience, freedom of the press, or trial by jury in criminal cases." This proposal was consistent with Madison's belief that the greatest dangers to rights would continue to arise within the states.

The remaining proposals formed the framework for the amendments that Congress ultimately sent to the states nearly four months later. One major change in format came at the repeated urging of Roger Sherman of Connecticut, who insisted that Congress must not tamper directly with the original Constitution that he, like Madison, had helped to draft. Rather than interweave the amendments in the existing text, as Madison had proposed, they should be treated as supplemental articles. Sherman, a dogged politician, had some difficulty getting his suggestion accepted, but eventually it prevailed. Turning the amendments into additional articles rather than interwoven ones made it easier over time to think of them as a bill of rights, each of whose separate articles addressed some distinct or integral realm of civil liberty or governance.

Records of the House debates on the amendments suggest that few members regarded their approval as an urgent priority. They did not discuss how the amendments, if ratified, would be enforced, nor did they speculate about the ways in which the constitutional entrenchment of rights might lead to an expanded judicial role in their protection. Mostly, they tinkered with Madison's language before sending the amendments on to the Senate in August. The Senate

did some editorial work of its own, and final revisions were made in a conference committee.

One especially noteworthy change occurred here. Madison had originally proposed a religion article, stating, somewhat awkwardly, "The civil rights of none shall be abridged on account of religious belief or worship, nor shall any national religion be established; nor shall the full and equal rights of conscience be in any manner, or on any pretext infringed." The House changed the second clause to read, more simply, "Congress shall make no law establishing religion." The Senate then narrowed that language to a mere prohibition on "laws establishing articles of faith or a mode of worship." The conference committee on which Madison sat took a much simpler tack still, rejecting these efforts at precision with a broad ban holding, "Congress shall make no law establishing a Religion, or prohibiting the free exercise thereof."

That broader and simpler wording has left ample room for continuing interpretation and controversy, but its original significance should not be overlooked. Religion was one realm of behavior that governments had always believed should remain subject to state support and public regulation. By approving the dual principles of nonestablishment and freedom of conscience, the adopters of the religion clause were endorsing the far-reaching principle that matters of religious organization and belief should henceforth fall entirely within the sphere of private activity, where individuals, acting freely for themselves or in free association with others, could be counted upon to decide what was best. Here was the most telling example of what the broader American commitment to individual liberty and private rights could mean in practice.

Beyond Ratification

For well over a century after its ratification, the Bill of Rights was not a significant element in American constitutional jurisprudence. The "Congress shall make no law" formula of the First Amendment did not prevent the enforcement of the Sedition Act of 1798, which criminalized seditious speech directed against the administration of John Adams. In 1833, the Supreme Court held, in *Barron v. Baltimore*, that the numerous protections of the first eight amendments applied only against acts of the national government, not those of the states. One noteworthy doctrinal development did take place in 1878. In *Reynolds v. U.S.*, a case involving the Mormon practice of plural marriage, the Court held that the free exercise clause of the First Amendment covered matters of religious belief but not all practices that followed from religious doctrine. In reaching this decision, the Court relied on the writings of Jefferson and Madison, the two Revolutionary-era leaders who had written most eloquently on the subject.

That decision came at a time, however, when the Court was blunting the potential reach of the

Fourteenth Amendment, framed as the Reconstruction of the South was just getting under way. Section 1 of the amendment declared, "No state shall make or enforce any law which shall abridge the privileges or immunities of citizens of the United States." It was entirely plausible to read "privileges or immunities" to include the clauses of the federal Bill of Rights. Some of the amendment's leading authors and supporters believed that the *Barron* case of 1833 had been wrongly decided, and if their views were accepted, the amendment could have been read as a basis for enforcing the federal guarantees against the states generally. But in the early 1870s, with support for Reconstruction visibly waning, the Court began adopting a more restrictive approach, and the promise of the Fourteenth Amendment remained unfulfilled.

Only after World War I did the Court gradually begin to develop the so-called Incorporation Doctrine, under which it held that many, though not all, clauses of the original Bill of Rights could act as restraints on the actions of state governments. Freedom of speech was arguably the first right to be nationalized in this way, beginning with the 1925 ruling in *Gitlow v. New York*. The leading proponent of a wholesale incorporation of the Bill of Rights was Justice Hugo Black, the former Alabama senator and New Deal supporter who became the mid-century Court's leading libertarian. Although his brethren on the Court initially shied away from adopting his broad views, by the 1960s, the animus to apply most of the protections of the Bill of Rights against the states became one of the defining features of the jurisprudence of the Warren Court. Decisions on a whole array of subjects, from school prayer to the "revolution in criminal justice" brought about by expansive interpretation of the numerous procedural rights enshrined in the Fourth, Fifth, and Sixth Amendments, helped make the Supreme Court a lightning rod for political criticism.

The Court's most controversial modern decisions were those promoting desegregation (beginning with *Brown v. Topeka Board of Education* in 1954) and a woman's right to abortion (*Roe v. Wade* in 1973). But the nationalization of the Bill of Rights also played a critical role in the denunciations of "judicial activism" that have resonated so deeply in American politics since the 1960s, and that show no sign of abating. Whether debating school prayer or the right to bear arms or the unusual cruelty of the death penalty, Americans treat the clauses of the Bill of Rights as subjects for political discussion as well as judicial definition and enforcement. This is a different notion of the political value of bills of rights than the one that Federalists and anti-Federalists disputed in the late 1780s. But it helps to explain why "rights talk" remains so prominent an element of our political discourse.

See also Articles of Confederation; civil liberties; Constitution, federal.

FURTHER READING. Akhil Reid Amar, *The Bill of Rights: Creation and Reconstruction*, 1998; Patrick T. Conley and John Kaminski, eds., *The Bill of Rights and the States: The Colonial and Revolutionary Origins of American Liberties*, 1992; Leonard Levy, *Original Intent and the Framers' Constitution*, 1988; Jack N. Rakove, *Declaring Rights: A Brief History with Documents*, 1997; Bernard Schwartz, *The Great Rights of Mankind: A History of the American Bill of Rights*, 1992.

JACK N. RAKOVE

bureaucracy
See regulation.

business and politics
For generations the United States has nourished the world's most potent capitalist economy. The United States is also the longest-lived democracy. Their coexistence would seem to suggest that capitalism and democracy, at least in America, go together like love and marriage. But their union has been far from harmonious. At critical moments, relations have deteriorated to the breaking point. Yet for even longer stretches of time, popular sentiment has tacitly endorsed President Calvin Coolidge's 1925 adage that "the business of America is business."

Faith in the inherent virtue of market society is less strictly mercenary than Coolidge's aphorism might suggest. From the origins of the republic to the present day, the free market has promised freedom, in particular, the liberty of the individual to pursue happiness, to dispose of his or her own powers and talents, and to amass private property unencumbered by government or other forms of social restraints. The conviction that the market is the passway to liberty has deep roots in American culture.

But some Americans have always dissented from this faith. Henry Demarest Lloyd, a widely read critic of the country's new plutocracy during the late nineteenth century, observed that "liberty produces wealth and that wealth destroys liberty." Lloyd was worried about the power of great industrial combines and financial institutions to exterminate their competitors, snuffing out the freedom the market pledged to offer to all. He was also bothered by the inordinate influence of these economic behemoths over the country's political institutions.

Capitalism and democracy, by their very natures, establish two rival sources of power and authority: one private, the other public. Large-scale corporations control and dispose of vast resources upon which the whole of society depends. The liberty associated with market society provides the rationale for this otherwise extraordinary grant of private empowerment over decisions that carry with them the greatest public import. Democracy operates according to a contradictory impulse, namely, that matters affecting the public welfare ought to be decided upon by popularly delegated and publicly responsible authorities.

It might be assumed that, in any showdown, democracy would trump capitalism, if only by virtue of sheer numbers. Quite the opposite has often been the case. Market society presumes the privileged position of private property as the vessel of liberty. Even a thorough-going liberal democracy like the United States has been reluctant to challenge that axiom. Precisely because business is so vital to the well-being of society, government has tended to bend over backward to encourage and promote the same business institutions that Lloyd cautioned were driven to destroy liberty.

Business and the Birth of the Nation

The fundamental question about the relationship between capitalism and democracy has been asked since the beginning of the nation. One of the most famous controversies about U.S. history was ignited by the historian Charles Beard in his 1913 book, *An Economic Interpretation of the Constitution of the United States*. Beard argued that the architects of the new nation who gathered in Philadelphia in 1787 were chiefly motivated by a desire to protect and further the interests of the country's dominant economic classes: merchants, bondholders, plantation owners, and the like. The Constitution they authored established a central government empowered to regulate interstate and foreign commerce, to secure the credit worthiness of the infant republic, to levy taxes, to implicitly legitimate chattel slavery, and to ward off overzealous assaults on the rights and prerogatives of private property—the sort of democratic upheavals, like Shays's Rebellion, that had made life under the Articles of Confederation too precarious for the well-off.

Beard's interpretation echoed a primal antagonism about the future of America that began with the country's birth and raged with great intensity all through the 1790s, turning founding fathers into fratricidal enemies. Alexander Hamilton, the first secretary of the treasury, envisioned a formidable commercial future for the new republic. He imagined a nation fully engaged in international trade, one with thriving manufacturing establishments and cosmopolitan urban centers where high culture and high finance would mingle. All this would happen thanks to the catalytic role of the federal government and under the guidance of the country's rich and well-born.

Three proposals in particular embodied the secretary's bold plan for the country's future: a "Report on the Public Credit," which called on the new federal government to assume at face value the nearly worthless revolutionary and postwar debt obligations of the Continental Congress and the states; the creation of a Bank of the United States; and a "Report on Manufacturers" that pledged the national government to

help jump-start industrialization. Each in its own way was designed to mobilize the capital resources and active participation of the country's wealthier classes (as well as to attract foreign investment) in turning an underdeveloped country into a rival of the great European powers. Hamilton's view prevailed during the administrations of Washington and Adams.

But some old comrades from the war for independence, men with whom Hamilton had jointly conceived the Constitution, detested the secretary's policies. Thomas Jefferson and James Madison were convinced his proposals would incubate a new moneyed aristocracy that would subvert the democratic accomplishments of the Revolution. They feared precisely what Hamilton desired, namely, a commercial civilization like the one characteristic of the Old World. For all its cultural sophistication and economic vigor, such a society, they argued, was also a breeder of urban squalor and of vast inequalities of wealth and income. It fed a mania about moneymaking and self-seeking that incited moral and political corruption and an indifference to the public welfare.

Jeffersonians, however, did not comprise some eighteenth-century version of back-to-the-land romantics. They too recognized the advantages, even the necessity of trade and commerce. Hardly hostile to the free market, they instead wanted to widen its constituency beyond those circles favored by Hamilton. The most notable accomplishment of Jefferson's presidency was the Louisiana Purchase, which enormously enlarged the potential territory open to freeholder agriculture.

Nor did Jefferson or his successors imagine these pioneering agrarians living in splendid, self-sufficient isolation. Every subsequent administration through the presidency of James Monroe sought to buttress the nation's agricultural foundation by opening up the markets of the world to the produce of American farms. This meant breaking down the restrictions on trade with the rest of Europe and the Caribbean imposed by the British Empire, a policy that led first to Jefferson's embargo on trade with European belligerents during the Napoleonic Wars and eventually to the War of 1812. These drastic measures indicated that the Jeffersonians considered international trade a vital component of a flourishing agrarian republic.

Over time, the infeasibility of the old Jeffersonian persuasion became apparent. Even its most dedicated proponents reluctantly grew to accept that a modern market economy would inevitably bring in its wake dense commercial networks and a complex division of labor, industries, and cities. What nonetheless kept the temperature of political animosity at fever heat for the rest of the nineteenth century was how these warring parties envisioned the role of the government in promoting economic development and keeping the channels of economic opportunity open to all. Even as agrarian republicanism faded from view, its profound suspicion of finance and industrial capitalism remained very much alive, a living indictment of big business as the defining institution of American civilization.

The Age of Jackson

Andrew Jackson, "Old Hickory," seemed the natural inheritor of the Jeffersonian tradition. Jackson waged a dramatic and protracted struggle against an institution that seemed to embody every Jeffersonian nightmare about the rise of a counterrevolutionary moneyed aristocracy. The Second Bank of the United States was better known during the 1830s as "the Monster Bank." It was run by Nicholas Biddle, a blue-blooded Philadelphian. He presided over a quasi-public institution that exercised decisive influence over the country's monetary resources but without a scintilla of public accountability. The president set out to the kill the Monster. Because the bank aroused enormous popular resentment, he eventually succeeded.

Yet it would be a mistake to conclude from the so-called Bank War that antebellum Americans, especially in the North, were hostile to the commercial development of the country in the same way their Jeffersonian ancestors were. On the contrary, they were men on the make. What they most resented about the Monster Bank was the way it limited commercial opportunity rather than opening it up to every man. While they remained wary of ceding the government too much power, they also believed it could and should help to nourish their entrepreneurial ambitions.

Beginning in the antebellum years, government at every level was dedicated to the promotion, not the regulation, of business. The country's whole transportation and communications infrastructure—its roads, turnpikes, canals, wharves, dockyards, bridges, railroads, and telegraph system—were, practically without exception, quasi-public creations. Governments granted them franchises, incorporated them, lent them money, invested in them, provided them with tax exemptions and subsidies and land grants, and even, at times, shared in their management.

Such leaders of the Whig Party as Henry Clay and Daniel Webster sought to make this practice of state-assisted business development the policy of the national government. For this reason, the party commanded the allegiance of the rising business classes, as did the newly created Republican Party, into which the Whigs dissolved. Clay's "American system" of internal improvements and a protective tariff to nurture infant industry also enjoyed significant support among Jacksonian Democrats, but only in the North. Most Southern planters cared strictly about the cotton trade and were hostile to a protective tariff, which could only increase the costs of manufactured necessities and invite retaliation from its trading partners abroad. Because the slave South held the whip hand in the Democratic Party, the American system remained stillborn until after the Civil War. But the general proposition that government ought to be a helpmate to business was already widely, if not universally, accepted.

The Gilded Age

No myth about American history has demonstrated greater durability than the belief that the late nineteenth century was the golden age of laissez-faire. It was then, so the story goes, that a hands-off policy by the government allowed the impersonal operations of the free market to work their magic and turn the United States into an industrial goliath. But actually all branches of the federal government were deeply implicated in that process. Not only did they actively promote the development of a national capitalist economy; they did so in a way that favored the interests of industrial and financial corporations. Thus, the rise of big business was due less to impersonal economic laws and more to man-made ones.

Railroads epitomized how the system worked. Without the land grants, loans, tax exemptions, and subsidies provided by the federal government, it is hard to imagine the extraordinary transcontinental network of rail lines that provided the skeletal framework of the national marketplace. Railroads were to the mid-nineteenth century what the steel industry was a generation later or the auto industry was during the mid-twentieth century: the engine of the national economy driven by the country's dominant business institutions. America's emergence as the world's foremost economy began in this hothouse relationship between business and government.

However, accompanying government largesse were well-documented instances of cronyism and corruption. During the Grant administration, a scandal involving the Crédit Mobilier company, responsible for helping construct the transcontinental railroad, implicated congressmen, cabinet members, and even the vice president in schemes to defraud the government. Similar outrages occurred locally, as with the Erie Railroad in New York, where city councilmen, state legislators, and judges were bought and sold by rival railroad speculators. Such transgressions, however lurid and even illegal, were exceptional. Still, they signaled a more general disposition on the part of the country's political class to align itself with the country's most powerful business interests.

The Republican Party pursued this course most single-mindedly and commanded the loyalty of the emerging class of manufacturers, who particularly applauded the party's staunch support for the protective tariff—a barrier against industrial imports that grew steadily higher as the century drew to a close. The promotion of business, however, was a bipartisan policy. New York merchants and financiers engaged in the export trade tended to be Democrats because they favored free trade rather than a protective tariff. But the leadership of the party, and its two-time president Grover Cleveland, were of one mind with their Republican opponents when it came to defending the gold standard as essential for economic stability.

The late nineteenth century witnessed the emergence of trusts and other forms of industrial combinations all across the economy, from steel and sugar production to the drilling and distribution of oil. These firms exercised extraordinary power over the marketplace and, inevitably, posed a dire threat to the American dream of entrepreneurial independence, inspiring a fierce resistance.

Beginning during the Gilded Age and lasting well into the twentieth century, the antitrust movement was a major influence on American politics. It enjoyed the support of small and medium-sized businessmen and of the growing class of urban middle-class consumers and white-collar workers. It also inspired the political mobilization of the nation's farmers, especially in the South and the Great Plains, who particularly resented the life-threatening power of eastern financiers, the owners of the great railroads that crisscrossed the country, and the commercial middlemen (grain elevator operators, wholesalers, and the like) who dictated terms of credit as well as the costs of shipping, storing, and distributing farmers' produce.

Together, these groups turned to the government for help. During the 1870s and 1880s, they were moderately successful, especially in state politics. Laws were passed regulating and restraining the operations of interstate corporations, particularly the railroads. But all three branches of the federal government were hostile to reform. In a series of landmark cases, the Supreme Court ruled that these regulatory attempts by state governments violated the rights of corporations to due process under the Fourteenth Amendment (which was originally passed to protect the civil rights of emancipated slaves) and also trespassed on the exclusive powers delegated to the federal government to regulate interstate commerce. At the same time, the Senate came to be known as "the Millionaires Club," because its members seemed far more solicitous of the needs of major corporations than they did of their ordinary constituents.

Finally, the executive branch made its most formidable resource—the coercive power of the armed forces—available for the protection of corporate property. In addition to the antitrust and farmer movements (most famously the Populist or People's Party of the 1890s), the other great challenge to the profits and preeminence of big business came from the labor movement. The main battle took place on the factory floor, where workers were subjected to a ruthless regime of wage cutting, exhausting hours, and a draconian work discipline. Strikes, some local, some nationwide, in dozens of industries swept across the country in several waves, beginning in the mid-1870s and continuing to the end of the century. Again and again, businesses were able to count on state and federal judges to issue injunctions that outlawed these strikes, and on governors and even the president of the United States to send in state militias and federal troops to quell them when they continued. President Cleveland's decision in 1894 to use the army to end the strike of the American Railway Union against the Pullman Company is the most famous instance of the latter; it convinced many people that big business had captured the government.

Ironically, most leading businessmen of the Gilded Age initially had no serious interest in politics. They were content to turn to the government for particular favors when needed but otherwise kept aloof from party politics. All that began to change, however, when antitrust, Populist, and labor resistance grew so sizable it could not be ignored.

In the end, the groundswell of popular sentiment in favor of some form of regulation proved irresistible. Frustrated at the state level, reformers redoubled their efforts to get some redress from the federal government. The Interstate Commerce Act was passed in 1887 to try to do away with rebates and other forms of railroad market abuse. And, in 1890, Congress approved the Sherman Anti-Trust Act. But in both cases business interests used their political influence to dilute the effectiveness of these laws. By necessity, the nation's commercial elite became more practiced in the arts and crafts of democratic politics.

Indeed, as the century drew to a close, the business community mobilized to defeat its enemies in the electoral arena as well. In 1896 the Democratic Party was captured by elements sympathetic to populism and to antitrust reform and nominated the charismatic William Jennings Bryan as its presidential candidate. But the victory of Republican William McKinley, lavishly supported by leading industrial and financial interests, seemed to put an end to the immediate threat to the economic and political supremacy of big business and to bury along with it the vision of an alternative political economy and social order.

Business and the Progressive Movement

Yet in the early twentieth century, the axis of American politics shifted direction. Once devoted to the promotion of business, government in the Progressive Era turned to its regulation. Odder still, important segments of business and finance welcomed this turn of events as often as they had resisted it. No longer indifferent to or contemptuous of the democratic process, the business community increasingly grew to believe its fate would be decided in that arena.

The presidencies of Theodore Roosevelt and Woodrow Wilson especially marked the era as progressive. Roosevelt was feared by the Republican old guard—figures like the industrialist and politician Mark Hanna and financier J. P. Morgan. And the president was not shy in making known his disdain for such "malefactors of great wealth." His administration initiated the first antitrust lawsuits against such major corporations as Northern Securities (a gigantic railroad holding company) and Standard Oil.

Antitrust prosecutions comprised only a small portion of his attempts at regulating business. Roosevelt's regime achieved such legislative milestones as the Pure Food and Drug Act, the Meat Inspection Act, and the Hepburn and Mann-Elkins laws strengthening the hand of the Interstate Commerce Commission to rein in the railroads. Meanwhile, municipal and state governments in dozens of big cities and states—egged on by muckraking journalists like Lincoln Steffens and Ray Stannard Baker—took on public utility and urban mass transit companies that had been looting government budgets for years.

Woodrow Wilson, elected in 1912, promised to extend the scope of business regulation. He and a chief adviser, future Supreme Court justice Louis Brandeis, were convinced that the rise of big business and finance had worked to choke off opportunity for would-be entrepreneurs, had aborted technological innovations, and, by blocking the pathways of economic mobility, had undermined the institutions of political democracy as well. Wilson took office amid a widely publicized congressional investigation of the so-called money trust, a purported clique of Wall Street investment banks that controlled not only a host of other financial institutions but also many industrial corporations, including United States Steel and General Electric. Soon after the hearings ended, the president signed into law the Federal Reserve Act. It established a quasi-public institution to oversee the nation's monetary system and presumably break the stranglehold of the money trust.

The Wilson administration and a Democratic Congress accomplished other notable reforms of the business system as well. The Clayton Act tried to strengthen the antitrust provisions of the Sherman Act and exempted labor unions from prosecution as conspiracies in restraint of trade, which had been the main use of the earlier law. The new Federal Trade Commission (FTC) broadened the powers of the national government to regulate interstate commerce. The Adamson Act established the eight-hour day for railroad employees. However, the reform momentum stalled when the United States entered World War I in 1917.

Many businessmen and some consumers viewed corporate consolidation of the economy at the turn of the century as a godsend rather than a curse. It would, they assumed, end the competitive anarchy that had produced numerous booms and busts and two severe and protracted depressions during the Gilded Age. Businesses had tried, on their own, to impose some order over the marketplace by forming pools and other informal agreements to control prices, limit production, and share the market among the chief competitors. But such private arrangements to rein in the free market failed as firms could not resist taking advantage of any shift in the market to get a jump on their competitors.

Thus, some industrialists began to look to the government as the only institution with enough authority and legitimacy to impose commercial discipline. The Interstate Commerce Commission and the Mann-Elkins Act drew support not only from smaller businessmen who hoped to get rid of rate discrimination but also from the railroads themselves—as long as they could exercise some control over what the commissioners did and forestall popular pressure for more radical reform. Similarly, major meatpacking corporations welcomed the Meat Inspection Act. By establishing uniform standards of hygiene that their smaller competitors would have to meet, they hoped the act would open up foreign markets that had grown increasingly leery of importing American beef.

All this signaled that businessmen were becoming more politically conscious and organized. Trade associations representing whole industries began lobbying in Washington. The National Civic Federation—organized by Mark Hanna, Andrew Carnegie, and other leading industrialists—tried to impart a more conciliatory mood into the brittle, often violent relations between labor and capital characteristic of the Gilded Age. Other national business organizations, including the United States Chamber of Commerce (USCC) and the National Association of Manufacturers (NAM), formed to represent the political desires of smaller business, especially to thwart legislation sympathetic to labor.

Thus, on the eve of World War I, many businessmen and politicians had come to accept the need for some degree of regulation to supplement government promotion of private enterprise. However, differences within the business community and between it and the government over the nature and extent of that regulation left many questions unresolved.

Then the war fatefully shifted the terrain on which this tense relationship unfolded. On the one hand, the country's need to mobilize its resources restored the social reputation of big business, which produced most of the munitions and other goods for the American Expeditionary Force and its European allies. On the other hand, such a massive mobilization of private assets demanded a level of coordination that only the government could impose. The War Industries Board, created by President Wilson and run by financier Bernard Baruch, initiated a degree of state intervention into the private sector that would have astonished most of the radical critics of the previous century. Although this apparatus was quickly dismantled once the war ended, the experience with economic planning and supervision left a legacy many would turn to during the next national emergency.

More immediately, however, it was the political rehabilitation of big business that left its mark on the Jazz Age following the war. The Republican administrations of Warren Harding, Calvin Coolidge, and Herbert Hoover deferred to the corporate world. Businessmen were hailed as the nation's wise men who seemed to have solved the age-old problem of the business cycle, ushering in a new era of permanent prosperity.

Antitrust prosecutions virtually ceased. The Supreme Court severely restricted the power of the FTC to define methods of unfair competition. The regulatory vigilance of the government was relaxed in what turned out to be a tragic turn of events.

The Great Depression and the New Deal Order

No crisis in American history, save for the Civil War, presented as grave a national trauma as did the crash of 1929 and the Great Depression that followed. The economic wisdom, social status, moral authority, and political weight of the business community collapsed in a hurry. Until that moment business had generally prevailed in its tug of war with the government and the forces of democracy. But, for a long generation beginning in the 1930s and lasting well into the 1970s, the balance of power was more equally divided.

President Franklin Delano Roosevelt's New Deal never amounted to a single, coherently conceived and executed set of economic policies. It was in a constant state of motion, tacking first in one direction, then in another, pursuing courses of action that were often contradictory. One fundamental, however, never changed: the government must act because economic recovery could not be left to the impersonal operations of the free market. A return to the laissez-faire approach of the old regime was, once and for all, off the table.

Indeed, the Roosevelt administration found itself under relentless pressure from various social movements to challenge the power of big business. A new and militant labor movement spread through the industrial heartland of the country, taking on the most formidable corporations and mobilizing in the political arena to support the New Deal. Small farmers, tenants, and sharecroppers in the Midwest and South defied banks and landlords to stop foreclosures and evictions. Charismatic figures aroused populist emotions against financiers and the wealthy. Huey Long, the demagogic governor and later senator from Louisiana, led a Share the Wealth movement that called for taxing away any income over a million dollars a year. Father Charles Coughlin, the "radio priest" broadcasting from a suburban Detroit Catholic church, electrified millions of listeners with his denunciations of parasitic bankers.

Such democratic upheavals reverberated within the Democratic Party and helped heighten the tension between the Roosevelt administration and major sectors of the business and financial world. They inspired the President's denunciation in 1936 of "economic royalists." Without these upheavals, it is hard to imagine the basic reforms accomplished by the New Deal.

New Deal innovations covered four broad areas affecting the material well-being of Americans: (1) economic security and relief; (2) financial and industrial regulation; (3) industrial reform; (4) economic planning.

The most enduring legislative legacy of the New Deal is the Social Security system. Passed in 1935 by an overwhelmingly Democratic Congress, the Social Security Act, for the first time, established government responsibility for protecting against the most frightening insecurities generated by the free market: a poverty-stricken old age and unemployment. In fits and starts, the New Deal also initiated a series of federal relief measures to address the plight of the jobless and dispossessed in both urban and rural America.

This ethos of social responsibility for the economic security of all citizens continued well beyond the New Deal years. The welfare state continued to expand after World War II, most memorably through the GI Bill, which committed the federal government to subsidizing the education and housing of returning veterans. In the mid-1960s, President Lyndon Johnson's Great Society programs included various antipoverty and urban redevelopment measures—especially Medicare and Medicaid, which addressed the health needs of the elderly and some of the poor. However limited and flawed, such programs represented a major shift in the country's political orientation. They indicated a recognition that the free enterprise system could not be relied upon, by itself, to assure the economic security of the American people.

Rightly or wrongly, most people blamed the Depression on Wall Street, in particular on the reckless speculation, insider trading, and fraudulent practices that allegedly led to the crash of 1929 and to the economic implosion that followed. The resulting demand for the government to closely monitor the behavior of business naturally focused on the financial system. Therefore, the Roosevelt administration and Congress targeted the banking and securities industries. The Glass-Steagall Act of 1933 made it illegal for the same establishment to function both as an investment and as a commercial bank on the grounds that there was an inherent conflict of interest between those two functions—one that had undermined the credibility of the whole banking structure of the country.

The suspect and secretive practices of the stock market were addressed by two securities acts, the second of which established the Securities and Exchange Commission. These reforms demanded of Wall Street a far greater transparency about its operations, outlawed certain kinds of insider dealings, and subjected the nation's chief financial markets to ongoing public supervision.

Business regulation under the New Deal was hardly confined to the financial sector. New agencies like the Federal Communications Commission were created, and transportation and public utility companies found themselves under more rigorous scrutiny. The Public Utility Holding Company Act attempted, without much success, to dismantle corporate pyramids in the electrical power industry that had fleeced consumers and left the underlying companies saddled with insupportable debt. This assault, while abortive, reflected a revving up of antitrust sentiment.

While the politics of antitrust would lose energy in the years ahead, the regulatory momentum of the New Deal order would only grow stronger. By the late 1960s and early 1970s, its emphasis would shift from regulating the abuses of particular industries to policing business in general. New environmental and consumer protection movements inspired deep popular distrust of the business community. Largely composed of middle-class, college-educated professionals, these public interest organizations demanded that corporations be held not only responsible but accountable for their actions. The Occupational Health and Safety Act and the Environmental Protection Act of 1970 and the Consumer Product Safety Commission created in 1972—followed by legislation to clean up the air and water and the toxins of industrial waste—were all passed during the Republican administration of President Richard Nixon, suggesting just how irresistible this regulatory impulse had become.

A third phase of New Deal economic intervention proved just as robust. It is hardly an exaggeration to describe the pre–New Deal system of industrial labor relations as a form of industrial autocracy, especially in heavy industry. Most workers endured long hours at low wages, conditions subject only to the unilateral whim of their employers, who could also hire and fire them at will. The rise of a militant labor movement and the growth of pro-labor sentiment within the Democratic Party during the early years of the Depression resulted in fundamental reform. The National Labor Relations Act (NLRA, or Wagner Act) of 1935 established a form of industrial democracy by inscribing workers' right to organize unions free of employer interference. It proscribed a range of employer behaviors as unfair labor practices and made companies legally obliged to engage in collective bargaining once a union had been established by government-supervised elections. The Wagner Act was supplemented in 1938 by the Fair Labor Standards Act, which set a national standard of minimum wages and maximum hours and outlawed child labor.

Many of those who supported the NLRA did so not just out of a sense of social justice. They believed that reforming the system of labor relations was part of a larger design for economic recovery in which the government would have to play a central role. Unions and minimum wages, they hoped, would restore the mass purchasing power of ordinary Americans and thereby spur production and employment. The idea that government had an overarching role to play in getting the economy moving again was hardly restricted to these areas, however. It inspired the fourth salient of New Deal innovation: economic planning.

The National Industrial Recovery Act (NRA) of 1933—the New Deal's first attempt at general economic recovery—created a form of federally sanctioned corporatism or cartelization, operating not unlike the old War Industries Board of World War I. The system effectively suspended antitrust laws so that big businesses in every industrial sector could legally collaborate in establishing codes of fair competition.

A similar form of government intrusion into the operations of the free market tried to address the depressed state of the agricultural economy. The Agricultural Adjustment Administration established government-sanctioned production controls and acreage allotments that were designed to solve the crisis of overproduction that had led to mass farm foreclosures and evictions all across the country.

At first, many businesses welcomed these forms of economic planning, because they amounted to a form of self-regulation that left big firms in effective control of the government machinery charged with doing the planning. But for just that reason, they were vociferously attacked by smaller businessmen and small farmers. In 1935, the Supreme Court ruled the NRA was unconstitutional. Its demise, however, gave life to different, more democratically minded strategies for government-directed economic recovery.

Members of the New Deal administration were convinced that only government intervention could restart the country's economic engine. The Tennessee Valley Authority (TVA) was created with an ambitious mission to transform the economic and social life of the deeply impoverished trans-Appalachian southeast region. Under the auspices of the TVA, the federal government itself entered the electrical power business, directly competing with private utilities and forcing them to make their own operations more efficient and cost effective. By making electricity available to millions of rural Americans, TVA planners hoped to bring them within the orbit of the modern economy, improving their standard of living and turning them into customers for manufacturers of electrical appliances.

Balancing the federal government's budget had been a central orthodoxy of the old order. In the face of this, the New Deal committed the sacrilege of deficit spending to help get the economy out of its protracted slump. Deficit finance was at the heart of a new economic policy associated with the famous British economist, John Maynard Keynes. Keynesianism located the origins of the Depression in the problem of insufficient demand and argued that this tendency was inherent in modern capitalism. To overcome it, the government had to resort to its powers over fiscal and monetary policy, especially the former. The government's tax policy would redistribute wealth downward, bolstering consumer demand. The "wealth tax" of 1935 was a first attempt to do this by raising taxes on corporations and the wealthy. The Roosevelt administration never fully committed itself to this strategic break with the past, but even its experiments in that direction were pioneering.

During World War II, a version of Keynesianism became the new orthodoxy. Much of the war economy operated under government supervision, was financed with federal loans and cost-plus contracts, and a sizable portion of the new plants and equipment was actually owned by the government. But by putting an end to the Depression, the war also restored the economic and political fortunes of the private sector. Consequently, after the war, the business community managed to rein in the more social democratic variant of Keynesian policy and replace it with a version friendlier to private enterprise. Commercial Keynesianism relied more on monetary policy, that is, on manipulating the money supply and interest rates in responding to the business cycle. The government backed away from any effective commitment to assuring full employment, grew more leery of deficit spending (except in the military sector) and investments in the public sector, and avoided—until the mid 1960s—a broad expansion of the social welfare state. Commercial Keynesianism relied on automatic stabilizers like unemployment insurance to stabilize the business cycle.

The New Deal's groundbreaking efforts at income redistribution and social welfare did inspire the early years of the Lyndon Johnson's Great Society during the 1960s. But the enormous financial burdens of the Vietnam War and America's other military commitments short-circuited those assaults on poverty. Inflation—always the latent danger of deficit spending—haunted the economy as the decade of the 1960s drew to a close. It was easier to cut budgets for poverty programs than to tackle the politically more potent military-industrial complex that President Dwight Eisenhower had warned about in his Farewell Address in 1961.

Business and the Rise of Modern Conservatism

Commercial Keynesianism made business first among equals in the postwar New Deal order. Moreover, some segments of American finance and business had always supported certain New Deal reforms, just as there were elements of the business community that had backed Progressive-Era legislation. Industries that relied on the consumer market and banks oriented to the small depositor were sympathetic to Keynesian approaches that bolstered demand. These businesses formed the Committee on Economic Development in 1942. There were also corporations that supported Social Security as politically inevitable and worked to make the program business friendly. Some northern-based manufacturers backed the Fair Labor Standards Act as a way of eliminating the wage differential that gave their southern-based competitors an advantage. Still, the main business lobbies—the NAM and the USCC—militantly opposed most New Deal reforms.

Then the Keynesian regime entered a terminal crisis at the end of the 1960s. It collapsed for many reasons: the costs of the Vietnam War; the inability of the government's economic managers to stem war-induced inflation; the unraveling of the postwar

system of fixed international exchange rates in 1971; the emergence of powerful industrial competitors in Germany and Japan; the rise of foreign oil-producing nations that hiked energy costs. A protracted period of what came to be called "stagflation" in the 1970s seemed the final refutation of the Keynesian outlook. After all, its adherents had always maintained it was impossible for the economy to suffer simultaneously from inflation and unemployment. By the late 1970s, however, it indubitably was.

Commercial Keynesianism had been a bipartisan persuasion. The reaction against it, however, formed mainly within the Republican Party and culminated in the election of Ronald Reagan to the presidency in 1980. If big business had been the bete noire of the New Deal, big government played that role for champions of the free market counterrevolution to reverse the New Deal.

Restoration of the old order proceeded in several directions at once. Supply-side economics, which in contrast to Keynesianism focused on encouraging investment rather than demand, became the theoretical justification for cutting taxes on corporations and the wealthy and for trimming the social welfare budget and public spending on infrastructure. Both occurred during the two Reagan administrations.

Deregulation became a key watchword of the new regime. It entailed both capturing and dismantling the regulatory apparatus of the federal government. Agencies were increasingly run and staffed by people either directly recruited from the industries they were charged with regulating or by civil servants with decided sympathies for the business point of view. So, for example, presidential appointees to the National Labor Relations Board, beginning under Reagan and continuing during the administrations of George H. W. Bush and his son George W. Bush, ruled repeatedly in favor of businesses charged with unfair labor practices, or they at least tolerated long procedural delays that effectively stymied union organizing and collective bargaining.

Rules were relaxed or not enforced or eliminated entirely in a host of specific industries, including airlines, trucking, telecommunications, and the financial sector. The lifting of rules governing the operations of savings-and-loan banks resulted in the collapse of the whole industry in the late 1980s and the largest government bailout of private enterprise in American history; until, that is, the massive rescue and partial nationalization of the country's leading financial institutions during the meltdown of the country's financial system in 2008.

The drive to deregulate was less successful in the arena of non-industry-specific social regulation, exemplified by the Environmental Protection Agency and the Occupation Health and Safety Administration. Here powerful middle-class constituencies resisted the deregulatory impulse. Still provisions of the Clean Air Act were weakened, the powers of the FTC reduced, and efforts to beef up consumer protections thwarted.

The Democrats put up little effective resistance to such changes. The influence of big business and finance within the Democratic Party had grown steadily after Reagan's 1980 victory. By the 1990s, leading elements within the Democratic Party also favored cuts in the welfare state, deregulation, and monetary and fiscal policies that were designed to please the business community.

Still, the politics of restoration went only so far; modern business had come to rely on the government in certain crucial respects. While paying lip service to the aim of a balanced budget, deficits grew under both Ronald Reagan and George W. Bush, sometimes enormously. In both cases this had to do with a considerable expansion of the defense budget. Even before the Republican counterrevolution, military spending had become big business and a permanent part of the country's political economy. Much of this military production is sustained by government-guaranteed, cost-plus contracts, insulated from the oscillations of the free market.

However, the assault on the New Deal order had accomplished a great deal. Substantial credit for its success must go to the remarkable ideological discipline, self-organization, and political savvy of the business community itself. Beginning in the 1970s, new organizations like the Business Round-table (founded in 1972 and made up the country's top CEOs) worked with established ones like the USSC and the NAM not only to affect public policy but also the underlying values that shaped such policy. Together with such well-funded think tanks as the Heritage Foundation and the American Enterprise Institute, they denounced the profligacy of "tax and spend" liberalism, exposed the "culture of dependency" encouraged by the welfare state, and extolled the virtues of the free market. If the New Deal had been premised on the quest for economic security and a sense of social obligation, the business-sponsored literature of the Reagan and Bush eras help create a large constituency for older values of individualism, risk taking, and self-reliance.

The heightened activities of corporate lobbyists and think tanks were supplemented by an equally spectacular growth of business involvement in elections. A 1976 Supreme Court decision—*Buckley v. Valeo*—established the right of corporations to make unlimited financial contributions to political parties and political action committees. Increasingly, the viability of candidates for public office came to depend on how much money they could raise to wage their campaigns. No one had more money to offer than big business. Even without engaging in corrupt or illegal practices, the machinery of American democracy came to be more and more lubricated by cold cash.

The relationship between capitalism and democracy in American history has been a tumultuous one. It began in mutual suspicion, but then passed through a period when the governing classes considered it their mission to promote the development of business and the national market. The dilemmas of late nineteenth-century free market capitalism led to widespread demands for reform, ushering in the next phase of that relationship in which the government took up the responsibility of regulating business, culminating in the New Deal order. At least until the presidency of Barack Obama, the latest stage shifted the balance of power back in favor of the private sector, but the contemporary business system relies on government intervention and support far more than its nineteenth-century predecessor. Arguably, this latest phase in the relationship between capitalism and democracy was less a return to some imaginary laissez-fair utopia than it was a return to the kind of elitist financial system that Alexander Hamilton proposed at the birth of the republic.

See also banking policy; economy and politics; labor movement and politics.

FURTHER READING. Edward Berkowitz and Kim McQuaid, *Creating the Welfare State*, 1988; Thomas Cochran and William Miller, *The Age of Enterprise*, 1942; Robert Collins, *The Business Response to Keynes, 1929–1964*, 1981; Steve Fraser, *Every Man a Speculator: A History of Wall Street in American Life*, 2005; John Kenneth Galbraith, *The Great Crash: 1929*, 1997; Charles Lindbloom, *Politics and Markets: The World's Political-Economic Systems*, 1977; Drew McCoy, *The Elusive Republic: Political Economy in Jeffersonian America*, 1982; C. Wright Mills, *The Power Elite*, 1956; Kevin Phillips, *Wealth and Democracy: A Political History*, 2002; David Vogel, *Fluctuating Fortunes: The Political Power of Business in America*, 1989; Robert Wiebe, *Businessmen and Reform: A Study of the Progressive Movement*, 1962.

STEVE FRASER

cabinet departments

The first three cabinet departments—the Departments of State, War, and the Treasury—were organized in 1789 by the U.S. Congress at President George Washington's urgent request. The addition of the Department of Homeland Security in 2002 brought to 15 the total number of cabinet departments created since then. Charting the emergence of cabinet departments provides a shorthand guide of sorts to American history. The westward expansion of settlement, the extension of agriculture into unfamiliar environments, industrialization, urbanization, the emergence of the United States as a world power, and the advent of twentieth-century social movements in pursuit of political equality and economic security for all American citizens—each of these trends in American history was eventually reflected in the president's cabinet. Indeed, in a nation with a political culture supposedly premised on a mistrust of "big government," the existence of 15 cabinet departments within the executive branch stands as a frank acknowledgment of reality: there are, in fact, matters that require oversight and management on the part of the federal government. The order in which the cabinet departments were created provides not just a rough indication of the general contours of American history, then, but also suggests how and when Americans arrived at a consensus that the role of the federal government ought to be expanded to address a particular problem.

Political scientists often refer to "inner" and "outer" cabinet departments. Inner cabinet departments are generally understood as those performing essential governmental tasks, including national defense, finance, and enforcement of the law. These were among the first cabinet departments formed. The outer cabinet departments, by contrast, emerged over the course of the nineteenth and twentieth centuries as new and unforeseen problems surfaced. The creation of these cabinet departments often met with controversy and delay, but most Americans have come to accept the role of the federal government in these areas as well.

The Inner Cabinet Departments

The inner cabinet departments perform functions nearly universally recognized as essential for any successful nation-state. These functions include forging relations with foreign nations, providing for the national defense, ensuring a sound financial system, and enforcing the law. Accordingly, during the first months of 1789, George Washington lobbied Congress successfully for the establishment of the Departments of War, State, and the Treasury. President Washington also established the Office of the Attorney General, forerunner to the Department of Justice and the fourth inner cabinet department. The Department of Homeland Security, created in the wake of the September 11, 2001, terrorist attacks on the United States, has arguably been the only addition made to the inner cabinet since 1789.

The Department of State. The Department of State was the first cabinet department created by Congress and is the oldest department in the executive branch. President Washington signed the law creating a Department of Foreign Affairs in July 1789 in order to formulate and carry out the new nation's foreign policy. After Congress placed a number of domestic duties into the new department's portfolio—including the administration of the census and the management of both the U.S. Mint and the nascent Library of Congress—the department was renamed the Department of State in September 1789. Although these domestic obligations were shuttled to other departments during the nineteenth century, the name stuck. Since its inception, the State Department has served as the primary representative of the American government and its citizens in the international community. It assumes responsibility for maintaining diplomatic relations with other nations and assists and protects U.S. citizens traveling or living overseas.

The office of the secretary of state was a prestigious position during the early years of the republic—Thomas Jefferson, James Madison, James Monroe, and John Quincy Adams all used the State Department as a stepping-stone to the presidency. But given its emphasis on foreign policy, it is not surprising that the department itself grew slowly during the early nineteenth century, when isolationism and a focus on continental expansion prevailed. As the United States became a leading exporter of goods in the decades following the Civil War, however, the State Department's consular functions became more important. And as the United States became more involved in hemispheric and then world affairs beginning in the late nineteenth century, the department grew accordingly. State Department officials also took steps to professionalize the department. Written examinations—complete with foreign-language tests—began in 1895. Secretary of State Philander Knox (1909–13) introduced geographic divisions into the organization of the department and encouraged area expertise among its employees. The Rogers Act of 1924 unified the department's diplomatic and consular services, thereby creating the modern Foreign Service of the United States. By World War II, the department was on its way to developing a career-oriented foreign service complete with improved salaries, merit-based promotions, and an increased emphasis on language and cultural training.

The development of the State Department during the World War II and cold war eras was even more notable. The number of employees at the department increased from 1,100 to nearly 10,000 between 1940 and 1950. In 1949, moreover, the department reorganized into geographic bureaus focusing on inter-American, Far Eastern, European, Near Eastern, African, and international organization affairs, reflecting the geographic scope of postwar American foreign policy.

Other additions, such as the Bureau of Economic Affairs (1944), the Bureau of Intelligence (1957), and the Bureau of Cultural Affairs (1960), indicated the wide range of interests that the shapers of U.S. foreign policy had in the rest of the world. And whereas the secretary of state position in the nineteenth century proved to be a prestigious perch from which to launch a bid for the presidency, during these immediate post–World War II years when State Department influence was at its apex, secretaries of state George C. Marshall (1947–49), Dean Acheson (1949–53), and John Foster Dulles (1953–59) pursued cold war policies that endured for more than a generation, profoundly affected the U.S. role in international affairs, and altered American domestic politics. Yet at the very height of its influence, the State Department lost its monopoly on foreign affairs. Three cold war era creations—the Defense Department, the Central Intelligence Agency, and the National Security Council—circumscribed the State Department's power to shape American foreign policy. Secretary of State Henry Kissinger (1973–77) wielded considerable influence in the administration of President Richard Nixon, for example, but this was due as much to his concurrent position as national security advisor as to the power inherent in the office of the secretary of state. Similarly, President George W. Bush's secretary of state, Colin Powell (2001–5), proved unable to restrain the administration's hawkish foreign policy in advance of the 2003 invasion of Iraq.

Nevertheless, the Department of State remains the primary agency in charge of implementing U.S. foreign policy, even if it now competes with other policy actors at the formulation stage. The State Department currently maintains relations with nearly 180 countries, and, in 2007, it had approximately 30,000 employees and a budget of $10 billion.

The Department of the Treasury. Established in September 1789, the Department of the Treasury is the second oldest cabinet department still in existence. The Treasury Department performs many different functions, unified by money. It functions as the chief manager of the nation's financial and economic policies and ensures the solvency of the U.S. government. Its domestic duties include overseeing the collection of taxes and tariffs, allocating budgeted funds, borrowing the money necessary to operate the federal government, safeguarding the integrity of the nation's banks, manufacturing the nation's coins and printing its currency, and advising the president on matters of domestic and international economics.

The Department of the Treasury has historically served as one of the largest law enforcement agencies in the federal government: it enforces federal tax laws and investigates counterfeiting and the evasion of taxes and customs. These responsibilities have remained relatively consistent since 1789, although the department's power to manage the nation's finances naturally increased commensurate with the increasing power of the federal government. The Treasury Department expanded considerably during the Civil War, for example, when secession led both to a precipitous drop in revenue and a costly war to reunite the Union. The Bureau of Internal Revenue (forerunner to the Internal Revenue Service) was established in July 1862 to ensure a steady stream of revenue during the war effort. Similarly, the increased role of the United States in world affairs in the aftermath of the World War II led to an expansion in Treasury Department activities. The department helped shape the 1944 United Nations Monetary and Financial (Bretton Woods) Conference and has remained one of the dominant influences on the International Monetary Fund and the World Bank.

On the other hand, more recent events have stripped the Treasury Department of many of its law enforcement functions. Heightened concerns surrounding national security in the twenty-first century led to the transfer of the U.S. Customs Service and the U.S. Secret Service to the new Department of Homeland Security in 2002; the law enforcement arm of the Bureau of Alcohol, Tobacco, and Firearms was transferred to the Department of Justice by the same Homeland Security Act. This reorganization left the modern Treasury Department with an $11 billion annual budget and 110,000 employees spread throughout the Alcohol and Tobacco Tax and Trade Bureau, the Comptroller of the Currency, the Bureau of Engraving and Printing, the Financial Crimes Enforcement Network, the Internal Revenue Service, the U.S. Mint, the Bureau of the Public Debt, and the Office of Thrift Supervision.

The Department of Defense. Perhaps the most readily identifiable cabinet department, the Department of Defense is responsible for training, equipping, and deploying the military forces that defend the security of the United States and advance the nation's interests abroad. The Defense Department is the largest cabinet department in terms of human resources. It manages 1.4 million active-duty military men and women and 1.2 million Army Reservists and National Guard members. The Defense Department also employs approximately 700,000 civilians. Its budget was $440 billion in 2007, although it remains unclear how much of the costs of the ongoing wars in Afghanistan and Iraq were included in that figure.

The Department of Defense is the direct successor to the War Department, which was originally established alongside the Foreign Affairs (State) Department in July 1789 and was in charge of all land military forces from 1789 until 1947. Concerns over disorganization and inefficiency grew as the Army, Navy, and Air Force developed into discrete military units and made coherent military planning increasingly difficult. Between 1920 and 1945, for example, over 50 bills called for the uniting of the armed forces into a single organization, and concerns about inefficiency and redundancy were only exacerbated by the nation's participation in World War II and the looming cold war.

These anxieties culminated in the National Security Act of 1947, which eliminated the War Department and subsumed the Departments of the Army, Navy, and Air Force under the newly created National Military Establishment (NME). A series of 1949 amendments to this National Security Act reconstituted the NME as the Department of Defense, stripped the service branches of department status, and centralized command and control of all branches of the armed forces under the secretary of defense.

The Department of Justice. Often described as "the largest law firm in the nation," the Department of Justice is charged with enforcing federal laws. As is the case with the Department of Defense, the Justice Department can be traced back to the events of 1789, even though the department itself did not come into existence until much later. In 1789 Congress established the office of the attorney general to represent the interests of the United States at the Supreme Court and to advise the president on legal matters. But the legal work of a growing nation quickly became more than the small office of the attorney general could manage. An avalanche of costly litigation during the Civil War era led to the creation of the Department of Justice.

As established by the Judiciary Act of 1870, the Department of Justice—led by the attorney general—was ordered to conduct the legal business of the federal government, including all civil and criminal cases in which the United States had an interest. The 1870 legislation also established the Justice Department as the primary agency responsible for the enforcement of federal law. This obligation to enforce federal laws has meant that as such laws have moved into new legal territory, so, too, has the department expanded: alongside the original Civil, Criminal, and Tax Divisions, the modern Justice Department also houses Antitrust, Civil Rights, Environment and Natural Resources, and National Security Divisions—all legacies of legal developments in the twentieth and twenty-first centuries.

Also included in the current Justice Department are the Drug Enforcement Administration, the Federal Bureau of Investigation, the Federal Bureau of Prisons, and the U.S. Marshals Service. Since 2003 the department has housed the Bureau of Alcohol, Tobacco, Firearms, and Explosives. In 2007 the Department of Justice employed 110,000 people and had a budget of $23 billion.

The Department of Homeland Security. The Department of Homeland Security's purpose is to safeguard the homeland against catastrophic domestic events, including acts of terrorism as well as natural disasters. The product of the largest governmental reorganization since the National Security Act of 1947 and an amalgam of 22 agencies and bureaus—such as the U.S. Customs Service and the U.S. Secret Service (both from the Treasury Department), the Immigration and Naturalization Service (from the Department of Justice), the U.S. Coast Guard, and the Federal Emergency Management Agency—Homeland Security instantly became the third-largest cabinet department, upon its creation in 2002, with approximately 200,000 employees. Early signs suggest that this reorganization has not been seamless. The department's hapless response to Hurricane Katrina in 2005 raised many questions about its readiness to handle similar natural disasters or a major terrorist attack. The Department of Homeland Security budget was $46.4 billion in 2008.

The Outer Cabinet Departments: 1849–1913

The cabinet departments created during the nineteenth and early part of the twentieth centuries—the Departments of the Interior, Agriculture, Commerce, and Labor—reflected the demands of a nation in the throes of westward expansion and economic upheaval.

The Department of the Interior. The Department of the Interior has been one of the more enigmatic cabinet departments. Proposals for a "home department" or a "home office" to manage federal territories, Indian Affairs, and internal improvements surfaced as early as 1789, but the Department of the Interior was not created until 1849 when the present-day southwestern United States became part of the national domain as a result of the U.S.-Mexican War. Yet even though the heart of the new Interior Department was the General Land Office, transferred from the Treasury Department in 1849, the department's identity as the nation's primary manager of the nation's public lands and natural resources remained partially obscured by the other tasks during much of the nineteenth century. In addition to the General Land Office, the department was given so many other miscellaneous offices—the Patent Office, the Office of Indian Affairs, a Pension Office serving Army veterans, the nation's first Office of Education, the first Federal Bureaus of Agriculture and Labor—that it became known as "the department of everything else." There seemed to be little coherence in the department's early mission.

But the history of the Department of the Interior from the late nineteenth century to the present is one in which it cast off many of these miscellaneous tasks and focused more intently on land management, natural resource use, and conservation—so much so that Secretary of the Interior Harold L. Ickes (1933–46) fought to reconstitute it as the Department of Conservation. If anything, though, the increased specialization on natural resource management only made the department's mission more complex: at times the Interior Department facilitated the development—even rank exploitation—of the country's natural resources; at other times it enforced strict conservation and preservation measures. The U.S. Geological Survey, for example, was created within the Interior Department in 1879 to survey the lands and mineral resources in order to facilitate the development of the U.S. West. But between the 1870s and the 1890s, the department also preserved lands that would eventually become Yellowstone, Yosemite, Sequoia, and Rainier National Parks.

The pattern of exploitation and conservation continued into the twentieth century: the department's Bureau of Reclamation rarely encountered a river it would not dam for irrigation and hydroelectricity, but the National Park Service and the Fish and Wildlife Service walled off millions of acres of land from future development. When the Interior Department tried to strike a balance between preservation and use, it did so with predictably controversial results. The Bureau of Land Management, for example, has closed remaining public lands to entry and offered instead to allow western ranchers to lease access. But ranchers were quick to complain that the department needlessly "locked up" resources, while conservationists decried "welfare ranchers" determined to use public lands on the cheap. The struggle among developers, conservationists, and preservationists for the control of the nation's public lands and natural resources is woven into the Interior Department's history.

Today the Interior Department consists of the Bureaus of Indian Affairs, Land Management, and Reclamation; the Minerals Management Service and the Office of Surface Mining; the National Park Service and the Fish and Wildlife Service; and the U.S. Geological Survey. The department manages over 500 million acres of public lands and nearly 500 dams and 350 reservoirs; oversees 8,500 active oil and gas operations on 44 million acres of the Outer Continental Shelf; operates nearly 400 national parks, monuments, seashores, battlefields, and other cultural sites, and over 500 national wildlife refuges; and conducts government-to-government relations with over 500 recognized Native American tribes. The Interior Department has 67,000 employees serving at 2,500 locations at an annual budget of $16 billion.

The Department of Agriculture. Unlike the Interior Department, the Department of Agriculture (USDA) began as a department that catered specifically to one economic interest—farmers. But over its century and a half of service, the USDA's mission has widened considerably to include not only the original goal of higher farm incomes through the promotion of agricultural research, businesslike farm management, the efficient use of the latest machinery, and better marketing practices, but also the improvement of the overall quality of life in the nation's rural areas, the protection of agricultural ecosystems through soil and water conservation programs, the promotion of U.S. agricultural goods in overseas markets, ensuring the safety of the U.S. food supply for consumers, educating the public about proper nutrition, and administering food stamp and school lunch programs to low-income Americans.

It is no surprise that suggestions for a Department of Agriculture can be traced back to the 1780s—a time when the United States was truly a nation of farmers. But early federal aid to agriculture was limited to a small seed collection and distribution program established in 1839 in the State Department's Patent Office. As agricultural settlement proceeded westward, however, and after years of lobbying on the part of agricultural societies, an independent Department of Agriculture was established in 1862 in order "to acquire and diffuse . . . useful information on subjects connected with agriculture."

At first, the USDA did little more than continue the seed collection program run by the Patent Office. But with the elevation to cabinet department status in 1889, the USDA embarked on a period of professionalization and expansion, particularly under Secretaries James Wilson (1897–1913) and David Houston (1913–20). During these decades the USDA engaged in more scientific research. The U.S. Forest Service was created in 1905 to professionalize the management of the nation's forest resources, for example, while bureaus or offices of entomology, soil chemistry, roads, weather, and agricultural economics were also established. The Smith-Lever Act of 1914 created the Cooperative Extension Service in order to disseminate the department's scientific and technological know-how to the nation's farmers.

Under the Depression-era management of Secretary Henry A. Wallace, the USDA's mission continued to expand. The Soil Conservation Service made the conservation of soils and water one of the department's tasks, while the Rural Electrification Administration and the Resettlement Administration sought to foster a better quality of life in the nation's rural communities. During the post–World War II era, the USDA turned its attention to issues of consumer safety, ensuring the safety and quality of the nation's food system, fighting hunger, and promoting proper nutrition.

These accumulated duties are now divided among the USDA's many bureaus and services. The Agricultural Marketing Service helps farmers market their products in domestic markets, while the Foreign Agricultural Service seeks to improve overseas markets for U.S. farm products. The Agricultural Research Service and the Animal and Plant Health Inspection Service provide farmers with research and information to increase productivity, aided by the Cooperative Extension Service. The Economic Research Service and the National Agricultural Statistics Service keep agricultural statistics and provide farmers with economic information. The Natural Resources Conservation Service helps farmers follow sound environmental practices. The Forest Service ensures the conservation and wise use of the nation's forest lands. The Farm Service Agency and Rural Development programs extend credit and federal aid to farmers and rural communities. The Food and Nutrition Service and the Food Safety Inspection Service ensure the safety of the nation's food supply, administer the federal government's antihunger programs, and seek to educate American consumers on matters of health and nutrition. The USDA had a budget of approximately $77 billion in 2007. It employs 110,000 people.

The Department of Commerce. The mission of the Department of Commerce is "to foster, promote, and develop the foreign and domestic commerce" of the United States. In other words, the Commerce Department exists to promote the conditions necessary for economic growth. To this end, it creates and disseminates the basic economic data necessary to make sound business decisions. It promotes scientific and technological innovation; facilitates foreign trade and tries to ensure the competitiveness of American businesses in international markets; and grants patents and registers trademarks.

The framers of the Constitution discussed the idea of creating a secretary of commerce and finance, with many of these tasks ending up as part of the Department of the Treasury's domain. But the advent of industrialization, the increase in American exports, and the overall growth in the size and scale of the American economy during the late nineteenth century led to increased demands on the part of business organizations such as the National Association of Manufacturers and the U.S. Chamber of Commerce for a separate cabinet department devoted exclusively to the needs of American business.

The Panic of 1893 served to underscore the need for better coordination and management of business conditions. In 1903 President Theodore Roosevelt signed a law creating the Department of Commerce and Labor; the two were divided into two separate cabinet departments in 1913. At the outset, the Commerce Department was charged with overseeing domestic and foreign commerce, manufacturing, shipping, the nation's fisheries, and its transportation systems.

The department peaked early. In its defining era under the leadership of secretary Herbert Hoover (1921–28), the Department of Commerce expanded by thousands of employees; its annual budget grew from approximately $1 million to $38 million; and the Building and Housing Division (1922), the Bureau of Mines and the Patent Office (1925), the Aeronautics Division (1926), and the Radio Division (1927) were established.

These functions are currently divided among the department's many offices and bureaus. The Economic and Statistics Administration and the Bureau of the Census provide business with data about the state of the economy. The International Trade Administration facilitates international commerce. The Economic Development Administration and the Minority Business Development Agency promote economic growth and business opportunity in economically troubled regions and underserved communities. The National Institutes of Standards and Technology, the National Oceanic and Atmospheric Administration, the National Technical Information Service, and the National Telecommunications and Information Administration each, in their own way, promote technological and scientific innovation among U.S. businesses. The Patent and Trademark Office seeks to encourage innovation through the protection of intellectual property rights. In 2007 the Commerce Department employed approximately 40,000 employees and had a budget of approximately $6.5 billion.

The Department of Labor. The culmination of nearly half a century of vigorous agitation for a "voice in the cabinet" on the part of organized labor, the Department of Labor was created in March 1913 in order "to foster, promote, and develop the welfare of working people, and to enhance their opportunities for profitable employment." It enforces federal laws governing workplace conditions, attempts to uphold the principle of collective bargaining, seeks to protect the solvency of retirement and health care benefits through regulation and oversight, administers unemployment insurance, helps displaced workers through retraining and educational programs, and tracks basic economic data relevant to the American labor force (such as changes in unemployment, prices, wages, and productivity). The department is also responsible for ensuring compliance with federal labor laws in the workplace, including safety and minimum wage regulations and freedom from discrimination.

These basic tasks have evolved over time. At its inception, the Labor Department consisted of a new U.S. Conciliation Service to mediate labor disputes, the Bureau of Labor Statistics, the Bureau of Immigration and Naturalization, and a Children's Bureau. Almost immediately, the demands of World War I meant that the department's primary responsibility was in the mediation of potential labor disputes—and this in turn meant that the department emphasized organized labor's right to collectively bargain with employers. That is, the Labor Department at times pushed for the organization of the workplace. But as health and safety regulations and rules governing the minimum hourly wage and overtime proliferated, the department's energies have focused on enforcing these governmental standards in American workplaces, regardless of unionization. Education, retraining, and reemployment programs grew in importance as deindustrialization began to plague traditional industries in the post–World War II era. The Area Redevelopment Act of 1961, for example, targeted unemployed workers in regions particularly hard hit by deindustrialization. The Comprehensive Employment and Training Act of 1973 underscored the department's increased emphasis on helping American workers survive in the "postindustrial" economy.

These functions are carried out today by the Bureau of Labor Statistics, the Employee Benefits Security Administration, the Employment Standards Administration, the Employment and Training Administration, the Mine Safety and Health Administration, the Occupational Safety and Health Administration, the Veterans' Employment and Training Service, and the Women's Bureau. The Labor Department's annual budget sits at roughly $60 billion, and the department employs 17,000 people.

The Outer Cabinet Departments
Established in the Post–World War II Era

Departments established during the postwar decades addressed broad structural problems in American life. Unlike the Departments of Agriculture, Labor, and Commerce, however, many of the outer cabinet departments established in this era enjoyed the support of no single interest group. Departments such as Health and Human Services, Housing and Urban Development, and Education served millions of Americans. But as the institutional embodiments of New Deal and Great Society liberalism, these departments also became a target of attack by small-government conservatives.

The Department of Health and Human Services. The Department of Health and Human Services (HHS) is the federal government's principal department working to ensure the health and welfare of all Americans, particularly those citizens least able to help themselves. HHS is by far the largest cabinet department in terms of budget—its 2007 budget was $707.7 billion.

In many ways, HHS embodied much of the economic reformism and the search for a basic sense of fairness and security that many historians argue was at the heart of New Deal liberalism. HHS began, in a sense, in 1939, when the Federal Security Agency was created to house the Public Health Service (from the Treasury Department), the Food and Drug Administration (from Agriculture), the Children's Bureau (from Labor), and the newly created Social Security Administration. The undeniable popularity of the New Deal state led Republican President Dwight D. Eisenhower to transform the Federal Security Agency into the cabinet-level Department of Health, Education, and Welfare in 1953. This department became the Department of Health and Human Services in 1979, after the Education Division was removed and sent to the new Department of Education.

Aside from its New Deal–era foundations, by far the most important development in HHS history was the expansion in departmental functions that occurred as a result of President Lyndon Johnson's Great Society programs, including Medicare, Medicaid, and the Head Start program for underprivileged preschoolers.

The department's 65,000 employees currently administer more than 300 programs that affect the lives of hundreds of millions of Americans. The National Institutes of Heath is the federal government's primary medical research organization. The Centers for Disease Control and Prevention works to prevent the outbreak of infectious disease. The Food and Drug Administration guarantees the safety of foods, pharmaceuticals, and cosmetics. The Health Resources and Services Administration provides basic medical care to Americans unable to afford health insurance. The Indian Health Service provides health care to nearly 2 million Native Americans and Alaskan Natives through a system of hundreds of health centers and village clinics. The department's Administration for Children and Families administers 60 programs designed to provide basic economic and social security for low-income families with dependent children. This administration also oversees Head Start. The Administration on Aging provides services to elderly Americans, including the Meals on Wheels programs that deliver food to the homebound.

The hallmark of HHS, though, is the Centers for Medicare and Medicaid Services, which provide health insurance to nearly 50 million elderly or disabled persons through the Medicare program, cover another 50 million low-income Americans through Medicaid, and insure millions of children through the popular State Children's Health Insurance Program. HHS is perhaps the cabinet department where ideological arguments against "big government" welfare programs collide most clearly with the reality that Americans now accept a role for the federal government in ensuring basic economic and health security for all Americans.

The Department of Housing and Urban Development. In addition to expanding the mission of HHS, Great Society initiatives also led to the creation of the Department of Housing and Urban Development (HUD) and the Department of Transportation (DOT). The establishment of HUD was an acknowledgment of the problems facing an increasingly urban nation during the 1960s.

The mission of HUD is to increase home ownership and provide access to affordable quality housing free from discrimination. Yet the department in many ways has been a house divided. During the mid-1960s, when HUD was created, the private housing construction and banking industries sought to restrict the new department's activities to the promotion of the construction of new housing. Urban reformers, civil rights activists, and planners, on the other hand, wanted to seize upon urban redevelopment as a way to promote broader social and economic change. But community development agencies such as Lyndon Johnson's Office of Economic

Opportunity were not placed within HUD. And in 1968, HUD lost jurisdiction over urban mass transportation systems to the newly created Department of Transportation—a truly crippling blow to its ability to engage in comprehensive urban planning.

Today the Department of Housing and Urban Development oversees hundreds of programs and is divided into three broad offices. The Office of Community Planning and Development tries to integrate affordable housing with expanded economic opportunity for needy families; the Office of Fair Housing and Equal Opportunity oversees the Fair Housing Act and other civil rights laws designed to ensure that all Americans have equal access to housing; and the Office of Public and Indian Housing provides affordable public housing for needy individuals. In 2008 the Department of Housing and Urban Development's budget was $35 billion.

The Department of Transportation. The Department of Transportation (DOT) is responsible for designing and carrying out policies to ensure the safety and efficiency of the nation's transportation systems. The creation of the DOT was signed into law in October 1966, and it began operations in April 1967 as the fourth-largest cabinet department, bringing together 95,000 employees then working in more than 30 existing transportation agencies scattered throughout the federal government.

The DOT is divided into 11 administrations: the Federal Aviation Administration, the Federal Highway Administration, the Federal Motor Carrier Safety Administration, the Federal Railroad Administration, the National Highway Traffic Safety Administration, the Federal Transit Administration (urban mass transport), the Maritime Administration, the St. Lawrence Seaway Development Corporation, the Research and Innovative Technologies Administration, the Pipeline and Hazardous Materials Safety Administration, and the Surface Transportation Board. Its 2008 budget was $68 billion.

The Department of Energy. The Department of Energy (DOE) became the twelfth cabinet department in October 1977 in the midst of the protracted energy crisis of the 1970s and was designed to consolidate existing energy agencies in order to promote efficiency and facilitate the research and development of new energy sources. To this end, the department assumed the responsibilities of the Federal Energy Administration; the Energy Research and Development Administration; the Federal Power Commission; the Southeastern, Southwestern, and Alaskan Power Administrations (regional hydroelectric projects); and a handful of other energy-related programs previously housed in the Departments of Defense, Commerce, and the Interior.

Since its creation, the DOE has been responsible for energy research and development, oversight and regulation of interstate transmission of natural gas, oil, and electricity, promotion of alternative energy, and managing the nation's nuclear weapons

development and the cleanup and disposal of nuclear waste from cold war programs. It also serves as the federal government's liaison with the International Atomic Energy Agency.

Yet not all of these goals have proven to be created equal. During the late 1970s, DOE emphasis was on research and development of new energy sources and on efficiency and conservation. During the 1980s, the DOE disproportionately focused on nuclear weapons development. During the late 1990s, a concern with renewable and alternative energy was again stressed. This interest in alternative energy has continued into the twenty-first century, although the conflation of energy and national security matters has set up a potential conflict within the DOE: Does national security mean all-out development of traditional sources of energy, or does it mean a long-term plan to develop alternative energy technologies? The Department of Energy employed 116,000 people in 2008, and its budget was $25 billion.

The Department of Education. Education in the United States has historically been the responsibility of state and local governments. The Department of Education notwithstanding, this remains the case. Even the 1979 enabling act that created the Education Department emphasized the fundamentally nonfederal nature of education in America, noting that "the establishment of the Department of Education shall not . . . diminish the responsibility for education which is reserved for the states and the local school systems." The Department of Education's primary contributions to education are the disbursement of money in the form of grants to states and school districts, funding student loan and grant programs for postsecondary education, and ensuring equal access.

The antecedents of the Department of Education go back to 1867, when an Office of Education was established in the Interior Department. With fewer than ten clerks on staff, the Education Office served as a statistical agency, although during the 1890s, it also assumed a supporting role in overseeing the nation's land-grant colleges and universities.

In 1939 the Office of Education was transferred to the Federal Security Agency before being incorporated into the Department of Health, Education, and Welfare (HEW) in 1953. But even within HEW the Office of Education led an austere existence until a dramatic increase in the federal presence in American education during the cold war. In an effort to compete with the Soviet Union, the 1958 National Defense Education Act provided support for college loans and also backed efforts to improve instruction in science, math, foreign languages, and area studies at all levels of the American education system.

The civil rights movement and the War on Poverty programs of the 1960s and 1970s also expanded the federal role in education. The 1965 Elementary and Secondary Education Act initiated programs for underprivileged children living in poor urban and rural areas. The Higher Education Act of 1965 provided financial aid programs for eligible college students. Civil rights legislation, such as Title IX of the Education Amendments of 1972, prohibited discrimination based on race, gender, and disability. Each of these responsibilities transferred to the Department of Education upon its creation in 1979.

The Education Department's elementary and secondary programs affect 56 million students in nearly 100,000 public schools and 28,000 private schools in 14,000 school districts across the nation. The department administers grant and loan programs that support 11 million postsecondary students. The Education Department has a staff of 4,100—45 percent fewer than the 7,500 employees in 1980, a testament both to the powerful tradition of local control in the American education system and to the fact that the Education Department has spent most of its life under the management of conservative Republican administrations generally opposed to the idea of a strident federal role in education. The department's 2008 budget stood at $68.6 billion.

The Department of Veterans Affairs. The mission of the Department of Veterans Affairs (VA), as taken from President Abraham Lincoln's second inaugural address, is "to care for him who shall have borne the battle, and for his widow and his orphan." With 58 regional offices, the VA's Veterans Benefits Administration distributes benefits to veterans and their dependents that include compensation for death or disability, pensions, educational and vocational training, and low-interest loans. The Veterans Health Administration oversees one of the largest health care systems in the United States, complete with over 150 hospitals and 350 outpatient clinics. The National Cemetery Administration offers burial and memorial services.

Although the nation has always made some provision for the care of veterans, it was not until 1930, in the aftermath of World War I, that the federal government created a Veterans Administration to bring order to the government services offered to the nation's veterans. This independent Veterans Administration was elevated to cabinet department status in 1988, in part due to the plight of disaffected Vietnam veterans. The annual VA budget is approximately $90 billion, and the department's 250,000 employees cause the department to be ranked second only to the Defense Department in number.

FURTHER READING. Anthony J. Bennett, *The American President's Cabinet: From Kennedy to Bush*, 1996; Jeffrey E. Cohen, *The Politics of the U.S. Cabinet: Representation in the Executive Branch, 1789–1984*, 1988; Richard F. Frenno, Jr., *The President's Cabinet: An Analysis in the Period from Wilson to Eisenhower*, 1959; Stephen Hess, *Organizing the Presidency*, 2002; R. Gordon Hoxie, "The Cabinet in the American Presidency, 1789–1984," *Presidential Studies Quarterly* 14, no. 2 (1984), 209–30; Shirley Anne Warshaw, *Power Sharing: White House–Cabinet Relations in the Modern Presidency*, 1996.

KEVIN POWERS

campaign consultants

The United States is the land of elections. Over any typical four-year cycle, there are more than a million elections, everything from the presidency, U.S. senator, and governor to big-city mayor, city council, and local school board bond issue. Americans vote into office approximately 513,000 elected officials and decide on thousands of ballot initiatives. No other country comes close to the number and variety of elections that are held in American states, cities, counties, and other political jurisdictions.

Most elections are low-profile, low-budget contests. For many voters, the first time they learn that an issue or some minor office is even being contested is when they close the curtain in the voting booth and see the official ballot. Candidates seeking office in these low-profile contests usually rely on their own shoe leather, pay for their own election expenses, and rely on assistance from family, friends, and other volunteers.

But in contests for big-city mayors, governors, members of Congress, and other contests, professional political consultants are used to help guide candidates, political parties, and interest groups through the complexities of today's elections. These are the expensive, often high-profile contests, where candidates and interested parties will raise hundreds of thousands, even millions of dollars to fund their races. It is not unusual for candidates for the U.S. Senate to raise and spend $10 to $15 million. It was once a rarity for candidates for Congress to spend $1 million; now it is commonplace. In some jurisdictions, candidates who are elected to the state supreme court might spend $5 or $8 million, while some school board candidates in big cities have been known to spend well over $100,000. Statewide spending in California presents a special case. In 2005 alone, with no governor, no state legislators, and no other state officials to elect, still over $500 million was spent by participants trying to defend or defeat ballot issues.

Where does the money go? Much of it, of course, goes to television advertising or direct-mail expenses, but a considerable portion goes to a battery of professionals who are hired by the campaigns to help win the public over to their side. Campaign consulting is a thriving business; no serious candidate in an important contest can do without consultants. Yet, campaign consulting is a relatively new business.

Through much of American electoral history, campaigns were run by political party machines and operatives. Parties recruited candidates, funded election drives, urged people to vote, and tried to generate excitement through mass rallies and torchlight parades. But by the middle of the twentieth century, the political party was no longer the focus of campaigning for many elections. Increasingly, the focus was on the individual candidate. The candidates relied on others to assist them, and increasingly, as campaigns became more complex and sophisticated, they turned to professionals skilled in public relations, survey research, media relations, and other specialties.

The Beginning of the Business of Political Consulting

The business of political consulting traces back to the mid-1930s, when a California husband-wife public relations team, Clem Whitaker and Leone Baxter, created a firm called Campaigns, Inc. Throughout their 25-year career, Whitaker and Baxter were enormously successful, providing public relations and communications services to a variety of candidates, ballot initiatives, and issue causes.

Others followed, but even by the early 1950s, most political consulting was still a sideline for public relations firms. One study showed that by 1957 some 41 public relations firms, located mostly in California, Texas, and New York, offered campaign services. But during the 1950s a new specialty was emerging: the professional campaign manager or political consultant. These were political activists who were making campaign work their principal business. By the 1960s the political consultant was becoming a fixture in presidential, gubernatorial, and U.S. Senate races.

The first generation of consultants included Joseph Napolitan, Walter De Vries, F. Clifton White, Herbert M. Baus, William B. Ross, John Sears, Stuart Spencer, and Joseph Cerrell. They tended to be generalists, who would handle a campaign's overall strategy, develop themes and messages, and run campaigns. Others were known for special skills. Louis Harris, Albert H. (Tad) Cantril, Oliver Quayle, William Hamilton, Richard Wirthlin, Robert Teeter were among those who focused on research; Matt Reese was known for his campaign-organizing skills. Media specialists Charles Guggenheim, Tony Schwartz, David Garth, Marvin Chernoff, and Robert Squier crafted television commercials for Democratic candidates, while Robert Goodman, Douglas L. Bailey, John D. Deardourff, and others worked on the Republican side.

The business of political consulting grew quickly in the 1980s through 2000, and in 2008 approximately 3,000 consulting firms specialized in political campaigns. A few political consultants have become widely known to the public, like Karl Rove, Dick Morris, and James Carville. But they are the rare exceptions. Most consultants work quietly, and comfortably, behind the scenes. Even at the presidential level, few Americans would recognize the names of principal consultants for 2008 presidential candidates Hillary Clinton, Barack Obama, Rudy Giuliani, or John McCain.

The Role of Political Consultants in Campaigns

What do consultants bring to the modern campaign? They bring skills, experience, and discipline to an essentially unruly process. Few events are as potentially chaotic, vulnerable, and unpredictable as a modern campaign. They are, by definition, contests, pitting one side (or more) against another. So much can go wrong. There is such a steep learning curve for the campaign, so many ways to make a mistake, an often inattentive public, and an opponent and allies doing their best to knock your candidate off track.

In some campaigns, no amount of skill or energy from a consultant would change the ultimate outcome. Winning (and losing) is contingent on a variety of factors, and many of those are beyond the control of consultants. But consultants can make the vital difference between victory and defeat when contests are close. Furthermore, consultants can help candidates avoid big, costly mistakes. They can bring order, discipline, focus, and consistency when things might otherwise be falling apart; they can keep a volatile situation from total meltdown and fire up a listless, drifting campaign that has lost its direction.

Campaign consultants come with a variety of skills and occupy different niches in campaigns. For an $8 million U.S. Senate race, a candidate might hire a bevy of consultants. The candidate will hire *strategists* (a general consultant, a campaign manager, pollster, direct-mail specialist, media expert) and *specialists* (candidate and opposition researchers, fund-raisers, lawyers and accountants with specialized knowledge of campaign finance law, speechwriters, television time buyers, electronic media specialists, telemarketers, micro-targeting specialists, and others). The campaign will also use campaign *vendors* (firms that supply voter files, campaign software, yard signs, and more).

Many consultants offer niche services, such as providing state and federal election law advice, buying time for radio and television advertising, providing voter and demographic databases, geo-mapping, and sophisticated targeting techniques, helping candidates in debate preparation, preparing their stump speeches, or providing that all-important cadre of fund-raisers who collect money that provides the fuel for the entire campaign.

New specialties have emerged just as new technologies have been introduced. No serious political campaign now would be without a Web site, e-mail, and blog. One of the newest job descriptions is that of director of electronic media: the person on the campaign responsible for maintaining the Web site, coordinating e-mails, and monitoring the campaign's blog. Particularly since the 2004 presidential campaign, candidates have found that online communications can be cost-effective and efficient ways to reach out to volunteers, collect campaign funds (usually in smaller denominations), and keep activists and others engaged in the campaign.

Campaign consultants provide services for more than the traditional candidate campaign, such as a gubernatorial race or big-city mayor's race. In fact, very few campaign consultants work on only election cycle campaigns. Many are involved in ballot issue campaigns, such as found in California and about 25 other states. Many too provide services in issue advocacy fights, such as the battle over national health insurance, immigration reform, gay marriage, and many other issues. Consultants will work for corporations, trade associations, and other business interests. Finally, American consultants have found a lucrative market during the past 30 years going abroad and working on campaign elections in other countries.

The Business of Political Consulting

The business of political consulting is just a small fraction of the commercial marketing world. Many of these firms have fewer than ten employees and generate $1 million or less in revenue. Private political survey research represents only about 2.5 percent (or $100 million) of the $4 billion annual revenues of the polling industry. Direct mail for political causes constitutes but 2 percent of the direct-mail commercial market, and political telemarketing is less than 1 percent of the overall telemarketing industry.

While citizens watching television during a heated presidential primary might think that there is nothing but political commercials dominating the airwaves, in fact, such commercials are just a tiny portion of the market. In recent presidential campaign years, for example, during the six months that preceded the general election, political commercials represented only about 1.0 to 1.5 percent of all commercials. In a typical presidential election year, mass-marketing companies like Procter & Gamble or General Motors will each spend about the same amount selling their own products as all presidential candidates combined.

In the early twenty-first century, political campaigns pose special problems for candidates, consultants, and their campaigns. It is so much harder to get people's attention. There has been a fundamental shift in where people get their news and how candidates can advertise. Newspaper readership is declining; weekly newsmagazines have become slimmer and less relevant in a 24-hour news culture; network television, which once dominated viewers' attention, has little of its former power. Communications outlets exploded with the advent of cable television in the 1970s, followed by the Internet, e-mail, mobile phones, and instant messaging. The communications marketplace is extraordinarily splintered, making it much harder for campaigns to reach voters with their messages. The mass market of three television networks has largely been supplanted by niche markets with hundreds of choices.

At one time, campaigns were much simpler: one candidate vying against another. Television, radio, and print advertising from one camp were pitted against the advertising from the other side. Since then, campaign communications have become much more complicated. Other voices added their messages and get-out-the-vote drives in the campaigns. For example, labor unions, political parties, trade associations, even private individuals have been willing to spend great sums of money to influence a contest. Then contests became nationalized. By the mid-1990s, congressional

races that once were considered only local contests were seeing advertising campaigns from abortion rights, pro-gun control, anti-NAFTA, and English-only advocates—national groups, all—trying to influence the outcome. On top of these influences has come the wide open, robust influence of citizen activists through blogs and Web sites, adding their voices to the mix. This makes it all the more necessary to have professional campaign help to fight through the clutter and competition in the contest and make the candidate's views and positions known.

Consultants often get blamed for the harsh, negative tone of campaign rhetoric, especially in television ads. They defend their craft by saying that they are providing useful information, albeit in stark and clear terms, about the differences between their candidates and the opponents. Academics and public citizen groups worry about the negative impact such ads might have on democratic behavior or voter turnout.

If anyone is to be blamed, it must be the candidate, who ultimately is responsible for the conduct of a campaign. An unfair, slash-and-burn campaign commercial, a "dirty tricks" stunt against the opponent, an embarrassing photo digitally pieced together, a cruel, salacious comment by a campaign staffer—all these unfair or unethical practices redound against the campaign and the candidate.

The negativity and the harsh words found in contemporary campaigns will likely only get worse. New voices, without the constraints of professional responsibility, have entered the picture. We should expect campaigns to get uglier and louder. Particularly with online campaigning, there are so many more voices filling cyberspace, from bloggers to e-mail rumors, to the online posting of sound bites and video clips. Professional media consultants, knowing they have reputations to uphold and are working for a candidate and a party or interest group, will use some semblance of caution. The really wild, outrageous comments or videos posted on the Web will come from outsiders, often anonymous, unfettered by constraints. The early twenty-first century may become the Wild West period of campaigning.

Challenges and Opportunities of Online Campaigning

Particularly since Howard Dean's run for the Democratic presidential nomination in 2003–4, we have seen a challenge to the dominant form of professional campaigning. Dean and his campaign manager touted a new approach to campaigning. That approach was to listen to the voices expressed on Dean's blog and other online sources and emerge with a bottom-up campaign, gaining ideas from the people, listening to (and presumably acting on) their concerns, rather than imposing a command-and-control, top-down campaign (with the implication that it did not listen to the people).

While the approach sounded promising, it was less than what it appeared. A critical ingredient in any successful campaign is top-down control: message discipline, a fixed but flexible strategy, the ability to cut through all the noise (electronic and otherwise) of a campaign, set a firm, clear direction, and plan to beat the opponent. This is what traditional, professional campaigning does best: it brings order out of chaos. But at the same time, successful campaigns are not out of touch with what voters want or feel. They conduct polls, run focus groups, and monitor blogs; candidates engage in "listening tours," greet voters in malls, coffee shops, and private homes. In short, they listen very carefully to what people think.

In recent election cycles, a thriving blogging community, both on the liberal/Democratic and conservative/Republican sides, has emerged. These bloggers, self-appointed activists, are also claiming a stake in the nature, content, and direction of campaigning. Bloggers, particularly from the progressive or liberal side, like to tout that they will break down the barriers between the people and the candidates. They boast that they are the future of campaigns and will invariably supplant the activities of campaign consultants.

Electronic democracy, citizen activism, and Web advocacy, however, have not supplanted old-fashioned, professionally run campaigns. Professional campaign consultants, above all, want their clients to win. They adapt to new circumstances, and increasingly have added electronic communications to their arsenal of tools. No current professionally run campaign would be without an e-communications team to run the Web site, monitor the campaign blog, and produce online versions of campaign videos, fundraising appeals, and other tricks of the trade. Consultants will adapt, endure, and prosper. They are indispensable to modern American campaigns, and, increasingly, in campaigns throughout the world.

See also campaigning.

FURTHER READING. David A. Dulio, *For Better or Worse? How Political Consultants Are Changing Elections in the United States*, 2004; Ronald A. Faucheux and Paul S. Herrnson, *The Good Fight: How Political Candidates Struggle to Win Elections without Losing Their Souls*, 2000; Paul S. Herrnson, *Congressional Elections: Campaigning at Home and in Washington*, 4th ed., 2007; Kathleen Hall Jamieson, *Packaging the Presidency: A History and Criticism of Presidential Campaign Advertising*, 1984; Dennis W. Johnson, *No Place for Amateurs: How Political Consultants Are Reshaping American Democracy*, 2nd ed., 2007; Dennis W. Johnson, ed., *Routledge Handbook on Political Management*, 2008; Stephen K. Medvic, *Political Consultants in U.S. Congressional Elections*, 2001; Bruce I. Newman, *The Mass Marketing of Politics: Democracy in an Age of Manufactured Images*, 1999; Daniel M. Shea and Michael John Burton, *Campaign Craft: The Strategies, Tactics, and Art of Political Campaign Management*, 3rd ed., 2006; James A. Thurber and Candice J. Nelson, eds., *Campaign Warriors: The Role of Political Consultants in Elections*, 2000.

DENNIS W. JOHNSON

campaign law and finance to 1900

Financing candidates' campaigns was simple and uncontroversial in the absence of mass parties and a complex economy. But with the demise of the relatively hierarchical, elite-driven politics of the eighteenth and early nineteenth century, men of limited means who had made politics their profession needed financial help to reach an expanded electorate. Through the nineteenth century, campaign finance raised questions about who should pay for politics and whether those who paid got an unfair return on their investment. Those questions, asked with both public spiritedness and partisan advantage in mind, remain with us.

In the early years of the republic, many campaigns were straightforward. Men of prominence and wealth "stood" for office, ideally approaching the exercise as a somewhat unwelcome civic duty, akin to jury service in the twentieth century. The rituals of electioneering—voice voting for the (usually) white propertied men who made up the electorate and the candidates treating the voters with food and drink—illustrated the hierarchical relationships. Voter turnout tended to be low. Costs were, too, and they were usually borne by the candidates.

Contentious elections required more desperate activity and more extensive methods. Newspapers devoted to parties and to factions, such as those organized around personal followings in the Middle Atlantic states, promoted candidates. The Federalists financed Noah Webster's *American Minerva* (later renamed *The Commercial Advertiser*); the Democratic-Republicans responded with Philip Freneau's *National Gazette*. So it went around the new nation: from 1790 to 1808, the number of newspapers, most of them partisan, more than tripled. Backed by wealthy patrons or government printing contracts, newspapers put out the partisan line, denigrating the godlessness of the Democratic-Republicans or the monarchical aspirations of the Federalists.

The party press remained an important cost of doing political business with the rise of mass parties in the 1830s. There were additional expenses: printing and distributing ballots, holding rallies, dispensing campaign paraphernalia, and getting out the vote of an electorate expanded to include most white men. Party activities were now nearly constant, reaching down from presidential campaigns to an expanded number of state and local races. All this exertion required a regular stream of funds, particularly since a new generation of men who made politics their profession lacked the means of more elite predecessors.

Part of a solution to the problem of funds emerged from the "spoils system" or "rotation in office," which followers of Andrew Jackson touted as a more democratic way to distribute government positions than the creation of a class of permanent officials. Replacing public employees, minor as well as major, with partisans of a new presidential administration—a practice repeated at the state and city levels—gave the executive branch loyal men to carry out the government's work. These workers could also be tapped for funds. The party in power expected the men holding patronage jobs—from upper-level administrators to postmasters—to show their gratitude and fealty by paying a percentage (generally 2 to 5 percent) of their salaries to their party. Such assessments became an alternative system of taxation or after-a-fashion public financing, in which those who benefited or hoped to benefit from the result of an election paid for it.

The assessment system generated controversy almost from the start, and like every attempt to regulate campaign finance to follow, proposed reforms were both partisan and principled. In 1837 Whig congressman John Bell of Tennessee introduced a bill that would have banned assessments and electioneering on the part of federal employees. This measure, as well as a hearing concerning abuses at a customs house, took aim at the Democrats. Proponents argued that the executive branch was using patronage to build a machine that interfered with legislative elections; they decried a system in which "partisan service is the required return for office, as office is to be the reward for public service." Opponents countered that everyone, including federal employees, had the right to participate in politics. The bill failed. But constituents received free copies of the debate and the hearing: the franking privilege was an important perk of incumbency.

Strains on the assessment system grew. Businessmen who relied on customs houses for import and export trade resented the sometimes inefficient service, which improved greatly with payoffs, provided by partisan employees. Workers who performed professional tasks increasingly wanted to be treated like professionals, rather than as patronage hacks. They came to resent paying taxes to their party. The cost of the Republican Party's effort to build party infrastructure in the South after the Civil War encouraged the GOP to nag public employees more tirelessly than usual. Democrats naturally grumbled, as did some Republicans. Appalled by the corruption of the Ulysses S. Grant administration and weary of Reconstruction, African Americans, and the South, Liberal Republicans offered civil service reform as a new issue and purpose for the party and a cure for corruption.

They felt strongly enough about the issue to form their own party in 1872; President Ulysses Grant responded by creating a civil service commission. Meaningful reform came with the passage of the Pendleton Act in 1883, given a final push by the mistaken idea that President James Garfield had been assassinated by a "disappointed office seeker," driven mad by patronage.

The campaign work and dollars of public employees continued to be a target of reform into the twentieth century, but assessments ceased to be a major source of funds for national party organizations by the late nineteenth century. Wealthy partisan individuals had pitched in throughout the nineteenth century, but as assessments dried up, business increasingly paid for elections. This money quickly sparked more controversy than assessments.

We know some of the names of the big spenders of the late nineteenth century—August Belmont, Jay Cooke, and Tom Scott, for example—and their interests in what government did in banking, tariffs, railroad subsidies, and regulation. The assumption of many, especially supporters of third parties, was that money blocked the path to reforms that were in the interests of those without huge wealth. Yet, business interests generally did not seek out political fundraisers—rather it was the reverse, except perhaps for cases like the 1896 election, when fear of what William Jennings Bryan would do if elected, inspired businessmen to give William McKinley more money than his campaign could possibly use. The question of what businessmen bought with their contributions would be central to the campaign finance debates of the twentieth century.

See also campaign law and finance since 1900.

FURTHER READING. Paula Baker, ed., *Money and Politics*, 2002; Robert E. Mutch, "Three Centuries of Campaign Finance Law," in *A User's Guide to Campaign Finance Reform*, edited by Jerold Lubenow, 1–24, 2001; Louise Overacker, *Money in Elections*, 1932, reprint, 1974; Clifton K. Yearly, *The Money Machines: The Breakdown and Reform of Governmental and Party Finance in the North, 1860–1920*, 1970.

PAULA BAKER

campaign law and finance since 1900

Concerns about campaign finance—the amount of money candidates and political parties raise and spend and the sources of those funds—have persisted through the twentieth and into the twenty-first century. The issue's appeal was and remains rooted in many Americans' suspicion of the influence of money on policy and fears for democracy itself. Anxiety has not produced satisfactory solutions. In contrast to the European model, American parties have no tradition of dues-paying members who support their activities, and American campaigns are long and require the purchase of increasingly expensive publicity. As campaign finance regulations have expanded, parties, candidates, and interest groups have adapted nimbly to the constraints, which they also helped to write. Regulations that control contributions and spending have been limited by constitutional protections of free speech. The structure of American politics and Supreme Court guidelines have allowed campaigns to raise and spend the funds they believe they need within each regulatory regime reformers have built, which leads inevitably to the next try at reform.

While fears about the impact of money on politics have been constant, the issue rarely has risen anywhere near the top of public concerns. The particular targets for reform have been driven by scandal and partisan politics. In the early twentieth century, large, secret corporate contributions, the mainstay of party fund-raisers in the 1890s, were the evil that most excited reformers' interest. The first federal legislation stemmed from Democratic presidential candidate Alton B. Parker's charges that his opponent, Theodore Roosevelt, collected big corporate contributions while threatening to regulate many of the same firms. Roosevelt successfully deflected the accusations, although his campaign had accepted substantial sums from financier J. P. Morgan ($150,000), Henry Clay Frick of U.S. Steel ($50,000), and railroad operator H. L. Harriman ($50,000, plus $200,000 raised from his contacts). A series of widely publicized scandals between 1904 and 1908—detailing campaign contributions and payoffs New York Republicans received from life insurance companies in return for favorable legislation, and benefits to utilities and railroads from legislators in the West and Midwest, among many others—appeared to confirm the suspicion that politicians catered to moneyed interests that made big contributions.

Federal Campaign Finance Legislation to 1970

The Tillman Act (1907) made it "unlawful for any national bank, or any corporation organized by authority of any laws of Congress, to make a money contribution in connection with any election to any political office." Corporations or their officers or board members who violated the law were subject to fines and up to one year in prison. While the final bill did not require the parties to disclose the sources of their funds, the Republican National Committee and Democratic National Committee began to voluntarily release financial records for the 1908 presidential election. The Tillman Act prevented firms from using stockholders' funds for campaign purposes but changed little in how campaigns raised money. There is record of only one prosecution, for a gift from the United States Brewers' Association to a House candidate.

Reformers were disappointed that the Tillman Act did not provide for the disclosure of contributions, and Congress responded with the 1910 Federal Corrupt Practices Act (FCPA) and amendments to it in 1911. The law required every House and Senate candidate and "political committee" to report the sources of their contributions and capped spending at $5,000 for a House seat and $10,000 for the Senate. Committees that operated in single states were excepted. The 1911 amendments required reports both before and after elections and extended spending limits to primary elections. The measure contained no enforcement mechanism; violators would have to be taken to court, where they would be subject to fines and up to two years in prison. The 1910 bill passed

the House without much debate; the 1911 amendments were adopted unanimously by the House and passed the Senate with only seven no votes, all from southern Democrats who opposed any extension of federal power over state election procedures.

The legislation had minimal effect on campaigns, due to loopholes and upward pressures on campaign costs. A close reading suggested that the spending limits applied to candidates, not committees formed to advance their campaigns, so only the most naïve candidates indicated that they had spent anything more than a nominal sum while "independent" committees raised the real money. Campaigns spent it because of Progressive Era changes in how the parties operated required that they do so. Primary elections could double campaign costs in competitive states. Nineteenth-century parties had controlled their own newspapers, but twentieth-century campaigns could not count on free fawning press coverage. Purchased advertising filled the gap. Advertising totaled between 25 to 50 percent of campaign budgets, depending on the expense of the market (in 1920, a full-page ad in the *New York Times* cost $1,539 and the *Chicago Tribune* $1,708). Election Day expenses, including hiring the workers who once had been patronage-hungry volunteers, were also substantial.

If the wish embodied in legislation could not control costs, the FCPA still had its uses. Congressional Democrats hoped spending limits might frighten wealthy Republican donors and lessen the GOP's fund-raising advantages. An opponent's spending could be made into a campaign issue. And a losing candidate could take a big-spending opponent to court or to Congress, in the hope of denying a seat to the winner. A few losing House candidates challenged the seating of winners, usually coupling charges of excessive spending with more traditional accusations of corruption. As the party balance in the Senate tightened in the 1910s and early 1920s, it became the site of numerous election challenges. The most consequential was Henry Ford's challenge to Republican Truman H. Newberry's 1918 victory in a close, nasty Michigan Senate race. The committee that promoted Newberry spent $190,000, almost all of it from his family and close friends, well above the apparent FCPA limits for candidates. The money bought the advertising deemed necessary to defeat the rich and famous automaker. Nearly four years of wrangling followed, including two grand jury hearings and one federal trial orchestrated by Ford that found Newberry guilty; a trip to the Supreme Court that reversed the conviction; and a Senate investigation that rehashed the legal proceedings. Newberry finally resigned in 1922 when that year's election brought in enough new Democrats to make a rehearing and his expulsion likely.

The Supreme Court had found fault in both Newberry's trial and the FCPA, but the majority opinion focused on the unconstitutional reach by Congress in regulating state primary elections. The 1924 and 1925 revisions of the FCPA removed coverage of primaries and increased the amounts candidates could spend, but otherwise left the law's vague provisions intact. The Senate could still refuse to seat members-elect it deemed to have spent too much. A coalition of progressive Republicans and Democrats succeeded in denying seats to Frank L. Smith, Republican of Illinois, and William A. Vare, Republican of Pennsylvania, who were elected in 1926 by the voters of their states in expensive races.

Attempts to deny seats to candidates over excessive spending disappeared when the Democrats gained solid control of Congress in the 1930s. But the campaign finance issue persisted, now with Republicans taking the lead. A coalition of southern Democrats and Republicans struck at some of the Franklin D. Roosevelt administration's sources of campaign labor and funds. The 1939 Hatch Act prohibited political activity by government workers, eliminating the threat of Works Progress Administration (WPA) recipients turning into the president's personal political workforce. Because of the prohibition against all but high-ranking federal officials participating in conventions, the president could not stack a convention. (In 1936 about half of the delegates were federal employees.) The law set spending and contribution limits of individual political committees at $3,000,000 per year and capped individual contributions at $5,000. Sure enough, numerous "independent" committees sprung up, each able to spend to the limit.

In 1940 Republicans spent five times the limit and the Democrats double, all the while staying within the letter of the law. Beginning with the 1936 election, organized labor became an important source of funds for Democrats, and southern Democrats and Republicans aimed to restrict its ability to fund campaigns. The Smith-Connally Act (1943) contained a provision that temporarily banned union contributions in the same language that the Tillman Act used against corporate donations; the 1946 Taft-Hartley Act made the restriction permanent. The Congress of Industrial Organizations responded by setting up the first political action committee (PAC) in 1944 that legally funneled money to pro-union candidates. Not until the 1960s did business PACs follow the labor model.

Although the Supreme Court had opened the way for Congress to regulate primary elections in 1941 and the cost of elections outstripped the nominal limits, the FCPA remained the basic, if ineffective, campaign finance law of the United States. The issue had not disappeared. New actors dedicated to campaign finance reform, including a handful of academics and foundations, tried to fire public concern and to sell Congress on new policies. In 1956 Senator Francis Case of South Dakota admitted he had been the target of an oil company deal offering cash in exchange for his vote on a pending bill. This scandal refocused enough interest in campaign finance reform to inspire an investigation headed by Senate Democratic liberals but not to generate new legislation.

The problem was conflicting goals and interests. Organized labor, one important Democratic constituent group that favored restrictions that might curb the advantages of business donors and their Republican recipients, opposed legislation that targeted PACs; many Republicans insisted on controls on PACs; television networks rejected proposals that required them to provide free time for short "spot" advertisements; some sitting officeholders worried about assisting challengers; and a number of powerful members of Congress, backed by public opinion, blocked proposals for public funding of campaigns. Meanwhile, campaign costs ballooned, a trend carefully tracked by new "public interest" groups such as the Citizen's Research Foundation and, by the late 1960s, Common Cause. Spending on the presidential elections of 1968 was up by 25 percent compared to that of 1964. Candidate- (rather than party-) centered campaigns, television, the consultants to coordinate the message, and fund-raising itself drove up the costs of congressional and statewide campaigns as well as presidential races.

Campaign Finance Legislation Since 1970

Rising costs got the attention of members of Congress, especially senators who could easily imagine facing well-financed challengers. With this prod, the logjam broke in 1971. The Federal Election Campaign Act (FECA) imposed much stronger disclosure requirements than those of the FCPA: candidates for federal office had to file quarterly reports detailing receipts and expenditures, with names, addresses, occupations, and businesses attached to each contribution over $100. It limited the contributions of candidates and their immediate families, spending on publicity and outreach, and the proportion of campaign budgets spent on radio and television advertising. The law thus treated media costs as the core problem and contained sufficient incumbent protection provisions to pass. But the FECA did not control overall costs. Richard M. Nixon's 1972 reelection campaign spent twice as much as his 1968 run; Democratic nominee George McGovern's race cost four times as much as Hubert H. Humphrey's 1968 campaign. That, together with the Watergate scandal, brought a major overhaul of the FECA in 1974, creating the current framework of campaign finance law.

Arguing that a renewed effort to divorce money from politics would revive American's sagging confidence in government (and, for Democratic liberals, promote their stalled policy agenda), the Senate bill provided public funds for primary and general election campaigns for federal offices and limits on what candidates could spend, even if using their own money. Restricted too were contributions to political parties and from independent groups, individuals, and PACs. The final bill kept the 1971 disclosure requirement and created the Federal Elections Commission, with commissioners evenly divided between the parties, to monitor compliance. It provided public funding for presidential elections, enabled by a $1 voluntary taxpayer checkoff, but no public support for congressional races. Even the most ardent champions of reform considered the bill not much better than a good first step toward clean elections.

The new regulations were immediately litigated. The major challenge came in *Buckley v. Valeo* (1976). A combination of left- and right-wing groups claimed that many of the FECA's provisions violated constitutional rights to free speech and association. The Court agreed, in part. Large contributions given directly to a campaign might be corrupt or create the appearance of corruption. Therefore, the FECA's $1,000 limit on individual donations and $5,000 for PACs to a single candidate fell within the federal government's interest. But spending was protected speech. "The First Amendment denies government the power to determine that spending to promote one's political view is wasteful, excessive or unwise," according to the Court. The decision struck down the restrictions on candidates' contributions to their own campaigns, mandatory spending limits (unless candidates voluntarily participated in the public financing system), and restrictions on expenditures by independent groups.

The FECA never succeeded in controlling campaign costs; it is doubtful that it would have done so even if the Court had ruled differently in *Buckley*. The law has required reams of paperwork but has only redirected the channels through which money reaches candidates. Raising enough money in small sums to run a credible campaign is expensive and time consuming. Internet fund-raising might lower the costs of finding small donors in future campaigns, but traditionally, only the most finely targeted and best maintained mailing and phone lists justified the considerable investment. Congressional and presidential candidates devote much more of their time to fundraising than before the FECA. To lessen their load, they use "bundlers," who locate caches of $1,000 contributions and PACs. The number of PACs grew from 608 in 1974 to 4,180 in 1990. Many of these were business PACs, which were responding to the expansion of federal regulations through the 1960s and 1970s by making sure they had access to both Democratic and Republican policy makers. New ideological PACs as well as officeholders' PACs also emerged to encourage candidates who mirrored their agendas. A 1978 FEC ruling allowed state parties to follow state rather than federal disclosure and contribution guidelines. This had the effect of strengthening party organizations badly weakened by the FECA, but it also opened the way for unlimited "soft money" contributions. Democrats have relied more heavily than Republicans on "soft money," since the Republicans constructed an effective database to generate "hard" money.

Soft money was the target of the next round of reform, which followed revelations about questionable donations to the Democratic National Committee and some unseemly fund-raising by President Bill Clinton and Vice President Al Gore. The Bipartisan Campaign Reform Act, commonly known as McCain-Feingold, blocked some of the soft money channels; others, especially the independent "527" groups (named after their place in the Internal Revenue Service code) remain. The FECA system continues to demand time and effort to ensure compliance, but since 1996 many presidential aspirants have opted out of the restrictive federal financing system. The American system of campaign finance remains tangled, intrusive, and complex, while reformers await the next scandal.

See also campaign law and finance to 1900; interest groups.

FURTHER READING. Anthony Corrado et al., *The New Campaign Finance Sourcebook*, 2005; Spencer Ervin, *Henry Ford vs. Truman Newberry: The Famous Senate Election Contest*, 1935; Alexander Heard, *The Costs of Democracy*, 1960; Louise Overacker, *Money in Elections*, 1932; James K. Pollock, *Party Campaign Funds*, 1926; Melvin I. Urofsky, *Money and Free Speech: Campaign Finance and the Courts*, 2005.

PAULA BAKER

campaigning

Campaigning for office is one of American democracy's most defining acts—yet many citizens find campaigns unruly, distasteful, demeaning. Most elections are shrouded in some mystery; even in the age of polling, surprises sometimes occur. But, especially in presidential campaigns, the complaints about campaigns being too long, expensive, demagogic, and frilly come as regularly as America's distinctive, scheduled election days, albeit more frequently.

The word *campaign* originated in the seventeenth century from the French word for open field, *campagne*. With contemporary soldiers fighting sustained efforts, often on the wide country terrain, the term quickly acquired its military association. The political connotation emerged in seventeenth-century England to describe a lengthy legislative session. In nineteenth-century America "campaign" was part of the barrage of military terms describing electioneering: as the party *standard bearer*, a *war horse* tapping into his *war chest* and hoping not to be a *flash-in-the-pan*—a cannon that misfires—*mobilized* the *rank-and-file* with a *rallying cry* in *battleground states* to vanquish their enemies.

American politicians needed to conquer the people's hearts because popular sovereignty has been modern Anglo-American government's distinguishing anchor since colonial days. In elitist early America, the ideal candidates stood for election; they did not run. Wooing the people was considered too ambitious, deceitful, undignified; passivity demonstrated the potential leader's purity. This posture lingered longest at the presidential level, and it continues to feed the national fantasy about disinterested, virtuous candidates wafting into the presidential chair by acclamation, rather than the stereotypical grubby, aggressive, blow-dried, weather vane politicians slithering into office today.

There are more than 500,000 elected offices in the United States, ranging from tree warden to president. Most are elected directly to serve locally. While senatorial, gubernatorial, and presidential campaigns require "wholesale" campaigning to mobilize blocs of voters, the typical campaign is a "retail," mom-and-pop, door-to-door operation pressing the flesh. This contact enables American citizens to meet, assess, scrutinize those who aspire to lead them. Even in today's high-tech, television-saturated age, the July Fourth meet-and-greet county picnic or the Election Day get-out-the-vote drive by carpooling neighbors more typifies campaigns than big-budget multistate advertising buys during presidential elections.

While presidential campaigning commands most Americans' attention, often setting the tone for campaigns at all levels, the presidential election remains indirect. As many Americans only first realized in 2000, when Al Gore won more popular votes than George W. Bush but lost the presidency, voters choose slates of electors, organized state by state, and pledged to vote for particular candidates when the Electoral College meets. This filtering of the people's voice reflects the Founding Fathers' fears of "mobocracy." The Electoral College today orients campaign strategy toward a few voter-rich, swing states. In 1960 Vice President Richard Nixon vowed to campaign in all 50 states. He lost, narrowly. Many Republicans grumbled that Nixon wasted precious resources fulfilling that imprudent pledge.

Campaigns are legitimizing and unifying democratic rituals, linking the leader and the led in a historic, tradition-rich rite of affirmation. Ultimately, campaigns involve the mystical alchemy of leadership and the practical allocation of power, cleanly and neatly. America's winner-take-all elections designate one winner, with no power sharing or booby prizes for losers. Campaigns also offer a clear narrative trajectory, with all the plots and personalities culminating on one day, when the people speak. As a result, the history of campaigning, on all levels, is a history of vivid clashes, colorful personalities, defining moments. Presidential campaigning history includes President John Adams clashing with his own vice president, Thomas Jefferson, in 1800; Republican Wide Awakes marching through northern cities before the Civil War; Grover Cleveland winning despite the mockery of "Ma, Ma, Where's my pa, gone to the White House, Ha, Ha, Ha" in 1884; William Jennings Bryan's valiant, superhuman speechifying in 1896; John Kennedy's elegance during the 1960 televised debates; Ronald Reagan's stirring Morning in America 1984 campaign; the geysers of baby boomer idealism that the honey-smooth Bill Clinton tapped

in 1992; George W. Bush's Karl Rove–engineered, play-to-the-base strategy in his 2004 re-election; and Barack Obama's 2008 mix of redemptive "Yes We Can" uplift and an impressive ground game mixing old-fashioned grassroots politics with cutting edge netroots outreach.

The First Three Historical Phases: The Republican, Democratic, and Populist Campaigns

Just as earth scientists debate whether humans evolved gradually or through occasional leaps called punctuated equilibrium, political scientists debate how campaigns developed. Historians traditionally focused on breakthrough campaigns pioneering particular techniques, celebrating 1840 as the first popular campaign that mobilized the masses and 1896 as the first mass merchandising effort organized bureaucratically. Historians also identified critical elections that realigned power, especially the 1800 revolution that empowered Thomas Jefferson's Democratic-Republicans, the 1828 Democratic Jacksonian revolution, the 1860 Republican antislavery revolution, the 1896 corporate Republican realignment, the 1932 Democratic New Deal ascension, and the 1980 conservative Republican Reagan Revolution.

In fact, campaigns evolved slowly, haphazardly, sometimes fitfully, responding to changing communication and transportation technologies, shifts in population and society, the parties' rise and fall, and the growth of the presidency. Technological innovations, including the railroad, telegraph, radio, television, and even the Internet, created necessary but not sufficient conditions for change. Sometimes, traditionalists resisted: throughout the 1800s, editorialists and opponents repeatedly denounced candidates who stumped—mounted speaking tours—claiming they acted in an undignified—and unprecedented—way. Sometimes, innovations failed until politicians figured out how to adapt the technology. Citizens in a democracy get the campaign they deserve; interested, overall, in winning strategies, successful candidates offer unsentimental reflections of what works, despite what people wish worked or imagine worked in the past.

The history of presidential campaigning can be divided into four phases: the republican, democratic, populist, and electronic. The republican phase, reflecting the founders' republican ideology, trusted the wisdom of the few and feared the passion of mobs while rooting government's legitimacy in consent of the governed. Politics' gentlemanly tone reflected the search for virtuous candidates who would neither conspire with cabals nor rabble-rouse demagogically. Campaigns emphasized the candidate's suitability, as candidates functioned as icons, ideal representations of the perfect gentleman and leader.

Candidate, from the Latin word for white, *candidus*, evoked the white togas that represented Roman senators' supposed purity. In that spirit, candidates were to stand for election and not run. Local campaigns were not always as sober as the group conceit hoped. Decades before the Populist and Progressive movements instituted the secret, "Australian" ballot, Election Day was a raucous occasion. On this day, grandees, sitting at the polls as people voted, asked their social inferiors for help, thanking them with libations. This momentary egalitarianism reflected the essential links between equality, liberty, and democracy.

Still, the ideal republican candidate was George Washington. Reflecting his reluctance, he stayed on his farm in humble repose, awaiting the people's call, before being elected president unanimously. In 1792, he was re-elected without touring around begging for votes.

Embodying national virtue, Washington was a demigod who set the bar unrealistically high for Americans—and his successors. As parties developed and as local candidates began campaigning, Washington's passive silence became a straitjacket his successors tried wriggling out of, campaign by campaign.

The rise of political parties, the lifting of voting restrictions on white males, and the move from farms to factories triggered a democratic revolution. Local campaigns became increasingly hard fought. In 1824, 1828, and 1832, Andrew Jackson, the charismatic, controversial war hero who became an assertive president, brought a new personality-based mass excitement to the campaign. Jackson's elitist Whig opponents copied, perfected, and outdid the Jacksonian Democrats' mass appeal tactics in their 1840 campaign for William Henry Harrison. This Whig hijacking proved that the democratic sensibility had become all-American.

The nineteenth-century democratic campaign mobilized the masses through their partisan identities. Politicking became the national pastime. Election days were mass carnivals, culminating months of pamphleting, marching, orating, editorializing in party newspapers, and bickering neighbors. The party bosses dominating the system sought loyal soldiers more than virtuous gentlemen. The primary ability parties prized was "availability," seeking pliant, appealing, noncontroversial candidates. Rather than lofty, passive icons, candidates were becoming actors, sometimes speaking, sometimes stumping, always following the party script. During this time, acceptance letters became increasingly elaborate policy statements, fitting the candidate's views to the party platform, rather than simple republican expressions of virtuous reluctance to plunge into politics.

While party bosses picked most local candidates, the national parties mounted elaborate quadrennial conventions to nominate a standard-bearer and define the party platform. These colorful, often rollicking affairs were way stations between republican elitist politics and today's popular politics. Party bosses lobbied behind the scenes to select candidates and set agendas, but the conventions' deliciously democratic chaos reflected America's drift away from hierarchical politics.

Seeking loyalists, these conventions nominated last-minute dark horses, like James Knox Polk or James Garfield; undistinguished party hacks like Millard Fillmore and Franklin Pierce; war heroes like Lewis Cass, deemed a "doughface" because he could mold himself to appear sympathetic to the North or the South; and relatively uncontroversial, compromise candidates like Abraham Lincoln. A one-term Whig congressman in a party dominated by the antislavery titans William Henry Seward and Salmon Chase, Lincoln followed the textbook strategy during this phase: "My name is new in the field, and I suppose I am not the first choice of a very great many. Our policy, then, is to give no offense to others—leave them in a mood to come to us if they shall be compelled to give up their first love."

As democratization, urbanization, industrialization, and the communications revolution intensified, American politics became more populist, and the presidency became more central. In this populist phase, candidates were more independent of party and more nationalist in orientation. The quaint gentlemanly postures vanished as candidates stumped, whistle-stopped, and prop-stopped on trains, planes, and automobiles. Candidates needed to demonstrate their popularity and their potential to lead the nation. The best candidates were master orators with just a tinge of demagoguery who could move thousands listening in person and millions of newspaper readers and, eventually, radio listeners. After Franklin Roosevelt made America into a superpower and 1600 Pennsylvania Avenue America's central address, Americans no longer sought mere actors but superheroes who could dominate their parties, the campaign, the presidency, and the national news cycle.

Presidential candidates stumped more and more intensely throughout the nineteenth century, and the acceptance letter developed into an elaborate notification ceremony featuring a candidate's address. In the 1880s and 1890s, torn between the tradition of passivity and pressures to be more active, James A. Garfield and other candidates mounted Front Porch campaigns, staying at home but greeting huge delegations of supporters from across the country who came to pay homage. Still, the 1896 campaign became one of those historical moments that consolidated and advanced various innovations. William Jennings Bryan's elaborate 18,009 mile, 600-speech, 27-state rear-platform campaign ended the charade that candidates did not stump for themselves. William McKinley's front porch campaign, whereby he greeted over 300 delegations consisting of 750,000 visitors from 30 states at his Ohio home, genuflected toward the past. Meanwhile, McKinley's campaign manager, Mark Hanna, mounted a modern campaign. Recognizing the growing overlap between consumerism and politics, he organized dozens of special-interest groups, deployed hundreds of speakers, raised millions of dollars, and distributed hundreds of millions of pamphlets.

Subsequently, the charismatic, candidate-centered campaigns of Theodore Roosevelt, Woodrow Wilson, and Franklin Roosevelt presented the candidate as poised to master what Theodore Roosevelt called the "bully pulpit." By 1948, even the mild-mannered Harry Truman felt compelled to run an aggressive, "Give 'em hell" Harry campaign crisscrossing America, despite the fact that he, following Franklin Roosevelt, was also dominating the airwaves thanks to radio's spread in the 1920s and 1930s.

By 1952, the heroic Dwight Eisenhower also campaigned actively and cut campaign commercials on the new medium of television. "Eisenhower Answers America" offered short, staged televised interactions between the general and "the people"—all-American types Eisenhower's advertising wizards selected from the queue at New York City's Radio City Music Hall. Between takes, Eisenhower muttered: "to think that an old soldier should come to this."

The Fourth Phase: The Electronic Campaign

The television revolution ushered in campaigning's electronic era. Most local candidates could not afford to broadcast television commercials, but the need for state, national, and some local candidates to raise big money favored entrepreneurial candidacies. Party discipline and loyalty faded as state primaries nominated most candidates. At all levels, outsiders could defy the bosses. Independent gunslingers with enough popularity could win the nomination and inherit the party apparatus. Movie stars could become California governors, billionaires could become New York City mayors. Losers then frequently faded into the sunset and winning candidates emerged less beholden to party powers. Media mastery, rather than virtue, loyalty, or oratory became prized, as candidates frequently traded on celebrity. Campaigns were no longer quests to emphasize a candidate's iconic virtue but to project an appealing image. In this electronic era, smooth-talking salesmen such as John Kennedy, Ronald Reagan, and Bill Clinton dominated.

Television debates offered some of the turning points in presidential campaigns, including when a tanned, confident John Kennedy bested a sweaty, shifty Richard Nixon in 1960, when Gerald Ford stumbled and declared Eastern Europe "free" even though Soviets still dominated in 1976, and when Ronald Reagan laughed off Jimmy Carter's criticisms in 1980, chuckling, "There you go again." Television commercials offered equally powerful defining moments: 1964's pro-Lyndon Johnson "Daisy" commercial suggesting Republican Barry Goldwater might blow up the world, 1984's "Morning in America" commercial praising Ronald Reagan's America as paradise recovered, and 1988's "Willie Horton" commercial maligning Michael Dukakis for furloughing a murderer who then raped and murdered again.

Most recently, some politicians welcomed the computer age as heralding a fifth, virtual era of campaigning. But in the first few national election cycles, the Internet and blogosphere extended the reach of the electronic campaign without yet fully transforming it. In 2008, Barack Obama exploited the Internet as a fundraising and friend-raising tool, raising unprecedented amounts from a huge base of small donors. Still, most of his $600 million war chest came from big money sources. The revolution will happen, gradually, haphazardly.

Meanwhile, many of the historic conundrums surrounding campaigning persist. Are voters fools, do they make what scholars called "low information rationality" decisions like choosing a toothpaste brand, or are they seriously assessing a job applicant's potential to lead in the world's superpower? Why is voter turnout so low: does it reflect America's stability or Americans' disgust with politics? What is the role of money in politics: are campaign costs and donor influence out of control, or are costs reasonable, considering that Procter & Gamble's advertising budget of $6.8 billion in 2006 puts into perspective the estimated $4.3 billion spent during the 2008 campaign to select the leader of the free world? Do Americans seek a president who can be king or prime minister, or could the criteria for those two different jobs be combined? And do America's greatest leaders win campaigns—or if not, why not?

Questions and grumbling continue—and will continue, considering how important the process is, and how messy. Still, American campaigns remain magical, from the contest for the most common to the highest office in the land. Leaders trying to converse communally with thousands, millions, or even hundreds of millions face daunting challenges. But the lack of violence during campaigns, their remarkable regularity through prosperity and depression, peace and war reveal the system's buoyancy. And the fact that even after the contested presidential election of 2000, most Americans accepted the declared winner as legitimate speaks to the Constitution's continuing power. That a document cobbled together hastily in the horse-and-buggy age of the 1780s still works today is a miracle most Americans take for granted, but that every campaign affirms, no matter how much mudslinging, grandstanding, and promiscuous promising there may be.

See also campaign consultants; campaign law and finance; elections and electoral eras.

FURTHER READING. Paul Boller, *Presidential Campaigns: From George Washington to George W. Bush*, revised ed., 2004; Richard Ben Cramer, *What It Takes: The Way to the White House*, 1993; Kathleen Hall Jamieson, *Packaging the Presidency: A History and Criticism of Presidential Campaign Advertising*, 3rd ed., 1996; Alexander Keyssar, *The Right to Vote: The Contested History of Democracy in the United States*, 2001; Richard P. McCormick, *The Presidential Game: The Origins of American Presidential Politics*, 1984; Joe McGinniss, *The Selling of the President*, 1988; Nelson Polsby and Aaron Wildavsky, with David A. Hopkins,

Presidential Elections: Strategies and Structures of American Politics, 12th ed., 2007; Gil Troy, *See How They Ran: The Changing Role of the Presidential Candidate*, revised ed., 1996; Theodore H. White, *The Making of the President 1960*, 1967.

GIL TROY

Caribbean, Central America, and Mexico, interventions in, 1903–34

In the first two decades of the twentieth century, the United States intervened in the Caribbean, Central America, and Mexico with a frequency and purpose that made earlier policy in the region seem haphazard. The interventions ranged from outright military occupations in Mexico, Haiti, and the Dominican Republic to less bellicose, but still coercive, efforts to control the finances of Honduras and Nicaragua. Despite their differences, the actions all aimed to force stability on the poor, weak, and politically volatile nations of the South while protecting U.S. security and promoting American economic interests. The wave of interventions gave U.S. foreign policy a formal new doctrine—the Roosevelt corollary to the Monroe Doctrine—as well as the informal, and at first pejorative, title "dollar diplomacy." While less dramatic than U.S. participation in the Spanish-American War and World War I, the interventions were highly controversial and had repercussions that echoed through the twentieth century and into the twenty-first.

U.S. Expansion in Global Context

The projection of American power in the Western Hemisphere in the early twentieth century was part of a larger global process by which advanced industrial nations—above all Great Britain and France, but also Germany, Italy, Belgium, and Japan—took direct or indirect control of less developed societies in Africa, Asia, and the Middle East. Many factors contributed to this New Imperialism, as it was called: the vast new military and technological power that the industrial revolution bestowed on a handful of advanced nations, the competition for raw materials, foreign markets and geopolitical advantage among these same powers, and the belief, supported at the time, that most non–European peoples were unfit for self-rule and thus needed to pass under the tutelage of one or another "civilized" nation—what Rudyard Kipling called the "White Man's Burden."

Similar factors encouraged the extension of American hegemony, or domination, over the Caribbean and Central America. The growing wealth, military power, technology, and trade of the United States meant that "more or less meddling on our part with the political affairs of our weaker neighbors seems inevitable," as one newspaper editorial put it in 1912. American leaders also looked over their shoulders at the relentless growth of Europe's colonial empires.

They worried most of all that Germany, a powerful industrial nation with few colonies, would ignore the Monroe Doctrine and make a grab for territory in the New World.

Creating Panama

Those fears increased after the first American intervention of the twentieth century brought the nation of Panama into existence in 1903. This came about when Colombia refused to accept an American offer of $10 million for the right to build a canal across the isthmus of Panama, that nation's northernmost province at the time. In November 1903, with the U.S. warship *Nashville* in place to keep Colombian troops from interfering, rebels in Panama declared their independence. Soon after, the tiny new nation leased the Canal Zone to the United States, and work on the great project began the next year. When the Panama Canal opened in August 1914, it channeled a significant share of world trade through Caribbean waters and allowed the United States to move warships quickly from the Atlantic to Pacific theaters. Given the economic and strategic importance of the canal, American policy makers feared that the "weak and tottering republics" of the Caribbean would emerge as the soft underbelly of the United States. As signs grew clearer that a major European war was imminent, U.S. officials fretted that the European powers would pressure one or another country near the canal to grant them coaling stations or naval bases. "The inevitable effect of our building the Canal," Secretary of State Elihu Root noted in 1905, "must be to require us to police the surrounding premises."

The Panama intervention gave the United States a 99-year lease on the Canal Zone, and American officials did not seek to acquire more territory in the region. Few Americans of the time favored creating a formal empire on the European model, especially after the United States resorted to brutal tactics to suppress the Filipino independence movement in the wake of the Spanish-American War. Anti-imperialists like Senator Carl Schurz of Ohio argued that the United States did not need to own the countries it wished to trade with, since American products could compete with the best industrial goods made. Racial prejudice also worked against creating a formal empire. Historically, Americans had allowed new territories to become states, granting full political rights to their inhabitants. If the United States annexed the Dominican Republic or Haiti, eventually those overwhelmingly nonwhite peoples might gain the right to vote, an abhorrent idea to most Americans in the early 1900s. Thus, while policy makers wished to impose stability in the Caribbean and Central America, they did so through what William Appleman Williams called "non-colonial but nevertheless imperial expansion"—the policy of dominating the region without the cost or political headaches of outright ownership.

Noncolonial Expansion:
The Dominican Receivership

President Theodore Roosevelt developed the center-piece of this nonterritorial imperialism in the Dominican Republic, which shares the island of Hispaniola with Haiti. By 1904 the Dominican government had defaulted on millions of dollars in loans from both European and American creditors. At first the State Department worked to ensure that American investors got their money back, but when European foreign ministries threatened to force repayment by seizing Dominican custom houses, Roosevelt ordered U.S. Navy officers to broker a deal. In January 1905, Dominican president Carlos Morales agreed to accept U.S. control of his government's finances. Under the customs receivership, as it was called, American officials took over the Dominican Republic's custom houses—the source of nearly all government revenue—and then paid 45 percent of the money to the Dominicans, with the rest going to foreign creditors. The plan followed from the view that the frequent Latin American revolutions were nothing more than squabbles over money. Roosevelt believed that, by denying Dominicans control of their own national treasury, he had hit on the perfect mechanism to end political instability and financial chaos.

As a complement to the customs receivership, Washington officials brokered a $20 million loan from American banks to help the Caribbean nation build the roads, wharves, and other infrastructure needed for economic growth. Thus, the receivership and loan had the added, and not accidental, benefit of transferring Dominican financial dependence from Europe to the United States. Historian Emily Rosenberg has argued that, by linking a loan agreement to financial supervision, the Dominican plan was a prototype for public-private development partnerships that in the post–World War II period would be "enshrined in the International Monetary Fund."

The Roosevelt Corollary

The Dominican intervention was also the occasion of Roosevelt's famous corollary to the Monroe Doctrine. The original doctrine, first announced in 1823, warned European powers not to try to carve colonies from the newly independent but feeble nations of Latin America. Through the corollary, Roosevelt now forbade European powers to bombard or occupy nations anywhere in the Americas, even to collect legitimate debts. In return, Roosevelt promised that "the United States, however reluctantly," would itself exercise "an international police power" to ensure that each nation "keeps order and pays its obligations." When Democrats and some progressive Republicans in the U.S. Senate objected to the extension of American power over the Caribbean republic, Roosevelt skirted their treaty-making power and had the U.S. Navy implement the receivership by executive fiat.

American leaders saw the customs receivership as an ideal solution to the problem of instability in the Caribbean and, for the first few years, the receivership seemed to live up to their hopes. The *New York Times* cheered that "Uncle Sam has waved the wand that produces National transformation, and lo! a republic has appeared where government is of the people, peace is assured, prosperity is perennial." Although the term would not be coined until a few years later, the Dominican receivership embodied the new policy of "dollar diplomacy," which promised to deploy financial control rather than troops to bring stability to the Caribbean region.

Dollar Diplomacy in Central America

American officials saw the Dominican receivership as such a success that they tried to replicate it elsewhere. After Roosevelt left office, President William Howard Taft and Secretary of State Philander C. Knox pressured Honduras to accept a receivership on the Dominican model, supplemented by loans from American banks. Honduran president Miguel Dávila waffled, fearing a nationalist outcry if he voluntarily gave control of his country's finances to a foreign power. At last, in 1911 he agreed to the plan—only to be driven from office a few months later. That same year, American diplomats pressed a similar arrangement on neighboring Nicaragua, where President Adolfo Díaz, formerly an employee of a U.S. mining company, fearfully accepted the receivership plan.

Both treaties ran into trouble in the U.S. Senate, however, where Democrats and some progressive Republicans objected to what they saw as an unholy alliance of Wall Street bankers and an overreaching president. Opponents worried that Taft would put the receiverships in place without Senate approval, as Roosevelt had done in the Dominican Republic. "They are trying to use the army and navy of the United States to accomplish that which we have specifically refused to give them authority to do," Senator Augustus Bacon, Democrat of Georgia, fumed in 1912. In the end, neither treaty won Senate approval.

Dollar diplomacy, conceived with the goal of ending military interventions, sometimes precipitated them. In Nicaragua, President Díaz faced an armed insurrection by opponents of the U.S. receivership and the American loans that came with it. To keep Díaz in power, the United States landed over 2,000 marines in Nicaragua in what newspapers at the time noted was a clear setback to dollar diplomacy. Once the revolt was quelled, some marines remained, ostensibly to guard the U.S. embassy but really as a tripwire—if violence broke out again, American boots would already be on the ground, justifying the dispatch of reinforcements. U.S. soldiers would return to Nicaragua in force in the late 1920s to crush the rebellion led by Augusto Sandino, who declared, "I want a free country or death."

The Haitian and Dominican Occupations

Even more disappointing to U.S. policy makers was the fate of the "model" receivership in the Dominican

Republic. In 1911 an assassin took the life of President Ramón Cáceres, a popular leader who had cooperated with the United States. The death of Cáceres unleashed several years of precisely the kind of instability that the receivership had supposedly ended. As Dominican presidents rose and fell, the United States began to interfere in day-to-day politics on the island, sending 750 marines to "protect" the U.S. embassy, ordering warships to cruise Dominican waters, and cutting off the receivership's payments to leaders that American diplomats disliked. It is noteworthy that these strong measures were taken by President Woodrow Wilson and his secretary of state, William Jennings Bryan, Democrats who had denounced the Latin American adventures of Republican presidents Roosevelt and Taft. Bryan, three times the Democratic candidate for president from 1896 to 1908, was indeed the symbol of anti-imperialism, once calling dollar diplomacy "a repudiation of the fundamental principles of morality."

It was, nevertheless, under Wilson that U.S. Marines invaded and occupied the Dominican Republic in 1916 (Bryan had resigned in mid-1915 over Wilson's increasing belligerence toward Germany). After repressing scattered resistance, the marines established a military government—no Dominican leader would give the occupation the fig leaf of local support—that imposed martial law, censored the press, and began confiscating arms from the local population.

The occupation lasted eight years. In that time, the American occupiers had some success improving infrastructure, education, and public health, despite unrelenting hostility from the Dominican people that grew into an armed resistance. In 1919 the Dominican president deposed by the U.S. Marines three years earlier traveled to the Versailles peace conference and called for an end to the occupation based on Wilson's pledge in the Fourteen Points to support "justice for all peoples . . . whether they be strong or weak." The Dominican plea had little effect beyond embarrassing American officials at the conference.

The Dominican intervention was not unique. Even before U.S. Marines landed in Santo Domingo, they had occupied the neighboring country of Haiti. Political instability in that country fed American fears of German intervention as World War I raged in Europe. Future secretary of state Robert Lansing justified the occupation of Haiti and other Caribbean nations as essential to "prevent a condition which would menace the interests of the United States . . . I make no argument on the ground of the benefit which would result to the peoples of these republics." The American occupation of Haiti lasted from 1915 until 1934. As in the Dominican Republic, it triggered violent popular opposition in the form of strikes, riots, and guerrilla warfare.

Wilson and Mexico

Wilson and Bryan also used military force to try to steer the course of the Mexican Revolution. The overthrow of Porfírio Díaz, the dictator who had ruled Mexico for over 30 years, led to a violent civil war in Mexico that began in 1911. By 1914 General Victoriano Huerta had defeated his opponents and taken the oath as Mexico's president, yet Wilson withheld official U.S. recognition and pressed for new elections.

When Huerta refused to resign, Wilson seized on a minor incident—Mexico's arrest of several American sailors—to force a showdown. Wilson ordered U.S. Marines to seize the port city of Veracruz, assuming there would be scant resistance and that the occupation would humiliate Huerta and force him to resign. Instead, the marines found themselves fighting street to street with Mexican forces while Huerta clung to power. Despite the casualties, Wilson would not abandon his plan "to help Mexico save herself and serve her people." Wilson at last withdrew the marines from Veracruz in November, after Huerta's rival Venustiano Carranza forced him from power. American meddling in Mexico was not over, however. After revolutionary leader Pancho Villa raided a border town in New Mexico, Wilson sent a 6,000-troop "punitive expedition" across the border in 1916. Wilson, the "anti-imperialist," intervened in Latin America more than any earlier U.S. president.

The receiverships, incursions, and occupations that characterized U.S. policy in the region left a bitter legacy of anti-Americanism throughout Latin America. Leading literary works of the early twentieth century, including Uruguayan intellectual José Enrique Rodó's essay *Ariel* and Nicaraguan poet Rubén Darío's bitter ode "To Roosevelt," cast the United States as a materialistic bully out to crush the romantic spirit of Latin America. In the wake of U.S. interventions in the region, many Latin Americans came to accept this view of their northern neighbor.

Political Repercussions of Intervention

The interventions in the Caribbean, Central America, and Mexico launched between 1903 and 1916 coincided with the high tide of progressivism in the United States. Political debate at home focused on critical economic issues, such as corporate power and labor unrest, in addition to perennial topics like the protective tariff. Those and other domestic issues, as well as the outsized personalities of Theodore Roosevelt, William Jennings Bryan, William Howard Taft, and Woodrow Wilson, dominated the presidential campaigns of 1904, 1908, and 1912. Although many Democrats and some Republicans objected to the way Roosevelt had "taken" Panama, a majority of voters favored building the canal and forgave the president's methods, returning him to the White House in 1904. By 1908, despite Bryan's efforts to make Republican foreign policy a campaign issue, the *New York Times* declared that "anti-imperialism is not an issue in this country, it is only a whine."

After Democrat Woodrow Wilson became president in 1913, Republicans accused him of "vacillating" in his defense of American lives and property in revolutionary Mexico. By 1914, however, World War I had dwarfed the issue of Mexico, and voters reelected Wilson in 1916 in large part for keeping the country out of what Democrats called the "carnival of slaughter" in Europe. While they never became decisive electoral issues, the U.S. interventions in Panama, the Dominican Republic, Nicaragua, Honduras, and Mexico triggered vigorous debate in the Senate, which was called on to approve treaties in the first four cases. The interventions thus became episodes in the long struggle between the executive and legislative branches over control of U.S. foreign policy.

The interventions in the Caribbean, Central America, and Mexico are arguably more relevant to U.S. foreign policy in the twenty-first century than larger conflicts like the two world wars, Korea, and Vietnam. The interventions raised stark questions about the constitutional limits of presidential power in foreign affairs, the effectiveness of using the military to promote stability, democracy, and nation building in less-developed regions, and the unanticipated consequences of overthrowing hostile leaders in manifestly weaker nations. The occupations of the Dominican Republic and Haiti ended by 1934, and Franklin D. Roosevelt formally abandoned dollar diplomacy and pledged to be a "good neighbor" to Latin America after he took office in 1933. Even so, in the second half of the twentieth century the United States resorted to overt and covert intervention in the greater Caribbean, with the Central Intelligence Agency's destabilization of the elected government of Guatemala in 1954, the U.S.-sponsored Bay of Pigs invasion of Cuba in 1961, military intervention in the Dominican Republic in 1965, and the invasion of Panama in 1990.

See also foreign policy and domestic politics, 1865–1933; presidency 1860–1932; progressivism and the Progressive Era, 1890s–1920; Spanish-American War and Filipino Insurrection; territorial government.

FURTHER READING. Bruce J. Calder, *The Impact of Intervention: The Dominican Republic during the U.S. Occupation of 1916–1924*, 1984; Julie Green, *The Canal Builders: Making America's Empire at the Panama Canal*, 2009; Robert E. Hannigan, *The New World Power: American Foreign Policy, 1898–1917*, 2002; John Mason Hart, *Empire and Revolution: The Americans in Mexico since the Civil War*, 2002; Walter LaFeber, *Inevitable Revolutions: The United States in Central America*, 1984; Lester D. Langley, *The Banana Wars: United States Intervention in the Caribbean, 1898–1934*, 2002; Emily S. Rosenberg, *Financial Missionaries to the World: The Politics and Culture of Dollar Diplomacy, 1900–1930*, 1999; Hans Schmidt, *The United States Occupation of Haiti, 1915–1934*, 1971; Lars Schoultz, *Beneath the United States: A History of U.S. Policy toward Latin America*, 1998; Cyrus Veeser, *A World Safe for Capitalism: Dollar Diplomacy and America's Rise to Global Power*, 2002; William Appleman Williams, *The Tragedy of American Diplomacy*, 1959.

CYRUS VEESER

cities and politics

City politics in the United States has a distinctive trajectory, characteristic competitors, and institutions different from national politics. Cities have been the entryway for immigrants to the United States and the destination of domestic migrants from the countryside; their arrivals have discomfited some and thus challenged local politicians to manage their accommodation into local politics. For most of U.S. history, the characteristic antagonists of city politics have been machine politicians and municipal reformers. Machine and reform politicians argued about the purposes and institutions of city government from the mid-nineteenth century until well after World War II. Over the same period, machine and reform politicians adapted their styles and organizations to the expanded purposes of governing the city and the changing demands of urban voters. In the last quarter of the twentieth century, local institutions were again changed to accommodate diverse and politically sophisticated constituents.

From Echo to Urban Politics

In the first decades after independence, city politics were largely an echo of national politics. When Whigs and Democrats debated internal improvements and small government, for example, local party leaders in the cities voiced the same arguments. Two sets of issues interrupted that debate. In the 1840s, and again in the 1850s, nativist politicians argued that the central problem in local politics was the presence of immigrant voters. In the late 1820s and the mid-1850s, organized workingmen campaigned for legal reforms and for assistance during hard times. Each of these challenges left its mark on city politics.

Nativists argued that recent immigrants, mostly Irish and German Catholics, did not fit well into American cities. Immigrants were costly to city government, as evidenced by their presence in local poorhouses and prisons. Worse, since they came from countries that did not enjoy republican government, they were new to political participation, and did not have the skills to bear the burdens of U.S. citizenship. That deficit was amplified by their religion, as Catholicism, nativists claimed, discouraged independent thinking. Nativists were organized into local "American" parties. In most places, Whigs were more receptive to nativist arguments, while Democrats were more likely to defend immigrants. In the 1850s, nativists came together in Know-Nothing parties, which elected representatives to city, state, and federal governments. Like the Whigs, the Know-Nothings foundered on the political divisions that led to the Civil War. Party politicians who defended immigrants denounced nativists as "traitors to the Constitution" and "bigots and fanatics in religion."

Workingmen's parties appeared in cities in the late 1820s and had a long political agenda. The "workingmen" for whom they spoke were artisans, skilled craftsmen working in small shops. The parties called for the abolition of imprisonment for debt, compensation for municipal office holders, improved public schools, and easing the obligations of the militia system. Some of these issues were also supported by farmers and small businessmen; as a result, the parties succeeded at abolishing imprisonment for debt, reform of militia systems, and enacting democratizing reforms. Issues peculiar to wage laborers—a legal limit to the workday, abolition of prison labor—found few supporters beyond their natural constituency and failed. By the 1850s, there were fewer artisans in the cities and many more wage workers. Workers organized in mutual aid societies, unions, and federations of unions; these functioned in prosperous times but could not survive the periodic "panics" (depressions) that plagued the nineteenth-century economy. During the depression of the mid-1850s, mass demonstrations loudly demanded "work or bread" from city halls in New York, Philadelphia, Baltimore, and Pittsburgh, as well as some smaller cities like Newark, New Jersey, and Lynn, Massachusetts. Although the protests briefly convinced some members of the elite that revolution was imminent, the same demands provided an opportunity for major party leaders to demonstrate their sympathy and support for workers. Party leaders in Boston, Philadelphia, New York, Philadelphia, and Trenton, New Jersey, responded with public works to provide employment, established soup kitchens, and endorsed many of labor's demands. In this decade, the first political bosses appeared in big cities. They led party organizations to which working class voters, especially the foreign-born, were fiercely loyal. Their opponents called the parties "machines" because they stamped out election victories as uniformly as machines created identical products.

Hardly had bosses appeared when municipal reformers challenged their rule. In the 1850s, municipal reform slates appeared in elections in Boston, Philadelphia, Baltimore, New York, and Springfield, Massachusetts. Reform politicians had good reasons for their discontent. First, party politics in the cities was corrupt. Second, as cities grew rapidly in the nineteenth century, their budgets grew with them. Even leaving aside the costs of corruption, the burgeoning cities needed streets, sewers, lighting, water, schools, and parks, and these required major investments. Given the incidence of municipal taxes in the nineteenth century—the rich could escape them and the poor were not taxed—growing municipal budgets rested squarely on the shoulders of a small, beleaguered urban middle class. Their disgruntlement provided followers and votes for municipal reform. Third, wealthy and middle-class citizens were not comfortable with the working classes, especially the immigrants, who were the foundation of party politics. Reformers denounced the reliance of party politicians on the unwashed, insisting that cities should be ruled "by mind instead of muscle." Reformers

were united by a belief that machine politicians and their immigrant constituents had corrupted democratic institutions in the cities; and they were united in their desire to upset the status quo and create order in city government. Thus, by mid-century, city politics had developed its own political antagonists and political arguments. Municipal reformers led small groups of activists and put forward candidates to compete in elections, but they rarely won. Party leaders defended workers as "the bone and sinew of the Republic," denounced nativists, and insisted that parties were the best defense of the many against the few. Like extended families or married couples, they repeated these arguments over and over again in the century to follow.

Twentieth-Century Reform

Over the last half of the nineteenth century, the antipathies and discontents of municipal reformers coalesced into an agenda for change. Reformers' opposition to the dominant parties led to a more general antiparty sentiment, and reformers endorsed nonpartisanship. Arguing that the concerns of national parties, necessarily focused on national issues, were irrelevant to city life, reformers were fond of saying that there was no Republican way to lay a sewer, no Democratic way to pave a street. Cities, reformers argued, should be run as businesses; they required fewer politicians and more management. For reformers, urban budgets called for retrenchment, city governments should be frugal, and tax rates should be cut. In addition, municipal reformers opposed cronyism and patronage, called for competitive bidding for city contracts and, toward the end of the century, for merit-based appointments (civil service) for government jobs. Party leaders rejected the reform agenda. Cities were not like businesses, they argued, but communities in which government had obligations to citizens. Party leaders claimed that meeting needs for relief, public health, building codes, "make-work" during recessions, and accepting differences of religion and even affinity for drink were all in the legitimate province of politicians.

Seth Low, mayor of Brooklyn (1882–85) and then New York (1902–3), was an exemplary municipal reformer of this sort. Low made every effort to bring business-like efficiency to city government, and succeeded at reforming New York's tax system and reducing its municipal debt. He opposed cronyism and patronage and argued for merit-based appointments to city jobs. Low did not attend to tenement reform and assistance to needy citizens.

At about the time Low was elected, another type of reformer appeared in the nation's cities: the social reformer. Social reformers agreed with other advocates of municipal reform that corruption and cronyism were destructive of city finances and city government but also saw that corruption took its toll on all citizens. These views soon became widespread. Muckraking journalists brought shocking revelations to the public in newspapers and magazines. Lincoln Steffens's essays, later published in the collection *The Shame of the Cities* (1904), exposed corruption across the country. He traced it not to the low character of immigrant voters but to the malfeasance of large interests and calculated its many costs to city coffers, ordinary citizens, and the moral standard of urban life.

Hazen Pingree, mayor of Detroit from 1890 to 1897, was a businessman transformed by his election. Once in office, Pingree became one of the nation's leading social reformers. Detroit, like many cities, suffered from high prices set by its utilities. Of these, the most costly to working-class residents was the street railway; for workers, even a slight increase in fares might devastate a family budget. Pingree led a campaign to maintain the three-cent fare and free transfers. Resistance by the company led to riots not only of workers but also by middle-class patrons. Pingree vetoed renewal of the company's franchise. Well before that, his efforts became a national crusade, followed in the press, to keep the three-cent fare. There were other social reform mayors, including Tom Johnson (Cleveland, Ohio) and Mark Fagan (Jersey City, New Jersey), who served their cities in similar ways.

In 1894 municipal reformers and leading progressives, including Theodore Roosevelt, founded the National Municipal League. In 1899 the league published its first model city charter, which proposed commission government for cities. In this innovation, citizens elected commissioners who individually served as administrators of city departments (streets, parks, etc.) and collectively served as both the legislative and the executive branch of city government. Although briefly popular, commission government was problematic, and in 1919 the National Municipal League endorsed a different model charter for city manager government.

The charter embraced nonpartisan, citywide elections for city council and the mayor. The council and mayor together appointed the city manager, a professional administrator who served as the chief operating officer of city government. The manager appointed the leaders of municipal agencies and monitored their performance. In addition, the manager was expected to advise the council about both its choice of policies and their implementation. The National Municipal League promoted the model charter in its journal, and supplied public speakers, pamphlets, advice, and boilerplate for newspaper editorials. By 1923, 240 cities had adopted city manager charters.

The changes endorsed by the National Municipal League were important for a second round of reform in the middle of the twentieth century. The Great Depression, and the U.S. effort in World War II, meant that cities across the country were neglected for almost a generation. Housing was not built, roads and other infrastructure not maintained, government conducted without change. After the war, one response to urban stagnation was the federal Urban Renewal program. Urban Renewal funds were eagerly sought by mayors and their city governments and drew support from downtown and real estate interests, construction workers, and low-income residents who hoped for better housing. Urban Renewal revitalized the downtowns of many cities but also displaced communities and did not fulfill the promise of increased housing for low-income families. Displacement provoked the tag "Negro removal" for the program, evidence of the bitterness left in its wake. Lingering black resentment at urban renewal joined demands for the integration of schools, anger at police brutality, resentment of job discrimination in the private sector, increased pressure for more candidates and public officials of color, and greater equity in law enforcement.

In the Southwest and the West, city governments responded to postwar challenges with a fresh campaign to reform city government. The goals of this latter-day reform movement were both to create new institutions and to staff them with new leaders. Between 1945 and 1955, charter change worked its way across the South and the West. This generation's efforts brought municipal reform to towns that grew to be among the nation's largest cities and mid-sized cities: Dallas and Austin, San Diego and San Jose, Phoenix, Albuquerque, and Toledo. In addition to renewed city manager governments, reformers in these cities created a counterpart to the political party, the Nonpartisan Slating Group (NPSG), which nominated candidates for office, agreed on a platform, placed advertisements in newspapers, and worked to get out the vote. In time, the local NPSGs were as successful as the political machines of earlier decades at winning elections, often without effective opposition. In the 20 years that followed World War II, the leaders of big-city reform governments achieved a great deal. They planned and oversaw unprecedented growth, recruited industry, and presided over enormous efforts to build housing, parks, roads, and schools for their cities' growing populations. NPSGs led governments unblemished by scandal or patronage and governed without effective opposition.

Civil Rights

As popular as big-city reform governments were, they had problems and failures alongside their great successes. The failures were not reported in the press and, in some cities, even politicians were blind to them. Two problems in particular could not be fixed without dramatic change. The first was fiscal. A central promise of reform governments was low taxes. Yet for a generation and more after World War II, cities in the Southwest enjoyed tremendous economic, population, and territorial growth. It was the territorial growth—aggressive annexation of outlying areas over many years—that sustained low taxes. As city government expanded to deliver services, annexation kept the taxable population growing even more rapidly, keeping taxes low. By 1970, however, the cities were reaching limits that could not be extended. Many could not annex more territory, as they bordered nature preserves, military installations, and Native American reservations. Municipal debt was on the increase as governments tried to maintain their level of services. Yet the size of these cities was so great that it was not possible to deliver adequate services to all the residents who had come to expect them.

The second problem was the restricted political communities big-city reform created. The institutions of reform—nonpartisan, citywide, and sometimes off-cycle elections, stiff voter registration requirements (sometimes required annually), and literacy tests, in some places well beyond the time they were declared unconstitutional, kept the electorate small. In Dallas, for example, fewer than 20 percent of adults over 21 voted in municipal elections from 1947 to 1963. Turnout in partisan cities was higher: in New Haven, the election with lowest turnout in the same years brought 51 percent of adults over 21 to the polls. Restrictions on voting particularly affected residents of lesser means and citizens of color. The candidates they supported were rarely if ever elected; city councils were remarkably uniform. Annexation of new communities almost always increased the Anglo population and electorate, but not the number of African American and Spanish-surnamed voters.

In 1975 San Antonio tried to annex an outlying suburb. Latino residents filed a suit to stop the annexation, claiming that its intent and consequence were to keep them a minority of the electorate just as Latinos were on the verge of becoming the majority. The U.S. Justice Department agreed with them, and gave San Antonio a choice: the city could annex the territory but had to elect city council members from districts rather than citywide, or the city could maintain citywide elections, but could not annex any more territory. The city chose the first option. San Antonio thus became the first in a long line of big-city reform governments toppled by civil rights activists and the Justice Department.

Big-city reform governments everywhere gave up citywide for districted elections to city councils. The most common consequence was a more equitable distribution of public services. In San Jose, San Diego, and Albuquerque, city council members have more authority assuring the delivery of services to their constituents. This is not trivial. Public services—libraries, roads, garbage collection, schools, police officers, and firefighters—are key to the quality of daily life, and they are what cities provide.

The legacies of political machines and municipal reform remain. The most important and widespread legacy of reform is the decline of patronage appointments for municipal employees, and their replacement by merit-based hiring and civil service. Civil service has delivered more competent city employees at the street level and in administration and in management, has increased the quality of services to citizens, and has created openness and fairness of employment opportunity for those seeking work in the public sector. The legacy of machine politics is the principles that the responsibilities of city government extend beyond business-like management, that urban governments are obliged to represent the interests and values of all of their citizens. At the beginning of the new millennium, U.S. cities were again host to many immigrants, and thus once again were required to rethink and revise municipal institutions, decide what is fair, and debate the appropriate functions and priorities of city government.

See also local government; suburbs and politics.

FURTHER READING. Amy Bridges, *Morning Glories: Municipal Reform in the Southwest*, 1997; Steven P. Erie, *Rainbow's End: Irish-Americans and the Dilemmas of Urban Machine Politics 1840–1985*, 1988; Melvin G. Holli, *Reform in Detroit: Hazen Pingree and Urban Politics*, 1969; David R. Johnson, John A. Booth, and Richard Harris, eds., *The Politics of San Antonio: Community, Progress, and Power*, 1983; Lincoln Steffens, *The Shame of the Cities*, 1904; Jessica Trounstine, *Political Monopolies in American Cities: The Rise and Fall of Bosses and Reformers*, 2008.

AMY BRIDGES

citizenship

At the time of the founding, the American conception of citizenship was marked by two profound contradictions that influenced the new nation's constitutional and legal history.

First, the concept of citizenship, which we associate with freedom, was actually derived from the English tradition of subjecthood, anchored in the feudal notion of obligatory allegiance to the lord for all within his domain. This was formulated most prominently by Sir Edward Coke in *Calvin's Case* (1608). At issue was whether persons born in Scotland after 1603, when the Scottish king James VI became king of England, were to enjoy the benefits of English law as subjects of the English king. Coke argued that, by virtue of the divine law of nature, they indeed did so. Once established in common law, the principle of jus soli was applied to all persons born on the king's domain.

The residual importance of this element of domain is visible in American adherence to the overarching rule of jus soli, most prominently in the constitutional requirement of citizenship by birth on American soil as a qualification for the presidency, but also in the granting of citizenship to children of visitors and even illegal immigrants. However, well before the Revolution the colonists diverged from Coke, contending, in response to their special circumstances, that under the law of nature, subjecthood was modified by the wholly opposite principle of consent. They insisted that this transformed citizenship into an implicit contract whereby subjects could legitimately deny their allegiance to a tyrannical ruler. Accordingly, the concept of citizenship by consent is at the root of American constitutional documents and jurisprudence. By the same token, Americans proclaimed the right of the English and other Europeans to voluntary expatriation and the right of American citizens to shed their citizenship as well.

The second contradiction arose from the ambiguity of the concept of *person*. To begin with, the law of nature did not preclude the practice of slavery—whereby certain human beings were in effect property that could be owned, traded, and disposed of at will—nor the exclusion of persons of African origin born on American soil, even those legally free, from the benefit of jus soli. Although some of the colonies refrained early on from the practice of slavery, or even actively opposed it, the fact that American slaves were overwhelmingly of African descent extended the ambiguous legal status to all African Americans, even those legally free. This contradiction remained unresolved throughout the first half of the nineteenth century.

Eventually highlighted in the debates over the Dred Scott affair, it contributed to the escalation of tensions between the states. In the case formally known as *Dred Scott v. Sanford*, Scott was the slave of an army surgeon who was taken in 1834 from Missouri to Illinois, where slavery had been forbidden by the Ordinance of 1787, and later to the Wisconsin Territory, where slavery was also illegal. Scott sued for his and his wife's freedom on the grounds of their residence in those locations. The case reached the U.S. Supreme Court, which ruled that neither Scott nor any person of African ancestry could claim citizenship in the United States and therefore could not bring suit in federal court under the diversity of citizenship rules. Moreover, Scott's temporary residence in Illinois and Wisconsin did not affect his emancipation under the Missouri Compromise, as this would deprive Scott's owner of his property. This contradiction was not resolved until after the Civil War and the enactment of the Fourteenth Amendment.

Ironically, a similar contradiction pertained to the status of those we now call Native Americans, in acknowledgment of their ancestral roots on American soil. In colonial times, independent unconquered tribes were dealt with as foreign nations; tributary tribes were considered subjects of His Majesty, but within a subordinate jurisdiction and with a separate legal status. In the first half of the nineteenth century, the United States dealt with organized tribes through treaties executed by the Department of War, after which jurisdiction passed to civilian control under the Department of Interior. Tribes gradually encompassed by white settlements exhibited the contradiction most acutely. American leaders viewed the barring of Indians from citizenship as a concomitant of their "peculiar" status: they were either members of "foreign nations," ineligible for naturalization by virtue of the "free, white" requirement legislated in 1790, or—if living among whites—members of a "separate inferior race" in a "state of pupilage" resembling the relationship of a ward to his guardian (as pronounced by New York's Chancellor Kent in 1825 and reaffirmed later at the national level by Chief Justice John Marshall).

The contradiction persisted until 1924, when Congress passed the Indian Citizenship Act, the same year in which it firmed up the blatantly racist National Origins Quota system of immigration regulation. In 1921, the United States had imposed an annual limit on the admission of immigrants from the "Eastern Hemisphere" (meaning Europe, as Asians were already largely excluded) and allocated a quota to each country based on the putative number of persons of that national origin in the current population of the United States. The legislation was designed to reduce immigration from eastern and southern European countries (notably Poland, many of whose immigrants were Jewish; Italy; and Greece). The quotas were further reduced in 1924. By the end of the 1920s, the number of Poles admitted shrank to 8.5 percent of the pre-quota level.

One important source of contention between the settlers and England, featured among the grievances expressed in the Declaration of Independence, was disagreement over the granting of privileges and immunities of citizenship to aliens by way of naturalization. Whereas England jealously guarded this as an exclusive royal privilege, to be allocated sparingly and only under special circumstances, the colonial settlers eagerly adopted an acquisitive stance, asserting their own authority in the matter and establishing a much lower threshold of eligibility. One reason for this was economic: citizenship created attractive and lucrative opportunities to buy and sell land, as the status of national was traditionally required for holding real property. Under English common law and throughout much of Europe, aliens could not pass on property to their heirs; at their death, it reverted to the king. The ability to grant citizenship, therefore, was crucial for American land promoters.

The doctrine of citizenship by consent was reflected in all the founding constitutional documents, at both the state and national levels. However, constitutional doctrine failed to specify precisely what privileges and immunities citizenship conferred, and which Americans were citizens. Adult white women were undoubtedly citizens, but it did not follow that they shared in the voting rights of white *male* citizens. Moreover, a woman could lose her citizenship by marrying an alien. In retrospect, the concept of citizenship was, in effect, limited to the legal sphere.

Until the Civil War, citizenship matters were complicated by the U.S. constitutional structure, which established a distinction between the relationship of persons to the several states and to the central government. The most important aspect of this distinction was that an African American could be a citizen of New York or Illinois but not of the United States (as the *Dred Scott* decision established). This was eliminated by the Fourteenth Amendment (1868), which declared that "all persons born or naturalized in the United States . . . are citizens of the United States and of the State wherein they reside," and that "No State shall make or enforce any law which shall abridge the privileges or immunities of citizens of the United States." Two years later, the Fifteenth Amendment broadened legal citizenship to encompass the political sphere by specifying, "The right of citizens of the United States to vote shall not be denied or abridged by the United States or any State on account of race, color, or previous condition of servitude." However, it took nearly a century for this amendment to move from prescription to practice. The struggle to extend political citizenship to women, launched in the final decades of the nineteenth century, was achieved only about half a century later with the ratification of the Nineteenth Amendment in 1920. Yet another half a century later, the Twenty-Sixth Amendment extended political citizenship to 18 year olds, down from the age of 21.

By the middle of the twentieth century, the concept of citizenship had expanded further in most western democracies to cover the social sphere, constituting what attorney Thurgood H. Marshall termed in 1950 "social citizenship." The United States made some important strides in this direction during the New Deal period, with the institution of unemployment compensation and Social Security. But after World War II it diverged significantly from the path followed by its European counterparts, as well as Canada and Australia, in the sphere of health insurance, the narrowing of income inequality, and the assurance of minimal means of subsistence to all citizens. In 1996 the United States did in effect acknowledge the broadening of the rights of citizenship to encompass the social sphere by enacting legislation to restrict important federal benefits, such as welfare, to U.S. citizens only and allow the states to do the same. In recent decades the concept of citizenship has begun to broaden further to encompass the cultural sphere: the acknowledgment of religious and linguistic diversity, as well as symbolic matters such as pictorial representations of "typical Americans" and references to their cultural heritage. However, in the United States this domain is largely relinquished to the private sector, leaving citizens to fend for themselves according to their varying resources.

Access to citizenship through naturalization figured prominently in the United States, as in other so-called immigrant nations. The dissolution of imperial bonds gave individual state governments the authority to admit members of the political community. Former British subjects were admitted without question on the basis of their participation in the revolutionary struggle. Beyond this, most of the states devised quite liberal rules for incorporating the foreign-born, either in their constitution or by statute. The northern states usually required good character, one year's residence, the renouncing of foreign

allegiances, and the taking of an oath of allegiance to the state. Maryland required, in addition, an oath of belief in the Christian religion (which could be taken by either Catholics or Protestants). For anyone seeking appointment or election to public office, however, most of the states required a more extended period of residence, thereby introducing gradations of citizenship. The southern states usually specified, in addition, that the person be free and white. Initially, "national" citizenship was derived from membership in a state and, except for the racial qualification, the states generally accepted one another's acts of naturalization. Nevertheless, ambiguities arose and fostered a growing sense that citizenship was a national matter. The idea of a more unified state took shape in the Philadelphia Convention's proposed federation, which would have authority to implement a "uniform rule of naturalization." The coupling of naturalization with the authority to establish "uniform laws on the subject of bankruptcies" highlights the prominence of economic concerns in the Founding Fathers' view of citizenship and in the overall process of nationalizing governance.

President George Washington placed citizenship on the agenda in his very first message to Congress, which acted promptly on the matter. Pennsylvania and the western states advocated quick and easy naturalization, especially for prospective buyers of land, to whom citizenship would assure secure property rights. The stance would also serve the interests of ethnic minorities. In the national elections of 1788, for example, Pennsylvania's German community, which had hitherto shied away from politics, demanded representation in proportion to its weight in the population, thereby prompting both the Federalists and their opponents to nominate appropriate ethnic candidates. Voting as a bloc, the Germans sent three representatives to the new Congress, where they firmly supported what today would be called the liberal side in the naturalization debate, thereby demonstrating the feedback effect of political incorporation on immigration and naturalization policy. The other side consisted of a coalition of unlikely bedfellows: New Englanders, who reflected their region's narrower view of national identity, and Southerners who, although in favor of immigration, feared that most of the new citizens would oppose slavery.

Overall, naturalization appears to have been conceived originally as a first step toward Americanization, somewhat akin to a secular baptism, rather than as the capstone of a process of incorporation. The Naturalization Act of 1790 provided that free white persons of satisfactory character would be eligible for naturalization after two years' residence in the United States, including one year within the state from which they applied. The qualifier *free* excluded numerous white immigrants bound in temporary servitude until their term expired. The requirement of satisfactory character, inspired by the Pennsylvania Constitution, was designed to exclude not only convicts and felons, but also "paupers," considered malefactors in need of discipline, much as with welfare cheats today. That said, the naturalization procedure was accessible: the law specified that it could take place in any common law court of record. The law also provided that the minor children of naturalized parents automatically became citizens by way of jus sanguinis and, conversely, that the children born abroad of American citizens be considered natural-born citizens.

Admission to the political community also required an oath of allegiance to the U.S. Constitution. Although applicants were not subject to political vetting, the Constitution did specify that foreign-born persons who had left the United States at the time of the Revolution could not become naturalized without the express consent of the states. Directed at repentant British-born Loyalists, this exclusionary provision constituted one more indication of the country's emerging assertiveness as a sovereign state and distinctive political régime.

Although the requirement of whiteness, which southern representatives insisted on, constituted a retreat from the inclusive notion of citizenship inscribed in the Northwest Ordinance enacted three years earlier, it evoked no debate whatsoever. Perennially restated in subsequent legislation down to the Civil War, this provision excluded not only persons of African descent, notably mulattoes from Saint-Domingue (now Haiti) who streamed into the United States as refugees from the island's revolution, but also American Indians, who could become citizens only by treaty. "White" clearly meant "white exclusively," and when Asians appeared on the scene in the 1840s, the courts quickly determined that they were ineligible as a matter of course. In the end, although the law confirmed the new republic's exclusionary racial boundary, the inclusiveness of all free Europeans of good character, regardless of nationality, language, religion, or even gender, constituted a unique assertion of republican universalism, no less remarkable for being driven by interests as much as principle.

Considered from an international perspective, the provision of routine access to American citizenship constituted a radical political innovation. It challenged the ruling European doctrine of "perpetual allegiance" and threatened to seduce subjects away from their sovereigns. Added to the marketing of land, the naturalization law encouraged immigration. As a counterpart of the naturalization procedure, Americans also insisted on the right to expatriation. At a time when Europe's population was still growing slowly and Europe adhered to Jean Bodin's mercantilist formula—"*Il n'y a richesse ni force que d'hommes*" (There is no wealth nor power but in men)—they actively recruited British subjects as well as foreign Europeans and intervened in the international arena to secure freedom of exit on their behalf. This entailed not only physical exit (i.e., emigration) but also political exit—those coming to America

had to renounce their original nationality, thereby challenging the prevailing doctrine of perpetual allegiance. Indeed, Britain's insistence that British sailors who had become U.S. citizens remained under obligation to serve the king shortly emerged as one of the sources of conflict leading to the War of 1812.

Despite America's generally acquisitive stance, public opinion on immigration swung sharply after 1792, when the crisis triggered by the French Revolution flared into war. The United States attracted a variety of dissenting groups, including aristocratic Frenchmen and German Pietists seeking to evade military service. Most of all, the radicalization of the revolution in France triggered widespread fear of Jacobins. The Federalists, now in power, sought to restrict immigration altogether on the grounds that it constituted a threat to national security. The intrusion of security considerations into the sphere of immigration and citizenship prefigured similar movements in response to the threat of anarchism at the turn of the twentieth century, of Bolshevism in the wake of World War I and the Russian Revolution, and communism at the outset of the Cold War, as well as the fear of Jihad terrorism in the wake of 9/11.

The Federalists lacked constitutional authority to restrict immigration directly, however, because control over persons fell within the sphere of police powers that were reserved to the states in order to protect slavery. Instead, they sought to achieve such restrictions by passing the Alien and Sedition Acts, which subjected both aliens and their American associates to governmental surveillance and criminalized certain forms of political protest. Naturalization emerged as a secondary line of defense against undesirable immigration. In 1795 the ruling Federalists amended the naturalization law to require 14 years' residence and the filing of a declaration of intention five years before undertaking naturalization proceedings. After the Jeffersonian Republicans gained power in 1800, they repealed the Federalist naturalization amendments: in 1802 the residency period for naturalization was set at five years, with a three-year delay for filing a declaration of intention.

These terms, founded on the notion that a substantial period of residence was necessary to infuse aliens with American values, marked a shift away from the idea of naturalization as a ritual starting point toward the notion that it constitutes the capstone of an apprenticeship. With the significant exception of the racial qualification, the terms of citizenship have changed little since 1802, with the addition of more or less demanding tests of language skills and political information to ascertain the candidate's qualification for naturalization. Although federal statutes excluded people of even partial African descent from ordinary naturalization (in keeping with the "one drop of blood rule"), the ruling doctrine of jus soli suggested they might claim citizenship by birthright. But this, in turn, threatened the founding's grand compromise that enabled the exemplary land of freedom to tolerate the existence of slavery. The resulting tension moved to the fore in the debates over the admission of Missouri in 1820 and remained unresolved throughout the first half of the century, culminating in the Supreme Court ruling in *Dred Scott v. Sanford* (1857).

At the end of the Napoleonic Wars in 1815, European emigration resumed quickly and encompassed a broader continental region, because the Congress of Vienna specifically authorized the departure of the inhabitants of the territory ceded by France, including most of present-day Belgium, for a period of six years, and also provided for free emigration from one German state to another, including the Netherlands. Once on the move, many "Germans" kept going until they reached the ports of embarkation for America. Numbers rose to at least 30,000 in both 1816 and 1817 and reached nearly 50,000 in 1818. The growing numbers found a warm welcome from America's budding manufacturing community hungry for labor as well as from land promoters. But they simultaneously stimulated public concern that the arrival of so many Germans, including numerous destitute persons and other undesirables that would burden state and municipal relief facilities, would dilute the nation's British heritage.

Lacking authority to restrict immigration directly, in January 1818 Congress adopted a motion to limit the number of persons carried by incoming ships according to the tonnage of the vessels. The proposal was modeled on the British Passenger Act of 1803, which had been designed to restrict emigration of sheepherders from Scotland. The measure prohibited ships of any nationality entering an American port from carrying more than two persons for every five tons of registry, and required them to deliver to the Department of State "a list or manifest of all the passengers taken on board," including each one's name, occupation, and place of origin. It further specified water and food requirements for Europe-bound ships departing from the United States.

The 1819 law, motivated by a combination of restrictionist and humanitarian concerns, stood as the sole federal enactment pertaining to European immigration until the late 1840s. In the broader perspective of American development, it can be seen as a block in the building of the "American system"—the ensemble of measures designed to promote the development of an autonomous American economy—in keeping with the continuing nationalization of major elements of economic policy. Five years later, the landmark 1824 Supreme Court decision in *Gibbons v. Ogden* granted Congress the power to regulate international commerce as well as immigration. Why 2.5 tons per passenger? Britain, it seems, had recently reduced the minimum from 5 tons per passenger to 3; therefore, 2.5 tons "would afford every necessary accommodation." This was in fact misinformation; Britain maintained a 5-ton requirement for U.S.-bound ships but had recently lowered it to 1.5 for the

traffic to British North America. In any case, the regulation significantly reduced the passenger-carrying capacity of all U.S.-bound ships but simultaneously gave American ships an edge over their British competitors. Immigration restriction, yes, but business is business.

At the time of Alexis de Tocqueville's field trip to America in the 1830s, half a century after independence, his hosts did not think of themselves as a "nation of immigrants." Reflecting the prevailing self-image, the French statesman characterized them as a thoroughly formed Anglo-American people whose political culture was founded on a collective character molded in the course of many generations of shared existence. In effect, he saw white Americans making up a more unified nation than his native France, which, despite centuries of monarchical centralization, remained a country of highly diverse provinces and localities. Although he did observe some immigrants, the foreign-born then constituted at most 5 percent of the white population, a minimal level not equaled again until the 1940s. However, in his second edition, Tocqueville added a last-minute footnote, undoubtedly inspired by information he received from his Whig friends, that deplored the undesirable impending changes likely to follow from the growing arrival of poor Europeans.

This was the first of the series of so-called immigration crises that have marked American history. Although the Know-Nothing Party and its sympathizers attempted to raise the residence requirement for naturalization to the Federalists' 14 years, or even 21 years—a symbolic term designed to subject newcomers to a thorough "re-maturing" process on American soil—they failed to achieve their goal, and had to satisfy themselves with the imposition of burdensome residence requirements for access to local elected and appointed offices. State and local measures of this genre were reenacted in the course of later crises as well, notably in the final decades of the nineteenth century and the first three decades of the twentieth, when they were supplemented by linguistic requirements, literacy tests, and demonstration of the candidate's knowledge of American history and governmental institutions. When these requirements were first imposed in the early decades of the twentieth century, public facilities existed to help applicants prepare. With the decline of immigration from the 1920s onward, however, these public facilities largely fell into disuse and were not fully revived when massive immigration resumed in the final third of the twentieth century.

When Asian immigrants appeared on the scene around 1850, the courts excluded them from naturalization by the long-standing statutory requirement of whiteness, ruling that this was in keeping with the Constitution. However, in the wake of the Civil War amendments, jus soli prevailed. In *United States v. Wong Kim Ark* (1898), a solid Supreme Court majority ruled that birth on American soil sufficed to make citizens of all people, even those of Chinese descent. Under the circumstances, the only way to prevent what many deemed the "racial pollution" of the citizenry was to minimize the likelihood of such births by redoubling efforts to exclude Chinese females, as well as by creating obstacles to miscegenation wherever possible. Consequently, the American population of Chinese origin declined steadily throughout the first four decades of the twentieth century, and Chinese and other Asians remained excluded from acquiring citizenship by naturalization. As a condition of China's participation in the war against Japan, Chinese were made eligible in 1943, but the last traces of racial qualifications for Chinese naturalization were eliminated only in 1952; ironically, the same law also reasserted the racist National Origins Quota system instituted in the 1920s. During World War II, the United States deliberately violated the rights of many citizens of Japanese descent by ordering them to move away from the West Coast on security grounds or interning them along with legally resident aliens.

Despite the doctrinal equality between native-born and naturalized citizens, in practice the naturalized were often subject to more demanding rules. For example, a citizen could lose his U.S. naturalization by returning to his native country and residing there for more than a year. Most of these discriminatory strictures were eliminated in the final decades of the twentieth century, restricting denaturalization to persons who engaged in willful misrepresentation in the filing process.

Not surprisingly, applications for naturalization rose steadily in the wake of the revival of immigration that followed the 1965 reform law. The average annual number of people who became naturalized American citizens increased from fewer than 120,000 during the 1950s and 1960s to 210,000 in the 1980s. Enactment of the Immigration Reform and Control Act of 1986, which provided an avenue to legalization for 2.7 million undocumented immigrants, stimulated an additional 1 million applications, boosting the annual average for the 1990s to 500,000. By 2005, the leading source country for newly naturalized citizens was Mexico, at 13 percent; followed by the Philippines, at 6.2 percent; India, at 6 percent; Vietnam, at 5.4 percent; and China, at 5.2 percent. Seventy-seven percent of immigrants were residents of ten states, with California in the lead, at 28 percent; followed by New York, at 14 percent; Florida, at 7 percent; and Texas, at 6 percent.

The growth of anti-immigrant sentiment from the 1990s onward, the denial of public benefits to noncitizens, and the costs of a newly imposed mandatory renewal of permanent residence permits ("green cards") prompted many eligible but hitherto unconcerned alien residents to apply for citizenship in order to be able to vote or to qualify for benefits. The swelling of applications quickly bogged down federal agencies and created lengthy delays.

Moreover, in the wake of 9/11, security concerns prompted U.S. authorities once again to tighten the borders and access to citizenship without resorting to statutory change. After the Immigration and Naturalization Service was relocated from the Department of Justice to the newly created Department of Homeland Security, its officials reassessed established procedures and concluded that FBI checks on applicants for citizenship were insufficiently thorough. Consequently, in 2002 the agency resubmitted 2.7 million names to be checked further. Rather than simply determining if the applicants were subjects of FBI investigations, the bureau was charged with ascertaining if their names showed up in *any* FBI files, even as witnesses or victims. Because many old documents were not electronic and were scattered throughout the agency's 265 offices, the process could take months, if not years. Further confusion and delays arose from the difficulty of sorting out individuals with common non-European surnames. Some 90 percent of the names submitted for rechecking did not appear in the FBI records. The 10 percent whose names did appear faced further delays, because "deep checks" often require access to records of foreign governments. Many of those stuck in the backlog were from predominantly Muslim countries, as well as from Asia, Africa, and the former Communist countries of Eastern Europe.

According to the official rules as of 2006, to be eligible for naturalization: an alien had to be over 28 years of age, a legal permanent resident of the United States for at least five years (three if married to a U.S. citizen and only one if a member of the armed forces), with absences totaling no more than one year; reside in one state for at least three months; demonstrate the ability to read, write, speak, and understand "ordinary" English (with some exemptions); demonstrate knowledge and understanding of fundamentals of U.S. history and government (special consideration given to applicants with impairments or older than 65 with at least 20 years of residence); take an oath of allegiance that includes renouncing foreign allegiances (although dual citizenship with countries deemed friendly to the United States is permitted); and pay an application fee (plus an additional fee for fingerprints).

Grounds for refusal included certain criminal offenses and failure by the applicant to demonstrate that he or she is "of good moral character." Individuals were permanently barred from naturalization if they had ever been convicted of murder or of an aggravated felony since November 29, 1990. Moreover, a person could not be found to be of good moral character if he or she had "committed and been convicted of one or more crimes involving moral turpitude"; had been convicted of two or more offenses for which the total sentence imposed was five years or more; had been convicted under any controlled substance law, except for a single offense of simple possession of 30 grams or less of marijuana. Other grounds for denial of naturalization included prostitution, involvement in the smuggling of illegal aliens, polygamy, failure to support dependents, and giving false testimony in order to receive a benefit under the Immigration and Nationality Act.

The number naturalizing grew 12 percent from 537,151 in 2004 to 604,280 in 2005, with Mexico the leading country of birth and the Philippines in second place. At the end of that year, more than half a million applications awaited decisions. Growth accelerated further in 2006 with an increase of 16 percent to 702,589. Mexico remained the leading source country, but India overtook the Philippines for second place. A decline in the median number of years in legal permanent residence of the newly naturalized from a recent high of ten years in 2000 to only seven in 2006 confirmed that legal permanent residents who met the residence requirement had become more eager to avail themselves of the rights and privileges of U.S. citizenship. Despite a further increase in naturalization fees and the introduction of a new, more difficult civic test in 2007, the number of naturalization petitions doubled that year to 1.4 million. The backlog was so great that receipt of applications filed in July 2007 was acknowledged only four months later.

Although applicants for naturalization are still required to renounce their allegiance to foreign states, in practice, the United States has become more tolerant of multiple nationality, thus falling in step with the general movement of liberal democracies toward a more flexible concept of citizenship less bound to the world of mutually exclusive territorial sovereignties.

See also immigration policy; voting.

FURTHER READING. Alexander Aleinikof and Douglas Klusmeyer, eds., *Citizenship Today: Global Perspectives and Practices*, 2001; James Kettner, *The Development of American Citizenship, 1608–1870*, 1978; Peter H. Schuck, *Citizens, Strangers, and In-Betweens: Essays on Immigration and Citizenship*, 1988; Daniel J. Tichenor, *Dividing Lines: The Politics of Immigration Control in America*, 2002; Aristide R. Zolberg, *A Nation by Design: Immigration Policy in the Fashioning of America*, 2006.

ARISTIDE R. ZOLBERG

civil liberties

Civil liberties are defined as the rights enjoyed by individuals over and against the power of government. The idea of civil liberties originated in English history, with the Magna Carta in 1215, and developed over the following centuries. By the time of the American Revolution, the list of individual liberties included habeas corpus, freedom of speech, and religious liberty, among others. Specific guarantees were incorporated into the U.S. Constitution (1787), the Bill of Rights (1791), and the constitutions of the individual states.

Civil liberties have had an uneven history in America. The freedoms enshrined in the Bill of Rights were largely ignored for much of American history. In the late eighteenth century, political thinkers did not debate complex rights issues; discussions of free speech, for example, did not address obscenity or hate speech. Serious consideration of such issues did not begin until the modern civil liberties era in the twentieth century.

Civil Liberties in Early American History

The first great civil liberties crisis in American history involved the 1798 Alien and Sedition Acts. The Sedition Act prohibited virtually any criticism of the government, and the administration of President John Adams prosecuted and jailed a number of its critics under the law. The two laws provoked strong protests, most notably the Kentucky and Virginia Resolves in late 1798, which were secretly written by James Madison and Thomas Jefferson, respectively. Both resolves denounced the laws as threats to freedom of speech and challenged the power of the federal government to enact such laws. The principal focus, however, was on the respective powers of the federal government and the states, not on freedom of speech; the resolves contributed to the debate over states' rights rather to the theory of the First Amendment. The crisis over the Alien and Sedition Acts passed when Thomas Jefferson was elected president in 1800 and pardoned all Sedition Act victims.

In the years preceding the Civil War, a major free speech controversy erupted over efforts by proslavery forces to suppress advocacy of abolition, specifically by banning antislavery material from the U.S. mail and by restricting debates on slavery in the U.S. Congress. These assaults on free speech raised public concern to the point where the independent Free Soil Party in 1848 adopted the slogan "Free Soil, Free Labor, Free Speech, and Free Men." The new Republican Party adopted the same slogan in 1856.

Civil War and Reconstruction Era Crises

The Civil War produced two major civil liberties crises. President Abraham Lincoln, in a controversial move, suspended the right of habeas corpus in certain areas controlled by the federal government, fearing that opponents of the war would undermine the war effort. The Supreme Court declared Lincoln's action unconstitutional on the grounds that civil courts were still functioning in those areas. Military authorities in Ohio, meanwhile, arrested and convicted Clement Vallandigham, a prominent antiwar Democrat, for a speech opposing the war, charging him with interfering with the war effort. President Lincoln, however, deported Vallandigham to the Confederacy to avoid making him a martyr. Lincoln also directed military authorities to drop prosecution of an antiwar newspaper in Chicago, believing that such prosecution violated freedom of the press.

The Reconstruction era following the Civil War produced major changes in civil liberties law. The

Thirteenth Amendment to the Constitution prohibited slavery, the Fourteenth Amendment forbade states from depriving persons of due process or equal protection of the law, and the Fifteenth Amendment guaranteed the right to vote. In practice, however, the Civil War amendments provided little actual protection to African Americans. The Supreme Court eventually interpreted the Fourteenth Amendment to invalidate social legislation to help working people, on the grounds that such laws violated individuals' right to freedom of contract (*Lochner v. New York*, 1905).

World War I and the Modern Era of Civil Liberties

The modern era of civil liberties began during the World War I years, when Woodrow Wilson's administration suppressed virtually all criticism of the war and also conducted massive illegal arrests of political dissidents. Such actions set in motion a national debate over the meaning of the Bill of Rights.

In the early twentieth century, the Supreme Court had issued a series of decisions on the First Amendment, all of which upheld the prosecution of antiwar critics. In the case of *Abrams v. United States* (1919), however, Justice Oliver Wendell Holmes, joined by Justice Louis Brandies, wrote a dissenting opinion arguing that the American experiment with democracy rested on the free expression of ideas. Holmes's dissent shaped the subsequent course of constitutional law on the First Amendment.

Another important development shortly after the war was the creation of the American Civil Liberties Union (ACLU) as the first permanent organization devoted to the defense of individual rights. The ACLU succeeded the National Civil Liberties Bureau, which had been created in 1917 to defend the rights of conscientious objectors and to fight violations of free speech during the war. Officially founded in 1920, the ACLU played a major role in advocating expanded protection for civil liberties in the decades that followed.

The legal and political climate in the United States was extremely hostile to civil liberties in the 1920s. The idea of free speech was associated with radicalism, and in the pro-business climate of the period, the freedom of speech and assembly rights of working people who sought to organize labor unions were systematically suppressed.

A 1925 controversy over a Tennessee law prohibiting the teaching of evolution in public schools had a major impact on public thinking about civil liberties. Biology teacher John T. Scopes was convicted of violating the law in a trial that received enormous national and international attention. Because Scopes's conviction was overturned on a technicality, there was no Supreme Court case on the underlying constitutional issues. Nonetheless, the case dramatized civil liberties issues for the general public and foreshadowed many subsequent battles over the role of religion in American public life.

The first important breakthrough for civil liberties in the Supreme Court occurred in the 1925 *Gitlow v. New York* case. The Court upheld Benjamin Gitlow's conviction for violating the New York State criminal anarchy law by distributing a "Left Wing Manifesto" calling for the establishment of socialism in America. In a major legal innovation, however, the Court held that freedom of speech was one of the liberties incorporated into the due process clause of the Fourteenth Amendment. By ruling that the Fourteenth Amendment incorporated parts of the Bill of Rights, the Court laid the foundation for the revolution in civil liberties and civil rights law in the years ahead.

Four Supreme Court cases in the 1930s marked the first significant protections for civil liberties. In *Near v. Minnesota* (1931), the Court held that freedom of the press was incorporated into the Fourteenth Amendment. In *Stromberg v. California* (1931), meanwhile, it held that the Fourteenth Amendment incorporated the free speech clause of the First Amendment. Two cases arising from the celebrated Scottsboro case, where nine young African American men were prosecuted for allegedly raping a white woman, also resulted in new protections for individual rights. In *Powell v. Alabama* (1932) the Court overturned Ozie Powell's conviction because he had been denied the right to counsel, and in *Patterson v. Alabama* (1935), it reversed the conviction because African Americans were systematically excluded from Alabama juries.

The Era of the Roosevelt Court

International events also had a profound impact on American thinking about civil liberties in the late 1930s and early 1940s. The examples of Nazi Germany and the Soviet Union provoked a new appreciation of the Constitution and the Bill of Rights in protecting unpopular minorities and powerless groups. The American Bar Association, for example, created a special Committee on the Bill of Rights in 1938, which filed amicus briefs in several important Supreme Court cases. President Franklin D. Roosevelt, in his 1941 State of the Union address, argued that the "Four Freedoms," which included freedom of speech and freedom of worship, defined American democracy and promoted liberty in a world threatened by totalitarianism.

President Roosevelt appointed four justices to the Supreme Court who were strong advocates of civil liberties, and the so-called Roosevelt Court created a systematic body of constitutional law protecting individual rights. Some of the Court's most important decisions involved the unpopular religious sect known as the Jehovah's Witnesses. In *Cantwell v. Connecticut* (1940), the Court incorporated the freedom of religion clause of the First Amendment into the Fourteenth Amendment, thereby protecting the free exercise of religion against infringement by state officials. In the most famous controversy, the children of Jehovah's Witnesses refused to salute the American flag in public schools as required by the laws in several states on the grounds that it violated their religious beliefs. The Supreme Court upheld their right, holding that the government cannot compel a person to express a belief contrary to his or her conscience (*West Virginia v. Barnette*, 1943).

World War II did not lead to the suppression of free speech that had occurred during World War I, but it did result in one of the greatest violations of civil liberties in American history. With Executive Order 9066, President Roosevelt ordered the internment of 120,000 Japanese Americans from the West Coast, 90,000 of whom were American citizens. They were held in "relocation centers" that were, essentially, concentration camps. Public opinion overwhelmingly supported the government's action, as did the Supreme Court. In *Hirabayashi v. United States* (1943) the Court upheld the constitutionality of a curfew on Japanese Americans, and in *Korematsu v. United States* (1944), it sustained the forced evacuation of Japanese Americans, although Justice Frank Murphy denounced the government's program as racist in his *Korematsu* dissent. In 1988 the federal government apologized for the Japanese evacuation and provided monetary damages to the surviving victims.

The Cold War Years

The anti-Communist hysteria of the cold war period resulted in sweeping assaults on civil liberties. Under President Harry Truman's 1947 Loyalty Program, a person could be denied federal employment for "sympathetic association" with a group or activities deemed subversive. The House Committee on Un-American Activities publicly investigated individuals alleged to be Communists or Communist sympathizers. In the atmosphere of the times, people could lose their jobs or suffer other adverse consequences if the committee simply labeled them as subversive. States, meanwhile, required teachers and other public employees to take loyalty oaths. Senator Joseph McCarthy made reckless and unsupported claims that the government was filled with subversives, and "McCarthyism" became part of the American political lexicon. By the mid-1950s, Senator McCarthy was discredited, and the Supreme Court began to place constitutional limits on many anti-Communist measures.

Racial Equality and Other Advances in Civil Liberties

The post–World War II years also marked significant advances in civil liberties in several areas. The civil rights movement challenged racial segregation in all areas of American life. The high point of this effort was the landmark Supreme Court case *Brown v. Board of Education of Topeka* (1954), which declared racial segregation in public schools unconstitutional. The decision marked the advent of the Warren Court (1953–68), named after Chief Justice Earl Warren, which issued many decisions expanding the scope of civil liberties and defending individual rights.

In response to changing public demands for greater freedom of expression, the censorship of books, magazines, and motion pictures came under steady attack. In *Burstyn v. Wilson* (1952), for example, the Supreme Court ruled that motion pictures were a form of expression protected by the First Amendment. In a series of subsequent decisions, the Court by the late 1960s struck down censorship of virtually all sexually related material except for the most extreme or violent forms, although it never succeeded in formulating a precise definition of pornography or what kinds of expression were outside the protection of the First Amendment.

With respect to the establishment of religions, the Court in 1947 (in *Everson v. Board of Education)* held that the establishment of religion clause of the First Amendment created a "wall of separation" between church and state. In 1962 the Court held that official religious prayers in public schools violated the establishment clause.

The Supreme Court also imposed constitutional standards on the criminal justice system. It placed limits on searches and seizures (*Mapp v. Ohio*, 1961) and police interrogations, ruling in *Miranda v. Arizona* (1966) that the police are required to inform criminal suspects they have a right to an attorney. The Court also held that all criminal defendants facing felony charges were entitled to an attorney under the Sixth Amendment. In *Furman v. Georgia* (1972), the Court held that existing state death penalty laws were unconstitutional as applied but did not declare the death penalty unconstitutional under the cruel and unusual punishment clause of the Eighth Amendment.

A New Rights Consciousness

The civil rights movement spurred a new consciousness about rights that affected virtually every aspect of American society and added a new and ambiguous element to thinking about constitutional rights. Although courts decided cases in terms of individual rights, the emerging rights consciousness increasingly focused on group rights. Decisions on equal protection and even the First Amendment rights of an African American, for example, became instruments for the advancement of African Americans as a group. As a consequence, political movements emerged in the 1960s to support the rights of women, prisoners, children, the mentally and physically disabled, and lesbian and gay people. Each group undertook litigation asserting an individual right as a device to advance the rights of the group in question and effect social change. The Supreme Court was sympathetic to many of these claims, and created a vast new body of constitutional law. The long-term result was the emergence of a new "rights culture" in which Americans responded to social problems by thinking in terms of individual and/or group rights.

The unresolved ambiguity between individual and group rights emerged in the controversy over affirmative action and other remedies for discrimination against particular groups. Traditional civil rights and women's rights advocates argued that group-based remedies were necessary to eliminate the legacy of discrimination. Their conservative opponents argued that group-based remedies violated the individual rights of groups who did not receive what they saw as preferential treatment.

The Vietnam War (1965–72) and the subsequent Watergate Scandal (1972–74) raised several important civil liberties issues. Some Americans argued that the Vietnam War was unconstitutional because Congress had never issued a declaration of war. After much debate, Congress enacted the 1973 War Powers Act, designed to reassert its constitutional authority over committing American military forces to combat. Most commentators, however, have argued that the law failed to achieve its objectives, and the war in Iraq in 2003 again raised difficult constitutional questions regarding the power of the president as commander in chief.

The Watergate scandal resulted in the first Supreme Court ruling on the concept of executive privilege. The Court ordered President Richard Nixon to turn over certain White House tape recordings (which quickly led to his resignation from office) but held that presidents could withhold material whose disclosure would jeopardize national security. The exact scope of this privilege remained a controversy under subsequent presidents. Watergate also brought to light the abuse of constitutional rights by the Federal Bureau of Investigation and the Central Intelligence Agency over many decades. Both agencies had engaged in illegal spying on Americans. To assert more effective legal control over the FBI, Attorney General Edward H. Levi in 1976 issued a set of guidelines for intelligence gathering by the Bureau. In 1978 Congress passed the Foreign Intelligence Surveillance Act (FISA) to control intelligence gathering related to suspected foreign spying or terrorist activities.

The most controversial aspect of the new rights culture involved abortion. In the 1973 *Roe v. Wade* decision, the Supreme Court held that the constitutional guarantee of a right to privacy included the right to an abortion. *Roe v. Wade* provoked a powerful political reaction that exposed a deep cultural division within American society over civil liberties issues related to abortion, prayer in school, pornography, and gay and lesbian rights. A powerful conservative movement led to the election of several presidents and the appointment of conservative Supreme Court justices who either took a more limited view of civil liberties or objected to particular remedies such as affirmative action.

The Supreme Court took a more conservative direction in the 1980s, backing away from the judicial activism on behalf of individual rights that characterized the Warren Court. The conservative orientation became particularly pronounced following the appointments of Chief Justice John Roberts in 2005 and Associate Justice Samuel Alito in 2006. Two important indicators of the Court's new orientation were the 2007 decisions disallowing race-based remedies for school integration (*People Involved in Community Schools, Inc. v. Seattle; Meredith v. Jefferson County*) and a 2008 decision striking down a Washington, D.C., gun control ordinance as a violation of the Second Amendment (*District of Columbia v. Heller*). Until the 2008 decision, the Court had ignored the question of whether the Second Amendment created an individual right to own firearms.

The War on Terrorism and Civil Liberties

The most significant development in civil liberties in the early twenty-first century involved the reaction to the September 11, 2001, terrorist attacks on the United States. The 2001 Uniting and Strengthening America by Providing Appropriate Tools Required to Intercept and Obstruct Terrorism Act (better known as the USA PATRIOT Act) included several provisions that critics argued threatened civil liberties. The law permitted secret searches of home or offices without a warrant (labeled "sneak and peek" searches) and authorized the FBI to collect information through "national security letters" that did not involve a judicial warrant and did not allow the person being investigated to reveal that the letter was even issued. President George W. Bush also authorized secret, warrantless wiretapping of American citizens by the National Security Agency, in violation of the 1978 FISA law. The administration also denied the right of habeas corpus to suspected terrorists held at the U.S. military base at Guantanamo Bay, Cuba. When the Supreme Court held that the president did not have constitutional authority to do this, Congress passed a law denying detainees the right of habeas corpus.

The controversies over habeas corpus, warrantless wiretapping, and other issues related to the so-called War on Terrorism represented what many observers regarded as the most serious constitutional crisis over civil liberties in American history, particularly with regard to the issues of separation of powers and presidential war powers.

See also anticommunism; civil rights.

FURTHER READING. David Cole and James X. Dempsey, *Terrorism and the Constitution: Sacrificing Civil Liberties in the Name of National Security*, 2nd ed., 2002; Edward J. Larson, *Summer for the Gods: The Scopes Trial and America's Continuing Debate over Science and Religion*, 1997; Paul L. Murphy, *World War I and the Origin of Civil Liberties in the United States*, 1979; Mark E. Neeley, Jr., *The Fate of Liberty: Abraham Lincoln and Civil Liberties*, 1991; Geoffrey Stone, *Perilous Times: Free Speech in Wartime from the Sedition Act of 1798 to the War on Terrorism*, 2004; Samuel Walker, *In Defense of American Liberty: A History of the ACLU*, 2nd ed., 1999.

SAMUEL WALKER

civil rights

African Americans waged the civil rights struggle to obtain first-class citizenship, not just on an individual basis but for the entire group. Initially, historians situated the movement between 1954 and 1965, from the landmark Supreme Court decision in *Brown v. Board of Education* to passage of the Voting Rights Act. According to this version, national civil rights organizations led protests to win legal decisions and secure federal legislation. More recently, historians have questioned the validity of this interpretation, especially its focus on national politics and leaders, and have uncovered the origins of the civil rights struggle in earlier periods, such as Reconstruction, the turn of the twentieth century, the Great Depression and New Deal of the 1930s, and World War II. Revisionists also shift the spotlight from the national arena to local communities. More than a struggle for equal rights and racial integration, they argue the civil rights movement aimed to gain freedom for African Americans from all forms of white supremacy—economic, social, and cultural as well as legal and political.

The civil rights movement contained several components. It had a liberationist ideology; participants possessed a consciousness of oppression and the belief that something could be done to overcome it; and it offered a purposeful agenda. Consensus existed among civil rights activists, though the movement allowed for multiple and conflicting objectives and tactics. Although internal tensions weakened the unity of the movement, its diversity provided for a useful division of labor and creative energy.

Prelude to the Civil Rights Movement

Reconstruction laid the basis for black civil rights. Framed by the Republican Party, the Fourteenth Amendment (1868) conferred citizenship on African Americans and guaranteed due process and equal protection of the law, and the Fifteenth Amendment (1870) prohibited racial discrimination against citizens entitled to vote. However, black political participation gradually ended after the Republican Party abandoned Reconstruction in 1877. From 1877 to 1901, the Reconstruction amendments proved inadequate for protecting black citizenship rights. After Congress passed the Civil Rights Act of 1875, which guaranteed equal access to public accommodations regardless of race, the United States Supreme Court in 1883 struck it down as unconstitutional. Once Democrats regained power in the South, they circumvented the Fifteenth Amendment by passing literacy tests and poll taxes as voting requirements. Southern Democrats also adopted the all-white primary, effectively denying African Americans suffrage in that one-party region. In addition, in 1896 the Supreme Court in *Plessy v. Ferguson* ruled that the Fourteenth Amendment did not prohibit segregation in public accommodations, specifically on railroad cars, so long as separate meant equal, thereby opening up the way for the establishment of segregation, albeit without equality, in all aspects of southern life.

African Americans developed several strategies to deal with second-class citizenship. In the 1890s, the educator Booker T. Washington, the most powerful black leader in the nation, accepted the reality of segregation and urged black Southerners to improve themselves economically before seeking civil rights. Opposition to this approach came from Ida B. Wells and W.E.B. DuBois. Wells campaigned against lynching, which had skyrocketed in the 1890s, and DuBois joined sympathetic whites to form the National Association for the Advancement of Colored People (NAACP) in 1909. The NAACP fought against racial discrimination primarily in the courts and in Congress. Headquartered in New York City, the organization was less a mass movement than a single-interest pressure group. It had branches in the South, but they were small in number because it was still too dangerous to challenge white supremacy there.

The Great Depression of the 1930s and President Franklin D. Roosevelt's New Deal stimulated the growth of black activism without tearing down segregation and disfranchisement. World War I had generated a great migration of African Americans from the South to the North in search of jobs and freedom. Though the majority of blacks still lived in the South, those relocating to northern cities now had the right to vote, and sometimes could wield as the balance of power in close local, state, and national elections. Since Reconstruction, the small percentage of African Americans retaining the vote had kept their allegiance to the Republican Party. However, the economic assistance offered by Roosevelt's New Deal persuaded the majority of black voters to switch to the Democratic Party starting in 1936. Roosevelt was no champion of civil rights, as he depended on southern white Democratic congressmen to support his economic programs. Nevertheless, mainly in response to labor organizing against the repressive treatment of industrial workers, the Roosevelt administration set up the Civil Liberties Unit (CLU) in the Justice Department, which focused on civil rights enforcement. From then on, civil rights advocates viewed Washington as an ally.

The New Deal also inspired the formation of interracial organizations in the South, such as the Southern Conference for Human Welfare (SCHW) and labor unions affiliated with the Congress of Industrial Organizations (CIO), that fought racial injustice and poverty. Along with the Communist Party, which actively recruited black members, these groups expanded the definition of civil rights to include economic justice. Their efforts, while significant, did not produce a successful mass movement for civil rights in the South or eradicate segregation, disfranchisement, and poverty.

The Second Reconstruction

More than any other event, World War II set in motion the forces that sparked the modern civil rights movement. The political ideology of freedom, democracy, and antiracism associated with the Allied fight against the Nazis gave African Americans ammunition in challenging repressive, undemocratic, and racist practices at home. In mid-1941, with U.S. participation in the war on the horizon, black labor leader A. Philip Randolph threatened to lead 100,000 African Americans in a march on Washington (MOW) to protest segregation in the armed forces and racial discrimination in industries receiving federal government contracts. Seeking to build a national consensus in favor of going to war and recognizing the political transformation of blacks from Republicans to Democrats, Roosevelt issued an executive order creating the Fair Employment Practice Committee (FEPC) to investigate complaints of racial discrimination by military contractors. Although nothing was done to integrate the armed forces, Randolph called off the march.

Wartime militancy among blacks increased as civil rights groups proclaimed a "Double V" campaign—victory abroad and victory at home against white supremacy. Membership in the NAACP increased tenfold, and the organization won an important Supreme Court victory in 1944 against the white primary, which chipped away at southern disfranchisement. Returning from the war instilled with pride, black veterans lined up to battle domestic forces that continued to deny them freedom. They received moral and political support from the large numbers of black migrants who had journeyed to northern and western cities during the war.

President Harry S. Truman responded to the political reality of the augmented northern black vote. Looking ahead to the 1948 presidential election, Truman set up a committee on civil rights and used its findings to introduce congressional measures to abolish employment discrimination and the poll tax. Truman recognized the balance of political power held by black voters, and in 1948, when his civil rights proposals fell into the deadly clutches of southern congressmen, the president issued an executive order desegregating the armed forces. Truman was also responding to the cold war confrontation with the Soviet Union. As the United States embarked on military preparedness, Randolph threatened demonstrations against the draft if the military remained segregated. Furthermore, in the propaganda war with the Communists, Truman needed all the foreign allies he could get, including newly emerging nonwhite nations in Africa and Asia. However, the cold war was a double-edged sword. It provided a stimulus for racial equality, but repression of domestic Communists and their sympathizers curtailed the contribution of radicals to the civil rights struggle.

Anti-Communist repression ensured the civil rights movement would be black-led, as African American ministers and secular organizations of black men and women formed the vanguard of the movement. Following *Brown v. Board of Education*, which overturned *Plessy*, black citizens in Montgomery, Alabama, launched a boycott against segregation on municipal buses. Beginning in December 1955, it lasted until November 1956, when the Supreme Court ruled in their favor. The boycott thrust its leader, the Reverend Dr. Martin Luther King Jr., into the limelight. He became the most charismatic leader in the civil rights movement and founded the Southern Christian Leadership Conference (SCLC), consisting of black ministers who mobilized African American communities in nonviolent protests against Jim Crow and disfranchisement.

In 1957 the NAACP and other liberal and labor organizations lobbied for passage of the first civil rights law enacted since Reconstruction. The Civil Rights Act of 1957 gave the federal government authority to seek injunctions against discriminatory voter registration officials in the South and created two new agencies to advance civil rights: the Civil Rights Division of the Justice Department (the heir to the CLU) and the U.S. Commission on Civil Rights. President Eisenhower, a lukewarm supporter of government action to promote civil rights, endorsed the measure for several reasons. He believed in the right to vote, saw it as tactic in waging the cold war, and hoped blacks would return to the Republican Party. This measure and another passed in 1960 did not remove all hurdles to black enfranchisement, but they persuaded civil rights proponents that the federal government was prepared to carry out a second reconstruction.

The Civil Rights Movement at High Tide

In the 1960s the civil rights struggle became a genuine mass movement and leaped to the forefront of domestic politics. Following sit-in protests by college and high school students against segregated lunch counters in Greensboro, North Carolina, in February 1960, young people who participated in these and subsequent demonstrations formed the Student Nonviolent Coordinating Committee (SNCC). This interracial group used nonviolent tactics to confront directly all forms of racial discrimination, not only in public accommodations but with respect to the right to vote. The group believed in community organizing and sent its field staff into some of the most resistant areas in Mississippi, Alabama, and Georgia to recruit local people to mount their own challenges to white supremacy. In addition, in 1961 the Congress of Racial Equality (CORE), originally formed in 1942, conducted freedom rides from Washington, D.C., to Mississippi, which ignited white brutality against the participants. President John F. Kennedy, fearing unfavorable publicity, tried to get the riders to call off their protests. When they refused, his administration persuaded the Interstate Commerce Commission to enforce existing desegregation decrees. Kennedy owed his presidential victory in no small part to black voters, who contributed to his margin of less than 1 percent of the popular vote. He had cemented the loyalty of black voters during the campaign by arranging the release of Dr. King from a Georgia jail.

However, Kennedy hesitated to propose antisegregation legislation for fear of alienating southern Democratic allies in Congress. Then, in June 1963, following civil rights demonstrations in Birmingham, Alabama, which led to bloodshed, the Kennedy administration proposed a comprehensive civil rights bill against segregation in public accommodations, schools, and employment. Before the measure became law in 1964, Kennedy was assassinated and replaced by Vice President Lyndon B. Johnson, a former segregationist lawmaker from Texas who had converted to the civil rights cause. In 1965, in response to demonstrations directed by the SCLC in Selma, Alabama, Johnson signed the Voting Rights Act. The measure finally gave the federal government adequate weapons to destroy the chief instruments of disfranchisement: literacy tests and poll taxes.

Civil rights activists had orchestrated the transformation of American politics in another significant way. A year before passage of the landmark Voting Rights Act, the civil rights coalition of SNCC, CORE, and the NAACP, known as the Council of Federated Organizations (COFO), sponsored Freedom Summer in Mississippi, the state with the lowest percentage of black voter registrants (6 percent). During June, July, and August of 1964, COFO recruited some 800 volunteers, mainly white and from the North, to encourage blacks to register to vote, expose brutal white opposition in the state to the rest of the country, and persuade officials in Washington to take action on behalf of Mississippi blacks. After coordinated suffrage drives and the creation of freedom schools, black Mississippians, along with a few white supporters, formed the Mississippi Freedom Democratic Party (MFDP). At the 1964 Democratic National Convention, the MFDP challenged the credentials of the regular state Democratic Party delegates, whose organization barred blacks from participation. Seeking to keep southern white delegates from walking out, President Johnson supported a compromise that gave the MFDP two at-large seats and recognized the Mississippi regulars who swore allegiance to the national Democratic Party. The compromise satisfied neither side, but it called for reforms to wipe out racism within party ranks. Keeping their promise at their next national convention in 1968, Democrats seated integrated delegations from Mississippi and other previously all-white state parties. Subsequently, the national party opened up representation to women and young people, demographic groups also underrepresented in state delegations.

Along with these reforms, Democratic Party identification with the civil rights movement initiated partisan realignment in the South. The once-solid Democratic South became the two-party South, with conservative voters drawn to the Republicans. The civil rights movement increased African American political clout, but it also turned the Democratic Party into a minority party in Dixie. This shift had national consequences. Since 1968, four of eight presidents have come from the South, but no Democratic candidate has won a majority of southern white votes. In addition, the party's identification with the cause of African Americans, especially after race riots and the rise of Black Power in the mid-1960s, pushed some traditionally Democratic groups in the North into Republican ranks. Many blue-collar workers and ethnic Americans of European origin viewed the party of Roosevelt as having abandoned them by favoring such programs as school busing and affirmative action, which they considered reverse racism. Some liberals became neoconservatives, dismayed with civil rights advocates for their apparent abandonment of color-blind principles in identity politics.

Civil Rights Legacies

The civil rights movement transformed politics for other exploited groups, such as women, Chicanos, Native Americans, the disabled, and homosexuals, who also demanded first-class citizenship. Each of these groups created its own freedom movement in the 1960s, benefiting from the ideology and tactics of the civil rights struggle. The feminist movement, in particular, profited from the black freedom movement. Young women working as freedom fighters in southern communities were inspired by older black women, such as Fannie Lou Hamer and Unita Blackwell in Mississippi, who constituted the backbone of grassroots organizing networks. Once Black Power pushed whites out of SNCC and CORE, white women civil rights veterans applied the emancipationist ideology of the black freedom struggle to the formation of the women's liberation movement. In addition, the 1964 Civil Rights Act, with its provision against racial and sexual discrimination in employment, provided one of the main weapons women's groups used to combat occupational and educational bias.

By the end of the 1960s, the coalition of civil rights groups had collapsed. Yet the civil rights movement continued in new forms, such as the election of black officials (an estimated 9,000 by 2007). Two generations after the heyday of the civil rights movement, black politicians and their white allies still had not solved all the problems of racial and sexual discrimination embedded in the economic, political, and social structures of the United States. But they had transformed southern and national politics by opening up decision making at the highest levels to African Americans and other suppressed groups. This achievement of first-class citizenship and erosion of white male supremacy constitute the greatest legacies of the civil rights movement.

See also homosexuality; race and politics; voting.

FURTHER READING. Jerold Auerbach, *Labor and Liberty: The La Follette Committee and the New Deal*, 1966; John Dittmer, *Local People: The Struggle for Civil Rights in Mississippi*, 1994; Mary Dudziak, *Cold War Civil Rights: Race and the Image of American Democracy*, 2000; Adam Fairclough, *Better Day Coming: Blacks and Equality, 1890–2000*, 2001; Peter Lau, *Freedom Road Territory: The Politics of Civil Rights Struggle in South Carolina during the Jim Crow Era*, 2002; Steven F. Lawson, *Running for Freedom: Civil Rights and Black Politics in America since 1941*, 2nd ed., 1997; Charles M. Payne, *"I've Got the Light of Freedom": The Organizing Tradition and the Mississippi Freedom Struggle*, 2007; Patricia Sullivan, *Days of Hope: Race and Democracy in the New Deal Era*, 1996; Nancy J. Weiss, *Farewell to the Party of Lincoln: Black Politics in the Age of FDR*, 1983.

STEVEN F. LAWSON

civil service

In most modern administrative states, the *civil service* consists of those nonpartisan and tenured civilian government employees who have been hired based on merit and technical expertise. Civil servants are the public administrators of government and, though not expressly responsible for making policy, they are charged with its execution. They are expected to be politically neutral. In the United States, civil servants work in a variety of fields such as teaching, health care, sanitation, management, and administration for the federal, state, or local government. As a rule, the civil service does not include elected officials, judicial officers, military personnel, or employees selected by patronage.

Most civil service positions are filled from lists of applicants who are rated in descending order of their passing scores on competitive written civil service examinations. The tests measure aptitude to perform a job. Promotional competitive examinations screen eligible employees for job advancement. Veterans of the armed services may receive hiring preference, usually in the form of extra points added to their examination scores, depending on the nature and duration of service. Legislatures establish basic prerequisites for employment, such as compliance with minimum age and educational requirements and residency laws. Once hired, an employee may have to take an oath to execute his or her job in good faith and in accordance with the law. Employees enjoy job security, promotion and educational opportunities, comprehensive medical insurance coverage, and pension and other benefits often not provided in comparable positions in the private sector.

The Early Civil Service Movement

The establishment of the modern civil service parallels the growth of centralized bureaucratic government and the decline of feudalism. Civil service systems probably originated in the earliest known Middle Eastern societies where rationalized administrations carried out the increasingly complex tasks of government. One of the oldest examples of a merit-based civil service existed in the imperial bureaucracy of China. Tracing back to 200 b.c., the Han dynasty adopted Confucianism as the basis of its political philosophy and structure, which included the revolutionary idea of replacing the nobility of blood with one of virtue and honesty, and thereby calling for administrative appointments to be based solely on merit. Later, the Chinese adopted the nine-rank system, which created a formal hierarchy based on power and expertise. Around a.d. 100, and about the same time paper was invented, the Han dynasty used competitive examinations to select civil officials. This system allowed anyone who passed an examination to become a government officer, a position that would bring wealth and honor to the whole family.

In part due to Chinese influence, the first European civil service did not originate in Europe but rather in India by the British-run East India Company during the early seventeenth century. Company managers hired and promoted employees based on competitive examinations in order to prevent corruption and favoritism. Indeed, today's Indian civil service attracts the best talent in that country, with officers selected through a tough examination system.

The modern European civil services date from seventeenth-century Prussia, when Frederick William and the electors of Brandenburg created an efficient public administration staffed by civil servants chosen competitively. In France a similar bureaucracy preceded the French Revolution and formed the basis for the Napoleonic reforms that converted the royal service into a professional civil service. Across Europe during the early nineteenth century, reformers established regulations intended to minimize favoritism and ensure a wide range of knowledge and skills among civil service officers.

The British Experience

In 1855 the British Parliament established the Civil Service Commission, which instituted a system of competitive examinations. After World War II, the influential Whitley Councils, representing both government employees and administrators, were created to deal with conditions in the civil service. In the British Civil Service, career employees are recruited and promoted on the basis of administrative skill and technical expertise. Civil servants are expected to be politically neutral and are prohibited from taking part in political campaigns or being members of Parliament.

The British Civil Service was at its largest in 1976, with approximately three-quarters of a million people employed. After falling to a record low of 459,600 in April 1999 due to privatization, outsourcing, and downsizing, the number of civil service employees has again risen. While it has been criticized for lack of flexibility and elitism in its upper ranks, the British system remains extremely powerful because of its permanency, extensive grants of power from Parliament, and a reputation for honesty.

The Civil Service Reform
Movement in the United States

The history of civil service in the United States is dominated by the struggle between a completely politicized spoils system and a predominantly merit-based system, a struggle spanning more than a hundred years and still being waged in some state and local jurisdictions. During the Federal period under President George Washington and his successors through John Quincy Adams, the civil service was stable and characterized by relative competence, efficiency, and honesty, although it was somewhat elitist and, over time, superannuated. After 1829 and the election of Andrew Jackson, however, the increasingly strong pressures of grassroots democracy abruptly transformed the civil service of the Founding Fathers. For more than a half century federal, state, and local public services were governed by a spoils system that gave little consideration to competence. During this period, the political party in power dominated the patronage, and changes in party control resulted in a wholesale turnover of government employees. In 1831 New York Senator William Marcy best characterized this chaotic period with his oft quoted adage, "To the victor belong the spoils."

Because the spoils system spawned widespread corruption, inefficiency, and incompetence during the Jacksonian era, the United States lagged far behind European nations in standards of civil service competence and integrity. Agitation for reform began soon after the Civil War, when unprecedented corruption and political chicanery generated calls for a professional, merit-based civil service. In 1871 Congress created the first Civil Service Commission and authorized the president to prescribe regulations for admission to the public service and to utilize examinations in the appointing process. However, Congress refused subsequent appropriations for the commission and allowed it to expire in 1874.

The civil service movement continued to gain momentum after the scandals of President Ulysses Grant's administration, and especially after the assassination of President James Garfield in 1881 by a disappointed office seeker. Spurred by efforts of the National Civil Service League and other reformers, Congress passed the Pendleton Act in 1883, which reestablished the Civil Service Commission after a nine-year lapse. The act remains the federal government's central civil service law and provides the rulemaking process for governing examinations for civil service positions. Successive presidents, requiring increasing professional expertise to carry out congressional mandates, continued and consolidated the reform. Significant expansions of the merit system occurred during the

presidencies of Grover Cleveland, Theodore Roosevelt, and Herbert Hoover. By 1900 the proportion of the federal civil service under the merit system reached nearly 60 percent. By 1930 it had exceeded 80 percent, and in the early twenty-first century, there were fewer than 15,000 patronage posts of any consequence in a federal civil service of 3 million.

In 1940 the Hatch Act attempted to divorce the civil service from politics by prohibiting federal civil service employees from participating in elections or making campaign contributions. A 1993 relaxation of the act allowed most civil servants to engage in political activity on their own time. Unlike workers in private employment, civil service employees may be prohibited from certain acts that would compromise their position as servants of the government and the general public. This is especially true of government employees involved in national defense activities or law enforcement and those holding security clearances.

Civil service reform took place in many state and local governments beginning in the late nineteenth century, although more slowly and less completely than in the federal government. In 1883 both New York and Massachusetts adopted the first state civil service acts. Many states followed after 1939, when the federal government ordered that merit systems be extended to those sections of state administration receiving federal grants. By the 1970s, over a million state and local positions fell within personnel systems closely monitored by the federal government. The proportion of states with comprehensive merit systems grew to one third by 1940 and to two thirds by 1970.

Civil service reform spread to large cities as well, beginning when New York City and Boston set up civil service commissions in the 1880s and followed by Chicago in 1895. Most large metropolitan centers and many smaller cities now have modern merit systems, especially for police and fire departments. In most jurisdictions, a bipartisan civil service commission provides administrative leadership, although single personnel director has become an increasingly popular model.

The Modern Civil Service in the United States

In 1978 Congress passed the Civil Service Reform Act, one of the major domestic accomplishments of the Carter administration. The act instituted a wide variety of management reforms, including the creation of the Office of Personnel Management, the Merit Systems Protection Board, and the Federal Labor Relations Authority. These new agencies replaced the former Civil Service Commission. In addition, the act established the Senior Executive Service (SES), composed of 8,000 top civil servants having less tenure but greater opportunity for productivity bonuses than under previous classification arrangements. This was seen as a step toward the creation of a senior management system allowing recruitment and compensation of top managers on a basis competitive with the private sector. The act also established a system of productivity-related merit pay for senior federal employees just below the SES levels and provided explicit protection for whistle-blowers and employees who call attention to government malpractices.

The Civil Service Reform Act expanded the functions of federal personnel management, which had consisted mainly of administering examinations and policing the patronage. Consequences included improved pay and fringe benefits, training and executive development, a search for first-rate talent, new approaches to performance rating, equal employment opportunity, improved ethical standards, loyalty and security procedures, incentive systems, and special programs for the handicapped. These developments and a system of collective bargaining between unions and managers characterize the transformation of the nineteenth-century merit system into an advanced public personnel regime.

The federal civil service has grown from an institution of a few hundred employees in 1789 to nearly 3 million. During major wars, the federal civil service doubled and even quadrupled. Its peak occurred in 1945, when civil service employees numbered nearly 4 million. There has been a similar growth in state and local services. By the 1970s, federal civil employees functioned almost entirely under merit system procedures, as did some 75 percent of those in state and local governments.

But since the 1980s civil service systems have come under increasing criticism. Critics charge that government has become too big and costly. In response, state legislatures have proposed and implemented significant budget reductions in many civil services. As a result, civil service officers at both the state and federal levels face the challenge of meeting growing obligations with declining resources. Critics also complain that the civil service has outlived its usefulness, stifles flexibility and creativity, and creates unresponsive, out-of-touch government bureaucrats who put their own narrow interests ahead of those of the American people. As calls for the modification or abolition of civil service systems have grown louder, the federal government and some states have adopted an incremental approach in relaxing the strictures of civil service by streamlining recruiting and testing, simplifying job classifications, and building more flexibility into compensation systems. The federal government also made it easier for states to relax civil service requirements when it modified a longstanding requirement that federally paid state workers be covered by a formal merit system. Instead, federal law now asks that state agencies with federally funded employees follow "merit principles" in their personnel management practices.

Modern Civil Service Reform

Three southern states abandoned their civil service systems outright. In 1985 Texas became the first state to cast aside its traditional civil service when its legislature abolished the Texas Merit Council. As a result, agencies hire and promote as they see fit, most written exams are eliminated, and supervisors have more discretion over employee pay. In 1996 Georgia removed merit system protections for all new employees and decentralized hiring authority to agencies and departments. Florida followed in 2001 with the most dramatic reform. Overnight, thousands of merit-protected employees were reclassified into at-will status. The state eliminated seniority and no longer allowed longstanding employees to "bump" newer staff members during downsizing. Florida collapsed thousands of job categories into a few dozen occupational groups and assigned each group a wide pay band that allowed management great discretion in determining individual employee compensation. Between 2000 and 2002, Florida reduced its state workforce by 24,000 positions.

Notwithstanding budget concerns and retrenchment, civil service in the United States remains a uniquely open system, in contrast to the closed career system common to other nations, where one enters at a relatively early age and remains for a lifetime, in a manner similar to a military career. The Pendleton Act of 1883 established this original approach, providing that the federal service would be open to persons of any age who could pass job-oriented examinations. Employees can move in and out of public service, from government to private industry and back again, through a process known as lateral entry. U.S. civil service policy provides a viable route for upward mobility, especially for women and minorities. The federal civil service, in particular, continues to serve as the "model employer" by setting high standards for employee health and safety, amenable labor relations, equal opportunity for women and minorities, and open access to persons with disabilities. Thus, the U.S. civil service has reflected the open, mobile nature of an American society that values individual employees' rights and, in turn, has done much to support it.

FURTHER READING. Ari Hoogenboom, *Outlawing the Spoils: A History of the Civil Service Reform Movement, 1865–1883*, 1961; Patricia W. Ingraham, *The State of the Higher Civil Service after Reform: Britain, Canada, and the United States*, 1999; Ronald N. Johnson, *The Federal Civil Service System and the Problem of Bureaucracy: The Economics and Politics of Institutional Change*, 1994; David A. Schultz, *The Politics of Civil Service Reform*, 1998; Paul Van Riper, *History of the United States Civil Service*, 1958.

RICHARD D. WHITE JR.

Civil War and Reconstruction

The Civil War (1861–65), in which Northerners and Southerners fought over the federal government's relationship to slavery and with the states, destroyed slavery and replaced constitutional ambiguity about secession with an understanding of the United States as an indivisible nation. Reconstruction (1863–77) re-admitted seceded states to the Union and redefined American citizenship to include African Americans. The Civil War and Reconstruction reshaped American government and politics by ending slavery, expanding federal power, inventing presidential war powers, establishing precedent for civil liberties in wartime, solidifying Republicans and Democrats as long-term players in a revitalized two-party system, and enlarging the American polity via constitutional amendment.

Collapse of the Two-Party System and the Coming of the War

Sectional conflict intensified in the 1840s and 1850s, leading to the collapse of the national two-party system, which for decades had discouraged secession and contained conflict over slavery. The question of slavery's extension into U.S. territories reconfigured political fault lines from partisan ones, in which Whigs opposed Democrats chiefly over economic issues, to sectional ones, in which Northerners and Southerners sparred over whether slavery should spread and what the federal government's relationship to slavery should be. In the 1850s, the slavery extension issue contributed to the downfall of the Whigs and the rise of the Republicans, an exclusively northern party opposed to slavery's expansion. In 1860 slavery split the Democratic Party between northern Democrats, who rallied behind Illinoisan Stephen Douglas and popular sovereignty (in which territorial voters, not Congress, determined slavery's status), and southern Democrats, who called for stronger federal commitment to slavery expressed through measures like formal recognition of slavery as a national (not local) institution, a federal slave code obligating federal forces to protect the extension of slavery into territories, and congressional invalidation of state personal liberty laws passed by some northern states to exempt individuals from helping recapture runaway slaves.

Four candidates ran for president in 1860. Southern Democrat John Breckinridge ran on a platform calling for increased federal commitment to slavery and a federal slave code. Stephen Douglas advocated popular sovereignty. John Bell ran as the candidate of the new Constitutional Union Party, which appealed to southern moderates by supporting slavery where it existed but avoiding the expansion question. Abraham Lincoln ran on a platform opposing slavery's extension. Lincoln won with 39 percent of the popular vote (none from southern states) and 59 percent of the electoral vote.

In the absence of national party organizations to temper sectional anger, Deep South states rejected the election results. The South Carolina legislature called a secession convention, which, on December 20, 1860, dissolved the Union between South Carolina and the United States. Mississippi, Alabama, Florida, Georgia, Louisiana, and Texas seceded by February. Delegates from the seceded states met in

Montgomery, Alabama, to select Jefferson Davis as president and Alexander Stephens as vice president of the Confederate States of America, and to draft a Constitution of the Confederate States, which echoed the U.S. Constitution in most places but added firmer protections for slavery. Davis's inaugural address compared the Confederacy to the 13 colonies declaring their independence when Great Britain no longer represented their interests, and he noted the need to prepare for war. The provisional Confederate Congress authorized 100,000 troops. As the new Confederate government formed, conventions in upper South states declined to secede but passed "coercion clauses" pledging to side with the seceded states if the U.S. government attempted to coerce them.

Northern public opinion split between those who called for compromise and those who advocated preserving the Union by whatever means necessary. Lame-duck president James Buchanan did not respond to secession, while Congress considered compromise measures. Most important was the Crittenden Compromise, which permitted the spread of slavery into territories south of the 36° 30′ north latitude line promised federal noninterference with slavery in Washington, D.C., and with the slave trade; and proposed an unamendable amendment to the Constitution that protected slavery. Denounced by Republicans who opposed the extension of slavery and the unalterable amendment, and by southern Democrats who objected to the lack of a federal slave code, the compromise failed.

As support for compromise faded, the Confederate seizure of forts and customs houses contributed to growing northern anger at the seceded states. In addition, many Northerners emphasized the international impact of the dissolution of the Union. Convinced that the American republic stood as an example to the world of self-government based on the egalitarian ideals stated in the Declaration of Independence, Northerners worried that to dissolve the Union over election results would doom the fate of self-government everywhere because other nations would conclude that republican government had failed.

Lincoln hoped to employ a strategy of "masterly inactivity," in which the federal government patiently waited until white Southerners renounced secession. But events intervened. Lincoln's inaugural address stressed the perpetuity of the Union, pledged not to provoke the seceded states, and vowed to preserve the Union. The following day, Major Robert Anderson informed the president that soldiers at Fort Sumter in Charleston Harbor were nearly out of food and other supplies. Lincoln notified Jefferson Davis and South Carolina officials that a U.S. ship with food but not arms would reprovision the fort. On April 12, 1861, acting on orders from Davis, General Pierre G. T. Beauregard and his troops shelled Fort Sumter, which surrendered on April 14. Lincoln called for 75,000 troops to put down the rebellion.

Interpreting the call as coercion, Virginia, Tennessee, Arkansas, and North Carolina seceded to create an 11-state Confederacy.

Emancipation

Emancipation freed 4 million people, destroyed one of the country's greatest sources of wealth, upset the social order of the South, and, by transforming the United States from a slaveholding to a free nation, altered the interests that dictated foreign policy. For these reasons, emancipation was the most important result of the Civil War alongside the survival of the Union. But in 1861, several factors made abolition appear unlikely. For its entire existence, the U.S. government had sanctioned slavery. The Constitution did not permit federal interference with slavery and protected the property rights of slaveholders. The border slave states (Delaware, Kentucky, Maryland, Missouri) stayed in the Union, but close decisions in Kentucky, Maryland, and Missouri meant that retaining the border states would require assurances for the protection of slavery. Moreover, Lincoln and many white Northerners initially believed that most white Southerners were loyal to the Union at heart and would return peacefully if assured that slavery would be safe.

At first, President Lincoln and Congress supplied such assurances. In his July 1861 message to Congress, Lincoln emphasized that he had "no purpose, directly or indirectly to interfere with slavery in the States where it exists." That same month Lincoln endorsed the Crittenden Resolutions, in which Congress claimed that Union war aims did not include abolition. In August, when Union General John C. Frémont sought to pacify portions of Missouri by emancipating secessionists' slaves, Lincoln overturned the proclamation; he also revoked General David Hunter's similar proclamation in South Carolina in May 1862. When New York abolitionist Horace Greeley harangued Lincoln for his apparent reluctance to emancipate, Lincoln answered, in a public letter, that his primary purpose was to save the Union, and any decisions about slavery would be made in service to that goal.

The actions of African Americans and the course of the war led to dramatic changes in Union policy. In May 1861 a Confederate officer demanded the return of three slaves who had fled to Fortress Monroe, Virginia, an encampment under the command of General Benjamin F. Butler. Butler refused, declaring that the rules of war gave him the right to confiscate enemy property as "contraband of war." As word of Butler's actions spread, "contrabands" throughout the seceded states flocked to Union camps, where their labor sustained the Union war effort and their physical presence demonstrated that ending the war would require the Union to face the issue of slavery. Meanwhile, as Northerners realized that the Confederacy would fight a prolonged war, civilians, soldiers, and political leaders warmed to policies designed to

rob the South of the valuable resource of slave labor. In August 1861 and July 1862, Congress passed Confiscation Acts permitting Union Army officers to confiscate and emancipate slaves owned by Southerners who supported the Confederacy. Also in 1862, Congress overturned the Crittenden Resolutions; abolished slavery in Washington, D.C., and U.S. territories; and passed the Militia Act, which authorized the enlistment of black Union soldiers and promised freedom to their families. In July of that year, Lincoln met with border state congressmen to urge the slaveholding Union states to emancipate within their own states.

When Lincoln's appeals to the border states failed, he made new plans. On July 23 the president announced to his cabinet that in his role as commander in chief, he would emancipate slaves in the rebelling states as an act of military necessity. Because Union armies had recently suffered setbacks (most notably, the failure of the army of the Potomac's elaborate Peninsula Campaign to capture Richmond), Secretary of State William H. Seward convinced Lincoln to wait for military victory to issue the proclamation so that the move did not appear to be an act of desperation. On September 22, 1862, five days after the Union Army repulsed a Confederate invasion of Maryland at the Battle of Antietam, Lincoln issued the preliminary Emancipation Proclamation, vowing to free slaves in areas still in rebellion on January 1, 1863. On January 1, Lincoln's final Emancipation Proclamation realized the promise. Though restricted in geographic scope and limited in moral fervor by its emphasis on military necessity, the Emancipation Proclamation nonetheless expanded the aims of the war to include abolition.

Because the Emancipation Proclamation's status as a war measure meant that, in peacetime, its authority might be questioned, Lincoln and a growing number of antislavery advocates looked to a constitutional amendment to permanently end slavery throughout the nation. A proposed amendment abolishing slavery got the necessary two-thirds vote to pass the Senate in June 1864 and the House in January 1865. By December 1865, enough states had ratified the Thirteenth Amendment to make it part of the U.S. Constitution. The document that had protected slavery now outlawed it.

Centralization, Civil Liberties, and Dissent

Constitutional abolition of slavery was just one of many ways in which the national government's power grew during the Civil War. To pay for the war, Congress authorized the first national paper currency with the Legal Tender Act in February 1862. The following month, Congress passed a progressive income tax and empowered the federal government, rather than state governments, to collect it. The Confederacy enacted military conscription for the first time in the nation's history in April 1862, but the U.S. Congress also passed a conscription bill in March 1863 to take effect in July. Unlike the Confederate draft, which mandated the enlistment of every white male of arms-bearing age, the Union draft consisted of a lottery system that placed a percentage of men into the ranks, but even the Union draft expanded the central government's ability to affect the lives of its citizens.

With Democratic representation reduced by the secession of solidly Democratic southern states, Republicans used their newfound congressional majority to increase government involvement in the economy. In 1862 the Homestead Act made public lands in the West available to settlers for a nominal filing fee, the Pacific Railroad Grant subsidized the construction of a transcontinental railroad, and the Morrill Land-Grant College Act used government land grants to increase access to higher education. After decades of low tariffs, Congress raised protective tariffs to promote domestic industry and, supporters argued, to raise workingmen's wages. In short, the Civil War Congress laid the foundations for a distinctly national economy and a view of capitalism as inherently democratic that would come to be seen as a mainstream American (rather than partisan) view in the late nineteenth and twentieth centuries.

The role and power of the president expanded even more significantly, especially with the creation of presidential war powers. Lincoln first used the term *war power* in his July 4, 1861, message to Congress. Since April, Lincoln had taken actions, such as blockading Confederate forts and expanding the armed forces, that seemed to violate Article 1 of the Constitution, which reserves to Congress the right to declare war and support armies. Lincoln's message argued that, with no Congress in session, the president's oath to preserve the Union and the Constitution necessitated that he "call out the war power of the Government." To detractors, the expansion made Lincoln a despot. To his supporters, and in his own mind, Lincoln's obligation to preserve the nation kept his actions aligned with the spirit of the Constitution, if not always its letter. Congress affirmed the idea of the president's war power when it ratified all of Lincoln's actions in July 1861, and the judicial branch gave tacit assent in March 1863, when the Supreme Court narrowly approved the president's blockade in the *Prize* cases. But precisely what "war power" meant would develop over the course of the conflict.

Lincoln used the concept of presidential war powers to take vigorous measures to keep the border states in the Union. Although Missouri and Kentucky remained in the Union largely due to Lincoln's hands-off approach, which respected Kentucky's initial "neutrality" and left matters in Missouri in the hands of state leaders, Maryland required more direct and immediate action because of its proximity to Washington, D.C. In April 1861, when Confederate sympathizers in Maryland effectively cut off the U.S. capital by destroying telegraph and rail lines and attacking a Washington, D.C.–bound Massachusetts regiment as it passed through Baltimore, Lincoln responded by suspending the writ of habeas corpus from Philadelphia to Washington. Because habeas corpus requires an arrested citizen to be promptly charged with and tried for a specific crime, its suspension permitted the indefinite imprisonment of suspected Confederate sympathizers without specific charges. A clear curb on individual liberty, the suspension was immediately tested when John Merryman, a wealthy Marylander and officer in a Confederate cavalry unit that cut telegraph lines, was imprisoned at Fort McHenry and petitioned for a writ of habeas corpus. The Union officer who imprisoned Merryman refused, citing the suspension of the writ; his refusal gave the federal circuit court judge Roger B. Taney (who also served as chief justice of the Supreme Court) the opportunity to rule the suspension unconstitutional because Congress, not the president, could suspend the writ. Lincoln ignored Taney's ruling and Congress later ratified the president's actions.

Lincoln also used the concept of presidential war powers, sometimes at the expense of civil liberties, to recruit and retain soldiers. As the number of men volunteering for military duty waned, Congress adopted measures to raise soldiers, at first by assigning enlistment quotas to states and later by delivering control over recruitment to the national government in the 1863 Conscription Act. Federal officials such as provost marshals and boards of enrollment oversaw the registration of men between ages 25 and 45 in communities throughout the North, and Lincoln issued several calls for troops to be filled by draft in 1863 and 1864. In areas where protesters threatened to interfere or where adversarial newspaper editors encouraged draft resistance, Lincoln suspended habeas corpus and limited freedom of the press. In the fall of 1862, when the requisitioning of troops from the states coincided with the announcement of the preliminary Emancipation Proclamation, Secretary of War Edwin Stanton issued an order subjecting "all persons discouraging volunteer enlistments, resisting militia drafts, or guilty of any disloyal practice affording aid and comfort to the rebels" to martial law, and Lincoln reinforced the order by suspending the writ of habeas corpus throughout the Union. Over the course of the war, about 5,000 civilian arrests were made under the suspension (the total number of individuals affected was smaller because many were arrested more than once), with most individuals released in a matter of weeks.

Emancipation, the expansion of federal power, and the abridgement of civil liberties generated fierce dissent. Antiwar Democrats decried federal overreaching on legal, constitutional, and racial grounds. Editors of some antiwar Democratic newspapers, such as Brick Pomeroy of the *La Crosse Democrat* in Wisconsin, railed against encroaching tyranny. In the fall 1862 elections, Democrats scored key victories in congressional and state contests in midwestern states, New York, and Pennsylvania. Ohio congressman Samuel Cox introduced a resolution denouncing Republican "usurpation of power," and Governor Horatio Seymour of New York chastised the administration for ignoring constitutional liberties. Outspoken antiwar Democrat Clement C. Vallandigham of Ohio lost his bid for reelection to Congress in 1862 but persevered as a vocal war opponent. Antiwar militancy divided the Democratic Party between "War Democrats," who supported the war effort, and "Peace Democrats," denounced by their detractors as "Copperheads"; the divide would not heal until after the war.

Dissent raged all over the North (the most dramatic outburst was the 1863 New York City Draft Riot), but it was particularly concentrated in southern Indiana, Illinois, and Ohio. In Indiana and Illinois, antiwar state legislatures clashed with Republican governors as secret organizations like the Knights of the Golden Circle were rumored to be plotting to overthrow governors, seize federal arms, and launch rebellions. Clement Vallandigham continued to militate against emancipation and the draft. In May 1863, when Vallandigham delivered a speech denouncing the administration and discouraging enlistment, Department of the Ohio Commander General Ambrose Burnside utilized Lincoln's suspension of habeas corpus to punish him. After Burnside ordered the arrest and trial of Vallandigham by military tribunal, Lincoln commuted the sentence to banishment to the Confederacy. Vallandigham escaped to Canada, then ran for governor of Ohio and lost decisively to War Democrat John Brough.

The presidential election of 1864 presented the Union with the biggest test of its ability to withstand dissent, as Lincoln faced challenges within his own party and from Democrats. Radical Republicans believed Lincoln had moved too slowly on emancipation and wanted to replace him with a stauncher abolitionist. Some Democrats portrayed Lincoln as an irresponsible radical intent on either elevating blacks over whites or, according to a pamphlet entitled *Miscegenation*, advocating racial mixing. Other Democrats focused their opposition on the president's conduct of the war. The convention adopted an antiwar and anti-emancipation platform and nominated General George McClellan for president. While party operatives hoped that McClellan's war credentials would mute charges of insufficient patriotism, vice presidential candidate George Pendleton's Copperhead reputation gave the Democratic ticket a decidedly antiwar cast. As the spring and summer of 1864 brought setbacks to Union arms and necessitated more drafts, McClellan and the antiwar platform grew so popular that Lincoln predicted his own defeat.

But the capture of Atlanta by General William Sherman in September 1864 shifted the military momentum of the war and the momentum of the presidential campaign. Aided by the fall of Atlanta and a resounding vote of confidence from Union soldiers, nearly 80 percent of whom voted for the incumbent, Lincoln defeated McClellan. The presidential contest was especially significant because its very existence in the midst of civil war helped quell doubts about the viability of self-government in wartime, validated the legitimacy of two-party politics, and so firmly embedded the Republican and Democratic parties in voters' consciousness that they would remain the dominant parties in a two-party system long after the initial issues that defined them had faded. More specifically, Lincoln's victory dashed Confederate hopes for a negotiated peace and contributed directly, though not immediately, to the conclusion of the war. The passage of the Thirteenth Amendment outlawing slavery temporarily reignited the Confederates' will to fight, but the relentless pressure of the Union Army eventually forced the Confederacy to capitulate in the spring of 1865.

Presidential and Congressional Reconstruction

After the war the United States needed to restore seceded states to the Union and determine the status of former slaves. Both tasks would proceed without the leadership of Abraham Lincoln. Shot by the actor John Wilkes Booth, Lincoln died on April 15, 1865. Struggles ensued between the president and Congress, and between former slaves and former Confederates, for control of Reconstruction.

The first stage, Presidential Reconstruction, in which control rested mainly with the president and the southern states, began in 1863. Aiming to turn internal southern disaffection with the Confederacy into pro-Union sentiment, Lincoln proposed the Ten Per Cent Plan, which offered lenient terms for readmission to the Union. Under Lincoln's plan, once 10 percent of the number of eligible state voters who had voted in the 1860 election took an oath of allegiance to the United States, the state could be readmitted to the Union upon drafting a state constitution abolishing slavery. Confederates, except for very high-ranking political and military leaders, would receive full amnesty and restoration of property except for slaves. Radical Republicans objected that the lenient terms offered insufficient safeguards for the rights of former slaves and would restore the prewar power structure that led to secession. Instead, they proposed the Wade-Davis Bill, which required a majority of eligible voters to take a loyalty oath and which prevented Confederate officials and soldiers from voting for delegates to the state constitutional conventions. Congress passed the bill, but Lincoln pocket-vetoed it. By April 1865 Lincoln recognized the need for a new approach and publicly supported voting rights for at least some African Americans, but he died before articulating a plan.

Lincoln's successor, President Andrew Johnson, shared his predecessor's determination to retain presidential control of Reconstruction but lacked Lincoln's political skill or sense of obligation to black

Americans. In May 1865 Johnson outlined a plan that restored full political, legal, and property (except slave property) rights to all Confederates, except for members of specific exempted groups, including very high-ranking political and military leaders and planters owning more than $20,000 in taxable property, who were required to apply personally to the president for amnesty. Johnson also recognized state governments in Arkansas, Louisiana, Tennessee, and Virginia, thereby approving the rights of those states to send delegations to Congress, and he established easy terms for the readmission of all remaining states as soon as conventions drafted constitutions nullifying secession, repudiating Confederate debts, and recognizing the end of slavery. Encouraged by Johnson's leniency, states asserted the legitimacy of secession, slavery, and white supremacy by repealing rather than nullifying secession and by passing Black Codes that reduced former slaves to conditions close to servitude. Meanwhile, voters elected staunch Confederates to state constitutional conventions.

Alarmed that growing white southern intransigence threatened both genuine restoration of the Union and the rights of former slaves, members of Congress began to maneuver for control of Reconstruction. In December 1865 congressional Republicans refused to seat southern delegations and established a Joint Committee on Reconstruction to review policies for readmission to the Union. Despite divisions between moderate Republicans (who aimed to prevent secessionists from regaining power and sought to protect basic civil rights for blacks with minimal social change) and Radical Republicans (who desired disfranchisement of rebels, full civil rights for former slaves, and the restructuring of southern society), congressional Republicans united to pass two important pieces of legislation. The Freedmen's Bureau Bill established the Bureau of Refugees, Freedmen, and Abandoned Lands, a government agency whose official mission included ministering to civilian war refugees white and black, but in practice the Bureau concentrated on easing former slaves' transition to freedom. The Civil Rights Act explicitly defined national citizenship as applying to black Americans and protected all citizens' rights to make contracts, sue in court, and hold property. The Civil Rights Act was a moderate bill in that it left enforcement primarily to the states, but it still marked an important shift in delineating citizenship rights and linking them to the federal government.

When Johnson vetoed both bills, Congress passed the Fourteenth Amendment in June 1866. The amendment defined all white and black native-born Americans and all naturalized immigrants as citizens of the United States and barred states from denying equal protection under the law to any citizen. It did not guarantee voting rights, but it reduced congressional representation for any state that withheld suffrage from male citizens. To achieve ratification, the Fourteenth Amendment required the approval of three-fourths of the states, which meant it needed the approval of at least some former Confederate states.

Johnson's reaction to the Fourteenth Amendment tipped the balance of power to Congress. The president publicly reiterated his own white supremacist convictions, encouraged white southern hostility toward former slaves, and urged southern states to reject the Fourteenth Amendment. Johnson also embarked on the "Swing Around the Circle" tour of the northeastern and midwestern states to urge Northerners to oppose the amendment and support his approach to Reconstruction. Before large crowds, Johnson harangued Congress, portrayed himself as a persecuted martyr, and taunted audience members. Alienated by Johnson's behavior, northern voters blamed the president when every former Confederate state except Tennessee rejected the Fourteenth Amendment and when race riots erupted in Memphis and New Orleans. They overwhelmingly elected Republicans in the 1866 congressional elections, giving them a veto-proof congressional majority, yet power remained divided between radicals and moderates.

Congress passed the Military Reconstruction Acts and in so doing ushered in a new phase, Congressional Reconstruction, which neither restructured southern society nor redistributed property, but it did prevent former Confederates from dominating state constitutional conventions and did provide some protection for freed people's most basic civil rights. Because Tennessee had ratified the Fourteenth Amendment and reentered the Union, it was exempt, but the remaining ten Confederate states were divided into five military districts by the First Military Reconstruction Act, passed March 1867 over Johnson's veto. Each district fell under the command of a major general who would supervise the registration of eligible voters, including blacks and excluding high-ranking former Confederates. Registered voters would elect delegates to state constitutional conventions. Once a state's convention framed a constitution that enfranchised blacks and barred the highest-ranking ex-Confederates from office, Congress would approve the constitution and the state could hold elections for state officials and members of Congress. Following the ratification of the Fourteenth Amendment by the newly elected state legislature, the state would be fully restored to the Union. Three additional Military Reconstruction Acts clarified ambiguous provisions. By June 1868 Alabama, North Carolina, South Carolina, Arkansas, Louisiana, and Florida had rejoined the Union under the terms of the Military Reconstruction Acts. Georgia, Texas, Virginia, and Mississippi followed by 1870.

The power struggle between Congress and Johnson over the Military Reconstruction Acts resulted in the nation's first presidential impeachment. Johnson replaced Republican generals in charge of military districts with conservative generals sympathetic to former Confederates and hostile to former slaves, and he dismissed cabinet officials until only Secretary of War Stanton remained from Lincoln's cabinet. Radicals pushed to impeach the president in early 1867, but moderates balked and instead Congress passed two laws. The Command of the Army Act, a provision of the Army Appropriations Act, required all orders to army commanders to be issued through General Ulysses S. Grant. The Tenure of Office Act prevented the president from removing federal officials, including cabinet members, without congressional approval until one month after the term of office of the appointing president had expired (April 1869 for officials appointed by President Lincoln).

Johnson tested both laws by removing Generals Philip Sheridan and Daniel Sickles and also by removing Stanton when Congress was not in session. Moderates still rejected impeachment, since by dismissing Stanton when Congress was unable to grant approval, Johnson technically had not violated the Tenure of Office Act. Congress reinstated Stanton, only to have Johnson remove him in February 1868, when Congress was in session. On February 24 the House of Representatives voted along strict party lines (126 to 47) to impeach the president. Johnson would stand trial in the Senate on eleven charges, nine concerning narrow violations of the Command of the Army Act and Tenure of Office Act and two concerning Johnson's broader obstruction of Reconstruction.

Moderate Republicans in the Senate faced a dilemma: they despised Johnson, but worried about the impact of impeachment on separation of powers, and distrusted the Radical Benjamin Wade, who would replace Johnson. After striking a deal in which Johnson pledged to enforce the Reconstruction Acts, stop criticizing Congress, and appoint the well-regarded general John Schofield as secretary of war, seven moderate Republicans joined twelve Democrats to vote against removing the president from office. The final vote, 35 to 19, fell one short of the two-thirds necessary to oust Johnson, who remained in office for the remainder of his term, embittered and unrepentant but with little power to prevent Congress from overriding his vetoes.

The election of 1868 laid the groundwork for a third constitutional amendment. Republican Ulysses S. Grant defeated Democrat Horatio Seymour, but by narrower margins than party operatives anticipated. Concerned that restored southern state governments would abridge black rights, and also looking to bolster their party's base, Republicans drafted the Fifteenth Amendment guaranteeing black men's right to vote. Congress passed the amendment in February 1869.

Following passage of the Fifteenth Amendment, northern white interest in Reconstruction waned, and former Confederates reclaimed power and reasserted white supremacy through violence. Semisecret groups such as the Ku Klux Klan terrorized all southern Republicans but especially former slaves to prevent them from voting or exercising civil rights. Congress passed and President Grant vigorously administered the Enforcement Acts of 1870–71, which succeeded in paralyzing the Klan and protecting at least some black Southerners' right to vote in the 1872 election. Grant won reelection, and Republicans held their own in Congress, paving the way for a final Reconstruction measure, the Civil Rights Act of 1875, which outlawed segregation.

An economic depression in 1873 deflected white Northerners' attention from Reconstruction toward economic issues, and scandals within the Grant administration soured voters on Reconstruction politics. A splinter within the Republican Party, the Liberal Republicans, steered the party away from racial issues toward concerns like governmental corruption and economic recovery. As Democrats regained control and curtailed gains made by black Southerners in the former Confederate states, northern voters and the Republican Party looked the other way.

The election of 1876 brought Reconstruction to an official close. Democrat Samuel J. Tilden won the popular vote, but the Electoral College remained contested because of disputed tallies in South Carolina, Florida, and Louisiana. Republican and Democratic operatives agreed to concede all three states, and thus the presidency, to the Republican candidate, Rutherford B. Hayes, in exchange for Republicans removing the last federal troops enforcing Reconstruction measures and withdrawing national support from southern state Republican Party organizations. Hayes was inaugurated, Republican state governments in the South crumbled, and "Redemption," or the return of southern state governments to the Democratic Party, ensued. Over the next decade, conservative Democrats consolidated power, and by the turn of the twentieth century, an era of solid white Democratic state governance in the South had begun, with poll taxes, literacy tests, and intimidation effectively robbing black Southerners of many civil rights, including the right to vote.

Expansion and Contraction

While the Civil War enabled the expansion of federal power, citizenship rights, and the American polity, the aftermath of Reconstruction reversed significant aspects of wartime expansion, leaving a mixed legacy. The invention of presidential war powers had an ambiguous impact. Some of Lincoln's actions inhibited civil liberties, but he exercised relative restraint, using the authority mainly in areas of Confederate guerrilla activity rather than to punish political enemies. For example, newspaper editor Brick Pomeroy was never arrested despite his calls for Lincoln's assassination. After the Civil War, the Supreme Court trimmed presidential wartime powers with rulings like *ex Parte Milligan* (1866), which found that trying civilians in military courts when civilian courts were operational was unconstitutional. Further, despite growth in Lincoln's power, the impeachment of Andrew Johnson in 1868 and consistent overriding of his vetoes by Congress restricted presidential authority.

The aftermath of Reconstruction also curtailed the expansion of civil rights, particularly through a series of Supreme Court decisions limiting the impact of the Fourteenth and the Fifteenth Amendments. The *Slaughterhouse Cases* of 1873 identified most civil rights as state rights, rather than national rights, and concluded that the Fourteenth Amendment prevented states from depriving citizens of only a few national rights, such as access to ports. *United States v. Cruikshank* (1876) and the *Civil Rights Cases* (1883) determined that the constitutional amendments and the Civil Rights Act of 1875 prevented only states, not individuals, from infringing on citizens' rights. Most famously, *Plessy v. Ferguson* (1896) asserted the constitutionality of state-mandated racial segregation.

The Civil War and Reconstruction did resolve the questions of secession and slavery. Union military victory kept the southern states in the Union, and in *Texas v. White* (1869) the Supreme Court declared secession unconstitutional. The Thirteenth Amendment outlawed slavery. Further, the Fourteenth Amendment and the Fifteenth Amendment extended citizenship and voting rights to black men, and established scaffolding on which the civil rights movement of the twentieth century would build. Yet the precise relationship between federal and state governments and the exact meaning of former slaves' freedom would remain contested long after the era ended.

See also Reconstruction era, 1865–77; slavery; South since 1877.

FURTHER READING. Michael Les Benedict, *The Impeachment and Trial of Andrew Johnson*, 1973; Ira Berlin et al., *Slaves No More: Three Essays on Emancipation and the Civil War*, 1992; Dan T. Carter, *When the War Was Over: The Failure of Self-Reconstruction in the South, 1865–1867*, 1985; Eric Foner, *Forever Free: The Story of Emancipation and Reconstruction*, 2005; Idem, *A Short History of Reconstruction*, 1990; William E. Gienapp, *Abraham Lincoln and Civil War America*, 2002; Allen C. Guelzo, *Lincoln's Emancipation Proclamation: The End of Slavery in America*, 2004; Steven Hahn, *A Nation under Our Feet: Black Political Struggles in the Rural South from Slavery to the Great Migration*, 2003; Frank L. Klement, *Lincoln's Critics: The Copperheads of the North*, 1999; James M. McPherson, *Battle Cry of Freedom*, 1988; Mark E. Neely, *The Last Best Hope of Earth: Abraham Lincoln and the Promise of America*, 1995; Idem, *The Union Divided: Party Conflict in the Civil War North*, 2002; James Oakes, *The Radical and the Republican: Frederick Douglass, Abraham Lincoln, and the Triumph of Anti-slavery Politics*, 2007; George Rable, *But There Was No Peace: The Role of Violence in the Politics of Reconstruction*, 1984; Heather Cox Richardson, *The Greatest Nation of the Earth: Republican Economic Policies during the Civil War*, 1997; Michael A. Ross, *Justice of Shattered Dreams: Samuel Freeman Miller and the Supreme Court during the Civil War Era*, 2003; Rebecca J. Scott, *Degrees of Freedom: Louisiana and Cuba after Slavery*, 2005; James F. Simon, *Lincoln and Chief Justice Taney: Slavery, Secession, and the President's War Powers*, 2007; Hans L. Trefousse, *The Radical Republicans: Lincoln's Vanguard for Racial Justice*, 1969; Michael Vorenberg, *Final Freedom: The Civil War, the Abolition of Slavery, and the Thirteenth Amendment*, 2001; Jennifer L. Weber, *Copperheads: The Rise and Fall of Lincoln's Opponents in the North*, 2006.

CHANDRA MANNING

class and politics to 1877

Since the nation's founding, Americans have sought to reconcile the principle of equal rights for all (at least for all white men) with the reality of significant social differences based on wealth with occupation. To the Founding Fathers, there appeared no inherent contradiction. The Declaration of Independence famously asserted that "all men" possessed "certain unalienable rights," including "Life, Liberty, and the pursuit of Happiness." Yet just because everyone enjoyed the same right to pursue happiness did not mean that everyone would achieve the same level of success, material or otherwise. The founders envisioned the United States as a meritocracy where individuals' social and economic standing would reflect their relative talents, industriousness, and virtue. But they also recognized that differences in wealth and occupation could undermine popular faith in the legitimacy of American government if they hardened into enduring class divisions passed along from one generation to the next. Much of American political history has revolved around the issue of what role government should play both in promoting equal rights and in protecting the unequal results that meritocratic processes can produce over the long term.

The Federal Constitution

Class proved a controversial topic at the Constitutional Convention in 1787. Charles Pinckney of South Carolina argued that America was essentially a classless society and destined to remain so for the foreseeable future. Perhaps because the gap between free whites and enslaved blacks in his home state was so immense, he viewed differences among whites as negligible. "The people of the United States are more equal in their circumstances than the people of any other Country," he affirmed. "The genius of the people, their mediocrity of situation & the prospects which are afforded their industry in a country which must be a new one for centuries are unfavorable to the rapid distinctions of ranks." Virginian James Madison disputed Pinckney. "It was true," he conceded, "we had not among us . . . hereditary distinctions, of rank . . . nor those extremes of wealth or poverty" that plagued European countries. "We cannot however be regarded even at this time, as one homogenous mass." In the future, tensions between rich and poor were bound to grow. "An increase of population will of necessity increase the proportion of those who will labour under all the hardships of life, & secretly sigh for a more equal distribution of its blessings," Madison predicted. New Yorker Alexander Hamilton agreed. "It was certainly true that nothing like an equality of property existed," he declared, "that an inequality would exist as long as liberty existed, and that it would unavoidably result from the very liberty itself. This inequality of property constituted the great & fundamental distinction in Society."

To contain the threat of an impoverished and jealous majority in a republican polity, the Founding Fathers designed a national government that would be dominated by men of substantial property and social distinction. Given the large size of federal electoral districts, only persons of prior renown—for the most part members of established elites—were likely to win election to the House of Representatives, the most democratic branch of the new regime. Both sides in the struggle over ratification of the Constitution grasped this logic. New York anti-Federalist Melancton Smith warned that the new system would award too much power to "the natural aristocracy of the country." He did not wish to keep all men of high achievement and reputation out of government, but he wanted the new Congress to be open as well to members of "the middling class." Although the campaign to block ratification of the Constitution failed, Smith framed a question that would recur periodically in American political history: what class of men should rule in a republic—the better sort or ordinary citizens?

Federalists, Republicans, and the "Revolution of 1800"

During the 1790s, political debate raged over the proper relationship between the populace at large and their representatives in the national government. Federalist leaders believed that natural aristocrats like themselves possessed a near monopoly on the wisdom necessary to identify the public good and guide the country in the right direction. When members of Democratic-Republican societies, many of them middling artisans and farmers, challenged administration policies on the grounds that they favored the rich and well-born, President George Washington denounced the societies as illegitimate "self-created" organizations bent on subverting the American republic. According to Federalists, qualified voters had a right and responsibility to elect virtuous gentlemen to Congress, but once elections were over, the common people should quietly abide by the policies prescribed by their social superiors.

Yet the natural aristocracy failed to consolidate into a cohesive ruling class under Federalist auspices. Soon after the new federal government got under way, a fierce quarrel broke out within the nation's upper echelons. Hamilton, as secretary of the treasury, sought to build a financial system modeled on the British example. He hoped to tie wealthy investors to the national project and to fuel economic development by establishing a national bank and by funding at par the combined public debt of the nation and the separate states. Hamilton's proposal deeply alienated his erstwhile ally Madison and Madison's good friend Thomas Jefferson. They feared that Hamilton meant to turn over control of the government to unscrupulous speculators and to prepare the way for a return to monarchy. In response, they formed the Republican Party and deployed class rhetoric to mobilize the middling sort against Hamilton's policies. The Federalists, Madison charged, "are more partial to the opulent than to the other classes of society; and having debauched themselves into a persuasion that mankind are incapable of governing themselves, it follows with them . . . that government can be carried on only by the pageantry of rank, the influence of money and emoluments, and the terror of military force."

The Republican triumph of 1800–1801—what Jefferson later called the "Revolution of 1800"—signaled an important shift in the class dynamics of American politics. Especially in the northern states, the Republican coalition challenged the political dominance of long-standing local elites. Jefferson, though by any measure a natural aristocrat, believed that, in a republic, sovereignty should reside actively in the people at large, with government—especially the federal government—interfering as little as possible in the "natural" processes of a free society. Yet Jefferson's policies as president proved more interventionist than his principles. By acquiring the huge Louisiana Territory, Jefferson safeguarded the economic opportunities of westward-heading farmers for generations to come. And by imposing the Embargo of 1807–9, he weakened New England commerce, stimulated American industrialization, and reenergized the partisan conflict between Federalists and Republicans. The result was a deepening sectional divide between the elites of the North and the South and a general rise in popular political participation. Despite the failure of Jefferson's embargo and the subsequent outbreak of the War of 1812, the Republicans succeeded in isolating northern merchants and financiers by consolidating their political base in the South and by attracting enough support among artisans and farmers in the middle states to dominate national politics. By 1820 the Federalist Party was moribund, and the eighteenth-century conception of rule by a natural aristocracy seemed passé.

The Missouri Crisis and the Rise of Jacksonian Democracy

Yet the uproar over Missouri's application for admission to the Union in 1819 revealed a serious cleavage within the Republican coalition. The most obvious line of division was sectional. Northerners opposed the extension of slavery while Southerners supported it. Underlying this difference were the parallel yet conflicting class dynamics of North and South. Even as the northern economy grew more diverse and many farmers' sons and daughters migrated to urban centers, other northern progeny sought to maintain an agricultural way of life by moving west. Their model of enterprise was the family farm, and they deeply feared competition from slaveholders whose ability to exploit black bondsmen made plantation agriculture more efficient. Southern farmers likewise looked westward for opportunity, especially as global demand for cotton soared in the early nineteenth century. Some large planters moved west, where land was comparatively cheap and the soil quite fertile, but the majority of southern whites who migrated were less affluent, including aspiring yeomen whose strategy for success was to climb into slaveholding ranks. The social goals of middling farmers in North and South had much in common, but their engagement in different labor systems tended to drive them apart.

During the late 1820s and 1830s, Andrew Jackson and his supporters were nonetheless able to build a Democratic Party composed mainly of northern and southern agriculturalists. To achieve this goal, Jacksonians muffled the debate over slavery as best they could. They also wooed middle-state manufacturing interests and disgruntled northern artisans, including veterans of short-lived Working Men's Parties based in the Northeast. Much of Jackson's appeal was personal: he was a self-made man and military hero whose rise from anonymity to fame and from rags to riches depended on his strength of will. He was not a natural aristocrat in the traditional sense, with its genteel connotations. He embodied a new variant of meritocracy, where those at the top of the social order were expected to resemble the middle class in temperament and opinion, only on a grander scale. As Alexis de Tocqueville observed in *Democracy in America*, "The men who are entrusted with the direction of public affairs in the United States are frequently inferior, both in point of capacity and of morality, to those whom aristocratic institutions would raise to power. But their interest is identified and confounded with that of their fellow citizens." In the public imagination, Andrew Jackson was the common man writ large.

Jackson's "war" on the Second Bank of the United States solidified the Democratic Party as a national organization. Like Jefferson, Jackson feared that an alliance between the federal government and large-scale financial interests—the so-called money power—would subvert the liberty of the American people. In his 1832 veto message aimed at the national bank, Jackson portrayed a situation in the United States bordering on class warfare. "It is to be regretted that the rich and powerful too often bend the acts of government to their selfish purposes," he wrote. "When the laws undertake to add to . . . natural and just advantages artificial distinctions, to grant titles, gratuities, and exclusive privileges, to make the rich richer and the potent more powerful, the humble members of society—the farmers, mechanics, and laborers—who have neither the time nor the means of securing like favors to themselves, have a right to complain of the injustice of their Government."

Jackson's opponents rejected his analysis root and branch. Calling themselves Whigs, they viewed the Second Bank of the United States as an economic engine that benefited all Americans. Whigs believed in class cooperation, not class conflict, and they thought a republican government, properly led, could and should maximize the public good by promoting balanced capitalist development. Unlike the Federalists before them, the Whigs did not believe in government by a natural aristocracy ruling the hoi polloi with aloof condescension. They celebrated self-made men as fervently as the Democrats and adopted modern forms of mass politics with enthusiasm. Yet they never fully escaped the charge that they cared more about business interests than the interests of ordinary people. Though studies of voting patterns have found significant variations from place to place and have demonstrated that factors such as ethnicity and religion were often as important as wealth and occupation, it appears that the Whigs drew their support mainly from those best positioned to gain directly from capitalist growth, while the Democrats drew their support primarily from those who feared they were losing out in a rapidly commercializing economy.

The Coming of the Civil War

While Democrats attacked federal intervention in the economy as an insidious plot to make the rich richer at the expense of everyone else, their laissez-faire policies served another, less egalitarian purpose: to protect slavery and the interests of southern slaveholders. The weaker the national government, the less chance it would interfere with the "peculiar institution"—an institution potentially at political risk as the proportion of slaveholders within the American population declined during the first half of the nineteenth century. In 1800 the demographic balance between free and slave states was roughly 50:50; by 1850 it was closer to 60:40. Moreover, within the slave states, slaveholders were a shrinking minority among the white population. Yet by leveraging their influence within the national Democratic Party, slaveholders captured a disproportionate share of high federal offices and exercised virtual veto power over congressional legislation. Between 1789 and 1850, slaveholders held the presidency four-fifths of the time, and, notwithstanding northern opposition to slavery's expansion, they greatly increased the amount of American territory open to human bondage. But when slaveholders demanded the repeal of the Missouri Compromise in 1854 and pushed for the introduction of slavery into Kansas—until then "free" territory under the Missouri accord—they overreached. In response to the Kansas-Nebraska Act, middle-class northerners turned against the so-called slave power with a vengeance and rallied with greater intensity than ever before to the antislavery appeal of "free soil" and "free labor."

Significantly, it was not New England's industrialists who led the campaign to end the slaveholders' control over national policy. Abolitionists angrily denounced the unholy alliance of the "lords of the lash" and the "lords of the loom." Nor did leading New York merchants wish to undermine the intersectional and trans-Atlantic trade in cotton that yielded them hefty profits. The new Republican Party of the mid-1850s found its strength elsewhere: among northern farmers, small-scale manufacturers, middling merchants, and a subset of wage earners. The Republicans cared less about the plight of southern slaves than the prospects of northern whites, but they earnestly deemed the slave power a font of evil.

Against the backdrop of Bleeding Kansas, the *Dred Scott* decision, and southern calls for a federal slave code, the Republican Party persuaded a majority of northerners that Democrats could not be trusted to safeguard northern rights. Likewise, against the backdrop of the Republicans' antisouthern rhetoric and John Brown's raid on Harpers Ferry, proslavery "fire-eaters" persuaded a large proportion of whites in the Deep South that the elevation of a Republican to the presidency would endanger their equal rights as American citizens. When Abraham Lincoln won the presidential election of 1860 with a clear-cut majority of the electoral vote, albeit only 40 percent of the popular vote, the stage was set for southern secession and the outbreak of civil war.

The Outcome of the Civil War and Reconstruction

After four years of bloodshed and devastation, the Union Army, helped by emboldened southern blacks and disaffected southern whites, defeated the slave power. Union victory opened the way for the liberation of America's most thoroughly exploited working class. Slaves were not the passive recipients of freedom but active agents in securing it. When peace came, they were eager to exercise their newly recognized rights, both as human beings and as American citizens.

The Thirteenth, Fourteenth, and Fifteenth Amendments to the federal Constitution promised an extraordinary transformation of the American social and political order. Not only would former slaves be guaranteed their freedom, they would enjoy the same civil rights as their former masters and voting rights on par with their fellow Americans regardless of "race, color, or previous condition of servitude." Although the postwar settlement did not include a large-scale transfer of land ownership from planters to the freed people, for a brief period in the late 1860s and early 1870s it looked like southern blacks might be able to rise out of poverty with the help of sympathetic Republican administrations at the state and national levels. Except for Haiti, no other country in the Western hemisphere experienced such a dramatic shift in class relations as the result of slavery's abolition. "The black man is free, the black man is a citizen, the black man is enfranchised, and this by the organic law of the land," exclaimed the ex-slave and radical leader Frederick Douglass in 1870. "One of the most remarkable features of this grand revolution is its thoroughness. Never was revolution more complete."

Unfortunately, this postwar settlement did not endure. Although some ex-slaveholders accepted the legitimacy of Union victory and the principle of black participation in the reconstructed polity, many more turned to terror and intimidation in order to regain control over local and state governments. They found collaborators among poor and middling southern whites whose social identities rested on their sense of racial superiority over blacks. This interclass racist alliance not only quashed the civil and political rights of black Southerners but also broke the will of middle-class white Northerners who had sought to impose a "free labor" vision on the South.

Abraham Lincoln had eloquently sketched the free labor vision in his annual message to Congress in 1861. "Labor is the superior of capital, and deserves much the higher consideration," he declared. Yet he emphasized, "A large majority belong to neither class—neither work for others, nor have others working for them." The epitome of success was the independent proprietor: "Men, with their families—wives, sons, and daughters—work for themselves on their farms, in their houses, and in their shops." The promise of America was that all free men could realistically aspire to this level of independence. "The prudent, penniless beginner in the world, labors for wages awhile, saves a surplus with which to buy tools or land for himself; then labors on his own account another while, and at length hires another new beginner to help him," Lincoln observed. "This is the just, and generous, and prosperous system, which opens the way to all—gives hope to all, and consequent energy, and progress, and improvement of condition to all."

But, in the aftermath of the Civil War, the chances of rising from wage labor to independent proprietorship seemed to diminish in the North. Mammoth capitalist enterprises—many of them corporations enjoying limited liability and legal immortality—came to dominate the fast-growing industrial sector, and small producers denounced the power that major railroad companies exercised over their livelihoods. While magnates like Andrew Carnegie of Carnegie Steel and John D. Rockefeller of Standard Oil were self-made men, their aggressive business strategies and huge fortunes set them far apart economically and socially from those in the middle and working classes. A new American aristocracy began to coalesce—one based mainly on capitalist calculation and the determination to corner markets by whatever means necessary. The new aristocrats did not boast formal titles, and unlike natural aristocrats of the late eighteenth century, they did not hold public office. But with unprecedented wealth at their disposal, they greatly influenced government policies. The muckraker Henry Demarest Lloyd wrote acerbically of Rockefeller's political machinations, "The Standard has done everything with the Pennsylvania legislature, except refine it."

As Northerners lost faith in the free labor vision, they also grew tired of the seemingly endless task of reconstructing the postwar South. Soon after taking office in 1877, President Rutherford B. Hayes, a Republican, removed federal troops from statehouse guard in Louisiana and South Carolina, thereby enabling ex-slaveholders to complete the "redemption" of former Confederate states. Over the next quarter century, the South, with little interference from Washington, would evolve into an apartheid social order. Yet while federal officials refused to intervene on behalf of blacks in the post-Reconstruction South, they proved eager to intervene on behalf of business interests in the North. Hayes established the precedent. When railway workers nationwide walked off their jobs in July 1877, he dispatched federal troops to break the strike and restore economic and social order. A decade and a half after Abraham Lincoln told Congress that "labor is the superior of capital, and deserves much the higher consideration," Hayes acted on a very different assumption: that the rights of workers to pursue their happiness were inferior to the rights of corporations to protect their property and to accumulate capital. A century after the nation's founding, there persisted a profound tension between the American ideal of equal rights and the reality of class inequities sustained by governmental power.

See also agrarian politics; business and politics; economy and politics; labor movement and politics.

FURTHER READING. John Ashworth, *"Agrarians" and "Aristocrats": Party Political Ideology in the United States, 1837–1846*, 1987; Eric Foner, *Free Soil, Free Labor, Free Men: The Ideology of the Republican Party before the Civil War*, 1970; Idem, *Reconstruction: America's Unfinished Revolution, 1863–1877*, 1988; Steve Fraser and Gary Gerstle, eds., *Ruling America: A History of Wealth and Power in a Democracy*, 2005; William W. Freehling, *The Road to Disunion*, 2 vols., 1990–2007; Steven Hahn, *A Nation under Our Feet: Black Political Struggles in the Rural South, from Slavery to the Great Migration*, 2003; James Oakes, *The Ruling Race: A History of American Slaveholders*, 1982; Heather Cox Richardson, *The Death of Reconstruction: Race, Labor, and Politics in the Post–Civil War North, 1865–1901*, 2001; Charles Grier Sellers, *The Market Revolution: Jacksonian America, 1815–1846*, 1991; Sean Wilentz, *The Rise of American Democracy: Jefferson to Lincoln*, 2005.

GARY J. KORNBLITH

class and politics since 1877

Mainstream pundits and politicians have long proclaimed the absence of class in modern American politics. Leftist scholars have responded by proclaiming the centrality of the working class in the political realm. Both sides have compelling claims. The United States has indeed been distinctive in the way that class has influenced politics, with—at times—a striking lack of a classical European conflict between bourgeoisie and proletariat. As German sociologist Werner Sombart famously put it, referring to the relatively prosperous standard of living for ordinary Americans, radical working-class politics in America have often foundered on "roast beef and apple pie." Yet said proletariat has, at critical moments, been a crucial player in American public life, whether by means of Gilded Age anarchist bomb throwing, Depression era sit-down striking, or the simple act of being a collective electoral presence.

The standard debate about class between mainstream editorial writers and leftists, however, obscures more than it illuminates. What is truly distinctive about American class politics is the strength of that great beast, the middle class. That said, "the middle class" is a creature easy to caricature but difficult to pin down because of its demographic and ideological complexity. And the moral of the story is not, as so many scholars have claimed, that the middle class means the end of "class"; rather, that entity is the crucial starting point for understanding the foundational significance of class in modern American politics.

The Gilded Age

The year 1877 was a time of intense class polarization that witnessed some of the most violent class conflicts in all of American history. With the close of Reconstruction, federal troops moved from South to North to patrol the powder keg that many industrial cities had become as the result of a national railroad strike. Dozens of workers were killed, and millions of dollars' worth of property was damaged from Baltimore to St. Louis, before federal troops ended the 45-day melee.

The display of railroad employees shot down in the street by what many believed were rapacious corporate elites and the minions provided a dramatic opening act to the Gilded Age. And the gilding of the period was indeed quite thick. A self-conscious national elite formed, perhaps for the first time in American history, as merchants and manufacturers, Northerners and Southerners, united across divides of political economy and region to unleash a world historic wave of corporate growth sponsored by both major political parties. Armed not only with guns but with the proud ideology of social Darwinism, these elites were intent on politically marginalizing those outside their charmed circle, particularly an increasingly immigrant-based working class. In turn, workers responded with the most impressive drive for unionization to date. The Knights of Labor organized upward of 700,000 workers, often across the divides of race, gender, and job skills, and appeared poised to move the political economy in a more small-scale and worker-friendly direction.

As the battle between workers and elites lurched toward a momentous bombing at Haymarket Square in Chicago on May 4, 1886 (where seven police officers and an unknown number of citizens were killed in the melee caused by a bomb of unknown origin), it seemed that intense class conflict would be the defining axis of social and political life in the late nineteenth century. Yet matters were not so simple. The Knights of Labor, for example, were as intent on defining themselves as hardworking—and middling—"producers" as they were in forging a proletarian consciousness. (It was actually members of the more cautious and conservative American Federation of Labor, founded by Samuel Gompers in 1886 as a response to the Knights, that articulated a hard-core identity as "workers," set apart from small business owners and other "nonworkers.") Similarly, the Populist Party—the chief expression of rural rebellion during the 1890s—also claimed to stand for those in the middle. Protesting banking, transportation, and monetary policies, the Populists argued in their 1892 Omaha Platform that "from the same prolific womb of governmental injustice we breed the two great classes—tramps and millionaires." During their brief limelight, the Populists elected (sometimes on a fusion ticket with Democrats or Republicans) ten governorships and 45 members of Congress and placed a number of measures, such as that of income tax, firmly on the national agenda.

The middling nature of American politics showed up even more powerfully in mainstream politics. While many voters continued to vote in an "ethnocultural" way, with religion in particular a key point of conflict, the presidential campaigns of candidates from James Garfield to Grover Cleveland were able to assume a fairly moderate middle-class consensus, even amid the class tumult of the period. William McKinley appealed more directly to workers in the 1896 election against William Jennings Bryan, but still did so as an upholder of self-conscious middle-class and Middle American values—the beginnings of a tradition that would hold considerable sway over American electioneering up to the present day.

The Progressive Era
That small farmers like the Populists, as well as exploited workers like the Knights of Labor, were claiming the mantle of *middle class* meant that an important part of the structure of political conflict going into the early twentieth century was a vigorous ideological battle over who should be included in that term and what it meant. Moreover, professions traditionally associated with the upstanding middle class—business owners, lawyers, doctors, and other white-collar workers—greatly expanded during the era of corporate modernization that lasted from 1877 to 1929. With such a wide range of occupations and experiences making up a culturally contested middle class, it is no surprise that those in the middle did not act in political unity.

This is especially important to recognize when reckoning with the politics of the early twentieth century—the period traditionally known as the Progressive Era. Scholars for more than a half century have argued that the middle class provided the impetus for progressive reform. Whether the anxious and antidemocratic middle class of Pulitzer Prize–winning Richard Hofstadter's *The Age of Reform* (1955) or the confident and modernizing middle class of Robert Wiebe's *The Search for Order* (1967), the middle class latched on to reform not just to stand with Theodore Roosevelt at Armageddon, battling for the Lord, but also to forge their own class identity against ethnic workers and old moneyed elites. Historians such as Hofstadter and Wiebe viewed the middle class as acting in lockstep, with "its" politics flowing out of a monolithic unity. Yet, in both local and national arenas, middling folks acted in quite disparate ways. In some cities, especially in the West, non-elite business owners formed the shock troops for a vigorous and often successful open shop and antiradical movement. In contrast, in places like San Francisco and Portland, Oregon, middling shopkeepers, printers, lawyers, and housewives joined with workers to forge a political culture that upheld the rights of unions and pressed for radical measures of direct democracy and economic equality.

Indeed, no matter how broadly the term is stretched, *middle class* does not cover a good portion of Progressive Era politics. It is applicable to a reformer like Jane Addams, who grew up in privileged circumstances in a small Illinois city but who was not a member of Chicago's upper class, no matter how much she associated with elites during her crusades for worker and immigrant rights. Yet the term cannot encompass one of the two most prominent political figures of the period, the ultra-upper-class Theodore Roosevelt, and it does not fit easily upon the shoulders of the other, Woodrow Wilson. The elite presence within progressive reform, and within Progressive Era politics more generally, was substantial. And, at the other end of the spectrum, the extreme class conflicts characteristic of the Gilded Age by no means disappeared in the generally more prosperous era before World War I. Poor and middling farmers, and their agrarian-oriented representatives in Congress, were a major reason for the rise of national regulatory power over business during the years 1910–20. Union membership also increased substantially with conflict intensifying to such peaks as a general strike in Seattle in 1919; workers also played an important role in campaigns such as those for accidental injury insurance. In tandem, a socialist movement, led by the charismatic (and middle-class) Eugene V. Debs, gained considerable strength. Debs twice gained close to a million votes in his race for the presidency, and Socialists took seats in Congress and plenty of political offices in cities ranging from Schenectady, New York, to Milwaukee, Wisconsin.

Despite the complexities of class politics during the Progressive Era, there was a substantial connection between the middle class and the politics of this period of reform. Middle-class outrage against corporate corruption helped fuel changes from limits on campaign contribution to the regulation of food and drugs. Middle-class concern about economic polarization also led to the passage of minimum wage and maximum hours laws (especially for women). Despite their support for the right to hold private property, ordinary Americans displayed considerable ambivalence about some of the basic structures of capitalism, ranging from the inequality of wealth to the exploitation of labor. Presidents Roosevelt and Wilson often expressed the same concerns as they engaged in a creative debate about the fate of the national economy; the result was the first systematic federal regulation of corporations and financial markets. Middling morality became a hurricane force in American politics, particularly in campaigns for Prohibition and against vice. And middle-class support was crucial for passage of the constitutional amendments of the period—regarding the income tax, the direct election of U.S. senators, Prohibition, and woman suffrage. The middle class never did any of this alone; in particular, much of the working class was attracted to "middle-class" political reform. Yet the middle class was clearly the star of the early twentieth-century political show.

From World War to World War

The period from 1914 to 1945 was an era in which American politics seemed to leapfrog rapidly between liberalism and conservatism. The glow of reform remained in the air from 1914 until the United States entered World War I in the spring of 1917. Immediately afterward, an intense period of reaction gripped the country, subsiding into a period of conservative "normalcy" until 1933—when Franklin D. Roosevelt abruptly switched gears and marched the country through the most sweeping moment of liberal reform in the nation's history.

A good portion of this leapfrogging can be explained by events that were related to but in many ways transcended issues of class: the rise of the United States to the status of a superpower, the greatest economic depression in world history, the growing threat of totalitarian powers in Europe and Asia. Yet part of the turbulence of American politics was also the result of the temporary decentering of the middle class. With the reform impulse of the Progressive Era stifled—even strangled—by the political consequences of World War I, middle-class concerns took a backseat as, first, elites took charge of American politics during the 1920s and then workers asserted power during the 1930s.

Woodrow Wilson feared that war would kill the spirit of reform, and he was right. While scholars have correctly pointed out that liberal and leftist politics survived during the war and into the 1920s,

Wilson himself launched a devastatingly effective campaign against any perceived radicalism, with the net cast quite widely. Socialists and other labor radicals were jailed, and leaders of organized labor had little choice but to announce a suspension of strikes during the course of the war—a war that, at home, was in many ways run by corporate elites. A massive strike wave immediately followed the war, and the birth of bolshevism in the United States led to ardent fears of the overturning of the social order. Yet the strikes were, in the main, put down—often violently—and unions hemorrhaged membership throughout the 1920s.

Workers played a role in politics during this decade, particularly in their successful advocacy of what was arguably its most important piece of legislation—the Immigration Act of 1924, which strictly limited migration from countries outside of northern and western Europe. Also, Protestant workers joined avidly with their middling and elite counterparts to form the backbone for the brief but troubling rise to power of the Ku Klux Klan in the North during the early 1920s. Yet, overall, the period saw a remarkably strong consensus that, in the words of President Calvin Coolidge, "the chief business of the American people is business." Corporate chieftains such as Andrew Mellon were major players during the Republican administrations of Warren Harding, Coolidge, and Herbert Hoover. While Hoover, in particular, had creative ideas about how to bring government and business leaders together, few in the 1920s mainstream questioned the primary purpose of politics: the nurturing of corporate growth.

The start of the Great Depression in 1929 did not immediately change that purpose, but the inauguration of Franklin Roosevelt did. Roosevelt was no radical, and indeed his own elite pedigree was as blue-blooded as it gets. Moreover, Roosevelt made no bones that his ultimate goal in reforming the economic system was to save capitalism. Still, Roosevelt, who by 1936 was denouncing "economic royalists," transformed the political system and became a symbol for the hopes of ordinary Americans that the national government could work for them.

The capstone of this effort to transform American society was, arguably, the National Labor Relations Act of 1935, or Wagner Act, which officially recognized the rights of most workers to organize unions and established federal machinery to uphold workers' right to representation. The national government went from its Gilded Age role of often violently repressing to becoming, in many ways, the chief enforcer of workers' rights. Of course, Roosevelt and other national politicians responded to labor out of more than a sense of patrician obligation. They recognized the newfound power of workers, many of whom were attracted to radical ideas and needed to be convinced that mainstream politics could serve their needs. Nor did these workers simply rely on the benevolent power of Washington, D.C. The Wagner

Act unleashed a historic set of strikes, with auto-workers taking over factories in Michigan and textile workers in South Carolina mobilizing their rural communities in support of unions. Employer response was often violent, but (at least in the North) just as often accommodating, and by the end of the 1930s, a markedly different political economy—one that actively incorporated unionization—had been born.

There were significant limits to this new New Deal order. The continued failure of unions in the South—the function of the power of white southern elites who skillfully wielded their economic as well as political power over disenfranchised African Americans—provided a substantial regional obstacle to the extension of liberalism. Even within successful New Deal legislation, there were significant restrictions to the empowering of "the working class." The Social Security Act of 1935—arguably the most important piece of New Deal legislation–provided pensions for millions of workers but left out the most exploited (and, not coincidentally, heavily nonwhite) laborers: in particular, agricultural workers and domestic servants.

The (Short) American Century

Class politics did not take a holiday during World War II, but they were generally suppressed in the global fight against fascism. They returned with a vengeance in the war's immediate aftermath, however, with another postwar strike wave accompanying an attempt by procorporate politicians to reverse the New Deal. The chief symbol of such reaction was the Taft-Hartley Act of 1947, which put significant restrictions on labor organization and required union officials to take loyalty oaths. Yet, despite the newly conservative legal and political environment, the overall pattern of class politics from the 1940s to the 1970s was far from traditional. Rather, at the height of "the American Century," many workers became so prosperous and secure that in many ways the divide between "the working class" and "the middle class" threatened to dissolve.

If Taft-Hartley symbolized the dreams of the most conservative of Republicans, the so-called Treaty of Detroit best epitomized the new class order. In 1950, United Auto Workers president Walter Reuther negotiated a five-year contract with the "big three" car manufacturers. Workers gave up hopes of control over the shop floor along with their rights to strike during the term of the contract. In exchange, they received generous benefits in areas ranging from health insurance to pensions, unemployment to vacations. Cost-of-living wage adjustments ensured that workers would remain prosperous in times of inflation. As a result of such contracts, union membership reached an all-time high during the postwar period. While this broad treaty left out plenty of workers, overall economic inequality declined substantially as the economy went through a prolonged expansion, driven in large part by mass demand for consumer goods.

As factory workers prospered, they increasingly moved to the suburbs. And while those who labored at manual and semiskilled tasks in gargantuan factories never stopped thinking of themselves as "workers" while on the job, they increasingly took on self-conscious identities as part of the "middle class" while living as homeowners, taxpayers, and members of neighborhood associations. Indeed, many contemporary intellectuals argued that all genuinely ideological problems were off the table, as the American political economy had produced the most inclusive middle class in world history. With the simultaneous rise of the civil rights movement, and the promise of a triumphant "color-blind" liberalism, it appeared that the American Dream was nearing fulfillment.

Deindustrialization, Globalization, and the Continuing Significance of Class

All too quickly the bottom fell out of this dream of a classless utopia. During the 1960s, the nation discovered that poverty, whether among whites in Appalachia or blacks in Watts, had not disappeared. A persistent strain of inflation, originating in President Lyndon Johnson's attempts to feed a war machine while also significantly expanding social programs, turned virulent in the late 1970s. Deindustrialization hit the Northeast and Midwest particularly hard during the 1960s and 1970s and was followed in succeeding decades by a globalization that moved much of American manufacturing outside the nation's borders. Union membership, particularly in the private sector, declined dramatically, with President Ronald Reagan (himself a former union chief) by 1981 taking on the mantle of proud union buster.

The promise of racial egalitarianism fell away as issues of class became increasingly intertwined with those of race. These abstractions had always been connected, and one popular argument among scholars holds that working-class revolution never came about primarily because of white workers' long-standing investment in their racial privilege. Yet it was not until the dismantlement of structures of legal racism that class became so visible within racial conflicts. The busing crises of the 1970s, which largely pitted white working-class ethnics against the black poor and working class in cities such as Boston, best symbolized a class conflict that took on the surface complexion of simple racial struggle. White workers who had previously been loyal to the New Deal order defected from the party of Roosevelt, becoming first "Reagan Democrats" and then volatile swing voters. In turn, members of a small but growing African American middle class joined their class brethren in a flight to the suburbs, where schools remained largely (and legally) segregated because of neighborhood residential patterns based on inequalities of wealth and income.

As the politics of prosperity and liberalism fell away, middle-class and working-class Americans began to increasingly practice the politics of populism. One of the longest-standing traditions in American civic life, populism could take many different forms, from Alabama governor George Wallace's and Pat Buchanan's implicit appeals to race when defending hard-working (white) "little" people against liberal elites and immigrants, to Ralph Nader's attempts to embrace racial egalitarianism while focusing on the depredations of big business. While some commentators have remarked that the language of populism in its invoking of "the people" has meant the abandonment of a hard-edged rhetoric of class, the opposite in fact seemed to be the case. When Democrats such as Bill Clinton and Al Gore spoke out on behalf of a neglected and forgotten middle class, for example, Republicans went to great lengths to charge their colleagues across the aisle with "class warfare."

These Republicans were more right than they knew. While much of this ideological battle played out as cynical and even duplicitous campaign rhetoric, the struggle over the middle class was the real thing, the authentic version of American class politics. And with the decline in socialism and social democracy in Europe, it now appears that the United States has not been "deficient" in the way that class has played out in its political history. Rather, with their own appeals to a populist middle class, politicians in the rest of the world may now be catching up to us.

See also business and politics; conservatism; labor movement and politics; populism; race and politics; socialism.

FURTHER READING. Sven Beckert, *Monied Metropolis: New York City and the Consolidation of the American Bourgeoisie, 1850–1896,* 2001; Lizabeth Cohen, *Making a New Deal: Industrial Workers in Chicago, 1919–1939,* 1990; Melvyn Dubofsky, *The State and Labor in Modern America,* 1994; Steve Fraser and Gary Gerstle, eds., *Ruling America: A History of Wealth and Power in a Democracy,* 2005; Richard Hofstadter, *The Age of Reform: From Bryan to FDR,* 1955; Robert D. Johnston, *The Radical Middle Class: Populist Democracy and the Question of Capitalism in Progressive Era Portland, Oregon,* 2003; Michael Kazin, *The Populist Persuasion: An American History,* 2nd ed., 1998; Matthew D. Lassiter, *The Silent Majority: Suburban Politics in the Sunbelt South,* 2006; Anthony Lukas, *Common Ground: A Turbulent Decade in the Lives of Three American Families,* 1985; "The Omaha Platform," downloadable from http://historymatters.gmu.edu/d/5361/; Robert Wiebe, *The Search for Order, 1877–1920,* 1967.

ROBERT D. JOHNSTON

cold war

See Korean War and cold war.

colonial legacy

At first glance, the colonial legacy for the political history of the United States seems obvious. Schoolbooks tell of the gathering in 1619 of Virginia's earliest representative assembly, which developed into the House of Burgesses, and of the Mayflower Compact two years later, establishing government among the settlers of Plymouth by mutual consent. Fast forward to the eve of independence, and it seems that the legacy of Virginia's gathering and the Pilgrims' agreement was fully worked out.

By the third quarter of the eighteenth century, each of the mainland British colonies south of newly founded Nova Scotia had its assembly. In all save Pennsylvania there was a council, which served as upper legislative house, court of appeals, and advisory body. Each colony had a governor, appointed by the king in most cases, named in Pennsylvania and Maryland (and formerly in New York, New Jersey, and the Carolinas) by the province's hereditary "proprietor," and locally chosen in Connecticut and Rhode Island. Election intervals and units of representation varied enormously: Massachusetts chose a new assembly every year, with all towns having the right to send a delegate if the town meeting chose. In neighboring New York, assembly elections could take place at intervals of up to seven years, and three of the province's quasi-feudal manors had the right to send their own delegates, which meant sending the landlord's choice. But there were elections everywhere from Georgia to New Hampshire, and those elections could be fought ferociously.

Above it all loomed the vaunted British government of king, lords, and commons, acting together as the king-in-Parliament. Colonials acknowledged the sovereign authority of the British monarch. In practice, they also acknowledged that Parliament could legislate for them, if the larger British good required it. Until 1763 neither Britons "at home" nor Britons in the American "dominions" gave serious thought to what Parliament could or could not do about America. Rather than worry, colonials basked in the half-formed thought that their local institutions served them well, protecting their "British liberties," much as Parliament served the realm. If anything, they placed greater trust in the crown than did metropolitan Britons.

Neither in Britain nor in the colonies could the king rule by decree. Louis XIV boasted that in France "l'état, c'est moi" (the state is myself) and a Spanish monarch could impose the royal will with the simple formula "yo, el rey" (I, the king). But the young Prince of Wales who was to become George III rejoiced that in Britain the king-in-Parliament, not the king alone, made laws, imposed taxes, and spent public money. This, thought the student prince, was the glory of the British crown and the secret of British liberty. His subjects-to-be agreed, in the metropolis and the colonies alike. So did envious continental Europeans, most notably the highly respected French political thinker Charles de Secondat, Baron de Montesquieu.

Fast forward again, this time a mere three decades, and the legacy of colonial political experience seems obvious. In place of a king named George, there was a president, also named George, whose public demeanor seemed kingly. He worked with two new institutions, a U.S. House of Representatives that clearly owed a great deal to Britain's House of Commons, and a U.S. Senate that resembled the House of Lords. The provinces had become states, with governors, state senates, and state assemblies. The continuity appears clear.

But Britain's North American empire had foundered on that very legacy. Had the colonial institutions existed "of right," fundamentally independent of Parliament's power and its will? Or had they been mere conveniences, to which Parliament could give orders and alter if it chose to do so? That question bedeviled colonial political thinkers after 1764, when Parliament began to assert its power over colonial life. When it proved to have no acceptable answer, the empire fell apart.

By 1790, the old order's fatal problems seemed resolved in two ways. One was that both the U.S. government and the separate state regimes drew their power directly from "the people" as codified in formal constitutions. No longer was there was any question of state institutions deriving power from the sovereign central government and being subject to its veto or its requirements, as Parliament had claimed to be the case with their colonial forebears. Federal and state governments were creatures of their respective peoples, where sovereignty lay.

The other issue that seemed settled was that the United States had its own colonial problem, including rebellion. Vermont declared its independence from New York in 1777, which called it a "pretended state" and its people "revolted subjects" until 1791. For a few years the "State of Franklin" tried to break free from North Carolina. Meanwhile settlers and enslaved black people were spilling west into country that they were seizing from its Indian owners. Like the original East Coast colonists, they required order and structure. But rather than form permanently subordinate colonies, they established "territories." These could win full statehood, with self-government and full participation in national politics. Except for Vermont, Kentucky, Tennessee, Texas, California, and West Virginia, all of the states from Ohio to Hawaii went through the process, which transformed what had been a major British problem into an American public ritual.

The Larger Politics of Colonial America

Despite these points, the legacy of colonial political life is neither simple nor straightforward. Historians have devoted a vast amount of energy to the study of East Coast, Anglophone, white, male institutional political life. The greatest political legacy of the colonial era was the creation of a robust, white, male-dominated republic that rapidly spanned the continent. But there is little point in simply updating previous writings that have dealt with it admirably.

Let us start instead with the "continental turn" that historians have taken in understanding "colonial America." Current understanding no longer restricts the subject to the Anglophone East Coast.

Instead, different European communities and native peoples created a colonial social formation across much of the continent as early as 1700. Ultimately, all of that formation's people were linked to distant European centers of power. The elements that bound them to Europe and to one another included the emerging idea of race; the uncertain boundaries of empire; the justified belief by native peoples that the land belonged to them; hostility among tribes; conflicting ideas about the ownership and use of land; enslavement; divergent religions; the damage wrought by unseen microbes; the impact of larger nonhuman species such as horses, swine, cattle, and wheat; and merchant-capitalist commerce that turned American products into commodities and introduced metallurgy, textiles, firearms, and alcohol to the American world. Colonial politics, including diplomacy and war, emerged from and dealt with all of these elements.

Politics is about the disposition of power, and of the resources, obligations, liabilities, and possibilities that power can command. From the very beginning of the permanent European presence, European "powers" that were becoming national states maintained that they could dispose of the American world and everything it contained, people and resources alike, all seeking to clothe their actions with legality.

The initial politics of empire was about turning a mere supposition of distant authority into a working imperial system, and it took two forms. One was to crush existing structures and impose new ones. That happened in the sixteenth century when the ruins of the Aztec capital Tenochtitlan became the foundation of Mexico City. It happened on a much smaller scale among the New England Indians who submitted to Puritan authority and became denizens of "praying towns." It happened, too, on Spanish missions in eighteenth-century California.

The other form was to link existing native ways to European ones in a hybrid fashion, which might be an informal but recognized pattern. Spaniards and Caddos in eighteenth-century Texas agreed that peace could come "in the form of a woman," meaning that women's presence at a parlay signified peaceful intentions in a world where war seemed to spread everywhere. Some arrangements congealed into de facto institutions, most notably the Covenant Chain. Developing out of the formal claims to neighboring spaces by the province of New York and by the Five Haudenosaunee (Iroquois) Nations, the Covenant Chain expanded from those two central links to include British provinces from Massachusetts to Virginia, together with many native groups. None of these arrangements was formal in the sense of being codified. All created some sort of "middle ground" between European and native ways. But exactly the same informality characterized the unwritten constitution of documents, usages, precedents, customs, and common law that set the rules of British political life.

The continent-spanning and culture-crossing politics of colonial America is apparent on the maps and other symbolic devices that imperial and provincial cartographers and native people produced. All of these were political in the sense that they expressed claims to power. None could display "definitive" lines in the manner of later political maps of the American republic and its separate states. Taken together, imperial, provincial, and native images show how geographical boundaries overlapped and how lines of political power tangled.

Perhaps the best-known case is the way that New France, Pennsylvania, and Virginia all claimed title to the forks of the Ohio River, where Pittsburgh now stands. To vindicate Virginia's claim, Governor Robert Dinwiddie sent the young Colonel George Washington there in 1754, instructing him to order the French to depart from their recently constructed Fort Duquesne. Virginia's northern boundary supposedly stretched indefinitely from the Potomac River to include the whole Ohio Valley, the western Great Lakes region, and beyond. On British maps, at least, the Old Dominion's southern boundary extended to the Pacific coast. So did the boundaries of the two Carolinas and Georgia. French, Spaniards, and native people of many sorts had other ideas. The politics of colonial empire emerged from those conflicting claims.

Within the supposedly British zone, Massachusetts, New Hampshire, and New York all claimed what is now Vermont. The Abenaki Indians disagreed. Massachusetts maintained that it overleaped New York's settled zone and had a claim to the Lake Ontario Plain, which the Iroquois nations understood to be their own. Writing to London in 1774, New York's final royal governor described how his province sprawled beyond Detroit, by virtue of an Iroquois deed to the Niagara Peninsula executed in 1702. But a very detailed map of the same province that was in preparation as the governor wrote his report placed New York's western boundary only a little west of Albany, where the country of the Iroquois Nations began.

Native people also tried to map the politics of American space. Their devices including Iroquois and Huron wampum belts and Catawba and Chickasaw maps traced on deerskin. The Iroquois Hiawatha Belt, now repatriated from the New York State Museum to the Onondaga Nation, shows the Five Nations linked to one another in a symbolic longhouse, with its eastern (Mohawk) and western (Seneca) doorkeepers. Hidden within its imagery is an elaborate pattern of relationships that the Iroquois had worked out before contact and which served them well. Some historians argue that what the Iroquois had wrought formed the original template for the U.S. Constitution. Others doubt the

point, but nobody denies the magnitude of the Iroquois achievement.

Other belts identified the 51 holders of hereditary Haudenosaunee sachemships and the members of the Covenant Chain, colonies and tribes alike. Seventeenth-century Huron Indians used wampum to depict the relationship among their four nations, and, later, their confederacy's relationship with the French.

The Catawba deerskin map of 1723, traced on a paper copy that now is in Britain's Public Records Office, shows the detailed arrangements among the people who form its center and the world around them. It signifies their own villages with circles, and whites' communities with squares. Nearby South Carolina is divided into smaller squares, probably indicating city blocks in Charles Town, together with a simply drawn ship at anchor. More distant Virginia is just a box. Chickasaws used similar imagery. Wampum belts and native maps alike located the centers of affairs and power among native peoples, not in Quebec, Boston, Albany, Philadelphia, Williamsburg, Charles Town, New Orleans, San Antonio de Bexar, or Santa Fe, let alone Paris, London, or Madrid.

Throughout the colonial era, white scribes recorded conferences between their leaders and native peoples. These written observations rank among the fundamental documents of colonial political history. Though taken down in a European tongue, the records show growing sophistication on both sides about the language and ritual of negotiations and about the subjects under discussion. Ultimately, the participants attempted to resolve what is perhaps the most fundamental of all political problems, how various groups of people are to deal with one another without violence.

This intensely political conversation dealt increasingly with the most basic and intractable of colonial problems, which was the ownership, use, and disposition of land. Talk could and did collapse into warfare. During the late seventeenth and early eighteenth centuries, trouble broke out from Maritime Canada to New Mexico. Abenaki fought with northern New Englanders; lower New England Algonquians with Puritans; Iroquois with Algonquians' Abenaki, and French; Susquehannocks with Virginians; Yamasees and Tuscaroras with Carolinians; and, far to the west, Pueblo Indians with Spaniards. These people were not strangers. The New England Algonquians knew that befouling the Bible would infuriate the Puritans; the Pueblos understood the same point about the sacred vessels of the Catholic Mass.

A new pattern gradually emerged, as people worked out lasting accommodations. Iroquois and French did so in 1701 at Montreal, creating neutrality for the battered Indians, whatever British officials said about the Five Nations "depending" on them as de facto British subjects. In 1692, 12 years after the Pueblo Indians had driven Spaniards out of their country, they allowed them to return. But no longer did the Spaniards attempt total domination. Kivas, representing traditional ways, shared village space with missionary churches.

At the heart of the informal but enduring colonial situation was the reality that neither colonizers nor natives enjoyed full power over either their own lives or the lives of the people they encountered. Ultimately, all of them were linked to distant Europe—some tightly, others loosely. Everyone was "colonial" in a more meaningful and profound sense than conventional images of quaint costumes and imitation Parliaments. All of them took part one way or another in colonial politics.

Slavery and Freedom

Two major events took place in Virginia in 1619. One was the gathering of a representative assembly. The other was the arrival of a Dutch warship bearing 20 people who were sold to Virginians for labor in their burgeoning tobacco fields. The records described those people as "Negars."

There is more than coincidence to the events. The people sold from the Dutch vessel did not enter formal slavery when they stepped onto Virginia soil. Quite possibly, their shipboard slavery ended, because neither Virginia nor any other British possession recognized enslavement. Formal servitude did exist, in a debased, often brutal form from its English counterpart, and labor-hungry masters used many tricks and devices to extend their servants' terms. But some servants, both black and white, survived their terms, and at least a few of those survivors prospered.

Elsewhere in America those people would have been slaves. Spaniards simply transferred their law of slavery, codified under the medieval King Alfonso X "the Wise," to their American realms. After some debate, the Spanish Crown forbade the enslavement of Indians, but Bartholeme de las Casas, the Dominican priest who successfully argued for that outcome before the king, had no doubt that Africans could replace enslaved Indians. The Dutch brought both the law and the practice of slavery to New Netherland when they founded it. But English colonizers did not bring slavery with them—they had to create it themselves.

Barbadians did so first, establishing a slave law in 1636 to govern the Africans whom they were starting to import as sugar emerged as the West Indies cash crop. Three decades later, the Barbadian founders of Carolina simply carried their island's slave law with them to the mainland colony. In 1641 Puritan Massachusetts created the earliest mainland slave law. The backhanded language in the statute read, "There shall never be any bond slaverie unles it be lawfull Captives taken in just warres, and such strangers as willingly selle themselves or are sold to us." They did enslave Indians, massively so after they defeated King Philip's forces in 1676. By that time, Carolina colonists were developing a sizable Indian slave trade that ultimately reached as far as the Great Plains. As late as 1776, South Carolina patriot leader William Henry Drayton was promising backcountry small farmers that they could seize Cherokee lands and enslave their former owners if the farmers joined the movement for independence from Britain.

Virginia, however, provides the most complex and probably most important case. Some evidence suggests that it treated black people unequally from the very start. In 1630 one Virginian was punished for "lying with a Negro." But we do not know the gender of that "Negro," so the punishment may have been for sodomy rather than a sign of black degradation. Virginia's slave law took shape slowly, as black servants lost such privileges as bearing firearms, intermarrying with whites, and owning personal property; as black escapees from servitude did not have their terms extended upon recapture, a clear indication that they already were serving for life; and as the condition of children came to follow the condition of their mothers, who were open to sexual exploitation.

What does seem clear is that, by 1700, Virginia slavery existed in both law and practice. It also seems clear that the emergence and consolidation of Virginia black slavery had a great deal to do with Virginia's transformation from a place where white colonists lived in mutual hostility to one where a local elite was able to rule through elected, representative institutions.

Perhaps this was aristocracy, since there was no question that the planter elite was in charge. Possibly it was democracy, since the elite ruled in the name of a larger population that gave its consent every time small-property-holding farmers and artisans gathered to elect a planter to speak for them in the House of Burgesses. Maybe the elite was secure, surrounded by rituals and customs that brought all white Virginians together. Conceivably, like its Carolina counterparts, the elite was beleaguered by discontented white folk as well as by native and black people with ample reason to be hostile. Perhaps the real point is that Virginia's elite ruled through the House of Burgesses, not through outright force. Whatever the explanation, the creation and stabilization of racially defined plantation slavery went hand in hand with the eighteenth-century Virginia political settlement that eventually produced George Washington, Thomas Jefferson, and James Madison.

North of the plantation zone, New York developed the largest slave population. Unlike Virginia's increasingly cohesive eighteenth-century rulers, New York's elite was factious to the point of outright enmity. But when it appeared in 1741 that a major plot was taking shape among slaves and bottom-of-the-population white people in New York City, members of the elite turned the rumors to their political advantage. They launched a series of show trials that led to exile for some of the accused, hanging for others, and, for certain slaves caught up in the terror, burning at the stake. This, too, was political. Both in the North and South a pattern of enduring racial politics was taking shape. In some ways, that pattern's legacy endures today.

British Liberties in America

On both sides of the Atlantic, Britons took great pride in the belief that they enjoyed greater freedom than any other people on earth. Others might have argued with them, given the chance. Spaniards construed *liberdades* (liberties) as specific exemptions and privileges, not as absolute rights, a meaning close to what English colonists also thought. South Carolina slaves who sought to escape from the misery of the rice swamps invariably headed south, where they knew they would find a welcome from Florida's Spanish rulers. Nonetheless, in the formal political realm the Britons had reason for pride. British America, like Britain itself, possessed an electoral politics unlike anything seen in Quebec or Paris, Havana or Mexico City. Here lay the segment of the larger colonial political structure that developed into the civic life of the United States.

Historians have pored over the formal politics of the elections and legislation of the Anglophone provinces. Some have pondered whether colonial politics was "democratic" or "aristocratic." That question now seems badly posed. Proportionately, far more white, adult colonial males were able to vote than in any other place on earth, but the "better sort" remained in charge. Others have asked which colony's public life was most "American." Setting aside the quintessentially American tangle of slavery and race, does that mean that a colony developed competitive, interest-group politics and perhaps even outright organized partisanship?

If so, Pennsylvania might qualify. Not happy about his province's politics, William Penn admonished its settlers, most of them fellow Quakers, to "be not so governmentish." The Penn family's hereditary proprietorship suggests that they were shopkeepers, but in reality they were lords, wielding more actual political power and enjoying greater potential wealth than any baron, viscount, earl, marquess, or duke in Britain.

Potentially, the Penns were the richest family on earth, thanks to their province's enormous resources of coal, iron ore, and oil. Southeastern Pennsylvania was so fertile that it, together with the northern Chesapeake Bay area, became the main supplier of wheat and flour to both the West Indies and Western Europe. Freehold farmers to whom the Penns sold the land—not rent-paying tenants—grew the wheat, and life among them could be good. But the farmers, together with many of Philadelphia's merchants, professional people, artisans, and ordinary laborers, came to resent Penn domination, as well as the Penns' refusal to allow the provincial assembly to tax the ruling family's own land, treating it instead as if it were sovereign property.

Tension mounted as religious and ethnic differences appeared. William Penn's sons left the Quaker faith for the Church of England, turning Quaker settlers from probable—albeit "governmentish"—allies into opponents. Attracted by Pennsylvania's reputation as "the best poor man's country" and a haven for religious dissenters, sectarian Protestants from Bohemia and Germany, and Scotch-Irish Presbyterians, migrated, together with a sprinkle of Catholics and Jews. Split by religion, ethnicity, and language; divided by the gulf between country and town; and broken again by issues of social class, Pennsylvanians were not a harmonious lot. Their public life was raucous and competitive from the province's founding until independence.

This was the milieu in which Benjamin Franklin emerged as a public figure. Franklin knew about elections in which armed mobs intimidated opponents and where Anglicans decried Presbyterians as "Piss-Brutearians." No fan of immigrants, Franklin dismissed German farmers (*Bauern*) as "boors." Aligning with the Quakers, he sought in 1765 to end the Penn family's rule and make Pennsylvania a royal province. Perhaps he had himself in mind for the office of governor. Indeed, his son William did become the final royal governor of neighboring New Jersey through the excellent connections that Benjamin Franklin had acquired as his own star rose. The father recovered from his faux pas of seeking direct royal government. In 1775, as the British Empire was collapsing, father and son found themselves bitterly emplaced on opposite sides. Their family tragedy, too, was a consequence of colonial political life, and the Franklins were not the only family to suffer such a split.

New York's political history under the English was even more vicious. After the Glorious Revolution, Captain Jacob Leisler seized power in 1689 in the name of the joint monarchs, William and Mary. But he could not consolidate his position, and a new royal governor had him tried and executed for treason. Years of partisan hatred resulted. The frequently told tale that Governor Edward Hyde, Lord Cornbury (in office 1701–8), was a public cross-dresser seems to be an urban legend. It developed out of hostile rhetoric about him "playing the Queen," a reference to his high-handed rule in the name of his cousin, Queen Anne. But Cornbury's political enemies jailed him the moment his successor arrived, and he lost the immunity that had gone with his office. Governor Danvers Osborne committed suicide within days of arriving in New York in 1753. The cause was a personal tragedy, but realizing what he had to govern could not have helped.

One of New York's enduring characteristics was its conquered Dutch population, which slowly adapted to English rule but which did not cohere as an ethnic bloc. Another of its qualities was great estates that legally possessed quasi-feudal standing. A third was New York City, with a public life that had been diverse, conflicted, and raucous from the very beginning. At the very least, New York was "factious," with no pretense of easy agreement among its elite or its various plebeians. At its worst, its public life could be lethal. The legacy of that public life was a disruptive, transforming revolution.

Was New England any more harmonious? Certainly its people were more homogeneous, being overwhelmingly English and largely Puritan in their ancestry and heritage. At the beginning, some Puritan villagers had cultivated harmony, showing by their behavior that they took seriously John Winthrop's advice to present a "model of Christian Charitie" to the world. But, from the start, Winthrop's own Boston was riven with division and it seems that, for every cohesive, placid village, there was another whose people seemed primed to argue with one another.

Connecticut, New Haven, and Rhode Island emerged from disputes as the supposedly unified Puritan founders of Massachusetts Bay found that they could not agree among themselves. As the founding generation was dying off in the mid-seventeenth century, Massachusetts disputed sharply about the requirements for church membership. Salem's notorious witchcraft trials have been so intensely studied that many explanations seem plausible. But the town of Salem failed completely to contain its internal tensions, spilling from what politics might have settled—had it worked—into bloodshed, particularly of its women.

Eighteenth-century New Englanders conflicted just as sharply. In town meetings and street gatherings alike, the wave of religious enthusiasm that historians call the "Great Awakening" broke congregations and whole towns open, on matters that emerged from Christian doctrine and practice and that had deep roots in social experience. Where non-Congregational churches emerged among New Englanders—be they Anglican, Presbyterian, Baptist, or Quaker—discord followed. The theory of town meetings was to create harmony, but Boston's town meetings turned raucous under popular leaders such as Samuel Adams. Prominent Bostonian Thomas Hutchinson, who spurned popularity for the sake of royal favor, became so disliked that when his elegant house caught fire in 1749, townsfolk tried to block volunteer firefighters, crying "Let it burn!" Sixteen years later, when Britain was trying to impose its Stamp Act, another Boston crowd invaded and wrecked Hutchinson's mansion, leaving it an empty, ruined shell.

"Regulators" in the North Carolina interior raised armed resistance to a provincial government that seemed not to serve them at all. In the mid-eighteenth century, land rioters wracked New Jersey, setting up a countergovernment with its own courts and "gaols" back "in the woods." Ethnic tensions among Protestant whites turned into racial hatred against Indians in central Pennsylvania. New York's Hudson Valley simmered with discontent between landlords and tenants and broke into a large rebellion of farmers in 1766. One reason was conditions on the great estates; another was belief that landlords

had defrauded the river's Indians, a point with which the Indians agreed and on which they took a protest all the way to London. A third reason was the uncertainty of New York's boundary with New England. During the last ten years under British rule, similar problems led to outright insurgency in North Carolina and in the Green Mountain zone between Lake Champlain and the Connecticut River claimed by both New York and New Hampshire. Given the contentious future of American electoral politics, there were few places in the English colonies that could not claim to be among its starting places.

The Colonial Legacy

Half a century ago, Clinton Rossiter called the colonial era the "seedtime" of the Republic. At the time it seemed to historians that there was a fundamental consensus among the white English-speaking males who seemed to be the only people who counted. Now historians perceive that far more early Americans—and not just the people who did not speak English—who were not free, male, or white were somehow "present." We understand that such people participated in a colonial order that spread far beyond what the different sorts of settlers claimed were their boundaries.

Adding the elements of that order together, we can see that it bore more than a passing resemblance to the European ancien régime that had spawned it. French historian Fernand Braudel has called it "a mosaic of a hundred different colours: modern, archaic, primitive, or curious mixtures of all these." Like early modern Europe, colonial America had simply grown. It comprised a whole, but it had no coherence. A large part of the story of its politics was a constant struggle for mastery among tribes, empires, provinces, and settler communities, a struggle that nobody actually won in any "definitive" way. Another large part of that story was the emergence of a politics in which the supposed contrast between "savagery" and "civilization" melded into a politics of race, and in which race could justify the oppression of slavery and the driving back of the land's first peoples.

In the colonial era, those peoples possessed enough political, economic, and—if necessary—military power to resist, and so they were driven back only slowly or not at all. But the long thrust of colonial politics was to simplify the tangle of the American political map. Swedes in the Delaware Valley, Dutch from there to the upper Hudson, and the French from the mouth of the St. Lawrence to the mouth of the Mississippi all fell to the surging power of dynamic Britain and its East Coast provinces. But their relationship, too, is best understood as part of the ancien régime's unwieldy tangle. Britain's attempt to assert its mastery provoked another great struggle, this time among people who had agreed proudly that they all were Britons.

That struggle led to a sizable group of those people concluding that they were Britons no longer, and to giving themselves the means to assert and achieve a mastery that nobody in the old order had been able to maintain. The republic they created completed the simplification that had long been under way. Its constitution established a "supreme law of the land." Its spreading political map gradually wiped out the overlapping, conflicting lines of possession and authority that colonial maps had shown. In this sense, the victorious revolutionaries were continuing a politics of expansion and consolidation that had run through the colonial era.

Colonial politics continued in two other ways. The American republican order only appeared to be similar to the British monarchical order that it overthrew and replaced. Washington was a president, not a king. Sovereign power in the United States lay among its people. But East Coast colonials had learned to compete in the public arena, and they carried what they had learned into their raucous republican future.

They also carried the colonial era's politics of race, reduced now to two propositions. The first, a direct continuation from colonial life, was that slavery was the normal condition in America of people whose ancestors had come, or who came themselves, from Africa. The second, different from colonial life, was that native people and their ways had no place in the new order, a point worked out in practice long before it became official public policy with the Indian Removal Act of 1830.

But there was another difference as well. The colonial version of politics had assumed human differences. John Winthrop, first governor of colonial Massachusetts, came close to theorizing the old order with his proposition that "God Almighty in his most holy and wise providence, hath soe disposed of the condition of mankind, as in all times some must be rich, some poore, some high and eminent in power and dignitie; others mean and in submission." In practice, that belief gave many sorts of people space in which to maneuver around one another, though it also meant that there was no intellectual problem with holding some people in the absolute meanness and submission that was slavery.

Theoretically, at least, the American Revolutionaries broke with that belief, asserting instead that "all men are created equal." Their practice, of course, fell far short of their theory. But the politics that their revolution inaugurated opened a new ground for contestation, a ground whose deep, continuing theme and enduring problem has been to resolve the contradictions between the theory and the harsh realities of American life.

See also era of a new republic, 1789–1827; slavery; war for independence.

FURTHER READING. Fred Anderson, *Crucible of War: The Seven Years War and the Fate of Empire in British North America, 1754–1766*, 2000; Bernard Bailyn, *The New England Merchants in the Seventeenth Century*, 1955; Idem,

The Ordeal of Thomas Hutchinson, 1955; Idem, *The Origins of American Politics*, 1968; Juliana Barr, *Peace Came in the Form of a Woman: Indians and Spaniards in the Texas Borderlands*, 2007; Carl Lotus Becker, *The History of Political Parties in the Province of New York, 1760–1776*, 1909; Richard R. Beeman, *The Varieties of Political Experience in Eighteenth-Century America*, 2004; Michael A. Bellesiles, *Revolutionary Outlaws: Ethan Allen and the Struggle for Independence on the Early American Frontier*, 1993; Robin Blackburn, *The Making of New World Slavery: From the Baroque to the Modern, 1492–1800*, 1997; Ned Blackhawk, *Violence across the Land: Indians and Empires in the Early American West*, 2006; Patricia U. Bonomi, *A Factious People: Politics and Society in Colonial New York*, 1971; Idem, *The Lord Cornbury Scandal: The Politics of Reputation in British America*, 1998; Daniel J. Boorstin, *The Americans: The Colonial Experience*, 1958; Terry Bouton, *Taming Democracy: "The People," the Founders, and the Troubled Ending of the American Revolution*, 2007; Paul Boyer and Stephen Nissenbaum, *Salem Possessed: The Social Origins of Witchcraft*, 1974; T. H. Breen and Stephen Innes, *"Myne Owne Ground": Race and Freedom on Virginia's Eastern Shore, 1640–1676*, 1980; John Brooke, *The Heart of the Commonwealth: Society and Political Culture in Worcester County, Massachusetts, 1713–1861*, 1992; Kathleen M. Brown, *Good Wives, Nasty Wenches, and Anxious Patriarchs: Gender, Race, and Power in Colonial Virginia*, 1996; Robert E. Brown, *Middle Class Democracy and the Revolution in Massachusetts*, 1955; Robert E. Brown and B. Katherine Brown, *Colonial Virginia 1705–1786: Democracy or Aristocracy?* 1964; Martin Brückner, *The Geographic Revolution in Early America: Maps, Literacy, and National Identity*, 2006; Richard L. Bushman, *From Puritan to Yankee: Character and the Social Order in Connecticut, 1690–1775*, 1968; Andrew Cayton and Fredrika Teute, eds., *Contact Points: American Frontiers from the Mohawk Valley to the Mississippi, 1750–1830*, 1998; Richard W. Cogley, *John Eliot's Mission to the Indians before King Philip's War*, 1999; Edward Countryman, "'Out of the Bounds of the Law': Northern Land Rioters in the Eighteenth Century," in *The American Revolution: Explorations in the History of American Radicalism*, edited by Alfred F. Young, 37–69, 1976; Idem, *A People in Revolution: The American Revolution and Political Society in New York, 1760–1790*, 1981; Idem, "'To Secure the Blessings of Liberty': Language, the Revolution, and American Capitalism," in *Beyond the American Revolution: Explorations in the History of American Radicalism*, edited by Alfred F. Young, 123–48, 1993; David Brion Davis, *The Problem of Slavery in Western Culture*, 1966; Cornelia Hughes Dayton, *Women before the Bar: Gender, Law, and Society in Connecticut, 1639–1789*, 1995; John Putnam Demos, *Entertaining Satan: Witchcraft and the Culture of Early New England*, 1982; Matthew Dennis, *Cultivating a Landscape of Peace: Iroquois-European Encounters in Seventeenth-Century America*, 1992; Richard S. Dunn, *Sugar and Slaves: The Rise of the Planter Class in the English West Indies, 1624–1713*, 1973; A. Roger Ekirch, *"Poor Carolina": Politics and Society in Colonial North Carolina 1729–1776*, 1981; William N. Fenton, *The Great Law and the Longhouse: A*

Political History of the Iroquois Confederacy, 1998; Thelma Wills Foote, *Black and White Manhattan: The History of Race Formation in Colonial New York City*, 2004; Alan Gallay, *The Indian Slave Trade: The Rise of the English Empire in the American South, 1670–1717*, 2002; Jack P. Greene, *The Quest for Power: The Lower Houses of Assembly in the Southern Royal Colonies, 1689–1776*, 1963; Idem, "The Reappraisal of the American Revolution in Recent Historical Literature," in *The Reinterpretation of the American Revolution, 1763–1789*, edited by Jack P. Greene, 2–74, 1968; Philip J. Greven, *Four Generations: Population, Land, and Family in Colonial Andover, Massachusetts*, 1970; Donald J. Grinde and Bruce E. Johansen, *Exemplar of Liberty: Native America and the Evolution of Democracy*, 1991; Sara Stidstone Gronim, "Geography and Persuasion: Maps in British Colonial New York," *William and Mary Quarterly*, 3rd ser., 58 (April 2001), 373–402; Ramon A. Gutierrez, *When Jesus Came the Corn Mothers Went Away: Marriage, Sexuality, and Power in New Mexico, 1500–1846*, 1991; Stephen W. Hackel, *Children of Coyote, Missionaries of St. Francis: Indian-Spanish Relations in Colonial California, 1769–1850*, 2005; Gilles Havard, *The Great Peace of Montreal of 1701: French-Native Diplomacy in the Seventeenth Century*, translated by Phyllis Aronoff and Howard Scott, 2001; Christine Leigh Heyrman, *Commerce and Community: The Maritime Communities of Colonial Massachusetts, 1790–1850*, 1984; A. Leon Higginbotham, *Shades of Freedom: Racial Politics and Presumptions of the American Legal Process*, 1996; Stephen Innes, *Labor in a New Land: Economy and Society in Seventeenth-Century Springfield*, 1983; Rhys Isaac, *The Transformation of Virginia, 1740–1790*, 1980; Francis Jennings, *The Ambiguous Iroquois Empire: The Covenant Chain Confederation of Indian Tribes from Its Beginnings to the Lancaster Treaty of 1744*, 1983; Idem, *Empire of Fortune: Crowns, Colonies, and Tribes in the Seven Years War in America*, 1988; Michael G. Kammen, *Deputyes and Libertyes: The Origins of Representative Government in Colonial America*, 1968; Carol F. Karlsen, *The Devil in the Shape of a Woman: Witchcraft in Colonial New England*, 1987; Marjoleine Kars, *Breaking Loose Together: The Regulator Rebellion in Pre-Revolutionary North Carolina*, 2002; Stanley Nider Katz, *Newcastle's New York: Anglo-American Politics, 1732–1753*, 1968; Milton M. Klein, *The Politics of Diversity: Essays in the History of Colonial New York*, 1974; Rachel N. Klein, *Unification of a Slave State: The Rise of the Planter Class in the South Carolina Back Country, 1760–1808*, 1990; Andrew Knaut, *The Pueblo Revolt of 1680: Conquest and Resistance in Seventeenth-Century New Mexico*, 1995; Lyle Koehler, *A Search for Power: The "Weaker Sex" in Seventeenth-Century New England*, 1980; Allan Kulikoff, *Tobacco and Slaves: The Development of Southern Cultures in the Chesapeake, 1680–1800*, 1986; Jane Landers, *Black Society in Spanish Florida*, 1999; James T. Lemon, *The Best Poor Man's Country: A Geographical Study of Early Southeastern Pennsylvania*, 1972; Jill Lepore, *The Name of War: King Philip's War and the Origins of American Identity*, 1998; Idem, *New York Burning: Liberty, Slavery, and Conspiracy in Eighteenth-Century Manhattan*, 2005; James Lockhart, *The Nahuas after the Conquest: A Social and*

Cultural History of the Indians of Central Mexico, Sixteenth through Eighteenth Centuries, 1992; Kenneth A. Lockridge, *A New England Town: The First Hundred Years, Dedham, Massachusetts, 1636–1736*, 1970; Brendan McConville, *The King's Three Faces: The Rise and Fall of Royal America, 1680–1776*, 2006; Idem, *Those Daring Disturbers of the Public Peace: The Struggle for Property and Power in Early New Jersey*, 1999; James K. Merrell, *Into the American Woods: Negotiators on the Pennsylvania Frontier*, 1999; Jane T. Merritt, *At the Crossroads: Indians and Empires on a Mid-Atlantic Frontier, 1700–1763*, 2003; Edmund S. Morgan, *American Slavery, American Freedom: The Ordeal of Colonial Virginia*, 1975; John M. I. Murrin, "Political Development," in *Colonial British America: Essays in the New History of the Early Modern Era*, edited by Jack P. Greene and J. R. Pole, 408–56, 1984; Helen Nader, *Liberty in Absolutist Spain: The Hapsburg Sale of Towns, 1516–1700*, 1990; Jerome J. Nadlehaft, *The Disorders of War: The Revolution in South Carolina*, 1981; David E. Narrett, *Inheritance and Family Life in Colonial New York City*, 1992; Gary B. Nash, *Quakers and Politics: Pennsylvania, 1681–1726*, 1968; Idem, *The Urban Crucible: Social Change, Political Consciousness, and the Origins of the American Revolution*, 1979; Gregory H. Nobles, *Divisions throughout the Whole: Politics and Society in Hampshire County, Massachusetts, 1740–1775*, 1983; Mary Beth Norton, *Founding Mothers and Fathers: Gendered Power and the Forming of American Society*, 1996; Idem, *In the Devil's Snare: The Salem Witchcraft Crisis of 1692*, 2002; Peter S. Onuf, *The Origins of the Federal Republic: Jurisdictional Controversies in the United States, 1775–1787*, 1983; J. R. Pole, "Historians and the Problem of Early American Democracy," *American Historical Review* 68 (1962), 626–46; Sumner Chilton Powell, *Puritan Village: The Formation of a New England Town*, 1963; Elizabeth Reis, *Damned Women: Sinners and Witches in Puritan New England*, 1997; Daniel K. Richter, *The Ordeal of the Longhouse: The Peoples of the Iroquois League in the Era of European Colonization*, 1992; Oliver A. Rink, *Holland on the Hudson: An Economic and Social History of Dutch New York*, 1986; Robert C. Ritchie, *The Duke's Province: A Study of New York Politics and Society, 1664–1691*, 1977; Clinton Rossiter, *Seedtime of the Republic: The Origin of the American Tradition of Political Liberty*, 1953; Darrett Rutman, *Winthrop's Boston: Portrait of a Puritan Town, 1630–1649*, 1972; Philip J. Schwarz, *The Jarring Interests: New York's Boundary Makers, 1664–1776*, 1979; Patricia Seed, *Ceremonies of Possession in Europe's Conquest of the New World, 1492–1640*, 1995; Judith N. Shklar, *American Citizenship: The Quest for Inclusion*, 1991; Nancy Shoemaker, *A Strange Likeness: Becoming Red and White in Eighteenth-Century North America*, 2004; Sheila L. Skemp, *William Franklin: Son of a Patriot, Servant of a King*, 1990; Alan Taylor, *American Colonies: The Settling of North America*, 2001; Bruce G. Trigger, *The Children of Aataentsic: A History of the Huron People to 1660*, 1976; Alan Tully, "Colonial Politics," in *A Companion to Colonial America*, edited by Daniel Vickers, 288–310, 2003; Idem, *Forming American Politics: Ideals, Interests, and Institutions in Colonial New York and Pennsylvania*, 1994; Idem, *William Penn's Legacy: Politics and Social Structure in Provincial*

Pennsylvania, 1726–1755, 1977; Daniel Vickers, ed., *A Companion to Colonial America*, 2003; Mike Wallace and Edwin G. Burrows, *Gotham: A History of New York City to 1898*, 1999; Gregory A. Waselkov, "Indian Maps of the Colonial Southeast," in *Powhatan's Mantle: Indians in the Colonial Southeast*, edited by Gregory A. Waskelov, Peter H. Wood, and Tom Hatley, 292–343, 1989; Wilcomb E. Washburn, *The Governor and the Rebel: A History of Bacon's Rebellion in Virginia*, 1957; David S. Weber, *The Spanish Frontier in North America*, 1993; Richard White, *The Middle Ground: Indians, Empires, and Republics in the Great Lakes Region, 1650–1815*, 1991; Robert A. Williams, *The American Indian in Western Legal Thought: The Discourses of Conquest*, 1990; Idem, *Linking Arms Together: American Indian Visions of Law and Peace, 1600–1800*, 1997; John Winthrop, "Christian Charitie, a Modell Hereof" (1630), reprinted in *The Founding of Massachusetts: Historians and the Sources*, edited by Edmund S. Morgan, 191–204, 1964; Gordon S. Wood, *The Americanization of Benjamin Franklin*, 2004; Idem, *The Creation of the American Republic, 1776–1787*, 1969; Idem, *The Radicalism of the American Revolution*, 1992; Peter H. Wood, *Black Majority: Negroes in Colonial South Carolina from 1670 through the Stono Rebellion*, 1974; Esmond Wright, *Franklin of Philadelphia*, 1986; Michael Zuckerman, "Authority in Early America: The Decay of Deference on the Provincial Periphery," *Early American Studies* 1 (2003), 1–29.

EDWARD COUNTRYMAN

communism

Communism, a movement inspired by the 1917 Bolshevik Revolution in Russia, never attracted many adherents in the United States, peaking in the late 1930s with 75,000 members. Nonetheless, over the years Communists played significant roles in a number of social movements.

Communism came to the United States in the fall of 1919, a year of revolutionary upheaval. Vladimir Lenin and Leon Trotsky, the leaders of the precariously established Soviet government in Russia, looked abroad for aid, hoping sympathizers in Europe and elsewhere would open new fronts in the international struggle against capitalism. In March 1919, Russian Communist leaders presided over the founding in Moscow of the Communist International (also referred to as the Comintern), a federation of pro-Soviet revolutionary parties. The Comintern was intended to supplant the old Socialist International, scorned by Communists for its failure to prevent the outbreak of World War I.

A Party of a New Type

Lenin had long before decided that the Bolsheviks should be a "party of a new type," governed by the principle of "democratic centralism." After the success of the Bolshevik Revolution, these became the central organizational principles of the ideology

known as Marxism-Leninism. Unlike the loosely organized socialist parties, the new Leninist parties would function as monoliths, whose members carried out decisions of their leaders without dissent. The Comintern's member parties were similarly required to carry out policies handed down from above.

No Americans attended the Comintern's founding meeting in Moscow, but there was strong sentiment within the left wing of the American Socialist Party (SP) and the radical labor federation, the Industrial Workers of the World (IWW), to affiliate. American journalist John Reed—who had been in the Russian capital of St. Petersburg during the revolution and whose 1919 account of the Bolshevik triumph, *Ten Days That Shook the World*, proved influential—was among those determined to create an American Communist Party. But faction fighting led in September 1919 to the creation of two rival Communist parties.

Soviet leaders regarded the Americans as squabbling amateurs, who would have to be taken in hand. Orders were dispatched from Moscow to end the division between the two Communist groups, but it was not until May 1921 that the merger was effected. Meanwhile, the Russian civil war drew to a close, and the Union of Soviet Socialist Republics (USSR) was founded, uniting most of the territory formerly part of the Czarist Empire. Another landmark event in Soviet history took place in 1922, when Joseph Stalin became general secretary of the Soviet Communist Party. Lenin suffered a stroke that year and played a diminished role in the affairs of the USSR until his death in January 1924.

Secrecy and Sectarianism

American Communists functioned as an underground movement in the early 1920s, partly in imitation of the prerevolutionary Bolsheviks and partly out of necessity. In 1917–18, the U.S. government cracked down on antiwar dissenters, sending hundreds to prison, including SP leader Eugene Debs. Attacks continued in the "Red scare" years after the war. Attorney General A. Mitchell Palmer launched a series of raids across the country on the second anniversary of the Bolshevik Revolution, November 7, 1919, resulting in the arrest of thousands of foreign-born Communists and anarchists, 200 of whom were deported to Russia aboard a ship dubbed the "Soviet ark."

American Communists began to emerge from underground in 1922, under the leadership of the Cleveland-born Charles E. Ruthenberg, with the formation of an open party, at first called the Workers Party, then the Workers (Communist) Party, and finally, in 1929, the Communist Party, USA (CPUSA). National headquarters were set up in Chicago but were moved to New York City, the center of the party's strength, in 1927. For the next two decades the party's activities were directed from the ninth floor of a building it owned at 35 East 12th Street. Secret financial subsidies from the Soviets helped pay for the CPUSA's operations.

Throughout the 1920s, factional struggles within the CPUSA mirrored those taking place among rival leaders of the USSR. In 1927 a group of American Communist leaders, including James P. Cannon, sided with Trotsky against Stalin. Trotsky was sent into exile, while the Trotskyists were expelled from the CPUSA.

Ruthenberg died in 1927 and was succeeded as general secretary (the party's leading post) by Jay Lovestone, a former student activist at the City College of New York. Lovestone's tenure in office was short-lived; he was deposed in 1929 on orders of the Comintern, having backed another soon-to-be-disgraced Soviet leader, Nicolai Bukharin. At the start of the 1930s, Stalin entrusted leadership of American communism to a hitherto obscure party functionary named Earl Browder, a former Kansas City bookkeeper. William Z. Foster, who in the 1920s headed the party's efforts to "bore from within" the American Federation of Labor (AFL) as leader of the Communist-organized Trade Union Education League (TUEL), had hoped to win the top spot for himself and became a bitter rival of Browder in the years to come.

In the 1920s most American Communists were foreign-born, with the largest groups coming from Finnish and Jewish backgrounds. The Communists launched a daily newspaper in Yiddish, the *Morgen Freiheit*, in 1922, two years before they started a daily newspaper in English, the *Daily Worker*. Although the party counted in its ranks some experienced labor organizers, like Foster, Communists had little influence in the broader union movement of the 1920s. In 1922 the party formed a youth affiliate, the Young Workers League, later renamed the Young Communist League (YCL), a group that gave Communists their first significant influx of native-born English-speaking members. Communists helped launch a monthly literary magazine, *New Masses*, in 1926 (which became a weekly in 1934); the magazine, along with a writers and artists organization called the John Reed Clubs, founded in 1929, began to give the Communists inroads among intellectuals and artists.

The Impact of the Great Depression

Stalin consolidated his control of the Soviet leadership in 1928, ending a period of relative moderation in the Soviet Union's political and economic life. He announced a crash industrialization program, to prepare the USSR for a new outbreak of "imperialist war." And he predicted a new wave of economic crisis and revolutionary activity in the capitalist world—a so-called third period. Communist parties around the world adopted this militant perspective, which seemed vindicated by the onset of the Great Depression of the 1930s. Instead of seeking united fronts with other radical parties around common aims, they denounced socialists as "social fascists."

And they bitterly opposed the new reform-minded administration of President Franklin D. Roosevelt. Communist trade unionists in the United States abandoned attempts to "bore from within" the AFL, and formed their own openly revolutionary unions. Communist efforts to turn their Trade Union Unity League (TUUL) into a revolutionary alternative to the AFL proved futile. They were somewhat more successful in organizing Unemployed Councils to demand relief payments for laid-off workers.

This ultrarevolutionary stance hindered the party's growth and influence, compared to their rivals on the Left. The Communists started the decade with about 7,500 members. That number doubled in the next two years to about 15,000, but during the same period, the Socialist Party grew to 25,000 members.

But in the mid-1930s, American Communists saw their membership and their influence increase dramatically as they once again shifted their political line. Following the accession to power of Adolf Hitler in 1933, Stalin grew increasingly concerned about the threat to the Soviet Union posed by Nazi Germany. Hoping to negotiate collective security treaties with the Western democracies, Stalin ordered Communists around the world to build broad antifascist alliances.

"Communism Is Twentieth-Century Americanism"

In the United States the new policy, known as the Popular Front, led to the abandonment of the slogan "Towards a Soviet America," and its replacement with the less threatening "Communism Is Twentieth Century Americanism." Communists no longer denounced Roosevelt and even lent him backhanded support in the 1936 election, although they ran Browder as their presidential candidate that year. Communist-organized Popular Front organizations like the League Against War and Fascism, the American Youth Congress, the American Student Union, the League of American Writers, and the National Negro Congress, among others, attracted many non-Communist adherents. Much of this growing influence was a product of the party's staunch antifascism, particularly during the Spanish Civil War of 1936–39, when 3,000 American volunteers, about 80 percent of them Communists, went to Spain to fight against fascists and in defense of the Spanish Republic in the Comintern-organized International Brigades. In the later 1930s, for the first time, a majority of American Communists were native-born. About 10 percent of the party was made up of African Americans, attracted by the CPUSA's vigorous support for civil rights.

From 1935 on, Communists also played an important role in labor organizing. Mine union leader John L. Lewis broke with the craft-union-oriented AFL in 1935 to form the Committee (later Congress) of Industrial Organizations (CIO). Although staunchly anti-Communist, Lewis hired Communist organizers to help build new industrial unions in mass production industries like steel, auto, and electrical manufacturing.

By 1938 the CPUSA was ten times the size it had been in 1930. But for all its apparent adaptation to American political life, the party remained firmly under Soviet control. CPUSA leaders traveled to Moscow on an annual basis to consult about political strategy. In the era of the Soviet purges, when millions were rounded up for prison, exile, or execution, the CPUSA defended Stalin as a benevolent leader. Some American Communists were recruited into clandestine espionage rings in the United States.

Wartime Gyrations

The CPUSA proved its loyalty to the Soviet Union in August 1939, when in a stunning reversal of policy, Stalin signed a "nonaggression pact" with Hitler. Within days, the Nazis invaded Poland, setting off World War II. American Communists dutifully denounced both sides in what they labeled the "Second Imperialist War." The vast array of Popular Front organizations they had created over the past half-decade collapsed in disarray. In a "little Red scare," Communists found themselves under legal attack. Communist teachers were fired from the City College of New York, while Browder was imprisoned in 1940 on a passport violation charge. Congress passed the Smith Act in 1941, giving the federal government the power to prosecute those who conspired to advocate the overthrow of the government through force and violence.

When the Nazis invaded the Soviet Union in June 1941, Communists switched from being antiwar isolationists to prowar interventionists. With the United States and the USSR allied against Nazi Germany after American entrance into the war in December 1941, the Communists' pro-Soviet sympathies ceased to stigmatize them as disloyal. In 1943, as a good-will gesture to his Western Allies, Stalin dissolved the Comintern. Browder, who had been released from prison, attempted a bold political experiment by dissolving the CPUSA and replacing it with a new and more loosely organized Communist Political Association (CPA). Despite such gestures, Communist loyalties to the Soviet cause remained undiminished; during the war, Soviet intelligence agents expanded their espionage efforts in the United States, recruiting American Communists to help penetrate the top-secret Manhattan Project in Los Alamos, New Mexico, where the atomic bomb was being developed.

During the war, Roosevelt met with Stalin on several occasions, and hopes for the continued postwar unity of the so-called Grand Alliance remained high through the spring of 1945. But tensions between the two countries were already rising when Roosevelt died in April. His successor, Harry Truman, was determined to stand up to Soviet expansionism in Europe and elsewhere. Before another year passed, the term *cold war* had come to describe the conflict between the United States and its allies, on the one hand, and the Soviet Union, its new Eastern European empire, and, after 1949, Communist China, on the other. Meanwhile, in June 1945 Browder was deposed as the American Communist leader for what was seen in Moscow as his heresy in dissolving the party. The CPUSA was restored with Browder's long-time rival Foster as chairman and Eugene Dennis as general secretary.

Cold War and McCarthyism

Under new leaders, the CPUSA veered leftward. The decision to launch a third-party campaign in 1948, with former vice president Henry Wallace as the presidential nominee of the new Progressive Party, would prove a disaster for the Communists. Wallace's Election Day showing was unimpressive and Truman was returned to the White House. Eleven Communist-led unions were expelled from the CIO in 1949 for breaking with the labor movement in endorsing Wallace. At the same time, the Communist Party was coming under fierce legal assault. The Truman administration initiated a loyalty review procedure for federal employees that resulted in the firing of several thousand suspected Communists. Private industries, including the Hollywood studios, fired or blacklisted hundreds of others for suspected Communist sympathies. The Federal Bureau of Investigation (FBI), under the directorship of J. Edgar Hoover, launched an intense campaign to infiltrate and disrupt the party. And federal prosecutors indicted 11 top Communists, including the party's general secretary Dennis, for violation of the Smith Act (between 1949 and 1956 over a hundred Communist leaders would be tried under the Smith Act and sentenced to lengthy prison terms). Sensational revelations about Soviet wartime espionage and the conviction and execution of Julius and Ethel Rosenberg for atomic espionage, reinforced public hostility to communism. Anticommunism provided the issue that launched the careers of some of the nation's most influential politicians, including Wisconsin senator Joseph McCarthy, and California congressman Richard M. Nixon.

By 1956 a battered Communist Party retained about 20,000 members. But that year the party was struck by two devastating blows from abroad. The first was the revelation in the spring of the text of a secret speech that Soviet premier Nikita Khrushchev had delivered to a Soviet Party congress in Moscow earlier in 1956 denouncing the bloody crimes committed by Stalin, who had died in 1953. The second was the outbreak of rebellion against Communist rule in Hungary in the fall of 1956, which was brutally suppressed by the Soviet Red Army. Thousands of American Communists resigned in disillusionment.

Fade to Irrelevance

The 1960s saw a minor revival of the CPUSA, under the leadership of Gus Hall, who became general secretary in 1959. The Communists' greatest asset in the 1960s was the young African American activist Angela Davis, who became famous for her fiery rhetoric and run-ins with the law. However, the CPUSA's decision to endorse the Warsaw Pact invasion of Czechoslovakia in 1968, overthrowing a reform-oriented Communist government, led to a new round of resignations. In an ironic twist, when reformer Mikhail Gorbachev took over the leadership of the Soviet Union in the 1980s, Hall and other orthodox Communists in the United States finally started to oppose Soviet policies. Following the collapse of the Soviet Union in 1991, the CPUSA split between the hard-liners and Gorbachev-influenced reformers, with the latter group, which included Davis, leaving to form the Committees of Correspondence for Democracy and Socialism. Hall remained the leader of the CPUSA until his death in 2000, when he was succeeded by Sam Webb.

See also anticommunism; radicalism; socialism.

FURTHER READING. Theodore Draper, *The Roots of American Communism*, 1957; John Haynes and Harvey Klehr, *Verona: Decoding Soviet Espionage in America*, 1999; Dorothy Healey and Maurice Isserman, *Dorothy Healey Remembers: The Life of an American Communist*, 1990; Maurice Isserman, *Which Side Were You On? The American Communist Party during the Second World War*, 1982; Harvey Klehr, *The Heyday of American Communism: The Depression Decade*, 1985.

MAURICE ISSERMAN

Confederacy

The Confederacy refers to the Confederate States of America, the nation that existed between 1861 and 1865 and fought the United States of America during the Civil War. It encompassed 11 states (Virginia, North Carolina, South Carolina, Georgia, Florida, Alabama, Mississippi, Louisiana, Texas, Arkansas, and Tennessee), though it laid claim to other, disputed, border states (Maryland, Missouri, and Kentucky). Although the Confederate state existed for scarcely more than four years, a sense of Confederate nationalism or identity persisted throughout the nineteenth century and, some might argue, well into the twentieth and twenty-first.

Politically, the Confederacy stood for several interrelated principles. First and foremost, its founders and citizens believed that their nation should be a slaveholding one, and they brooked no opposition to the "peculiar institution." Underlying that belief in the rightness of slavery were other ideas, including a staunch belief in states rights, a desire for a nonpartisan government, and a conviction that the Confederacy, not the United States, represented the perfection of the Founding Fathers' vision.

Creation

The Confederacy was born out of the secession of southern slaveholding states, but secession itself preceded the Confederacy. Abraham Lincoln's election in November 1860 gave longtime southern nationalists the excuse they needed to secede from the Union. South Carolina, long the home of the most fervent proslavery and states' rights ideologues, seceded first on December 20, 1860. The other Deep South states quickly followed, and by February 1, 1861, seven states had left the Union (in order: South Carolina, Mississippi, Florida, Alabama, Georgia, Louisiana, and Texas).

Secessionists were sensitive to criticism of their actions as illegitimate and were careful to provide constitutional justifications for their actions. They saw secession not as revolution but as an alternate and, in their minds, correct reading of constitutional provisions. Secessionists subscribed to the "compact theory" first elucidated in the Virginia and Kentucky Resolutions of 1798. According to this theory, the individual states delegated their authority to the federal government when they ratified the Constitution and could therefore withdraw it through another convention. In general, the secession ordinances passed at these conventions rescinded ratification of the Constitution. The secessionists believed themselves to be the true heirs of the Founding Fathers, and their rhetoric frequently hearkened back to 1776. They argued that the Republicans were the true revolutionaries, citing as evidence Lincoln's "A house divided" speech and William H. Seward's "irrepressible conflict" speech. Secession and its rhetoric also took on an air of emotionalism and celebration, particularly in the lower South. Southerners had felt under siege for over a year, and secession provided a sort of catharsis or relief. Standard manifestations of nineteenth-century political culture, like parades, fireworks, and celebrations, accompanied each secession convention. Additionally, as each state seceded, it sent commissioners to sitting conventions, encouraging the slaveholding states still in the Union to jump on the bandwagon as well.

There were, however, opponents to secession within the slaveholding states and particularly in the border states of the upper South, the same regions that voted for the Constitutional Unionist John Bell in the 1860 election. These Unionists counseled moderation and urged their southern brethren to wait until Lincoln took overt action against them. Unlike in the lower South states, many of these conventions had Unionist majorities, until the firing on Fort Sumter and Lincoln's call for troops in April 1865. Many Unionists hoped to broker a compromise between the Lincoln administration and the new Confederacy.

The Confederate nation appears to have been born almost fully formed. On February 4, 1861, delegates from the seven seceded states met in Montgomery, Alabama, essentially to create their new nation. In large part because they believed themselves to be the heirs to the Founding Fathers, they drew heavily on the U.S. Constitution. This served a double function: first, it allowed them to create a nation quickly, without having to build everything from scratch. Second, and more importantly, it also gave the Confederate people a ready-made myth of national origin and eased the shifting of their allegiances from the United States to the Confederate States.

The Confederate Constitution adopted in March 1861 in Montgomery was almost identical to the U.S. Constitution, with a few differences that highlighted the Confederacy's shifts in ideological emphasis. In the preamble, it omitted the general welfare clause and added that each ratifying state was acting "in its sovereign and independent character," thus signaling that this was a true confederation of states. It prohibited protective tariffs and congressional appropriations for internal improvements, thus addressing a perennial source of southern resentment and complaint. Interestingly, the Confederate Constitution limited the president to one six-year term but gave him a line-item veto.

The greatest differences regarded slavery. The Confederate Constitution explicitly guaranteed slavery in both states and territories, charging that "no bill of attainder, ex post facto law, or law denying or impairing the right of negro property in slaves shall be passed." It did, however, ban the importation of slaves from outside the Confederacy. This may seem surprising, for many of the same men (especially South Carolinians) who had been agitating for secession during the 1850s had also been pushing for a reopening of the international slave trade. But the delegates to the Montgomery convention were also well aware that eight slaveholding states had not yet seceded and that the residents of these border states would not support the importation of slaves. Thus, banning the international trade was seen as a necessary measure to gain the support of the upper South states and ensure their eventual secession.

A similar impulse was at work in the selection of the Confederate president. The Montgomery convention was the site of considerable jockeying for political position, especially over the choice of president. The convention eventually selected Jefferson Davis, of Mississippi, a compromise candidate who was not even in attendance at Montgomery. Davis was clearly experienced in both foreign and domestic matters, as he had been secretary of war under Franklin Pierce as well as a senator and congressman. He was also more of a moderate, and this too appealed to the upper South. Extremists like William Lowndes Yancey of Alabama and South Carolina's Robert Barnwell Rhett were largely left out of the government. The vice presidential slot went to Alexander Stephens of Georgia, head of the Constitution-drafting committee. The process was also important to the Confederates: they liked the fact that Davis was chosen by consensus, no unseemly elections, no outright dissent. In this, they saw themselves returning to an earlier model, without dangerous factionalism. Whether a nation could survive based on states' rights and nonpartisanship remained to be seen.

On April 12, 1861, Confederate forces fired on Fort Sumter, a Union holdout on an island in Charleston Harbor. Thirty-four hours later, on April 14, the Union forces surrendered. On April 15, President Lincoln declared South Carolina in rebellion against the United States and issued a proclamation calling 75,000 state militiamen into federal service for 90 days in order to put down the insurrection. In the North, his call was answered eagerly, and a fever of excitement swept through the populace. Nearly every northern state sent more than its quota of men. The remaining slave states were placed in a more difficult position.

The eight slave states remaining in the Union (Delaware, Maryland, Virginia, Tennessee, North Carolina, Missouri, Kentucky, and Arkansas) were generally horrified by Lincoln's request that they take up arms against their "southern brethren." All but Maryland and Delaware rejected Lincoln's request. Most of the people in these border states had been conditional Unionists, and this was simply too much for them to accept. Within a matter of days, Virginia's convention voted to secede and offered Richmond as the new site of the Confederate capital. Within a matter of weeks, Arkansas, North Carolina, and Tennessee seceded from the Union, and the Confederacy was complete.

Nationalism

The vast majority of white Southerners, even those who had been Unionists throughout the winter of 1860–61, transferred their allegiance to the Confederacy with few backward glances. In large part, this transition was eased by the ways that Confederates drew on staples of American political culture and made them their own. Confederates carefully cast themselves as their heirs of the American Revolution and often drew explicit comparisons between the spirits of '76 and '61. George Washington's image adorned the Great Seal of the Confederacy and Confederate postage stamps. By drawing on the Revolutionary past, Confederates rejected antebellum bursts of southern sectionalism as exemplified in the nullification crisis and the debates over the Compromise of 1850, in favor of an image with more broadly based appeal. Discussions of Revolutionary antecedents rarely mentioned slavery, and Confederates seemed to like it this way. A war fought to protect the founders' values—however nebulously defined—would appeal to nonslaveholders and former Unionists as well as longtime fire-eaters.

Confederates also imbued their political culture and identity with a healthy dose of Christian rhetoric. They believed themselves to be God's chosen people, and they saw confirmation of that in their early victories of 1861–62. Of course, as the tide of battle increasingly turned against them in 1863–64, Confederates shifted their rhetoric, and believed that God was testing or chastening them.

As much as Confederates argued that their nation was based on constitutional principles, Revolutionary antecedents, and Christianity, it also included a potent mix of fear and rage. The fear was of the end of slavery, couched often in the language of so-called black rule or race-mixing; the rage was against invading Yankees, demonized to the point of dehumanization. White supremacy and the protection of slavery were integral to the Confederacy, and even nonslaveholders understood that benefits and status accrued to them by virtue of their white skin. Thus, discussions of slavery per se appeared only rarely in public forums. For the most part Confederates took slavery as a given, albeit a sometimes problematic one, subject to neither challenge nor discussion.

Confederates had a second reason to keep silent on the subject of slavery, for they worried constantly about how their nation would be perceived by foreign countries. The ever-present search for diplomatic recognition, a sort of national status anxiety, underlay Confederate calls for indigenous schoolbooks and literature and influenced the language in which Confederates framed their national aspirations. While hoping that the Confederate monopoly on cotton production would force Europeans to help the Confederacy, they were also sensitive to foreign, particularly British, opposition to slavery. By deemphasizing bondage as a cause of secession, stressing instead states' rights and political domination, Confederates were able to shift the terms of debate, thus making their cause more palatable to conditional Unionists, nonslaveholders, and foreign nations.

Collapse

The Confederacy struggled mightily as the war went on, pressured externally by the Union Army and internally by both slaves and its own structural instabilities. Confederates rather quickly discovered that states' rights (particularly when guarded jealously by state governors) was not a strong foundation from which to launch a nation and fight a war. Thus, each time President Jefferson Davis attempted to increase centralization—whether through taxation, impressment, or conscription—he faced considerable internal opposition. But because of the Confederacy's avowed anti-partyism (perhaps compounded by the six-year presidential term), there was no real channel for that opposition. Anger, resentment, and disenchantment became focused on Jefferson Davis personally. At the same time, while all Confederates struggled with shortages of foodstuffs and runaway inflation, lower-class whites were hit especially hard. Shortages and the perception inspired by the 20 slave exemption (a law that allowed one white man to stay home on plantations of over 20 slaves, ostensibly to help grow food and keep the peace) alienated even supportive yeomen. In 1863 there were bread riots in cities around the South, with the worst one in Richmond, as working-class women stormed stores and government warehouses to get food for their families. Family interests might take precedence over national interests, as illustrated by letters from women begging their husbands and sons to desert. The South also had the problem of slaves who ran away or would simply refuse to work. A combination of labor unrest, slowdowns, and escape all rendered the southern economy much less efficient and contributed to a general sense that the Confederates' world was falling apart.

Some historians charged that the Confederacy ultimately lost the Civil War because of failures of will—essentially claiming that Confederate patriotism was not strong enough to sustain a viable nation and that a withdrawal of public support at home ultimately led to defeat on the battlefield. More recently, however, historians have discounted that view, arguing instead that the Confederacy was defeated by the North's superior resources, both material and personnel. These historians have sought to change the questions being asked from "Why did the Confederacy lose?" to "Why was the Confederacy able to exist for as long as it did?" The Confederacy, for all of its shortcomings, did possess the necessary apparatus of government—an executive, a legislature, a judiciary, a treasury, a postal service, a state department. Most importantly, for the Confederacy had no real existence apart from war, it raised and kept an army in the field. These may not have always functioned well or efficiently—indeed in many cases they barely functioned at all—but they did exist.

Furthermore, while the Confederate nation-state ceased to exist in April 1865 (although President Jefferson Davis was not captured by Union troops until May 10, 1865, and some Confederate troops remained in the field until late May 1865), a sense of allegiance to the Confederacy continued in the hearts of white Southerners for generations. During the late nineteenth and early twentieth centuries, veterans and descendants groups, most notably the United Daughters of the Confederacy, flourished. These groups helped to recast the Confederate experience into a noble "lost cause," from which slavery and white supremacy were almost entirely excised. Confederate flags, specifically the Army of Northern Virginia's battle flag, began to fly again throughout the South during the 1950s and 1960s in response to the civil rights movement. The 1990s and early 2000s saw renewed controversy over these flags and their meanings, demonstrating the degree to which the Confederacy, or at least an idealized, sanitized version of it, still holds a degree of cultural power in the United States.

See also Civil War and Reconstruction; race and politics; slavery.

FURTHER READING. David W. Blight, *Race and Reunion: The Civil War in American Memory*, 2001; William C. Davis, *"A Government of Our Own": The Making of the Confederacy*, 1994; Paul D. Escott, *After Secession: Jefferson Davis and the Failure of Confederate Nationalism*, 1978; Drew Gilpin Faust, *The Creation of Confederate Nationalism: Ideology and Identity in the Civil War South*, 1988; George

C. Rable, *The Confederate Republic: A Revolution against Politics*, 1994; Anne Sarah Rubin, *A Shattered Nation: The Rise and Fall of the Confederacy, 1861–1868*, 2005; Emory M. Thomas, *The Confederate Nation: 1861–1865*, 1979.

ANNE SARAH RUBIN

conservatism

No coherent conservative political movement existed before the twentieth century. Until the late nineteenth century, the principles of laissez-faire and classical republicanism were integral to the American political tradition. Essential to this tradition was an inherent distrust of centralized government, and this distrust found its classic expression in the U.S. Constitution. Its famous beginning, "We the people," asserted that the source of its authority rested in the citizenry rather than in the state.

The tradition came under challenge in the late nineteenth century with the rise of corporations, mass manufacturing, international agricultural markets, and business malfeasance and exploitation of labor. Progressive reformers called for the federal government to expand its regulatory powers through legislation, the courts, and the marshaling of scientific expertise.

Conservatives developed two main responses to the changing political and social order. The first was social Darwinism, the application of Darwinian biology to promote laissez-faire ideas articulated by English author Herbert Spencer, Yale University professor William Graham Sumner, and steel mogul Andrew Carnegie. Social Darwinists supported laissez-faire capitalism, free trade, and anti-imperialism. The second response, conservative nationalism, drew upon long-standing Republican Party policies of high tariffs, government support for American business, the expansion of American economic interests abroad, and an adherence to strict constitutional interpretation. In the late nineteenth and early twentieth centuries, laissez-faire ideology was on the defensive. Conservative nationalism, however, remained crucial to Republican political success well into the 1920s in the presidential administrations of Warren Harding, Calvin Coolidge, and Herbert Hoover.

Conservatism in the early twentieth century was not a political movement per se. There was no self-identified political vehicle for conservative ideas. Many of the most important conservatives in the 1920s and 1930s were only peripherally concerned with politics; instead, they lamented what they saw as the cultural decline of Western civilization and criticized what Spanish political philosopher José Ortega y Gasset called "the revolt of the masses."

During the 1920s, the "new humanists," led by Irving Babbitt and Paul Elmer More, excoriated any literature published after the eighteenth century. The architect Ralph Adams Cram fought against the modern world in his own work designing Gothic cathedrals and buildings, and expressed a belief that human nature had not changed since the Neolithic era. Such views were hardly equipped to build a conservative political majority.

In the next decade, conservative commentators such as Garet Garrett and Albert Jay Nock condemned Franklin D. Roosevelt's New Deal for furthering the decline of individualism. Meanwhile, in 1934, businessmen hostile to the expanded power of the federal government founded the American Liberty League to challenge Roosevelt's view that "money changers in the temple of civilization" and the free enterprise system in general were responsible for the Great Depression, and that only government intervention could cure the broken economy. The Liberty League hoped to influence the midterm congressional elections, but the Democrats expanded their majorities in Congress; in 1936 Roosevelt won a landslide reelection, and the Liberty League soon disbanded.

Only in the late 1930s did conservatives in Congress from both parties succeed in opposing the New Deal through such agencies as the House Committee on Un-American Activities, which investigated the influence of Communists in federal programs. Then, during World War II, a revitalized conservative coalition of Republicans and southern Democrats managed to terminate New Deal relief programs, although the most important liberal reforms—Social Security and the Wagner Act—remained impervious to change.

Groups like the National Association of Manufacturers, with individuals like Sun Oil chairman J. Howard Pew leading the way, revitalized the free enterprise message throughout World War II. Business recovered much of its damaged social authority during the war years by securing the economic and military power necessary to defeat Germany and Japan. Pew encouraged ideological combat against the New Deal, securing funds to help publish such seminal conservative works as Friedrich Hayek's *The Road to Serfdom* and Henry W. Wriston's *Challenge to Freedom*. The conservative weekly *Human Events* also began publishing in 1944. Initially critical of interventionist foreign policy—it was edited by former supporters of the antiwar group America First—*Human Events* would soon be a strong supporter of the cold war. After a long period in the political wilderness, conservatives had resurrected their ideas.

The Conservative Revival

Conservatism in the post–World War II period became intertwined with the Republican Party. This is not to say that all conservatives were Republicans: many conservatives, especially in the South, were aligned with the Democratic Party or voted, at various times, for third-party candidates. Nonetheless, in the postwar period, conservatives launched a movement to transform the Republican Party.

Many of the key intellectuals who reinvigorated conservatism in the postwar period were émigrés from Europe: Ayn Rand, from Russia; Friedrich Hayek and his fellow economist Ludwig Von Mises, from Austria; and the philosophers Eric Voegelin and Leo Strauss, from Germany. They were joined by such young American intellectuals as William F. Buckley Jr., who founded the conservative *National Review* in 1955; the historian Russell Kirk; the philosopher Richard Weaver; and the journalist Frank Meyer.

Fundamental philosophical differences separated these thinkers. Concern about communism intensified debate over an array of questions: Should the right compromise its principles of small government in support of the cold war? Did the United States have the right to intervene militarily and politically in the affairs of another country to prevent a perceived Communist takeover? Should government restrict the civil liberties of Communists in the United States? These debates were largely philosophical and, until the 1960s, usually did not involve specific pieces of legislation. But they lent vitality to the right and appealed to a new generation of students and activists dissatisfied with the Freudianism and existentialism fashionable among liberal intellectuals of the day.

Much of this debate occurred in conservative journals, particularly the *National Review*. In founding the magazine, Buckley sought to present different perspectives on the right and to expand its readership beyond the only other mass-circulation conservative publication, *Human Events*, whose audience was mostly drawn from grassroots anti-Communists. Buckley gathered an impressive editorial board including James Burnham, former Communist Frank Meyer, Whittaker Chambers, Russell Kirk, novelist John Dos Passos, Buckley's brother-in-law L. Brent Bozell Jr., Yale University political scientist Willmore Kendall, corporate lawyer William Rusher, and libertarian Frank Chodorov.

The vitality of the conservative intellectual movement paralleled the growth of a mass grassroots anti-Communist movement organized primarily through local community, religious, and business groups. The movement reflected profound fears about the Soviet threat abroad and Communist subversion at home. Australian physician and evangelist minister Fred Schwarz organized the Christian Anti-Communist Crusade, which conducted seminars and lectures that drew tens of thousands of participants. In Texas, former Federal Bureau of Investigation agent Dan Smoot published a widely read newsletter and hosted a syndicated radio program. Leonard Read headed the Foundation for Economic Education, which promoted free enterprise and warned about the dangers of communism and socialism. In 1958 candy manufacturer Robert Welch founded the John Birch Society, which attracted a large national membership. Welch's accusation that Dwight D. Eisenhower was a conscious Soviet agent, however, stunted the growth of the society, and Welch later retracted his statement.

Within the Republican Party, conservatives sought to replace what they saw as the dominance of the eastern liberal wing, symbolized by Nelson Rockefeller, with an uncompromising anti–New Deal faction. Many conservatives had been disappointed by the failure of Ohio Republican Robert Taft to win the GOP presidential nomination in 1948 and 1952. Conservative Republicans had generally supported Eisenhower's presidency, but discord within the party had increased.

Goldwater, 1964, and Civil Rights

As the 1960 election approached, conservatives hoped that Senator Barry Goldwater, a Republican from Arizona, would win the GOP nomination for president.

In 1959 Clarence Manion, former dean of the Notre Dame Law School, organized a Goldwater for President group. As part of the campaign, he arranged for Buckley's brother-in-law, Bozell, to write a political manifesto under Goldwater's name. Published in 1960, *Conscience of a Conservative* became a national best-seller, even though Richard Nixon secured the GOP nomination and went on to lose the election to John F. Kennedy. That same year, college-age supporters of Goldwater organized Young Americans for Freedom on the Buckley family estate in Sharon, Connecticut, proclaiming, "In this time of moral and political crisis, it is the responsibility of the youth of American to affirm certain eternal truths."

Conservatives believed that, if they could secure Goldwater's nomination in 1964, the GOP had a chance of winning the White House. The entire race changed, however, when President Kennedy was assassinated in Dallas, Texas, in November 1963. His successor, Lyndon Johnson, drew upon the tragedy to push an aggressive liberal agenda through Congress. Although Goldwater believed it would be impossible for any Republican to win in 1964, out of loyalty to his followers he remained in the race and defeated Nelson Rockefeller, the governor of New York, in a bitter fight for the GOP nomination.

Goldwater's vote against the Civil Rights Bill of 1964 as an unconstitutional interference in private matters drew heavy criticism from moderates within his own party as well as from northern Democrats. His acceptance speech, which contained the lines, "Extremism in the defense of liberty is no vice. Moderation in the pursuit of justice is no virtue," widened the gap even further.

The *National Review* did not help his cause. The magazine harshly criticized the civil rights movement and opposed federal enforcement of equal access to public accommodations and protection of black voting rights in the South, reinforcing perceptions that conservatives were racists. The magazine's editorial rhetoric often overstepped the bounds of civility and was racially offensive. Years later Buckley would apologize for the tone the magazine had set.

Lyndon Johnson won by a landslide, and Democrats gained huge majorities in Congress. Conservatives found some signs of hope, however. Goldwater

Republicans won Senate races in California with former movie star George Murphy and in Nebraska with Roman Hruska. Most significantly, the Republicans won most states in the Deep South for the first time since Reconstruction. This reversal of fortune persuaded southern Democrats to become more conservative and, often, more vocal in their support for segregation.

Nixon, Ford, and Frustration of Conservatives

In 1968, with the Democratic Party sharply divided over the Vietnam War, Richard Nixon narrowly won the presidency. Most conservatives had supported him, albeit reluctantly, in hopes of gaining influence over his policies. Few Republicans could stomach the third-party campaign of Alabama governor George Wallace, whose rage-filled populist message gained 13.5 percent of the popular vote. But Nixon came into office with big Democratic majorities in both houses of Congress. Even if he had wanted to move to the right, he would have been unable to do so. Instead, Nixon pursued a rather liberal agenda at home, expanding the welfare and regulatory state. He intensified the bombing in Vietnam, while his national security adviser, and later secretary of state, Henry Kissinger, opened negotiations with North Vietnam. At the same time, Nixon entered into a new arms-control agreement with the Soviet Union, the Strategic Arms Limitation Talks. Then, shortly before the 1972 election, Nixon announced he planned to open relations with mainland China.

These policies dismayed many GOP conservatives. But the primary challenge to Nixon mounted by the new American Conservative Union failed miserably. Nixon easily won renomination and went on to swamp George McGovern, his Democratic opponent. Two years later, Nixon's involvement in the Watergate scandal forced his resignation. New president Gerald Ford followed a moderate course that made him seem impervious to the rumblings of the right wing in his party.

In the mid-1970s, conservatives were a distinct minority within the Republican Party, but they were beginning to build an institutional foundation for their movement. They expanded the American Enterprise Institute, founded in the early 1940s, to provide conservative policy analysis. In 1973 conservative foundations such as the Scaife Fund, the John M. Olin Foundation, and the Bradley Foundation, and wealthy benefactors such as beer magnate Joseph Coors supported the establishment of the Heritage Foundation. These think tanks added intellectual firepower to the conservative resistance to the modern liberal state.

The founding of the magazine *Public Interest* by New York intellectual Irving Kristol in 1965 helped fuel the intellectual challenge to liberalism. Kristol viewed the *Public Interest* as an antidote to what he considered the increasing utopianism of leftist thinkers. The magazine attracted contributors who had become disgruntled with Johnson's Great Society, including Daniel Moynihan, Nathan Glazer, James Q. Wilson, Edward C. Banfield, and Aaron Wildavsky. These scholars, many of them social scientists, criticized programs devised by what they called the "new class" of fashionable leftists and government bureaucrats. Similar criticisms emerged in the Jewish opinion magazine *Commentary*, edited by Norman Podhoretz.

Although not uniformly conservative in their political outlooks, the most prominent writers for the *Public Interest* and *Commentary* became known as "neoconservatives," former liberals who rejected social experimentation, affirmative action, and moral relativism. They also supported a vigorous American foreign policy backed by a strong national defense to meet what they perceived as a heightened Soviet threat.

More traditional conservatives built a powerful movement to oppose the equal rights amendment (ERA) that Congress had passed in 1972—a victory for feminists. The ERA seemed to be headed toward easy ratification by the states until veteran right-wing activist Phyllis Schlafly organized a movement to stop it. She argued that the amendment would allow the drafting of women into the military, provide abortion on demand, legalize gay marriage, and weaken legislation protecting women in the workplace and in marriages. Schlafly organized a coalition of traditionalist Catholics, evangelical Protestants, Mormons, and orthodox Jews into a grassroots movement that helped stop the ERA from being ratified.

Other conservative activists—including Paul Weyrich, fund-raiser Richard Viguerie, Howard Phillips, and Republican strategist Terry Dolan—saw potential in Schlafly's success. They mounted a challenge to the GOP establishment through grassroots action on other "social issues," such as opposition to abortion and gay marriage, and support for school prayer. Calling themselves the New Right, these activists brought new organizing and fund-raising prowess to the conservative cause.

With conservative activism growing, Ronald Reagan challenged Ford for the presidential nomination in 1976. He was unsuccessful, but Ford's narrow defeat by Jimmy Carter that year put Reagan in position to win the party's nomination four years later. White evangelical voters moved away from Carter, a southern Baptist Democrat, during his presidency; a key turning point was the Internal Revenue Service's 1978 ruling to deprive all private schools established after 1953 of their tax-exempt status if they were found guilty of discriminatory racial practices. Along with Carter's support for abortion rights, this decision rallied many evangelicals into supporting ministers Jerry Falwell and Tim LaHaye, who headed a new organization, the Moral Majority, that vowed to bring "traditional morality" back to government.

Conservatives exerted their influence in the 1978 midterm elections through the Committee for the Survival of a Free Congress and the National

Conservative Political Action Committee. Although the South did not go fully Republican that year, history professor Newt Gingrich won election in Georgia, and, in Texas, Ron Paul won back a seat in Congress he had lost to a Democrat in 1976. At the same time, in California, voters ratified the Jarvis-Gann initiative, Proposition 13, cutting property taxes.

The Reagan and Bush Years

In 1980 Reagan won the Republican nomination and defeated Carter in the general election. The conservative standard bearer carried every region and every major constituency except Hispanics and African Americans. He won most southern states by 5 percentage points, and cut heavily into the blue-collar vote in the North. Republicans also won a majority of Senate seats for the first time in almost 30 years and made big gains in the House of Representatives. It was a significant victory for conservatives after 35 years of struggle.

During the next eight years, Reagan redefined the tone and nature of political discourse, although he had to compromise with a Democratic House throughout his term in office. Reagan failed to reshape the federal bureaucracy that sheltered liberal programs but did accomplish a good deal that delighted conservatives. The Economic Recovery Tax Act provided the largest tax decrease in history by reducing capital gains taxes and inflation-indexed tax rates. He continued Carter's policy of deregulation, enacting major monetary and banking reform. He ordered staff cuts in the Consumer Product Safety Commission, the Occupational Safety and Health Administration, and the Environmental Protection Agency. Reagan's administration supported efforts to restrict legalized abortion and to allow prayer in public schools, but these measures failed to pass in Congress. Reagan also initiated a massive increase in the defense budget and, in 1983, announced the Strategic Defense Initiative, an antimissile defense system based in outer space, which drew widespread protests from peace activists and liberal columnists.

The conservative president also waged what was, in effect, a proxy war against the Soviet Union. With the support of the AFL-CIO, the Vatican, and European trade unions, the United States assisted the anti-Communist labor movement Solidarity in Poland. The Reagan administration also aided "freedom fighters" in Central America, Southeast Asia, Africa, and Central America, and provided training and military assistance to Islamic forces opposed to the Soviet invasion of Afghanistan.

Reagan's policy toward the Soviet Union combined militant engagement and arms reduction. This policy, which appeared inconsistent to his opponents, followed a conservative strategy captured in the slogan "peace through strength." In pursuit of this aim, Reagan opposed calls by peace activists for a "nuclear freeze" on the development of new weapons and the deployment of Pershing II intermediate missiles in Europe. In a series of bilateral summit meetings from late 1985 through late 1988, Reagan and Soviet leader Premier Mikhail Gorbachev reached agreements that essentially brought an end to the cold war.

Conservatives found in Reagan an articulate and popular spokesman for their principles. While they sometimes criticized him as being overly pragmatic—raising taxes in 1983 and 1984, and failing to push for antiabortion legislation—he still left office as the hero of their movement. Reagan had succeeded in making conservatism a respectable political ideology in the nation as a whole.

Reagan's successor, George H. W. Bush, sought to turn the Republican Party to the center while maintaining his conservative base. This proved to be a cumbersome political act that betrayed a lack of principle. Bush seemed more involved in foreign than domestic policy: he ordered a military incursion in Panama to overthrow a corrupt dictatorship and then mobilized international support for military intervention in Iraq following its invasion of neighboring Kuwait. At home, Bush supported such Democratic measures as a ban on AK-47 assault rifles, the Americans with Disabilities Act, and a large tax hike for wealthy Americans. To fill two openings on the Supreme Court, he named David Souter, who turned out to be a liberal stalwart, and Clarence Thomas, a conservative whose nomination became controversial when a former employee, Anita Hill, accused him of sexual harassment.

The Clinton and George W. Bush Years

In the general election of 1992, Bush sought desperately to regain his conservative base. He invited conservative columnist Patrick Buchanan, who had challenged him in the primary campaign, to address the Republican convention. Buchanan's speech declared that the Democratic Party nominee Bill Clinton and his wife, Hillary Rodham Clinton, would "impose on America . . . abortion on demand, a litmus test for the Supreme Court, homosexual rights, discrimination against religious schools, women in combat. . . ." Buchanan's talk of a "culture war" was received enthusiastically by evangelical conservatives, but it alienated mainstream voters and probably helped defeat Bush's bid for reelection that fall.

Conservatives viewed Clinton as a baby boomer who had protested the war in Vietnam, repelled the military, and supported abortion. Conservatives seized on Clinton's proposal, as president-elect, to lift the ban on gay men and lesbians in the military, a quiet campaign promise he had to back away from under a barrage of criticism from the right. This proved to be the opening round in a well-orchestrated conservative assault that put the Clinton administration on the defensive and defeated the president's proposal for a universal health care system that the first lady had largely devised.

As the midterm election of 1994 drew near, conservatives led by Representative Newt Gingrich of

Georgia organized a group of young Turks in the House to retake Republican control of that body for the first time since 1952. They drafted the Contract with America, which pledged 337 Republican candidates to a ten-part legislative program, including welfare reform, anticrime measures, a line-item veto, regulatory reform, and tax reduction. The contract notably ignored such emotional issues as abortion, pornography, and school prayer. The Contract with America drew enthusiastic response from the conservative media, especially Rush Limbaugh, whose radio program appeared on 600 stations with 20 million weekly listeners. On Election Day, Republicans captured both houses of Congress with a 230–204 majority in the House and eight new Senate seats.

Clinton nonetheless won reelection in 1996 against the weak campaign of Senator Robert Dole and survived a sexual scandal involving a White House intern that led the Republican House to impeach him. The Senate failed to convict, and Republicans lost seats in the 1998 election, shocking conservatives who had assumed that "immorality in the Oval Office" would benefit their cause. Many Republicans blamed Gingrich for the loss, and shortly after the election, he resigned from the House.

The Clinton scandal carried into the 2000 presidential race, in which Republican Texas governor George W. Bush defeated Democratic Vice President Al Gore in the closest election in modern U.S. history. Bush lost the popular vote, but he gained Republican support among observant conservative Christians, especially evangelical Protestants and Roman Catholics. Although Pat Robertson's Christian Coalition had waned in influence, a strong religious network made direct contact with voters through voter guides and pastoral commentary. Much of this strategy of targeting key voters was the brainchild of political consultant Karl Rove.

The world of politics—and the fate of Bush's presidency—was transformed by the terrorist attacks of September 11, 2001. Bush's resolute stance won him enormous popularity, and Congress passed a series of emergency measures, including the Combating Terrorism Act and the Uniting and Strengthening America by Providing Appropriate Tools Required to Intercept and Obstruct Terrorism (USA PATRIOT) Act, which expanded the surveillance powers of federal agencies. Civil libertarians worried that this legislation extended too much power to the federal government at a cost to personal liberties. But it underlined the Republican advantage on the issue of national security and helped the party gain seats in Congress in the 2002 election—and also gave the president the political support he needed to invade Iraq in early 2003. Although the war did not proceed as planned, Bush won a second term in 2004 against Democrat John Kerry, due in large part to his image as the leader of the so-called War on Terror. For the first time in decades, conservative Republicans were in firm control of the White House and Capitol Hill.

The triumph was brief, however. Soon after Bush's reelection, the continuing bloodshed in Iraq and the administration's fumbling of relief efforts following Hurricane Katrina led to the beginning of his steep decline in approval polls, and he never recovered. A series of lobbying and fund-raising scandals involving Republican leaders in Congress and a well-organized grassroots campaign allowed Democrats to regain control of the House and the Senate in 2006. The Republican decline continued in 2008, when Democrat Barack Obama was elected to the White House and Democrats retained control of Congress. Although Obama only won 1.5 percent more of the popular vote than George W. Bush had in 2004, Republicans were soundly defeated. Especially disturbing for the party was the defection of nearly 20 percent of Republicans who had voted for Bush. Moreover, Obama won among independents, women, and the young, while white males, white Catholics, and seniors barely supported the GOP presidential candidate, John McCain. No longer were the Republicans a majority party.

Conservatism in Defeat

Conservatism has been a dynamic political movement through most of the twentieth and early twenty-first centuries, continually shaped both by new ideas and ideological tensions. Before World War II, it consisted mainly of a defense of the cultural traditions of Western civilization and of laissez-faire and free markets. Pre–World War II conservatives staunchly defended localism, a strict adherence to the Constitution, and distrust of strong executive power in the face of profound technological and political change.

The cold war altered conservatism profoundly. Most conservatives supported cold war containment and extended the fear of communism into the domestic arena. In order to combat liberalism at home and communism abroad, it was necessary for conservatives to enter politics and not just to plead for their views in the intellectual realm. From the 1950s to the end of the cold war, conservatives constructed a political movement based on firmly opposing state-building tendencies at home while fighting communism abroad. There were inherent contradictions in such a policy, but conservatives focused on policies and programs designed to fulfill these two goals. The end of the cold war deprived conservatives of an enemy and left those critical of cold war conservatism, such as journalist Patrick Buchanan, to revive Old Right isolationism in the post-9/11 world.

Modern liberalism proved to be a formidable opponent; despite Republican victories, the modern welfare and regulatory states were not easily dismantled. Nonetheless, the conservative ascendancy within the Republican Party and in the electorate during the last half of the twentieth century led to significant political and policy changes. Conservatives were able to mobilize large number of voters to their cause. Even as late as 2008, when conservatives appeared to be in a downswing, nearly 35 percent of the electorate identified themselves as "conservative." More important, while conservatives acting through the Republican Party were not able to scale back Social Security, Medicare-Medicaid, education, or environmental protection, they won notable victories in strengthening national defense, reforming welfare policy, restricting reproductive rights, reinvigorating monetary policy, deregulating major industries, and appointing conservative federal judges.

As conservatives sought to regroup after the 2008 defeat, they could take little consolation in the historical reminder that Republican success often followed Democratic mistakes in office. Given the severity of the financial meltdown and the international threats of rogue nations, oil shortages, nuclear proliferation, and military involvement in the Middle East and Afghanistan, even the most partisan-minded Republicans hoped that their return to office would not be built on a failed Obama presidency. While partisan differences would not be ignored, Democrats and Republicans, progressive and conservatives alike, understood that above all else, as Abraham Lincoln said in 1858, "a house divided against itself cannot stand."

See also anticommunism; anti-statism; economy and politics; liberalism; Republican Party.

FURTHER READING. Donald T. Critchlow, *The Conservative Ascendancy: How the GOP Right Made Political History*, 2007; Brian Doherty, *Radicals for Capitalism: A Freewheeling History of the Modern American Libertarian Movement*, 2007; Lee Edwards, *The Conservative Revolution: The Movement that Remade America*, 1999; Bruce Frohnen, Jeremy Beer, and Jeffrey O. Nelson, eds., *American Conservatism: An Encyclopedia*, 2006; F. A. Hayek, *The Road to Serfdom*, 1944; Steven F. Hayward, *The Age of Reagan: The Fall of the Old Liberal Order, 1964–1980*, 2001; George H. Nash, *The Conservative Intellectual Movement in America: Since 1945*, 3rd ed., 2006; Gregory L. Schneider, *The Conservative Century: From Reaction to Revolution*, 2009; Jonathan M. Schoenwald, *A Time for Choosing: The Rise of Modern American Conservatism*, 2001; Henry M. Wriston, *Challenge to Freedom*, 1943.

DONALD T. CRITCHLOW AND GREGORY SCHNEIDER

conservative ascendancy, 1980–2008

In 1984 President Ronald Reagan cruised to reelection in the second largest electoral landslide in American history. The next year, before a cheering crowd of conservatives, Reagan declared, "The tide of history is moving irresistibly in our direction. Why? Because the other side is virtually bankrupt of ideas. It has nothing more to say, nothing to add to the debate. It has spent its intellectual capital." It was a bold proclamation by a leader who had proved beyond debate that conservative ideas could have mass appeal.

But was Reagan right? On the one hand, liberals had apparently lost the war of ideas. By the mid-1980s, conservatives had amassed an impressive stockpile of ideological weapons thanks to a well-financed and well-coordinated network of private foundations, policy journals, and think tanks. On the other hand, Reagan's explanation downplayed a host of other political, historical, economic, personal, and structural factors. And whether the "tide of history" was irresistible or irreversible was by no means a foregone conclusion.

Nevertheless, conservatives became dominant in the two decades immediately following 1984, at least in electoral terms. The Republicans won five of the seven presidential elections after 1980, when they also captured the Senate for the first time since 1952. The Democrats recaptured the Senate in 1986, but, eight years later, the Republicans reclaimed it and, for the first time since 1954, also took command of the House. For most of the next decade, the GOP had effective control of Congress. Moreover, by 2004 the party as a whole had veered sharply to the right, with conservatives in charge and moderates on the verge of extinction.

The conservative ascendance was not, however, preordained. Few could or would have predicted it in the wake of the Watergate scandal. An assassination attempt against Reagan in March 1981 dramatically boosted his popularity and contributed significantly to passage of his tax bill, the signature achievement of his first term. The terrorist attacks in September 2001 transformed the presidency of George W. Bush and restored national security as the preeminent issue in American politics. They also enabled the Republicans to extend their control of Congress in 2002 and made possible Bush's narrow reelection in 2004.

Nor was the conservative ascendancy complete by 2004. By some measures, public opinion had shifted to the right since 1980. President Bill Clinton, for instance, was the first Democrat since Franklin Roosevelt to win consecutive terms. But he also achieved his greatest popularity after he proclaimed "the end of welfare as we know it" and "the era of big government is over." By other measures, the country had remained in place or moved to the left. Even on controversial social issues like homosexuality, the data were mixed, with greater tolerance counterbalanced by strong opposition to gay marriage. On balance, the evidence suggests that while most Americans object to big government in principle, in practice they accept and approve of federal programs like Social Security that benefit the great majority. As a result, the bureaucracy has grown steadily, which in turn has led to a debate among conservatives between "small-government" purists, who are usually not elected officials, and "big-government" politicians like George W. Bush, who supported a major expansion in Medicare benefits.

By 2004 no mass or permanent realignment of partisan preferences had taken place. The conservatives had won many electoral victories since 1980, but the nation remained divided and polarized. In a sense, the situation was little changed from 2000, when Bush and Vice President Al Gore, the Democratic nominee for president, fought to a virtual stalemate, the Senate was split 50-50, and the Republicans retained a slim majority in the House. Nonetheless, the New Right had eclipsed the New Deal political coalition and brought the Democratic era in national politics to a clear end. What made the conservative ascendance possible, and what sustained it?

Immediate Causes

Scholars disagree as to whether the New Deal political coalition of white Southerners, urban workers, small farmers, racial minorities, and liberal intellectuals was inherently fragile or whether the 1960s was the moment of reckoning. But the immediate causes of Reagan's victory in 1980 are less debatable. Most important was the failure of the Carter presidency. At home, the "misery index" (the combined rates of inflation and unemployment) stood at more than 20 percent. Abroad, Soviet troops occupied Afghanistan, and American hostages were held captive in Tehran. The future seemed bleak, and the president appeared to be unable to provide confident or competent leadership. What the White House needed was a new occupant—the main question was whether Reagan was a conservative ideologue or capable candidate.

Reagan's personality proved critical during the campaign. A gifted and affable performer, he was able to cross the "credibility threshold" in the presidential debates and reassure Americans that he was a staunch anti-Communist, not an elderly madman bent on nuclear confrontation with the Soviet Union. On the contrary, Reagan appeared vigorous, warm, principled, and optimistic—he promised that America's best days lay in the future, not the past. He also asserted that the weak economy was the fault of the government, not the people. Above all, Reagan was the smiling and unthreatening face of modern conservatism.

A third cause of conservative ascendancy was the tax revolt of the late 1970s. As inflation mounted, the middle class was trapped between stagnant incomes and rising taxes. In 1978 California voters approved Proposition 13, which slashed property taxes and triggered a nationwide movement toward such relief. The tax issue helped unite a contentious conservative coalition of libertarians, traditionalists, and anti-Communists. It also crystallized opposition to the liberal welfare state and gave Republicans a potent weapon to aim at government programs previously viewed as politically untouchable. In the coming decades, tax cuts would become conservative dogma, the "magic bullet" for growing the economy, shrinking the bureaucracy, and harvesting the votes of disgruntled citizens.

A final cause was the emergence of religious conservatives as a significant bloc of Republican voters. Prior to the 1960s, many evangelical Christians either avoided the political world or divided their votes between the parties. But in 1962, the Supreme Court ruled in *Engel v. Vitale* that the First Amendment banned even nondenominational prayer in the public schools. Then the sexual revolution and the women's movement arrived amid the social upheaval of the decade. In 1973 *Roe v. Wade* made abortion an important issue, and in 1978 the Internal Revenue Service threatened to repeal the federal tax exemption for racially segregated Christian schools. The latter action outraged evangelicals, especially the Reverend Jerry Falwell, who in 1979 founded the Moral Majority, which quickly became a powerful force within the New Right. In 1980 Reagan received 61 percent of the fundamentalist vote; by comparison, Jimmy Carter (a born-again Christian) had received 56 percent in 1976. By 2004 the most reliable Republican voters were those Americans who went to church more than once a week.

Sustaining Factors

At first the conservative momentum continued under Reagan's successor, Vice President George H. W. Bush, who easily won election in 1988. But he lacked the personal charisma and communication skills that had enabled Reagan to attract moderates and bridge divisions on the right. The end of the cold war also removed a unifying issue from the right's repertoire and shifted the political focus from national security (a Republican strength) to economic security (a Democratic strength). The fall of the Soviet Union meant, moreover, that conservatives could no longer paint liberals as soft on communism—a deadly charge in American politics since the 1940s. Finally, Bush made a critical political error in 1990 when he broke his "read my lips" campaign pledge and agreed to a tax hike. According to most economists, the increase was not a significant factor in the recession of 1991–92. But many conservatives today trace the start of what they see as the betrayal or repudiation of the "Reagan Revolution" to that fateful moment.

In 1992 Clinton focused "like a laser beam" on the poor state of the economy and, thanks in large measure to the presence of independent candidate Ross Perot on the ballot, defeated Bush. Then the Democrat rode peace and prosperity to reelection in 1996. Clinton infuriated conservatives because he usurped what they saw as their natural claim to the White House, he seemed to embody the counterculture values of the 1960s, and was a gifted politician who co-opted many of their issues. In many respects, Clinton truly was a "New Democrat," who supported free trade, a balanced budget, and the death penalty. Nevertheless, even he was unable to reverse the conservative ascendance—at best, he could only restrain it after the Republicans took control of Congress in 1994.

In the 1990s, conservatives continued to set the political tone and agenda by demonstrating that they were masters of coordination and discipline. In Washington, they gathered every Wednesday at a breakfast sponsored by Americans for Tax Reform and a lunch sponsored by Coalitions for America to discuss issues, strategies, and policies. At the same time, the Club for Growth targeted moderates (deemed RINOs—Republicans in Name Only) and bankrolled primary challenges against them. And after 1994, members of Congress received committee chairs based on loyalty to the leadership, not seniority, a change spearheaded by House Speaker Newt Gingrich of Georgia. By 2000 conservative control and party discipline were so complete that Bush never had to employ the veto in his first term—a feat not accomplished since the presidency of John Quincy Adams.

The conservative movement was also flush with funds. Much Republican money came in small contributions from direct mailings aimed at true believers, but large sums came from two other sources. The first was corporate America, which in the 1970s found itself beset by foreign competition, rising wages, higher costs, and lower profits. In response, it created lobbying organizations like the Business Roundtable, formed political action committees, and channeled campaign contributions in ever larger amounts to conservative politicians, who in turn made government deregulation, lower taxes, and tort reform legislative priorities in the 1980s. The second source of funds was lobbyists, who represented many of the same corporations. After the GOP rout in 1994, House Majority Whip Tom DeLay of Texas initiated the "K Street Project," whereby lobbyists hoping to do business on Capitol Hill were pressured into making their hiring practices and campaign contributions conform to Republican interests.

At the same time, corporate boards and private foundations invested heavily in institutions like the American Enterprise Institute and the Heritage Foundation, which had immense influence in policy design, both domestic and foreign. These think tanks constituted a veritable shadow government for officials between positions or awaiting an opportunity. They also acted as incubators of ideas and command posts for policy research in the ideological war that conservatives fought against liberals.

The struggle was waged on several fronts. On the ground, conservatives proved expert at mobilizing their base, which became increasingly important to both parties as the number of undecided voters shrank in the highly partisan political climate of the 1990s. In 2004, for example, George W. Bush won largely because the Republicans recruited 1.4 million volunteers, who boosted the president's popular vote by 20 percent (including 4 million Christians who had voted in 1996 but not in 2000). By comparison, in 2004 the Democrats raised their vote totals by 12 percent over 2000, which was impressive but insufficient. On the air, the conservatives also exploited every advantage at their disposal. In 1987 the abolition of the Fairness Doctrine, which had required broadcasters to provide "equal time" to alternative views, opened the door to right-wing talk radio. Enter Rush Limbaugh, a disk jockey from Missouri, who by the

mid-1990s had inspired countless imitators and was reaching 20 million devoted listeners (known as "dittoheads") daily on 660 stations across the nation. And, by 2000, FOX News, with a strong conservative slant, had surpassed CNN to become the most popular news channel on cable television.

Another source of strength for Republicans was the weakness of the Democrats, who lacked a clear vision or coherent set of core principles. The party was deeply divided between "upscale Democrats" (well-educated professionals who were more socially liberal) and "downscale Democrats" (economically marginal workers and minorities who were more socially conservative). Moreover, historical memories had faded—by 2002 less than one in ten voters could personally recall the Great Depression and New Deal. Labor unions, a pillar of the party, had also eroded in size and influence. In 1960, 40 percent of the workforce was unionized; by 2000, the figure was 14 percent and falling. In addition, the once Solid South was now reliably Republican. In the seven presidential elections between 1980 and 2004, Republican candidates lost a combined total of just five southern states to Democratic candidates.

Even the much touted "gender gap" provided little solace to the Democrats. Since 1980, when it first appeared, the party attracted women in growing numbers. By 2004, the Democrats were majority female and the Republicans were majority male. The problem for Democrats was that the exodus of men, especially working-class white Southerners, exceeded the influx of women. That was the real cause of the gender gap, which in 2004 was also a marriage gap (55 percent of married women voted for Bush, while 62 percent of single women voted against him). Nevertheless, if men and women had switched partisan allegiances at the same rate after 1980, Bush would have lost in both 2000 and 2004.

Future Considerations

After 2004 many Democrats were in despair. Bush, whom few experts had predicted would win in 2000, had again defied the odds by surviving an unpopular war, a weak economy, and soaring deficits. The Republicans had also extended their control of Congress and built a well-financed party structure. In the aftermath of the 2004 election, White House political adviser Karl Rove boasted that the United States was in the midst of a "rolling realignment." Eventually, the Republicans would become the dominant party, he predicted, as they had in 1896 and the Democrats had in 1932. It was merely a matter of time, especially if the terrorist threat continued to make national security a priority.

Some Democrats, however, were not disheartened. Both elections were close calls, and in 2004 Bush had a considerable advantage as an incumbent wartime president. Moreover, some long-term demographic and technological developments seemed to favor the Democrats. The Internet had filled their war chest with vast sums, and bloggers had reenergized intellectual debates among the party faithful, even if new groups like MoveOn.org and America Coming Together were less successful at mobilizing voters on election day. The increasing number of well-educated working women and Latino voters also seemed to bode well for the Democrats, as did the steady growth in unmarried and secular voters, who seemed to be more liberal in their outlook.

Nevertheless, the Republicans continued to have structural and ideological advantages. In the Electoral College, the less populated "red states" still had disproportionate influence, raising the bar for Democratic candidates. And in congressional districts, partisan gerrymandering kept most Republican districts intact. In 2004, for example, Bush carried 255 districts—almost 59 percent—compared with his popular vote total of less than 52 percent. In addition, the Republican Party's moral conservatism and entrepreneurial optimism seemed likely to appeal to a growing number of Latino voters, assuming that the immigration issue did not prove divisive in the long term.

But, in 2006, the Democrats surprised themselves and the pundits by retaking the House and Senate, as undecided voters punished the party in power and negated the base strategy of the Republicans by overwhelmingly blaming them for political corruption and the Iraq War. Then, in 2008, the Democrats solidified their control of Congress and recaptured the White House when Senator Barack Obama defeated Senator John McCain in a presidential race dominated by voter discontent with the Bush administration and the most serious financial crisis since the Great Depression. The tide of history that Reagan hailed in 1985 had ebbed. Republican hopes for a major realignment had faded. But it was too soon to tell whether the conservative ascendancy had come to a lasting end.

See also conservatism; Democratic Party, 1968–2008; Republican Party, 1968–2008.

FURTHER READING. Donald Critchlow, *The Conservative Ascendancy: How the GOP Right Made Political History*, 2007; Thomas B. Edsall, *Building Red America: The New Conservative Coalition and the Drive for Permanent Power*, 2006; Jacob S. Hacker and Paul Pierson, *Off Center: The Republican Revolution and the Erosion of American Democracy*, 2005; John Micklethwait and Adrian Wooldridge, *The Right Nation: Conservative Power in America*, 2004; Michael Schaller and George Rising, *The Republican Ascendancy: American Politics, 1968–2001*, 2002; Thomas F. Schaller, *Whistling Past Dixie: How Democrats Can Win without the South*, 2006.

MICHAEL W. FLAMM

conservative interregnum, 1920–32

The years between World War I and the New Deal are popularly known as the Roaring Twenties because of the era's tumultuous social and cultural experimentation and spectacular economic growth. The cultural upheaval—from the Harlem Renaissance to jazz, and from flappers to speakeasies—stands in contrast to the period's conservative politics. The decade witnessed a muting of the Progressive Era voices that had sought to end the abuses of unregulated capitalism through industrial regulation and reform. Presidents Warren Harding, Calvin Coolidge, and Herbert Hoover emphasized a limited role for the regulatory power of the federal government and the importance of efficiency, individualism, as well as support for business. Calvin Coolidge summed up the dominant ethos in the White House with his statement, "The business of America is business."

Despite the support for business fostered in the halls of the White House and a broad segment of Congress, the 1920s did not simply represent a discontinuous period sandwiched between two eras of reform (the Progressive Era and the New Deal). Indeed, the decade opened with major victories for two important reform movements. With the passage of the Nineteenth Amendment in 1920, women's rights advocates had won their long battle for suffrage. The national electorate expanded dramatically with female citizens no longer excluded from the right to vote on the basis of gender. In the wake of woman suffrage, advocates for women's equality struggled to define their movement. Alice Paul and the National Women's Party battled for the passage of an equal rights amendment, while other activists pressed on for protective legislation, winning a victory in 1921 when Congress passed a bill providing funds for prenatal and child health care. A second reform movement, that of temperance, triumphed with the ratification of the Eighteenth Amendment, outlawing the sale, manufacture, and transportation of liquor, to take effect in January 1920. The radical experiment with national Prohibition, the law of the land until 1933, helped to lay the groundwork for the expansion of the federal government that took place during the New Deal. In addition, Hoover's conservative variant of progressivism included an important role for the federal government in providing knowledge, expertise, and information to business to shore up economic growth. Indeed, Franklin D. Roosevelt's first New Deal had much in common with Hoover's effort to utilize the state in cooperation with business to mitigate the severe economic crisis that shook the nation during the Great Depression.

After the upheavals of the "Great War," the tumultuous global ramifications of the Russian Revolution, and the defeat of Woodrow Wilson's postwar internationalism, Warren Harding's calls for a "return to normalcy" resonated with many voters. In November 1920, Harding won a lopsided victory over Democrat James M. Cox of Ohio, and the Republicans solidified the hold on Congress that they had won in 1918. Harding came to the presidency with a long record of public service but an undistinguished record as a senator. The policies of his administration, however, as well as those of the Supreme Court, demonstrated a strong orientation toward the business community. With the federal government's pro-business· orientation, emboldened industrialists undertook a successful counterattack against the gains labor had made during World War I. The great labor strikes that rocked the nation in 1919 had ended in defeat. By 1923, union membership fell to 3.6 million from more than 5 million at the end of the war.

Falling union membership mirrored developments in political participation more broadly. Voter turnout rates were low throughout the decade, averaging around 46 percent. Progressive innovations such as nonpartisan elections undercut party organization and weakened party identification. The nonvoters tended to be the poor, and new voters such as women, African Americans, and naturalized immigrants. Only in 1928 did participation rise to 56 percent as the volatile issues of religion, ethnicity, and Prohibition mobilized the electorate.

With Harding's death on August 2, 1923, Vice President Calvin Coolidge succeeded to the presidency. His reserved New England demeanor marked a sharp break from Harding's outgoing midwestern charm, but their different personalities belied a common approach toward government. As Harding before him, Coolidge emphasized efficiency, limited government, and strong praise for capital. Coolidge summed up this ethos when he remarked, "The man who builds a factory builds a temple. The man who works there worships there." These notions seemed to resonate with large numbers of Americans in a period of economic expansion and growing affluence. While the decade had opened in recession, from 1922 to 1929, national income increased more than 40 percent, from $60.7 billion to $87.2 billion. Automobiles, construction, and new industries like radio fueled an economic boom. The number of passenger cars in the United States jumped from fewer than 7 million in 1919 to about 23 million in 1929. Radio, getting its start in 1920, was a household item for 12 million Americans by 1929. The availability of new products, installment buying, and an increasingly national advertising industry fueled a mass consumption economy just as increased leisure, radios, and movies generated a mass culture.

Economic growth and mass consumption went hand in hand, however, with the increasing maldistribution of wealth and purchasing power. Indeed, about one-third of families earned less than the minimum income estimated for a "decent standard of living." Those Americans working in what were then known as the "sick industries," such as textile and coal, along with the nation's farmers, failed to benefit from the economic gains of the period. Progressive reformers continued to criticize the consolidation of private capital and the inequalities of income. Eugene Debs, sentenced to ten years in prison under the Seditions Act of 1918, ran as Socialist Party candidate for president in 1920 (from federal prison) and won close to a million votes. In 1924, Robert F. Lafollette, a senator from Wisconsin, led the third-party Progressive ticket, mobilizing reformers and labor leaders as well as disgruntled farmers. The Progressive Party called for the nationalization of railroads, the public ownership of utilities, and the right of Congress to overrule Supreme Court decisions. Lafollette won 5 million popular votes but carried only his home state of Wisconsin.

While progressives and radicals chipped away at the sanctified praise of business voiced by three Republican administrations, their criticisms were shadowed by far more powerful reactions against the tide of urbanization, secularization, and modernism. Protestant fundamentalist crusades against the teachings of Darwinism and modernism in the churches culminated in the *State of Tennessee v. John Thomas Scopes* trial (better known as the "Scopes Monkey Trial") in 1925. Riding a tide of backlash against urban concentrations of immigrants, Catholics, and Jews as well as militant Prohibitionist anger with the unending flow of illegal drink, the Ku Klux Klan mushroomed throughout the nation, becoming a significant force in politics in such states as Indiana, Ohio, and Colorado.

During its heyday in the mid-1920s, between 3 to 5 million people joined the ranks of the hooded Klan, making it one of the largest and most influential grassroots social movements in twentieth-century America. Systematically targeting African Americans, Catholics, Jews, and foreigners as threats to Americanism, the Klan drew from a broad group of white Protestant men and women throughout the Midwest, West, and South through its promises to stave off a drift away from the values of small-town Protestant America. The Klan sold itself as an organization devoted to "law and order" by promising to rid America of liquor. Prohibition intersected closely with the Klan's larger nativist, anti-Catholic agenda since many ethnic Catholic immigrants blatantly flouted the law. By organizing drives to "clean up" communities and put bootleggers out of business, the Klan became a popular means of acting on militant temperance sentiments.

Prohibition was a radical experiment and, not surprisingly, it sharpened key cultural divides of the era. The Eighteenth Amendment became effective on January 17, 1920, after ratification of all but two states (Connecticut and Rhode Island). Outlawing the sale, manufacture, and transport of alcohol, it was, one contemporary observed, "one of the most extensive and sweeping efforts to change the social habits of an entire nation in recorded history." It was an astonishing social innovation that brought with it the greatest expansion of federal authority since Reconstruction. While the Republican and Democratic parties had avoided taking official positions on the subject, during the 1920s, national Prohibition became a significant bone of contention, particularly for the Democratic Party, solidifying divisions between the Democratic Party's rural, "dry," Protestant wing and its urban, Catholic "wet" wing. The party's two wings fought over nativism, the Klan, and Prohibition at its 1924 Convention. And by 1928, the party's urban wet wing demonstrated its newfound strength when Alfred E. Smith became the Democratic presidential nominee.

For many of the nation's immigrants, Prohibition was an affront to personal liberty, particularly since their communities were the special targets of law enforcement efforts to dry up the flow of bootleg liquor. As a result, it ignited a growing politicization of ethnic immigrant workers. While Prohibition made immigrant, urban, and ethnic workers aware of the dangers of state power, it had the far greater effect of leading many of these workers into the national Democratic Party. Catholic immigrant and New York governor Al Smith carried the country's 12 largest cities, all rich in immigrants, and all of which had voted Republican in 1924. The Smith campaign forged an alignment of urban ethnic workers with the Democratic Party that was solidified during the New Deal. In their turn, the nation's rural Protestant and dry Democrats dreaded the specter of a Catholic and wet urbanite in the White House. Their disdain for Smith led many to abandon their allegiance to the Democratic Party to vote for Hoover. As a result, Hoover won in a landslide, receiving 58 percent of the popular vote and 447 electoral votes to Smith's 87. Hoover cut heavily into the normally Democratic South, taking the upper tier of the old confederacy, as well as Florida.

The third straight Republican to dominate the era's national politics, Hoover had won the support of many progressive reformers, including settlement house leader and international peace advocate Jane Addams. Hoover championed a conservative variant of progressivism that flourished in the 1920s. While he refused to countenance public authority to regulate business, he hoped to manage social change through informed, albeit limited, state action. He championed the tools of social scientific expertise, knowledge, and information in order to sustain a sound economy. His desire to organize national policies on a sound basis of knowledge resulted in a major study called *Recent Social Trends*, a 1,500-page survey that provided rich data about all aspects of American life. As this social scientific endeavor suggests, Hoover drew from a broad font of progressive ideas but remained firm in his commitment to what he called "American Individualism."

Hoover's strong belief in limited government regulation went hand in hand with his embrace of federal authority to shore up Prohibition enforcement. To make clear that the federal government would not tolerate the widespread violations apparent almost everywhere, Hoover signed the Jones Act in 1929, a measure strongly backed by the Anti-Saloon League. The act raised a first offense against the 1929 Volstead Act to the status of a felony and raised maximum

penalties for first offenses from six months in jail and a $1,000 fine to five years and a $10,000 fine.

An outpouring of protest undermined support for the Eighteenth Amendment. William Randolph Hearst, once a strong backer of national Prohibition, now declared that the Jones Law was "the most menacing piece of repressive legislation that has stained the statute books of this republic since the Alien and Sedition laws." As the reaction to the Jones Act suggests, the "noble experiment" sounded a cautionary note about using the power of the state to regulate individual behavior.

But Prohibition's repeal did not signify a broad rejection of federal government regulation. Rather, the great debate over the merits of Prohibition throughout the decade helped lay the ground for a greater legitimacy of state authority: The debate did not challenge the government's right to regulate as much as it raised important questions over what its boundaries should be. Prohibition helped draw a thicker line between the legitimate arena of public government regulation and private behavior.

In the face of the increasingly dire economic circumstances at the end of the decade, the nation's preoccupation with moral regulation appeared increasingly frivolous. The stock market, symbol of national prosperity, crashed on October 29, 1929. By mid-November, stock prices had plunged 40 percent. The crash intensified a downward spiral of the economy brought about by multiple causes: structural weaknesses in the economy, unequal distribution of income, and the imbalanced international economic system that had emerged from World War I.

Hoover put his conservative progressivism to the test during the downturn, and it proved inadequate for the scope of the crisis. He called on business to cooperate by ending cutthroat competition and the downward spiral of prices and wages. He proposed plans for public works to infuse money into the economy. And in 1932, he established the Reconstruction Finance Corporation to provide emergency loans to ailing banks, building and loan societies, and railroads. Hoover's embrace of government action was tethered, however, to his strong belief in voluntarism and, as a result, provided too little too late. His efforts, moreover, were directed for the most part toward business. While he did support federal spending to shore up state and local relief efforts, the sums were not enough. In 1932 a bitter and recalcitrant Hoover was trounced by the gregarious Franklin D. Roosevelt, whose declaration that the American people had "nothing to fear but fear itself" ushered in a new relationship of citizen to state and a new period of economic reform.

One of Roosevelt's first acts in office was to sign the Beer and Wine Revenue Act, anticipating the repeal of national Prohibition and effectively ending the radical experiment. The experience of national Prohibition had highlighted the real danger posed to personal liberty by the linkage of "morality" and politics. By the 1930s, the federal government's effort to dry up the nation and alter personal habits appeared increasingly absurd. Facing a grave economic crisis, the nation's chastised liberals now concerned themselves with using the state to regulate capitalism and provide a minimal security net for Americans against the vagaries of the marketplace. During the New Deal, state regulation focused on economic life, replacing an earlier era of regulation of public "moral" behavior that had marked the Roaring Twenties.

See also Americanism; conservatism; consumers and politics; New Deal Era, 1932–52; Prohibition and temperance.

FURTHER READING. David Burner, *The Politics of Provincialism: The Democratic Party in Transition, 1918–1932,* 1986; Norman H. Clark, *Deliver Us from Evil: An Interpretation of American Prohibition,* 1976; Lizabeth Cohen, *Making a New Deal: Industrial Workers in Chicago, 1919–1939,* 2nd ed., 2008; Alan Dawley, *Changing the World: American Progressives in War and Revolution,* 2003; Lynn Dumenil, *Modern Temper: American Culture and Society in the 1920s,* 1995; Ellis Hawley, *The Great War and the Search for a Modern Order,* 1979; David Kennedy, *Freedom from Fear: The American People in Depression and War, 1929–1945,* 1999; David Kyvig, *Repealing National Prohibition,* 2000.

LISA MCGIRR

Constitution, federal

The oldest of the world's effective written constitutions, the U.S. Constitution was designed in a convention in the summer of 1787, made public on September 17, and formally adopted with the ratification of New Hampshire on June 21 of the following year. It serves as the fundamental law determining the scope and limits of the federal government. But its origin lies in a perceived need to reform the "firm league of friendship" that held together the 13 original colonies in one nation, with "a more perfect Union."

Union and Liberty

The Articles of Confederation, drafted during the opening stages of the war for independence, had established the first American Union. Less than a decade later, they were widely regarded as a failure. In the 1780s, the United States faced a number of critical international and interstate issues arising from the Revolution and the ensuing separation of the colonies from the British Empire. State governments refused to adhere to the peace treaty with Britain; Britain refused to give up military posts on U.S. territory; public creditors went unpaid; Indians attacked settlers and squatters occupied public lands; Spain closed the Mississippi to American commerce; and Britain banned American ships from trading with the West Indies and the British Isles.

Congress—the central government established by the Articles of Confederation—was unable to address these issues. It had neither money nor soldiers, only minimal administrative departments, and no court system. The Constitution aimed to change this situation. It was therefore a practical solution to immediate problems. But this should not detract from the achievement of the founders, for the difficulties were pressing and the stakes were high. In the minds of the reformers, the American Union had become so weak that the future of the nation as an independent confederation of republics was in doubt. Because republican rule on the scale attempted in the United States was a novel political experiment, the outcome of the American crisis had global significance. The success or failure of the reform would decide whether republican government—that is, popular self-rule for the common good—was viable. Ultimately, therefore, the framing and ratification of the Constitution should be understood as an attempt to secure republican government by means of a stronger union.

The reform of the Union was based on two fundamental premises: first, that the civic liberties and rights that Britain had threatened and the American Revolution defended could only be safeguarded under a republican form of government; second, that the American states could only be guaranteed a republican form of government by union. Union and liberty were therefore intimately linked in the political imagination of the founding generation as the preservation of liberty was the raison d'être of the Union.

In the present world of stable democracies and superpower republics, the notion that republics are inherently weak and unstable, and therefore difficult to maintain, does not come naturally. Early modern political theory, however, taught that republics were prone to internal dissension and foreign conquest. Republican citizens were freer than the subjects of monarchs, but this freedom made them hard to control and made it difficult for the government to command the social resources and popular obedience necessary to act forcefully against foreign enemies and domestic rebellion. Monarchies were therefore held to be better equipped than republics for securing the survival of the state. But the strength of monarchical rule rested on centralization of power at the cost of popular liberty. Political theory also taught that republican rule could be maintained only in states with a limited territory and a small and homogeneous population. Thus, the republic's weakness came both from a necessary small size and the form of government.

Confederation provided a way out of this predicament. In the words of eighteenth-century French writer Baron Montesquieu, by joining together, republics could mobilize and project "the external force of a monarchy" without losing "all the internal advantages of republican government." Confederation also provided protection against internal dissension, the other great threat to the republic. "If sedition appears in one of the members of the confederation," noted Montesquieu, "the others can pacify it. If some abuses are introduced somewhere, they are corrected by the healthy part." In important respects, the U.S. Constitution is the practical application of Montesquieu's lesson.

The American states assumed independence and entered into union in a single political process. Work on an act of union was already under way when the states declared independence, but the Articles of Confederation were not finished until 1777 and took effect only with ratification by the thirteenth straggling member, Maryland, in 1781. Like the Constitution, the articles were both an agreement of union between the states and a charter for the central government created to realize the purposes of union. They aimed to provide the states with "common defense, the security of their Liberties, and their mutual and general welfare" (Article III). To this end, the states delegated certain enumerated powers to the central government. These powers were those that the English political philosopher John Locke termed "federative" and which he defined as "the Power of War and Peace, Leagues and Alliances, and all the Transactions, with all Persons and Communities without the Commonwealth." These powers had been invested in the imperial government under the colonial system, and, under the articles, the central government was to assume them.

Although in theory, the state governments would not exercise the powers they had vested in the central government, in practice, they retained complete control over the application of these powers. This was a reflection of the fear of central power that to a great extent had inspired the American Revolution. Thus, Congress possessed neither the right to collect taxes nor to raise an army, and it had neither a judiciary nor an executive. Therefore, the central government could declare and conduct war but not create or supply an army; it could borrow money but not provide for its repayment; it could enter into treaties with foreign powers but not prevent violations of international agreements. On paper, its powers were formidable, but in reality, Congress depended completely on the cooperation of the states.

Historians have emphasized the many conflicts during the reform process, first in the Constitutional Convention and later during the ratification struggle. Nevertheless, there was, in fact, a widely shared consensus on the essential features of the reform. Most Americans agreed on the necessity and ends of union; on the propriety of investing federative powers in the central government; and on the need to strengthen Congress. There was relatively little debate on the purposes of the union. Commentators agreed that the central government was intended to manage interstate and international affairs. Congress should provide for the defense against foreign nations; prevent violations of international law and treatises; regulate interstate and international commerce; appoint

and receive ambassadors; preserve peace among the states by preventing encroachments on states' rights; and ensure domestic peace and republican liberty by providing for defense against sedition in the states. The last of these duties has occasionally been interpreted as an undue involvement in the internal affairs of the states in order to quell popular movements. In fact, it originated in the need to maintain stability and republican government in the composite parts in order to guarantee the strength of the Union as a whole. In addition to these duties, some reformers had a more expansive agenda and wanted the central government to take an active role in governing the states. Chief among them was James Madison, who wanted Congress to guarantee "good internal legislation & administration to the particular States." But this was a minority view that had little influence on the final Constitution.

If there was consensus on the Union's objectives, there was also agreement that the Articles of Confederation had not met them. Three issues in particular needed to be addressed: Congress had to have the right to regulate trade; it needed a stable and sufficient income; and it had to possess some means by which it could ensure that the states complied with Congress's requisitions and resolutions.

Economic recovery after the war for independence was hampered by discrimination against American trade. The most serious restrictions were the closing of the Mississippi River and the exclusion of American ships from the British West Indies and British Isles. In order to retaliate against these measures, Congress needed the right to regulate commerce, including the right to tax imports and exports.

The Articles of Confederation had not entrusted Congress with power over taxation. Instead, the central government was expected to requisition money from the states, which would handle the administration of taxation. The system never worked, making it difficult to pursue the Revolutionary War efficiently and provide for the postwar debt. If states neglected or ignored Congress's legitimate demands, it had no way to enforce compliance. It was therefore necessary to reform the articles so as to provide the central government with power to enforce congressional resolutions.

The framing and adoption of the Constitution had been preceded by several reform initiatives originating in Congress, which sought to correct deficiencies by amending the Articles of Confederation without modifying the organization of the Union. One after another these attempts failed, however, and the reform initiative passed from Congress to the states. In 1785 Virginia negotiated an agreement with Maryland over the navigation of the Chesapeake Bay, and in the following year, Virginia invited all the states to a convention to meet in Annapolis, Maryland, to consider the Union's commerce. The convention adjourned almost immediately because of insufficient attendance (only five state delegations were present).

But the convention also issued a report that spoke of "important defects in the system of the Foederal Government" a political situation that was serious enough "to render the situation of the United States delicate and critical." The report recommended calling a new convention with a broadened mandate to "take into Consideration the situation of the United States, to devise such further Provisions as shall appear to them necessary to render the constitution of the Foederal Government adequate to the exigencies of the Union." Congress and the states agreed to the proposal and a convention was called to meet in Philadelphia on May 14, 1787, "for the sole and express purpose of revising the Articles of Confederation."

The Constitutional Convention

In all, 55 delegates from 12 states attended the Constitutional Convention (only Rhode Island did not send delegates). They belonged to the political leadership of their respective states; many had served in Congress or held a commission in the Continental Army. A majority of delegates were lawyers (34), and almost half were college educated (26). If they were not the assembly of demigods they have sometimes been made out to be, they were nonetheless a group highly qualified to address the ills of the American union.

The convention did not reach a quorum until May 25, 1787, and the delay allowed the Virginia delegation to prepare a set of opening resolutions that set the agenda for the convention. The acceptance of these resolutions on May 30 was the most important decision of the convention, because it superseded its mandate to revise the Articles of Confederation in favor of establishing "a national government . . . consisting of a supreme legislative, judiciary and executive." The novelty of the Virginia Plan, as the resolutions are known, lay not in an expansion of the powers delegated to the central government but in a reorganization of the structure of the union that would make it possible to use those powers effectively. According to the plan, the projected government would inherit all "the Legislative Rights vested in Congress by the Confederation." In addition, it would have the right "to legislate in all cases to which the separate States are incompetent, or in which the harmony of the United States may be interrupted by the exercise of individual Legislation"—a broad grant that included both the power to tax and to regulate trade. The plan did not question the aims of the Union, however, stating that like the Articles of Confederation it was created for the "common defence, security of liberty and general welfare" of the member states.

The Virginia Plan was largely the brainchild of James Madison, who came to Philadelphia best prepared of all the delegates. Madison was disappointed with important aspects of the finished Constitution, and his reputation as "Father of the Constitution" rests on his success in determining the basic thrust of the convention's work by means of the Virginia Plan.

Madison had thoroughly analyzed the shortcomings of the Union under the Articles of Confederation and had identified the crucial defect to be the reliance on voluntary compliance of state governments to Congress's resolutions and the lack of "sanction to the laws, and of coercion in the Government of the Confederacy." Rather than providing Congress with an instrument of coercion, however, Madison suggested a reorganization of the central government. It would no longer be a confederated government that depended on state governments for both its upkeep and the implementation of its decisions, but a national government legislating for individuals and equipped with an executive and a judiciary to enforce its laws. It was a simple and ingenious solution to a critical problem: how to enable the central government to exercise its powers efficiently.

The basic idea of the Virginia Plan was to create two parallel governments that were each assigned a separate sphere of government business. As was the case under the Articles of Confederation, the business that would fall on the lot of the central government was foreign politics and interstate relations, whereas the state governments would manage their own internal affairs. The two governments would both derive their legitimacy from popular sovereignty and be elected by the people. Each government would be self-sufficient in the sense that it could provide for its own upkeep, legislate on individuals, and have its own governmental institutions for implementing its legislation.

If the line of demarcation that separated the central government from the state governments seemed clear enough in theory, there was a risk that each would encroach on the other. Madison and his supporters in the convention were convinced that the only real risk was state encroachment on the central government, and the Virginia Plan thus provided for its extensive protection. Other delegates were more concerned with the danger of central government encroachment on state interests and rights. In the course of the Constitutional Convention, such critiques of the plan led to important modifications intended to safeguard state interests.

Opposition to the Virginia Plan first came from the delegations of New York, New Jersey, Delaware, and Maryland, which, at critical points, were joined by Connecticut. During the convention and afterward, these delegations were called "small-state members." Gradually, concern for the protection of state interests came to be a common concern for almost all the delegates.

At times, objections to the Virginia Plan were so strong that the convention came close to dissolution, and only compromises and concessions saved it. Opposition first arose over the plan's provision that the "National Legislature" be elected by the people rather than the states and that "the rights of suffrage" in the legislature "ought to be proportioned to the Quotas of contribution [i.e., taxes], or to the number of free inhabitants." The "small-state" men were not ready to accept this change in the principle of representation but struggled to retain the rule of one state, one vote, as was the case under the Articles of Confederation. Concern for state interests reappeared in demands for protection of specific state rights and disagreement over the mode of electing the president. Conflicts over the status of the states dominated the convention's business and have tended to overshadow the consensus that existed on the fundamentals of the plan. Thus, the need for stronger central government was not challenged, nor were the concepts of separate spheres of government business and of two self-sufficient governments acting on the same citizens.

The small-state men first offered an alternative plan to that of the Virginia delegation. Presented by William Paterson of New Jersey (on June 14, 1787), the New Jersey Plan agreed to many of the provisions of the Virginia Plan, but left the principle of representation in Congress untouched. Had the plan been accepted, Congress would have continued to be an assembly appointed by and representing states in which each state had one vote. When the convention rejected the New Jersey Plan on June 19, the small-state members fell back on their second line of defense: demand for state appointment to, and state equality in, one of the two branches of the legislature. They secured this goal in the so-called Connecticut Compromise on July 16, whereby the states were to appoint the members of the Senate and have an equal number of representatives in this branch. Senators were to vote as individuals and not as state delegations, however. After this victory, the small-state opposition dissolved.

It was replaced by concern for specific state interests, chiefly emanating from southern delegations. State equality in the Senate meant that the southern states would now be outnumbered eight to five, which made encroachment on southern interests a distinct possibility. Whereas the small-state men had spoken in general and abstract terms of state rights, state interests now took concrete form. As Pierce Butler of South Carolina commented, "The security the Southn. States want is that their negroes may not be taken from them which some gentlemen within or without doors, have a very good mind to do." Eventually, several demands of the southern states made it into the finished Constitution, among them the Three-Fifths Compromise (which counted three-fifths of the slave population toward representation in the House of Representatives); the prohibition on interference with the slave trade before 1808; the Fugitive Slave Clause (which required that escaped slaves be apprehended also in free states and returned to slavery); and the ban on federal export duties. Concern for state interests also influenced the intricate rules for the election of the president, which were intended to balance the influence of small and large states, both in the North and the South.

Opposition to the Virginia Plan reveals much about conceptions of the Union at the time of its founding. Proposals to create new jurisdictions by means of a subdivision of the states were not seriously considered. Despite their recent and contingent history, the existing states had become political entities whose residents ascribed to them distinct interests arising chiefly from economic and social characteristics. The delegates to the convention further believed that the interests of different states were sometimes conflicting, something that had been repeatedly demonstrated in the 1780s when congressional delegations fought over western lands and commercial treaties. The founders grouped the states into sections of states sharing basic interests, the most important of which were the slave states in the South and the nonslave states in the North. Concern for protection of state interests grew not so much from a fear that the central government would pursue its own agenda to the detriment of the states collectively as from fear that the central government would come under the control of one section that would use it as an instrument to promote its own interests at the expense of another.

State interests were a reality in the minds of the American people and could hardly have been transcended, even if the delegates had wished to do so. Opposition to the Virginia Plan provided a necessary correction to the purely national government first envisioned by Madison. States were now protected from central government encroachment on their interests by state representation in the Senate and by guarantees for specific state interests. The central government was protected from state government encroachment primarily by being made self-sufficient and therefore able to act independently of the states, but also by making the Constitution and federal laws and treatises the supreme law of the land. All state officers and state courts were now bound to obey and uphold the Constitution and federal legislation.

It is often said that the Constitution was the result of a compromise that created a government, in Oliver Ellsworth's words, "partly national, partly federal." In comparison to the Virginia Plan, this seems accurate enough. But compared to the Articles of Confederation, the Constitution created a government much more national than federal, able to act in almost complete independence of the state governments. When Madison reflected on the Constitution in *The Federalist* he remarked, "If the new Constitution be examined with accuracy and candor, it will be found that the change which it proposes, consists much less in the addition of *New Powers* to the Union, than in the invigoration of its *Original Powers*." This is the best way to understand the achievements of the convention. By a radical reorganization of the Union that provided for a separate and self-sufficient central government acting on individuals rather than states, the Constitutional Convention had correctly diagnosed the Union's fundamental malady and provided for its cure.

The Struggle over Ratification

The finished Constitution was signed on September 17, 1787, and in a dramatic gesture, three of the delegates—Elbridge Gerry, George Mason, and Edmund Randolph—refused to sign the document. Gerry and Mason feared that the convention had gone too far in creating a strong central government and had failed to safeguard basic civic rights and liberties. Their objections foreshadowed a prominent critique that would soon be directed against ratification of the Constitution.

Framing the Constitution was only the first step toward re-forming the Union. An important part of the reorganization was the establishment of the federal government by an act of popular sovereignty, whereby it would be placed on par with the state governments. It had therefore to be accepted by the people and not the states. To this end, the Constitutional Convention had proposed that the states call ratifying conventions, whose delegates would be chosen by the electorate in each state. Despite some complaint in Congress and some of the states that the convention had exceeded its mandate, ratifying conventions were eventually called in all states except Rhode Island.

The ills arising from the defunct Union had been widely experienced, and the new Constitution stirred enormous interest. Within a few weeks, 61 of the nation's 80 newspapers had printed the Constitution in full; it also was printed in pamphlets and broadsides. The public debate that followed is impressive in scope, even by modern standards. The Federalists, who supported the Constitution, controlled most of the newspapers and dominated the debate. Yet the opposition, branded Anti-Federalists by their opponents, was nevertheless distinctly heard in both print debate and ratifying conventions.

Although states' rights comprised an important theme in Anti-Federalist rhetoric, the opposition was even more concerned with the dangers to republican liberty that would flow from an overly strong federal government. Apart from the last-minute objections by Gerry and Mason, such fear had not been a marked feature of the deliberations in the Constitutional Convention. The majority of Anti-Federalists accepted that the central government had to be strengthened, but also believed that the Constitution had gone too far in creating a government with unlimited power to raise armies and taxes, regulate the militia, borrow money, and to pass any law "deemed necessary and proper." By establishing a strong president, a small House of Representatives, and a Senate with a six-year mandate, the convention had set up a government that would be unresponsive to the wishes of the common people and beyond the effective control of the citizens. It was bound to fall under the control of the rich and "wellborn," who would use the new government to oppress the people and to increase their own riches and prestige. Although the federal government would be able to act with energy against foreign nations, this ability would come

at the price of a centralization of power that would eventually put an end to liberty.

Federalists never accepted that analysis of the Constitution. They maintained that representation would work and government would be exercised for the benefit of the people. They also argued that reorganization of the Union was necessary for the preservation of liberty. The main strategy of Federalist rhetoric was to contrast the blessings of union with the horrors of disunion. The choice before the American people was presented as a choice not between different ways to reform the Union but between adopting the Constitution or inviting certain disunion. According to the Federalists, disunion would result in the creation of mutually antagonistic regional confederacies. These confederacies would build up their military strength and enter into alliances with Europe's great powers. War was certain to follow, and in its train, political centralization and the decline of liberty. Wars gave rise to standing armies, heavy taxes and large public debts, a "trinity of evil" that Madison once described as the bane of republics and the maker of monarchies. Adoption of the Constitution, in contrast, promised to secure the future of the Union and thereby to banish war from the North American continent.

Federalists also urged critics of the Constitution to accept that the American republic existed in a world of predatory monarchies. If the self-rule of the American people was to be maintained, their government had to be able to defend the independence and interests of the United States. Ultimately, this defense rested on the ability to project military power, which required the federal government to have unlimited powers of mobilization. If left to themselves, the states could only mobilize sufficient resources to defend their interests by exerting a heavy pressure on their citizens. By joining forces, however, states could establish enough strength to warn off hostile powers with a minimum imposition on the people. Thus, the Constitution promised the benefits of government with little cost.

Despite control over the press and support from the majority of the social and political elite, ratification of the Constitution was not a foregone conclusion. From the Federalist perspective, the ratification process began well: Delaware, Pennsylvania, New Jersey, Georgia, and Connecticut ratified the Constitution between December 7, 1787, and January 9, 1788, and only Pennsylvania's ratifying convention witnessed any real opposition. Although outnumbered, Pennsylvania Anti-Federalists were influential in shaping critical responses to the Constitution in other states. With the meeting of the Massachusetts convention in January, easy Federalist victories came to an end. Massachusetts finally ratified with a narrow margin of 187 to 168. Even this slight majority could be secured only after the Federalists had accepted that the Constitution be adopted with amendments. This practice was followed in all of the remaining states save Maryland. The next convention to meet was that of New Hampshire, where the Federalists avoided defeat only

Table 1

Delegates Appointed to the Constitutional Convention (with Signers in Italics)

State/ Name	Comment	State/ Name	Comment
New Hampshire		**Maryland**	
John Langdon		*James McHenry*	
Nicholas Gilman		*Daniel of St. Thomas Jenifer*	
John Pickering	Did not attend	*Daniel Carroll*	
Benjamin West	Did not attend	Luther Martin	Left before adjournment
Massachusetts		John Francis Mercer	Left before adjournment
Nathaniel Gorham		Robert Hanson Harrison	Declined appointment
Rufus King		Charles Carroll of Carrollton*	Declined appointment
Elbridge Gerry*	Nonsigner	Thomas Sim Lee	Declined appointment
Caleb Strong	Left before adjournment	Thomas Stone*	Declined appointment
Francis Dana	Did not attend	Gabriel Duvall	Declined appointment
Connecticut		**Virginia**	
William Samuel Johnson		*George Washington*	
*Roger Sherman**		*John Blair*	
Oliver Ellsworth	Left before adjournment	*James Madison*	
Erastus Wolcott	Declined appointment	Edmund Randolph	Nonsigner
New York		George Mason	Nonsigner
Alexander Hamilton		George Wythe*	Left before adjournment
John Lansing Jr.	Left before adjournment	James McClurg	Left before adjournment
Robert Yates	Left before adjournment	Patrick Henry	Declined appointment
New Jersey		Thomas Nelson*	Declined appointment
William Livingston		Richard Henry Lee*	Declined appointment
David Brearley		**North Carolina**	
William Paterson		*William Blount*	
Jonathan Dayton		*Richard Dobbs Spaight*	
William C. Houston	Left before adjournment	*Hugh Williamson*	
Abraham Clark*	Declined appointment	Alexander Martin	Left before adjournment
John Nielson	Declined appointment	William R. Davie	Left before adjournment
Pennsylvania		Richard Caswell	Declined appointment
*Benjamin Franklin**		Willie Jones	Declined appointment
Thomas Mifflin		**South Carolina**	
*Robert Morris**		*John Rutledge*	
*George Clymer**		*Charles Pinckney*	
Thomas FitzSimons		*Charles Cotesworth Pinckney*	
Jared Ingersoll		*Pierce Butler*	
*James Wilson**		Henry Laurens	Declined appointment
Gouverneur Morris		**Georgia**	
Delaware		*William Few*	
*George Read**		*Abraham Baldwin*	
Gunning Bedford Jr.		William Pierce	Left before adjournment
John Dickinson		William Houston	Left before adjournment
Richard Bassett		George Walton*	Did not attend
Jacob Broom		Nathanael Pendleton	Did not attend

*Signer of the Declaration of Independence

Sources: Farrand 3, 557–59, 596–90; Jensen et al., 1, 76, 230.

by securing a four-month adjournment before voting on the Constitution. Momentum seemed lost and ratification uncertain. However, Maryland and South Carolina ratified in April and May 1788 with solid majorities in favor of the Constitution. Eight out of the nine states required for the Constitution to take effect had now accepted the new compact of union. On June 21, New Hampshire became the ninth state to adopt the Constitution.

Without acceptance by Virginia and New York, the Union nevertheless had slight chance of success. In Virginia Anti-Federalism was strong, and in New York, it was overwhelming. Eventually, both states ratified the Constitution by narrow margins, ten votes in Virginia and only three in New York. Their acceptance can be explained by the late hour of their conventions. When the Virginia and New York conventions met, eight states had already ratified the

Constitution and the two states' conventions were still in session when the news came of New Hampshire's vote. Rejecting the Constitution in this situation would have meant separation from the other states in the Union. With Virginia and New York in favor, it mattered little that North Carolina and Rhode Island at first rejected the Constitution and adopted it only in 1789 and 1790, respectively. Three years after the Philadelphia Convention adjourned, all of the states had accepted the new Constitution.

A Federal Republic

The new federal government convened in the spring of 1789. As had been universally anticipated, George Washington was elected the first president, and both the House of Representatives and the Senate had Federalist majorities. The first Congress continued the work begun in the Constitutional Convention by transforming the clauses of the Constitution into government institutions and policies that would address the Union's problems. Only when these were in place would the Constitution truly be "adequate to the exigencies of the union" and the promise of the framers and the Federalists be fulfilled. For this reason, the first Congress may also have been the most important, and, overall, it was remarkably successful. It created three administrative departments to deal with foreign affairs, finances, and defense. It set up a postal service, an Indian Department, and a Land Office responsible for selling federal lands. The Judiciary Act of 1789 organized the federal judiciary and further specified its jurisdiction. Within six years under the new federal government, the United States had achieved a number of political successes. The Indian nations in the Ohio territory had been defeated and neutralized and the government earned revenue from public land sales. The fiscal apparatus was remodeled to secure a steady income from customs duties. Public finances were reformed and public credit restored. In 1795, major commercial treaties were entered into with Britain and Spain.

In the short run, the clearest evidence of the Founding Fathers' success in reforming the Union is that their rebuilt ship of state managed to sail unharmed, if not altogether untroubled, through the storm of the French Revolution and the ensuing quarter century of worldwide war. This period brought down kings and empires on both sides of the Atlantic, and it placed great stress on the Union, not the least of which came during the War of 1812. But the Union endured. The founders' work did not eliminate the tension that resulted from conflicting sectional interests; to the contrary, the Constitution facilitated the articulation of sectional interests through the representation of the states in the Senate and the guarantee to protect state interests such as the preservation of slavery. Eventually, internal tension came close to dissolving the Union during the Civil War. Yet despite such conflicts, the Constitution provided the institutional basis on which the nation would grow

Table 2
Ratification of the Constitution by the States

State	Date	Vote	Amendments
Delaware	7 Dec. 1787	30–0	No
Pennsylvania	12 Dec. 1787	46–23	No
New Jersey	18 Dec. 1787	38–0	No
Georgia	31 Dec. 1787	26–0	No
Connecticut	9 Jan. 1788	128–40	No
Massachusetts	6 Feb. 1788	187–168	Yes
Maryland	26 Apr. 1788	63–11	No
South Carolina	23 May 1788	149–73	Yes
New Hampshire	21 June 1788	57–47	Yes
Virginia	25 June 1788	89–79	Yes
New York	26 July 1788	30–27	Yes
North Carolina	2 Aug. 1788	84–184	Yes
	21 Nov. 1789	194–77	Yes
Rhode Island	29 May 1790	34–32	Yes

in territory, population, and riches. In the long run, therefore, the framers of the Constitution demonstrated that republics were not forever destined to weakness and instability but could become powerful and achieve world domination.

See also Articles of Confederation; Bill of Rights; federalism.

FURTHER READING. Lance Banning, *The Sacred Fire of Liberty: James Madison and the Founding of the Federal Republic*, 1995; Jacob E. Cooke, ed., *The Federalist*, 1961; Max M. Edling, *A Revolution in Favor of Government: The U.S. Constitution and the Making of the American State*, 2003; Max Farrand, ed., *The Records of the Federal Convention of 1787*, 4 vols., 1937; Alan Gibson, *Understanding the Founding: The Crucial Questions*, 2007; David C. Hendrickson, *Peace Pact: The Lost World of the American Founding*, 2007; Willam T. Hutchinson and William E. Rachal, eds., *The Papers of James Madison*, 17 vols., 1962–91; James J. Hutson, ed., *Supplement to Max Farrand's Records of the Federal Convention of 1787*, 1987; Merrill Jensen, John P. Kaminski, and Gaspare J. Saladino, eds., *The Documentary History of the Ratification of the Constitution*, 20 vols., 1976–; Leonard W. Levy and Dennis J. Mahoney, eds., *The Framing and Ratification of the Constitution*, 1987; Peter S. Onuf, *The Origins of the Federal Republic: Jurisdictional Controversies in the United States*, 1983; Peter Onuf and Nicholas Onuf, *Federal Union, Modern World: The Law of Nations in an Age of Revolutions, 1776–1814*, 1993; Jack N. Rakove, *Original Meanings: Politics and Ideas in the Making of the Constitution*, 1997; Gordon S. Wood, *The Creation of the American Republic, 1776–1787*, 1969.

MAX M. EDLING

consumers and politics

The history of consumers and American politics dates back to the founding of the country and has three distinct strands. First, since the American Revolution, Americans have used the boycott of consumer goods as a political tool. Second, beginning in the late nineteenth century, Americans have made political demands as consumers for a higher standard of living. Finally, in the twentieth century, especially in the postwar period, an organized movement has pushed for greater regulation of the quality and safety of consumer products.

From the Revolution to the Gilded Age

The American Revolution traced its origins, in part, to a consumer boycott, the famous Boston Tea Party on December 16, 1773, when rebelling colonialists dumped British tea in the harbor to protest the crown's imperial policies. This was not an isolated event. Before the American Declaration of Independence in 1776, colonists boycotted British goods to demonstrate their displeasure with England's tax policies. After the Seven Years' War, the British government sought to raise money to pay war debts by taxing its colonial subjects. At the time, the North American mainland purchased 25 percent of English exports. In that context, the colonialists' nonimportation strategy was a powerful political tool, one intended to put economic pressure on the British government to repeal the Stamp Act of 1765, the Townshend duties, and the Tea Act as unconstitutional violations of the principle of no taxation without representation. Colonial merchants organized boycotts, which led to a decline in British exports by two-thirds. This strategy gained support from ordinary colonists, from the Daughters of Liberty who held spinning bees and encouraged the wearing of homespun clothes to crowds who mobilized to intimidate customs officials and importers. This new kind of mass politics based on organized popular resistance and everyday political participation culminated in the Boston Tea Party. At stake were fundamental questions of Britain's public power over its colonial subjects that led to the American Revolution. Colonialists not only achieved independence but also created a new notion of direct representation premised on popular participation in politics.

In the century that followed independence, Americans based their participation in politics on their producer identity as hardworking, virtuous independent farmers, small merchants, or artisans. As more Americans became wage earners, trade unions emerged to represent their collective interests and preserve a sense of autonomy and freedom at the workplace.

In the late nineteenth century, however, Americans began to embrace a consumer identity as the basis of political action. Between 1870 and 1920, the number of Americans living in cities doubled to over 50 percent. By 1920 more people worked in factories than on farms, and less than one-quarter of the workforce was self-employed. At the same time, people were now purchasing basic necessities, from prepared food to ready-to-wear clothing to store-bought tools and furnishings, rather than producing them at home. Moreover, the emergence of department stores, mass retailers, and mail-order catalogs, along with the rise of brand-name goods, created a new consumer ethos of satisfaction guaranteed. Amusement parks, nickelodeons, and commercial dance halls arose as forms of cheap amusement. In that context, Americans started to make demands as consumers entitled to a higher standard of living.

With a rise in productivity, organized labor insisted on a shortening of the workday and the right to leisure time. "Eight hours for work, eight hours for rest, eight hours for what we will!" was the slogan. In 1886 hundreds of thousands of workers staged an unsuccessful general strike to demand the eight-hour day. The eight-hour movement won a victory in 1916 with the passage of the Adamson Act, which limited hours for railroad workers. But only in 1938 did labor succeed in getting Congress to pass the Fair Labor Standards Act to make the eight-hour day the national standard.

In the late nineteenth century, organized labor also demanded higher wages as another crucial aspect of a sense of entitlement to an "American standard of living." Workers began to abandon their critique of wage labor as an extension of slavery. Becoming less critical of capitalism, instead they argued they had a right to earn a "living wage," by which advocates like American Federation of Labor (AFL) president Samuel Gompers meant enough money to buy a home of at least six rooms with indoor plumbing, furniture, pictures, carpets, and books. Rather than dulling political activism, the prospect of better living standards propelled labor agitation. As Gompers explained in an 1887 political speech, "Continual improvement, by opening up new vistas, creates new desires and develops legitimate aspirations. It makes men more dissatisfied with unjust conditions and readier to battle for the right."

From the Progressive Era to the 1920s

As nineteenth-century deflation gave way to twentieth-century inflation, a preoccupation with the cost of living led to an activist consumer politics. Between 1897 and 1916, the cost of living rose 30 percent. New sites of consumption, from streetcars to storefronts, became sites of protests with slight fluctuations in price. The early twentieth century witnessed countless rent strikes, beef boycotts, and other fights over the "high cost of living," led by housewives who understood their actions in the marketplace as the counterpart to their husbands' wage campaigns at the union hall and factory. For example, Pauline Newman, who became well known as a leader of the 1909 "uprising of 20,000," when tens of thousands of teenage New York garment workers went on strike, first cut her teeth by leading rent strikes around the city.

A consumer identity could cross class lines and be a unifying force in the Progressive Era fight against corporations. Contemporary Americans understood rising prices as the product of a conspiracy by big trusts. President Woodrow Wilson captured that antimonopoly sentiment when he said, "The high cost of living is arranged by private understanding." The fight against rising prices united workers and the growing segment of the white-collar middle class on fixed salaries, who shared the belief that trusts were to blame. Progressive journalist Walter Lippmann identified what he saw as a rising "consumer consciousness." In his 1914 book *Drift and Mastery*, he explained, "The real power emerging today in democratic politics is just the mass of people who are crying out against the 'high cost of living.'" That consumer sensibility was especially true for women, who were thought to be responsible for the vast majority of purchasing. "The mass of women do not look at the world as workers," said Lippmann. "In America, at least, their primary interest is as consumers."

Playing on that sentiment, reformers founded the National Consumers League (NCL) in 1898 as a lobbying group of middle-class women who would push for greater regulation of consumer goods and the conditions under which they were made. Under the leadership of Florence Kelley, the NCL led union-label campaigns to persuade women to purchase garments made only in union factories under safe and fair labor conditions. Kelley argued, based on germ theory, that consumers should be concerned about the health of workers and the potential spread of diseases like tuberculosis. Through boycotts, Kelley sought to transform women's purchasing power into a political force for labor reform. The NCL also pushed, sometimes successfully, for state-level minimum-wage legislation for women workers. Massachusetts passed the first law for minimum wages for women in 1912. Several other states followed until the U.S. Supreme Court declared such legislation unconstitutional in 1923.

Protests over high prices came to a head in World War I, when the cost of living doubled. The Wilson administration worried that high prices would trigger labor unrest as the cost of living outpaced wages. Indeed, organized labor justified its strikes by claiming the right to a living wage. Wilson appointed Herbert Hoover to head the Food Administration and lead the campaign to restrain inflation—or war profiteering, as it was popularly known. Hoover appealed to Americans for patriotic conservation with requests for "meatless Tuesdays and wheatless Wednesdays"; at the same time, he engaged in a massive propaganda effort that legitimized notions of "fair prices" and the rights of consumers and put pressure on businessmen to moderate price increases. In the absence of price controls, which ultimately doomed his efforts, Hoover mobilized housewives to investigate local prices as a way to keep inflation in check.

The notion that shoppers had rights in the marketplace evolved in the 1920s when America became a modern consumer society. The publication of Upton Sinclair's *The Jungle* (1906), with its description of the horrible conditions in packinghouses, had earlier led to the passage of the Pure Food and Drug Act and the Meat Inspection Act, bringing the government into the business of regulating product standards for the safety and health of consumers. But the number of mass-produced products and the advertising of those products vastly expanded in the 1920s and were largely unregulated. In the 1920s, Stuart Chase and F. J. Schlink published scathing critiques of the tactics used by manufacturers to produce and sell their goods in books with titles like *Your Money's Worth* and *100,000,000 Guinea Pigs*. Without standardization of weights, sizes, and materials, and without sufficient product information, consumers could not judge value. In addition, these reformers worried about adulterated and even harmful products and called for stiffer government regulation of production and advertising. Their books became best sellers and led them to form Consumers' Research as an agency to test branded goods.

Reformers like Chase worried not only about consumer safety but also about inadequate consumer income. In the 1920s, the gross national product increased by 40 percent as a result of the application of mass production techniques to many industries, from automobiles to appliances. Reformers argued that the new economy required a better distribution of income so that more Americans could actually afford to purchase the new consumer goods. Organized labor claimed that living wages were not only morally and politically necessary but also essential to sustaining a mass consumption economy. Edward Filene, the department store magnate, articulated this vision best at a 1925 meeting of progressive reformers: "Mass production can live only through mass distribution, and mass distribution means a mass of people who have buying power." As he put it, "Production cannot be profitable unless it produces, first of all, consumers." In 1926, at an AFL annual convention, AFL president William Green explained, "If America's prosperity is to be maintained, it must be possible for the masses of workmen to buy and use the things they have produced." Henry Ford had argued for the importance of working-class consumption when he introduced the five-dollar day and cut the prices of his cars. But the labor movement and their allies believed that only unions and federal regulation of wages would enable sufficient redistribution of income to sustain the economy.

The New Deal and World War II

This argument gained traction in the 1930s, when reformers pointed to the problem of underconsumption to explain the Great Depression. Though capital spending fell far more than consumption, the idea of underconsumption as the major economic problem had widespread appeal. In his Commonwealth Club speech in September 1932, Franklin D. Roosevelt said, "Our task now is . . . meeting the problem of underconsumption, of adjusting production to consumption, of distributing wealth and products more equitably." Once in office as president, Roosevelt used the language of consumers and consumption to justify a range of measures, often even contradictory, that would boost the purchasing power of Americans and thereby restore prosperity.

When Roosevelt introduced the New Deal in 1933, he promised an expansion of governmental authority to increase purchasing power: "The aim of this whole effort is to restore our rich domestic market by raising its vast consuming capacity." But the National Industrial Recovery Act (NIRA) and the Agricultural Adjustment Act (AAA), the two key measures of the early New Deal, were necessarily inflationary, enabling producers to cut production and raise prices as a way of restoring profits. Section 7a of the NIRA was intended to increase wages by legalizing collective bargaining, but industry noncompliance rendered this measure ineffective. Both the NIRA and AAA led to higher prices without substantially increasing national income. Those higher prices threatened to undermine public support for the New Deal. As a result, Congress created new bodies to look out for consumers' interest and to contain protest. In the spring of 1935, housewives across the country formed "high cost of living committees," demanding price cuts on meat, milk, and bread.

The Great Depression led to the creation of new governmental agencies dedicated to protecting consumers. The National Recovery Administrations's (NRA) Consumer Advisory Board and the AAA's Consumers' Counsel pushed for three programs. First, they sought to organize county consumer councils to create a grassroots consumer movement. These local groups distributed new government publications like *Consumers Guide* that listed average prices of basic goods like meat, milk, and bread and urged consumers not to pay more. Second, consumer advocates pushed for an end to price fixing in NRA codes. Finally, they called for a government system of quality standards to provide consumers with essential product information. Their efforts culminated in the Food, Drug, and Cosmetic Act of 1938.

The key moment of injecting a consumer rationale into New Deal legislation came with the passage of the National Labor Relations Act in 1935. New Dealers looked to organized labor as the way to challenge corporate power and redistribute income. When Roosevelt took office, only 10 percent of the industrial workforce was organized. In introducing his measure to Congress in 1935, Senator Robert Wagner of New York explained that unionization of workers was essential for economic recovery:

"When employees are denied the freedom to act in concert, . . . they cannot participate in our national endeavor to coordinate production and purchasing power." The solution was to let workers organize and bargain collectively for higher wages.

By the election of 1936, Roosevelt cemented his coalition of farmers, workers, and middle-class voters, often using consumer rhetoric to justify his programs. Farm supports boosted agricultural purchasing power, unionization boosted labor's purchasing power, and Social Security would boost purchasing power for millions of unemployed and retired Americans. When the economy declined in 1937–38, Roosevelt announced a Keynesian deficit spending measure, saying that the government had a responsibility to increase national purchasing power during a recession. In the postwar period, politicians would continue to use Keynesian fiscal tools to stabilize the economy.

World War II ended the Depression, and inflation returned as the key economic problem. To fight it, the government created the Office of Price Administration (OPA). As in World War I, the wartime administration mobilized the nation's housewives to prevent profiteering. But this time Congress passed mandatory federal price controls and rationing. Influenced by the New Deal, the wartime government was committed to preserving mass purchasing power by an expansion of state power. By setting ceilings on millions of products, the OPA successfully restrained business; simultaneously, it got 20 million women to sign the Home Front pledge not to pay more than ceiling prices. Hundreds of thousands volunteered for "little OPAs" in each county, and millions more reported price violations. The OPA remained in place more than a year after the war ended, with broad popular support, including that of organized labor. Having agreed to no-strike pledges and wage freezes, labor supported price controls to protect its members. The war, with a strong activist state, was the high point of a public policy committed to protecting mass purchasing power by regulating prices and wages.

The Postwar Years

In 1962 President John F. Kennedy announced his commitment to a "consumers' bill of rights." But unlike during the first two-thirds of the twentieth century, consumer issues now had little to do with prices or income. Instead of regulating wages and prices, government relied on taxing and spending to stabilize the economy. In the 1960s and 1970s, the modern consumer movement led by activist Ralph Nader focused on health and safety issues. In 1962 Congress passed the Truth in Lending Act to protect credit borrowers and the Truth in Packaging Act to require better labeling, and created the Consumer Protection Safety Commission. Nader's *Unsafe at Any Speed* (1965) led to the National Traffic and Vehicle Safety Act of 1966. Nader launched the public interest movement in which lawyers pushed for greater government regulation of safety and health in the environment and at the workplace.

By the 1970s, liberals no longer saw greater consumption as the solution to the nation's ills but pointed to abundance and an ethos of indulgence as the problem. President Jimmy Carter made that point of view clear during the energy crisis. "In a nation that was proud of hard work, strong families, close-knit communities, and our faith in God," said Carter in his famous 1979 "malaise" speech, "too many of us now tend to worship self-indulgence and consumption. Human identity is no longer defined by what one does, but by what one owns. But we've discovered that owning things and consuming things does not satisfy our longing for meaning. We've learned that piling up material goods cannot fill the emptiness of lives, which have no confidence or purpose."

Since the energy crisis of the 1970s, critics have taken sharply different views about consumption. Most liberals have called for restraint and conservation, whereas the business community and conservatives have pushed for relaxing regulations to make it easier to exploit the country's natural resources and productive potential. During the 1980s, while the left condemned displays of conspicuous consumption and ridiculed the "yuppie" lifestyle, the right took up the consumer mantle, using arguments about consumer choice to call for an end of government regulation and a return to free-market policies. President Ronald Reagan signed the largest tax cut in the nation's history in 1981, claiming that a reduction in taxes would unleash the nation's creative genius and result in greater economic growth. While the number of jobs in the high-tech and service industries grew, income inequality also increased. To maintain consumer lifestyles and make ends meet, Americans took on unprecedented amounts of consumer debt made possible by the explosion of the credit card industry.

At the beginning of the twenty-first century, the largest corporation in the United States is Wal-Mart. The company appeals to American consumers by offering everyday low prices, which it stocks through a global supply chain. Whereas reformers a century earlier sought to regulate sweatshops in American cities, most production of consumer goods is now located in "third world" countries, especially China. There are periodic campaigns to prevent Wal-Mart stores from expanding into neighborhoods, spearheaded either by unions who fear the corporation's low wages and non-union workforce or by local retailers who fear the retail giant's low prices. The success and proliferation of global corporations like Wal-Mart have largely undercut the century-long effort for government regulation of prices and wages. But as long as America remains a consumer society, political struggles about the means and meaning of consumption will occur.

See also business and politics; economy and politics; labor movement and politics; New Deal Era, 1932–52.

FURTHER READING. Lizabeth Cohen, *A Consumers' Republic: The Politics of Mass Consumption in Postwar America*, 2003; Lucy Black Creighton, *Pretenders to the Throne: The Consumer Movement in the United States*, 1976; Gary Cross, *An All-Consuming Century: How Commercialism Won in Modern America*, 2002; Lawrence B. Glickman, *Buying Power: A History of Consumer Activism in America*, 2009; Idem, *Consumer Society in American History: A Reader*, 1999; Meg Jacobs, *Pocketbook Politics: Economic Citizenship in Twentieth-Century America*, 2005.

MEG JACOBS

conventions, political
See party nominating conventions.

crime
The United States has long been distinctive among industrial societies for both its high level of violent crime and the harshness of its criminal justice systems. The paradox of great reliance on penal coercion to ensure social order in a society founded on the idea of individual liberty was noted early on by Gustave de Beaumont and Alexis de Tocqueville, who wrote in the 1830s that while society in the United States "gives the example of the most extended liberty," its prisons "offer the spectacle of the most complete despotism." In the late twentieth century, this difference became magnified, as the United States increasingly diverged from other advanced societies in the degree to which its citizens suffered from interpersonal violence and, simultaneously, in the degree to which it imprisoned an ever growing proportion of its citizens. By the turn of the twenty-first century, the United States stood as an outlier among advanced societies, with both the highest rates of homicide in the advanced industrial world and the highest proportion of its population behind bars of any country, advanced or otherwise.

At the start of the twenty-first century, the United States incarcerated its population at a rate five times that of its closest Western European counterpart, England; eight to nine times that of more typical European countries like Germany, France, or Sweden; and twelve times that of Japan. Yet the American death rate from homicide was six times that of Germany, eight times that of the United Kingdom, and ten times that of Japan.

Measured by the risks of death by violence, the United States more closely resembles some countries of the former Soviet bloc and the third world than it does other advanced societies. Measured by levels of incarceration, only Russia now comes close, among major countries, to the United States. One of the world's richest societies is also one of its most violent: one of the most militantly individualistic of nations also has more of its people under state confinement than any country in the world.

Moreover, at the turn of the twenty-first century, the United States stood almost alone among industrial democracies—and indeed among many less-developed countries—in continuing to use the death penalty on a regular basis. (Some other industrial democracies, including Japan and Taiwan, have also maintained the death penalty, though on a smaller scale.)

These patterns, however, have varied considerably across different regions in the United States. In some ways, it is misleading to speak of an "American" crime problem—or an "American" response to crime. Imprisonment rates have been especially high in some of the southern states in recent years, and far lower in parts of New England and the Midwest—a pattern that partly reflects differences in the underlying rate of serious crime, but also long-standing regional differences in political culture and social policy. In the early twenty-first century, Mississippi imprisoned its citizens at a rate nearly four times that of Minnesota. The use of the death penalty varies even more sharply: the vast majority of executions have taken place in a handful of southern states, with Texas alone accounting for more than a third of all executions in the United States since the mid-1970s.

Entrenched Problems, Failed Reforms

This situation would have been hard to predict from the nature of American approaches to criminal justice at the nation's beginnings. American attitudes toward crime and justice were diverse in the seventeenth and eighteenth centuries, but they were often shaped by a reaction against the harshness of British policy. The colonies used the death penalty relatively sparingly by English standards, for example, and Enlightenment ideas stressing the reformability of offenders flourished, at least in some places in the eighteenth and early nineteenth centuries (notably in Pennsylvania, center of a Quaker-inspired reform movement to prevent crime and rehabilitate criminals), American reformers invented the penitentiary (in Pennsylvania in the 1830s) and probation (in Massachusetts in the 1840s).

Yet, in what was to become an enduring pattern, early efforts at reform were generally short-lived and confined to certain states. Moreover, the reformers' vision was problematic—and doomed to failure—from the start. The belief that hard labor, religious instruction, and strict discipline—the foundations of the penitentiary system—could tame the unruly and desperate products of an unequal and disruptive society lent itself to extraordinary harshness in the best of times, and many of the "reformed" institutions ultimately devolved into places of routine official brutality and inmate rebellion. By the middle of the nineteenth century, the United States had built many prisons, but the reform impulse was hard to discern: the prisons generally warehoused offenders under conditions of sometimes horrific brutality.

Those conditions sparked another reform movement in the years just after the Civil War. Once again, reformers argued that a combination of severe discipline with industrial training (or domestic training for female offenders) could transform the volatile (and heavily immigrant) "dangerous classes" into productive and docile citizens of the emerging industrial order. There were some enduring changes in this period—notably the creation of the first juvenile court at the turn of the century. But on the whole, the reform movement again failed, as the belief that a divided and dangerous society could be held together through its penal institutions ran up against social and economic realities. Offenders turned out to be far more intractable than the reformers had hoped: urban crime remained rampant (and far worse than in foreign cities; New York's homicide rate was several times higher than London's throughout the nineteenth century). By the turn of the century, the reformers' emphasis on the malleability of offenders was increasingly replaced by a more pessimistic view, informed by the biological determinism of Cesar Lombroso and other European theorists, whose ideas found considerably greater traction in the United States than in their countries of origin.

Throughout this period, the South presented a different pattern, both with respect to crime and the response to it. The economics of slavery worked against the widespread use of incarceration in southern states: corporal punishment, supplemented by both formal and informal strategies of terror, was more appealing to slaveholders as a means of social control, since they stood to lose the labor of slaves if they went behind bars. The post–Civil War years brought a shift toward a peculiarly southern blend of state and private control of offenders, based on the leasing of convicts to private employers—a system that destroyed the bodies and lives of thousands of convicts but did nothing to lessen the stunningly disparate levels of violent crime in much of the South. (Journalist H. V. Redfield wrote in 1880 that "the number of homicides in the Southern states is proportionately greater than in any country on earth the population of which is rated as civilized.")

Explaining the American Exception

The distinctive American pattern of unusual harshness toward offenders coupled with unusually high levels of violence is sometimes attributed to the nation's "frontier" history. But other settler societies show a very different trajectory when it comes to crime and punishment. Australia, another nation with a long frontier tradition (and one settled partly by convicts), had an average homicide death rate roughly one-fourth that of the United States throughout the second half of the twentieth century, and, by the twenty-first, had an incarceration rate one-sixth that of the United States.

The growing gap in crime and punishment between the United States and other advanced societies is rooted in a broader set of developments in political culture and public policy that have increasingly distinguished the nation from its counterparts in the developed world. These differences had been apparent at least since the industrial revolution but sharpened after World War II, and particularly after the 1960s. The central difference is the degree to which the United States hewed to a Darwinian vision of social policy with minimal attempts to narrow social and economic inequalities. In contrast to many other industrial societies, political movements to challenge the dominance of market principles were relatively weak. This had a twofold impact on crime and punishment in America, simultaneously aggravating the conditions that breed violent crime and constricting the range of politically feasible responses to it.

Social and economic policies driven by market principles contributed to the distinctive American pattern of crime and punishment in several mutually reinforcing ways. These policies widened economic inequalities, deepened poverty, and fostered community disintegration—all conditions that are known to breed violent crime—and also produced a massive trade in illicit drugs that, particularly after the 1980s, became inextricably entwined with the problem of violence. (Hard drugs were illegal in other developed countries as well, but in none of them was drug abuse as severe as in the United States, or the illegal drug trade as extensive.) The same principles simultaneously crippled the ability of public authorities to address those conditions by minimizing preventive public social spending and by fostering an ideology that placed the blame for crime and other social ills on the shoulders of individuals.

In contrast to other advanced societies, too, the sale of firearms remained largely unregulated in the United States. While some nations—including England and Australia—moved toward even tighter restrictions on gun availability in the late twentieth century, the United States moved, on the whole, in the opposite direction—relaxing already minimal restrictions on the individual right to own and carry firearms. The gap between the United States and other advanced industrial societies in homicide is notably higher than the gap for other violent crimes or property crime, and the wide availability of guns is an important part of the explanation.

The Eclipse of Alternatives

During a pivotal period in the 1960s, a movement for reform challenged the traditional reliance on the criminal justice system to maintain order in the face of these structural pressures toward violent crime. It was widely argued among social scientists, as well as many criminal justice practitioners, that relying on an expanded prison system to control crime was inherently ineffective, as well as costly. There was increasing criticism of the drift toward warehousing offenders while neglecting their rehabilitation and ignoring the social conditions that predictably bred crime, especially in the inner cities. There were calls for limiting the scope of the criminal law and for

reducing the role of the prison as a first line of defense against crime—particularly by removing nonviolent offenders and juveniles from confinement. But with the partial exception of the reform of juvenile justice, most of these tentative efforts were derailed in the 1970s and 1980s and replaced by a new insistence on deterrence and incapacitation as the only effective strategies against crime.

While many countries in Europe and Asia kept rates of incarceration within a relatively narrow historical range (and a few enjoyed actual declines in imprisonment rates), the United States saw a relentless increase beginning in the 1970s, which continued even during periods when crime rates fell overall. The American prison and jail population increased sevenfold during the last three decades of the twentieth century, a rise that was unprecedented in U.S. history and, in terms of sheer size, unparalleled anywhere in the rest of the world. Prison populations also rose significantly in some other countries—including England and, especially, the Netherlands—after the 1990s. But in no country did the expansion of the penal system take place on such a massive scale as in the United States.

The reasons why this shift took place when it did, and why it was maintained through every national administration—whether Democratic or Republican—since then are complex. The Vietnam War diverted public resources from the domestic social programs and promising criminal justice alternatives that could have made a difference in crime rates. Simultaneously, the 1970s and 1980s saw the growing dominance of conservative views stressing the limits of government intervention in addressing the problems from which urban violence grew. The argument that "liberal" solutions like fighting poverty or providing job programs had failed were widely accepted, not only among the right but across much of the political spectrum. Influential conservative scholars began to argue that the liberal belief in the potential for rehabilitation of criminal offenders was an illusion, and that argument became widely influential among legislators, criminal justice practitioners, and the media. Many factors fed this ideological shift, including the very real stubbornness and persistence of violence, particularly in the cities, and, from another angle, the relative weakness of expert opinion in influencing public policy, which tended to be driven to a degree unusual in advanced societies by specific political interests and popular fears.

By the 1980s, both major parties shared a self-consciously "tough" approach to crime that included support for the death penalty, stiffer sentences, and increased investment in incarceration. The tendency for party positions on crime to become blurred was accelerated during the administration of President Bill Clinton, which worked energetically to pass legislation expanding the number of crimes eligible for the death penalty and to use federal authority (and federal money) to coerce state governments into keeping offenders behind bars for longer periods.

By the early twenty-first century, indeed, crime and the state of the criminal justice system had nearly disappeared from national political debate and from presidential election campaigns—in sharp contrast to the 1960s, when concern over "crime in the streets" helped elect Richard Nixon to the presidency. This was not because the problems had receded: after a period of decline in the 1990s, violent crime had stabilized at a level that remained extraordinarily high by international standards—and in many places was increasing (especially among the inner-city young), despite the unprecedented growth in imprisonment during the past several decades. The criminal justice system had swollen to the point where maintaining it cut deeply into other public expenditures and, arguably, lowered the quality of life for much of the population. Rather, the near disappearance of these issues from the national political stage reflected the fact that the major parties no longer differed significantly in their approach to them; therefore no political advantage could be gained by invoking the continuing crisis of violence in the streets or the social and fiscal strain of an increasingly dysfunctional correctional system.

Paradoxically, this has meant that the United States, despite the pervasive rhetoric about "getting tough" on crime, routinely tolerates a degree of public fear and insecurity that does not exist in other advanced societies. Part of the reason for this paradoxical acceptance of violence, as well as the lack of broad social or political concern with the consequences of a swollen penal system, is that both violence and incarceration have become increasingly concentrated in low-income minority communities with little political influence or public voice. The most serious forms of street violence, as well as violence in the home, had always been more severe among the poor and became more so in the late twentieth century. High levels of homicide death among the poorest fifth of the population, for example, were a key reason why the overall gap in life expectancy between affluent and poor Americans widened after the 1960s.

The racial dimension of this concentration is inescapable: at the beginning of the twenty-first century, 17 percent of black men then living (more than one in six) had spent some time in a state or federal prison, versus less than 3 percent of whites. Moreover, the growing army of the formerly incarcerated came disproportionately from a relatively few neighborhoods in the inner cities. But this pervasive presence of prison in the lives of black men did not make them safer. Homicide death rates among young black men in some states exceeded those of their counterparts in many of the most violent countries in the third world: young black men in Louisiana were more likely to die by violence than young men in Brazil or El Salvador. The continuing danger of everyday life had not diminished for inner-city minority residents, especially the young, but inner-city minority residents had little influence on the preoccupations of national politics.

There have been a number of recent exceptions to the generally punitive drift of American criminal justice policy—most of them launched at the state (and sometimes local) levels. In the early years of the twenty-first century, certain states moved, with some success, to divert minor drug offenders from incarceration; others explored a variety of strategies to remove some of the least dangerous offenders from prison. These developments were often driven by the fiscal burden placed on state budgets by increased spending on prisons. But on the national level, where debate on criminal justice policy was shaped less by hard fiscal realities and more by ideology, there was little change in almost 40 years of reliance on criminal sanctions to deal with social ills.

In the absence of a sustained set of policies to address the roots of violent crime, the criminal justice system in the United States has, by default, come to take on an unusually pervasive role—in effect becoming the social policy instrument of first resort for dealing with the multiple troubles of low-income communities. The tacit commitment of both major political parties to this general strategy—with occasional exceptions—means that there is little to suggest that the shape of American crime policy will change much anytime soon, or that the United States will relinquish its place as both the most violent and the most punitive of advanced societies.

FURTHER READING. Stuart Banner, *The Death Penalty: An American History*, 2003; Katherine Beckett, *Making Crime Pay: Law and Order in Contemporary American Politics*, 1999; Elliott Currie, *Crime and Punishment in America*, 1998; Lawrence M. Friedman, *Crime and Punishment in American History*, 1994; Marc Mauer, *Race to Incarcerate*, revised and updated ed., 2006; Eric Monkkonen, *Murder in New York City*, 2001; Jonathan Simon, *Governing through Crime*, 2007; Bruce Western, *Punishment and Inequality in America*, 2007; James Q. Whitman, *Harsh Justice; the Widening Divide between America and Europe*, 2003.

ELLIOTT CURRIE

Declaration of Independence

The Declaration of Independence, issued by the Second Continental Congress on July 4, 1776, publicly proclaimed 13 of Great Britain's colonial provinces in North America to be independent, sovereign states, and formally styled their union "The United States of America." In justifying the act of separation, the Declaration enumerated numerous grievances the 13 colonies had against King George III of Great Britain while it appealed to natural law, corporate and individual liberty, and the right to revolution—concepts widely accepted in the eighteenth-century European world generally and the Anglophone world in particular. The Declaration marked the end point of a debate in the American colonies over the pursuit of independence from Britain. After the American Revolution, the Declaration became one of the most important American state papers, cited repeatedly by political leaders, activists, and commentators in the United States and in the wider world.

Prelude to the Declaration

The Declaration of Independence resulted from two overlapping political discussions in the North American colonies of the British Empire, one beginning in 1763, the other in 1775. The first discussion was the series of debates that took place in the colonies and in Britain itself over various measures Parliament had passed after the conclusion of Seven Years' War in 1763—debates historians collectively refer to as the "imperial crisis." Between 1764 and 1774, Parliament passed numerous laws designed to raise revenue in the American colonies. The Sugar Act (1764), the Stamp Act (1765), the Townshend Duties (1767), and the Tea Act (1773) all met with protests, each increasingly widespread. The leadership in the colonies disputed Parliament's right to levy taxes on the colonial population for a variety of reasons. At the beginning of the crisis, many colonists disputed Parliament's right to enact taxes on commerce or activities within a colony's borders (so-called internal taxes), but supported Parliament's right to regulate imperial commerce (so-called external taxes). Other colonists disputed Parliament's right to collect any taxes or enact any laws affecting the colonies. Although the latter was a minority viewpoint in the mid-1760s, it gained an increasing number of supporters by the early to mid-1770s. Parliament consistently asserted its right to legislate for the colonies (and all of the British Empire), doing so explicitly in the Declaratory Act (1766) and implicitly in subsequent revenue legislation, as well as in its response to the colonial protest that became known as the Boston Tea Party, the

punitive Coercive Acts (1774). The Declaration of Independence came at the end of this long constitutional discussion: Parliament's insistence on legislating for the colonies drove the colonial leadership to abandon hope for compromise and to seek recognition of their independence as sovereign states.

At the same time, the Declaration of Independence came at the end of a shorter but just as heated discussion that marked the final phase of the imperial crisis. After the military confrontation between British regulars and Massachusetts militia at Lexington and Concord in April 1775, the debate among the colonists increasingly focused not on whether to declare independence but on when and how. The Second Continental Congress convened on May 10, 1775. Almost immediately it began to consider how it and the colonies should respond to the violence at Lexington and Concord. While a vocal minority believed that the colonies should seek independence from Great Britain immediately, a majority of delegates hoped to improve the situation through the existing mechanisms of the British government—appealing to Parliament and the ministry of Lord Frederick North or to King George III. At the same time, a majority of delegates also believed that the colonies should coordinate their resistance to measures of the North Ministry. On July 6, 1775, the Continental Congress issued the Declaration of the Causes and Necessity for Taking Up Arms, a justification for the Continental Army created just weeks earlier. The tone of this declaration was strident and uncompromising. Yet two days later, the Congress issued a petition to King George III, colloquially known as the "Olive Branch Petition," that identified the North Ministry and Parliament as the parties responsible for the controversy and called on the king to mediate the dispute. George III rejected the "Olive Branch" as soon as it arrived in Britain, refusing to officially receive or respond to the document. Even months after Lexington and Concord, however, the desire in the colonies to pursue independence was not unanimous.

With many members of the Continental Congress and a large segment of the colonial population lukewarm on the prospect of American independence, the Congress enacted a series of measures that quietly moved the colonies toward a position where independence became tenable. In mid-June, the Congress had created the Continental Army to coordinate the colonial siege of Boston. Congress also created continental currency and issued £4 million of it by the end of 1775. On July 6, Congress not only issued the Declaration of Causes but also created a continental post office and appointed Benjamin Franklin as postmaster. In October, George III, during his speech opening the new session of Parliament, declared the

American Congress to be leading "a desperate movement" to "establish an independent empire." At the end of November 1775, Congress created the Committee of Secret Correspondence to communicate independently with foreign powers, the precursor to the Committee on Foreign Affairs. Congress was thus performing many activities of an independent sovereign. In December, Congress rejected allegiance to Parliament, while still claiming allegiance to the crown. Weeks later, on December 22, Parliament issued the Prohibitory Act, which closed off British trade with the colonies. It was in this environment, in January 1776, that Thomas Paine published *Common Sense*. Paine's plainspoken argument against monarchy and in favor of American independence proved very popular; within a month more than 100,000 copies had been published. Circulated throughout the colonies, *Common Sense* did more than any other publication to put American public opinion squarely on the side of independence. In the months that followed the publication of *Common Sense*, groups of Americans at the town, county, and state levels issued petitions and resolutions calling on the Continental Congress to declare American independence from Britain. In March, Congress dispatched a secret diplomatic agent, Silas Deane, to France; in April, Congress opened American ports to foreign commerce; and on May 10, Congress issued a resolution, written by John Adams, calling on the individual colonies to draft new constitutions. It was not surprising when, just three weeks later, Congress found itself pondering a declaration of independence.

Proposal and Drafting

The Continental Congress began formal discussion of a declaration of independence on June 7, 1776, when Richard Henry Lee, speaking on behalf of the Virginia delegation, declared, "That these United Colonies are, and of right ought to be, free and independent States." He called on Congress to proclaim that reality, to formulate a plan for contracting foreign alliances, and to prepare articles of confederation to bind the 13 independent states together. Congress resolved itself into the Committee of the Whole and took up discussion of Lee's resolution the following day. Again, the sentiment for American independence was far from unanimous; a group led by delegates John Dickinson, Robert Livingston, Edward Rutledge, and James Wilson held fast to the notion that the time was still not right for a declaration, that the public needed more time to come around, and that the questions of confederation and foreign alliances should be resolved *before* Congress issued a declaration. But a majority of delegates favored independence at this point, and on June 11, 1776, Congress appointed a committee composed of John Adams (Massachusetts), Benjamin Franklin (Pennsylvania), Thomas Jefferson (Virginia), Robert Livingston (New York), and Roger Sherman (Connecticut) to draft a declaration of independence. As

is well known, the primary responsibilities of drafting the declaration fell to Jefferson, who wrote at least three drafts during the 17 days he devoted to the declaration's composition. Franklin and the rest of the committee made only minor alterations before sending the draft of the declaration to the Congress on June 28.

An initial vote in the Committee of the Whole found nine colonial delegations in favor, South Carolina and Pennsylvania opposed, Delaware deadlocked, and New York abstaining. After a series of eleventh-hour reconsiderations by South Carolina, the last-minute arrival of Delaware's Caesar Rodney to break the tie in his delegation, and the abstention of Pennsylvania's two anti-independence delegates (Dickinson and Robert Morris), the vote on July 2 was 12–0–1 in favor of independence. (The New York legislature subsequently approved independence later in the month, making the decision unanimous.) Congress spent the next two days debating and revising the text of the declaration, agreeing to a series of changes, and approving a final version on the evening of July 4.

The president of Congress, John Hancock, signed the declaration immediately, and it was quickly printed and then reprinted throughout the now independent United States. The parchment copy of the Declaration of Independence that modern Americans recognize as the official Declaration of Independence (the copy on display at the National Archives in Washington, D.C.) was completed on August 2, and the delegates signed it when they could, as they moved in and out of Philadelphia during the remainder of the summer. Answering the other two elements of Lee's resolution, as well as the concerns of critics, in September, Congress resolved on a "plan of treaties" that would guide American diplomats during the Revolution. The drafting of the Articles of Confederation would continue into 1777. The 13 colonies declared independence as a united whole, but left the exact nature of their union (a singular sovereignty? a confederation? an alliance?) unresolved at the moment of the Declaration. (The lack of capitalization of the term "united" in certain parts and copies of the Declaration likely has more to do with the vagaries and idiosyncrasies of eighteenth-century penmanship than any attempt by the framers at a definitive statement on American federalism.)

Contents and Influences

When asked about the Declaration of Independence late in his life, Thomas Jefferson told one correspondent that its contents were "the genuine effusion of the soul of our country at that time." In other words, in drafting the Declaration, Jefferson attempted to express the conventional wisdom of the majority of Americans at that moment. Politically, the Continental Congress needed to issue a document that would justify the movement to independence using language and ideas that most Americans would support.

The Declaration thus lists a multitude of grievances against King George III that would have appealed to Americans from all sections of the union and orders of society. The Declaration was also couched in language designed to appeal to the public in Britain and the British Empire, and also to the publics and governments in other European states. The Declaration is beholden to several overlapping currents of early modern political thought, although historians and political scientists continue to debate which political philosophers and schools of thought most influenced the Declaration.

The Declaration is structured into three major parts: the preamble or introduction, which lays out the principles under which the United States are issuing their declaration; the body, which lists the grievances against King George III that have compelled the declaration; and the conclusion. The preamble has become the most famous and oft-quoted section of the Declaration, although the body arguably was the most crucial section for contemporaries, as the revolutionaries were quite sensitive about justifying so drastic an action as breaking with king and country. The body is of note in that it was the part of the Declaration in which the Committee of the Whole committed one of major pieces of editing—removing the entire clause in which Jefferson had blamed the king of England for the institution of the slave trade, a passage that has been construed as an attack on the institution of slavery by Jefferson (although this is a subject of debate). The conclusion contains the actual declaration (from Lee's resolution) that the colonies are now "Free and Independent States," as well as several phrases that are also often quoted during American patriotic celebrations.

The Declaration's preamble lays out in broad strokes the political theories under which the Americans were justifying their action of declaring independence. The preamble presents the framework within which political society had come into being, the circumstances under which overturning an established political authority was justified, and the assertion that British North Americans had found themselves in such a position.

The preamble blends two major strains of early modern Anglophone political thought: Enlightenment-era natural law and Lockean contractualism. Eighteenth-century British political thinking was defined by a consensus that emerged from the English revolutions of the seventeenth century that human beings possessed rights innately, as a product of their existence in nature as created beings. These rights were known as natural rights, and the system that supported them was known as natural law. While the idea of natural law traced its antecedents to antiquity and to medieval scholasticism, Enlightenment-era natural law writers downplayed or outright rejected the theological implications of rights and laws rooted in nature and took the mechanistic cosmos of the scientific revolution as a model. The notion was that natural rights—the rights of human beings—conformed to the same inherent set of principles that Isaac Newton's laws of motion did, and thus could be studied, articulated, and understood.

Natural law served as the fundamental building blocks for human governments and polities. This was the message of John Locke's *Second Treatise of Government*, in which he described how "Governments are instituted among men"—human beings labored in the earth, creating property, and then surrendered most of their total and absolute freedom to a government in order to protect that property and their remaining, unceded rights. Government relied on this implied contract between the governors and the governed, and Locke outlined, in the *Second Treatise*, justifications of when a people could undo the contract, abolish their existing government, and seek to establish a new one. It was to this conventional wisdom of British political thought that Jefferson and the Americans were appealing in the Declaration's preamble. It was almost the exact same form that English subjects had used in the 1689 Declaration of Rights that had overthrown James II, asserted Parliamentary supremacy, and set the stage for the installation of William and Mary on the English throne.

Most historians, political scientists, and commentators have pointed to the Declaration's origins in seventeenth- and eighteenth-century English Enlightenment thought. The classic modern statement of this interpretation was the scholarship of Carl Becker, particularly his 1922 book *The Declaration of Independence: A Study in the History of Political Ideas*. Becker's work remains the standard account of the Declaration's intellectual origins, although in recent years other historians have argued for emphasizing other potential intellectual antecedents to the Declaration. Essayist Garry Wills argued in *Inventing America* for locating the bulk of the intellectual history of Jefferson's Declaration of Independence in the writings and thinkers of the Scottish Enlightenment, such as Francis Hutcheson, Thomas Reid, David Hume, and Adam Ferguson. While few Jefferson scholars would argue with the notion that Jefferson was influenced by the Scottish Enlightenment, Wills controversially argued that Locke played a small role in shaping the Declaration as opposed to the Scots. Ronald Hamowy disagreed with Wills, pointing to the fact that Locke's writings influenced much of the Scottish Enlightenment, and that much of the thinking behind the Declaration can be observed in both Locke and Hutcheson. This insight further demonstrates how Jefferson was working within a framework of British political conventional wisdom in laying out the intellectual framework for the American declaration.

As important as the preamble, if not more so, to contemporaries was the body of the Declaration. The list of grievances began with a set of general accusations accusing the king of poor governance and subverting the system of divided powers that characterized the English Constitution and then moved toward specific complaints about laws and policies that the British government had enacted. The first set of grievances accused King George of undermining the English Constitution. He was accused of being a bad executive, in that he refused to either enact or assent to laws designed to promote "the public good." The king was then accused of undermining the legislative and judicial bodies of government—suspending colonial legislatures, calling them at inconvenient times and in inconvenient places, or refusing to call them at all, while also making colonial judges "dependent on his will alone" for both their time of service and their salaries. The Declaration then moved from a general indictment to a list of more specific grievances. These included the placing of standing armies within the colonies and subordination of the civilian to the military power (a reference to Massachusetts, where General Thomas Gage served as both governor and commander in chief of the king's forces); the enactment of the punitive Intolerable Acts against Massachusetts in the wake of the Boston Tea Party; the Quebec Act, which expanded Quebec's boundaries and protected the rights of French Catholics; and the Prohibitory Act, which had suspended commerce between the 13 colonies and the rest of the British Empire. The final grievances referred to the recruitment and deployment of German mercenaries against the colonies, the recruitment of American Indian allies against the colonies ("the merciless Indian savages"), and the "excitement of domestic insurrections among us," which referred to the offers of freedom extended to slaves who would support the British cause.

The grievances were all directed at King George III, even though many of them were the responsibility of Parliament or the joint responsibility of both Parliament and the king. Congress had absolved itself of allegiance to Parliament in December 1775, so the king was the only person and office toward which the Americans could legitimately direct their complaints. While the Intolerable Acts and the actions of the king, ministry, and their officers since those acts—including the events at Lexington and Concord and Lord Dunmore's proclamation—formed most of the complaints, a number stretched back to the beginning of the imperial crisis. By and large, though, the Americans rooted their Declaration in the violations of their rights and liberties that had occurred in the previous two to three years. The grievances were important since they were the justification for the separation—something that required justification not so much for domestic consumption (where the violations were well known) nor for British consumption (where the Declaration would be dismissed outright by most), but for an international audience. As historian David Armitage has shown, the Declaration served as what diplomats referred to as a "general manifesto"—that is, a state paper issued by one government to others to justify

a particular course of action. As the United States hoped to achieve equality with and recognition from the other European states ("to assume among the separate powers of the earth"), the justification for their separation from Britain and reasons for entry into the wider community of states were important, if for no other reason than to allow the other European states to justify future agreements with the United States.

The body of the Declaration was the place where Congress deleted the entire passage in which Jefferson accused the king of supporting the introduction of the slave trade into the American colonies and actively refusing its abolition. Congress not only found this statement inaccurate, but the antislavery tone of the complaint also was deleted in order not to offend the sensibilities of the southernmost states, especially South Carolina, which remained involved in the slave trade.

The Declaration's conclusion contains the actual affirmative declaration of the independence of the 13 states, their rejection of allegiance to Britain and the British, and their declaration that they could perform all the activities of independent, sovereign states.

Publication and Reception

Shortly after its approval on July 4, 1776, the Declaration was sent to Philadelphia printer John Dunlap. Official copies were printed as broadsides and sent by John Hancock, as president of the Congress, to the governors of each of the states and to General George Washington as commander in chief of the Continental Army. Washington ordered his officers to read the Declaration to their soldiers on July 9. Similar public readings were held throughout the United States. As historian Jay Fliegelman observed, Jefferson wrote the Declaration to be read aloud, indicating on one of his handwritten drafts "reading marks" that indicated where readers should take pauses. These marks were transferred onto the first typeset proof that Dunlap prepared, and although they were removed from subsequent printings, the Declaration still became the publicly read document it was intended to be. Public readings usually were accompanied by celebrations that often included the defacement or removal of symbols of royal authority, such as portraits and statues of the king. The Declaration was subsequently reprinted in at least 30 American newspapers (including a German-language newspaper in Pennsylvania) by the end of July 1776.

While independence was greeted with enthusiasm in most of the states in the summer of 1776, the Declaration itself was met with a more lukewarm reception. Looking at declarations of independence, constitutions, and bills of rights enacted at state levels in the years following July 1776, historian Pauline Maier found that the rhetoric and particular phrasing of the Declaration of Independence were copied little, if at all, and other contemporary documents, such as George Mason's draft of the Virginia Declaration of Rights, proved to be more influential. In Great Britain, the Declaration was officially ignored, and American independence was not recognized until negotiations for the peace treaty to end the American Revolutionary War began in 1782. However, the North Ministry did silently commission a lawyer named John Lind to write *The Answer to the Declaration of the American Colonies*, which, after an initial round of revisions, was published in several editions by the end of 1776. Lind offered a point-by-point refutation of all the Americans' listed grievances. Lind, like many other Britons who opposed the American cause, criticized the Americans for issuing a declaration proclaiming that "all men are created equal" while they continued to hold African slaves. Criticisms of the Declaration, such as those by Jeremy Bentham, continued to appear in the British press through the end of the war. The Declaration was greeted with more enthusiasm in France, where American diplomats Silas Deane and Arthur Lee could point to the document as a sign of the seriousness of the American people and Congress to the cause for which they were seeking French support.

Legacy

The Declaration of Independence has become, along with the Constitution, the most important of American state papers. Its effects have been various. Most basically, the day on which the Declaration was published, July 4—and not the day on which the vote for independence was taken and approved (July 2)—is commemorated as Independence Day in the United States. The "Fourth of July" and "The Fourth" have become synonymous with Independence Day in the American vernacular, and it can be argued that the usage of these colloquialisms is more widespread and common than the official name, Independence Day. During the partisan battles of the 1790s, adherents to the Jeffersonian Republican Party began to emphasize the text of the Declaration, Jefferson's authorship of it, and the universality of its principles to distinguish their nationalism from the pro-British and anti-French leanings of the Federalist Party. Public readings of the Declaration took on a partisan tone, which faded in the aftermath of the War of 1812 along with the Federalists. Readings of the Declaration then became, and continue to be, the centerpiece of many public celebrations of Independence Day, and expressions of a desire for national unity. Beyond defining an American national holiday, the Declaration has served as a touchstone for American national identity, and the sentiments in its preamble are nearly universally regarded as an expression of the bedrock principles of American political organization.

Throughout the lifetime of the United States, groups or individuals protesting against a perceived injustice sanctioned by American federal, state, or local governments, and protestors have used the text of the Declaration to turn public opinion to their cause.

One of the earliest and most famous examples was the publication of the "Declaration of Sentiments" by the Seneca Falls Convention for women's rights in July 1848. Authored principally by Elizabeth Cady Stanton, the Declaration of Sentiments rephrased the Declaration of Independence to include both men and women and went on to list rights that the established American political and legal order had denied to women—most important, the right to vote, the right to own property without qualification, and the right to equal citizenship. The Declaration of Sentiments and the Seneca Falls Convention marked what most historians consider to be the starting point of the modern American women's movement. One attendee at the Seneca Falls Convention, former slave and abolitionist Frederick Douglass, would argue in an 1852 Independence Day oration ("What to the Slave Is the Fourth of July?") that the Declaration's promise would remain unfulfilled as long as slavery existed in America. This was a theme President Abraham Lincoln seized on as he implicitly referenced the Declaration as the starting point of the American ideal in the Gettysburg Address of November 19, 1863, when he located the birth of the American nation "four score and seven years ago." A century later, in one of the defining episodes of the civil rights movement, Martin Luther King Jr.'s "I Have a Dream" speech to the August 28, 1963, March on Washington for Jobs and Freedom quoted the Declaration to great effect. Historians regard that speech and march as a defining moment leading to the Civil Rights Act of 1964 and the Voting Rights Act of 1965.

The Declaration of Independence has also had a life beyond the borders of the United States. Issuing a declaration of independence became an important act for colonial peoples seeking to win independence from an imperial power. In his international history of the Declaration, historian David Armitage identified over a hundred declarations of independence issued by national groups between 1776 and the early 1990s. Many nations borrowed rhetoric or form or both from the American declaration in issuing theirs. Following the American actions against Britain, the Latin American colonies of Spain issued declarations of independence as either a prelude or part of their revolutions against colonial rule—beginning with Colombia and then including Venezuela, Mexico, Argentina, Chile, and Central America. Declarations of independence would proliferate in the wake of the First and Second World Wars as the European colonial empires were broken up. Among the most famous of the postcolonial declarations of independence was Ho Chi Minh's "Proclamation of Independence of the Democratic Republic of Vietnam," which was issued on September 2, 1945, in the wake of the collapse of the Japanese Empire and explicitly (and ironically, given later events) quoted the American Declaration of Independence. Following the collapse of the Soviet bloc between 1989 and 1991, many of the former republics of the Soviet Union issued their own declarations of independence. Thus, the influence and legacy of the Declaration of Independence continue into the twenty-first century.

See also Articles of Confederation; war for independence.

FURTHER READING. David Ammerman, *Under the Common Cause: American Responses to the Coercive Acts of 1774*, 1974; David Armitage, *The Declaration of Independence: A Global History*, 2007; Carl Becker, *The Declaration of Independence: A Study in the History of Political Ideas*, 1922; Jay Fleigelman, *Declaring Independence: Jefferson, Natural Language, and the Culture of Performance*, 1993; Ronald Hamowy, "Jefferson and the Scottish Enlightenment: A Critique of Garry Wills's *Inventing America: Jefferson's Declaration of Independence*," *William and Mary Quarterly*, 3d ser., 36 (October 1979), 503–23; John Locke, *Two Treatises of Government*, 1690, edited by Peter Laslett, reprint, 1988; Pauline Maier, *American Scripture: Making the Declaration of Independence*, 1997; Jerrilyn Greene Marston, *King and Congress: The Transfer of Political Legitimacy, 1774–1776*, 1987; Garry Wills, *Inventing America: Jefferson's Declaration of Independence*, 1978.

LEONARD J. SADOSKY

democracy

Democracy is one of the most significant of the essentially contested keywords of American politics—second only, perhaps, to "freedom." Any effort to define its meaning is bound to strike some as preemptory and partisan. The whole of American political history might well be narrated as a struggle, often bitter, over what democracy can and should mean. Since the early nineteenth century, few Americans have been so bold as to suggest that the nation should shelve democracy altogether, but this consensus has hardly quieted conflict over its meaning.

But one could do worse, by way of a helpful working definition, than Abraham Lincoln's lapidary formulation in his Gettysburg Address (1863): democracy is "government of the people, by the people, for the people." At least Lincoln's definition provides us with the critical questions at the heart of the American contest over democracy's meaning: Who are (and who are not) the sovereign people? How might the sovereign people govern themselves? And how might the interests of all citizens be given equal consideration by the policies of their government? That is, American contests over democracy have centered on matters of inclusion, participation, and distributive justice.

Those many Americans who have taken pride in their democracy over the last two centuries have, again and again, had to answer to other Americans who have objected that their democracy is not democratic enough. The adversarial edge to "democracy" lies in its tie to the ideal of political equality. Some of the most significant students of American democracy

have, to be sure, pressed for an even more expansively egalitarian, less strictly political understanding of the term. Alexis de Tocqueville argued in *Democracy in America* (1838–40) for a conception of democracy as a "habit of the heart" grounded in an "equality of social conditions." John Dewey went even further, contending in *The Public and Its Problems* (1927) that, at bottom, democracy was a moral ideal that should govern "associated living" of all sorts, "a wider and fuller idea than can be exemplified in the state even at its best. To be realized, it must affect all modes of human association, the family, the school, industry, religion" (325). But even if we set aside the controversies engendered by these more expansive understandings of democracy, we are still left with a disruptive ideal.

As an ideal, political equality dictates that democracies manifest some common features. These include an equal and effective opportunity for all adult citizens to express their views in the making of public policy, to offer a vote of equal weight on public decisions, to inform themselves on matters of public moment, and to participate in determining the agenda of public decision. These common features prescribe for all citizens of democracies a set of fundamental political rights.

Before the late eighteenth century, the widespread assumption was that a strictly democratic government meant direct rule and face-to-face participation by an entire citizenry. It was a regime suitable, if at all, only to very small polities, such as the city-states of ancient Greece. The genius and the challenge of modern democracies, among which the United States has played a pivotal role, has been to pursue the ideals of political equality in large, populous nation-states by means of representative institutions, in which most political decisions are made not directly by citizens themselves but by their agents.

As a consequence of this ambition, modern democracies—despite a host of different constitutional arrangements—have developed some common institutions widely conceived to be necessary, if not sufficient, for a representative democracy. These include placing the making of public policy in the hands of officials subject to popular election; fair and fairly frequent elections in which all adult citizens are entitled to participate; the right of every citizen to seek election to public office, subject only to minimal requirements of age and residence; the right of every citizen to free expression on matters of public concern; the presence of independent and competing sources of information readily available to all citizens; and the right of all citizens to participate in relatively independent associations and organizations (such as political parties) through which they might pursue political interests. Each of these institutions is linked to one or more features of an ideal democracy: universal inclusion, effective participation in public decision making and agenda setting, voting equality, and equal opportunity for the development of informed views on public issues.

The regulative ideals of political equality are just that, regulative ideals against which to measure the political institutions and practices of putative democracies, none of which has yet to register a perfect score. Even if one doubts that any actual democratic polity could ever fully realize these ideals, they have set a horizon against which we may measure the history and momentum of each of them.

The Founding

The intention of American revolutionaries in 1776 was not to erect the world's first modern democracy but to launch a confederation of republics. Republics, as they saw it, were like democracies, governments "deriving their just powers from the consent of the governed." But unlike democracies, they held in check the destabilizing, anarchical effects of undue popular participation in politics. Ideally, republican government rested in the hands of virtuous elites capable of a disinterested discerning of the common good. The role of the people was periodically to hand over their power to some of their betters, who "virtually" represented them.

Nonetheless, as once-loyal British subjects, the revolutionaries believed that a measure of popular participation in government was necessary to prevent tyranny, and, for a century and a half, Americans had developed a taste for it. The ideal constitution was one, like that of Great Britain, that balanced or mixed a "democratical" element with those of monarchy and aristocracy. Although suffrage in both the metropole and the colonies was exceptionally narrow by modern democratic standards, Britons believed that in electing representatives to bodies such as the House of Commons and the colonial assemblies, ordinary voters played an essential role in government as bulwarks for the protection of liberty. In the context of the controversies leading up to the Revolution, American patriots, outraged by imperial controls, argued that "virtual" representation in Parliament by legislators whom they had not elected was insufficient. Representation, they contended, must be "actual"—a decidedly democratic sentiment.

In writing their revolutionary state constitutions, Americans attempted to replicate the balanced government of the three social estates, even without the presence in the revolutionary polities of two of them. Most revolutionaries crafted state governments that, in the absence of a monarch or a hereditary aristocracy, attempted to mirror the British ideal by establishing the office of governor and an upper house of a bicameral legislature as expressions of the principles of monarchy and aristocracy, respectively, leaving popular representation to the lower house alone.

The portentous exception was Pennsylvania, where a largely plebian convention led by Thomas Paine and Benjamin Franklin argued in 1776 that, in the absence of a king and aristocracy, mixed government made no sense. "There is but one rank of men in America," they contended, "and therefore . . . there should be only one representation of them in government." Their constitution provided for a much simpler government: a single legislature of elected representatives with no governor or upper house. Although Pennsylvanians would replace this constitution in 1790 with a more typical alternative, the constitution of 1776, crafted just down the street from where a more genteel gathering was declaring independence, suggested the democratic ferment bubbling beneath the surface of the Revolution.

Critics of the first Pennsylvania Constitution were legion. It seemed to more conservative republicans a dangerously democratic deviation, a lurch beyond popular sovereignty to unconstrained popular rule. But these critics and defenders of balanced constitutions were hard pressed to meet the radicals' argument. Eventually, though, they arrived at an exceptionally original and immensely significant counterargument. They reconceived of American republican governments in their entirety as representative of the people—all elected officials, governors, and state senators as well as members of the lower houses were, by these lights, popular agents. The branches and divisions of the government were not the mirror of distinctive social estates but necessary *functional* divisions of a people's government, designed by virtue of the checks and balances among them to protect liberty (and property) from overweening power—including that of the people themselves.

As Gordon Wood has shown, "Because the so-called houses of representatives had lost their exclusive role of embodying the people in government, democracy as Americans had understood it in 1776 disappeared from their constitutions. The people ruled everywhere, or, from a different perspective, they ruled nowhere." The "true distinction" of American republicanism, James Madison wrote approvingly in *Federalist 63*, lay in its "*total exclusion of the people in their collective capacity* from any share" in government. Representation was the "pivot" on which American republicanism turned, and if it was "democratic" republicanism, it was so in a new sense that promised to address the shortcomings of popular rule and render it suitable for an expansive nation-state. Although many late eighteenth-century American republicans continued to regard democracy as little more than a synonym for mob rule, a decidedly less threatening reconstruction of its meaning had begun to emerge, one that, ironically, rested substantially on virtual representation.

This conceptual breakthrough guided Madison and other elite republicans in the drafting of the federal Constitution in 1787. The result was a framework for the national government that opened with a bold declaration of popular sovereignty and authorship ("We the People of the United States . . . do ordain and establish this Constitution for the United State of America"), and then proceeded to leave no constitutionally authorized space for the subsequent exercise of democratic citizenship.

Many are the ways that the original Constitution fell short of the ideals of democratic egalitarianism held by subsequent generations. It tacitly legitimated chattel slavery; it entrusted the election of the president in a body of worthies, the Electoral College, intended to be insulated from congressional or popular control; it entrusted the selection of senators not to the electorate but to state legislatures; it provided for the equal representation in the Senate of each state, whatever its population; and it opened the door to the review of legislation by the least democratic branch, the judiciary. Of particular note was the manner in which the Constitution left perhaps the most important attribute of full democratic citizenship, suffrage, to the states—authorizing exclusions that would leave American democracy long bereft of universal suffrage.

The constraints that the Constitution placed on popular participation did not go unremarked. The most democratic of the founders, Thomas Jefferson, was inclined to collapse the distinctions between republicanism and democracy, and he found early American constitutions troublingly undemocratic. As Jefferson saw it, a republic "means a government by its citizens in mass, acting directly and personally, according to rules established by the majority; and that every other government is more or less republican, in proportion as it has in its composition more or less of this ingredient of the direct action of citizens. . . . The further the departure from direct and constant control by the citizens, the less has the government of the ingredient of republicanism." By these lights, he concluded, "it must be agreed that our governments have much less of republicanism than ought to have been expected; in other words, that the people have less regular control over their agents, than their rights and their interests require."

The Course of American Democracy

If the original Constitution constrained the democratic impulses that the Revolution unleashed, it could not altogether contain them. In the longer term, the Revolution was a radical revolution of dramatic proportions, one that would invest considerable power in the hands of yeoman farmers, artisans, and other citizens of modest means once thought undeserving of a significant political role. American republicanism, as Gordon Wood has observed, "contained the seeds of its own transformation into democracy. The equality that was so crucial to republican citizenship had a permissive significance in America that could not be restrained, and ordinary people, whose meanness and need to labor had made them contemptible in the eyes of the superiors from the beginning of history, found in republican equality a powerful justification for their self-esteem and self-assertion. As a consequence, the important age-old distinction between leisured gentlemen and common working people, which the revolutionary leaders continued to try to honor, was repeatedly blurred and eventually dissolved."

In the wake of the Revolution, American democrats, like Jefferson, devised extraconstitutional means to inject a fuller measure of participatory democracy into the nation's politics. Chief among them was the political party.

In the face of the bitter conflict over the financial and foreign policy initiatives of Alexander Hamilton and other Federalists in the 1790s, Jefferson and his chief lieutenant Madison (ironically, the author of the oft-quoted denunciation of "factions" in *Federalist 10*) organized the opposition into the aptly named Democratic-Republican Party, the first political party to feature the organization of a grassroots electorate. Extraconstitutional democratic politics made further advances under the aegis of the even more aptly named Democratic Party of Andrew Jackson and Martin Van Buren. Jacksonians attacked the remaining property restrictions on suffrage, established widespread patronage networks that rewarded the loyalty of party workers, and lent vocal support to a popular constitutionalism that challenged judicial supremacy, if not judicial review.

From the 1830s through the 1890s, American political parties served as the basis for a vibrant, participatory public sphere. Mobilizing partisan "armies," they provided their "soldiers" with well-lubricated rallies, parades, and barbecues. They printed a vast array of campaign literature, dressed their supporters in buttons, ribbons, and hats, and armed them with banners and posters. Turnout was the key to victory in nineteenth-century elections, which were held year-round, and party members engaged in constant cajoling of the faithful. Between 1840 and 1872, turnout in presidential elections averaged 69 percent, and from 1876 to 1900, 77 percent.

This was, however, an exclusive and ritualized politics in which considerably less than half of the adult population and a bare majority of the free adult population could take part and in which participation was less deliberative than ceremonial. Although, by 1830, most states had committed to universal white male suffrage, women, slaves, many free blacks, and Native Americans were, to one degree or another, denied full citizenship. But for men enclosed within these exclusive boundaries, this period marked the height of participatory politics.

The course of American democracy since the mid-nineteenth century might be described as a bumpy, winding road toward the ideal of government *of* the people (inclusion), accompanied by a long and continuing detour away from government *by* the people (effective participation). In turn, the story of American democratic thought in this period can perhaps best be construed as a vigorous debate over whether this detour has best served the interests of government *for* the people.

The path toward a more inclusive and egalitarian representative democracy can be traced in the amendments to the federal Constitution. If it would be mistaken to characterize many of the anti-Federalists as radical democrats invested in widening and deepening political equality, they were responsible for the addition to the Constitution of the Bill of Rights, some provisions of which would subsequently serve the cause of political equality. The later Reconstruction amendments ended slavery and denied states the rights to limit suffrage on racial grounds. The most significant of these three amendments for the political equality of all Americans was the Fourteenth, which nationalized citizenship and guaranteed all citizens "the equal protection of the laws," a potentially powerful lever for extending democratic rights. Other later amendments provided for the direct election of senators, for women's suffrage, for electoral votes to residents of the District of Columbia, and for suffrage for citizens 18 years of age or older.

As the Twenty-Fourth Amendment abolishing the poll tax suggests, states and localities found a host of ways to make democracy less inclusive—so much has rested on the shifting interpretation of the Constitution by the courts. African American suffrage, supposedly authorized by the Fifteenth Amendment (1870), was not secured until nearly a century later with passage of the Twenty-Fourth Amendment and the Voting Rights Act of 1965. Today, the most significant exclusionary state laws are those that do not allow convicted felons to vote. These laws, which originated as part of the many late nineteenth-century Southern measures designed to disenfranchise African Americans (including poll taxes and literacy tests), continue to have a racially discriminatory effect, given the disproportionately African American percentage of the felon population. Estimates are that 31 percent of the black men who live in Alabama and Florida have been disenfranchised in this fashion. And, of course, some of the undemocratic provisions of the original Constitution remain in force. (As Robert Dahl observes, a resident of California on one side of Lake Tahoe can increase the worth of her senatorial vote by a factor of seventeen by moving to Nevada on the other side of the lake.)

If American democracy slowly became more inclusive in the twentieth century, at the same time it became decidedly less participatory. Presidential election turnout fell to an average of 65 percent from 1900 to 1916, and to only 52 percent in the 1920s. Behind these figures lay dramatic structural changes in American politics that, as Robert Wiebe put it, took shape as a simultaneous "sinking of the lower class" and the "raising of new hierarchies." That is, the period between 1880 and 1920 witnessed a steady constriction of popular political participation, particularly by the least advantaged Americans (including millions of new immigrants from eastern and southern Europe), and the rise of the elite, managerial rule by the modern industrial corporation. The growing hole in the electorate defined an emptied plebian space.

Democratic government, once intensely local, became increasingly centralized and insulated from popular scrutiny and control—much of it in the hands of unelected experts recruited from a new, college-educated middle class. The political party was first supplemented and then, to a large degree, supplanted by the specialized interest group as the extraconstitutional means of popular participation in government. Popular politics did enjoy a modest resurgence in the midst of the Great Depression, thanks in large measure to the prominence of labor unions in the councils of the Democratic Party. But the decay of union power after the 1960s again limited the collective political power of the working class, which lacked the clout and the resources available to other interests. Finally, the formidable national security state created to project American power overseas during the cold war shrouded in secrecy a host of exceptionally significant public decisions, not least the decision to go to war.

In this new context, democratic citizenship, once raucously collective, became increasingly atomized. An electorate once mobilized as active armies of partisan soldiers was now seen as individual consumers, targeted in the privacy of their homes with advertising that was guided by opinion polling and mediated by radio, television, and, of late, the Internet. "As the People dissolved," Wiebe observed, "the state thrived. . . . As the modern state solidified, it filled the spaces that a disintegrating People vacated, then rolled on to create empires of its own."

Market Capitalism and Political Equality

If American democracy began with a political revolution in the service of small property owners, it was thus transformed by an economic and social revolution led by large-scale manufacturers and finance capitalists, one that remade yeoman farmers and artisans into tenant farmers and industrial laborers. The relationship between market capitalism and American democracy has been particularly important in shaping the fate of political equality in the United States.

As Dahl has observed, the relationship between capitalism and democracy is one of "antagonistic symbiosis." They are "like two persons bound in a tempestuous marriage that is riven by conflict and yet endures because neither partner wishes to separate from the other." All modern democracies have market-capitalist economies (though not all nations with market-capitalist economies are democracies). A market economy, which decentralizes control over production and consumption, has proven more accommodating to egalitarian politics than the centralizing alternatives, such as fascism and state socialism. A market economy, which diffuses economic power to a greater degree than state-managed command economies, seems necessary, if not sufficient, to political democracy.

Yet, at the same time, capitalism generates deep economic and social inequities that threaten democracy by producing enormous disparities in wealth, income, status, prestige, information, organization, education, and knowledge. As Dahl writes, "Because of inequalities in political resources, some citizens gain significantly more influence than others over the government's policies, decisions, and actions. . . . Consequently, citizens are not political equals—far from it—and thus the moral foundation of democracy, political equality among citizens, is seriously violated."

Dahl's concerns are hardly new. Anxiety about the effects of economic inequality on political equality date from the earliest days of the republic. In 1792 James Madison, who had moved closer since 1787 to his friend Jefferson's equation of republicanism and democracy, proposed that Americans could go a good way toward ensuring political equality "by withholding *unnecessary* opportunities from a few, to increase the inequality of property by an immoderate, and especially unmerited, accumulation of riches," as well as "by the silent operation of the laws, which, without violating the rights of property, reduce extreme wealth towards a state of mediocrity, and raise extreme indigence toward a state of comfort."

American citizens afflicted by political inequality have followed Madison's advice, often turning to the state for interventions and regulations to deter the inequitable effects of capitalism, seeking to sustain the benefits of a market economy while addressing the harm it does to political equality. The results have included not only reforms, such as campaign finance regulations that directly target the effects of economic inequities on political democracy but also measures such as public education, progressive income taxation, and social welfare legislation that do so indirectly.

In Theory

Since Jefferson's time, Americans have played a significant role in the history not only of democratic practice but of democratic thought. They not only provided raw material for Tocqueville's great meditation on democracy but have made important contributions to democracy's intellectual legacy, some of them fit to stand with his. The history of democratic thought would be much the poorer were it not for Jefferson, Madison, Frederick Douglass, Elizabeth Cady Stanton, Walt Whitman, Henry George, Jane Addams, Herbert Croly, Dewey, Walter Lippmann, Reinhold Niebuhr, Martin Luther King Jr., Hannah Arendt, Christopher Lasch, John Rawls, Richard Rorty, and Robert Dahl—to name but a few American democratic thinkers of distinction.

Not surprisingly, American democratic theory has been closely attuned to American democratic practice. For all its variety, much of American democratic thought, particularly since the late nineteenth century, can be construed as a debate in which the nation's practical detour from the ideal of robust and effective democratic participation is either a necessary accommodation to circumstance or a contingent and unhappy U-turn away from political equality.

Pitting those who might be termed democratic realists against those who might be called democratic idealists, this debate remains important for the future of American democracy.

Walter Lippmann made the characteristic realist case in *Public Opinion* (1922). Most citizens, he wrote, were incapable of grasping the dynamics of a complex, interdependent, modern world, and should not be expected to do so: "the common interests very largely elude public opinion entirely, and can be managed only by a specialized class." Most democrats had erred in placing an emphasis on self-government. Men do not desire "self-government for its own sake. They desire it for the sake of results." Modern democracies were better served by a minimum of public participation in political life; too much participation gummed up the works, or worse. The criterion to assess a government was thus not the extent to which citizens were self-governing but "whether it is producing a certain minimum of health, of decent housing, of material necessities, of education, of freedom, of pleasures, of beauty." In sum, government *for* the people did not require much government *by* the people.

John Dewey responded with an idealist counter a few years later. He acknowledged that Lippmann's was "perhaps the most effective indictment of democracy as currently conceived ever penned." Yet in light of this indictment, he argued, the task for democrats was not to lower their sights, as Lippmann advised, but to figure out a way to rematerialize the "phantom public" and provide it with a much more substantial governing role in democratic politics. "The old saying that the cure for the ills of democracy is more democracy is not apt if it means that the evils may be remedied by introducing more machinery of the same kind as that which already exists, or by refining and perfecting that machinery," Dewey said. "But the phrase may also indicate the need of returning to the idea itself, of clarifying and deepening our sense of its meaning to criticize and re-make its political manifestations." And the "idea itself," as Dewey saw it, was in the broadest sense that of self-government. As he put it in 1888 at the outset of his long career as an oft-disappointed but never daunted democrat, "the ethical ideal is not satisfied merely when all men sound the note of harmony with the highest social good, so be it that they have not worked it out for themselves." Government *for* the people was inextricable from government *by* the people.

In the concluding pages of *Democracy in America*, Tocqueville suggested that "the kind of oppression with which democratic peoples are threatened will resemble nothing that has preceded it in the world." He imagined a democratic citizen oxymoronically invested largely in private life: "As for dwelling with his fellow citizens, he is beside them, but he does not see them; he touches them and does not feel them; he exists only for himself and for himself alone, and if a family still remains for him, one can at least say that he no longer has a native country." Such citizens would be subject to a state less tyrannical than protective:

It would resemble paternal power if, like that, it had for its object to prepare men for manhood; but on the contrary, it seeks only to keep them fixed irrevocably in childhood; it likes citizens to enjoy themselves provided that they think only of enjoying themselves. It willingly works for their happiness; but it wants to be the unique agent and sole arbiter of that; it provides for their security, foresees and secures their needs, facilitates their pleasures, conducts their principal affairs, directs their industry, regulates their estates, divides their inheritances; can it not take away from them entirely the trouble of thinking and the pain of living?

This is not a scenario that cost democratic realists much sleep at night. They are minimalists, wedded to Joseph Schumpeter's definition of democracy as little more than "that institutional arrangement for arriving at political decisions in which individuals acquire the power to decide by means of a competitive struggle for the people's vote"—a return to strictly virtual representation by elite "deciders." But Tocqueville's vision is the specter that haunts the nightmares of democratic idealists who refuse to admit that the ideals of political equality have fallen over the horizon.

See also Constitution, federal; Declaration of Independence; liberalism; republicanism.

FURTHER READING. Robert A. Dahl, *How Democratic Is the American Constitution?* 2001; Idem, *On Democracy*, 1998; Russell L. Hanson, *The Democratic Imagination in America*, 1985; Alexander Keyssar, *The Right to Vote*, revised ed., 2009; Michael McGerr, *The Decline of Popular Politics: The American North, 1865–1928*, 1986; Alexis de Tocqueville, *Democracy in America*, translated by Harvey Mansfield and Delba Winthrop, 2000; Robert B. Westbrook, *John Dewey and American Democracy*, 1991; Robert Wiebe, *Self-Rule: A Cultural History of American Democracy*, 1995; Sean Wilentz, *The Rise of American Democracy: From Jefferson to Lincoln*, 2005; Gordon S. Wood, *The Radicalism of the American Revolution*, 1992.

ROBERT WESTBROOK

Democratic Party, 1800–2008

Any party that endures for more than two centuries must learn to adapt to shifting historical circumstances. The Democratic Party has existed in some form since the 1790s, and its influence on American politics has been as long and profound as that of any private institution. That influence has always depended upon the party's ability to shift its ideology, policies, and leaders when necessary to win or hold power at every level of government.

Only 16 of the 43 presidents elected in competitive elections have been Democrats, but 5 of those chief executives—Thomas Jefferson, Andrew Jackson, Woodrow Wilson, Franklin Roosevelt, and Lyndon Johnson—altered the shape of American politics and of their party in lasting ways. One can trace those changes in three significant areas: *ideas, policies*, and *constituent groups*.

The Party of Jefferson and Jackson

Unlike most political organizations, the Democratic Party was not created on a specific date. Partisans of Andrew Jackson first adopted the name in the mid-1820s, but the seeds of "the Democracy" were planted in the 1790s. It was then that Democratic-Republican societies proliferated to support the views of Thomas Jefferson, who was engaged in conflict with Alexander Hamilton over what powers the new federal government should wield and whether it should take a friendly or hostile stance toward the French Revolution. By the time Jefferson won the presidency in 1800, most of his allies were calling themselves Democratic-Republicans as well. His victory and reelection relegated the opposition party, the Federalists, to the status of a permanent minority before it expired altogether during the War of 1812.

Into the 1820s, the Democratic-Republicans sought to keep faith with their founding leader's advocacy of states' rights and a weak federal role in the economy. As Jefferson had stated in his first State of the Union address, "the States themselves have principal care of our persons, our property, and our reputation . . . agriculture, manufactures, commerce, and navigation" are "most thriving when left most free to individual enterprise." He also left a legacy of informality in office—he sometimes greeted visitors in a dressing gown and slippers—and a creed of religious tolerance at a time when some states still had an established church to which all residents had to pay taxes.

But it took the partnership of Martin Van Buren and Andrew Jackson to transform the party now called the Democrats into an efficient electoral machine that competed successfully in a new era when most white men had the right to vote. This change began during the second half of the 1820s. In the election of 1824, Jackson lost the election for president, although he had received more popular votes than the victor, John Quincy Adams. In the aftermath Van Buren, "The Little Magician" from New York State, secured the allegiance of influential politicians up and down the East Coast and helped establish pro-Jackson newspapers from New England down to Louisiana. In 1828 Jackson swept to victory, as voter participation more than doubled from the previous campaign.

From that watershed year until the eve of the Civil War, Democrats won all but two presidential elections and usually controlled both houses of Congress. They espoused policies that managed to please a broad coalition of white immigrants in the cities, southern planters, and Americans of every region who favored conquering and settling the entire continent. Democrats welcomed Catholic immigrants, opposed laws to prohibit alcohol or ban the use of languages other than English in public schools, and wanted to keep taxes, especially on imports, as low as possible. In vetoing a bill to recharter the (Second) Bank of the United States, Jackson aligned the party with anyone who resented powerful financial interests. Every Democratic president before the Civil War defended slavery on the basis of both states' rights and white supremacy. But party leaders had no solution to the deepening sectional crisis of the 1850s. In the election of 1860, Democrats split apart along the North-South divide and ran two opposing national tickets. Their rift virtually ensured the election of Abraham Lincoln, the first Republican president. It would be more than seven decades before the Democrats regained their status as the majority party.

Although the party elected just one president—Grover Cleveland, twice—during the remainder of the nineteenth century, Democrats were not without power. They remained strongly entrenched in the commercial metropoles of New York, Chicago, and San Francisco as well as in the South and most border states. The swelling of immigration from Catholic Europe to the urban North and fear of "Negro domination" in Dixie strengthened the party's appeal in both regions. One consequence was that the Democrats controlled the House of Representatives through much of the 1870s and 1880s and kept the GOP's majority in the Senate to a handful of seats.

The Gilded Age Democracy was a lively party indeed. Urban machines, while they made their bosses rich, also bestowed jobs and charity on working-class residents at a time when federal welfare payments went mainly to veterans of the Union Army and their nearest kin. Tammany Hall, the largest and most notorious of the machines, was a prodigious font of municipal jobs and contracts; in the late 1870s one of every twelve family men in New York held a position with the city. During each campaign, Tammany and its counterparts in cities across the nation held massive street parades, fireworks displays, and free banquets.

Democrats after the Civil War, however, had done little to alter their ideology or policies. With few prominent exceptions, they continued to preach a doctrine better suited to a decentralized, agrarian society than to a nation filling up with industries and big cities. Party stalwarts still tried to safeguard the powers of individual states, to curb federal spending, and to oppose agitators for such reform causes as prohibition, woman suffrage, and the redistribution of wealth. After helping to end Reconstruction, Democrats rebuilt a base in the Solid South, where ex-Confederates erected a "redeemed" social order that terrorized black voters it could not control and eviscerated funding for education and medical care. Critics of the party dubbed its leaders "Bourbons,"

a reference to the last kings of France, about whom a diplomat quipped that they "had learned nothing and forgotten nothing."

The Bryan-Wilson Shift

In the 1890s, the Democrats finally made a change. Across the South and West, movements of farmers and workers were demanding relief from what they saw as corporate domination of the economy and politics. They called on the government to protect union organizing, to create public works jobs for the unemployed, and to establish a flexible money supply that could give relief to debtors and small businesspeople. Some of the disgruntled joined the new People's Party which espoused this ambitious agenda. As the economy fell into depression, President Grover Cleveland, who had been elected to a second term in 1892, opposed all those demands and sent federal troops to break a national railroad strike. "Though the people support the government," Cleveland intoned, "the government should not support the people." In the midterm elections of 1894, the party lost 121 House seats, the worst drubbing in its history.

Many Democratic officeholders realized their survival was at stake, and they repudiated Cleveland and the laissez-faire tradition he was struggling to uphold. In 1896 the party nominated for president William Jennings Bryan, a 36-year-old former congressman from Nebraska who identified himself with the agrarian and labor insurgencies. In a dramatic speech at the party's national convention, Bryan claimed, "The Democratic idea" was to "legislate to make the masses prosperous" and "their prosperity will find its way up through every class which rests upon them." He lost the election that fall to William McKinley, a far better organized and financed candidate. But Bryan persuaded most Democrats to endorse a progressive, interventionist state, and the party never reverted to Cleveland's philosophy.

In 1912 the Republicans split into warring camps, allowing Woodrow Wilson to win the presidency and the Democrats to build large majorities in both houses of Congress. During his eight years in office, Wilson spearheaded passage of a legislative program, known as the New Freedom, which assumed the need for an active state to counterbalance the power of big business. The program included a new antitrust act, the creation of the Federal Reserve System, and some protection for unions—most of which had become part of the Democratic coalition.

Only in their ideas and policies about race did Bryan, Wilson, and most of their fellow Democrats remain true to the views of Jefferson and Jackson. In the South legislators rammed through Jim Crow laws that confined African Americans to a separate and unequal sphere of both public and private life and effectively disenfranchised millions of black citizens. One of Wilson's first acts as president was to segregate most jobs in the federal government, and he raised no objection to anti-Asian laws that

Democrats on the West Coast were enacting. Most Democrats remained proud of belonging to a party for whites only.

Under Wilson, Americans also began to pay income taxes that made new federal programs possible, as well as raising funds for the troops who helped the United States and its allies win the World War I. In eloquent calls for a new democratic world order, the president also convinced his fellow Democrats that only international cooperation could stop future armed conflicts. However, many Americans resisted Wilson's demand that the United States join the new League of Nations he had proposed. They also feared the new immigrants from eastern and southern Europe, most of whom voted for Democrats. As a result, Republicans won three straight presidential elections during the 1920s, landslides every one.

FDR's Nation

Democrats returned to power with unprecedented force during the Great Depression of the 1930s. In winning four consecutive races for president, Franklin D. Roosevelt established his party as the majority in every region of the country except for northern New England and the rural Midwest. To their older bases among white Southerners and urban Catholics, the Democrats under FDR added millions of workers in a booming labor movement as well as Jews and African Americans—the latter deserted the party of Lincoln in gratitude for public works jobs and the antiracist commitment of First Lady Eleanor Roosevelt. Most intellectuals also gave their allegiance to a party that welcomed their ideas and participation in policy making.

Their electoral dominance enabled the Democrats to institute a New Deal order that greatly expanded the power of the federal government in the lives of its citizens. The political scientist Samuel Lubell once wrote that the major parties in the United States are not "two equally competing suns, but a sun and a moon. It is within the majority party that the issues of the day are fought out; while the minority party shines in the reflected radiance of the heat thus generated." During the 1930s and early 1940s, the Democrats who ruled Congress wrangled constantly but ended up passing such landmark programs as Social Security, the National Labor Relations Act, the Wages and Hours Act, and the GI Bill—while their Republican opponents could only grumble from the cooler margins.

Even though Dwight Eisenhower twice won the presidency in the 1950s, he made no attempt to repeal these popular policies. Ike was in position to occupy the White House only because he had been one of the top military commanders during World War II—a conflict most Republicans had wanted the United States to avoid before the Japanese attack on Pearl Harbor. Although FDR died just before the war ended, he had ensured that Democrats would continue to uphold his Wilsonian vision. Under President Harry Truman, the party became an enthusiastic promoter of the United Nations, as well the creator of a multinational alliance that waged a cold war against communism everywhere in the world. In 1948 Democrats endorsed a civil rights plank at their national convention; in protest, white delegates from the Deep South walked out of the hall and ran their own States' Rights, or "Dixiecrat," ticket.

Kennedy, Johnson, and the Watershed of the 1960s

In the early 1960s, most liberals were confident they could lead the United States into a new era of sweeping change under the aggressive, idealistic leadership of President John F. Kennedy. Apart from those southern whites who were hostile to the black freedom movement, the New Deal coalition held intact, and close to 60 percent of voters nationwide identified themselves as Democrats. Kennedy's assassination in 1963 helped Lyndon Johnson win reelection by a landslide the following year and give the Democrats majorities of 2 to 1 in both the House and Senate. Wielding the club of power like a wand, LBJ got Congress to enact a Great Society program as ambitious as the New Deal and one that, unlike in FDR's day, was committed to racial equality. Medicare, Medicaid, the National Endowment for the Humanities, the Voting Rights Act, a major change in immigration policy, and Head Start and other antipoverty initiatives all became law during Johnson's presidency. He also continued the cold war policies of JFK when he sent thousands of troops to combat a Communist-led insurgency in Vietnam.

But the new dawn of liberalism proved ephemeral. Beginning in 1965, events tore apart the coalition that had kept the Democrats on top during most of the years since the Great Depression. Riots in black communities scared white wage earners and convinced them to vote for candidates who promised to restore "law and order." Students on elite liberal campuses who protested the Vietnam War and reveled in drug taking and sexual promiscuity alienated many older Americans who revered the military and had not attended college. The enemy in Vietnam fought the United States to a standstill, while inflationary pressures and overseas competition began to stall the economy that had grown through most of the decade. Suddenly, Democrats appeared to be the party of failure. In 1966 they lost almost 50 seats in the House of Representatives; in 1968, after coverage of Chicago police beating up antiwar demonstrators on live TV, they also lost the presidency, as Vice President Hubert Humphrey received less than 43 percent of the popular vote.

During the next four decades, party activists struggled to accommodate themselves to a more conservative era. Republicans won all but three of the presidential contests held between 1968 and 2004. The Democratic exceptions—Jimmy Carter in 1976 and Bill Clinton in 1992 and 1996—did not call themselves liberals and triumphed in part because as

Baptists from the South, they were able to win back a large number of white Protestants from that region who had deserted their ancestral political home. Clinton was also a leader of the Democratic Leadership Council, a group founded in 1985 that was determined to steer the party to the ideological center.

Nationally, from the 1970s through the 1990s, Democrats rarely descended to minority status and controlled Congress more often than did their Republican opponents. Most Americans continued to favor the limited welfare-state programs that Democrats had advocated throughout the twentieth century and enacted, whenever possible. Many citizens also gradually warmed to gender equality, environmental protection, and even homosexual rights—all of which liberal Democrats had helped to pioneer. Still, a majority of voters tended to give the benefit of the doubt to any politician who railed against big government and embraced "traditional values," and most of those were Republicans. As the percentage of union members in the workforce declined, well-educated professionals and African Americans became the most reliable elements in the Democratic coalition. Because those two groups were concentrated in just a few big states, it was difficult for the party's nominees to gain a majority in the Electoral College.

But during President George W. Bush's second term, Democrats again began to think that they could wrest control of the political agenda. Bush's perceived failures both at home and abroad made conservatism itself seem an ideology whose time had passed. Young people, in particular, had begun to register and vote Democratic in large numbers even before the party nominated Barack Obama for president in 2008. Latino Americans were increasingly rejecting the GOP as well, due in part to the nativist views of many Republican officeholders. In 2006 the Democrats regained control of both houses of Congress for the first time since the early 1990s. Loyalists in America's oldest political party seemed poised for another era in the sun.

Indeed, in 2008, the Democrats won their most impressive victory since the Johnson landslide of 1964. After a long and, at times, bitter primary campaign, Barack Obama won the presidential nomination and went on to gain an easy victory in the fall. Obama, the only African American ever to be nominated by a major party, outpaced his Republican rival, John McCain, by almost 200 electoral votes and close to 10 million popular votes. And he won three important states—Indiana, North Carolina, and Virginia—that no Democrat had carried since Lyndon B. Johnson 44 years earlier. Obama's triumph was one of party as well as personality. Democrats padded their majorities in both houses of Congress.

But the elation—in much of the world as well as at home—that followed Obama's victory was coupled with fear about the deep recession that had soured most voters in the United States on the probusiness

Republican Party. The opportunity for Obama and his fellow Democrats to preside over a new New Deal probably depended on their ability to solve the economic crisis and to convince Americans that the federal government could once again be trusted to improve the fortunes of ordinary citizens.

See also elections and electoral eras; presidency.

FURTHER READING. John Ashworth, *Slavery, Capitalism, and Politics in the Antebellum Republic*, 2 vols., 1995, 2007; Steven Gillon, *The Democrat's Dilemma: Walter F. Mondale and the Liberal Legacy*, 1992; Richard Hofstadter, *The Idea of a Party System*, 1969; David Sarasohn, *The Party of Reform: Democrats in the Progressive Era*, 1989; Arthur Schlesinger, Jr., *The Age of Roosevelt*, 3 vols., 1957, 1958, 1960; Sean Wilentz, *The Rise of American Democracy*, 2005.

MICHAEL KAZIN

Democratic Party, 1800–28

The Democratic Party, or Democratic-Republican Party as it first called itself, began to form early in George Washington's first administration (1789–93). Led by Thomas Jefferson in the cabinet and James Madison in the House of Representatives, the party opposed Alexander Hamilton's financial measures: the funding of the national debt in a way that benefited speculators, the assumption of state debts, the chartering of the first Bank of the United States, and the levying of numerous taxes. This division was further deepened by foreign policy and personality conflicts. Hamilton and his followers wanted the United States to align itself with Great Britain during the wars of the French Revolution, while Jefferson and Madison were anti-English and argued that the United States should live up to its treaty obligations with France, which dated back to 1778. By the end of the 1790s, the division had gone beyond specific policy issues to include differences over how to interpret the U.S. Constitution, the nature of the Union, and the kind of country America should become.

Actually, the Founding Fathers did not believe that political parties had any legitimacy or value. The Constitution made no provision for political parties. Moreover, they were generally viewed as dangerous to the stability of the Republic. The Federalists denounced the opposition associated with Jefferson and Madison as misguided, self-interested, obstructionist, and encouraging anarchy by opposing the authority of the government. The Democratic-Republicans portrayed the Federalists as essentially tyrants and monarchists intent on undermining the Republican principles of the American Revolution, and therefore determined to overthrow them. In the beginning of Washington's administration, the differences between the political combatants were confined to disputes within the government itself, to cabinet meetings and debates in Congress. But soon each side established newspapers to criticize its opponents and advocate its points of view to the broader public. When Washington left office in 1797, he denounced the development of political parties.

As the 1790s wore on, the Democratic-Republicans, especially in the Middle Atlantic states of Pennsylvania, New York, and New Jersey, increasingly resorted to public meetings, parades, demonstrations, and the establishment of various committees to direct their election campaigns by publishing addresses to the voters, circulating handbills and leaflets, and holding meetings. Following the Democratic-Republican victory in 1800 and the ascendancy of the Jeffersonians during the first few decades of the nineteenth century, many of these organizations remained active. Nonetheless, the Jeffersonians never fully embraced party development. Thus, when James Monroe was reelected president with only one vote cast against him, they celebrated it as an indication that the country had returned to the consensual ideal that had manifested itself in Washington's unanimous elections as president. Not until the very late 1820s and 1830s were political parties accepted as a development and a permanent fixture on the political scene.

With the exception of a brief period (1793–95) when the Democratic-Republicans captured control of the House of Representatives, they were a minority party throughout the 1790s. Following Washington's retirement from politics in 1796, the first contested election for the presidency took place, but the Federalist candidate John Adams defeated Jefferson by 71 electoral votes to 68. Since the Constitution at that time required the vice presidency to go the person with the second highest number of electoral votes, Jefferson assumed the position of presiding officer of the United States Senate, and while he had no influence on the making of policy, he continued to lead the opposition.

The Democratic-Republican Party finally gained control of both the presidency and Congress in the election of 1800. Geographically, its support was mainly in the Middle Atlantic and southern states, as well in large parts of northern New England (New Hampshire and Vermont; and what is now Maine, then still part of Massachusetts). It also had support in the new western states of Kentucky and Tennessee. The party included former Anti-Federalists, who called themselves Old Republicans because they strongly believed in a weak central government and limited executive power—the prevailing view at the time of the Revolution, but one the Old Republicans believed had been abandoned with the adoption of the U.S. Constitution in 1787–88. Support for the Democratic-Republican Party came from different classes that included slaveholding Virginia tobacco growers and South Carolina rice planters, but also most self-sufficient farmers and others who had at best only tenuous connection with the market. Also in the Democratic-Republican camp were most Baptists, Methodists, and members of other evangelical protestant denominations, along with Deists, Unitarians, and Universalists. Many of these people, unlike the Old Republicans, were not necessarily against the Constitution per se but objected to the specific policies implemented under its authority.

The Democratic-Republicans did not promulgate a formal platform in the election of 1800. But they did make their beliefs known by means of resolutions issued by the states of Kentucky and Virginia (1798) disputing the constitutionality of the Alien and Sedition Acts and arguing that the Constitution was a compact made by the states in which the powers not specifically granted to the federal government belonged to the states. They also found expression in pamphlets, essays in newspapers, campaign handbills, and private letters. In addition to strong support of states' rights, Democratic-Republicans advocated a frugal and simple central government, opposition to a standing army, and a reduction of the national debt.

The presidential election of 1800 turned out to be much more complicated than anyone anticipated. Jefferson defeated Adams's bid for reelection by eight electoral votes, 73 to 65. However, Jefferson's vice presidential candidate, Aaron Burr, also received 73 electoral votes. The tie meant that the election would be decided by the lame duck Federalist-dominated House of Representatives that had been elected in 1798, with each state having one vote. Although some Federalists failed to swing the election to Burr, they did manage to prevent Jefferson from getting the requisite majority. Jefferson was elected when a number of key Federalists withdrew their opposition, perhaps with the understanding that they would not be persecuted nor Hamilton's economic policies repudiated in a Jefferson administration.

Jefferson was sworn in as the third president of the United States on March 4, 1801. This was a particularly significant development because it was the first time under the U.S. Constitution that the out-party had peacefully assumed power with the cooperation of its defeated opponents. Equally significant, the Democratic-Republicans gained control of Congress, thus beginning a 24-year period of hegemony over the federal government that lasted through the administrations of Jefferson (1801–9), James Madison (1809–17), and James Monroe (1817–25).

Jefferson's assumption of the presidency raised important constitutional and even ideological issues. Was there simply to be a change in the personnel and policies of the new administration, or were changes to be made to the Constitution itself? To what extent was the Democratic-Republican victory in 1800 a popular mandate for the new administration to do whatever it wanted? Since the election had been particularly bitter, did the incoming administration need, in some way, to consider the interests and feelings of the defeated minority and make an effort to heal the wounds of the country? How, in particular, was Jefferson to reconcile his position as president of all the people with his position as a party leader?

In the quarter century that followed, not all Democratic-Republicans agreed on the answers to these questions. At the most important level, the Old Republicans wanted basic changes to the U.S. Constitution in order to weaken the powers of the central government and executive branch and to shorten the terms of office of senators. On the other hand, the more nationalist members of the Democratic-Republican Party, led by James Madison—who more than anyone else had helped create the Constitution—feared and opposed such changes. Sharp internal differences existed within the party over such issues as whether to repudiate Hamilton's financial measures and what to do about Federalist control of the national judiciary. Although Jefferson had some sympathy with the concerns of the Old Republican wing of the party, he opted for a policy of moderation and reconciliation.

But the Democratic-Republican Party, having achieved power, did not "out-Federalize" the Federalists. It reduced the size of the army and navy, significantly lowered internal taxes, and generally cut government spending to ensure the accumulation of surpluses that were used to pay off the national debt. Most important, the Democratic-Republicans acquired additional territory for the United States through wars and treaties with Native Americans, the Louisiana Purchase, and the buying of Florida. They encouraged settlement of the West by allowing people to buy land on credit.

During the first two decades of the nineteenth century the Democratic-Republicans effectively shifted the attention of the country from its involvement in the Atlantic economy to its own internal economic development. The most concrete manifestation of this was the number of new states admitted to the union between 1800 and 1820: Ohio (1803), Louisiana (1812), Indiana (1816), Mississippi (1817), Illinois (1818), Alabama (1819), Missouri (1820), and Maine (1820). This was also a period of rapid economic growth. Older urban areas like New York, Philadelphia, Baltimore, and New Orleans grew rapidly during these years, and various boomtowns like Pittsburgh, Pennsylvania; Lexington and Louisville, Kentucky; Cincinnati, Ohio; St. Louis, Missouri; Nashville, Tennessee; Rochester, New York; and Huntsville, Alabama, also emerged.

Madison's election to the presidency was a major victory for the commercial and national wing of the Democratic-Republican Party. He helped secure the independence of the federal judiciary by threatening to use force against Pennsylvania when it tried to resist a controversial Supreme Court decision, *United States v. Peters* (1809), compelling the state to back down. His appointments of Joseph Story and Gabriel Duvall to the high court were also important because the two men became firm allies of Chief Justice John Marshall. It is no accident that the most important economic and constitutional decisions made under Marshall's leadership occurred following Madison's assumption of the presidency.

At the same time, the numerous diplomatic problems created by the events that led to the War of 1812 brought difficulty and confusion to the Democratic-Republican Party. Jefferson's embargo policy proved controversial and unenforceable, and the drift and confusion that characterized Madison's foreign policy during his first term in office led to a temporary revival of Federalist strength in Congress. Madison also faced various personality and policy conflicts within his cabinet, and the failure of a measure he supported, the rechartering of the first Bank of the United States in 1811, created numerous economic problems and an unstable currency.

Madison was barely reelected president in 1812. The War of 1812 found the country unprepared militarily, and was characterized by chaos, inefficiency, and frequent military defeats, including the burning of Washington, D.C. Still, the results of the War of 1812 worked to Madison's and the Democratic-Republican Party's benefit: a spirit of nationalism prevailed in most parts of the United States, aided and magnified by Andrew Jackson's belated but significant victory at New Orleans.

As a result, during the last two years of his second administration, Madison and his followers were unusually popular and powerful. Significantly, the Federalists who had engaged in obstructionist activities during the war were now discredited as a national party, while the Old Republicans were also in disarray. As a consequence, a protective tariff and a second Bank of the United States were adopted in 1816, and a federal program of internal improvements failed when Madison opposed it for constitutional, not policy, reasons. These measures were later referred to as the American System because their purpose was to develop the domestic economy by making the nation less dependent on foreign trade.

The years immediately following the end of the War of 1812 were ones of agricultural prosperity in most parts of the country outside of New England. Following the Napoleonic Wars, bad weather in Europe created a heavy demand for American meat and grain products. At the same time, British manufacturing interests were willing to pay ever higher prices for American cotton. Within the United States, major transportation changes, which included the building of turnpikes and canals and the development of the steamboat, allowed goods to be shipped to market more quickly and cheaply than ever before and led to a quickening of communication among different parts of the country. During the early decades of the nineteenth century, a legal system that encouraged and protected the country's economic development also evolved. Perhaps most important, the United States underwent a major financial revolution built on the proliferation of banks, which made capital easily available and increased the money supply, lubricating the economy and replacing the older barter system used by small farmers in economic transactions.

James Monroe's presidency is frequently referred to as the "era of good feeling." At best, the term is misleading. While no formal opposition party existed on the national level and the various constitutional and ideological struggles of the prewar period were muted, politics now involved struggles for power, the control of patronage, and special privileges on the local level. The result was that, with a few exceptions (mainly in New York and Pennsylvania) popular participation in politics tended to be low between 1815 and 1819.

This development did not disturb many Democratic-Republicans because they did not believe in a robust two-party system in which issues could be debated openly and the mass of the people could make the final decision at the polls. Most Democratic-Republicans believed political leaders were chosen because of their demonstrated superiority in education, experience, and achievement. They stressed consensus, compromise, and for the most part—at least outwardly—a harmony of interests. They also stressed a separation between the making of public policy by elites and participation in the development of a market economy by the mass of people that had been the object of their economic policies.

For the Democratic-Republicans, the congressional nominating caucus was the most important manifestation of how politics should operate. It consisted of members of the party from both houses of Congress, which selected the party's presidential candidate. The practice had started during the election of 1800 and continued through 1824. This nomination was the most important step in a presidential race because, with the exception of the election of 1812, selection by the caucus was tantamount to election during the first two decades of the nineteenth century. The caucus played a key role in 1808, selecting Madison over Monroe despite opposition by a number of important Old Republicans lead by John Randolph, John Taylor, Nathaniel Macon, and George Clinton, who were critical of Madison's constitutional nationalism and believed he had not been sufficiently extreme in his opposition to the Hamilton-inspired financial system after Jefferson's election. Madison was renominated in 1812, but DeWitt Clinton, an important Democratic-Republican from New York, openly aligned himself with a number of New England Federalists and other discontented Democratic-Republicans to oppose Madison's reelection. The election was extremely close, but Madison won. From that point, Clinton, who remained a major force in New York politics, was effectively barred from the national arena. In fact, Madison and Monroe used their control of the federal patronage to aid Clinton's opponents in New York. In 1816 Monroe received the caucus nomination, defeating William H. Crawford of Georgia by a vote of 65 to 54.

Unlike Clinton, Crawford accepted the caucus decision and supported Monroe, who went on to an easy victory. For his part, Crawford accepted an appointment as secretary of the treasury in Monroe's cabinet, and was generally considered to be his heir apparent: he was expected to receive the caucus nomination for president in 1824 after Monroe served his two terms in office.

But, by 1824, when Crawford did receive it, the caucus nomination meant little. The Democratic-Republican Party had begun to disintegrate under several pressures: the Panic of 1819 and the depression that followed, the states' rights reaction to the U.S. Supreme Court's nationalist decisions, the debate over the growth and expansion of slavery and the Missouri Compromise, and the emergence of Andrew Jackson as a national political figure. The Panic of 1819 was particularly important because it increased interest in politics among enfranchised white males who believed the making of economic policy should no longer be left in the hands of elites. As a consequence, the congressional caucus had become outdated by 1824, attended by less than one-third of its members. Instead, the various other candidates for the presidency (Andrew Jackson, John Q. Adams, Henry Clay, and John C. Calhoun) were selected by various state nominating conventions or by local resolutions.

The 1820s was also characterized by the development of sectionalism. It was linked in part to the growth of slavery, for the development of the cotton culture in the Old Southwest (Alabama, Mississippi, central and western Tennessee, and Louisiana) undercut the Jeffersonian view that slavery was a dying institution. But economic issues were the main focus of sectionalism. The struggle over a protective tariff and the push for a national bankruptcy law divided the country primarily along North-South lines, but the debate over a federal program of internal improvements and national land policy involved a contest between the East and West. As a consequence, the sectionalism of the 1820s tended to be kaleidoscopic, shifting from issue to issue and therefore different from the sectionalism that developed during the 1850s between the free and slave states.

In the ensuing presidential election of 1824, Jackson received a plurality of both the electoral and popular vote, but the House of Representatives chose Adams, who came in second in each category, on the first ballot. As president, Adams continued to espouse the American System and the older elitist view of politics, going so far at one point as to urge Congress not to be "palsied by the will of our constituents." During his administration, the Democratic-Republican Party divided into two groups. Adams and his supporters, led by Clay, became known as the National Republicans, which became the core of the Whig Party in the 1830s. Jackson's supporters became known as the Democratic Party and took most of their values from the Old Republicans.

There is no connection between the Democratic-Republicans and the Republican Party that emerged in 1854. There are, however, very real organizational ties between the Democratic-Republicans and the Democratic Party of today.

See also Republican Party to 1896.

FURTHER READING. Noble E. Cunningham, Jr., "The Jeffersonian Republican Party," in *History of U.S. Political Parties*, vol. 1, edited by Arthur M. Schlesinger Jr., 1973; Richard E. Ellis, *Aggressive Nationalism: McCulloch v. Maryland and the Foundations of Federal Authority in the Young Republic*, 2007; Idem, "The Market Revolution and the Transformation of American Politics, 1801–1837," in *The Market Revolution in America: Social, Political, and Religious Expressions, 1800–1880*, edited by Melvyn Stokes and Stephen Conway, 1996; William W. Freehling, *The Road to Disunion: Secessionists at Bay, 1776–1854*, 1994; Daniel Walter Howe, *What God Hath Wrought: The Transformation of America, 1815–1848*, 2007; Merrill D. Peterson, *The Great Triumvirate: Webster, Clay, and Calhoun*, 1987; Charles Sellers, *The Market Revolution: Jacksonian America, 1815–1846*, 1991; Leonard White, *The Jeffersonians: A Study in Administrative History, 1801–1829*, 1951; Sean Wilentz, *The Rise of American Democracy*, 2005.

RICHARD E. ELLIS

Democratic Party, 1828–60

The Democratic Party was the dominant political organization of the antebellum republic. Although never entirely united and in fact prone to periodic schism and fracture, it commanded a degree of loyalty and reverence that made it more like a church than a political party. To its most dedicated supporters it was indissolubly linked to American democracy and freedom, and to the nation itself.

The party nevertheless presents the historian with some problems. As the splits and divisions that punctuate its history confirm, it was never monolithic. Moreover, it went through major changes in the generation between the election of Andrew Jackson and the republic's collapse in 1861: the issues of the 1850s were, for the most part, not those of the 1820s, and the party responded accordingly, despite continuities of personnel and policy and the ideological assumptions governing both.

Early Years

A sharp ideological focus was not apparent when the party came into existence in the 1820s. Andrew Jackson, its standard-bearer in that decade, first acquired fame not for the principles he propounded but for the triumphs he had secured on the military battlefield. As a slayer of Native Americans and the British (most conspicuously at the Battle of New Orleans in 1815), Jackson attracted public attention and—even more important—the attention of politicos who wished to find a winning candidate for the presidential election of 1824. Jackson was bolstered by disparate groups, with different motives in different sections and even

states of the Union, but among his core supporters were some who feared that speculation and a newly emerging financial and political elite threatened the traditional values of the republic. Some had been disturbed by the Panic of 1819, which suggested that the commercial growth of the era had been purchased at the expense of the rural simplicity that Thomas Jefferson had extolled and that many believed essential to the preservation of American democracy. These groups and these perceptions would come to dominate the Democratic Party later, but they were merely one element among many in the party's earliest days.

In the presidential election of 1824, Jackson received a plurality of both popular ballots and votes in the electoral college. But with no outright winner, the election went into the House of Representatives and John Quincy Adams of Massachusetts, son of former president John Adams, was elected, thanks to support from a third group, the supporters of Henry Clay. When Adams then appointed Clay secretary of state, Jackson's supporters, together with the "Old Hero" Jackson himself, were outraged by what they believed had been a "corrupt bargain" that had cheated the American public of their rightful president. The election of 1824, together with the corrupt bargain charge, was of enormous importance to the Democratic Party. Partisans repeated the charge ad nauseam for the next four years while Jackson and his supporters identified their cause with that of American democracy itself. This identification would remain in place for a generation. The Democratic Party was confirmed, in the eyes of its members and even some of its enemies, as the party of American democracy.

As yet, however, Jackson was identified with few specific policies. He favored little more than "retrenchment" (a reduction in federal spending), and "reform" (the principle of rotation in office). On the issue of a protective tariff, he was largely uncommitted, and he had no specific policy toward the second Bank of the United States, which had been chartered in 1816.

The Jackson and Van Buren Presidencies

Having defeated Adams in 1828, however, the party of Jackson began to acquire a more distinctive identity. Four events in the 1820s and early 1830s were decisive. The first, the election of 1824, confirmed Jackson's majoritarianism (despite his failure to obtain a majority of the votes cast). Believing that the electorate had been cheated, he assumed a natural conflict between the people and the elites of the nation.

The second event that played a key role in the creation of a Democratic Party identity concerned Native Americans. By the time Jackson came to office, the Indians in the South and Southwest presented a barrier to the expansion of white America—or so men like Jackson believed. The new president accordingly suggested the "voluntary" removal of Indians in Georgia and elsewhere in the South to west of the Mississippi River. The scheme was tantamount to forced relocation, since the pressures on those who chose to remain would soon become unendurable. During his administration, Jackson and his officials signed dozens of treaties with Native Americans, obtaining in the process some 100 million acres of land. In its impact on the Indians this dispossession and forced relocation constituted one of the greatest tragedies of the antebellum era, such was the suffering endured by its alleged beneficiaries. For the Democratic Party, however, Indian removal contributed to the great strength that Jackson enjoyed in most of the states concerned. When combined with his personal popularity (resting in part upon his earlier military victories against Indians as well as Englishmen), it made his presidency almost unchallengeable in the states most directly affected. On balance, Indian removal was a tremendous vote winner for the Democratic Party in general and for Jackson in particular. Moreover, it reinforced a cardinal tenet of the Democratic creed: the party would advocate "equal rights"—but not for those whose skin was the "wrong" color.

The third major event of Jackson's presidential career concerned the politics of slavery. In the early and mid-1830s, the slavery controversy, relatively quiet since the early 1820s, entered a new era. Some agitators demanded immediate abolition; others insisted that slavery was perpetual in the Union, guaranteed by the Constitution, and, as such, deserving of special protection. The acknowledged leader of the proslavery forces was, by the early 1830s, John C. Calhoun, who had been elected Jackson's vice president but broke with his running mate. He argued that any state, within its own boundaries, had the right to nullify a federal law of which it disapproved. Clearly this was the principle of states' rights driven to its farthest reaches. Jackson's reply to the nullifiers was equally extreme. Unable to see any real threat to slavery, and concluding that Calhoun was driven by the basest of motives, the president condemned nullification as treason. He went further: insisting that the Union was perpetual, he refused to acknowledge that states possessed the right of secession. Indeed, he implied, secession—like nullification—was treason. To remove any ambiguity about his intentions, Jackson asked Congress for a "force bill" allowing him to use troops, if necessary, to collect the federal revenue.

The effect on southern opinion was immediate. Many of the president's supporters in the South balked at the Force Bill of 1833, and his previously unassailable position became vulnerable. His critics now came out into the open. Throughout most of the Middle and Deep South, where Jackson had run so strongly in 1828 and 1832, the results were similar. While most Southerners applauded Jackson's view of nullification, many were reluctant to endorse his view of secession, and, in some cases, the majoritarianism upon which it rested. Though the nullification crisis was soon over, in the next few years, abolitionists

flooded the South with pamphlets, and controversy raged over the reception in Congress of antislavery petitions. The result was a new set of problems for Northerners and Southerners alike. In his presidential campaigns, Jackson had not had to contend with these difficulties, but in 1836, they would pose a severe test for all parties and for statesmen on both sides of the Mason-Dixon Line.

The fourth event to exercise a major influence on the Democratic Party was the war with the Bank of the United States. For many years, historians were reluctant to acknowledge the basic—and obvious—fact that Andrew Jackson disliked all banks on ideological grounds. These sentiments were not prominent in his election campaigns of the 1820s, but by the time of the Annual Message of 1829, Jackson was expressing serious misgivings about the bank. A year later, he proposed important modifications to any new charter it might receive. When its president, Nicholas Biddle, applied for a rechartering in 1832, Jackson not only vetoed the bill but expressed what would become classic Democratic hostility to "the rich and powerful," whose influence on government, he declared, posed an ever present threat to the well-being of the masses. In 1832 Jackson was triumphantly reelected; the masses seemed to have endorsed his view of the Bank of the United States.

Even more controversial was Jackson's next move in his war against the Bank of the United States: the removal of government deposits. In justifying this action, the president once again expressed his suspicion of the nation's elites, now both commercial and political. Here the ultimate goal of the president and those who shared his views could be glimpsed: he wanted to force smaller bills out of circulation entirely. Although paper money would continue to be used in larger commercial transactions, many Americans would encounter throughout their lives only specie—coins made of gold or silver. With the same goal in mind, Jackson in 1836 insisted that government agencies receive only gold and silver in payment for public lands. In his Farewell Message, he went far beyond attacks on a single commercial institution, however large. Excoriating the "money power" and the "paper system," the president warned that they engendered speculation, corruption, and inequality. Jackson posited an unending struggle between "the agricultural, the mechanical, and the laboring classes" on the one hand, and the "money power" on the other. Here was the pure milk of Jacksonian Democracy. By the time of Jackson's Farewell Message, Democratic principles were as clear as they would ever be.

In the next few years, the bank war entered its most critical phase. No sooner had Old Hickory's chosen successor, Martin Van Buren, taken office than news of a financial crisis broke. By May a panic had set in, and banks across the nation suspended specie payments. The new president made a crucial decision. He would follow Jackson's lead and establish an Independent Treasury, an institution that would hold and disburse government funds but would not act like a bank in other ways. In effect, Van Buren was, as his supporters claimed, "divorcing" the government from the banks.

Still more important was the course of the bank war in the states. The late 1830s and early 1840s marked the high point of agrarian radicalism, not only in the Jacksonian era but in the entire history of the United States. They also signaled the eclipse of sectional hostilities. Banking overshadowed the slavery question throughout the nation. The hard-money Democrats, the heirs of Andrew Jackson, now brought the Jacksonian era to its culmination. In almost every state of the Union, the Democratic Party took action against the banks. In the West, where the financial turbulence had been most severe, hard money Democrats frequently aimed to destroy all banks; in the East, where the banking system was more mature and stable, reform was the order of the day. How successful were they? The configuration of political forces varied from state to state. A minority of (conservative) Democrats objected vigorously to the attacks on the banks and, in some states, were able to effect an alliance with the Whig opposition that prevented the hard-money Democrats from achieving their goals. In many states and territories, however, abolition of all banks was official party policy, and, in some, it was actually implemented.

A Changing Agenda: The 1840s

In the 1840s, however, the political agenda shifted decisively, and the nature and priorities of the Democratic Party changed accordingly. Early in the decade, even though the Bank war was still raging in some states, sectional issues resurfaced. For most of the 1840s, the Democratic Party managed to combine a muted version of its original appeal with a new responsiveness to the demands of southern slaveholders. Democratic attacks upon the rich and powerful had been directed against those whose wealth was mercantile, financial, or industrial. Those who had prospered instead by exploiting the labor of African American slaves had escaped censure and indeed were viewed as part of the farming interest that Democrats had pledged to uphold. Nevertheless, in the 1840s, some slaveholders demanded more. Fearing that British antislavery pressure soon would be brought to bear upon the newly independent republic of Texas, some Southerners, with John C. Calhoun once again at their head, urged the immediate annexation of Texas. The Democratic Party succumbed to this pressure, as Northerners and Southerners alike presented this expansionist drive as evidence of the nation's Manifest Destiny to occupy the entire North American continent. Democrats were thus able to call for similar accessions of territory in the North, specifically in Oregon.

The problem was that these accessions of territory, when they could be secured, reopened the question of the extension of slavery. In the 1840s and 1850s, Democrats in the South spearheaded the drive for more slave states, and most Democrats in the North were more willing to countenance these demands than were members of other political parties, whether Whigs, Know-Nothings, or Republicans. In the mid- and late 1840s, Democrats were most keen to wage war with Mexico and most keen to allow slavery into the lands thus acquired, despite the Democratic affiliation of Representative David Wilmot, whose famous Proviso of 1846 sought to prevent the spread of slavery into new areas. Then in 1850, under the leadership of Illinois senator Stephen A. Douglas, Democrats championed the policy of "popular sovereignty," which denied to Congress, but conferred on the inhabitants of the territory in question, the right to determine the fate of slavery there.

These concessions to the South and the slaveholding interest were made only at the expense of a damaging split within the party in the North. Wilmot himself was from Pennsylvania, but the deepest intraparty division was probably in New York. Here the radical Democrats, dubbed "barnburners" by friend and foe alike, led a crusade to prevent the party becoming the vehicle for the expansion of slavery. In 1848 an outright breach occurred when their leader, Martin Van Buren, accepted the Free Soil Party's nomination for president. Van Buren, in common with virtually all Democrats north and south, had traditionally been hostile to abolitionism on the grounds that it threatened national unity. But the extension of slavery awakened fresh concerns that had more to do with the injustices allegedly suffered by white labor than with the iniquities of enslavement itself. Although these northern Democrats repudiated the proslavery policies of the 1840s, others took their cue from Stephen A. Douglas and acquiesced in them.

Toward the Civil War: 1850–61

Similarly, it was northern Democrats, again under Douglas, who took the lead in extending the policy of popular sovereignty to the territories of Kansas and Nebraska. The Kansas-Nebraska Act of 1854, perhaps the most portentous legislative measure in the history of the republic, repealed the Missouri Compromise and thus created the possibility that Kansas (and Nebraska, though climatic considerations made this highly improbable) might enter the Union as slave states. The Democratic goal here, or at least the northern Democrats' goal, however, was not to spread slavery but instead to open up the West to settlement and to link the existing states of the Midwest to those recently established on the Pacific Coast.

The impact of the Kansas-Nebraska Act was immense. It played a major role in weakening the Democrats in the North while confirming and extending their influence in the South. Moreover, it created in Kansas conditions that were ripe for a rapid descent into near civil war as pro- and antislavery settlers repeatedly clashed.

In the mid-1850s, however, these were not the only issues to achieve prominence. The crusade for a governmental prohibition of alcohol, though focused entirely on state and local governments, polarized many communities, especially in the North. Democrats had traditionally frowned upon such governmental activism, partly on the grounds that it eroded individual liberty, and that it seemed to confer dangerous powers upon a self-constituted moral elite. These attitudes persisted into the 1850s, but some states and localities modified or abandoned them as the temperance movement gained strength. More important was the Know-Nothing crusade, which rose to meteoric prominence in late 1854 and 1855. Once again, traditional Democratic values mandated a defense of the immigrant, and of the right to vote of even the recently arrived immigrant, but those values were modified or even renounced in some localities.

By the time of the presidential election of 1856, however, both the temperance and the anti-immigrant crusades had subsided, leaving the slavery question at the top of the nation's political agenda. By now the political geography of the nation had changed markedly. In the heyday of the Second Party System in the late 1830s and early 1840s, the Democrats had been strong throughout the nation, but especially in the West, the lower North, and the Deep South. By the mid- to late 1850s, on the other hand, the South, apart from the border states, was solidly Democratic, whereas the North as a whole had been lost, apart from Pennsylvania, Illinois, Indiana, and the then underpopulated states of Oregon and California.

By now, too, the agrarian radicalism of Jacksonian times had largely disappeared from view. A financial panic in 1857 allowed it to reemerge but on a much smaller scale and, as far as most of the nation was concerned, for only a matter of months. In contrast, by 1860 the Democrats' southern orientation was more evident than ever and resulted in a split in the party in 1860. Northern Democrats, having been saddled with the defense of unpopular measures or actions like the Kansas-Nebraska Act, the subsequent unrest in Kansas, and the beating of Charles Sumner in the U.S. Senate in 1856, now refused to bend the knee once more in subjection to the southern demand for a slave code in the territories (by which Congress would be required to protect slavery in any territory until the moment of statehood). This Democratic split was probably not responsible for the Republican victory of 1860, but it did reveal the inability of the party to come to terms with the dominant issues of the day.

The Democratic Party Balance Sheet
The Democratic split of 1860 both mirrored and anticipated the split in the nation that would usher in four years of slaughter and carnage. Since the time of Andrew Jackson, the party had enjoyed extraordinary political success, achieving victory in all but two presidential elections between 1828 and 1859.

Democrats had controlled Congress for most of this time, and they had also controlled a majority of the states. What had the party accomplished? Its policies had—until the 1850s, at any rate—been crowned with success. As Democratic ideology implied, the federal government had withdrawn from the activities that it had once pursued: a national bank had been dismantled and a low-tariff policy instituted; and Congress had even renounced its control over slavery in the territories. Equally important, the populistic political practices inaugurated in the 1820s by the Jacksonians had become standard by 1860, and were adopted enthusiastically by the Republicans that year. Ironically, this played a major part in bringing about the collapse of Democratic control.

The Democratic balance sheet contains many liabilities. Democratic economic policies were, on the whole, triumphant. But by midcentury, they resulted not in the triumph of Jeffersonian agrarianism but instead in economic development and diversification that more closely resembled the vision of those in the anti-Democratic tradition. Moreover, the party utterly failed to deal with the slavery question. It increasingly became the vehicle for southern proslavery militancy, and—first in the North, and then in the nation as a whole—paid a high electoral price as a result.

For a generation, the party had claimed to be the party of American democracy and of the republic. In a sense, this claim was still valid in 1860. Within Republican ranks, the former Democrats were famed for their inflexible unionism, their refusal to contemplate any major concessions to the slaveholding interest. Even those who had not defected to the Republican Party rallied to the Union, with few exceptions, once the first shots had been fired at Fort Sumter. But by now northern Democrats were bit players in the great national drama that was unfolding. Southern Democrats, by contrast, were essentially in charge of events south of the Mason-Dixon Line but had little enthusiasm for party forms, little affection for the vast majority of their onetime northern allies, and little pride in the traditions of the Democratic Party. The days of Democratic hegemony were over. But in one sense, this confirmed the connections among the party, American democracy, and the nation itself. The marginalization of the party signaled the failure of the democratic process. It also announced the deepest crisis ever to face the American republic.

See also abolitionism; agrarian politics; banking policy; Jacksonian era, 1828–45; slavery.

FURTHER READING. John Ashworth, *Slavery Capitalism and Politics in the Antebellum Republic*, 2 vols., 1995, 2007; Lee Benson, *The Concept of Jacksonian Democracy: New York as a Test Case*, 1961; Robert W. Johannsen, *Stephen A. Douglas*, 1973; Roy F. Nichols, *The Disruption of American Democracy*, 1948; Robert Remini, *Andrew Jackson*, 3 vols., 1977–84; Arthur M. Schlesinger, Jr., *The Age of Jackson*, 1945.

JOHN ASHWORTH

Democratic Party, 1860–96

In 1860 the Democratic Party suffered the most disastrous defeat in its entire history. The party split apart, running two separate tickets, one headed by Senator Stephen Douglas of Illinois and the other by John C. Breckinridge of Kentucky, the sitting vice president. The Democrats lost not just the election but also half of their membership, which left to join the southern Confederacy. From this low point, the party managed to revive and then, by the mid-1870s, return to its former position as the rival of the nation's other major party, the Republicans. How did it manage to achieve such a remarkable recovery?

Throughout the first half of the nineteenth century, the Democratic Party, and its predecessor, the Democratic-Republican Party of Thomas Jefferson and James Madison, had assumed the role of watchdog over American politics, making sure that the power and authority of the federal government were kept under control. To offset federal authority, the Democrats mobilized the power of state and local government and the ideas associated with them, states' rights and localism. To counter attempts by Federalists, or Whigs, or Republicans to impose cultural or religious orthodoxy or to marginalize particular ethnic or social groups, the Democrats insisted on the promotion of cultural and social diversity and the protection of civil liberties. As the *New York Herald* complained in 1860, Democrats had to fight against "the evils of political meddling with morals, religion and the rights of communities." Opposition to federal interference and government meddling, whether in the economic, social, or cultural sphere, was the Democratic Party's assigned role in American party politics. As long as it maintained this oppositional tradition, the party would continue to be both necessary and viable.

But a political party is held together by more than ideology and identity. It also consists of an electoral coalition of interests and groups. By the outbreak of civil war in 1861, the Democrats' base of support was well established. Its geographic center lay in the southern slaveholding states, along with the border states and the lower portions of the Midwest that were populated by migrants from the nearby South. In the northern states, it relied primarily on the immigrant population, mainly Irish and German, as well as the growing numbers of Catholics, most of them Irish. Living in the cities, these religious and ethnic groups tended to be organized by the Democratic bosses and machines that were proliferating there. Also reliably Democratic were New York and New Jersey, both of which contained important economic sectors engaged in commerce and finance. Although one of their hallmarks was a tolerance of ethnic and religious differences, the Democrats were nevertheless hostile toward nonwhite races, African Americans in particular but also Native Americans and later the Chinese. White supremacy, in fact, continued to be a defining feature of Democratic identity after the war. Therefore, those whites who responded to racist appeals and racial fears were a basic component of the Democratic coalition.

Possessing a well-established ideology, or creed, and a broad electoral coalition, the Democrats could probably withstand the calamity of 1860 as long as they hewed to their recognized role in American politics as the party of opposition whose task was to prevent political centralization and cultural homogenization. Abandonment of this traditional stance would risk losing the party's identity and courting electoral disaster.

Phase One: Upheaval, 1861–74

The prospects for the Democratic Party when war broke out looked gloomy indeed. Once the overwhelmingly Democratic Southerners had withdrawn, the party became a distinct minority in Congress. As the party that had collaborated with the men who were now rebels and traitors, the Democrats might have faced extinction. That possibility threatened when the Republican Party renamed itself the Union Party and succeeded in drawing into its inclusive tent a number of what were soon called "War Democrats" when the other wing of the party, consisting of the "Peace Democrats," or "Copperheads," began to oppose the war and call for a negotiated peace. But the main body of the Democratic minority decided to assume the role of a vigorous opposition so as to maintain "the Constitution as it is, the Union as it was," even though it lacked the votes to prevent or change the Republicans' policy initiatives.

In assuming this stand, the regular Democrats opposed the dominant Republican Party in several arenas of public policy during the war. First, they challenged the Republicans when they took advantage of their wartime majority in the Thirty-eighth Congress and promoted their activist, partisan agenda, consisting of a protective tariff, a transcontinental railroad, homestead legislation, land-grant colleges, and a uniform national system of banking and currency. Democrats also reacted strongly to many of the Republicans' civil measures for prosecuting the war, such as their Confiscation Acts of 1861 and 1862, as well as periodic action by the executive branch and the military to curb seditious activities by curtailing civil liberties. Also generating Democratic opposition were the Republicans' efforts to finance the war by means of taxes, loans, and paper money (greenbacks), all involving dangerous economic intervention and change. And, finally, Republican attempts to expand war aims beyond the limited objective of saving the Union provoked Democratic ire, most notably over the introduction of emancipation of the slaves in the fall of 1862.

The Democrats' function as an unwavering opposition and their routine votes against most Republican measures during the war seemed to resonate with an electorate fearful of federal activism and innovation. Party leaders calculated accurately the extent of the electorate's primordial resistance to central authority as well as their own party's ability to benefit politically from it. In the 1864 presidential election, 45 percent of voters cast a ballot for the Democrats, despite their nomination of a failed Union general, George B. McClellan, who ran on a platform calling for a negotiated peace after "four years of failure" to restore the Union through war. New York's governor, Horatio Seymour, hailed this strong Democratic showing as evidence of "our numerous strength."

With the end of the war in April 1865, sectional conflict did not cease, nor did the Democrats become more cooperative. Instead, the formulation of policy for the defeated South became an arena for the Democrats to continue to challenge the Republicans, though they now shifted their stance from instinctive opposition to willful obstruction. If Lincoln's successor, Andrew Johnson, had not chosen to resist the Republicans' determined efforts to introduce a new political order in the South, the Democratic minority in Congress might have taken a different and more pragmatic course. But the ensuing struggle between Johnson and Congress over Reconstruction policy provided the Democrats with an influential and stubborn ally in their attempt to revitalize their party. So they voted solidly, often unanimously, against all the major Reconstruction legislation enacted by the Republicans—the Civil Rights Act of 1866, the Fourteenth Amendment, and the Reconstruction Act of 1867. And they provided eager and reliable support for Johnson's steady stream of truculent vetoes.

Although this strategy of resistance did not prevent the Republicans from enacting their vital measures for reconstructing the South, it still polarized the differences between the parties, giving the Democrats a clearly defined posture that, they were convinced, would ensure their viability as a needed check on radical federal policies. Democrats stood for conciliation toward the former Confederates and a speedy reunion of the divided country, and they objected to an externally imposed reconstruction of the South. They also encouraged white hostility to Republican efforts to provide blacks with legal and physical protection in the South and to guarantee them equal rights and suffrage throughout the nation. Sectional reconciliation and white supremacy would resonate, so the Democrats hoped, with northern voters tired of conflict and eager for stability and order. The sharp contrast between the major parties was dramatized during the 1868 presidential contest, when the Democrats selected a well-known Peace Democrat, Horatio Seymour, whose running mate, Francis Blair Jr., denounced the Reconstruction Acts as "null and void" and made his distaste for African Americans abundantly clear.

During the two-term Grant administration from 1868 to 1876, the Democrats continued to vote as a bloc against further measures to sustain Reconstruction in the South, such as the Enforcement Acts of 1870–71, as well as against additional civil rights legislation like the Fifteenth Amendment and the Civil Rights Act of 1875. But, after 1870, they shifted their position somewhat by pledging formally that, if it should return to power nationally, the Democratic Party would not overturn any federal statute or amendment expanding black rights. This initiative, called the New Departure, prepared the way for the party to move on to other issues, which it did in 1872, when the Democrats endorsed the presidential nominee of the Liberal Republican Party, which had just been formed by a sizable group of Republican dissidents opposed to the renomination of Grant. This maneuver was intended to broaden the Democrats' support as well as to proclaim their changed stance, away from obstruction and back to opposition.

Even though this scheme failed when Horace Greeley lost decisively to President Grant, the party's fortunes revived dramatically over the next few years. The new Republican governments elected and installed in the South after 1868 had encountered difficulties from the outset, and, by the 1870s, they were struggling to stay in control. Simultaneously, their opponents, the former Confederates and their allies who had aligned themselves with the Democrats, were returning to power in the region, sometimes by fair means, usually by foul.

After the nation's economy plunged into a depression in 1873, the Democrats blamed their Republican opponents for the ensuing hard times and were rewarded with a majority in the House a year later. The Republicans' 102-seat majority was replaced by a Democratic majority of 60 seats, the largest electoral swing at the national level in the nineteenth century. Significantly, two-thirds of the South's congressional seats were now held by Democrats. Meanwhile, all but a few states in the Lower South had come under Democratic control as the Reconstruction governments collapsed under their opponents' onslaught. Of course, the national Democrats stood to gain immensely from the return of their southern base. By 1876, when Reconstruction formally ended, they actually enjoyed near parity with the Republicans (149 to 130 in the House and 36 to 39 in the Senate).

Phase Two: Stalemate, 1874–96

After the turmoil of the Civil War and Reconstruction, the political system experienced deadlock for the next 20 years. In sharp contrast with the dramatic growth of large-scale industries and big cities that were transforming American life, the political arena was static. Turnout at elections was extremely high (around 75 percent), but voter efforts proved disappointing because they produced a balance between the two major parties so close and so precarious that neither party was prepared to take risks or act forcefully. For the Democrats, whose traditional approach was oppositional and whose preference was for limited and inactive government, such a situation was almost ideal. Even though the Democrats won the presidency only twice in that period (in 1884 and 1892, each time with Grover Cleveland of New York), they controlled the House for all but eight years. By contrast, they enjoyed only four years of dominance in the Senate. Congress was therefore divided, and the majorities in both houses were razor thin. Similarly in equipoise was the presidency. Despite the Republicans' seeming stranglehold, the executive branch was also closely contested. The popular vote was always so tight that a Democratic victory in New York, or Indiana, or Ohio could prevent the Republicans from winning.

Contributing to the electoral stalemate were the powerful identities each party represented in the minds of voters. As a result, anxiety over expected close elections was compounded by awareness of dire consequences if the enemy were to seize control. Democrats were still tarnished by their identification with the Confederacy, and so their Republican opponents constantly reminded voters of this by "waving the bloody shirt." Moreover, by the 1880s, it was difficult for the Democrats to refute this charge since the party's heartland had once again become the South, while southern Democrats were back in control of most committees in the Democratic-controlled House.

This sharp cleavage was supplemented by several other distinctive differences. Democrats, both northern and southern, could be expected to denounce racial equality and oppose civil rights for blacks, as their party continued to identify itself as the upholder of white supremacy. Further distinguishing the parties was the Democrats' persistent laissez-faire approach to governance. As Thomas "Czar" Reed, the Republican House Speaker in the 1800s, once observed contemptuously, "The Republican party does things; the Democratic party criticizes." And, finally, one policy issue clearly differentiated Republicans from Democrats. The Republicans advocated a protective tariff, and they clung firmly to that issue, claiming that it developed the economy and protected workers' wages. Naturally, Democrats countered with their traditional support for a tariff "for revenue only." But they were not as adamant or consistent about reducing the tariff as their rivals were about maintaining or increasing it.

In fact, the Democrats' stance on a number of prominent issues of the late nineteenth century was more equivocal and imprecise than the Republicans. The primary reason for this was the diversity of the Democratic coalition. Those Democratic districts where manufacturing and mining interests were influential wanted tariff protection against foreign competition. Consequently, when Democrats in both Cleveland administrations tried to lower the tariff, they found themselves having to concede to protectionist demands, and so they failed on each occasion. And while the party generally wanted a more

flexible currency and an increased money supply, New England and New York Democrats who were engaged in banking and commerce favored currency contraction and maintenance of the gold standard.

But this alignment of the parties changed dramatically when the electoral equilibrium was suddenly shattered in 1888 and again in 1892. In 1888 the Republicans won the presidency and both houses of Congress and proceeded to enact the party's campaign platform. Four years later, the Democrats did the exact same thing and met with the same result—defeat at the next national election. The Republicans returned to power between 1894 and 1896 and stayed there until 1932.

This definitive outcome occurred for two reasons. First, another depression struck in 1893, soon after Cleveland's second term began, but it was far worse than its predecessor in 1873–74. In response, the president contracted the money supply by getting Congress to repeal the Sherman Silver Purchase Act of 1890 and return the nation to the gold standard, an action that undoubtedly aggravated the economic distress. Also seriously damaged were the Democrats' chances of winning the 1896 election. Second, the 1896 contest forced the Democrats to take a clear-cut position on the money question. Repudiating the sound money/gold standard wing of the party, they aligned decisively with free silver and currency expansion by nominating William Jennings Bryan, a young and popular silverite, for president. Instead of trying to balance its gold and silver factions (as it had also balanced its protectionist/reductionist elements on the tariff), the party committed itself unequivocally to free silver and its determined advocates in the South and West. Simultaneously, the Republicans endorsed gold equally decisively after having tried to appease the pro-silver forces in the West during the Benjamin Harrison administration (1888–92) by means of the Silver Purchase Act. The election of 1896 became a "battle of the standards," gold versus silver, hard money versus soft.

Beset by a serious economic crisis, the two parties had been forced to identify themselves clearly with one or the other of the economic panaceas currently in fashion. In the election, the Republicans won, partly because of their own well-run campaign and partly because of a confusing campaign by the Democrats, whose nominee was also backed by the new, insurgent People's Party. Although it totaled a mere 4 percent of the votes cast, the Republican margin of victory amounted nevertheless to a larger electoral shift than in any presidential election since 1872. As a result, both the electoral stalemate and the policy logjam ended. The lifting of the economic depression a few years later suggested that perhaps the Republican policy, and therefore the Republican Party, had got it right.

Not until another even more severe depression in the 1930s did the Democrats develop a winning alternative. During the intervening 30 years, the party found itself once again defeated and discredited, as it had been after 1860. This time, however, the Democrats would revive, not by preserving their traditional issues and identity, as they had done since 1860, but by transforming themselves into a very different party, one that was predominantly liberal, urban, northern—and barely recognizable.

See also Democratic Party, 1828–60; Gilded Age, 1870s–90s; Reconstruction era, 1865–77; sectional conflict and secession, 1845–65; tariffs and politics.

FURTHER READING. Peter H. Argersinger, "The Transformation of American Politics: Political Institutions and Public Policy, 1865–1910," in *Contesting Democracy: Substance and Structure in American Political History, 1775–2000*, edited by Byron E. Shafer and Anthony J. Badger, 117–47, 2001; Richard Franklin Bensel, *The Political Economy of American Industrialization, 1877–1900*, 2000; Charles W. Calhoun, *The Gilded Age: Essays on the Origins of Modern America*, 1996; Robert W. Cherney, *American Politics in the Gilded Age, 1868–1900*, 1997; David Herbert Donald, Jean Harvey Baker, and Michael F. Holt, *The Civil War and Reconstruction*, 2001; Eric Foner, *Reconstruction: America's Unfinished Revolution, 1863–1877*, 1988; Joel H. Silbey, *A Respectable Minority: The Democratic Party in the Civil War Era, 1860–1868*, 1977.

MICHAEL PERMAN

Democratic Party, 1896–1932

Unlike many other political changes, the modern history of the Democratic Party began with a speech. When William Jennings Bryan gave one of the most famous speeches in American history to the 1896 Democratic convention, he not only boosted his own nomination for president, he also began the reshaping of a party of mixed and murky motivation into a party of persistent themes of activist government, reform, and regulation. Later Democrats might not identify with Bryan's issues and attitudes, but they could recognize his instincts.

Since the Civil War, the Democratic Party had been an outsiders' alliance led by white Southerners and urban machines, often winning control of the House but usually losing the White House and the Senate. The party included some elements challenging the nation's new industrial conditions and corporate power, but it also contained northern leaders close to business and Jeffersonians (frequently southern) committed on principle to weak government, especially weak federal government. The people support the government, explained Grover Cleveland, the only Democratic president between Buchanan and Wilson, but that did not mean the government should support the people.

Bryan's Party

The massive depression of the 1890s, crushing to both farmers and workers, challenged this attitude.

Western and southern Democrats echoed the calls of the Populist Party for expanding the money supply with silver (creating inflation and benefiting debtors) and regulating railroads and business. At the 1896 Democratic convention, the long-shot candidate Bryan, a former Nebraska congressman, captured the nomination with a speech warning, "Thou shalt not crucify mankind upon a cross of gold." The speech displayed both the eloquence and passion that would make him a national leader for decades and the heartland Protestant religiosity that would persistently discomfit immigrant and urban voters.

As the voice of the western and southern challenge, Bryan became the Populist as well as the Democratic nominee, taking on former Ohio governor William McKinley in a high-stakes race that was one of the most exciting in U.S. history. Republicans waged a multimillion-dollar campaign in which thousands of speakers warned against the dangers of Bryan, who pioneered modern campaigning by barnstorming the country and making hundreds of speeches. Bryan lost the presidency because he was unable to break into the Northeast and Great Lakes states, a problem for Democratic White House candidates for years to come and an alignment that kept the Democrats in mostly minority status until the Great Depression.

But the party influence of the Commoner, as Bryan came to be called, endured and strengthened. In 1900 he was renominated easily, and in the wake of the Spanish-American War, his opposition to imperialism in the Philippines won back some Cleveland conservatives. An improved national economic situation, however, knocked off enough of his original supporters that he actually lost some ground. Even in 1904, when Cleveland conservatives briefly recaptured the party to nominate New York judge Alton Parker against President Theodore Roosevelt, Bryan controlled the platform process.

By his third unsuccessful run, in 1908, Bryan was clearly the national leader of the party, sweeping convention delegates from every region, as he called for business regulation, an income tax, direct election of senators, the right of labor to organize, and a lower tariff—the issue that bound even Bryan and Cleveland Democrats together. Bryan's campaign also produced a direct endorsement by the American Federation of Labor, an alliance that would shape the Democratic Party ever after.

Partly because of the lack of other national leaders or governors and senators from northern states during this time, Democratic newspapers became particularly influential. The *New York World* was considered a national party voice, even after the death of Joseph Pulitzer in 1911, and William Randolph Hearst, with his chain of newspapers spreading across the country, was perhaps the only powerful party figure throughout the entire 1896–1932 period—even if he never achieved his personal goal of winning high office.

Besides Bryan, the party's foremost negotiable asset during this time was the South. During Bryan's years the region became solidly Democratic, with disfranchisement of African Americans embedded into state constitutions, succeeding—although not entirely ending—the tactics of violence and fraud previously used against blacks (and Populists). From 1900 the 11 states of the former Confederacy would not elect a single Republican senator until 1961. In the earlier part of the century, many southern Democratic leaders combined economic reformism with virulent racism, as the white supremacist South remained the most thoroughly Bryanized part of the country. As late as the 1960s, South Carolina had a congressman named William Jennings Bryan Dorn.

That economic outlook shaped southern Democratic voting in Congress through years when Democrats were out of the White House and during Woodrow Wilson's New Freedom years. Democrats, overwhelmingly from southern and border states, strongly supported Theodore Roosevelt's reform efforts and voted with insurgent Republicans during William Howard Taft's presidency, taking on tariff, regulation, and labor issues in an alliance of mutual mistrust. Progressive Republicans, heavily from west of the Mississippi with old-stock and Scandinavian backgrounds, distrusted both Southerners and urban immigrants, while congressional Democrats felt that progressives, like Roosevelt himself, often used them mostly as leverage to cut deals with the conservative GOP leadership.

After 1910—when Taft's problems and a wave of reform agitation gave the Democrats the House, ten Senate seats, and a raft of governorships in a widely overlooked harbinger of 1912 victory—the House launched widely covered investigations of corporate excesses and passed extensive legislation from the party platform. Most of it died in the Senate, although Democrats and Progressive Republicans did pass through Congress the Seventeenth Amendment for direct election of senators, improving Democrats' chances in many northern states. The record of the House made presidential contenders of its two leaders, Speaker Champ Clark of Missouri, an old Bryanite, and Majority Leader Oscar Underwood of Alabama.

Wilson Recreates the Democrats

Clark and Underwood would lose the 1912 nomination, in 44 ballots, to one of the new Democratic governors, Woodrow Wilson of New Jersey. The former president of Princeton University, Wilson had been a traditional Cleveland Democrat but had moved steadily and repeatedly left to achieve political credibility in his party—first in New Jersey and then nationally. Still, he was about to lose the presidential nomination to Clark, who had a majority of delegates until Bryan broke the Baltimore convention apart, declaring he could not support any candidate backed by New York—a move intended either to enforce progressive purity or to create chaos that might yield him a fourth nomination.

As the Democratic nominee, Wilson faced a shattered Republican Party, with Theodore Roosevelt running on the new Bull Moose Progressive ticket. The GOP split ensured Wilson's victory (and a massively Democratic House), but had historically obscured trends that had been already running in the Democrats' direction.

During the campaign, Wilson advocated a New Freedom, based largely on the thinking of reformist lawyer Louis Brandeis. The Democrat emphasized breaking up combinations of corporate power rather than trying to control them, the goal of Roosevelt's New Nationalism. The campaign was hardly a philosophical exchange, but it did send Democrats into complete control of Washington—for the first time in 20 years and only the second time since the Civil War—with a clear program and mandate.

In office, Wilson and the Democrats compiled an extensive record of reform legislation, including tariff reduction (with an income tax, now permitted by the Sixteenth Amendment); a new antitrust act, including some legal protections for labor unions; and the creation of the Federal Reserve, a distant descendant of the currency question of 1896. Wilson's bonds with the mostly southern congressional Democrats were bolstered by the Virginia-born president's sympathy for their racial attitudes, as he expanded segregation through the federal government.

Approaching reelection in 1916, Wilson—to the applause of most congressional Democrats—moved to a more aggressively interventionist stance. He backed legislation enforcing an eight-hour day for railroad workers and banning child labor in interstate commerce, and filled a Supreme Court vacancy with Louis Brandeis, the most activist reformer and the first Jew ever named to the high court. Brandeis's appointment was a major step in attracting Jews, previously uncomfortable with Bryan's assertive Protestantism and Irish Catholic city machines, into the Democratic Party. This two-decade evolution was symbolized by Henry Morgenthau, Wilson's fundraiser and ambassador to Turkey, and his son, Henry Jr., Franklin D. Roosevelt's secretary of the treasury.

The strategy worked just well enough; Wilson drew heavily from former Bull Moosers, Socialists, and unionists in the West to win a narrow, improbable reelection and to establish enduring Democratic roots in the Rocky Mountains. Republicans, and some subsequent historians, have argued that only persistent GOP divisions, and the claim that Wilson had kept the country out of World War I, allowed Wilson to slip through. But Democrats could also claim that low-level support among Irish and German voters, angry over friendliness to Great Britain, kept Wilson from a more resounding victory.

The Great War continued to produce great problems for the party. In 1920 anger over the postwar peace agreements, which frustrated the wishes of many immigrants and dismayed other voters, produced a Republican landslide, with Ohio senator

Warren Harding smashing the Democratic ticket of Ohio governor James Cox and Assistant Secretary of the Navy Franklin D. Roosevelt. Never again would a Democratic candidate follow Wilson in supporting U.S. membership in the League of Nations.

But Wilson's ideal in foreign affairs, of a U.S. advocacy for democracy exercised through international organizations and alliances, shaped the Democratic view long afterward. Both President Franklin D. Roosevelt and his secretary of state Cordell Hull were Wilsonians—Roosevelt in the administration and Hull in the House—an experience shaping their commitment to a United Nations, spurring a Democratic belief in multilateral efforts extending as far as John F. Kennedy and Bill Clinton. Wilson remained an iconic figure among many Democrats; Alben Barkley of Kentucky (Franklin D. Roosevelt's Senate majority leader and Harry Truman's vice president) concluded in his memoirs that Wilson was the greatest man he had ever known.

Cultural Clashes and Reconciliation

The ethnic strains in the Democratic Party, reflected in foreign policy issues in 1916 and 1920, exploded across domestic policy throughout the 1920s. Immigrant groups' prominence in the party rose steadily, as urban machines that had for decades nominated old-stock Protestants for statewide offices increasingly claimed governorships and Senate seats for members of their own ethnic groups. Their rise was symbolized by New York governor Alfred E. Smith, who became the first Catholic to contend for the White House. From 1919 to 1929, Smith's success expanding reach, protections, and efficiency in the state government made him one of the great governors in American history, providing concepts and officials to later Democratic national administrations.

But the changing dynamics of the party and of 1920s America, dismayed the party's Bryanite rural and small-town roots in the South and West. The nation's cultural and political conflicts were reflected in the rise of the Ku Klux Klan outside the South during the 1920s, the battle over Prohibition, and congressional struggles over immigration quotas. During the 1920s, especially in presidential politics, cultural strains overshadowed economic interests to a degree not seen again until the 1970s.

The strains exploded at the 1924 convention in New York in a 103-ballot death struggle between Smith's Northeast and Midwest supporters and the southern and western core of former treasury secretary (and Wilson son-in-law) William Gibbs McAdoo. During the weeks-long battle, the convention divided in half over condemning the Ku Klux Klan and an equally divisive final appearance by Bryan. To run against Calvin Coolidge, the convention ultimately issued a by-then worthless nomination to conservative John W. Davis, spurring a third-party run by Senator Robert La Follette, Republican of Wisconsin. The Democratic ticket won less than 30 percent of the vote, running third in much of the West and Midwest.

By 1928 most of the party concluded that Smith was inevitable, but his nomination led to the loss of half of the South to Herbert Hoover and a national GOP landslide, in a time of national prosperity and a blizzard of anti-Catholic agitation. The New York governor also alienated many traditional party supporters with his prominent Wall Street supporters, his opposition to (and personal defiance of) Prohibition, and his difficulty in connecting with rural voters.

Still, Smith ran better than any presidential Democratic candidate in memory among urban voters, a group that would provide the party core for decades to come. Later, pollster Samuel Lubell, in one of the most famous assessments in political history, would pronounce, "Before the Roosevelt Revolution, there was an Al Smith Revolution."

Moreover, quadrennial White House disasters were not the sole indications of the party's strength during the 1920s. In 1922, 1926, and 1930, off-year congressional elections produced sizable gains and displays of party potential. Allied with insurgent Republicans from the Midwest and West, Democrats managed to pass legislation for farm relief and labor protection, frequently vetoed by Republican presidents.

With the stock market crash in 1929 and the ensuing depression, Democratic chances in 1932 seemed highly promising. But the same stresses that had broken apart the Democrats in three previous campaigns surfaced again. New York governor Franklin D. Roosevelt, a former Smith ally, emerged as the leading candidate after his overwhelming 1930 reelection. He arrived at the Chicago convention with a majority of the delegates, but was kept short of the necessary two-thirds by a loose alliance of favorite sons, House Speaker John Nance Garner of Texas and Smith, embittered by the bigoted religious rhetoric of 1928 and his displacement by Roosevelt.

Despite his Albany address, Roosevelt's delegates were largely from southern and western Bryanite territories. A former Wilson subcabinet official, the candidate connected deeply with earlier party roots. In a preconvention message Roosevelt assured delegates, "I am a progressive in deed and word, in the truest and most Democratic sense." He won the nomination by allying with and offering the vice presidency to Garner, whose own House service extended back into Bryan's and Wilson's times.

On a platform vague about plans to treat the Great Depression—but explicit on re-legalizing beer—Roosevelt won the first of four landslide victories that would define the Democrats as the nation's majority party for half a century. To the traditional Democratic alliance of the South and urban ethnic voters, Roosevelt locked in the party's alliance with labor and added Western progressives who had been dubious about Democrats since 1916.

During the course of Roosevelt's New Deal, many of its elements—business regulation, protection of union-organizing rights, federal insurance of bank deposits, and even going off the gold standard—had roots in Bryanism.

The Democratic outsiders' alliance, now a majority, would persist through most of the twentieth century, until over the course of decades it shattered on the entry of the nation's ultimate outsiders, African Americans. But almost a hundred years later, the persistent Democratic themes of activist government at home and multilateralism abroad can still be traced to the party of Bryan, Wilson, and Smith.

See also conservative interregnum, 1920–32; Democratic Party, 1860–96; progressivism and the Progressive Era, 1890s–1920.

FURTHER READING. David Burner, *The Politics of Provincialism: The Democratic Party in Transition 1918–1932*, 1968; Douglas B. Craig, *After Wilson: The Struggle for the Democratic Party, 1920–1934*, 1992; J. Rogers Hollingsworth, *The Whirligig of Politics: The Democracy of Cleveland and Bryan*, 1963; Michael Kazin, *A Godly Hero: The Life of William Jennings Bryan*, 2006; Arthur Link, *Wilson*, 5 vols., 1947–65; Robert K. Murray, *The 103rd Ballot: Democrats and the Disaster in Madison Square Garden*, 1976; Richard Oulahan, *The Man Who . . . The Story of the 1932 Democratic National Convention*, 1971; Michael Perman, *Struggle for Mastery: Disfranchisement in the South, 1888–1908*, 2001; Elizabeth Sanders, *Roots of Reform: Farmers, Workers, and the American State, 1877–1917*, 1999; David Sarasohn, *Party of Reform: Democrats in the Progressive Era*, 1989; Robert A. Slayton, *Empire Statesman: The Rise and Redemption of Al Smith*, 2001.

DAVID SARASOHN

Democratic Party, 1932–68

On March 4, 1933, in Washington, D.C., standing hatless and coatless on a dreary, windswept inauguration day, Franklin D. Roosevelt placed his hand on an old family Bible and recited the oath of office. Afterward, he turned to face the 100,000 spectators somberly gathered in front of the Capitol. The faces staring back at him were lined with despair. One in four Americans were without a job. Each month, thousands of farmers and business owners went bankrupt. A Roosevelt adviser, Rexford Guy Tugwell, wrote in his diary, "Never in modern times, I should think, has there been so widespread unemployment and such moving distress from cold and hunger."

Roosevelt's first task as president was to restore hope in the future and confidence in government. In a firm and confident voice, he promised to ask Congress for "broad executive power to wage a war against the emergency, as great as the power that would be given to me if we were invaded by a foreign foe." Over the next few years, Roosevelt backed up his words with a bold and ambitious reform agenda designed to revive the economy and the nation's spirit. The New Deal, along with the dozens of alphabet agencies it spawned, redefined the relationship between the federal government and its citizens and forged a new political coalition that would sustain the Democratic Party and dominate American politics for the next three decades.

Roosevelt's landslide victory in 1936 institutionalized the New Deal political coalition. That year Roosevelt swept every state but Maine and Vermont, and carried with him into Congress unprecedented Democratic margins of 331 to 89 in the House and 76 to 16 in the Senate. Six million more people voted in 1936 than had cast ballots in 1932, and the bulk of these new voters supported the Democratic Party. Economic need served as the glue binding together the New Deal coalition. Hardship fused the interests of millions of rural farmers and urban workers, both skilled and unskilled, native-born and foreign-born, white and nonwhite, male and female. The disparate coalition included rural Protestants and urban Catholics; white segregationists and African Americans; liberal intellectuals and tradition-minded conservatives.

The journalist Samuel Lubell argued that the United States had a "sun" party, whose light dominated the landscape, and a "moon" party that reflected the sun's rays. Roosevelt's New Deal, and the coalition that sustained it, provided much of the energy that would illuminate American politics for the next three decades. By the 1960s, however, larger social and demographic changes eroded popular support for government activism, at the same time that a controversial war in Vietnam, combined with racial conflict at home, weakened old loyalties and exposed deep fissures in the New Deal coalition. By 1968 fear and uncertainty had eclipsed much of the light from the Democratic "sun."

The New Deal and Congressional Conservatism: 1938–52

While Roosevelt had created a new coalition in presidential elections, he was less successful in sustaining the congressional majorities needed to support his vision of a more activist federal government. A couple of uncharacteristic Roosevelt blunders—a misconceived plan to reform the Supreme Court and an effort to "purge" the party by campaigning in the 1938 primaries against conservatives who had opposed New Deal measures—allowed Republicans to make major gains in Congress. During the 1940s, wartime prosperity and the emergence of foreign policy issues further diluted the New Deal agenda. By 1944 the Republicans controlled 209 House seats—only 13 fewer than the Democrats. Since most of the Democratic losses came in the North and Midwest, the Republican gains enhanced the southern balance of power within the Democratic Party. In the House, representatives from 15 southern and border states claimed 120 of the 222 Democratic seats; in the Senate they held 29 of 57 seats. This "conservative coalition" placed a break on major new reforms until Lyndon Johnson's landslide in 1964.

Roosevelt's death in April 1945 left behind a powerful but weakened coalition, lacking a clear sense of how to deal with the economic pain of reconversion to a peacetime economy or the growing rift with the Soviet Union. While Republicans fed on public worries about inflation and unemployment, Democrats fought over how to deal with the cold war. When Harry Truman chose a confrontational course with the Soviet Union, many liberals rallied around former vice president Henry Wallace, who advocated maintaining a "popular front" with America's wartime ally. Republicans took advantage of the confusion, making major gains in the 1946 congressional elections and taking control of the House for the first time since 1930.

The cold war was only one of the new questions facing Truman and threatening the Democratic Party. When the Democratic Party included an endorsement of civil rights in its 1948 platform, southern delegates stormed out of the convention, formed the States' Rights Democratic, or "Dixiecrat," Party, and nominated J. Strom Thurmond, governor of South Carolina, for the presidency. "We stand for the segregation of the races and the racial integrity of each race," the platform declared.

In 1948, with his party deeply fractured over both the cold war and civil rights, observers gave Truman little chance of winning against popular New York governor Thomas E. Dewey. While Dewey tried to stay above the partisan fray, Truman waged a tough, bare-knuckled campaign, tying himself to Roosevelt's legacy, reminding voters that the Democratic Party had led the nation through depression and world war.

On Election Day, Truman scored the most dramatic upset victory in the history of presidential elections, winning 24.1 million votes to Dewey's 22 million. The election demonstrated the enduring appeal of the New Deal. "I talked about voting for Dewey all summer, but when the time came I just couldn't do it," confessed one farmer. "I remembered the Depression and all the other things that had come to me under the Democrats." The Democrats, by picking up 9 seats in the Senate and 75 in the House, regained control of Congress. "[T]he party that Roosevelt formed has survived his death," the journalist Walter Lippmann observed, "and is without question the dominant force in American politics."

From the Fair Deal to the New Frontier: 1948–63

Truman had promised the nation a "Fair Deal," and he managed to push some reforms through a reluctant Congress. By 1952, however, public attention had moved away from the economic concerns that had defined the New Deal and carried Truman over the finish line in 1948. With the administration burdened by an unpopular war in Korea, charges of corruption, and accusations of coddling Communists, the public turned to Republican war hero Dwight Eisenhower in 1952. Not only did Eisenhower win in

a landslide, Republicans won control of the House and Senate, although by slim margins.

Their poor showing on Election Day revealed that the Democrats faced serious problems as they tried to update the New Deal agenda to a new political environment. During the 1950s, the Democratic Party found itself trapped between the growing aspirations of African Americans and the increased intransigence of the white South. The Supreme Court raised the stakes in 1954, when, in a unanimous decision popularly known as *Brown v. Board of Education of Topeka, Kansas*, the justices declared segregation in public schools to be illegal. The historic decision triggered massive resistance to ending Jim Crow among state and local Democratic politicians in the South. Nineteen southern senators and 77 representatives signed a manifesto in 1956 that bound them to "use all lawful means to bring about a reversal of this decision which is contrary to the Court and to prevent the use of force in its implementation."

Race was dividing the Democrats at the same time that prosperity was eroding the common sense of economic grievance that united the disparate coalition. The United States experienced an unprecedented economic boom following World War II. Between 1940 and 1960, the gross national product (GNP) more than doubled from $227 billion to $488 billion. The median family income rose from $3,083 to $5,657, and real wages rose by almost 30 percent. How could a party born during a period of economic crisis adapt to a new age of prosperity?

In a series of articles written throughout the decade, liberal historian Arthur Schlesinger Jr. argued that liberalism born during the Depression needed to adjust to a new age of abundance. Instead of a quantitative liberalism "dedicated to the struggle to secure the economic basis of life," Schlesinger called for a "qualitative liberalism dedicated to bettering the quality of people's lives and opportunities." The Democratic Party had sowed the seeds of its own demise, he argued, by creating a satiated middle-class society.

Despite these challenges, the party turned anxiety over a struggling economy and worry about Soviet advances into a major victory in 1958. Indicting a failure of leadership in Washington, Democratic congressional candidates won 56 percent of votes cast—the highest figure since 1936. Democrats increased their majority in the House from 235 to 282. Democratic victories on the state level gave them control of 34 governorships, including those in traditional Republican strongholds like South Dakota, Wisconsin, and Nebraska.

Two years later, the Democrats turned to the youthful and attractive John F. Kennedy to head the party's ticket. The 42-year-old Massachusetts senator was the first Catholic to contend for the presidency since Al Smith in 1928. Realizing he needed a running mate who could provide regional balance, Kennedy asked Texas senator Lyndon Johnson to join the ticket. The Democratic ticket won by promising to "get the nation moving again," but Kennedy's razor-thin victory revealed the divisions within the party.

The new president's youthful style and soaring rhetoric inspired the nation, although his actions, especially on the home front, seemed timid by comparison. His tragic assassination in November 1963 turned the party over to Johnson, who used the shock of Kennedy's death to score a decisive victory in 1964. Johnson's percentage of the popular vote, 61.1 percent, matched Roosevelt's in 1936. Congressional Democrats coasted to victory on the president's coattails, providing the administration with large majorities in both houses: 68 to 32 in the Senate and 295 to 140 in the House

The Rise and Fall of the Great Society: 1963–68

Johnson reforged the New Deal coalition and promised to fulfill the unrealized legislative program of the New Deal and Fair Deal. His goal was to emulate his hero, Franklin D. Roosevelt, whom he once described as "like a daddy to me." In the spring of 1964, Johnson coined a phrase meant to define his vision for the presidency, announcing that he hoped to build a "Great Society," "where men are more concerned with the quality of their goals than the quantity of their goods." Johnson had built his vision of a Great Society on the belief that America had forged a new national consensus around shared goals of economic growth, anticommunism, and activist government.

Events over the next four years would expose the fragility of the New Deal coalition. The racial dividing line in the Democratic Party grew wider after Johnson signed into law the Civil Rights Act of 1964 and the Voting Rights Act of 1965. "I think we just gave the South to the Republicans for your lifetime and mine," Johnson confessed to an aide after signing the Civil Rights Act.

The racial rioting that ripped through the nation's cities in the 1960s added to the divisions. Between 1964 and 1968, the United States experienced the most intense period of civil unrest since the Civil War. Most whites responded to the riots and the new black militancy with fear and anger. In 1966 Republicans campaigning on a tough "law-and-order" platform gained 47 House seats and 3 in the Senate. The Democrats lost more seats in 1966 than they had won in 1964. After November 1966, there were 156 northern Democrats in the House, 62 short of a majority.

While the debate over civil rights and riots exposed the racial divide in the Democratic Party, the Vietnam War split it into rival camps of hawks and doves, and pushed millions of young people to take to the streets to protest the war. The draft system, which placed an unfair burden on the poor and working class, added to the frustrations that were tearing the party apart. A large number of working-class Americans opposed the war, but they disliked privileged student protesters even more. "We can't understand," lamented a blue-collar worker, "how all those rich kids—the kids with the beads from the fancy suburbs—how they get off when my son has to go over there and maybe get his head shot off."

The conflicting currents of the decade converged during the 1968 presidential election year. After Minnesota senator Eugene McCarthy, campaigning as an antiwar candidate, scored a symbolic victory in the New Hampshire primary, Senator Robert Kennedy entered the race. Many people believed that Kennedy offered the best opportunity for the party to reforge its tattered coalition. His tragic assassination in June, however, ended that hope and left the nomination to Vice President Hubert Humphrey.

The Democrats who gathered in Chicago that summer for their convention were members of a party in disarray. President Johnson, who did not attend, was determined to see the party support his Vietnam policy, thus denying Humphrey the ability to make peace with the antiwar forces. A small but vocal group of radical activists traveled to Chicago intent on provoking a violent confrontation with the police. The city's powerful mayor, Richard Daley, was just as determined to demonstrate that he was in control of the streets, turning the area around the convention hall into an armed fortress. The combustible mix produced a violent explosion, captured by news cameras and projected into the homes of millions of Americans. The images of baton-wielding police officers clubbing young people in the streets of Chicago contributed to the impression that the Democrats were a party in disorder, incapable of effective governing.

Two other major presidential candidates that year helped reinforce that message. American Independence Party candidate George Wallace, whose symbolic stance in a university doorway had made him a hero to southern whites, appealed to many northern Democrats angry over the party's association with protest and integration. Joining Wallace in pursuit of the hearts and minds of America's angry white voters was the Republican nominee, Richard Nixon, who appealed to the "forgotten Americans."

Nixon achieved a narrow victory on Election Day. While the Democrats maintained healthy majorities in Congress and many statehouses across the nation, the election exposed the deep fault lines in the New Deal coalition. Nearly as many people voted for Wallace and Nixon as had supported Johnson in 1964, revealing a growing conservative trend in American politics. Racial tensions made it difficult for Democrats to sustain a biracial coalition, and geographical differences between North and South threatened the very fabric of the party. Humphrey, who won only 10 percent of the vote among white Southerners, carried just one state in the ex-Confederacy, Texas. Franklin Roosevelt still cast a long shadow over American politics and policy, but the coalition he created was showing its age.

See also conservative interregnum, 1920–32; era of consensus, 1952–64; New Deal Era, 1932–52; presidency, 1932–2008.

FURTHER READING. Thomas Edsall, *Chain Reaction: The Impact of Race, Rights, and Taxes on American Politics*, 1992; David Farber, *Chicago '68*, 1994; Alonzo Hamby, *Beyond the New Deal: Harry S Truman and American Liberalism*, 1976; Samuel Lubell, *The Future of American Politics*, 1965; Allen J. Matusow, *The Unraveling of America: A History of Liberalism in the 1960s*, 1984; James T. Patterson, *Congressional Conservatism and the New Deal*, 1967.

STEVEN M. GILLON

Democratic Party, 1968–2008

Democratic Crack-up: 1968–76

When Lyndon B. Johnson succeeded to the presidency in November 1963, the Democratic Party was still dominated by a latter-day version of New Deal liberalism and a cold war commitment to the containment of international communism. By the time Johnson declined to seek another term in March 1968, both of these creeds were under attack. The intervening years had brought an overwhelming victory in the 1964 presidential and congressional elections, a major expansion of the welfare state called the Great Society, a less well-funded but still significant War on Poverty, and civil rights legislation that opened the way to full legal equality for African Americans. Starting in early 1965, while offering assurances that the booming economy could provide both "guns and butter," the Johnson administration steadily expanded the war in Vietnam.

These political developments, in confluence with such broader trends as the revival of feminism, increasing violent crime, loosening of sexual mores, and growing black militancy divided the country in general and the Democratic Party in particular. By 1964 there were signs of a "white backlash," a reaction against rising taxes, urban crime, and African American militancy. Segregationist governor George Wallace of Alabama won a large protest vote in three northern presidential primaries. Four years later Wallace ran for president on his own American Independent Party ticket.

The 1968 campaign occurred during the most tumultuous year for Americans since 1919. In January the Communist Tet Offensive in Vietnam undermined the administration's recent predictions of imminent victory. In March Senator Eugene J. McCarthy of Minnesota, an antiwar candidate, won 42 percent of the vote against Johnson in the New Hampshire primary. Then Senator Robert F. Kennedy of New York entered the race as a critic of the war. Vice President Hubert Humphrey became the de facto candidate of the Democratic establishment (even though Johnson dreamed of being drafted to run). After Kennedy's assassination in June, Humphrey received a nomination thought to be worthless. Outside the convention hall, Chicago police beat bystanders as well as angry antiwar demonstrators.

Humphrey ran 500,000 votes behind Republican Richard Nixon, while the Democrats retained control of Congress. He came so close to winning only because the anti-Democratic vote (57 percent) was split; Wallace won 13.6 percent. Humphrey received less than one-third of the southern vote.

The 1968 convention highlighted problems with party structure as well as ideological divisions. The Democrats began searching for a formula that would balance the interests of both party elites and grassroots movements. All factions agreed on the need to democratize the presidential selection process and increase the number of minority, female, and young delegates. The most important of several commissions created to find remedies was headed by Senator George McGovern of South Dakota. In 1971, despite opposition from organized labor, numerous members of Congress, and white Southerners, the Democratic National Committee adopted the McGovern commission "guidelines" and related reforms. Even prominent officials would not be guaranteed seats at the next national convention unless they were selected fairly. Moreover, all delegations had to take "affirmative steps" to include women, minorities, and the young.

McGovern used both the reforms he had recommended and the connections he had cultivated as commission chair to win the presidential nomination in 1972. Skeptical of cold war premises and enthusiastic about expanding the welfare state, McGovern was the most liberal major party nominee in the twentieth century. His closest rivals for the nomination were Hubert Humphrey, who now claimed to represent a responsible center, and Senator Henry Jackson of Washington, an unreconstructed cold warrior. McGovern's nomination was the product of a genuine grassroots movement. Fifteen percent of the convention delegates were black and 40 percent women, triple the percentages in 1968; 21 percent were under 30. Many in McGovern's "new politics" constituency wanted to change prevailing American ways of life as well as government policies. For instance, the convention considered a platform plank supporting abortion rights, which was rejected at McGovern's behest.

Nixon's shrewd combination of grudging liberalism and populist conservatism made him a formidable opponent. As president, he had agreed to expansion of the welfare state, pursued détente with the Soviet Union, normalized relations with the People's Republic of China, removed most ground troops from Vietnam, evaded enforcement of school desegregation, appointed conservative Supreme Court justices, and mobilized "square America" in opposition to cultural liberalization. A likely Democratic defeat was turned into a rout when McGovern chose Senator Thomas Eagleton of Missouri as his running mate. Eagleton was nudged from the ticket after reports surfaced that he had received electroshock treatment for clinical depression. The whole affair made McGovern look incompetent. Nixon won more than 60 percent of the vote, including 75 percent of erstwhile Wallace supporters, a majority of Catholics, and 30 percent of Jews. The Democrats nonetheless retained control of Congress.

The Carter Interlude: 1976–80

The most consequential act of the 1972 campaign did not affect the outcome. Burglars with ties to the White House broke into the Democratic national headquarters at the Watergate office building. This botched exercise in political espionage came to symbolize Nixon's high-handed presidency. He resigned on the verge of impeachment in 1974. Two years later Jimmy Carter, a former governor of Georgia, won the Democratic presidential nomination and general election in large part because the electorate, reeling from the Vietnam War as well as the Watergate scandal, craved an ostentatiously moral "outsider" in the White House. Other decisive factors were less amorphous than Carter's promise of a "government as good as the people": division among his economically more liberal Democratic rivals between chastened cold warriors and unreconstructed cold warriors; support from a growing constituency of evangelical Protestants who embraced this "born-again" Baptist as one of their own; and "stagflation" (a combination of high unemployment and high inflation) that Gerald Ford's administration could not cure. Carter's victory represented no resurrection of a predominantly liberal version of the New Deal coalition. Although Carter carried standard, if sometimes skeptical, Democratic constituencies, his narrow margin over Ford also reflected support from 44 percent of independents and 30 percent of self-described conservatives.

Carter's relations with a Democratic Congress began badly and got worse. Most congressional Democrats wanted to expand the welfare state while Carter, drawing on a pre–New Deal version of liberalism, emphasized efficiency, conservation, and consumer protection. This agenda reflected political calculation as well as the president's worldview. As the blue-collar workforce shrunk along with membership in labor unions, Carter sought to cultivate a new constituency among middle-class suburbanites. Almost all party leaders acknowledged that recent social and political developments made some adaptations necessary. For instance, Senator Edward Kennedy of Massachusetts, the president's foremost Democratic rival, joined forces with Carter to deregulate passenger air travel.

Any rapprochement between congressional welfare-state liberals and efficiency liberals in the White House was doomed by circumstances beyond their control. Indeed, during Carter's presidency, chronic domestic and international problems that had been building for years became acute. The most important of these were the inherent instability of détente combined with fears of the Soviet advances;

growing militancy in the third world; economic stagflation exacerbated by the rising cost of petroleum; and the increasing prominence of cultural issues like abortion.

In this context, most of Carter's victories proved to be pyrrhic. Ratification of the treaties that ultimately returned the Canal Zone to Panama revitalized Republican conservatives. Advocacy of human rights in the Third World looked like weakness to Carter's foes at home and abroad. Legislation lifting price controls on oil and natural gas in order to increase supply split the Democrats along ideological, regional, and class lines. Carter's acceptance of abortion as a constitutional right convinced evangelicals that he was more liberal than he had appeared in 1976.

The president's unique coalition was already disintegrating in November 1979 when his decision to admit the deposed Shah of Iran to the United States for medical treatment precipitated the seizure of the American embassy in Tehran. In December the Soviet Union invaded Afghanistan. These events widened another Democratic division—between advocates of international conciliation and proponents of an assertive foreign policy. The latter faction increasingly included the president himself.

After winning a bitter battle for renomination against Edward Kennedy, Carter lost a three-way race to Republican Ronald Reagan in 1980. Frightened liberals in their retrospective analysis emphasized Reagan's strong support among evangelical Protestants, many of whom had been mobilized by a new Christian right. A working-class willingness to become "Reagan Democrats" was at least as significant; a majority of white union members voted for the Republican nominee. Carter barely won a plurality among Jews. The most prominent Jewish defectors were neoconservative "Henry Jackson Democrats," who rejected the conciliatory side of Carter's foreign policy. The Republicans also captured the Senate for the first time since 1952. In sum, Reagan, a former Democrat who had voted for Franklin Roosevelt four times, detached important elements from the residual New Deal coalition.

Defeat and Confusion: 1980–92

President Reagan proved to be more flexible and popular than his opponents anticipated. A few congressional "blue dog" Democrats, most of them from the South, supported his conservative economic program. Seeking ways to forestall the emergence of a national Republican majority, Democratic leaders as a whole spent the Reagan years tinkering with party structure and exploring ideological adjustments. Many inferred from the nominations of McGovern and Carter that presidential selection had become too democratic. In accordance with the recommendation of another rules commission in 1982, members of Congress and other high officials would automatically serve as "superdelegates" to national conventions. Meanwhile, grassroots party organization was allowed to disintegrate in places where Reagan had strong support, including those southern states where native son Carter had run fairly well in 1980.

Throughout the 1980s, many prominent Democrats went along with the Republican caricature of liberalism. Except for the black activist Jesse Jackson, all major presidential contenders said that past Democratic administrations had ignored the merits of the market, wasted taxpayers' money, and slighted national defense. As appeals to the working class ebbed, the party cultivated newly influential constituencies and trendy rhetorical motifs. Women seemed an especially promising bloc because the Reagan administration attacked the welfare state and opposed abortion. To exploit the "gender gap" in 1984, presidential candidate Walter Mondale chose Representative Geraldine Ferraro of New York as his running mate. Trying to reclaim the center in 1988, presidential nominee Michael Dukakis, the governor of Massachusetts, waged his campaign on the basis of "competence" rather than "ideology."

With the possible exception of the Democratic recapture of the Senate in 1986, these tactical shifts rarely worked. Mondale received only 41 percent of the vote against Reagan, who won majorities among working-class whites, Catholics, and women. In 1988 George H. W. Bush, a weaker Republican candidate, turned the election into a referendum on patriotism. Although Dukakis received 46 percent of the vote, he too lost among Catholics, blue-collar workers, and white Southerners.

Governor Bill Clinton of Arkansas joined the effort to re-brand the Democrats as a "centrist" party during the early 1980s. When Clinton defeated President Bush and independent candidate Ross Perot in 1992, a majority of voters polled viewed him as a "new kind of Democrat." He won a plurality of Catholics and carried four southern states. Clinton also profited from evolving cultural attitudes. Many swing voters—especially single women—now favored abortion rights and feared the Christian right's influence among Republicans; four female Democrats were elected to the Senate in 1992. Amid a recession, however, a sign in Clinton's campaign headquarters summarized the main reason for his victory: "It's the economy, stupid."

"A New Kind of Democrat": 1992–2000

Clinton's initial agenda as president mixed old and new Democratic goals. He successfully pushed congressional Democrats to reduce the budget deficit and to promote international commerce by ratifying the North American Free Trade Agreement (NAFTA). Much more liberal on cultural issues than Carter, he tried unsuccessfully to lift the ban on gays in the military. He put his wife, Hillary Rodham Clinton, in charge of a failed effort to pass national health insurance, a liberal Democratic dream since the New Deal. Aided by an economic downturn in 1994, Republican conservatives led by Representative

Newt Gingrich of Georgia captured both houses of Congress in a landslide. Clinton fought back effectively with his characteristic ideological mix of new and old. On the one hand, he fulfilled a 1992 campaign promise to "end welfare as we know it" by signing legislation to abolish a New Deal entitlement, Aid to Families with Dependent Children (AFDC). On the other hand, he defended programs popular among swing voters, especially Medicare, environmental protection, gun control, and abortion rights. Running against Republican Robert Dole and Reform Party candidate Ross Perot in 1996, Clinton won 50.1 percent of the three-party vote. The Republicans not only retained control of Congress but also gained two Senate seats.

Whatever small chance Clinton had of turning his personal triumph into further legislative or ideological victories was destroyed by the scandal that dominated national politics from January 1998 to February 1999. Congressional Republicans tried to remove Clinton from office primarily because he lied under oath about having had sex with Monica Lewinsky, a young government employee. Most Americans doubted that Clinton's misbehavior rose to the level of an impeachable offense, as was demonstrated by Democratic gains in the 1998 congressional elections. Even so, the Lewinsky scandal left the party much weaker than it otherwise would have been. Vice President Al Gore, the presidential candidate in 2000, tried to distance himself from Clinton's personal flaws while sharing credit for the administration's successes as well as a revived economy.

Ambiguous Defeat and Revival: 2000–2006

Although Gore led Republican George W. Bush by 540,000 popular votes, the outcome in the Electoral College turned on disputed returns from Florida. In the end, Bush was certified the winner by 537 votes. Gore's loss of Florida had many causes, including support drawn away by Green Party candidate Ralph Nader, confusing ballots in key districts, a U.S. Supreme Court decision halting a recount, and perhaps intimidation of African Americans at the polls. But the Florida situation also reflected the Democrats' long-term inattention to grassroots organization. The old kind of Democrats in the New Deal coalition would have supplied poll watchers to explain confusing ballots and protect party faithful from intimidation.

Foreign policy and military action dominated politics after al-Qaeda terrorists attacked the United States on September 11, 2001. A majority of congressional Democrats favored the war to destroy the al-Qaeda sanctuary in Afghanistan. With greater reservations, they also supported the intervention begun in 2003 to overthrow Saddam Hussein's dictatorship in Iraq. The characteristic inclination of voters in wartime to follow a president's lead helped Republicans to recapture the Senate in 2002 (after a brief interlude under Democratic control because a Republican senator declared himself an Independent).

In 2004 former governor Howard Dean of Vermont sought the Democratic presidential nomination as a strong critic of the Iraq war. The Dean campaign resembled the grassroots movement that had supported Eugene McCarthy in 1968, and it too fell short. The Democrats nominated Senator John Kerry of Massachusetts, who had recently begun to criticize the intervention he had earlier voted to authorize. The electorate's continuing willingness to back a wartime president was the chief reason Bush defeated Kerry by 3 million votes. In an electoral landmark, Kerry, a Catholic, lost the Catholic vote. Still, his relatively narrow defeat by an incumbent president during wartime revealed growing public impatience with the Iraq intervention.

In 2006 the Democrats won a decisive majority in the House of Representatives and, joined by two independents, also gained control of the Senate. Disenchantment with the Iraq War, which had now become widespread, was the main cause of this sweep. Worries about a sagging economy also played an important role. In addition, the Democrats had begun to rebuild their grassroots organization even in conservative areas. The party's worst ideological wounds from the 1960s and 1970s finally had been healed by the passing of cold war issues, defection of conservatives to Republican ranks, and shared dislike of the Bush administration. In 2008 Barack Obama, an African American first-term senator from Illinois, used a brilliantly conceived and geographically extensive campaign to win the presidency. For the first time in 15 years, Democrats controlled the presidency and both houses of Congress.

See also Democratic Party, 1800–2008.

FURTHER READING. Gerald M. Pomper et al., *The Election of 1984: Reports and Interpretations*, 1985; Idem, *The Election of 1988: Reports and Interpretations*, 1989; Idem, *The Election of 1992: Reports and Interpretations*, 1993; Idem, *The Election of 1996: Reports and Interpretations*, 1997; Idem, *The Election of 2000: Reports and Interpretations*, 2001; Theodore H. White, *America in Search of Itself: The Making of the President 1956–1980*, 1982; Jules Witcover, *Party of the People: A History of the Democrats*, 2003.

LEO P. RIBUFFO

E

economy and politics to 1860

Before the Civil War, the central impetus for economic development was the growth of markets.
Simply put, people bought and sold more on regional, national, and international markets than they
had done in the colonial period. In the eighteenth
century, high transportation costs, low population
densities, and shortages of cash kept many Americans from participating in these markets. A wave of
nineteenth-century transportation projects (known
to contemporaries as "internal improvements")
made it far easier to exchange goods and services
with more distant places. Farmers took advantage of
turnpikes, canals, river improvements, and railroads
and produced greater surpluses of cash crops. Farmers specializing in cash crops demanded more textiles, furniture, clocks, books, and other consumer
goods. Demand from the countryside created a large
market for merchants and manufacturers that fueled
the growth of cities and industries. Scores of newly
chartered banks provided capital to entrepreneurs
taking advantage of these new opportunities. Historians have called the great expansion of commerce
the "market revolution." Economists have labeled
the process "Smithian growth," after the famous
eighteenth-century economist Adam Smith. Smith
argued that economic specialization and the division
of labor—the crux of what he called the "wealth of
nations," the title of his classic treatise—crucially depended on large markets.

The expansion of markets rested as much on political decisions as on economic actions. Scholars have
increasingly viewed "institutions"—what might be
thought of as the myriad formal and informal rules
that shape economic behavior—as a central component of market exchanges. Nineteenth-century
Americans self-consciously adopted rules that favored the creation of markets, whether these were
permissive policies toward corporate chartering or
the removal of barriers to interstate trade. The "rules
of the game" that Americans chose reflected a consensus that commercial and technological progress
generated widespread benefits. If Americans generally agreed that commercial progress was important,
they disagreed on precisely how national, state, and
local governments would shape commercial markets.
Two distinct visions dominated economic policy.
One called for large-scale federal involvement—
including national banks, national internal improvements, and a high tariff—while the other favored a
decentralized approach in which state and local governments would take the lead in encouraging economic development. These two different visions of

economic change would help shape political parties
and economic policy before the Civil War.

Economic Issues and the First Party System

When ratified in 1788, the Constitution established a
favorable framework for the growth of markets. The
Constitution prohibited the states from establishing
trade barriers and thus established a large internal
"free-trade zone" that allowed commerce to flourish.
Contracts, including debts, made in one state were
enforceable in another, giving businesses confidence
to engage in interstate commerce. The Constitution
also authorized a patent system that protected the
rights of inventors. During the nineteenth century
the federal government made patents cheap to obtain and easy to enforce—at least relative to European nations—which encouraged inventive activity
among thousands of individuals, from humble mechanics to professional inventors. While generally favorable to development, the Constitution was also
ambiguous about the role of the federal government
in promoting economic development. Could the
federal government establish a central bank to help
stabilize the nation's financial system? Could the federal government build roads, canals, and other internal improvements? Could the federal government
enact tariffs to protect domestic industry from foreign competition?

The Federalists, led by nationalists such as Alexander Hamilton and John Adams, believed that
strong national institutions could bind the fragmented republic together. A large national debt,
for example, ensured that the prominent financiers
and merchants who owned government securities
would have a vested interest in the security and prosperity of the nation. In similar fashion, a national
bank that would handle the business of the federal
government, including the deposit of tax receipts,
would give merchants and manufacturers a source
of capital while regulating state and local banks.
The Federalist vision of a strong, activist state had
an undeniable modernizing element, but it sprang
from a decidedly eighteenth-century view of politics
and society. The Federalists self-consciously sought
to concentrate economic and political power in the
hands of a small group of wealthy men with the experience, expertise, and leadership to run the nation's
economy. In the Federalist vision ordinary voters
would act as a check to ensure that these men did
not abuse these powers, but Federalists presumed
that most men of modest means would defer to their
economic and social superiors.

The Federalists prevailed in the 1790s, and with
Hamilton's leadership they nationalized the Revolutionary War debt (some of which had been owed by

individual states), levied new taxes, and established a national bank. In the pivotal election of 1800, however, Thomas Jefferson's Republican Party triumphed and would dominate electoral politics for the next quarter century. Republicans advocated a decentralized approach to economic policy, leaving most power in the hands of states and localities. Jefferson and his adherents interpreted the Federalist program as a ploy to centralize power within the hands of a power-hungry cabal of would-be aristocrats. Republicans believed, for example, that a national bank would use its considerable financial resources to reward its friends and punish its enemies, thus setting into motion a cycle of corruption that threatened the very existence of the republic. Republicans tied their support for expanding democracy (at least for white males) with their critique of Federalist economic policies: ordinary farmers and artisans, not elitist financiers, should be the real drivers of economic development. Once in power, Jefferson cut taxes, decreased government spending, and reduced the size of the government debt. President James Madison, a close friend of Jefferson and a stalwart Republican, allowed Hamilton's Bank of the United States to expire in 1811.

Political Economy and the Second Party System

Despite the success of the Jeffersonians in limiting the economic role of the federal government, conflict with Great Britain (culminating in the War of 1812) led some Republicans to embrace elements of economic nationalism, albeit without Hamilton's overt elitism. The fusion of economic nationalism with Jeffersonian democracy is best represented by Henry Clay's "American System." Clay argued that protecting American industry from foreign manufacturers would create large internal markets for cotton, foodstuffs, and other agricultural products. Clay and other advocates of the American System argued that high tariffs would benefit all sectors of the economy. Manufacturers would flourish, safely protected from cheap foreign goods. Farmers and planters would also prosper as a safe, dependable home market replaced uncertain foreign markets as the major outlet of American agricultural products. Merchants who coordinated the exchanges between cities and the countryside would see their business grow as well.

By 1832, Clay added two other major elements to the American System: a government-financed system of transportation improvements and a national bank. As committed nationalists, Clay and his allies—who eventually became known as National Republicans and then Whigs—believed that federal funding of roads, canals, and railroads would connect all American localities to the domestic market. Clay and his allies also vigorously defended the Second Bank of the United States, which they believed would regulate state banks, ensure a stable currency, and supply businesses with much-needed capital. A national system of internal improvements and a national bank

would also strengthen commercial ties and provide a shared set of common economic interests that would transcend regional loyalties. The economic and nationalistic appeals of the American System became an important part of Clay's platform during his presidential bids in 1824, 1832, and 1844. The nationalistic wing of the Jeffersonian Party embraced the American System in the 1820s. The National Republicans became a core constituency of the Whig Party, which formed in the early 1830s to oppose Andrew Jackson. Influential editors and writers such as Hezekiah Niles and Henry Carey strongly supported the Whig agenda, which also found considerable support in commercially developed areas with substantial manufacturing interests.

Much as Clay sought to revitalize elements of Hamilton's nationalistic program, Andrew Jackson resuscitated the Jeffersonian critique of activist government. Elected in 1828 on a populist appeal to democracy, Jackson aggressively attacked elements of Clay's American System. In 1830 Jackson vetoed the Maysville Road Bill, which would have provided federal funding for an important project in Clay's own state of Kentucky. Even more important, Jackson vetoed, in 1832, a bill to recharter the Second Bank of the United States. Jackson soundly defeated Clay in the presidential election of 1832, effectively dooming the American System. Most voters (especially those in the South and West) apparently shared Jackson's fears that the Whig economic program, in mixing economic power with political centralization, would invite political corruption. Traditional fears of political corruption reflected concerns that state activism was a zero-sum game in which some interests won and other interests lost. Such a political environment made it especially difficult for the federal government to fund transportation projects. Cities, states, and regions perceived to be on the short end of federal funding became a powerful voting bloc to oppose government investment. Federal funding thus proceeded on an ad hoc basis with little systematic planning.

A distinctly regional critique of activist government developed in the South. High tariffs were especially unpopular there: planters opposed paying higher prices for manufactured goods for the benefit of northeastern manufacturers. Some Southerners also feared that the centralization of power inherent in the American System presented a long-term threat to slavery. If the federal government had the power to protect industry, build canals, and regulate banking, they reasoned, then it might have the power to abolish slavery as well. During the winter of 1832–33, South Carolina took the dramatic step of nullifying the Tariff of 1828, which was known in the state as the "tariff of abominations." South Carolina eventually backed down, but the state's response indicated that Southerners saw an activist national government as a threat to slavery. As debates over slavery became more intense during the 1840s and 1850s, southern opposition to activist policies (at least those emanating from the federal government) hardened, resulting in a legislative deadlock that eliminated any real hope of passing the Whig's economic agenda.

Economic Development at the State Level

Jeffersonians and Jacksonians, however critical of national initiatives, eagerly supported economic development at the state and local level. Leaving most economic policy in the hands of state and local governments, in fact, helped democratize institutions such as the corporation. European nations tended to tightly restrict corporate chartering, often giving established corporations monopoly privileges in return for sweetheart deals with government officials. In the United States, though, intense competition between states and cities worked to loosen corporate chartering, as legislatures sought to please a variety of influential local interests. The more decentralized and democratic political culture in the United States encouraged logrolling rather than legislative monopoly. Banking is an excellent example. The number of state-chartered banks accelerated sharply so that, by 1820, the United States was well ahead of Great Britain and other European nations in bank capital per capita. These state banks were hardly the exclusive domain of wealthy financiers. Tens of thousands of ordinary individuals—including a good many prosperous farmers and artisans—invested in state-chartered banks. Political institutions in the United States, in short, managed to channel powerful "bottom-up" forces into economic development.

The decentralized nature of economic policy in the United States sometimes led to greater government involvement in the economy. Transportation improvements are a case in point. Fearing that private investors would avoid the risk associated with large-scale projects, the New York legislature authorized the construction of the Erie Canal as a state-run enterprise in 1817. The canal, built along a 363-mile route from Albany to Buffalo, promised an all-water route from the Great Lakes region to New York City. Completed in 1825, the Erie Canal was a stunning success. The bonanza of canal revenues allowed New York to finance politically popular branch lines. Prodded by New York's example, state governments in Pennsylvania, Maryland, and Virginia attempted to build their own canal systems to improve links with the Trans-Appalachian West. From 1817 to 1844 Americans invested nearly $131 million to build 3,360 miles of canals. Most of the investment came from state governments eager to spur economic development, either directly from canal revenues or indirectly via property taxes on rapidly appreciating land.

The failure of most canals to meet the grandiose expectations of their supporters led to fiscal retrenchment in many states. Part of the problem was that the Erie Canal proved exceptionally profitable. Most other canals, traversing more mountainous terrain or serving smaller populations, barely covered the cost of upkeep and repairs. Heavy investments in canals created large state debts that led to a backlash against state investment. In the 1840s and 1850s, important northern states such as New York, Pennsylvania, and Ohio adopted constitutional amendments that banned government investment in private corporations. The backlash against state canal investment—combined with the continued development of financial centers such as New York City and Philadelphia—left most railroad construction in private hands. Faster and more flexible than canals, railroads captured the imagination of both private capitalists and the general public. By 1840 Americans had built 2,818 miles of track; by 1860 that figure ballooned to 30,626 miles.

Although private capital financed much of the nation's railroad network, railroads were hardly examples of free enterprise. In the North, municipal and county governments often purchased railroad stock to encourage local companies. In the South, the region's slave economy prevented the growth of large financial centers that might finance railroad construction. State investment thus remained the norm. The public character of railroads, even when they were privately financed, generated a host of disputes that courts and local governments often decided. Should eminent domain compensation be determined by local juries (which often favored landowners) or special commissioners (which often favored companies)? Should railroads compensate farmers when locomotives struck livestock that were crossing tracks? Could cities regulate railroad operations to reduce noise, congestion, and pollution? Judges and legislators typically attempted to strike compromises that mediated the government's considerable interest in encouraging railroad construction with individual and public rights.

For the most part, the federal government played a secondary role to state and local governments in the proliferation of transportation companies. National policies—especially land policy—nevertheless had an important indirect impact. The federal government made land grants to various canals and railroads in the West and South. Although small compared to the investment of state governments, these land grants nevertheless aided individual enterprises, such as Indiana's Wabash and Erie Canal. More important, federal policy regarding land sales affected the rate of western settlement, thus had an important impact on internal improvements and the rest of the economy. Some easterners (including Northerners and Southerners) feared that rapid western expansion would undermine their own political influence. They therefore supported relatively high prices for the vast tracts of western land that the U.S. government owned. Not only did high prices slow western settlement, but they also provided an important source of revenue for the federal government. Popular pressure for cheap western land, though, led to the passage of the Land Act of 1841, which allowed settlers the right to buy a 160-acre homestead for as low as $1.25 per acre.

In the 1850s, the emerging Republican Party embraced the nationalistic ideas of Hamilton and Clay. Abraham Lincoln and many other Republicans had long admired Clay and his ideas. Republicans eagerly supported generous land grants to transcontinental railroads, a highly protective tariff, and a new national bank. Unlike Clay, the Republicans made slavery an economic policy issue. Believing that slavery inevitably discouraged hard work and enterprise, Republicans blamed the institution for the South's lack of development. While southern slaveholders often generated large profits from plantation agriculture, the South lagged behind the North in urbanization, manufacturing, and other benchmarks of economic development. Republicans, fearing that slavery would poison the national economy if allowed to spread, thus opposed the extension of slavery into the West. They instead supported a homestead act that would allow free-labor households to acquire federal land at little or no cost. Debates over federal land policy played a crucial role in the coming of the Civil War.

See also business and politics; economy and politics since 1860.

FURTHER READING. Naomi R. Lamoreaux, *Insider Lending: Banks, Personal Connections, and Economic Development in Industrial New England*, 1994; John Lauritz Larson, *Internal Improvement: National Public Works and the Promise of Popular Government in the Early United States*, 2000; John Majewski, *A House Dividing: Economic Development in Pennsylvania and Virginia before the Civil War*, 2000; David R. Meyer, *The Roots of American Industrialization*, 2003; Winifred Barr Rothenberg, *From Market-Places to a Market Economy: The Transformation of Rural Massachusetts, 1750–1850*, 1992; Gavin Wright, *Slavery and American Economic Development*, 2006.

JOHN MAJEWSKI

economy and politics, 1860–1920

Since the founding of the republic, Americans have debated about how to make the economy work for the general welfare. Making it work, however, has always been a means to larger social and political ends. Growing the economy has never been an end in itself.

Liberty was, at the founding, construed as a simple function of property ownership: if you owned property, you were economically independent of others, and thus could be a self-mastering individual—a citizen. Americans have since redefined liberty, equality, and citizenship, but most still conceive of "real politics" in terms of their economic status.

The politics of the period from 1860 to 1920 can be viewed as a debate about how to reorganize or reject an Atlantic economy, then as a way of imagining the political future of a more cosmopolitan, a more inclusive—maybe even a global—economy. Thus conceived, the politics of the period became an argument about how, not whether, to include the federal government in the sponsorship and supervision of economic arrangements.

The nonmilitary legislation of the 1860s, for example, which enacted the Republican platform on which Abraham Lincoln ran for president, was a detailed blueprint for industrialization on a continental scale. It could be implemented only because the South had removed its representatives from the national legislature. The Morrill tariff of 1861 was the first step. It reversed the trend toward free trade, which began under President Andrew Jackson in 1832 and culminated under President James Buchanan in 1857. The new tariff imposed specific duties on imports such as steel rails and thus allowed American manufacturers to undersell their more efficient British competitors.

Other steps included the Homestead Act, which excluded slavery from the territories by encouraging white settlers to head for the new frontier in the trans-Mississippi West; the National Banking Acts of 1863 and 1864, which, by forbidding state and private banks to issue money, created a uniform national currency and a new stratum of bankers with vested interests in manufacturing and transportation; the Immigration Act of 1864, which flooded the late-nineteenth-century American labor market with exactly the kind of ornery, adventurous, and ambitious individuals who might have led the class struggle back home; and the Aid to Railroads Acts of 1864–68, which subsidized the construction of transcontinental trunk lines, thus building the necessary infrastructure of a tightly knit national market for both finished goods and investment capital. Finally, the three "freedom amendments" to the Constitution—the Thirteenth, Fourteenth, and Fifteenth Amendments—abolished slavery, guaranteed due process of law to all persons (regardless of race), and armed the freedmen with the vote. Together they created a unitary labor/property system and prevented the restoration of the South to its prewar political preeminence.

This last step, a result of Radical Reconstruction, was more important than it may seem, because the repeal of the Republican Party's blueprint for modern America was a real possibility. Indeed, it was a programmatic imperative of the Democratic Party in the North. Even moderate Republicans with constituencies in the seaboard cities of the Northeast were anxious to restore, not reconstruct, the abject South, because the merchants and bankers who had organized and financed the antebellum cotton trade from their offices in New York, Philadelphia, and Boston wanted an immediate return to a free-trade Atlantic economy in which the pound sterling and the gold standard ruled. Many thousands of other Northerners who had been employed in and by this trade wanted the same thing.

When a majority of these merchants and bankers realized that there were more lucrative outlets for their capital in the "great and growing West" than in the restoration of the South and the resurrection of the cotton trade, the possibility of a return to a free-trade Atlantic economy was dead. So, too, was the Democratic Party's preference for "do-nothing government" (or "laissez-faire"). So, finally, was the related notion that the future of the American economy would be determined by the scale and scope of British demand for agricultural raw materials. In this sense, the abdication of merchant capital, the political power behind King Cotton's throne, turned agriculture into a mere branch of industry. As a result, the once regnant, even arrogant South had to reinvent itself as a political supplicant and a colonial appendage of the northeastern metropolis.

Politics in the late nineteenth century was mostly a matter of answering the money question, the labor question, and the trust question, as they were then called. Of course, party coalitions were based as much on ethnic loyalties and rivalries as on class allegiances. In the United States, race and ethnicity are never absent, or even distant, from the calculations of politicians. But the public discourse of the period 1860–1920 was a language of class conflict that kept asking not whether but how to use the powers of the state and federal governments to promote *equitable* economic development.

The political stalemate of the post–Civil War period had both a class component and a regional one. The regional component was a continental version of imperial politics. The northeastern metropolis stretching from Boston to Chicago could not simply impose its will on the South or the West in the 1880s and 1890s. Too many states and too many people resisted the juggernaut of industrial capitalism, sometimes with electoral initiatives and sometimes with extra-electoral activity that involved armed struggle, as in the terrorist campaigns of white supremacists in the South during Reconstruction and after.

The class component of the "great stalemate" was more important, however, because it had more profound intellectual as well as political effects. The short version of the argument is that the workers were winning the class struggle of the late nineteenth century, and the capitalists knew it. Certainly the rise of "big business" was a crucial phenomenon in the period, but corporations could not translate their obvious market power into political legitimacy without a struggle. When workers went on strike, for example, local populations usually sided with them.

Many observers of the economic scene proposed, therefore, to change things, so that labor and capital could share more equitably in the benefits of industrial accumulation. From the standpoint of capital, this change would mean that labor relinquished its control over machine production and allowed for greater efficiency and for a more minute division of labor. From the standpoint of labor, this change would mean that capital relinquished or reduced its claim to a share of national income, on the grounds that it produced nothing—that capital merely deducted its income from the sum of value produced by others.

This was the labor question of the late nineteenth century: how to allocate the benefits of economic growth in such a way that all social classes, all social strata—not just capital, not just labor—might benefit. It shaped political discourse because the answers determined where the parties stood but also where other organizations and institutions situated themselves, including state governments and federal courts.

The subtext was a political question: Could republican government survive the eruption of class conflict and the emergence of class society? Arthur T. Hadley, a Yale University economist who was also a member of the Pennsylvania Railroad's finance committee, answered this way: "A republican government is organized on the assumption that all men are free and equal. If the political power is equally distributed while the industrial power is concentrated in the hands of the few, it creates dangers of class struggles and class legislation which menace both our political and our industrial order."

The pacification of the epic class struggle of the late nineteenth century, a struggle that was more open, violent, and sustained in the United States than anywhere else, occurred only when the labor movement accepted capital as a legitimate claimant on a share of national income. This accomplishment was largely, but not only, the result of the American Federation of Labor (AFL), founded in 1886, and it was not complete until 1914, with the Clayton Act (which is usually interpreted as a concession to labor). Even then, labor was still the junior partner of capital, and would remain so until 1935, when the Wagner Act gave the federal government the power to punish businesses for refusing to deal with unions.

The money question was more complicated, and reached more constituencies, but it addressed the same problem: how to equitably allocate the benefits of economic growth. Was the money supply a cause or an effect of economic growth? What did money represent, anyway?

From the standpoint of capital, the money supply had increased in the late nineteenth century because substitutes for cash and coin had supplemented these meager (and shrinking) means of exchange—substitutes like checks, drafts, bills, securities, futures—all the financial devices that people called "credit" and understood as the foundation of a new, corporate economy. From the standpoint of labor and farmer activists, the money supply had shrunk because, after 1873, silver was no longer a precious metal to be treated as the backing for currency or the stuff of coins. The volume of national banknotes did, in fact, decline during and after the 1880s, but the procapitalist position was correct—the money supply had increased in spite of this decline.

For the critics, money was merely a means of exchange. To increase its quantity was to increase demand for goods, thus employing more labor and growing the economy and to make sure that price deflation didn't force borrowers to pay off their loans in money that was worth more than they originally took from the bank. From the standpoint of capital, money was multifarious, mysterious—it was credit, a system unto itself. As Edward Bellamy explained in *Looking Backward* (1888), his best-selling utopian novel that created something of a political cult, "Money was a sign of real commodities, but credit was but the sign of a sign."

Close regulation of the money supply and the ability to manage economic crises with such financial devices as interest rates and reserve requirements were finally accomplished with the creation of the Federal Reserve System in 1913. The answer to the money question, like the resolution of the labor question, was an adjunct to the trust question, for it made the corporation the central problem, and promise, of the politics of the period.

The trust questions went like this: Can we regulate and discipline these large corporations? Are they natural monopolies or unlawful restraints of trade? (The common law made this distinction, and the political discourse of the time seized on it.) Do they signify industrial serfdom? Can we be mere employees of their huge bureaucracies and still be free men and women? If they are artificial persons, fragile artifacts of the law, does that mean we are, too?

The turn of the wheel—the end of the Great Stalemate—came in the late 1890s, when the AFL could provide its new answer to the labor question and when Democrat-Populist William Jennings Bryan lost his bid for the presidency in 1896. "Free silver" became something of a joke, and the money question was resolved in favor of a gold standard.

Progressivism and Imperialism

After 1896, the urban industrial area of the nation was the primary scene of political discourse and party conflict. The relation between the corporations and the larger society was the question that shaped, even dominated, the Progressive Era. Some historians argue that, ironically, procorporate ideologues, executives, intellectuals, and journalists wrote a lot of the legislation that regulated the new corporations—the products of the great merger movement of 1898–1903. But there is no irony in the simple fact that large business enterprises need stability and predictability, and therefore want regulation of market forces.

The anarchy of the market is anathema for all participants, in capital as well as in labor. The issue was not whether but how to regulate it, through public agencies such as the Federal Reserve and the Federal Trade Commission (FTC) or through private organizations such as trade unions.

The Progressive Era was a time when the corporation was finally "domesticated," to borrow historian Richard Hofstadter's term. It was finally recognized as a normal part of economic and political life in the United States. By 1920 it was subject to close regulation, juridical supervision, and consistent public scrutiny. Woodrow Wilson had successfully split the difference between William Howard Taft and Theodore Roosevelt in the 1912 campaign by rejecting both Roosevelt's program of statist command of the market and Taft's program of fervent trust-busting in the name of renewed competition. The FTC was the emblem of his different answer to the trust question, combining executive power, antitrust law, and regulatory zeal without a trace of nostalgia for the small business owner.

The "domestication" of the large corporation in the Progressive Era also changed the world. For if imperialism was possible in the absence of corporate capitalism, the new corporate order could not survive in the absence of imperialism. The corporations were simply too efficient in reducing costs and increasing output without a comparable increase of labor inputs. Their "scientific" managers redesigned the shop floors to economize on the costs of skilled labor (the advent of electric power helped), and improved productivity to the point where the growth of the industrial working class ceased by 1905. What then? Where would the surplus go?

By the 1880s, the domestic market was saturated with the output of American industry. New overseas markets were imperative. Industry leaders and intellectuals were trying, by the 1890s, to think through an imperial model that would avoid the idiocies of European colonialism. The point was to avoid military conquest and occupation.

At the end of the nineteenth century, U.S. policy makers and a new stratum of such "public intellectuals" as Charles Conant, Arthur T. Hadley, and Jeremiah Jenks were inventing a new kind of imperialism, so new that it inaugurated the "American Century." With the international circulation of John Hay's *Open Door Notes* in 1899–1900, there was a doctrine to go with the new thinking.

The doctrine had six core principles. First, all people, all cultures, were capable of development—there were no racial barriers to advanced civilization. Second, in view of the insurrections staged in the American South and West in the late nineteenth century, as well as the Boxer Rebellion in China, economic development was the key to creating modern social strata where there were none. It was a risky strategy because rapid growth always displaces vested interests and creates new ones, but the alternative was recurrent insurrection on behalf of people deprived of the fruits of development. Third, development meant direct investment in, or transfers of technology to, less-developed parts of the world. Trade was important, but nowhere near as important as investment.

Fourth, the sovereignty of every nation, including China, then a large but crumbling empire, was inviolable. The American experience of the nineteenth century had taught U.S. policy makers like John Hay, the secretary of state under Presidents William McKinley and Theodore Roosevelt, that a nation could absorb enormous quantities of foreign capital and still thrive as long as its political integrity was kept intact. Fifth, the seat of empire was shifting to the United States. The question was, could this shift be accomplished without war?

Yes, Hay and others said, and their answer was the sixth core principle—that of an anticolonial, open-door world. If economic growth was the means to pacify domestic class conflict and avoid international conflict over the allocation of *shares* of world income, they claimed, then a world without barriers to trade and investment was a world of peace. If the *volume* of world income grew quickly enough, there would be no fighting about respective *shares*. An open-door world—without exclusive "spheres of influence," without colonies—was then the way to a *postimperialist* future.

The Politics of War and the Shape of the Future

This is the world for which the United States, under President Woodrow Wilson, went to war in 1917. It was not the world that resulted; the European victors were not about to give up their colonial possessions because the United States asked them to. But it is the world that American policy makers described as their goal until the end of the twentieth century, when neoconservatives proposed to go back to a military definition of power.

American entry into World War I was predicated on the politics of the new imperialism, which would have been almost entirely economic in nature. With U.S. troops in battle, the stalemate between the warring sides would be broken. A socialist revolution could be forestalled and German victory prevented. So, too, would the reinstatement of European colonialism proposed by the Allies, for the United States would no longer be a neutral party and could negotiate an early version of decolonization through a system of mandates.

The results were as good as could be expected in the absence of a prolonged American military presence in Europe, something that was unthinkable in 1919, when the war ended. For that reason, the United States could never have joined the League of Nations: enough senators refused to deploy American military power, such as it was, to sustain empires already in place.

Still, the future was written in the second decade of the twentieth century. An open-door world became the aim of American foreign policy. Organized labor came of age during and after the war; it waned and it waited in the 1920s, to be sure, but it was ready for power when depression struck in the 1930s. Finally, the problem of structural unemployment became crucial to the thinking of economists and politicians alike.

Here, the issue of corporate efficiency was again the driving force. The new corporations could increase output without any increase of inputs—whether of labor or of capital. So the pressing questions became how to employ a growing population and what would happen to the intellectual and political status of profit. If employment can't be provided to a growing population through private investment, what justification is there for profit? And, how else could people be employed? Public spending? These were the questions that surfaced in the second decade of the twentieth century, and we are still trying to answer them.

See also banking policy; business and politics; labor movement and politics; tariffs and politics.

FURTHER READING. Richard Bensel, *The Political Economy of American Industrialization, 1877–1900*, 2002; Alfred D. Chandler, Jr., *The Visible Hand: The Managerial Revolution in American Business*, 1977; Richard Hofstadter, *The Age of Reform*, 1955; James Livingston, *Pragmatism and the Political Economy of Cultural Revolution, 1850–1940*, 1994; Michael McGerr, *The Decline of Popular Politics: The American North, 1865–1928*, 1986; Elizabeth Sanders, *Roots of Reform: Farmers, Workers, and the American State, 1877–1917*, 1999; Martin J. Sklar, *The Corporate Reconstruction of American Capitalism, 1890–1916*, 1988; Robert Wiebe, *The Search for Order, 1877–1920*, 1966.

JAMES LIVINGSTON

economy and politics, 1920–45

In 1920 Republican presidential candidate Warren Harding announced that "America's present need is not heroics, but healing; not nostrums, but normalcy; not revolution, but restoration." Spoken after an alarming year of widespread labor unrest, the vicious Red Scare, and a bruising congressional battle over the country's postwar foreign commitments, the promise of "normalcy" soothed his constituents' jangled nerves and provided them with hope for a swift end to the dislocations stirred up by the Great War. Yet Harding's neologism signaled more than an assurance of domestic peace and a commitment to shut down the international adventures. Not only should Americans put the war and its unsettling aftermath behind them, his words suggested; so, too, should the country dispense with the previous decade of dangerously socialistic economic experimentation.

The Republican Party, as most business conservatives saw it, had been rudely unseated from national power by Democrat Woodrow Wilson's presidency from 1913 to 1921. During that time, an unexpected alliance of rural representatives and urban labor interests had provided the congressional muscle for a sweeping array of federal regulatory legislation, transferring the Progressive reform energy of the states and municipalities to the national level and there consolidating its reach and permanence. Even more jarring to the self-appointed protectors of property and sound money in both parties was the specter of a political coalition of reform-minded Theodore Roosevelt Republicans joined in unholy partnership with agrarian inflationists indoctrinated by the Democratic-populist credos of William Jennings Bryan.

But for the next ten years, party standpatters could put these worries to rest. A decade of unsurpassed prosperity muted the previous era's concerns for economic justice and responsive government. Both Harding and his successor, Calvin Coolidge, brought to the White House a political philosophy oriented toward private accumulation and proud of governmental inaction. "The chief business of the American people is business," Coolidge famously intoned, a dictum perfectly matched to the country's diminished concern with corporate concentration. Big businesses, now depicted in splashy advertisements, provided valuable and essential services that distributed everyday comforts and conveniences, brought families closer together, and satisfied the individual tastes of discerning consumers.

Indeed, after a brief recession that ended in 1921, the American economy certainly appeared capable of raising living standards quickly and dramatically, and without government interference. By 1930 manufacturing output had increased fourfold over 1900 levels. Real industrial wages, which rose almost 25 percent during the 1920s, put a portion of the accompanying productivity gains directly into the worker's pocket. The technological and organizational feats of Fordist mass production turned out low-cost consumer durables at prices average Americans could afford. High wages and low prices most famously brought automobile ownership within the reach of millions; at decade's end, one out every five Americans was driving a car. But they were not only crowding the roads with their modern marvels; by 1930 almost two-thirds of the nation's homes received electric service. Electrical appliances—refrigerators, ovens, radios, and vacuum cleaners—had become regular features of domestic life.

The nation's rapidly growing urban areas, which housed a majority of the population after 1920, provided the primary setting for such dizzying consumption. The decade's very prosperity, in fact, pushed the economic questions of the Progressive Era to the back burner and brought to the political forefront a simmering cultural divide between small-town America and the cities with their bustling immigrant communities, beer-soaked politics, and increasingly cosmopolitan tastes. Nothing showcased these geographical frictions better than the Democratic Party, reduced during the 1920s to infighting between its urban, working-class members and a Protestant, native-born, and prohibitionist wing. Furthermore, the party's rural faction was anchored—even dominated—by the segregationist, antiunion South, whose cotton barons and low-wage employers suppressed the region's populist heritage, warily eyed the big-city machines, and accrued ever

more congressional seniority. Fistfights broke out on the 1924 Democratic Party convention floor over a petition to condemn the Ku Klux Klan and brought the proceedings to a days-long standstill. Irish Catholic Alfred E. Smith, backed by New York City's Tammany Hall and an emblem of all the Klan reviled, lost that nomination, only to claim it four years later and to suffer a humiliating national defeat in 1928.

Rural Issues during the 1920s

The culture war falls short as a guiding framework for the political world of the 1920s, however. What separated the town and the country was not merely a mismatch of values and social customs but a gaping economic imbalance. Industrial America had not yet vanquished its agrarian past. Farmers still constituted nearly one-third of the nation's workforce, but earned, on average, one-fourth the income of industrial workers. While other Americans experienced rising wages and dazzling consumer choices, farmers received an unwelcome taste of the Great Depression to come. Emboldened by high prices and government encouragement, they had expanded production during World War I, often pushing into marginal lands where success was far from certain. Agricultural incomes dropped precipitously when overseas demand plummeted after 1920. Besieged by the postwar contraction, farmers found themselves caught between the low prices they received for farm products and the high prices they paid for nonfarm items; wheat and other commodity markets suffered from overproduction throughout the decade.

This agricultural distress prompted urgent calls for national assistance from a new congressional bloc of southern Democrats and farm-state Republicans. Their discontent found concrete expression in the McNary-Haugen Farm Bills, the focal point of farm relief legislation during the 1920s. The legislation proposed to raise domestic prices directly by selling surplus stocks abroad. Its proponents believed that this two-price system would not entail special protection for agriculture; it would simply extend the benefits of the tariff (already enjoyed by American manufacturers) to farmers. New Deal policy makers would soon criticize this export dumping and prescribe a purely domestic agricultural rescue package, but not before the bills faced decisive opposition from President Coolidge as well as Herbert Hoover, his Republican successor.

The political significance of the agricultural depression, though, lay not in the farm bloc's defeats during the 1920s but in the growing potential to resurrect an alliance between rural Democrats and Progressive Republicans. The absence of farm prosperity and the search for a method to address the economic imbalance kept alive an issue tailor-made for uniting rural representatives of all political stripes: public power. Private utilities and electric companies had decided that most farmers simply did not have the income to put them in the customer class; it was far more profitable to serve more densely populated urban areas. No one represented the progressive's passion for public power more than Nebraska Republican George Norris, who battled to bring the nation's rivers and waterways under state-sponsored, multiple-purpose control. Throughout the 1920s, Senator Norris labored to keep the government's World War I–era hydroelectric facility at Muscle Shoals, Alabama, in public hands and to use it as the starting point for a more ambitious scheme to develop the entire Tennessee River basin—a project realized eventually in the creation of the Tennessee Valley Authority. However, like the proponents of the McNary-Haugen Bills, the proponents of public power also faced decisive presidential opposition before the New Deal.

Onset of the Great Depression

While the agricultural depression aroused Progressive-like calls for government assistance during a decade whose governing ethos rejected such intervention, it also contributed to the Great Depression. Of the many domestic causes of the Depression's length and severity, the inequitable distribution of wealth ranks very high. The maladjustment was not only apparent in the disparity between rural and urban incomes; workers' wages, despite their increase, had failed to rise in step with industrial output or with corporate profits, thus spreading too thinly the purchasing power required to run the motors of mass production. The lower 93 percent of the population actually saw their per-capita incomes drop during the latter part of the 1920s. Furthermore, far too many excited buyers had purchased all of those consumer durables on installment plans. Entire industries balanced precariously on a shaky foundation of consumer debt.

The automobile and construction sectors felt the pinch as early as 1925, and by the end of the decade, businesses struggled with unsold inventories that had nearly quadrupled in value. A speculative frenzy on Wall Street ended with a stock market crash in the autumn of 1929. Less than 5 percent of the population owned securities in 1929, but many more Americans held bank deposits, and lost those in the wave of bank failures that followed. Still, the Depression was not merely the result of income inequality or credit-fueled overexpansion. It also emerged from a complicated tangle of domestic and international circumstances—an undercapitalized banking system with too few branch operations; a Federal Reserve that restricted the money supply instead of easing credit; an unassisted Europe that defaulted on its war debts; and a world trading system that fell prey to fits of economic nationalism. Much of the blame, in fact, could be placed on the doorstep of the United States, which emerged from World War I as the world's leading creditor nation but evaded the responsibilities of this leadership. Instead, during the 1920s, the U.S. government hindered the repayment of European debt and restricted the global movement of labor,

goods, and capital by halting immigration and raising tariffs to astronomically high levels—even while aggressively promoting its own products overseas. The president to whose lot the economic emergency first fell was Herbert Hoover, a widely respected engineer who had orchestrated European food relief efforts during World War I and who had served as secretary of commerce under Harding and Coolidge. Unlike his predecessors, Hoover was no orthodox disciple of laissez-faire. He claimed that the increasing complexity of modern society required the federal government to gather information and suggestions for the nation's improvement. He insisted, though, that these tools be used primarily to assist the voluntary activities of those people, businesses, and local governments interested in collective self-help.

By the spring of 1933, nearly 25 percent of the labor force was unemployed, and millions more worked only part-time. Construction had slowed, manufacturing had stalled, and new investment had virtually come to a halt. Traditional sources of assistance—mutual aid societies, municipal treasuries, even national charities—were crippled by such unprecedented need. Unlike his treasury secretary, Andrew Mellon, whom Hoover later criticized as a "leave-it-alone liquidationist," the president at first demonstrated considerable flexibility—he cajoled industrial leaders to resist lowering wages; requested public works funds from the U.S. Congress; persuaded the Federal Reserve to ease credit (though, as events would prove, not by nearly enough); and set up the Reconstruction Finance Corporation to provide billions of dollars to banks and businesses. On a few critical issues, however, Hoover dug in his heels: he refused to sanction direct federal assistance for either farmers or unemployed people, and he opposed any proposal that required the government to produce and distribute electricity without the assistance of private business.

Franklin D. Roosevelt and the New Deal

Into this political opening marched Franklin D. Roosevelt, the Democratic governor of New York, who challenged Hoover for the presidency in 1932. Roosevelt not only pledged relief to the urban unemployed but—unlike his gubernatorial predecessor Alfred E. Smith—also demonstrated remarkable acuity for rural issues. During his governorship, Roosevelt had begun a statewide program of soil surveys and reforestation, and attempted to provide rural New Yorkers with inexpensive electricity from government-run hydroelectric power facilities. In his lustiest presidential campaign rhetoric, he promised federal development of prime hydroelectric sites across the country. The federal government would not only build the required infrastructure but would distribute the electricity to the surrounding communities at the lowest possible cost. Roosevelt also committed his party to a program of direct farm assistance that would combine production control with higher prices and natural resource conservation.

Roosevelt put rural issues up front in his campaign not simply to distinguish his record from Hoover's but because he and his advisors attributed the Depression to an absence of farm purchasing power. Low agricultural incomes, they argued, kept factories idle and urban workers unemployed. Roosevelt had addressed the question of the urban unemployed as governor by instituting work relief and welfare benefits, anticipating the similar programs of the New Deal as well as the federal government's recognition of organized labor. Still, the model of the Depression that he initially adopted cast the farm sector as the primary problem, with the low purchasing power of the working class a complementary concern. Whatever the genuine economic causes of the Depression—and Roosevelt can certainly be faulted for embracing an exclusively domestic analysis, especially an agrarian fundamentalist one—the underconsumptionist model was political gold. The president intended to use the nation's economic distress to transcend the poisonous cultural divide between the country and the city and to create a more lasting reform coalition within the Democratic Party.

In the election of 1932, Roosevelt won a significant plurality of votes in the nation's major cities, swept the South and the West, and polled his largest majorities in the farm regions. Congress, pressured by constituents at home to do something quickly, submitted to executive leadership and engaged in a remarkable flurry of legislative energy. It first passed measures repairing the country's money and credit. To restore confidence in the financial system, Roosevelt authorized the federal government to reorganize failing banks and to issue more currency. Congress also created the Federal Deposit Insurance Corporation (FDIC) to insure regular Americans' savings accounts. The rural wing of the Democratic Party had historically agitated for inflation so that farm prices might rise and debts be repaid with easier money. Roosevelt moved in this direction by partially severing the currency from the gold standard, which had provided a basis of trust for international financial transactions but impeded domestic growth. Funneling assistance to those in need was an equally urgent task, and the administration set up aid programs that distributed cash grants through state relief agencies, put the unemployed directly to work with government jobs, and employed needy Americans indirectly by investing in public works projects.

The primary new departure in federal policy was the New Deal's attempt to raise prices and wages simultaneously—to get farms and businesses producing again and to supply consumers with the incomes to assist in that recovery. The Agricultural Adjustment Administration (AAA) sought to curb overproduction and raise prices by restricting the acreage planted in key commodities, providing farmers with support payments collected from taxes on agricultural processors. Such intervention was necessary, the AAA argued, to increase farm purchasing power and spur national economic recovery. On the industrial end, the National Recovery Administration (NRA) sought to foster cooperation among government, management, labor, and consumers, empowering planning boards to issue regulatory codes governing wages, prices, and profits. The NRA's enabling act, the National Industrial Recovery Act, also included funds for the Public Works Administration (PWA). The theory was that public works money would operate alongside the AAA's cash benefits to increase the total number of purchases nationwide, while the NRA would see to it that labor and capital shared the fruits of recovery. Policy makers initially embarked on such intricately managerial experiments because they never seriously considered the socialist alternatives—nor, for that matter, other liberal options such as massive government spending or aggressive taxation and redistribution. For most of the 1930s, balanced budgets remained the orthodoxy among New Dealers, including the president, and long-standing traditions of limited government and self-help continued to shape the beliefs of most liberals. Such ideas also continued to shape legal opinion; the Supreme Court overturned the NRA in 1935 and the AAA in 1936.

Rural issues remained central to New Deal policy. Congress enacted the creation of a second AAA, now financed with revenues from the general treasury. The government purchased thousands of acres of marginal and tax-delinquent farmland and added it to the national preserves and forests. Farmers also received cash benefits and technical assistance to halt soil erosion—a cause soon rendered even more urgent after the nation absorbed shocking images of the Dust Bowl—and the government financed construction of massive hydroelectric dams, irrigation facilities, and power distribution systems. Beginning with the Tennessee Valley Authority Act of 1933, every public dam-building agency (such as the TVA, the Bureau of Reclamation, and the Army Corps of Engineers) was required to produce and distribute power to serve surrounding rural areas, a task accomplished with the assistance of other New Deal creations such as the Rural Electrification Administration and the PWA. Such generous financing for rural development especially benefited the South and the West, the "Sunbelt" regions that emerged in the postwar era as economic counterweights to the Northeast and the Midwest.

While agriculture and rural resource policy remained central to New Deal policy, farm politics quickly gave way to a more urban orientation within the Democratic Party. Beginning with Roosevelt's landslide reelection in 1936, urban majorities became decisive in Democratic victories. Roosevelt's urban appeal lay in the federal government's work relief and welfare benefits, and in the New Deal's recognition of formerly marginalized religious and cultural groups. Though some reformers denounced the Democratic Party's ties to city machines, municipal officials and urban constituencies often liberalized the party, pushing to the forefront questions of workplace justice and civil rights. Nothing better signaled the urban liberal turn in national politics than the rise of the labor movement, officially sanctioned in 1935 by the National Labor Relations Act, which guaranteed workers' right to organize, hold elections, and establish closed shops. While business leaders resisted labor organizing, unions won enormous victories in the nation's major industrial centers. Legal recognition and government-mandated bargaining between labor and management put the nation's industrial policy on a more lasting footing: the government would set labor free as a countervailing power to business, rather than attempt to dictate industrial relations or to redistribute wealth directly to the working class.

End of Reform and World War II

The New Deal's initial political partnership between rural and urban America assumed that each party well understood its interdependence and the need to raise purchasing power among both farmers and workers. But the urban liberal tilt in national affairs—especially the rapid escalation of labor strikes and challenges to management—reignited long-standing divisions between countryside and city. Many southern Democrats and western progressives disdained what they viewed as the nonemergency New Deal: public housing experiments, relief for the "shiftless," unnecessary government projects, and programs that helped the rural poor—programs that only occasionally benefited African Americans but nonetheless convinced white Southerners that a direct federal assault on Jim Crow could not be far behind. The rising prices that accompanied the nation's agricultural and industrial policies also irked middle-class consumers. After Roosevelt's ill-judged attempt in 1937 to "pack" the Supreme Court, these tensions crystallized in Congress with the formation of a conservation coalition composed of Republicans and anti–New Deal Democrats (mainly Southerners, whose seniority granted them a disproportionate number of committee chairs). An antilynching bill backed by civil rights leaders and urban representatives drove a wedge further into the Democratic Party. Roosevelt declined to back the bill, citing the irate Southerners' strategic positions in Congress, and instead attempted to "purge" the conservatives from his party by intervening personally in the primary elections of 1938. Not only did this effort fail miserably, but voters all over the country also rebuked the president by replacing a significant number of Democratic representatives and governors with Republicans.

Compounding the political stalemate was an economic downturn that began in the autumn of 1937. Though the economy had never regained pre-Depression levels of employment and investment, enough progress had been made after 1933 that the administration could claim some success, however uncoordinated or dictatorial the New Deal appeared to its critics. But the recession shook this confidence. As in 1929, it began with a crash in the stock market and prompted unwelcome comparisons between Roosevelt's stalled agenda and the political fumbles of Hoover before him. More significant, it set off a debate within the administration over the causes of the downturn and the proper methods for economic revival. Some liberals blamed businesses for failing to invest; others intended to launch new legal actions against corporate monopolies. Still others drew lessons from the previous year's budget cuts, arguing that government spending had shored up consumer purchasing power from 1933 to 1937 and that its recent reduction posed the problem. In a line of economic argument that became known as "Keynesian" after British economist John Maynard Keynes, these liberals put forward the idea that consumption, not investment, drove modern industrial economies, and that public spending was the best vehicle for stimulating demand in a downturn. This analysis probably owed more to domestic champions of consumer purchasing power than to Keynes himself, whose complicated ideas Americans embraced only gradually and partially. Still, the reasoning nudged the New Deal in a different and less reformist direction. Roosevelt authorized increased spending programs in 1938 and justified these as important in their own right rather than as needed benefits for particular groups. No doubt Roosevelt also anticipated the political appeal of fiscal policy, which demanded less government intervention in the private decisions of firms, farmers, or consumers.

Public expenditures in 1938, only 8 percent of the national gross domestic product (GDP), were timid by later standards. Not until World War II, when federal spending reached 40 percent of the GDP, would public funds really ignite economic recovery. Between 1940 and 1944, the United States enjoyed the greatest increase of industrial output in its history—almost overnight, full employment returned and wages rose without government prodding. Clearly, the New Deal alone did not restore prosperity, nor had it substantially reduced income inequality. But it did remove much of the risk from market capitalism, providing a certain measure of security to farmers and businesses, homeowners and financiers, employers and employees.

This security was built along distinctly American lines. The New Deal's signature triumph, Social Security, departed from other models of universal social insurance by financing its benefits with regressive payroll taxes and dividing its assistance into two tiers: the retirement pensions, administered at the national level and pegged to national standards; and the unemployment and supplemental welfare programs administered by the individual states, which set their own eligibility requirements and benefit levels. Along with union recognition, laws regulating hours and wages, and World War II–era support for home purchases and education, Social Security provided a framework for the upward mobility of the postwar American middle class. But this framework also operated along distinctly American lines. African Americans were denied many of these benefits owing to the continued power of southern congressmen, who excluded from protection the occupations in which blacks were most represented, insisted on local administrative control, and prevented the passage of antidiscrimination provisions.

During the Depression, it was not uncommon for Americans to quest99ion the national faith in unlimited expansion. Some analysts had even wondered whether the idea of a "mature economy" might not describe the country's predicament; perhaps it was time to come to terms with an economic system that had reached the limits of its capacity to grow. But the lightning-quick recovery generated by World War II altered this mind-set fundamentally and permanently. Migrants streamed across the nation to take up work in the booming defense centers in the West and Midwest, many settling in the new suburbs spreading outward from urban cores. African Americans, eager to share in the promise of economic mobility but prevented from joining this workforce on equal terms, threatened a march on Washington to protest the injustice. Emboldened by Roosevelt's subsequent executive order forbidding discrimination in defense industries, blacks launched a "double V" campaign to fight for victory over enemies both at home and abroad. While victory on the home front would remain far more elusive than victory over Germany and Japan, the war energized a new, more assertive generation of civil rights activists.

Wartime mobilization also strengthened the conservative coalition in Congress, which targeted "non-essential" spending and dismantled relief agencies such as the Works Progress Administration, the National Youth Administration, the Civilian Conservation Corps, and the Farm Security Administration. Conservatives combined these attacks with more pointed critiques of government planning, drawing exaggerated parallels between the New Deal and the fascist regimes that had fomented the war. They also grew bolder in challenging organized labor, which faced diminished public and political support owing to unauthorized wildcat strikes. Wartime opportunities had raised labor's hopes for rising wages and perhaps even an equal share of managerial authority, but pressured by government officials, labor lowered its sights and agreed to a "no strike" pledge and to wage increases that rose in step with inflation but not higher. Now on the defensive along with their liberal allies, union leaders adapted to the anti-statism of the war years by more firmly embracing a Keynesian model of government intervention that steered clear of micromanaging private economic institutions and instead used macroeconomic fiscal tools to support mass consumption.

The war not only swept away any lingering doubts about the economy's ability to expand; it also buried the agrarian analysis of the Depression's origins. Suddenly policy makers grappled with commodity shortages, rising prices, and a labor deficit in the countryside—a sharp turnaround from earlier questions of overproduction, low prices, and a potentially permanent labor surplus. Rural policy makers moved away from the idea that the nation's economic health depended on stabilizing the existing rural population and instead defended a less reformist but still aggressive government role in expanding the country's industrial base and increasing its aggregate purchasing power. Clearly the future was in the factories and defense plants that were running at full capacity, not on America's small farms. But if the nation's economic future lay in urban and suburban America, politics at the end of the war still reflected long-standing divisions between the country and the city. The Democratic Party would emerge from the war as the majority party, but one nonetheless destined to rediscover its historic fault lines of region and race.

See also banking policy; business and politics; tariffs and politics; taxation.

FURTHER READING. Anthony J. Badger, *The New Deal: The Depression Years, 1933–1940*, 1989; Alan Brinkley, *The End of Reform: New Deal Liberalism in Recession and War*, 1995; Lizabeth Cohen, *Making a New Deal: Industrial Workers in Chicago, 1919–1939*, 1990; Meg Jacobs, *Pocketbook Politics: Economic Citizenship in Twentieth-Century America*, 2005; Ira Katznelson, *When Affirmative Action Was White: An Untold History of Racial Inequality in Twentieth-Century America*, 2005; David M. Kennedy, *Freedom from Fear: The American People in Depression and War, 1929–1945*, 1999; William E. Leuchtenberg, *Franklin D. Roosevelt and the New Deal, 1932–1940*, 1963; Idem, *The Perils of Prosperity, 1914–1932*, 1958; James T. Patterson, *Congressional Conservatism and the New Deal: The Growth of the Conservative Coalition in Congress, 1933–1939*, 1967; Sarah T. Phillips, *This Land, This Nation: Conservation, Rural America, and the New Deal*, 2007; Eric Rauchway, *The Great Depression and the New Deal: A Very Short Introduction*, 2008; Bruce J. Schulman, *From Cotton Belt to Sunbelt: Federal Policy, Economic Development, and the Transformation of the South*, 1991; Jason Scott Smith, *Building New Deal Liberalism: The Political Economy of Public Works, 1933–1956*, 2006.

SARAH T. PHILLIPS

economy and politics, 1945–70

The political economy of the United States during the first three decades after World War II can best be characterized as a liberal Keynesian regime. From the 1940s through the 1970s, the living standards of both the working class and the middle class doubled in an era that also experienced relatively rapid economic growth. This achievement rested on several key pillars: a legal framework favoring strong trade unions, a liberal welfare state entailing government promotion of economic security and labor standards, large expenditures for both the military and civilian infrastructure, and an interventionist state that regulated finance, investment, and trade. These policy initiatives were largely upheld during both Democratic and Republican administrations. As the income gap between the rich and poor narrowed—and social movements successfully extended citizenship rights to African Americans and other excluded groups within the population—the United States became a place of much greater social equality.

The New Deal created the terrain on which all post–World War II political struggles took place. It put *security*—economic security—at the center of American political and economic life. The enactment of federal mortgage assistance, bank deposit insurance, minimum wages, Social Security, and laws bolstering labor's right to organize created social and economic entitlements that legitimized the modern state and vitalized an expansive citizenship within new strata of the population. New Dealers identified economic security as a grand national project, "a great cooperative enterprise" among "the citizens, the economic system, and the government." Security necessarily entailed an element of public power. Though Roosevelt-era policy makers initially excluded many women, Latinos, and African Americans from the new entitlement state, President Lyndon Johnson's Great Society did much to expand the social citizenship concept, even as it engendered a fierce, debilitating backlash.

Moreover, Keynesians believed that such policies would generate high levels of employment by boosting aggregate demand in the economy. Through manipulating government spending and the money supply, the federal government could stimulate the economy when it lagged or slow growth when inflation threatened. The booms and busts that had been a routine feature of American economic life would instead be turned into steady growth and more widely shared benefits.

World War II mobilization policies completed social tasks begun in the Great Depression and set the stage for a postwar social Keynesianism. In exchange for labor's unimpeded participation in continuous war production, the federal government settled labor disputes through a National War Labor Board and facilitated union growth with a "maintenance of membership" policy that required every worker in a unionized workplace to join the union and pay dues. With millions of workers pouring into industrial manufacturing, national union membership soon jumped to 15 million, about 30 percent of nonfarm employment.

For American workers the fight against fascism during World War II had significance at home as well as abroad. As the new union movement, the Congress of Industrial Organizations (CIO), put

it, their hard work and sacrifice could also be seen as a struggle to "Insure Your Future . . . For Peace–Jobs–Security." Urging American workers and their families to "vote for Collective Bargaining and Full Employment, Lasting Peace and Security," the CIO saw the rights of the National Labor Relations Act (NRLA), Social Security, and the international struggle for democracy as inseparable: "The broad problems of world security and the personal problems of individual security seem to merge." President Franklin Roosevelt further legitimized the idea of a right to security when, in 1944, he proposed a Second Bill of Rights, protecting opportunity and security in the realms of housing, education, recreation, medical care, food, and clothing.

During the war the government kept a cap on both wages and prices as part of its anti-inflation strategy. American business flourished and productivity leaped forward, the consequence of nearly five years of government-subsidized investment in plant, machinery, scientific research, and physical infrastructure. Not unexpectedly, workers were ready to demand their share of wartime profits and prosperity. This demand took on particular urgency once it appeared that President Harry Truman planned to end government price controls, thereby unleashing an inflationary pulse that threatened to reduce real income for most working-class wage earners.

A huge strike wave swept through manufacturing industries in 1945 and 1946. America's workers had also gone on strike at the end of World War I, but at that time employers, relying on the armed force of the state, crippled the postwar union movement in steel, meatpacking, and coal mining, and on the railroads. But after World War II, unions were far more secure, with almost 35 percent of nonfarm workers enrolled. The frontier of trade unionism did not advance into agriculture, domestic service, the lower ranks of factory supervision, southern textiles, nor most white-collar occupations. Throughout the manufacturing, transport, utility, and construction sectors, however, legally sanctioned collective bargaining became a permanent feature of the U.S. political economy. Along with the New Dealers now in seemingly permanent command of the government policy-making and regulatory bureaucracy, union leaders contended that the key to economic growth must rest upon a regime of mass consumer purchasing power. Workers throughout the economy should be able to buy all the new goods the economy could produce, including housing, medical care, leisure, and entertainment.

In the late 1940s, labor and its New Deal allies saw the movement for greater purchasing power and security as a battle on two fronts: economic and political. Facing corporate employers, labor demanded not only higher wages, protections against inflation, and job security but also "fringe benefits": paid vacation, sick leave, health insurance, and pensions. The National Labor Relations Board (NLRB), created by the New Deal NLRA in 1935, eventually sustained by the Supreme Court, endorsed this bargaining strategy, thus forcing management to accept a widening sphere for collective bargaining. The strategy proved most successful in oligopolistic sectors of the economy (auto, steel, tire and rubber, airplane manufacturing), where the market power of the corporations and the bargaining clout of the unions made it possible to take wages out of competition. This generated "pattern bargaining": when a leading corporation signed a new contract, the other top companies in the sector agreed to almost all of its main provisions. Moreover, companies that did not want to become unionized but sought to maintain stable workforces, such as Kodak, DuPont, Johnson & Johnson, and Colgate Palmolive, also followed the pattern established by the big unions. Consequently, the presence of a strong, dynamic union movement helped drive wages up in primary labor markets across the economy. As inflation ebbed and women entered the workforce in a proportion that exceeded even that at the height of World War II, median family incomes rose in dramatic fashion, doubling in just over a generation.

Labor had a partner in the New Deal state. The Keynesian approach to economic management was embodied in the 1946 Employment Act. The federal government would be responsible for promoting "maximum employment, production, and purchasing power." Rather than waiting for economic crisis to provoke a government response, a new Council of Economic Advisors would have a continuing role developing macroeconomic policy aimed at these goals. The federal government also drove economic growth through investment in an interstate highway system, hospitals and medical schools, universities, and hydroelectric power. Economic modernization was not to be achieved at the expense of the working class or middle class. Building on the national welfare state of the New Deal, the Servicemen's Readjustment Act of 1944 (known more commonly as the GI Bill) offered veterans government support for home mortgages, vocational or university education, and small business start-up. The act was administered locally, however, and black and female veterans were often passed over for these benefits.

Harry Truman had initially sought to extend the New Deal welfare state as soon as the war was over, pushing forward a comprehensive agenda that included a higher minimum wage, federal commitment to public housing, increased unemployment insurance, and national health insurance. Although the Democrats lost badly during the 1946 congressional elections, Truman and a broad-based coalition of labor, liberals, and small farmers demonstrated the majority status of the Roosevelt coalition during the 1948 elections. Interpreting his surprising reelection as a vindication of the New Deal project, Truman declared early in 1949, "Every segment of our population and every individual has a right to expect from our government a fair deal." But a congressional bloc of Republicans and southern Democrats, known as "Dixiecrats," turned back many Fair Deal proposals. Dixiecrats, increasingly wary that Fair Deal labor policies and civil rights initiatives would threaten white supremacy in the states of the Old Confederacy, formed a generation-long alliance with anti–New Deal Republicans.

In the eyes of American business leaders, Truman's endorsement of a strong alliance between labor and the state smacked of European-style social democracy. They did not want to see further erosion of what they considered "managerial prerogatives," nor a further expansion of the welfare state. American employers recognized the social and political premium placed on security—economic security—as vividly as did the Democratic Party, the labor movement, and the proponents of national Social Security. While they were willing to accede to workers' demands for security, the link between union power and the federal government would have to be severed. As *Business Week* warned in 1950, "management, for the first time, is faced with a broad social demand—the demand for security. But if management does not use it wisely, the worker is likely to transfer his demands from the bargaining table to the ballot box." In order to outflank the political mobilization of labor, especially in its demands for health insurance and greater social security, corporate executives imitated the state: companies would now provide social security through private pensions and insurance benefits. Mimicking the standards set by the state, American business firms and commercial insurance companies became partners in creating and expanding private alternatives to public social insurance and community-controlled social welfare institutions. "The American working man must look to management," Ford Motor Company vice president John Bugas told the American Management Association.

This viewpoint reached fruition in 1950, when General Motors (GM) signed an unprecedented five-year contract with the powerful United Automobile Workers, an agreement that *Fortune* magazine dubbed "The Treaty of Detroit." GM agreed to assume health insurance and pension obligations for its workers, blue collar and white collar, forging an employment template that many other U.S. corporations soon followed. Henceforth paid vacations, sick leave, health insurance, and pension became standard features of blue-collar and white-collar employment. GM president Charles Wilson claimed to have achieved "an American solution for the relations of labor and industry." The government agreed. A 1956 Senate report labeled employee benefits programs "a tribute to the free enterprise system." By extending such security to employees, America's largest companies headed off political alternatives, including national health insurance, more progressive public pensions, and even union control of firm-based benefits.

Those elements of the Fair Deal that stayed within the parameters of the welfare state already set—minimum wage, means-tested public housing for the poor, improvements in Social Security pensions—passed into law. Proposals that would expand the welfare state in scope and curtail emerging private markets, like health insurance, went down to permanent defeat.

Also stymied in the immediate postwar years was the government's commitment to racial justice. African Americans had begun to make economic progress during World War II through the CIO, a newly aggressive NAACP, President Franklin D. Roosevelt's nondiscrimination executive order for defense work, and the Fair Employment Practices Committee (FEPC). With the FEPC, the federal government legitimized African American demands for equal opportunity and fairness at work. Although the FEPC itself had little power, African Americans mobilized around it and used it to pry open the previously insulated realms of segregated employment. After the war, CIO leaders and the NAACP pushed for a permanent FEPC. Some states did establish commissions on fair employment, but the Dixiecrats made sure the U.S. Congress never did. Instead, it took a massive, direct-action social movement, sweeping through the South two decades later to force Congress and the president to prohibit employment discrimination, on the basis of sex as well as race, with Civil Rights Act of 1964.

By the time Republican Dwight Eisenhower took office, the New Deal welfare state, labor reforms, and state regulatory policies were firmly established. Although a Republican with strong ties to corporate elites, Eisenhower shared the essential premises of liberal Keynesianism and the New Deal order. He signed a raise in the minimum wage, oversaw new amendments to Social Security that added disability pensions and expanded old-age coverage to new groups, including agricultural and domestic workers, and created a new cabinet department, Health, Education, and Welfare.

Eisenhower, however, viewed with skepticism the rapid expansion of another pillar of the Keynesian state, the military-industrial complex. After a brief period of demobilization at the end of World War II, national security affairs became the largest, fastest growing sector of the American government. Truman not only turned the War Department into the Defense Department but created domestic national security agencies. As tensions with the Soviet Union heightened in the late 1940s, and the United States took on an increasingly interventionist role in Western Europe, Greece, Turkey, Korea, and elsewhere, defense spending became a permanent, rising part of the federal budget. The defense budget hit $50 billion a year—half the total federal budget—when the United States went to war in Korea. For the first time, the United States maintained permanent military bases in over three dozen countries. The militant

anti-Communist agenda abroad also translated into political purges of leftists at home.

Liberals and conservatives alike let go of their sacrosanct commitment to balanced budgets and instead came to believe that by pumping money into the economy, Americans could have "guns and butter too." Defense spending in southern California and the Southeast—on military bases, weapons production, scientific research—built up entire local and regional economies. Military spending drove suburbanization, well-paid employment, and mass consumption in places like Orange County, California, during the 1950s and 1960s.

The American South, while eagerly digesting government largesse for military bases, defense contracts, and universities, contested the liberal political economy based on rising wages and labor rights. Through the New Deal and especially the war, Southerners had finally experienced a vast improvement in their standard of living. The Fair Labor Standards Act (which established the national minimum wage and 40-hour workweek), rural electrification, wartime spending, and economic modernization brought southern wages and consumer purchasing closer than ever to northern standards. Southern textiles plants continuously raised wages in order to stay a step ahead of the Textile Workers Union of America, primarily based in the North but seeking to organize the South. After 1948, however, southern states took advantage of the Taft-Hartley Act to ban the union shop through so-called right-to-work laws, while southern employers quickly made use of Taft-Hartley's grant of "free speech" for management during union elections. Within a few years, southern employers had stopped the postwar union movement in its tracks. By the latter half of the 1950s, it was clear the South would remain a lower-wage region. American business took the cue and began moving plants south of the Mason Dixon Line. Over the next decade and a half, leading corporations like Westinghouse, DuPont, and RCA and a wide range of smaller companies making textiles, light fixtures, chemicals, and auto parts relocated production to southern areas where states promised lax regulation, minimal taxation, low wages, and a union-free environment.

For new migrants to American cities, such as African Americans, Puerto Ricans, and Native Americans, capital flight had frustrating and devastating effects. Five million African Americans had migrated from South to North, and now industrial jobs went to precisely the repressive and impoverishing places they had recently fled. Companies like General Motors and Ford Motor relocated plants to suburbs and small communities where African Americans were shut out by racial exclusion. In places such as Detroit, the "arsenal of democracy" that had drawn so many black migrants, black unemployment shot up as high as 18 percent by 1960. Federal "termination" and "relocation" programs moved Indians off reservations to cities like Chicago, while Chicago lost over

90,000 jobs. This new urban working class ended up in low-wage service sector jobs, as janitors, domestics, or hospital workers, or in public sector jobs, as sanitation workers, school custodians, and home-care aides.

Cresting with the civil rights movement of the 1960s, though, public sector workers, long-excluded from the NLRA, began to win union organizing rights. Two decades of public investment had dramatically expanded the government workforce at all levels. President Johnson's War on Poverty and Great Society created even more social service jobs—in health care, education, job training. In a wave of union militancy not seen since the 1930s, public sector workers struck and won unions for teachers, hospital workers, police, social workers, and sanitation workers. These new unions fought for higher wages, better working conditions, dignity, and respect for tens of thousands of female and minority workers but also for expanded public services and social welfare. This movement created 4 million new union members, but it marked the last period of sustained union growth in the twentieth century.

For two generations, the public and private welfare state grew in tandem. Yet critical observers, journalists, liberal economists like John Kenneth Galbraith, civil rights activists, and feminists insisted with increasing urgency in the early 1960s that many Americans had been left out of this postwar prosperity—that poverty persisted amid plenty. John F. Kennedy, a cold warrior, focused his attention on foreign policy, although he had begun to take programmatic steps to address unemployment through job-training programs. Lyndon Johnson, however, was a New Deal liberal. When he became president after Kennedy's death, Johnson saw an opportunity to complete the project of the New Deal—and this time, to ensure that racial justice would not be pushed to the sidelines. Declaring "unconditional war on poverty" in 1964, LBJ oversaw the passage of the Economic Opportunity Act, which established Job Corps, Neighborhood Youth Corps, Adult Education Program, Volunteers in Service to America (VISTA), and Work Experience for those on AFDC. Believing that macroeconomic policy had solved the problems of economic growth, War on Poverty liberals more often sought to reform workers than to restructure the labor market. Poverty and unemployment, they argued, could be overcome through expanding individual opportunity without substantial redistribution. More broadly, Johnson's Great Society program included national health insurance for the elderly, Medicare, and medical assistance for the poor, Medicaid; public housing; Fair Housing to overcome decades of racial discrimination in housing markets; education funding and college grants and loans; and the elimination of national origins quotas for immigrants.

It also stressed a kind of participatory democracy. Through War on Poverty grants, community action agencies pressured city governments for better services, jobs, and housing. The Office of Economic Opportunity's Legal Services mobilized welfare rights activists to press for due process, supplemental grants, and basic citizenship rights for public assistance recipients; in California, it teamed up with United Farm Workers to win civil rights for Mexican Americans. Women and African Americans acted through collective mobilization and unions to achieve the promises of affirmative action and Title VII of the 1964 Civil Rights Act declaring discrimination based on "race, color, religion, sex, or national origin" to be an "unlawful employment practice," and backed it up with new means for redress. In the following decade, domestic workers won inclusion in the Fair Labor Standards Act. Women's groups used class-action lawsuits to force colleges and universities to change employment and admissions policies. The enactment of the Occupational Safety and Health Act (OSHA) brought the reach of the New Deal regulatory state into toxic and dangerous workplaces where many minorities worked. OSHA represented the last gasp of the New Deal.

The Keynesian New Deal order foundered in the 1970s, as economic growth slowed significantly, corporate profitability stagnated, energy costs soared, and inflation took off unabated. Manufacturing firms, which had already spent two decades shifting production to lower wage areas within the United States, sought yet another spatial fix, moving production out of the country. Unemployment hit levels not seen since the Depression, reaching 8.5 percent in 1975. High oil prices, unemployment, and inflation produced a new toxic brew—"stagflation"—and Keynesian policies of economic stimulus did not seem to work. Thus, in part, the conditions that had sustained the liberal Keynesian order changed.

But there was an increasingly successful political assault on it as well. A new conservative political movement had been taking shape and coalescing throughout the 1960s—in corporate boardrooms, new think tanks and foundations, and churches; among suburban housewives in the Sunbelt and college students in Young Americans for Freedom. Conservative activists began shifting the Republican Party rightward with the presidential nomination of Barry Goldwater in 1964 and the election of Ronald Reagan as California governor in 1966. Inspired by Friedrich Hayek and Milton Friedman, they set out to liberate the free market from the shackles of the welfare state, regulation, and labor unions. In the 1970s, conservatives successfully chipped away at the New Deal. Employers hired anti-labor management "consulting" firms to disestablish unions. The U.S. Chamber of Commerce launched aggressive campaign financing and lobbying operations and, along with new corporate political action committees, stopped liberal reforms in Congress. President Richard Nixon attempted to check the growing tide of welfare state spending. At the same time, wages and incomes stagnated, fueling well-orchestrated tax revolts. A Democratic president, Jimmy Carter, helped set the mold for the "Reagan revolution" of the 1980s—initiating deregulation and workers' concessions at the bargaining table, through the federal rescue plan of the ailing Chrysler Corporation. A path had been cleared for the rise of a new free-market ideology.

See also business and politics; era of confrontation and decline, 1964–80; era of consensus, 1952–64.

FURTHER READING. Martha Biondi, *To Stand and Fight: The Struggle for Postwar New York City*, 2003; Dorothy Sue Cobble, *The Other Women's Movement: Workplace Justice and Social Rights in Modern America*, 2004; Joshua B. Freeman, *Working-Class New York: Life and Labor Since World War II*, 2000; Meg Jacobs, *Pocketbook Politics: Economic Citizenship in the Twentieth Century*, 2004; Jennifer Klein, *For All These Rights: Business, Labor, and the Shaping of America's Public-Private Welfare State*, 2003; Nelson Lichtenstein, *Walter Reuther: The Most Dangerous Man in Detroit*, 1997; Nancy MacLean, *Freedom Is Not Enough: The Opening of the American Workplace*, 2006; Timothy Minchin, *What Do We Need a Union For? The TWUA in the South, 1945–1955*, 1997; Kimberly Phillips-Fein, *Visible Hands: The Making of the Conservative Movement from the New Deal to Reagan*, 2009; Robert Self, *American Babylon: Race and the Struggle for Postwar Oakland*, 2003.

JENNIFER KLEIN

economy and politics since 1970

The political economy of the United States has been hugely transformed in the years since 1970. In 1970 the United States had a largely insular economy, with trade accounting for just over 10 percent of gross domestic product (GDP). Major sectors of the economy, such as banking and finance, transportation, communications, and energy, were subject to extensive regulation covering both prices and product offerings. Unions were a major force in the economy, with close to one-third of the private sector workforce being represented by a union.

By 2005, trade accounted for almost 30 percent of GDP. Most major industries had been partially or whole deregulated, with corporations free to charge whatever prices the market would bear and enter and exit sectors as they pleased. In 2005, just over 7 percent of the private sector workforce was represented by a union, with membership still declining. These changes in the economy were driven by deliberate policy decisions that in turn transformed the face of politics in the United States.

A number of factors came together to bring about this transformation. In 1970 the United States was still in the midst of its long post–World War II boom. The boom was characterized by rapid productivity growth, which was passed along in rapid wage growth. This led to rising living standards, which sustained demand growth and led to further gains in productivity.

The End of Prosperity

This virtuous circle came to end in the mid-1970s. First higher oil prices, due to the assertiveness of the Middle Eastern countries in OPEC and later a cutoff in oil exports stemming from the Iranian revolution, ended the era of cheap energy. Higher food prices, resulting from large grain sales to the Soviet Union, also added to inflationary pressure. And most importantly, the long postwar productivity boom came to an end. For reasons that are still not fully understood, the annual rate of productivity growth slowed from more than 2.5 percent to less than 1.5 percent. This contributed further to inflation, since slower growth in productivity means that goods and services cost more to produce than if productivity growth was faster.

The economy suffered its worst recession of the postwar period in 1974–75 as the Federal Reserve Board raised interest rates sharply to try to contain inflation. By raising interest rates, the Fed hoped to slow economic growth and thereby reduce the rate of job growth. Slower job growth translates into higher unemployment. The Fed hoped that higher unemployment would slow wage growth, which would in turn slow cost pressures and reduce the rate of price growth. The recession occurred because the Fed went too far, with the unemployment rate eventually rising to 9 percent at the worst of the recession in 1975.

Even though it was painful in terms of throwing people out of work and reducing the rate of wage growth, the Fed's policy did have the desired effect of slowing the rate of inflation. However, this benefit proved to be short-lived. In 1979 the cutoff of oil from Iran again sent oil prices soaring. It also forced car owners to wait in gas lines; price controls often caused shortages, since gas prices could not just rise to their market clearing levels. Inflation went into double digits for the first time since the removal of price controls in the immediate aftermath of World War II. The Fed again slammed on the brakes, bringing on a short but steep recession in the spring of 1980.

This timing proved to be disastrous for the sitting president, Jimmy Carter, who faced reelection that fall. Ronald Reagan, the Republican presidential candidate, highlighted the country's economic problems in making his pitch for the White House. He repeatedly referred to the "misery index," the sum of the inflation rate and the unemployment rate, which reached its highest level in the postwar era in 1980.

The Sharp Right Turn

Reagan promised a new economic policy that would be a sharp departure from the policies pursued by previous administrations of both parties. At the center of this new policy was a 30 percent cut in income taxes. Reagan argued that a tax cut of this size would produce so much economic growth that it would actually pay for itself. For this reason, Reagan claimed that he could both cut taxes and balance the federal budget.

Reagan also promised to cut what he described as wasteful government social programs. In his campaign he repeatedly presented dubious examples of people defrauding welfare programs. He promised to put an end to such "waste, fraud and abuse." This promise had considerable appeal, especially among conservative white voters who perceived the prime welfare abusers to be African Americans.

In addition, Reagan promised to curtail regulation in a wide variety of areas. This agenda included measures like ending price controls on oil. It also meant promoting the deregulation of major industries like airlines, trucking, and banks. Reagan also promised to rein in what he described as abusive environmental and safety regulations.

Reagan's economic agenda, coupled with the promise of a more muscular foreign policy, proved sufficiently popular to earn him a solid victory in the presidential race and to sweep the Republicans into control of the Senate, the first time that they had controlled a house of Congress for almost three decades.

Reagan quickly sought to implement his agenda. He managed to push a large tax cut through Congress before the end of his first year in office. He also set about fulfilling other campaign promises. He cut back a wide range of social programs, most notably in the areas of job training, housing, and community development. Pushing his deregulatory agenda, Reagan reduced or eliminated regulations in a number of industries, accelerating a process that had begun under Jimmy Carter.

Early in his administration, President Reagan picked a fight with the Professional Air Traffic Controllers Union (PATCO) that proved to have enormous significance for the labor movement. PATCO reached a bargaining impasse with the Transportation Department and went out on strike. Reagan told the workers that if they did not return to work, they would be fired and replaced by military controllers. When the union ignored the warning, Reagan carried through on his threat, firing more than 10,000 striking controllers.

While Reagan had the legal authority to fire the striking controllers (strikes by federal employees are illegal), this marked a sharp departure from past practices. Employers in both the private and government sector almost always sought to negotiate with striking workers. Even when public sector workers were engaged in arguably illegal strikes, a solution to the dispute would usually paper over any legal issues. However, following the PATCO firings, it became routine for employers to use the threat of replacement workers. Suddenly, going out on strike meant that workers risked losing their jobs. This made strikes a far less effective weapon.

This was not the only action by the Reagan administration that weakened unions. President Reagan appointed members to the National Labor Relations Board (NLRB) who were far more supportive of management than appointees of previous administrations. The NLRB also developed a large backlog of cases, which made it far less useful to workers seeking redress for illegal actions by employers, such as firing workers for organizing.

Reagan's policies hit unionized workers in other ways. Following the election, the Federal Reserve Board again began to raise interest rates in an effort to quell inflation. This led to an even worse recession in 1981–82, with the unemployment rate reaching almost 11 percent. Heavily unionized industries like automobiles and construction were especially hard hit.

The Fed's high interest rate policy also led to a sharp rise in the value of the dollar against other major currencies. A higher dollar makes imported goods less expensive for people in the United States, which means that consumers are more likely to buy imported cars, clothes, and other items than goods produced in the United States. For this reason, the high dollar of this period provided yet another source of pain for many of the same industries that were hard hit by the recession.

While most workers did not do very well in the Reagan years (after adjusting for inflation, wages for most workers actually fell in the 1980s), more highly educated workers did see reasonable wage growth. Most workers also benefited from the fall in interest rates from the high inflation years at the end of the 1970s and the beginning of the 1980s. Lower interest rates made it much easier to buy a home or new car.

The big winners from the Reagan era were those who held considerable amounts of stock. The shift from wages to profits, coupled with the decline in both individual and corporate tax rates, sent the stock market soaring. Adjusted for inflation, the stock market rose by more than 90 percent between 1979 and 1989.

The Reagan era also left the country with a serious deficit problem. The size of the federal debt had been falling relative to the size of the economy since the end of World War II. This pattern reversed sharply as a result of President Reagan's tax cuts and military buildup. (The tax cuts did not generate enough growth to increase revenue.) Deficit reduction became a major priority for his immediate successors, George H. W. Bush and Bill Clinton.

The Rise of the Bubble Economy

Under President Bush, a modest tax increase coupled with spending controls helped to contain the deficit, but the 1990–91 recession, coupled with a weak recovery, left a large deficit in place by the time Bill Clinton entered the White House. During his campaign, Clinton had laid out an ambitious platform of public investment in education, job training, and infrastructure. This platform was quickly abandoned after he took office.

Clinton had drawn considerable support from the financial industry and he was determined to pursue policies with which that industry was comfortable, even if this risked alienating unions and other traditional Democratic constituencies. The priority on deficit reduction was very much in keeping with this Wall Street focus.

In addition, Clinton decided to make the inclusion of Mexico in a North American Free Trade Agreement (NAFTA) a top agenda item of his first year in office. A main purpose of NAFTA was to make it as easy as possible for U.S. manufacturers to relocate their operations to Mexico, thereby putting U.S. manufacturing workers into direct competition with much lower paid workers in Mexico. Using the full power of the presidency, including promises to fund pet projects (or threats to block such projects for NAFTA opponents), President Clinton was able to narrowly secure a victory for NAFTA in Congress.

Clinton used similar arm-twisting for approval of the Uruguay Round of the World Trade Organization and later trade agreements with China and other countries. The effect of such deals was to place a major source of downward pressure on the wages of the 70 percent of the U.S. workforce that lacked a college degree. This impact was heightened by the extraordinary run-up in the dollar that began in the mid-1990s. The dollar had drifted lower, partly as the result of conscious policy, since the mid-1980s. However, in the mid-1990s, under Robert Rubin, Clinton's second Treasury secretary, the United States again pursued a "strong dollar" policy.

The immediate force driving the dollar upward was the stock market bubble, which drew in foreign investors at a rapid pace. While the stock market soared, the strong dollar made U.S. goods less competitive in the world economy, leading to the loss of millions of manufacturing jobs. As was the case in the 1980s, the lost manufacturing jobs were disproportionately union jobs in traditional industrial states like Michigan and Ohio.

By 2006, manufacturing employment accounted for just over 10 percent of total employment. This compared to more than 25 percent in 1970. Just over 12 percent of manufacturing workers were unionized in 2006, compared to almost 40 percent in 1970. This means that the once powerful sector of unionized manufacturing workers accounted for just over 1 percent of the workforce.

If unionized manufacturing workers were obvious losers over this period, the financial sector was the most obvious winner. It expanded from just 12 percent of domestic corporate profits in 1970 to almost 30 percent by 2006. Its political power reflected this extraordinary growth as the financial sector could insist that both major parties adopt platforms that reflected its interests.

These policies include a commitment to low inflation, even if this is at the cost of high unemployment. The financial industry also vigorously pursued a policy of deregulation even when this led to instability and government bailouts. The collapse and bailout of the savings-and-loan industry in the 1980s is the most obvious example of poorly planned deregulation. More recently, inadequate regulation allowed hundreds of billions of questionable mortgages to be issued to homeowners who lacked the ability to repay them. This debt was then passed along in secondary markets through a variety of exotic financial instruments.

The financial industry's political agenda also included a willingness to ignore the economic distortions and disruptions associated with financial bubbles. The stock bubble and the housing bubble both led to enormous distortions in the economy. In the case of the stock bubble, tens of billions of dollars were pulled away from potentially productive uses and instead thrown into ill-conceived Internet schemes. The housing bubble led to huge investments in housing that may remain underutilized for many years to come. Both bubbles had the effect of distorting individuals' saving decisions, as many people assumed that the bubble-inflated prices of stock and housing would persist. As a result, they saved far too little for retirement or other needs. Many pension funds made similar mistakes. With the collapse of the housing bubble and the plunge in the stock market in 2008, tens of millions of families approaching retirement had little or no wealth accumulated, and traditional defined benefit pension plans faced enormous shortfalls.

The changes in the country's economy and politics since 1970 had the effect of shifting wealth and power upward. Since World War II, unions had been by far the most important institution supporting the interests of moderate-income and middle-income families. The policies of this period were intended to weaken their influence and were quite successful. Partly as a result, those in the middle and bottom of the income distribution enjoyed less economic security than they had through most of the post–World War II period.

The growing insecurity for those at the middle and the bottom coincided with an upward redistribution of income and wealth to those at the top. By the early twenty-first century, the richest 1 percent of the population owned a larger share of national wealth than at any time since the Great Depression. The sharp downturn brought on by these policies offered President Barack Obama an enormous opportunity to place the economy on a fundamentally different course.

See also business and politics; labor movement and politics.

FURTHER READING. Dean Baker, *The United States since 1980*, 2007; Barbara Ehrenreich, *Nickel and Dimed: On (Not) Getting By in America*, 2001; Jacob Hacker, *The Great Risk Shift: New Economic Insecurity and the Decline of the American Dream*, 2006; Larry Mishel, Jared Bernstein, and Sylvia Allegretto, *The State of Working America, 2006–2007*, 2007; Louis Uchitelle, *The Disposable American: Layoffs and Their Consequences*, 2007.

DEAN BAKER

education and politics

Politics in its various guises has always shaped educational ideals, whether in Plato's *Republic* or in recent federal initiatives such as No Child Left Behind. From the days of the founders to the present, Americans have generally agreed that "knowledge is power," and they have invested considerable time, money, and emotion in educating the young. Since the nineteenth century, they have increasingly focused those efforts on tax-supported public schools, whose nature, character, and quality have long been the subject of political commentary and the object of scorn or favor by the major political parties. When faced with everyday, seemingly intractable problems, from poverty to racial segregation, from poor nutrition to teenage pregnancy, Americans often turn to education and schooling as a panacea. Educational credentials for most decent jobs and careers have also risen considerably over the last half century. So it is not surprising that many governors seeking the presidency (whether Bill Clinton or George W. Bush) helped establish their bona fides as advocates of school improvement.

American Revolution to the Civil War

Education and politics have been intertwined since the birth of the nation. In colonial America, families and churches were the primary educators, supplemented, in New England, by a range of tax-assisted schools. The leaders of the Protestant Reformation and the majority Protestant population in British North America stressed the importance of literacy to enable everyone to read the Bible, thus liberating individuals from the church authority associated with Roman Catholicism. Independence, however, meant that the new nation had to determine the relative influence of federal, state, and local authority in most aspects of life, including education. Thorny questions about how to ensure good citizenship and nation building loomed large in public discourse.

Many political leaders in the late eighteenth and early nineteenth centuries fretted over the fragility of the republic; historically, most republics were small and short-lived, and, as classical history taught, often fell prey to tyranny. By the early 1800s, white citizens almost enjoyed almost universal literacy, which was applauded as a foundation for good citizenship. Contemporaries believed that literacy and properly trained minds would help ensure that voters would choose wisely at the polls, mothers would rear virtuous children, and commercial transactions based on uniform means of communication and calculation would flourish. But a common faith in education and literacy—unchallenged except with regard to slaves—did not mean that Americans rushed to build a system of free schools for all or agreed about the ultimate purposes of education.

The Constitution, in fact, ignored the subject of education. Instead, newly created states, like some colonies before them, encouraged the spread of knowledge and the establishment of schools. In the early 1800s, schools were a small part of most people's experience, and the options for education included a hodgepodge of one-room schools in the countryside and tuition-dependent schools and academies for those who could afford them. Schools gradually rose in importance in the coming decades, especially in the northern states, serving both ongoing secular concerns such as training for citizenship, exposure to the expanding world of print, and older religious needs, including Bible reading. The federal government also encouraged literacy and learning through generous postal rates, thereby subsidizing the spread of cheap print and newspapers. But the idea that there should be a significant federal role in education on any level ran into strong opposition.

Several Founding Fathers engaged in extended debates on the place of education and schools in the national polity. Advocates of a strong federal government, such as George Washington, called for the establishment of a national university to help train future leaders, an idea that never gained support. In contrast, fellow Virginian and anti-Federalist Thomas Jefferson wrote eloquently on behalf of state-financed schools; in his plan, schools would help identify the best and the brightest, allowing some poor but bright boys to enjoy a subsidized education at his alma mater, William and Mary. But the Virginia legislature rejected his plans, believing that families, churches, and existing educational arrangements sufficed. While some lands were set aside for sale under the provisions of the Northwest Ordinance of 1787 to encourage education, public schools by law and custom would long remain the province of states, whose constitutions encouraged or mandated their establishment. In practice, these schools were largely locally controlled and funded through property taxes and other fees.

Members of the major political parties continued to battle over education and schooling in the antebellum period. The Whig Party, heir to the Federalist ideal of strong centralized authority, led most campaigns to build public school systems in the 1830s and 1840s. Horace Mann, Henry Barnard, and most male school reformers were Whigs, often holding a wide range of political offices. Support for Whigs proved strongest among native-born Protestants and Northerners and especially those living in areas undergoing commercial and industrial development. Writing from Massachusetts, Mann affirmed that public schools trained children in proper moral values, good citizenship, and basic Christian virtues, all taught through the ubiquitous McGuffey Readers and other school texts. Democrats, reflecting the views of southern slaveholders, Irish immigrants, and northern Catholics, typically opposed strong centralized authority; Southerners even opposed the creation of state school systems for all white children, and Catholics often favored state subsidies for their own parochial systems. Public school textbooks were laced with anti-Catholic sentiments. Violent riots in Philadelphia in 1844 over the use of the King James Bible in local schools testified to the intense political world of which education was an integral part. Everywhere, local school committees, elected to office on political tickets, routinely used their patronage positions (from hiring teachers to awarding school contracts for supplies and construction) to enrich party members.

Civil War to World War II

During the Reconstruction period, schooling for African Americans became a major political issue for the Republican Party, especially its radical wing. The Republican and unionist battle cry of free men, free labor, and free soil was joined with the older Whig demand for more free schools. The short-lived federal Freedmen's Bureau helped protect educational initiatives sponsored by blacks themselves and by various northern missionary societies that sent teachers south to teach the freedmen. The very civil rights of black Americans thus became wedded to access to quality education. While federal protection for black civil rights declined in the 1870s, southern states were forced to include provisions in newly written constitutions to establish public schools for all races as a condition of readmission to the Union. Though ex-slaves shared the Republican conception of knowledge as power, the Democratic Party revived to rule the South with a heavy hand, denying many blacks access to any schools and allowing only some to attend inferior, poorly funded, segregated ones.

While public school enrollments, especially on the elementary level, continued to grow in all regions after the Civil War, exclusionary policies toward blacks in the South (and often in the North) and Asian immigrants on the West Coast demonstrated that local politics, based on white supremacy, compromised the ideal of all-inclusive public schools. Republicans not only withdrew federal protection for the ex-slaves, but in the 1870s they also helped rewrite northern state constitutions to tighten restrictions on the use of public monies for parochial schools. Nativist Republican politicians in Illinois and Wisconsin late in the century also tried to require children in all schools to use only English as the language of instruction, which led Catholics and Lutherans to rally at the polls to beat back the draconian measure.

Until the post–World War II era, the Republican Party remained the most important organized political party that endorsed public education. Championing the emergence of a more urban, industrial, corporate America, Republicans often favored political changes that proved influential and enduring. During the early decades of twentieth century, school boards underwent dramatic transformation, especially in urban areas. Urban school boards had traditionally been large, ward-based, and intimately tied to local party politics. But Republicans especially

sponsored legislation that dramatically reduced the size of school boards, often eliminating ward-based representation and replacing it with at-large, "non-partisan" positions, which consolidated power in the hands of elites. This also helped professionalize schooling, since board members, resembling a corporate board of directors, increasingly hired superintendents and other experts to take more formal control over curricular and other educational programs.

While removing politics from schools was the ostensible aim of these reforms, battles over curriculum and the purposes of education remained contentious. In the early 1900s, labor unions and socialists often fought to elect their own representatives to school boards and lobbied business-dominated boards to expand social services such as free breakfasts and lunches for poor children, playgrounds, and after-school and summer programs. John Dewey and other left-leaning intellectuals also protested the use of intelligence tests to sort working-class children and the poor generally into new, nonacademic vocational programs. Dewey famously criticized the sing-song teaching methods common in most schools and endorsed more democracy in school decision making, in contrast to the prevailing corporate-style models of administration, which emphasized efficiency and testing. As high school enrollments exploded, debates intensified over who should benefit from academic instruction and what should be taught (the biology curriculum became the subject of national attention at the Scopes trial in Dayton, Tennessee, in 1925). About 6 percent of all adolescents entered high school in 1890, while about half attended in 1930.

Schools in the first half of the twentieth century thus were embroiled in numerous political battles. Fundamentalists demanded the exclusion of Darwinian theory from science class, and they successfully eviscerated the teaching of evolution from many classrooms in the coming decades, despite their presumed defeat at Dayton. In the 1920s, reviving an old nativist demand, patriotic groups and the Ku Klux Klan tried without success to force parochial schools to teach pupils in English only. African Americans in turn fought against incredible odds to increase educational opportunities for their children; as late as 1930, 230 counties in the former Confederate states lacked any public high school for blacks, and those who attended any schools were often enrolled in inferior buildings with hand-me-down textbooks. The National Association for the Advancement of Colored People (NAACP), founded in 1909, successfully defeated Jim Crow in several momentous lawsuits, culminating in the famous *Brown v. Board of Education* case in 1954.

World War II to the Present

Throughout the 1950s and 1960s, political conflicts over education and the schools resurfaced on many fronts. Since secondary education had become nearly universal, more citizens had attended high school, and they increasingly voiced opinions on the character and problems of the institution. Rising expectations characteristic of the baby boom era, when the economy grew dramatically and the civil rights movement blossomed, also meant that schools were held accountable for America's failure to provide every citizen with access to the American dream of social mobility and justice for all. Civil rights activists faced uphill struggles against Jim Crow after *Brown*, and President Dwight D. Eisenhower only reluctantly deployed federal troops to help integrate Central High in Little Rock, Arkansas, in 1957. White resistance to racial integration was powerful, often violent, and widespread, and only about 1 percent of all southern blacks attended school with any whites by 1961.

More middle-class parents now expected their children to attend college, and they demanded the elevation of high school standards—especially for their children—an effort that intensified after the passage of the National Defense Education Act (NDEA) in 1958. Following the launching of the Soviet *Sputnik*, the NDEA (which emphasized among other things improved math, science, and foreign language instruction) brought cold war concerns directly to bear upon educational policy. Cold warriors also accused teachers of being too soft, progressive, and child-centered, and many districts demanded that teachers toe the line when it came to loyalty to God and country. Duck-and-cover drills taught children that the world teetered on the precipice of nuclear annihilation.

Modern liberalism flourished in the 1960s, despite the existence of countercurrents of conservatism that grew powerful by the end of the decade. The Great Society of Lyndon B. Johnson represented the new face of the modern Democratic Party, which had coalesced during the New Deal. While Republicans had traditionally been the prime champions of public education, Johnson and his allies, seizing the moment, used the federal government to advance reform in unprecedented ways. Legislation ranging from the Civil Rights Act, which empowered the Justice Department to sue southern districts that refused to desegregate; the Elementary and Secondary Education Act (ESEA), which led to major federal funding of schools; the Economic Opportunity Act, which created Head Start; the Higher Education Act; the Bilingual-Bicultural Act; and numerous other initiatives placed the Democratic Party in the vanguard of educational change. Because of the unpopularity of some of these reforms, especially in the area of civil rights, Johnson rightly predicted that the South would shift rightward toward the Republican Party. The liberal Warren Court, which ruled state-sponsored prayer and the banning of the teaching of evolution unconstitutional, also proved unpopular, fueling even more political dissent against public education.

Culture wars, an old feature of American society and common enough in the schools, reignited in the 1980s. Following the election of Ronald Reagan to the presidency in 1980, the failures of public education again grabbed the nation's attention, and the liberalism of the 1960s was routinely held accountable for educational failures. Reagan promised to restore prayer in the schools and abolish the new Department of Education (created during the Carter administration in 1979); he did neither, though he dramatically cut federal spending on education. Republicans also weakened federal support for busing to achieve racial integration, adding to their popularity. Ironically, the Department of Education enabled Republicans to regain their traditional eminence in framing debates about education and the schools. The department sponsored a commission that produced the most important educational document of the late twentieth century, *A Nation at Risk* (1983). Permeated with cold war rhetoric, the report claimed that low academic standards in the schools had weakened the American economy. In times of crisis, someone or something is usually held accountable, and instead of corporate boardrooms, it was the schools.

By the 1980s, governors in many states made educational reform integral to their political campaigns. While only roughly 7 percent of school funding came from Washington, Reagan's successor, George H. W. Bush, asserted that he wanted to become the "education president." Working with moderate Democrats, including Bill Clinton, a prominent champion of school reform while governor of Arkansas, Bush organized a major educational conference in 1989 in Charlottesville, Virginia, that led to successive federal initiatives (America 2000, then Goals 2000) that promised to end violence in the schools, improve graduation rates, and raise test scores, especially in math and science.

Very few successful politicians who wore the mantle of school reformer since the Reagan years called for more racial integration or equalization of school funding between city and suburb, showing the clear connections between politics and educational policy. Conservative times led many Democrats to move to the right, downplaying concerns about equality and equity. In addition, since the 1980s, Republicans in particular have advocated market competition, tax incentives, or vouchers for private schools, enabling tax dollars, in some cases, to flow to religious-based schools. Democrats, with major support from teachers' unions, have tended to favor choice within the public school system, reflected in the spread of magnet schools in the 1970s and 1980s and in charter schools during the early twenty-first century.

Raising standards is the ubiquitous goal of most politicians concerned with educational policy. The revision of ESEA, No Child Left Behind, enjoyed initial bipartisan support when enacted in 2002, and it reflected widespread concerns about low academic standards. But whether in liberal Connecticut or conservative Utah, states sometimes protested against federal intervention, reflecting age-old support for state and local control over the schools. Characteristically, each state set the standard for academic norms under No Child Left Behind. Americans want neither a national curriculum nor federal control, but they do support higher standards.

Politics and education remain inseparable. Schools teach values as well as subjects, and most educational issues concerning race (including court-ordered busing), or religion (including school prayer or the teaching of "intelligent design"), or finance (including redistribution of resources to the poor) inevitably lead to political controversy and dissent. These issues embroil local communities far more than standardized test results. Compared with most western nations, America has weak national authority over its schools (which are still governed by over 13,000 independent school districts), and education remains subjected to various federal, state, and local political pressures.

Most educational policies and practices are rooted in decisions about power and authority, so all education is inherently political. Even if political parties disappeared, every decision facing every teacher in every school would remain in the broadest sense political. Every debate about curriculum, pedagogy, or the values taught to pupils involves questions of whose ideas will triumph.

George Washington discovered how entangled education and politics were when he endorsed the creation of a national university; Thomas Jefferson realized it when he called for free schools for all white children in the slave South; and the intermingling was given broad attention when John T. Scopes became a symbol of the right of teachers to teach evolution. While defending an educational ideal, these men quickly learned that, at least in their lifetime, what seemed desirable and defensible to them lacked widespread political legitimacy and public sanction.

FURTHER READING. David L. Angus and Jeffrey E. Mirel, *The Failed Promise of the American High School, 1890–1995*, 1999; Samuel P. Hays, "The Politics of Reform in Municipal Government in the Progressive Era," *Pacific Northwest Quarterly* 55 (October 1964), 157–69; Daniel Walker Howe, *What Hath God Wrought: The Transformation of America, 1815*, 2007; Carl F. Kaestle, *Pillars of the Republic: Common Schools and American Society, 1780–1860*, 1983; William J. Reese, *America's Public Schools: From the Common Schools to "No Child Left Behind,"* 2005; David B. Tyack, *The One Best System: A History of American Urban Education*, 1974.

WILLIAM J. REESE

elections and electoral eras

Scholars have partitioned American history into distinct electoral eras, each of which is marked by stability in competition between political parties, the issues confronting the nation, and the composition of voter blocs. The constant feature of American politics that runs through these historical periods is a relatively stable two-party system, with shifting constellations of third parties introducing new ideas and leaders. Although most other democratic societies developed multiparty systems in the nineteenth and twentieth centuries, several factors account for persistent two-party dominance in the United States. Most critically, American elections are winner take all. Third parties lack the means to win a majority of Electoral College votes or to win the pluralities needed to secure other national, state, or local positions. Third parties also lack financial resources, established local organizations, and experienced leadership. In the twentieth century, restrictive state laws made it difficult for third parties to place their candidates on the ballot, and party primaries have shut members of third parties out of the nominating process in many states.

The First Party System: 1787–1804

In his farewell address of 1797, George Washington warned against the dangerous "spirit of Party," which he said "serves always to distract the Public Councils and enfeeble the Public Administration. It ignites the Community with ill founded Jealousies and false alarms, kindles the animosity of one part against another, foments occasionally riot & insurrection." Yet in opposing the formation of political parties, Washington was voicing a vain hope. During Washington's first term as president, his treasury secretary, Alexander Hamilton, had already formed the Federalist Party and his secretary of state, Thomas Jefferson, had founded the opposition Democratic-Republican Party. Hamilton intended to build a Federalist Party committed to strong central government, sustained by commercial interests. In contrast, Jefferson favored limited central authority, states' rights, and agrarian over commercial interests. Jefferson also opposed Hamilton's objective of building ties with England rather than with revolutionary France. To Jefferson, England was a corrupt, repressive society that still threatened the survival of American liberty.

As early as 1792, party-line voting emerged in Congress, local and national partisan allegiances took shape, and both the ruling and opposition parties cultivated partisan newspapers, with no lines drawn between news and opinion. In 1800 the first turning-point election in U.S. history, Federalist president John Adams—George Washington's successor—lost to Jefferson, and the Democratic-Republicans gained control of Congress. In his later years, Jefferson looked back on this contest as "the Revolution of 1800." He said that the election "was a real a revolution in the principles of our government as that of 1776 was in its form; not effected indeed by the sword, as that, but by the rational and peaceable instrument of reform, the suffrage of the people." Despite the hyperbole, Jefferson was essentially correct. The election of 1800 firmly established the two-party system as the norm in American politics. It set a precedent for the peaceful transfer of political power and changed the course of public policy. As president, Jefferson promoted states' rights, economy in government, a pared-down military establishment, lower taxes, and elimination of the national debt. In foreign policy he tilted more toward France than Britain.

The election also corrected a flaw in the system for electing presidents. Under the Constitution of 1787, members of the Electoral College cast two votes for president. The leading vote-getter, provided that he received a majority of the electoral vote, was elected president. The second leading vote-getter was elected vice president. If no candidate received a majority or if two candidates tied, the House of Representatives would choose the president, with each state casting a single vote. In 1800, Jefferson and his putative running mate, Aaron Burr, each received 73 electoral votes. The House that chose the president was not the new, heavily Jeffersonian House elected in 1800, but the lame-duck House that was closely divided between Federalists and Jeffersonians. It took 36 ballots for the House finally to elect Jefferson as president, with Burr becoming vice president. To avoid the problem of future tied votes, the Twelfth Amendment in 1804 created the modern ticket system, with separate balloting for president and vice president in the Electoral College.

The election of 1800 also set a precedent for two centuries of negative campaigns. Neither Adams nor Jefferson campaigned personally, in deference to George Washington's belief that presidents should be called to service. Still, Adams's Federalist backers attacked Jefferson for his alleged atheism, radicalism, and lack of moral standards. One propagandist warned that, with Jefferson as president, "murder, robbery, rape, adultery, and incest will be openly taught and practiced, the air will be rent with the cries of the distressed, the soil will be soaked with blood, and the nation black with crimes." Jefferson's backers responded with smears of their own, charging that Adams planned to marry one of his sons to the daughter of the king of England, start an American monarchy, and finally reunite America and England.

One-Party Dominance: 1804–24

Although nominal two-party competition persisted after Jefferson's victory, the Federalist Party would never again come close to winning the presidency or to controlling either house of Congress. The Federalists were caught up in the old politics of officeholding as nonpartisan service and of public deference to the nation's supposedly "natural" leaders. They never adjusted to the new era of electioneering and the mobilization of public opinion. To control the process of presidential succession, the Democratic-Republican Party relied on the congressional caucus to sort out the ambitions of competing candidates and nominate a single chosen leader.

Nomination by "King Caucus" was tantamount to election, given the weakness of the Federalist opposition. The system worked well until 1824, when it broke down internally and externally. With the end of the administration of James Monroe—the last of the Revolutionary-era presidents—the caucus could not control the ambitions of competing candidates. Moreover, elite control over elections was declining as states eliminated property qualifications for voting and increasingly chose electors by popular vote rather than the vote of state legislatures.

More than in any prior presidential campaign, the supporters of competing candidates in 1824 engaged in efforts to mobilize public opinion. A weak congressional caucus, attended by a minority of Democratic-Republican members of Congress, nominated a weak candidate, an ailing William Crawford, Monroe's secretary of the treasury. Three other candidates also contended for the presidency. The first candidate was John Quincy Adams, James Monroe's eight-year secretary of state and the main author of the Monroe Doctrine. The second candidate was Henry Clay, the Speaker of the House and architect of the Missouri Compromise of 1820, which temporarily quieted sectional conflict over slavery. The final candidate was the war hero Andrew Jackson, the first presidential candidate from the growing West. Jackson ran as an outsider who would clean out the corrupt political establishment that festered in the capital.

Jackson won a plurality of the popular and electoral votes. But his failure to win a majority of electoral votes meant that the House of Representatives would choose the president from among the top three finishers—Jackson, Adams, and Crawford. Jackson's supporters argued that in deference to the mandate of the people, the House should choose the first-place finisher. But the argument failed to convince Speaker of the House Clay, whose lobbying for Adams helped the secretary of state win election by the House. Although Jackson did not challenge the result, he was later outraged when Adams appointed Clay secretary of state, charging that "bargain and corruption" had combined to produce his defeat.

The Second Party System: 1828–56

In 1828, when Jackson made a second bid for the presidency, he began the transition to a new and more balanced system of two-party competition. In another high-stakes election with abusive charges coming from both sides, Jackson easily defeated Adams in both the popular vote and the Electoral College. Jackson inspired a broad and diverse following— diehard pro-slavery and states' rights advocates like John C. Calhoun of South Carolina, practitioners of the new patronage politics like Martin Van Buren of New York, Tennessee businessmen, western agrarians, and influential editors—that became the core of his new Democratic Party. The centerpiece of Jackson's two terms as president was a war against the Bank of the United States, which he regarded as representing the privileged interests that he had come to Washington to drive out of power. In his 1832 message vetoing legislation that would have granted the bank a new charter, Jackson declared that "we must stand against all new grants of monopolies and exclusive privileges, against any prostitution of our Government to the advancement of the few at the expense of the many."

Although Jackson easily swept to a second term in 1832, that election marked the emergence of America's first significant third party, the Anti-Masonic Party, dedicated to opposing the Masons and other secret societies that the party claimed imposed elite rule on the United States. The Anti-Masons gained a credible 8 percent of the popular vote and held the first national presidential nominating convention. The Anti-Masons represented one of three variants of third parties that would emerge in the United States: the single-issue third party. Other single-issue parties included the antislavery Free Soil of 1848 and the Prohibition Party that anti-alcohol activists founded in 1869. A second type of third party advanced a broad ideology. Examples included the People's Party, which agrarian reformers founded in the late nineteenth century; the Socialist Party of the early twentieth century; and the Libertarian Party of the late twentieth century. Finally, some third parties served primarily as vehicles for the presidential aspirations of particular candidates, such as Theodore Roosevelt in 1912, George Wallace in 1968, and Ross Perot in 1992 and 1996.

In 1834 Jackson's opponents coalesced into a new Whig Party, led by Clay and Senator Daniel Webster of New Hampshire. In contrast to the Democrats' philosophy of limited government and states' rights, the Whigs backed federal intervention to protect domestic industries through tariffs, promote education, build the nation's infrastructure, and enforce moral standards. The Whigs also opposed the Democrats' aggressive approach to the territorial expansion of the United States. Democrats and Whigs would compete on relatively equal terms nationally and in nearly every state of the union. Unlike later party systems, partisan allegiances were not sharply divided along sectional lines. From 1836 to 1852, Democrats won the presidential elections of 1836, 1845, and 1852, whereas Whigs prevailed in 1840 and 1848. During these years, neither party gained a decisive advantage in Congress. Close partisan competition, a rising number of elected offices, and new forms of popular mobilization greatly increased voter turnout in federal, state, and local elections. The election of 1840 also contributed to the rise of popular politics, with the Whigs shrewdly, if misleadingly, marketing the wealthy planter and war hero William Henry Harrison as the "log cabin and hard cider" candidate, a man of the people from the rough and tumble West. They organized log cabin clubs and distributed log cabin mugs and medallions and flyers showing Harrison seated beside a log cabin and a barrel of cider.

The Whigs led songfests that celebrated Harrison as the hero of the common man and lampooned their Democratic opponent, President Martin Van Buren, as an effete eastern dandy addicted to French wine.

The presidential election of 1844 between the Democrat James K. Polk and the Whig Henry Clay was pivotal to the Second Party System. This election was the last contest in which different states held elections on different days. In 1845 Congress passed a law establishing Election Day as the first Tuesday after the first Monday in November. Members of Congress viewed Polk's narrow victory over the anti-expansionist Clay as a mandate for the annexation of Texas, and Congress passed a joint resolution to accomplish that end, which outgoing President John Tyler signed. Polk's election portended additional expansion that he achieved by settling a boundary dispute with Britain over the northwest territory that became Oregon and Washington and acquiring what became California, Utah, Nevada, and parts of other states through war with Mexico. Had Clay prevailed in 1844, American history would likely have followed a profoundly different course.

At the time that Americans were proclaiming their Manifest Destiny to expand across the continent, the United States was also deeply divided by the presence of slavery in the newly acquired territories. The Second Party System unraveled in the 1850s under the pressure of sectional conflict over the expansion of slavery. The Whig Party included moderate but generally proslavery Southerners as well as northern Protestants in the vanguard of the antislavery, temperance, and anti-immigrant movements. This amalgam did not hold. During the 1850s, southern Whigs deserted the party as antislavery Northerners sought, in vain, to keep the party united in their region. After the Whigs decisively lost the presidential election of 1852, Whig representative Lewis Davis Campbell of Ohio prophetically said, "We are slayed. The party is dead-dead-dead!" By the next presidential election in 1856, the Whigs had disintegrated and two new parties had arisen to compete with the ruling Democrats. The American, or Know Nothing, Party was based on opposition to Catholics and immigrants. The Republican Party opposed the expansion of slavery and, like the defunct Whigs, backed an activist government that promoted industry, commerce, and education. Although the Republican nominee for president, the famed explorer John C. Frémont, lost to Democratic nominee James Buchanan in the presidential election of 1856, he finished in second place, well ahead of the Know Nothing nominee, former president Millard Fillmore. The results of the 1856 elections for the presidency and Congress established the fledgling Republican Party as the alternative to the Democratic Party in a new two-party system.

The Third Party System: 1860–96

The Third Party System marked the first of several distinct eras of competition between Republicans and Democrats. Unlike the Whigs, the Democrats withstood sectional divisions and endured to oppose Republican president Abraham Lincoln's commitment to military victory in the Civil War as well as Republican efforts to establish political and civil rights for the freed slaves during the postwar Reconstruction. Partisan conflict over racial issues in the 1860s would give Republicans a sizable advantage in northern states, create a solidly Democratic South after the demise of Republican-run Reconstruction governments, and define voter loyalties for another 70 years. The Republicans were the party of activist government in the late nineteenth century, whereas Democrats continued to defend limited government and states' rights.

In the pivotal election of 1860, Abraham Lincoln prevailed over a field of candidates that included Senator Stephen Douglas of Illinois, the regular Democratic nominee; Vice President John Breckinridge, the candidate of bolting southern Democrats; and former senator John Bell of Tennessee, the candidate of the compromise Constitutional Union Party. Although Lincoln won only 40 percent of the popular vote, he carried every northern state and gained a substantial majority of Electoral College votes. Just six years after its birth, the new Republican Party had won control over the national government. Abraham Lincoln, elected because of the dissolution of the old political order, would have the cheerless task of presiding over the near dissolution of the nation itself. The selection of a Republican president was unacceptable to many Southerners. Even before Lincoln took the oath of office on March 4, 1861, seven southern states had seceded from the Union. On April 12, 1861, the Civil War began with the bombardment of Fort Sumter in South Carolina.

The war dragged on for four long years and transformed the nation. When Lincoln issued the Emancipation Proclamation, which freed all slaves still held by the Confederacy, he committed the federal government for the first time to a decisive stand against slavery. The Lincoln administration also instituted a graduated income tax, established a national banking system, facilitated the settlement of western lands, and began the nation's first draft of soldiers. Lincoln won reelection in 1864 and, with the South still out of the Union, his Republican Party gained decisive majorities in both houses of Congress and passed the Thirteenth Amendment, which ended slavery in the United States. The election also ensured that the Republicans would dominate the reconstruction of the Union after the guns fell silent. "I earnestly believe that the consequences of this day's work will be to the lasting advantage, if not the very salvation, of the country," Lincoln said. But Lincoln's assassination in April 1865 meant that he would not live to fulfill his prophecy.

At the time of Lincoln's death, the big questions of Reconstruction were still unresolved. Under what terms would the South be restored to the Union?

To what extent would the federal government act to provide civil rights, civil liberties, economic security, and political rights to the newly freed slaves? In the face of opposition from Lincoln's successor, the former Democrat Andrew Johnson, Congress enacted a fairly ambitious program of Reconstruction. It included civil rights laws; the Fourteenth Amendment, which guaranteed "equal protection under the law"; and the Fifteenth Amendment, which prohibited the denial of voting rights on grounds of race, religion, or previous servitude. Still, in the late 1860s and 1870s, Republicans would be unable to prevent the unraveling of Reconstruction and the "redemption" of southern states by Democratic leaders committed to white-only government and to the exploitation of cheap black labor.

The disputed presidential election of 1876 marked the end of Reconstruction. Although Democratic candidate Samuel J. Tilden, the governor of New York, won the popular vote against Republican governor Rutherford B. Hayes of Ohio, the outcome of the election turned on disputed Electoral College votes in Florida, South Carolina, and Louisiana. With the Constitution silent on the resolution of such disputes, Congress improvised by forming a special electoral commission of eight Republicans and seven Democrats. The commission voted on party lines to award all disputed electoral votes to Hayes, which handed him the presidency. The years from 1876 to 1892 were marked by a sharp regional division of political power growing out of Civil War alignments and a national stalemate between Republicans, who dominated the North, and Democrats, who controlled the South. White Southerners disenfranchised African Americans and established an all-white one-party system in most of their region. The stalled politics of America's late nineteenth-century Gilded Age resulted in a seesaw series of close elections: with neither party able to gain a firm hold on government or the electorate, the White House would change hands in every contest of the era except 1880, when Republican James A. Garfield won by some 2,000 votes. During this period the difference between Democratic and Republican percentages of the national popular vote for president averaged only about 1 percent, whereas differences in the vote between the North and the South averaged about 25 percent.

This combination of major-party stasis and electoral uncertainty left the nation unable to cope with the deep depression of the mid-1890s, which shattered the second administration of Democratic president Grover Cleveland. In 1884 Cleveland became the first Democrat to win the White House since Buchanan in 1856. Four years later he narrowly prevailed in the popular vote but lost in the Electoral College to Republican Benjamin Harrison. Becoming the only American president to serve two nonconsecutive terms, Cleveland defeated Harrison in 1892. With Cleveland declining to compete for a third term in 1896, the insurgent Democratic candidate William Jennings Bryan was unable to shake off the legacy of Cleveland's failures. With his candidacy endorsed by the People's Party, Bryan embraced such reform proposals as the free coinage of silver to inflate the currency, a graduated income tax, arbitration of labor disputes, and stricter regulation of railroads—policies that were at odds with his party's traditional commitment to hands-off government. Despite Bryan's defeat by Republican William McKinley, his nomination began to transform the political philosophy of the major parties. By vigorously stumping the nation in 1896, Bryan also helped introduce the modern style of presidential campaigns. In turn, the Republicans, who vastly outspent the Democrats, pioneered modern fund-raising techniques.

The Fourth Party System: 1896–1928

The Republican Party dominated American politics from 1896 through 1928. Except for the two administrations of Woodrow Wilson, from 1913 to 1921, the GOP controlled the presidency throughout this period, which was marked by foreign expansionism and the rise and fall of progressive reform. Although William Jennings Bryan emerged as the reformist leader of the Democratic Party, it took the ascendancy of Theodore Roosevelt and a new generation of Republican progressives to add domestic reform to the expansionist policies begun by President McKinley during the Spanish-American War of 1898. Roosevelt became president through four unpredictable turns of fate. First, President William McKinley's vice president, Garret A. Hobart, died in 1899. Second, Republican boss Thomas C. Platt saw his chance to rid New York of its reformer governor, Theodore Roosevelt, by promoting him for vice president on McKinley's ticket in 1900. Third, McKinley defeated Bryan in a rematch of 1896, and fourth, Roosevelt became president six months into his vice presidency when McKinley died of a gunshot wound inflicted by anarchist Leon Czolgosz. During two terms in office, Roosevelt put his progressive stamp on the presidency. His sustained McKinley's expansionist foreign policies and gave concrete expression to his idea that government should operate in the public interest by steering a middle course between unchecked corporate greed and socialist remedies.

After stepping down from the presidency in 1908, Roosevelt was so disappointed with his hand-picked successor, William Howard Taft, that he sought a third term as president. In 1912 Roosevelt, Taft, and Senator Robert M. La Follette of Wisconsin fought the first primary-election campaign in American history, battling one another in the dozen states that had recently established party primaries. Although Roosevelt garnered more primary votes than Taft and La Follette combined, most convention delegates were selected by party bosses, who overwhelmingly backed Taft. The disgruntled Roosevelt launched an insurgent campaign behind the new Progressive Party that advocated reforms such as women's suffrage, tariff reduction, old-age pensions, and laws prohibiting child labor. Roosevelt siphoned off about half of the voters who had backed Taft in 1908. Democratic candidate Woodrow Wilson, the governor of New Jersey, held the Democrats together and won the election with only 42 percent of the popular vote. Roosevelt finished second in the popular vote with 27 percent, compared to 23 percent for Taft. It was the largest vote ever tallied by a third-party candidate.

During his two terms in office, Wilson pioneered the modern liberal tradition within the Democratic Party. Under his watch, the federal government reduced tariffs, adopted the Federal Reserve System, established the Federal Trade Commission to regulate business, and joined much of the Western world in guaranteeing voting rights for women. Wilson also increased America's involvement abroad and led the nation victoriously through World War I. Wilson had a broad vision of a peaceful postwar world based upon America's moral and material example. He became the first president of any party to advocate a strong internationalist program that centered on America's leadership in a League of Nations. He would not realize this vision, although it would be largely achieved under Franklin Roosevelt and Harry Truman after World War II.

The reaction that followed World War I and Wilson's failed peace plans led to the election of conservative Republican Warren G. Harding in 1920. Republicans won all three presidential elections of the 1920s by landslide margins and maintained control over Congress during the period. Republican presidents and congresses of the 1920s slashed taxes, deregulated industry, restricted immigration, enforced Prohibition, and increased protection tariffs. In 1928, when Commerce Secretary Herbert Hoover decisively defeated Governor Al Smith of New York—the first Catholic presidential candidate on a major party ticket—GOP senator William Borah of Idaho said, "We have an opportunity to put the Republican Party in a position where it can remain in power without much trouble for the next twenty years." But Democratic weakness concealed the party's resilient strength. The Democrats' pluralism, which melded diverse voters from outside America's elite—whites in the South, working-class Catholics and new immigrants in the North, and reformers in Mountain States—helped the party weather adversity, evolve with changing circumstance, and survive in contests for congressional and state offices. The Democrats' 1924 presidential candidate, John W. Davis, said after the election: "I doubt whether a minority party can win as long as the country is in fairly prosperous condition. . . . Some day, I am sure, the tide will turn."

The Fifth Party System: 1932–80

The tide turned after the crash of 1929 began the nation's longest and deepest depression and led to a two-tiered realignment of the American party system. First, between 1930 and 1932 the Democrats benefited from a "depression effect" that swelled the ranks of party voters throughout the United States but neither restored the Democrats to majority status nor reshuffled voter coalitions. Second, after Franklin Roosevelt won the presidential election of 1932, the "Roosevelt effect" completed the realignment process. FDR's liberal New Deal reforms and his inspirational leadership created a positive incentive for loyalty to the Democratic Party.

In 1936, after losing badly in four consecutive presidential and midterm elections, Republicans seemed nearly as obsolete as the Whigs they had displaced in 1854. Since 1928 the party had lost 178 U.S. House seats, 40 Senate seats, and 19 governorships. The GOP retained a meager 89 House members and just 16 senators. As Democrats completed the realignment of party loyalties, they recruited new voters and converted Republicans. From 1928 to 1936, the GOP's share of the two-party registration fell from 69 percent to 45 percent in five northern states and from 64 to 35 percent in major cities. The durable new Democratic majority—the so-called Roosevelt coalition—consisted of white Protestant Southerners, Catholics and Jews, African Americans, and union members.

Republicans recovered sufficiently in the midterm elections of 1938 to regain a critical mass in Congress and to join with conservative southern Democrats to halt the domestic reform phase of the New Deal. However, Republican hopes to regain the presidency and Congress in 1940 were dashed by the outbreak of war in Europe. A nationwide Gallup Poll found that respondents preferred Roosevelt to any challenger, although most said that they would have backed a Republican candidate in the absence of war abroad. Roosevelt won an unprecedented third term and led the nation into a war that largely ended America's traditional isolation from foreign entanglements.

In the first postwar election, held in 1946, the GOP's new slogan, "Had Enough?" evoked scarcity, high prices, and labor strife under Harry Truman, who had become president after Roosevelt's death in April 1945. In postwar Britain, voters defeated Winston Churchill and his conservative majority in Parliament. Americans, however, could not dispatch the Democrats in a single blow. The midterm elections of 1946 issued no policy mandate to Republicans in Congress, who had to confront a president armed with veto power, the bully pulpit, and the initiative in foreign affairs. After leading America into the cold war against communism, Truman unexpectedly won the election of 1948, and Democrats regained control of Congress.

Four years later, in the midst of disillusionment over a stalled war in Korea and Democratic corruption, the war hero Dwight David Eisenhower became the first Republican president in 20 years. But Eisenhower had no intention of turning back the clock to the 1920s. Instead, he governed as a "modern Republican" who steered a middle course between Democratic liberals and the right wing of the Republican Party. However, modern Republicanism neither stole the thunder of Democrats nor attracted independents to the GOP. Although Eisenhower remained personally popular, Democrats controlled Congress during his last six years in office. When he stepped down in 1960—the Twenty-Second Amendment, ratified in 1951, barred presidents from seeking third terms—a Democrat, John F. Kennedy, became America's first Catholic president by defeating Eisenhowers' vice president, Richard Nixon.

Kennedy and his successor, Lyndon Johnson, presided over a vast expansion of the liberal state. These Democratic presidents embedded the struggle for minority rights within the liberal agenda and, in another departure from the New Deal, targeted needs—housing, health care, nutrition, and education—rather than groups, such as the elderly or the unemployed. Its civil rights agenda would eventually cost the Democratic Party the allegiance of the South, but in the near term the enfranchisement of African Americans under the Voting Rights Act of 1965 offset losses among white Southerners. Still, the Johnson administration unraveled under pressure from a failing war in Vietnam and social unrest at home. In 1968 Richard Nixon became the second Republican to gain the White House since 1932. Although Nixon talked like a conservative, he governed more liberally than Eisenhower. Nixon signed pathbreaking environmental laws, backed affirmative action programs, opened relations with mainland China, and de-escalated the cold war.

The Watergate scandal and Nixon's resignation in 1974 dashed any hopes that Republicans could recapture Congress or pull even with Democrats in party identification. However, conservative Republicans began rebuilding in adversity. They formed the Heritage Foundation to generate ideas, the Eagle Forum to rally women, new business lobbies, and Christian Right groups to inspire evangelical Protestants. Although Democrat Jimmy Carter won the presidential election of 1976, his administration was unable to protect its constituents from the ravages of "stagflation"—an improbable mix of slow growth, high unemployment, high inflation, and high interest rates. Carter also exhibited weakness in foreign affairs by failing to gain the quick release of American hostages seized by militants in Iran or to halt the resurgent expansionism of the Soviet Union.

The Sixth Party System: 1980–2008

After defeating Carter in 1980, Republican Ronald Reagan, the former actor and governor of California, became the first conservative president since the 1920s. The election of 1980 did not match the shattering realignment of 1932. Republicans did not gain durable control of Congress, long-term domination of the presidency, or an edge in the party identification of voters. Nonetheless, the election profoundly changed American politics. It brought Republicans into near parity with Democrats, enabled Reagan to implement his conservative ideas in domestic and foreign policy, and moved the national conversation about politics to the right. In 1980 Republicans gained control of the Senate and held an ideological edge in the House. In his first year as president, Reagan cut taxes, reduced regulation, shifted government spending from domestic programs to the military, and adopted an aggressive approach to fighting communism abroad. Although Reagan won reelection after a troubled economy recovered in 1984, the "Reagan revolution" stalled in his second term. Still, Reagan presided over the beginning of the end of the cold war, a process completed by his vice president, George H. W. Bush, who won the presidency in 1988.

Republican progress stalled when moderate Democrat Bill Clinton of Arkansas defeated Bush in the presidential election of 1992. However, conservatives and Republicans rebounded in 1994, when the GOP regained control of both houses of Congress for the first time in 40 years. Although Republicans failed to enact their most ambitious policy proposals or prevent Clinton's reelection in 1996, the congressional revolution of 1994, no less than the Reagan revolution of 1980, advanced conservative politics in the United States. The elections gave Republicans unified control of Congress for most of the next dozen years, established Republicans as the dominant party in the South, polarized the parties along ideological lines, and forestalled new liberal initiatives by the Clinton administration.

In the disputed presidential election of 2000, Republican George W. Bush, the governor of Texas, trailed Vice President Al Gore in the popular vote by half a percent. But the Electoral College vote turned on contested votes in Florida. On December 12, the U.S. Supreme Court stopped a recount of Florida's votes with Bush ahead by 537 votes out of 6 million cast. Bush won a bare majority of 271 Electoral College votes, including all in the South and about one-third elsewhere. He won overwhelming support from white evangelical Protestants and affluent voters.

Bush's conservative backers in 2000 brushed aside suggestions from media commentators that the president-elect fulfill his promise to be "a uniter, not a divider" and emulate Rutherford B. Hayes, who governed from the center after the disputed election of 1876. Dick Cheney, who was poised to become the most influential vice president in American history, added, "The suggestion that somehow, because this was a close election, we should fundamentally change our beliefs I just think is silly." Bush advanced the conservative agenda by steering major tax cuts and business subsidies through Congress, advancing a Christian conservative agenda through executive orders, and aggressively opposing foreign enemies abroad.

Although Bush won reelection in 2004, under his watch conservatism, like liberalism in the 1970s,

faced internal contradictions. Conservatives had long opposed social engineering by government, but in Iraq and Afghanistan the Bush administration assumed two of the largest and most daunting social engineering projects in U.S. history. Conservatives have also defended limited government, fiscal responsibility, states' rights, and individual freedom. Yet the size and scope of the federal government and its authority over the states and individuals greatly expanded during the Bush years. These contradictions, along with the Republicans' loss of Congress in 2006 and Democrat Barack Obama's victory in the 2008 presidential race, suggest that the conservative era that began in 1980 had come to an end.

See also Democratic Party; Republican Party.

FURTHER READING. Walter Dean Burnham, *Critical Elections and the Mainsprings of American Politics*, 1970; John Gerring, *Party Ideologies in America, 1828–1996*, 1998; Allan J. Lichtman, *White Protestant Nation: The Rise of the American Conservative Movement*, 2008; David R. Mayhew, *Electoral Realignments: A Critique of an American Genre*, 2004; Albert J. Nelson, *Shadow Realignment, Partisan Strength and Competition, 1960 to 2000*, 2002; Theodore Rosenof, *Realignment: The Theory That Changed the Way We Think about American Politics*, 2003; Byron E. Shafer, *End of Realignment? Interpreting American Electoral Eras*, 1991; Joel Silbey, *The American Political Nation, 1838–1893*, 1991.

ALLAN J. LICHTMAN

Electoral College

In many ways, the history of the Electoral College reflects the evolution of a persistent problem in American politics, one summarized in political scientist Robert Dahl's succinct question "Who governs?" The answers Americans have given have changed throughout the nation's history. The framers of the Constitution believed the college would balance tensions among the various states and protect the authority of the executive from the influence of Congress and the population at large. More recently, however, debates over the college have centered upon whether it performs these functions too well, and, in so doing, hampers democratic values increasingly important to Americans.

Origins

Many of the delegates to the Constitutional Convention in 1787 initially were convinced that the president should be chosen by majority vote of Congress or the state legislatures. Both these options steadily lost popularity as it became clear the Convention did not want to make the presidency beholden to the legislature or to the states. However, many delegates also found distasteful the most viable alternative—direct election by the populace—due to fears that the public would not be able to make an intelligent choice and hence would simply splinter among various regional favorite-son candidates.

On August 31, 1787, toward the end of its third month, the convention created the Committee on Postponed Matters, or the "Committee of Eleven," to solve such problems. Chaired by David Brearley of New Jersey and including Virginia's James Madison, within four days of its organization, the committee proposed that electors, equal in number to each state's congressional delegation and selected in a manner determined by the state legislatures, should choose the president. These electors would each choose two candidates; when Congress tabulated the votes, the candidate with the "greatest Number of Votes" would become president and the runner-up vice president. In the case of a tie, the House of Representatives would choose the president and the Senate the vice president. This plan proved acceptable to the convention because it was a compromise on many of the points that had rendered earlier proposals unworkable—it insulated the president from the various legislatures but preserved the process from undue popular influence. Similarly, in basing its numbers on the bicameral Congress, the college moderated the overwhelming influence of the populous states. Though the phrase "Electoral College" was not included in the Constitution, the plan was encoded in Article II, section I.

The College and the States: Solving Problems

Over the first few presidential elections, states experimented with various means of choosing their electors. In the first presidential election, for example, 11 states participated. Four held popular elections to select electors; in five the legislature made the decision. The remaining two combined these methods; the legislature chose individuals from a field selected by general election.

Despite this carefully constructed compromise, the practicalities of electoral politics gradually overtook the college's system. Most influential was the surprisingly quick emergence of political parties that coalesced around individual candidates. By 1800, the Democratic-Republican Party and its rival Federalist Party had gained control of many state governments and began to manipulate local methods for selecting electors; the Federalist parties of Massachusetts and New Hampshire, for example, were in command of those states' legislatures and reserved to those organizations the right to select electors. In the next presidential election, the legislature, doubting its ability to secure the states' electors for the Federalists, switched to a system in which each congressional district selected one elector, only to revert back to legislative control in 1808. Similarly, in Virginia the Democratic-Republican Party shifted the authority to a winner-take-all general election, where favorite-son candidate Thomas Jefferson was assured to gain a majority and sweep the state's electoral votes. Thus, despite the original expectation that independent

electors would gather and deliberate over the most qualified candidate, they were increasingly selected to represent their parties and to cast their votes accordingly.

The 1800 election also revealed perhaps the greatest flaw in the Electoral College as established by the Constitution. The Democratic-Republican electors chosen in 1800 obediently voted for their party's choice for president, Jefferson, and vice president, New York's Aaron Burr. However, the convention had not anticipated such party-line voting, and the tabulation of the electors' votes revealed an inadvertent tie. In accordance with the Constitution, the election was thrown to the House, where Federalist representatives strove to deny their archenemy Jefferson the presidency. It took 36 ballots before the Virginian secured his election. As a result, in 1804 the Twelfth Amendment was added to the Constitution, providing that electors should cast separate ballots for the president and vice president. Despite several recurrences of such crises in the system, only one other constitutional reform of the college has been adopted; in 1961, under pressure from citizens complaining of disenfranchisement, the Twenty-Third Amendment was added to the Constitution; it granted the District of Columbia three electoral votes.

As the nineteenth century progressed, such manipulations as occurred in Massachusetts and New Hampshire gradually faded in favor of assigning electors to the winner of the general election. The combination of new styles of mass politics that presidential contenders like Andrew Jackson embodied and the allure that the winner-take-all system held for confident parties meant that by 1836 South Carolina was the only state in the Union that clung to legislative choice against popular election, and even that state capitulated after the Civil War. Despite the occasional crisis in which states have resorted to legislative choice—such as Massachusetts in 1848, when a powerful bid by the Free Soil Party meant that no party gained a majority of the popular vote, or Florida in 2000, when the legislature selected a slate of electors in case the heated contest over the disputed popular vote was not resolved—this system has remained ever since.

The Problem of the Popular Vote

This does not mean, however, that it has always worked perfectly. As concerns over regional balance and the fitness of the electorate have receded, debate has centered on the awkwardness of the combination of popular ballots and state selection. For example, the winner-take-all system ensures that the minority in each state is disenfranchised when the electors cast their votes. Indeed, despite the universal desire to empower the general electorate, it remains quite possible for the president to be chosen by a minority of the popular vote. In the three-way election of 1912, for example, Democrat Woodrow Wilson won more than 80 percent of the electoral vote despite winning only a plurality of the popular vote—barely 41 percent. Similarly, Democrat Bill Clinton was elected in 1992 when his 43 percent of the popular vote—a plurality—translated into nearly 70 percent in the Electoral College. Though neither of these elections was in danger of being thrown to the House of Representatives, a similar three-way election in 1968 raised such fears; indeed, the independent candidate George Wallace hoped to gain enough electoral votes to force such an event and gain concessions from either Republican Richard Nixon or Democrat Hubert Humphrey. Nixon, however, gained a close majority in the Electoral College.

Despite earning the appellation "minority president" from their weak showing in the popular election, Nixon, Wilson, and Clinton did at least receive pluralities. Several other times, the uneven correlation between the popular vote and the Electoral College resulted in the loser of the former attaining the presidency. In 1888, Republican Benjamin Harrison defeated the incumbent Democrat Grover Cleveland in the Electoral College despite losing the popular vote; Cleveland's graciousness, however, assured a smooth transition of power. The other such elections—1824, 1876, and 2000—were met with discontent and protest from the losing party. Indeed, though correct constitutional procedure was followed in each case, all three elections were tainted with accusations of corruption and manipulation, allegations exacerbated and legitimated by each eventual president's failure to win the majority of the popular vote.

In 1824 the presidential election was a contest among several Democratic candidates, and a situation the Convention had hoped to avert occurred: the nation split along regional lines. Andrew Jackson gained a plurality of the popular and electoral vote, primarily in the South and middle Atlantic. Trailing in both totals was John Quincy Adams, whose base was in New England. The other candidates, Henry Clay and William Crawford, won only three and two states, respectively (though both also won individual electoral votes from states that divided their totals). Despite his plurality, Jackson was unable to gain a majority of the electoral vote, and the election was again, as in 1800, thrown to the House of Representatives. There, Clay threw his support to Adams, who was selected. Despite the fact that correct procedure was followed, Jackson denounced Adams and Clay for thwarting the will of the people and subsequently swept Adams out of office in 1828.

In 1876 Democrat Samuel Tilden led Republican Rutherford B. Hayes by more than a quarter million popular votes. However, the results in four states, Oregon and the southern states of Florida, South Carolina, and Louisiana—all three of which were expected to easily go for Tilden—were disputed. Without the electoral votes of these states, Tilden found himself one vote short of a majority. All four states sent competing slates of electors to the session of Congress that tabulated the votes. In 1865 Congress had adopted the Twenty-Second Joint Rule, which provided that contested electoral votes could be approved by concurrent votes of the House and Senate. However, the rule lapsed in January 1876, leaving Congress with no means to resolve the dispute. In January 1877, therefore, Congress passed the Electoral Commission Law, which established—for only the particular case of the 1876 election—a 15-member commission, consisting of 5 members of the House, 5 of the Senate, and 5 justices of the Supreme Court, which would rule on the 15 disputed electoral votes. Seven seats were held by members of each party; the remaining seat was expected to go to David Davis, an independent justice of the Supreme Court. However, Davis left the commission to take a Senate seat, and his replacement was the Republican justice Joseph Bradley. Unsurprisingly, the commission awarded each disputed vote to Hayes, 8 to 7. Hayes thus edged Tilden in the college, 185 to 184. Though Democrats threatened to filibuster the joint session of Congress called to certify the new electoral vote, they agreed to let the session continue when Hayes agreed to end Reconstruction and withdraw federal troops from the South. The Hayes-Tilden crisis resulted in the 1887 Electoral Count Act, which gave each state authority to determine the legality of its electoral vote but also provided that a concurrent majority of both houses of Congress could reject disputed votes.

The act was invoked to resolve such a dispute in 1969 and again in the first two presidential elections of the twenty-first century. The 2000 election mirrored the Hayes-Tilden crisis; as in 1876, the Democratic candidate, Al Gore, held a clear edge in the popular vote, leading Republican George W. Bush by half a million votes. However, the balance in the Electoral College was close enough that the 25 votes of Florida would decide the election. Initial returns in that state favored Bush by the slimmest of margins but recounts narrowed the gap to within a thousand. Finally, however, the Supreme Court affirmed Bush's appeal to stop the recounts; the Republican was awarded a 537-vote victory in the state and consequently a majority in the Electoral College. Democrats in the House of Representatives attempted to invoke the 1887 law to disqualify Florida's slate of electors but failed to gain the necessary support in the Senate to put the matter to a vote. Bush's successful 2004 reelection campaign against Democrat John Kerry also sparked discontent, and concerns about the balloting in Ohio prompted House Democrats to again invoke the law. This time, though, they were able to gain enough Senate support to force a concurrent vote; it affirmed Ohio's Republican slate of electors by a large margin.

These controversies have highlighted growing discontent with the intent and function of the Electoral College, and the reasoning behind the Constitutional Convention's adoption of the institution has been increasingly marshaled against it. While the founders hoped that electors would select the president based on reasoned discussion, 24 states now have laws to punish "faithless electors" who defy the results of their states' popular election and vote for another candidate, as has occurred eight times since World War II. While the founders hoped the Electoral College would create a presidency relatively independent of public opinion, it has come under fire since Andrew Jackson's time for doing exactly that.

Possible Solutions

Multiple measures have been proposed to more closely align the Electoral College with the popular vote. One of the more commonly mentioned solutions is proportional representation; that is, rather than the winner of the presidential election in each state taking all that state's electoral votes, the state would distribute those votes in proportion to the election results. Such a reform would almost certainly enhance the chances of third parties to gain electoral votes. However, since the Constitution requires a majority of the Electoral College for victory, this solution would most likely throw many more presidential elections to the House of Representatives. For instance, under this system the elections of 1912, 1968, and 1992 would all have been decided by the House. Thus, proportional representation would undo two of the Framers' wishes, tying the presidency not only closer to the general public but perhaps unintentionally to Congress as well. The Colorado electorate rejected a state constitutional amendment for proportional representation in 2004.

A similar policy is often referred to as the "Maine-Nebraska rule," after the two states that have adopted it: Maine in 1972 and Nebraska in 1996. It is reminiscent of the district policy that states such as Virginia and Massachusetts implemented in the early years of the republic. Maine and Nebraska allot one electoral vote to the winner of each congressional district, and assign the final two (corresponding to each state's two senators) to the overall winner of the state's popular vote. While this technique seems to limit the potential chaos of the proportional method, it does not actually solve the problem: if every state in the Union adopted the Maine-Nebraska rule, it would still be possible for a presidential candidate to lose the election despite winning the popular vote.

A third state-based reform of the Electoral College system gained significant support in April 2007, when the Maryland legislature passed a law calling on the rest of the states to agree to assign their electors to whichever presidential candidate wins the popular vote. This would effectively circumvent the Electoral College, while retaining the elector and Congress's tabulation of the vote as a symbolic, constitutional formality.

Finally, many commentators have called for a constitutional amendment simply eliminating the Electoral College entirely, arguing that, in addition to the possibility of presidential victors who have lost the popular vote, the electoral system artificially inflates the value of votes in small states (due to the constitutionally mandated minimum of three votes to every state), discourages minority parties, and encourages candidates to ignore states they believe they cannot win. However, the college is not universally unpopular; its supporters counter that the system maintains political stability and forces candidates to expend effort on states with small populations that they might otherwise bypass. Additionally, supporters of the Electoral College maintain that it is an important connection to the federal system envisioned by the framers of the Constitution.

Some observers have noted that disputes over the college tend to follow fault lines already existing in American politics. Gore's loss in the 2000 election inspired many Democrats to look at the college with a critical perspective; additionally, more rural states, small in population, that oppose losing the influence the Electoral College gives them tend to support Republican candidates. Heavily urban states with more concentrated populations tend to vote Democratic. Thus, the regional differences the Convention hoped to moderate through the Electoral College have been effectively translated into partisan differences that the college exacerbates. However, the constitutional barriers to removing the college likely ensure it will remain on the American political landscape for the foreseeable future.

See also elections and electoral eras; voting.

FURTHER READING. Richard McCormick, *The Presidential Game: The Origins of American Presidential Politics*, 1982; Arthur Schlesinger, Jr., *The History of American Presidential Elections, 1789–1968*, 1971; Paul D. Schumaker and Burdett A. Loomis, eds, *Choosing a President: The Electoral College and Beyond*, 2002.

MATTHEW BOWMAN

energy and politics

For most of its history, the United States has depended on its own abundant supply of energy resources. If there is a common political theme in the history of American energy and politics, it is the desire to maximize domestic production and to stabilize competition between private firms. Although these imperatives dominated the energy policies of the nineteenth and twentieth centuries, events in the 1970s caused a dramatic reversal of direction. This article traces the development of public policies in the coal and oil industries, since these commodities supplied the bulk of American energy throughout the nation's history and were the primary target of state and federal policy makers. This necessarily excludes important developments in the political history of utilities, electrification, and the development of nuclear power, but it allows for a long-range perspective on American energy policy.

Policy Making and the Rise of Coal

At the time of the American Revolution, the predominant forms of energy came from human or animal power and firewood. Coal was in limited use, but American policy makers viewed the domestic coal trade as vital to the young nation's future. To encourage the growth of a coal industry the federal government moved to protect American colliers from foreign competition. The original tariff on coal imports in 1789 was 2 cents per bushel. It increased gradually over the years, until in 1812 it reached 10 cents a bushel, or about 15 percent of the wholesale price of British coal. After the War of 1812, tariff rates on coal dropped in 1816 to 5 cents a bushel, which ranged between 10 and 25 percent of the price of foreign coal in New York, and remained at about that range until 1842. British imports bounced back after 1815, but they never again exceeded more than 10 percent of American production. Tariff levels did not completely push British coal out of American markets, but they did severely restrict its ability to compete with the domestic product. By the postbellum decades, the federal government had eliminated the tariff on anthracite, and levels on bituminous coal bottomed out at 40 cents a ton in 1895. Domestic production dominated American coal markets, and the United States became a net exporter of coal in the 1870s.

Under the umbrella of federal protection, state governments encouraged the rapid development of coal mining in the antebellum period. First, in the 1830s, Pennsylvania's legislature exempted anthracite coal from taxation and promoted its use in the iron industry through a liberal corporate chartering law. As anthracite use increased, Pennsylvania officials refused to grant exclusive carrying or vending rights to any company engaged in transporting anthracite to urban markets. As a result, a diverse group of canals and railroads served Pennsylvania's relatively compact anthracite fields. Competition between the Schuylkill Navigation Company's all-water route and the Lehigh Coal and Navigation Company's rail and water connections to Philadelphia, for example, ensured that anthracite prices remained low. To expedite the exploitation of new coalfields, many states commissioned geological surveys. North Carolina employed a state geologist to catalog the state's mineral resources in 1823; by 1837, 14 states had followed suit. The annual reports and final compilation of the state geological surveys served to underwrite the cost of finding viable coal seams and marking valuable mineral deposits for entrepreneurs. In some cases, such as Pennsylvania and Illinois, the state geologist specifically targeted coalfields as the primary emphasis of the survey. In others, a more general assessment of mineral resources occurred. Although state geologists would find, label, and survey the coalfields, it

was up to private firms to mine, carry, and sell the coal to domestic and industrial consumers. Pennsylvania's leadership in this field was apparent, as that state boosted coal production levels to nearly 6.5 million tons, or about three-fourths of U.S. production, by 1850.

The period following the Civil War saw a heightened role for railroads in American energy policy. Railroad companies appealed to state legislatures for the right to buy or lease coal lands—a combination of mining and carrying privileges that many antebellum policy makers were unwilling to tolerate. In Pennsylvania an 1869 law authorized railroad and canal companies to purchase the stocks and bonds of mining firms. By the 1870s the Philadelphia and Reading Railroad embarked on an ambitious plan to purchase enough anthracite coal lands to set prices. The Philadelphia and Reading failed in its attempt to monopolize anthracite, but it and other regional railroads became increasingly powerful in the late nineteenth century. The nation's bituminous fields were too large for any significant concentration of power, but in the more compact anthracite fields, a distinct combination of large mining and carrying companies formed during the 1880s to keep prices high even as they forced small-scale colliers to sell their coal at rock-bottom prices. State-level attempts to impose rates on railroads, as well as early attempts by federal authorities to regulate the coal trade under the auspices of the Interstate Commerce Commission (1887) or the Sherman Anti-Trust Act (1890), fell flat, as policy makers at both state and federal levels remained focused on maintaining high production levels, keeping prices low, and bringing new coalfields into production. For example, Congress created the United States Geological Survey in 1879, an agency charged with the topographic and geological mapping of the entire nation. This institution combined several surveys that had been created for military and scientific purposes in order to catalog valuable mineral resources of the nation just as the antebellum surveys did for their respective states.

The relations between labor and capital in energy production also became a concern for policy makers by the late nineteenth century. Prior to the Civil War, coal mining was done on a relatively small scale. Individual proprietorships could survive with a few skilled miners who exerted total control over the hiring of laborers, the construction of the shafts and tunnels, and the cutting and hauling of the coal from the mine. Experienced miners thus acted as independent contractors throughout most of the nineteenth century. The corporate reorganization of coalfields created new pressures on firms; now they needed to increase production and cut costs at every turn. Many mine operators sought to use the autonomy of miners for their own benefit by pressing tonnage rates down, docking miners for sending up coal with too many "impurities," and paying miners in scrip rather than cash. Although the transformation of work at the coal seam itself with the introduction of machine cutters would not occur until the 1890s, labor relations aboveground changed rapidly during and after the Civil War. Small-scale unions formed in individual coalfields and struck, with varying effectiveness, for higher wages. Since the largest variable cost in coal mining is in labor, colliers insisted on the ability to control wages and fought to keep unions from organizing in American coalfields. In 1890, however, a national trade union, the United Mine Workers of America (UMWA), formed in Columbus, Ohio. For the next half century, the UMWA struggled to win collective bargaining rights in the nation's geographically diverse and decentralized coal trade.

Federal authorities were drawn into the regulation of the nation's coal trade during the early twentieth century. In the anthracite fields of Pennsylvania, for example, labor disputes and an attempt by a handful of railroad operators to manipulate prices provoked federal action. When miners in the anthracite fields sought the aid of the UMWA to secure an eight-hour day, decent wages, and safe working conditions, managers of coal companies responded with intimidation, lockouts, and violence. The long and crippling strike of 1902, which threatened energy supplies across the eastern seaboard by shutting down anthracite production, drew President Theodore Roosevelt into the fray. By declaring that he would negotiate a "square deal" between labor and management, Roosevelt set a precedent for federal intervention. A square deal, however, did not create a federal mandate for collective bargaining rights for coal miners; nevertheless, it did offer some modicum of governmental oversight. In 1908 the Justice Department, under the authority of the Interstate Commerce Commission (ICC), filed a major lawsuit against anthracite railroads accused of manipulating prices and intimidating independent colliers. Results were mixed; the Supreme Court upheld the "commodities clause" of the ICC, which banned the direct ownership of coal mines by railroads, but informal relationships between large coal companies and railroads continued to dominate the region. Finally, the U.S. Bureau of Mines, created in 1910, enforced safety regulations on reluctant coal operators. Mine safety remained a concern for the industry, but miners in this period did at least see a modest increase in protection from hazardous working conditions. In all these cases, federal intervention in the nation's coal trade preserved the nineteenth-century focus on high levels of production, even as new legislation and policy decisions produced minor victories for small colliers and mine workers.

The Rise of Federal Policy Making and the American Oil Industry

Throughout most of the nineteenth century, the U.S. government's energy policy consisted of tariff protection and the promotion of new coalfields, either actively by creating agencies like the U.S. Geological Survey or passively by refusing to regulate the coal trade. At the advent of the twentieth century, however, federal policy makers found themselves drawn into major conflicts over competition and labor, as well as the rise of oil and natural gas as new sources of energy. The era between 1880 and 1920 truly was the reign of "King Coal": production soared from 80 million tons to 659 million tons, an increase of more than 800 percent, and coal accounted for 70 percent of the nation's energy consumption. Crude oil production increased seventeenfold, from 26 million barrels in 1880 to 443 million in 1920; yet American refineries still focused on illumination and lubrication products, rather than fuel, throughout the late nineteenth and early twentieth centuries. The discovery of massive reserves in the Spindletop oil field in southeastern Texas, the Mid-Continent Field of Kansas and Oklahoma, and southern California during the decade before World War I all pointed toward American oil's bright future as a source of energy.

Natural gas also became a significant energy source in the early twentieth century. Producers pumped 812 billion cubic feet by 1920, an increase from the 128 billion cubic feet they secured in 1900. As nationwide reserves came into production, interstate railroads and pipelines made state-level oversight difficult, and the bulk of energy policy shifted to the federal level throughout the twentieth century. The rise of oil and gas, moreover, created more challenges for policy makers and forced them to regulate production, competition, and price setting in unprecedented ways.

The specific crises brought by World War I created a new kind of regulatory regime and signaled the growing importance of oil in the nation's energy economy. In response to the anticipated coal shortage triggered by the American declaration of war in 1917, the Federal Trade Commission explored the possibility of federal controls over prices and distribution. Although initial attempts to coordinate the nation's coal trade failed when the Council for National Defense's Committee on Coal Production folded in the summer of 1917, Congress granted President Woodrow Wilson broad authority over energy production and consumption, including the right to set the price of coal. This resulted in the creation of the United States Fuel Administration, a wartime agency designed to coordinate coal, petroleum, and railroad operations in both military and civilian sectors of the economy. Its director, Harry Garfield, was unfamiliar with the vagaries of the well-organized anthracite and vast decentralized bituminous coal industries; attempts to fix prices failed, and a coal shortage crippled the American economy in the winter of 1917–18. To boost production levels, the USFA encouraged the opening of new mines and restricted coal consumption among non-war-related industries and households. Wartime demand for petroleum boosted production but also created headaches for the USFA's Oil Division. Petroleum shortages during the war were less debilitating, however. The price stability caused by the artificially high demand provoked much needed conservation and storage reforms among private petroleum producers and put new oil fields into production. Some USFA officials advocated a continuation of the command-and-control approach to energy policy after the war ended in November 1918. Pre-war energy markets had faced debilitating gluts and shortages, coupled with unstable prices. Since energy reserves in the United States were still abundant, they argued, public oversight might help stabilize both production and consumption of vital commodities like coal, oil, and natural gas.

Despite calls for a continued presence of federal authority, Congress cut appropriations for the USFA at the war's end. By 1919 the coal trade was experiencing serious problems. Wartime demand had boosted the number of American coal mines from 6,939 in 1917 to 8,994 in 1919. When new orders for coal waned, mine operators reduced wages and laid off miners at the same time that millions of American soldiers returned in search of work. A series of strikes rocked the bituminous and anthracite industries in the 1920s as the UMWA continued its efforts to organize the nation's miners, now 615,000 strong. By 1932 the number of miners dropped to less than 400,000 and the American coal industry was in disarray. The creation of the National Industrial Recovery Act (NIRA) the following year set up price codes for coal and helped stanch the bleeding. The UMWA also benefited from Section 7(a) of the NIRA, which provided for collective bargaining. By 1935 federal support for unionization swelled the ranks of the UMWA to more than half a million. But when the Supreme Court declared the NIRA unconstitutional in that same year, the short-lived stability faded. Federal support for collective bargaining continued, but the American coal trade returned to its old familiar pattern of decentralized, uncoordinated production, which kept prices relatively low for consumers but profit margins razor-thin for mine operators. Labor relations became even more heated, as the UMWA, under the leadership of its forceful president John L. Lewis, challenged attempts to cut wage rates at every turn.

Oil and gas producers also suffered during the Great Depression, even as production levels reached all-time highs of nearly a billion barrels of crude petroleum in 1935. In Texas, state regulation, under the aegis of the Texas Railroad Commission, helped maintain some price stability by limiting production. Oil producers also had price and production codes under the NIRA, but without the labor conflicts of their counterparts in coal, no controversy over collective bargaining hit the industry. With the termination of the NIRA, no broad regulatory agency appeared in the petroleum industry. Instead, a consortium of six major oil-producing states formed to regulate production and stabilize the industry. The 1935 Interstate Compact to Conserve Oil and Gas joined Colorado, Kansas, Illinois, New Mexico, Oklahoma, and Texas together to replicate the state-level programs of the Texas Railroad Commission in a national setting. Natural gas came under federal control with the passage of the Natural Gas Act of 1938, which regulated interstate trade in gas, including the nation's growing network of pipelines for shipping natural gas. In oil and gas the control of interstate traffic remained an essential, and ultimately effective, way to ensure price stability without radically expanding government oversight.

By the advent of World War II, coal had declined to about 50 percent of the nation's energy consumption, even though reserves of coal showed little sign of depletion. When the UMWA's 400,000 coal miners struck in 1943, federal officials seized some mines and reopened them under government control. Coal remained important, but the increasing popularity of automobiles, oil for heating, and electric motors in industry made petroleum the dominant element of the American fuel economy. The Petroleum Administration for War, under the leadership of Secretary of Interior Harold Ickes, coordinated the flow of oil for civilian and military uses. Some rationing occurred to avoid costly shortages, but most significant for long-term growth were the thousands of miles of new pipelines to connect the oil fields of the Southwest to the rest of the nation. Following the war, the Oil and Gas Division of the Department of the Interior was established to stabilize the oil industry through price data sharing, pipeline policies, and consulting trade organizations such as the National Petroleum Council. The World War II years also introduced nuclear power into the nation's energy future, although the use of nuclear power was not widespread immediately after the war.

As the consumption of energy skyrocketed in the post–World War II decades, oil continued to grow in importance. Most significant for energy policy, the United States became a net importer of oil in 1948. As the booming postwar economy grew, American producers attempted to stem the flow of foreign oil by persuading President Dwight D. Eisenhower to set up mandatory oil import quotas. A year later a cartel of major oil-producing nations such as Saudi Arabia, Iraq, Iran, Kuwait, and Venezuela formed the Organization of Petroleum Exporting Countries (OPEC). OPEC had little impact on American energy markets, and the extent to which the United States depended upon foreign oil remained untested, until the Arab-Israeli conflict of 1973 triggered an embargo by Arab nations on exports to the United States. By early 1974 the price of oil had nearly quadrupled, triggering the first "oil shock" in the American economy. The embargo ended that same year, but throughout the 1970s American dependence on Middle Eastern oil became a political issue, coming to a head with the overthrow of the pro-American regime in Iran in 1979. From that point on, energy policies became intertwined with foreign policy, particularly in the Middle East.

The 1970s brought a major reversal in American energy policy, the repercussions of which are still shaking out today. Nuclear power, once considered a major source of energy for the future, became politically toxic after the 1979 partial meltdown of a reactor core at the Three Mile Island facility in Pennsylvania. The oil shocks of that decade, moreover, suggested that traditional policies directed at maximizing domestic production of energy sources were no longer adequate for the United States. In response to this new challenge, Congress passed the National Energy Act in 1978, which aimed to reduce gasoline consumption by 10 percent, cut imports to make up only one-eighth of American consumption, and increase the use of domestic coal—about one-third of American energy consumption in the early 1970s—to take advantage of abundant reserves. President Jimmy Carter also created the Department of Energy (DOE) in 1978 and promoted the further exploration of alternative energy sources such as solar, wind, and wave power. Although the DOE's emphasis on traditional versus alternative energy sources seemed to wax and wane with changes in presidential administrations, alternatives to the well-established fossil fuel sources of energy have demanded the attention of policy makers in Washington. In this regard, energy policy in the twenty-first century will take a different course from the first two centuries of the nation's history.

See also business and politics; environmental issues and politics; transportation and politics.

FURTHER READING. Sean Patrick Adams, *Old Dominion, Industrial Commonwealth: Coal, Politics, and Economy in Antebellum America*, 2004; William Childs, *The Texas Railroad Commission: Understanding Regulation in America to the Mid-Twentieth Century*, 2005; John Clark, *Energy and the Federal Government: Fossil Fuel Policies, 1900–1946*, 1987; Martin Melosi, *Coping with Abundance: Energy and Environment in Industrial America*, 1985; David Nye, *Consuming Power: A Social History of American Energies*, 1997; David Painter, *Oil and the American Century: The Political Economy of US Foreign Oil Policy, 1941–1954*, 1986; Joseph A. Pratt, "The Petroleum Industry in Transition: Anti-Trust and the Decline of Monopoly Control in Oil," *Journal of Economic History* 40 (December 1980), 815–37; Richard Vietor, *Energy Policy in America since 1945*, 1984.

SEAN ADAMS

environmental issues and politics

Today, the phrase "environmental issues and politics" invariably refers to debates about problems such as pollution, species extinction, and global warming. But the United States had environmental policies long before the rise of the modern environmental movement. Indeed, the modern movement is partly a rejection of earlier American ideas about government and nature.

From the founding of the nation, government at all levels encouraged the development of land. To promote the real-estate market, New York City created a street grid in 1807. States built canals—"artificial rivers"—to facilitate commerce. Beginning in 1862, the federal government gave land to settlers willing to improve the landscape by establishing farms. In the 1930s, the federal government sought to promote economic development in the South and the West by constructing vast systems of dams. In many ways, state and federal policy has encouraged exploitation of natural resources, from timber to oil. The federal government also has helped individuals and businesses to conquer nature: federal agencies have predicted the weather, controlled wildfires, protected cattle and sheep from predators, and kept floodwaters at bay.

The first challenges to the nation's pro-development spirit came in the decades before the Civil War. A small group of artists and writers began to celebrate the undeveloped countryside as a romantic escape from civilization and a sublime source of national pride. In some states, farmers began to complain about dwindling stocks of fish. Though a few of the fish defenders were concerned about pollution, most argued that the principal threats to fisheries were dams built to power mills. Residents of a few cities also took legal action to rid their neighborhoods of manufacturing smoke and stenches.

The Formative Period

The antebellum questioning of development was limited to a tiny minority. In the period from 1865 to 1915, however, many more Americans sought government action to address what we now call environmental problems. They organized to stop pollution, conserve natural resources, and preserve wild places and wild creatures. Many urban Americans also sought to renew their relationship with nature.

The activism of those formative years was a response to the profound environmental changes brought by unprecedented urbanization, industrialization, and immigration. Hundreds of towns became congested, polluted industrial cities. The vast forests of the Great Lakes region were cut down. Millions of acres of grassland were transformed into farms and ranches. Many creatures that once were important parts of the landscape were driven to the edge of extinction or beyond.

To many Americans, the industrial city seemed to be a great experiment, a new form of civilization that promised much but that might prove unsustainable. Many of the doubts were environmental. The urban environment was far less healthy than the rural or small-town landscape. Would cities ever become places where births exceeded deaths? Many observers also feared the moral and social effects of separating so many millions from contact with nature.

Without remedial action, the rapid transformation of the countryside also portended harm as well as good. Would the United States continue to have the resources necessary to grow richer and more powerful and to take its ordained place on the world stage? The symbolic closing of the frontier in 1890 led many Americans to conclude that the nation no longer could take superabundance for granted.

Municipal governments felt the greatest pressure to assume new responsibilities. In 1865 most cities had no sanitary infrastructure. The explosive concentration of people and industrial activity threatened to turn urban areas into environmental hellholes. The leaders of many cities responded by greatly expanding the power of municipal government. They created boards of health. They also built sewer systems, took responsibility for collecting garbage and cleaning streets, established parks, protected sources of drinking water, and regulated "the smoke nuisance."

The urban environmental reforms of the Gilded Age and Progressive Era had mixed consequences. The new sanitary infrastructure greatly reduced mortality from epidemic diseases, especially cholera and typhoid. In most cities, the parks became valuable oases. But the antismoke regulations did little to improve air quality. Though most cities were able to improve their drinking water, many forms of water pollution continued unabated, and some grew worse: most cities dumped untreated sewage into nearby rivers and harbors.

At the federal level, the concern about the nation's environmental future led to a dramatic change in land policy. After decades of trying to privatize the public domain, the government decided that millions of acres never would be sold or given away. Those lands instead were to be national forests, parks, and wildlife refuges. To manage the forest reserves, the government established a new kind of bureaucracy, run by scientifically trained experts. The parks initially were the responsibility of the U.S. Army, but the government established the National Park Service in 1916, and the agency soon became a powerful promoter of outdoor recreation.

State governments also responded to new environmental demands. Many established boards of public health, fish-and-game departments, and forest commissions. At a time when the federal government had limited capacity, states also took the initiative in studying environmental problems. Massachusetts undertook the first systematic surveys of river pollution in the 1870s. In the 1910s, Illinois pioneered the study of environmental hazards in the workplace, and these investigations led to a deeper understanding of the health effects of air pollution.

Many of the new laws and agencies met resistance. In debates about pollution, business leaders often argued that environmental degradation was the price of progress. Immigrants sometimes resisted sanitary and conservation regulations. In national parks and forests, officials were challenged by people who no longer could use those areas for subsistence.

The support for environmental initiatives in the Gilded Age and Progressive Era came largely from the well-to-do. Many professional men supported conservation, preservation, and antipollution efforts. To progressives, social and environmental reform went hand-in-hand. The reform cause always had some backing from the business community. In sheer numbers, however, the greatest support came from middle- and upper-class women. Because so many environmental issues involved the traditionally feminine concerns of beauty, health, and the well-being of future generations, women often argued that they were especially equipped to address environmental problems. That argument became a justification for suffrage as well as a rationale for professional careers.

New Deal Conservation

Until recently, scholars paid little attention to environmental issues and politics from the end of the Progressive Era until the first stirrings of the modern environmental movement in the 1950s. But a number of new works make clear that the age of Franklin D. Roosevelt deserves more attention from environmental historians. Though grassroots activism was relatively limited, government and university research on environmental problems in the interwar period provided a foundation for future reform efforts. Federal environmental policy also became much more ambitious in the New Deal years.

Among the many agencies established by New Dealers, several had conservation missions, including the Soil Conservation Service, the Tennessee Valley Authority, and the Civilian Conservation Corps. The new agencies were partly a response to natural disasters. In the 1930s, dust storms devastated the Great Plains, while floods wreaked havoc on much of the eastern third of the continent. In addition to providing relief, the government undertook to prevent a recurrence of such disasters. That preventive effort depended on a new recognition that dust storms and floods were not entirely acts of nature: in both cases, federal policy makers concluded, human action had turned climatic extremes into economic and social tragedies.

The new conservation agencies were not conceived together, yet all became part of the New Deal attempt to end the Depression. Like the conservationists of the Progressive Era, the New Dealers believed that conservation would ensure future prosperity. But their joining of environmental and economic goals was more explicit. The Tennessee Valley Authority (TVA) was a development agency for the nation's most destitute region. By controlling the South's rampaging rivers, the TVA would stimulate industry and improve rural life. The Civilian Conservation Corps (CCC) put 3 million men to work on conservation and economic development projects:

The corps reclaimed denuded landscapes by planting trees, worked with farmers to protect soil from erosion, and built outdoor-recreation facilities, including parks, trails, and roads, to attract visitors.

In contrast to the Progressive Era, when the federal government sought to influence private decision making by demonstrating "wise use" of resources in public forest reserves, many of the New Deal conservation initiatives sought to have a direct impact on the management of privately owned land. The Soil Conservation Service encouraged the formation of thousands of county conservation districts and provided financial and technical assistance to millions of farmers. For the first time, the New Dealers sought a role for the government in land-use planning. The Taylor Grazing Act of 1934 greatly strengthened the ability of federal officials to control the way ranchers used millions of acres of the public domain. Though a New Deal effort to plan development on the Great Plains failed, the TVA had a far-reaching impact on the South.

New Dealers also spread the conservation gospel more than any previous adminstration. Government photographs of the dust bowl and the rural South became iconic images. Two government-sponsored films—*The Plow That Broke the Plains* and *The River*—publicized the New Deal argument about the social causes of the period's great natural disasters. The 3 million men who joined the CCC were instructed in conservation principles. Almost all the enrollees came from cities, and the government hoped that CCC work would strengthen their bodies and persuade them that contact with nature had many benefits. Historians now credit the CCC with broadening the constituency for environmental protection.

In other ways, however, New Deal policy left a mixed legacy. Though officials hoped to revitalize rural America, many New Deal measures ultimately encouraged large enterprises rather than small farms. The soil conservation effort checked some of the worst agricultural practices, but few farmers truly accepted a new land ethic. In the decades after World War II, environmentalists often argued that New Deal conservation put economic development ahead of ecological balance.

The Environmental Age

The modern environmental movement became a major political and social force in the 1960s. The great symbol of the movement's emergence was the inaugural Earth Day in 1970, when approximately 20 million Americans gathered in thousands of communities to seek action in addressing "the environmental crisis." It was the biggest demonstration in U.S. history.

Three broad developments explain the rise of environmentalism after World War II. First, the unprecedented affluence of the postwar years encouraged millions of Americans to reject the old argument that pollution was the price of economic progress.

Instead, they argued that the citizens of a rich nation should be able to enjoy a healthy and beautiful environment. Second, the development of atomic energy, the chemical revolution in agriculture, the proliferation of synthetic materials, and the increased scale of power-generation and resource-extraction technology created new environmental hazards. From atomic fallout to suburban sprawl, new threats provoked grassroots and expert protest. Third, the insights of ecology gave countless citizens a new appreciation of the risks of transforming nature. Rachel Carson's 1962 best-seller *Silent Spring*—a powerful critique of chemical pesticides—was especially important in popularizing ecological ideas.

Even before the first Earth Day, government at all levels had begun to respond to new environmental demands. In 1964, for example, the federal government created a system of "wilderness" areas. But the explosion came in the 1970s—the environmental decade. A series of landmark federal laws addressed such critical environmental problems as air and water pollution, endangered species, and toxic waste. The federal government and many states established environmental-protection agencies. A "quiet revolution" gave state and local officials unprecedented power to regulate the use of privately owned land. In many communities, Earth Day led to the creation of ecology centers, some short-lived and some enduring. The early 1970s brought new national environmental organizations with different goals than the conservation and preservation groups established in the late nineteenth century. Colleges and universities established environmental studies programs. The 1970s also saw the first attempts to create environmentally friendly ways of organizing daily life, from recycling to efforts to grow organic food.

The sources of support for the new movement were varied. Many Democrats concluded that a liberal agenda for affluent times needed to include environmental protection. Middle-class women often saw environmental problems as threats to home and family. Young critics of the nation's institutions were especially important in the mobilization for Earth Day. To varying degrees, old resource-conservation and wilderness-preservation organizations took up new environmental issues in the 1950s and 1960s. Many scientists warned the public about the environmental dangers of new technologies. The environmental cause also depended on the institutional support of many professional groups, from public-health officials to landscape architects. Though still based largely among white, well-to-do residents of cities and suburbs, the modern movement was more demographically diverse than its predecessors.

Despite the popularity of the environmental cause in the early 1970s, the new movement had powerful opposition. The coal industry organized a coalition to try to defeat or weaken the Clean Air Act of 1970, while the National Association of Homebuilders led a successful campaign against national land-use legislation. Though a handful of unions supported antipollution initiatives, many labor leaders sided with management in opposing environmental regulation. The successes of environmentalists also provoked a backlash. In the so-called Sagebrush Rebellion, Western timber and cattle interests challenged federal management of forest and grazing lands. The revolution in state and local regulation of land use soon sparked a "property rights" movement.

The opposition grew stronger after the oil crisis of 1973. Because the production and distribution of oil comes at a steep environmental cost, environmentalists already had begun to lobby for the development of alternative forms of energy, and the crisis might have made that case more compelling. But the sudden scarcity of a critical resource instead strengthened the position of those who saw environmentalism as a terrible drag on the economy. The oil crisis was perhaps the final blow to the postwar boom. Both inflation and unemployment worsened, and the hard times brought a revised version of the old argument about jobs and environmental protection: The nation could have one or the other, but not both.

The backlash against environmentalism helped Ronald Reagan win the presidency in 1980. Reagan promised to remove restrictions on energy development, eliminate thousands of environmental regulations, and privatize millions of acres of the public domain. But he was only partly successful. The resurgence of conservatism forced environmentalists to give up any hope of expanding the federal government's power to protect the environment. The Reagan administration was unable, however, to undo the environmental initiatives of the early 1970s. In the 1980s, the membership of environmental organizations reached new highs.

The rise of concern about global warming in the late 1980s did not change the basic political dynamic. The federal government undertook few important environmental initiatives in the generation after Reagan left office. Though scientists, environmentalists, and many others called with increasing urgency for bold action to limit human-induced climate change, their efforts did not break the political stalemate at the federal level. But the environmental movement was more successful in other arenas. Environmental ways of thinking and acting are more common now in many basic American institutions, from schools to corporations.

See also energy and politics.

FURTHER READING. Richard N. L. Andrews, *Managing Nature, Managing Ourselves: A History of American Environmental Policy*, 2nd ed., 2006; Stephen Fox, *The American Conservation Movement: John Muir and His Legacy*, 1985; Robert Gottlieb, *Forcing the Spring: The Transformation of the American Environmental Movement*, revised and updated ed., 2005; Samuel P. Hays, *Beauty, Health, and Permanence: Environmental Politics in the United States, 1955–1985*, 1987; Martin V. Melosi, *The Sanitary City: Urban Infrastructure in America from Colonial Times to the Present*, 2000; Carolyn Merchant, *The Columbia Guide to American Environmental History*, 2002; Adam Rome, *The Bulldozer in the Countryside: Suburban Sprawl and the Rise of American Environmentalism*, 2001; Adam Rome, "'Give Earth a Chance': The Environmental Movement and the Sixties," *Journal of American History* 90 (September 2003), 525–54; Ted Steinberg, *Down to Earth: Nature's Role in American History*, 2002; Thomas R. Wellock, *Preserving the Nation: The Conservation and Environmental Movements, 1870–2000*, 2007.

ADAM ROME

era of a new republic, 1789–1827

In 1789 the United States was a new republic on multiple levels. The new nation represented the first attempt at a continent-sized republic in the history of the world. Regarding organized competition for national power as both immoral and likely to bring on civil war or foreign intervention, the founders designed the constitutional system to prevent the development of political parties, then lined up unanimously behind the country's most revered public figure, General George Washington, as the first occupant of the powerful new presidency.

On a more substantive level, the question of what kind of nation the United States would become was completely open. Despite their commitment to unity, American political leaders turned out to have very different ideas about the future direction of the country. To northeastern nationalists like Alexander Hamilton, America was "Hercules in his cradle," the raw materials out of which they hoped to rapidly build an urban, oceangoing commercial and military empire like Great Britain. Upper South liberals like Thomas Jefferson hoped for a reformed version of their expansive pastoral society, gradually purged of slavery and gross social inequality, and sought to stave off traditional imperial development. Less enlightened planter-politicians in the more economically robust lower South looked forward to building new plantation districts on rich lands just becoming available and to acquiring the slave population they expected to build and work them. Still other Americans who were relatively new to politics—artisans, immigrants, and town dwellers of the middle and lower ranks—held to the radicalism of 1776 and saw America as the seedbed in which the most democratic and egalitarian political visions of the Enlightenment would flower.

"Monarchical Prettinesses"

All these potential futures were predicated on a distinctive role for the American state and different policies. With Alexander Hamilton ensconced as Washington's treasury secretary and de facto prime minister, his option got the first trial. Proceeding on the assumption that ample revenues and stable credit were the "sinews of power," Hamilton set up a British-style system of public finance, with a privately owned national bank and an interest-bearing national debt. Secretary of State Jefferson and Hamilton's old ally Representative James Madison protested the resulting windfall profits for northern financial interests and bristled at the freedom from constitutional restraint with which Hamilton acted—there was no constitutional provision for a national bank or even for creating corporations. Hamilton's reading of the Constitution's "necessary and proper" clause as allowing any government action that was convenient or conducive to its general purposes horrified Jefferson and Madison as tantamount to no constitutional limitations at all.

Despite his own rapid social climb, Hamilton's expansive approach to government power went along with a dismissive attitude toward popular aspirations for political democracy and social equality. This attitude was quite congenial to the wealthiest men in every region, merchants and planters alike, and these elites formed the backbone of what became the Federalist party. As long as they held power, the Federalists did not consider themselves a party at all, but instead the nation's rightful ruling elite. While admitting that republican government was rooted in popular consent, they favored strict limits on where and when consent was exercised. Political contention "out of doors" (outside the halls of government) should stop once the elections did.

Slaveholding democrats such as Jefferson and Madison stood in a more ambiguous relation to popular democratic aspirations than their northern followers realized, but they shared in the distaste aired in the press for the "monarchical prettinesses" built up around President Washington to strengthen respect for the new government. These included official birthday tributes, a magnificent coach and mansion, and the restriction of access to the presidential person to official "levees" at which guests were forbidden the democratic gesture of shaking the president's hand. This monarchical culture sparked the first stirrings of party organization, when Jefferson and Madison recruited poet Philip Freneau to edit the *National Gazette*, a newspaper that first named and defined the Republican (better known as Democratic-Republican) opposition and became the model for the hundreds of partisan newspapers that were the lifeblood of the early party system.

A Postcolonial Politics

From the inward-looking modern American perspective, it may be surprising that the catalyst for full-scale party conflict actually came from outside the republic's borders. Yet the early United States was also a new nation in the global order of its time. The great political upheavals of Europe during the 1790s elicited tremendous passions in America and reached out inexorably to influence the nation's politics, often through the direct manipulations of the great powers.

As was the case in other former colonies, U.S. politics inevitably revolved partly around debates over the nation's relationship with the mother country. Respecting Great Britain's wealth and power, Hamilton and the Federalists generally favored reestablishing a relatively close economic and political relationship with the British; Democratic-Republicans were less quick to forget their revolutionary views and sought to forge some completely independent status based on universal republicanism and free trade.

Then there was the question of the old alliance with France. Initially, the French Revolution was uncontroversial in the United States, but as the French situation became more radical and bloody it divided the rest of the Atlantic World. Just as Washington began his second term, France was declared a republic, King Louis XVI was executed, and Great Britain joined Austria and Prussia's war against France, setting up a conflict that would involve the young United States repeatedly over the next 20 years. Both sides periodically retaliated against neutral American shipping and sought to push American policy in the desired direction.

Hamilton and the Federalists recoiled from the new French republic. Yet, despite its violence and cultural overreach (rewriting the calendar, closing the churches, etc.), the radicalized French Revolution was wildly popular in many American quarters, especially with younger men and women who had been raised on the French alliance and the rhetoric of the American Revolution. When Edmond Genet, the first diplomatic envoy from the French republic, arrived in America in April 1793, he found enthusiastic crowds and willing recruits for various projects to aid the French war effort, including the commissioning of privateers and the planned "liberation" of Louisiana from Spain.

The political response to Genet was even more impressive. A network of radical debating societies sprang up, headed by the Philadelphia-based Democratic Society of Pennsylvania. The societies were modeled on the French Jacobin clubs and opened political participation to artisans and recent immigrants. While not founded as party organizations, they provided a critical base for opposition politics in Philadelphia and other cities. Genet's antics flamed out quickly, but it was the Democratic-Republican Societies that struck fear into the hearts of the constituted authorities. President Washington denounced the clubs as "self-created"—extra-constitutional and illegitimate—and blamed them for the western troubles known as the Whiskey Rebellion.

The Democratic-Republican Societies as such withered under Washington's frowns, but the opposition grew even stronger when Chief Justice John Jay brought back a submissive new treaty with Great Britain at a time when the British navy was seizing neutral American ships and impressing American sailors by the score. French minister Pierre Adet bought a copy of the secret document from a senator and saw that it fell into the hands of printer and Democratic Society leader Benjamin Franklin Bache. Bache disseminated it widely, helping to evoke the biggest demonstrations America had seen since the Stamp Act crisis. Once Washington reluctantly signed the treaty, the opposition forces shifted their focus to the House of Representatives, where they tried to deny the appropriation of funds needed to implement certain provisions of the treaty. This effort asserted a right of popular majorities to influence foreign policy that the Framers had tried to block by vesting the "advise and consent" power in the Senate only. This tactic narrowly faltered in the face of a wave of pro-treaty petitions and town meetings skillfully orchestrated and funded by the heavily Federalist merchant community—an early example of successful public lobbying by business interest groups.

By the middle of 1796, the only constitutional alternative the opposition seemed to have left was electing a new president. Washington desperately wanted to retire, but with only the unpopular Vice President John Adams available as a plausible replacement, Hamilton convinced Washington to delay his farewell until a month before the 1796 presidential voting was scheduled to take place. Though hampered by a fragmented electoral system in which only a few states actually allowed popular voting for president, the Republicans mounted a furious campaign that framed the election as a choice between British-style monarchy or American republicanism. These efforts propelled Thomas Jefferson to a second-place finish that, under the party-unfriendly rules of the Electoral College, made him Adams's vice president. Unfortunately, Jefferson's victory in the swing state of Pennsylvania was clouded by published French threats of war if Adams was elected.

The Federalist "Reign of Terror"

Federalists were in a vengeful mood and unexpectedly dominant when the next Congress convened. French diplomatic insults and prospective French attacks on American shipping stoked a desire to deal harshly with the new nation's enemies, within and without. Amid the "black cockade fever" for war against France, the Federalists embarked on a sweeping security program that included what would have been a huge expansion of the armed forces. The enemies within were a wave of radical immigrants, especially journalists, who had been driven from Great Britain as the popular constitutional reform movement there, another side effect of the French Revolution, was ruthlessly suppressed.

The Federalists' means of dealing with the new arrivals and the problem of political opposition more generally were the Alien and Sedition Acts. The Alien Acts made it easier for the president to deport noncitizens he deemed threats, such as the aforementioned refugee radicals, and lengthened the delay for immigrants seeking citizenship. The Sedition Act made criticism of the government a criminal offense,

imposing penalties of up to $2,000 and two years in prison on anyone who tried to bring the government or its officers "into contempt or disrepute; or to excite against them the hatred of the good people of the United States." Of course, it was almost impossible to engage in the normal activities of a democratic opposition without trying to bring those in power into some degree of public "contempt or disrepute."

The power grab backfired badly. Ignored by his own cabinet, Adams belatedly decided to make peace with France. Despite prosecuting all the major opposition editors, jailing a critical congressman, and backing legal persecution with occasional violence and substantial economic pressure, the Federalists found themselves dealing with more opposition newspapers after the Sedition Act than before, and a clearly faltering electoral position. Leaning heavily on a politicized clergy, Federalists defended their New England stronghold with the first "culture war" in American political history, painting Jefferson as an effete philosopher, coward, and atheist who might be part of the international Illuminati conspiracy to infiltrate and destroy the world's religions and governments. Voters were invited to choose "God—and a Religious President; Or impiously declare for Jefferson—and No God!!"

By the end of 1800, all that was left was scheming to avoid the inevitable: Pennsylvania Federalists used the state senate to block any presidential voting in that banner Republican state, while Alexander Hamilton tried to torpedo Adams with a South Carolina stalking horse for the second election in a row. When strenuous partisan campaigning produced exactly equal electoral vote totals for Jefferson and his unofficial running mate, Aaron Burr, congressional Federalists toyed with installing the more pliable Burr as president. As angry Democratic-Republicans prepared for civil war, the Federalists backed down and accepted Jefferson's election after 35 ballots were cast.

After the Revolution of 1800

The 1800 election permanently resolved the question of whether popular democratic politics "out of doors" would be permitted, but Jefferson and his successors did not regard the party conflict itself as permanent or desirable. Jefferson's goal was not so much total unity as a one-party state in which the more moderate Federalists would join the Democratic-Republicans (as John Adams's son soon did) and leave the rest as an irrelevant splinter group. Though Jefferson believed the defeat of the Federalists represented a second American revolution, his policies represented only modest changes. Few of the working-class radicals who campaigned for Jefferson found their way into office. Hamilton's financial system was not abolished but only partially phased out, with the national debt slowly repaid and the national bank preserved until its charter expired.

In contrast, Jefferson's victory had a profound impact on the democratization of American political culture. Though the electoral system had been fragmented and oligarchic in 1800, it became much less so once "the People's Friend" was in power. Jefferson self-consciously dispensed with "monarchical prettinesses" in conducting his presidency, receiving state visitors in casual clothing, inviting congressmen in for "pell-mell" dinner parties, and personally accepting homely tributes from ordinary Americans such as the Mammoth Cheese from the Baptist dairy farmers of Cheshire, Massachusetts. Putting the French machinations of 1796 behind them, the Democratic-Republicans had successfully taken up the mantle of patriotic national leadership, and one of their most successful tactics was promoting the Jefferson- and democracy-oriented Fourth of July as the prime day of national celebration, over competitors that commemorated Washington's birthday or major military victories. Rooted in celebrations and mass meetings knitted together by a network of newspapers, the Jeffersonian politics of patriotic celebration proved a powerful form of democratic campaigning. Using these methods, vibrant though fractious Democratic-Republican parties took control in most of the states, moving to win areas (such as New England, New Jersey, and Delaware) that Jefferson had not carried in 1800 and posting some of the highest voter turnouts ever recorded.

In response, the Federalists began behaving more like a political party, dropping self-conscious elitism, intensifying their culture war, and putting more money and effort into political organization as they fought to hold on. Hamilton suggested organizing Christian constitutional societies to better promote the idea of a Federalist monopoly on religion. New England Federalists amplified their claims to include the suggestion that Jefferson and his followers were libertines who wanted to destroy the family. From 1802 on, Federalists also began to bring up slavery periodically, not to propose abolishing the institution, but instead to use it as a wedge issue to keep northern voters away from Virginia presidential candidates. The revelations about Jefferson's relationship with his slave Sally Hemings were used as another example of his libertinism and disrespect for social order, while the three-fifths clause of the Constitution was decried as evidence that Southerners wanted to treat northern voters just like their slaves.

While there was no direct foreign interference after 1800, postcoloniality remained the dominant fact of American political life through the end of the War of 1812. Though wildly popular and serving Jefferson's larger agenda of agricultural expansion without heavy taxation or a large military, the Louisiana Purchase owed much to Napoleon's desire to destabilize the United States and set it against Spain and Britain, and he achieved that goal. Jefferson and his two successors lived in fear of territorial dismemberment at the hands of European powers allied with Indians, slaves, and disloyal American politicians, among them Jefferson's first vice president, Aaron Burr, who was courted as a possible leader by both western and eastern disunionists.

Beginning late in Jefferson's second term, the Napoleonic Wars subjected the country to renewed pressures, as both the British and French took countervailing measures against American shipping. It was now the Republicans' turn to clamor for war, this time against Great Britain. Having largely dismantled the Federalist military buildup and loath to violate his small military/low taxation principles, in 1807 Jefferson unleashed a total embargo on all foreign trade. In so doing, he hoped to impel the belligerent powers to treat American ships more fairly by denying them needed raw materials, especially food, and markets for their manufactured goods. The embargo policy failed miserably and brought disproportionate economic suffering to commercial New England, but it proved a godsend for the Federalists.

Beginning in 1808, the Federalist party stormed back to competitiveness in much of the North and stabilized itself as a viable opposition party, despite never managing to field a national candidate who could seriously challenge Madison or Monroe. New York's De Witt Clinton came the closest, but rather than a Federalist he was an independent Democratic-Republican sometimes willing to cooperate with them. State and local Federalists did better once Madison and Congress finally broke down and declared war in 1812. The hapless nature of the American war effort soon lured the Federalists to their death as a national party, or at least the sickness unto death. In 1814 the once-again firmly Federalist New England states called a special convention at Hartford that was widely perceived as disunionist.

Andrew Jackson's shocking, lopsided victory at New Orleans in January 1815 revolutionized the war's public image. The Battle of New Orleans placed the Federalists in a dangerously ignominious light. It also made many of the existing postcolonial issues irrelevant, with Jackson having shown the great European powers that further intervention on the North American mainland would be costly and fruitless. "Hartford Convention Federalist" became a watchword for pusillanimity and treason. Federalist political support retreated to its strongest redoubts and declined even there. In 1818 even Connecticut, a "Land of Steady Habits" that neither Jefferson nor Madison had ever carried, fell to the Democratic-Republicans.

The Era of Mixed Feelings

The Federalists' decline went along with a collapse of the key distinctions of the old party conflict. Most Republican officeholders were gentlemen attorneys and planters who had long since broken with the old Jacobin radicals and joined the ruling elite themselves. At the same time, the war had convinced many younger Republican leaders that a more powerful and prestigious federal government was necessary to keep the country safe and united. During Madison's second term, a second Bank of the United

States was created, and ambitious plans were made for federally funded improvements in the nation's transportation facilities and military capabilities. Before leaving office, Madison—citing constitutional qualms—vetoed a Bonus Bill that would have spent some of the money earned from the new bank on the planned internal improvements.

Though once the fiercest of partisans, James Monroe faced only token regional opposition in the 1816 election and arrived in the presidency ready to officially call a halt to party politics. He toured New England, and many former enemies embraced him, but what a Federalist newspaper declared an "Era of Good Feeling" was rather deceptive. While Democratic-Republican officials in Washington accepted a neo-Hamiltonian vision of governing, and squabbled over who would succeed to the presidency, powerful and contrary democratic currents flowed beneath the surface. Popular voting was increasingly the norm for selecting presidential electors and ever more state and local offices, and property qualifications for voting were rapidly disappearing. This change had the side effect of disfranchising a small number of women and African Americans who had hitherto been allowed to vote in some states on the basis of owning property.

Republican radicals in many states, often calling themselves just Democrats or operating under some local label, refused to accept the partisan cease-fire and battled over economic development, religion, the courts, and other issues. Pennsylvania Democrats split into New School and Old School factions, with the former controlling most of the offices but the latter maintaining the Jeffersonian egalitarianism and suspicion of northern capitalism. Divisions over debtor relief following the Panic of 1819 left Kentucky with two competing supreme courts, and civil war a distinct possibility. When Congress tried to upgrade member living standards in 1816 by converting their $6 per diem allowance to a $1,500 yearly salary, backlash among voters and the press forced 80 percent of the members who voted for the pay raise out of office.

The collapse of national party lines also permitted a number of other threatening developments as politicians operated without the need or means to build a national majority. For example, General Andrew Jackson was allowed to seize Spanish territory in Florida to aid the expansion of the southern cotton belt. Jackson's actions were then repudiated by the Monroe administration and pilloried by House Speaker and presidential candidate Henry Clay, only to be vindicated in the end by another contender, Secretary of State John Quincy Adams, and his Transcontinental Treaty with Spain.

Slavery also emerged as a major national issue when the northern majority House of Representatives voted to block Missouri's entry into the union as a slave state. Though slavery had existed in every state at the time of the Revolution, the North had

largely, though gradually, abolished it by the 1820s. Coming seemingly out of nowhere, the proposal of New York congressman James Tallmadge (a Clintonian Democrat) sparked one of the fullest and most honest debates on slavery that Congress would ever see, with various members adopting the sectional positions that would eventually bring on the Civil War. Nationalists led by Henry Clay and President Monroe worked out a compromise to the Missouri Crisis, but a group of Democratic leaders centered around New York's Martin Van Buren, already disturbed by the rampant crossing of party lines, concluded that the old Jeffersonian coalition of northern workers and farmers with southern planters would have to be resurrected if the union was to survive. Unfortunately, that meant limiting further congressional discussions of slavery, along with additional national development programs that might break down the constitutional barriers protecting slavery and southern interests.

Van Buren's first try at executing his plan was doomed by the lack of party institutions possessing any semblance of democratic authenticity. Though for many years the congressional caucus system of nominations had been under attack from radical democrats, in 1824, Van Buren and his allies still used it to nominate their favorite, Treasury Secretary William Crawford, despite the fact that Crawford was gravely ill and most members of Congress refused to attend the caucus. In the presidential election, with no clear party distinctions operating, Crawford and fellow southern contender Henry Clay were beaten by surprise candidate Andrew Jackson and Secretary of State John Quincy Adams. Jackson's sudden political rise, launched by cynical western Clayites but then supported by "Old School" Democrats back east, had already swamped the candidacy of John C. Calhoun, who stepped into the vice presidency. Jackson appeared to have attracted the most popular votes, in a light turnout. But with no Electoral College majority, Congress elected the younger Adams in a "corrupt bargain" with Clay that was permissible within the existing constitutional rules but flew in the face of an increasingly democratic political culture.

The "Lurid Administration" and the Origins of the Second Party System

The deal that made Adams president also played into the hands of those looking to resuscitate the old Jeffersonian coalition at his expense. Van Buren and his allies somewhat grudgingly decided that the popular but excitable General Jackson could supply the electoral vitality they needed. Denied the presidency, Jackson vowed revenge on Clay and Adams, and his supporters in Congress set out to turn the Adams administration into a lurid caricature that would ensure Jackson's election in 1828.

Though among the most far-sighted and conscientious of men, John Quincy Adams was a failure as a president. A useful ally of Jackson and the South before 1824, he assumed that his good intentions toward all sides were understood. so he forged ahead with a continuation and expansion of the Monroe administration's nonpartisan approach and nationalist policies. In his first presidential speeches, Adams urged Congress to literally reach for the skies, proposing not only an integrated system of roads and canals but also federal funding for a national university, a naval academy, and for scientific exploration and research, including geographic expeditions and astronomical observatories—"those light-houses of the skies," as Adams called them in a much-lampooned turn of phrase. Knowing that such an ambitious expansion of government would meet public resistance in a still largely rural nation, Adams made one of the more tone-deaf comments in the history of presidential speechmaking, urging Congress not to be "palsied by the will of our constituents" in pursuing his agenda. This remark, and the imperious attitude behind it, was a gift for enemies who were already bent on depicting Adams's election as a crime against democracy.

After that the Jacksonian onslaught never ceased and Adams's every action was ginned into a scandal by a hostile Congress and a burgeoning Jacksonian press. Adams's decision to send a U.S. delegation to Panama for a meeting of independent American states sparked a congressional fracas that lasted so long the meeting was over before the Americans could arrive. This labored outrage over the Panama Congress was partly racial in nature because diplomats from Haiti would be present. Though Adams undoubtedly ran one of the cleanest, least partisan administrations, refusing to fire even open enemies such as Postmaster General John McLean, Jacksonians also mounted cacophonous investigations of malfeasance and politicization in the president's expenditures and appointments.

Like the election of 1800, the 1828 election was both a democratic upheaval and a nasty culture war. This time the anti-intellectual shoe was on the other foot, as relatively unlettered new voters were urged to identify with Old Hickory's military prowess over Adams's many accomplishments. The slogan was "John Quincy Adams who can write/and Andrew Jackson who can fight." At the same time, Adams drew support from the forces associated with the emerging "benevolent empire" of evangelical Christianity. With an eye on evangelical voters, Adams partisans muckraked Jackson's life relentlessly for moral scandal. The general probably deserved the "coffin handbills" calling him a murderer for his dueling and several incidents of his military career, but the detailed eviscerations of his staid, respectable marriage, in which Jackson was accused of seduction and his dying wife Rachel of wantonness and bigamy, have few equals in the annals of American political campaigning. Such aggressive moralizing failed to save Adams's presidency, but it did help define one of the enduring boundaries of the Second Party System, pitting middle-class evangelicals against more secular-minded democrats, immigrant workers, and slaveholders.

See also Democratic Party, 1800–28; federalism; Federalist Party; slavery; War of 1812.

FURTHER READING. Norma Basch, "Marriage, Morals, and Politics in the Election of 1828," *Journal of American History* 80 (1993), 890–918; George Dangerfield, *The Awakening of American Nationalism, 1815–1828*, 1965; Stanley Elkins and Eric McKitrick, *The Age of Federalism*, 1993; Richard E. Ellis, *The Jeffersonian Crisis: Courts and Politics in the Young Republic*, 1974; Philip S. Foner, ed., *The Democratic-Republican Societies, 1790–1800: A Documentary Sourcebook of Constitutions, Declarations, Addresses, Resolutions, and Toasts*, 1976; Robert Pierce Forbes, *The Missouri Compromise and Its Aftermath: Slavery and the Meaning of America*, 2007; Richard Hofstadter, *The Idea of a Party System: The Rise of Legitimate Opposition in the United States, 1780–1840*, 1969; Jeffrey L. Pasley, "The Tyranny of Printers": Newspaper Politics in the Early American Republic*, 2001; Jeffrey L. Pasley, Andrew W. Robertson, and David Waldstreicher, eds., *Beyond the Founders: New Approaches to the Political History of the Early American Republic*, 2004; Kim T. Phillips, "The Pennsylvania Origins of the Jackson Movement," *Political Science Quarterly* 91, no. 3 (Fall 1976), 489–508; C. Edward Skeen, "*Vox Populi, Vox Dei*: The Compensation Act of 1816 and the Rise of Popular Politics," *Journal of the Early Republic* 6 (Fall 1986), 253–74; Alan Taylor, "From Fathers to Friends of the People: Political Personas in the Early Republic," *Journal of the Early Republic* 11 (1991), 465–91; David Waldstreicher, *In the Midst of Perpetual Fetes: The Making of American Nationalism, 1776–1820*, 1997.

JEFFREY L. PASLEY

era of confrontation and decline, 1964–80

Addressing a grieving nation on November 27, 1963, five days after the assassination of President John F. Kennedy, Lyndon B. Johnson offered a simple message of reassurance. In his inaugural address in January 1961, Kennedy had declared, "Let us begin." President Johnson amended that injunction to "Let us continue." But if there was one quality that characterized neither his presidency nor those that followed over the next decade and a half, it was continuity. The years between 1964 and 1980 brought wrenching political, social, economic, and cultural changes to the United States.

Johnson had sound political reasons to position himself as caretaker of Kennedy's legacy. He feared being seen as an interloper, an illegitimate successor to a martyred hero. Accordingly, he presented his legislative agenda for 1964 as the fulfillment of his predecessor's work. He actually hoped to go far beyond Kennedy's domestic record: "To tell the truth," Johnson confided to a prominent Kennedy associate in early 1964, "John F. Kennedy was a little too conservative to suit my taste."

Liberalism at High Tide

Nineteen sixty-four turned into a year of triumph for Johnson and for a resurgent American liberalism. In his January State of the Union address, the president announced plans for an "unconditional war on poverty." In May, in a speech to students at the University of Michigan, he offered an even more ambitious agenda of reforms, under the slogan "the Great Society," promising "an end to poverty and racial injustice," as well as programs to improve education, protect the environment, and foster the arts. Two days before the Independence Day holiday in July, he signed into law the Civil Rights Act, the most significant federal legislation advancing the rights of black citizens since the Reconstruction era, with provisions outlawing segregation in public facilities and discrimination in employment and education. In August he signed the Economic Opportunity Act, the centerpiece of his war on poverty, funding local antipoverty "community action agencies," and programs like the Job Corps (providing vocational training to unemployed teenagers) and VISTA (a domestic version of the Peace Corps).

Rounding out his triumphant year in November, Johnson soundly defeated conservative challenger Barry Goldwater. Strengthened Democratic majorities in the eighty-ninth Congress gave the president a comfortable margin of support for his reform agenda. Johnson went on to send 87 bills to Congress in 1965, including such landmark measures as Medicare and Medicaid, the Voting Rights Act, the Clean Water Act, and the Immigration Reform Act.

Dark Shadows in Vietnam

But other events in 1964–65 had troubling implications for the future of American liberalism. The war in South Vietnam was another Kennedy legacy that Johnson inherited, and it was not going well. Communists were making military gains in the countryside, and in Saigon one unpopular regime followed another in a series of military coups. On November 22, 1963, just under 17,000 U.S. servicemen were stationed in South Vietnam; a year later, under Johnson, the number had grown to 23,000. During the election campaign, Johnson sought to downplay the war, promising not to send "American boys nine or ten thousand miles away from home to do what Asian boys ought to be doing for themselves." But there was an ominous sign of a widening war in August, when North Vietnamese PT boats allegedly attacked American destroyers in the Gulf of Tonkin, and Johnson authorized a retaliatory air strike against North Vietnamese naval bases. He also secured passage of the Gulf of Tonkin Resolution, a joint congressional resolution providing him open-ended authorization for the use of U.S. military force in Southeast Asia.

Vietnam turned into a major war six months later, in February 1965, when Johnson ordered the start of a massive and continuous bombing campaign against North Vietnam. A month later he began sending ground combat forces to South Vietnam. By the end of 1965, there were close to 185,000 U.S. troops in South Vietnam, and more than 2,000 Americans had died in the war.

Racial Justice and Racial War

At home in 1965, the civil rights movement led by Dr. Martin Luther King Jr. reached its high point in the spring with a campaign for voting rights in Selma, Alabama. Johnson had not originally intended to bring a voting rights bill before Congress in 1965, but public outrage at bloody attacks by Alabama authorities on King's nonviolent followers changed his mind. On August 6, 1965, the President signed the Voting Rights Act, fulfilling the long-deferred promise of democracy for African American citizens in the South, perhaps the greatest achievement of the Johnson administration.

But just five days later, the poverty-stricken black neighborhood of Watts in Los Angeles exploded in rioting. Before police and National Guardsmen were able to suppress the outbreak 34 people were killed and more than 250 buildings burned down. Nineteen sixty-five proved the first of a series of "long hot summers" of similar ghetto conflagrations. America's racial problems were now a national crisis, not simply a southern issue. The political consequences were dramatic. White Southerners were already switching their allegiance to the formerly unthinkable alternative of the Republican Party, in reaction to Democrats' support for civil rights. Now white working-class voters in northern cities were departing the Democratic Party as well, to support candidates who promised to make the restoration of "law and order" their highest priority. The New Deal coalition of the Solid South, the industrial North, and liberal intellectuals that had made the Democratic Party the normal majority party since the 1930s was unraveling.

Thunder on the Left

Liberalism was coming under attack from another and unexpected quarter, the nation's campuses. Inspired by the civil rights movement, a new generation of radical student activists, the New Left, had been growing in influence since the early 1960s. In the Kennedy years New Leftists had regarded liberals as potential allies in tackling issues like racism and poverty. Johnson's escalation of the war in Vietnam now led New Leftists, centered in the rapidly growing Students for a Democratic Society (SDS), to view liberals as part of the problem instead of part of the solution. Within a few years the New Left embraced a politics of militant confrontation that had little in common with traditional liberalism. Young black activists in groups like the Student Non-Violent Coordinating Committee (SNCC) abandoned both nonviolence as a philosophy and integration as a goal, as they raised the slogan "Black Power."

Meanwhile, the war in Vietnam escalated. By the end of 1967, there were almost a half million U.S. troops fighting in South Vietnam and nearly 20,000 Americans killed in action. The U.S. military commander in Vietnam, General William Westmoreland, sought to shore up shaky public support for the war by proclaiming in November 1967 that "the light at the end of the tunnel" was in sight.

Things Fall Apart

Nineteen sixty-eight was the year that many things fell apart, not least the American public's belief that victory was at hand in Vietnam. The Communists' Tet Offensive, launched at the end of January, proved a great psychological victory. At the end of March, following a near defeat at the hands of antiwar challenger Eugene McCarthy in the New Hampshire primary, President Johnson announced a partial halt in the bombing campaign against North Vietnam and coupled that with a declaration that he would not run for reelection in the fall. Five days later, Martin Luther King Jr. was assassinated in Memphis, Tennessee, sparking riots in a hundred cities. In June, after winning the California Democratic primary, Robert Kennedy was assassinated in Los Angeles. Eugene McCarthy continued a dispirited race for his party's presidential nomination, but Vice President Hubert Humphrey, who did not compete in a single primary, arrived in Chicago at the Democratic National Convention in August with enough delegates to guarantee his nomination. The convention would be remembered chiefly for the rioting that took place outside the hall as antiwar protesters and police clashed in the streets.

In the presidential campaign in the fall, Humphrey was crippled by his inability to distance himself from Johnson's Vietnam policies. Many liberal voters chose to sit out the election or cast their votes for fringe candidates. Former Alabama governor and arch-segregationist George Wallace, running as a third-party candidate, also drained conservative Democratic votes from Humphrey. In the three-way race, Republican candidate Richard Nixon won the White House with a plurality of popular votes.

Thunder on the Right

Following his election Nixon promised Americans that his administration would "bring us together," but that was neither his natural instinct as a politician nor his strategy for building what one adviser called an "emerging Republican majority." George Wallace's strong showing in the election suggested the advantages of pursuing a "southern strategy," raising divisive issues of race and culture to peel off traditional Democratic voters in the South and Southwest and in working-class neighborhoods in the North.

During the 1968 campaign, Nixon had spoken of a "secret plan" to end the war in Vietnam. In private conversations with his closest adviser, Henry Kissinger (national security adviser 1969–72 and thereafter secretary of state), Nixon would speak of the war as a lost cause. But his policies suggested that he hoped against reason that some kind of victory could still be achieved, and he would not become "the first American president to lose a war." His problem was to find a way to prosecute the war while giving the American public the reassurance it sought that the war was in fact winding down. His solution was to begin a gradual withdrawal of American ground combat forces from South Vietnam in 1969, while stepping up the air war, including launching a secret bombing campaign against Cambodia.

Meanwhile, American soldiers continued to die (a total of 22,000 during Nixon's presidency). The antiwar movement grew in size and breadth; in November 1969 half a million Americans marched in Washington, D.C., to protest the war. In May 1970, when Nixon broadened the role of U.S. ground forces, sending them into Cambodia in what he called an "incursion," nationwide protests on and off college campuses forced him to back down, although he argued that a "silent majority" supported his policies.

Nixon Self-Destructs

In the end, Nixon's combative style of governing and his penchant for secrecy proved fatal to his presidency and historical reputation. In the first months after taking office, he ordered the illegal wiretapping of some of Kissinger's aides to find out who had leaked news of the secret bombing of Cambodia to the press. Later he would authorize the creation of an in-house security operation, known as the "Plumbers," to stage break-ins against and play dirty tricks on political opponents. Some of the Plumbers were arrested in a bungled break-in at the Democratic National Committee headquarters in the Watergate complex in June 1972. The subsequent Watergate scandal attracted little attention during the campaign, and Nixon coasted to easy reelection over his Democratic opponent, George McGovern. And in January 1973, with the signing of the Paris Peace Accords, the war in Vietnam was formally ended.

But in the months that followed, as the Watergate burglars were brought to trial, the cover-up initiated by the White House unraveled. The Senate launched a formal investigation of Nixon's campaign abuses. Indictments were handed down against top Nixon aides and associates, including former attorney general John Mitchell. Vice President Spiro Agnew resigned after pleading no contest on unrelated corruption charges and was succeeded in office by House minority leader Gerald Ford. Finally, in August 1974, facing impeachment, Nixon resigned.

Nightmare Ended?

On taking office, President Ford attempted to reassure the nation that "our long national nightmare" had ended, but soon after he saw his own popularity plummet when he offered a blanket pardon to President Nixon for any crimes committed while in the White House. The Democrats did very well in the fall 1974 midterm elections, and liberals hoped that the whole Nixon era would prove an aberration rather than a foretaste of an era of conservative dominance. But the overall mood of the country in the mid-1970s was one of gloom, rather than renewed political enthusiasm, either liberal or conservative. The most striking feature of the 1974 elections had been the marked downturn in voter turnout. The country's mood worsened the following spring, when the Communists in Vietnam launched a final offensive leading to the fall of the U.S.-backed regime in Saigon. It was now apparent to many that 58,000 American lives had been wasted. Some Americans feared that a resurgent Soviet Union had the United States on the run throughout the world, not just in Southeast Asia.

And there now seemed to be new foreign opponents to contend with, among them the Arab oil-producing nations that launched a devastating oil embargo in the aftermath of the 1973 Arab-Israeli War. The subsequent leap in energy prices was but part of the economic woes of the late 1970s, including the loss of manufacturing jobs overseas, rising unemployment, declining real wages, soaring inflation, and a mounting trade deficit. Americans had come to take for granted the long period of prosperity that followed World War II, and now it was clearly coming to an end.

One Last Chance for Democrats
The immediate political beneficiary of this doom and gloom was a self-defined political outsider, Jimmy Carter, a one-term former governor of Georgia, who promised voters in 1976 a "government as good as its people," and beat out a field of better-known rivals for the Democratic presidential nomination. As a Southerner and a born-again Christian, Carter hoped to embody a return to a simpler and more virtuous era; he was deliberately vague in campaign speeches as to his preference in political philosophy and policies. With the economy in tatters and the memory of Watergate still strong, it was a good year to run against an incumbent Republican president, but Carter barely squeaked out a victory in November over Gerald Ford, in an election in which just over 50 percent of eligible voters turned out to vote, the lowest level in nearly 30 years.

Carter's outsider status did not help him govern effectively once in office. He disappointed traditional Democratic interest groups by showing little interest in social welfare issues. And Republicans attacked him for what they regarded as his moralistic and wishy-washy foreign policy. The economic news only worsened in the later 1970s, with increased unemployment and inflation. And in 1979, when Islamic militants seized the American embassy in Teheran and took several dozen embassy staff members

as hostages, Carter's political fate was sealed. The hostage taking provided the perfect issue for the Republican presidential nominee in 1980, former movie star and California governor Ronald Reagan, who vowed that in a Reagan administration America would "stand tall" again. In a three-way race that included independent Republican John Anderson, Reagan handily defeated Carter, and the Republicans regained control of the Senate for the first time since 1952. This political landslide was the beginning of a new era known as the "Reagan revolution."

See also civil rights; liberalism; New Left; Vietnam and Indochina wars; voting.

FURTHER READING. Robert Dallek, *Flawed Giant: Lyndon Johnson and His Times, 1961–1973*, 1999; George C. Herring, *America's Longest War: The United States and Vietnam, 1950–1975*, 4th ed., 2001; Maurice Isserman and Michael Kazin, *America Divided: The Civil War of the 1960s*, 3rd ed., 2008; James T. Patterson, *Grand Expectations: The United States, 1945–1974*, 1997; Rick Perlstein, *Nixonland: America's Second Civil War and the Divisive Legacy of Richard Nixon, 1965–1972*, 2008; Bruce Schulman, *The Seventies: The Great Shift in American Culture, Society, and Politics*, 2001.

MAURICE ISSERMAN

era of consensus, 1952–64
The years between 1952 and 1964 have long been viewed as an era of consensus. During this period, the fierce struggles over political economy that had dominated the country during the 1930s and 1940s receded, as the Republican Party under the leadership of President Dwight D. Eisenhower accepted the reforms of the New Deal and Fair Deal years. Both political parties agreed about the positive role that government could play in ensuring economic growth and security. Labor unions abandoned radical politics, while most critics of capitalism had been silenced by the anticommunism of the McCarthy years. And many leading political and intellectual figures celebrated the country's ability to transcend destructive conflicts of ideology or politics.

Yet when we look at the period more closely, it is clear that in many ways the consensus was far from complete. Under the surface, many business leaders and conservative activists already dissented from the New Deal order. Leading industrial companies had begun their migration from northern and midwestern cities to the southern United States. A significant conservative political subculture that organized around a reaction against the New Deal order began to emerge. Long before the turn toward black power, the civil rights movement was already meeting with great hostility, even in the North. Today, many historians see the period as one of continued, if at times submerged, political and economic conflict more than genuine consensus.

Dwight D. Eisenhower, elected in 1952, presided over many of the consensus years. Eisenhower was a genial and popular World War II military leader, and his victory in the Republican primary over Senator Robert Taft of Ohio, who had been a stalwart opponent of the New Deal since the 1930s, seemed to mark a dramatic shift on the part of the Republican Party. Eisenhower viewed fighting the changes of the New Deal as a political dead end; as he wrote to his more conservative brother, "Should any political party attempt to abolish social security, unemployment insurance, and eliminate labor laws and farm programs, you would not hear of that party again in our history." He advocated "modern Republicanism," a new fiscal conservatism that nonetheless accepted the transformations of the 1930s and 1940s. Eisenhower was not a liberal. He generally refused further expansion of the welfare state; he reduced the federal budget, gave oil-rich lands to private companies for development, and opposed national health insurance. But he also maintained and expanded Social Security, raised the minimum wage, and distanced himself from the anti-Communist paranoia of Senator Joseph McCarthy of Wisconsin (although he was reluctant to challenge McCarthy openly). Business and labor, he believed, needed to come together in a common program, united in opposition to communism and confidence in the ability of the state to bring about consensus in areas that, left to the private economy alone, would be fraught with conflict.

The declining opposition of the Republican Party leadership to the New Deal program helped bring the two political parties together. And, more than anything else, what they came to agree about was economic growth. The age of consensus was defined by its leaders' abiding confidence in the idea that the government could and should intervene in the economy in certain circumscribed ways in order to ensure the continued expansion of national wealth. The resulting material abundance, they believed, would permit the resolution of virtually all social problems. Many different thinkers from across the political spectrum argued that economic growth and the constant expansion of material wealth made class conflict obsolete, and that the mass-consumption economy emerging in the decade was fundamentally different from the old, exploitative capitalism of the pre–New Deal years. Government intervention in the economy through fiscal and monetary policies—as suggested by British economist John Maynard Keynes—could tame the frenetic cycle of recession and expansion, ensuring a smooth and steady economic course. Such involvement by the state in economic life did not need to challenge private property or capitalism; on the contrary, by reducing poverty, it would lessen social unrest.

Indeed, the high proportion of the workforce represented by labor unions—over one-third, a high point for the century—caused many commentators to argue that the working class itself no longer

existed, having been replaced by a broad middle class. Suburban homeownership, made possible by new federally subsidized loans for veterans and the construction of highways, extended to working-class Americans the possibility of participation in what historian Lizabeth Cohen has called a "consumers' republic." Televisions and movies and the rise of a national mass culture—especially a youth culture—helped create the image of a single, unified middle class. The class divisions of the early years of the century had been transcended by a broad consensus organized around continued material expansion and mass consumption; the old era of economic conflict was over.

If there seemed to be a new consensus around the basic virtue of a capitalism regulated and managed by strategic government intervention, the two political parties and most leading intellectual and economic figures shared an equally powerful hostility to communism and the Soviet Union. Senator McCarthy's mudslinging career came to a close in 1954, when he accused the U.S. Army of harboring spies in a set of televised hearings that made clear to the country that the senator from Wisconsin had lost whatever support he had once had in Washington. But the Red Scare that had dominated American politics in the late 1940s and early 1950s—peaking with the electrocution of Julius and Ethel Rosenberg in 1953 for giving the Soviets atomic secrets in the 1940s—had already reshaped the country's political culture.

In this context, the number of people willing to publicly affiliate themselves with the radical left dwindled greatly. Membership in the Communist Party (never very high to begin with) collapsed, and the radical political scene that had flourished in the party's orbit dried up. The liberal establishment, no less than conservatives, joined in making anticommunism central to national politics. In the late 1940s, liberal historian Arthur Schlesinger Jr. identified the struggle against communism as the preeminent issue defining liberalism in the postwar period. Labor unions sought to expel Communists from their ranks. Virtually no one was openly critical of the underlying assumptions of the anti-Communist worldview in the 1950s.

The cold war and fear of nuclear holocaust helped cement the anti-Communist consensus in foreign policy. The threat of a third world war in which nuclear weapons might annihilate all of humanity deepened the broad agreement about the necessity of fighting communism. Even after the Korean War ended in 1953, the United States remained an active supporter of anti-Communist governments throughout the decade. The CIA helped engineer coups against leftist leaders in Guatemala and Iran; the American government supported Ngo Dinh Diem's anti-Communist regime in Vietnam and then later acquiesced in his overthrow. In the atmosphere of broad agreement about the necessity of containing communism, few objected to such actions.

Although many of them viewed the consensus warily, intellectuals during the 1950s did much to create the idea that fundamental political conflicts were a relic of the past in the modern United States. They gave various diagnoses for what they saw as a new quiescence. Some thinkers, like sociologist Daniel Bell and theologian Reinhold Niebuhr, believed that Nazism, Stalinism, and the end of science in the atomic age had all helped to create a sense of the limits of ideas and of reason in guiding human affairs. As Bell put it in his 1960 book *The End of Ideology*, the sharply confrontational political ideas of the 1930s and 1940s—socialism, communism, fascism, traditional conservatism—had been "exhausted" in the America of the 1950s: "In the West, among the intellectuals, the old passions are spent." American historians such as Richard Hofstadter and political scientists like Louis Hartz argued that a basic agreement about the principles of laissez-faire capitalism had endured throughout the nation's past. Others, like sociologist David Riesman, suggested that the rise of a consumer society sustained personality types that sought assimilation to the norm rather than individuality, terrified to stand out and constantly seeking to fit in. And C. Wright Mills wrote that the rise of a "power elite" limited the range of collective action available to the rest of the nation, leading to a stunned apathy in political life.

The election of John F. Kennedy in 1960 over Richard Nixon (Eisenhower's vice president) seemed to mark a new political direction, as his calls to public service contrasted with the private, consumer-oriented society of the 1950s. But in other ways Kennedy's administration did not diverge significantly from the politics of the earlier decade. He delivered the first major tax cuts of the postwar period, and while he justified them by talking about the incentives that they would offer to investment, the cuts were crafted along Keynesian lines in order to stimulate the economy. He continued to advocate a fierce anticommunism, speaking of a struggle between "two conflicting ideologies: freedom under God versus ruthless, godless tyranny." The ill-fated Bay of Pigs invasion of Cuba in 1961 (followed by the showdown with the Soviet Union over the stationing of nuclear weapons on Cuba the next year) showed that he was more than willing to translate such rhetoric into military action.

In all these ways, Kennedy's administration—which was cut short by his assassination in November 1963—was well within the governing framework of the era of consensus.

Yet by the early 1960s, the limits of the consensus were also becoming clear. The most important challenge to consensus politics was the civil rights movement, which called into question the legitimacy of the image of the United States as a land of freedom opposed to totalitarianism and Fascism. The legal victory of the National Association for the

Advancement of Colored People in *Brown v. Board of Education*, the 1954 Supreme Court decision that ruled segregation of public schools unconstitutional, helped to expose the harsh inequalities that African Americans faced throughout the country. Starting with the boycott of segregated public buses in Montgomery, Alabama, the following year, African Americans began to engage in new political strategies, most importantly that of nonviolent civil disobedience, which embodied a politics of moral witness and protest that was deeply at odds with the political style of consensus. Martin Luther King Jr. emerged as a national leader out of the bus boycott, and his Southern Christian Leadership Council was the largest organization coordinating the movement's strategy. In the early 1960s, civil rights activists engaged in sit-ins at department store counters that refused to serve black people, registered black voters in the South, and resisted the system of Jim Crow legislation in countless other ways.

Although the roots of the civil rights movement were in the South, the image of ordinary people taking charge of their lives through direct action also inspired white students and others in the North. In 1962 a small group of students gathered in Port Huron, Michigan, to write the Port Huron Statement, which would become the founding manifesto of Students for a Democratic Society, the largest organization on the New Left. In the same year, Michael Harrington published *The Other America*, a book that called attention to the persistence, despite two decades of economic growth, of deep poverty within the United States—in the inner cities, in Appalachia, and among the elderly.

As the consensus began to fray from the left, it also came under increased criticism from the right. In the business world, many corporate leaders continued to resent the new power of labor unions and the federal government. While the unions and the idea of the legitimacy of the state were too powerful to challenge openly, some corporations did donate money to think tanks and intellectual organizations (such as the American Enterprise Association, later the American Enterprise Institute) that criticized Keynesian liberalism. Others, like General Electric, adopted hard-line bargaining strategies in attempts to resist their labor unions, a tactic that caught on with companies such as U.S. Steel at the end of the 1950s, when a brief recession made labor costs more onerous. And some corporations, including RCA and General Motors as well as countless textile shops, sought to flee the regions where labor unions had made the most dramatic gains in the 1930s and 1940s, leaving the North and Midwest for the southern and southwestern parts of the country, where labor was much weaker.

In the late 1950s, organizations like the John Birch Society and Fred Schwarz's Christian Anti-Communism Schools flourished, especially in regions such as southern California's Orange County, where affluent suburbanites became increasingly critical of liberalism. The civil rights movement met with massive resistance from white Southerners, who removed their children from public schools to start separate all-white private academies, insisted that segregation would endure forever, and turned to violence through the Ku Klux Klan in an attempt to suppress the movement. In the North, too, white people in cities like Chicago and Detroit continued to fight the racial integration of their neighborhoods, revealing the limits of the New Deal electoral coalition.

These varied forms of conservative rebellion came together in the 1964 presidential campaign of Arizona Senator Barry Goldwater. Goldwater, a Phoenix businessman and department store owner, was a leading critic of what he called the "dime store New Deal" of Eisenhower's modern Republicanism. His open attacks on labor unions, especially the United Auto Workers, won him the respect of anti-union businessmen. He had supported a right-to-work statute in Arizona that helped the state attract companies relocating from the North. And his opposition to the Supreme Court decision in *Brown v. Board of Education*, as well as his vote against the Civil Rights Act of 1964, won him the allegiance of whites in the North and South alike who were afraid of the successes of the civil rights movement. Lyndon B. Johnson defeated Goldwater soundly in the 1964 election, which at the time was seen as the last gasp of the old right. In later years, it would become clear that it was in fact the first campaign of a new conservatism, which would be able to take advantage of the crisis that liberalism fell into later in the 1960s and in the 1970s.

The reality of the "era of consensus" was sustained struggle over the terms of the liberal order. But despite such continued conflicts, the two major political parties, along with many intellectual figures, continued to extol the ideal of consensus in ways that would become impossible only a few years later.

See also anticommunism; civil rights; communism; conservatism; foreign policy and domestic politics since 1933; Korean War and cold war; labor movement and politics; liberalism.

FURTHER READING. Taylor Branch, *Parting the Waters: America in the King Years, 1954–1963*, 1988; Lizabeth Cohen, *A Consumer's Republic: The Politics of Mass Consumption in Postwar America*, 2003; Robert M. Collins, *More: The Politics of Economic Growth in Postwar America*, 2000; Elizabeth Fones-Wolf, *Selling Free Enterprise: The Business Assault on Labor and Liberalism, 1945–1960*, 1994; Gary Gerstle, "Race and the Myth of the Liberal Consensus," *Journal of American History* 82, no. 2 (September 1995), 579–86; Robert Griffith, "Dwight D. Eisenhower and the Corporate Commonwealth," *American Historical Review* 87, no. 1 (February 1982), 87–122; David Halberstam, *The Fifties*, 1993; Godfrey Hodgson, *America in Our Time*, 1976; Lisa McGirr, *Suburban Warriors: The Origins of the New American Right*, 2001; James Patterson, *Grand Expectations: The United States, 1945–1974*, 1996; Richard Pell, *The Liberal Mind in a Conservative Age: American Intellectuals in the 1940s and 1950s*, 1985; Rick Perlstein, *Before the Storm: Barry Goldwater and the Unmaking of the American Consensus*, 2001; David Stebenne, *Modern Republican: Arthur Larson and the Eisenhower Years*, 2006; Thomas Sugrue, *The Origins of the Urban Crisis: Race and Inequality in Postwar Detroit*, 1996; Wendy Wall, *Inventing the "American Way": The Politics of Consensus from the New Deal to the Civil Rights Movement*, 2008.

KIM PHILLIPS-FEIN

exceptionalism

See liberal consensus and American exceptionalism.

executive branch

See cabinet departments; presidency.

F

federalism

The foundations of federalism were laid in the colonial period, when power was shared between governments in the American provinces and the British metropolis. The sources and limits of political authority in the empire were increasingly controversial in the years leading up to independence, and the failure to resolve these constitutional issues led to the revolutionary-era outburst of state constitution writing. Abjuring their allegiance to King George III, revolutionary constitutionalists invoked the "sovereignty" of the people. But relocating legitimate authority did not clarify the distribution of authority in an extended republican polity. Pressed by the exigencies of war making on a continental scale, revolutionaries sought to cement the alliance of the states under the Articles of Confederation (drafted by Congress in 1777 and finally ratified when Maryland acceded in 1781) and the Constitution (drafted in 1787 and ratified by 11 states in 1787–88).

In theory, the sovereign people, acting through their state republics, delegated strictly defined powers to a central government exercising sovereign powers in the international system. In practice, however, the location of sovereignty remained controversial. The process of constitution writing taught Americans that the actual distribution of power was subject to their political will. The bitterly contested constitutional politics of the Revolutionary years culminated in the debate over the Constitution between Federalist proponents and anti-Federalist opponents, thus preparing the way for the vicious party battles of the 1790s and subsequent struggles over the character of the federal union. The constitutional ambiguity was never fully resolved before the victory of Union forces in the Civil War and the imposition of a new federal regime through Constitutional amendments and the Reconstruction of the seceding southern states.

The crisis that destroyed the British Empire in North America resulted from a constitutional deficit—from the failure of the British government to negotiate terms of union that would have secured provincial autonomy and guaranteed colonists the rights of Englishmen. Antebellum Americans suffered no such deficit. Quite the contrary, the destruction of their federal union was the result of a contentious, highly polarized political culture—a surfeit of constitutionalism—that inspired politicians and theorists to raise fundamental questions about the sources of legitimate authority and its proper distribution. From crisis to crisis, the union survived only through a series of increasingly tenuous compromises: in 1820–21, over admitting Missouri; in 1832–33, over South Carolina's nullification of the tariff; and in 1850, over the future of the West, the rendition of fugitive slaves, and other related issues. Every compromise left a legacy of bitterness for principled constitutionalists.

Forging the Federal Union

Security issues had prompted the colonists to consider forming intercolonial alliances before the Revolution, most notably in the abortive Albany Plan of Union in 1754, drafted by Benjamin Franklin. His plan to manage Indian relations under the aegis of an American grand council and a crown-appointed governor general was rejected both by provincial governments, wary of curbs on their autonomy, and by imperial authorities. In the subsequent war with France and its Indian allies (1757–63), the British ministry made no further effort to tamper with colonial constitutions, instead promoting colonial cooperation though large-scale spending and generous financial guarantees. Led by provincial assemblies determined to defend traditional privileges and liberties, patriotic Americans thus linked loyalty to king and empire with expansive conceptions of colonial autonomy; primed to resist postwar reforms that jeopardized the constitutional status quo, defenders of British American rights looked to their king, George III, to protect them against encroachments by the British Parliament.

Before the empire's final rupture, the idea that the American colonies were distinct dominions, or "kingdoms," was embraced by John Adams, Thomas Jefferson, James Wilson, and other forward-looking patriots. Through their allegiance to a common sovereign, the American provinces constituted a federal union. When George III definitively rejected this extraordinary conception of his authority and unleashed massive force against his recalcitrant American subjects, reluctantly independent Americans had to forge bonds of union on an entirely new basis. Although they had improvised ad hoc extraconstitutional structures, from local committees through the Continental Congress and the Continental Army, the protracted mobilization against imperial authority systematically undercut the legitimacy of imperial—or continental—governance. The great challenge for American constitutionalists was to reverse these centrifugal tendencies and find a way to superimpose a strong executive power capable of making war and of securing peace, over a loose federation of independent republics. The first step was for delegates from the respective states to symbolically kill the king and to assert their own authority—or, rather, the authority of the sovereign peoples they represented.

Americans did not resist British imperial authority with the intention of creating unconnected, independent state republics that would exercise full sovereign powers. The Declaration of Independence, Jefferson later recalled, was "the fundamental act of union of these States." But the war effort itself led many Americans to fear they might be creating a monster in their own midst. The drafting and ratification of the Articles of Confederation *followed* the wartime exercise of unprecedented governmental power over the lives of ordinary Americans, imposing strict limits on a central government and securing the residual "sovereignty" of member states. Defenders of the subsequent Constitution attempted to resolve this conceptual incoherence; sovereignty, they claimed, remained in the people—whoever (and wherever) they were. But clever rhetoric could not make the problem go away. Conditioned by the imperial crisis to see a fundamental tension between provincial liberties and imperial authority, Americans struggled to create and preserve a tenuous federal balance among legitimate—that is, sovereign—authorities.

Federal union was supposed to secure the protection that the American colonies had formerly enjoyed under the empire. But Americans feared that an energetic central government would jeopardize their liberties; they also feared that some states would gain the advantage over others, reducing them to subject provinces. State equality was therefore the fundamental premise of the confederation, an alliance that would protect the states from each other as well as from external threats. Though the Constitution introduced the principle of proportional representation in the lower house, the state equality principle survived in the senate as well as in Article IV, Section 3, providing for the equality of new states. Expansion would also stabilize the union by mitigating power imbalances among the original states.

Because the invention of American federalism reflected various—sometimes conflicting—imperatives, the Constitution has been subject to an extraordinary range of interpretations. On one hand, American constitutionalists sought to construct a regime that would secure a place for the United States as an independent nation in the system of Atlantic States. This "nationalist" impulse emphasized energetic administration and state building on the federal level, drawing inspiration from Britain's powerful fiscal-military state. In response, advocates of states' rights harked back to the defense of provincial liberties against imperial reform efforts in the run-up to the American Revolution: the Articles of Confederation struck the original federal balance and remained the benchmark for strict constructionists even after the Constitution's ratification.

Concerns about the new nation's faltering position in the postwar period—the Confederation's inability to raise revenue, service its debts, or negotiate effectively with other powers—led to a new push for energetic government, but reformers had to accommodate widely shared concerns about the dangers of centralized, "consolidated" authority. Federalists thus presented the Constitution as a "peace plan" that would guarantee collective security and protect the states from one another, thus enabling them to enjoy the full benefits of their republican governments. Federalist assurances that the new regime would secure, not destroy, the states constituted the first great exercise in constitutional interpretation (however disingenuous), buttressed by the subsequent implementation of campaign promises to adopt amendments that would protect states and citizens from federal overreach. James Madison pushed ten amendments (collectively known as the Bill of Rights) through the first federal Congress, demonstrating the reformers' good faith and providing skeptical oppositionists with potentially useful lines of defense.

Far from clarifying the character of the new federal regime, the proliferating commentaries on the Constitution initiated by the ratification debate generated massive interpretive confusion. To some extent, controversy over the limits of federal authority had a stabilizing effect, channeling political conflicts into the courts and promoting the formation of broad political party coalitions. But, in the 1790s, clashing views on the constitutionality of the first Bank of the United States and other key planks of Treasury Secretary Alexander Hamilton's ambitious state-building program also gave new life to fundamental questions about the distribution of authority that had destroyed the British Empire and chronically jeopardized the American union. Hamiltonian "loose constructionists" betrayed impatience with—if not contempt for—the Constitution as a mere text, seemingly confirming anti-Federalist skepticism about the Federalists' good faith. For their part, Jeffersonian "strict constructionists" convinced themselves that the whole point of the Constitution was to limit federal authority and secure states' rights, thus turning the original reform impulse on its head.

The party battles of the 1790s thus perpetuated the constitutional politics of the ratification debate, with controversy centering on how to interpret the Constitution and party mobilization focused on maintaining or gaining control of the federal government. Jeffersonian Republicans promoted state sovereignty claims, intimating during the darkest hours of High Federalist oppression during the undeclared war with France of 1798–1800 that liberty-loving states might have to exercise their primal exit rights and leave the union. But their goal was to redeem the union from hypercentralization and reinforce the consensual bonds that, Jefferson later asserted, made the government of the union "the strongest on earth." Meanwhile, High Federalists invoked patriotic sentiments to build a powerful war-making federal state, implementing direct taxation, curbing seditious speech, and taking controversial steps to contain the alien menace (all in 1798): at best, the states would have only a subordinate, administrative role under the new dispensation. The Republican response, articulated in Jefferson's Kentucky Resolutions (1798), Madison's Virginia Resolutions (1798), and Madison's report to the Virginia legislature (1800), became the new orthodoxy—"the principles of 1798"—in the wake of Jefferson's "Revolution of 1800." Recognition of the states' foundational role, their original sovereignty and continuing autonomy, was the hallmark of the new orthodoxy. Yet the character of American federalism would remain incoherent and controversial in subsequent decades—until the union finally collapsed in 1861.

Political Economy

Beginning in 1801, Republicans controlled Congress and the presidency but not the federal court system. The Jeffersonians' subsequent campaign to purge the Federalist-dominated judiciary was foiled, as Federalist Chief Justice John Marshall beat a prudent retreat. Marshall went on to establish the Supreme Court's role as the ultimate arbiter of constitutionality under the new regime in *McCulloch v. Maryland* (1819) and other landmark federalism cases. Yet notwithstanding the charges of orthodox Jeffersonians, Marshall was no High Federalist intent on dismantling the states. To the contrary, the thrust of Marshall's jurisprudence, and particularly of his expansive readings of the Commerce Clause (in Article I, Section VIII), was to promote mobility and market exchange in a continentwide free trade zone and so foster the interdependent interests that Republicans agreed were the most durable bonds of union.

Marshall's long tenure as chief justice (1801–35) coincided with a period of extraordinary economic growth in which *state* governments played the most crucial role. Freed from the crippling tax burdens of the confederation years by the new federal government's assumption of Revolutionary War debts, the states responded to popular pressure for internal improvements, banks, and state-sanctioned business enterprises. The "commonwealth" period of mixed enterprise and aggressive state promotion of market development was the heyday of early American federalism, with governments at all levels demonstrating increased capacity in an expanding economy. The federal government guaranteed free trade at home, regulated overseas commerce, acquired new territory, and secured the states against foreign threats; it also subsidized the circulation of news and financial information through the postal service; sponsored a wide range of improvements, from lighthouses to post roads, that were related (sometimes only very loosely) to its primary security functions; removed Indians from their homelands; privatized public lands; and promoted political and economic development in western territories (most importantly by opening the Southwest to slavery).

The federal balance was not well defined in the antebellum decades, though periodic crises would revive old arguments about the source and location of legitimate authority. What is most remarkable about the period is the generally high level of tolerance for theoretical ambiguity and the ability of politicians to foster good working relations between state and federal governments. Intergovernmental cooperation was helped by the circulation of party elites from the local to the national level, from the more or less distant periphery to the center of action in Washington, D.C., the republican metropolis. The overlap and interpenetration of governments through the "corruption" of party politics—loaves and fishes to the politicians, and pork to their constituents—made federalism work, substituting a virtuous circle of expanding benefits for the vicious cycle of escalating threats that periodically threatened the union. Theorizing about federalism, whether in the British Empire or in the antebellum United States, tended to culminate in irreconcilable sovereignty claims.

State Rights and Sectional Nationalisms

The Constitution created a "more perfect union" that periodically threatened to fall apart. Major economic interests vying for advantage were concentrated in particular sections: for example, southern cotton producers sought free trade with foreign trading partners while northern manufacturers pressed for a protected home market. Struggles over national commercial policy led in turn to new controversies over constitutional interpretation. Opponents of protection argued for a narrow construction of the Commerce Clause, insisting high tariffs distributed benefits unequally and thus threatened to subvert the union; protectionists responded that collective security depended on achieving economic independence and balanced development in an expansive home market. Differing assessments of risk and opportunity in a world trading system that had been chronically wracked by war pitted economic "nationalists" who preached preparedness against cosmopolitan free traders who began to question the value of the union. Discounting the threat of foreign war, strict constructionists instead emphasized the danger of concentrated power *within* the union: their Constitution, seen as a more perfect version of the Articles of Confederation, was supposed to guarantee the rights of states against the "foreign" power of a corrupt and despotic central government.

In the federal arena, policy disputes tended to rise (or descend) to fundamental questions about the character of the union. Depending on changing calculations of costs and benefits, combatants shifted grounds, sometimes embracing federal authority, sometimes resisting its supposed encroachments. The "slave power" was notoriously changeable, first using the federal government to guarantee slave property, secure foreign markets, and remove Indians from productive western lands. Then, debates over the tariff transformed John C. Calhoun and other southern "nationalists" into defenders of states' rights who feared that *any* exercise of federal authority jeopardized their peculiar institution. Yet even as they threatened to bolt the union, Southerners pressed for constitutional protections of slavery throughout the union—and a new federal regime strong enough to enforce them.

Radical Southerners, determined to perpetuate the institution of slavery talked about strict construction and state sovereignty in order to justify secession, but they envisioned the creation of a powerful new slave-holding nation that would assume a prominent place in the world. For northern nationalists, America's future greatness depended on preserving and strengthening the union, with or without slavery. Northerners mobilized to block slavery's expansion only when the Republicans emerged as a strictly sectional party, but even then few challenged the institution where it already existed.

Yet, despite the limited appeal of antislavery, slavery proved to be the polarizing, nonnegotiable issue that destroyed American federalism. As Southerners and Northerners embraced incompatible conceptions of American (or southern) nationhood, the founders' provisions for union and collective security seemed less and less compelling. The threat of sectional domination—whether by the slave power or by a prospective antislavery majority—came from within, not from abroad. For growing numbers of alienated or principled Americans, North and South, the intersectional party coalitions that made federal policy making possible increasingly reeked of corruption: majority rule threatened minority rights. The virtuous circle of federal politics, fueled by the growing capacity of governments at all levels to deliver benefits, now lurched into reverse. Efforts to mend the system accelerated its collapse. As the sectional crisis deepened, increasingly desperate unionists proposed to amend or rewrite the Constitution, thus depriving the union of its last shred of legitimacy and preparing the way for disunion and war.

Americans talked themselves into Civil War. Alienated by the tariff and fearful of moves against slavery by Constitutional majorities, Southerners moved from strict construction to first principles, bringing the sovereignty question back to the fore: if sovereign states had made the union, they could also unmake it. In response, Northerners embraced an increasingly robust conception of union as nation, but also moved away from the original understanding of "the union as it was." The destiny of the United States was to be a great nation, humankind's best hope. Pledging to uphold "our national Constitution," Abraham Lincoln thus promised his fellow Americans in his first inaugural address that "the Union will endure forever." Of course, it only endured because the rump Union was finally able to impose its will on the Confederacy.

Before the Civil War, Joseph Story and other nationalists had countered the orthodox Republican claim that the states had exercised their original, sovereign powers in creating the union, insisting instead that the "nation" had come first. The war resolved any lingering ambiguity on the question of origins, confirming a new orthodoxy: the nation had created—and continued to sustain—the union. The Civil War Amendments (1865–70) constitutionalized U.S. rule over the defeated Confederacy. They outlawed slavery, defined national citizenship, and promised to uphold freedmen's voting rights, thus overturning slave state constitutions and transforming the character of the old federal union. In the Supreme Court case *Texas v. White* (1869), Chief Justice Salmon Chase echoed Lincoln in concluding that the Constitution had created "an indestructible Union, composed of indestructible states." The national polity would thus preserve constitutionally subordinate jurisdictions: if the precise distribution of authority sometimes generated controversy, the practical business of federalism now focused on politics, administration, and intergovernmental relations. The sovereignty issue had been definitively resolved.

Yet if the Civil War seemed to resolve the fundamental theoretical questions that had finally destroyed the antebellum Union, the perpetuation of multiple jurisdictions offered subsequent generations of American politicians and lawyers continuing opportunities to promote and protect particular interests, sometimes in apparent defiance of the national will—as in the case of segregated "Jim Crow" regimes in the South. During the early twentieth century, progressive reformers would also seek to recalibrate the federal balance in favor of the states, celebrating them as "laboratories of democracy." And, during the first year of the Obama administration, some conservative Republicans asserted a right to "state sovereignty," based on their reading of the Tenth Amendment. The legacy of antebellum conflicts over the nature of the Union thus persists in both opportunistic and principled efforts to renew or redefine American federalism.

See also Civil War and Reconstruction; Constitution, federal; era of a new republic, 1789–1827; state constitutions.

FURTHER READING. Max M. Edling, *A Revolution in Favor of Government: Origins of the U.S. Constitution and the Making of the American State*, 2003; Jack P. Greene, *Peripheries and Center: Constitutional Development in the Extended Polities of the British Empire and the United States, 1607–1788*, 1986; Oscar Handlin, *Commonwealth: A Study of the Role of Government in the American Economy: Massachusetts, 1774–1861*, revised ed., 1969; David Hendrickson, *Peace Pact: The Lost World of the American Founding*, 2003; Michael F. Holt, *The Political Crisis of the 1850s*, 1978; Harold M. Hyman, *A More Perfect Union: The Impact of the Civil War and Reconstruction on the Constitution*, 1973; Peter Knupfer, *The Union As It Is: Constitutional Unionism and Sectional Compromise, 1787–1861*, 1991; Forrest McDonald, *States' Rights and Union: Imperium in Imperio, 1776–1876*, 2000; Edmund S. Morgan, *Inventing the People: The Rise of Popular Sovereignty in England and America*, 1988; Nicholas Onuf and Peter

Onuf, *Nations, Markets, and War: Modern History and the American Civil War*, 2006; Peter S. Onuf, "Federalism, Republicanism, and the Origins of American Sectionalism," in *All Over the Map: Rethinking Region and Nation in the United States*, edited by Edward L. Ayers, Patricia Nelson Limerick, and Stephen Nissenbaum, 11–37, 1996; Idem, *Jefferson's Empire: The Language of American Nationhood*, 2000; Edward G. White, *The Marshall Court and Cultural Change, 1815–1835*, 1991.

PETER S. ONUF

Federalist Party

Disagreements over domestic and foreign policy within George Washington's cabinet, then within Congress, brought on the emergence of the first two political parties in the world with recognizably modern attributes. One of those parties was the Federalist Party.

The party was not a product of earlier divisions over ratification of the Constitution. Nor were its adherents, who always championed a vigorous national government, the direct descendants of those, also called "federalists," who had championed the writing and ratification of the new Constitution in 1787 and 1788. To be sure, the party's leaders had led that movement to replace the Articles of Confederation. Yet, so had many others, like James Madison, who, after joining the new government, soon formed the core of the Federalists' opposition, the Democratic-Republican Party. Both original parties thus came into being because of new circumstances of government and new policy issues after 1789.

The Federalist Party as Political Party

What justifies calling the Federalist Party a "party" in the first place, when, considered as a political party, it was a pale image of what have since become continuing, clearly defined popular organizations with large staffs, impressive fund-raising capacities, and office seekers and officeholders at all levels of government? The justification is that the Federalist Party had many of the characteristics possessed by modern parties in nation-states with open societies governed under popular constitutions by freely elected representative assemblies and executive officers. The party put up candidates who engaged in competition for public office. It built the capacity to define public issues, educate the public about its policies, and mobilize people to vote by holding election rallies. By printing political handbills, pamphlets, and sermons; founding newspapers; and raising funds, the party created what we know of as political campaigns. It worked to get out the vote from qualified male voters, and even from women in those few places where, for a time, women could vote. It developed a rudimentary kind of organization—with a rough leadership hierarchy from congressional and legislative caucuses to state, town, and ward committees and with responsibilities

distributed among adherents. It took over existing nonpartisan institutions, like volunteer militia companies, to make them accessories of the party. "Membership" was open to anyone who wished to support the party. In that respect, it was a voluntary association, not an emanation of the national state, and it operated under the rule of public law. It also developed a clearly defined political ideology, many of whose elements, like the championship of strong federal intervention in the economy and opposition to the spread of slavery, had enduring consequences in American history.

The Federalist Party was a party in a modern sense. It was not, for instance, a "faction" or "interest," a group of like-minded men—long characteristic of British government, the Continental states, and the colonies—who protected each other's interests and sought preferment on personal, regional, or class grounds rather than for policy ends. Nor was it a closed association—one that required its members to pass a kind of test for entry. No coercion or state sponsorship (like that exhibited in totalitarian, Communist, and some post-Communist nations like Russia) were involved in its creation or development. It was not the expression of a tribal identity or clan affiliation, as in many parts of the Middle East and Africa. Nor was it a kind of family possession, as was the case with some parties in, for example, Pakistan. Instead, the Federalist Party was an institution, recognized as such, with whom anyone could freely associate as compatriots whose principal aim was to put up candidates to contest and win elective offices and thus gain the power to enact legislation and steer bureaucratic policies in particular directions.

But why did the United States and not another nation give birth to modern parties? The Constitution created a national arena in which each contest for the presidency, the principal elective national office, had to be organized and waged. Unlike parliamentary systems, in which the largest party or a coalition of smaller parties elect a prime minister, under the Constitution, a majority of electoral votes cast in all the states was made to decide the presidential contest, and so the electoral outcome in no state could be left to chance. Control of Congress also depended on fielding candidates of like political mind in every state. Under electoral methods prevailing in the nation's early years, state governments usually elected each state's senators, and thus control of the state legislatures themselves was imperative if a party was to gain control of Congress. Finally, since American elections were—as they are today—single winner-take-all contests in which a plurality of votes, not a majority, was necessary for election (with no second-chance, runoff elections as in, for example, France), each contest was a deciding struggle between candidates. It did not, therefore, take long for the generation of the framers and those who staffed the early administrations and served in the early congresses to realize that, despite their dislike of parties, partisanship, and political discord, the realities of the constitutional government they had created and of the world into which they had launched the new constitutional system called for national political organization.

The Federalist Party Emerges

Signs of partisan division appeared soon after the new government came into being in 1789. Washington himself, while disdaining parties and disclaiming party affiliation, was, by political view and personal inclination, a Federalist and the party's great figurehead, and he drew to himself other leading figures—John Adams, Alexander Hamilton, John Jay, and John Marshall—who were of like mind. Policy differences within Washington's cabinet originated after Hamilton, the first secretary of the treasury, in 1790 proposed a set of bold, strategic, precedent-setting steps to stabilize the nation's finances. Hamilton urged the federal government to assume the states' Revolutionary War debts, pay those debts at their par value rather than at their depressed market value, and charter a national bank. Because, if enacted, these proposals would reward speculators in federal and state debt instruments and significantly boost the power of the national government over the nation's financial system, Secretary of State Thomas Jefferson argued vigorously within the cabinet against the initiatives, and Virginia congressman James Madison led opposition to Hamilton's plan in the House of Representatives, where he was then serving. This opposition was confined more or less to circles in the capital (then New York, soon, until 1800, Philadelphia) and did not spread much beyond. Moreover, the opposition failed, and Hamilton's proposals were enacted into law in 1791.

The Federalist Party began to take more organized shape and gain a larger set of adherents within the general public. In 1794 the administration called up troops to quell the "Whiskey Rebellion" in western Pennsylvania, and in 1795 and 1796 Congress debated the ratification and implementation of a new treaty with Great Britain (known as Jay's Treaty, after Chief Justice John Jay, its American negotiator). Under Hamilton's leadership, the party began to gain its historic identity as a champion of strong national government; decisive executive leadership; domestic order, maintained if necessary by military force; wide-ranging judicial oversight of legislation; a preference for commercial links with Britain; and a deep suspicion of French policies (especially after the commencement of the French Revolution in 1789). The classic statement of the party's views, prepared with Hamilton's help, was Washington's celebrated Farewell Address of 1796. The president's valedictory deplored partisan division and urged the avoidance of all permanent alliances with foreign powers (a veiled attack on the 1778 wartime alliance, still in force, with France).

While Washington had avoided openly identifying himself with the Federalist Party, Vice President John Adams, who succeeded Washington in 1797, was the first president to be an avowed partisan. Adams initially maintained Washington's cabinet members and policies, and his administration engaged in a popular undeclared naval war with France, the so-called Quasi War. Adams also supported and implemented the Alien and Sedition Acts after congressional Federalists, having gained control of both the House and Senate in the 1798 elections, enacted them. Their passage marked the Federalists' political high watermark.

Soon the party came under withering attack for implementing these laws, which limited free speech and put immigrants under suspicion of disloyalty. As a result of a popular backlash, never again would the Federalists control both the presidency and Congress. In fact, the party began to splinter in 1799 as Hamilton's wing of the party attacked Adams for opening negotiations with France to end the Quasi War. The Hamiltonians finally broke with Adams when he reorganized the cabinet with men loyal to himself and not to Hamilton. These actions, taken in part to strengthen Adams's own political position, proved insufficient to gain him reelection. Nevertheless, before handing over the presidency to Thomas Jefferson, Adams concluded peace with France and saw his nominee, John Marshall, confirmed as chief justice of the Supreme Court. Through Marshall's court, Federalist principles became the foundation of American constitutional law and extended the party's influence and principles well into the future.

The Federalists in Opposition

In the minority after 1801, Federalists had to accept the need to create a system of state party organizations and adopt more democratic electoral practices to parallel and compete with those of their Democratic-Republican rivals. Even with such a system in place, Federalists remained a minority party whose following was found principally in the commercial Northeast, especially in Massachusetts and Connecticut, and in Delaware and sections of Virginia, North Carolina, and South Carolina among the commercial elite. The party also attracted workingmen attached to commercial interests and adherents of established religious bodies, like Congregationalists and Episcopalians. But it lacked appeal among the nation's largest bloc of voters, small farmers in the South and West, as well as among religious dissenters (like Baptists) and slaveholding plantation owners in the South, especially once the party began to attack the overrepresentation of slave states in Congress and the Electoral College because of the Constitution's three-fifths clause.

Federalist policies appealed principally to those who supported a strong national government to counterbalance state governments, an economic system controlled by a national bank, tariffs to protect American commerce, and a military force capable of protecting the nation and, if necessary, putting down domestic disorders. And, although they were forced by circumstances to adopt popular methods of campaigning and to encourage the gradual broadening of the electorate, the party's leaders, whose style was generally elitist, opposed as long as possible the general spread of political and social democracy. Not surprisingly, Federalist ideology and policies, plus the resulting geographic limitations on the party's support, led to its repeated defeats (save in a few states), its inability to mount successful national candidacies, and its eventual demise.

Jefferson's election in 1800 and the popularity of his administration made the Federalists' chances of regaining the presidency with Charles Cotesworth Pinckney in 1804 difficult at best. But their opposition in 1803 to the popular Louisiana Purchase, because it threatened the influence of northeastern states and was too costly, resulted in Federalists' resounding defeat in that election. Hamilton's death in a duel with Vice President Aaron Burr the same year cost the party its most energetic, if divisive, leader. Those setbacks might have been enough to destroy the party, but the Jeffferson administration's 1807 embargo on all foreign trade, which seriously injured the economy, gave Federalists a new lease on political life. Yet they failed once again to win the presidency when Secretary of State James Madison defeated the Federalist candidate, again Charles Cotesworth Pinckney, in the 1808 presidential election. Even after Madison's administration declared war against Great Britain in 1812, the Federalists could not mount an effective challenge to his reelection that year, when the party carried only New York, New Jersey, and some of Maryland, in addition to New England. The party's days seemed numbered.

With another approach, Federalist leaders might have built upon their renewed popularity after the embargo of 1807 and given the party a fighting chance at a new majority. Instead, by choosing to oppose the War of 1812 and then to obstruct it— the kind of strategy always tempting but usually dangerous for opposition parties in time of war— the Federalists sealed their political doom. Convening in Hartford in 1814 to discuss how to affect the course of the war by legal means, Federalists instead faced charges, however unjust and inaccurate, that they had secessionist and treasonous aims. It did not help that the report of the Hartford Convention appeared just as news of the war-ending Treaty of Ghent arrived in the United States in early 1815. Facing ridicule, the party never recovered. In the 1816 presidential election, Secretary of State James Monroe swamped Federalist candidate Rufus King, who carried only Massachusetts, Connecticut, and Delaware. This was the last time the party would contest a presidential election.

Following that defeat the party could only hold on for a while in Congress and in some states and cities. With Monroe's administration and Congress enacting many measures (such as chartering a second national bank) urged earlier by the Federalists, and with the emergence of new issues in the 1820s that brought about a general reorganization of American politics, the Federalist Party was no more. Finding a home in both the Democratic Party and the Whig Party, Federalists thereafter transferred their energies into civic, charitable, professional, historical, and cultural organizations and into corporations and banks, where in many places, especially in cities, they had lasting influence.

The Federalist Party Assessed

How are we to assess the history of the first American political party to die? Its death surely was due in large part to its inability, despite its adoption of many popular political and electoral methods, to adjust its views, strategies, words, and tone to the nation's increasingly democratic culture. Federalist resistance to democracy, while gaining some support among workingmen in the nation's commercial towns and cities, could not appeal to the majority of Americans who, as farmers, were suspicious of the government and its influence over the economy and were increasingly less inclined to accept the political dominance of members of the wealthy elite. Federalist attacks on slave representation made the party in effect a regional party of the Northeast. In addition, the party's close association with British interests, both commercial and strategic, gradually eroded its popularity. When it then opposed war with Britain, it seemed to be nothing more than an opposition party—one without commitment to the national interest. Not for the last time did a party opposing a popular war cast its future into doubt.

Nevertheless, the Federalist Party left an enduring legacy to the nation. Its principles—an energetic executive, a vigorous federal government, a national economy comparatively free of internal restraint, and a judiciary capable of interpreting law and Constitution—eventually became bedrocks of American government and politics. A reluctance to get involved in troubles overseas, especially in Europe, classically expressed in Washington's Farewell Address, became the fundamental, if not always honored, theme of American foreign policy. By even briefly, if not with full commitment, seeking and accepting the votes of women, the party recognized (more so than the Democratic-Republicans) the political agency of that part of the population that would not be fully enfranchised until the twentieth century. And by introducing into partisan politics many issues about slavery—its immorality, the excess political strength it gave the South, and its further spread westward, issues subsequently taken up by the Whig, and then Republican, parties—the Federalists laid the groundwork for defining northern politics as distinct from those of the South and for the political abolitionism that would ineluctably lead to the Civil War.

See also federalism.

FURTHER READING. James M. Banner, Jr., *To the Hart-ford Convention: The Federalists and the Origins of Party Politics in Massachusetts, 1789–1815*, 1970; Doron Ben-Atar and Barbara B. Oberg, eds., *Federalists Reconsidered*, 1998; Stanley Elkins and Eric McKitrick, *The Age of Federalism: The Early American Republic, 1788–1800*, 1993; Albrecht Koschnik, *"Let a Common Interest Bind Us Together": Associations, Partisanship, and Culture in Philadelphia, 1775–1840*, 2007; Shaw Livermore, Jr., *The Twilight of Federalism: The Disintegration of the Federalist Party, 1815–1830*, 1962; Matthew Mason, *Slavery and Politics in the Early American Republic*, 2006; James Roger Sharp, *American Politics in the Early Republic: The New Nation in Crisis*, 1993; Rosemarie Zagarri, *Revolutionary Backlash: Women and Politics in the Early American Republic*, 2007.

JAMES M. BANNER JR.

feminism

The word *feminism* comes from the French word *feminisme*, which was coined in the nineteenth century by followers of communitarian socialist Charles Fourier to denote their women's rights stance. By the end of that century, feminism in Europe became associated with an emphasis on enlightened motherhood as a key to social reform and on establishing national welfare programs to provide financial support to unmarried mothers so that they could stay home to raise their children. The word feminism and the ideas associated with it first appeared in the United States in 1910. They especially appealed to younger women who wanted both careers and families and who were critical of older women's rights leaders for not marrying, being antimale, and focusing on political and legal issues above maternal and psychological ones. Until 1910 the terms *woman's rights* and *women's rights* denoted the drive for equality for women in the United States. From this perspective, the use of the word feminism to apply to earlier women's rights endeavors in the United States is technically inaccurate, although the usage has become standard among historians. By the 1960s, feminism was adopted as an umbrella term for a variety of intellectual positions that called for gender equality.

The Wave Metaphor: A Framework

Historians often use the metaphor of a wave to categorize three major periods of feminist advocacy in the history of the United States. Many women in the 1960s and 1970s described their conversion to feminism in terms of an ocean "wave" crashing over and carrying them along in its wake. In the historical framework based on this metaphor, the first wave occurred between 1848 and 1920; the second in the 1960s and 1970s; and the third in the 1970s and 1980s. In 1848 a convention held in Seneca Falls, New York, launched the women's rights movement, and in 1920 the Nineteenth Amendment, giving the vote to women, became law. In the 1960s, groups of women discovered that discriminatory laws and practices against women existed on the local, state, and national levels. They worked to eliminate them, inspired by the civil rights movement of the 1950s and 1960s and the student movement of the 1960s. The term *third wave* is sometimes applied to the "postfeminists" of the 1970s and 1980s who, paralleling their predecessors in the 1910s, launched an attack on the previous generation of feminists as antifamily, antimale, and, in this instance, puritanical about sex.

Within the wave framework, the period from 1920 to 1960 is usually viewed as an interlude between first wave and second wave feminism. According to this interpretation, once the suffrage amendment became law, the energy of the women's movement dissipated and it factionalized into different groups, while the political and social conservatism of the 1920s and the national focus on the sexual revolution of the decade hampered its progress. A revisionist interpretation by younger historians, however, stresses greater continuity between historical periods and questions the use of the wave metaphor.

From the Seneca Falls Convention to the Woman Suffrage Amendment

Even before the Seneca Falls Convention marked the formal beginning of the equal rights movement, individual women—like communitarian socialist reformer Frances Wright—had called for legal and social rights for women equal to those of men. In addition, women had been leaders in antebellum reform groups, such as ones organized to eliminate prostitution and alcoholism, both seen as male vices. Some historians use the term *social feminism* to denote women's participation in general reform movements that advanced women's position. The Seneca Falls Convention, however, focused on gaining legal, political, and social rights for women at a time when married women were defined as legal appendages of their husbands—with no right to their property, their earnings, their children, and even their bodies—and when most colleges and professions were closed to them. They did not have voting rights. The famed Seneca Falls Declaration of Sentiments detailed such wrongs visited on women and called for their elimination.

During the 1850s and 1860s, the women's rights movement took a backseat to the militant antislavery movement and to issues raised by the Civil War. After the war, and especially after antislavery leaders refused to include women under the terms of the Fifteenth Amendment, which enfranchised black men, the women's movement focused on attaining woman suffrage. In 1868 a woman suffrage amendment was introduced into Congress. At the same time, groups of feminist women (and men) in municipalities and states throughout the nation secured women's entry into higher education and into the professions, while significant advances were made in overturning legal codes that discriminated against women. By the end of the nineteenth century, in most states women had rights to their property and earnings, and in cases of divorce, mothers usually were awarded custody of their children.

Women's involvement in social feminism soared in the late nineteenth and early twentieth centuries, as women helped initiate and lead the Progressive reform movement of that era. Women—both black and white—participated in community and state efforts throughout the nation to provide public services like paved roads, sewage systems, playgrounds, and parks. They joined organizations like the many settlement houses located in urban ghettos that were designed to help the impoverished improve the conditions of their lives, and they established local and national organizations like the General Federation of Women's Clubs and the National Association of Black Women. They lobbied for pure food and drug acts, subsidized housing for the poor, and legislation to provide payments to unmarried women with children. To justify these reform endeavors, women used the Victorian argument that they were "morally superior" to men combined with the new "feminist" emphasis on the moral superiority of motherhood and Jane Addams's proposal that women's experiences as domestic managers of homes could translate into an ability to become effective "municipal housekeepers."

Women's reform efforts supported the growing campaign for a woman suffrage amendment to the constitution. That campaign dated from the Reconstruction Era, when women were excluded from the Fourteenth and Fifteenth Amendments. For more than 40 years, national woman suffrage organizations lobbied legislatures and organized electoral campaigns to achieve women's right to vote. They finally secured that right in 1920 with ratification of the Nineteenth Amendment.

From 1920 through the 1950s

Some historians of women argue that the period between 1920 and 1960 was not static with regard to women's advance. Indeed, organizations like the women's clubs, the National Parent-Teachers Association, and the League of Women Voters had sizable memberships, while all worked to a greater or lesser degree to further a woman's rights agenda. In the face of a strong conservative backlash, however, women's organizations expended considerable energy maintaining the advances that had been won, giving the incorrect impression that they were ineffectual. Both conservatives and the media caricatured feminism as out of date and unnecessary, while the term itself was less and less used. An equal rights amendment guaranteeing women's equality was introduced into Congress in 1923, but it failed to pass either house in the interwar period. The sexual revolution of the 1920s and its flagrant consumerism also gave the false impression that women had achieved all the rights they desired. In the 1930s, the economic depression occupied the attention of the nation, and strong leftist

organizations like the Communist Party focused on issues concerning labor and class, and overlooked gender. Yet some historians contend that feminism remained sufficiently strong in the interwar years that the wave metaphor as the paradigm for the history of women in the United States should be abandoned altogether.

During World War II, men joined the armed services and journeyed overseas, while women entered the workforce in large numbers. Yet this participation did not spark a new feminist movement. Once the war ended, many women returned to the home, and the domestic ideal of the 1950s, which drew strong distinctions between masculinity and femininity and viewed women's proper place as in the home, undermined any desire on the part of women to agitate for rights that were still denied them. On the other hand, some historians argue that the women's organizations in existence pursued a proto-feminist agenda, while the very domesticity of many 1950s women may have inspired their daughters in the 1960s to demand equal rights and social participation.

The 1960s

Once the civil rights movement emerged in the 1950s and the student movement followed in the early 1960s, it was probably inevitable that women would follow suit, especially since numerous women involved in the civil rights and student movements found that their male colleagues treated them as second-class citizens. Such treatment led them to identify with the disadvantaged groups whose goals they were furthering and to realize that they also were oppressed. At the same time, a number of women in the leadership ranks of labor unions and in government service grouped around Eleanor Roosevelt to persuade John F. Kennedy to call a presidential commission on the status of women soon after he was elected president. That commission, which identified existing discriminations against women, implicitly publicized the goals of feminists.

Second-wave feminists, doing their own research in books and magazines, studies and reports, found widespread evidence of discrimination against women. Professional schools enforced quotas on the number of women they admitted, as they did on blacks, Hispanics, and Jews. Women in business were relegated to the clerical pool or low-level management, while the entire workforce was segregated by gender into women's and men's occupations, with women's occupations, like airline stewardess, paying less than similar jobs for men. Under the law, women could not serve on juries; they did not have access to credit in their own names; they could not join the regular military forces; and men had control over the family in the case of divorce. Antiabortion laws were strictly enforced, and in the case of rape, women were usually considered the instigators. Men dominated municipal governments, state legislatures, and the federal government.

Feminist Perspective: 1960s and 1970s

In response to discrimination, women formed national and state organizations—like the National Organization for Women, founded in 1966—to right these wrongs. Laws were passed extending government protections to women—like Title VII of the Civil Rights Act of 1964, which extended to women the concept of affirmative action, under which sex discrimination in hiring became illegal. In 1972, under pressure from women marching in the streets and organized in the National Abortion Rights Action League (NARAL), the Supreme Court in *Roe v. Wade* made abortion legal throughout the nation.

With many adherents on college campuses and in radical study groups, the feminist movement of the 1960s and 1970s generated a number of theoretical perspectives. Many of them were grounded in the major male intellectual paradigms of the previous century. Eight dominant strains of feminism emerged: liberal, Marxist, radical, spiritual, psychoanalytic, eco-feminist, women of color feminism, and post-feminism. Liberal feminists, grounded in the equal rights traditions of the eighteenth-century Enlightenment and of John Stuart Mill in the mid-nineteenth century, focused on changing laws, equalizing education, and opening the professions and politics as equally to women as to men. Marxist feminists, whose theories were based on the ideas of Karl Marx, grounded the oppression of women in their economic exploitation, while they related women's oppression to the oppression of social class. Psychoanalytic feminists revised Sigmund Freud's doctrine that women suffered from "penis envy" to argue that men, in fact, had a more difficult time developing an adult identity than did women.

Radical feminists located the oppression of women in the objectification of their bodies under the domination of a male "gaze," while they contended that a male patriarchy controlled both women and the social order. Spiritual feminists who belonged to Christian, Buddhist, Jewish, and Islamic religions worked for the ordination of women as ministers and rabbis and produced feminist versions of traditional liturgies. Other spiritual feminists eschewed traditional religion and developed woman-centered religions like Wicca (witchcraft) and goddess worship. Eco-feminists interpreted both the oppression of women and the oppression of nature as part of the general system of patriarchal oppression. Women of color often sided with black men over white women as their natural allies, attacked the entire feminist enterprise as disregarding their concerns, and accused it of treating women of all races, ethnicities, and sexual orientations as the same, ignoring major differences that existed among them.

The post-feminists of the 1970s and 1980s, influenced by the theoretical perspectives of postmodernism and deconstruction, seconded the critique advanced by women of color, by accusing mainstream feminists of "essentialism"—or of positing the existence of universalizing constructs like patriarchy, which, they argued, varied widely over time and by geographic location. Yet some of them, influenced by the theories of Antonin Gramsci and Michel Foucault, contended that women internalized their oppression and enforced it on their own bodies. At the same time, responding to the fall of communism, the end of the cold war, and the seeming triumph of capitalism, some post-feminists proposed advancing the cause of women by the subversion of cultural styles through dress, music, and behavior, and they argued that women's true freedom lay in reinvigorating femininity by sexualizing their bodies and behaviors in order to attain power through manipulating men.

Conflict Between Generations

Throughout U.S. history, the definition of feminism—whether as a concept or just a word—has changed, as in 1910, when a new generation of women adopted the word to challenge the ideology of the previous generation of women's rights reformers, as did the post-feminists in the 1970s and 1980s. Indeed, changes in the meaning of feminism often have been motivated by conflict between generations. This recurring conflict may provide the grounding for a cyclical interpretation of the history of feminism that might replace the wave concept. Historians have stretched the definition of feminism to cover a variety of historical phenomena. Thus, some historians have identified a "domestic" feminism that grew out of women's attempts to exert themselves through their experiences in the home, as in the dramatically lessened birth rates over the course of the nineteenth century, which may have indicated a drive on the part of women to take control over their lives. Then there is social feminism, which refers to women's involvement in general reform movements. Finally, some historians have coined the term maternal feminism to apply to the movement for financial aid to unmarried women with children, which culminated in the Aid to Dependent Children provision of the Social Security Act of 1936.

Backlash

Since the 1980s, the successes of second-wave feminism have occasioned a backlash. Especially troubled by the legalization of abortion, the religious right waged a campaign to overturn *Roe. v. Wade* and to impose constraints on women's bodies. Political conservatives focused on ending affirmative action, and an increasingly conservative Supreme Court decreased its effectiveness. The equal rights amendment finally passed both houses of Congress in 1973, but it subsequently failed to achieve the votes of two-thirds of the state legislatures that were necessary for its passage. Identifying second-wave feminists as "man-haters" and "lesbians," many in the media successfully convinced younger generations of women that the feminists of the 1960s and 1970s were unthinking dissenters whose actions were irrelevant to the opportunities they possessed. Even within the feminist movement, alternatives to the word feminism were proposed, such as "womanist," which many African American activists prefer, or "humanist," which, some individuals argue, might more explicitly include men within any movement for gender equality. Once before in the history of the United States, a major movement for women's rights took a new direction with the aging and then the death of its original members, as first-wave feminists aged and then died. As second-wave feminists undergo the same life cycle realities, feminism itself may once again disappear—or take on new forms.

See also civil rights; woman suffrage.

FURTHER READING. Lois W. Banner, *Women in Modern America: A Brief History*, 4th ed., 2005; Nancy Cott, *The Grounding of Modern Feminism*, 1987; Josephine Donovan, *Feminist Theory: The Intellectual Traditions of American Feminism*, 2006; Myra Marx Ferree and Beth H. Hess, *Controversy and Coalition: The New Feminist Movement Across Four Decades of Change*, 2000; Estelle Freedman, ed., *The Essential Feminist Reader*, 2007; Elizabeth Frost-Knappman, *Women's Suffrage in America*, 2005; Barbara J. Love, *Feminists Who Changed America, 1963–1975*, 2006; Sally McMillen, *Seneca Falls and the Origins of the Women's Rights Movement*, 2008; Ruth Rosen, *The World Split Open: How the Modern Women's Movement Changed America*, 2000.

LOIS BANNER

foreign observers of U.S. politics

Foreign observers of the United States were preceded by those who developed an idea of America during the Age of Discovery. Indeed, long before the idea of America broke upon the general consciousness of the world, originally as a place to immigrate and eventually as a power whose military, movies, music, and money spanned the globe, European elites were aware of what they called the New World. *Mundis novis* and *de orbe novo* were the terms the educated literate classes in Western Europe used to describe the Americas after Christopher Columbus's voyages of discovery. The idea of America gripped the imaginations of both rulers and thinkers. Rulers envisioned it as a place rich in resources and territory that could add strength and grandeur to their empires; thinkers viewed it as a dramatic challenge to established ways of knowing about the human condition. As J. Martin Evans argues in *America: The View from Europe*, the discovery of the Americas challenged the notion of limitation, which was simply assumed to be a characteristic of the human condition.

The discovery of America not only required that maps of the world be redrawn, but also that ideas about humankind be rethought and recentered. The leading intellectuals of Europe quickly invested the New World with idealistic meaning. It was paradise, a tabula rasa, a place of innocence, regeneration, and new beginnings. After Columbus, it was no longer possible to contemplate the human condition and its possibilities without taking America into account. Before America became a place to be fought over and plundered by the Old World and a destination for its emigrants, it was already an idea. The mythic significance of America to the elite classes preceded its practical significance on the world stage.

For the masses in Europe, however, America represented something different. Emigration on a significant scale did not begin before the early 1600s, and even then it was small compared to the huge migrations of the nineteenth and twentieth centuries. For these millions, the attraction of America had little to do with a philosophical idea of the place and more to do with a dream of opportunity, an exile from misfortune, or flight from religious persecution. It is doubtful that many of the millions who emigrated did so because they had read accounts like St. Jean de Crèvecoeur's "What is an American?" (published in England in 1782 in *Letters from an American Farmer*, and a year later in France). Crèvecoeur extolled the freedom, egalitarian spirit, and opportunities for material betterment and personal dignity that America offered the European masses. Hundreds of European observers visited the United States during the period from the War of Independence to the early twentieth century, a period during which roughly 30 million immigrants arrived. Some, such as Alexis de Tocqueville and James Bryce, published famous accounts of their visits.

Among the hundreds of accounts written by foreign visitors to America during the early decades of the republic, many dealt with the subject of the Indian population. One of the best known and most influential of such accounts was François René de Chateaubriand's *Travels in America* (1827). Chateaubriand did not subscribe to the uninformed romanticism of Jean-Jacques Rousseau, for whom the Indians were "noble savages." Instead, he argued that "The Indian was not savage; the European civilization did not act on the pure state of nature; it acted on the rising American civilization . . . it found manners and destroyed them because it was stronger and did not consider it should mix with those manners." The fate of the Indian population in the face of America's expanding western frontier was, Chateaubriand believed, tragic and inevitable. This judgment was shared by his more famous compatriot, Alexis de Tocqueville. In Book I of *Democracy in America* (1835) he observed, "Before the arrival of white men in the New World, the inhabitants of North America lived quietly in their woods, enduring the vicissitudes and practicing the virtues and vices common to savage nations. The Europeans having dispersed the Indian tribes and driven them into the deserts, condemned them to a wandering life, full of inexpressible sufferings." The Scottish writer Robert Louis Stevenson included the Indians with the Chinese as what he called the "despised races" in America. In *Across the Plains* (1892), an account of his journey from New York to San Francisco, Stevenson wrote, "If oppression drives a wise man mad, what should be raging in the hearts of these poor tribes, who have been driven back and back, step after step, their promised reservations torn from them one after another as the States extended westward, until at length they are shut up into these hideous mountain deserts of the centre—and even there find themselves invaded, insulted, and hunted out . . ."

The Civil War that threatened to bring the American union to an end was also a subject of considerable interest for many of Europe's most prominent intellectuals. In a letter written in 1864 to President Lincoln, Karl Marx made clear that he believed the defeat of the Confederacy would be a victory for the working class: "The working men of Europe feel sure that, as the American War of Independence initiated a new era of ascendancy for the middle class, so the American Anti-Slavery War will do for the working classes." Most of the British press commenting on the Civil War saw in it nothing more than an economic struggle between a protectionist industrializing North and a pro–free trade, agricultural South. Slavery, most British observers argued, had little or nothing to do with the conflict. Charles Dickens, who returned to visit the United States shortly after the war, agreed with this assessment. And, like many of his British contemporaries, he characterized Lincoln as a brutal tyrant. Although British opinion leaders were, in the main, supportive of the South, they opposed the institution of slavery. Harriet Martineau, one of the most prominent British feminists and social reformers of the nineteenth century and a longtime abolitionist, was among the few prominent defenders of Lincoln and the North.

Mass and Elite Perceptions of America

"[W]ithout an image of America," Hannah Arendt observed in 1954, "no European colonist would ever have crossed the ocean." That image, she argued, was never homogeneous across class and ideological lines. Among the lower classes, America represented the dream of opportunity and material betterment. Among liberal and democratic thinkers, it represented the promise of greater freedom and equality. Yet for the traditional European bourgeoisie, the aristocracy, and what might be described as anti-modern intellectuals, America represented a sort of nightmare, the "evening land" of human civilization, as D. H. Lawrence put it in 1923.

Outside of Europe, foreign elites have not always given a great deal of thought to America. The Muslim world paid little attention to the United States before the middle of the twentieth century, and in such parts of the world as China, India, Japan, and Africa, little was written about America before the

United States emerged as a world military power at the end of the nineteenth century.

Many Latin American intellectuals, however, at first viewed the independence of the United States with optimism. They saw the Americas, including the United States, as what Greg Grandin calls a "renovating world force distinct from archaic Europe." But by the mid-nineteenth century, a particular form of anti-Americanism arose in reaction to the Mexican-American War, the invasion of Nicaragua, and the growing economic influence of American business in Latin America. It was characterized by mistrust of American motives, disappointment over what was seen as U.S. abandonment of the democratic ideals it had represented only a generation or two earlier, and resentment toward what was perceived as the tendency of the new nation to impose its values, institutions, and preferences on other peoples.

By the middle of the twentieth century, the criticisms Latin American intellectuals had long expressed toward the United States were largely replaced by a more widespread anti-Americanism based on the perception of the nation as an imperialist power. As in other regions of the world, some of this anti-Americanism was the product of what Alan McPherson calls "elite opportunism." But the record of American involvement in Latin American countries, particularly during the cold war era, made it both easy and often plausible to portray the United States as the cause of every problem from political instability to poverty and weak economies. The slogan "Yankee go home!" resonated throughout the region, from Mexico to Argentina, although it did not entirely submerge admiration for some perceived attributes of Americans and American society.

In Europe, the idea of America has long been an obsession among many national elites, for reasons that early on had nothing to do with the military or economic power of the United States. Among French elites, the idea of America has shaped the way they understand their own society, the human condition, and world history since the time of Alexis de Tocqueville, but particularly and less sympathetically since Georges Duhamel's extremely negative portrait of American civilization in *America: the Menace* (1930). Simone de Beauvoir, Jean Baudrillard, Jean-François Revel, Régis Debray, and Bernard-Henri Lévy were among the prominent French thinkers who, since Duhamel, attempted to understand the meaning of America in world history.

There is some disagreement over whether the preponderance of European elite observation and interpretation of America has been, historically, mainly favorable or antipathetic. In a collection of foreign writings on the subject, *America in Perspective* (1947), Henry Steele Commager notes that the European view of America was mainly flattering. But Andrei Markovits argues that European elites have long held a mainly negative image of America. He uses the term *ressentiment*—the French word for resentment, but with connotations of a deeper, more passionate emotion—to characterize the hostility that Western European elites have long expressed toward the United States. Markovits places emphasis on the holders of hostile sentiments rather than their object, arguing that anti-Americanism has long operated as a sort of prejudice in that its holders prejudge the object of their hostility based on what they believe America signifies, rather than on the actual characteristics and actions of the United States and its citizens.

Chinese perceptions of the United States appear to have moved through a number of phases since the mid-nineteenth century, when Chinese visitors first arrived in America and recorded their impressions. These phases, as described by R. David Arkush and Leo Lee, begin with a period of exotic wonder, lasting until roughly 1900, followed by a half century during which admiration of an idealized America was mixed with criticism of what were seen as serious flaws in its culture and social institutions. A long period of state-orchestrated, anti-American propaganda followed (though not in Taiwan, where the United States was viewed as a friend and protector). Since the 1980s and the liberalization of the Chinese economy, both official and popular attitudes toward the United States and American society have lost the virulent and paranoid qualities that continue to characterize North Korean propaganda. Nevertheless, the continued high degree of state censorship and control over the media ensure that Chinese public opinion is strongly influenced by whatever image of the United States the political authorities wish to project.

There is, of course, no single or simple image of America held by opinion leaders from Paris to Beijing. The image of America held by the members of a national population is often quite complex and segmented. In some countries, including Canada and the United Kingdom, the idea- and information-generating class has long been divided in how it portrays and assesses the United States. In a country like South Korea, there is a considerable divide between generations when it comes to public opinion toward America. And in virtually all countries it is important to recognize conflicting ideas, beliefs, and sentiments toward different aspects of America. Admiration for what are thought to be particular American traits, values, historical figures and events, or accomplishments can coexist with a lively dislike or even hatred of other traits or motives ascribed to America or its government, particular policies or actions, and specific influences believed to be exerted by American governments, businesses, culture, or other institutions.

The systematic comparative study of mass perceptions of America may date from William Buchanan and Hadley Cantril's 1953 publication, *How Nations See Each Other*, which drew upon survey data carried out for UNESCO in 1948–49. The images of America that emerged were overwhelmingly positive and were also, in most cases, quite different from the way these populations were inclined to see themselves or other nations. *Progressive, practical, hardworking,* and *generous* were among the words most often selected by foreigners as describing Americans.

As is also true of national elites, the perceptions of mass publics include a mixture of positive and negative beliefs and images. The negative elements have gained influence during certain periods, particularly when American foreign policies were seen as harmful for world peace or inconsistent with the values that its citizens claimed to represent and that other nations expected of American behavior. During the Vietnam War, and again in the 1980s when the Reagan administration accelerated spending on missile defense, mass publics throughout the world followed the lead of their elites in becoming less positive toward the United States. Most commentators suggest that these occasional downdrafts in America's image abroad involve foreign perceptions of the U.S. government or of corporate interests.

Ambivalence and Anti-Americanism

A sharp international decline in popular sympathy for and admiration of the United States occurred in 2002, leading up to and continuing after the invasion of Iraq. But even as the image of the United States was taking a drubbing, a 2003 survey of 11 countries revealed that national populations continued to admire such aspects of America as its scientific and technological innovation, economic opportunities, and, to a lesser degree, its respect for freedom of expression and its democratic institutions. This corroborated the findings of a 43-country survey conducted in 2002 by the Pew Center's Global Attitudes Project, which in addition to reporting widespread admiration for what were seen as America's technological and scientific accomplishments also found that American popular culture and American ideas about democracy were widely admired.

In an empirical analysis of ambivalence in foreign perceptions of America, Giacomo Chiozza observes that "contradictory perceptions coexist in people's minds because America is an inherently multidimensional 'object' to which individuals relate in different manners." Muslim foreign observers of America are often thought to be the least sympathetically disposed toward American values and actions, but, even in this case, Chiozza maintains that a love-hate relationship more accurately describes the Muslim world's perception of America. "Muslim respondents are not systematically opposed to all aspects of America," he asserts. "The appreciation of American political and societal ideals coexists in the minds of the highly informed with the rejection of America's foreign policy choices in the Middle Eastern political arena."

In Western European populations, Chiozza found that widespread dislike of President George W. Bush and his administration's foreign policies did not produce a corresponding decline in the generally warm sentiments toward American political values and America as a positive symbol. It appeared that in many countries throughout the world, national populations were quite able to separate their perceptions of the American government from those of the American people and society.

Recent attempts to understand what foreigners believe about America have focused on anti-Americanism. This, according to Josef Joffe, is the inevitable result of the United States occupying the role of "Mr. Big" on the world stage and thus being the focus for the resentments, grievances, and criticisms of opinion leaders and populations in societies as diverse as Russia, Iran, and France. Joffe argues that what America actually *does* is less important than what America *is* or is seen to be.

Casting the United States as "the Great Satan" has proved an influential tool for mobilizing public opinion and maintaining popular legitimacy in parts of the Muslim world since the Iranian Revolution of 1979. Bernard Lewis argues that the rise of militant and fundamentalist Islam in the last half century is largely due to resentment over the undeniable decline of Islam's stature in the contemporary world and the effort to locate the source of this deterioration in the actions and values of the West. As the obvious embodiment of what the West is understood to represent, the United States has been the chief target of this anger and resentment.

Anti-Americanism has performed a rather different ideological function in Western Europe, argues Markovits. He contends that the construction of a European identity centered on the institutions of the European Union, a project embraced by most Western European elites, requires a measure of hostility toward America and is built on a foundation of anti-Americanism. "History teaches us," he notes, "that *any* entity—certainly in its developing stages—only attains consciousness and self-awareness by defining itself in opposition to another entity." Anti-Americanism has become a necessary part of the construction of a European identity and the idea of America serves as a measure against which those engaged in this enterprise of identity construction define what they maintain is a more human, civilized, and just alternative.

The View from Abroad

Foreign observers of the United States continue to be gripped by ideas of America, as was the learned elite of Western Europe five centuries ago. Some of the meanings attributed to America during this earlier time—as a place of new beginnings, opportunity, regeneration, and freedom from limits—remain important in foreign perceptions of the United States. But the view from abroad has become much more complex and ambivalent as the characteristics of American society, and the role of America in the world, have changed enormously through history.

See also transnational influences on American politics.

FURTHER READING. R. David Arkush and Leo O. Lee, eds., *Land without Ghosts: Chinese Impressions of America from the Mid-Nineteenth Century to the Present*, 1990; Stephen Brooks, *As Others See Us: The Causes and Consequences of Foreign Perceptions of America*, 2006; James Bryce, *The American Commonwealth*, 1888, reprint, 1959; William Buchanan and Hadley Cantril, *How Nations See Each Other: A Study in Public Opinion*, 1953; François René de Chateaubriand, *Travels in America and Italy*, 1828 (originally published in 1827 as *Voyages en Amérique et en Italie*); Giacomo Chiozza, "Disaggregating Anti-Americanism: An Analysis of Individual Attitudes toward the United States," in Peter J. Katzenstein and Robert O. Keohane, eds., *Anti-Americanism in World Politics*, pp. 93–126, 2007; Henry Steele Commager, ed., *America in Perspective: The United States through Foreign Eyes*, 1947; J. Martin Evans, *America: The View from Europe*, 1979; Greg Grandin, "Your Americanism and Mine: Americanism and Anti-Americanism in the Americas," *American Historical Review* (October 2006), 1042–66; Paul Hollander, *Anti-Americanism*, 1992; Josef Joffe, "Who's Afraid of Mr. Big?" *The National Interest* 64 (Summer 2001), 43–52; Peter J. Katzenstein and Robert O. Keohane, eds., *Anti-Americanism in World Politics*, 2007; Bernard Lewis, *What Went Wrong? The Clash Between Islam and Modernity in the Middle East*, 2002; Andrei Markovits, *Uncouth Nation: Why Europe Dislikes America*, 2007; Alan McPherson, *Yankee No! Anti-Americanism in U.S.–Latin American Relations*, 2003; Jean-François Revel, *Anti-Americanism*, 2003; Robert Louis Stevenson, *Across the Plains*, 1892; Alexis de Tocqueville, *Democracracy in America*, 1994 (originally published as 2 vols., 1835 and 1840).

STEPHEN BROOKS

foreign policy and domestic politics to 1865

During the first century of its existence, the United States pursued a foreign policy that had three main goals. During the Revolutionary War and its aftermath, it engaged with foreign powers to confirm its existence as an independent nation-state and to preserve this freedom during international crises caused by the French revolutionary wars and the Napoleonic Wars. With independence secure, the United States then pursued two further goals: to ensure prosperity for American elites and the bulk of the enfranchised American public by diplomatically opening foreign markets to American producers and consumers on favorable terms, and to expand the territorial size of the United States on the North American continent through both diplomacy and the use of military force. The desire for expansion culminated in a war with Mexico in the mid-1840s and the acquisition of new territory that vastly increased the size of the United States. This territorial expansion fueled internal debates about the expansion of the institution of slavery, which culminated in the Civil War, during which the United States of America and the Confederate States of America pursued diametrically opposite foreign policies, with the Confederacy seeking international recognition of its independence and the Union doing all it could to prevent such recognition. Keeping foreign powers out the Civil War facilitated the defeat of the Confederacy and allowed the federal government to retain control over the entire nation.

The American Revolution: 1775–83

The primary goals of American foreign policy during the Revolutionary War were straightforward: the United States wanted foreign powers to recognize its independence and to assist materially, financially, and militarily in its war against Great Britain. The Continental Congress began to look for foreign assistance in its resistance to British policy months before the formal Declaration of Independence. On November 29, 1775, the Congress created the Committee of Secret Correspondence, with the stated mission of communicating with the "friends" of the American cause in Britain, Ireland, and "other parts of the world." The committee initially made discreet inquiries to known friends of the American cause in Europe and also made contact with one the few colonial agents (the colonies' lobbyists to Parliament) in Britain who still supported the congressional cause, Virginian Arthur Lee. In December 1775, the committee received a clandestine agent of the French government, Julien-Alexandre Archard de Bonvouloir, dispatched from his official post in the Caribbean by the French foreign minister, Charles Gravier, Comte de Vergennes. Bonvouloir made it clear to the Continental Congress that France was prepared to support the American effort against Britain, at least with some material and financial assistance. In early March 1776, the Continental Congress dispatched Connecticut merchant Silas Deane to Paris to work with Arthur Lee and began to make more formal inquiries for French assistance. Although Vergennes was eager to support the American cause in order to weaken Britain, until the American colonies formally declared independence French assistance had to be secret and, of necessity, small in scope.

With the Declaration of Independence of July 1776, the United States formally sought recognition of its sovereignty from other powers as well as foreign assistance. Although Vergennes was predisposed to direct King Louis XVI to recognize and support the United States, he knew that such recognition meant open war with Great Britain, and he thus wished to wait until an ongoing French military and naval buildup was close to complete. In the interim, Vergennes employed writer Pierre Augustin, Caron de Beaumarchais, to head a dummy corporation, known as Roderigue Hortalez and Company, to funnel arms and other war materiel to the Americans. The arrival in early 1777 of a third American minister to France, Benjamin Franklin, assisted the American cause in giving the United States a famous public face in that country, and helped sway French public opinion

toward favoring the Americans. By the autumn of 1777, the French government was disposed toward formal recognition of the United States. When word of American General Horatio Gates's victory over Britain's General John Burgoyne at Saratoga reached Europe, the negotiations between Vergennes and the American ministers moved into high gear, and two treaties—the Treaty of Alliance and the Treaty of Amity and Commerce—were concluded between the United States and France on February 6, 1778.

The need for a formal alliance with France was disturbing to some of the political leadership in America. Shortly after the Declaration of Independence, the Continental Congress had approved a blueprint for American diplomacy with the European powers, known formally as the Plan of Treaties but sometimes called the Model Treaty. Drafted largely by John Adams, the Plan of Treaties called for the United States to seek out commercial connections with all of the European states but to avoid political connections. America would replicate its colonial economic relationship with Britain with the rest of Europe. The United States would send agricultural produce and other raw materials to Europe and to colonies in the Caribbean in exchange for European manufactured goods. U.S. diplomats were thus called on to negotiate commercial treaties that would open foreign markets but not political alliances that would draw the United States into the European balance of power. The French Alliance—rooted in both a political and a commercial treaty—thus went against this cardinal principle. Diplomatic historians point to the unwillingness of the French to agree to the terms of the Plan of Treaties as a reflection of the foreign policy idealism that informed it. Despite this, American policy makers continued to hope for commercial treaties and relationships with the European powers without committing to formal political alliances.

The French Alliance proved crucial in securing American victory in the Revolutionary War. Many French officers volunteered for service in America even before the alliance had been concluded. In May 1780, the Expeditionary Force under General Jean-Baptise de Vimeur, Comte de Rochambeau departed France and arrived in Newport late the next month. By 1781 Rochambeau and Washington were conducting joint operations around New York City, and in late summer, the forces of both men hurried to Virginia to trap British General Charles Cornwallis at Yorktown, following victory over the British fleet of French Admiral François-Joseph-Paul, Comte de Grasse-Rouville. The Comte de Grasse's victory and the subsequent successful capture of Cornwallis were both products of the French-American alliance and of the larger coalition that Vergennes had built.

After the Treaty of Alliance between France and the United States was concluded, the Comte de Vergennes began to negotiate a treaty of alliance between the kingdoms of Spain and France. Although the Spanish kingdom of Carlos III did not recognize the independence of the United States, Spain joined France in the fight against Britain. A formal alliance was concluded with the Treaty of Aranjuez in April 1779. When Great Britain declared war on the Netherlands in December 1780, it too joined Vergennes's coalition against Great Britain. It would not be until April 1782 that the Dutch would formally recognize American independence, when they received John Adams as minister. Adams was able to negotiate a Treaty of Amity and Commerce between the United States and the Netherlands, which was concluded in October 1782. As diplomatic historian Jonathan Dull has argued, this alliance of France, Spain, and the Netherlands put to sea a combined navy far larger than that of Great Britain. Forced to defend itself against three major European powers, Britain's resources available for returning the former American colonies to its empire were severely diminished. The alliance thus paved the way for the Comte de Grasse's victory, as well as the inability of the British government to send another army to America after Cornwallis's was captured.

The United States commissioned ministers Benjamin Franklin, John Adams, John Jay, and Henry Laurens to negotiate a peace treaty with the British government. After the collapse of Frederick North, Lord North's ministry, and the death of his successor the Marquis of Rockingham, the prime ministership fell to William Petty-Fitzmaurice, Earl of Shelburne, who favored a quick and generous peace treaty with the Americans. Shelburne appointed a Scots merchant, Richard Oswald, to lead the negotiations in Paris with the Americans; they concluded a preliminary peace treaty on November 30, 1782. The Preliminary Peace, as it was known, was generous to the Americans: the United States was given title to North American territory that included not only the first 13 states but land bounded to the west by the Mississippi River, to the north by the Great Lakes, and to the south by the Floridas. Americans were also granted rights to fish the Grand Banks of the Atlantic Ocean. Controversially, the American commissioners agreed to language in the treaty that the Continental Congress would "recommend" to the individual states that they restore the property of loyalists that had been seized. Similarly, the British committed to restoration of property (including slaves) that was taken from American citizens. Neither of these promises were honored in full. An additional controversial element about the treaty between the United States and Great Britain was that it was done without consulting the French government, a violation of the Treaty of Alliance. Vergennes, however, did not publicly voice displeasure with the Americans; France and Spain concluded an armistice with Great Britain on January 30, 1783. The final peace treaties were signed between Britain and the United States on September 3, 1783, in Paris, with Spain and France signing their treaty with Britain the same day at Versailles. The first objective of American foreign policy during the Revolution—recognition of American independence—had been achieved. The second foreign policy goal of the United States—the opening of foreign markets to American commerce—would prove to be much more elusive.

The Confederation Period and the Constitution: 1783–89

The primary goal of American foreign policy during the years under the Articles of Confederation was to negotiate commercial treaties that would open European and colonial markets to American agricultural produce and other raw materials, and in turn secure favorable terms for importing foreign manufactures and other goods. American diplomats had only limited success in achieving these goals, as the United States was seen as having a weak government that could not enforce the treaty provisions it signed. Few European powers were willing to sign commercial agreements with the United States. The weakness of the confederation government in conducting foreign policy was a major impetus behind the moves to reform the Articles of Confederation, a measure that culminated in the Philadelphia Convention of 1787, and the new Constitution.

In the years following the Revolutionary War, securing favorable treaties with foreign powers proved a difficult task for the men charged with managing U.S. diplomacy. Upon his return from negotiating the Treaty of Paris, John Jay was appointed the Continental Congress's secretary for foreign affairs in December 1784. When the Spanish government closed the mouth of the Mississippi River to American shipping in 1784, Jay opened negotiations with the Spanish minister to the United States, Don Diego de Gardoqui. Conducted during 1785, the Jay-Gardoqui negotiations put forward a controversial compromise: Spain proposed to allow American merchants and shippers open access to commerce with Spain and the Canary Islands (but not Spanish America) in exchange for granting Spain the exclusive right to navigate the Mississippi River for 25 years. Although Jay moved forward with negotiations, delegates to the Continental Congress from the states with western interests (especially in the South) were horrified by the proposal, which promised to retard the growth of western settlements and only benefit northern shipping interests. Congress ordered Jay to suspend negotiations, but word of the proposed treaty inflamed nascent sectional tensions.

The U.S. ministers to Great Britain and France after 1784, John Adams and Thomas Jefferson, respectively, found diplomacy with the European powers equally difficult. After his formal reception as the U.S. minister to the Court of St. James on June 1, 1785, Adams was unsuccessful in negotiating a new commercial treaty with the British government. From the conclusion of the Preliminary Peace Treaty, British policy toward the United States was informed by a set of principles known as neomercantilism. The

British government encouraged essentially free trade within the British Empire, but offered most-favored-nation status to only a few other foreign nations. Neomercantilist commentators—most notably, John Holroyd, Lord Sheffield—had posited that the newly independent United States would continue to engage in the majority of its commercial activity with Britain and the British Empire. The British government could therefore withhold most-favored-nation status and still capture the bulk of American commerce. This assessment proved accurate. There was little Adams could do to change British policy.

At the same time, Jefferson faced a difficult situation in France. French commerce was theoretically open to Americans under the terms of the 1778 Treaty of Amity and Commerce, but the realities of the legal regime and economic order of France made trade problematic. The French government's practice of tax farming (delegating the collection of all taxes) resulted in the body with the privilege of collecting most taxes—the farmers-general—having enormous power to decide which goods could enter and leave France and who could engage in this trade.

Jefferson's lobbying to change this system met with little success. Although he won an opening in the French market for American whale oil, he was only able to open the tobacco market for a minority of American planters. Jefferson's greatest success came in late 1788, when he completed negotiations on a new consular convention between France and the United States. Notably, this new convention made consuls subject to the laws of the land in which they operated, not where they were appointed. All told, in dealing with the most powerful nations in Europe in the 1780s—Great Britain and France—U.S. diplomats found themselves with very little power and legitimacy, and their ability to affect positive changes in the position of the United States vis-à-vis these European states was quite limited.

The weakness of the United States in the realm of diplomacy was a primary motive among those who wished to reform and strengthen the Articles of Confederation. Under the articles—although Congress had the power to appoint diplomats and conclude treaties—commercial regulations were left to the individual states. Several states sent delegations to the 1786 Annapolis Convention to discuss new commercial regulations for all of the United States, and the delegates quickly concluded that a full revision of all of the Articles of Confederation would be necessary. This became the Philadelphia Convention of May–September 1787. Of all of the issues that animated debate during the ratification process of the Constitution, among the least controversial was that of foreign policy. The Constitution put all the powers involved in making foreign policy in the hands of the central, or federal, government. Within the federal government, the bulk of foreign policy powers was given to the executive branch. The president had the power to appoint a secretary of state, subordinate diplomats, and to negotiate treaties. Treaties required a two-thirds vote of the Senate in order to be ratified, and the Senate also had to approve presidential diplomatic appointments. The extent to which the Senate's power to provide "advice and consent" to the president allowed it, and Congress as a whole, to participate in the treaty-making process would be a subject of heated debate during the early years of the federal government and beyond.

The Federalist Era: 1789–1801

The Electoral College overwhelmingly chose George Washington as the first president of the United States. After taking the oath of office on April 30, 1789, Washington and his administration were almost immediately confronted with a series of foreign policy crises. With the rechristening of the French Estates General as the French National Assembly in June 1789, the French Revolution began. The majority of Americans supported the French Revolution during its early years, as the creation of a constitutional monarchy, the abolition of feudalism, and the promulgation of a Declaration of the Rights of Man were all seen as developments either related to, or an extension of, the American Revolution. In September 1792, the government of the National Assembly was replaced by the more radical National Convention. This new government proceeded to abolish the monarchy, and then tried and executed King Louis XVI in January 1793. Already at war with Prussia and Austria, France declared war against Great Britain, the Netherlands, and Spain. The American reaction to the execution of Louis was divided. Also unclear was the question of whether the 1778 Treaty of Alliance bound the United States to assist France in its war against the rest of the European powers. Washington's cabinet was divided on both counts. Representing the emerging pro-administration party known as the Federalists, Secretary of the Treasury Alexander Hamilton did not approve of the radical turn of the French Revolution and believed that the execution of Louis XVI rendered the Treaty of Alliance null and void, since the treaty had been between the United States and him. Speaking for the emerging opposition known as the Republicans, Secretary of State Thomas Jefferson lamented the bloodshed in France but continued to approve of the larger revolution. He believed that treaties existed between nations, and therefore the alliance was still in effect. Washington split the difference between the two viewpoints. He chose to formally receive the new French government's minister, Edmond Genêt, but issued the Proclamation of Neutrality on April 22, 1793, declaring that the United States would remain neutral in the conflict between France and its enemies. The Proclamation of Neutrality was an important milestone—it confirmed the ability of the president to interpret treaties, and the controversy helped coalesce the Federalist and Republican movements into something resembling political "parties"—although historians debate to extent to which this first "party system" resembled that of later, more modern political parties.

The ongoing wars of the French Revolution continued to affect the United States during the remainder of the 1790s. Although the United States maintained its neutrality, Great Britain began seizing American merchant ships bound for the European continent, claiming a broad definition of contraband goods that justified the seizures. Washington dispatched John Jay to Britain to negotiate a compromise, and the resulting Treaty of Amity and Commerce became known as the Jay Treaty. Under the terms of the treaty, commerce between the United States and Great Britain would now exist on a most-favored-nation basis, and Britain would evacuate posts in the American West it continued to occupy. But commerce between the United States and the British islands in the West Indies would be restricted—Americans could only employ vessels of under 70 tons, and the export of several staple crops to the Indies was forbidden. These restrictions promised to affect the planters and farmers of the South and West greatly, and to secure a pro-ratification vote, the Senate struck out the West Indies article. The treaty still barely passed. Before Washington could sign it, public opposition—led by Jefferson and James Madison's Republican Party—grew. Washington ultimately signed the treaty after the British government leaked intercepted French documents that implicated Jefferson's successor as secretary of state, Edmund Randolph, as secretly favoring France over Britain. Although there was nothing substantial to the accusations, the controversy gave Washington political cover to sign the Jay Treaty, which he did on August 18, 1795.

Not all of Washington's diplomatic efforts were controversial. A treaty with Spain negotiated by Thomas Pinckney and ratified in early 1796 clarified the southern boundary of the United States with Spanish Florida, and also gave Americans the right to navigate the Mississippi River and transship their goods onto oceangoing vessels at the Port of New Orleans; this was known as *the right of deposit*. As Washington prepared to leave office at the close of his second term as president, he issued his now-famous Farewell Address, which restated the principle of the Plan of Treaties—that the United States should seek out commercial connections with foreign powers while avoiding political connections.

Avoiding foreign entanglements proved difficult for Washington's successor, John Adams. In the wake of the Jay Treaty's ratification, France (now being governed by an executive council called the Directory) interpreted the new treaty as an American alliance with Britain, and began interdicting American shipping. Adams sent a team of three ministers—John Marshall, Elbridge Gerry, and Charles C. Pinckney—to negotiate with the Directory's foreign minister, Charles Maurice de Talleyrand-Périgord. Before formal negotiations began, agents of Talleyrand solicited bribes from the American ministers and asked them to arrange an American loan for the French government. The commissioners balked at this offer, and when word of the proposed bribes reached the United States and was published (Talleyrand's agents were code-named X, Y, and Z in the public dispatches), a clamor for war with France swept through much of American public opinion. Following the lead of Congress, Adams signed authorization for an expansion of the U.S. Army, the creation of a navy, and the controversial Alien and Sedition Acts. An undeclared naval war—the Quasi-War—between France and the United States ensued. Rather than ask Congress for a formal declaration of war, however, Adams pursued further negotiations that culminated in the September 1800 Convention of Mortefontaine. Word of the peace treaty reached the United States after the presidential election, which Adams lost to Thomas Jefferson.

The Jeffersonian Era and the War of 1812: 1801–15

During his two terms as president, Jefferson sought to keep the United States out of the European wars between Napoleonic France and the various coalitions against it led by Great Britain. During Jefferson's first term, American neutrality, combined with a brief peace between France and Britain, allowed American commerce to flourish. The only exception was American commerce in the Mediterranean, which was subject to seizure by pirates sponsored by the state of Tripoli (one of the "Barbary States" of North Africa). Although he campaigned on drydocking the blue-water force of frigates of the U.S. Navy in favor of relying on smaller, short-range gunboats for coastal defense, Jefferson put aside those plans and dispatched the Navy against the Tripolitan forces. During operations in 1803, a frigate, the USS *Philadelphia*, ran aground in Tripoli harbor and surrendered; its crew was taken hostage. A subsequent operation bombarded Tripoli, and a small force of U.S. Marines captured the smaller Tripolitan port of Derna, forcing the pasha of Tripoli to sign a treaty with the United States and return the prisoners.

Jefferson's pragmatic abandonment of his campaign promises was also evident in his acceptance of Napoleon Bonaparte's 1803 offer to sell the United States the French territory of Louisiane (Louisiana). The offer to purchase Louisiana came after the Spanish intendant of New Orleans suspended the American right of deposit in late 1802. Hearing of the eminent transfer of New Orleans and Louisiana from Spain to France, Jefferson dispatched James Monroe to assist Robert R. Livingston in negotiating with Napoleon's government and gave both diplomats explicit instructions to offer to buy New Orleans and the Floridas from France. Having lost an army in a futile attempt to reconquer the former French colony of Haiti and build an empire in the Americas, Napoleon responded with an offer of Louisiana (Spain had retained the Floridas), which Monroe and Livingston accepted. Although the diplomats had technically violated their instructions, and Jefferson was uncertain whether the Constitution allowed the annexation of new territories, he sent the treaty to the Senate anyway, where its ratification was approved and the sale confirmed by the end of 1803. Although Haitian military success paved the way for the sale of Louisiana, Jefferson refused to recognize Haiti when it formally declared its independence on New Year's Day, 1804. Not wanting to support an independent nation born of a successful slave rebellion, American administrations would refuse to recognize Haiti until 1862.

The Louisiana Purchase was the final time the events of the Napoleonic Wars would redound to the advantage of the United States. At the end of 1803, war between France and the British-led coalition resumed. Between 1805 and 1807, Napoleon defeated Austria, Prussia, and Russia, leaving Britain and France the only belligerents locked in what both saw as a war for survival. Both countries imposed blockades on the other's trade, and the French and British navies were soon seizing American merchants who attempted to trade with the opposite power. At the same time, the British government extended the use of the policy of impressment, under which the Royal Navy searched American ships looking for deserted British seamen and other British subjects, who when found would be forced into the British service. In addition to the humiliation this practice caused to American honor, many American citizens were inadvertently caught up in this gauntlet and the British government was slow to respond to their complaints, if it did at all. The height of humiliation came in 1807, when the HMS *Leopard*, looking for British deserters, fired on the USS *Chesapeake* within sight of the American shore. Public opinion called for war, but Jefferson demurred, preferring to suspend American commerce altogether in an attempt to force Britain and France to comply with American understandings of neutral rights. The embargo lasted for the final two years of Jefferson's presidency and did little to change the policies of France or Britain.

When James Madison succeeded Jefferson as president in 1809, he convinced the Congress to abandon the embargo and adopt a policy of nonimportation of British and French goods, with the promise that the United States would open its ports to the first power to rescind its restrictions on American commerce. When in late 1810, a back-channel communication from a French diplomat indicated that Napoleon was considering repealing his restrictions (the Berlin and Milan Decrees), Madison removed restraints on American commerce with France, and only nonintercourse with Britain remained. Impressments and interdictions by the British navy continued through 1811. The British were also blamed as tensions rose in the trans-Appalachian West, with the emergence of a large American Indian resistance movement against American expansion, led by the Shawnee war chief Tecumseh. Madison asked Congress for a declaration

of war against Great Britain on June 1, 1812, and both the House and Senate voted to declare war, although the votes were very close, with all the Federalists and several Republicans voting against war.

The War of 1812 formally lasted from June 1812 until the Treaty of Ghent of December 24, 1814. The slow speed of communication, however, meant that the war continued into the early months of 1815. The United States attempted multiple invasions of British Canada—the intention being to seize as much of British North America as possible to force concessions in maritime and commercial policy at the bargaining table. The American invasions of 1812 were thwarted by British forces. The American campaigns of 1813 were a little more successful—the United States established naval superiority on the Great Lakes by the end of the year, and Tecumseh was killed at the Battle of the Thames in October 1813. By the summer of 1814, Napoleon had been defeated, and Britain brought its naval superiority to bear on the American coast, capturing and burning Washington in August 1814 and briefly shelling Baltimore's outer fortifications weeks later. By the end of the year, the British Navy was engaged in a similar campaign of harassment on the Gulf of Mexico coast.

The relative stalemate between British and American forces, and a desire on the part of both parties to end the war brought diplomats from both countries together in Ghent, Belgium, in August. The Ghent negotiations came after an 1813 offer by the Russian government to mediate the conflict, which the British government turned down, and an offer in early 1814 by British foreign minister Robert Stewart, Viscount Castlereagh, to engage in direct talks with the Americans. Madison had commissioned John Quincy Adams, Albert Gallatin, Henry Clay, James Bayard, and Jonathan Russell to negotiate for the United States; Britain sent three relatively minor officials: Dr. William Adams, an admiralty lawyer; Lord Gambier, a naval officer; and Henry Goulburn, an undersecretary in the Colonial Office. Goulburn took charge of the British delegation, while Adams, Clay, and Gallatin were the dominant voices for the Americans. The negotiations dragged on for months; although both sides dropped discussion of the issue of impressments, the British negotiators presented a series of demands that infuriated most of the American delegation, including a proposal to create an American Indian buffer state in the Great Lakes region, and a proposed reworking of American rights to the Canadian fisheries.

However, as the talks at the more important Congress of Vienna dragged on, the British government instructed its diplomats to agree to a treaty that simply restored the prewar status quo. The Americans jumped at this opening. British plans for an American Indian buffer state were dropped, and American Indian nations within U.S. borders lost their last major remaining European diplomatic partner, clearing a path for American westward expansion. Other outstanding issues, such as the boundary between the United States and Canada, would be settled by subsequent commissions. The Treaty of Ghent allowed Britain to focus on European diplomacy and the Americans to claim a peace with honor. News of the treaty reached the United States at the same time that word was spreading of Andrew Jackson's victory at New Orleans—allowing the War of 1812 to be remembered as an American victory even though its result was as equivocal as any war in U.S. history.

Antebellum Foreign Policy: The Monroe Doctrine, the Quest for Markets, and Manifest Destiny: 1815–45

Following the War of 1812, American foreign policy was directed toward opening foreign markets to American commerce, keeping European political interference in the Americas to a minimum, and increasing the territorial size of the United States. The war transformed the domestic political scene. First, it spelled the end of the Federalists as a national political force. Between December 1814 and January 1815, New England Federalists had convened a special Congress called the Hartford Convention to discuss difficulties caused by the war. Although the convention ultimately called for some policy changes by the Madison administration and Congress in the conduct of the war, and proposed seven amendments to the Constitution, the body's secret meetings allowed Republican opponents to smear its activities as treasonous. Outside New England, Federalism had acquired the taint of disloyalty.

Second, the setbacks the United States had faced during the war in terms of mobilization, materiel, transportation, and, most of all, funding prompted a split within the Republican Party. Many, including Henry Clay and John C. Calhoun became known as National Republicans, who advocated federal government funding of a system of internal improvements, coastal fortifications, a standing army, and a national bank. These were measures that the so-called Old Republicans like James Madison and James Monroe balked at, as they had a whiff of the old Hamiltonian program about them. These basic divides would inform the ultimate split of the Republicans into Andrew Jackson's Democrats and Henry Clay's Whigs in the 1830s.

These different visions extended to approaches to foreign policy. Although the embargo and the War of 1812 and the resulting disruptions in trade helped facilitate the growth of an American manufacturing sector (a process that had begun in the 1790s), the United States remained an overwhelmingly agricultural nation in the late 1810s and 1820s. Planters and farmers desired to ship their foodstuffs and staples to Europe and the European colonies in the Americas and wanted diplomacy devoted to ensuring the continued flow of transatlantic commerce. This became the policy position of the Old Republicans and the Jacksonian Democrats. The National Republicans,

and then the Whigs, had a different vision: they hoped the federal government could spur the expansion of the American industrial and financial sectors and wanted to develop internal transportation and markets. Under Henry Clay's leadership in Congress, this became known as the "American System." Its most controversial aspect was high protective tariffs, which passed Congress in 1828 during John Quincy Adams's presidency. In 1832 the so-called Tariff of Abominations almost split the Union, as South Carolina threatened nullification of the law. A compromise was reached, but the crisis showed how central commercial and foreign policy was to the domestic political scene.

No matter what the tariff rates, the United States still actively sought to expand its access to world markets during this period. Under the initiative of merchant John Jacob Astor and others, Americans expanded the scope of the fur trade in the American West and Pacific Northwest, and regular shipping to the Pacific Coast soon extended to Hawai'i and across the Pacific to East Asia. American trade with China, begun in the 1790s, increased in scope in the first half of the nineteenth century, and the U.S. Navy was operating across the Pacific by the late 1840s; under the expedition of Commodore Matthew Perry, the United States forced open trade with Japan with the 1854 Treaty of Kanagawa. American merchants and financiers also seized the opportunities provided by the collapse of the Spanish Empire, and American trade with the newly independent republics of the Americas increased during the 1820s and 1830s as well.

Responding to the end of the Spanish Empire and the various Latin American independence movements provided the United States with its first great diplomatic challenge of the post–War of 1812 world. The bulk of the Spanish colonies had experienced a de facto independence of sorts during Napoleon's occupation of Spain. Although the particulars varied from country to country, Latin American settler elites generally resisted the attempts of the Spanish government to reimpose direct imperial rule after Napoleon's fall.

While many Americans were sympathetic to the various Latin American revolutionaries (especially South America's Simón Bolívar), the Monroe administration held off recognizing Latin American independence while Spain still wielded a modicum of power. This allowed Monroe's secretary of state, John Quincy Adams, to conclude the 1819 Transcontinental Treaty with Spain, which established a firm western border between the United States and New Spain (Mexico), and also to broker the purchase of the Floridas from Spain at the same time. The acquisition of the Gulf Coast was a boon to the states to the Deep South, as it guaranteed their access to Atlantic markets and abetted the ongoing expansion of the Cotton Belt. In 1822, following military successes on the part of Bolívar's forces in South America and a successful revolution in Mexico, the Monroe administration finally recognized the independence of four Latin American republics—Mexico, Peru, Colombia, and Rio de la Plata (Argentina).

When it appeared that Spain's European allies would support an attempt to send another expedition to reconquer the republics, Secretary of State Adams and President Monroe drafted a proclamation declaring that the United States was opposed to any attempts by the European powers to recolonize the Americas, and would resist attempts to draw the Americas into the European balance of power. This statement, issued on December 2, 1823, became known as the Monroe Doctrine, and would be used to justify American diplomacy and military activity in the Western Hemisphere for the rest of the nineteenth century and into the twentieth.

The Monroe Doctrine was also significant in that Monroe and Adams rejected an opportunity to issue a joint declaration on Latin American affairs with the British government, despite the fact that both governments shared the same policy. British-American relations evolved in a generally amicable direction during the 1820s and 1830s, as trade between the two countries remained vital to the economies of both. However, tensions over the U.S.-Canadian border flared in the late 1830s, and the Americans had tended to be recalcitrant in providing naval vessels to assist with British efforts to interdict the African slave trade (which Britain had abolished in 1807, with the United States following in 1808). Both issues were resolved by a treaty negotiated by Secretary of State Daniel Webster and British Minister Alexander Baring, Baron Ashburton, in August 1842. The Webster-Ashburton Treaty formalized the contested boundary between Maine, New Brunswick, and Quebec (the Revolutionary Era maps the boundary had been drawn on in 1783 proved highly inaccurate) and committed the United States to a more robust presence in assisting the British West Africa Squadron in slave trade interdiction.

With the expansion of American access to overseas markets came a desire to increase the amount of American territory under settlement and cultivation and to increase the size of the United States in total. This desire for expansion was felt by most white Americans, but under the term *Manifest Destiny* (coined by a Democratic newspaper editor named John L. O'Sullivan) it became a hallmark of the Democratic Party's platform. The notion that it was the Manifest Destiny of the United States to extend from the Atlantic to the Pacific (and even beyond) informed the presidential election of 1844. Running against Whig Henry Clay, Democrat James K. Polk wanted to follow up the successful Webster-Ashburton Treaty of 1842 with negotiations (or belligerence) that would compel Britain to cede the United States all of the so-called Oregon Country (modern-day Oregon, Washington, and British Columbia). More important, Polk called for the immediate annexation of the Republic of Texas, a breakaway province of Mexico that had declared and won its independence in 1836. Mexico, however, refused to recognize Texas's independence. The issue proved immensely popular in the South and the West, and spurred Polk to victory in 1844. His belligerence, however, put Mexico and the United States on a collision course for war.

The Mexican-American War: 1845–48

Polk's predecessor, John Tyler, had begun to pursue the annexation of Texas as early as 1843, and negotiated an annexation treaty that finally passed in Congress days before Polk took office. Almost immediately after Polk's inauguration, Mexico suspended diplomatic relations with the United States. Polk sent a special envoy with extensive knowledge of Mexico, John Slidell, as a fully accredited minister to negotiate with the Mexican government. Controversy ensued over Slidell's credentials as a normal minister plenipotentiary, which caused Mexican officials to believe that if they received Slidell it would indicate their acquiescence in the Texas annexation. Also factoring into Mexico's response was an ongoing internal political debate between conservative centralizers and liberal federalists that made compromise on Texas very difficult.

As Slidell's mission was failing, Polk dispatched the bulk of the U.S. Army under General Zachary Taylor to the disputed borderland between the Nueces River and the Rio Grande. A violent confrontation ensued between U.S. and Mexican forces, and war formally began in May 1846.

The war dragged on longer than expected. For all his success as a polemicist, Polk proved to be a poor war president. He withheld support for Taylor during the latter part of his successful campaign in northern Mexico, fearing his Whig-leaning general was becoming too popular. Polk then allowed Mexico's exiled president and military leader Antonio Lopez de Santa Anna to return to Mexico; rather than negotiate an end to the conflict, Santa Anna took charge of the Mexican war effort. It fell to General Winfield Scott to defeat Santa Anna, which he did, landing at Veracruz in March 1847 and capturing Mexico City in September of that same year. During the winter of 1847–48, Nicholas Trist, a State Department clerk who had accompanied Scott, negotiated with delegates from the Mexican Congress (now in charge after Santa Anna's resignation).

Although Polk hoped for the acquisition of most, if not all, of Mexico, Trist was less ambitious. The Treaty of Guadalupe Hidalgo confirmed American control of Texas, a boundary at the Rio Grande, and granted the United States the territories of Upper California and New Mexico in exchange for a $15 million payment and the assumption by the United States of the claims of all American citizens against the Mexican government. Polk was unhappy with the treaty but did not want to prolong the war and feared that he could not negotiate a better treaty. The Senate voted to ratify the treaty on March 10, 1848.

The Sectional Crisis and the Civil War: 1848–65

The acquisition of the Mexican Cession moved the question of the extension of the institution of slavery into western territories to the forefront of American political debate. The number of states that would be carved from the new territory and the question of whether they would be slave states or free states vexed American politics until the Compromise of 1850; the desire on the part of Southerners to add territory that could be open to slavery did not abate, however.

The southern cause was pursued by a small number of private adventurers known as filibusters—men who gathered small forces of mercenaries and attempted to conquer several Latin American states and eventually incorporate them into the United States. A Venezualan-born Cuban exile named Narisco López sought American support for his plans to capture Cuba from Spain and annex it to the United States; he led three unsuccessful invasions of Cuba between 1849 and 1851. Another notable filibuster was a Tennessee doctor named William Walker who launched a private invasion of Mexico in 1853 and actually succeeded in controlling Nicaragua during a filibuster between 1855 and 1857. Driven out by the local population, Walker made three more expeditions to Central America before being captured and executed in Honduras in 1860.

More legitimate were attempts by the U.S. government to acquire Cuba, where Spain had remained in charge and where slavery remained legal. President Franklin Pierce made several attempts to purchase Cuba from Spain to placate southern Democrats. Meeting secretly at Ostend, Belgium, the U.S. ministers to Britain, France, and Spain vowed to work together to acquire Cuba by purchase or force. When word of this secret plan (known as the "Ostend Manifesto") leaked, controversy ensued, and Pierce was forced to recall the most controversial of the diplomats, Louisiana's Pierre Soulé.

Attempts to increase American territory did not placate the South and only served to exacerbate sectional tensions. With the formation of the new Republican Party in 1856 (a party committed to halting the extension of slavery and the protection of free labor) and the election of its presidential candidate Abraham Lincoln in 1860, the process of secession began and the United States was at war with itself by April 1861. The Confederate States of America sought foreign recognition of its independence and foreign assistance for its war against the federal government. The United States sought to prevent European powers from recognizing and assisting the Confederacy. The U.S. Navy blockaded the ports of the South. Most controversially, in November 1861, the commander of the USS *San Jacinto* boarded the British mail ship HMS *Trent* and captured two Confederate diplomats bound for Britain. The seizure provoked a minor diplomatic incident, but the U.S. minister to Great Britain, Charles Francis Adams, succeeded in keeping Britain from recognizing the Confederate government and thus out of the war. Starved for materiel and unable to sell its cotton crop abroad, the Confederacy capitulated in April 1865.

See also Articles of Confederation; Civil War and Reconstruction; Constitution, federal; federalism; Mexican-American War; War of 1812; war for independence.

FURTHER READING. Samuel Flagg Bemis, *The Diplomacy of the American Revolution*, 1935; Jerald A. Combs, *The Jay Treaty: Political Battleground of the Founding Fathers*, 1970; Alexander DeConde, *Entangling Alliance: Politics and Diplomacy under George Washington*, 1958; Idem, *The Quasi-War: The Politics and Diplomacy of the Undeclared War with France, 1797–1801*, 1966; Idem, *This Affair of Louisiana*, 1976; Jonathan R. Dull, *A Diplomatic History of the American Revolution*, 1985; Idem, *The French Navy and American Independence: A Study of Arms and Diplomacy, 1774–1787*, 1975; Donald R. Hickey, *The War of 1812: A Forgotten Conflict*, 1989; Daniel Walker Howe, *What Hath God Wrought? The Transformation of America, 1815–1848*, 2007; Thomas G. Paterson, J. Garry Clifford, and Kenneth J. Hagan, *American Foreign Relations: A History*, 1995; Bradford Perkins, *Prologue to War: England and the United States, 1805–1812*, 1968; J.C.A. Stagg, *Mr. Madison's War: Politics, Diplomacy, and Warfare in the Early American Republic, 1783–1830*, 1983; Gerald Stourzh, *Benjamin Franklin and American Foreign Policy*, 2nd ed., 1969.

LEONARD J. SADOSKY

foreign policy and domestic politics, 1865–1933

In foreign policy as in domestic politics, if the period before the Civil War concerned itself with *whether* the United States would remain a nation, then 1865–1933 helped determine *what kind* of nation it would be. The themes of this contest for national self-definition included the limits to continental and extracontinental expansion; the role of industry in expansion and vice versa; the power of the executive; the debate over "imperialism"; the sharpening markers of race, religion, and gender; and the definition of citizenship.

As presidents, secretaries of state, members of congress, business lobbyists, missionaries, journalists, and other opinion makers wrestled with these themes, patterns emerged. On one hand, a powerful majority of Americans supported expansion beyond the continental limits of the nation as an outlet for commercial and moral energies. On the other, a smaller but not negligible group called for restraint in the exercise of global power. Interestingly, both the dominant expansionists and the so-called isolationists articulated arguments based on similar domestic pressures and ideologies.

Manifest Destiny and
Continental Expansion: 1865–90

In the area of westward expansion, there was relatively strong consensus. The ideals of Manifest Destiny gained ever-greater currency after the Civil War. Both political parties sided with President Andrew Johnson's desire to speed up the readmission of the former Confederate states into the Union so as to move on to what they considered the more pressing matter of developing the West. The end of the war also worsened the odds for tribes beyond the Mississippi, because in 1871 the Supreme Court ruled that Congress could override the traditional treaty system and consider tribes "local dependent communities" to be controlled, rather than independent nations. This led to a cycle of violence ending in the confinement of most Native Americans on reservations by the 1890s.

The "winning of the west," as Theodore Roosevelt called it, shaped future U.S. conquests of nonwhites. Starting with the War of 1898, U.S. troops overseas referred to the enemy as "Indians" and called hostile territory "Indian country." Eighty-seven percent of American generals who fought against Filipinos after 1898 were seasoned "Indian chasers." Native American wars also produced land laws that would be redrafted for overseas possessions, drew a blueprint for the "Americanization" of foreign cultures, prepared U.S. military tacticians for guerrilla tactics, and inoculated enlisted men against the brutality of race war. In 1902 Elihu Root, corporate lawyer and soon-to-be secretary of state, justified taking the Philippines thusly: "Without the consent of hundreds of thousands of Indians whom our fathers found in possession of this land," he said, "we have assumed and exercised sovereignty over them." He prescribed the same for "the ignorant and credulous Filipinos."

Early Overseas Acquisitions and Failures: 1865–97

Policy makers after the Civil War were much less united in their desire for overseas possessions. Among the expansionists, Secretary of State William Henry Seward (1861–69) was a visionary. He understood that "political supremacy follows commercial ascendancy," and argued against European-style colonization. His plan, rather, was to secure naval bases in the Pacific and a canal in the Caribbean to create a "highway" for U.S. commerce with Asia. Against those who derided Alaska as "Seward's Icebox," the secretary purchased the barren land from the Russians for $7.2 million in 1867. The same year he annexed the Midway Islands for a possible way station and cable point in the Asian trade.

Those who pressed to end the post–Civil War feud with London shared Seward's imperial optimism. Many Americans remained outraged that British ships used by the Confederacy had destroyed or disabled about 250 Union ships, and they asked for millions in what were called the *Alabama* claims. Anti-British sentiments even ensured a GOP victory

in 1872. Against this crowd, expansionists felt that settling these claims would strengthen the bonds of "Anglo-Saxonism." Equally important, it would keep England and America out of each other's empire. Eventually, deals struck in 1872 and 1893 resolved the claims peacefully. "I feel very strongly that the English-speaking peoples are now closer together than for a century and a quarter," wrote a relieved Theodore Roosevelt to a friend.

Other expansionists issued calls for strengthening U.S. military power. After the Civil War, the Union army and navy demobilized and, by the 1880s, they respectively ranked a lowly thirteenth and twelfth in the world. The army was so depleted that even the Pinkerton Detective Agency was larger. In 1890, Captain Alfred Thayer Mahan published *The Influence of Sea Power upon History, 1660–1783*, which convinced many that the path to global power lay with the military. In response, the navy, described by its secretary, John D. Long, in 1885 as "an alphabet of floating wash-tubs," won appropriation after appropriation from the Congress until, by the end of the century, the United States ranked sixth in the world in battleships commissioned or under construction. All the while, officer colleges sprang up and the diplomatic corps grew more professional, ridding itself of its most embarrassing political appointees and finally using the rank of ambassador, as of 1893.

A countervailing force of antiexpansionists was more powerful in the Gilded Age than at any time since. Few of them, however, cited moral qualms against expansion. Instead, domestic politics motivated many objections. The House, for instance, refused to pass the Alaska appropriations in 1867 until it moved to impeach Johnson. Others thought overseas expansion too expensive. The *New York Evening Post* cited the "unprofitableness" of empire, and, in 1867, the Senate thought $7.5 million to be too steep a price for the Virgin Islands. When Seward moved on Hawai'i, the Senate defeated his treaty on the basis that it would hurt the tariff. Still others used racist arguments *against* empire. In 1869, when President Ulysses S. Grant negotiated the annexation of the Dominican Republic, opponents in the Senate countered that the United States could not absorb such a mixed-race people, and ratification fell short of the two-thirds needed.

Economic Growth and Party Politics

The extraordinary industrial boom of the late nineteenth century fueled an expansionist surge. U.S. share of world trade climbed from 6 percent in 1868 to 16 percent in 1929, producing a century-long trade surplus starting in 1874. Transnational corporations such as Singer Sewing Machines and Eastman Kodak appeared in the 1880s, and industrialists such as John D. Rockefeller, Cyrus McCormick, and J. P. Morgan became shapers of foreign policy. By 1929, with only 6 percent of the world's population, the United States accounted for about half of its industrial goods and gold reserves. The railroad, steamship, telephone, and transatlantic cable eroded the cherished insularity of Americans. In 1901 President William McKinley marveled at "how near one to the other is every part of the world. Modern inventions have brought into close relations widely separated peoples. . . . The world's products are being exchanged as never before . . . isolation is no longer possible or desirable."

Despite booms and busts affecting all regions—at century's end, 70 to 80 percent of the South's cotton was exported—until 1913 Republicans tended to favor Republican foreign policies and Democrats, Democratic ones. Diplomatic posts were largely political footballs. For instance, Republicans defeated an important Canadian fisheries agreement in 1888 because it had been reached by Democrats, and when Grover Cleveland gained the presidency—the only Democrat to do so during the Gilded Age—he rolled back Republican actions on a Nicaraguan canal (1885) and on the Congo (1885), Hawai'i (1893), and Samoa (1894). Regional interests also mattered, as when Republicans from the interior voted against a bigger navy while seacoast Democrats voted in favor.

The tariff was the most divisive partisan issue. High tariffs, erected during the Civil War to raise revenue, remained high afterward for protectionist reasons. Groups interested in the tariff were many and complex, but the general fault lines had the Republicans mostly in favor because they protected infant industries and held workers' wages high, and the Democrats less in favor because high tariffs elicited countertariffs against crops such as cotton. Allegiances ebbed and flowed: industrialist Andrew Carnegie once said he got into the business of steel because its tariff was high, but by 1885 he argued for lowering tariffs to enable the purchase of cheap raw materials. The McKinley Tariff of 1890 and the Dingley Tariff of 1897 lowered rates somewhat, but U.S. rates remained far higher than those in Europe. The power of the tariff was a testament to the hold on foreign policy enjoyed by Congress in the nineteenth century.

Farmers also had their own foreign policies. To be sure, farmers shared in the export boom. But agrarian reformers organized as the Populist Party to protest farmers' shrinking piece of the export pie and the downward pressure on prices exerted by agricultural powerhouses Russia, Canada, Argentina, and India. Populist sympathizers such as Democrat William Jennings Bryan wished to disengage from the world and merely stand as an example of "the glory that can be achieved by a republic," and Populist leader Tom Watson railed that the War of 1898 benefited only the "privileged classes." In the end, Populists faded partly because their signature foreign policy issue—the free coinage of silver—went down in flames with the defeat of Bryan as a presidential candidate in 1896 and the passage of the Gold Standard Act in 1900, which declared the gold dollar the only currency standard.

Crises in the 1890s

The year 1893 witnessed the most serious recession in U.S. history to that point, sparking crises whose solution would be perceived to be more, not less, expansion. Some industrialists reasoned that domestic consumers were too few to buy the nation's output. As a result, many organized in 1895 into the National Association of Manufacturers (NAM) to promote exports. "We have the Anglo-Saxon thirst for wide markets growing upon us," said NAM president Joseph C. Hendrix in 1898. Hendrix, like others, saw mounting threats: the workers might revolt; immigrants multiplied; Europeans raised tariffs; and a new power in the Far East, Japan, defeated China in 1895 and now threatened the greatest potential U.S. market. Fear of a "glut" in exports was exaggerated, but plenty of farmers and factory owners shared it.

Many also believed that land had run out. Although there remained millions of unclaimed acres on the mainland, historian Frederick Jackson Turner's 1893 essay "The Significance of the Frontier in American History" fueled the crisis atmosphere by arguing that the disappearance of the frontier out West threatened the yeoman democracy and rugged individualism that graced American character. The solution, he said in 1896, was "a vigorous foreign policy . . . [and] the extension of American influence to outlying islands and adjoining countries."

Several groups heeded his words, starting with Protestant missionaries. In 1869 there had been only 16 American missionary societies. By 1900 there were 90, and by 1910, Americans outpaced even the British in financing missionaries. With the rise of Darwinian science, Protestant churches feared losing social status and compensated by sending thousands of missionaries abroad, the large majority to China. Their chief propagandist was Josiah Strong, a Congregationalist minister whose 1885 best-seller, *Our Country*, argued that the spread of American religion would advance the cause of American foreign policy. Protestants abroad exposed locals to U.S. goods and preached a morality that helped sell those goods, for instance, covering naked bodies with New England's textiles. Hoping to produce what the Student Volunteers for Foreign Missions called "the Evangelization of the World in This Generation," millions joined missionary societies in the United States. In 1890 women made up 60 percent of the movement. One woman explained that missionary work "should appeal to every broad-minded Christian woman who is interested in education, civics, sanitation, social settlements, hospitals, good literature, and the emancipation of children, the right of women to health, home and protection; and the coming of the Kingdom of our Lord."

Just as missionary work filled a void in the 1890s, so did a renewed sense of racial superiority that arose from domestic developments. Social Darwinism had already raised the profile of racism in the United States, southern supremacists had encoded racial segregation for African Americans into law, and xenophobes warned of the "yellow peril" in the West. Americans now integrated visions of domestic and foreign race relations in the dozen or so international expositions of the Gilded Age. The World's Colombian Exposition in Chicago in 1893, for instance, displayed all the supposed races of the world on its main strip, from least to most civilized, starting with Africans and moving on to Indonesians, Pacific Islanders, other Asians, on up the ladder to Anglo-Saxons. As the century turned, race justified expansion. "We are a conquering race," argued Senator Albert Beveridge, Republican of Indiana. "We must obey our blood and occupy new markets, and, if necessary, new lands."

But racism was not simply for conquering. The "White Man's Burden," as British poet Rudyard Kipling called it in 1899, posited a moral, paternalistic obligation to uplift inferior races. Theodore Roosevelt shared it fully, explaining "it is our duty toward the people living in barbarism to see that they are freed from their chains." Race and racism, moreover, could be themselves changed by the experience of empire. Americans occupied the Philippines in 1898 with a racial ideology that held that Filipino "niggers" were unredeemable savages but then came out years later with a more subdued view that Filipinos had a "capacity" for self-government if properly directed.

Less obvious was the domestic crisis of gender. Late-century American men felt emasculated by urbanization and modern life. Roosevelt argued that adventures abroad could help men relive "the strenuous life." "Oversentimentality, oversoftness . . . , and mushiness are the great danger of this age and this people," he complained. He wanted to revive "barbarian virtues" and yearned for a war that would do so. "You and your generation have had your chance from 1861 to 1865," he told Civil War veteran and anti-imperialist Carl Schurz. "Now let us of this generation have ours!"

The War of 1898 and Its Consequences

As if responding on cue to the domestic martial spirit, the United States fought Spain in 1898 and joined the club of great powers. "From a nation of shopkeepers we became a nation of warriors" is how Democratic Party boss Henry Watterson described the transition. However, while between 1870 and 1900 Great Britain added 4.7 million square miles to its empire and France added 3.5 million to its own, the United States annexed only 125,000. This was not because Americans were "reluctant" imperialists but because they preferred informal control of foreign lands rather than formal colonization.

The struggle over Cuba helped define the U.S. preference for informal empire. The explosion of the USS *Maine* and the death of 266 American sailors in February 1898 punctuated an already tense situation in which U.S. observers sympathized with Cubans rebelling against corrupt Spanish rule. Even

after this tragedy, however, U.S. opinion was by no means united behind war. The "yellow press" and religious publications wanted war on nationalistic and humanitarian grounds, but others warned against the cost of fighting even a weak empire like Spain. U.S. planters in Cuba and trade journals back home were hawkish, but the American Federation of Labor (AFL) feared the island's cheap labor. President McKinley moved for war in April only after the Congress insisted on a promise of nonannexation though the Teller Amendment, named for Senator Henry Teller of Colorado, who acted to protect his state's beet sugar from Cuba's cane sugar. In the end, McKinley asked for war not to pander to a jingoistic public but to stop a Cuban revolution that could threaten U.S. property and to stem charges of cowardice from Democrats. The "splendid little war," as Rough Rider Theodore Roosevelt called it, ended quickly, prompting the *New York Sun* to declare, "We are all jingoes now," and giving Washington control over Cuba, Puerto Rico, the Philippines, and Guam. The Platt Amendment, strong-armed into the Cuban Constitution of 1901, gave oversight of the island's foreign policy to the United States and confirmed the apparent wisdom of informal empire.

The war in the Philippines—the other major former Spanish colony—garnered far less consensus. Easily defeating Spain, the United States then entered into a years-long brutally racist guerrilla war with Filipino rebels, led by Emilio Aguinaldo. "Civilize 'em with a Krag," went a popular army song, as Americans administered the "water cure" and other tortures to captured Filipinos. "I want no prisoners," General Jacob Smith instructed his troops. "I wish you to kill and burn, the more you kill and burn the better you will please me." The war took 4,165 American lives and more than 200,000 Filipino lives. McKinley justified the carnage with a classic euphemism: "benevolent assimilation" meant the desire to uplift Filipinos through Americanization, a program that began in earnest after the war.

But while it lasted, the carnage stirred the period's greatest domestic debate about foreign policy. Anti-imperialism made for strange bedfellows: writers and editors such as Mark Twain, E. L. Godkin, and William Dean Howells joined industrialists like Carnegie, social reformers like Jane Addams, the AFL's Samuel Gompers, and politicians of both parties. Opponents formed the Anti-Imperialist League in Boston in June 1898, and its arguments largely reflected domestic politics. Civil rights leader Moorfield Storey, for instance, saw parallels between the treatment of Filipinos and African Americans; and women identified with Aguinaldo's fury at being governed without his consent. Others feared "the incorporation of a mongrel and semibarbarous population into our body politic," as a South Carolina senator expressed it. As one observer noted, all the posturing, abroad like at home, achieved little: "Democrats howling about Republicans shooting negroes in the

Philippines and the Republicans objecting to Democrats shooting negroes in the South. This may be good politics, but it is rough on the negroes."

Besides the takeover of Cuba and the Philippines, the War of 1898 had other important consequences. One was the annexation of Hawai'i. By the 1890s, planters, missionaries, navy planners, whalers, and traders on their way to China had long advocated U.S. control of the islands. A treaty from the mid-1870s boosting sugar made Hawaiians "practically members of an American Zollverein in an outlying district of the state of California," said Secretary of State James G. Blaine. A believer in economic imperialism, Blaine championed annexation as "a purely American form of colonization." By 1893 Americans made up only 5 percent of Hawai'i's population but owned 65 percent of its land. That year, they led a coup against a strong-willed Queen Liliuokalani that paved the way for full annexation in the heat of the war with Spain, on August 12, 1898.

Hawai'i foreshadowed another consequence of 1898: the rising power of the executive. When McKinley could not carry two-thirds of the Senate for a Hawaiian treaty, he achieved it through a joint resolution, which required only simple majorities. McKinley and his successor, Theodore Roosevelt, especially overpowered Congress in foreign policy. McKinley was the first chief executive with cabinet officers who had few political bases of their own and so were more loyal to him. He was also first to appoint a "secretary to the president," who assumed the duties of today's press secretary: holding daily meetings with reporters, issuing press releases, and putting together press scrapbooks. During the war, the president imposed harsh rules on war reporting and had three telegraph wires and 25 telephone lines running into the White House. With such expanded powers, McKinley took unprecedented license. He responded to China's Boxer Rebellion of 1900, for instance, by sending troops without congressional permission. Meanwhile, Roosevelt penned several "executive agreements" that could supplant treaties and circumvent Congress. It was not clear, however, if a stronger White House meant an expanded voice for the people in foreign policy. The Oval Office often defied popular sympathies, for instance, when it sided with the British in South Africa's Boer War. And besides, McKinley and Roosevelt believed the president's role was not to follow but to "educate," in the style of the Progressive movement. To Roosevelt, public opinion was "the voice of the devil, or what is still worse, the voice of a fool."

World War I: Wilsonianism Abroad and at Home

The Great War of 1914–18, more commonly known as World War I, sparked yet another debate, this one over U.S. involvement in Europe. Americans greeted the news of war with a reflexive reluctance, and as late as August 1917, one journalist assessed that two-thirds of the nation was still against the war. Antiwar

groups included Irish Americans who hated the British Empire and German Americans who disapproved of fighting their *Heimat* (homeland). The Socialist Party made gains with its rhetoric of peace, and the Selective Service Act, or draft, passed the House by a slim margin of 199 to 178, with 52 abstentions. President Woodrow Wilson won reelection in 1916 with the motto "He Kept Us Out of War." In fact, neutrality paid off: before they joined the war, Americans sold some $2.2 billion in arms to the British and their Allies.

Yet the moralistic internationalism advocated by Wilson and fellow progressives led logically to war. Herbert Croly, in his 1909 book *The Promise of American Life*, had linked progressivism to foreign relations by calling for a centralized Hamiltonian state, a stronger military, and lower tariffs that would promote democracy and capitalism abroad. When Wilson called for war in the spring of 1917, he articulated aims in the "fourteen points" speech of January 8, 1918. Its major principles included self-determination for small nations, freedom of the seas, reduction of armaments, adjustment of colonial claims, open treaties, and a vaguely defined League of Nations. "There are American principles, American policies," explained the president. Wilson presented a democratic alternative to the specter of communism engulfing Russia as of 1917. "The spirit of the Bolsheviki is everywhere," he warned.

Wilson's democratic spirit was a hit with European audiences. Parisians lined their streets under banners that read "*Vive Wilson*" and Italians welcomed him as the *Redentore dell'Humanità* (Redeemer of Humanity). But negotiations over the Treaty of Versailles and the League of Nations faced opposition from European victors and crippling criticism at home. Republicans who now controlled the Senate organized as the "reservationists" and "irreconcilables." The latter wanted nothing to do with the treaty or the league, while the former, headed by Henry Cabot Lodge, the chairman of the Senate Foreign Relations Committee, were wary of surrendering U.S. sovereignty. "Are you willing to put your soldiers and your sailors at the disposition of other nations?" Lodge asked rhetorically. Wilson refused to give Congress oversight over such matters and embarked on an 8,000-mile, 22-day, cross-country speaking tour that worked him into a paralyzing stroke. The tour was in vain. Congress kept the United States out of the treaty and the league.

War also affected domestic groups. African Americans "over here," as the popular song called the homeland, still lived overwhelmingly in a South that lynched 382 of their own from 1914 to 1920, and met with hostility that often boiled over into race riots when they migrated to the North. Four hundred thousand joined the military but were assigned to camps often segregated with "whites only" signs. Leaders such as W.E.B. Du Bois took a respite from encouraging "black nationality" among those of

African descent and argued for standing "shoulder to shoulder" with whites in a common struggle for democracy. Du Bois organized a Pan-African Congress in conjunction with the Versailles conference, but his advocacy fell on deaf ears with the Great Powers. Women, too, mobilized for food campaigns, child welfare work, and Liberty bond and loyalty drives. "The Girl Behind the Man Behind the Gun" is how one poster described their influence. For women, patriotism brought concrete political gain: the Nineteenth Amendment securing the vote was ratified in 1920.

For those not deemed patriotic enough, repression came swiftly. Respectively passed in 1917 and 1918, the Espionage Act and the Sedition Act interpreted any criticism of the war as subversive, and as a result some German-born residents of the United States fell victim to vigilante mobs. In 1919 war's end brought not only racial but labor strife. When terrorists exploded a bomb outside the home of Attorney General A. Mitchell Palmer, the state rounded up thousands of pacifists and labor leaders, leading to the deportation of more than 500 aliens. Even Eugene Debs, the Socialist Party's standard-bearer, was imprisoned under Wilson, against whom he had run for the presidency in 1912.

Empire in the Caribbean and Central America

Despite the rejection of European postwar settlements, the United States did not turn inward. Quite the contrary, it expanded its presence around the world, especially when unopposed by other Great Powers. Cultural and economic radiance were especially intertwined. Marketers spread the "American Dream" of material wealth, and exporters satisfied those urges with the automobile, motion pictures, and the radio. "Foreign lands are feeling the benefit of American progress, our American right thinking," automaker Henry Ford believed. "Both Russia's and China's problems are fundamentally industrial and will be solved by the application of the right methods of thinking, practically applied." Americans also sent themselves abroad; passport holders multiplied almost tenfold in the 1910s and 1920s. Finally, Americans increasingly imported the world's goods. French salons, English libraries, Japanese designs, and folk objects from American Indians or Latin America became *de rigueur* in chic homes.

In the Caribbean area, however, imposing "right thinking" did not go smoothly. Especially after 1898, president after president sent U.S. troops to occupy Latin American ports, negotiate loans in exchange for financial supervision—an arrangement called "dollar diplomacy"—and remake what they perceived to be unstable political cultures into havens for U.S. security, foreign investment, and moral reform. In 1903, when Theodore Roosevelt encouraged the separation of Panama from Colombia through French and U.S. private promoters, it showed the convergence of the U.S. Navy's need for a canal with American merchants' desire for increased trade. The result was the opening of the Panama Canal in 1914, built by a multinational workforce and managed by thousands of U.S. citizens living in a ten-mile-wide colony bisecting the Central American Isthmus.

The canal engendered another need: securing Caribbean routes leading to it. In 1904, when he signed an agreement with Dominicans to take over their customs houses, Roosevelt declared the need for the United States to exercise "international police power" in its "backyard." Racist paternalism again mixed with security and business interests to send U.S. troops to invade Caribbean countries at least 34 times in the 30 years after 1903. Wilson's interventions in the Mexican Revolution were especially contradictory, since he rejected conquest yet sent soldiers so that the Mexican government could "be founded on a moral basis." A desire to minimize criticism of these adventures, especially by the "peace progressives" in Congress, led Presidents Herbert Hoover and Franklin D. Roosevelt in the late 1920s and early 1930s to call for the end of military interventions, what FDR coined the Good Neighbor Policy.

Puerto Rico fit oddly into this pattern. U.S. troops took it over in 1898 but met no armed resistance. In 1900 the Foraker Act made the island an "unincorporated territory" led by a U.S.-appointed governor and subject to congressional laws, thus taking away Puerto Ricans' independence but not granting them rights as U.S. citizens. In decisions from 1901 to 1910 known as the Insular Cases, the Supreme Court ratified this state of legal limbo. In 1917 the Jones Act gave Puerto Ricans U.S. citizenship—just in time to draft them into the war—but awarded the island neither statehood nor independence.

Citizenship and Immigration

Immigration and foreign policy were closely related in 1865–1933 because defining citizenship was key to U.S. relationships with the world. So while the era was a high point for immigrants from Europe, it was not so for Asians. In 1882 Congress passed the Chinese Exclusion Act, banning practically all Chinese from entering the United States and marking the first such restriction based on race or nationality. In 1907 Roosevelt signed a "Gentlemen's Agreement" with Tokyo, sharply cutting back Japanese immigration in return for putting pressure on the California legislature not to segregate Japanese students. Such xenophobic actions went hand-in-hand with Jim Crow laws in that they relegated nonwhites to a separate, second-class citizenry. Meanwhile, "Americanization" movements aimed to assimilate Europeans into a "melting pot" that allowed them to minimize differences and emphasize their common whiteness.

The Johnson-Reed Immigration Act of 1924 solidified this narrowing of citizenship. It established the first numerical limits for immigrants of every nation, nonwhites such as those from China and India being limited to 100 per year. Supreme Court decisions in the 1920s went further, barring Japanese and Asian Indians from claiming whiteness and therefore citizenship. Hardened racial lines created the "alien citizen," or U.S. citizen now seen as alien by most Americans.

For Mexican Americans—the large majority of Latin American immigrants before the 1960s—the process was different but equally revealing of domestic politics. From 1900 to 1930, more than 1 million Mexicans came into the United States, nearly all to work in the fields of the Southwest. The 1924 law did not apply to Mexicans because farmers needed cheap labor, but by the late 1920s, calls for restriction grew more strident. Mexicans did compete for some jobs and housing with U.S. citizens, and were often called ignorant, dirty, lazy, and criminal. Ominously, the 1930 U.S. Census for the first time defined Mexicans as a separate race. When the Great Depression hit, the U.S. government forced half a million Mexicans in America, nearly one in five, back to their homeland.

Defining America

The Depression caused a sharp downturn in U.S. engagement with the world. Exports declined 60 percent, and Americans virtually stopped investing overseas. In 1930 the protectionist wall, eroded slightly since Wilson, went back up with the Smoot-Hawley Tariff. Two years later, some 25 nations had retaliated. It would take another war in Europe to reinvigorate U.S. leadership in world affairs.

From the Civil War to the Great Depression, proponents and opponents of expansion tied themselves to the word *Americanism*, suggesting that they were expressing the best of the country's values through its behavior abroad. That debate, perhaps more than anything, marked the era. Now that issues such as trade openness, military expansion, and immigration are again debated, the importance of defining America through its foreign relations speaks to the seminal nature of the 1865–1933 period.

See also Alaska and Hawai'i; Americanism; business and politics; Caribbean, Central America, and Mexico, interventions in, 1903–34; immigration policy; race and politics; tariffs and politics.

FURTHER READING. Robert L. Beisner, *From the Old Diplomacy to the New, 1865–1900*, 2nd ed., 1986; Idem, *Twelve against Empire: The Anti-Imperialists, 1898–1900*, 1992; Joseph A. Fry, "Phases of Empire: Late Nineteenth-Century U.S. Foreign Relations," in *The Gilded Age: Essays on the Origins of Modern America*, edited by Charles W. Calhoun, 261–88, 1996; Andrew Gyory, *Race, Politics, and the Chinese Exclusion Act*, 1998; Kristin L. Hoganson, "Cosmopolitan Domesticity: Importing the American Dream, 1865–1920," *American Historical Review* 107, no. 1 (February 2002), 55–83; William R. Hutchison, *Errand to the World: American Protestant Thought and Foreign Missions*, 1987; Akira Iriye, *The Globalizing of America, 1913–1945*, Vol. 3 of *The Cambridge History of American Foreign Relations*, 1993; Matthew Frye Jacobson, *Barbarian Virtues: The United States Encounters Foreign Peoples at Home and Abroad, 1876–1917*, 2000; Paul Kramer, *The Blood of Government: Race, Empire, the United States, and the Philippines*, 2006; Walter LaFeber, *The American Search for Opportunity, 1865–1913*, Vol. 2 of *The Cambridge History of American Foreign Relations*, 1993; Eric T. L. Love, *Race over Empire: Racism and U.S. Imperialism 1865–1900*, 2004; Mae Ngai, *Impossible Subjects: Illegal Aliens and the Making of Modern America*, 2005; John L. Offner, "United States Politics and the 1898 War over Cuba," in *The Crisis of 1898: Colonial Redistribution and Nationalist Mobilization*, edited by Angel Smith and Emma Dávila-Cox, 18–44, 1999; Mary Renda, *Taking Haiti: Military Occupation and the Culture of U.S. Imperialism, 1915–1940*, 2001; Serge Ricard, ed., *An American Empire: Expansionist Cultures and Policies, 1881–1917*, 1990; Emily S. Rosenberg, *Financial Missionaries to the World: The Politics and Culture of Dollar Diplomacy, 1900–1930*, 2003; Idem, *Spreading the American Dream: American Economic and Cultural Expansion, 1890–1945*, 1982; Robert W. Rydell, *All the World's a Fair: Visions of Empire at American International Expositions, 1876–1916*, 1984; Elliott P. Skinner, *African Americans and U.S. Policy toward Africa, 1850–1924: In Defense of Black Nationality*, 1992; Neil A. Wynn, *From Progressivism to Prosperity: World War I and American Society*, 1986.

ALAN MCPHERSON

foreign policy and domestic politics since 1933

Bookended by moments of far-reaching global and national crisis, the period from 1933 through the early twenty-first century opened with the United States in economic depression and enforced retreat from the bold internationalism espoused by President Woodrow Wilson. The long-standing isolationism that dashed Wilson's global aspirations ended abruptly when the United States entered World War II, and when the country emerged from the war as the ascendant global power, with European colonialism collapsing in the wake of wartime challenges. After the Allied Forces' victory over global fascism, the United States competed for the next 40 years with the Soviet Union for the hearts, minds, and resources of the more than 40 new nations then emerging from decades of European colonial rule. That history of conflict—of the aspirations of formerly colonized peoples seeking national independence, control of their resources, and an independent course for their economic development pitted against cold war policies—remains resonant. By the end of the U.S.-Soviet conflict, both sides had poured millions of dollars and tons of weapons into Africa, Asia, Latin America, and the Middle East, setting the stage for contemporary ethnic conflicts and the rise of al-Qaeda and global terrorist groups. Moreover, by the early twenty-first century, the United States would be engaged in costly protracted wars in Iraq and Afghanistan while facing the greatest national and global crisis since the Great Depression.

Consuming the World

The United States emerged from World War II as the dominant military and economic power amid proclamations of the "American Century." Several decades later, the demise of the Detroit automotive industry that had served as the nation's arsenal during wartime would symbolize the end of American supremacy in manufacturing. Once the world's wealthiest creditor, the United States became a debtor nation (with, in mid-2008, a national debt of $9.5 trillion and a federal budget deficit of $410 billion). The export of manufacturing jobs, the decline of the dollar in relation to foreign currencies, the nation's dependency on foreign-produced oil, and the nation's borrowing from China to finance its deficit spending have made connections between U.S. foreign policy and the nation's domestic life and politics visible to many Americans. Many undoubtedly recall with nostalgia how the U.S. entry into World War II pulled the country out of a prolonged economic crisis. But other aspects of the relationship between foreign policy and the way Americans live have remained mysterious to many Americans. How many know, for example, that the unprecedented expansion of wealth in the 1950s and the benefits of a consumer society depended on U.S. domination of strategic and manufacturing resources?

Conceptualizations of connections between domestic politics and U.S. foreign relations—military, economic, and diplomatic—have changed dramatically over time. At moments defined by national crisis, such as restrictions on civil liberties during the cold war, or more recently, during the "war on terror" after the 9/11 attacks, the connection between domestic and foreign affairs seems abundantly clear. Less well known are the more routine socioeconomic ties that have historically bound the United States to foreign peoples and their societies. The material abundance of a domestic U.S. consumer society founded on cheap energy, industry's access to raw materials, and foreign sweatshop labor has fostered in many Americans an innocence about the relationship between inflated military spending and a neglected national infrastructure and public sphere. Similarly, this innocence of past ties between foreign relations and domestic politics emerges in the unwillingness of anti-immigration forces to consider the impact of past U.S. foreign wars and economic policies as a catalyst for immigration. Yet it is impossible to consider U.S. politics and culture outside of the history of the United States on the world stage.

The relationship between U.S. foreign and domestic policy tends to enter the American political arena and public consciousness primarily in times of war or crisis, while significant realms and operations of U.S. power remain on the periphery of public discourse

and awareness. One reason is that some momentous foreign policy actions were carried out covertly, such as the 1953 CIA overthrow of the Iranian elected government of Muhammad Musaddiq and the installation of Shah Reza Pahlevi's U.S.-friendly dictatorship. Beyond this, the actions of powerful nonstate actors who are nonetheless sanctioned or promoted by the government—from the Hollywood film industry in the twentieth century, which accepted State Department guidelines for cinematic content in exchange for the global distribution of films, to corporations contracted to secure the occupation and rebuilding of Iraq—remain hidden to most Americans, and beyond the reach of U.S. legal and regulatory authority.

Although contemporary historians of the United States have vigorously challenged earlier tendencies to separate the foreign and domestic spheres and have raised awareness of America's intricate global connections, the story of the post–World War II economic boom, demographic and social shifts such as the growth of the suburbs, the population shift to the Sun Belt, and the unprecedented material affluence experienced by that generation of Americans is often told without considering how profoundly these shifts depended on U.S. policies that aggressively promoted a globally integrated, U.S.-led capitalist economy. Americans simply would not have had the automobiles, refrigerators, and air conditioning that enabled these massive demographic shifts without ready Western access to resources in southern Africa, the Middle East, and Latin America. The growth of commercial air travel would not have developed without cobalt, an essential material for jet engines. Like uranium, diamonds (without which computers could not operate), and countless other metals, the vast majority of cobalt reserves were in southern Africa. Then, as now, the classic American freedom of the open road depended on Middle Eastern oil production. The 1970s energy crisis exposed U.S. oil dependence, a dependency again well in evidence as the world market price of oil and unprecedented gas prices reached new highs in the aftermath of the U.S. invasion and occupation of Iraq.

Global dependencies structured daily consumption as well as fundamental economic and social shifts. In the 1950s and 1960s, Americans consumed millions of frozen TV dinners, no doubt for the most part unaware of the origins of the aluminum tins in Jamaican bauxite mines, acquired during World War II by the U.S.-based Reynolds Metals corporation; the fried chicken processed under the dismal working and living conditions of the undocumented immigrants in southern poultry farms; and the fruit dessert harvested by migrant farm workers in the West. Today, the U.S. presence within a web of global labor relations, including past and present wars and global entanglements, is reflected in myriad seemingly mundane consumer decisions such as whether to order Vietnamese or Cambodian food for takeout. Many American cultural and culinary tastes are shaped by the history of the nation's expansive global involvement, as well as its high consumption of energy and natural resources.

Wilsonian Internationalism and the American Century

In 1933 the global economic depression temporarily stalled America's earlier imperial expansions and disrupted the Wilsonian project of making the world safe for American democracy and institutions. During World War I, Wilson had waged explicit and fierce economic competition with America's military allies, and changed the United States from a debtor nation to a creditor nation with legislation that freed U.S. banks and corporations from Progressive Era restrictions. The establishment of the Federal Reserve and its central banking system provided U.S. industries with a competitive global advantage. Wilson's missionary zeal for reshaping the world in America's image was further reflected in his response to the 1917 Russian revolution and Vladimir Lenin's call for a worldwide revolution against imperial powers. In response to Lenin, Wilson's "Fourteen Points" speech offered an anticolonial politics that challenged Europe's privileged access to markets and investment.

Compelled to focus on the domestic crisis of the Great Depression, Franklin D. Roosevelt also looked outward as the first president to recognize the Soviet Union, and through his attempts in the face of isolationist opposition to build new alliances in aiding opponents of Japanese and German aggression. World War II sparked social conflict within the United States, notably in the forced internment of Japanese American citizens and in the widespread white resistance to the movement of African Americans into cities and the West with the opening of factories and jobs. At the same time, the wartime alliance with the Soviet Union enabled a second flowering of the popular front culture of the 1930s, as leftist-inspired labor and social movements vigorously debated the appropriate character of U.S. internationalism. The period of World War II through the early cold war marked the ascendance of the United States as a global superpower at precisely the moment that European colonialism collapsed, and in the midst of a related cold war with the Soviet Union. Both superpowers struggled to win the allegiance and resources of formerly colonized peoples. Many Americans, including such black radicals as Paul Robeson and W.E.B. DuBois, and Roosevelt's first vice president, Henry Wallace (the Progressive Party candidate in the 1948 election), envisioned a worldwide New Deal in which future peace and prosperity hinged on ending colonialism and raising the standard of living of colonized peoples as well as continued cooperation between the United States and the Soviet Union.

Others revived the ambitious Wilsonian internationalism of World War I to argue that the priority in a new American-led internationalism was the safety

of American investments and America's access to resources needed for economic growth. For Time-Life publisher Henry Luce and his allies, the "American Century" would usher in a world where American values, culture, and consumer products peacefully conquered the world. This vision profoundly influenced U.S. wartime and postwar objectives, as U.S. policy makers envisioned an American-led, globally integrated capitalist economy. Committed to ensuring the West's privileged access to the world's markets, industrial infrastructure, and raw materials, this group embraced President Harry Truman's ambitious declaration that the United States had the right and responsibility to intervene in external and internal threats everywhere across the globe.

The Cold War and U.S. Global Ambitions

Scholars generally agree that despite Joseph Stalin's notorious brutality toward the Soviet people, the Soviet Union was not expansionist in the early years of the cold war, forced instead to rebuild internally after the enormous casualties and destruction of infrastructure during World War II. (This would change dramatically in the 1960s under Soviet Premier Nikita Khrushchev, who declared support for national liberation movements worldwide.) Yet at the end of World War II, with conservatives throughout Europe tarnished by collaborations with the Nazis, and Communists and Socialists hailed as the core of resistance to fascism, the European left emerged from the war greatly strengthened, and anticapitalist ideologies had enormous appeal for anticolonial movements. In the eyes of many U.S. policy makers, this represented a serious threat to American economic and political objectives.

The Truman Doctrine, announced before Congress on March 12, 1947, specifically funded beleaguered anti-Communist governments in Greece and Turkey but more broadly asked Americans to accept the "great responsibilities" entailed in a global struggle against communism. The Attorney General's List of Subversive Organizations and the Loyalty Oath declared the criticism of American foreign policy beyond the pale of acceptable discourse. The cold war repression of political dissent intensified during the early 1950s, under the leadership of Wisconsin senator Joseph McCarthy, who used the spotlight of nationally televised hearings to promote the idea of a conspiracy of Communists who had infiltrated the nation's foreign policy establishment. McCarthy's witch hunts had a far-reaching, intimidating influence on critical institutions such as the press and education from the elementary to university level, and in setting up a bipartisan cold war foreign policy consensus.

After decades of careful documentation of cold war repression within the United States, some scholars have more recently contended that the cold war's impact on the narrowing of political and cultural expression has been overemphasized. Certainly, some social processes and intellectual and political traditions transcended cold war divides. But a fundamental issue remains: despite sometimes heated debates over strategy, such as Eisenhower's critique of Truman's execution of the Korean war, the United States consolidated its position as the world's dominant power largely without scrutiny of means or ends. For 20 years following the announcement of the Truman Doctrine in 1947, the ruling assumptions and objectives of American foreign policy to contain communism went unopposed in Congress or within any significant sector of the American people. The substantially narrowed anti-Communist political discourse during the 1950s helped account for the episodic nature of American citizens' engagement with foreign affairs, as well as the explosive social conflict that occurred in the 1960s. Most important, the institutional patterns of secrecy and lack of democratic accountability established in the early cold war years posed profound challenges to not only the broader vibrancy of a democratic culture where citizens feel engaged and empowered in matters that affect their lives, but the most basic tenets of liberal procedural democracy.

Anticolonialism, Civil Rights, and the Cold War

The leading international alternative to the cold war's bipolar vision of global politics, the nonaligned movement of newly independent Afro-Asian nations, had little traction within U.S. politics. The most far-reaching demands for political and economic equality of the World War II era, including the linking of civil rights to anticolonial struggles abroad, were abruptly altered and in many cases thoroughly repressed in the early cold war. While such radical advocates of anticolonialism as Robeson and DuBois were prosecuted and had their passports seized, others, such as the NAACP's Walter White, became architects of a new anti-Communist liberalism, promoting an anticolonialism that was justified by anticommunism, arguing that the abuses of colonialism opened the doors to Communists and that Asia and Africa must remain in the Western orbit.

Despite strong rhetoric denouncing the abuses of domestic racism, such as Secretary of State Dean G. Acheson's warning that the United States could not neglect the "international implications of civil rights violations," advocates for civil rights and desegregation found the range of debate sharply constrained, despite the Truman administration's unprecedented endorsement of a civil rights agenda. Truman's embrace of civil rights acknowledged Acheson's understanding of civil rights as a national security issue. But in focusing more on the cold war than on civil rights, Truman presided over the contraction of public debate and the collapse of the left during the early cold war years. As early as 1946, with the formation of Truman's Committee on Civil Rights, White and others began to craft the dominant argument of the anti-Communist civil rights liberals. The

new argument seized on international criticism, in the world press, of American racism to argue that antidiscrimination measures were vital for the United States in its struggle against communism. The dominant liberal argument against racial segregation, using anticommunism to justify the fight against racism and for civil rights, conceded the high ground to anticommunism.

Scholars have traced a powerful remobilization of business between 1946 and 1948, which afforded anti-Communist labor leaders power within the circles of the corporate elite and blocked the radical social agenda of labor and civil rights evident during World War II. The growing conservatism of the labor movement and the narrowing of labor's agenda had a critical impact on global politics. As Communists and progressives were expelled from unions in America, American labor supported anti-Communist unions abroad even when that meant collaborating with former Nazis and other fascists. In 1949 CIO unions left the World Federation of Trade Unions (WFTU), and both the AFL and CIO took the lead in setting up the new anti-Communist International Confederation of Free Trade Unions. CIO support for African labor during World War II had been an important feature of the globally inflected civil rights activism that had also supported anticolonial movements. But after the CIO's departure from the WFTU, the role of U.S. labor in Africa, as well as in the well-documented European cases, would be filtered through a close collaboration between the AFL-CIO (under director George Meany) and the State Department—with covert support from the CIA.

The Hot Battle for Hearts and Mines

The debate over the significance of the cold war in shaping American politics rests in part on the very definition of the term *cold war*. To grasp the implications of U.S. cold war policies it is necessary to look beyond the bipolar U.S.-Soviet conflict. From the U.S. entry into World War II through the early cold war, the United States ascended as the hegemonic power while competing with the Soviet Union for the allegiance and resources of formerly colonized peoples. In theory, colonialism had no place in the vision of American democratic capitalism. U.S. policy makers not only objected to the resources and markets that colonialism afforded the European powers but also came to see American race relations as the Achilles' heel in the cold war battle for hearts and minds overseas, and sought to distinguish themselves from European colonizers.

Thus, for the most part, U.S. policy makers did not seek to take over European models of colonialism as they withered in the face of anticolonial challenges and the straitened conditions of wartime. Asserting instead the right of the United States to lead the "free world," they pursued global economic integration through modernization and development. American policy makers committed themselves to making sure that the West had privileged access to the world's markets, industrial infrastructure, and raw materials. And like the Wilsonian promotion of self-determination that had no trouble reconciling the invasions of Haiti and Mexico when U.S. interests and investments were at stake, policy makers in the post-1945 period interpreted democracy to mean capitalism first and foremost, and consistently supported dictatorships friendly to capitalism over democratically elected nationalist governments in Asia, Africa, and the Middle East or U.S. economic imperialism in Latin America.

In the face of persistent attempts by formerly colonized peoples to regain control of their resources, U.S. policy makers made repeated use of (often covert) military force; the "cold" war was in fact a bloody and protracted conflict for the peoples of Asia, Africa, Latin America, and the Middle East, where democratic challenges often met with violent suppression by either U.S. proxies, covert operatives, or both. By the mid-1950s, the CIA had already carried out covert actions to oust elected leaders in Iran and Guatemala, and by the mid-1960s, had waged counterinsurgencies in Indonesia, Syria, the Congo, Cuba, Guyana, and Vietnam. Certainly many policy makers viewed these actions as a necessary evil. The "common sense" of covert action depended on a worldview of the Soviet Union as a dangerous enemy that fundamentally threatened "the American way of life." But in confronting a seemingly ubiquitous Soviet threat, American policy makers repeatedly conflated nationalism and communism. Moreover, U.S. opposition to leaders throughout the Middle East, Africa, Asia, and Latin America often reflected ethnocentric and paternalistic assessments of non-Western leaders that prohibited American policy makers from viewing them as independent political agents. From the CIA overthrow of Muhammad Musaddiq in Iran to the ouster and assassination of Patrice Lumumba in the Congo in 1961, U.S. officials tended to see leaders in these regions as pawns or potential pawns of the Soviets. Despite the complexity of America's global relationships, when control over crucial strategic resources such as oil and uranium were at stake American officials brooked no ambiguity in assessing the allegiances of national leaders.

The enormous reach of U.S. foreign policy entailed highly porous boundaries between the government and purportedly private corporations and cultural industries. As the Soviet Union sent classical orchestras and ballet companies around the world and the United States responded with jazz, dance, and other cultural forms, the circulation of culture became part of the cold war battle for hearts and minds. The United States Information Agency produced and distributed films, radio programs, and vast numbers of pamphlets and news releases aimed at showing the world the superiority of the American way of life and American democracy. By 1955 the Voice of America brought American music and culture to an estimated

30 million people in more than 80 countries. In the next decade, that number would triple. The State Department sponsored cultural presentations involving a multitude of artists, from jazz musicians Louis Armstrong, Duke Ellington, and Dizzy Gillespie to dancers and choreographers Martha Graham, Alvin Ailey, and Paul Taylor to the Cleveland Orchestra, high school marching bands, and rhythm and blues and soul groups. While such tours were highly publicized, the CIA clandestinely funded cultural institutions from the Museum of Modern Art in New York City to radio, newspapers, and the motion picture industry. Touring jazz ensembles closely followed an itinerary tracking the cold war commodities of oil and uranium; some appearances occurred practically simultaneously with U.S. backed coups and interventions. As the U.S. government courted neocolonial elites, musicians traveled with remarkable frequency to places where the CIA operated, from Iran and Iraq to the Republic of the Congo to other areas of America's northern perimeter defense zone across Afghanistan, Pakistan, and Turkey.

As the U.S. government secured access to oil for American companies by means from coups to concerts, precursors of Texaco, Chevron, Exxon, and Mobil exported U.S. segregationist race relations in their worker-management relations throughout the Western hemisphere. In the segregated workforces the oil companies assembled in Mexico and Venezuela, workers were paid differently according to race. These same companies owned the conglomerate Arabian American Oil Company, which styled itself as a private enterprise version of the Marshall Plan as it extended such arrangements into former parts of the British and French empires, transplanting segregationist labor and housing laws to the oil fields and refineries of Saudi Arabia, where Arab workers labored under Jim Crow–style discrimination.

As these private enterprises thrived throughout Central America and the Middle East, in the many areas where the accelerated anticolonial activity of World War II carried into armed conflict between independence movements and colonial powers, ultimately the United States nearly always backed up its colonial allies when they faced challenges to their rule. Only in rare cases—such as Indonesia, where the United States judged the Dutch to be so intransigent as to be driving the Indonesians into the hands of the Communists, and the 1956 Suez Canal crisis, in which the United States defied Britain and France and eventually forced them to withdraw troops they had amassed to challenge Gamel Abdel Nasser after he nationalized the canal—did the United States directly challenge its European allies in matters of colonial control.

Vietnam and Deepening Militarism

The case of America's longest war, in Vietnam, starkly illustrates the tendency of the United States to ultimately back up its colonial allies. Historians have struggled to explain America's participation in the Vietnam War, a war that would shape the character of American politics and society for decades to come. Scholars have analyzed the war as an inevitable by-product of cold war assumptions and even as an example of the sheer excess of liberal cold war ideology. While both of these views are important, historians have less often considered the war as an ill-advised by-product of the U.S. commitment to colonial France. With the United States initially sympathetic to Ho Chi Minh's revolutionary nationalism, when the French government of General Charles de Gaulle found itself both embattled by the Communist left and incapable of defending its colonial empire, the United States reversed its position and came to its aid, propping up successive South Vietnamese governments tottering precariously atop an inherited colonial state structure.

In his Farewell Address, President Dwight Eisenhower expressed concern that what he labeled "the military industrial complex" might imperil American democratic institutions. Over time, antiwar critics would extend this observation to charge that America had overinvested in military sectors at the expense of basic industry, manufacturing, and infrastructure. The most radical critics of U.S. participation in the Vietnam War linked the war to U.S. imperialism throughout the globe.

Protest and National Nervous Breakdown

Scholars have discussed the irony of a government defending democracy from communism by creating a secret government accountable to no one. Certainly, the fact that so much U.S. foreign policy remained under the radar in the early cold war—such as the order by John F. Kennedy to depose President Ngo Dinh Diem of South Vietnam in 1961, and the 1964 Tonkin Gulf incident that led President Lyndon Johnson to ratchet up U.S. intervention in the war—contributed enormously to the outrage of the 1960s antiwar movement, as many Americans who had generally trusted their government and shared in the hopeful optimism projected by Kennedy began to discover that they did not have the whole story, and indeed, had been lied to. In 1965 high school students in Des Moines, Iowa, braved suspension and even death threats by wearing black armbands in an antiwar demonstration. Four years later the Supreme Court upheld the First Amendment Rights of students (and teachers) at school. Americans inundated by humanitarian appeals to sponsor impoverished children because poverty would lead them to communism now saw those children slaughtered by American troops. In 1967, the year of the My Lai Massacre in Vietnam, Americans also learned that the CIA had illegally funded such American organizations as the National Students Association and the American Society of African Culture, in addition to a multitude of foreign cultural organizations.

By 1968 the violence—whether covert or military—that had become integral to the pursuit of U.S. objectives abroad seemed endemic in U.S. society as well. In February of that year, police fired on African American students protesting segregation in Orangeburg, South Carolina. Domestic and international opposition to U.S. participation in the Vietnam War became a polarizing force, further undermining the liberal consensus for civil rights reform, fracturing the Democratic Party and sowing the seeds for the demise of the New Deal Coalition and the rise of the New Right. Martin Luther King Jr.'s antiwar speech on April 4, 1967, and his opposition to racism, poverty, and militarism divided the civil rights movement. In 1968 the unpopular war had forced President Johnson to withdraw his campaign for reelection. The assassination of King, and shortly afterward of Robert Kennedy, the leading antiwar contender for the Democratic nomination for president, hurled the nation into chaos.

President Richard M. Nixon, who parlayed the nation's racial and antiwar conflicts to gaining the presidency in 1968, ordered the expansion of the conflict to Laos and the secret bombing of Cambodia. The term *imperial presidency* usually refers to Nixon's use of unchecked executive power in his conduct of American involvement in the war, and his disregard for legislative oversight. The Watergate scandal, caused by the administration's cover-up of the burglary of Democratic National Committee offices before the 1972 presidential campaign, proved to be Nixon's undoing. He resigned when his claims of executive privilege on the withholding of evidence related to Watergate were rejected by the Supreme Court. And by firing Archibald Cox, the special prosecutor appointed by Congress, who investigated the scandal, Nixon had outraged critics by causing a constitutional crisis. To be sure, Nixon was a complex figure, a paranoid and mean-spirited politician eager to destroy his critics on the eve of his 1972 reelection campaign, but also an astute statesman whose policy of détente opened up relations with the China and the Soviet Union. But the view of Nixon and his National Security Advisor Henry Kissinger that managing superpower relations was the key to resolving all global conflicts extended the cold war conflation of nationalism and communism and failed its greatest test in Vietnam. The Nixon-Kissinger foreign policy favored aggressive protection of U.S. access to key strategic and economic resources at the expense of democratic governments and movements. The administration supported military dictatorship in Pakistan in its war with India and its genocide in Bangladesh. Nixon supported the right wing dictatorship of Portugal in its colonial war in Angola, and backed white supremacist governments of southern Africa. Nixon and Kissinger also directed CIA support for the bloody 1973 military coup that overthrew Salvador Allende, the democratically elected Socialist president of Chile. The coup, led by General Augusto

Pinochet, killed more than 3,000, including Allende himself. Pinochet's military dictatorship, marked by detention, torture, and murder, lasted until 1990.

Debating U.S. Power

Nixon's use of executive power led to demands for transparency and congressional oversight. The War Powers Act (1973), passed over Nixon's veto, called for congressional authorization of the president's deployment of the armed forces. After a series of revelations, including the U.S. Army surveillance of civilians and covert CIA activities reported by Seymour Hersh in 1975, a Senate Select Committee on Intelligence Activities chaired by Senator Frank Church (D-Idaho) unearthed extensive information on covert intelligence and counterinsurgency programs, including FBI domestic surveillance and CIA operations, plots to assassinate foreign leaders ordered by presidents, and a shared CIA-FBI program involving the surveillance of the mail of American citizens. The Church Committee inspired regulatory restraints, including an executive ban on U.S.-sanctioned assassinations of foreign leaders. In addition, the Federal Intelligence Surveillance Act (FISA) established court procedures and oversight for surveillance of foreign intelligence agents. The Church Committee's efforts to impose limits on the CIA and executive authority were strongly resisted by President Gerald Ford's advisors, including Kissinger and Donald Rumsfeld.

The fact that Congress never debated, voted on, or declared an official U.S. war in Vietnam meant that its financing was concealed from public oversight. The high cost of the war led to the "stagflation" and economic crisis of the 1970s, unveiling longer patterns of global interdependence. The 1973 oil embargo led by the Organization of Petroleum Exporting Countries, the cartel of oil-producing nations, unmasked America's dependence on foreign oil. The triple shocks of the Vietnam War, Watergate, and the oil crisis revealed the Western Fordist industrial economy to be in precipitous decline, with shrinking social welfare benefits for workers in Western industrial societies and the rise of new transnational corporations and financial institutions with rapidly diminishing accountability to states and nations. The long-term U.S. economic dependence on the extraction of raw materials in dangerous and exploitative conditions may not have been apparent to most Americans, but the loss of 500,000 auto jobs between 1978 and 1982, leading to widespread hardship, was highly visible.

Popular discontent at the failure in Vietnam, economic troubles, and the exposure of government improprieties led to the election of Georgia Democrat Jimmy Carter to the presidency in 1978. Carter advocated U.S. foreign policy guided by concern for human rights and urged Americans to accept limits to the easy access to resources that many had taken for granted. Leading by example, Carter promoted energy conservation as a means of reducing America's dependence on foreign oil. Carter's challenges to the American public provoked a backlash. And to many, Carter appeared generally inept at foreign policy, powerless to stop the erosion of the gains of détente and the escalation of the cold war as the Soviets invaded Afghanistan and stepped up support for leftist governments and opposition groups. In 1979 the Iranian Revolution sent the U.S.-backed shah into exile, creating a vacuum filled by the Islamic cleric Ayatollah Ruholla Khomeini. When young Iranian militants seized 52 U.S. diplomats as hostages, Carter staged a military rescue mission that failed. While Carter brokered the hostages' release before the end of his term, the 444-day national ordeal had doomed his reelection campaign.

A Supernova Burning Brightest at the Moment of Its Demise: The Last Years of the Cold War

Republican Ronald Reagan ran on two simple premises: getting the "monkey of government" off people's back and restoring U.S. might and right. Although Reagan ran against big government, his administration increased military spending while scaling back the welfare state.

During the 1980s, with the nation deeply divided over U.S. foreign policy, the Reagan administration accelerated the cold war, particularly through support of anti-Communist counterinsurgencies in Latin America. Through the continuing and new proxy wars of the 1980s, the Reagan administration supported right-wing insurgencies in El Salvador and Nicaragua. When the Boland Amendment blocked Reagan's support of the contras in Nicaragua, the White House, led by National Security Council staff member Lieutenant Oliver L. North, secretly funneled support to the contras as they sought to overthrow the democratically elected Sandinistas. The disclosure of North's "shadow government" led to the Iran-Contra Affair, in which North diverted to the contras the proceeds of arms sales to moderates in Iran in exchange for the release of Americans held hostage there.

Ironically, as a president who presided over a dramatic escalation of the cold war, Reagan ended his second term benefiting from Soviet Premier Mikhail Gorbachev's campaign of Glasnost and Perestroika—political openness and economic reform—and the formal dissolution of the Soviet Union in 1991. The collapse of the Soviet Union and the fall of Communist governments in the Eastern Bloc states led to profound changes in global politics. While activists demanded a "peace dividend" of investment in domestic social programs, in 1989 one commentator, Francis Fukuyama, proclaimed "the end of history" marked by the universal triumph of Western liberal democracy and the demise of all ideological alternatives. Many U.S. policy makers shared Fukuyama's thesis and believed that the fall of Communist states vindicated the values of free-market capitalism. But this triumphalist view of the cold war mitigated against an examination of failed policies on all sides of the conflict. Many have tended to view present dangers with nostalgia for the supposed stability of the cold war era. But one cannot neatly classify the wars and challenges of the twenty-first century as those of a distinct post–cold war moment with entirely new dynamics. State and nonstate wars, the U.S. occupation of Iraq, political violence in Africa, and the "war on terror" all suggest the limitations of Fukuyama's bipolar cold war perspective.

The Reagan administration opposed the Soviet occupation of Afghanistan by supporting the anti-Soviet Mujahadeen fighters in that country (including Osama bin Laden). Reagan also enlisted Iraq and its dictator Saddam Hussein as an ally against Iran after the overthrow of the shah of Iran. The arming of Africa and the Middle East by the United States and Soviet Union, and the dubious alliances between western powers and third world "strongmen," contributed to continued instability in Africa and later electoral victories of leftist governments in Latin America, including those of Brazil, Venezuela, and Bolivia. The alliance with Pakistan in the "war on terror" was part of a longer history of U.S. military support for Pakistan that reaches back to partition and U.S hostility toward India and its nonaligned foreign policy.

Cold War Continuities and the War on Terror

The George W. Bush administration's responses to the terrorist attacks of September 11, 2001, and the U.S. invasion and occupation of Iraq not only marked a return to the government secrecy of the cold war but also deployed U.S. armed forces in the region where the United States first engaged in cold war–era covert operations. Some of the ardent cold warriors of the Reagan era, including Elliot Abrams, Donald Rumsfeld, and Dick Cheney, resurfaced in the administration of George W. Bush, implementing their "ends justify the means" vision of unchecked executive power in the pursuit of war and intelligence gathering. The publication of photographs taken by U.S. troops engaging in the torture of detainees in the Abu Ghraib prison in Iraq sparked public outrage and congressional scrutiny. Further investigations revealed that despite widespread opposition within the administration itself; from members of Congress in both parties; and from people within the Justice Department, the State Department, and the CIA, a small but powerful group led by Vice President Dick Cheney extended a network of secret prisons and secret torture unprecedented in U.S. history in its scope and disregard for both the U.S. Constitution and international law.

In a sense, every presidential election since the end of U.S. participation in the Vietnam War has served as a referendum on American foreign policy and America's place in the world. The crises of the early twenty-first century suggest that the country has yet to overcome the institutionalized patterns of secrecy and lack of democratic accountability established in the early cold war years. Many have argued that such patterns have profoundly damaged democratic institutions within the United States. For many citizens and elected officials, the use of torture, the erosion of civil liberties, and widespread electoral fraud of the 2000 and 2004 elections called into question the legitimacy of the electoral system, the basic functioning of procedural democracy, and the survival of the Constitution. Some hoped that the severity of the crisis would present a historic opportunity to restore transparency and democratic accountability, and to rethink U.S. foreign policy, the country's dependence on global resources, and the future of the United States in a multilateral world.

See also anticommunism; globalization; immigration policy; war and politics.

FURTHER READING. Thomas Borstelmann, *The Cold War and the Color Line*, 2003; Mahmood Mamdani, *Good Muslim, Bad Muslim: The Cold War and Roots of Terror*, 2004; Elaine Tyler May, *Homeward Bound: American Families in the Cold War Era*, 1988; Jane Mayer, *The Dark Side: The Inside Story of How the War on Terror Turned into a War on American Ideals*, 2008; Frances Stoner Saunders, *The Cultural Cold War: The CIA and the World of Arts and Letters*, 1999; David F. Schmitz, *The United States and Right Wing Dictatorships, 1965–1989*, 2006; Robert Vitalis, *America's Kingdom: Mythmaking on the Saudi Oil Frontier*, 2007; Penny Von Eschen, *Race against Empire: Black Americans and Anticolonialism*, 1997; Idem, *Satchmo Blows Up the World: Jazz Ambassadors Play the Cold War*, 2004; Odd Arne Westad, *The Global Cold War and the Making of Our Times*, 2005.

PENNY M. VON ESCHEN

gender and sexuality

Debates over gender and sexuality have been central to American politics since the days of the Founding Fathers. At stake have been conflicting definitions of men's and women's proper roles, both in the family and in relation to state and nation. These disputes are significant, in part, for their enduring rhetorical appeal: few politicians have sought to depict themselves as "antifamily," while many have criticized their male opponents as weak and effeminate or, conversely, violent and piratical. In a deeper sense, recurring conflicts over public policy—over the outcome of politics—have also had crucial gender dimensions. Over two centuries, the accepted model of American family life moved from a patriarchal model to one centered on domesticity and women's indirect moral influence, then gradually, in the twentieth century, toward an egalitarian ideal. Political parties and movements not only responded to these long-term shifts, they helped articulate and advance them.

The centrality of aggressive masculinity in U.S. empire building has had a critical impact on the nation's politics at many junctures, from at least the 1840s through the cold war. Masculine "toughness" has served as a potent rallying cry for military mobilization and, at moments of crisis, has proven difficult for both male and female peace advocates to counter. Consistently, calls for manliness have been racially charged, a phenomenon that has had clear domestic racial parallels in, for example, the era of "Redemption," when Southern white supremacists called upon white men to overthrow Reconstruction by armed force, in the name of protecting white womanhood. Women, meanwhile, have steadily gained a place within party organizations and electoral campaigns beginning as early as the antebellum era. But women remain a minority among convention delegates, candidates, and decision makers. Exclusion from power has prompted politically active women to develop a rich array of extrapartisan strategies and organizations. Both inside and outside the parties, women have often cultivated a politics of moral zeal that has drawn upon domestic ideology, perceptions of female purity and selflessness, and women's very real status as political outsiders.

The Revolution and Its Aftermath

The American Revolution, grounded in an Enlightenment vision of human equality, opened new possibilities for both men and women in politics. The victory of the new United States established the world's first modern republic, with political power vested in the individual citizen. Americans viewed voters'

"civic virtue" as crucial for the nation's survival. Though the vast majority of Americans considered citizenship a male prerogative, prominent thinkers like Judith Sargent Murray argued that American women had a special role to play in promoting civic virtue. As "republican mothers," they should educate themselves and take an interest in political affairs, in order to raise their sons to be virtuous citizens and their daughters to become republican mothers in the next generation.

With suffrage confined at first to property-holding white men (except for a brief extension of the franchise to propertied women in New Jersey), the very core of American politics lay in a gentlemen's code of honor. Within that code, hierarchies of wealth, family connections, and reputation pitted men against one another. Early American politics relied on personal networks of friendship, obligation, and gossip. When a man's honor was attacked, political duels were not uncommon. While a few women became partisan writers and editors, most who exercised political influence did so informally, through social networks. As parties developed, the more elite-based Federalists proved particularly welcoming to female participation in campaign work. While Democratic-Republicans achieved a more radical vision in class terms, granting full citizenship rights to nonpropertied men by the 1820s, they were hostile to women's participation. The fading of Revolutionary radicalism and the Federalist Party's demise caused women's place in politics to decline by the 1810s.

Militant Manhood in the Antebellum Era

The election of Andrew Jackson in 1828 ushered in a vibrant era of mass-based party politics. Drawing first on Jackson's public persona as a military hero and aggressive Indian fighter, Democrats celebrated a "white man's democracy" with overt gender dimensions as well as racial ones: they defended the authority of white men over all dependents in their households, including wives, children, bound laborers, and slaves. Patriarchal manhood helped unite Democrats across class and regional lines and informed the party's small-government stance. Consistently, Democrats attacked "paternalistic" government policies as intrusions on the rights of white male citizens. During the Jacksonian era, when most states extended suffrage to all white men, politicians gradually began to cultivate a folksy style and depict themselves as "men of the people." Slaveholding complicated this pattern in the South, where political power continued to be equated with mastery, and thus to some extent with wealth. In a region that disciplined labor through direct, brutal violence rather than through the exigencies of survival through wage work, duels and physical violence persisted longer than in the North.

In the meantime, a powerful domestic ideology began to emerge in the growing northern cities and factory towns. Increasingly, prosperous urban men worked outside the home, while wives and mothers, responsible for a domestic space that had allegedly been stripped of its productive role, came to be seen as conservators of morality and noncommercial values. For men, domesticity prescribed temperance, self-control, and deference to womanly moral influence. Political conflicts over such issues emerged as early as 1828, when Jackson's opponents caricatured him as a violent man, prey to the vices of lust and liquor, and alleged that he had seduced his wife Rachel into bigamy. After Rachel's death, Jackson's opponents lamented that she could no longer "control the violence of his temper" or serve as a "restraining and benign influence" over the new president. Domesticity quickly spread beyond the northern urban middle classes to many other sectors of American society. It filtered into politics, predominantly through the vehicles of the Whig and Republican parties, and it is hard to overemphasize its significance in American politics thereafter. Seeking to build a "benevolent empire" for reform, Whigs embraced an ideal of manly restraint and a cautious acceptance of indirect female influence in the public sphere. Domesticity had overt class dimensions: Whigs criticized undisciplined, poor men who allegedly drank, brawled, and failed to support their families. By the late 1840s, such critiques included a strong streak of anti-Irish prejudice. The Democrats, meanwhile, championed working-class manhood and largely opposed and ridiculed female political participation.

By the 1840s and 1850s, race and gender became intertwined in an array of political issues, as Americans debated Manifest Destiny and the seizure of lands from native peoples. Democrats, in particular, justified military aggression through appeals to manhood, urging "Anglo-Saxon" men to seek their destinies on the frontier and in Latin America. Such arguments had special appeal for Southerners, who sought to expand the empire of slavery, and for white working-class men, many of whom were losing ground in the new commercial economy. On the other hand, proponents of masculine restraint and self-control, who tended to be Whigs, deplored violent conquest and criticized expansionists as bullies and pirates.

Gendered conflicts between an aggressive, racialized manhood on the Democratic side and restrained manhood and domesticity among their opponents also played a central role in debates over slavery. Radical abolitionists, strongly committed to domesticity, emphasized slavery's perversion of both white and black family life. The Liberty Party and Free Soil Party carried these ideas into the electoral arena, with female editors playing a major role in shaping arguments against slavery. While Free Soil men depicted themselves as moderate compromisers who merely sought to prevent the extension of slavery into federal territories, Free Soil women took the role of moral crusaders: outsiders demanding immediate, unconditional abolition. At the same time, the most radical abolitionists began to call for equal rights for women. These women's rights abolitionists began to move beyond domesticity, critiquing its glorification of "women's sphere" and arguing that female citizens had not only a right but a duty to act as public speakers, writers, and voters.

In gender terms, meanwhile, the new Republican Party of the 1850s inherited and expanded the Whigs' passion for domesticity. Republican leaders drew on the gendered rhetoric of Free Soil men, for example, to oppose extension of slavery into the territories. In some areas, Republicans also attacked immigrant men for their supposed violence and intemperance, arguments that were also made in the 1850s by the short-lived American (or Know-Nothing) Party. Across the North, Midwest, and West, Republicans vigorously attacked the Mormon practice of plural marriage. The party's first presidential candidate, John Frémont, was hailed as "Jessie's choice" because his young and attractive wife, Jessie Benton Frémont, was rumored to have antislavery sympathies. Republicans simultaneously denounced Frémont's opponent, James Buchanan, as an aging bachelor and possibly a homosexual.

From Domesticity to Imperialism

During and after the Civil War, the rise to power of the Republican Party brought a revolution in many aspects of national politics, including gendered political values. As part of their commitment to expanded government power, Republicans vested manhood in the state rather than in the authority of autonomous, patriarchal heads of household, as Democrats had done. Party leaders and rank-and-file members celebrated both Union victory and emancipation as defeats for a violent, tyrannical aristocracy of slaveholders. Though few yet conceived of a modern welfare state, they did lay the foundations for that development in a modest "breadwinner" state. For example, Republicans provided generous Union pensions to widows and disabled Union veterans, and after 1890 to all Union veterans, in legislation that modestly prefigured Social Security. Republicans also defended their economic policies—especially high protective tariffs—on the grounds that they extended domesticity to millions of Americans, helping working-class breadwinners earn a family wage to support their wives and children.

Republicans sought to extend or enforce domesticity among African Americans and native peoples, viewing male breadwinning and female domesticity as the keys to "race uplift" and civilization. Many freedmen and freedwomen in fact embraced domesticity, and African American editors and political leaders preached the gospel of homemaking for women and temperance and self-discipline for men. The late nineteenth century thus represented a kind of apex of political domesticity, exemplified by such models of hearthside happiness as First Lady Lucy Webb Hayes, a temperance advocate who was widely viewed as the force behind her husband's ban on liquor at the White House. The term *first lady* itself, as a semiofficial title for the president's wife, came into use near the end of the Civil War, a sign of the increasing symbolic importance of presidents' wives and families.

But the patriarchal manhood of the antebellum era did not remain defeated after the Civil War, and by 1900 Republicans also proved susceptible to its appeal. It reemerged most obviously in the South, as ex-Confederates and their allies engineered the violent overthrow of Reconstruction. In so doing, they appealed directly to white men in gendered terms, claiming falsely that enfranchised black men were responsible for an epidemic of rape against white women. The extension of voting rights to African American men was frequently cited as the alleged cause of interracial rape, suggesting the continued political and psychological link that many men drew between voting, sexuality, and men's control over their female dependents. (Several historians have observed that the struggle over "long ballots" versus "short ballots" in this era had phallic overtones; party loyalists who organized campaign pole raisings celebrated the rapidity with which they raised their poles, and they often accused opponents of not being able to raise their poles or failing to keep them "in an upright position.")

"Martial manhood" also reemerged in the Spanish-American War, especially in the figure of Theodore Roosevelt. Yet, departing from the antebellum model of martial manhood, turn-of-the-century imperialists also gave prominent attention to the role of white women as civilizers. They argued that inferior races needed to see the example set by white Christian wives and mothers, in order to adopt domesticity and uplift themselves. Such arguments were advanced not only by government agents in the U.S.-occupied Philippines but on Indian reservations, where missionaries and agents tried to force Native Americans to conform to the model of male breadwinning and female domesticity.

Progressive Politics

The era of Republican dominance paved the way for many other uses of domesticity in politics. The mantle of moral and economic reform passed first to the Prohibition and Populist parties, both of which called for women's political rights while appealing for Americans to "protect the home" by increasing government intervention in the economy. Proposals to protect, support, or supplement family incomes abounded between the Civil War and the New Deal, especially during the Progressive Era. These were often championed by coalitions of politically active women who appealed to their maternal roles as justification to engage in "municipal housekeeping." After the Civil War, these powerful grassroots women's movements became fixtures in national politics. The most popular, the Woman's Christian Temperance Union (WCTU), counted over a million members at its peak and advanced an explicitly nativist, Christian agenda with its appeal for women to work for "God and Home and Native Land." Despite its initial focus on liquor, the WCTU undertook an array of reform activities, from soup kitchens to the creation of kindergartens; its charismatic leader, Frances Willard, became a strong ally of labor and advocate for the eight-hour workday.

Between 1865 and 1920, women's clubs and missionary societies joined the chorus of female-led groups active in politics. Such groups succeeded, for example, in getting legislators to raise the age of sexual consent in many states, which had been as low as 10 years of age in 14 states and 7 in Delaware. They also helped pass laws to restrict women's working hours and grant mothers' pensions for "deserving" women who found themselves bereft of a breadwinner. Reformers succeeded in adding a Women's Bureau and Children's Bureau to the national Department of Labor. The broad scope of these agencies' work is suggested by the mandate Congress gave the Children's Bureau upon its creation in 1912. The bureau was instructed to investigate child labor and working conditions and to make recommendations on "infant mortality, the birth-rate, orphanages, juvenile courts, desertion, dangerous occupations, and accidents and diseases of children."

The woman suffrage movement, still small at the end of the Civil War, flourished in the Gilded Age and Progressive Era. Women began voting in some western states and territories as early as 1869, and by the early 1910s, most women in states west of the Mississippi had achieved full suffrage. By that same decade, suffrage had become a mainstream cause with widespread support across class and regional lines. The exception, unsurprisingly, was in the South, where suffragists made little headway even when they argued that white women's votes would help sustain white supremacy. When the federal woman's suffrage amendment achieved ratification in 1921, it did so with the support of only one legislature in an ex-Confederate state—that of Tennessee.

The Progressive Era thus offered new opportunities for women in the public sphere, including full voting rights, but it also vividly demonstrated the limits of women's power, especially on subjects such as foreign policy, where calls to martial manhood still had a powerful appeal. When the United States entered World War I, proponents of war mobilization fiercely attacked women who worked for disarmament and arbitration through groups like the Woman's Peace Party. (Theodore Roosevelt, still on the national scene, declared that the place for such women was "in China—or by preference in a harem—and not in the United States.") At the same time, reformers who appealed for government action on the basis of motherhood and domesticity reinscribed the very outsider status that made it hard for women to implement laws in the first place.

Breadwinners and Consumers

With the passage of national woman suffrage after World War I, candidates at all levels faced new pressures to tailor their appeals to both women and men. Anxious party leaders began including women more fully in their organizations and worked for passage of national Prohibition. In cities like Chicago, African American women who had worked for racial justice used their new clout as voters to bring pressure for change. Many candidates appealed to women as housekeepers and shoppers. Herbert Hoover, who had coordinated domestic conservation and food aid during and after World War I appealed directly to female voters. In the 1928 campaign, Republicans recruited "Hoover Hostesses" who invited friends into their homes to hear Hoover's radio campaign speeches.

But equality in voting and representation proved elusive despite the achievement of suffrage. Though women accounted for over half the U.S. population, their voting turnout was low and did not exceed 50 percent until 1980. Those women who did vote were, despite suffragists' hopes, divided along geographic, economic, racial, and religious lines. Advancement of women's rights suffered a serious blow in the 1920s in struggles over the first proposed equal rights amendment (ERA). Progressive reformers who had achieved gender-based protective labor legislation limiting women's working hours, helped defeat the ERA, fearing it would undermine such laws. Meanwhile, despite suffrage, many states refused to permit women to serve on juries, and an array of other discriminatory practices remained legal.

The onset of the Great Depression intensified conflicts between the old ideal of domesticity and the realities of an increasingly urban and industrial society. It became obvious in the 1930s that, through no fault of their own, millions of men could not support their families. The election of Franklin D. Roosevelt in 1932 firmly established Democrats as the party of government activism, and reformers who sought to protect workers and families gained tremendous clout. The substantial welfare initiatives of the New Deal followed earlier gendered patterns. Programs that aided breadwinners, such as Social Security, provided direct entitlements, while mothers who sought government support had to prove their "moral fitness" to receive aid. Gender and racial exclusion moved, again, in tandem: at the insistence of southern Democrats in Congress, the Social Security Act excluded agricultural and domestic workers, who in the South were overwhelmingly black. African American women thus suffered a double exclusion, both from welfare programs that denied coverage to most black workers and from a "breadwinner model" of government aid that refused to recognize women as wage earners with equal status to men.

Despite Americans' continued faith in the domestic ideal and their widespread blindness or indifference to the needs of wage-earning women, industrialization and urbanization kept issues of sexuality and gender in the political arena. The percentage of married women working outside the home rose to 30 percent by 1960, as women entered the paid workforce in enormous numbers. Urban neighborhoods witnessed a day-care crisis. Unequal pay, gender-segregated job markets, glass ceilings, and sexual harassment gained increasing recognition among working women but negligible attention from political leaders. Instead, Americans publicly celebrated women's "return to domesticity" during the baby boom era. But the number of women working outside the home, including married women with children, continued to climb, and grassroots women's organizations, along with their allies in government agencies like the Women's Bureau, kept alive issues of women's rights.

These efforts culminated in President John F. Kennedy's appointment of a Presidential Commission on the Status of Women (PCSW), which played a high-profile role in calling attention to women's issues between 1961 and 1963. The commission, chaired by Eleanor Roosevelt, considered numerous legislative measures to enhance women's rights. Members of the PCSW, galvanized by their experiences on the commission, played a central role in the creation of the National Organization of Women (NOW) in 1966. In the meantime, when Congress debated the 1964 Civil Rights Act, a conservative southern representative tried to derail the bill by adding language that prohibited discrimination on the basis of sex; the law passed with this language included, providing a basis for federal prosecution of both race- and gender-based discrimination. By the time NOW came into existence, most states had created their own commissions to investigate such issues as domestic violence, unequal pay, female poverty, and sexual harassment in the workplace.

The Cold War, Civil Rights, and Feminism

Urgent domestic needs had been long neglected, in part, because the United States had remained on a war footing after the defeat of Germany and Japan. Fear of Soviet power abroad and communism at home had a chilling effect on both political dissent and domestic reform. Cold war politicians, like their predecessors who advocated aggressive exploits on the frontier or overseas, perceived a need for "toughness" in both their public stances and internal decision making. Belligerent anticommunism ran as a connecting thread through a long line of otherwise diverse administrations during the cold war, from that of Harry Truman through those of Richard Nixon and Ronald Reagan. Like the Woman's Peace

Party of the 1910s, antinuclear and peace advocates regularly faced charges that they were effeminate or "soft." The civil rights movement offered a strikingly different model of manhood, centered on courageous nonviolence. The movement achieved early successes in the 1960s through appeals to Christian theology and principled civil disobedience. By late in that decade, however, poverty and growing anger among younger, poor urban African Americans, as well as growing unrest over American militarism abroad, led to the rise of a militant Black Power stance. Black Power advocates critiqued America's involvement in Vietnam, identified with postcolonial black nationalists in Africa, and urged black men to engage in aggressive self-defense. Like earlier African American men, civil rights leaders struggled between seeking access to the masculine prerogatives of American politics and critiquing the highly racialized prerogatives and distinctive models of political manhood.

By the 1970s, national grassroots coalitions were pressuring politicians to address the long-deferred issues of day care and workplace equity as well as sex education, contraception, and abortion rights. Despite the political uses of domesticity, a majority of American families had never achieved the "domestic ideal" of a male breadwinner whose earnings enabled his wife to refrain from productive labor. Feminists proposed sweeping measures to address poverty and the needs of families with children, as well as a vigorous campaign to end discrimination against women. Feminism faced its most crucial public test over the second equal rights amendment, which failed to win ratification by a margin of only one state. Opponents of the ERA rallied on the basis of domesticity, arguing that the ERA would weaken families, undermine women's central identities as wives and mothers, usher in a military draft for women, and lead to such unacceptable innovations as unisex toilets.

In the decades that followed, preservation of traditional gender roles remained a central concern of many conservatives who feared a breakdown of older social mores, especially domesticity. These arguments played a critical role in the rise of the New Right, but the women who joined this movement were hardly united. One group, libertarian women, emphasized the protection of individual rights; like patriarchal Democrats of the antebellum years, they mistrusted government intrusion, but they applied that argument to themselves as women, rather than to men's prerogatives as household heads. The second group, evangelical or social conservatives, focused on enforcing traditional marriage laws, ending abortion, and opposing homosexuality. In some ways these two groups recapitulated gendered political divisions that had emerged in the 1920s, over whether government should protect women or leave them alone, and whether "free markets" or antidiscrimination laws would best ensure women a level playing field.

Probably due to the impact of feminism by the 1980s, social scientists began to identify for the first time differences in the voting patterns of women and men. The so-called gender gap actually appeared less often on obviously gender-based issues such as abortion and marriage law and more often on issues of social welfare and national security. From the Reagan era onward, more women than men favored antipoverty initiatives, opposed the death penalty, and sought reductions in military spending. Another long-term change was the growing success of the gay rights movement. Men and women who identified themselves as gay or lesbian not only gained increasing public acceptance, but they began to run as political candidates and win. While the prospect of gay marriage provoked many of the same anxieties and debates that domesticity did in an earlier era, the emergence of gays and lesbians into public life was one of the clear triumphs of the movement for equal gender rights.

Certain themes have emerged repeatedly in the history of gender and sexuality in American politics. On the domestic front, the parties that have sought more robust government intervention in the economy (Federalists, Whigs, and Republicans), and in the twentieth century enhanced social welfare programs (most often Democrats), have tended to seek women's support and participation more eagerly than their opponents—whichever party has been, at that moment, resisting the growth of domestic government power. Meanwhile, defense of the patriarchal family model has consistently been associated with white supremacy and racialized nationalism in both domestic and foreign affairs. With a few notable exceptions, parties that have advocated an aggressive foreign policy have tended to be those less committed to government intervention in the domestic economy and on behalf of social welfare.

This perhaps explains why the cause of women's rights advanced rapidly after the Civil War and World War I, when women demonstrated that, in times of extreme national crisis, they had shown courage and patriotism—a kind of "martial womanhood." In both the Civil War and the civil rights era, proto-feminism and feminism emerged out of grassroots movements for racial justice, and the party more sympathetic to African American rights has tended to show more sympathy to women's rights, as well.

At critical junctures, women have mobilized on behalf of political causes ranging from "free soil" to Prohibition and for and against equal rights amendments in the 1920s and 1970s. As longtime outsiders to formal politics, women frequently adopted the stance of moral crusaders, from Free Soil women's call for immediate and unconditional abolition, to the temperance movement's call to "protect the home." Since 1920, tensions between women's new status as partial insiders and the power they have long drawn from domesticity and their "outsider" status have continued to resonate among both feminists and neoconservatives. Calls to preserve domesticity and "protect the home" still arise in debates over such issues as day-care funding, abortion, and gay marriage.

Among the many implications of gender and sexuality in American politics is the continuing struggle of public officials and their families to reconcile the realities of political life with the domestic ideal handed down from the nineteenth century. Americans still want their political leaders to display normative gender behavior: no unmarried man became a major presidential candidate in the twentieth century, and marital fidelity has long been a presumed measure of a president's character. The public exposure and resignation of New Jersey governor James McGreevy in 2004, when he revealed that he was gay, suggest that old assumptions had not vanished. Even when polls indicate that a majority of voters are not concerned about private sexual matters—as in the celebrated case of President Bill Clinton's affair with White House intern Monica Lewinsky—such perceived misbehavior remains a powerful tool for opponents when it becomes publicly known.

Meanwhile, political wives are pressured to demonstrate proper wifely and motherly qualities, and Americans continue to show profound ambivalence over the appropriate role for First Ladies. Eleanor Roosevelt served as a transitional figure, playing an influential part in internal debates during her husband's presidency but achieving her greatest political impact after his death. Later First Ladies who took outspoken political positions included Betty Ford, who supported the equal rights amendment and was widely admired for her frankness about her personal struggles with drug dependency and breast cancer. Former First Lady Hillary Rodham Clinton pursued a political career, as a U.S. Senator and then as a leading presidential candidate in 2008.

During the Ohio Democratic primary in the 2008 race, Hillary Clinton's campaign produced an advertisement depicting a sleeping white woman and her children, imperiled by an unseen force. Viewers were invited to ask themselves, when such dangers loomed, who should answer the "red telephone" in the White House. It is both ironic and significant that such an ad—a staple of cold war political campaigns, in its appeal to both executive toughness and white female vulnerability—should resurface in the campaign of the first woman to become a major presidential candidate. The episode, like others in recent years, suggests that gender and sexuality, as well as the underlying hopes and fears on which those constructions rest, will continue to play a central role in both political campaigns and public policy.

See also homosexuality; race and politics; woman suffrage.

FURTHER READING. Rebecca Edwards, *Angels in the Machinery: Gender in American Party Politics from the Civil War to the Progressive Era*, 1997; Joanne B. Freeman, *Affairs of Honor: National Politics in the New Republic*, 2001; Linda Gordon, *Pitied but Not Entitled: Single Mothers and* the History of Welfare, 1890–1935, 1995; Amy S. Greenberg, *Manifest Manhood and the Antebellum American Empire*, 2005; Melanie Gustafson, Kristie Miller, and Elisabeth Israels Perry, *We Have Come to Stay: American Women and Political Parties, 1880–1960*, 1999; Kirstin Hoganson, *Fighting for American Manhood: How Gender Politics Provoked the Spanish-American and Philippine-American Wars*, 1998; Robyn Muncy, *Creating a Female Dominion in American Reform, 1890–1935*, 1991; Michael D. Pierson, *Free Hearts and Free Homes: Gender and American Antislavery Politics*, 2003; Catherine E. Rymph, *Republican Women: Feminism and Conservatism from Suffrage through the Rise of the New Right*, 2006; Louise A. Tilly and Patricia Gurin, eds., *Women, Politics, and Change*, 1990; Elizabeth R. Varon, *We Mean to Be Counted: White Women and Politics in Antebellum Virginia*, 1998; Lois Duke Whitaker, *Voting the Gender Gap*, 2007; Rosemarie Zagarri, *Revolutionary Backlash: Women and Politics in the Early American Republic*, 2007.

REBECCA EDWARDS

Gilded Age, 1870s–90s

The Gilded Age, a descriptive label for the period from the end of Reconstruction to the start of Theodore Roosevelt's presidency in 1901, came into general use during the middle of the twentieth century. In political history these decades carry a pejorative connotation that has persisted despite much scholarly work on the complexity of the period's public life. Broadly speaking, the Gilded Age is regarded as a time when politicians failed to engage the issues of industrialism, urbanization, and agricultural discontent. Instead, so the argument runs, Republicans and Democrats wasted their time and energies on such peripheral issues as the protective tariff and civil service. By 1901, according to this interpretation, the United States was no better off than it had been when Ulysses S. Grant left the presidency in March 1877.

Historical scholarship has challenged this pejorative view of the late nineteenth century, but the stereotype remains powerful. The term *Gilded Age* itself derives from a novel of the same name by Mark Twain and Charles Dudley Warner, published in 1873, that depicted economic life as a speculative excess where fraud and chicanery abounded. More than half a century later, the phrase seemed to capture the essence of the period between Reconstruction and the emergence of the reform spirit called progressivism.

Americans faced daunting challenges in the fast-moving era of the Gilded Age. The United States industrialized, became more urban, settled the West, and expanded overseas. Racism marred the way citizens interacted. Workers, farmers, and city dwellers faced major inequities and struggled to exist on meager salaries. Ample social problems demanded solutions, and politicians struggled to find useful answers to new dilemmas.

But the Gilded Age, in the minds of its critics, had a larger failing. The men in power and the electorate who supported them should have known that future generations would criticize the record of those in authority between 1877 and 1901. The centers of power in the society should have adopted the reform measures of the New Deal half a century before the presidency of Franklin D. Roosevelt. This lack of prescience about the direction of American life created, with deliberation and malice, an unjust society at the end of the nineteenth century.

There is much that is unhistorical about these generalizations. By projecting twentieth-century assumptions back to nineteenth-century Americans, critics have imposed on the Gilded Age the impossible task of correctly predicting the future. In the process, the real contributions and limitations of national politics during these years have become obscured. Much of the way Americans view politics now stems from the evolution of public life after 1877. When the polemical aspects of the era are removed, the political importance of the Gilded Age can be judged with more accuracy.

The Electoral System

The most salient features of this time period were the high degree of voter involvement in politics and the relatively even balance of the two major parties. The figures indicating a substantial level of electoral participation are striking. Turnout in state, congressional, and presidential contests far exceeded what was common during the twentieth century. In 1896, when William McKinley ran against William Jennings Bryan, some 78 percent of eligible voters outside of the South cast ballots. Of course, African Americans, Hispanics, and women were denied the right to vote throughout much of the country. (It is worth noting that African American men had been granted the right to vote by the Fifteenth Amendment, but that right had been stripped away in a campaign of terror and disenfranchisement culminating in the 1890s. Those African American men who managed to continue to vote through the end of the century almost all supported the Republican Party.) Nonetheless, the extent of voter mobilization during the 1870s, 1880s, and 1890s reflected the strong partisan identifications among Americans.

Within this political universe, Democrats and Republicans battled on equal terms. Neither party achieved an absolute majority in the four contests for president from 1880 through 1892. On Capitol Hill, it was rare for a single party to control both houses (though it did occur on four occasions from 1874 to 1896). In the battleground states of the Middle West, elections often turned on a small percentage of the vote, with the outcome hinging on which party's adherents came to the polls on voting day. Participants at the time believed that the fate of the nation turned on the outcome of voting.

During the Gilded Age, Americans debated with passion an issue that had dominated domestic politics for most of the century: the extent to which

government should promote the growth of the economy. The question of regulating the economy and society through government action was not yet a mainstream concern. But the two major parties took positions on the questions at odds with modern perceptions of their ideological differences.

The Republicans were then the party of an active government. They believed that protective tariffs to develop native industries could diffuse the benefits of a prosperous economy through all levels of society. In the arguments of men such as James G. Blaine and William McKinley, the tariff fused economic appeals with nationalistic pride. The doctrine served the interests of the business community, but protectionism also appealed to labor, small business, and farmers who faced competition from Mexico and Canada. For some adherents, the tariff acquired an almost religious significance.

Republican activism carried over into other areas of economic and cultural life. The party favored subsidies to railroads, land grants to farmers, and federal support of public education. It put in place an elaborate, expanding, and expensive program of pension payments to Civil War veterans and their families. Pensions became one of the largest expenditures of the federal government. While there were regional differences about money and banking policy, the Grand Old Party (as it became known) endorsed the gold standard and opposed inflation. On social issues, most Republicans favored laws against entertainment on the Sabbath, supported the prohibition of alcohol, and sought to have public schools teach all students in English. These positions aroused opposition from immigrant groups. Above all, the Republicans saw themselves as the party of progress and the Democrats as advocates of obstruction.

The Democratic Party (or the Democracy as it was often called) still believed in the core principles that Thomas Jefferson and Andrew Jackson had advanced earlier in the century. The smaller the government and the closer to the people in its operations the better off the country would be. Democrats stood for the rights of the states against the power of the federal government. Since the South was a major bastion of Democratic strength in elections, the ability of white Southerners to maintain racial supremacy was a key element in the appeal of "the party of the fathers." Democrats also supported a smaller government role in the cultural issues of Prohibition and Sunday closings that Republicans favored.

On the tariff, the Democrats identified with the interest of consumers, doubted the constitutionality of customs duties, and stood for freer trade. The most that the party would accept as an official doctrine was "a tariff for revenue only." Since Democrats wanted the government to remain small, in practice, they believed that tariff rates should be as low as possible. Some elements of the party in industrial states favored a degree of protection. Nonetheless, the tariff issue represented a major dividing line between the parties throughout these years.

With the Civil War and Reconstruction a tangible memory for most politicians, the two parties reflected the lingering consequences of that conflict. The Republicans stood for political equality for African Americans, although their fervor for that position waned as the years passed. By the 1890s, many members of the Grand Old Party (GOP) believed that the racial issues of the war and its aftermath should be muted or abandoned.

The Democrats, on the other hand, were unapologetic champions of white domination in the South. A belief in states' rights and the rule of white men was a quasi-religious conviction among southern Democrats. These party members tolerated the Fourteenth and the Fifteenth Amendment because they had no choice. In their true convictions, they believed that all such legislation should be repealed. As a result, African Americans had at most a marginal position in the public life of the Gilded Age.

Both major parties felt the pressure from reform elements in society to professionalize politics and reduce the impact of partisanship. Calls for changing the ways in which public officials were chosen for government offices became known as civil service reform, and the idea gained popularity in the 1870s and early 1880s. The Pendleton Civil Service Act of 1883 began the process of diminishing the role of parties in the appointment process.

The Party Battles

Stalemate characterized the first ten years of the Gilded Age. The Republicans elected Rutherford B. Hayes in 1876 over Samuel J. Tilden in a disputed contest that reflected the even balance between the parties nationally. Hayes served one reasonably successful term and was succeeded by James A. Garfield, who carried the Republicans to victory in 1880. The president's assassination in the summer of 1881 put Chester Alan Arthur in the White House. After 24 years of successful elections to office, the Republicans were losing their ascendancy in national politics. They nominated their most popular leader, James G. Blaine, in 1884. But the taint of scandal that surrounded him put their chances in serious doubt.

The Democrats selected the governor of New York, Grover Cleveland, to oppose Blaine. In an election notable for its emphasis on personal issues, such as whether Cleveland had fathered an illegitimate child and whether Blaine was corrupt, the Democrats won in a close vote. Cleveland served a solid if undistinguished term and faced uncertain prospects for reelection. In late 1887 he made the issue of the tariff the centerpiece of his impending campaign. Delighted Republicans jumped at the opportunity to wage a presidential race on that topic. Making a unified campaign, the GOP nominated Benjamin Harrison of Indiana, who proved effective in delivering the party's message. Although Cleveland prevailed in the popular vote, Harrison triumphed in the electoral count. The Republicans also controlled both houses of Congress.

In the two years that followed, the Republicans implemented a program of governmental activism with the passage of the McKinley Tariff to raise rates and the Sherman Antitrust Act. Their effort to protect the voting rights of African Americans in the South through a federal elections bill failed in the face of opposition from the Democrats. Most voters turned against the Republicans and repudiated their initiatives.

By the election of 1890, long-simmering discontent among farmers in the South and West produced a third party in the congressional races. Low crop prices and a heavy burden of debt impelled many agrarians to support candidates for the Farmers Alliance and the People's, or Populist, Party. These candidates spoke out for inflating the currency by coining silver into money on an equal basis with gold. This strategy would, they believed, raise prices and make debts easier to pay back. Congress had enacted the Sherman Silver Purchase Act in 1890 to provide support for silver, but Populists argued that the measure did too little to address the problem. In the 1890 elections, the Republicans lost control of the House as the Democrats and the Populists made impressive gains.

The resurgent Democrats continued their success in the presidential contest in 1892. Cleveland won an impressive victory over Harrison, and his party now controlled both the House and the Senate. The Populists had fielded their own presidential ticket, which carried four states in the West. The new third party had produced significant gains in its effort to become a viable alternative to the Republicans and Democrats.

Economic hard times hit in the spring of 1893 with a panic in the banking sector that soon spread across the nation. Cleveland called Congress into special session in August to repeal the Sherman Silver Purchase Act, which the president blamed for the economic crisis. He achieved his goal but split his party into two warring factions. The situation then deteriorated further for the Democrats. Beyond the monetary issue, the Pullman Strike in the summer of 1894 and other examples of social unrest during hard economic times gave both the Republicans and the Populists an opportunity to capitalize on pervasive discontent.

The congressional elections in 1894 brought dramatic Republican gains. The Democrats lost more than 100 seats in the House and lost their majority. The GOP also gained in the Senate. The Populists saw their vote totals rise to a limited extent. The outcome in 1894 signaled a probable Republican victory in 1896 and also suggested that the appeal of the People's Party was limited to the agrarian regions of the South and West. As it turned out, the Republican triumphs in 1894 proved enduring, and the party held control of the House for the next 16 years.

The political climax of Gilded Age politics came in the presidential election of 1896 in the race between William McKinley for the Republicans and William Jennings Bryan for the Democrats and Populists. Bryan stood for free silver; McKinley defended the gold standard. Voter turnout was very high in the North and Middle West. McKinley won a decisive victory with a nearly 600,000-ballot majority in the popular vote. The stalemated politics that had characterized the Gilded Age had come to an end with the Republicans triumphant.

During McKinley's administration, the nation went to war with Spain over the independence of Cuba, and, in the process, acquired the Philippine Islands in 1898. This overseas adventure sparked debate about the nation's future as an imperial power. At the same time, with the return of prosperity after 1897, concerned citizens argued that the growth of big business required expanded government power to regulate the economy. There was a sense that, for all the material achievements of the late nineteenth century, political and economic reform had become imperative. In 1900, McKinley's second victory over Bryan confirmed Republican dominance, even as there were calls for lowering the tariff, addressing the power of big business, and redressing social injustice. In waging the war with Spain and administering the colonial empire that ensued, McKinley became the first president to administer the United States as a world power. His assassination in September 1901 brought his vice president, Theodore Roosevelt, to the White House. Soon there was talk of "progressive" change and a need to depart from the ideas and policies of the late nineteenth century. The reputation of the Gilded Age sagged and has never recovered.

What did these decades mean for American politics? The intensive voter interest in elections of that time has never been repeated. The issues of the tariff and money have survived in other forms but have never again dominated political discourse. Debate over the role of government in regulating the economy has supplanted the controversy over promoting national growth. The processes of choosing candidates became more democratic with woman suffrage, direct election of U.S. senators, and procedural changes such as the direct primary, the initiative, and referendum. In many respects, the Gilded Age seems a lost world in national politics.

But, the period had a significant legacy. Racial segregation, established after the Civil War and solidified in the Gilded Age, took years to address and still shapes voter attitudes in the South. The power of corporations to influence policy and finance politics has survived all attempts at reform. The two-party system that emerged intact from the late nineteenth century still precludes alternatives. While the Gilded Age may seem a receding era in the political history of the United States, its impact endures.

See also banking policy; Democratic Party, 1860–96; economy and politics, 1860–1920; elections and electoral eras; Republican Party to 1896; Spanish-American War and Filipino Insurrection; tariffs and politics.

FURTHER READING. Charles W. Calhoun, *Conceiving a New Republic: The Republican Party and the Southern Question, 1869–1900*, 2006; Charles W. Calhoun, ed., *The Gilded Age: Perspectives on the Origins of Modern America*, 2nd ed., 2007; Robert W. Cherny, *American Politics in the Gilded Age, 1868–1900*, 1997; Rebecca Edwards, *New Spirits: Americans in the Gilded Age, 1865–1905*, 2006; Lewis L. Gould, *The Presidency of William McKinley*, 1980; H. Wayne Morgan, *From Hayes to McKinley: National Party Politics, 1877–1896*, 1969; H. Wayne Morgan, ed., *The Gilded Age: A Reappraisal*, Revised ed., 1970; Mark Wahlgren Summers, *The Gilded Age or, the Hazard of New Functions*, 1997; Robert Wiebe, *The Search for Order, 1877–1920*, 1967; R. Hal Williams, *Years of Decision: American Politics in the 1890s*, 1993.

LEWIS L. GOULD

globalization

Globalization refers to the process of increasing the ease with which goods, people, and money move across borders or, in the more precise language of economic historians, the integration of international markets in commodities, labor, and capital. These markets depend on the support of political institutions, and in turn, the operation of these markets affects political institutions—often in such a way as to create a backlash against globalization.

Trade, migration, and investment across borders characterize the modern world, and so *globalization* becomes a useful term of historical analysis only when we can identify a marked increase or decrease in the volume of these international movements during a particular period and track its effects on politics and culture. We might therefore say that globalization meaningfully shaped the Islamic civilizations of the eleventh-century Near East, whose peoples traded spices, silver, and silks to Europe; salt and swords to Africa; and horses and gold to Asia while a similar claim about the eleventh-century civilizations of North America would necessarily rest on much slimmer evidence. So globalization waxes and wanes, and we need to speak as precisely as we can about its magnitude and local influence if we wish meaningfully to discuss its effects.

The Americas first became important to the history of globalization during the era of European discovery, when the flow of riches from the New World affected the shape of the Old World. Despite the early establishment of Iberian empires, the Dutch benefited greatly from colonial loot because their cities served as entrepôts for colonial trade. Likewise, this early process of globalization dramatically affected the peoples of the Americas, who died off in quantity from war and disease, which frequently go along with globalization. Moreover, the arrival of European goods, including horses, swine, and firearms, turned the Americas into what the historian Alfred Crosby identifies as ecological "Neo-Europes," easing the transplantation of European institutions and politics into a new hemisphere.

With the establishment of European colonies in the Americas and the extension of European trade with Africa, the triangle trade in slaves from Africa, finished goods from Europe, and staple products from America—particularly sugar, tobacco, and cotton—altered the arrangement of power on all three continents. The trade fueled British textile mills, enabling the consequent technological innovation so important to the industrial revolution. It accounted for the forcible removal of around 11 million Africans over the two and a half centuries of the Atlantic slave trade. It built up the wealth and power of the southern colonies (later states) in the United States, permitting Virginia to dominate the new nation's politics and planting the seeds of national self-immolation in the contradictions between racism and the republic's professions of devotion to liberty. And these contradictions in turn provided the earliest instance of international skepticism about the new nation's claims to virtue, often repeated in subsequent centuries: How, the British ministry-approved *Answer to the Declaration* asked, could rights be inalienable if "denied to 'these wretched beings'"?

After the American Revolution, the wars of the French Revolution and their attendant blockades and embargoes slowed the processes of globalization considerably and for a period of some decades. Britain and France tried to keep each other from getting precious metals out of the New World. In the United States, the Nonimportation, Embargo, and Nonintercourse Acts of 1807–9 cut off trade to the belligerent nations. Thus barred from importing finished European goods, Americans began to manufacture ever more products for themselves. And as U.S. factory owners grew used to doing business without foreign competition, they began to lobby Congress—often successfully—for continued protective tariff legislation. Protectionism prevailed in Europe as well, with French manufacturing interests lobbying for tariffs and the Corn Laws largely keeping grain imports out of Britain until 1846.

A new era of increased globalization opened in the middle of the nineteenth century. Technological improvements pushed steamship costs downward, making it cheaper to ship goods and for people to book passage over oceans; the Suez Canal opened; new populations of migrants began streaming into the New World; and the lure of profitable expansion into frontiers drew investment from overseas, into the canals, roads, and railroads of new nations.

This early era of international investment in the development of America's frontier ended poorly owing to the peculiar federal structure of the United States. Although Albert Gallatin and other statesmen of the early republic envisioned the government in Washington paying for a transportation network tying the country together, their plan foundered on the objections of Southerners and others already eager to promote the doctrine of state sovereignty. And so the states borrowed money—often from international investors—to build out their frontiers, each in their own way. Initial success, as in the case of the Erie Canal, which paid off its millions of dollars in debts to London, yielded to later failure; by 1841, eight states plus the territory of Florida were in default. "U.S. security" became a byword for worthless paper and fodder for jokes in England.

The institution of federalism coupled with the defaults had long-term consequences, including the rise of powerful American banks on Wall Street. As economic historians Lance Davis and Robert Gallman note, "Governments with good reputations, Australia and Canada for example, did not have to draw on the services of international financial syndicates to underwrite and market their bonds. In the case of the United States such syndicates were required." These syndicates included American banks with close ties to European banks, including Morgans, Brown Brothers, and Kuhn Loeb, and these American banks learned to intervene where American states had failed.

Meanwhile, the many unanticipated consequences of globalization included the chain of events by which the Irish potato famine helped spark the U.S. Civil War. Together with the failed revolutions of 1848, the famine spurred Irish migration to the United States. The nativist reaction and the short-lived American Party split and destroyed the Whig Party, making way for the rise of the antislavery Republican Party. The subsequent election of a Republican president, Abraham Lincoln, led to the secession of the South. Global trade scuttled the hopes of southern leaders that they could bring European countries to heel by choking off their supply of cotton; instead, other cotton-producing nations, like Egypt and India, increased their output and scuttled the thesis that American cotton was king of world trade.

The war itself contributed further to the rise of American investment banks. As is often the case during war, the effects of globalization diminished: few people wished to migrate to a country at war; blockades stopped trade; international investors shied away from betting on the bonds of a nation that might, in a few years' time, have vanished or at least have repudiated the obligations of a war government. American financial syndicates also learned from this experience how to raise money and how to cloak themselves in patriotism: as Jay Cooke romantically insisted, just as the war freed slaves from their masters, so might it free Americans from the punishing "whip" of foreign capitalists.

Americans emerged from their wrenching sectional crisis into a new era of global openness.

Money, people, and goods moved with increased freedom across borders. American banking syndicates channeled British pounds into railroads and ranches in the West, nearly unrestricted immigration let European laborers find better wages in American cities than they could at home, and—even considering the continuing pressure for tariff legislation—international trade ensured that the prices of commodities like wheat, bacon, coal, coffee, copper, cotton, hides, pig iron, tin, and wool converged in markets around the world. As open borders begot a global similarity in the basic stuff of commerce, the midcentury predictions of Karl Marx and Friedrich Engels in the *Communist Manifesto* appeared to be coming true: "The need of a constantly expanding market for its products chases the bourgeoisie over the whole surface of the globe. It must nestle everywhere, settle everywhere, establish connexions everywhere. . . . [W]e have intercourse in every direction, universal inter-dependence of nations. . . . National one-sidedness and narrow-mindedness become more and more impossible . . ."

Marx and Engels turned out to be wrong about this; globalization did not proceed smoothly to create cosmopolitan cultures but rather swiftly begot a backlash against it that, translated into policies, encouraged national one-sidedness. As Engels himself later observed with respect to the American working class, great diversity on the shop floor tended to suppress class consciousness and increase tribal feeling. With increasing energy and effectiveness, Americans lobbied for restrictions on immigration, securing the first of a series of Chinese Exclusion Acts in 1882. The second such act, in 1892, instituted a presumption of illegal presence for persons of Chinese appearance and began the process of requiring documentation for apparently racially different peoples. For decades, various groups including the American Federation of Labor lobbied for the restriction of immigrants by class background, finally getting a literacy test—coupled with further Asian exclusions—passed over President Woodrow Wilson's veto in 1917. The economic crisis after World War I strengthened the forces opposing globalization, leading to a rise in tariffs and immigration quotas. This early postwar legislation saw firmer establishment in the Fordney-McCumber and Smoot-Hawley tariffs, as well as the National Origins Act of 1924. In addition, various states passed laws to prevent foreign ownership of land.

Apart from these efforts to shut globalization down and thus shield themselves from foreign competition, Americans reacted in other, less predictable ways. Some moved out of the cities of the East, where immigration from Europe was heaviest, into the new states of the West. The more such internal migrants the new states had, the more likely their voters were to support the Socialist Party of Eugene Debs. In American cities that became home to larger populations of immigrants, taxpayers responded with policies of self-defense, both cultural (through increased support for public education) and material (through increased support for public health programs). As a result of such investments, particularly in water purification and waste treatment, the American city finally became a healthier place to live than the countryside. Thus, the fear of immigration and its consequences sometimes led indirectly to an overall improvement in well-being.

American policies that slowed globalization in the 1920s must often shoulder at least part of the blame for the Great Depression. The British economist John Maynard Keynes predicted in his 1919 forecast of the *Economic Consequences of the Peace* that a massive depression would result from the failure to reassemble the nineteenth-century global economy, noting that the world before the war, in allowing movement across borders, had helped relieve economic pressures: the unemployed could seek opportunity elsewhere rather than stay and suffer. But, Keynes noted, the postwar settlement included "no provisions for the economic rehabilitation of Europe . . . or to adjust the systems of the Old World and the New." American unwillingness to help rehabilitate Europe or adjust relations to the Old World might not have mattered, had the Old World, in working off wartime debt, not depended so thoroughly on continued loans from the New World. When those loans began to dry up in 1928–29, countries around the world slid into depression, and the United States followed.

During the Depression, globalization stood at low ebb. Immigrants had no place worth going, even if laws permitted them entry. Nations traded within autonomous blocs. Each country acted, as Franklin Roosevelt wrote in his telegram to the London Economic Conference of 1933, as if "[t]he sound internal economic system of a Nation is a greater factor in its well being" than its international economic relations. Barring a few gestures like the Anglo-American Trade agreement of 1938, the United States carried out its New Deal with (as Isaiah Berlin observed about FDR) "a minimum of relationship with the outside world." During this period of relative isolation from the international arena, the Democratic Party put through some of America's most clearly class-conscious legislation. It is possible, some historians suggest, that this correlation represents causation: with immigration restriction (and its attendant racial hierarchy) firmly in place, it might have been easier to appeal to class solidarity.

After World War II, the United States, with some help from Keynes, worked with its allies to create the system the world had lacked in 1919, to rehabilitate Europe and keep the Old World and the New World in balance. The Bretton Woods institutions—the World Bank and the International Monetary Fund—especially as augmented by the European Recovery Program (or Marshall Plan), of 1947 created a degree of international stability while allowing countries the freedom to set their own economic policies. They created the conditions for Americans to invest in the reconstruction and development of the war-torn world and promote the sale of U.S.-manufactured goods overseas. They enabled the growth of trade worldwide, and of non-Communist labor movements in industrialized countries. During these institutions' peak period of operations, per-capita incomes around the globe grew more than under previous or subsequent frameworks for international economic affairs.

In the later twentieth century, a new era of accelerated globalization began. After the Hart-Celler immigration act of 1965, the United States saw renewed immigration from non-European nations, and a new wave of anti-immigrant sentiment to greet it. The United States ran large current-account deficits, buying imports from developing countries, contributing to the growth of manufacturing in the historically poorer parts of the world. Central banks in the developing world—particularly in Asia—increasingly financed the U.S. deficit by buying federal debt. Under such circumstances, Americans could afford, at least for the near term, to save little money and run large government deficits. In the early twenty-first century, the dollar dropped in value, creating an incentive for individual investors in American debt to stop financing the United States, even as collectively their interest lay with continued support for the dollar. In the early years of the new century, there came a growing perception that as the Euro grew more attractive as an alternative investment, the long-standing arrangement might fail, and America might shift away from its historically fortunate place in the center of the global economy. While the world has generally favored the United States with a willingness to invest capital and labor within American borders, these inflows have depended more on historical incident—including reigning American policy and circumstances in the rest of the world—than on general laws.

See also banking policy; economy and politics; federalism; tariffs and politics.

FURTHER READING. Michael D. Bordo, Alan M. Taylor, and Jeffrey G. Williamson, "Introduction," in *Globalization in Historical Perspective*, edited by Michael D. Bordo, Alan M. Taylor, and Jeffrey G. Williamson, 1–10, 2003; Alfred W. Crosby, *Ecological Imperialism: The Biological Expansion of Europe, 900–1900*, 1993; Lance Edwin Davis and Robert E. Gallman, *Evolving Financial Markets and International Capital Flows: Britain, the Americas, and Australia, 1870–1914*, 2001; J. Bradford DeLong and Barry Eichengreen, "The Marshall Plan: History's Most Successful Structural Adjustment Programme," in *Postwar Economic Reconstruction and Lessons for the East Today*, edited by Rüdiger Dornbusch, Wilhelm Nölling, and Richard Layard, 189–230, 1993; Barry Eichengreen, *Global Imbalances and the Lessons of Bretton Woods*, 2007; Ronald Findlay and Kevin H. O'Rourke, "Commodity Market Integration, 1500–2000," in *Globalization in Historical Perspective*, edited by Michael D. Bordo, Alan M. Taylor, and Jeffrey G. Williamson, 13–62, 2003; Idem, *Power and Plenty: Trade, War, and the World Economy in the Second Millennium*, 2007; Gary Gerstle, *American Crucible: Race and Nation in the Twentieth Century*, 2001; Kevin H. O'Rourke and Jeffrey G. Williamson, *Globalization and History: The Evolution of a Nineteenth-Century Atlantic Economy*, 1999; Eric Rauchway, *Blessed among Nations: How the World Made America*, 2006.

ERIC RAUCHWAY

Great Depression

See economy and politics, 1920–45; New Deal Era, 1932–52.

Great Plains, the

The Great Plains—a relatively flat, semiarid region along the east side of the Rocky Mountains—include the eastern parts of Montana, Wyoming, Colorado, and New Mexico, and the western parts of North and South Dakota, Nebraska, Kansas, Oklahoma, and Texas. Though none of these states are wholly in the Great Plains, all will be treated here.

Before Europeans arrived on the Great Plains, politics there were largely local and focused on authority within bands or tribes of Native Americans and with disputes between or among them. Europeans introduced new dimensions. After the United States acquired the plains in the early nineteenth century, politics there evolved into a regional variant of national patterns. The most distinctive aspects of plains politics appeared between 1890 and World War II, in the form first of Populism and then of progressivism. Since 1945 plains politics have moved close to national patterns.

Before Assertion of U.S. Authority

Before the arrival of Europeans and horses, most indigenous people of the plains lived in villages along streams and rivers. A few were nomadic hunters. For most, the basic political unit was the village. The Pawnee, for example, consisted of four independent bands that formed a confederation, with the internal organization of each band based on villages. Village chiefs met periodically as a tribal council.

Patterns of leadership differed among the plains tribes, but the position of village chief was typically hereditary within certain lineages. A chief's actual authority rested on his ability to resolve disputes, deal with traders, distribute goods, allocate farmlands, and negotiate with outsiders. Those from other families could exercise other forms of leadership. Thus, a village might have one or a few main chiefs, several shamans, and separate leaders for war, buffalo-hunting expeditions, and men's societies. Occasionally, a woman became a shaman, but women did not hold other political roles.

In 1541 Vasquez Coronado and his men became the first Europeans to venture onto the Great Plains. French explorers and traders entered the plains by the early eighteenth century. The Treaty of Paris (1763) gave Spain title to the region between the Mississippi River and the crest of the Rocky Mountains, but in 1800 Spain sold to France the entire Louisiana country north of the Red River. Neither Spain nor France sought to exercise real political authority on the plains.

Though few Europeans came to the region, plains Indians experienced the consequences of European settlement elsewhere. The Pueblo Revolt of 1680, in what became New Mexico, brought horses to the plains. European settlers along the Atlantic traded with nearby Indian peoples, providing guns and manufactured goods. As European expansion pushed Indian people west, they, in turn, armed with guns and iron weapons, pressured the peoples into whose lands they moved. Such pressures bred conflict between plains tribes and westward migrating tribes and among plains tribes themselves. For example several Lakota bands and the Cheyenne moved onto the plains in the late eighteenth century, became nomadic, and came into conflict with the Crows. Horses and guns combined to populate the plains with bands of nomadic buffalo hunters.

Among nomadic plains tribes, the basic political unit was the band, comparable to the villages of the sedentary peoples. The band traveled, camped, hunted, and made war as a unit. Political leadership was typically fluid, with different leaders for different purposes, none with supreme authority. Bands of the same tribe or closely related tribes came together for religious ceremonies, councils, hunting, or war. As of about 1800, for example, the Cheyenne had ten bands, each with four chiefs. All ten came together each spring, and the four chiefs of each band plus a few other elders formed a tribal council.

The experience of Sitting Bull (Tatanka Iyotake) provides both example and exception. In 1857, when Sitting Bull was about 26 years old, the Hunkpapa Lakota named him a war chief in recognition of his bravery and his victories over the Crows. He also gained a reputation as a holy man, given to prophetic visions. In 1869 Sitting Bull's supporters brought together a group of Lakotas and Cheyennes who named him to an unprecedented position: war chief of the Lakota nation. Given the fluidity of leadership among the Lakotas, however, not all Lakotas accepted this action.

After the United States purchased Louisiana from France in 1803, more explorers ventured onto the plains, notably the Lewis and Clark expedition of 1804–6, intended not only to explore but also to assert U.S. authority in the northern plains and lay claim to the region west of it. By the 1820s, the United States had planted small military posts along the Missouri River and had established a limited military presence on the plains. Federal policy makers considered the region a "permanent Indian frontier," however, and political authority there still rested with villages, bands, and tribes. Eastern tribes were moved to the eastern parts of the plains states beginning in the 1830s.

Through the annexation of Texas (1845), war with Mexico (1846–48), and the Treaty of Guadalupe Hidalgo (1848), the United States acquired territories that included the southern plains. The new state of Texas claimed most of the area, but the residents of New Mexico contested that claim. In 1850 Congress attempted to resolve these and other issues through an elaborate compromise that, among other provisions, set the western boundary of Texas and established territorial government for New Mexico.

The Compromise of 1850 left most of the plains unorganized, even though they formed a vital part of the major land routes to California, Oregon, and New Mexico territories. Stephen Douglas, senator from Illinois, seeking to have a railroad built from Chicago to the Pacific, wanted to establish territorial organization on the plains, but Southerners opposed territorial status anywhere the Missouri Compromise of 1820 banned slavery. Douglas crafted a compromise in 1854, creating Nebraska and Kansas Territories, with each to decide whether to permit slavery. The Kansas-Nebraska Act provoked a great national debate over slavery, precipitated the emergence of the Republican Party, and contributed significantly to a major national political realignment. The organization of Kansas, in turn, initiated a miniature civil war.

From the Civil War to 1890

Kansas became a state in 1861, Nebraska in 1867, and Colorado in 1876. Beginning in 1861, Congress promoted the rapid economic development of the West through land grants to railroads, the Homestead Act, and similar distributive programs. And Congress created Dakota and Colorado Territories in 1861, Montana Territory in 1864, and Wyoming Territory in 1868.

Late into the nineteenth century, much of the plains remained territories, due to sparse population and sometimes also to congressional jockeying for partisan advantage. Montana and the Dakotas became states only in 1889 and Wyoming in 1890. Oklahoma and New Mexico remained territories into the twentieth century. Residents of territories could not elect their governors or participate in presidential elections, and their delegates to Congress commanded little attention. Political patronage often was allocated in faraway Washington. Some historians have suggested that party organizations and loyalties were stunted by the low stakes in territorial politics.

In the plains states, partisanship developed along regional lines. Kansas, Nebraska, and Colorado were initially Republican strongholds, often under the leadership of Union veterans who constantly reminded voters that Republicans promoted western economic development. Party politics in Texas followed from that state's participation in the Confederacy, as westward-moving southern whites assisted the Democrats in redeeming the state from Republican rule in 1873 and keeping it securely Democratic until the 1960s.

Advocates of woman suffrage were active on the northern and central plains. In 1867 Kansas became the first state to vote on the issue, but its voters rejected suffrage. The first session of the Wyoming territorial legislature, in 1869, approved suffrage for women—the first state or territory to take such a step and one of the first political entities in the world to do so. Some attributed that decision to Wyoming males' expectation that woman suffrage would attract more women to the plains but others have pointed to diligent lobbying by suffrage advocates. Wyoming achieved statehood in 1890 and became the first state to fully enfranchise women. Colorado, in 1893, became the first state whose male voters approved woman suffrage. Despite repeated agitation and several referenda, the other plains states continued to reject suffrage until the 1910s, even as women won statewide elective office in North Dakota and Oklahoma.

With or without suffrage, plains women helped to lead reform movements, especially Prohibition. In 1878 Kansans banned the importation, manufacture, and sale of alcohol, but the law was widely violated. Despite referenda in several other plains states, before 1907 laws banning liquor passed only in North and South Dakota, and South Dakotans soon reversed that decision.

On the northern plains, the political battle over alcohol reflected broader ethno-religious differences. Old-stock Americans and immigrants affiliated with the Methodist, Baptist, Congregational, or Presbyterian denominations, along with Norwegian and Swedish immigrants and their offspring, usually condemned as sinful any use of alcohol, and often censured gambling and dancing as well. Catholics and many German Protestants found no sin in a stein of beer, a dance, or a lottery. Thus, referenda on Prohibition and woman suffrage (closely connected in many voters' minds) often turned on the ethno-cultural values of voters. Identification with the Democratic Party and Republican Party on the northern plains often had ethnic dimensions, for northern Democrats adamantly opposed Prohibition and courted German and Irish voters. Republicans usually tried to duck the issue but sometimes issued cautious endorsements.

While Prohibition formed a highly divisive political issue on the northern plains, Texas politics sometimes revolved around race. Texas experienced radical reconstruction beginning in 1867, and a coalition of black and white Republicans held control until 1873, when the Democrats won a gubernatorial election characterized by widespread fraud and intimidation of black voters. The Democrats then wrote a new state constitution, severely limiting the legislature but not disfranchising black voters.

In the plains states, as elsewhere, African Americans aligned themselves with the dominant Republicans. In Kansas and Nebraska, some received political patronage in return, and a few were elected to local or state office, including state auditor in Kansas. In Kansas and Nebraska, and later in Oklahoma Territory, black migrants from the South created all-black towns and exercised local political authority.

Only in New Mexico, in the late nineteenth and early twentieth centuries, did Mexican Americans exercise significant political power. There, the long-established *Hispano* communities (most not on the plains), along with the slow pace of in-migration by other groups, meant that Mexican culture dominated many areas. Voters elected Mexican Americans as local officials, territorial legislators, and territorial delegates. Mexican Americans also secured federal patronage posts, including territorial secretary and governor.

In the 1880s, Congress moved toward a new Indian policy with important implications for the plains. The Great Sioux Reservation, in Dakota Territory, was reduced in size in 1877 and broken into smaller units in 1889. Officials of the Bureau of Indian Affairs, committed to a policy of assimilation, sought to eliminate traditional practices, including structures of authority and governance. The Dawes Act of 1887 directed that reservations be divided among Indian families and the land be owned in severalty (i.e., individually). Remaining land was to be taken out of the reservation system.

On the southern plains, much of what is now Oklahoma became home to the "Five Civilized Tribes"—the Cherokee, Chickasaw, Choctaw, Creek, and Seminole—in the 1830s, when they were moved from their previous homes in the Southeast and were promised permanent reservations in the new territory. During the Civil War, some or all of these tribes in the new territory sided with the Confederacy and, as punishment, were deprived of their western lands. Those lands, in turn, became reservations for tribes from the southern plains. In 1890 Congress created Oklahoma Territory in the western part of what is now Oklahoma, leaving the eastern region as Indian Territory.

Populism and Silver

By the 1880s, political agitators on the plains were condemning both Republicans and Democrats for failing to counteract declining prices for farm products and to regulate railroad rates. Most such agitators were on the margins of politics, but not in Texas. John Reagan, a member of Congress from that state, consistently advocated regulation and contributed significantly to passage of the Interstate Commerce Act in 1886. James Hogg, Texas's attorney general and governor in the late 1880s and early 1890s, also built a following by attacking the railroads.

In 1890, in the central and northern plains states, new political parties emerged, claiming to speak for hard-pressed farmers and laborers. First organized as state parties, they came together as the People's Party, or Populists, in 1892. The new party called for federal action to restrict the great corporations that had developed since the Civil War. Those corporations, Populists argued, limited the economic opportunities and political rights of ordinary citizens. On the plains, Populists drew their greatest support from farmers on marginally productive land, often with large mortgages at high interest rates, for whom the prevailing deflation proved especially ruinous.

The Populists called for government ownership of the railroads; sweeping changes in federal monetary and banking policies, especially currency expansion to counteract deflation; structural reforms to make government more responsive to voters, including the secret ballot and the initiative and referendum; the eight-hour workday; a graduated income tax; and other reforms. Populists won election as local officials, state legislators, governors, and members of Congress. In most places in the central and northern plains states, the Democrats were reduced to a tiny third party and often threw their support behind Populist candidates. Such fusions brought gubernatorial victories in 1892 in Colorado, Kansas, and North Dakota, and in Nebraska in 1894.

In 1896 William Jennings Bryan, a Democrat from Nebraska, won the Democratic presidential nomination on a platform that stressed currency inflation through silver coinage and called for an income tax and other reforms. Most western Populists gave Bryan enthusiastic support, and he secured their party's nomination. Leading western Republicans broke with their party, formed the Silver Party (or Silver Republicans), and also nominated Bryan.

Bryan lost the presidency but did well throughout much of the West. The Populist Party and the Silver Republican Party survived only a few more years. For many former Populist voters, however, party loyalties seem to have significantly weakened. Republicans and Democrats were closely competitive in Nebraska, Colorado, and Montana over the next 20 years. Kansas and the Dakotas, however, usually voted Republican.

Racial issues became prominent in Texas politics in the 1890s, when the state's Populists made a strong appeal to black voters and, fusing with the Republicans, registered a strong vote for their gubernatorial candidate in 1896. Texas adopted a poll tax in 1902 but never followed other former Confederate states in creating a more elaborate set of legal or constitutional restrictions on black participation in politics. Texas Democrats accomplished much the same thing extralegally, however, by barring African Americans from Democratic primaries (and eventually writing that provision into law) and by coercing blacks who insisted on exercising the franchise.

Progressivism

Every plains state experienced progressive reform during the two decades before World War I, and those reforms significantly changed most state governments. George W. Norris, a Nebraska Republican, became an important national leader of progressivism, leading the "revolt against Cannonism"—a reduction in the powers of the Speaker of the House, then Joseph Cannon—in 1910 and continuing as a leading progressive in the U.S. Senate until 1943. Other plains progressives also drew national attention.

"Direct democracy"—efforts to increase the role of voters in the political process—flourished on the plains. In 1898 South Dakota Populists adopted the nation's first initiative and referendum process. Most plains states also adopted the initiative and referendum, though not through Populists' efforts. Other widely adopted direct-democracy reforms included the direct primary and recall. States adopted other structural reforms, including nonpartisan offices, limits on political parties, the merit system for appointing state employees, and rationalization of the structure of state government.

Plains progressives added new functions to state government as they promoted regulation of railroads and public utilities, abolition of child labor, employer liability and workers' compensation, and protections for consumers. Four states set up insurance funds for deposits in state-chartered banks. Under Republican governor Peter Norbeck (1917–21), South Dakota launched several state-owned enterprises, including a coal mine, cement plant, hail insurance fund, and hydroelectric plants. When Oklahoma became a state in 1907, its constitution included many progressive innovations, including restrictions on corporations, a graduated income tax, and the initiative and referendum. Oklahoma Democrats also enacted racial segregation and a literacy test aimed at disfranchising African American voters.

Renewed efforts by woman suffrage and temperance advocates finally brought victories. Kansas adopted woman suffrage in 1912 and Montana followed in 1914. In 1916 Montana elected the first woman to serve in the House of Representatives, Jeannette Rankin, a progressive Republican. South Dakotans and Oklahomans adopted woman suffrage in 1918. Oklahomans voted their state dry in 1907, and, by 1918, all the plains states but Texas had done the same.

Plains progressivism differed in important ways from progressivism in eastern states. Like other western progressives those on the plains were more likely to favor direct democracy, woman suffrage, and Prohibition than their eastern counterparts. Some, like Norbeck, promoted state-owned enterprise, especially those devoted to economic development. Other plains progressives were more isolationist regarding foreign policy.

In some plains states, groups to the left of the progressives attracted a following. In Oklahoma, the Socialist Party, espousing government ownership of key industries, won 21 percent of the vote for governor in 1914. Socialists developed strength elsewhere in the plains states, electing local officials in several places, but failed to win any office higher than state legislator. In North Dakota, Arthur C. Townley, a former socialist organizer, created the Nonpartisan League (NPL), which worked within the Republican Party to win the governorship in 1916 and the state legislature in 1919. They enacted much of its program, including a state-owned bank and terminal grain elevator.

World War I and the Depression

Rankin and Norris were among those in Congress who voted against the declaration of war in 1917. But throughout the plains, World War I stimulated intense patriotism, encouraged by the federal government, state Councils of Defense, and extragovernmental bodies. Suspicion, hostility, and sometimes vigilante action greeted those of German birth or descent, pacifists (including Mennonites, who were also of German ancestry), and radicals, especially the NPL, Socialists, and the Industrial Workers of the World.

The summer of 1919 brought racial conflict in several parts of the nation, as white mobs lynched African Americans or attacked black sections of cities. Three riots took place in Texas. In Longview a mob killed several people and burned buildings in the black section of town before National Guard troops arrived. In Omaha, Nebraska, some 4,000 whites intent on lynching a black man accused of raping a white woman attacked police and deputy sheriffs guarding the courthouse, set it on fire, nearly lynched the mayor, beat any black people they found on the streets, and finally lynched the accused man. Ultimately U.S. troops put down the riot. In 1921 Tulsa, Oklahoma, was the scene of the worst race riot in U.S. history. As in Omaha, the riot began with an effort to lynch a black man accused of assaulting a white woman. In Tulsa, however, a group of armed African Americans attempted to assist the sheriff, who was determined to prevent a lynching. A gun battle between blacks and whites left several dead. A white mob then attacked the black commercial and residential section of town, called Greenwood. African Americans fought back. Before the National Guard could arrive, an estimated 300 African Americans and 13 whites were killed. Greenwood was destroyed by fire—more than a thousand buildings worth nearly $2 million.

The war had created a huge demand for wheat and meat. At the end of the war, agricultural prices fell, initiating an agricultural depression that persisted when the rest of the economy began to roar with the prosperity of the 1920s. The economic distress of farmers contributed to the development of a congressional "farm bloc" in 1921. Members of Congress from both parties, including many from the plains states, joined to support regulation of stockyards and grain exchanges, exempting farm cooperatives from antitrust laws, and easing credit for farmers. Despite such efforts, the farm economy continued to slump.

In 1922 agricultural distress and reversals for organized labor, especially railroad workers, sparked political protests among farmers and workers. Organized through the Conference on Progressive Political Action (CPPA), protesting voters put Democrats into the governorship in several states and elected Burton K. Wheeler, a progressive Democrat from Montana, to the Senate. In 1924 the independent presidential candidacy of Robert La Follette drew significant support from plains farmers and organized labor. He failed to win any plains state but carried many counties across the northern and central plains.

In 1924 two plains states elected the nation's first female governors. In Wyoming the death of the incumbent shortly before the election led to the nomination and election of his widow, Nellie Tayloe Ross. Miriam A. "Ma" Ferguson won the governorship in Texas but was widely seen as a surrogate for her husband, James E. Ferguson, who was ineligible because he had been impeached from the office in 1917.

Ma Ferguson won the Texas Democratic primary over the opposition of the Ku Klux Klan. Anti-black, anti-Catholic, anti-Semitic, and anti-immigrant, the Klan presented itself as the defender of old-fashioned Protestant morality and became a significant force in plains politics. Klan-endorsed candidates won local and state offices across Colorado, Kansas, Oklahoma, and Texas in the early and mid-1920s. The Klan tried to influence elections elsewhere but its authority swiftly declined by the end of the decade.

The Depression that began in 1929 was a serious blow to farmers, who had not shared in the prosperity of the 1920s. Shortly after, drought turned large areas of the southern plains into the dust bowl. Political repercussions appeared in some plains states as early as 1930, when voters elected governors and senators who promised to solve their economic problems. In 1932 Franklin D. Roosevelt became the first Democrat to sweep every plains state. He also carried Democrats into Congress, statehouses, and state legislatures. In North Dakota, a revived NPL won control of the state government.

Roosevelt's New Deal addressed farmers' problems with the Agricultural Adjustment Act, which included provisions for paying farmers and stock growers to reduce production. Relief rolls, both state and federal, grew to include a quarter or a third of the population in some plains states, and sometimes two-thirds or more of those in dust bowl counties.

Other New Deal programs ranged from construction of schools and bridges to rural electrification, from tree planting and flood control to Social Security. One New Deal project, the Fort Peck Dam in Montana, was the largest earthen dam in the world when it was completed in 1939.

By the mid-1930s, several plains states had experienced efforts by Democratic governors and legislatures to create "Little New Deals," but most were modest and unimaginative. Nearly everywhere, governors and legislatures drastically cut state spending to provide property tax relief. Seeking alternatives to property taxes, several states enacted sales taxes or income taxes.

In a few instances in the 1930s, states went beyond budget cutting, tax reform, and participation in New Deal programs. In 1936 Colorado voters approved a pension program for those over 60; the program proved so costly it absorbed most of the new sales tax. In Nebraska, Senator Norris convinced voters in 1934 to amend the state constitution to create a unicameral, nonpartisan legislature. Norris also inspired the development of Nebraska's public power districts, most of which used federal funds to construct electrical generating and distribution systems. By 1945 the state's entire electrical power system was publicly owned.

The New Deal brought important changes to the governance of Indian reservations. Roosevelt appointed John Collier commissioner of Indian affairs. A long-time critic of previous federal Indian policies, Collier closed many boarding schools and ended efforts to suppress traditional religious practices. His "Indian New Deal" included as its centerpiece the Indian Reorganization Act (1934), which promised to end allotments, restore tribal ownership of unalloted lands, and encourage tribal self-government. Not all were persuaded of the value of the new approach, and some tribes rejected the reforms.

In 1936 Republicans nominated Alfred Landon of Kansas for president, but he was defeated in a Roosevelt landslide that continued Democratic dominance in most plains states. Soon after, however, leading Democrats, notably Burton Wheeler, became increasingly critical of Roosevelt. In 1938 and after, plains voters expressed their disaffection from the New Deal, as most of the northern plains states returned to the Republicans and the southern plains states turned to conservative Democrats.

The mid- and late 1930s saw isolationism at high tide on the northern plains. Senator Gerald Nye (Republican) of North Dakota led investigations into the munitions industry and sponsored neutrality legislation. After the 1941 attack on Pearl Harbor isolationism receded, but Senator William Langer of North Dakota (Republican and NPL), was one of the two senators who voted against joining the United Nations, and both North Dakota senators opposed the North Atlantic Treaty Organization.

Plains Politics since 1945

Prosperity returned to the plains during World War II. Then and after the war, liberals continued on the defensive in most places, as conservative Republicans held most governorships in northern and central plains states and equally conservative Democrats held those in Oklahoma and Texas. Except for Montana and sometimes North Dakota, the northern and central plains states usually sent conservative Republicans to represent them in Washington. Between the late 1950s and the 1980s, however, all the plains states moved toward more competitive two-party systems.

In the late 1950s the nation entered a recession. Economically distressed farmers and urban dwellers elected liberal Democrats in most northern and central plains states. By 1959 George McGovern of South Dakota, Quentin Burdick of North Dakota (elected following a fusion of the Democratic Party with the NPL in 1956), Gale McGee of Wyoming, and Mike Mansfield and Lee Metcalf of Montana made the northern plains appear to be a center of congressional liberalism. Since then, Montana and North Dakota have usually elected Democratic senators. South Dakota, Nebraska, and Colorado have been competitive in senate races, and Wyoming and Kansas have usually elected Republicans. All the northern plains states have been competitive for governor except South Dakota, which has usually elected Republicans. Underneath those highly visible offices, however, significant majorities of the voters of most northern and central plains states identified as Republicans, especially in the counties that are part of the Great Plains.

As Democrats won elections in northern and central plains states, Republicans made gains in the southern ones. In 1961 Texans sent a Republican, John Tower, to the U.S. Senate for the first time since Reconstruction, and Republicans have won both Texas Senate seats since 1990. In 1962 Henry Bellmon became the first Republican ever to win the Oklahoma governorship, and since then that office has often alternated between the parties. Republicans and Democrats also alternated winning senatorial contests in Oklahoma in the 1970s and 1980s; both Oklahoma Senate seats have gone Republican since 1992. Not until 1978 did a Republican, Bill Clements, win the Texas governorship. That office then alternated between the parties until 1994, when Republicans began a winning streak. New Mexico has been competitive for governor since the 1950s, and the two parties have won almost equal numbers of Senate contests.

The plains states usually voted Republican for president between 1952 and 2004. There have been only a few exceptions: New Mexico in 1960, 1992, 1996, and 2000; Texas in 1960, 1968, and 1976; and Colorado and Montana in 1992. In 2008, Colorado and New Mexico voted Democratic, and Montana and North Dakota were considered "battleground" states. Nebraska law provides that a candidate who carries a congressional district receives one electoral vote, and the candidate who carries the state wins two votes in addition to those earned in the congressional districts. In 2008, for the first time, this law resulted in Nebraska splitting its electoral votes when Barack Obama carried the second congressional district (Omaha and its suburbs to the south).

Republican gains in southern plains states, like Republican gains in the South more generally, came in part in response to Democratic support for civil rights. The civil rights movement had its most direct impact in the southern plains, even though *Brown v. Board of Education* (1954) concerned Topeka, Kansas. Earlier, the Supreme Court had struck down the Texas white primary law (1944) and had ordered Oklahoma and Texas to integrate their state graduate and professional schools (1950). There were, however, relatively few African Americans in most plains counties, so the direct political impact of the civil rights movement was more pronounced in the eastern, non-plains portions of those states. One important exception was Colorado, where Denver residents fought a brutal and occasionally violent battle over school integration between 1969 and 1974. Earlier, Latino veterans returning from World War II had organized the American GI Forum and the Mexican American Legal Defense and Education Fund. These groups took the lead in fighting discrimination against Latinos and made important gains.

The 1970s saw increased politicization of ethnic groups on the plains. In South Dakota, the American Indian Movement, first organized in Minneapolis in 1968, demanded equal treatment and autonomy and challenged existing tribal leadership. A confrontation at Wounded Knee in 1973 resulted in two deaths. In New Mexico a violent, but not deadly, confrontation in 1967 brought the end to the Alianza, a group seeking the return of land grants. In the early 1970s in Texas, Mexican Americans formed the Raza Unida party and won a number of local offices.

During the last quarter of the twentieth century, politics in several plains states achieved a greater measure of racial and gender diversity. New Mexicans, to be certain, have elected Mexican Americans throughout their history. In 1978 Nancy Landon Kassebaum of Kansas won the first of three terms in the U.S. Senate. That same year, Coloradians elected the nation's first black lieutenant governor since Reconstruction, and, in 1992, they sent Ben Nighthorse Campbell, an American Indian, to the U.S. Senate. Patricia Schroeder, member of Congress from Colorado, established a national reputation. In Nebraska in 1986, two women faced each other as the major party candidates for governor.

Throughout most of the Great Plains counties, net out-migration began after World War II and has persisted in most rural places. States consequently became more urban, though most cities were located on the fringe of the Great Plains. Local and state governments faced a variety of problems resulting from a diminishing population base, but education often drew the greatest attention. Declining population and increasing accreditation standards caught rural schools in their pincers. Although school consolidation often proved politically divisive, most plains states witnessed sharp reductions in the number of school districts—by 72 percent in Wyoming between 1952 and 1984 and by 67 percent in Nebraska between 1949 and 1965. In 2008, Arthur County, Nebraska, with an estimated population of 372, had fewer than 70 students in all grades in the entire county. In such places population decline has sometimes made it difficult to fill county and local offices.

Since the 1980s, preachers in evangelical Christian megachurches in such places as Wichita, Tulsa, and Colorado Springs have allied themselves closely with the Republicans and have pushed the party in those states toward the Christian Right by focusing on issues like abortion and gay rights. By the early twenty-first century, however, the evangelical tide within the region's Republican Party seemed to be receding. In Kansas between 1999 and 2007, the state board of education reversed itself repeatedly on the teaching of evolution in the public schools, as first one side then the other won majorities in elections for board members. In South Dakota in 2006, a referendum on a state law banning abortions voided the law by a margin of 52 to 48 percent, and a similar statewide vote in 2008 failed by a slightly larger margin.

The political history of the Great Plains has much in common with its surrounding regions. Many, even most, of its distinctive features are shared with other western or middle-western states. One feature, federal policies aimed at promoting economic development, has been common throughout much of the West. Populism, early approval of woman suffrage, and the western variety of progressivism were, perhaps, the most distinctive aspects of plains political development, but they were not unique to plains states. Populism and progressivism left most plains states with a legacy of direct democracy and a few plains states with state-owned enterprises. Populism and western progressivism, born of agricultural adversity and, in the 1920s at least, nurtured by a political alliance of farmers and labor, grew out of a social and economic situation now largely vanished. The substantial decline in the proportion of farmers and stock growers on the plains has reduced the potential base for such politics, and the emergence of an agribusiness attitude among many of the survivors seems to have given them a different political outlook.

The emergence of two-party competition throughout most of the plains states since the late 1950s suggests that plains political subcultures are being homogenized into larger national patterns. Similarly, the half-century pattern of support for most Republican presidential candidates throughout much of the plains suggests a blending into larger patterns of western politics. Finally, the decline in party loyalty in the East and South suggests that even that aspect of western politics is no longer unique.

See also Pacific Coast; populism; progressivism and the Progressive Era, 1890s–1920; race and politics; Rocky Mountain region; taxation; woman suffrage.

FURTHER READING. Norman D. Brown, *Hood, Bonnet, and Little Brown Jug: Texas Politics, 1921–1928*, 1984; Robert W. Cherny, *Populism, Progressivism, and the Transformation of Nebraska Politics, 1885–1915*, 1981; Gene Clanton, *Kansas Populism: Ideas and Men*, 1969; Chandler Davidson, *Race and Class in Texas Politics*, 1990; Juan Gómez-Quiñones, *Chicano Politics, Reality and Promise, 1940–1990*, 1990; Lewis L. Gould, *Progressives and Prohibitionists: Texas Democrats in the Wilson Era*, 1973; Paul Kleppner, "Politics without Parties: The Western States, 1900–1984," in *The Twentieth-Century West, Historical Interpretations*, edited by Gerald D. Nash and Richard W. Etulain, 317–21, 1989; Richard Lowitt, *The New Deal and the West*, 1984; Robert L. Morlan, *Political Prairie Fire: The Nonpartisan League, 1915–1922*, 1955; Theodore Saloutos and John D. Hicks, *Agricultural Discontent in the Middle West, 1900–1939*, 1951; James E. Wright, *The Politics of Populism: Dissent in Colorado*, 1974.

ROBERT W. CHERNY

health and illness

For much of American history, matters of disease prevention and health promotion were neither the concerns of the national government nor matters of political discourse. One of the critical tropes of American political history is the evolving sense of government authority and responsibility at the local, state, and federal levels for protecting society from disease and promoting individual and community health in the context of an increasingly pluralistic society. Government interventions in different eras have included quarantining the sick, conducting medical inspections of immigrants, sterilizing those defined as mentally defective, providing the public clean water and air, regulating the contents of food and drugs, seeking cures and therapies for disease through medical research and epidemiology, creating institutions for the care of the ill, and preventing disease through inoculation and education. Politicians rarely spoke of such matters until the early years of the Progressive Era, when the pressures of urbanization, industrialization, and immigration threatened to undermine the health and vitality of American citizens and stymie local economic development. In the decades to come, and especially following World War II, battling disease and improving the public's health and access to medical care increasingly became federal priorities and the stuff of national political debate.

What Makes People Sick?

Governments have long acted to protect their communities from foreign diseases. Regulations in medieval Venice required returning seamen who were ill to remain isolated from their neighbors for 40 days. The Italian word for 40, *quarentenaria*, was the origin of the word *quarantine*, the practice of separating the ill from the well for a specified time. In eighteenth-century North America, each colony had quarantine procedures that became state statutes after the American Revolution.

In the eighteenth century, aside from quarantine enforcement and local regulations designed to promote public hygiene, government officials could offer physicians little assistance. A 1744 New York City ordinance stated that "the health of the Inhabitants of any City Does in Great measure Depend upon the Purity of the Air of that City and that when the air of that City is by Noisome smells Corrupted, Distempers of many kinds are thereby Occasioned." The ordinance reflects physicians' beliefs that disease resulted from effluvia or miasmas, noxious gases arising from decaying organic matter. In the mid-nineteenth century, sanitarians would argue that filth caused disease, leaving public sanitation the best form of prevention. In the 1880s, Germany's Robert Koch and France's Louis Pasteur demonstrated that specific diseases were not simply the result of filth but were caused by specific microorganisms, or germs that invaded the body.

Disease and Therapy in Colonial America

Long before most physicians accepted germ theory, however, many understood that contact with a disease, if not fatal, often rewarded victims with immunity. Inducing smallpox immunity via inoculation by placing some diseased matter under the skin was likely taught to the Puritans in the seventeenth century by African slaves. Some thought the procedure the practice of the devil because the slaves were heathens, but others, including the influential minister Cotton Mather, believed in its efficacy and inoculated his family members. Such injections were not without their dangers, because an inoculated individual, even if immune, could still pass smallpox to another who was uninoculated. By 1760, laws regulated the practice and provided for a minimum quarantine period for those inoculated.

Colonial Americans also sought to protect patients from irresponsible medical practitioners. In 1736 the Virginia legislature enacted a law specifying fees for medical services. University-trained physicians could charge more than apprentice-trained doctors. Physicians' bills had to specify what drugs they had prescribed. However, the measure lapsed after two years and was never repassed. True regulation began in New York in the 1750s. By 1760 New York's Provincial Assembly passed the first colonial medical licensure law for New York City, requiring that applicants for a medical license be examined by government officials assisted by respected physicians. Still, quacks and charlatans were ubiquitous.

Government Power in Support of Public Health

Under the U.S. Constitution the new government possessed powers to "promote the general Welfare," powers hardly ever invoked in matters of health and disease. Seamen's health was the exception. Merchant seamen, often without families or permanent abodes, created a burden on public hospitals where they existed and aroused public sympathies. On July 16, 1798, Congress passed and President John Adams signed a bill establishing the United States Marine Hospital Service (USMHS, renamed the U.S. Public Health Service in 1912), a uniformed service for "the temporary relief and maintenance of sick or disabled seamen in the hospitals or other proper institutions . . . in ports where no such institutions exist. . . ." The first hospital built with Marine Hospital funds was in Boston. Soon, America's westward expansion prompted the building of hospitals near rivers in ports such as New Orleans, Chicago, Cleveland, St. Louis, and Louisville. In these hospitals all the surgeons, stewards, matrons, and nurses were political appointees.

In the nineteenth century, state and local governments and private voluntary organizations protected community health with limited funding. Most well-off individuals loathed spending money on the health of strangers, especially those who were nonwhite or from other countries. However, two great epidemic diseases, yellow fever and Asiatic cholera, demanded a cohesive public response. In the South, yellow fever epidemics in the 1850s aroused state legislatures to use their quarantine regulations to keep ships with sick passengers or crew out of their ports. The wealthy could temporarily flee stricken cities, but yellow fever was bad for business. There were passionate political debates over how to keep cities fit for investment and trade. Because of yellow fever, Louisiana became the first state with a permanent board of health. After 1900, when Dr. Walter Reed and his U.S. Army Commission in Havana, Cuba, discovered that yellow fever was spread by a mosquito vector, states funded mosquito control.

In northern cities, Asiatic cholera and poor immigrants, especially the Irish, often arrived simultaneously. In 1832, 1849, and 1866, major cholera epidemics swept the East Coast of the United States. Nativists blamed the immorality and ignorance of Irish Catholic newcomers for the cholera epidemic of 1832. In New York, a Special Medical Council was formed by the politically appointed Board of Health and manned by seven of the city's leading physicians. However, when the epidemic receded in the autumn, the Board of Health regressed into its apathetic state. When New York clergy petitioned President Andrew Jackson to appoint a day of national fasting, prayer, and humiliation to mark the devastation of the epidemic, he refused, affirming his belief in the efficacy of prayer but citing the separation of church and state. Not until 1866 did New York finally launch a permanent Municipal Board of Health removed from the choke hold of politicians and given over to physicians. New York gradually improved urban sanitation and hygiene, the price of industrialization and population congestion.

After the Civil War, the Bureau of Refugees, Freedmen and Abandoned Lands, popularly known as the Freedmen's Bureau, offered medical attention and constructed hospitals to serve newly emancipated black slaves and displaced whites. By 1872 racism and corruption within the bureau had undermined these efforts. Medical research did not become a routine federal endeavor until 1887, when Surgeon General John Hamilton opened the Hygienic Laboratory in one room of the Marine Hospital on Staten Island. There, director Dr. Joseph Kinyoun studied cholera, yellow fever, and the bacterial content of the waters in New York Bay. In 1891 the laboratory moved to Washington, evolving into the National Institutes of Health under the Public Health Service in the next century.

Doctors at the Gate: Immigration, Industrialization, and Disease Prevention in Progressive America

When the federal government assumed responsibility for immigration in 1891, USMHS physicians examined all newcomers at depots such as New York's Ellis Island. Those deemed physically or mentally unfit to support themselves were not admitted. In San Francisco Bay, a depot on Angel Island was the entrance for many Chinese and Japanese arrivals as well as some Europeans, all of whom also underwent physician inspection. An 1893 law gradually transferred quarantine authority from state to federal officials. At Ellis, there were two hospitals to treat newcomers, one a contagious disease facility. Immigrants who recovered were eventually allowed to leave the island and enter the country.

These safeguards proved insufficient for immigration's critics. Nativists, including many eugenicists seeking to improve human stock by encouraging some individuals to procreate while discouraging others, advocated the 1924 Johnson-Reed Immigration Act and its highly restrictive quota system. A broader eugenical concern about the number of children born to those defined as mentally defective, especially retarded persons, criminals, and the insane, resulted in passage of state laws permitting involuntary sterilization of institutionalized persons. These laws were found to be constitutional by the Supreme Court in *Buck v. Bell* (1927), and many remained in force until the late twentieth century.

In unhealthy, congested cities, immigrant workers were felled by such infectious diseases as tuberculosis. Illnesses and injuries from unsafe working conditions abounded. Progressive reformer Dr. Alice Hamilton investigated conditions in tenements and factories where lead in paints and phosphorus on matches were poisoning workers and their families. In public schools, the children of the poor received health education and sometimes even health care, including minor surgeries. Often only labor union agitation or tragedies, such as the 1911 Triangle Shirtwaist factory fire, resulted in state legislation improving health and safety. At the federal level, the Food and Drug Act of 1906 defined food adulteration and the misbranding of products and regulated the interstate shipment of food, penalizing violators. The act was superseded in 1938 by the stricter Food, Drug, and Cosmetics Act.

Government intervention was at times tainted by racism and ethnocentrism. In 1900 several cases of bubonic plague were identified in San Francisco's Chinatown. Local citizens blamed immigrants for their unsanitary living conditions. The government response smacked of anti-Chinese bias, including San Francisco's imposition of quarantine on all

Asian residents of Chinatown but not Caucasians and, at the suggestion of USMHS officials, the state's forced inoculation of Asians with an experimental serum. The courts offered relief, lifting the quarantine under the equal protection clause of the Fourteenth Amendment.

Federal Power, Prejudice, and the Public Health

When they had nowhere else to go for assistance, urban immigrants often turned to political machines, such as the New York Democratic Party's Tammany Hall. Tammany, dominated by Irish political bosses, pushed for municipal hospitals and helped individuals gain access to physicians or hospital admission in exchange for votes. In the 1930s, President Franklin Roosevelt's New Deal sounded urban bossism's death knell. Government agencies began to offer health services once obtainable only as political patronage, increasing the federal role in health care. The American Medical Association (AMA), founded in 1847, continued its long-standing opposition to government involvement in such matters. However, the Farm Security Administration's rural health programs provided more than a million migrant workers and some 650,000 others in rural America with medical care. Republicans condemned it as "socialized medicine."

The 1930s was also the time when the U.S. Public Health Service's efforts to treat syphilis in African American communities of the South had to be abandoned because of the economic pressures of the Depression. Instead, in 1932, the PHS, in collaboration with the Tuskegee Institute, embarked on an investigation of untreated syphilis involving hundreds of Alabama blacks that lasted until 1972, long after the discovery that syphilis could be treated with penicillin and long after any medically useful results had been produced. The episode remains synonymous with American medical racism.

A more benign episode of federal investigation and experimentation was the PHS pellagra study under federal physician Dr. Joseph Goldberger, who established that pellagra was a dietary disease. By the 1930s, researchers identified niacin as the missing element in pellagrins' diets. Bread and dairy products were enriched with niacin by presidential order during the war and by state law afterwards.

Federal Aid Improves Health
Care in Postwar America

Following World War II, federal funds and regulation had a major impact on research and the provision of health care. The Hospital Survey and Construction Act of 1946 (Hill-Burton Act) funded hospital construction in underserved communities, largely rural and suburban, creating a proportion of 4.5 hospital beds per 1,000 individuals. Prior to the war, Vannevar Bush, director of the Office of Scientific Research and Development, had recommended $15 million for medical research to investigate the therapeutic value of penicillin, the development of insect repellents

and insecticides, and the use of serum albumin as a blood substitute—all valuable in wartime. His 1945 report, *Science, the Endless Frontier*, pressed for more funding in science and medicine to establish the National Science Foundation and energize agencies such as the Public Health Service at the National Institutes of Health. Extramural federal funding supported research at medical schools and universities.

Soon a vast federal health bureaucracy developed. In 1953 the Department of Health, Education, and Welfare was created, redesignated the Department of Health and Human Services in 1979. It oversees the Public Health Service, which itself has 42 divisions, including NIH for medical research, Food and Drug Administration (FDA) to implement public health measures, and the Centers for Disease Control and Prevention (CDC), which battle the spread of disease.

Health care became more accessible when President Lyndon Johnson and a Democratic Congress passed Medicare and Medicaid legislation in 1966 to assist elderly and poor citizens, respectively, with medical bills driven higher by an increasing array of drugs and sophisticated medical technologies. However, along with these programs came red tape and regulations that contributed to the escalating cost of medical care.

The Politics of Health Care
in the Twenty-First Century

At the beginning of the twenty-first century, issues of health and illness occupied center stage in American politics. Immigration amplified demands for political action in the name of public health. Concern about swine flu crossing the Mexican border increased demand for government expenditures to develop new influenza vaccines. Data collected by the New York City Board of Health tracing spikes in drug resistant tuberculosis to migrants from China and Mexico raised concern about the adequacy of federal health restrictions and immigration procedures. Health care for racial and ethnic minorities and the native-born poor remained inadequate. State governments increasingly offered free DPT vaccinations to children whose parents could not afford them and provided other health care services, as well.

The HIV-AIDS crisis occasioned virulent debates over cultural values but also increased levels of federal funding for research on this disease as well as on cancer, heart disease, and obesity. The federal genome project redefined the future of medical research, stimulating the search for the genetic origins of various diseases. Debates over the morality of stem cell research divided conservatives, especially those on the Christian Right, from their opponents on the liberal left.

Issues of health and disease have long been debated in the political arena. Until the twentieth century, partisan conflict over such matters was largely state and local, but the expanded use of federal power in the twentieth century allowed some Americans to argue that promoting "the general Welfare" should include battling disease, promoting preventive public health measures, and perhaps providing health insurance to every American. The degree of responsibility the federal government ought to assume to conquer disease and in defense of the public's health has become a political perennial.

See also cities and politics; nativism.

FURTHER READING. John Duffy, *From Humors to Medical Science: A History of American Medicine*, 1993; Michael Grey, *New Deal Medicine: The Rural Health Programs of the Farm Security Administration*, 1999; Gerald N. Grob, *The Deadly Truth: A History of Disease in America*, 2002; Victoria A. Harden, *Inventing the NIH*, 1986; James H. Jones, *Bad Blood: The Tuskegee Syphilis Experiment*, revised ed., 1993; Daniel J. Kevles, *In the Name of Eugenics: Genetics and the Uses of Human Heredity*, 1985; Alan M. Kraut, *Silent Travelers: Germs, Genes, and the "Immigrant Menace,"* 1994; Roy Porter, *Blood and Guts: A Short History of Medicine*, 2002; George Rosen, *A History of Public Health*, revised ed., 1993; Charles E. Rosenberg, *The Cholera Years: The United States in 1832, 1849, and 1866*, revised ed., 1987; Paul Starr, *The Social Transformation of American Medicine: The Rise of a Sovereign Profession and the Making of a Vast Industry*, 1982; Rosemary Stevens, *The Public-Private Health Care State: Essays on the History of American Health Care Policy*, 2007.

ALAN M. KRAUT

homosexuality

Although the modern concept of "homosexuality" did not emerge until the late nineteenth century, characteristics associated with this category—same-sex desire, same-sex sexual acts, and nonconformist gender performance—have been contested within American political culture since the colonial period in two critical ways. The first involves political struggles over policy, including the legality of same-sex sexual acts, and, by the latter half of the twentieth century, civil rights protections for those who identify as gay, lesbian, bisexual, and transgendered. Second, homosexuality has served a powerful function within American political discourse. Especially in the arena of electoral politics, sodomy and homosexuality have functioned as rhetorical markers of weakness and subversion to social order and American values.

The Politics of Sodomy in Early America

In the seventeenth century, all American colonies adopted sodomy—or "buggery"—laws that prohibited nonprocreative sexual acts between men, as well as between men and women and between men and animals. However, not all forms of nonprocreative sex met with the same level of condemnation or prohibition; in New England, for example, governmental and ministerial officials characterized such

sexual acts between men as more sinful and socially dangerous than those committed between men and women. Although religious authorities also condemned sex between women, the crime of sodomy typically required evidence of penetration, so such acts were rarely prosecuted in colonial courts (the sodomy code of the New Haven Colony proved exceptional in its explicit prohibition of sex between women). Colonies imposed a range of punishments for sodomy, from the imposition of fines to execution. However, sodomy laws were unevenly enforced, and severe forms of punishment were relatively rare; historical evidence suggests that American colonists responded to sodomy in more pragmatic ways, carefully weighing their religious opprobrium against the social disruption of legal prosecution.

This disinclination to prosecute sodomy, even more pronounced in the eighteenth century, did not evince true tolerance, however. Indeed, colonial authorities interpreted evidence of male same-sex acts and other forms of sexual "deviance" as grave threats to social and political order. In 1642 Plymouth governor William Bradford ascribed an outbreak of "sodomy and buggery (things fearful to name)" to the arrival of migrants to New England who did not share the Puritan goal of establishing a shining and moral "city on the hill." The linking of sodomy to political subversion became more common in the 1700s when the "sodomite"—a male person who desired sex with other men—emerged as a category of personhood in the transatlantic world. In 1726, for example, a Boston newspaper, reporting on the raids of a number of "sodomitical clubs" in London, linked sodomy to the dangers of a growing and threatening urban commercialism; sodomites and financiers alike conducted secretive and illegal deals that threatened social stability. Sodomy and commercial exchange also evinced European dissoluteness and corruption, as did Freemasonry. Anti-Masonic Massachusetts satirists used phallic homoerotic imagery to recast ostensibly civic-minded Masonic fraternal rituals as corrupt and emasculating. Such aspersions were intended to counter the political prominence of Freemasons in the colony.

This predilection for defining both the practice of sodomy and effeminate gender performance as distinctly foreign—as violating the foundations of American character—continued into the Revolutionary and early national eras. An ascendant Enlightenment ethos was manifested in the revocation of capital punishment for sodomy, but it also produced a model of white American national manhood that emphasized independence and self-governance, a hallmark of which was the control of sexual desire and intensified stigmatization of nonmarital sexual practices. This prescriptive model, espoused by northern elites, took as a foil the stereotype of the decadent and corrupt European "fop," a figure associated with sexual profligacy if not always sodomy. The sodomitical qualities of this figure grew more explicit in the middle of the nineteenth century when American newspapers began to report on groups of urban men who engaged in same-sex relations. The first such known report, appearing in the New York paper *The Whip* in 1842, attributed the appearance of a sodomitical subculture to foreign influences and condemned this development as antithetical to the purity of the young American nation.

Homosexuality and Political Subversion

By the end of the nineteenth century, the figure of the sodomite had been replaced by the "homosexual," a modern category defined by an inversion of gender role and by same-sex desire. The homosexual—alternatively referred to as someone of the "third sex" or an "invert"—emerged from sexology, a new field of medical science that had originated in Europe. Yet, antecedents to this modern figure can be found in nineteenth-century American political culture. Critics of those who advocated radical reforms of the American political system, such as abolitionism and woman suffrage, had been pilloried as improperly gendered. The pejorative name "Miss Nancy" was applied to male abolitionists and male prostitutes alike, for example. Proponents of civil service reform and of third-party movements acquired such descriptors as "third sex" and "political hermaphrodite." This conflation of sexual and political subversion is evinced by the first published American analysis of homosexuality, neurologist Edward Spitzka's "A Historical Case of Sexual Perversion" (1881), which retroactively diagnosed Lord Cornbury, the colonial governor of New York and New Jersey who was alleged to have dressed as a woman, as sexually inverted, anathema to the American ethos of masculine individualism, and as a threat to national strength.

The negative political meanings attached to homosexuality grew more vociferous in the twentieth century, as homosexual men and women were pathologized by medical professionals and further criminalized within the law. In the 1920s, critics used a stigmatizing psychological model of homosexuality to impugn politically active "New Women" who had formed lifelong intimate relationships with other women—including the leading social reformer Jane Addams—as unnatural and perverted "short-haired women." During World War II, homosexuality functioned as grounds for exclusion or discharge from military service; more than 10,000 lesbians and gay men were discharged for "undesirable habits or traits of character" between 1941 and 1945. The policing and persecution of homosexuality intensified after the war. In 1953 President Dwight D. Eisenhower signed Executive Order 10450, which excluded those deemed to be homosexual from federal employment on the grounds that they represented a threat to national security. An array of American thinkers and politicians, including liberal historian Arthur Schlesinger Jr., conflated homosexuality and communism, interpreting both as threats to a masculinist

tradition of American pragmatic centrism. Zealous cold warriors, including Senator Joseph McCarthy, viewed both homosexuality and communism as anti-American and embarked on a systematic effort to root out gay men and women from the civil service and to smear their political opponents on the left. The resulting "lavender scare" ruined careers and lives and undermined the 1952 presidential candidacy of Democrat Adlai Stevenson.

Homosexual Rights and Conservative Backlash

The postwar period also saw the rise of the modern American homosexual rights movement, beginning with the founding of homophile organizations in the postwar years. Although the first to form a sustained movement, homophile leaders drew on an older leftist political discourse that resisted a dominant pejorative American conception of same-sex desire. An array of late-nineteenth-century intellectuals and bohemians, influenced by the poet Walt Whitman's vision of homoerotic democratic "adhesiveness" and the sex radicalism of European freethinkers like Edward Carpenter, had maintained that same-sex desire might be directed toward the civic good. This position was argued most forcefully by American anarchists, including Leonard Abbott and Emma Goldman, who viewed state efforts to regulate homosexuality as a violation of individual freedom and an unjust expression of state power. Early homophile leaders—notably, Harry Hay, who founded the Mattachine Society in 1950—spoke for this tradition within the Communist Party in the 1930s. Although American Communists ultimately proved hostile to homosexuality, Hay and others brought the organizational skills and political commitments developed within the Communist Party to the cause of "homosexual liberation."

Influenced by the civil rights movement, Hay and his homophile comrades conceptualized homosexuals as a minority group "imprisoned within a dominant culture." The 1950s saw the formation of similar groups, including the first lesbian political organization in the United States, the Daughters of Bilitis, in 1955. Although homophile activists struggled over organizational strategies, and many sought to distance themselves from the early leaders' Communist roots, the movement gained strength and engaged in more militant forms of activism by the 1960s. In 1964 members of the East Coast Homophile Organizations coalition staged a demonstration in New York City to protest military policy toward homosexuals. In 1965 the Washington, D.C., Mattachine chapter, led by Frank Kameny, a scientist who had been fired from his government post during the lavender scare, picketed the White House, Pentagon, and Civil Service Commission to protest antigay employment practices.

By the late 1960s, members of the growing homophile movement allied themselves with black power and other radical liberation movements as well as with New Left student and anti–Vietnam

War efforts. This radicalization found expression in new slogans like "Gay Power" as well as in more confrontational forms of protest, especially in relation to police harassment in burgeoning urban gay enclaves like New York City's Greenwich Village and the Tenderloin and Castro neighborhoods of San Francisco. Two such dramatic and spontaneous acts of rebellion catalyzed a more radical movement: the 1966 Compton's Cafeteria riot in San Francisco, led by transgender women and gay hustlers, and the more famous 1969 Stonewall rebellion in New York City. These pivotal events set the stage for a dizzying proliferation of gay and lesbian activism, including the 1969 founding of the Gay Liberation Front, inspired by third-world liberation movements, and the lesbian feminist groups Radicalesbians (1970) and Salsa Soul Sisters (1974), which protested both the misogyny of gay male activists and the antilesbian positions of the National Organization for Women.

The mid-1970s saw two key developments in the politics of homosexuality. First, a reform-oriented model of gay activism began to dominate the movement, finding institutional expression in such organizations as the National Gay Task Force (founded in 1973); these organizations achieved significant successes in the legal arena, including the repeal of state sodomy statutes and the passage of antidiscrimination legislation at the local level. Reformist efforts also led to the election of gay and lesbian candidates, notably Harvey Milk as San Francisco city supervisor in 1977. However, the successes of the gay rights movement also engendered a political backlash led by religious conservatives who, calling on the established trope of homosexuality as subversive to American values, waged a vociferous and well-funded battle against "the gay agenda." In 1977 religious singer and orange juice pitchwoman Anita Bryant, arguing that homosexuality posed a threat to American children and families, led an effort to repeal a gay rights ordinance in Dade County, Florida. Her campaign found significant national support, especially among evangelicals, and laid the foundation for the antigay activism of New Right organizations like the Moral Majority, established by Jerry Falwell in 1979.

With the election of Ronald Reagan as president in 1980, culture warriors like Jerry Falwell and Pat Robertson attained considerable influence in the Republican Party, which identified homosexuality as an effective wedge issue in state and national elections. In the 1980s, when the Reagan administration all but ignored the suffering and devastation of the new AIDS epidemic, some gay activists turned to a more confrontational and performative mode of activism, exemplified by ACT UP (the Aids Coalition to Unleash Power), which charged that federal neglect amounted to complicity in the suffering and deaths of those afflicted with AIDS. With the availability of medications that mitigated the effects of HIV (at least for those with access to health care) in the 1990s, the political struggle over gay rights shifted

to issues of marriage and military service. Although many had viewed the presidential election of Democrat Bill Clinton in 1992 as a favorable development for the gay rights movement, the failure of the administration to implement a nondiscriminatory military service policy and Clinton's endorsement of the 1996 Defense of Marriage Act, which prohibited federal recognition of same-sex marriages, attested to the continued political opposition to the aims of the movement.

The politics of marriage rights have remained especially contentious into the twenty-first century; by 2008, judicial gains had been countered by restrictive legislation and ballot referenda at the state level. That opponents of same-sex marriage framed their position as "defending" a foundational social institution points to the resilience of an understanding of homosexuality as threatening to social order.

See also gender and sexuality.

FURTHER READING. Barry D. Adam, *The Rise of a Gay and Lesbian Movement*, 1987; John D'Emilio, *Sexual Politics, Sexual Communities: The Making of a Homosexual Minority in the United States, 1940–1970*, 1983; Lisa Duggan and Nan Hunter, *Sex Wars: Sexual Dissent and Political Culture*, 1995; Thomas A. Foster, ed., *Long Before Stonewall: Histories of Same-Sex Sexuality in Early America*, 2007; David K. Johnson, *The Lavender Scare: The Cold War Persecution of Gays and Lesbians in the Federal Government*, 2004; Jonathan Katz, *Gay American History: Lesbians and Gay Men in the U.S.A.*, 1976; Terence Kissack, *Free Comrades: Anarchism and Homosexuality in the United States, 1895–1917*, 2008; Molly McGarry and Fred Wasserman, *Becoming Visible: An Illustrated History of Lesbian and Gay Life in Twentieth-Century America*, 1998; Kevin P. Murphy, *Political Manhood: Red Bloods, Mollycoddles and the Politics of Progressive Era Reform*, 2008; James T. Sears, *Behind the Mask of Mattachine: The Hall Call Chronicles and the Early Movement for Homosexual Emancipation*, 2006; Carroll Smith-Rosenberg, *Disorderly Conduct: Visions of Gender in Victorian America*, 1985.

KEVIN P. MURPHY

House of Representatives

The House of Representatives is often considered to be America's most democratic institution. Since the founding of the American government in 1789, the House has been populated by a more diverse range of individuals than the Senate or the White House. Legislators have been required to face reelection every two years. To win election to the House, the Constitution requires only that a candidate be a minimum of 25 years of age and a U.S. citizen for 7 years. Candidates also have to reside in their district. The founders decided that membership in the House would be proportionate to the size of the population so that the delegations from each state corresponded, albeit imperfectly, to demographic realities. The sheer number of members has required negotiation and compromise. In this respect, the House lived up to George Mason's aspiration that it would be the "grand depository of the democratic principle of the government."

The Constitution bestowed three important responsibilities on the House: the power over revenue and spending, the power to impeach an elected official, and the power to elect the president if the Electoral College was deadlocked. This authority reflected how highly the nation's founders valued the House as an antidote to the British monarchy.

There are four different eras in the history of the House of Representatives, each defined by the procedural framework—the informal and formal rules—through which legislators operated.

The Founding Period
The first three decades of the House were the founding period, during which legislators established the basic mechanisms through which decision making would take place.

In the founding period, legislators developed the committee system and party organizations, as well as procedures that enabled individual legislators to influence decision making from the floor. Initially, the relative importance of each procedure remained unclear. Most legislation would be worked out on the floor and then given to a committee that was temporarily convened to deal with the issue. But some committees became regular components of the House, such as the Rules Committee (created in 1789), which made decisions about scheduling legislation and about the rules through which bills would be debated. Procedural decisions had a big impact on the character of the House. In 1811, for example, an important rules change ensured that the House would become a majoritarian institution by allowing half of the chamber to end debate. This procedural change limited the potential for minority obstruction (in contrast to the Senate filibuster).

One of the most influential legislators in the founding period was Henry Clay of Kentucky. During his tenure as Speaker, Clay, first a Democratic-Republican and later a Whig, elevated the institutional status of the Speaker by using his power to keep members in line. While the speakership was the only position mentioned in the Constitution, its actual status in the House had remained unclear. When he became Speaker at the start of the congressional session in 1812, just after being elected to the House, Clay headed a coalition of war hawks who mounted pressure for military action against Great Britain. Clay also pushed for an expanded role of government in promoting the economy through public works, tariffs, and road construction. To achieve his objectives, Clay took responsibility for deciding which committees would deal with legislation, and he made appointments to key committees.

Even as legislators tried to determine how the House would function, they confronted a series of major challenges. In 1801, for example, the House had to decide a deadlocked presidential election after the electors cast an equal number of votes for Thomas Jefferson and Aaron Burr. The vote went to Jefferson. In 1825 the House was required again to settle a presidential election when none of the candidates received a majority from the Electoral College. The House then chose John Quincy Adams to be the next president of the nation.

In the era, house majorities also voted for a significant expansion of the federal government. Through the Alien and Sedition Acts (1798), the House strengthened the authority of government to crack down on the political activity of aliens and to prosecute opponents of the Federalists. Although Democratic-Republicans such as Albert Gallatin of Pennsylvania and Edward Livingston of New York derided the Alien and Sedition Acts as a violation of state and individual rights, Federalists pushed the bills through the House by narrow margins. Additional legislation strengthened the administrative capacity of government to conduct war, regulate banking and currency, and improve networks of internal communication. Pork barrel spending was central to financing the construction of roads, railroads, and canals. Tariffs protected industrial goods such as cotton and iron.

Even when not explicitly discussed, slavery was extremely influential throughout the founding period. When considering most issues—as wide ranging as direct taxation, territorial expansion, and diplomacy—legislators always weighed the potential impact of a decision on the slaveholding economy. This was not surprising. Between 1788 and 1850, according to the historian Robin Einhorn, a slaveholder served as Speaker 66 percent of the time and as chairman of the powerful Ways and Means Committee, which controlled revenue and trade, 68 percent of the time.

The Party Period
Despite the fear that the founders expressed about the dangers of political parties and partisanship, a party system slowly took form. In the founding period, Federalists faced off against the Democratic-Republicans. Parties became even more important during the second era in the history of the House—the party period—which lasted from the 1830s to the 1900s. Even though the formal organization of parties remained tenuous before the Civil War, parties influenced House politics in a number of ways, as was evident from the large number of party-line roll call votes in this period. Partisan electorates and state legislators weighed heavily on the decision making of congressmen. Informal norms discouraged mavericks from challenging party leaders. Subsequent speakers followed Henry Clay's precedent by making committee assignments on the basis of party loyalty

in voting and sometimes punished those who defied them. Speakers controlled floor debate to protect their party. Party bosses relied on patronage to ensure that lower-ranking legislators remained loyal.

From the 1830s to the 1850s, Whigs competed against the Democrats. The Whigs supported national programs to promote economic growth, protective tariffs, the creation of a national bank, and moral reform. In contrast, Democrats championed presidential power, protection for southern slaveholders, territorial expansion, and local and state over federal power. Third parties, such as the Anti-Masons, the Liberty Party, and the Know-Nothings, formed to promote issues when neither the Whigs nor Democrats seemed responsive.

By the 1850s, the pull of section in the House became stronger than the pull of party. Each time that the federal government acquired a new territory, legislators fought over whether slavery should be allowed. The tension worsened with congressional passage of the Kansas-Nebraska Act (1854). Whigs and Democrats divided along sectional lines. Although a coalition of northern Whigs, northern Democrats, and Free-Soilers had attempted to block the measure, southern Whigs helped remove the bill from committee. In May 1856, sectional tension became so severe that Representative Preston Brooks of South Carolina beat Senator Charles Sumner of Massachusetts with his walking stick. Brooks was furious about a statement that Sumner, an opponent of slavery, had made about his uncle.

The Civil War of 1861–65 severed the nation. The secession of southern states and the departure of southern politicians were followed by brutal battles on the home front. Toward the end of the conflict, Congress responded to the crisis through legislation. In 1865 the House passed the Thirteenth Amendment (approved by the Senate the previous year), which abolished slavery within the United States. Throughout the war the Republican House remained active on a number of fronts in addition to slavery. For example, the House passed the Pacific Railway Act, created land-grant colleges, and enacted a national income tax. House Republicans also conducted investigations into how the Lincoln administration handled the war.

During Reconstruction, House Republicans pushed for an expanded role for the federal government to rebuild the nation and improve race relations, although the party divided between moderates and radicals over how far the policies should go. In 1866 the House passed the Fourteenth Amendment, which guaranteed due process and equal treatment before the law to all Americans, and, in 1869, the House passed the Fifteenth Amendment, which protected the right of every male citizen to vote. Congress also created the Freedmen's Bureau, which provided food, education, and other forms of assistance to freed African Americans. During Reconstruction a significant number of African Americans were elected to the House. President Andrew Johnson, who opposed most Reconstruction initiatives, attempted to capitalize on divisions among congressional Republicans. His efforts to split moderate and Radical Republicans, however, backfired. In February 1868, the House voted to impeach Johnson. Following a lengthy trial in the chamber, the Senate acquitted him by one vote. Support for Reconstruction diminished by the 1870s.

After Reconstruction the parties regained their strength. Republican legislators captured support in the northern industrial sector by promoting policies to expand national markets, preserve the gold standard, and provide generous Civil War pensions. Meanwhile, Democratic legislators retained their hold on the South by pushing farm assistance, inflationary monetary policies, free trade, and states' rights. These years were competitive for the parties. Republicans tended to control the Senate and Democrats the House between 1875 and 1897. Majorities in both chambers were razor thin. Congress passed legislation in 1872 that required all elections for the House to be held the same day.

Parties were important because they offered platforms to members, but also because they provided some organizational coherence in an era of high turnover. According to *Congressional Quarterly*, 145 out of 243 members of the House were new in 1869.

Members of the House were at the forefront of efforts to expand the federal government beyond policies related to Reconstruction. Democratic House representative John Reagan of Texas, for example, headed attacks against the railroads throughout the 1870s. Reagan's main goal was to protect the interests of farmers, whose distrust of national corporations he shared. He called on the House to impose regulations through legislation rather than rely on independent commissions. He feared that corporations would capture control of a regulatory commission and subvert agrarian interests. This was a widespread fear among southern Democrats. In 1876 Reagan used his seat on the House Commerce Committee to expose the activities of railroad magnates and build support for legislation. He introduced a bill that would prohibit pooling—where the railroads pooled their revenue so that no individual company would have an incentive to lower its charges and be able to undercut competition—and guarantee fair rates for shippers. Teaming up with the moderate Shelby Cullom of Illinois, Reagan won the support of southern and western legislators, who voted for his bill in 1885. Although the final legislation in 1887 created the Independent Commerce Commission rather than relying on legislative regulations, Reagan's efforts had spearheaded one of the biggest expansions of federal power into the economy.

Toward the end of the party period, the Republican leadership in the House added procedural muscle to their influence. In 1890 Republican speaker Thomas Bracket Reed of Maine won support from his caucus for a rules change that allowed the majority party to block obstructive tactics of the minority. The most important was the "disappearing quorum," whereby Democrats in the House had refused to answer roll calls even while present in order to prevent a quorum. Reed ended this practice by announcing that those physically present were in attendance. After becoming Speaker in 1903, Republican Joseph Cannon of Illinois further strengthened the office. He used his power to stifle progressive legislation and frustrate President Theodore Roosevelt.

However, just as legislative parties started to gain more organizational cohesion, the strength of parties as national political institutions weakened. While parties remained a crucial component of American political life, their influenced vastly diminished. Electoral reforms increased the prevalence of split-ticket voting and precluded many of the tactics that parties had traditionally used to influence voters. National and state civil service reforms, such as the Pendleton Act of 1883, sharply curtailed the parties' ability to ensure loyalty through patronage. Moreover, both parties were forced to compete with organized interest groups, whose leaders promised they could deliver solid votes and ample campaign assistance. The partisan press disintegrated as a new medium arose, a system of professional journalists with an adversarial outlook who maintained weaker allegiances to elected officials. Americans did not vote as much, and electoral politics lost its salience with many citizens, who were more enthralled with amusement parks than with campaigns. Dramatic scandals in the Gilded Age that involved the parties had also spurred reforms that weakened the hold of parties. Partisan roll calls declined.

The high turnover in House membership on which parties had thrived diminished as rates of incumbency increased and legislators started to conceive of serving in the House as a full-time occupation. Seniority took hold as legislators obtained committee assignments by remaining in office for the longest amount of time rather than by displaying party loyalty. Committees themselves gained greater autonomy. Strong party leaders came under attack. In 1909 and 1910, a coalition of insurgent Republicans and Democrats who were unhappy about repeated failures in the legislative process—and about how Cannon had treated them—revolted against the Speaker. Representative George Norris of Nebraska led the attack for the Republicans, working closely with Victor Murdock and Edmund Madison of Kansas as well as John Nelson and Irvine Lenroot of Wisconsin. Missouri's Champ Clark and Alabama's Oscar Underwood led the Democratic part of the team. The coalition removed the Speaker from the Rules Committee and ended his control over committee assignments. It also passed reforms that allowed chairs to bring bills directly to the floor if they were bottled up in the Rules Committee. Finally, legislators agreed to delegate more governance responsibilities to independent commissions. Further reforms in the 1910s facilitated this trend. In 1911, for instance, the Democratic caucus empowered the Ways and Means Committee to handle committee assignments, thereby taking this responsibility away from the Speaker. Promotions in the chamber revolved around seniority. Formal rules and informal norms discouraged younger members from challenging committee chairmen.

The Committee Period

The committee period constituted the next stage in the evolution of the House and lasted from the 1910s through the early 1970s. The committee chairs retained tight control over proceedings. Access to information was restricted to the chairs and a few select senior members. Most deliberations were closed to the public. Legislative negotiations were dominated by tight-knit policy communities composed of committee chairs, representatives from the executive branch and agencies, powerful interest groups, and policy experts. Committee chairs rarely spoke to the national media.

The committee period had several pillars beyond the sheer power and autonomy of chairmen. At the electoral level, states preserved outdated district lines that favored rural constituencies and failed to reflect the growth of urban and suburban populations. The campaign finance system required legislators to cultivate a handful of prominent families, corporations, and unions that were willing to make large contributions. As parties with strong ties to the electorate weakened, interest groups offered legislators a resource to deliver blocs of voters and money. Striving to be objective, the media generally did not adopt an adversarial stance toward the House leadership.

During the committee period, party caucuses refrained from removing committee members for party disloyalty or incompetence. The weak Democratic and Republican caucuses rarely met, and they avoided taking strong positions or imposing them on members. The most influential party leaders were successful because they deferred to committee chairs rather than dominating them.

The committee process did not take hold automatically. Even after the historic revolt against Speaker Cannon, party caucuses remained influential throughout most of the 1910s. During World War I, to the frustration of Republicans, President Woodrow Wilson operated through a partisan alliance with congressional Democrats. He depended on Ways and Means Chairman Claude Kitchen of North Carolina, a progressive who initially opposed American intervention, to move much of the wartime legislation through the House in exchange for reforms. Yet by the Great Depression, the committee system was in place.

By the advent of the New Deal, southern Democrats and the committee process came to be seen as inseparable. While some Northerners, such as New York's Emanuel Celler, thrived in the committee process, Southerners claimed the greatest rewards in the House since they came from noncompetitive districts and thus retained their seats for longer periods of time. Southerners also constituted a disproportionate part of the Democratic Party. Southern Democrats held over 50 percent of the key committee chairs after the party regained control in 1933.

At the height of the New Deal, Congress responded to the Great Depression and often initiated policies before President Franklin D. Roosevelt did. House Democrats crafted legislation that preserved the alliance between Southerners and Northerners in the party who agreed on many areas of economic policy but disagreed on race relations and unionization. The House leadership included Speaker Henry Rainey of Illinois and Majority Leader Joseph Byrnes of Tennessee. Legislators such as Sam Rayburn of Texas and David Lewis of Maryland were instrumental in passing New Deal legislation.

But the committee process became a subject of contention for New Deal liberals. President Roosevelt had taken the unusual step of campaigning against five conservative Democrats in the 1938 election. He was able to unseat only one of those Democrats: New York representative John O'Connor, chairman of the House Rules Committee. Republicans also scored major victories in 1938. Conservative Democrats replaced liberals and moderates in a number of southern districts. Following the election, tensions escalated between southern chairs and northern Democrats. Southerners were not opposed to the expansion of government in general, but they did oppose unionization in their region and civil rights protection for African Americans.

When northern liberals began to support these issues in the 1940s, the committee process in the House became a major obstacle to twentieth-century liberalism. Southern Democrats, allied with Republicans, could rely on procedures to influence the House. Besides procedural power, southern Democrats and Republicans formed a potent voting bloc on the floor of the House. They could also count on southern Democrats in the Senate to use the filibuster, as they did with an antilynching bill in 1937, to block any civil rights legislation that the House passed.

Throughout World War II and the cold war, the committee-period House continued to produce legislation that expanded government. During World War II, the House agreed to a vast expansion of the tax base as well as a withholding system that enabled the government to collect taxes directly from paychecks. A decade later, the House voted to fund scientific research, highway construction, and civil defense. The House Un-American Activities Committee, founded in 1939, was at the forefront of the congressional investigations of suspected Communists.

By the 1950s, there were enough proponents of civil rights to produce legislation in the House, even though southern power in the Senate remained formidable. House liberals became pivotal players as they continued to force senators to grapple publicly with racial issues many preferred to ignore. The 1960s offered another burst of government activity. Almost 90 years after the end of Reconstruction, the House passed the Civil Rights Act of 1964 and the Voting Rights Act of 1965. Under the banner of the Great Society, the House passed legislation dealing with the environment, health care for the elderly, urban decay, and the War on Poverty.

A majority of Democrats and Republicans in the House also agreed to an expanded international role for the United States. During World War II and the cold war, the House supported a vast mobilization of resources and manpower in the effort to combat fascism and communism. But the Vietnam War broke that concensus apart. Although many members of the House voiced their doubts about intervention in 1964 and early 1965, they allowed President Lyndon Johnson to expand America's involvement in Vietnam. The vote for the 1964 Gulf of Tonkin Resolution was unanimous. By the late 1960s, however, many Democrats and Republicans joined colleagues in the Senate to build pressure on President Richard Nixon for a gradual withdrawal.

Many liberals came to believe that success could only occur if northern legislators worked around the committee system. One of the foils of the 1960s House was Virginia's Howard Smith. Elected in 1938, Smith had taken over the House Rules Committee in 1955 and used the power of his chairmanship to stifle liberal legislation.

As the federal government expanded, so too did the executive branch. Some observers believed this was the period of the "imperial presidency." But many legislators felt differently. Congress continued to exert influence on national politics. In the creation of domestic and international programs, committee chairs retained a tight grip over the government. Wilbur Mills, the Arkansas Democrat who chaired the Ways and Means Committee, caused enormous problems for President Johnson in 1968, when he forced the president to accept domestic spending cuts in exchange for higher taxes.

The Supreme Court had made a series of decisions between 1962 and 1964 that affected the composition of the House because they forced it and state legislatures to create voting districts with equal populations. In *Wesberry v. Sanders* (1964) the Court ruled that Georgia's federal districting system was unconstitutional. Plaintiffs from Georgia's district alleged that they were unjustly treated, since their population was three times as large as the population of the ninth, the smallest district in the state. The fifth district was the most underrepresented in the nation. The Court ruled 6 to 3 that populations in each congressional district must be roughly equal so that the vote of each citizen carried the same weight. In the short term, the decisions put conservative Democrats on notice. One of the earliest victims was Howard Smith. He lost in the 1966 primaries to a Democrat who was more popular in the suburbs but who became part of Smith's district as a result of the "one man-one vote" Supreme Court rulings. In the long term, the Court decisions opened up the opportunity for Republicans to make gains in the South and end the region's one-party monopoly.

Public hostility toward the House intensified in the 1960s, as did the frustration with all government institutions. Liberals denounced Congress for being too timid in its support for the Great Society and for allowing Presidents Kennedy, Johnson, and Nixon to fight the Vietnam War. At the same time, conservatives attacked the House for being inefficient and corrupt. Public interest reformers attacked Congress for failing to represent average citizens and stifling democratic participation. Although the Watergate scandal focused on the abuses of the presidency, reformers believed that Congress could only regain its stature by dismantling the committee process.

During the early 1970s, congressional reformers obtained support for procedures that aimed to weaken committee chairs. The reforms simultaneously centralized power by granting more decision-making authority to the party caucuses and decentralized power through the Subcommittee Bill of Rights in 1973. The House voted for reforms that constrained the power of the president in budgeting and war making. After the 1974 midterm elections, the "Watergate babies" (an influx of newly elected Democrats following Nixon's resignation) deposed four powerful House committee chairs, further weakened the autonomy of committees, and opened more proceedings to the public.

As the committee period ended, the House became fractured and unstable. Freed from the dominance of committee chairs, individual legislators, specialized caucuses, subcommittees, and the congressional minority pursued their own electoral and ideological interests. Although committee chairs lost power, party leaders were not yet able to impose order on the House. For instance, legislators constantly amended committee bills after they reached the floor, in contrast to the previous period when such activity was rare. Several scandals also shook the House, including sexual scandals that brought down Democratic congressmen Wilbur Mills and Wayne Hays as well as the ABSCAM scandal in 1980, when legislators were videotaped accepting bribes. The House reprimanded its first member since the Civil War.

The Partisan Period
In the most recent period, elite partisanship took hold of the House. Although most Americans were not strongly partisan, party caucuses became more influential in the House in two ways. First, Democrats and Republicans became more homogenous ideologically. As the number of southern conservative Democrats diminished and moderates lost power in the Republican Party, Democrats moved to the left and Republicans to the right. Facing more

cohesive membership, party leaders were more willing to use procedural tools that they had gained in the 1970s to expand their role. Between 1987 and 1989, for instance, Speaker James Wright of Texas intimidated members of his own party and manhandled Republicans. On one occasion, he extended the time for voting after Democrats could not find a sufficient number of members to vote for a tax package. Democrats used the extra time to round up more legislators outside the chamber. Younger Republicans such as Newt Gingrich of Georgia rejected the bias of older moderates who favored compromise. Gingrich publicly broke with President George H. W. Bush in 1990 who broke his campaign pledge by agreeing to a tax hike. When Republicans elected Gingrich Speaker after the GOP gained control of the House, he excluded Democrats from deliberations and enhanced the power of party leaders.

The new partisanship in the House differed from that of the nineteenth century. The nineteenth-century parties lacked strong centralized organization in the House but maintained deep roots in the electorate. But after the 1980s, political parties were organizationally strong within the House but lacked meaningful connections to the electorate. American voters thus witnessed a more partisan institution to which they did not feel connected. Instead of mechanisms of political participation, parties increasingly became fund-raising devices and organizational tools.

Partisan fighting was fierce in the partisan period, since neither Republicans nor Democrats were able to maintain solid control over Congress, and the leadership passed back and forth several times. In 1980 Democrats retained control of the House but Republicans gained control of the Senate until 1986. Republicans won both chambers of Congress in 1994, lost the Senate in 2001, and regained control of both chambers in the 2002 midterm elections. In 2006 Democrats regained control of both chambers. Although control of the House remained relatively stable after 1994, razor-thin margins during much of the 1990s fostered insecurity among those in power.

While the reforms of the 1970s had promised to make Congress the dominant branch of government, legislators were still working under tremendous constraints. There were multiple and competing centers of legislative power, with none achieving absolute dominance and none conducive to producing legislative compromise. Many reformers had hoped to ensure that no part of Congress developed the kind of singular strength that committee chairs had; the reformers succeeded in this respect. The proliferation and empowerment of subcommittees and specialized caucuses produced small fiefdoms that became obstacles to party leaders and committee chairs. Furthermore, new rules and norms encouraged mavericks and freshmen to take action when they felt an issue was being ignored by the party leadership. Every legislator from senior party leaders to lower-ranking representatives was subject to new ethics regulations and norms. Scandals brought down powerful leaders, including Speakers Wright, Gingrich, and Tom DeLay.

Public policy was a second constraint on legislators in the partisan period. Since the 1970s, the federal budget loomed large over every congressional decision. The tremendous increase in pre-committed spending, as well as sizable federal deficits and debt, meant there was less money for legislators who wanted to construct new types of government programs outside of national emergencies. By the 1980s and 1990s, almost half of the federal budget went to entitlement programs such as Social Security and Medicare. For most of these years, the federal government spent more than it took in in taxes. In an environment of fiscal constraint, it was hard to create new programs. The nature of the federal budget also made it difficult to dismantle programs.

When conservatives took power in the 1980s, culminating in the 1994 congressional elections, they discovered it was hard to alter most programs, except for federal taxation. Republicans could not touch items like Social Security without severe electoral consequences. This left conservatives with the unattractive option of cutting modestly priced programs like welfare that came with the high cost of antagonizing active interest groups or attacking programs important to their own supporters. Even after the 2000 election, with a staunchly conservative president in office, federal spending grew. The war on terrorism increased the size of government. Conservatives railed against Republicans by 2006, accusing the party of having accepted "big government." In reality, however, cutting the size of the state was virtually impossible.

The news media constituted a third constraint on the power of representatives. In contrast to the committee period, the news media had a hostile relationship with elected officials. Trust and cooperation evaporated. The rise of adversarial journalism in the 1960s and 1970s had produced a new generation of reporters and editors determined to expose corruption. This outlook would continue to shape the print media as well as television. Cable television added to this volatile environment. Producers worked on exposés to attract large television audiences. Even though ownership became concentrated, the number of stations multiplied. Cable television created a 24-hour news cycle, which made controlling the flow of news more difficult since stories could go on the airwaves within seconds. Media organizations looked for shocking material to fill the airwaves and generate high ratings. In a period when most Americans distrusted government, scandals became a favorite topic. Legislators responded by honing their media skills. Some relied on C-SPAN, created in 1979, two years after the House authorized televised proceedings, to communicate directly to voters without the filter of reporters.

It was not just that the media had changed. Another challenge facing legislators in the partisan period was the fractious world of interest groups, think tanks, and political activists. While all these organizations were present throughout the twentieth century, their numbers grew after the 1960s. The expansion of federal regulations and domestic policies since the 1960s increased the incentive for them to lobby legislators. Moreover, campaign finance reforms of the 1970s required legislators to expand their base of financial support. Public interest groups also formed lobbying organizations. The number of think tanks proliferated. This hyper-competitive environment resulted in a situation in which legislators were constantly scrambling to secure their links to a greater number of interest groups, none of which was dominant.

Divided government through much of this era made it difficult for legislators who sought dramatic policy change. Although divided government did not prevent Congress from passing legislation, it no longer offered a hospitable climate for major innovations like the Great Society.

The Supreme Court and the president also remained strong. The Court continued to take an active stand on issues such as legislative redistricting and states' rights. The presidency continued to remain a dominant institution, as when Ronald Reagan used his office to advance conservative aims. The War Powers Act seemed almost irrelevant when Reagan authorized military operations in Nicaragua and El Salvador without congressional approval. Presidents relied on international bodies to legitimate military action. While Congress responded with litigation, investigation, and legislation, the president usually had his way.

Despite all these obstacles, the House still passed significant legislation. In 1990, the House agreed to a deficit reduction plan that increased taxes and lowered spending. Following the terrorist attacks of September 11, 2001, Congress restructured airline security, put money into public health research, and created the Department of Homeland Security. Congress also created a prescription drug benefit for Medicare.

With all the uncertainties that legislators faced, a high rate of incumbency provided a form of personal security. The trend toward incumbency that started in the late nineteenth century never abated. While the Supreme Court had forced the elimination of congressional districts with unequal populations, it never tackled political gerrymandering. As a result, state legislatures were able to draw district lines to protect incumbents. After 1949, the majority of elections brought only 80 new members to the House. Campaign finance rules, moreover, favored those who already held office, since they could raise large sums of money quickly and receive free media exposure. Citizens also tended to like their representatives, even though they disliked Congress as an institution.

As George Mason hoped, the House has energized and preserved America's democratic aspirations. Commentators like to joke that legislation resembles sausage in that the taste may be good, but people do not want to see how the product was made. Yet the messiness and complexity of deliberations in the House, which are often criticized, reflect tensions and divisions that exist in the country. The House has struggled to forge compromises in response to the nation's biggest challenges. Sometimes the institution has failed in this task, but, at other times, the House has sent the Senate legislation that ended up transforming America. At the same time, the history of the House reminds us of some of democracy's biggest weaknesses, including corruption, destructive partisanship, and the lack of accountability on the part of elected officials.

See also Senate; state government.

FURTHER READING. Congressional Quarterly Press Electronic Library, http://library.cqpress.com/; Robin L. Einhorn, *American Taxation, American Slavery*, 2008; Lewis L. Gould, *The Most Exclusive Club: A History of the United States Senate*, 2006; Robert V. Remini, *The House: The History of the House of Representatives*, 2006; Eric Schickler, *Disjointed Pluralism: Institutional Innovation and the Development of the U.S. Congress*, 2001; Julian E. Zelizer, *On Capitol Hill: The Struggle to Reform Congress and Its Consequences, 1945–2000*, 2004; Idem, ed., *The American Congress: The Building of Democracy*, 2004.

JULIAN E. ZELIZER

immigration policy

Immigration policy has long been one of the most contentious and ultimately transformative issues on the American public agenda, evoking intense political struggles over how to regulate the flow of newcomers. Rival interests and ideals lie at the heart of these profound political conflicts. For more than two centuries, Americans have argued about the impact of new immigrants on jobs and economic growth, demography, culture, social welfare, the distribution of political power, foreign relations, and national security.

The United States may be a nation built upon immigration, but it has long been ambivalent about new arrivals. From Benjamin Franklin's eighteenth-century fears that Pennsylvania Germans would never assimilate to Samuel Huntington's more recent warnings that a growing Latino population imperils cultural harmony, many Americans have celebrated their sojourner past while dreading the immigrant present and future. For others, especially those in the labor movement, fresh waves of immigration have been perceived as anathema to workplace standards and economic security. By contrast, cosmopolitans such as Jane Addams and John F. Kennedy have championed broad immigrant admissions and rights as consistent with the American Creed, while capitalists like Andrew Carnegie have praised immigration as "a golden stream" that fortifies U.S. prosperity. In short, the choices raised by immigration policy have spurred vibrant debate since the founding and have served as a bellwether for larger political conflicts over changing economic opportunities, the status of ethnic, religious, and racial minorities, and the nation's evolving role in international diplomacy and warfare.

The polarizing politics of immigration reform, both past and present, has made policy making arduous but not impossible. Indeed, it has produced strange political bedfellows over time and yielded marked shifts from one period to the next between national policies that have significantly stimulated or discouraged immigration. The federal government only gradually and reluctantly took control of regulating immigrant admissions over the course of the nineteenth century. Since then, American immigration policy has assumed both restrictive and expansive forms. Whereas the creation of national origins quotas and an Asiatic Barred Zone in the 1920s effectively closed the gates, immigration reforms since 1965 helped trigger the nation's fourth major wave of migration, predominantly originating in Latin America, the Caribbean, and Asia. Few policy areas

have left a more profound mark on the development and present character of American social, economic, political, and cultural life. Even when immigration reform has had unintended results or when the best-laid plans of lawmakers have been defied by migratory behavior—such as dramatic increases in both unauthorized immigration and undocumented populations living in the United States—the policy outcomes have reshaped the nation.

At the time of the founding, due to early waves of immigration and the importation of slaves, the United States was already a remarkably diverse country in terms of religion, race, and ethnicity. Less than half of the new republic's white population could be described as English when the Revolution began. Anglo-Americans remained the dominant group in the former English colonies, but British newcomers increasingly came from Scotland, Wales, and Ireland. Moreover, one-third of the country's white inhabitants claimed German, Swedish, French, Swiss, or Dutch origins. Southern importation of African slaves was the principal engine of racial diversity in the early American republic. Finally, the United States was more religiously diverse than any country in Europe. Although immigration slowed to a trickle during the era of the American Revolution (no more than a few thousand per year), some national leaders remained wary of future inflows. In his *Notes on the State of Virginia* (1781), Thomas Jefferson criticized the new nation's member states for their "present desire to produce rapid population by as great importations of foreigners as possible." Most newcomers, he feared, would prove incapable of shedding their loyalties to the "absolute monarchy" of the Old World, or prone to material and anarchical temptations of the new one. The French Revolution and subsequent Napoleonic warfare in Europe delayed robust immigration to the United States until well after the 1820s. Nevertheless, new state governments wasted little time in establishing their own immigration and naturalization policies soon after the nation's founding. Most of these policies were designed to entice new European settlers and to extend broad membership rights to white male newcomers.

Immigration and the New Republic

With the ratification of the Constitution, the young nation embraced a laissez-faire federal policy toward European immigration and authorized Congress "to establish a uniform Rule of Naturalization." During Philadelphia deliberations in 1787, James Madison observed that those states which most encouraged European immigration were the strongest in population, agriculture, and the arts, and he warned against restrictions on immigrant rights that might "give a tincture of illiberality" to the new republic. The first Congress in 1790 enacted a naturalization law that granted citizenship to "free white persons" who lived in the United States for as little as two years.

During the 1790s, support for immigration was eroded by the Anglo-French conflict and partisan polarization at home. For the dominant Federalists, new French and Irish immigrants were untrustworthy because of their celebration of French revolutionary ideals and their support for the Democratic-Republican opposition. Federalist majorities in Congress passed a new naturalization law in 1795 that increased the residency requirement for citizenship to five years. Responding to security jitters in 1798 associated with the French conflict, Federalist lawmakers enacted the Alien and Sedition Acts. The legislation made immigrants eligible for citizenship only after 14 years of residency, and all aliens were required to register with federal officials. The Alien Act empowered the president to arrest and deport any alien "whom he shall judge dangerous to the peace and safety of the United States." The Alien Enemies Act, passed the same year, authorized the president to confine or remove male enemy aliens age 14 years or older during times of war. The Alien and Sedition Acts proved to be short-lived, as the victory of Jeffersonian Republicans in 1800 led to a repeal of alien registration requirements and the restoration of a five-year residency requirement for naturalization. With future elections and economic development in mind, Jefferson proclaimed that the United States represented a New Canaan where "those whom the misrule of Europe may compel to seek happiness in other climes" would "be received as brothers."

Immigrants, Nativists, and Nation Building: 1820–60

From the 1820s until the start of the Civil War, roughly 5 million European immigrants came to the United States. During the 1820s, immigration accounted for only 4 percent of the steady increase in American population; by the 1850s, immigration accounted for nearly one-third of U.S. population growth. The national government remained all but silent on European immigration during this period. Federal law required that new arrivals be counted after 1819 to maintain uniform statistics, and it mandated minimum living standards for vessels carrying immigrant passengers to the country. However, the task of regulating immigration continued to fall to state and local governments. In practice, the modest structures governing immigrant traffic in antebellum America were the creation and responsibility of a few states with large ports, such as New York (where most immigrants landed), Maryland, Massachusetts, Pennsylvania, and South Carolina. State immigration laws authorized exclusion of immigrants with criminal records, contagious illnesses, or other undesirable qualities, but few were turned away. Coastal states charged ship masters small head taxes on their immigrant passengers, a practice affirmed by the Supreme Court in 1837. The 1848 *Passenger Cases* reversed this holding, asserting that state head taxes violated federal prerogatives, but states made minor adjustments and maintained primacy in this area.

The dramatic expansion of U.S. territory with the Louisiana Purchase and the Mexican-American War created a strong demand for new immigrants to settle a large frontier. Territorial governments actively recruited European newcomers, hiring agents to recruit immigrants overseas or as they landed in port cities. The rise of an industrial economy also required an expanded labor force that European immigration helped realize. Grassroots nativism accompanied the unprecedented immigration of the antebellum decades, with Irish Catholic newcomers the most frequent targets of xenophobic hostility. Whereas Germans, who dominated immigration in these years. exemplified religious, class, and ideological diversity, the Irish were almost invariably poor and Roman Catholic. Anglo-American angst over the Irish Catholic influx, which soared during the Irish potato famine of the 1840s, was exacerbated by competition for jobs and housing in northeastern cities, struggles over public and parochial education, and the marriage of powerful urban party machines and Irish voters. Anti-Catholic books, newspapers, and magazines flourished in the antebellum period, offering lurid accounts of sinister Roman Catholic crimes and plots that fed Protestant antipathy. Sometimes the dark tales promulgated by this anti-Catholic literature spurred mob violence, from the 1834 burning of the Ursuline convent near Boston to the 1844 Bible Riots in Philadelphia that led to 20 deaths and the destruction of more than 100 Catholic churches, schools, and homes. The ranks of secret anti-Catholic associations swelled in seaboard cities. The nativist leader Samuel Morse, a newspaper editor and future inventor of the telegraph, organized an anti-immigrant party and ran for New York City mayor in 1836. He also fed anti-Catholic venom through popular and incendiary writings such as *Foreign Conspiracy* (1841), warning readers that "the evil of immigration brings to these shores illiterate Roman Catholics, the obedient instruments of their more knowing priestly leaders."

Because of the nation's insatiable appetite for immigrant labor and the clout of Irish voters, political nativists enjoyed little success until the 1850s. In 1849 secret nativist societies formed the Order of the Star Spangled Banner to furtively organize electoral support for its anti-Catholic and anti-immigrant agenda in cities around the country. The movement's rank and file included Anglo-American workers, artisans, and small entrepreneurs. Their secrecy led Horace Greeley to mock their members in *New York Tribune* as "know-nothings"—a label soon applied to political nativists who sought to restrict immigration and Catholic influence. The Know-Nothing movement formed a new American Party in the 1850s devoted to strict limits on immigrant admissions, 21-year waiting periods for citizenship, and restricting voting rights and officeholding to the native-born.

The Know-Nothings benefited enormously from a political vacuum created by the gradual demise of the Whig Party and balkanization of the Democrats. During the 1854 and 1855 elections, the American Party elected seven Know-Nothing governors, controlled eight state legislatures, and established a strong presence in Congress. In 1856, the party nominated Millard Fillmore for president, and he won 22 percent of the popular vote. The movement's meteoric rise transcended the ballot box. Know-Nothing candy, tea, and other merchandise were successfully marketed, while buses, stagecoaches and clipper ships soon bore the popular name. The decline of the American Party was as swift and dramatic as its ascent. The new Republican Party siphoned away nativist voters more devoted to excluding slavery from the territories than the Know-Nothings' "war to the hilt on Romanism." By 1860 the movement had collapsed. Ironically, the same slavery controversy that helped elevate anti-Catholic xenophobia in antebellum America was the driving force behind its rapid demise.

Expansion and Exclusion in the Gilded Age

To the chagrin of nativists, European immigration flourished in the last half of the nineteenth century. Fueled by federal recruitment efforts in Europe, the Homestead Act, and industrialization, inflows from Europe reached record levels in the post–Civil War decades. Immigration soared to 2.3 million in the 1860s, 2.8 million in the 1870s, 5.2 million in the 1880s, 3.6 million in the 1890s, and 8.8 million in the first decade of the twentieth century. The vast majority of new arrivals landed in New York, where they were channeled through a central immigration depot, Manhattan's Castle Garden. The nationalization of U.S. immigration policy began in 1875, when the Supreme Court nullified state efforts to regulate alien inflows as unconstitutional encroachments on exclusive congressional power. The Immigration Act of 1882 essentially legitimized state policies governing immigration that had been struck down by the Court. It excluded "any convict, lunatic, idiot" or anyone deemed likely to become a public charge, while assessing head taxes on each entrant to fund inspections and welfare provision for needy arrivals. In 1885 the Knights of Labor persuaded Democratic majorities in Congress to enact a ban on the importation of foreign contract labor. Legislation in 1891 created a new federal bureaucracy in the Treasury Department to supervise the screening of immigrants, with a corps of federal immigration inspectors stationed at the nation's major ports of entry. Within the year, Castle Garden was replaced by a new federal facility in New York harbor, Ellis Island. Screening nearly three-quarters of new arrivals, Ellis Island became the largest and busiest inspection station for years to come.

Compared to its European counterparts, Chinese immigration of the late nineteenth century was miniscule (4 percent of all immigration at its zenith), but it inspired one of the most brutal and successful nativist movements in U.S. history. Official and popular racism made Chinese newcomers especially vulnerable; their lack of numbers, political power, or legal protections gave them none of the weapons that enabled Irish Catholics to counterattack nativists. Chinese workers were first recruited to California from the 1850s through the 1870s as cheap contract labor for mining, railroad construction, manufacturing, and farming. They inspired hostility among white workers for allegedly lowering wages and working conditions, while newspapers and magazines portrayed the Chinese as a race of godless opium addicts, prostitutes, and gamblers. Labor leaders in San Francisco organized large anti-Chinese clubs in every ward of the city during the 1860s, and comparable associations followed in cities and towns throughout the state. California politicians also learned that anti-Chinese speeches and policies translated into votes. The state's first Republican governor in 1862, Leland Stanford, promised "to protect free white labor" from the "degraded" Chinese while, at the same time, his own farming and railroad enterprises employed them.

Economic distress inflamed the anti-Chinese movement in the 1870s, as the closing of unproductive mines, the completion of the transcontinental railroad, and a flood of new settlers to the Pacific Coast led to rampant unemployment. San Francisco union leaders again spearheaded Sinophobic organizational efforts, initiating a grassroots network of Chinese Exclusion Leagues that spread across California and the Far West to elect sympathetic candidates. From 1871 onward, California politicians raced to claim credit for a steady stream of anti-Chinese reforms that included state-level barriers to Chinese entry, segregation laws, and special taxes on Chinese businesses. One of the anti-Chinese movement's most effective firebrands was Denis Kearney, an Irish immigrant who blamed Chinese immigrants for his personal failure at mining. His demagogic campaign, which began with race-baiting speeches in the San Francisco sandlots, drew white laborers into a new Workingmen's Party of California, dedicated to the proposition that "the Chinese must go!" Kearney spurred a state constitutional convention in 1878 targeting the "Chinese menace," as well as an 1879 state referendum that endorsed Chinese exclusion by a 150,000-to-900 vote. When the Supreme Court struck down state-level efforts to restrict Chinese immigration, the Sinophobic movement pressed Congress to enact sweeping exclusions.

Fierce party competition in presidential elections of the post-Reconstruction era transformed the anti-Chinese movement into a national political juggernaut. As the *New York Times* queried in 1880, "Which great political party is foolish enough to risk losing the votes of the Pacific States by undertaking to do justice to the Chinese?"—neither, as it turned out. Large bipartisan majorities in Congress suspended Chinese admissions for ten years with passage of the Chinese Exclusion Act of 1882. Some of the worst anti-Chinese riots erupted in subsequent years, as Sinophobes sought to purge Chinese communities altogether across the Far West. Forced expulsions were initiated almost wherever Chinese numbered in the hundreds in cities and towns of the Pacific Northwest and Mountain States. During the 1885 Rock Springs, Wyoming, massacre, 28 Chinese were murdered and every Chinese-owned building except one was destroyed. In Tacoma and Seattle during 1885 and 1886, Chinese residents were given "deportation" deadlines. They suffered looting, arson, and violent riots until few remained. In subsequent election years, national Democrats and Republicans curried favor with the Sinophobic movement by enacting increasingly draconian restrictions on the "Chinese race." The 1888 Scott Act, for instance, denied readmission of Chinese who left U.S. territory; 20,000 were not allowed to return under the law and many were separated from their families. The Sinophobic fervor did not subside until the early 1900s, when a significantly reduced Chinese population was concentrated in a few self-sufficient Chinatowns.

As western nativists put their final touches on Chinese exclusion, a new anti-Catholic movement emerged in the nation's heartland. The American Protective Association (APA) was founded in Clinton, Iowa, in 1887 by Henry Bowers, an attorney aggrieved by a friend's mayoral defeat and the decline of public schools, both of which he attributed to malevolent Catholic influence. An ardent Mason, Bowers made the APA into a secret fraternal order with an anti-Catholic political agenda that drew heavily upon the rituals, organization, and membership of Masonic lodges. The APA spread in the early 1890s to larger midwestern and Rocky Mountain communities where Catholics were gaining political and social clout; its support came primarily from Protestant businessmen, disaffected union workers, and those competing with cheap Irish labor.

In 1893 the ranks of APA faithful surged to more than a half million. Its growth owed much to new leadership by William "Whiskey Bill" Traynor, a former saloon owner with considerable experience promoting anti-Catholic causes and publishing nativist newspapers. During the depression of 1893, he and his APA lieutenants roused crowds by blaming the economic crisis on Irish Catholic immigrants who allegedly stole jobs, started a run on the banks, and encouraged labor militancy.

Rather than form a third party, APA organizers established local and state "advisory boards" to endorse candidates, almost invariably Republican, who demonstrated strong anti-Catholic credentials. In 1893 and 1894, APA voters were credited with electing anti-Catholic Republicans in municipal, school board, and congressional elections in midwestern and Rocky Mountain States. Yet the importance of immigrant labor and votes led many national Republican leaders to challenge the APA's nativist agenda. In 1896 William McKinley's presidential campaign actively courted immigrant and Roman Catholic voters while purging the APA from Republican ranks. Cut loose from its partisan moorings, the APA quickly faded from the political landscape.

Closing the Gates: 1917–44

As the APA crusade dissipated, a new anti-immigrant movement led by the upper-class Immigration Restriction League (IRL), the American Federation of Labor, and patriotic societies distanced itself from anti-Catholic nativism. Embracing the scientific racism of Social Darwinism and the eugenics movement, these reformers argued that southern and eastern Europeans arriving in record numbers from countries like Italy, Greece, Russia, Hungary, and Poland were biologically inferior to immigrants from Western and Northern Europe. Their chief goal was a literacy test for admission, based on the presumption that most immigrants lacking Anglo-Saxon lineage were unable to read. They enjoyed a prominent champion in Massachusetts senator Henry Cabot Lodge, who warned that "new" European immigration posed "nothing less than the possibility of a great and perilous change in the fabric of our race." Progressive Era nativists also spurned party politics in favor of mass publicity campaigns, biased research, and full-time Washington lobbying. Their efforts paid dividends when the 1911 Dillingham Commission, led by IRL allies, including Lodge, produced 42 volumes of findings that purportedly vindicated nativist claims about southern and eastern Europeans. Despite these inroads, a counter-mobilization of immigration defenders led by employer and ethnic groups yielded policy stalemate. President Woodrow Wilson denounced the nativist agenda as inconsistent with "the humane ardors of our republic."

The onset of World War I broke the logjam. Immigration restrictionists seized upon wartime anxieties to win passage of an immigration literacy test in 1917, arguing that southern and eastern Europeans were inherently disloyal and dangerous. While the IRL and its allies were closing the gates, an Americanization movement attacked any hint of divided loyalties among the foreign-born already in the country. Theodore Roosevelt led the charge for "100% Americanism," denouncing "hyphenated" Americans as guilty of no less then "moral treason." Patriotic conformity was pursued by a government-sponsored network of local defense and patriotic associations, including 250,000 badge-wearing volunteers of the American Protective League (APL). German Americans, celebrated for decades as the model ethnic group, endured the harshest treatment. They were targets of vandalism, mob violence, surveillance, and harassment by APL watchdogs; job discrimination; and arrest for unpatriotic speech. By 1918 public burnings of German books were common, dozens of German American newspapers and organizations were forced to dissolve, and several states prohibited speaking German or playing German-composed music in public.

After the war, the immigration restriction movement mobilized for new reforms when the literacy test failed to curb southern and eastern European inflows. As European immigration soared to 800,000 in 1920, a sharp leap from the meager numbers of the war years, a State Department report warned that the country faced an inundation of "filthy" and "unassimilable" Jews, displaced by persecution in eastern and central Europe. At the same time, the House Immigration Committee employed its own "expert eugenics agent," Harry Laughlin, to illuminate racial differences among immigrants. "We in this country have been so imbued with the idea of democracy, or the equality of all men," Laughlin testified, "that we have left out of consideration the matter of blood or natural inborn hereditary mental and moral differences. No man who breeds pedigreed plants and animals can afford to neglect this thing." During the first "Red scare," immigration restrictionists pressed for "emergency" legislation to fend off a foreign influx that would compromise national security. The Quota Act of 1921 established annual limits of 3 percent of each nationality living in the United States at the time of the 1910 census. These quotas were applied to immigration from all countries except those of the Western Hemisphere. The free flow of Western Hemisphere immigration was a concession that lawmakers made to southwestern growers who lobbied vigorously to retain access to cheap Mexican farm labor. Southern and eastern European inflows were the chief target of the new law, restricted by quotas to less than one-fourth of annual admissions before World War I.

The Immigration Act of 1924 marked the crowning achievement of the immigration restriction movement. It created a 165,000 ceiling on annual immigrant admissions, refined national origins quotas to reserve 84 percent of annual visas for northern and western Europeans, and reaffirmed an Asiatic Barred Zone that excluded virtually all Asian immigrants and most other nonwhites. "To the national dishonor of the 'assisted' immigration of slave trade days," Jane Addams sadly noted, "we are adding another chapter." But immigration restrictionists exalted as southern and eastern European immigration slowed to a trickle. "The United States is our land," Congressman Albert Johnson proclaimed. "The day of unalloyed welcome to all peoples, the day of indiscriminate acceptance of all races, has definitely ended." Legislation in 1928 made the national origins quota system fully operative, but it also continued to allow unfettered Western Hemisphere migration as a bow to powerful southern and western lawmakers

and economic interests. The result was a bifurcated system imposing draconian restrictions on European and Asian immigration while remaining open and flexible toward labor inflows from Mexico and other Western Hemisphere countries.

Mexican immigration increased substantially during the 1920s, but neither legal nor illegal Mexican inflows prompted great concern among national policy makers. Efforts by the American Federation of Labor to impose 1,500 annual quotas on Mexican immigration went nowhere because of resistance from southwestern growers and their supporters in Congress. The onset of the Great Depression changed public perceptions of Mexican labor migration considerably, leading to a mass deportation campaign that reinforced notions of Latino workers as a "returnable" labor force. At the same time, U.S. consular offices denied visas to those deemed "likely to become a public charge," with the effect that many quota slots went unfilled. During the 1930s, immigration reached the lowest levels in a century and the total number of people leaving the country exceeded those entering for the first time in its history. From the rise of the Nazi regime until the end of World War II, powerful members of Congress and State Department officials blocked efforts to grant refuge to European Jews and others fleeing fascist regimes. In the early 1940s, by contrast, agribusinesses and other employer groups won White House support for a new Mexican temporary worker program, the Bracero Program, to address wartime labor shortages. This guest worker program would bring 4.2 million temporary Mexican laborers to the United States before it was terminated at the urging of organized labor in 1963.

Refugees, Cold War, and Reform: 1945–65
During the 1940s and 1950s, pro-immigration reformers attempted to chip away at the national origins quota system. Eager to strengthen a wartime alliance with China, Congress repealed Chinese exclusion statutes in favor of a token annual quota. Symbolic quotas were extended to other Asian nations a few years later. Lawmakers also enacted the War Brides Act in 1946 that waived quota limits for the alien wives and children of U.S. servicemen. The cold war imperatives of global leadership and anticommunism led to other departures from the quota restrictions. President Harry Truman took unilateral action in 1945 to give 40,000 people from various European countries displaced by the war preferential consideration for visas. At Truman's urging, Congress later passed the Displaced Persons acts of 1948 and 1950 to permit European refugees from countries with severe visa limits to be included in future quotas.

Despite these modest breaks in the restrictionist wall, cold war anxieties fueled passage of the Internal Security Act of 1950, which authorized the exclusion or deportation of aliens who had ever been

Communists or members of any group deemed to be a "front" organization. In a nation that had fallen under the spell of McCarthyism, immigration restriction continued to enjoy a deep reservoir of both popular and congressional support. The McCarran-Walter Act of 1952 retained national origins quotas as the cornerstone of U.S. immigration policy and expanded the government's alien surveillance and deportation powers. Receiving solid backing from southern and western members of Congress, it is little wonder that the 1952 law also contained a "Texas proviso" that exempted employers of undocumented aliens from any form of legal sanction. A year later, the Eisenhower administration persuaded lawmakers to open the door temporarily for 200,000 European refugees. In 1956 the White House used emergency powers to admit refugees from the failed Hungarian Revolution. During the same period, the federal government cracked down on illegal immigration. Supported by local police and federal troops, the Immigration and Naturalization Service (INS) launched "Operation Wetback" in 1954 to quiet public concerns about a growing population of undocumented aliens. Dragnet raids led to the capture and summary expulsion of more than a million Mexican noncitizens.

The postwar decades witnessed the rise of a new movement for immigration reform that included a broad array of ethnic, human rights, religious, business, and even labor groups like the Congress of Industrial Organizations. During the early 1960s these reformers found champions in Presidents John Kennedy and Lyndon Johnson. In 1964 Johnson called on Congress to "lift by legislation the bars of discrimination against those who seek entry into our country." A product of the Great Society, the Immigration Reform Act of 1965 dismantled the national origins quota system in favor of a new preference system that gave primacy to reuniting families while reserving a limited number of visas for skilled workers and refugees. In its aftermath, an unexpected wave of Asian, Latin American, and Caribbean immigrants came to the United States, with European immigration falling by the early 1970s to only 10 percent of all legal admissions. The 1965 law also placed a 120,000 annual ceiling on Western Hemisphere visas that, along with the 1963 termination of the Bracero Program, spurred illegal Mexican inflows.

Reopening the Golden Door: 1966–present

The issue of illegal immigration inspired more media attention, public concern, and remedial proposals by policy makers than did any other migratory issue of the 1970s. At the heart of early efforts to control porous borders was a proposal by organized labor and congressional Democrats like Peter Rodino to penalize employers who knowingly hired undocumented aliens. Employer sanctions bills met staunch resistance, however, from southwestern growers and various business groups opposed to new regulation

as well as Latino and civil rights groups concerned that sanctions would lead employers to discriminate against anyone who looked or sounded foreign. An effort by the Carter White House to enact a compromise reform package in 1977 drew fire from all sides and ultimately died.

As efforts to address illegal immigration became mired in rancorous debate in the late 1970s, Congress created a Select Commission on Immigration and Refugee Policy to broadly review U.S. immigration policy. Its 1982 report endorsed large-scale legal immigration, highlighting the social benefits of family reunification, the economic value of immigrant laborers and taxpayers, and the diplomatic and moral imperatives of admitting refugees. It also concluded that illegal immigration had an adverse affect on American society and recommended a reform package of employer sanctions, enhanced Border Patrol resources, and a legalization program for most of the undocumented population already living in the country. After protracted legislative wrangling, Congress finally took action to curb illegal immigration with enactment of the Immigration Reform and Control Act of 1986 (IRCA). The new law was a compromise package of watered-down employer sanctions, legalization for undocumented aliens living in the country since 1982, and a new Seasonal Agricultural Worker Program to appease growers. The measure proved highly successful in granting legal status to nearly 3 million undocumented aliens, but employer sanctions proved to be a "toothless tiger."

By the late 1980s, it was clear to national policy makers that the IRCA had done virtually nothing to discourage illegal immigration. But legislators were eager to shift their attention to the politically painless task of expanding legal immigration. A welter of advocacy groups clamored for specific expansions in legal immigration opportunities. A "family coalition" of Asian, Latino, and other ethnic and human rights groups won an increase in the number of visas available for family reunification. A "business coalition" secured new preferences and visa allocations for employer-sponsored and skills-based immigration. At the end of the day, the Immigration Act of 1990 unified cosmopolitans and free market expansionists behind a 40 percent increase in annual visa allocations that benefited both family-based and employment-based immigration.

During the early 1990s, a grassroots movement in California mobilized against illegal immigration by advancing a measure, Proposition 187, that was designed to deny unauthorized migrants and their children welfare benefits, health care, and public education. Republican governor Pete Wilson and the state Republican organization threw their support behind the measure during the 1994 campaign, transforming it into a partisan issue. Proposition 187 carried the state with 59 percent of the vote. For the first time since 1952, Republicans gained control of both houses of Congress in 1994. New immigration subcommittee leadership and a special task force on immigration reform, chaired by California Republican Elton Gallegly, called for restrictive policy challenges. Their agenda included new crackdowns on criminal aliens and illegal immigration, denial of welfare benefits to immigrants, and new limits on legal admissions. The first two of these goals were secured in 1996 with passage of the Illegal Immigration Reform and Immigrant Responsibility Act (IIRIRA) and the Personal Responsibility and Work Opportunity Act (PRWOA). Efforts to reduce legal immigration were defeated in the Senate by a cross-party alliance of cosmopolitans and free market expansionists.

In 1995 several prominent Republican congressional leaders expressed optimism behind closed doors that the immigration issue would cost Democrats blue-collar votes. At the start of the 1996 election, Pete Wilson made immigration control the defining issue of his short-lived presidential campaign; Pat Buchanan assailed third world immigration as a source of economic and cultural insecurity at home; and Bob Dole, the eventual Republican standard-bearer, associated himself with the stringent immigrant measures then working their way through Congress. The 1996 Republican platform pledged support for national legislation barring children of undocumented aliens from public schools.

Yet the results of the 1996 election left little doubt about two crucial developments: immigrants comprised the nation's fastest growing voting bloc and Democrats were the immediate beneficiaries of their unanticipated electoral clout. Naturalization rates soared after 1995, as record numbers of aliens became citizens. More than 1 million people became naturalized in 1996 alone. At the same time as unprecedented numbers of aliens petitioned for naturalization in the mid-1990s, President Clinton instructed the INS to implement the so-called Citizenship USA initiative. In the words of the agency, the initiative "was designed to streamline the naturalization process and greatly increase naturalizations during 1996." Voter registrations among Latinos grew by 1.3 million, or 28.7 percent, between 1992 and 1996; the percentage of Latinos on the voter rolls rose from 59 percent of those eligible in 1992 to 65 percent in 1996. The Latino Democratic vote increased from 60 percent in the 1992 presidential election to 72 percent in 1996. Asian voters, a smaller yet important swing bloc, increased their support for the Democratic ticket in the same years from 29 to 43 percent. Dole became the first Republican presidential candidate to lose Florida since Gerald Ford in 1976.

In the 2000 election, Republican national and state organizations drew up plans to attract new Asian and Latino voters. Texas governor George W. Bush was hailed by party leaders as the ideal candidate to court new immigrant voters, and he reminded Latinos throughout the campaign that early on he had "rejected the spirit of Prop 187," opposed "English-only" proposals, and refused "to bash immigrants" when it

was popular. Once in the White House, Bush created a special task force, led by Secretary of State Colin Powell, to address illegal immigration anew. These efforts were preempted by the terrorist attacks of September 11, which created a new sense of urgency about the security risks posed by newcomers and porous borders. Soon after the attacks, the Justice Department prescribed special registration requirements for male noncitizens aged 14 years or older from Arab and Muslim countries. The USA Patriot Act of 2001 eased deportations and restricted admission for those with potential ties to terrorist organizations or those who may have the intention of committing a terrorist act. Bush's efforts to relaunch comprehensive immigration reform in his second term, including a guest worker program, earned legalization, employer sanctions, and strengthened border enforcement—went nowhere. While the proposal was assailed by labor leaders and immigrant advocacy groups, the harshest attacks came from fellow conservatives both in Washington and at the grassroots who saw undocumented aliens as threats to national sovereignty, security, and identity.

In the winter of 2005, a punitive bill focused on border enforcement narrowly passed the Republican-controlled House of Representatives. It proposed for the first time to make illegal presence in the United States a felony, and made it a crime for any persons or organizations to lend support to undocumented immigrants. The bill was also a direct attack on day laborer centers. From March through May 2006, demonstrations against the bill by largely Latino immigrants and their supporters, unprecedented in number and size, took place in cities and towns across the United States. These nationwide rallies, protests, and boycotts drew negative reactions from most Americans: just 24 percent had a favorable view of people who marched and protested for immigrant rights in major cities while 52 percent expressed unfavorable opinions. Overall, however, public opinion remained open to varied policy solutions: majorities favored legal status and earned citizenship for undocumented immigrants, stricter employer penalties, and tougher enforcement.

In the spring and summer of 2007, the Bush administration and a bipartisan Senate coalition led by Edward Kennedy negotiated "a grand bargain" that included significant new funding for border security and other interior enforcement measures. It imposed criminal penalties for illegal entry, which had previously been a misdemeanor offense, and proposed to replace the current family and employment–based admissions system with a "merit-based" system. The bill provided a new Z visa for undocumented immigrants that covered "a principal or employed alien, the spouse or elderly parent of that alien, and the minor children of that alien" currently living in the United States. The visa provided they pay fees and penalties that could total as much as $8,000 and a "touchback provision" requiring the leader of the household to return home before applying for legal permanent residency status. The bill also contained a temporary Y worker program that would allow about 200,000 workers to be admitted for a two-year period that could be renewed twice, as long as the worker spent a period of one year outside of the United States between each admission.

The compromise Senate immigration plan was subject to intense media scrutiny and commentary, and the public response ranged from hostile to tepid. Many members of Congress were deluged with angry phone calls, emails, and letters from constituents and other activists. Surveys indicated that most Republicans, Democrats, and Independents opposed the measure, with only 23 percent in favor. Significantly, most Americans opposed the initiative not because they opposed "amnesty" or other proposals for legalizing millions of undocumented immigrants in the country (roughly two-thirds supported earned citizenship options over deportation), but rather because they had little trust that it would provide genuine border security. More than 80 percent in surveys said that they did not believe that the Bush-Senate compromise bill would reduce illegal immigration or enhance border control. Ultimately, the forces arrayed against this last-ditch reform effort were overwhelming, from the grassroots to the halls of Congress. The political minefield of immigration reform was shelved until after the 2008 election.

In the early twentieth century, the United States was in the midst of a "fourth wave" of immigration unprecedented in terms of its extraordinarily diverse origins and the dominance of newcomers from Latin America, the Caribbean, and Asia. Wealthy democracies all face thorny policy challenges when they try to stimulate or restrict the flow of people across their borders. For Americans, immigration policy has long stirred ambivalence and political conflicts that defy the standard liberal-conservative divide, inspire battles among fellow partisans, and produce strange and fleeting bedfellows. The laissez-faire, restrictive, and expansive policies that have emerged from these political struggles over the course of U.S. history have had profound implications for the character and development of the nation.

See also anticommunism; citizenship; nativism.

FURTHER READING. Kitty Calavita, *Inside the State: The Bracero Program, Immigration and the I.N.S.*, 1992; Roger Daniels, *Coming to America: A History of Immigration and Ethnicity in American Life*, 2002; David Gutierrez, *Walls and Mirrors: Mexican Americans, Mexican Immigrants, and the Politics of Ethnicity*, 1985; John Higham, *Strangers in the Land: Patterns of American Nativism, 1860–1925*, 2002; Hiroshi Motomura, *Americans in Waiting: The Lost Story of Immigration and Citizenship in the United States*, 2007; David Reimers, *Still the Golden Door: The Third World Comes to America*, 1985; Daniel Tichenor, *Dividing Lines: The Politics of Immigration Control in America*, 2002; Aristide Zolberg, *A Nation by Design: Immigration Policy in the Fashioning of America*, 2006.

DANIEL J. TICHENOR

impeachment

Impeachment is one of the most potent and sharply debated powers of Congress. It is formidable because it is the principal, if not only, means through which Congress may remove presidents, Supreme Court justices, and certain other high-ranking federal officials for misconduct. While the popular understanding of this power has largely been shaped by the notable impeachment efforts against Presidents Andrew Johnson, Richard Nixon, and Bill Clinton and Associate Justice Samuel Chase, it is not possible to understand impeachment generally, much less its high-profile deployments, without analyzing the distinctive features of its application throughout U.S. history.

Impeachment Clauses: Text and Original Meaning

The text and original meaning of the Constitution illuminate the distinctive features of the federal impeachment process. In designing it, the founders distinguished the Constitution's federal impeachment process from that which had been in existence in Britain and the colonies. Whereas the king was not subject to impeachment or removal, Article II, section IV of the Constitution explicitly makes the president, among others, subject to the impeachment process. Article II expressly narrows the range of people subject to impeachment from what it had been in England, where any citizen (other than a member of the royal family) could be impeached. This article explicitly restricts impeachment to "[t]he President, Vice-President and all civil officers of the United States."

Article II further narrows the range of impeachable offenses to "Treason, Bribery, or other high Crimes or Misdemeanors." Although the framers of the Constitution discussed "high Crimes or Misdemeanors" only in abstract terms as referring to political crimes or "great offenses" or "breaches of the public trust," they hoped to restrict the scope of impeachable offenses to deviate from the parliamentary practice, which recognized no limit to the grounds for which people could be removed from office.

Conviction became more difficult than it had been in Great Britain, where the House of Lords could convict with a bare majority. In contrast, the founders divided the impeachment authority between the House and the Senate; gave the House the "sole power to impeach," which required majority approval; and required at least two-thirds concurrence of the Senate for conviction and removal. The Senate was vested with trial authority, because the founders believed that senators would be better educated and more virtuous, well suited to making difficult judgments about procedures and removal, and resistant to majoritarian pressures than members of the House of Representatives.

Whereas the British Parliament could impose any punishment upon conviction, including death, Article I of the Constitution restricts the Senate's power in impeachment trials "to removal from Office, and disqualification to hold and enjoy any Office of honor, Trust, or Profit under the United States." Article II expressly forbids the president from pardoning an individual for the offenses committed, while the king could have pardoned any person convicted in an impeachment trial. In contrast to Great Britain, where impeachment was understood to be a criminal proceeding, Article I provides that "the Party convicted [in an impeachment trial] shall nevertheless be liable and subject to Indictment, Trial, Judgment and Punishment, according to law." Article III explicitly grants federal judges the special tenure of serving "during good Behavior." The founders required the chief justice to preside over presidential impeachment trials to avoid a potential conflict of interest for the vice president, who usually presided over the Senate, in presiding over the trial of the one person standing between him and the presidency. The Constitution further requires senators to be "on oath or affirmation" when sitting in presidential impeachment trials. These requirements underscore the solemnity of such proceedings.

Impeachment Practice

The founders left the scope of the federal impeachment power to be worked out by Congress over time. Since ratification, the House of Representatives has formally impeached 16 officials, including one Supreme Court justice (Samuel Chase) and two presidents (Andrew Johnson and Bill Clinton). President Richard Nixon resigned shortly after the House Judiciary Committee approved three impeachment articles against him. In the course of these proceedings and other occasions on which the House has conducted or considered initiating impeachment inquiries, Congress has faced several significant constitutional questions. Historical patterns are important because they illuminate Congress's deliberate judgments on the major constitutional questions arising in impeachment proceedings. Indeed, the impeachment judgments of Congress are effectively final, because they are not subject to judicial review—as held by the Supreme Court unanimously in *Walter Nixon v. United States* (1993)—or presidential veto. The realization that they have the final word on impeachment matters encourages most if not all members of Congress to make impeachment judgments that will withstand the scrutiny of history.

The first noteworthy pattern in Congress's impeachment practices clarifies the meaning of "other high Crimes and Misdemeanors" as the basis for removal. Most scholars believe that this language refers

to "political crimes" or abuses of power or injuries to the Republic. While they agree that not all indictable crimes are "political crimes" and vice versa, they disagree over how to identify which breaches of the public trust ought to qualify as grounds for removing high-ranking officials from office.

It is suggestive that, of the 16 men whom the House formally impeached, only five were impeached primarily or solely for indictable crimes, and one of the five (Alcee Hastings) had been formally acquitted of bribery prior to his impeachment and removal for that crime and for perjury. The House's impeachment articles against the other 11 included misconduct for which anyone could be criminally punished. Four of the seven impeached officials convicted by the Senate were charged with nonindictable offenses. The remaining three (Harry Claiborne, Alcee Hastings, and Walter Nixon) were charged with indictable crimes. Both Claiborne and Nixon had been indicted, convicted in federal court, and exhausted their criminal appeals prior to their impeachment proceedings.

A second significant pattern in historical practices clarifies the related questions of whether impeachment is the exclusive means for removing judges and justices and whether Article III conditions judicial tenure on "good Behavior" and therefore allows judges or justices to be removed not only for "Treason, Bribery, or other high Crimes and Misdemeanors" but also for any misbehavior, including bad or erroneous decisions. A minority of scholars and members of Congress have argued that the "good Behavior" clause may also establish an alternative mechanism to impeachment for disciplining judges. But most scholars and members of Congress have maintained that a natural inference from the structure of the Constitution, backed by original meaning, is that the impeachment process is the exclusive means by which Congress may remove judges or justices. The "good Behavior" clause vests Article III judges with life tenure and thus protection from political retaliation for their judicial decisions, and impeaching and removing justices and judges for mistaken decisions would completely undermine their judicial independence.

The principle of judicial independence was vindicated in the only impeachment of a Supreme Court justice to date. In 1804, the House, controlled by Democrat-Republicans, impeached Associate Justice Samuel Chase, a fiercely partisan Federalist, based on claims that he had rendered flagrantly partisan rulings in the trials of two Republicans charged with violating the Federalist-backed Alien and Sedition Acts. A bare majority vote in the Senate to convict Chase fell short of the required two-thirds for conviction and removal. Much later, Chief Justice William Rehnquist construed Chase's acquittal as a seminal decision upholding the "complete independence of federal judges from removal because of their judicial decisions."

Subsequently, impeachment resolutions have been introduced in the House against two other Supreme Court justices: Chief Justice Earl Warren and Associate Justice William O. Douglas. In quickly dismissing inquiries against both justices, the House followed the principle initially laid down by Chase's acquittal. On another occasion, President Nixon's attorney general John Mitchell and other White House aides successfully managed in 1969 to force Justice Abe Fortas to resign from the Supreme Court rather than face public embarrassment and possible impeachment because of a contract into which he briefly entered after joining the Court to provide legal counsel to a former client who had been subsequently convicted for securities fraud.

A third pattern in past impeachment practices suggests that the paradigmatic case for impeachment and removal has three elements: (1) a bad act such as serious abuse of power, (2) a bad or malicious intent, and (3) a link between the official's misconduct and his official duties. Though Richard Nixon was not formally impeached, convicted, and removed from office, scholars agree that all these elements were evident in the misconduct charged against him by the House Judiciary Committee—using the powers of his office to obstruct investigations into his involvement in authorizing or covering up a burglary of the Democratic National Committee headquarters; ordering the FBI and IRS to harass his political enemies; and refusing to comply with a legislative subpoena requesting taped White House conversations, which the Supreme Court had unanimously ordered him to turn over to a special prosecutor. In contrast, many commentators and several senators explained President Clinton's acquittal in 1998 on the absence of one or more of these three elements. Most historians also agree that in acquitting President Andrew Johnson on charges he had abused his powers by not complying with a federal law requiring him to get Senate approval before firing a cabinet member whom it had confirmed, the Senate had determined that Johnson's misconduct was merely a policy difference with Congress for which removal was inappropriate.

A fourth pattern of impeachment practices reinforces the inference, derived from the specific requirement of at least two-thirds concurrence of the Senate for removal, that removal is only possible with widespread bipartisan support in the Senate. A supermajority is difficult to achieve in the Senate, particularly when the stakes are high, as they were in the impeachment trials of Presidents Johnson and Clinton and Justice Chase. Statistics bear this out, given that most people impeached by the House have been acquitted by the Senate (the 16 House impeachments have resulted in only seven Senate convictions). Indeed, the uniform opposition of all 45 Senate Democrats to President Clinton's conviction for perjury and obstruction of justice highlights the enormous difficulty of securing a conviction in a presidential

impeachment trial as long as the senators from the president's party unanimously, or largely, support him. Since a political party rarely controls more than two-thirds of the Senate, presidential removal is only possible if the misconduct is sufficiently compelling to draw support for conviction from senators from both parties.

Fifth, historical practices supplement other sources of constitutional meaning to support the constitutionality of censure as an alternative to impeachment. For instance, the provision that "Judgment in Cases of Impeachment shall not extend further than to" removal from office or disqualification suggests that Congress may take any action against impeachable officials falling short of either of these sanctions, as seems to be the case with censure. Indeed, the House passed resolutions criticizing John Tyler, James Polk, James Buchanan, and several other high-ranking officials, while the Senate passed two resolutions critical of officials other than the president in the nineteenth century and censured Andrew Jackson for firing his treasury secretary for refusing to take actions undermining the national bank. While the Senate later expunged its censure of Jackson, neither the censure nor its subsequent expunging is binding authority on whether senators today may censure impeachable officials.

The historical records further suggest that impeachment is a relatively ineffective check against a popular president's misconduct, particularly in the age of the 24-hour news cycle. If the enormous ramifications of removing a president dissuaded a hostile Senate from doing so with the hugely unpopular Andrew Johnson, as was the case, it should not be surprising that a later Senate would hesitate before removing a popular one who used the bully pulpit of the presidency to defend himself, as was the case with Bill Clinton. The congressional investigation into Watergate took more than two years before the discovery of the "smoking gun"—taped White House conversations—that led to Nixon's resignation. The Clinton impeachment proceedings took roughly six months, among the shortest in history. Yet, throughout the constant media coverage of the proceedings, Clinton's popularity increased while the popularity of, and support for, the Republican majority in the House and Senate seeking his ouster declined.

Indeed, Clinton's case raises the issue of how serious the misconduct of a popular president must be to convince a majority of Americans or a supermajority in the Senate to support his ouster from office. Future members of Congress could hesitate before engaging in a prolonged investigation of a president's misconduct for fear of alienating the public. They might further believe that the failure of the House to do any independent fact-finding prior to impeaching Clinton (one of only three instances when the House failed to do so) was a mistake that cost the House a valuable opportunity to cultivate the public's confidence in its nonpartisan intent. Consequently, what

Clinton's acquittal may show is that, in the future, impeachment will be effective only in the rare circumstances in which the wrongdoing is so severe (and so clearly proven) as to galvanize the public and demand the president's ouster or resignation.

A seventh significant pattern in impeachment practices concerns the nonreviewable decisions by the House and Senate on critical procedural issues. In its proceedings against President Clinton, the House held a final vote on the impeachment articles in a lame-duck session, to forego adopting a uniform standard for defining the impeachability of certain misconduct, and not to call witnesses or otherwise engage in independent fact-finding. In Clinton's impeachment trial, senators resolved that each could decide for himself or herself on the applicability of the Fifth Amendment due process clause, burden of proof, rules of evidence, and the propriety of closed-door meetings. The senators also allowed three colleagues to vote on Clinton's removal even though they had voted on his impeachment in the House before being elected to the Senate.

A final set of historical practices is the two instances in which the chief justice presided over presidential impeachment trials. In 1867 the House impeached President Andrew Johnson for illegally obstructing Reconstruction and the Tenure of Office Act, which required Senate approval prior to dismissal by the president of any officials whom he had nominated and the Senate had confirmed. Chief Justice Salmon Chase declared, at the outset, that "the Constitution has charged the Chief Justice with an important function in the [impeachment] trial . . . of the President." Chase helped shape the rules adopted by the Senate to govern the president's impeachment trial, which continue to this day and which include one that empowered him to rule initially on every procedural issue, subject to override by a majority of the Senate. Subsequently, the Senate overrode Chase's evidentiary rulings 17 times. But most of his procedural rulings were upheld by the Senate even though they usually favored Johnson's defense.

In 1999 Chief Justice Rehnquist presided over President Clinton's trial. Whereas many senators had questioned Chief Justice Chase's impartiality (and suspected he wanted to use the proceedings to further his presidential ambitions), Rehnquist commanded the respect of all senators, and there were no Senate challenges to or overrides of any of his procedural rulings.

Since President Clinton's acquittal, the House has not initiated any impeachment proceedings. Some members of Congress and scholars insist justices may be impeached and removed for their decisions. And some insisted that President George W. Bush and Vice President Dick Cheney should have been impeached and removed for their aggressive actions in the wake of the terrorist attacks against the United States on September 11, 2001. But Congress does not appear eager to use its impeachment power. Instead, it seems resigned to employ it, as many founders expected, only as a last resort to deal with severe presidential and judicial misconduct.

See also House of Representatives; Senate; Supreme Court.

FURTHER READING. Raoul Berger, *Impeachment: The Constitutional Problems*, 1973; Charles L. Black, *Impeachment: A Handbook*, Revised ed., 1998; Michael J. Gerhardt, *The Federal Impeachment Process: A Constitutional and Historical Analysis*, 2nd ed., 2000; Peter Charles Hoffer and N.E.H. Hull, *Impeachment in America, 1635–1801*, 1984; William H. Rehnquist, *Grand Inquests: The Impeachment Trials of Justice Samuel Chase and President Andrew Johnson*, 1992.

MICHAEL GERHARDT

interest groups

The U.S. Constitution designated voting as the primary link between citizens and government, yet it also protected the politically salient rights of free speech, a free press, free assembly, and the right to petition. This framework recognized a broad arena of political activity outside of formal governmental institutions—one that would be funneled through individual voting in periodic elections to select legislators and presidential electors. Yet even before the Constitution was adopted, commentators were well aware that citizens' political activity with formal government was not likely to be limited to the casting of ballots. In Federalist Paper number 10, James Madison famously warned of the dangers of faction, by which he meant "a number of citizens, whether amounting to a majority or minority of the whole, who are united and actuated by some common impulse of passion, or of interest, adverse to the rights of other citizens, or to the permanent and aggregate interest of the community."

The Problem of Faction

Faction was not defined by the character of the group but by the relationship of its interest or passion to the rights of others or to the public good. Under Madison's formulation, a majority could constitute a faction and, therefore, protections against the tyranny of the majority were also protections against these large factions. Although one could not extinguish the causes of faction without extinguishing liberty itself, Madison argued that a system of representative government within a large republic offered the best protection from the dangers of faction, a protection that would be impossible in a pure democracy. Consequently, the lineage from Madison's "factions" to contemporary interest group politics is entwined with a succession of efforts by citizens, firms, and all varieties of organized interests to influence decisions made by representative institutions and executive agencies.

New Forms of Group Politics

The historical development of interest group politics may be traced by following each element of this threefold name: *politics* is modified by *group*, *group* by *interest*. By extension, *group politics* differ in some important way from other kinds of politics, just as *interest groups* are distinct from other sorts of social groups. The emergence of recognizably modern interest group politics required the mobilization of groups outside of electoral politics, the development of methods by which such groups could influence policy outcomes, and the legitimation of these interests as recognized elements of a political system that extended beyond the boundaries of the formal political institutions themselves. Although the presence of organized interests near to government has steadily expanded throughout American history, opinions differ over whether these groups support democracy by expanding citizens' access to politics or undermine it by allowing representatives of narrow interests to control policy making.

For the first half century of the nation's existence, much political energy focused on the invention of "group politics." One important stream of developments gave rise to political parties; another produced the distinctive breed of "private organizations with public purposes" that are the ancestors of the modern nonprofit sector. Yet, as discussed by Alexis de Tocqueville, voluntary associations were particularly intriguing as a vehicle for "shadow government" and for the shaping and mobilization of political opinion. Tocqueville arrived in the United States in 1831, when such large-scale voluntary associations were a relatively novel phenomenon. Fueled by religious revivals, large-scale missionary movements had forged a new "confessional politics" in which individual sins were linked to the sins of the nation. Focused on moral issues from the protection of the Sabbath through temperance and, most consequentially, abolition, this fusing of religious revival to national policy created a powerful template for doing politics not only outside of formal institutions but also outside political parties. Even where the specifically religious impulse was muted, such popular movements made use of the protected freedoms of speech, press, petition, and assembly to mobilize popular support and bring pressure on elected representatives. These new forms of "group politics" remained controversial, exemplified in the 1830s and 1840s by congressional refusal to accept petitions in support of the abolition of slavery.

The People's Lobby

While the abolitionist movement itself eventually entered party politics, for the remainder of the nineteenth century, mobilized groups continued their efforts to influence the outcomes of formal governmental processes. Often, the most direct path led directly into electoral politics, so state and local campaigns saw periodic insurgencies by new parties

that championed the concerns of labor, of farmers, of anti-Catholics, or of anti-Masons, along with many other causes. "Group politics" could become "third-party politics" with relative ease, but there was not yet a model for a stable, legitimate, nonelectoral alignment of extrapartisan groups with formal governmental institutions.

That model was elaborated at the turn of the twentieth century, in part by activists who were veterans of the failed third-party efforts of the 1870s and 1880s. While the Populist Party led another surge along the path from social movements to political parties, fusing with the Democratic Party in the elections of 1896, other organized groups explored different kinds of alignments with legislatures and government officials. Some of these efforts centered on influencing those who ran for office, notably by supporting the introduction of primary elections and then seeking to "pledge" candidates to support specific policies if elected. Incumbents were also subjected to new forms of accountability as labor and agrarian groups developed the technology of "roll call vote" scoring, a process that required a group to determine which issues were specifically in its interest and then to identify the precise vote that would provide the most meaningful evidence of a candidate's position. To accomplish this, labor unionists, clubwomen, and agrarian activists immersed themselves in the intricacies of parliamentary rules, recognizing that seemingly obscure procedural votes were often the most consequential ones. As pledges were extracted and votes tabulated, organized movements would then make use of speeches and publications to educate their members about which politicians were most worthy of support and which should be opposed.

This educational component of popular politics did not end with elections. As organized groups became more familiar with the process of policy making they also recognized the advantages of expertise that could be used in the context of legislative hearings or as support for drafting bills. The intensification of interest group activity is evident in the numbers of groups testifying in congressional hearings. According to Daniel Tichenor and Richard Harris, the number of interest groups and private corporations grew almost fourfold in the first decade of the 1900s, from roughly 800 to 3,000. Beyond the growth in numbers, the differences between corporation and interest group representatives was also striking: corporations tended to present narrow, local concerns while other groups were more attuned to broad policy issues. Even with the growing presence of trade associations representing industrywide concerns, various kinds of citizens groups and trade unions continued to account for roughly half of congressional appearances through 1917.

During the Progressive Era, a wide variety of groups developed new methods for influencing political outcomes, both through new provisions for primary elections and direct democracy (initiative, referendum, and recall), and by inserting themselves within legislative investigations and deliberations. The rise of this seemingly new kind of "pressure politics" was linked to the declining role of political parties. This popular mode of policy making reached a zenith with the adoption of constitutional amendments establishing prohibition and enfranchising women. Yet for all these accomplishments, the legitimacy of these extrainstitutional interventions in political decision making was far from established.

The Problem of Legitimacy

Madison's original definition of the term *faction* turned on the issue of whether collective pursuit of interests or passions was "adverse to the rights of other citizens, or to the permanent and aggregate interest of the community." Even movement activists had hesitated in the face of this concern; in 1892, for example, the California State Grange explicitly rejected a proposal that the convention consider proposed amendments to the state constitution and that it inform the state's farmers of where their interests lay in these matters. Such matters were to be left to the consciences of individual voters who, at least according to republican theory, were to vote for "the best man" who would then make legislative decisions in light of the common good rather than in terms of the consequences for his own constituents. Organized groups were thus reluctant to move into pressure politics, particularly when they could not make encompassing moral claims grounded in moral virtue or national destiny. The efforts of individuals and companies to secure favorable legislative action were often enmeshed with the "old lobby" of the nineteenth century, which later commentators portrayed as a web of corruption and, at times, seduction. Not surprisingly, some legislatures responded by adopting policies to limit these extralegislative influences, often appealing to the *Trist v. Child* (1874) ruling in which the Supreme Court declined to enforce a contractual claim for a contingency fee for lobbying Congress for relief related to the Mexican-American War. By the late nineteenth century, some state legislatures began to adopt laws requiring lobbyists to register and regulating campaign contributions, indeed prohibiting such contributions from corporations in some cases.

By the early twentieth century, facts on the ground had outrun theory. Political scientists were staking a disciplinary claim to "group politics," arguing, as Arthur F. Bentley did, that "if a law is in question, we find that our statement of it in terms of the group of men it affects . . . we can state its actual value in the social process at the given time in terms of the groups of men for whose sake it is there: a group of politicians and a number of groups of voters holding the prominent places." Others distinguished the "new lobby" from the old, noting, as E. Pendleton Herring expressed it, the "Washington offices of the associations, societies, leagues, institutes, boards, and federations organized on a nationwide scale to-day for the great lobbies in the capital. By comparison the representatives of corporations, the patronage brokers, the 'wire-pullers,' the crows of old-style lobbyists pale in significance. The men with the power are these spokesmen of organized groups."

As business relationships with the federal government were increasingly mediated by industry associations, the lineages of group politics and the business lobby began to merge into what would come to be labeled *interest group politics*. With the intensification of the federal government's role in the economy, driven by both Depression-era regulatory politics and mobilization for World War II, these ties would grow still stronger. They inspired new labels such as "iron triangles" and President Dwight D. Eisenhower's "military-industrial complex" (which, in its first formulation, was the "military-industrial-congressional complex").

Yet, if political scientists had begun to normalize this development, these groups still drew considerable condemnation. Congressional efforts to regulate lobbyists repeatedly failed and their numbers continued to multiply to an estimated 6,000 by the late 1930s. This "small army," in the words of journalist Kenneth Crawford, was "busy in Washington burning the bridges between the voter and what he voted for." This contrast between interest groups that advanced selfish corporate interests and those that promoted public interests bedeviled the efforts of postwar political science to develop a general theory of interest group politics.

Following the Second World War, political scientists mounted repeated efforts to document both the population of organized interests and their implications for democratic politics. These studies addressed questions of which interests became organized and which remained latent, which techniques were used by organized groups to influence policy outcomes, and whether such efforts actually had political consequences. Particular attention focused on if and how the expansion of government led either to increases in the numbers of organized interests or changes in their character. Although the precise magnitude of these changes depended heavily on the sources and methods used by researchers—directories of groups headquartered in Washington, D.C., or records of congressional testimony—there was consensus that the numbers of organized groups were increasing. One analysis found that the total (listed) population of associations had increased from 5,843 in 1959 to 23,298 in 1995. Within this total, trade associations had accounted for 39 percent in 1959 but only 18 percent by 1995. In the interim, categories such as those of public affairs and social welfare had increased their share of the total interest group population. Studies also explored the consequences of organized business interests, large membership organizations, and advocacy organizations for policy formation. Policy domains were documented as distinctive networks of elected officials, public agencies, organized interests, and private organizations.

The diversity of organized interests, as well as the divergent assessments of their role in American democracy, remains an obstacle to the development of either systematic evidence or theoretical consensus. The relationship between interest groups and political decision making continues to be closely—and often ineffectively—policed, with new variations on lobbyist registration, limits on campaign contributions, and time-limited prohibitions on former officials lobbying their own agencies or one-time colleagues. Yet because the constitutional framework of elections and legislatures provides no institutionalized access for "faction"—mobilized groups with shared yet less than universal interests or passions—interest group politics will continue to function as an "extralegal" mode of political activity.

See also campaign law and finance.

FURTHER READING. Frank R. Baumgartner and Beth L. Leech, *Basic Interests: The Importance of Groups in Politics and in Political Science*, 1998; Arthur F. Bentley, *The Process of Government: A Study of Social Pressures*, 1908; Elisabeth S. Clemens, *The People's Lobby: Organizational Innovation and the Rise of Interest Group Politics in the United States, 1890–1925*, 1997; Kenneth G. Crawford, *The Pressure Boys: The Inside Story of Lobbying in America*, 1939; Alexander Hamilton, James Madison, and John Jay, *The Federalist Papers*, 1961; E. Pendleton Herring, "Group Representation before Congress," Ph.D. diss., Johns Hopkins University, 1929; Edward O. Laumann and David Knoke, *The Organizational State: Social Choice in National Policy Domains*, 1987; Kay Lehman Schlozman and John T. Tierney, *Organized Interests and American Democracy*, 1986; Daniel J. Tichenor and Richard A. Harris, "Organized Interests and American Political Development," *Political Science Quarterly* 117 (2002–3), 587–612; David B. Truman, *The Governmental Process: Political Interests and Public Opinion*, 1951; Jack L. Walker, Jr., *Mobilizing Interest Groups in America: Patrons, Professions, and Social Movements*, 1991; Michael P. Young, *Bearing Witness against Sin: The Evangelical Birth of the American Social Movement*, 2006.

ELISABETH S. CLEMENS

Iraq wars of 1991 and 2003

In 1990, following an eight-year war against Iran, Iraq President Saddam Hussein sought to rebuild his battered nation by pressuring neighboring Sunni Arab states into raising international oil prices and forgiving Iraq's substantial war debts. Hussein's attention focused primarily on Kuwait. The Iraqis had long coveted Kuwait, both for its oil and access to the Persian Gulf. Furthermore, Hussein alleged that the Kuwaitis had stolen oil from Iraq through illegal "slant-drilling" in the Rumaila oil field and by exceeding production quotas established by Organization of Petroleum Exporting Countries. When the Kuwaitis rejected Iraqi demands for compensation, Iraq began massing troops along its border with Kuwait.

Previously, the administration of President George H. W. Bush had attempted to maintain friendly relations with Iraq by providing, in the words of National Security Directive (NSD) 26, "economic and political incentives for Iraq to moderate its behavior and to increase our influence with Iraq." During a meeting with Hussein on July 25, 1990, U.S. Ambassador April Glaspie conveyed the U.S. desire for peaceful resolution of Iraq's differences with Kuwait. The United States did not take additional steps to prevent an invasion of Kuwait because other Arab leaders and the Central Intelligence Agency had assured President Bush that Iraq would not invade Kuwait. Consequently, the United States was caught completely unprepared when Iraqi troops overran Kuwait on August 2 and annexed it six days later.

President Bush's national security team agreed that Iraq could not be allowed to remain in Kuwait, since that would give Iraq control of approximately 20 percent of the world's total oil reserves and leave it in a position to threaten Saudi Arabia. This affirmed the Carter Doctrine of 1980, which committed the United States to preventing any power from dominating the Persian Gulf and its oil reserves. After securing the consent of the Saudi royal family, the Bush administration initiated Operation Desert Shield on August 7 and immediately began deploying the first of 250,000 U.S. troops and their equipment to Saudi Arabia.

Disagreement arose over the question of using force to evict Iraq from Kuwait. The chairman of the Joint Chiefs of Staff, General Colin Powell, initially opposed military action and argued that UN sanctions could achieve the same end. Bush's national security advisor, Brent Scowcroft, and his secretary of defense, Richard Cheney, disagreed with Powell and convinced the president not to accept "another Munich." Bush warned Iraq on August 5 (the day before the United Nations imposed a complete embargo on Iraq), "This will not stand, this aggression against Kuwait." On August 20, the president signed NSD 45, which, in light of U.S. "vital" interests in the Persian Gulf (most notably "access to oil and the security and stability of key friendly states in the region"), called for the "immediate, complete, and unconditional withdrawal of all Iraqi forces from Kuwait." By October, Powell and the commander of U.S. Central Command (CENTCOM, which is responsible for planning and conducting U.S. military operations in the Middle East), General Norman Schwarzkopf, had developed Operation Desert Storm, an ambitious air, land, and sea plan that called for more than 500,000 U.S. troops to evict Iraq from Kuwait.

On November 29, 1991, the UN Security Council passed Resolution 678, giving Iraq a deadline of January 15, 1991, to evacuate Kuwait and authorizing the U.S.-led multinational coalition of over 30 nations (many of which, such as Saudi Arabia, Great Britain, Egypt, and France, provided large numbers of combat troops; others, such as Germany and Japan, provided financial assistance) to use any measures it deemed necessary to enforce compliance. The only remaining obstacle for the Bush administration was the U.S. Senate, which was controlled by the Democratic Party. Scarred by the experience of the Vietnam War and reluctant to give the president carte blanche, most Democrats supported a policy of coercive diplomacy, as embodied by Security Council Resolution 661, adopted on August 6, which imposed a total embargo against Iraq. Such sanctions, Democrats hoped, would eventually compel Iraq to abandon Kuwait without the need for force.

In spite of such opposition and Cheney's insistence that the administration did not need legislative authorization to proceed, the president was determined to secure congressional approval. Following three days of debate, a resolution authorizing the use of force narrowly passed both houses of Congress, thanks largely to the support of Democrats such as Senator Al Gore (Tennessee). Eleven years later, Gore would again make headlines when he condemned the administration of George W. Bush's march to war. The 2004 presidential campaign of Democratic Senator John Kerry (Massachusetts), on the other hand, would be hamstrung by the fact that he opposed the 1991 Gulf War but voted in favor of the use of force in 2003.

Desert Storm commenced on January 17, 1991, with a bombing campaign against Iraqi military and civilian targets and was followed by a land invasion on February 24. After coalition forces outflanked the Iraqi military and threatened to cut off their line of retreat, the Iraqis began falling back on February 26, setting fire to Kuwaiti oil wells along the way. Lacking air cover, however, large numbers of Iraqis were slaughtered by coalition planes along the "highway of death" toward Iraq. At the urging of General Powell, President Bush declared a unilateral ceasefire the following day. By war's end, the United States had suffered a total of 293 dead, while Iraq suffered well over 20,000 military and civilian fatalities. Although coalition casualties during the fighting were light, tens of thousands of veterans later suffered from a variety of aliments that are collectively known as Gulf War Syndrome.

The postwar situation presented problems for the United States. For one thing, the Iraqis used the ceasefire to evacuate substantial portions of their elite Republican Guard divisions from Kuwait. Schwarzkopf also assented to an Iraqi request that they be allowed to use helicopters to ferry troops from Kuwait. In fact, the Iraqis used their remaining army units and aircraft to brutally suppress an uprising by Iraqi Shiites, who had been urged to rebel by the United States. While many in the U.S. government wanted to use the Shiites to destabilize the Ba'ath regime, leading figures such as Scowcroft, Powell, and

Cheney opposed any move to assist the Shiites or march on Baghdad, since they did not want to re- sponsible for establishing a new government in Iraq and rebuilding the country. Furthermore, they feared that if Hussein were toppled, Iraq would break apart. The main beneficiary of that situation would be Iran, which would extend its influence into the primarily Shiite provinces of southern Iraq, an area that contained most of Iraq's oil reserves and bordered both Kuwait and Saudi Arabia.

In one of the war's great ironies, Hussein, despite his catastrophic military defeat, managed to remain in power for another 12 years. His primary opponent, President Bush, fared less well. Although he enjoyed high approval ratings for his handling of the Gulf War, Bush's popularity sagged due to a stagnating economy. As a result, he was defeated in the 1992 presidential election by Bill Clinton, whose campaign revolved around the memorable expression, "It's the economy, stupid."

The Interlude of Sanctions: 1991–2001

For the next 12 years, the United States pursued a policy containing Iraq. U.S. and British warplanes enforced "no fly zones" over northern and southern Iraq and the UN Special Commission on Iraq (UN-SCOM) was established to verify that the nation had dismantled its substantial programs for weapons of mass destruction (WMD). Despite Iraqi interference, UN weapons inspectors managed to dismantle most of Iraq's WMD infrastructure before withdrawing in December 1998, after the chief of UNSCOM reported that Iraq was not complying with inspections. Shortly thereafter, the United States and Britain launched Operation Desert Fox, a three-day campaign of aerial bombardment and cruise missile attacks against suspected Iraqi WMD sites and military installations. Although the Clinton administration was criticized for taking only limited action against Iraq in 1998, following the conclusion of the second Iraq war, the Iraq Survey Group (an Anglo-American-Australian team of weapons inspectors established in 2003 to find Iraq's WMD) discovered that UN weapons inspections had been more successful than previously thought. Since Western intelligence services lacked an effective espionage network within Iraq, they had no way of knowing this.

Throughout the 1990s, the consensus of U.S. policy makers was that containment was the most effective policy for dealing with Iraq. Some outspoken opponents, such as Paul Wolfowitz (one of Cheney's deputies at the Pentagon in 1991), however, argued strongly in favor of regime change. In January 1998, an organization called the Project for a New American Century sent a letter to President Clinton asserting that the United States could no longer rely on UN inspections or containment to prevent Hussein from threatening the Middle East. Among the signatories of the letter were numerous prominent "neoconservatives" and future members of the second

Bush administration. Their recommendations did not receive significant support within the American foreign policy establishment, however, and when the second Bush administration came to power in January 2001, it initially pursued a policy of "smart sanctions" designed to ease the humanitarian burden on Iraq's civilian population.

A New Administration and a New War: 2001–8

The U.S. government's attitude changed completely following the terrorist attacks of September 11, 2001. The attacks proved to be the catalyst for the invasion of Iraq for fear that state sponsors of terrorism—such as Iraq—could provide radical Islamic terrorists with WMD. Accordingly, by the summer of 2002, the administration of George W. Bush publicly embraced the concept of preventive war. In a speech that June at the United States Military Academy at West Point, the president stated that the United States would "confront the worst threats before they emerge." Furthermore, even before the 2001 terrorist attacks, proponents of regime change in Iraq had argued that prior U.S. foreign policy in the Middle East had created the popular basis for the rise of terrorist organization such as al-Qaeda through its support for authoritarian regimes, and that the United States needed to aggressively promote democratization in the Middle East.

The administration formally unveiled its new foreign policy on September 20, 2002, when it published the *National Security Strategy of the United States*, whose tenets came to be known as the Bush Doctrine. Among its highlights was an explicit repudiation of the cold war concept of deterrence in favor of "preemptive" and, if necessary, unilateral military action.

The Bush administration began warning of the threat posed by Iraqi WMD before the 2001 military campaign in Afghanistan had even ended, and throughout 2002. In his 2002 State of the Union address, President Bush named three nations—Iran, Iraq, and North Korea, which he collectively called the "axis of evil"—that were actively developing WMD and might supply such weapons to terrorists. In August, Vice President Richard Cheney unequivocally stated that "there is no doubt that Saddam Hussein now has weapons of mass destruction; there is no doubt that he is amassing them to use against our friends, against our allies, and against us." Quoting President Bush, Cheney warned, "Time is not on our side," and that the "risks of inaction are far greater than the risks of action."

The tipping point came in October, when the government distributed a national intelligence estimate concerning Iraq's "continuing" WMD programs. With a majority in the Senate, congressional Democrats could have derailed the president's plans, but the terrorist attacks of the previous year had left them on the defensive. With midterm elections quickly approaching, and the president's popularity soaring in the wake of the terrorist attacks and the seemingly successful war in Afghanistan, congressional Democrats reckoned that they could not wage an effective campaign on national security and sought to shift the emphasis back to domestic issues such as health care and corporate scandals by supporting the Bush administration's stance on Iraq. Consequently, on October 16, 2002, Congress authorized Bush to "defend the national security of the United States against the continuing threat posed by Iraq." This electoral gambit failed, however, and Democrats were defeated in the 2002 midterm elections.

The Bush administration faced a stiffer challenge at the United Nations. The Security Council unanimously passed Resolution 1441 in November 2002, which declared that Iraq was in material breach of previous resolutions and that it had 30 days to accept the reentry of weapons inspectors. Months of inspections failed, however, to turn up evidence of an illicit Iraqi WMD program. In spite of Secretary of State Colin Powell's speech before the Security Council on February 5, 2003, describing alleged Iraqi violations of existing Security Council resolutions and cooperation with Islamist terrorist groups, several members, most notably France and Germany, remained opposed to military action. Consequently, the United States and the 48 other nations that comprised the "coalition of the willing" (of which only four actually provided combat troops for the invasion) moved to the next stage. On March 16, the United States ordered all UN weapons inspectors to leave Iraq and, the following day, gave Hussein and his family 48 hours to seek exile. On the morning of March 20, the United States and its allies began Operation Iraqi Freedom with a massive aerial bombardment of Baghdad and a land invasion from Kuwait.

It soon became apparent that U.S. war planning was flawed for two reasons: it relied on too few troops to occupy Iraq, and it ignored the question of postwar planning. As early as November 2001, CENTCOM had been charged with drawing up a plan. At the time, Secretary of Defense Donald Rumsfeld pushed for a small, highly mobile invasion force, over the objections of senior officers such as Army Chief of Staff General Eric Shinseki, who warned that the United States would require a large presence in Iraq for an indefinite period in order to guarantee postwar peace and security. Deputy Secretary of Defense Wolfowitz publicly ridiculed such concerns and asserted that the U.S. occupation of Iraq would be self-financing through Iraqi oil exports. In fact, U.S. government expenditures during the first four years of the war exceeded $2 billion per week.

Although the small force envisaged by Rumsfeld (145,000 U.S. and British soldiers) quickly routed the Iraqi Army, it was unable to stabilize the country after the collapse of Hussein's Ba'ath regime. Following the fall of Baghdad on April 9, widespread looting broke out across the city in front of helpless U.S. troops. The scene was repeated across the country, with dire consequences for U.S. forces, since insurgents looted arms depots and secured large supplies of small arms and explosives.

After President Bush declared an end to "major combat operations" on May 1, 2003, the United States created a Coalition Provisional Authority to govern Iraq. The original head of the CPA was retired General Jay Garner, who planned to quickly transfer the responsibility for governing Iraq to local authorities and rely on the Iraqi Army to maintain order. Garner also clashed with Ahmed Chalabi, the leader of a prominent Iraqi exile group (the Iraqi National Congress) that had provided much of the flawed evidence of Iraqi WMD to the U.S. government who aspired to high political office in post-Ba'ath Iraq. Garner soon fell afoul of the leadership in Washington and was replaced by a former diplomat, L. Paul Bremer, in May. Bremer subsequently made two momentous decisions. On May 16, he issued an order expelling all Ba'ath Party members from Iraqi civil service. One week later, he demobilized the Iraqi Army and laid off the staff of the Interior Ministry and Hussein's personal security forces. These disgruntled soldiers and Ba'ath Party members provided the nucleus for an insurgency that claimed the lives of thousands of coalition soldiers and untold numbers of Iraqi soldiers, police, and civilians.

While it was hoped that the capture of Hussein in December 2003 would stabilize Iraq, two events in early 2004 shattered any such illusions. First, on March 31, a convoy carrying four private U.S. military contractors was ambushed by insurgents in Fallujah, and the contractors' charred remains were later hung from a nearby bridge. Much of the city was subsequently destroyed, and its population displaced, when U.S. Marines stormed it at great cost in November. Second, at the end of April, reporter Seymour Hersh revealed the torture of Iraqi detainees by U.S. Army guards at the Abu Ghraib prison. The U.S. government claimed that the excesses had been committed by only a handful of soldiers and were not the result of official policy. Nevertheless, the sexually explicit nature of the offenses, as well as the fact that they took place in a prison that had been used by the Ba'ath regime, stripped away much of the U.S. occupation's moral legitimacy, both in Iraq and abroad.

Despite the deteriorating the situation in Iraq, President Bush won reelection against John Kerry in 2004 by the narrowest margin for a sitting president since Woodrow Wilson in 1916. The war in Iraq was probably not the decisive issue during the campaign, since matters such as terrorism, same-sex marriage, the economy, and health care also received much attention. Furthermore, Kerry did not advocate a withdrawal from Iraq. Rather, he criticized the president for poor management of postwar Iraq and argued that the United States needed allies to help stabilize that nation. Kerry's initial support of the resolution authorizing the use of force, and the fact that he

continued to argue as late as August 2004 that "it was the right authority" for a president to have, left him vulnerable to withering attacks by the Republicans, who derided him as an opportunistic "flip-flopper."

The political costs of the war for the Republican Party only became evident during the 2006 congressional midterm elections. In November 2005, Democrat John Murtha (Pennsylvania), a senior congressman with close ties to the U.S. military, withdrew his support for the war and offered a plan to withdraw U.S. troops from Iraq at the "earliest practicable date." Although Democrats remained divided over how quickly any withdrawal should proceed, most rallied around Murtha's call for a "strategic redeployment." Sagging popular support for the war, combined with a series of scandals involving high-ranking Republicans and Bush's unpopularity following his failed bid to privatize Social Security and his administration's botched response to Hurricane Katrina, handed the Democrats an electoral triumph as spectacular as that of the Republicans in 1994.

Although President Bush acknowledged that the results of the 2006 election reflected substantial public discontent over his handling of the war and accepted the resignation of Defense Secretary Rumsfeld, he remained adamantly opposed to withdrawal from Iraq. Consequently, in May 2007, Bush vetoed a bill funding U.S. military operations in Iraq and Afghanistan because it included a timeline for withdrawal. It was only the second time he had used that power since becoming president.

As an alternative to the "redeployment" plans advocated by Democrats and the Iraq Study Group (a bipartisan panel created by Congress in 2006 to provide recommendations on future policy concerning Iraq), in January 2007, Bush unveiled a new counterinsurgency strategy that featured the deployment of an additional 20,000 troops to Iraq to "clear and secure" insurgent-controlled areas in Baghdad, under the direction of the newly installed commander of Multi-National Force–Iraq, General David Petraeus, a noted expert on counterinsurgency warfare and author of the U.S. Army/Marine Corps *Counterinsurgency Field Manual*. The aim of the 2007 "troop surge" was not, however, to achieve a decisive military victory over the Sunni insurgency. Rather, it was to provide enough stability within Baghdad to promote political reconciliation between rival sectarian and ethnic factions within the Iraqi government and prevent a civil war. Since congressional Democrats lacked the votes either to override a presidential veto concerning withdrawal or to cut off spending for the war, the questions of when and how the United States would eventually withdraw from Iraq were left to be settled after the 2008 presidential election.

See also foreign policy and domestic politics since 1933; war and politics.

FURTHER READING. Andrew J. Bacevich and Efraim Inbar, eds., *The Gulf War of 1991 Reconsidered*, 2003; Rajiv

Chandrasekaran, *Imperial Life in the Emerald City: Inside Iraq's Green Zone*, 2006; William Cleveland, *A History of the Modern Middle East*, 2004; James Fallows, *Blind into Baghdad: America's War in Iraq*, 2006; Lawrence Freedman, *A Choice of Enemies: America Confronts the Middle East*, 2008; Lawrence Freedman and Efraim Karsh, *The Gulf Conflict, 1990–1991: Diplomacy and War in the New World Order*, 1993; Lloyd C. Gardner and Marilyn B. Young, eds., *The New American Empire: A 21st Century Teach-In on U.S. Foreign Policy*, 2005; Michael R. Gordon and Bernard E. Trainor, *Cobra 2: The Inside Story of the Invasion and Occupation of Iraq*, 2006; Gary R. Hess, *Presidential Decisions for War: Korea, Vietnam, the Persian Gulf, and Iraq*, 2009; Michael Klare, *Blood and Oil: The Dangers and Consequences of America's Growing Petroleum Dependency*, 2004; Douglas Little, *American Orientalism: The United States and the Middle East since 1945*, 2008; James Mann, *Rise of the Vulcans: The History of Bush's War Cabinet*, 2004; National Security Council, *The National Security Strategy of the United States of America*, downloadable from http://georgewbush-whitehouse.archives .gov/nsc/nss/2002/index.html; Clayton R. Newell, *The A to Z of the Persian Gulf War, 1990–1991*, 2007; George Packer, *The Assassins' Gate: America in Iraq*, 2005; Thomas E. Ricks, *Fiasco: The American Military Adventure in Iraq*, 2006; Ian Rutledge, *Addicted to Oil: America's Relentless Drive for Energy Security*, 2005; Micah L. Sifry and Christopher Cerf, eds., *The Gulf War Reader: History, Documents, Opinions*, 1991; Tim Weiner, *Legacy of Ashes: The History of the CIA*, 2007; Bob Woodward, *Plan of Attack*, 2004; Idem, *State of Denial*, 2006; Idem, *The War Within: A Secret White House History, 2006–2008*, 2008; Steve A. Yetiv, *The Persian Gulf Crisis*, 1997.

ANAND TOPRANI

Jacksonian era, 1828–45

The Jacksonian era was the period in American political history dominated by the influence of the seventh president, General Andrew Jackson (1767–1846), who served two terms between 1825 and 1837. An exuberantly egalitarian political culture for white men, divisive political reactions to economic change, the development of a mass-based two-party electoral system, and the growing importance of the slavery issue in national politics all marked the period. Jackson and his associates pushed American politics from an older republican tradition in the direction of democracy but saw their work as restoration rather than innovation.

A Changing Society

From the end of the eighteenth century, a series of linked economic and technological changes, sometimes referred to as the Market Revolution, framed the social and economic context of the Jacksonian era. Faster and cheaper forms of transportation, including turnpike roads, steamboats, canals, and ultimately railroads, spread from the Northeast across the country, hastening passenger travel and cutting freight costs. This made it much more feasible to make goods in one place while selling them in another. Once-isolated farmers increased their production of staples like wheat, corn, and pork for the world market, while entrepreneurs replaced traditional artisanal manufactures with new means for making and distributing cheap consumer goods like shoes, hats, and clothing. The invention of the cotton gin (1793) opened the way for large-scale cotton production in the southern interior, fed the movement of planters and slaves to the Southwest, and furnished raw material to a generation of newly mechanized textile factories in Britain and New England.

A rapid increase in the number and size of chartered banks facilitated this active commerce. The first American bank opened in 1782 (Robert Morris's Bank of North America), and the numbers of banks grew to 28 in 1800 and 729 by 1837. Often operating on slender capital reserves, these banks provided credit-hungry borrowers with loans in the form of paper notes that served as the medium of exchange for an increasingly monetized economy. Eager to foster economic development, state governments frequently protected banks and internal improvement companies with the privilege of corporate charters. The largest and most privileged corporation of all was the second Bank of the United States, chartered for 30 years in 1816, with a capital of $35 million, a monopoly of the banking business of the federal government, and the size and strength to discipline the note issue of the state banks.

Americans reacted to commercial growth with a mixture of optimism and anxiety. Farmers who profited from the sale of commodities welcomed the changes, unless the purchase of new lands and new equipment for market production put them periously in debt and subjected them to market swings. Customers certainly welcomed cheaper consumer goods, but new forms of inequality, including new class structures and new gender roles, also accompanied the new economy. Cultural tension was reflected in the so-called Second Great Awakening, a wave of religious revivals that offered reformed ways of life to converts who suffered from social and spiritual upheaval from frontiers to big cities.

State decisions to relax property requirements and other restrictions on white men's right to vote amplified political reactions to economic, social, and cultural change. The new voters did not cast their ballots consistently along class lines, and many did not vote at all initially, but the broadened franchise created a mass electorate that skilled political operatives would soon learn to mobilize. Roused by compelling rhetoric and public spectacles, the new voters would form the mass membership for Jacksonian-era political parties.

Jackson's Life

Andrew Jackson's dramatic personal story greatly contributed to his popular appeal and sharply contrasted with the privileged upbringings of earlier presidents. He was born under modest circumstances in a backcountry settlement on the border of the two Carolinas. Jackson's father died before his birth, so his mother raised her three sons with relatives. The future president received some schooling in the neighborhood but never attended college.

During the war for independence, 13-year-old Andrew Jackson was captured as an American messenger when the British invaded the Carolina backcountry in 1780. He received lifelong scars when he refused to clean his captor's boots and the furious officer slashed him with a saber. Jackson also survived an attack of smallpox he contracted in captivity, but war took the lives of his mother and two brothers, leaving the youth seemingly marked by providence as the only member of his immediate family to survive the American Revolution. He would become the last U.S. president to have served in that conflict.

With iron determination, Jackson managed to overcome his difficult adolescence by reading law, moving to Nashville, Tennessee, and rapidly rising in his profession. There he married Rachel Donelson Robards, leading to a later scandal when enemies revealed that the couple had married before the bride was divorced from her first husband. Jackson also succeeded in land speculation, won a duel, and joined the region's nascent planter elite. Entering politics, he briefly served in the U.S. House, the U.S. Senate, and the Tennessee Supreme Court, but he preferred his work as major general of the state militia.

Military distinction brought the frontier general to national attention. During the War of 1812, Jackson's troops honored his toughness with the nickname "Old Hickory," as he crushed an uprising of the Creek Indians, occupied Spanish Florida in pursuit of the survivors, executed their British advisors, and repelled the British invasion of New Orleans. At war's end, Jackson pursued warring Seminoles into Florida again, which provoked international outrage but also pressured Spain to sell the vulnerable province to the United States in 1819. After cementing U.S. rule as first territorial governor of Florida, Jackson retired to the Hermitage, his plantation outside Nashville.

Jackson's rise coincided with serious national stress. In 1819 a postwar boom collapsed in a disastrous "panic," or depression. Collapsing prices for land and crops bankrupted countless farmers and speculators who had borrowed heavily to purchase public lands. Banks, especially the Bank of the United States, roused widespread resentment when they pressed their borrowers relentlessly but refused to honor their obligations to pay specie (gold or silver) for their notes. The federal government could not act in the crisis but plunged into bitter sectional controversy when northern congressmen tried to limit the growth of slavery as a condition for the admission of Missouri to the union. Temporarily eased by the Missouri Compromise, the slavery dispute threatened serious long-term disruption and frightened the aging Thomas Jefferson "like a fire-bell in the night."

Seeming to ignore these dangers, national leaders intrigued instead to succeed retiring President James Monroe in the election of 1824. Four major candidates emerged, three of them from Monroe's own cabinet: Secretary of State John Quincy Adams, Secretary of the Treasury William H. Crawford, and Secretary of War John C. Calhoun. A fourth, Speaker of the House Henry Clay of Kentucky, supposedly led the administration's friends in Congress.

The triumphant Tennessean seemed to offer a stark contrast to these bickering and self-interested insiders. While government insiders scoffed at his inexperience, lack of polish, and pugnacious, highhanded temperament, Jackson appealed to ordinary voters, especially in the West and South, as the embodiment of bold action and old-fashioned republican virtue.

Nominated by the Tennessee legislature, Jackson led in both the popular and electoral vote without gaining a majority, so the House of Representatives had to choose between Jackson, Adams, and Crawford, the three highest vote-getters. Jackson believed that his plurality, plus state legislative instructions in his favor, gave him the moral right to win. Instead, Henry Clay threw his support to Adams and gave him the victory. Soon afterward, Adams made Clay his secretary of state, rousing furious charges by Jacksonians of a "corrupt bargain" to defeat the "will of the people." Determined on vindication, Jackson and his supporters launched an immediate and ultimately successful campaign to gain the White House in 1828, putting claims for majority rule and the moral superiority of "the people" over "aristocrats" at the ideological core of his movement.

Jackson's Presidency

As president, Jackson repeatedly invoked the republican principles of the Revolution, but he actually turned American political culture toward democracy by identifying the people themselves, not an enlightened elite, as the greatest source of public virtue. Seeing his movement as the majority's legitimate voice, however, Jackson rarely saw a difference between the people's welfare and the good of his own party. His first major initiative, for example, was to replace long-established federal officeholders with his own supporters, insisting that the incumbents were often incompetent or corrupt, but also arguing that holdovers from previous administrations were out of step with the people's will. Jacksonians strongly defended this so-called spoils system, but advocates of an independent civil service struggled against it for most of the nineteenth century.

Jackson also took office determined to remove the eastern Indian tribes to lands beyond the Missisippi. The Indian Removal Act of 1830 authorized the president to exchange lands in modern Oklahoma for tribal lands within existing states. Occupying extensive tracts in Georgia, Alabama, Mississippi, and Florida, the Cherokees, Creeks, Choctaws, Chickasaws, and Seminoles were quite unwilling to move. The Cherokees were promised partial protection in two Supreme Court decisions, *Cherokee Nation v. Georgia* and *Worcester v. Georgia*, but the decisions proved unenforceable. All the major eastern tribes, with as many as 100,000 members, were eventually deported by a combination of bribery, fraud, intimidation, and coercion. Corruption and neglect led to the death of about one Indian in four along the so-called Trail of Tears.

When South Carolina, worried about the viability of its slave-based economy, followed John C. Calhoun's proposal to nullify the federal tariff in 1832, Jackson threatened military action to restore federal supremacy, arguing that the state's actions were an intolerable rejection of majority rule. In 1835 South Carolinians defied federal law again when a mob seized and burned a shipment of abolitionist tracts from the Charleston post office. Supporting the mob's goals but opposing its methods, Jackson called for federal legislation to exclude "incendiary" materials from the

U.S. mail. The proposal foundered, so the administration tolerated informal mail censorship by local vigilance committees.

Andrew Jackson's war against the Bank of the United States (BUS) was the central political struggle of his presidency. Partly inspired by the eighteenth-century British radicals who underpinned the republican tradition and also denounced privileged corporations like the Bank of England and the South Sea Company, Jackson distrusted all banks. He especially distrusted the Bank of the United States for allegedly using its immense powers and legal privileges for private gain at public expense. Drawing energy from Americans' ambivalent feelings about the new economy that banks had abetted, the Bank War revived the two-party system and defined American politics for the decade following Jackson's presidency.

When Congress granted the bank a new charter in the summer of 1832, Jackson vetoed the bill with a ringing denunciation of wealthy men who misused government "to make the rich richer and the potent more powerful." Supporters denounced the veto as ignorant madness, but the message was wildly popular among voters who shared Jackson's misgivings about unrestrained private power, and Jackson was resoundingly reelected with a larger majority than before. Soon after, Jackson went further and pulled the government's funds from the bank, an arguably illegal move that crippled it both politically and financially. In a related policy, Jackson favored state control of internal improvements and vetoed the use of federal funds for local transportation projects.

The Second Party System

Deposit removal galvanized the president's opponents, who argued that his high-handed actions defied Congress and threatened a dictatorship. Denouncing Jackson as "King Andrew I," they organized themselves as the Whig Party, adopting the name from the British opponents of centralized royal power. Led by congressional magnates like Henry Clay and Daniel Webster, the Whigs became a formidable political force after Jackson left office and another powerful panic swept the United States in 1837. Jacksonians responded by reviving Jeffersonian party lines, shortening the older name "Democratic-Republicans" to "Democratic Party," and portraying the Whigs as resurrected Federalists. Each party solidified its identity and its organization by blaming its opponents for the panic of 1837, creating a competitive political structure that scholars have called the Second American Party System, to distinguish it from the First Party System of Federalists and Democratic-Republicans.

Both parties became national institutions that contested elections at the federal and local level in every state except South Carolina, which remained aloof from both. Democrats generally embraced party organization with vigor and finesse; Whigs retained more antipartisan principles and weaker gifts

for organization. A Washington newspaper spelled out doctrine for each party—*The Globe* for the Democrats and *The National Intelligencer* for the Whigs—while a host of state-level prints adapted the message to local conditions. Each party also embraced an ascending network of local, district, state, and national party conventions to convey opinions and decisions between bottom and top, to adopt platforms, and to nominate candidates for public office.

For presidential elections, each party organized a national campaign committee to distribute pamphlets and special campaign newspapers to corresponding networks of state, county, and local committees. Successful office seekers rewarded followers with government patronage and enforced party discipline by threatening to revoke it if crossed. Historians Glenn C. Altschuler and Stuart M. Blumin have questioned voters' genuine emotional involvement in Jacksonian elections, but most scholars note that voting turnout rates often approached and sometimes exceeded 80 percent, and conclude that colorful spectacles and lively debates between rival candidates successfully drew the connections between party doctrines and local concerns.

In their platforms, Democrats typically denounced federal measures to promote the new economy, including the national bank, high tariffs, and public funding for internal improvements, and all restraints on the liberty of common white men, including moral reforms favored by revivalists, like Sunday blue laws and restrictions on the sale of alcohol. After the panic of 1837, many Democrats shared Jackson's own desire to prohibit paper money banking altogether and return the country to an all-metallic currency. Party rhetoric denounced class privilege and stressed the equality of all white men, sometimes underscored with a fierce antiblack racism. Whigs were more likely to champion personal and public improvement over unrestrained liberty, and favored banks, internal improvements, the rights of corporations, evangelical moral reforms, and philanthropic causes like public schools and benevolent institutions. Though business conservatism often sent the largest southern planters into Whig ranks, Whigs across the nation were somewhat more tolerant of black rights and antislavery opinions than their rivals. Some Whigs and Democrats were found within all social classes, but voting studies have found that leading urban businessmen were more likely to be Whigs, while working-class wards usually leaned to the Democrats, and Whig counties were more closely linked to the market economy than their Democratic counterparts.

The Democratic Party and the Whig Party did not monopolize contemporary Americans' political reactions to the challenges of their era. An Anti-Masonic Party channeled popular resentment in northeastern states before absorption by the Whigs. Trade union movements and workingmen's parties briefly flared in large cities, before succumbing to hard times and

Democratic blandishments after the panic of 1837. Women entered public life through allegedly nonpartisan religious and reform movements and also found supportive partisan roles, especially among Whigs. Rebuffed by mainstream politicians, radical black and white abolitionists agitated outside party structures, though some eventually embraced politics through the Liberty Party and its successors. The example of Jacksonian politics proved irresistibly attractive, even to those it rigorously excluded.

Jackson's immediate successors competed within the political and ideological framework established during his presidency. In 1836 Vice President Martin Van Buren succeeded Jackson in the presidency but struggled unsuccessfully with the panic of 1837 and its aftermath. In 1840, the Whigs created a storm of popular enthusiasm for William Henry Harrison of Indiana, their own popular frontier general. Soon after being inaugurated, Harrison died and his vice president, John Tyler of Virginia, alienated both parties and proved that party support had become essential to a functional presidency. By 1844, however, the opportunity for western expansion through the acquisition of Texas and Oregon had eclipsed older issues. Martin Van Buren lost the Democratic nomination to James K. Polk of Tennessee when he fumbled the territorial issue. As president, Polk echoed Jacksonian themes in his veto of the Rivers and Harbors Bill, but the Mexican War dominated his term, and the territorial expansion of slavery preoccupied his successors.

Polk's election sent American politics in new and dangerous directions. In 1845 the annexation of Texas led to war with Mexico, conquest of the Far West, and a steadily intensifying national quarrel over the future of slavery there. That controversy would eventually destroy the Whig Party and other specific features of the Jacksonian political system, but subsequent generations of Americans would find the strong presidency, the rhetoric of democracy, and the institutions of party politics that Jacksonians had introduced to be indispensable to public life.

See also banking policy; Democratic Party, 1828–60; economy and politics to 1860; Republican Party to 1896; Whig Party.

FURTHER READING. Glenn C. Altschuler and Stuart M. Blumin, *Rude Republic: Americans and Their Politics in the Nineteenth Century*, 2000; Michael F. Holt, *The Rise and Fall of the American Whig Party: Jacksonian Politics and the Onset of the Civil War*, 1999; Daniel Walker Howe, *What Hath God Wrought: The Transformation of America, 1815–1848*, 2008; John Lauritz Larson, *Internal Improvement: National Public Works and the Promise of Popular Government in the Early United States*, 2001; Robert V. Remini, *Andrew Jackson and the Course of American Democracy, 1833–1845*, 1984; Idem, *Andrew Jackson and the Course of American Empire, 1767–1821*, 1977; Idem, *Andrew Jackson and the Course of American Freedom, 1822–1832*, 1981; Mary P. Ryan, *Women in Public: Between Banners and Ballots, 1825–1880*, 1990; Charles Sellers, *The Market Revolution: Jacksonian America, 1815–1846*, 1991; William G. Shade, "Political Pluralism and Party Development: The Creation of the Modern Party System, 1815–1852," in *The Evolution of American Political Systems*, edited by Paul Kleppner, 77–112, 1981; Harry L. Watson, *Liberty and Power: The Politics of Jacksonian America*, 2nd revised ed., 2006; Sean Wilentz, *The Rise of American Democracy: Jefferson to Lincoln*, 2005.

HARRY L. WATSON

judicial branch

See Supreme Court.

Korean War and cold war

The Korean War (1950–53), sometimes considered the forgotten war, was the first military confrontation between U.S. and Communist forces in the cold war era. It began on June 25, 1950, when armed forces of the People's Democratic Republic of Korea (PDRK, or North Korea) attacked across the thirty-eighth parallel, the line that divided Communist North Korea, led by Kim Il Sung, from the non-Communist Republic of Korea (ROK, or South Korea), led by Syngman Rhee.

North Korea's objective was to unify the two Koreas as a single Communist state. The United States led a military force under the auspices of the United Nations to repel North Korea's assault on the South. The UN troops successfully cleared North Korean troops from South Korea by October. Thereafter, the Truman administration changed its war aims. The U.S. commander of the UN forces, General Douglas MacArthur, led his army across the thirty-eighth parallel in order to unify Korea under the leadership of the Rhee government. In November the Communist-led People's Republic of China (PRC) entered the war to counter the advance of UN forces toward the Yalu River, the border between China and North Korea. The war continued for another two-and-a-half years until July 27, 1953, when the United States and the United Nations signed an armistice with China and North Korea.

Origins of the War

The Korean peninsula had a long history of invasion and war. Japan occupied Korea from 1910 until its defeat in 1945 in World War II. U.S. forces replaced the Japanese south of the thirty-eighth parallel, and Soviet troops occupied the northern part of the country. These occupations ended in 1947, when the United States and the Soviet Union withdrew their military forces. The United States installed Rhee as president of South Korea, and the Soviets sponsored Kim Il Sung as the leader of North Korea. Both Rhee and Kim declared that there was a single Korean state, of which he was the legitimate leader.

The political climate and geopolitical balance of power in East Asia changed dramatically in 1949, when the Chinese Communist Party, under the leadership of Chairman Mao Zedong, won the Chinese civil war against the Nationalists, led by Jiang Jieshi, and founded the People's Republic of China. Mao's victory represented a serious challenge to the U.S. political and military position in East Asia. U.S. policy makers had hoped that Chiang's Republic of China (ROC) would help the United States impose regional stability. President Harry Truman and Secretary of State Dean Acheson considered Mao a partner of Soviet leader Joseph Stalin, interested in fomenting Communist-inspired revolutions throughout East Asia. Faced with the new reality of the PRC in control of the Chinese mainland and a greatly diminished ROC on the island of Taiwan, Acheson, in January 1950, defined a defense perimeter for the United States in East Asia running through the Philippines, Taiwan, and Japan. South Korea was not included under this shield, because Acheson believed only the three island states he had mentioned were of paramount strategic importance to the United States.

The situation on the Korean peninsula became increasingly tense. After the creation of South Korea and North Korea in 1947, armed forces on each side conducted raids across the thirty-eighth parallel to harass and destabilize the other regime. Early in 1950, Kim asked Mao for support should the North Korean leader decide on a full-scale attack against South Korea. Mao did not explicitly warn Kim against an attack; instead, he offered vague assurances of future support. Mao consulted with Stalin about potential Soviet backing for a North Korean attack on the South Koreans. Stalin urged restraint but promised Mao military support should the United States threaten the PRC.

Outbreak of the War

North Korean forces attacked across the thirty-eighth parallel on June 25. They quickly overcame the poorly armed and outmanned South Korean army and captured Seoul, the capital of South Korea, within days. The Truman administration was shocked by the assault. Truman was already under severe political attack: his critics accused him of having allowed the Communists to win the Chinese civil war. North Korea's attack appeared to be another sign of Communist power in Asia. The Truman administration had not expected North Korea to move, but when it did, U.S. officials believed Stalin was behind the assault. The president ordered General Douglas MacArthur, the commander of U.S. armed forces stationed in Japan, to send troops to Korea to reinforce the battered South Korean army.

The United States brought the issue of North Korea's attack before the UN Security Council. Within days, the Security Council labeled North Korea's actions unacceptable aggression, called on it to withdraw north of the thirty-eighth parallel, and authorized member states to use armed force to help South Korea repel the invasion. The resolution passed without an expected Soviet veto, because the Soviet Union had boycotted the Security Council meetings over the UN refusal to seat the Communist PRC as the official representative of China.

Truman's firm response to the North Korean attack led to a sharp increase in his public approval, from 36 percent to 46 percent, in early July. Yet the military situation in South Korea was bleak throughout the summer. North Korean forces continued to push South Korean, United States, and allied forces fighting under UN auspices southward until they held only a small semicircle of territory around the southern port of Pusan. Then, on September 15, UN forces under MacArthur landed by sea at Inchon, northwest of Seoul. They surprised and quickly overwhelmed the North Koreans. The UN forces quickly recaptured Seoul, and by early October, they crossed the thirty-eighth parallel and marched into North Korea.

The Truman administration now changed its war aims from repelling aggression from the North to unifying Korea as a non-Communist state. As the UN forces continued their advance into North Korea, Kim became desperate for his future and Mao worried that the United States intended to attack China. The Chinese warned the United States not to approach the Yalu River separating Korea and China, or China would enter the war. MacArthur dismissed these warnings and assured Truman that China would not intervene. The president allowed UN troops to proceed north. As the UN forces approached the Yalu in mid-November, China sent an army of more than 300,000 across the river to attack the approaching troops. The Chinese outnumbered the UN forces and made them retreat south of the thirty-eighth parallel. North Korean troops once more occupied Seoul.

On November 30, Truman stated that the use of atomic weapons in Korea had "always been" under consideration. Such speculation alarmed British leaders whose troops fought alongside the Americans. After Prime Minister Clement Attlee complained, Truman backed away from the threat to use atomic weapons against Chinese or North Korean forces.

In the first three months of 1951, UN forces regrouped, retook Seoul, and advanced to positions near where the war had begun. Truman and his principal foreign policy and military advisors now favored pursuing a limited war in Korea, one that would assure the future of South Korea without sparking a larger conflagration with the Soviet Union.

MacArthur, on the other hand, continued his provocative rhetoric toward North Korea and China. Truman became increasingly angry and frustrated with MacArthur's belligerent tone. In April MacArthur telegraphed Republican House minority leader Joseph Martin, demanding that Truman "open a second front in Asia" by permitting him to attack China. Truman called this "rank insubordination" the last straw in his tense relationship with the general, and he fired MacArthur. The dismissal ignited a firestorm of public protest against the president, whose approval rating fell to an abysmal 23 percent. MacArthur received a hero's welcome in Washington and New York when he returned home. Truman's opponents called for the president's impeachment, but

the political storm subsided. More people came to believe that MacArthur's incessant demands for victory over North Korea and China might lead to a third world war.

Peace Talks

Peace talks between the UN and North Korea began in July 1951, but the war continued unabated. U.S. involvement in a stalemated conflict became increasingly unpopular at home, and Truman announced, in March 1952, that he would not seek reelection. The Korean War became a major issue in the 1952 presidential election campaign. Democratic presidential nominee Adlai Stevenson, the governor of Illinois, supported Truman's policy of containment and waging limited war in Korea. General Dwight Eisenhower, the Republican nominee, criticized Truman's handling of a war that had gone on for too long. His campaign adopted a slogan, K1C2 (Korea, Communism, and Corruption), as a way to tap popular discontent with the stalemate in Korea, fear of communism, and anger at scandals involving administration officials. Eisenhower promised that, if elected, he would go to Korea, survey the state of the war, and recommend ways to end it.

Eisenhower, the popular victorious commander in the European theater during World War II, easily defeated Stevenson. The public was looking for a change of parties after 20 years of Democratic control in the White House and eagerly awaited an end to the Korean War. Eisenhower did go to Korea after the election and returned convinced that the war needed to end quickly. He concluded that both North and South Korea were intransigent in their demands, and that the United States needed to apply pressure on both sides to end the fighting.

After Eisenhower became president, the world political environment changed. Soviet leader Stalin died in March 1953, and his passing offered the promise of reducing cold war tensions. The new U.S. administration threatened both North and South Korea in order to produce movement in the stalled peace negotiations. Washington again hinted that it might use atomic weapons against North Korea, and American officials demanded that South Korea drop its requirement that North Korean prisoners of war held in South Korea be permitted to remain there after the war if they chose. The pace of negotiations quickened.

South Korea released more than 100,000 North Korean POWs rather than forcibly repatriate them. The United States, the United Nations, China, and North Korea signed an armistice on July 27, but South Korea refused to join on the grounds that North Korea had not acknowledged its aggression. The armistice divided North and South Korea by a line between the opposing military forces, roughly along the thirty-eighth parallel. A 10-kilometer-wide demilitarized zone separated the two Koreas. Over the next half-century, this border became the most heavily fortified area in the world. Armed with artillery and tanks, hundreds of thousands of troops from North and South Korea and the United States faced each other. Intermittent negotiations failed to transform the temporary armistice into a full peace agreement.

Aftermath of War

Cold war tensions between the United States and the PRC remained high during and after the Korean War. The question of "who lost China" became a powerful and divisive issue in American politics. Anti-Communists accused Foreign Service officers, who had reported on the strength of Mao and the Communists and the weakness of Chiang and the Nationalists, of having contributed to the Communists' victory in the civil war. Between 1951 and 1953, many of these "China Hands" were fired from the State Department.

The Eisenhower administration provided more support for the Nationalist government of Taiwan than Truman had done. Early in the Korean War, the Truman administration had sent the U.S. Navy's Seventh Fleet into the Strait of Taiwan separating the island from the mainland. The aim was to protect Taiwan from a Communist attack but also to discourage the Nationalists from attacking the mainland. Eisenhower lifted the naval defense of Taiwan in 1953. A year later, Jiang sent 70,000 troops to the islands of Quemoy and Matsu, three miles off the coast of mainland China. In September the Chinese Communists began shelling these islands, and in November Communists planes bombed the Tachen Islands in the Taiwan Strait.

During this first Taiwan Strait Crisis, the Joint Chiefs of Staff recommended using atomic weapons against the mainland, and political pressure mounted on Eisenhower to send U.S. troops to protect the offshore islands. In the fall of 1954, the president decided against direct U.S. military involvement in the crisis. Instead, the United States signed a defense treaty with the Republic of China. Under this agreement, the United States promised to protect the island of Taiwan but was silent about the offshore islands. The first Taiwan Strait Crisis intensified in April 1955 when the president said that "A-bombs might be used . . . as you would use a bullet." China said it was willing to negotiate with the United States over the islands and the future of Taiwan. On May 1 China stopped shelling the islands.

Ambassadorial talks between the United States and Communist China began in the summer of 1955 and continued, off and on, mostly in Warsaw, for the next 16 years, until President Richard Nixon announced that he would visit Beijing. These conversations made no progress on the future of the Republic of China in Taiwan, but they did lead to the repatriation of U.S. and Chinese citizens who had been stranded in China or the United States, respectively, during the Chinese civil war and the Korean War. A second Taiwan Strait Crisis began in August 1958, when the Communists resumed shelling Quemoy and Matsu. Eisenhower asserted that the shelling was part of a plan "to liquidate all of the free world positions in the Western Pacific." China stopped shelling the offshore islands on January 1, 1959.

Tensions persisted, and the United States continued to see Communist China as a major threat. During the 1960 presidential campaign, Democratic candidate John F. Kennedy accused the Eisenhower administration of sending mixed signals to China, which had encouraged its aggressive moves in the Taiwan Strait. The growing split between Mao and the Soviet Union, under the leadership of Nikita Khrushchev, ratcheted up the cold war competition. In January 1961, Khrushchev, responding to Mao's accusation that the Soviet Union had retreated from its earlier revolutionary fervor, pledged his country's support for "wars of national liberation" around the world. The new Kennedy administration considered Khrushchev's promise a direct challenge to the United States and its support of pro-western governments. Kennedy increased U.S. support to the government of the Republic of Vietnam, or South Vietnam, as a way to counter Soviet and Communist Chinese influence in Southeast Asia.

The memory of the Korean War and Chinese intervention in it was ever present as the United States deepened its involvement in the Vietnam War during Kennedy's administration and the first 18 months of Lyndon Johnson's presidency. Democratic presidents were haunted by fear that their opponents would resurrect the cry "who lost China?" and charge them with "losing" Vietnam to the Communists. U.S. policy makers believed that the preservation of South Vietnam as an anti-Communist bulwark against what they considered to be a newly aggressive Communist North Vietnam was essential. Kennedy and Johnson administration officials both drew analogies between South Vietnam and South Korea and between North Vietnam and North Korea. They also drew sobering lessons from the Korean War and wished, at all costs, to avoid Chinese intervention in Vietnam.

See also era of consensus, 1952–64; Vietnam and Indochina wars.

FURTHER READING. Jian Chen, *China's Road to the Korean War: The Making of Sino-American Confrontation*, 1994; Rosemary Foot, *The Wrong War: American Policy and the Dimensions of the Korean Conflict*, 1985; John Lewis Gaddis, *The Cold War: A New History*, 2006; David Halberstam, *The Coldest Winter: America and the Korean War*, 2007; Yuen Foong Khong, *Analogies at War: Korea, Munich, Dien Bien Phu, and the Vietnam Decision of 1965*, 1992; Michael Schaller, *Douglas MacArthur: The Far Eastern General*, 1989; William Stueck, *The Korean War: An International History*, 1995; Idem, *Rethinking the Korean War: A New Diplomatic and Strategic History*, 2002; Nancy Bernkopf Tucker, *Taiwan, Hong Kong, and the United States, 1945–1992: Uncertain Friendships*, 1994; Odd Arne Westad, *The Global Cold War: Third World Interventions and the Making of Our Times*, 2005.

ROBERT SCHULZINGER

L

labor movement and politics

On July 23, 1788, New York City artisans organized a parade to support the ratification of the U.S. Constitution. Marching behind banners of their crafts, artisans mobilized to defend their interests in the nation's emerging political order. As this episode suggests, organized workers have been active in American politics since the founding of the republic. More than 200 years after the New York parade, Web sites, phone banks, campaign contributions, and sophisticated canvassing operations had become labor's favored methods of political mobilization, but the aims of workers' organizations were unchanged: organized labor still mobilized politically around policies in the interest of wage earners.

The 200-year history of labor's political activism reveals a paradox. No nation produced a labor movement with a longer history of concerted electoral activity than the United States. Yet no labor movement had expended as much electoral energy without institutionalizing its political experience in a labor party. Indeed, it was the failure of American workers to develop an enduring labor party that led scholars to periodically ruminate on American exceptionalism.

Many factors worked against a successful American labor party. Some were political: a federal system that dispersed power among federal, state, and local jurisdictions and made it difficult for workers to win enough power to enact policies; winner-take-all elections that undercut minority representation; a court system that often undermined workers' legislative gains. Other factors were social: slavery and its legacy, a racial caste system that made it difficult to unite white and nonwhite workers behind a common political program; and waves of immigration that made the American working class unusually fractious along religious and ethnic lines. Other factors were economic: a vast and competitive national market that fostered an exceptionally anti-union ethic among employers; and a perennial shortage of skilled labor that created opportunities for skilled workers at the expense of working-class solidarity. Still other factors were cultural: in no industrializing nation did an ethic of individualism and social mobility sink deeper roots than in the United States. Together these factors created profound obstacles to the institutionalization of labor's political voice.

Yet despite the factors that inhibited the formation of a labor party, political activism was a continuous theme in the history of organized labor in America. Over two centuries, the form of workers' organization changed from journeymen's societies to craft unions, then to industrial unions, and ultimately to huge organizations encompassing public sector, service, and industrial workers in one union. Over time, union membership expanded beyond its original base among skilled, male, native-born whites and western European immigrants to include women and previously excluded groups of blacks, Asians, and Latinos. Labor's political philosophy moved from an early-nineteenth-century emphasis on anti-monopoly to a late-nineteenth-century brand of anti-statist voluntarism, and it ultimately evolved into support for a welfare state in the twentieth century. Yet in every era, the vast majority of organized workers believed that no matter what form their organizations took, what demographics characterized their membership, or what goals they sought to achieve, if they were to advance their interests they would have to engage in political action as well as workplace organization.

Indeed, if there was a form of "exceptionalism" in the American labor movement, it was represented by those few organizations like the Industrial Workers of the World (IWW) that rejected political action. The case of the ephemeral IWW, founded in 1905 and largely destroyed by combined government and employer repression in 1918, was not atypical: labor organizations that rejected politics altogether tended to have short histories. Thus, while the perennial frustrations and disappointments of American politics nursed a disdain for parties and politicians that waxed and waned among labor's activists from age to age, few labor leaders or organizations ever believed they would gain more by rejecting politics than by engaging in it. Most unions thus constantly sought to maximize their influence on the shifting terrain of American politics.

An analysis of labor's political strategies over the course of two centuries permits three generalizations. First, unions tended to find it more difficult to achieve solidarity at the ballot box than on the job. Not only did labor fail to create its own party, but for much of their history, unions also found it difficult to deliver their members as coherent blocs to one of the mainstream political parties. Second, in part due to the difficulty of constructing political solidarity, unions tended toward pragmatism and opportunism rather than ideological clarity and unity, especially in local and state politics. And third, labor organizations found that their political fortunes rarely rested in their own hands alone. Labor required coalitions, and the success or failure of those efforts was often outside of labor's control alone.

Despite these problems, labor continually found ways to express its political voice, and often exerted political influence that far exceeded its membership. Labor activism helped turn crucial elections, generate popular reform ideas, and mobilize new constituencies. If labor's political power operated under significant constraints, unions nonetheless helped shape American political history, as an examination of labor's activism in four distinct periods illustrates.

The Era of Party and Union Formation: 1780s–1880s

The formation of unions in the United States actually preceded the formation of parties. Philadelphia journeymen's societies began to negotiate with master craftsmen in the 1780s, even before Hamiltonians and Jeffersonians created the first party system. Yet parties grew faster and soon outstripped unions in scope and sophistication. By the mid-1880s, the United States had a well-established two-party system in which political professionals fused local machines into statewide and national coalitions to vie for power. Workers were only then beginning to construct their first broad-based national union federation capable of withstanding an economic downturn. The unequal development of parties and unions over this century was crucial: it meant that no matter how avidly labor experimented with independent political action, workers were never organized well enough to match party professionals in the creation of national organizations.

Nonetheless, workers were politically active in the early nineteenth century. Indeed, labor's first partisan political activity can be traced to the Jeffersonian Democratic-Republicans, a movement in which New York and Philadelphia artisans played a significant role. Yet before the 1820s, labor's political activism was limited. It was the upsurge of union organization during the economic boom of 1824–37 that saw the first great experiments with labor-based political activism. During the union upsurge of these years, roughly 44,000 workers joined unions. This unionization led to the first city-wide labor federations, a necessary precursor to significant political activism. In 1827 Philadelphia tradesmen founded the Mechanics' Union of Trade Associations, through which they advocated for a ten-hour workday, argued that wealth belonged to those who produced it, and demanded equal rights for workers. The Philadelphia organization inspired the creation of "city central" federations in 13 other cities by 1836, including New York, where the General Trades' Union included 52 organizations. This organizational impulse eventually led to the creation of the National Trades' Union, a short-lived national labor federation.

As Andrew Jackson was consolidating his Democratic Party during these years, workers also turned to politics. Jackson found allies among trade unionists in cities like New York. But the agitation of the 1820s also produced the first instances of independent labor political action as the trades helped form "workingmen's parties" in several states. The first was launched in New York City in 1829, where it attracted talented leaders like labor editor George Henry Evans, reformer Thomas Skidmore, and radicals Robert Dale Owen and Fanny Wright. The workingmen's parties were short-lived, often succumbing to factionalism or absorption into the emerging two-party system, but they succeeded in making a number of issues—including the demand for free universal public education—central to the politics of the Jacksonian era.

When the depression of 1837 struck, labor's thriving organizational structures suddenly collapsed. During the 1840s, unions played an insignificant role in mobilizing workers, as Whigs and Democrats fought increasingly sophisticated campaigns against each other. Instead, the locus of labor activism shifted to the National Reform Association, established in 1845, and the "industrial congresses" that convened in several states. These initiatives helped to put land reform and homesteading on the national political agenda but yielded no independent political vehicle for workers. Such vehicles would not reemerge until after the Civil War.

It was the emergence of national trades unions that made post–Civil War political action possible. The first national unions, the National Typographical Union and the National Molders' Union, arose in the 1850s. By the 1860s, railroad workers, stonecutters, machinists, shoemakers, and plumbers had formed unions and begun to collect dues and establish strike funds. When the Civil War ended in 1865, some 200,000 workers had been unionized, and by 1872 at least 30 national trade unions had been set up.

This upsurge allowed labor to revive independent political action through a national union federation called the National Labor Union (NLU), formed in 1866. The NLU advocated the eventual replacement of waged labor by a cooperative commonwealth, the exclusion of Chinese contract labor from the United States, and the enactment of eight-hour workday laws. In 1868 iron molder William Sylvis led the NLU's effort to create a national political party to realize this vision. But like the workingmen's parties, the NLU was short-lived. Sylvis's death in 1869, the NLU's abortive attempt to field a presidential candidate in 1872, and the economic depression that struck the next year combined to destroy the NLU.

The social turbulence unleashed by the depression of 1873 soon gave rise to several labor-backed political initiatives. In the space of a few years, three different parties were launched around appeals to labor: the Greenback-Labor Party (1874) advocated currency reform and appealed to farmers and workers alike; the Socialist Labor Party (1877) advocated Marxian socialism and drew support from European immigrant communities; and the Workingmen's Party of California (1877) campaigned for Chinese exclusion. All three parties left a mark: California's workingmen helped bring about the Chinese Exclusion Act of 1882; the Greenback-Labor Party helped win some modifications in the nation's monetary policy and sowed the seeds for the later Populist movement; and the SLP helped incubate the more popular Socialist

Party of America (founded in 1901), which would become America's most successful socialist party.

Yet by the 1890s, organized labor began to pull back from independent political action. Labor's reluctance to launch its own party became clear in the aftermath of a great contest between two divergent union tendencies: one represented by the Noble and Holy Order of the Knights of Labor, an inclusive union that organized women and men, skilled and unskilled, black and white, founded in 1869; the other by the American Federation of Labor (AFL), founded in 1886 by a group of skilled craft unions, whose members were overwhelmingly white and male. Like the NLU, the Knights hoped to supplant the wage system with a cooperative commonwealth; its local assemblies often engaged in political activity and, in many locations, made alliances with Greenbackers and other third parties. Indeed, Terence V. Powderly, who served as Grand Master Workman of the Knights during its peak years of 1879–93, was elected to three terms as mayor of Scranton on the Greenback-Labor ticket beginning in 1878. The AFL, by contrast, favored the organization of workers by craft and the improvement of their wages, hours, and working conditions through collective bargaining, strikes, and union control of access to jobs. AFL leaders tended to have less faith in political action than did most Knights. AFL president Samuel Gompers, for one, had experienced firsthand the frustrations of political action when legislative compromises and judicial hostility undermined a multiyear campaign by his union, the Cigar Makers International Union, to eliminate tenement-house cigar production. Gompers believed that workers could not count on the state or political parties to deliver reform, and that only strong unions could win lasting gains for workers.

As the AFL grew and the Knights declined by the 1890s, a discernable pattern emerged in organized labor's political practice. The range of independent political initiatives that characterized labor activism in the 1870s gradually gave way to a system of "political collective bargaining" in which unions increasingly forsook independent political action in favor of pragmatic alliances with Democratic or Republican candidates.

The Emergence of Political Collective Bargaining: 1880s–1932

The period between the mid-1880s and the late-1890s saw decisive shifts in both the national party system and the labor movement, the results of which reinforced the new pattern in labor's political activism. If Republicans and Democrats competed on a relatively equal footing in the 1880s, Republicans achieved a decisive national advantage following the election of 1896, in which William McKinley defeated the Democratic-Populist fusion ticket headed by William Jennings Bryan. As Republicans consolidated their power, the AFL's trade unionism supplanted the failing Knights of Labor. The AFL's political approach soon became labor's predominant strategy.

The AFL steered clear of formal alliances with parties. Most of its leaders believed that the loyalties of many workers were already cemented to the Democratic or Republican parties by family tradition, regional or religious affiliations. These leaders never believed that workers would unite in a third party and thus resisted the two significant third parties that tried to attract workers in the years between the 1890s and World War I: the People's (Populist) Party and the Socialist Party of America. Populists tried hard to cultivate ties to labor: the Southern Farmers' Alliance rechristened itself the National Farmers' Alliance and Industrial Union in an effort to link farmers and workers, and Populists organized food shipments from farmers to striking steelworkers in Homestead, Pennsylvania, in 1892. Nonetheless, the AFL rejected populism. "Party politics, whether they be Democratic, Republican, Socialistic, Populistic, Prohibition, or any other shall have no place in the conventions of the American Federation of Labor," resolved the AFL at the height of the Populist agitation. Nor did the AFL reconsider during the climactic 1896 election. "Let the watchword be: No political party domination over the trade unions; no political party influence over trade union action," Gompers announced.

The AFL was equally opposed to an alliance with the Socialist Party of America. Although the Socialists built a strong following among workers, elected mayors in dozens of smaller cities, claimed the support of a significant minority of delegates to AFL national conventions, and perennially nominated the beloved former railroad union leader Eugene V. Debs as a presidential candidate, the AFL steadfastly rejected them.

AFL nonpartisanship did not mean that the organization was nonpolitical. Unlike the syndicalist radicals of the IWW, AFL members were active in partisan politics, especially on the local level. Rather than allying with one party, however, they tended to follow Gompers's dictum that unions should "reward our friends and punish our enemies." Local unions thus tended to engage in political collective bargaining in which they helped those politicians who offered them support on key issues—regardless of their party affiliation.

Even the AFL's nonpartisan approach was flexible. Indeed, in the decade before World War I, the AFL slowly revised its nonpartisanship without ever formally renouncing it. The impetus for this change was the increasing harassment of unions by the courts. In the early twentieth century, judicial injunctions became the bane of trade unionists. Judges' orders regularly barred unions from picketing and disrupted their boycotts and sympathy strikes. In frustration, the AFL drew up a Bill of Grievances in 1906 demanding an anti-injunction law and other measures. In 1908 the AFL presented its demands to both major party conventions. When the Democrats and their presidential nominee, again William Jennings Bryan, responded more favorably, the AFL inched toward an alliance with the Democrats. Still, important elements of the AFL's leadership and membership continued to vote Republican. Given this resistance, and Republican William H. Taft's 1908 election to the presidency, the consummation of an alliance between the AFL and the Democratic party was postponed until Democrat Woodrow Wilson unseated Taft in the 1912 election.

As Wilson took office, both he and AFL leaders saw much to be gained from an alliance. Wilson took the advice of Gompers in making appointments to the U.S. Commission on Industrial Relations, which recommended reforms in the nation's labor practices. Wilson also signed legislation granting an eight-hour workday for the nation's train crews and labor rights to the nation's merchant seamen, as well as the Clayton Anti-Trust Act, which Gompers mistakenly hoped would protect unions from injunctions. By the time Wilson ran for reelection in 1916, the AFL unions were actively working for him. Indeed, labor's help was instrumental in helping Wilson retain control of the White House in that close election.

But the Wilson-AFL alliance was itself cut short by the fallout from World War I. The war initially seemed to strengthen the relationship between labor and the Democratic Party. Even before the United States declared war, the AFL pledged to support Wilson's war policy. In return, the administration created war labor policies that encouraged collective bargaining and repressed the Socialists and the IWW, the AFL's chief rivals. With tacit federal support, the AFL saw its membership nearly double between 1916 and 1919. Yet these gains were fleeting: once the armistice was declared, federal support was withdrawn, and a ferocious anti-union backlash gathered strength. Democrats lost control of Congress in the 1918 elections—in part due to dissatisfaction with Wilson's wartime labor and economic policies—and unions lost a series of strikes in steel, coal, and textiles amid the rising fears of the "Red Scare" of 1919. In the 1920 elections, Republicans regained the White House, leaving the AFL-Democratic alliance in disarray.

The political backlash led to a brief revival of interest in independent labor political action. In 1922 a number of union leaders formed the Conference for Progressive Political Action (CPPA). The CPPA claimed credit for the defeat of dozens of anti-labor U.S. representatives that year, and hoped to launch a national party in 1924. But factional differences frustrated this vision. Senator Robert M. La Follette ran for president as a Progressive in 1924, with support from many unions. However, La Follette's defeat and the death of Samuel Gompers after the election left labor without a clear political strategy. In the 1928 elections, labor divided: Democrat Al Smith garnered the support of some union leaders, while others, including John L. Lewis, president of

the United Mine Workers of America (UMW), supported Republican Herbert Hoover. American labor may have distanced itself from the independent political initiatives so prevalent in the nineteenth century, but labor still lacked a coherent political program as the 1920s came to an end. It would take a major economic calamity and political upheaval for labor to fashion an alternative.

The Heyday of the Labor-Democratic Alliance: 1932–72

The 1932 election of Democrat Franklin D. Roosevelt in the midst of the Depression transformed labor's politics. Roosevelt's election allowed labor and the Democrats to rebuild a national political alliance, this time on a more solid footing. Labor support for Roosevelt in 1932 had not been unanimous; Herbert Hoover still commanded the allegiance of William Hutcheson of the Carpenters and other Republican-leaning union leaders. But once in office, Roosevelt cultivated ties with labor more assiduously than any previous president and his legislative programs earned him the enduring loyalty of rank-and-file unionists. The Wagner Act of 1935 guaranteed most private-sector workers the right to organize, gave the National Labor Relations Board (NLRB) the power to enforce that right, and compelled employers to recognize unions when the majority of their workers wanted to be represented by a union. The 1935 Social Security Act, which created a national retirement program and funded state programs of unemployment insurance and aid to dependent children, laid the basis of an American welfare state (and swept away most lingering resistance to state-administered welfare among the nation's unions). The Fair Labor Standards Act of 1938 finally banned child labor and created a minimum wage.

The enactment of such policies not only transformed labor's orientation to national politics and the state, but changed the union movement. By 1935 the legal and political context for union organizing had improved profoundly, forcing to the surface a long-simmering disagreement within the AFL between craft unionists and industrial unionists over how best to organize in this favorable environment. Led by Gompers's successor, William Green, craft unionists favored continuing the traditional AFL model. But an emerging faction led by UMW president Lewis, Sidney Hillman of the Amalgamated Clothing Workers, and others called for big new industrial unions in each of the nation's basic industries. When the AFL balked at this plan, Lewis and allies plunged ahead. In 1935 they formed the Committee for Industrial Organization, an initiative that soon evolved into a rival labor federation: the Congress of Industrial Organizations (CIO). These unions began recruiting thousands of auto, steel, and rubber workers in 1936.

Although labor was divided on the best method for organizing, the movement remained united politically behind the effort to reelect Roosevelt in 1936. Teamster union leader Daniel Tobin, a CIO opponent, helped coordinate Roosevelt's reelection campaign, even as the CIO also supported Roosevelt. Indeed, John L. Lewis transferred $500,000 from the UMW treasury to Roosevelt's campaign (the largest single contribution to a political campaign in that era). In 1936 Lewis and Hillman also helped launch Labor's Non-Partisan League in an effort to unify labor behind Roosevelt's reelection. George Berry of the AFL's Printing Pressmen's union ran the initiative, which raised $1.5 million for Roosevelt's reelection. Developments on the left aided the budding labor-Democratic alliance. New York labor leaders launched the American Labor Party in 1936, nominating Roosevelt as its presidential standard-bearer, and thus providing lifelong Socialists with a way to vote for Roosevelt without becoming Democrats. Meanwhile, the Communist Party of the United States, which had vocally opposed Roosevelt's policies before 1935, entered its Popular Front phase and encouraged members to support the CIO and New Deal initiatives.

Roosevelt's victory over Republican governor Alf Landon of Kansas in 1936 seemed to seal the emerging alliance between labor and the Democrats on the national level. Labor played a crucial role in the "New Deal political coalition" that emerged in these years. Unions proved especially important in mobilizing millions of second-generation immigrant urban voters.

Yet the national-level labor-Democratic alliance was not without tensions, and it was put to the test repeatedly in its formative years, 1936–48. While Roosevelt's administration relied on labor support in its conflicts with Republicans and conservative Democrats, Roosevelt viewed labor as just one component in a broad governing coalition. He was reluctant to expend political capital for labor. Thus, the president remained neutral during the CIO's failed 1937 "Little Steel" strike even as he asked John L. Lewis to support his failed "court-packing" initiative. Lewis came to mistrust Roosevelt's intentions and later broke with the president on foreign policy. Meanwhile, some anti-Communist trade unionists became suspicious of radical influences in the CIO and New Deal agencies. Still, most labor voters remained Roosevelt loyalists, as Lewis learned in 1940. When Lewis unsuccessfully opposed Roosevelt's election to a third term, he was compelled to turn over leadership of the CIO to Roosevelt ally Philip Murray of the Steelworkers.

American entry into World War II reinforced labor's alliance with Roosevelt while creating new problems for that alliance. Both the AFL and the CIO offered "no strike pledges" and cooperated with the war mobilization; the administration, in turn, supported unionization through the policies of the National War Labor Board. The union movement emerged from the war larger and more powerful. In turn, labor lent its help to Roosevelt's effort to win an unprecedented fourth term. In 1944 Sidney Hillman helped launch the CIO's Political Action Committee (arguably the first modern PAC). The AFL followed suit, creating a PAC called Labor's League for Political Education in 1947. Yet as labor emerged as a key organizational component of Roosevelt's Democratic party, it also became a target for political attacks. In 1944 an invigorated Republican Party ran its best campaign against Roosevelt by arguing that labor had too much influence in his administration. Although Roosevelt prevailed, the results of the vote indicated that Republicans and conservative southern Democrats had begun to contain the labor wing of the party.

The real test of the labor-Democratic alliance, though, was whether it could weather three transitions that came in rapid succession between 1945 and 1948: the elevation of Roosevelt's successor, Harry S. Truman; conversion to a peacetime economy; and the emergence of the cold war. After Roosevelt's death and the end of World War II, a strike wave swept the nation as unions fought to make up ground lost to wartime inflation. Many labor leaders felt that President Truman, a moderate Missourian, offered tepid support to labor during this tumultuous period, and they resented Truman's threat to draft railroad strikers into the Army during one particularly bitter postwar battle. When Republicans recaptured control of Congress in 1946 and passed the anti-union Taft-Hartley Act over Truman's veto in 1947, labor's dissatisfaction with Truman flared. Left-wing unionists opted to abandon the Democrats and support the Progressive Party candidacy of Henry Wallace, a labor ally and a critic of Truman's emerging anti-Communist foreign policy. Most unions, however, stuck with Truman. Two factors ensured this. First, unions feared that Wallace would divide the Democratic vote and help elect Republican Thomas E. Dewey, a defender of Taft-Hartley. Second, most union leaders and members shared Truman's anticommunism stance and rejected Wallace's contention that the Soviet Union posed no threat to the United States. Ultimately, the AFL and most CIO unions and their members rallied behind Truman and helped him defeat Dewey. There was much truth in Truman's often-quoted reaction to the surprising election results: "Labor did it." Labor's support of Truman in 1948 sealed the national-level alliance between unions and the Democratic Party. But the alliance exacted a high price: the unions that supported Wallace were expelled from the CIO for alleged Communist domination of their leadership.

The postwar labor-Democratic alliance was founded on the principles of cold war liberalism, the belief that the extension of the New Deal and resistance to Soviet communism were inseparable. Between 1948 and 1972, this shared commitment held the alliance together despite the opposition of southern Democrats, who fought unions and liberal social programs, and liberal Republicans, who courted (and occasionally won) union support, especially on the state or local level.

As the postwar Red Scare faded, labor liberalism emerged as a fragile juggernaut. The AFL and CIO reunited in 1955 to form the AFL-CIO and created the Committee on Political Education (COPE) to channel their political activism. COPE soon became a major source of political contributions and experienced campaign volunteers. Its support was instrumental in electing John F. Kennedy in 1960 and lobbying on behalf of the social programs of Kennedy's successor, Lyndon B. Johnson. The mid-1960s marked a high point for labor's political influence as the AFL-CIO became a powerful force in Lyndon Johnson's Democratic Party. Yet southern Democrats continued to act as a counterweight to labor's influence. Moreover, liberal Democrats, like Walter Reuther of the United Automobile Workers, were reluctant to appear to hold too much sway within the party. Any threatened labor "takeover" of the party, Reuther believed, would instigate a backlash, destroy the party's broad base, and leave labor politically isolated. Moreover, Reuther understood that no union could "deliver" its rank and file as a unified voting bloc. Indeed, Reuther was disturbed to find that a significant minority of his union's white members supported segregationist George Wallace's third-party campaign for the presidency in 1968. Ever conscious of the limited nature of electoral solidarity, unions thus pressed their political agenda without trying to control the Democratic Party, occasionally supporting sympathetic Republicans when it was advantageous. Overall, labor made important strides in the 1960s, including winning local, state, and federal policies that allowed government workers to unionize (government union membership grew tenfold between 1955 and 1975).

Labor in the Era of Post-Liberal Politics: 1972–2008

Before the 1960s ended, the Vietnam War and the civil rights movement—both of which labor supported—divided the Democratic coalition. Labor lobbyists helped pass the Civil Rights Act (1964) and Voting Rights Act (1965), but these laws accelerated the mass departure of southern whites from the Democratic Party over the next 20 years. Nor did labor's influence within the party grow as conservatives departed. In part this was due to labor's support of the Vietnam War. The staunchly anti-Communist AFL-CIO and its president George Meany favored U.S. military intervention in Vietnam in 1965. However, the disastrous war that resulted triggered a Democratic Party rebellion that brought down the Johnson presidency in 1968 and left labor isolated from the growing ranks of antiwar Democrats. Tensions between the AFL-CIO and advocates of the New Politics were exacerbated when the AFL-CIO refused to endorse the presidential candidacy of George McGovern in 1972,

helping to ensure the liberal Democrat's crushing defeat by incumbent Richard M. Nixon.

The economic crises of the 1970s helped prevent labor-liberalism from rebounding in that decade as "stagflation" (the simultaneous surge of inflation and unemployment), plant closings, and declining union membership sapped labor's strength. Although unions and the Democrats revived their alliance in Jimmy Carter's successful 1976 campaign, the Carter administration disappointed labor. Carter was too concerned about inflation to back the aggressive economic stimulus programs unions desired and was weak in his support for labor law reform. Thus, several unions endorsed Senator Edward Kennedy's unsuccessful primary challenge to Carter in 1980. Even though labor reunified behind Carter in the general election, many union members voted for Republican Ronald Reagan.

Ironically, labor experienced a nadir of its influence under the administration of the only union leader ever to become president (Reagan had once headed the Screen Actors Guild). Reagan undercut union power by breaking a nationwide strike of air traffic controllers, appointing anti-unionists to the NLRB, and implementing a host of policies inimical to labor. The AFL-CIO fought back by working to rehabilitate the Democratic Party. Labor officials helped redesign the Democratic nominating process in 1984 in a way that created unelected "superdelegates"—including union leaders—who would be empowered to cast votes for the party's presidential nominee. Yet when the AFL-CIO tried to exert its influence by endorsing of Walter Mondale in 1984, the former vice president was attacked for being the candidate of "special interests." Mondale won the nomination only to be trounced by Reagan in 1984. Labor's influence slipped further when centrist Democrats created the Democratic Leadership Council (DLC) in 1985 in an effort to distance the party from its labor and liberal wings.

The ascendance of conservative politics forced labor to become increasingly adept at political action and to search more pragmatically for allies. In 1992 labor helped elect Arkansas governor Bill Clinton, a charter member of the DLC, to the presidency. Clinton rewarded union allies by supporting a higher minimum wage and stricter occupational health and safety policies. But he also defied labor by signing the North American Free Trade Agreement. When Republicans won control of Congress in 1994, internal dissatisfaction with labor's waning influence resulted in the first contested election for the AFL-CIO presidency in 1995. John Sweeney won that election, promising to retool labor's political operation and revive union organizing.

Sweeney's record was mixed during his first ten years in office. Despite their development of increasingly sophisticated voter mobilization techniques, unions were unable to help the Democrats recapture Congress or help Vice President Al Gore defeat Republican George W. Bush in the controversial 2000 presidential election. At the same time, the share of workers organized continued to fall, reaching 13 percent by 2005. These failures contributed to the most significant labor schism since the 1930s, when five unions, led by the Service Employees International Union (SEIU) and the Teamsters, left the AFL-CIO in 2005 to form a new federation, Change to Win (CTW), promising to shift their emphasis from political action to workplace organizing. Such promises notwithstanding, CTW unions devoted significant resources to politics. Like the founders of the AFL, CTW concluded that it had no choice but to do so. Indeed, no union spent more on political action during 2005–8 than the SEIU. Although they continued to squabble, the AFL-CIO and CTW devoted millions of dollars and mobilized thousands of volunteers to help Democrats recapture Congress in 2006. Unions also played a vital role in the victory of Democratic presidential candidate Barack Obama in 2008.

The 2006 congressional victory and Obama's election heartened labor activists. Yet, tellingly, most unions discounted predictions of the dawn of a new era of liberalism and labor influence amid the economic turmoil of 2008. A century of labor history since the AFL's Bill of Grievances had taught union leaders to temper their expectations. They knew that no labor movement had a longer history of electoral success. American labor had undeniably left its mark on U.S. political development, but no labor movement anywhere had found the mobilization of working-class political power to be a more Sisyphean task.

See also Democratic Party, 1932–68; interest groups; liberalism.

FURTHER READING. Robin Archer, *Why Is There No Labor Party in the United States?* 2007; Kevin Boyle, ed., *Organized Labor in American Politics: The Labor-Liberal Alliance 1894–1994*, 1998; Idem, *The UAW and the Heyday of American Liberalism, 1945–1968*, 1995; David Brody, *Workers in Industrial America: Essays on the Twentieth Century Struggle*, 1980; Alan Dawley, *Class and Community: The Industrial Revolution in Lynn*, 1976; Melvyn Dubofsky, *The State and Labor in Modern America*, 1994; Leon Fink, *Workingmen's Democracy: The Knights of Labor and American Politics*, 1983; Peter L. Francia, *The Future of Organized Labor in American Politics*, 2006; Julie Greene, *Pure and Simple Politics: The American Federation of Labor and Political Activism, 1881–1917*, 1998; Marc Karson, *Labor Unions and Politics, 1900–1918*, 1958; Michael Kazin, *Barons of Labor: The San Francisco Building Trades and Union Power in the Progressive Era*, 1987; John H. M. Laslett and Seymour Martin Lipset, eds., *Failure of a Dream? Essays in the History of American Socialism*, Revised ed., 1984; Nelson Lichtenstein, *State of the Union: A Century of American Labor*, 2002; Seymour Martin Lipset, *American Exceptionalism: A Double-Edged Sword*, 1996; Theodore J. Lowi, "Why Is There No Socialism in the

United States? A Federal Analysis," in *The Costs of Federalism*, edited by Robert T. Golembiewski and Aaron Wildavsky; Gary Marks, *Unions in Politics: Britain, Germany, and the United States in the Nineteenth and Early Twentieth Centuries*, 1989; Gwendolyn Mink, *Old Labor and New Immigrants in American Political Development: Union, Party, and State, 1875–1920*, 1986; David Montgomery, *The Fall of the House of Labor: The Workplace, the State, and American Labor Activism, 1865–1925*, 1987; Karen Orren, *Belated Feudalism: Labor, Law, and Political Development in the United States*, 1991; Howard Rock, Paul A. Gilje, and Robert Asher, eds., *American Artisans: Crafting Social Identity, 1750–1850*, 1995; Michael Rogin, "Voluntarism: The Political Functions of an Antipolitical Doctrine," *Industrial and Labor Relations Review* 15, no. 4 (July 1962), 521–35; Richard Schneirov, *Labor and Urban Politics: Class Conflict and the Origins of Modern Liberalism in Chicago, 1864–97*, 1998; Kim Voss, *The Making of American Exceptionalism: The Knights of Labor and Class Formation in the Nineteenth Century*, 1993; Sean Wilentz, *Chants Democratic: New York City and the Rise of the American Working Class, 1788–1850*, 1984; Robert Zieger, *Republicans and Labor, 1919–1929*, 1969.

JOSEPH A. MCCARTIN

legislative branch
See House of Representatives; Senate.

liberal consensus and American exceptionalism

The idea of liberal consensus took hold of the historiography of the 1950s and in some ways reflected the apparent tranquility of the Eisenhower years. After the tumultuous 1930s, which saw the radicalization of American intellectual life, and the arduous 1940s, in which the American people endured World War II, the 1950s seemed to welcome a healthy return to the sane and normal. The moderation in politics matched the homogenization in historical scholarship, which denied all that had been contentious and conflictual in the American past in order to uphold the "the vital center" that the poet W. B. Yeats once wrote "cannot hold."

Liberal consensus had also been associated with the cold war, and here the chronology needs to be questioned. The first major book that launched the consensus school of thought, Richard Hofstadter's *The American Political Tradition*, appeared in 1948, and the author had been composing it years earlier, before the cold war surfaced with the Soviet invasion of Czechoslovakia and the fall of China toward the end of the decade. But consensus theory did have something to do with communism. Hofstadter, Daniel J. Boorstin, and Louis Hartz had all been Communists or Trotskyists in their college years in the 1930s, and they became convinced that American capitalism would most likely not survive the stresses of the war against Adolf Hitler and the Third Reich. The assumption was that the United States must move toward the left by collectivizing the economy or risk succumbing to some form of fascism in which the U.S. Constitution would be scrapped and liberty lost. When America survived World War II with its political and economic institutions intact, historians Hofstadter, Boorstin, and Hartz, together with the sociologists Daniel Bell and Seymour Martin Lipset, set out to explain what it was that kept the country together when many intellectuals believed it would fall apart. The idea of conflict, especially class conflict, no longer seemed a viable concept, and out of such reconsiderations was born the idea of consensus.

Closely related to consensus was the idea of American exceptionalism, and this, too, had its origins in the 1930s. The term was first coined by the followers of Jay Lovestone, a Communist leader who opposed the official Communist Party of the USA and claimed, against those willing to take orders from Moscow, that America had a different historical experience from Europe and thus had a right to formulate its own policies independently of the Comintern. Among the realities America had to deal with that set it apart from Europe and the rest of the world were the absence of a revolutionary proletariat and a strong socialist tradition, the influx of immigrant populations, and the presence of African Americans, which meant that ethnic cultures and race must be dealt with apart from the class question. Such issues that America had to face confounded Marxism and rendered the country unique and exceptional.

The idea of exceptionalism now has various meanings in different fields, sometimes with disastrous consequences. Political leaders like to invoke America as the "city upon a hill" to claim that their country enjoys the blessings of providence and is somehow morally superior to the rest of the world—forgetting that the seventeenth-century Puritan who first uttered the phrase, John Winthrop, saw the New World as corruptible as the Old World unless it shunned "the sins of the flesh." The idea of exceptionalism has also been invoked in recent discussions of international relations, especially to argue that America has a right to be exempted from rulings of the United Nations and the Geneva Convention.

In the buildup to the war in Iraq in 2003, the idea was also cited to persuade the American people that they had a responsibility to bring democracy to the Middle East. Here the concept of exceptionalism turned into a misleading conceit. Advocates of the war quoted Abraham Lincoln describing his country as the "last best hope" for liberty, as though America could bring its message to any other country for which it wanted a "regime change." But Lincoln was warning, in the 1860s, that if the Union broke apart, liberty would die on native ground. In opposing the war with Mexico in 1848, Lincoln could not believe that America could bring democracy beyond its borders even to its next-door neighbors. Properly understood, the idea of American exceptionalism could reinforce isolationism far more than interventionism.

The three exponents of liberal consensus, the historians Hofstadter, Boorstin, and Hartz, rarely wrote about diplomatic history as they sought to explain the unique structure of American society where many of the conditions of the Old World were lacking. But in the final passage of Hartz's *The Liberal Tradition in America*, the reader may appreciate the connection between liberal consensus and American exceptionalism. America had experienced no great social conflicts in its history, including even the Civil War, which was more a sectional struggle over the issue of slavery and state sovereignty than of a class conflict between labor and capital that would be solved by revolution. Thus Americans, Hartz pointed out, are unprepared to sympathize with the need for radical change at home and revolutions abroad because they have enjoyed freedom almost as a birthright: "Can a people 'born equal' ever understand peoples elsewhere that have to become so? Can it ever understand itself?" To those who regard liberal consensus as part of what sociologist C. Wright Mills called the "great American celebration," Hartz must represent an exception, a historian who saw little to praise about the past. America offered few answers to the problems facing the country because the pervasiveness of consensus soothed over issues and left people untroubled, completely contented with a life of bovine consumption. In the 1950s, with the "end of ideology" proclaimed, historians began to argue whether there was anything to argue about. Not so Hartz, who wondered how Americans could ever become conscious of themselves as a people with a coherent identity rather than a series of aimless desires. "Instead of recapturing our past, we have got to transcend it," he exhorted. "There is no going home for America."

Hartz followed his own advice. Teaching at Harvard University, he suffered a mental breakdown in the 1960s and, upon retiring, left America, never to return. He set out to discover the third world and spent years studying the non-Western religions of Islam, Confucious, Buddhism, and Hinduism. He died in Ankara, Turkey, in 1986. His last book, *A Synthesis of World History*, verges on mysticism as it advocated humankind to "be free to be Chinese one day, Indian the next, and European the next."   .

The three historians of consensus each approached their subject differently. Hofstadter dealt with the unrelenting continuity of the American value system expressed by political leaders and presidents. Hartz examined the structural implications of a country that lacked clear-cut class divisions in society and ideological divisions in the American mind. Boorstin, in contrast, was happy to report that historians need not deal with the American mind since the American people had successfully lived without big ideas or ideologies. In reasoning somewhat like the pragmatists and contemporary neopragmatists, Boorstin argued that it was the philosophy of America to have no philosophy, no metaphysical foundations, no grounding in first principles, no truths upon which beliefs depend. Americans, Boorstin insisted, lived more by doing than by thinking.

Hofstadter, one of the bright "New York intellectuals," lived by thinking, and his *The American Political Tradition and the Men Who Made It* came to a conclusion that Boorstin reached by other means. As evidenced by the positions and speeches taken by their political leaders, the American people did think, but all they thought about was their own materialistic concerns that viewed liberty as the "pursuit of happiness." In the preface to the book, Hofstadter specified the values Americans live by: "The sanctity of private property, the right of the individual to dispose and invest it, the value of opportunity, and the natural evolution of self-interest and self-assertion, within broad legal limits, into a beneficent social order." The conflicts and antagonisms in American history should not be allowed to mislead us, he argued, for individuals and groups compete for the same ends even with different means, whether it be wages or profits, or land prices or financial investment, or the modern trade union or the corporate law firm: "Even when some property right has been challenged—as it was by the followers of Jefferson or Jackson—in the name of the rights of man or the rights of the community, the challenge, when translated into practical policy, has actually been urged on behalf of some other kinds of property." Hofstadter traced this mentality from Thomas Jefferson to Franklin D. Roosevelt, with each and every president committed to bourgeois values that frustrated any possibility for the success of socialism in America. Hofstadter wrote the book as a democratic socialist, and he made readers aware of Wendell Phillips, the New England radical who believed that the abolition of slavery required the redistribution of property in the South to assure that free blacks would enjoy self-sufficiency. But in capitalist America, property remained sacrosanct, the very foundation of the liberal consensus.

In *The Liberal Tradition in America*, Hartz traced that consensus to two factors, the absence of feudalism and the presence of Lockeanism. In the 1830s, Alexis de Tocqueville visited America and was astonished to discover (erroneously) that, in their revolution, all Americans fought on the same side, and he attributed this to the absence of class traditions in an America that had skipped the feudal stage of history and thus had no aristocracy to struggle against and no proletariat to worry about. Hartz drew upon Tocqueville, as did Bell, Lipset, and other sociologists, to explain the implications of a consensual political culture that lacked class tensions.

He also delineated the implications of John Locke's political philosophy that had pervaded America in the colonial era. Whereas the classical and Christian traditions of the past had condemned self-interest as betraying the ideals of civic virtue or the laws of God, Locke hailed it as liberating, giving men the right to property and women the right to divorce, and making labor the source of value in a new environment of possessive individualism. Americans, Hartz observed, had little respect for history and tradition and, unlike the British conservative Edmund Burke, rarely looked to custom to bind generations together in an organic compact with the dead, the living, and those about to be born.

Yet what Hartz discovered within American liberalism turned out to be a conservative time bomb. Although his book was written in the 1950s, it anticipated the President Ronald Reagan of the 1980s, especially the conservative exhortation that Americans should not look to government for a solution to their problems since government itself is the problem. The message would be repeated by Democratic president Bill Clinton, who declared in his second inaugural address, "The era of big government is over." Such stances are what political philosophers call "negative liberty," the Lockean assumption that humankind is free to the extent that the government is diminished—or, as Jefferson put it, "That government is best which governs least"; or, as Henry David Thoreau added, "which governs not at all."

The most intriguing of the consensus historians may have been Boorstin, an uncanny thinker who was a member of a Communist cell while at Harvard University as an undergraduate, a barrister in England after studying law at Oxford University, a "friendly witness" who testified before the House Un-American Activities Committee about his political activities, and then became an eminent scholar at the University of Chicago and later the Librarian of Congress. Perhaps because Boorstin had been seduced by communism's sparkling glitter of ideas, he decided to write a history to argue that America had no need of ideas, especially ideologies and abstract concepts that deflected the mind from the practical tasks of the day. In *The Genius of American Politics*, he insisted that Americans had always been guided by the "givenness" of ideas and values, by thoughts that required no reflection or mediation but were simply acted upon as the country encountered problems to be solved. Boorstin believed that America has almost instinctively resolved one of the greatest issues in philosophy, how to get from factual detail to moral knowledge, from the "is" to the "ought." He argued that moral values were embedded in everyday existence, and thus life as it is "gave the outlines of life as it ought to be, that values were implicit in experience."

One wonders what Lincoln would have thought about Boorstin's explanation of America's "genius." Lincoln insisted that experience itself was the problem, especially the experience of slavery, and, to deal with it, America must look to the Bible and return to the values of the Declaration of Independence, the "sheet anchor" of the republic. But the amazing aspect of Boorstin's conservative position of the 1950s is that it anticipated radical positions taken in the 1980s, especially the neopragmatism of the literary scholar Stanley Fish and the philosopher Richard Rorty. They, too, insisted that history and society have no foundation in philosophy or reason, that we are not what we think in any deep reflective sense but simply what we do, and what we do we do culturally not intellectually, simply following the contingencies of convention. That conservatives and radicals can partake of the same mental outlook could very well be called the cunning of consensus.

The consensus school of history was challenged during the 1960s as students took to the streets to protest the Vietnam War; a decade or so later, after the same radical students went to graduate school and received PhDs, they challenged the idea of consensus in the classroom and in their scholarship. Everywhere in American history they found enclaves of resistance and episodes of opposition, continuing moments of conflict that discredited the idea that America could have ever been held together by a set of core values, especially capitalist values. Everything from a labor strike to a hip-hop album was interpreted as subversive and transgressive, as though the worker had no desire for higher wages and the musician could hardly be motivated by money. While professors told their students how radical America was, the polls continually proved how conservative the country was. Professors proved conflict by teaching it; the masses of people proved consensus by heading for the shopping mall.

See also era of consensus, 1952–64; liberalism.

FURTHER READING. Daniel J. Boorstin, *The Genius of American Politics*, 1953; David S. Brown, *Richard Hofstadter*, 2006; John Patrick Diggins, *On Hallowed Grounds: Abraham Lincoln and the Foundations of American History*, 2000; Louis Hartz, *The Liberal Tradition in America: An Interpretation of American Political Thought since the Revolution*, 1955; Idem, *A Synthesis of World History*, 1984; John Higham, *Writing American History*, 1970; Richard Hofstadter, *The American Political Tradition: And the Men Who Made It*, 1989; Seymour Martin Lipset, *American Exceptionalism: A Double-Edged Sword*, 1996.

JOHN PATRICK DIGGINS

liberalism

Liberalism has been a word of multiple meanings and valences ever since the late medieval introduction of the word *liberal* to English from Latin. On the one hand, liberal has indicated an inclination toward freedom, open-mindedness, generosity, and the cultivation of intellect; on the other, a shortage of discipline and practicality. As that cluster of disparate meanings suggests, liberalism has been an essentially contested concept, a problem made even more nettlesome for historians by its constantly changing significance over the last four centuries.

Puritan Origins

The Puritans bound for America on the *Arbella* in 1630 heard John Winthrop urge them to practice a "liberality" of spirit consistent with the Hebrew prophet Nehemiah's exhortations and St. Matthew's rendering of the Christian ideal of benevolence. Winthrop instructed his flock, as God's chosen people, to balance a prudent concern for their families with an unrestrained generosity toward those in need of help. Against the temptation of "selfishness," he counterposed Christ's injunction of unrestrained love and cheerful "liberality" to the poor as the surest sign of God's grace. The Puritans must be "knitted together in this work" and "must be willing to abridge ourselves of our superfluities for the supply of others' necessities." If instead they were "seduced" and served "other Gods," such as "our pleasures and profits," Winthrop warned, they would "surely perish."

Thus began the American liberal project. The tensions between the narrow concern for kin and a broader interest in the community, between the sin of selfishness and the divine injunction to generosity, have persisted ever since. Puritans left England to escape religious constraints and to establish communities governed by rules devised according to their understanding of God's will. In laying those foundations, they demonstrated the inextricable ties between liberality and democracy in America. They also showed the artificiality of separating "negative" from "positive" freedom, an empty and misleading but influential distinction made familiar in recent decades after its introduction in 1958 by the Russian-émigré English philosopher Isaiah Berlin. The Puritans fled from the constraints of Anglicanism, but their escape was meaningful only because it enabled them to establish their own religious and civic institutions. As astute American advocates of liberality from Winthrop until today have understood, freedom from restraint exists only when individuals possess a real opportunity to exercise that freedom within self-governing communities. Fantasies of individual rights independent of the capacity of people to exercise them, or outside the boundaries of law that both constitute and constrain their use, have no foundation in American history.

The tensions between selfishness and generosity marked American colonial development up and down the Atlantic seaboard. Everywhere in Europe's American colonies—as everywhere in Europe—women, the poor, and members of racial and religious minorities were subjected to harsh discipline and excluded from decision-making processes. In this world, hierarchy was taken for granted as God's will. Despite his injunctions to generosity, even Winthrop assumed that there would continue to be rich and poor, powerful and powerless. Free men with property existed at one end of a spectrum; slaves at the other; women, children, artisans, servants, religious minorities, native peoples, and the few free people of color fell somewhere in between. Open-mindedness toward those unlike oneself marked a liberal sensibility, but in the seventeenth and early eighteenth centuries, such toleration existed within rigid frameworks that dictated what types of treatment suited what sorts of people. Sharp distinctions, enforced between slave and free, nonwhite and white, women and men, members of religious minorities and majorities, and those without and with property, curtailed the exercise of the benevolence enjoined by Winthrop.

Rights and Duties in the Age of Democratic Revolutions

Beginning with the Revolution of 1688 in England and continuing through the ratification of the U.S. Constitution a century later, a whirlwind of cultural change uprooted many of these hierarchical patterns and transformed others. These ideas, which provided the ammunition for Americans to construct a new national political culture on the foundations of earlier colonial thought and practice, derived from multiple sources.

In American writers' contributions to transatlantic debates during the age of democratic revolutions, diverse traditions of dissenting Protestantism blended with arguments by Samuel Pufendorf and John Locke concerning the relation between individual rights and God's will, with eighteenth-century Scottish common sense moral philosophy, and with varieties of republican political theory drawn from the ancient world and updated by Renaissance humanists. Attempts to disentangle the religious, liberal, and republican strands of the arguments woven during the eighteenth century are futile and counterproductive. Americans involved in these furious debates cited authorities promiscuously, hijacked arguments for their own particular purposes, and did not always see the differences between traditions that now seem evident to many scholars.

The American discourses of independence and constitution making displayed the full range of meanings contained in the idea of a liberal disposition. A passionate commitment to freedom from British rule inspired the local and state declarations of independence on which Thomas Jefferson drew. Versions of that commitment also surfaced in the early rumblings of antislavery sentiment among African Americans, Quakers, and New Englanders and in the scattered calls for women's rights from writers such as Abigail Adams and Judith Sargent Murray. A commitment to open-mindedness manifested itself in the distinctive American idea of amendable constitutions, a federal structure, independent branches of limited government that quickly contested each other's authority, and provisions to protect personal property and the freedom of speech and religious belief. Reminders of the importance of benevolence and generosity coursed through countless speeches, learned treatises aimed at persuading an international reading audience, and informal pamphlets directed toward ordinary people. In their efforts to balance the unquestionable desire to prosper and the equally genuine concern with advancing what they called the "general interest," Americans drew on the Hebrew Bible and the Christian scriptures, philosophical and legal tracts on history and ethics, and new-fangled British and French economic ideas about a self-regulating market.

Among the state constitutions that appeared during the war for independence, the Massachusetts constitution drafted by John Adams in 1779 proved the most influential; it manifests impulses persisting in the American colonies from their early seventeenth-century origins. Adams proclaimed the rights to life, liberty, property, free expression, and trial by jury; he balanced those rights against citizens' duty to worship God, obey the law, and contribute to an educational system that extended from elementary schools to the university in Cambridge. In a republic, Adams insisted, duties matter as much as rights, because "good morals are necessary to the preservation of civil society." A government founded on popular sovereignty could flourish only through the general diffusion of "wisdom and knowledge, as well as virtue." Without "the principles of humanity and general benevolence, public and private charity, industry and frugality," some individuals would be tempted to look to their own "private interest" instead of the proper end of government, "the common good." Unself-consciously echoing John Winthrop, Adams concluded that republican government must "inculcate the principles of humanity and general benevolence" and inspire "generous sentiments among the people."

Easy agreement on a few principles, however, including the rights to self-government and to life, liberty, and the pursuit of happiness, masked deeper divisions. No sooner had Americans won their independence than citizens of the new nation began to squabble. Those who invoked "justice and the general good," or "the common good of society" against the dangers of selfish factions, as James Madison did in *The Federalist*, were charged with elitist leanings poorly masked by their genuflections to popular government. Many of those who resisted the U.S. Constitution claimed it would empower a rising metropolitan elite. But the backwoodsmen and farmers in western regions, who joined with some urban artisans to oppose the new Constitution, were themselves accused of advancing their own narrow self-interest against the broadly shared goals of political stability and commercial expansion. Thus, the multiple meanings of a "liberal" sensibility became apparent as early as the debates that raged over proposed state and national constitutions in the 1780s.

The Puzzle of Parties

With the outbreak of the French Revolution in 1789, centuries-old charges that self-government might prove undisciplined and ultimately impractical persuaded increasing numbers of anxious Americans. The first U.S. party system resulted from the contrasting reactions of Americans to their erstwhile ally's dramatically different experience with democracy. Federalists reacted in horror to the assault on individual rights they saw in the Reign of Terror, whereas Jeffersonian Republicans embraced the cause of *liberté*, *égalité*, and *fraternité* as their own and saw their enemies' embrace of England as treasonous. Both groups embraced ideals of liberality such as freedom, equality, and national self-determination. But only a few years after George Washington warned that political parties would erode Americans' shared commitments to the general good, Jefferson ascended to the presidency in a bitterly contested election that was dubbed a Second American Revolution by his partisans—and by their enemies.

Were either the Federalists or the Jeffersonian Republicans, or were the Whigs or the Jacksonian Democrats that followed them several decades later, more "liberal" than the other? For nearly two centuries, ever since the word *liberal* itself entered Anglo-American discourse with a specifically political meaning during the early nineteenth century, American historians have debated that question. If liberalism is thought to involve generous support for the disfranchised, including African Americans, Indians, and women, and to involve extending educational opportunities and enforcing public authority in the economic sphere for the sake of the common good, then first the Federalists and later the Whigs might deserve to be designated liberals. But if liberalism instead means advancing farmers' and workers' interests against the plutocracy and asserting decentralized local authority against national elites threatening to monopolize political and economic power, then the followers of Jefferson and Jackson ought to be considered the liberals of the antebellum years. To complicate matters even further, many Federalists and Whigs worried about the danger of lawlessness and defended the principle of privilege, hardly a liberal quality, whereas many Jeffersonians and Jacksonians exhibited antiliberal tendencies of their own, ignoring the rights of blacks, Indians, and women as they trumpeted their commitment to white-male democracy.

As those contrasts make clear, both sets of early-nineteenth-century American parties invoked principles and championed programs that drew on some of the original meanings—both favorable and pejorative—of liberality. Only by shoehorning these parties anachronistically into categories that emerged later in American history can either group be made to embody liberal sensibilities, as these were later understood, more fully than the other. The solution to this problem is not to invoke a "liberal" litmus test but to concede that different Americans understood the constellation of liberal commitments toward freedom, toleration, benevolence, cultivation, and popular government in strikingly different ways. Perhaps the French visitor Alexis de Tocqueville's idea of "self-interest properly understood," capturing both Americans' concern with individual rights and the robust sense of social responsibility that inspired them to create countless voluntary organizations, best conveyed the unstable amalgam of American values.

At no time did a unitary "liberal tradition" ever exist in America. The dynamics of antebellum American public life reflected instead racial, gendered, economic, religious, and ethnocultural tensions that increasingly divided the nation along sectional lines. That process culminated in the emergence of Abraham Lincoln, the towering figure of nineteenth-century American politics, the individual who cemented the nation's enduring commitment to the ideals of liberty, equality, and democracy.

Lincoln's Legacies

Only after the Civil War did some American writers and politicians enthusiastically and self-consciously embrace the designation *liberal*. Those who called themselves liberals first clustered around Lincoln's party, the Republican Party that formed in the 1850s from the ashes of the Whigs, an awkward fact for those committed to the idea that Jackson's Democratic Party was the authentic carrier of a continuous American liberal tradition that began with Jefferson and culminated in Franklin Roosevelt. Post–Civil War Republicans called themselves liberals to signal several commitments. First, they embraced and even extended Lincoln's plans for reconstructing the South. They fought to secure the Fourteenth and the Fifteenth Amendments because they judged the extension of social, economic, and political rights to the freedmen crucial to consolidate the triumph of the Union and transform race relations forever. The unyielding force of racism, a tragic legacy of centuries of slavery, doomed their plans to failure.

Second, they embraced the cause of education and aesthetic cultivation. Together with English liberals such as John Stuart Mill, American liberals reasoned that the promise of democracy could be redeemed only if all citizens, black and white, women and men, ordinary workers and college-educated professionals, could read and write and participate in public deliberation. Charges of elitism limited the effectiveness of their program of cultural uplift.

Third, many of those who embraced liberalism sought to exchange the strident sectarianism of American religious denominations with a less doctrinaire and more open-minded emphasis on spirituality. Fierce loyalties to particular religious traditions persisted, however, and manifested themselves in fervent critiques of liberalism as a new species of godlessness masquerading as broadmindedness.

Fourth, liberals championed civil service reform. Liberals worked to end the spoils system and the reign of party bosses and urban machines, not because they hated immigrants but because they judged political corruption among the gravest sins of the republic, a flaw that some of them hyperbolically equated with slavery as an abomination of democracy. But the Democratic Party loyalty of immigrants in northern cities—and of Southerners who hated Lincoln as deeply as these liberals revered him—combined to thwart their efforts.

Finally, liberals imported the British and French idea of laissez-faire. Opposing the legacies of feudal practices and the stifling mercantilist policies of the nation-state on behalf of a free-market economy made sense in Europe in the eighteenth and early nineteenth centuries. But in the United States, economic regulation had been practiced primarily by local and state authorities for the benefit of ordinary people, whether by protecting their neighborhoods against "noxious trades" or by regulating the flow of goods according to the principle *salus populi* (the people's welfare). So the late-nineteenth-century American campaign to restrict government authority did not liberate the energies of shackled entrepreneurs from the stranglehold of monarchies and landed aristocracies, as British and French liberals had sought to do decades earlier. Only in the economic sphere did late-nineteenth-century American liberals succeed, thereby unleashing a wave of unregulated economic activity that soon swamped agricultural and industrial workers alike.

The New Liberalism

Given the failure of liberals to achieve color-blind democracy in the South or defeat bosses in the North, and given the success of their campaign for laissez-faire, the aging liberal Republicans of the Gilded Age came under fire from a new generation of political and social reformers at the end of the nineteenth century. Emerging first in the radicalism of the Knights of Labor, then in diverse forms of rural discontent that assumed the name of populism, these forms of insurgency gave way to a new coalition of reformers who gradually coalesced around the label *progressives*. Allied as their liberal Republican predecessors had been with like-minded English reformers, these progressives likewise adopted a program similar to that advanced by their early-twentieth-century English counterparts, which they dubbed the "new liberalism."

The new liberalism shared with the older version a commitment to cultural reforms such as education, temperance, and campaigns against prostitution. American new liberals also called for democratic reforms like a nonpartisan civil service, the initiative, referendum, recall, and the direct election of U.S. senators. Some new liberals—though not all—favored woman suffrage. As new liberals continued their predecessors' calls for democratic reform, some understood that commitment to mean the elevation of the electorate's judgment rather than the expansion of its size. In the American South, self-styled progressives sold the exclusionary practices of Jim Crow legislation as a form of democratic "purification," just as some English "liberal imperialists" justified the expansion of empire and the denial of home rule to Ireland as versions of the "White Man's Burden." On the question of extending American power in the Spanish-American War, American liberals old and new divided bitterly. Some, including aging veterans of the Civil War and radical Reconstruction such as New England reformer Thomas Wentworth Higginson and cultural critic Charles Eliot Norton, and others, including the writer Samuel Clemens and the philosopher William James, condemned American expansionism as a repudiation of the nation's most precious democratic ideals. Certain liberals, such as Theodore Roosevelt, interpreted American empire as the natural extension of Americans' reformist energies. The Spanish-American War would not be the last time liberals would divide over the issues of war and peace.

The sharpest departure of the new liberalism from the old, however, came in the domain of economic regulation. Empowered by a conception of economics brought back from Germany by a new generation of scholars such as Richard T. Ely and his student John Commons, reformers denied the timelessness of classical economics and asserted that economic ideas, like all others, develop historically and must be scrutinized critically. The rise of the social gospel shifted the emphasis of prominent Protestant clergymen such as Washington Gladden and Walter Rauschenbusch from the afterlife to the injustices endured by the poor in this life. A new generation of women, often college-educated, sought to exert pressure in various domains. Some justified their reformist activities as a form of "social housekeeping" for which women were uniquely well suited. Others, such as Jane Addams in the settlement house movement, Florence Kelley in the realms of industrial regulation and consumer protection, and Charlotte Perkins Gilman in the broader campaign for women's equality, worked to reconceive and expand women's roles by reassessing their capacities.

In place of laissez-faire, most new liberals called for the federal government to intervene in order to restrain corporate power and restore the rights and freedoms ostensibly secured by law but effectively limited by economic inequality. Progressives created a new apparatus, the regulatory agency, with procedures patterned on the model of scientific inquiry. The officials who staffed regulatory agencies were expected to use their expertise to find and enforce a nonpartisan public interest. Inspired (or shamed) by muckrakers such as Lincoln Steffens, Upton Sinclair, and Ida Tarbell, prominent legislators experimented with new forms of government authority designed to address particular economic and social problems.

Many members of the judiciary abandoned the doctrine of laissez-faire and embraced a conception of law as a flexible instrument, an orientation that jurists like Oliver Wendell Holmes Jr. and Louis Brandeis developed from the premises of the philosophy of pragmatism developed by William James and John Dewey. The principle animating these reforms descended from the eighteenth-century conception of balancing rights and duties. As Theodore Roosevelt put it in 1910, "Every man holds his property subject to the general right of the community to regulate its use to whatever degree the public welfare may require it." These programs were to be financed by the graduated income tax, which many considered the quintessential progressive reform because it tied the obligation owed to the capacity to contribute. The implementation of these programs, however, left much to be desired. Both legislators and regulatory commissions proved susceptible to capture by those they were empowered to restrain. Business interests proved as creative in eluding government oversight as they were in exploiting new resources and new markets.

Despite its failures, the new liberalism permanently transformed American politics. Affirming the principle that government may intervene in the economy to protect the interest of consumers, workers, and other disadvantaged groups remained a pillar of liberal doctrine throughout the twentieth century, as did a more or less self-consciously pragmatist commitment to flexible experimentation in public policy. Whereas the old liberalism had calcified by 1900 around an unyielding commitment to laissez-faire, the new liberalism substituted what Walter Lippmann called "mastery" for now-discredited "drift." Many new liberals saw in the open-endedness of pragmatism not a threat to stability but the key to fulfilling what another central theorist, Herbert Croly, called "the promise of American life," the use of democratic means to attain a great national end of active government devoted to serving the common good.

Toward a Second Bill of Rights

World War I constituted a cultural watershed in American life, but politically the changes were more subtle. The war and its aftermath, especially the failure of the United States to join the League of Nations, soured many progressives such as Lippmann on the possibilities of democracy. So did the fracturing of the progressive coalition between its urban and rural factions. Many evangelical Christians supported the prohibition of alcohol and opposed new ideas such as evolution; those passionate commitments divided them sharply from many of their erstwhile progressive allies and opened a new rift between increasingly secular and enduringly religious Americans previously linked by a shared commitment to principles both groups considered liberal. An equally fateful rift opened between those who embraced government power and sought to silence critics of Woodrow Wilson's war effort and those who, like the founding members of the American Civil Liberties Union, considered freedom of speech inviolable. Both the division between progressive and conservative religious groups and the division between civil libertarians and those wary of unregulated speech and behavior have become increasingly deep—and more debilitating both politically and culturally for liberalism—over the last century.

In the 1920s, liberals' pre–World War I interest in bringing scientific expertise to government continued unabated. The most celebrated hero of the war, the "great engineer" Herbert Hoover, abandoned Woodrow Wilson's internationalism but continued to think of himself as a progressive keen on efficient management. First as secretary of commerce and then as president, Hoover oversaw a modified regulatory regime that purported to extend the progressives' approach to government-business relations while surrendering decision making to the private sector. When that experiment in corporatism failed dramatically and the nation sank into depression, Franklin D. Roosevelt stumbled into half-hearted versions of progressive economic regulation while forging a coalition of voters that sustained his unstable brand of liberalism for several decades. Some members of Roosevelt's administration embraced much more aggressive schemes of economic planning that would have expanded public control over the private sector to an unprecedented degree. But their efforts, like those of the most ambitious new liberals before them, crumpled in Congress under the assault of critics who characterized such plans as utopian, medieval, Communist, or Fascist.

When the United States was forced into World War II by Pearl Harbor, doctrinal disagreements no longer mattered as much. Spurred by the urgent need to produce military supplies as fast as possible, informal arrangements between government and business facilitated unprecedented economic growth. In the face of never before seen military dangers, government authorities curtailed the civil liberties of many Americans, particularly those of Japanese descent. At the end of the war, the United States faced a new world. Now the richest economy as well as the most powerful military in the world, the nation had to decide how to use its wealth and power. For several years Roosevelt had been developing a plan to meet that challenge, which he outlined in his 1944 State of the Union address and on which he campaigned for reelection that fall.

The Second Bill of Rights, as Roosevelt called his plan, was to include the right of every American to a job at a living wage, adequate food, clothing, housing, medical care, education, and "protection from the economic fears of old age, sickness, accident, and unemployment." Similar programs of social provision took shape throughout the industrialized world. In almost all western European nations, through the efforts of liberal and social democratic coalitions, they came to fruition. Roosevelt griped to Secretary of Labor Frances Perkins that the most visible of these schemes, England's Beveridge Plan, which served as the blueprint for Clement Atlee's postwar Labour government, should have been called the Roosevelt Plan. But the same forces that had stymied earlier liberal programs did the same to the Second Bill of Rights, which Congress dismantled in the wake of Roosevelt's death. Only a remnant of the plan survived in the form of the G.I. Bill. The benefits provided by even that limited measure fueled a sustained wave of prosperity that lasted three decades, and scholars of the Second Bill of Rights have been left wondering about its effect had Roosevelt lived to shepherd it into law.

Cold War Transformations

The postwar period never saw the resurrection of Roosevelt's ambitious plan, the unrealized ideal of one strand of twentieth-century liberalism. The onset of the cold war transformed American politics even more dramatically than had the Red Scare after World War I. Harry Truman presented his Fair Deal as the culmination of Roosevelt's liberal plan for generous social provision, a benevolent discharging of comfortable Americans' duties to their less fortunate fellow citizens. But, given the perceived threat from an expansionist Soviet Union, such programs were vulnerable to the charge that they had become un-American. After three centuries in which Americans had worked to balance their rights against their responsibilities and the sin of selfishness against the divine command of benevolence, property rights metamorphosed under the shadow of communism into the essence of America and concern with the poor into almost a sign of disloyalty. Consumption replaced generosity in the national pantheon. New Dealers shifted from redistributionist schemes to the stabilizing ideas of English economist John Maynard Keynes; conservatives embraced the free-market principles of Ludwig von Mises and Friedrich Hayek. Confusingly, both Keynesians who emphasized government intervention through monetary and especially fiscal policy and conservatives who prized laissez-faire called themselves liberals, as European champions of free-market capitalism do to this day. But whereas the heirs of FDR continued to invoke the principle of equality alongside their commitment to liberty, American conservatives increasingly branded egalitarian ideals as socialist and exchanged the term *liberal*, which they rejected as tainted by its association with progressives' and New Dealers' economic programs, for the new label *libertarian*.

Not all American liberals retreated before the widespread enthusiasm for salvation by consumption. Many followed the neo-orthodox Protestant minister Reinhold Niebuhr. Counterposing a newly chastened realism to the ostensibly naïve reformism of earlier liberals such as Dewey and his followers in the New Deal (many of whom remained committed to the possibilities of radical democracy), Niebuhr urged Americans to acknowledge the pervasiveness of sin and the ubiquity of evil. Tough opponents called for tough-mindedness, and although Niebuhr did not entirely renounce Rauschenbusch's social gospel, many liberals' shift in emphasis from possibilities to dangers, and from pragmatic problem solving to ironies and tragedies, was unmistakable. Whereas Roosevelt had called Americans to an expansive egalitarian mission, liberals such as Arthur Schlesinger Jr. instead urged them to cluster around "the vital center." For many liberals, as well as most libertarians, ambitious egalitarian plans took a backseat to hard-headed geopolitical maneuvering.

Beneath the tone of cold war realism, though, a more subtle shift in liberal focus was taking place. Despite a rhetoric of free-market triumphalism, many ostensibly conservative mid-century Republicans shared liberals' belief that some version of a government-business alliance was in the interest of all Americans. Just as informal gentlemen's agreements had enabled war production to go forward, so new treaties were struck with labor unions, interest groups, and government regulatory agencies in the hope that some new American hybrid would emerge to dissolve the tensions between labor and management. Many liberals shared the confidence that a new, university-trained, non- or post-ideological managerial elite could staff the ramparts of the private and public sectors. Where earlier progressives had seen inevitable conflict, new corporate liberals trumpeted a professionally engineered consensus forged by voluntary accommodation.

So placid (or constricted) did such visions seem that some American observers projected them backward across American history. Many scholars argued that Americans had always agreed on basic principles, but they disagreed in evaluating that consensus. Historian Daniel Boorstin deemed it "the genius of American politics." Political scientist Louis Hartz considered it a tragedy. Unfortunately, one of the most influential books ever written about American politics, Hartz's *The Liberal Tradition in America*, was also among the most misleading. Not only did Hartz's account minimize the significance of the nonwhites and women who were still ignored by many white male writers in the 1950s, it also papered over the fierce battles that had characterized public life in America ever since the founding of the English colonies. Hartz's portrait of a one-dimensional and stifling consensus flattened a much more conflictual and dynamic record of constant struggles. Liberals grappled with their opponents over the meanings and purposes of American democracy, a conflict that flared into violence and culminated in a bloody Civil War, and even those who assumed the mantle of liberalism frequently disagreed about its meaning.

Indeed, no sooner had sociologist Daniel Bell and other liberals proclaimed "the end of ideology" than dramatic conflicts began breaking out over competing principles. The first battleground was the South. African Americans radicalized by the rhetoric of democracy, by the experience of military life, or by knowledge of a world outside the segregated South mobilized to challenge the stifling regime of Jim Crow. This racial crusade began decades earlier, as signaled by the founding of the National Association for the Advancement of Colored People (NAACP) in 1909. Booker T. Washington had already emerged by then as a prominent educator and writer, and his critic W.E.B. DuBois, the only African American among the founders of the NAACP, had offered profound analyses of "the problem of the color line" as the central challenge of the twentieth century. After simmering for decades without attracting the attention of the mainstream press, the African American campaign for civil rights at last awakened the consciences of white liberals. When the combustible combination of post–World War II agitation, the Supreme Court's 1954 decision in *Brown v. Board of Education of Topeka, Kansas* (which declared segregation of public facilities unconstitutional), and the Montgomery, Alabama, bus boycott inspired by Rosa Parks and led by Martin Luther King Jr. came together, the scattered efforts of many activists ignited into a national movement.

Earlier accounts, which centered on the heroic struggles of King and a few visible leaders, have been replaced by broader histories of a "long civil rights movement" that stretched unbroken from the early twentieth century and extended through the efforts of countless foot soldiers who challenged norms of racial subjugation across the nation. Coming as it did at the same time that social scientists and literary scholars were constructing a new paradigm of "human"—as opposed to "national" or "racial" or "ethnic" or "gendered"—characteristics, the civil rights movement rode a wave of universalism that most American liberals took as the harbinger of a transformed set of social relations across earlier chasms of race, class, and gender. From linguistics to sociology, from anthropology to the study of sexuality, from biology to philosophy, liberal scholarly investigators joined the quest for a common denominator that would link all humans.

These heady ambitions fueled forms of liberal social and political activity that left a permanent imprint on American culture and American law. Under pressure from liberal and radical reformers, race, gender, and labor relations gradually shifted. These changes—piecemeal, partial, and incremental—rarely satisfied impatient liberal activists, yet they nevertheless transformed the American cultural landscape. Campaigns in the 1960s and 1970s on behalf of American women, workers, prisoners, and those who were poor, mentally or physically disabled, gay, lesbian, or aged changed the ways in which employers, police, judges, school officials, architects, engineers, social workers, and physicians worked. In another domain, a chorus of environmentalists assailed smug assumptions about the consequences of Americans' profligate use of natural resources and worked to nurture alternative environmentalist sensibilities. Visionaries saw the dawn of a new age.

Challenges from Right and Left

Within little more than a decade, however, such hopes had evaporated. Struggles within the movements for black liberation, women's liberation, the labor movement, and against the war in Vietnam began to seem almost as bitter as the struggles fought by the partisans in those conflicts against their conservative foes. By the time the prolonged economic expansion of the postwar decades ended with the oil crisis of 1973–74, liberals' cultural confidence had been shattered. They found themselves assailed not only from the right but from a new, and more radical, left. A newly energized conservative movement found a modern leader in the governor of California, Ronald Reagan, and additional support from disgruntled white ethnics, suburbanites anxious about their cultural and religious values and their future, and an increasingly vocal segment of Americans antagonized by blacks, women, and gay and lesbian Americans demanding equal rights. Critics on the left began to assail liberals for their alleged complicity in the forms of racism, sexism, and exclusion practiced internally and in the nation's imperialist atrocities abroad, all of which were said to derive from the Enlightenment's shallow confidence in a narrow form of "reason" that promised liberating fulfillment but delivered only confinement. By the time Reagan was elected president in 1980, liberalism had become a term of opprobrium for critics on the left as well as the right.

In recent decades liberals have struggled to escape the dismissive caricatures of both radicals and conservatives. Liberals' egalitarian dreams were judged unrealistic and their cultural leanings elitist, their generosity counterproductive and their confidence in reasoned debate faintly comic. Liberals' commitment to freedom of expression also came under attack. By excluding religion and tolerating obscenity, critics charged, liberals made possible a degrading competition between pornography and banality in the value-free zone of popular culture. According to critics left and right, liberals were responsible for all that was wrong with America—even though those groups offered diametrically opposite diagnoses of the nation's maladies.

When the Soviet Union and its satellite states collapsed in 1989–91, and when the domestic U.S. economy began to lose ground relative to both the industrialized and the developing world, liberal confidence was shaken. Without a Communist menace or a socialist alternative, which had provided the fixed points against which many liberals could measure their economic policies, navigating the new terrain of domestic and international politics became more treacherous. Free-market champions and their allies in academic disciplines who were attracted to models proclaiming self-interested behavior as the consequence of "rational choice" increasingly set the terms of social scientific debate. The particularistic agendas of identity politics challenged the integrationist programs of the civil rights movement and the post–World War II wave of feminism. The earlier liberal emphasis on freedom and toleration remained, but in the absence of a compelling agenda of economic reforms premised on the ideal of equality or the older virtue of benevolence, the new liberal critique of a naturalized and thus unassailable free-market model seemed vulnerable to libertarians' charges of impracticality.

By the twenty-first century, few candidates for public office embraced the label of liberalism— not surprising given that fewer than 25 percent of voters identified themselves as liberals. Clearly the momentum had shifted: 50 years earlier Boorstin and Hartz had declared all of American history a species of the genus liberalism, and liberals confidently proclaimed that the future belonged to them as well. Partisan squabbles seemed to be subsiding. New nations were emerging from colonial childhood into full membership in the United Nations. As partialities and particularities appeared to be giving way to a new universalism, a reign of liberal toleration, benevolence, generosity, and cultural cultivation seemed visible on the horizon. One decade into the twenty-first century, that world seemed very far away.

Opposition to the war in Vietnam had prompted liberals to associate flag-waving patriotism with their hawkish opponents, a strategic disaster that enabled conservatives to identify their own aggressive foreign policy with the national interest and to portray liberals as traitors. Particularly after September 11, 2001—and with disastrous consequences—the charge stuck, which was odd given the commitments of earlier American liberals. From the birth of the nation through the Civil War to World War II, most liberals had rallied to legitimate assertions of American power. Relinquishing that tradition proved catastrophic, both culturally and politically. Likewise from the dawn of the United States through the height of the civil rights movement and the opposition to the Vietnam War, liberals mobilized alongside—not against—people of faith. Surrendering religion to the right proved as damaging to the political prospects of liberalism as the widespread concern that liberals were insufficiently patriotic because they disagreed with conservatives over issues of foreign policy.

Yet if liberals were able to recover from those strategic blunders or correct those misperceptions, they might find their fortunes changing in the twenty-first century. Opinion polls demonstrate that the ideals associated with liberalism for the last four centuries retain a grip on the American imagination. If liberals could regain the confidence to embrace and reassert those ideals, and if they could abandon commitments to failed policies and programs and construct a new cultural and political agenda to advance the principles they embrace, they might yet see a brighter horizon. From the early seventeenth century until the present, many of those attuned to liberality have distrusted selfishness and parochialism and embraced the idea that popular sovereignty could enable Americans to replace inherited practices of oppression and hierarchy with open-mindedness and generosity. Achieving those goals remains the challenge facing liberals today.

See also conservatism; democracy; radicalism.

FURTHER READING. Joyce Appleby, *Liberalism and Republicanism in the Historical Imagination*, 1992; Isaiah Berlin, *Four Essays on Liberty*, 1969; Elizabeth Borgwardt, *A New Deal for the World: America's Vision for Human Rights*, 2005; Howard Brick, *Transcending Capitalism: Visions of a New Society in Modern American Thought*, 2006; Alan Brinkley, *The End of Reform: New Deal Liberalism in Recession and War*, 1995; Leslie Butler, *Critical Americans: Victorian Intellectuals and Transatlantic Liberal Reform*, 2006; Lizabeth Cohen, *A Consumers' Republic: The Politics of Mass Consumption in Postwar America*, 2003; Eric Foner, *The Story of American Freedom*, 1998; J. David Greenstone, *The Lincoln Persuasion: Remaking American Liberalism*, 1993; Louis Hartz, *The Liberal Tradition in America*, 1955; David A. Hollinger, *Postethnic America: Beyond Multiculturalism*, 3rd ed., 2006; Daniel Walker Howe, *What Hath God Wrought: The Transformation of America, 1815–1848*, 2007; Meg Jacobs, Julian E. Zelizer, and William J. Novak, eds., *The Democratic Experiment: New Directions in American Political History*, 2003; Neil Jumonville and Kevin Mattson, eds., *Liberalism for a New Century*, 2007; Laura Kalman, *The Strange Career of Legal Liberalism*, 1996; Michael Kazin, *The Populist Persuasion: An American History*, revised ed., 1998; Linda Kerber, *No Constitutional Right to Be Ladies: Women and the Obligations of Citizenship*, 1998; Alexander Keyssar, *The Right to Vote: The Contested History of Democracy in America*, 2000; Richard King, *Civil Rights and the Idea of Freedom*, 1992; James T. Kloppenberg, *The Virtues of Liberalism*, 1998; Idem, *Uncertain Victory: Social Democracy and Progressivism in European and American Thought*, 1986; John Rawls, *Political Liberalism: The John Dewey Essays in Philosophy*, 1993; Daniel Rodgers, *Contested Truths: Keywords in American Politics since Independence*, 1987; Michael Sandel, *Democracy's Discontent: America in Search of a Public Philosophy*, 1996; Rogers Smith, *Civic Ideals: Conflicting Visions of Citizenship in U.S. History*, 1997; Sean Wilentz, *The Rise of American Democracy: Jefferson to Lincoln*, 2005; John Winthrop, "Christian Charity, A Model Hereof," in *Puritans in the New World, A Critical Anthology*, edited by David D. Hall, 165–80, 2004; Gordon Wood, *The Creation of the American Republic, 1776–1787*, 2nd ed., 1998.

JAMES T. KLOPPENBERG

lobbying
See interest groups.

local government

For four centuries Americans have remained devoted to grassroots rule and organs of local government. They have deemed that government closest to the people as most representative of the popular will and thus have jealously protected and perpetuated local power. In Canada and Great Britain as well as the continental European nations, central lawmakers have been able to revise and reform local government without submitting their measures to the veto of local referenda. In the United States, however, voters have repeatedly blocked the path to change, fearful that the destruction of inherited local units would diminish their political voice and open the door to dreaded centralization. Perhaps more than any other nation, the United States is a land of local satrapies, a prevailing fear of big, distant government preserving a complex structure of local rule. State governments have increasingly imposed a degree of supervision over localities. But local institutions persist as perceived bulwarks against central authority, and the defensive instincts of the local electorate remain strong.

Local Rule 1607–1900

During the colonial era, Americans fashioned the primary units of the future nation's structure of local rule. In New England the town was the chief governing unit, exercising responsibility for schools, poor relief, and roads. Policy-making power rested with the town meeting, a conclave of all enfranchised townspeople, though popularly elected selectmen assumed primary authority for day-to-day governance. In the South the county court and parish vestry of the established Church of England were the chief units of local government. Dominated by the local gentry, the county courts served both judicial and administrative functions, hearing legal suits as well as maintaining county roads. The parish vestry was generally responsible for poor relief. The middle colonies of Pennsylvania, New Jersey, and New York combined the governmental forms of New England and the South, assigning a large share of local responsibility to counties but also maintaining town or township governments. In this hybrid mix, counties were less powerful than in the South, but towns or townships exercised less authority than their New England counterparts.

To govern their emerging cities, the middle and southern colonies applied the institution of the municipal corporation inherited from Great Britain. Some municipalities such as Philadelphia, Williamsburg, and Norfolk were closed corporations in which the incumbent board of aldermen filled any vacancies in their governing body; the local citizenry had no voice in the selection of city officials. In Albany, New York City, and the municipal corporations of New Jersey, however, popular election of the governing aldermen prevailed. New England eschewed the institution of the municipal corporation, its more populous communities retaining the town form of rule and the town meeting.

The American Revolution wrought some changes in the system of local government. New municipal charters granted by state legislatures replaced the closed corporations ruled by a self-chosen elite, with government by popularly elected city councils. The disestablishment of the Church of England also deprived the parish vestry of its responsibility for poor relief; henceforth, secular overseers of the poor assumed charge of the least fortunate members of society. Yet there was also great continuity in the forms of local rule. The town remained the principal unit of local government in New England, though in the 1780s five communities in Connecticut, including Hartford and New Haven as well as Newport in Rhode Island, accepted city charters. Not until 1822 did Boston finally abandon town rule and the town meeting, accepting a city form of government with a mayor and municipal legislature. In the middle states, counties and towns continued to exercise local authority, and the county courts remained supreme in the South.

The new western states adopted the established forms of their eastern neighbors. Ohio, Indiana, Illinois, Michigan, and Wisconsin embraced the hybrid form of county-township rule characteristic of Pennsylvania and New York, whereas in the new southern states of Kentucky, Tennessee, Alabama, and Mississippi the county was the focus of local authority. The town or township never took root in the South. During the late nineteenth century, the states west of the Rockies also found diminutive township units unsuited for their sparsely settled rural areas. Consequently, the town or township remained primarily a northeastern and midwestern unit. In these regions, it administered local roads, cemeteries, and poor relief while township justices of the peace handled minor offenses and disputes.

One new unit of local government that proliferated during the nineteenth century was the school district. Elected school boards administered education in miniscule districts across America. For example, the number of school districts in Michigan rose from 3,097 in 1850 to 7,168 in 1890. By the latter date, there was one school district for every 60 pupils enrolled in the state. Over 1,000 districts could claim less than 25 pupils. In many areas of the nation, there was a unit of school government for every one-room schoolhouse, each a diminutive educational republic charged with bringing reading, writing, and arithmetic to its youth.

Meanwhile, municipal corporations had to adapt to burgeoning centers of urban population. As New

York City, Philadelphia, Chicago, and scores of lesser metropolises attracted millions of migrants from Europe and rural America, their city governments assumed new and expanded duties. In the mid-nineteenth century professional fire departments supplanted the volunteer forces of the past, and a professional police bureaucracy developed to preserve the urban peace. An emerging corps of professional engineers applied their expertise to water supply and sewerage, constructing elaborate systems of aqueducts, reservoirs, and drainage tunnels. A body of pioneering landscape architects led by Frederick Law Olmsted laid out great urban parks, the most notable being New York City's Central Park.

The adoption of universal manhood suffrage in the early nineteenth century shifted the political advantage to plebeian leaders who cultivated the loyalty of the immigrant masses flooding the cities. Tammany Hall, New York City's Democratic organization, became known for its steadfast support among Irish immigrants who benefited from the public jobs and favors that Tammany could bestow. Sober citizens who deemed themselves the respectable class grew increasingly troubled by the rising power of such partisan organizations and launched repeated campaigns to reform the structure of municipal rule. Consequently, in the latter half of the nineteenth century, city councils dominated by neighborhood leaders, some of them local saloonkeepers, lost power to mayors who were generally respected businessmen.

Twentieth-Century Reform

Reform demands mounted in the early twentieth century, resulting in a major restructuring of many city governments. In 1901 Galveston, Texas, pioneered the commission form of government, which lodged all executive and legislative authority in a small board of elected commissioners, each commissioner charged with responsibility for one area of municipal administration. This city commission plan eliminated the ward-based councils deemed the source of much local corruption; by carefully defining the responsibilities of each commissioner, the plan also heightened official accountability. By the end of 1913, 337 American municipalities had adopted the commission plan.

The commission scheme, however, did not ensure professional, expert administration of municipal services. Consequently, during the second decade of the twentieth century reformers increasingly turned to another alternative, the city manager plan. First adopted in Staunton, Virginia, in 1908, the city manager plan lodged policy-making authority in an elected city council, but the execution of policy and administration of the city was the job of an appointed city manager. Expected to be nonpartisan professional administrators, city managers were supposed to apply their expertise and guarantee optimal efficiency in the operation of their municipalities. By the close of 1923, 269 cities employed city managers,

and the number would increase throughout the twentieth century, as the manager plan supplanted commission rule as the preferred reform alternative.

Meanwhile, some reformers were also turning their attention to the antiquated structure of county government. Traditionally, elected boards of supervisors or county commissioners had exercised both executive and legislative authority at the county level, and a long list of elected officials such as county treasurer, auditor, clerk of courts, and sheriff had performed specific administrative functions. The concept of separation of powers did not exist at the county level, and popularity at the polls rather than professional credentials determined who would administer these local units. Proponents of the manager plan proposed extending it to counties, but not until 1927 did Iredell County, North Carolina, appoint the nation's first county manager. By 1950 only 16 of the nation's more than 3,000 counties had hired administrators with duties akin to those of the city manager. In the 1930s two populous New York counties, Nassau and Westchester, sought to rationalize local rule by creating the elected office of county executive to serve basically as mayor of the county. Not until the late twentieth century, however, did large numbers of counties create the post of elected executive or hire a professional administrator charged with broad managerial supervision of county affairs.

Structural reformers also targeted New England's venerable town meetings. By the early twentieth century, only a small proportion of those eligible actually attended the meetings in New England's largest towns. Consequently, an unrepresentative and self-interested minority appeared to be determining town policies. To correct this problem, in 1915 reformers in the populous suburban town of Brookline, Massachusetts, secured adoption of the representative town meeting form of government. Henceforth, Brookline voters would elect 240 town meeting members who were to represent them at the meetings. Every town voter could attend the meetings and participate in discussion, but only the elected members could vote. By 1930, 18 Massachusetts towns had opted for the representative town meeting form.

Local Rule in Metropolitan America

Rationalization of local government attracted increasing attention from the 1920s onward, as rapid suburbanization produced a bewildering array of new governmental units in metropolitan areas throughout the nation. During the nineteenth century, states had adopted permissive incorporation procedures, allowing virtually any community to become an independent municipality. As Americans moved to the suburbs, they took advantage of this to create a mass of new municipalities tailor-made to serve the interests of their residents. In the 1920s American municipalities acquired zoning powers in order to protect the interests of homeowners and upscale-housing developers. Now municipalities not only could provide traditional policing, ensure street maintenance, and offer water and sewer services, they could also restrict who and what moved into a community. For the growing corps of home-owning suburbanites, this constituted a strong incentive to incorporate. In suburbanizing Nassau County on Long Island, the number of municipalities soared from 20 in 1920 to 65 in 1940, and in suburban Saint Louis County, Missouri, the municipal head count rose from 20 in 1930 to 84 in 1950.

Meanwhile, Americans organized thousands of special district governments to provide certain services. Unlike multipurpose municipalities or townships, special districts usually provided only a single service. From 1920 to 1933, the number of such units in Nassau County climbed from 87 to 173; this latter figure included 38 districts charged with water supply, 52 fire protection districts, and 53 lighting districts responsible for the provision of street lights. Each special district had separate taxing powers, and their proliferation markedly augmented the number of hands reaching into taxpayers' pockets.

Some metropolitan residents deplored the confusion and fragmentation of authority resulting from this multitude of counties, townships, municipalities, and special districts. But in the 1920s and early 1930s campaigns for the consolidation or federation of local units failed in the seriously divided Pittsburgh, Cleveland, and Saint Louis metropolitan areas. Localism posed a formidable barrier to unification, and a renewal of metropolitan government crusades in the 1950s again produced no significant results. Any consolidation or federation of units in the United States required voter approval, and this was not forthcoming. Repackaged as the new regionalism, in the 1990s metropolitan cooperation stirred renewed interest among scholars and civic reformers but yielded few results. During the latter half of the twentieth century in a few metropolitan areas such as Jacksonville, Nashville, and Indianapolis, civic leaders secured a consolidation of city and county governments, thereby attempting to streamline local administration and achieve some unity in policy making. But consolidation was the exception, not the rule. A myriad of township, village, and city governments survived, and the number of special districts soared.

In contrast, states were successful in reducing the number of school districts. Whereas village and township governments could adapt and provide minimal services for twentieth-century small towns and rural areas, school districts designed to govern one-room schools were outmoded in a nation where a good education was perceived as necessary to personal success. Claiming that consolidation of districts would improve schooling and offer rural residents advantages formerly enjoyed only in city schools, state departments of education coerced or cajoled Americans to eschew the miniscule districts of the past. The number of school districts in the United States thus dropped from 127,531 in 1932 to 15,781 in 1972.

By the last decades of the twentieth century, states were also forced to intervene and prop up some faltering central-city municipal regimes as well as distressed inner-city school governments. As business investment abandoned aging central cities for the suburbs, tax bases shrank; at the same time, the expense of providing services for the remaining impoverished residents increased. In 1975, New York State took charge of the finances of a virtually bankrupt New York City, and, until the mid-1980s, the state carefully monitored fiscal decision making in the nation's largest city. Cleveland, Philadelphia, Buffalo, and Pittsburgh also became fiscal wards of their state governments. Financial difficulties as well as poor academic performance resulted in state takeovers of some city school systems, with state-appointed administrators superseding the authority of locally elected school board members.

Yet such heavy-handed state intervention was not the norm. Americans continued to place their faith in local elected officials, preferring grassroots rule to centralized dictation. At the beginning of the twenty-first century, there were 87,849 units of local government in the United States. In the late twentieth century the number of counties remained stable, whereas the figure for municipalities increased slowly. For decades so-called experts had criticized townships as unnecessary relics of the horse-and-buggy era, yet there remained 16,506 of these units in 2002, the number falling only 2 percent in the previous quarter-century. The traditional New England town meeting survived, with only 38 of the 300 Massachusetts towns opting for the representative town meeting. The last half of the twentieth century also witnessed a sharp rise in special districts, their number almost tripling from 12,340 in 1952 to 35,356 in 2002. Owing to innovations in transportation and communication, the lives of most Americans were no longer confined to the narrow boundaries of localities. In this increasingly cosmopolitan nation, however, the government of the village and town remained a jealously guarded political legacy.

See also cities and politics; suburbs and politics.

FURTHER READING. David R. Berman, ed., *County Governments in an Era of Change*, 1993; John C. Bollens, *Special District Governments in the United States*, 1957; Alexander B. Callow, *The Tweed Ring*, 1966; H. S. Gilbertson, *The County: The "Dark Continent" of American Politics*, 1917; Robert M. Ireland, *The County Courts in Antebellum Kentucky*, 1972; Bradley R. Rice, *Progressive Cities: The Commission Government Movement in America, 1901–1920*, 1977; John Fairfield Sly, *Town Government in Massachusetts, 1620–1930*, 1930; Jon C. Teaford, *City and Suburb: The Political Fragmentation of Metropolitan America, 1850–1970*, 1979; Idem, *The Municipal Revolution in America: Origins of Modern Urban Government, 1650–1825*, 1975; Idem, *The Unheralded Triumph: City Government in America, 1870–1900*, 1984.

JON C. TEAFORD

Mexican-American War

Often called America's "forgotten" war, the 1846–48 conflict with Mexico was brief, bloody, and a great short-term success for the United States. After a string of impressive military victories under General Zachary Taylor in Texas and Mexico's northeast between May 1846 and February 1847, General Winfield Scott's troops completed an amphibious assault on the port of Vera Cruz in Mexico's south and marched west to the capital, ultimately occupying Mexico City in September 1847. In early 1848, Mexico ratified the Treaty of Guadalupe Hidalgo, transferring 500,000 square miles, almost half of its territory, to the United States in exchange for $15 million. The U.S. states of California, New Mexico, Nevada, and Utah, as well as parts of Arizona, Colorado, and Wyoming are all products of the Mexican cession. The ratified treaty arrived in the United States on the Fourth of July in 1848 to ecstatic celebration. That the nation had "won an empire" in this war seemed providential to many Americans, proof of the country's Manifest Destiny to expand across the continent.

The long-term implications of the war were less than positive, however. The question of the status of slavery in the newly acquired territories greatly exacerbated sectional tensions and eventually contributed to both the collapse of the Second Party System and southern secession. The war with Mexico was the first war fought by America for reasons other than self-defense; it set a precedent for military action in Latin America in the name of American interests, and permanently damaged relations with Mexico. This little-remembered war had far-reaching effects, ultimately transforming America's foreign relations and internal politics almost as dramatically as it altered the nation physically.

The Road to War

Hostilities between the United States and Mexico officially erupted when President James K. Polk ordered General Taylor to move his army in Texas into a disputed area between the Nueces River and the Río Grande. After the Texas rebellion of 1836, both Mexico and the newly independent Republic of Texas claimed this area, although Texas's claims were somewhat speculative (the republic also claimed Santa Fe, the capital city of Mexico's province of New Mexico). In fact, Mexico refused to recognize the independence of Texas, considering it a rebel province. Although most Texans favored joining the United States, attempts to annex Texas in the late 1830s and early 1840s failed because both Democrats and Whigs

recognized that annexation would inflame sectional tensions and likely result in a war with Mexico. President John Tyler, a Whig in name but Democrat in policy, fastened on the idea of annexing Texas in the hope that this stance would win him the presidency in 1844. It did not, but his proposal was met with an outpouring of popular and congressional support. Tyler invited Texas to join the union at the close of his presidential term in 1845.

Democrat James K. Polk entered office immediately after on an explicitly expansionist platform and pledged himself to gaining Mexico's Alta California. During his first year as president, he unsuccessfully attempted to buy California and New Mexico for more than twice the amount the United States eventually paid in 1848. After Mexican cavalry crossed the Río Grande and attacked a U.S. patrol, Polk addressed Congress on May 11, 1846, and reported that "Mexico has passed the boundary of the United States, has invaded our territory and shed American blood upon the American soil." Although many representatives had serious doubts about Polk's claims and suspected that the president had provoked war by moving U.S. troops into an area rightfully claimed by Mexico, Congress overwhelmingly supported the declaration of war.

Dissent

The Whig minority in Congress opposed territorial expansion generally and expansion into potential new slave territories in particular. But with memories of the disastrous collapse of the Federalist Party over the War of 1812 firmly in mind, the vast majority of congressional Whigs supported Polk's call for volunteers and voted for funds to fight Mexico. Only 14 members of the House, all of whom represented heavily antislavery constituencies in the Northeast and upper Midwest, voted against the declaration of war.

The American public, schooled in the ideology of Manifest Destiny and firmly convinced of the racial and cultural inferiority of Mexicans, largely embraced this war. But a vigorous antiwar movement, centered in New England and led by abolitionists, offered sharp critiques of its morality. Antiwar activists argued that the war was unjust, that might did not make right, and that the conflict was evidence of a "slave power" manipulating the government in order to expand slavery. These positions would ultimately emerge as the consensus view by the late nineteenth century.

During the first year of the war, the antiwar movement had a limited impact. But as war dragged on, dissent became widespread. By late 1847, mainstream congressional Whigs, including some from southern and western districts, openly protested the war and called for its immediate end. Freshman representative Abraham Lincoln demanded to know the "exact spot" where American blood had supposedly been shed. Presidential hopeful Henry Clay gained national attention when he called for mass protests against the war. The antiwar movement has been discounted by some scholars as ineffective, but it played a clear role in pressuring President Polk to come to terms with Mexico at the close of the war.

Soldiers and the Military Front

Polk's initial call for troops resulted in an outpouring of volunteer enthusiasm, but most soldiers found service in Mexico disillusioning. The Mexican-American War had the highest casualty rate of any American conflict, almost 17 percent of the 79,000 American soldiers who served in it died, mainly from disease. Although the regulars in the army did most of the hard fighting and both Taylor and Scott regularly condemned the volunteers for lack of discipline (they were responsible for most of the atrocities committed against Mexican civilians), it was the volunteers who won most of the acclaim back home. The working men who made up the bulk of both army regulars and volunteers may have believed that service in Mexico would result in an increase in their class status at home, but their harsh treatment by officers tended to reinforce their subservient position in industrializing America. Desertion rates were high, particularly among Catholic immigrants who felt divided loyalties fighting a Catholic country under an army openly hostile to their faith. Some of these men joined the San Patricio Battalion and fought for Mexico. Many more American soldiers embraced the "free soil" political movement upon returning home, convinced that democracy and economic opportunity could flourish only for working men in slavery-free territories.

At the outset of the war, most European observers predicted that Mexico, fighting at home with a large standing army, would easily defeat the invaders from the north. But General Stephen W. Kearny's troops easily conquered New Mexico, Taylor's troops prevailed in a number of bloody clashes in northeastern Mexico, Scott battered his way to the capital, and an initial revolt of Anglo settlers under the command of Captain John C. Frémont in California (known as the Bear Flag Revolt) culminated in the surrender of Mexican *Californios* to American forces in January 1847. Factors internal to Mexico greatly aided the U.S. cause. Chronic political instability, a series of popular uprisings against national and state governments, wars between Mexican settlers and independent Native Americans in the border region, and the inept military leadership of General Antonio López de Santa Anna all hampered Mexico's ability to repulse the invaders.

Polk had secured the northern half of Mexico by the end of February 1847, and dispatched diplomat Nicholas Trist to negotiate a treaty of peace soon after. But the incensed Mexican government refused to come to terms, even after the fall of Mexico City. American forces in the capital were subject to brutal attacks by guerrilla partisans, and General Scott came to believe that the long-term occupation of central Mexico by the United States was untenable. But extreme Democratic expansionists increasingly called for the annexation of all of Mexico as spoils of war, and Polk recalled Trist in the fall of 1847 in hopes of gaining a larger settlement from Mexico than he had originally authorized. With the support of General Scott, and in sympathy with Mexico's plight, Trist disobeyed the president and negotiated a treaty on his own. Polk agreed to the terms of the Treaty of Guadalupe Hidalgo, both because of growing antiwar sentiment at home and because the annexation of the densely populated southern part of Mexico was opposed on racial grounds by many in both the North and South.

War and the Democratic Party

There was initial support for the war among northern Democrats who believed expansion was healthy for democracy, desired California's ports in order to commercially expand into Asia, and saw the annexation of Texas and California as the best means of preventing British encroachment in North America. Yet many came to view Polk's war with Mexico with suspicion, born of the belief that the war was being waged in the interest of southern slaveholders. When Pennsylvania Democratic congressman David Wilmot offered a rider to a war appropriations bill in August of 1846 on the floor of the House that banned slavery from any territory won from Mexico, he revealed the increasing sectional rift and growing power of free soil ideology in the North.

Democrats faced other struggles during "their" war. Polk had pledged to serve only one term in office, and there was no clear front-runner for the Democratic nomination in 1848. The two heroes of the engagement, Zachary Taylor and Winfield Scott, were Whigs. Despite Polk's attempts to brevet Democratic generals, including Franklin Pierce, the president's fears were realized when the Whigs won the presidency in 1848 with Taylor at the head of the ticket. This was the second and last time the Whigs would win the presidency before the party collapsed over the issue of slavery in the 1850s. Winfield Scott, the Whig Party's final presidential candidate, was defeated by Pierce in 1852.

Popular Reception of the War

In the eyes of many U.S. citizens, virtually every battle in the Mexican-American War made manifest the heroism and superior fighting abilities of the North American. In the battle of Buena Vista, less than 5,000 U.S. soldiers defeated a Mexican army of 15,000. At Cerro Gordo, U.S. forces flanked and drove a much larger Mexican army out of a defensive position, clearing the way to march on the capital, where they successfully stormed Chapúltepec Castle, which guarded Mexico City.

The first war covered by newspaper correspondents was closely followed at home, and these victories became cultural events, celebrated not only in the press, but also in fiction, music, and art. This war marked the first encounter of most white Americans with Mexicans and disrupted the reigning division between black and white that structured American racism. Dime-novel accounts of the war celebrated romance between U.S. soldiers and light-skinned Mexican women, while casting dark-skinned Mexican men as villains. The years following the war saw an explosion of filibustering expeditions by American men into Mexico, the Caribbean, and Central America. American filibusters were motivated to invade foreign countries without governmental sanction by a belief that the continued territorial expansion of America was God's will, by greed for land, and by visions of international romance. For these mercenaries, the key lessons taught by the Mexican-American War were that violence was an acceptable means to gain new territory, and that victory was inevitable over the racial inferiors of Latin America.

Sectional Crises

The status of slavery in the Mexican cession led to repeated sectional crises. Despite its support among northern representatives of both parties, the Wilmot Proviso never became law because of southern strength in the Senate. The question of whether to allow slavery in the new territories took on concrete importance when California applied for statehood in 1849. When President Zachary Taylor proposed outlawing slavery from all the new territories, including California, furious Southerners threatened to secede from the Union. Only Henry Clay's Compromise of 1850 calmed the storm by offering Southerners a strict fugitive slave law and the possibility of a new slave state in the unorganized New Mexico territory through the doctrine of "popular sovereignty."

But this compromise was only temporary. The Second Party System was yet another casualty of the war. The platforms of both major parties, which studiously avoided discussing slavery, began to seem increasingly irrelevant to voters in both the North and South, opening up room for the new Republican Party to make a strong showing in the North in 1856 with presidential candidate John C. Frémont, hero of the Bear Flag Revolt.

Lasting Memory and
Hemispheric Impact of the War

Both supporters and opponents agreed that the Mexican-American War marked a turning point in the nation's history. In 1848 Captain James Henry Carleton wrote that "the Battle of Buena Vista will probably be regarded as the greatest ever fought on this continent." The Civil War quickly proved him

wrong, however, and completely overshadowed the war in Mexico. While in Mexico La Invasíon Norteamericana exerted a powerful force in the political realignment of the late nineteenth century, the creation of a centralized state, and the forging of a common Mexican identity, the half-life of this war north of the border was remarkably short. Representations of even the most dramatic victories of the conflict disappeared after 1860, and veterans of the 1848 conflict struggled to gain public recognition and financial support from a society that had no heart for revisiting the Halls of the Montezumas.

In 1885 former president Ulysses S. Grant, who like most Civil War generals had gained key military experience in the Mexican conflict, described the war with Mexico as "one of the most unjust ever waged by a stronger against a weaker nation." He declared the Civil War "our punishment" for that "transgression." At the time this view was a mainstream one. While Grant had been a member of the pro-war Democratic Party in the 1840s and 1850s, he was a Union general and Republican president and accepted the antiwar Whig Party as his party's forebear. Although the Democrats promoted and won the war with Mexico, it was a pyrrhic victory for the party. Ultimately the views of Whigs, who maintained that the war was unjust, immoral, and part of a land grab on the part of slaveholders, held sway. The 1847 resolution by the Massachusetts House of Representatives that "an offensive and unnecessary war is one of the highest crimes which man can commit against society; but when is superadded a war for the extension of slavery, its criminality stands out in the boldest possible relief" had become the dominant belief among Republicans after the Civil War.

But white Americans of all parties and all sections of the country in the later nineteenth century tried to forget the Mexican conflict and to reimagine the bloody 1840s as a peaceful period, when sectional harmony and common purpose advanced Manifest Destiny. By the fiftieth anniversary of the war in 1898, politicians and historians seemed comfortable writing a history of America's military past in which the war with Mexico and its veterans were absent. Congress debated whether to fight a war for empire in 1898 without acknowledging that it was the fiftieth anniversary of the successful conclusion of the first war for empire. The 1848 war posed some difficulties for those who endorsed a history in which Americans always behaved from selfless motives. In 1898 both supporters and opponents of imperialism maintained that the United States had always firmly and consistently disavowed empire.

Since many scholars now explain the war fought by the United States in 1898 as part of a regional struggle for dominance, a process that started with the Monroe Doctrine, this amnesia was significant. Some historians have suggested that the war with Mexico was unnecessary: Polk could have gained

Mexico's northern territories through steady diplomatic negotiations and without either the loss of life or principle that the war entailed. In either case, many would now consider Ralph Waldo Emerson prophetic for predicting in 1846 that "the United States will conquer Mexico," but that "Mexico will poison us."

See also sectional conflict and secession, 1845–65.

FURTHER READING. Brian DeLay, *War of a Thousand Deserts: Indian Raids and the U.S.-Mexican War*, 2008; Paul Foos, *A Short Offhand Killing Affair: Soldiers and Social Conflict during the Mexican-American War*, 2002; Amy S. Greenberg, *Manifest Manhood and the Antebellum American Empire*, 2005; Richard Griswold del Castillo, *The Treaty of Guadalupe Hidalgo*, 1990; Thomas Hietala, *Manifest Design: American Exceptionalism and Empire*, 2003; Irving W. Levinson, *Wars within War: Mexican Guerrillas, Domestic Elites, and the United States of America*, 2005; David Pletcher, *The Diplomacy of Annexation: Texas, Oregon, and the Mexican War*, 1973; Andrés Reséndez, *Changing National Identities at the Frontier: Texas and New Mexico, 1800–1850*, 2005; Cecil Robinson, *The View from Chapultepec: Mexican Writers on the Mexican-American War*, 1989; John H. Schroeder, *Mr. Polk's War: American Opposition and Dissent, 1846–1848*, 1973; Richard Winders, *Mr. Polk's Army: The American Military Experience in the Mexican War*, 2001.

AMY S. GREENBERG

Middle Atlantic, the

Just three Middle Atlantic states, among the most populous in the nation between 1820 and 1940 and industrial leaders for much of American history, have wielded huge potential influence in American politics, particularly in the election of presidents and the make-up of Congress. Yet they have realized this potential only intermittently, as great wealth and diverse populations have made them notorious for political corruption and the politics of compromise.

Leading banks, industries, and railroads were the glue that held these diverse states together. From the Civil War until the mid-twentieth century, Pennsylvania was dominated politically by the Pennsylvania Railroad, Standard Oil, the great steel and coal companies, the Mellon Bank interests (including the Aluminum Corporation of America), and the Pennsylvania Association of Manufacturers. In New York during the same period, the New York Central and Erie Railroads, along with Wall Street bankers, notably J. P. Morgan, wielded the most influence. In New Jersey, the Camden and Amboy Railroad before the Civil War and the Pennsylvania Railroad afterward came to dominate the state. In each state, the enormous discrepancy between private and public wealth ensured that state legislators were almost invariably willing to do the bidding of the capitalists.

New York

New York was founded as New Netherland in 1624 by the Dutch East India Company for two purposes: sending furs, especially for beaver hats, to Holland, and supplying the newly acquired Dutch colony of Brazil with provisions such as fish and grain. Peter Minuit, the first governor, instituted the patroon system in 1629, which the English continued under the name of proprietary estates, in which wealthy men who brought at least 50 settlers to the colony received large tracts of land that they leased to tenants.

New Netherland was governed autocratically by a series of governors, none of whom could maintain order effectively among the diverse population of Dutch, English (on eastern Long Island), and, after 1654, Swedes in the Delaware Valley, whom Governor Pieter Stuyvesant conquered. Stuyvesant was so unpopular that when an English fleet arrived in 1664, the population refused to fight. The renamed New York was then ruled as a proprietary colony by the Duke of York, the future King James II. Conflict between the influential English and Anglican minority and the Dutch characterized New York politics until the mid-1730s, when the proprietary Livingston family of upstate New York and the French Huguenot merchant Delanceys of New York City became leading rivals until the American Revolution.

New York anticipated the party politics that did not develop elsewhere until the 1790s or later. Each faction ran complete slates of candidates, distributed literature, held rallies, and articulated specific policies.

As with Pennsylvania and New Jersey, New York's assembly never supported the American Revolution, and leadership before 1775 fell to New York City merchants and sea captains, who, in 1766, led the fight against British soldiers at what became known as the Battle of Golden Hill. But New York's revolution did not lead to a major class conflict because members of the elite, such as the intermarried Jay and Livingston families, took a strong stand for resistance and independence. In 1777 John Jay (governor, 1795–1801) drafted most of a constitution that gave equal political rights to all citizens regardless of religion. But until 1795, the anti-Federalist supporters of states' rights dominated New York, with George Clinton holding the governorship for 18 years. Alexander Hamilton and John Jay, along with James Madison, wrote the *Federalist Papers* to convince New Yorkers to support the U.S. Constitution, but only the threat to remove heavily Federalist New York City from the state and join the union convinced the upstate opposition to support ratification. New York was the eleventh state to ratify.

New York continued to lead the nation in political mobilization in the nineteenth century. Aaron Burr (senator, 1791–97) earned his spot as vice president on Thomas Jefferson's 1800 ticket when he was a principal organizer of the nation's first urban political machine, known as Tammany Hall after the meeting place of New York Democrats. On the state level, Martin Van Buren (senator, 1821–28; president, 1837–41) did likewise, earning a similar position from Andrew Jackson in 1833. Van Buren wrote the first theoretical defense of the two-party system as well, arguing that a legitimate opposition encouraged voter participation, especially in an era when nearly every government job was a political appointment.

During the Civil War, New York State, especially the New York City area, was the most pro-southern in the North. The city was the center of the cotton export trade, and by 1860, its population was three-fourths immigrant or first-generation (mostly Irish) American—poor workers who had little sympathy with southern slaves and competed for jobs with local African Americans. Mayor Fernando Wood hoped the city would secede and form the state of Islandia to join the South. In 1863 the city descended into chaos for seven days after the draft was instituted on July 4, and between 100 and 1,000 people died in the ensuing riots. Only the arrival of Union troops from Gettysburg, Pennsylvania, ended the disturbances; had Lee won that pivotal battle, Union control over its largest city might have ended.

With the most patronage positions up for grabs, the New York Republican and Democratic parties led the nation in corruption. William M. "Boss" Tweed, a Democrat who dominated the city in the 1860s, had a Republican counterpart in Senator Roscoe Conkling (1867–81), who persuaded his party to nominate the former head of the New York customhouse, Chester Arthur, for vice president in 1880. Republican president Rutherford Hayes had dismissed Arthur for his willingness to overlook corruption where more of the nation's imports landed than anywhere else. Earlier, New Yorkers of both parties had joined together and nominated Republican editor of the New York *Tribune* Horace Greeley to run for president in 1872 against the scandal-ridden administration of Ulysses S. Grant. The Democratic Party endorsed him as well. New York Governor Grover Cleveland was the only Democratic president between the Civil War and Woodrow Wilson, who would become president in 1913: in 1884 Cleveland defeated the notoriously corrupt James G. Blaine, a Maine senator, despite having admitted to fathering and supporting an illegitimate child. When a New York Republican minister denounced the Democrats as the party of "Rum, Romanism, and Rebellion," his speech backfired, giving Cleveland a minuscule margin in his home state.

With Theodore and Franklin Roosevelt and Alfred E. Smith (governor, 1923–29), New York became a national leader in progressive reform in both political parties. Laws that protected women and children at work, supported labor unions, provided old-age and disability insurance, and furthered public education were a model for the New Deal; Governor Herbert Lehman (1933–44) was a firm friend of Franklin Roosevelt and his policies. New York public housing

and road construction led the nation: by the 1930s, New York City had five times the highway mileage of any other city, as well as the largest city and regional railroad system.

Following World War II, New York continued to lead the nation in expenditures, including a huge highway system, state university, and capitol complex in Albany built under Governor Nelson Rockefeller (1959–73), which greatly expanded the state's debt. In the 1960s, New York and many of the state's older cities were plagued by poverty, riots, and a flight to the suburbs. New York City went bankrupt in 1975 and had to be bailed out by the state government. Under Mayor Ed Koch (1978–89), the city regained much of its prosperity by promoting international tourism and investment, but at the expense of the poor and the middle class, who found it increasingly hard to pay the astronomical city rents. The suburbs continued to grow while urban and rural areas of upstate New York declined in population.

In the twentieth century, New York was the only state to have important liberal and conservative parties that ran candidates of their own as well as endorsing those of the major parties. Liberal Republican John Lindsay won election as mayor of New York City (1966–73) when conservative Republicans ran candidates—including columnist William F. Buckley Jr.—who took votes away from the Democratic machine's choice. Lindsay ran on the Republican-Liberal ticket to win his first term and Democratic-Liberal for his second. When Buckley's brother James (senator, 1981–87) defeated longtime liberal Republican senator Jacob Javits (1957–81) in the 1980 primary, Javits refused to give up his Liberal Party line, taking enough votes away from Democrat Elizabeth Holtzman to cost her the election.

New York also attracted celebrity candidates from other states: the Buckleys from Connecticut, Senator Robert F. Kennedy from Massachusetts, and Senator Hillary Rodham Clinton from Arkansas. In the late twentieth and early twenty-first centuries, New York voters were independent and unpredictable: they elected two Republican mayors, Rudolph Giuliani (1994–2001) and Michael Bloomberg (2001–), in heavily Democratic New York City and a conservative Republican governor, George Pataki (1995–2006), to succeed the liberal Democrat Mario Cuomo (1983–94). Until the Democrats' victory in the election of 2008, the state senate had been in Republican hands, the assembly in Democratic, since the 1960s. Candidates for judges were almost invariably endorsed by the Democratic, Republican, Conservative, and Liberal parties.

Pennsylvania

Pennsylvania began in 1682, when William Penn became the proprietor of the colony. Penn recruited English Quakers as well as German pacifists to receive freeholds in a colony that would grant religious toleration to all peaceful inhabitants (although only

Christians could vote and hold office before the constitution of 1790). Penn recruited whole communities, which settled together, thereby preventing serious internal conflict until the Scots-Irish settled the western frontier in the 1750s. He bought the western land fairly from the Indians, although the "treaty" made famous in Benjamin West's 1771 painting was actually 12 treaties with small groups in the Philadelphia area.

Penn's colonists did not appreciate his largesse. They opposed his design for an appointed council and did not want to pay rents or taxes without an assembly's consent; Penn lost so much money on Pennsylvania that when he tried to sell it in the 1690s to pay off his debts, there were no buyers. After 19 constitutions or instruments of government either proposed or attempted, in 1701 Penn and the colonists finally settled on a system unique among the 13 colonies in having a one-house legislature, the assembly. With representation set by county, the three original counties that favored the Quaker Party dominated the legislature; their opponents, the Proprietary Party, supported the Penn family interests and mostly consisted of Presbyterians and Anglicans.

When warfare broke out in 1754 over whether the French or British should rule what is now western Pennsylvania, the Indians from whom Pennsylvania had purchased land attacked all along the frontier, driving settlement back beyond the Susquehanna River and turning Lancaster, York, and Reading into refugee centers. The assembly insisted the proprietors pay taxes for frontier defense; eight pacifist Quakers resigned in 1756 rather than approve funds for war, but the party kept control. It sent Benjamin Franklin to London to lobby for Pennsylvania's becoming a royal province; during the 1760s and 1770s, when most colonies were resisting British taxes and commercial regulation, leaders of both Pennsylvania factions were trying to impress the home government with their loyalty.

As a result, Philadelphia artisans and politicized Pennsylvania German farmers, led by notable Philadelphians including Franklin, Thomas Paine (author of *Common Sense*), painter Charles Willson Peale, astronomer David Rittenhouse, and Dr. Benjamin Rush, took control of the revolution, ousted the assembly, and drew up a new constitution in 1776. Abolishing the office of governor for a mere "president," who simply presided over the assembly, the document was both the most and least democratic of all the state constitutions: most democratic in that tax-paying men could vote and the assembly was reapportioned to favor the previously underrepresented backcountry, but least democratic in that only those who swore an oath to the government on the Bible could participate in the new order. Pennsylvania also adopted the nation's first system of rotation in office (no one could serve in the assembly more than four out of seven years), authorized the Council of Censors to judge whether laws violated the constitution, and required two consecutive assemblies to pass nonemergency legislation, to give people a chance to look over the new laws. But the new government proved both tyrannical in suppressing opponents and enforcing price fixing and ineffective in collecting taxes and keeping order. Businessmen headed by U.S. superintendent of finance Robert Morris formed the Republican (later Federalist) Party to oppose the Constitutionalists (later anti-Federalists). Bringing fiscal stability to the state with the first bank on the North American continent in 1781, they also supported commercial and industrial development. After they took over the state in 1786, they brought it into line for the U.S. Constitution, and replaced Pennsylvania's own constitution in 1790, restoring a strong senate and governor.

Aside from the struggle over the nature of its government, Pennsylvania endured more unrest than any other state between 1750 and 1800. It had fought with three of its neighbors—Maryland in the south, Virginia in the west, and Connecticut in the north—over its boundaries, and only settled them in 1763, 1781, and 1786, respectively. Two of the three "rebellions" in the early republic (more accurately, cases of tax resistance)—the Whiskey Rebellion of 1794 and Fries's Rebellion in 1799—occurred in Pennsylvania when the federal government appointed unpopular individuals to collect new taxes.

Between 1800 and the Civil War, Pennsylvanians of every political persuasion dedicated themselves to economic growth. They strongly favored government support for internal improvements, differing primarily over whether this should occur through legislative grants, borrowing, or assistance to banks. Pennsylvania staked its industrial growth on high tariffs, but by the 1850s, after most of the schemes for canals and railroads failed, the state was controlled by the pro–southern Democratic machine headed by James Buchanan.

Buchanan's disastrous presidency and the invasion of Pennsylvania twice by Confederate forces (at Gettysburg in 1863 and Chambersburg in 1864) led to a Republican ascendancy that even the Great Depression barely interrupted, and which ultimately survived until the 1950s. The state legislature became notorious as the servant of business interests: Pennsylvania was the only state in the union that allowed corporations to recruit government police forces (the infamous "coal and iron police") and allowed the Pennsylvania Railroad to create corporations, such as John D. Rockefeller's South Improvement Company, which drilled and processed most of western Pennsylvania's oil. Tom Scott, President of the Pennsylvania Railroad, helped negotiate the deal that in 1876 made Republican Rutherford B. Hayes president in a disputed election with Samuel Tilden; the next year, Hayes ordered federal troops to break the national railroad strike. Even Pennsylvania Democratic reformers such as lawyer J. Mitchell Palmer could not defeat boss Boies Penrose in the first direct election of a senator held in the state in 1914; six years later, Penrose solved an impasse at the Republican National Convention and secured the presidential nomination for Warren Harding, with his chief supporter Andrew Mellon of Pittsburgh becoming secretary of the treasury. Nor could William Wilson, secretary of the United Mine Workers—in whose northeastern Pennsylvania strike of 1903 the federal government intervened on the workers' behalf for the first time—defeat William Vare, the boss of Philadelphia, in the dishonest senate election of 1926. Vare had previously arranged for his wife to be the first woman in the Pennsylvania state legislature as a sop to women's rights. Ultraconservative Pennsylvania supported neither woman suffrage nor Prohibition.

Only in 1922 and again in 1930 was a reformer, Gifford Pinchot, elected governor. Pinchot had won the support of the Mellons and the Pennsylvania Association of Manufacturers, which, represented by its president Joseph Grundy, ran the state most of the time between Penrose's death in 1921 and his own (at the age of 99) in 1961. The first chief of the National Forest Service, Pinchot pushed for conservation of the formerly magnificent woods that had allowed Pennsylvania to lead the nation in lumber production during the 1860s and 1870s. He also favored employment projects, especially roads and public construction, during the New Deal, as did his successor Democrat George Earle (1935–39): both men supported unions and the right of workers to strike. But the Republican legislature refused even to set up a system for distributing much of the New Deal monies to which the state was entitled, just as, in the 1920s, it had refused to enforce Prohibition, leading Pinchot to rely on funds from the Women's Christian Temperance League. The Pennsylvania Turnpike, the nation's first limited access high-speed highway, was built only when President Roosevelt approved $20 million in federal funds to do so.

After World War II, Pennsylvania became a two-party state. Popular governors included Democrats George Leader (1955–59), David Lawrence (1959–63), and Ed Rendell (2003–) as well as Republicans William Scranton (1963–67) and Tom Ridge (1995–2001). Once a leader in American industry, Pennsylvania now confronted deindustrialization: numerous small cities as well as Pittsburgh and Philadelphia lost one-third to one-half of their population between 1960 and 2008.

New Jersey

New Jersey began as two colonies: East Jersey, with its capital at Perth Amboy, opposite New York City, and West Jersey, with its capital at Burlington opposite Philadelphia, in 1676. Although the colony united in 1702, its economy and politics reflected this geographic divide. West Jersey was heavily Quaker, settled with freehold farms, and used Philadelphia as its major port; East Jersey was settled largely by Scots, had large proprietary estates, and fell within New York's orbit.

At first New Jersey was considered too insignificant to have its own royal governor, and shared one with New York until 1738. During the 1750s, Scottish proprietors attempted to collect their rents and control the settlement on their estates, which led to land riots. Only the American Revolution and the ousting of the largely loyalist owners settled the problem. New Jersey accepted the U.S. Constitution with alacrity, fearing that otherwise it would be swallowed by its stronger neighbors. But the divisions continued: the state had to pass a law in 1790 preventing people from bringing their guns to polling places.

New Jersey set up one of the weakest state governments in the nation: the executive had no appointive powers, it was the next to last state to have free public education, and, as late as 1960, had neither a sales nor an income tax. In the nineteenth century, it was overwhelmingly Democratic until the Republicans supplanted the Democrats after William McKinley defeated William Jennings Bryan in the presidential election of 1896. Conservative New Jersey gave African American men the vote only when compelled to, along with the South, by the Fifteenth Amendment to the Constitution in 1870. Republican rule was briefly interrupted when a division between Republican reformers and conservatives permitted the election of Woodrow Wilson, a Democratic governor (1911–13) who supported such innovations as the direct primary, laws protecting workers, and regulation of public utilities. Wilson had won election as the choice of Boss James Smith of Newark, and infuriated Democratic regulars when he decided to become a reformer.

In later years, New Jersey, like New York, behaved unpredictably in state elections, although consistently in presidential races, voting Democratic in every national contest between 1992 and 2008. Republican moderates won election as governor, including Tom Kean (1982–90) and Christine Todd Whitman (1994–2001). Democratic governor James Florio (1990–94) generated a backlash against his party when he raised taxes significantly to improve public services. As in Pennsylvania, state taxes were low (New Jersey had some of the lowest gasoline prices in the nation), which put the burden of solving urban problems on cities. Many New Jersey residents lived in suburban areas and were more closely linked, economically and psychologically, with the communities in Pennsylvania and New York, especially Philadelphia and New York City, where they worked.

Compromise and Corruption

New Jersey and Pennsylvania, and frequently New York, have been bastions of corruption and compromise through much of their history, from their refusal to endorse independence in 1776 to the vast influence corporations and railroads exercised over state legislatures. As the nation moved to a service economy, representatives of urban ethnic groups, middle-class suburbs, business interests, farmers, and post-industrial cities all had to cooperate to solve the problems of a region that had lost national importance to the South and the West. Nevertheless, all three states proved capable of electing energetic officials whose civic commitment extended beyond enriching corporations and satisfying the wishes of political machines. Mayors Giuliani (1994–2001) and Bloomberg (2002–) of New York City and Governor Jon Corzine (2006–) of New Jersey won national attention for their efforts to control fiscal expenditures, promote economic growth, and improve some of the nation's most polluted environments. At the same time, perpetual squabbling in the state legislatures continued to stymie meaningful advances in educational reform and improved health care.

See also local government; state government.

FURTHER READING. Paul D. Beers, *Pennsylvania Politics: Today and Yesterday*, 1980; Thomas Fleming, *New Jersey: A History*, 1984; Richard Hofstadter, *The Rise of a Party System: The Growth of the Idea of Legitimate Opposition in the United States, 1780–1840*, 1969; Milton M. Klein, ed., *The Empire State: A History*, 2005; Philip Klein and Ari Hoogenboom, *A History of Pennsylvania*, 1980; Richard Lehne and Lana Rosenthal, eds., *Politics in New Jersey*, 1979; Randall Miller and William Pencak, eds., *Pennsylvania: A History of the Commonwealth*, 2002; John F. Reynolds, *Testing Democracy: Electoral Behavior and Political Reform in New Jersey, 1880–1920*, 1988; William Riordan, ed., *Plunkett of Tammany Hall*, 1963; Barbara G. Salmore and Stephen A. Salmore, *New Jersey Politics and Government: The Suburbs Come of Age*, 3rd ed., 2008; Edward V. Schneier and Brian Murtaugh, *New York Politics: A Tale of Two States*, 2001; Jack M. Treadway, *Elections in Pennsylvania: A Century of Partisan Conflict*, 2005.

WILLIAM PENCAK

Midwest, the

In his recent polemic *What's the Matter with Kansas?* Thomas Frank examined that state to discover "how conservatives won the heart of America." For many Americans, Frank's assessment that the Midwest is fundamentally conservative, unprogressive, and even backward politically is self-evident. An earlier generation, however, saw the Midwest as a laboratory for democratic ideas and causes. John Barnhart, author of a 1953 history on the settlement of the Ohio River Valley, applied historian Frederick Jackson Turner's emphasis on the frontier's importance for democracy to that region. Barnhart's thesis was that in Ohio's territorial period, democracy triumphed over the elitism of the Federalist Party. Although it is no longer fashionable among historians to see a causal connection between the settlement of the frontier and the advance of democracy, many of the issues and problems of U.S. politics have been worked out in the Midwest. Even William Allen White, the newspaper editor who first asked the question "What's the matter with Kansas?" in an 1896 editorial, was ridiculing a movement—populism—that many contemporary historians view as a radical solution to the economic ills of the late nineteenth century. And Frank's maligned conservatives were, in the 1980s, part of a revolution to remake American society and politics. Far from being backward, the Midwest has been at the forefront of political debate in the nation.

Native and Euro-Americans

The first political systems of the Midwest were the consensus-based tribal politics of the Native Americans. The collective decision making and noncoercive nature of the Native American political tradition ran contrary to the European colonizers' hierarchical systems. As European alliances became important to the tribes, tribal politics began to revolve much more around diplomacy and trade relations. Historian Richard White has posited a "middle ground" in which Native Americans and Euro-Americans accommodated and adapted to each other. That relationship eroded, however, when Euro-Americans achieved dominance in the early nineteenth century. Rather than accommodate Native Americans, Americans sought to expel them.

The removal period of the early 1800s saw some tribes displaced from certain areas of the Midwest, often to more western parts of the region. In states that had undergone removal, the families and bands that remained often lost their tribal status. Some, such as the Miami, engaged in a long political struggle to regain that status. Even among current Native Americans with tribal status, resentment at government encroachments on tribal sovereignty conflicts with fears that government moves toward "self-determination" will mean the end of the federal aid the tribes receive.

For Euro-Americans in the Midwest, the American Revolution brought new forms of government. The national government, under the Articles of Confederation, possessed a vast colonial territory: the region between the Appalachian Mountains and the Mississippi River. Congress resolved the issue of governance through the Northwest Ordinance, which established the Northwest Territory and provided for stages of government as the territory grew in population. In the earliest stages, government was autocratic under a federally appointed governor and judges. As population increased, the territory acquired an elected legislature, but the governor retained absolute veto power. When the population reached a certain level, voters could elect a constitutional convention and apply for statehood. If admitted, the new state entered on an equal footing with its predecessors. The ordinance acknowledged both the democratic underpinnings of the American system and a good deal of distrust in the pioneers' capabilities to govern properly. It also, however, laid the groundwork for territorial government not only in the Midwest but in all regions of future U.S. expansion. As well, the trend from the earliest settlement of Ohio was for autocratic features to erode in favor of democracy. The population benchmarks required for the government to move to the next stage were often waived, governors of future territories lost their absolute veto, and the presumption became that settlers were fit for statehood as soon as they desired it. In fact, the national government, or political parties that sought to gain electoral votes, would often push for statehood before many settlers felt ready to bear the financial burden of extra taxation that statehood entailed.

Creating the Midwest

The Midwest achieved statehood during the nineteenth century, a period when expanding democracy was the norm. James H. Madison, an expert in Midwestern history, includes the following states in the region: Ohio (which achieved statehood in 1803), Indiana (1816), Illinois (1818), Missouri (1821), Michigan (1837), Iowa (1846), Wisconsin (1848), Minnesota (1858), Kansas (1861), Nebraska (1867), South Dakota (1889), and North Dakota (1889). State constitutions provided for strong legislatures and weak governors. Ohio's 1803 constitution did not even give the governor a veto. Some early state constitutions gave the legislature extensive control over appointments or required frequent elections of both the legislative and executive branches. Frequent elections gave the people more control over their representatives. Nineteenth-century notions of democracy, however, were limited only to white men. When Indiana revised its constitution in 1851, it specifically limited suffrage to white males. Many Midwestern states had black exclusion laws that forbade blacks to settle in them or required the posting of a bond. Although these laws were often flouted, they demonstrated the pervasive hostility to African Americans and became the basis for harassing blacks who incurred community wrath—often for abolitionist activity.

Attitudes toward African Americans depended in part on sectional differences. New England migrants who settled Ohio's Western Reserve formed abolition societies and voted Whig or Republican, while the Kentuckians in the lower North favored the Democrats. In general, regional differences in housing styles, foodways, and political culture would be subordinated to a general sense of American westernness. Stephen A. Douglas and Abraham Lincoln demonstrated the subordination of region of origin to party politics when they clashed in the 1858 Illinois senatorial race. The Democrat, Douglas, a Vermont native, rejected the East's confining morality and deference to hierarchy. The Republican, Lincoln, a Kentucky native, rejected the South's economic backwardness and embraced the very movements Douglas abhorred—temperance and antislavery. Both men, of course, considered themselves Westerners and believed their positions represented the best interests of the Midwest. The place where this emphasis on westernness failed, perhaps, was the Kansas Territory. Since Kansas was at the center of a sectional storm over slavery, settlers from New England, the Midwest, and Missouri were unable to forget their regions of origin and forge a common western identity. Rather, they adhered to free soil or proslavery political positions, keenly aware of region.

The Midwest was at the forefront of disputes over democracy during the Civil War. The Peace Democrats, or Copperheads, took their nickname from a poisonous snake indigenous to the Midwest. The Copperheads advocated constitutional liberty, which they believed the administration of President Abraham Lincoln threatened. They opposed military arrests and trials of civilians, the suspension of habeas corpus, and the suppression of free speech and the press. Deeply racist, they also opposed emancipation, as well as civil and political rights for African Americans. Many Midwesterners believed that Copperhead objections to Republican wartime policy constituted active support of the Confederacy. In 1863 the military's arrest of the leading Peace Democrat, former congressman Clement Vallandigham of Ohio, became a cause célèbre. Because Vallandigham had spoken against the war, he was arrested and tried by a military tribunal. President Lincoln commuted his sentence to exile to the Confederacy. While never a threat to the war effort, the Copperheads represented deep discontent in the white Midwest with many of the Lincoln administration's policies, particularly on civil liberties and race.

African Americans

Although the Midwest had long been hostile to blacks, African American migration to the Midwestern states increased after the Civil War. The suppression of African American political rights at the end of Reconstruction prompted a migration of so-called Exodusters (so named because of their exodus from the increasingly repressive southern states). Segregation of schools, workplaces, housing, and social venues existed formally and informally in the Midwest, but voting was nonetheless allowed. By the early 1900s, industrialization stimulated black migration. Factory owners sometimes recruited black workers as strikebreakers, but, in general, the availability of jobs just as surely brought African Americans from the South. Race riots occasionally marred the Midwest's reputation as a refuge from the Jim Crow South. In 1908 a race riot erupted in Springfield, Illinois—Abraham Lincoln's hometown—when whites attacked blacks in reaction to their growing presence. During World War II, a terrible race riot occurred in Detroit, where black and white workers clashed. By contrast, race riots during the 1960s were more often associated with black frustration at poor housing and menial jobs, as was the case with a Detroit riot in 1967.

Civil rights leaders worked to improve conditions in the Midwest as well as in the South. The lead case in the U.S. Supreme Court's groundbreaking school desegregation case, *Brown v. Board of Education of Topeka*, was that of an African American family, the

Browns, against the school board of Topeka, Kansas. In the all-white Chicago suburb of Cicero, Martin Luther King Jr. drew attention to segregation in the North by means of a peaceful march. By 2008 the rise of Illinois senator Barack Obama to the U.S. presidency indicated the progress that Midwestern African Americans had achieved.

Ethnocultural versus Economic Issues

After the Civil War, the Midwest became a political battleground. Several Midwestern states possessed both divided electorates and considerable electoral votes. Moreover, government's growing involvement in regulating the economy was of special interest to residents of the region. As a heavily agricultural area, but also one of growing industry, the Midwest faced the social and economic changes of the age. The temperance, Greenback (labor), and grange or populist movements all drew great attention in the Midwest.

Quantitative analyses of Midwestern politics in the late nineteenth century argue that voters split along ethnic and religious—rather than along class—lines. In this formulation, pietists (evangelical Protestants) backed the Republican Party, and ritualists (Catholics) backed the Democrats. The 1896 presidential election between William McKinley and William Jennings Bryan, both Midwesterners, shifted the dynamic. Pietists embraced the Presbyterian Bryan, but ritualists were repelled from the Democratic Party. The result was a new ascendancy for the Republican Party in the Midwest as the "party of prosperity."

However, pietism was not dead, and soon saw results in the Prohibition movement. Both major anti-alcohol organizations, the Women's Christian Temperance Union and the Anti-Saloon League, originated in the Midwest. The Eighteenth Amendment to prohibit alcohol was ratified by most Midwestern state legislatures, and the enforcement legislation, the Volstead Act, took the name of Minnesota congressman Andrew Volstead.

The Midwest also became a center of resistance to Prohibition. Al Capone, a Chicago gangster, gained notoriety as a supplier of bootleg liquor. Because the legalization of alcohol not only promised to undermine this flourishing criminal subculture but also to stimulate a flagging economy, the Midwest decisively supported repealing Prohibition in the early years of the Great Depression.

Ethnicity was an important element of the struggle over Prohibition. Among the bootleggers' customers were ethnic, urban voters who supported the repeal of Prohibition, while native-born, rural Protestant Midwesterners opposed it, embracing the crusade against alcohol. These ethnic voters resulted from the waves of migration into the Midwest from the early nineteenth century on. Irish, Germans, and Scandinavians came first, followed by the late-nineteenth- and twentieth-century migration of southern and eastern Europeans. Democrats welcomed the immigrants, but the Whig Party, and later the Republican Party—although attractive to some immigrant groups such as the Germans—were more hesitant to embrace the new constituencies.

Issues such as slavery, alcohol, and economics helped determine the partisan split of immigrant groups. German voters were more receptive to the middle-class aspirations of Republicans than were the Irish. Although German voters might have disliked Republican temperance proclivities, they were more likely to appreciate Republican moral qualms about slavery and invocations of the superiority of a free-labor society. In the post–Civil War period, Democrats continued to appeal to immigrants for their defense of cultural traditions, such as drinking alcohol, and their closer identification with the working class, to which many immigrants belonged.

More recently, many political alliances have been reshaped by Hispanic migration, especially from Mexico, and by migration from Asia, Southeast Asia, Africa, and the Mideast. Federal immigration legislation in 1965, which removed quotas that favored western and northern Europeans, coincided with shifting patterns of migration by bringing more persons from developing nations. As immigrants became more involved in civic life, their presence often provoked a nativist backlash. Political movements to deny immigrants the right to hold office, to enforce the legal prohibition of alcohol, or to deny amnesty for illegal immigrants have all grown from nativist sentiment.

The increasing presence of women on the Midwestern public stage in the late nineteenth and early twentieth centuries dovetailed with the growing movement for their own rights. Although the women's rights movement originated in the northeast, Midwestern women took part in meetings before the Civil War. It was at an Akron, Ohio, women's rights gathering that Sojourner Truth delivered her famous "Aren't I a Woman?" speech, reminding the audience that nineteenth-century gender roles made no allowance for the situation of black women. Clarina Nichols took a notable role at the convention that wrote Kansas's constitution.

Nonetheless, women's activism was still seen as an extension of their role in the home. During the Civil War, women supported the war effort through aid societies, sanitary fairs, and nursing. Although Mary Livermore, a Chicagoan and organizer of sanitary commission fairs, became a suffrage advocate, the movement was not as strong in the Midwest. In the post–Civil War period, many women turned their activism toward temperance. Midwestern women joined the Women's Christian Temperance Union (WCTU) and participated in its crusades against the saloon. Kansan Carrie Nation and her hatchet became national symbols of the WCTU's campaign against alcohol.

Their battle against the liquor interests persuaded many women of the need for the vote. Midwestern states began to permit women to vote, often in local elections, before the passage of the Nineteenth

Amendment. The leader of the campaign for the woman suffrage amendment was an Iowan, Carrie Chapman Catt. A generation later, the feminist movement would also have Midwestern roots. Betty Friedan from Peoria, Illinois, was living the life of a suburban housewife and mother when she wrote her protest against women's isolation in the home, *The Feminine Mystique*, in 1963. All the Midwestern states except Illinois ratified the equal rights amendment, although Nebraska and South Dakota later rescinded their ratifications. After the expansion of women's rights to include reproductive rights, the National Abortion Rights Action League was founded in Chicago to protect against attacks—both political and physical—on abortion rights.

Women had, of course, never been entirely isolated in the domestic sphere. Economic necessity as well as the desire for a career often drove women to work outside the home. During the nineteenth century, certain occupations such as teaching and nursing had become feminized. But women also worked in the emerging factories.

The new industrial order, in fact, stimulated some of the most important political developments in Midwestern history. Early factory labor was dangerous, subject to the boom and bust periods of the business cycle, and largely unregulated. Manufacturers' reliance on holding companies and trusts allowed them to build near monopolies in certain industries. Amid a political culture of lax ethics, politicians took money and gifts from industrialists, thereby compromising their ability to speak for the people. Some of the most famous protests against the new industrial order arose out of the Midwest. In 1894 Jacob Coxey, an Ohio manufacturer, led an army of the unemployed in a march on Washington, D.C. Although they drew attention to the hardships created by the Panic of 1893, they gained little from the government except arrest for walking on the grass.

Industrialization stimulated the political movement of progressivism. Progressives sought to ameliorate its worst effects through social reform and government regulation. Jane Addams pioneered the settlement house movement when she and Ellen Gates Starr opened Hull House in an immigrant neighborhood in Chicago in 1889. Settlement houses provided social services for their neighbors, such as day care and vocational training, but they also played an active role in civic life. Settlement house workers helped immigrants prepare for naturalization and campaigned for regulation and services from city government. Midwestern mayors such as Hazen Pingree of Detroit, Samuel Jones of Toledo, and Tom Johnson of Cleveland led early reforms against the boss-dominated politics of their cities. Samuel M. "Golden Rule" Jones, a Christian Socialist, advocated public ownership of utilities. Robert M. "Fighting Bob" La Follette of Wisconsin, the great leader of Midwestern progressivism, began his career by winning election against his state's Republican

machine. By 1900 the machine was broken, and La Follette and his followers were implementing the "Wisconsin idea" of expanded democracy, whose major reforms included direct primaries, initiative and referendum, campaign finance, civil service, and antilobbying laws; government regulation of transportation, public utilities, industry, and banking; state income and inheritance taxes; child labor, industrial safety, pure food and workmen's compensation laws. Although La Follette lost influence in the national party, the Wisconsin reforms became a model for national progressivism.

Radicalism versus Reaction

While Progressives accepted the capitalist economic order, some Midwesterners rebelled against it. The Midwest was the site of labor unrest that galvanized the nation. Chicago, a major railroad hub, was caught up in the national railroad strike of 1877. In 1886 strikes in Chicago for the eight-hour day panicked middle-class residents, who feared the violent rhetoric of many in the labor movement. When police fired into a crowd of strikers at the McCormick Harvester plant, labor leaders organized a protest meeting at the Haymarket. A bomb was thrown among the police who came to the meeting, and the police opened fire. Eight anarchists were convicted of conspiracy for murder, although little evidence connected them to the bomb.

During the depression of 1893–94, workers in Pullman, Illinois—who built railroad cars—went on strike over wage cuts. The strike became national when the American Railway Union agreed to support the Pullman workers. Eugene V. Debs, the leader of the American Railway Union, converted to socialism while in jail during the Pullman strike. Debs emerged from prison determined to change the economic system. A Hoosier, Debs pioneered an indigenous, American version of socialism, but socialism still was too radical and—despite Debs—too foreign for most Midwesterners.

Industrial workers were not the only people turning to organization to resolve their economic difficulties. Farmers also adopted cooperative arrangements, such as those offered by the Patrons of Husbandry (also known as the Grange) or the Farmers' Alliance. The Granger laws, aimed at regulating the railroads on which farmers relied, were passed in many states. The Farmers' Alliance, which began in Texas, took hold in the Midwest with a program of cooperative marketing and proposals for a government-run subtreasury that was intended to expand the money supply. Unable to achieve these reforms through the two-party system, the Alliance turned to political action with the creation of the Populist Party in 1892. It was the strength of the Populists in Kansas that provoked White to pose the question "What's the Matter with Kansas?" for the first time. However, the Populists' venture as a third party was short-lived: when they decided to fuse with the Democrats in

1896, they lost both the election and their identity as an influential party.

But Midwestern radicalism did not expire with the demise of the Populists. Before World War I, North Dakota farmers responded to the monopoly practices of grain elevators and railroads by forming the Non-Partisan League. Radicalism spread to other parts of the Midwest, where the Farmer-Labor party allied farmers with miners and industrial workers. During the war, the party lost power because adherents were accused of being pro-German.

A reactionary movement saw surprising growth in parts of the Midwest with the rise of the Ku Klux Klan in the 1920s; this second Klan movement was as much anti-immigrant and anti-Catholic as it was antiblack. Klansmen, ostensibly representing moral rectitude and Americanism, enforced the vice laws, such as Prohibition, that immigrants often flouted. The Klan reached its apex of political power in Indiana, where the governor had ties to the group. Ironically, the Indiana Klan collapsed under the weight of a sex scandal when its leader kidnapped and raped a young woman who then committed suicide.

The Klan was one manifestation of another side of Midwestern politics. In contrast to the discontent and push for reform demonstrated by farmers and laborers, there were powerful impulses of conformity. The pioneering sociological study by Robert S. Lynd and Helen Merrell Lynd, *Middletown*, found the Klan to be an offshoot of that impulse. Muncie, Indiana—the site of *Middletown*—possessed a business class that promoted civic boosterism, local and national patriotism, and encouraged voting a straight ticket. In this environment, citizens knew less and less about their candidates and their local government. Peer pressure kept those who might dissent from the local ethic quiet. In Middletown, the emphasis was on "getting a living," not on political activism.

While the Midwest saw much protest against the emerging industrial-capitalist order, it also saw the rise of powerful conservatives who were part of that order. William McKinley, the Ohio Republican who concentrated on tariff reform, was bankrolled by Mark Hanna, the epitome for many in the Progressive Era of the money bag–carrying plutocrat. Herbert Hoover, a self-made man, championed a philosophy of "rugged individualism." Conservative or so-called Bourbon Democrats, such as J. Sterling Morton of Nebraska, were more comfortable with industrialization than their Populist-oriented counterparts. In some parts of the Midwest, a more symbiotic than antagonistic relationship existed between farm and factory. Midwestern industrial centers such as Chicago and Omaha, Nebraska, provided markets for farmers' output.

The Midwestern protest tradition reasserted itself during the Great Depression. The Farm Holiday Association dramatized the plight of farmers through farm strikes and by pouring milk onto roads in an attempt to raise its price. President Franklin D. Roosevelt's New Deal brought Midwestern farmers the Agricultural Adjustment Act, which paid farmers not to plant and formed the basis of much modern farm policy. The American Farm Bureau emerged as spokesman for the farm interest. Although its roots were in the cooperative movements of the nineteenth century, it came to represent the farmer as small businessman. The Farm Bureau became a powerful lobbying force, closely allied to the Farm Bloc—congressmen and senators from farm states who have a major say in agricultural policy. The New Deal thus turned agrarian activism in a more conservative direction.

The Great Depression also renewed labor activism, which had been crushed by government suppression during and after World War I, and had remained dormant during the affluence of the 1920s. Flint, Michigan, home to a General Motors factory, became the site of a major sit-down strike that inspired similar labor actions across the country. Through such strikes, and New Deal legislation, labor won the right to organize.

World War II brought prosperity that continued into the postwar period, and that prosperity brought increased conservatism. As white workers could afford a middle-class income, they became increasingly concerned with rising taxes that redistributed income to the poor and to African Americans. By the 1980s, they became known as Reagan Democrats, traditionally working-class Democratic voters who voted for Republican Ronald Reagan because they liked his antitax stance and anticommunism. Ironically, the emergence of Reagan Democrats coincided with the decline of industry and working-class affluence. Filmmaker Michael Moore caught the emergence of the Rust Belt in *Roger & Me*, a profile of Flint's decline as General Motors closed its plants there. Industry's decline crippled labor's political power.

Liberals and Conservatives

During the post–World War II period, the Midwest was home to both a vibrant liberalism and a rising conservatism. Iowan Henry A. Wallace, who had a long career as secretary of agriculture under President Franklin D. Roosevelt and then as his vice president, would run for president himself in 1948 as the candidate of the left-wing Progressive Party. Conservatism would see its triumph with the election of Illinois-born Ronald Reagan in 1980.

Some of the best-known national spokesmen for postwar liberalism were from the Midwest. Throughout his long career as mayor of Minneapolis, senator from Minnesota, vice president, and presidential candidate, Hubert Humphrey worked for the ideals of the New Deal and the Great Society, a social safety net, and civil rights. Humphrey, along with the 1972 Democratic presidential candidate, South Dakota senator George McGovern, embodied the big-government liberalism that conservatives attacked. In addition, McGovern was identified with a youth movement that wanted to legalize marijuana and end the Vietnam War.

The student movement had its birth in the Midwest with the Port Huron Statement, which was issued by Students for a Democratic Society (SDS) in 1962. With roots in the Old Left, SDS initially focused on civil rights but quickly moved to antiwar protest. Student rallies against the Vietnam War at campuses throughout the country became a hallmark of the era. On May 4, 1970, a protest at Kent State University in Ohio turned deadly when National Guardsmen fired on protesters and bystanders, killing four and wounding several others.

At the same time, the Midwest was home to much dissatisfaction with the direction of liberalism. The cold war's animus toward radicals undermined progressivism in the Midwest. Senator Robert Taft of Ohio, known as "Mr. Republican," viewed government as the source of oppression not social welfare. He not only opposed the New Deal but also voted against U.S. entry into the North American Treaty Organization. Taft's fellow senator, Joseph McCarthy of Wisconsin, gave his name to the era's anti-Communist preoccupations, making exaggerated charges of Communist infiltration into the federal government and the Hollywood entertainment industry. One manifestation of the New Right was the John Birch Society, founded in Indianapolis in 1958, which advanced theories of left-wing subversion and claimed, for a time, that President Dwight Eisenhower was a Communist.

Although the "Birchers" might be dismissed as cranks, the conservative ideals of small government and anticommunism went mainstream with the election of Ronald Reagan in 1980. Although Reagan built his political career in California, he always acknowledged his Midwestern upbringing as key to his individualistic values. As president, he presided over major tax cuts, a military buildup, and cuts in social welfare programs. Many Midwestern politicians carried out Reagan's philosophy at the state level. Governor Tommy Thompson of Wisconsin, for example, became nationally known for innovative conservative stands on welfare reform, for support of school choice and voucher programs, and for using the line-item veto—a power Reagan continually lamented the president lacked—to cut state spending.

As the history of the Midwest in the period after World War II reveals, it is a misconception to see the region as monolithically liberal or conservative. Just as the famous 1896 presidential election pit William McKinley of Ohio against William Jennings Bryan of Nebraska, who were styled as standard-bearers of money power versus the people, respectively, late-twentieth-century elections have featured Midwesterners of very different viewpoints. The witty Adlai Stevenson, governor of Illinois and defender of liberal "eggheads," was twice defeated for the presidency by Dwight D. Eisenhower of Kansas. In 1984 Ronald Reagan defeated a protégé of Hubert Humphrey, Minnesota's Walter Mondale, who crippled his chances by pledging to raise taxes.

In addition, Midwestern politics is still capable of producing its share of candidates who are not easily categorized. Former independent Minnesota governor—and former professional wrestler—Jesse Ventura supported tax rebates when the state was running a surplus, but vetoed a bill to promote recitation of the Pledge of Allegiance in public schools—a key test of patriotism for many conservatives in the 1990s.

Once a stronghold of Republican "red states," electoral maps of the Midwest offer only a superficial understanding of political divisions. Since World War II, Indiana usually voted Republican for president, but Minnesota was a Democratic stronghold. At the turn of the twenty-first century, the region became increasingly competitive. Minnesota, Michigan, and Ohio were battlegrounds during the 2000 and 2004 elections. In the Midwest, Democratic U.S. Senate candidates were successful almost two-thirds of the time in the last third of the twentieth century, while House of Representative seats split fairly evenly between the two parties. In the 2008 presidential primary race, two of the leading Democratic candidates, Barack Obama and Hillary Clinton, had ties to Illinois, while Republican candidate Mitt Romney originally hailed from Michigan. In addition, the Midwest still plays a crucial role in selecting candidates via the primary and caucus system. Iowa, by virtue of its first-in-the-nation place in the presidential selection process, has a disproportionate say in picking the major party nominees.

Indiana, which had not given its electoral vote to a Democrat since 1964, went for Obama in 2008. This deviation from its staunchly Republican record may be temporary. It remains to be seen whether Obama will emphasize pragmatism or progressivism, but the election of the first Midwestern president in a generation reaffirms the centrality of the region in the nation's politics.

See also Great Plains; Rocky Mountain region.

FURTHER READING. John D. Barnhart, *Valley of Democracy: The Frontier versus the Plantation in the Ohio Valley, 1775–1818,* 1953; William C. Berman, *America's Right Turn: From Nixon to Clinton,* 1998; Allen F. Davis, *Spearheads for Reform: The Social Settlements and the Progressive Movement,* 1967; Thomas Frank, *What's the Matter with Kansas? How Conservatives Won the Heart of America,* 2004; Lawrence Goodwyn, *The Populist Moment; A Short History of the Agrarian Revolt in America,* 1978; R. Douglas Hurt, *American Agriculture: A Brief History,* 1994; Paul Kleppner, *The Cross of Culture: A Social Analysis of Midwestern Politics, 1850–1900,* 1970; Robert S. Lynd and Helen Merrell Lynd, *Middletown: A Study in American Culture,* 1929; James H. Madison, ed., *Heartland: Comparative Histories of the Midwestern States,* 1988; Stephen Middleton, *Race and the Legal Process in Early Ohio,* 2005; Peter S. Onuf, *Statehood and Union: A History of the Northwest Ordinance,* 1987; Richard White, *The Middle Ground: Indians, Empires, and Republics in the Great Lakes Region, 1650–1815,* 1991.

NICOLE ETCHESON

nativism

Fear of "the other," of minority groups seen as alien peoples threatening a dominant population, is present in many lands. *Nativism* is the term used to describe this hostile view of such alleged outsiders. Scholars have identified nativist movements in Nigeria and Australia, Japan and Brazil, Iran, China, Zimbabwe, and across the planet and history. But it is in the United States that the term emerged, and it is there that nativism has had it most profound impact. This should not be surprising, for the United States is the world's preeminent example of a great multiethnic, multireligious, multiracial society. It is the continent-sized "land of immigrants," a democracy that for much of its history has been the great magnet for those seeking a better life in a New World. And so inevitably it also has been the setting for resistance to these waves of newcomers, seen as incapable of being assimilated, as destructive and dangerous to the stable order created by the heirs of the earlier settlers, the "real Americans."

These real Americans, of course, were not Native Americans, dismissed by the first nativists as primitives, aboriginal peoples who must be pushed aside and later fit only for reservations. Native Americans were seen as racial inferiors, a breed apart. Certainly this was also true—and most profoundly the case—with African slaves and their heirs. Surely, African Americans, Native Americans (and some other "people of color") would be the objects of particular fear and contempt across history. They would be the victims of racism. And racism, while linked to nativism, has had its own peculiar characteristics and chronology in the story of America.

But so powerful has been the heritage of racism in this nation that some recent historians have suggested that nativism should be seen only as a relatively minor subtext of the racist past. The objects of nativist animus, it is argued, needed only to calculate how they could use America's real hatred of the feared "other," racism, to overcome their own ethnic and/or religious outsider status. Thus, there are works that describe how the Irish, the Italians, or the Jews "became white." But these works, while useful correctives to simplistic explanations concerning the fate of anti-alien movements, can be misleading if used to denigrate the enormous impact of nativist attitudes and nativist actions on millions of Americans across much of the nation's history. Such attitudes and actions darkened the lives of Catholics for centuries. They also created severe obstacles to social, economic, and political mobility for Irish, Italian, Jewish, and Slavic immigrants—and their descendents—for generations.

Nativism became the dark underbelly of the American dream of equality and opportunity beckoning immigrants to the New World. Yet it was the decline of nativism—at least in the ways it affected the lives of the Catholic and Jewish white ethnic groups who were traditional objects of such hatred—that can offer encouragement, not only for those groups still victimized and marginalized in American society but also for such groups in other nations troubled by religious, ethnic, and racial hostilities.

American nativism, which one scholar has defined as "the intense opposition to an internal minority on the grounds of its allegedly un-American characteristics," affected not only the lives of its victims but also of the victimizers, the nativists. By attacking the "other," some people were able to identify themselves by what they were not; the alien enemy was crucial to their self-image. The common foe, the "un-Americans" in their midst, allowed many anti-aliens to find community, for in polarization there was bonding. Here was a way to overcome other differences inside the favored circle of "real" Americans, people who did not carry the mark of religious or ethnic inferiority. Moreover, by projecting or displacing anger and hatred on the enemy within, nativists could more easily deal with the tragic dissonances in their own lives and in their moment in history.

Yet to view nativism only as a psychological crutch for hostile bullies and unexamined bigots does an injustice to the complexity of this American story. Many anti-aliens perceived real threats to the health and comity of their national community. The newcomers brought wrenching social and economic problems to the New World. Many nativists seriously grappled with the question of what it meant to be an American, and their fears were not merely the product of arrogance, ignorance, and hatred. The history of nativism in America is a complex story that begins with the very dawn of white settlement in the New World.

In Colonial America

The earliest targets of anti-alien hostility were Roman Catholics. Anti-Catholicism was widespread in England for decades before the first colonists arrived in America. It was the product of the rival imperial ambitions of Catholic Spain and France and was a continuous feature of English society across the late sixteenth and seventeenth centuries, after the Elizabethan Acts of Supremacy and Uniformity had put the kingdom permanently in the Protestant camp. The colonists arrived in the wilderness across the ocean having spent their lives with "no-Popery" laws proscribing the role of Catholics.

Particularly in the Massachusetts Bay Colony, where Calvinists would build a "city upon a hill," the goal was a church "purged of Romish corruptions." Catholicism was a destructive element that threatened "God's American Israel." These settlers had despised the Anglican Church because they saw it as a mirror image of the Church of Rome.

In the seventeenth century, the Catholic mass could not be celebrated anywhere except Pennsylvania. All Englishmen save Roman Catholics enjoyed the franchise in several colonies, and there were repeated anti-Catholic demonstrations in many places. In the Bay Colony, Catholics were banished and priests returned only on pain of execution. Even Roger Williams, founder of Rhode Island, the great enemy of religious persecution and the man who had demanded freedom of worship for Quakers, conducted his dispute with Puritan divines of Massachusetts in the terminology of antipapal hatred, writing of the "Romish wolf gorging herself with huge bowls of the blood of saints."

There was no toleration for Catholics in colonial America, and the eighteenth century brought new assaults on religious freedom. In Maryland, founded by a Catholic who had encouraged Catholic settlement before the proprietor's charter was voided and it became another royal colony with an established Anglican church, the governor in 1704 assailed the "Irish Papists" and their "false . . . superstitious worship." In New England, Elisha Williams, a famously learned figure who had supported religious conscience, wrote of "the Pope, who has deluged the Earth with the Blood of Christians and is the most detestable Monster the Earth ever had upon it."

In a land where wars against France and Spain had led to rumors of Catholic conspiracy, the papist was seen as an enemy agent. Nativism became firmly rooted in the conventional wisdom. In communities where children learned to write by use of rhymed couplets beginning with the letter "A," public school primers instructed them to "abhor that arrant Whore of Rome and all her Blasphemies." "Pope Night" festivals showed how the Devil was aligned with the Catholics. Fireside games bore such names as "Break the Pope's Kneck."

It was bizarre that so many felt so threatened by such a tiny minority. There were fewer than 35,000 Roman Catholics, half of them in Maryland, among the 3 million Americans at the end of the colonial period.

But the coming of the Revolution ameliorated the hostility. If anti-Catholic activism in the colonial era served to unite a disparate people, creating a sense of community in a vast and threatening continent, the conflict with England suddenly made all this counterproductive. The Revolution was a great unifying force for "true" patriots; the test of loyalty was whether one supported the new government or the Crown, not whether one practiced Catholicism or some other

"false" religion. General George Washington quashed the Pope Day festivals in 1775.

In fact, success in the Revolutionary War seemed to signal an end to anti-Catholic nativism. In 1790 President Washington told clerical and lay leaders in Maryland that he believed America would become an example to the nations of the world in advancing justice and freedom, noting that "your fellow-citizens will not forget the patriotic part which you took in the accomplishment of their Revolution and the establishment of their Government, or the important assistance which they received from a nation [France] in which the Roman Catholic faith is professed." But it was not to be. The next century would bring the most intense nativist activities in American history.

Nineteenth-Century America:
Immigration Leads to Nativism

In the period just after the birth of the new United States and through the depression of 1819, immigration to the new nation remained relatively low. But by 1830 conditions had changed. At least 60,000 foreigners a year arrived through the mid-1830s and the numbers escalated in the early 1840s. By 1840 there 660,000 Roman Catholics in the United States, and this number tripled in the next decade. More than a third of the new arrivals were from Ireland.

The newcomers arrived in an expanding nation undergoing political and social upheaval. The Jacksonian era was a time of opportunity but also a disorienting one. In grappling with its challenges, many sought community in zealous new Protestant groups caught up in the revivalism of the age. Soon, anti-Catholic newspapers proliferated, with such titles as *Anti-Romanist, Priestcraft Unmasked,* and *Downfall of Babylon, or Triumph of Truth over Popery.* The fear was that Catholics could not be citizens of a democracy because they owed fealty to a foreign sovereign, the "Pope in Rome."

There were widespread clashes between Protestant and Catholic, native and "foreigner." In 1834 the imposing brick Ursuline Convent in Charlestown, Massachusetts, was attacked by an angry mob of Protestant workmen shouting anti-Catholic slogans; furniture was smashed and the vast building sacked and set aflame. The convent burners were acquitted. In New York City, Protestant gangs—the True Blue Americans, the American Guards—fought street battles with Irish rivals.

In these years, Samuel F. B. Morse, inventor of the telegraph, wrote two books warning of an international conspiracy by European Catholics to infiltrate Jesuits into the trans-Mississippi region, with plans to annex the land and deny America expansion to the west. Meanwhile, publications in the East printed Catholic immigration statistics, sounding alarm at an influx of foreign criminals and paupers.

Catholic priests and nuns—such as those in the Ursuline Convent—were seen as particularly despicable deviants, as sadists and murderers. In 1836 a slim volume published in New York became an immediate sensation, the best-selling book in American history (save the Bible) until *Uncle Tom's Cabin. The Awful Disclosures of Maria Monk* purported to tell the story of a Protestant girl converted to Catholicism and, after entering a convent, brutally abused by nuns and priests. The work sold 300,000 copies and, with its explicit detail of torture and sexual assault, became a classic in pornographic literature. Yet it was only one of a growing number of "convent books" with similar messages printed during the nineteenth century. And its fabricated tales were widely believed. When nativists gained control of the Massachusetts legislature in the succeeding years, their "nunnery committee" demanded access to convents, digging up cellars in hopes of locating the bleaching bones of babies who had been killed and buried following the rapes of innocent girls by Jesuits secretly brought to the convents by evil nuns.

In this context, nativist party organizations emerged to check the power of the newcomers. The American Republican Party's leaders talked of election fraud, voting by noncitizens, corrupt political machines manipulating the votes of credulous, dull-witted Irish Catholics. When the issue became the "school controversy," that perennial nativist fear of new parochial schools educating children in a doctrine imposed by "a foreign ecclesiastical power," the party played a major role in an 1845 Fourth of July confrontation in Philadelphia. Thousands of nativists clashed with groups of Irish laborers and fire brigades; buildings were set ablaze, cannons exchanged fire, and the city was ravaged by intergroup violence.

All this occurred months before the huge wave of Irish immigration that began in 1847. It was in that year that the Great Famine—the failure of the potato crop, with its devastating impact on millions in Ireland and Europe—sent a huge wave of starving Irish immigrants to America. In 1844 there were 75,000 immigrants; in 1847 the number swelled to 234,000, and by 1851 it reached 380,000. In an eight-year period, 2.75 million newcomers arrived, the vast majority of them Roman Catholic. While many came from Germany, most were from Ireland. And they brought with them what the nativists saw as critical and dangerous social problems.

There was some substance to nativist concerns. The immigrants arrived at port cities in the Northeast in desperate straits. The vessels were filled with the sick and the dying—victims of "ship fever" (a form of typhus), smallpox, cholera, and dysentery. Epidemics erupted in all ports of disembarkation, and quarantine hospitals had to be financed. Most newcomers were postfeudal peasants, people who knew only farming and lacked the capital or skills to head west; they found themselves housed in some of the first (and worst) slums in the history of urban America.

In New York City, Boston, Philadelphia, and other communities where the immigrants settled, crime rates immediately escalated (half of those arrested in New York by 1850 were of Irish ancestry) and state penal institutions had to be expanded. The number of "paupers"—those in need of "pecuniary assistance" or refuge in almshouses—grew apace and there was a striking rise in the number of "truant and vagabond children." *The Report on Insanity and Idiocy in Massachusetts* charted a huge increase of "foreign lunatics" in state asylums. And everywhere the new immigrants settled, the number of "gin houses" and arrests for public drunkenness skyrocketed.

Nativists clearly linked the social problems of the immigrant ethnic group to their ancient fears of religious difference. Irish Catholics were seen as a cancer in the New World. They were penniless alien intruders, sick, drunk, violent, and dangerous. They had come to steal American jobs and bring dirt and chaos to communities. An ignorant and illiterate mob of fist-fighting thugs, the Irish were aggressive and clannish and would stay that way because they were controlled by priests who opposed the public school system.

The response was the creation of new nativist organizations. A series of secret societies were shaped, and from one—the Organization of the Star Spangled Banner—a new political party emerged, bearing a name "real Americans" could rally to: the American Party. But so fearful were its leaders of the secret power of "Jesuitical conspirators" that members were instructed to say "I Know Nothing" if asked about the party.

Because this was the critical decade in which the slavery issue would rip apart so many American institutions, including mainline Protestant churches and the major political parties, the Know-Nothing Party would gain in strength beyond the appeal of its potent nativist rhetoric. As the Whig Party was sundered into northern and southern factions and the Democrats were stretched to the breaking point, many political leaders and members of the older organizations found refuge in a new party insisting that the real division in America was not between those who differed on the questions of free soil and abolition but on the threat of alien immigrants.

The Know-Nothings were briefly the second largest political party in America, their presidential candidate a formidable contender in 1856. But the growth was an illusion. Soon the Know-Nothing Party was split apart by the same intractable forces dividing the nation North and South. By 1860 the party had appeal only in some border states. Fear of the alien "other" had enormous impact in the 1850s, but the great crisis that led to the Civil War swept everything aside—including nativism.

As the Civil War neared its end, Abraham Lincoln, no friend of the nativists, seemed to promise the immigrant Catholic population what Washington had at the conclusion of the Revolutionary War. Perhaps anti-alien hostility would soon fade away. But, as in decades past, nativism would find new life in the years following a great and unifying struggle.

Once again, a floodtide of new immigrants stimulated nativist activism. From 1870 to the middle of the next decade, new settlers headed to a booming, postwar America. Most newcomers were from familiar locales, including large numbers from Germany and Ireland. But by 1887 the "new immigration" began, and by 1900, southeastern European émigrés were by far the dominant element in the huge waves transforming the nation. Three-quarters of the almost 450,000 arrivals in 1900 were from Italy, the Russian Empire, or Austria-Hungary (the Hapsburg Monarchy); by 1907 of the 1.2 million immigrants, 285,000 were from Italy, 258,000 from Russia, 338,000 from the Hapsburg Monarchy—many of them south Slavs or Jews. Between 1880 and 1915, when the Great War in Europe arrested the process, more than 20 million had arrived, the majority "new immigrants." Most were Catholics, many were Jewish, and few spoke English. They represented almost a quarter of the population of a nation that had doubled in size from 50 million to 100 million in those years.

Violent resistance to newcomers flared in some areas. In California, fear of the "Yellow Peril" marked anti-Chinese and anti-Japanese activism. But the émigrés from Asia were a tiny population compared to those arriving from southeastern Europe and settling in the East and Midwest. These new immigrants became the target of hostility by intellectual and social elites as well by as the ordinary folk—merchants, laborers, small farmers—who were the traditional members of anti-alien groups.

Princeton professor Woodrow Wilson contrasted the "men of the sturdy stocks of the north of Europe" with the "more sordid and hopeless elements which the south of Europe was disburdening . . . men out of the ranks where there was neither skill nor energy nor quick intelligence." Other major academic and political figures, some of whom would become leaders of the Progressive movement, shared his contempt. Stanford professor E. A. Ross wrote of "their pigsty mode of life, their brawls and criminal pleasures, their coarse, peasant philosophy of sex." One writer noted that Italians were "largely composed . . . of the most vicious, ignorant, degraded and filthy paupers with an admixture of the criminal element . . . the lowest Irish are far above these creatures." Other prominent writers described Jews as "dirty, bearded, lecherous, foreign degenerates"; this "squat Slavonic" people were "pushy, money-grubbing materialists."

With the huge numbers of new immigrants came poverty, crime, and teeming urban slums—and renewed interest in nativist fraternal organizations. Dozens of anti-alien associations were organized, with such names as Patriotic Order of the Sons of America, the American Patriotic League, the Red, White and Blue Organization, and United Organization of the Pilgrim Fathers. Some had were little more than a few passionate activists, but many had growing memberships and boasted dozens or even hundreds of chapters. One organizaion, the American Protective Association (APA), would become a national phenomenon.

Founded in a small Iowa railroad and mill town in 1887, the APA was created to combat "political Romanism." As it grew through the 1890s, it continued to focus on anti-Catholic themes but also assailed, in the words of one of its publications, the "pauper and criminal riffraff of Europe . . . every ignorant Dago and Pole, Hun and Slav." APA writers warned of the "Jews who have been brought in to wage war with Rome against America and Americans."

The APA—and the other nativist sects—lost members and influence after 1896. New political and social forces were stirring across the land: the Populist movement and progressive reformers in state and local government as well as in the media. Populism, with its concern for the struggle against predatory economic interests, created a dramatic new cause that made the anti-alien crusade suddenly seem much less significant. Its emergence helped ensure that the APA and the entire resurgent nativism of the post–Civil War era—which never enjoyed the political success of the Know-Nothings—would pass into history.

Although the Populist Party declined in the late 1890s, with the Progressive movement dominating the national scene in the first decade and a half of the new century, it would be a generation before even a modest revival of nativism occurred.

Into the Twentieth Century

The most notable progressive leaders, including presidents Theodore Roosevelt and Woodrow Wilson, believed in the natural superiority of Teutonic, Anglo-Saxon people. They accepted the fashionable views of European writers like Count Gobineau and Houston Stuart Chamberlain as well as the American Madison Grant, who insisted on the inferiority of those "degraded savages" who had arrived at nineteenth-century immigration stations. But the reform agenda of the Progressive movement, with its goal of adjusting capitalism to democracy after the excesses of industrial expansion, made nativism seem irrelevant.

World War I changed that. When America entered the Great War on the side of the Allies in 1917, German Americans suffered. Before the Civil War, it had been Irish, not German, immigrants who were the central focus of the most virulent anti-alien activity. Now, German Americans were accused of poisoning food, spoiling medical supplies, and undermining public support for the war effort. German names were changed, German dishes disappeared from restaurants, German-language newspapers were burned in the streets. Private "patriotic" groups, the Knights of Liberty and the American Protective League, played a role in the harassment of German Americans.

The end of the war in November 1918 brought an end to much of this hysteria. But 1919 was a time of social upheaval in America. Postwar inflation led to massive strikes and brutal repression by corporate managers, some of whom blamed "these foreigners" for the widespread labor unrest. The Bolshevik Revolution in Russia had rekindled fears of radical activists and when a series of anarchist bombs were discovered, the "Red Scare" led to wholesale violations of civil liberties. With President Wilson disabled by a stroke, hundreds of alleged "un-Americans" were arrested in Palmer Raids, named after the attorney general, A. Mitchell Palmer. Palmer, defending his action in an article entitled "Where Do the Reds Come From? Chiefly Imported and So Are Their Red Theories," pointed to the new immigrants from southeastern Europe, "these aliens, not of our sort," particularly a "small clique of autocrats from the East Side of New York." He was referring, of course, to Jewish radicals.

The Red Scare was over by the summer of 1920. Labor unrest receded and the postwar era boom would soon be underway. But nativism did not disappear in the Roaring Twenties. Across much of the decade, anti-Jewish rhetoric was found in the pages of the *Dearborn Independent*, the newspaper purchased by billionaire auto pioneer Henry Ford, a fanatical anti-Semite. Ford's efforts had limited impact; the major nativist development in the 1920s was the growth of the Ku Klux Klan.

The modern Klan, founded in 1915 by fraternal organizer William J. Simmons, had little to do with the post–Civil War Ku Klux Klan (KKK), whose hooded vigilantes repressed black freedmen and helped to restore native white supremacy in the South. After a period of slow growth and little interest, this new Klan grew to enormous size in the 1920s.

Simmons soon lost control of the organization to shrewder promoters. The KKK prospered as an anti-Catholic, anti-Semitic, and anti-ethnic immigrant crusade. Using the white garb and the bizarre titles of the old Klan (the magical "K" for ranks such as Klud, Kluxter, Klabee), the organization soon spread across America. It had strength in the South, but it was stronger still in the Midwest and had many active chapters in several western states as well as some urban areas in the Northeast. The Klan left fragmentary local records and no national archives; estimates of its total membership at the high point of its meteoric rise range from 2.5 to 5 million.

The Klan offered community to many left behind or left out in the boom years of the Roaring Twenties. It was a fraternal movement that sponsored picnics, ballgames, and "konklaves" for the like-minded. It attacked the decline of traditional values in the "modern Sodoms and Gomorrahs" that were the skyscraper cities of the new age, and assailed the immigrant drinking masses violating Prohibition and the urban elites with their depraved sexual practices. The old convent tales found a new readership. Hiram Wesley Evans, the imperial wizard, explained: "We are a movement of the plain people . . . we demand a return to power of the everyday, not highly cultured, not overly intellectualized but entirely unspoiled and not de-Americanized average citizens of the old stock."

There were only a few notable instances of repressive violence involving this KKK. While it had a powerful political presence in some areas and played a role in checking the early presidential aspirations of Al Smith (a Catholic who was governor of New York), the Klan had limited political influence on the national scene. But it attracted many ambitious and unsavory figures, men who saw in it a road to wealth and influence. And it disappeared rapidly after allegations of corruption in some states weakened its appeal. The final blow was a sex scandal involving the most powerful Klan state leader (in Indiana) in mid-decade, which put a lie to the organization's defense of traditional family values. After the Klan's collapse, no powerful new nativist movements would emerge in the twentieth century.

The Decline of Nativism

The Great Depression was not a fertile ground for nativism. Extremist groups that offered to save Americans facing economic ruin by emulating the work of European Fascists, blaming Jews and foreigners for the crisis, attracted only tiny followings.

Then, during World War II and the postwar era, nativism in America seemed to fade away. What explains its decline? The first important factor was the end of unlimited immigration. Since a series of congressional actions passed from 1917 to 1924, over a generation had passed in which the golden door was essentially closed. Millions of newcomers no longer arrived yearly, with their poverty and language difficulties. Earlier arrivals had settled in, and many were beginning to achieve mobility and realization of their own American success story. As assimilation proceeded, the reasons for anti-alien movements withered away.

President Franklin D. Roosevelt also played a key role. He shrewdly appealed to groups that had been victimized in the past by nativists, offering support and political patronage in the difficult Depression decade. It was the "Roosevelt coalition," embracing Catholics, Jews, and a variety of former immigrant subcultures, that not only empowered ethnic political constituencies and "minority" religious groups but celebrated the glories of the melting pot.

The programs of Roosevelt's administration also helped to bury the old hatreds. In earlier eras, the anxieties and dislocations accompanying economic and social upheaval had led many to displace or project their anger onto "the aliens," symbolic scapegoats for the troubles of the moment, the New Deal insisted it was not villains but the vagaries of the capitalist system that had placed so many at economic risk. There was no need this time to blame Catholics or Jews, Irish, Italians, or Asians for the crisis; strong federal policies would save America.

There were also other factors at work. In the prewar decade, the menace of Hitler helped discredit fashionable racial theories that had influenced elites and others in previous years. The work of a new generation of influential academics, led by anthropologist Franz Boas, assailed the "scientific" racism of Gobineau, Grant, and others. In a series of resolutions passed at national meetings of sociologists, psychologists, and biologists as well as anthropologists, racist ideologies were reviled by a vast cross section of scientific professionals. They demolished the argument that certain people were destined to be inferior, that Anglo-Saxons were intellectually superior, that there were "racial" cultures or racial "moralities." By the 1940s, nativist ideas could no longer be defended in rational discourse.

Another critical factor in the decline of nativism was the impact of World War II. Not only was the war a bonding experience for many Americans, but it also provided a full-employment boom during the conflict and the setting for postwar prosperity, removing some of the economic anxieties in which the old anti-alienism had taken root. More important, perhaps, the war marked the accelerated growth of a more complex business and professional culture that had been emerging in America for years before Pearl Harbor.

Significant changes transformed finance, marketing, law, medicine, advertising, and other specialized fields. Large corporations increasingly were directed not by the risk-taking entrepreneurs who had given them birth but by a new class of managers trained and certified to handle complex problems of a new age. In the war—when it was essential to get the job done right—and in the postwar era, a person's occupational credentials, not religion or ethnicity, increasingly became the central variable in judging acceptability. Skills, not culture, became the standard of admission to elites. And the G.I. Bill allowed many to move more quickly on the path to such status.

The toleration of ethnic diversity widened as strict professional rules took hold. Making it in America more and more became a matter of not who you were but how skilled and educated you appeared to be. In a new age of access and opportunity after the war, barriers to entry into elite colleges and professional schools weakened. Opinion leaders turned to pluralism in their definition of success. Ethnic difference soon seemed to be disappearing everywhere. In food and clothing, in language and even religion, distinctions were blurred and the old animus seemed out of place, even un-American. As the twentieth century neared its conclusion, nativism had all but disappeared. But in the next decade, some would argue it found renewed life in a time of terrorist threats and a new wave of immigration.

Toward a New Millenium: A Return of Nativism?

In the last years of the twentieth century, a few extremist sects with miniscule membership continued to focus on the old hatreds. There were fragmentary Klan chapters, unconnected to the great Klan of the 1920s. Christian identity groups such as Aryan Nations and the Order viewed Jews as children of the Devil who dominated the nation through a Zionist Occupied Government. Their rhetoric had only marginal impact, and only in a few remote areas.

Nativist-inspired restrictions on immigration, in place for over 40 years, were finally eliminated in 1965, with the abolition of the national origins quota system that created overt discrimination against Asian immigrants and a historic preference for western Europeans. But then large numbers of illegal aliens arrived in the 1970s and 1980s, and there were efforts to arrest this flow. Opponents of such modest but restrictive legislation characterized it as grossly nativistic, inspired by "the spirit of the Know-Nothings." However, even large numbers of Hispanic Americans supported the successful passage of the Simpson-Rodino Act in 1986, which sought—unsuccessfully—to deal with illegal immigration through employer sanctions.

Into the new millennium, nativist animus seemed a thing of the past. But the 2001 terrorist attack on 9/11 was followed by the U.S. Patriot Act. New immigration restrictions were put in place. Some Muslim Americans complained of harassment by law enforcement agencies. There were reports that Muslim men and women had been insulted and shunned in the weeks following the attack. Still, with an unpopular war in Iraq dragging on for over five years, and no further terrorist incidents in the United States during this period, fear of widespread anti-Muslim discrimination waned.

Yet, at the same time, there was renewed debate about undocumented aliens. Early in 2008, with the numbers of such immigrants in the nation reaching over 12 million, with thousands of people from Asia, Central America, and—most significantly—from Mexico illegally crossing the southern border daily, immigration became a major political issue. Certain media commentators and members of Congress used inflammatory nativist rhetoric. But many who endorsed immigration restriction avoided and condemned such arguments. Some of the old fears mixed with new concerns: newcomers had broken the law, had not waited to be included in an immigration quota, would not be assimilated and insisted on speaking Spanish, were stealing American jobs, and were illegally using services provided by U.S. taxpayers.

Of course, there were powerful counterarguments by those calling for immigration reform that would not result in draconian sanctions on those already in the United States. And, during the 2008 election campaign, the immigration issue was eclipsed by other concerns. Even the brief touch of nativist rhetoric disappeared from public debate. Nativism, it seemed, was no longer a meaningful issue in America.

See also immigration policy.

FURTHER READING. David H. Bennett, *The Party of Fear: The American Far Right from Nativism to the Militia Movement*, 2nd ed., 1995; Ray Allen Billington, *The Protestant Crusade, 1800–1860*, 1964; Karen Brodkin, *How Jews Became White Folks*, 1998; Gary Gerstle, *American Crucible: Race and Nation in the Twentieth Century*, 2001; John Higham, *Strangers in the Land: Patterns of American Nativism, 1860–1925*, 2nd ed., 1963; Noel Ignatiev, *How the Irish Became White*, 1995; David R. Roediger, *The Wages of Whiteness*, 1991.

DAVID H. BENNETT

New Deal Era, 1932–52

By 1932 the United States was in the third year of the worst economic depression in its history. Industrial production stood at half the level of 1929. Nearly one in four Americans was unemployed. For those lucky enough to still be employed, average weekly earnings dropped from $25 to $15. Under such circumstances, the outcome of the 1932 presidential election was never in serious doubt: voters would hold the party in power responsible for the economic debacle. On Election Day, the Democratic challenger, New York State governor Franklin D. Roosevelt, handily defeated the incumbent Republican in the White House, Herbert Hoover, with 57.4 percent of the popular vote and the electoral votes of 42 of the 48 states. The previous summer, accepting the nomination for the presidency, Roosevelt had pledged to his audience to devote his administration to securing "a new deal for the American people." But what a "New Deal" would mean in practice was something neither the voters nor even the candidate himself had a very clear idea of on Election Day.

A Crisis of Abundance

The New Deal is often associated with the ideas of British economist John Maynard Keynes, who in 1932 urged policy makers to recognize that the worldwide economic downturn was "not a crisis of poverty, but a crisis of abundance." Modern capitalism, Keynes argued, had in a sense become too efficient by producing vast quantities of consumer goods that, due to inequalities in income distribution, outstripped effective demand—a "crisis of abundance." In Keynes's view, it was irresponsible for a government to rely on market forces alone to restore prosperity, which might require years of mass suffering and political and economic instability. Instead, he advocated increasing demand by consumers through government spending on public works projects and relief programs. This strategy was known as "pump-priming." It would be costly, and rather than raise taxes (which would decrease demand), Keynes also advocated the government embrace deficit spending.

Yet there was nothing like a coherent economic theory or plan guiding Roosevelt's policy choices. If in time he became a Keynesian in practice, FDR was never a committed one in theory. Raymond Moley, a Barnard College economist, served as a campaign adviser to Roosevelt and briefly as a member of his administration, before leaving over political differences. In a critical memoir of his experiences with Roosevelt, published in 1939, Moley complained about the president's eclectic approach to ending the Depression, noting, "To look upon [Roosevelt's] policies as the result of a unified plan was to believe that the accumulation of stuffed snakes, baseball pictures, school flags, old tennis shoes, carpenter's tools, geometry books, and chemistry sets in a boy's bedroom could have been put there by an interior decorator."

Such criticisms did not bother Roosevelt, a self-assured politician who prided himself on pragmatism, not ideological or intellectual consistency. His willingness to embrace varied and even contradictory policies, keeping those that worked and discarding those that failed, proved a hallmark of his administration.

Two New Deals

Some historians of the 1930s, in an effort to bring at least a measure of order to the "boy's bedroom" concept of Roosevelt's policies, speak of two New Deals: the first an attempt to end the Depression from the top down, the second an attempt to end it from the bottom up. At the risk of oversimplification (because policies and periods overlapped), the first New Deal could be said to have run from Roosevelt's inauguration in March 1933 to mid-1935. It was represented in the policies of the National Recovery Administration, and the Agricultural Adjustment Administration, new federal agencies that encouraged large producers in industry and agriculture to restrict production and fix prices to restore profitability, and thus encourage increased production and the rehiring of laid-off workers. The second New Deal, which came to the fore from 1935 through 1938, was represented in the policies of the Public Works Administration, the Works Progress Administration (WPA), the Civilian Conservation Corps, and the Farm Security Administration. These agencies followed what amounted to a Keynesian strategy of putting money into the pockets of the unemployed through federally sponsored work projects and the like, intended to end the "underconsumption" that since 1929 had kept consumer demand low.

There were important political as well as policy differences between the two New Deals. The language of the early New Deal stressed "unity"—"We Do Our Part" was the slogan of the National Recovery Administration. The language of the later New Deal shifted toward an acknowledgment of the conflicts and divisions in American society; in his 1936 reelection campaign, Roosevelt directed his appeal to the "ill-housed, ill-clothed, ill-fed" of the nation while denouncing his Republican opponents as "economic royalists." Despite this whiff of rhetorical class warfare, and despite the fanatical hatred the president inspired among some wealthier Americans, Roosevelt was no radical. His goal was to save capitalism from its own excesses through the judicious application of a combination of government regulation and economic stimulus.

Revolution or Reform?

Of course, some Americans in the 1930s—Socialists, Communists, and other left-wing activists—did actively seek the downfall of capitalism. The Depression brought them some political gains, at least in the short run. Socialist Party presidential candidate Norman Thomas received nearly 900,000 votes in the 1932 election. Communists led demonstrations of the unemployed that often ended in clashes with the police but also brought them new recruits. And, beginning in 1935, a powerful new trade union federation, the Committee of Industrial Organizations, began organizing mass-production workers in the auto, steel, electrical manufacturing, maritime, and other major industries. The most devoted organizers, and some of the leaders of those new unions, were often radicals of one stripe or another. The new union militancy was certainly one factor that pushed the New Deal "leftward" in the mid-1930s, and helped bring passage of new laws ensuring the right of workers to collective bargaining (the National Labor Relations Act), and securing old age pensions (Social Security) and unemployment insurance.

However, those who hoped that such reforms were merely the prelude to a socialist transformation of the United States (either through peaceful or violent means), would be disappointed. American politics were indeed transformed in the 1930s— but by a realignment, not a revolution. Political scientists use the term *realignment* to describe a decisive and long-term shift in political power from one party or coalition to another in a democratic electoral system. From the mid-1890s through the end of the 1920s, the Republican Party had been the majority party in U.S. politics, winning all but two presidential elections in those years. Roosevelt's 1932 victory, which also saw the Democrats gain control of both houses of Congress for the first time since 1916, ushered in several decades when the Democratic Party took over as the majority party. Roosevelt's sweeping reelection victory in 1936, when he won 60.8 percent of the popular vote, and the electoral votes of all but the two rock-ribbed Republican states of Maine and Vermont, illustrate the extent of the dramatic political changes brought by the Great Depression. Voter turnout increased dramatically in the 1930s, with most of the new voters supporting the Democratic Party. For the first time, white, urban working-class voters in the big industrial states in the Northeast and Midwest, many of them immigrants or the children of immigrants, overwhelmingly backed the Democrats. To give one example, in 1928 Democratic presidential candidate Alfred E. Smith received 19 percent of the vote in the auto-producing city of Flint, Michigan; in 1936 Roosevelt got 72 percent of Flint's vote. Black voters, traditionally suspicious of Democrats (historically the party of white supremacy in the South), gave three-quarters of their votes to Roosevelt in 1936. The white South remained solidly Democratic, as it had since the Civil War. These three broad groups of voters—white workers, blacks, and white Southerners, were the core of the New Deal coalition that propelled the Democrats to the White House and control of both houses of Congress in the 1930s and for some years thereafter.

Second Term Blues

During Roosevelt's second term in office, he secured some significant reforms, including the Fair Labor Standards Act of 1938 that established a minimum wage and a 40-hour workweek and curtailed the employment of child labor. But the pace of reform slowed in the later 1930s, in part because of Roosevelt's own political and fiscal miscalculations. In his first term in the White House, the president had frequently clashed with the conservative majority of the Supreme Court, who declared his National Industrial Recovery Act unconstitutional in 1935. After his reelection, he retaliated with an ill-fated proposal to expand the number of Supreme Court justices, widely condemned as a "court-packing" scheme that failed in Congress (although it did push the Supreme Court to take a more lenient attitude toward the New Deal, as a majority of justices subsequently upheld the constitutionality of the Social Security and National Labor Relations Acts).

In what amounted to a self-inflicted political wound, Roosevelt decided to cut spending in 1937 on social welfare and public works programs. Here was another example of the contradictions at the heart of the New Deal. Despite the sizable sums appropriated for his New Deal programs, Roosevelt was still no Keynesian. He remained a fiscal conservative uncomfortable with the idea of deficit spending. As soon as a more favorable economic climate began to develop, he was determined to balance the budget by getting government out of the role of employer of last resort. And by 1937, New Deal programs like the WPA had succeeded in rolling back the worst effects of the Depression: between 1933 and 1937, the economy expanded by an annual rate of 9 to 10 percent, and the unemployment rate dropped from 25 percent to 14.3 percent of the workforce. But when Roosevelt pushed through cuts in spending for programs like the WPA, it quickly became apparent that the Depression had not yet run its course, and that the private sector remained incapable of provide anything like full employment. Between 1937 and 1938, unemployment jumped back up to 19 percent in an economic downturn dubbed the "Roosevelt recession." His popularity suffered, and he seemed to be losing his political touch.

Foreign Challenges

Yet Roosevelt would go on to serve an unprecedented third term in office and be elected to a fourth one, chiefly because of ominous developments overseas. Nazi leader Adolf Hitler came to power in Germany in 1933. He had rebuilt Germany's military might, and by 1938, was using it to force territorial concessions in central and eastern Europe. The Germans invaded Poland in 1939, precipitating World War II. Meanwhile, in Asia the imperial Japanese government was waging a brutal military campaign to extend its power over mainland China. In 1940 Germany, Japan, and Italy (led by fascist dictator Benito Mussolini, who had his own territorial ambitions) joined together in a military alliance known as the Axis powers.

Although the United States remained officially neutral at the beginning of World War II, Roosevelt was determined to do all he could to shore up the Allied powers, while building up American military forces. In doing so, he finally managed to end the Depression. American factories converted from producing civilian consumer goods to military weapons, and hired millions of formerly unemployed workers, with millions more joining the armed forces. As Keynes wrote from an embattled Britain in an article for an American magazine in July 1940, "Your war preparations . . . far from requiring a sacrifice, will be the stimulus, which neither the victory nor the defeat of the New Deal could give to you, to greater individual consumption and a higher standard of life."

Dr. Win the War

On December 7, 1941, the Japanese attacked Pearl Harbor, and the United States went to war, both in the Pacific Ocean and in Europe. President Roosevelt announced that "Dr. New Deal" was being replaced for the duration by "Dr. Win the War." New Deal agencies like the WPA were shut down. Full employment in defense industries, combined with growing trade union strength, brought dramatic gains in the living standards of American workers, even with wartime rationing and higher taxes.

Many Americans feared that when the war ended the Depression would resume. To forestall such a possibility, Roosevelt oversaw one final expansion of federal social welfare spending. In a 1943 speech, he declared that America's "gallant men and women in the armed services . . . must not be demobilized . . . to a place on the breadline or on a corner selling apples." The following year Congress passed the GI Bill of Rights, which guaranteed financial assistance to returning veterans seeking to pursue an education, purchase a home, or start a business. With over 13 million men and women serving in the U.S. military during the war, that represented a commitment to expanding opportunities for ordinary Americans larger than any undertaken during the New Deal (the WPA, at its height, had never employed more than 3.5 million people).

Truman's Fair Deal

President Roosevelt died on April 12, 1945, just weeks before the Allies prevailed over Nazi Germany. His successor, Harry S. Truman, sought to protect and expand the reform legacy of the New Deal. But in doing so, he faced stiff political opposition. In 1946 American voters signaled their impatience with lingering wartime austerity and government regulation by electing a Republican majority to both houses of Congress. Their success proved short-lived; in a hard-fought campaign in 1948, the Democrats regained control of Congress, and Truman was elected to the presidency in his own right.

In his 1949 State of the Union address, Truman announced plans for a "Fair Deal" that would expand the existing American social welfare state to include new programs like a system of national health insurance. But that proposal went down to defeat, along with other reform measures. Since the late 1930s, southern Democrats (labeled "Dixiecrats") had grown increasingly unreliable as partners in the New Deal coalition, and often made common cause with conservative Republicans. White Southerners feared that a more powerful federal government would inevitably try to extend full civil rights to African Americans in the South (indeed, in 1948 Truman issued an executive order desegregating the armed forces). Increasingly, conflict about race rather than economics became the new dividing line in American politics.

President Truman also had to contend with another world crisis, the cold war between the United States and the Soviet Union. Republicans exploited fears that the Soviets were winning that conflict, supposedly aided by spies and subversives within the Truman administration. In 1952 Truman chose not to run for reelection. Republican presidential candidate Dwight D. Eisenhower swept into office, bringing along with him Republican majorities in the House of Representatives and the Senate. And here is where the durability of the New Deal became apparent, because during his two terms in office neither President Eisenhower nor congressional Republicans made any serious effort to dismantle the social welfare programs instituted under Roosevelt. The New Deal had become a seemingly permanent part of the American political landscape.

See also Democratic Party, 1932–68; Republican Party, 1932–68.

FURTHER READING. Alan Brinkley, *The End of Reform: New Deal Liberalism in Depression and War*, 1995; Steve Fraser and Gary Gerstle, eds., *The Rise and Fall of the New Deal Order, 1930–1980*, 1990; David M. Kennedy, *Freedom from Fear: The American People in Depression and War, 1929–1945*, 1999; Raymond Moley, *After Seven Years*, 1939; Eric Rauchway, *The Great Depression and the New Deal: A Very Short Introduction*, 2008; Robert Zieger, *The CIO: 1935–1955*, 1995.

MAURICE ISSERMAN

New England

New England is America's most clear-cut region, hanging appendage-like into the North Atlantic. Maine, whose top-heavy bulk dominates the region geographically, is precariously bolted to the nation by only one state, New Hampshire. Maine is thus the only contiguous state that borders but one state. Similarly, the entire six-state region is attached to the United States by a single state, New York. Thus America's only land route to or from New England is through but one state. The only other way in or out of New England is by Canada or by sea.

New England is only about the size of the state of Washington and accounts for only 2 percent of the land mass of America. Fewer than 5 of every 100 Americans live there. Yet in New England, history runs deep: back to the very beginnings of America, the United States, and the New England town meeting, the Western world's first real democracy since the experiment in ancient Athens. In New England, the sinews of culture have been toughened by the natural adversity of a hard land and a still harder sea. Patterns of human events have been defined by rhythms of ethnic settlement that, in microcosm, reflect those of the nation as a whole.

New England is a geography set apart, but its human base and its politics have traditionally been as eclectic as the nation's. Here the boredom and the drama, the growth and the decline, the despair and the hope of the American experiment in self-government are laid bare.

The Connecticut River valley, which splits the region, from the Canadian border to Long Island Sound, marks the complexity of New England in ways political as well as economic. West of the river in Connecticut and Massachusetts, the land is apt to be rolling and hilly in the south, growing more mountainous as one goes north into Vermont. Its towns west of the river are accordingly smaller and more defined and its culture tends to be more rural and radical. From this region of Connecticut came Ethan Allen, who published the first anti-Christian book on the continent. From the hills of western Massachusetts came Daniel Shays and his agrarian revolutionaries. And when convention (in Shays's case, made manifest by an army from eastern Massachusetts) drove these men out, they didn't go west in what was to become the American way of radicalism. They went *north* and stayed on the same side of the river—Allen to agitate in and Shays to hole up in western Vermont.

Although in the north the Connecticut River valley on both sides was settled by more conservative churchgoers from southern New England, by 1840 the river marked important political divisions—mainly, the border between Vermont and New Hampshire. During the presidential election of that year, in what historian Richard McCormick calls "a conundrum

for political analysis," Whig William Henry Harrison received a 2 to 1 majority in Vermont and Democrat Martin Van Buren a 3 to 1 majority in New Hampshire. By the end of the twentieth century, no two adjacent American states were more different politically than Vermont, to the west of the river, and New Hampshire, to the east. Vermont's southern border abuts Massachusetts' Berkshire Hills (an extension of Vermont's Green Mountains) where town meetings are still strong and local currencies seek to compete with the dollar. New Hampshire's southern border abuts metropolitan Boston and the northern end of the vast East Coast megalopolis, where cities, casinos, and commerce abound.

Moreover, important divisions exist within the six states themselves. Southeastern Maine is profoundly dissimilar from the thick, wet, and rolling timberlands to the northwest or the fertile open potato fields of Arrostic County to the northeast. Vermont's Green Mountains divided the state's development and politics for a century; today its Northeast Kingdom remains a place apart where one can still find the older Vermont, ungentrified, hard-sledding, sometimes defiant. Northeastern and southwestern Connecticut are cultures apart. Its two major cities are oriented in different directions: Hartford looks toward Boston, New Haven toward New York City. Southern New Hampshire has always been an extension of industrial New England, which thrust itself northward from Boston along an axis of small factory cities like Nashua, Manchester, and the state capital, Concord. Less than an hour north of Concord abruptly rise the White Mountains, cold, lonely, and dangerous. Following them the great northern hardwood forest region stretches uninterrupted to the Canadian border.

Then there is Boston itself; its massive metropolitan presence creating its own region—a cultural overlay, which affects all six states. Boston is to New England what Chicago is to the Midwest—and more. In the little towns of northern New England radios are often set to WTIC hundreds of miles away in Hartford, Connecticut, to hear (almost eerily—so far the distance and so rugged the topography in between) baseball games of the Boston Red Sox. For New England, especially northern New England, there is something important and accurate in the euphemism "Red Sox Nation."

Even so, when Robert Frost—clearly New England's (and perhaps America's) greatest poet of the twentieth century—titled his famous book of poems *North of Boston*, he identified the most important division of all in New England. One is in the north, the other south. One is old; one is new. One contains the three states north of Boston and the other Massachusetts and the two states below it, Connecticut and Rhode Island. Above the line is postcard New England, below it is urban-industrial New England. In the northern half one is most likely to be "Yankee"; in the southern half one is more likely to be "ethnic."

In 1960 the six-state region of New England contained three of the ten most urban states in America and two of the ten most rural. The two most urban states in America (Rhode Island and Massachusetts) along with the eighth most urban (Connecticut) were in southern New England. Of the two most rural states in the nation, two were in northern New England: Vermont (the most rural) and Maine (the ninth most rural). Political differences—north to south—also prevailed. Before the landslide election of Franklin D. Roosevelt in 1936, Maine was called the bellwether state: "As Maine goes, so goes the nation." In 1936, when Maine and Vermont were the only two states to vote against Roosevelt, the phrase was changed to "As Maine goes, so goes Vermont." At midcentury the three New England states classified as "two-party competitive" were in southern New England, and the three one-party states in northern New England.

By the 1980s, however, along with the completion of the interstate highway system and during the beginnings of the information superhighway, the north-south distinction was fading like a September morning fog along the Connecticut River.

The decline of the north-south division began in earnest with the passage of the Interstate Highway Act of 1958. Since then, the federal government has squeezed four north-south interstate highways into the area north of Boston that hook the two New Englands together. These highways have changed the regional character of northern New England profoundly. A key component of New England's current political culture took the highway north so that many could live rural, clean, and easy lives—and still be within three hours' driving distance of Boston.

New England's Political Past

In its mix of peoples, in the variety of their social and economic arrangements, in the kinds of issues that arise, and in the political expression of all three, New England has long been (in varying degrees and with the inevitable nuisances) a microcosm of America. This development is reflected in the dynamics of its political past. Bernard De Voto called it "the first finished place" in America.

The Revolution began in New England. But New England had begun there a century and a half earlier. Indeed, as much American history transpired in that time as transpired between the adoption of the U.S. Constitution and the end of World War II. Prior to 1789, New England had worked through a westward expansion (from the Atlantic Ocean to the Connecticut River), settled a northern frontier (up the Connecticut to Canada), and endured a series of wars with native populations, which in their viciousness to civilian and combatants alike on both sides make the battle Little Bighorn seem tame. Had the dime novel existed in the mid-seventeenth century, Robert Rogers, not Buffalo Bill, would be the first popular male American frontier hero and

Susanna Johnson, not Annie Oakley, the first female hero.

Most of all during this time, before the beginning of the United States, New England planted and then cultivated democracy in North America. The transition from fundamentally democratic economic arrangements like the Mayflower Compact and religious institutions like Puritanism to a secular, liberal institution of governance still operating democratically—the town meeting—was in all its agony, its fits and starts, and its warts and roses the most unique contribution America has made to the science of governance. Indeed, political historians agree that the representative republic fashioned in Philadelphia owes its creation to the mind of Europe as much or more than to the mind of America.

But the Greeks were *not* to New England what the English theorists, especially John Locke, were to America. Moreover, no genetic connection between town meeting and Athens exists. And while the antecedents of the town meeting, especially the English vestry tradition, were obviously European, their transition into a purely political structure was worked out in the wilderness during the settlement of New England. In fact, the origins of the Constitutional Convention can be traced in part to the actions of town meeting democracies in western New England as, indeed, was the American Revolution itself a result of town meetings in eastern New England. When the king's secretary for the colonies, Lord Germaine, heard about the Boston Tea Party, his response was: "This is what comes of their wretched town meetings—these are the proceedings of a tumultuous and riotous rabble, who ought, if they had the least produce, to follow their mercantile employment and not trouble themselves with politics and government, which they do not understand."

The town meeting, this uniquely American institution in which every voting citizen is a legislator and laws are made in face-to-face assemblies of the whole, remained the fundamental governing institution in New England for the first three centuries of its existence. In his classic *The City in History*, Lewis Mumford called the "American failure" to incorporate town meeting democracy "in both the federal and state constitutions" a "tragic oversight in postrevolutionary political development." Thus the most *unique* thing about New England as a political region in America is its town meeting tradition—a tradition that did not spread westward.

The first impediment to the westward expansion of the New England town meeting was the aristocratic New York county system. This roadblock appeared as early as 1644 with the attempt to carry the town meeting across the Long Island Sound and implant it in Hempstead, New York, where it withered and died under the influence of first the Dutch and then the Duke of York. Over a century later, opposition to the county system was an important ingredient in the conflict between Vermont and

New York over the latter's land claims. The eastern towns of Vermont, which were more sympathetic to New York than the western towns led by Ethan Allen, became very concerned when the proposed New York county system failed to recognize town meeting government.

The second and ultimately more significant factor in the failure of the New England town meeting to take hold elsewhere in America was the face of the land west of New England. It was too broad, too flanked by distant horizons, lacking the ups and downs, the nooks and crannies of topography that typify most of New England. Where was the natural bumpiness essential to communal governance in village and town? Representation was the solution and face-to-face democracy, even in the places where attempts to transplant it were energetic, did not survive in meaningful measure. In short, most of the Midwest, the middle border, and the Far West were simply physically inhospitable to deliberative, communal enterprise.

Within New England, town meetings remained dominant until the urban industrial revolution took firm hold of the region. Then they began to fall to the one variable they could not accommodate: numerical size. This dynamic had begun modestly in Connecticut in 1784 when Hartford and New Haven adopted city councils within the towns themselves. It continued with a jolt when, in 1822, Boston deliberated for three days to abandon its town meeting. Providence, Rhode Island, followed suit in 1830 and Portland, Maine, in 1832.

Still, town meetings defined the great majority of local governance in New England throughout the nineteenth century, remained strong during the first half of the twentieth century, and continue to govern most small towns in the region. And although the great majority of New Englanders no longer practice town meeting democracy because they live in cities, the spirit of the face-to-face original meaning of democracy pervades the region's consciousness. As late as 1948, a town meeting in a southwestern Connecticut town thwarted an attempt to place the headquarters of the United Nations within its town boundaries.

New England's politics are tied to its past via the town meeting in several other ways beyond the political culture of face-to-face communal decision making. Most important is the structural heritage of the town. Since the town and its town meeting were sacrosanct, they received institutional protection. Towns were given geographical representation *as towns* in the state legislatures. This meant that several New England states violated the democratic principle of "one person, one vote" in the extreme. By 1950, in Vermont and Connecticut, the situation was as bad as it got in America. In both these states, only 12 percent of the population held 51 percent of the seats in the lower body of the legislature. In Rhode Island, 18 percent of the population could control the state

senate. Since the towns of New England tended to be so powerful in the legislatures, these bodies felt little need to protect the towns with "home rule" provisions in their state constitutions. Town representation also meant that state legislatures were huge. In 1950, 4 of the 50 state legislatures with more than 200 members were in New England.

Moreover, the constitutions of New England, being examples of late-eighteenth-century constitutions in this, America's "most finished" region, were short, difficult to amend, and gave great power to the legislature. In turn, the legislatures, which represented towns or at least combinations of towns (the counties are very weak in New England), were happy to leave local politics alone. For example, the organizing bases of the political parties themselves were apt to be town-based. There were exceptions, of course, but by the middle decades of the twentieth century (as Duane Lockard put it), the "town meeting and the concomitant emphasis on local autonomy" were still unique New England phenomena.

It is no accident, therefore, that the phrase "all politics is local" was made famous by a New Englander, Thomas Phillip "Tip" O'Neill, who, when he said it, was speaker of the House of Representatives in Washington. By the end of World War II, these localities in New England represented a profound mix of ethnic populations, rural and urban lifestyles, topographical settings, commercial enterprises, and socioeconomic class structures. This complexity was (and remains) manifest in the region's politics. The passion of these politics was most often found in the locality, and the spark that most often triggered it was ethnicity.

Beginning in 1620, New England experienced two centuries of nearly universal Yankee/Puritan homogeneity. But aggressive commercial growth and diversification and the resulting need for labor, followed by the Irish potato famine in the middle decades of the nineteenth century, brought newcomers in increasing numbers and from increasingly varied places. At the same time, many Yankees headed west (often preceded by a trip south in blue uniforms). By 1850 only one in ten New Englanders was foreign born. By 1920 almost 25 percent were. No other region in America had become more ethnically diverse.

Vermont, the coldest, most isolated state of the region and the only one without a seacoast, places the ethnic base of New England and its linkage to politics in sharp relief. Prior to the 1960s, the Democratic Party in New England's (indeed, America's) most rural and most one-party (Republican) state was almost exclusively located in the larger towns and tiny (by national standards) cities. And it was securely tied to ethnic politics. In the city of Winooski, French Canadian Catholic Democrats worked in the mills; in the city of Barre, the Italian Catholic Democrats quarried and carved granite; in other larger towns and little cities, the Irish Catholic Democrats did what they could.

Elsewhere in New England, this urban, ethnic, Catholic base, first united against the "Yankee Stock" and then taking the form of interethnic rivalry, was, throughout the first half of the twentieth century, the prime source of political and partisan conflict in New England. In its intensity and longevity, ethnicity has been to New England what water has been to the West.

In Maine and New Hampshire, the Democratic Party was strengthened by French Canadians and the Irish in the cities. In the southern half of the region, the Democrat-urban-ethnic versus the Republican-rural-suburban relationship was starkly more powerful. By 1950 ethnic names outnumbered Yankee names among Democrat representatives 78 percent to 22 percent in the lower body of Rhode Island's legislature. Among Republican legislators, however, the percentages were Yankees 84 percent and ethnics 16 percent. In Connecticut in 1951, ethnic names outnumbered Yankee names in the lower chamber of the state house 72 percent to 28 percent among Democrats, while, among Republicans, Yankees outnumbered ethnics 84 percent to 16 percent.

Nowhere was ethnic politics more dramatically played out than in Massachusetts. Beginning in 1884, when the Irish Catholic James Michael Curley was elected mayor of Boston, and continuing beyond his career (portrayed in Edward O'Connor's *The Last Hurrah*), the struggle between the Yankee Republicans (most notably represented by the "Boston Brahmins") and ethnic minorities within the Democratic Party dominated politics. By the 1950s, only 9 percent of the Republicans serving in the Massachusetts house of representatives had either Irish or Italian surnames, while 64 percent of the Democrats did. It would be a mistake, however, to believe that the "ethnic" alternative was totally monolithic. The conflict between eastern and western Democrats in Massachusetts, for instance, is reflected in the important division between David Walsh from the western part of the state, who was the first Irish Catholic elected governor, and Curley himself to the east. The rise of the Kennedy family as "Green Brahmins" is symbolized by the graduation of Joseph Kennedy (father of John F. Kennedy) from Harvard University. His subsequent penetration of many Yankee economic and cultural institutions also speaks to the complexity of ethnic politics in Massachusetts and throughout New England.

Political Transition

Locating political watersheds in time is a tricky business, but several factors emerged during the first two decades following World War II that, in (rough) combination, contributed to a new politics in New England.

First, a series of U.S. Supreme Court decisions beginning with *Baker v. Carr* in 1962 forever changed the nature of locality in American state politics, and especially in New England. These decisions demanded that geographical representation in *both* houses of all state legislatures (unlike the U.S. Congress) must be based on the principle of "one person, one vote." This decision democratized state politics in that it gave those living in cities their rightful share of political power. In New England, the decision's effect was to shift power away from places that practiced town-meeting, communitarian, and face-to-face politics to those that practiced big-city, liberal, and representative politics. It also shifted power away from the Republican Party and toward the Democratic Party.

In Connecticut in 1960, the city of Hartford had a population of 177,397 and two seats in the state's house of representatives. The town of Union, with a population of 261, had one seat. In Vermont, the largest city, Burlington, had one seat in the legislature representing 35,531 people and the town of Victory, with a population of 46, also had one. By 1970, however, all this had changed. Local units everywhere received representation based on their population in *both* houses of the legislature. The partisan impact of what was then called "the reapportionment revolution" did not happen overnight and varied from state to state. But no doubt exists that a region in which the partisan balance was often defined in rural-versus-urban terms was significantly affected when the cities got their fair share of the votes in the legislatures. In New England (as elsewhere in America), the partisan advantage was to the Democrats and the cultural advantage was to the cities, and perhaps more importantly to the growing suburbs attached to them.

Second, the New Deal Democratic coalition that dominated national politics—especially in Congress—beginning with the Great Depression and featuring the urban-industrial north in combination with the "Solid South" disappeared when the Deep South shifted sides and began voting Republican in 1964. New England's involvement in this coalition, called "Austin to Boston" ticket balancing (John F. Kennedy and Lyndon Johnson in 1960 and Michael Dukakis and Lloyd Bentsen in 1988), began when the tactic was still strong and ended as it became weaker. As New England has increasingly become a Democrat/liberal region and the national pattern has shifted to a bicoastal/heartland split, the region's national leverage has declined accordingly.

Third, the electronic revolution, which replaced the mechanical urban-industrial revolution, has diminished the importance of planetary variables in politics: rivers, oceans, mountains, valleys, watersheds, soil, and—most important—climate. In short, as air conditioning changed the politics of the Deep South, so too has central heating changed the politics of New England—especially northern New England. Moreover, variables tied to people matter more than variables tied to place. Within states, regions have become less important politically as they have become more culturally homogenized. This has tended to weaken traditional factional patterns within the political parties. This is especially important in New England, where geography traditionally played such an important role in political organization.

Fourth, no pattern has declined more sharply as a result of these changes than ethnic politics. Duane Lockard, in his seminal work on New England politics through the 1950s, proclaimed that ethnic names on the ballot were important only when the quality of the candidates was near equal and the election close. In such cases "the right kind of name" might be "the fillip needed for success." Two decades later, Neal Peirce would write, in regard to Massachusetts, that "everyone seemed to agree that a lot of the juice had been drained out of the old ethnic issue."

Democrats Become Dominant

Against this backdrop, and as the twenty-first century began, more specific sources of conflict had developed that are more typical of politics everywhere in America: energy, land use, an increasingly isolated low-income working class and wider issues of growth and environmental protection. Although these problems add to the decline in the importance of ethnic politics—especially the spatial (urban/rural) distribution of its core components—the current debates over social issues such as civil unions for same-sex couples (first allowed in Vermont) and same-sex marriage (first instituted in Massachusetts) demonstrate that ethnicity (when it is linked to traditional religious identities) still can play a role in New England. Yet whatever the issue, it seems increasingly likely that a solution will need to please Democrats and/ or liberal causes.

It was only symbolic at the time but it mattered. In 1972, when 49 of the 50 American states cast their electoral votes for the soon-to-be-disgraced president Richard Nixon, the lone dissenting state was in New England. Soon after the Watergate scandal forced Nixon to resign, bumper stickers appeared on automobiles with Massachusetts license plates reading "Don't Blame Us!"

In national politics, New England had held forth as a bastion of Republicanism after the party's imprint was embedded by America's most profound and enduring political realignment—which itself was caused by the first serious national crisis, the Civil War. Although New England *as a region* had itself posed an early and dangerous secessionist threat to the Union during the War of 1812, New England had subsequently become the epicenter of abolitionism. Antislavery and recurrent economic differences had made it a fierce enemy of the South by 1860; the election of Abraham Lincoln sealed the deal.

It took a century for New England's attachment to the Republican Party to change. The key moment was the election of New Englander Kennedy in 1960. Kennedy's Catholicism reflected the ethnic component of Yankee New England. Prior to Kennedy's victory, the only other time New England exceeded

the national percentage for the Democrat candidate for president was in 1928, when the first Catholic to run for president, Alfred E. Smith, lost to Herbert Hoover. Smith actually carried Massachusetts and Rhode Island, the first two New England states in the twentieth century to cast more than half their votes for a Democrat. Yet, despite New England's significant urban base and ethnic diversity, it lagged behind the realignment triggered by the second national apocalypse, the Great Depression—the "New Deal/Solid South/urban-industrial North" Democratic coalition.

Kennedy closed this gap. His victory nationally, however, was based in part on the old (and soon to disappear) north-south alignment of strange political bedfellows. Yet in New England, the old coalition was more a catalyst than a cause. By the end of the twentieth century, the New Deal Democratic Coalition was only a memory. The Republicans had walked off with the Solid South. As they did, New England continued to unify against them. It had cast its lot with the Democrats.

The key to this regional transformation is the northern half of the old "two New Englands." Whereas in 1936, Vermont and Maine would buck the nation as the only two states to vote against Roosevelt, now these two states vote solidly Democratic. Indeed, in the last four presidential elections the six New England states have had in the aggregate 24 chances to cast their votes for the Republican candidate. They did so only once, when New Hampshire cast its votes for George W. Bush in 2000. Of the three northern New England states, only New Hampshire trails behind. Vermont and Maine voted more heavily Democratic than Connecticut in the last four presidential elections, although Rhode Island and Massachusetts (so close in so many ways) tip the Democratic totals in favor of southern New England. Since 1988, of the six New England states, Vermont (which stuck with the GOP without a hitch from 1860 to 1960) now ranks third in its percentage-point differential for Democratic presidential candidates in New England.

In the 1980s, the New England delegation in the U.S. Senate was almost perfectly balanced between Democrats and Republicans. Since 2000 the Democrats have gained only a slight advantage there. In the House, however, Republicans have taken a severe hit since the 1980s. In that decade they averaged 37 percent of the New England delegation. Since the turn of the century this percentage has dropped to 18.

More important, perhaps, is the New England trend in state legislative elections; it clearly favors the Democrats. Of these 1,290 state representatives serving in 2008, 875 (over two-thirds) were Democrats. None of the 12 legislative chambers in New England had a Republican majority. The closest the GOP came to controlling even 1 house of the 12 is in the Maine senate, where they lacked but one seat. In all the other states Democratic majorities are substantial to massive. Even in New Hampshire, the Democrats controlled the state senate 14 to 10, and in the New Hampshire house of representatives, numbering 400 members, they had a 237 to 158 majority.

As is the trend across America, New England voters seem more apt to elect Republicans to governorships than they are to legislative offices. In 61 different gubernatorial elections between 1980 and 2007, New Englanders chose 32 Republicans, 26 Democrats, and 3 independents. Between 2000 and 2007, they chose 9 Republicans and 7 Democrats. Thus, the New England states often experience divided government. In 2007 Connecticut, Rhode Island, and Vermont had Republican governors facing Democratic legislatures.

But the New England shift in partisanship is only part of the story. New England's political ideology is changing as well. Between 1996 and 2006 public opinion polls demonstrate that, while the percentage of Americans identifying themselves as liberals held steady, five of the six New England states increased their liberal scores. In short, New England was significantly more liberal than the nation in 1996 and, by 2006, this gap had widened. Moreover, the percentage of New Englanders identifying themselves as conservatives decreased an average of 6 percentage points while, at the national level, conservatives have declined by only 1 percentage point.

Another, perhaps more poignant, measure of the political character of the New England states is how the region votes in the U.S. Congress, especially in the Senate. The composite voting index of political ideology prepared by the *National Journal* (which combines key votes on social, economic, and foreign policy issues) documents the solid and increasing liberal posture of the New England region. In nine of ten years of voting in the Senate (1998–2007), the New England average for liberalism was above the 60th percentile of all the senators combined. Moreover the New England delegation's liberal position is rising dramatically (see figure 1).

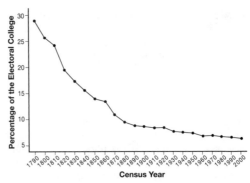

Figure 2. New England's Percentage of the Electoral College Vote.

The shift in New England's partisan and ideological balance away from the American mainstream (becoming increasingly liberal) coupled with New England's downward slide in Electoral College votes in national elections may spell an increasing marginalization of New England's influence in national politics. Indeed, it may mean a return to the midpoint of American life (1860–1960), when New England became so Republican it was taken for granted by the prevailing majority.

When the Census of 1790 was taken, New England controlled 29 percent of the electoral votes. The Census of 2000 gave it 6 percent (see figure 2). Electoral votes reflect power in Congress. With the closing of the continent and the statehood of Alaska and Hawaii, New England's share of Senate seats has ceased to decline. But its share of House seats still drops slowly downward. Clearly there is a bottom limit that precludes precipitous losses in the future. Yet it is likely New England will lose another seat with the 2010 Census.

This decline in New England's mathematical share of the republic and its increasing ideological marginalization is revealed by the success rates of presidential and vice presidential candidacies from the region in the last half century. Since the success of Kennedy, none of the ten presidential or vice presidential candidates who (like Kennedy) were both *of* New England and ran *from* New England were successful. Nor were the candidacies of Howard Dean or Mitt Romney, who were born elsewhere but ran from New England. Thus, Kennedy was the last president of the United States who was a child of New England and stayed in New England.

Establishing causality in matters political is a dangerous business. The linkage between the blending of the two New Englands and the region's increasing political homogeneity as a Democratic stronghold is far from clear; nor is the longevity of this new political posture. Most problematic of all is the extent to which regional historical habits and cultural imperatives can withstand the overarching changes (both national and global) caused by third-wave, postindustrial, electronic technology.

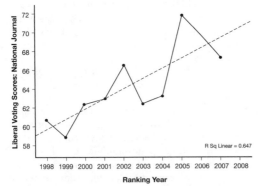

Figure 1. Liberal Voting: New England Senators (1998–2007). Rankings: Percentage of senators voting less liberal than average New England senator on key social, economic, and foreign policy votes.

What is clear, however, is that if regional values can survive the present technological revolution, then New England's heritage featuring classical liberalism (equal rights for all under law) and classical democracy (citizens making law face-to-face) may be a useful model for the future. No other region in America had as much to do with the formation of the American liberal, national enterprise (its representative and federal republic) as did New England. At the same time, only New England created and preserved America's most profoundly important local institution, the town meeting. Thus, as an architect of the machinery to operate a continental government and provider of a local means to train a citizen base to sustain it, New England's endowment for the future of American democracy is precious indeed.

See also liberalism; state government.

FURTHER READING. James Truslow Adams, *The Founding of New England*, 1921; Idem, *New England in the Republic 1776–1850*, 1926; Idem, *Revolutionary New England, 1691–1776*, 1923; Van Wyck Brooks, *The Flowering of New England*, 1936; Idem, *New England: Indian Summer 1865–1915*, 1940; Jonathan Daniels, *A Southerner Discovers New England*, 1940; Judson Hale, *Inside New England*, 1982; Ronald J. Hrebenar and Clive S. Thomas, eds., *Interest Group Politics in the Northeastern States*, 1993; Merrill Jensen, ed., *Regionalism in America*, 1951; Duane Lockard, *New England State Politics*, 1959; Josephine F. Milburn and Victoria Schuck, eds., *New England Politics*, 1981; Charlene Mires, "The Lure of New England and the Search for the Capital of the World," *New England Quarterly* 79 (March 1, 2006), 37–64; Lewis Mumford, *The City in History*, 1961; Garrison Nelson, "Running from New England: Will It Ever Lead the Nation Again?" Paper presented at the conference *The State of New England*, Easton, MA, March 29, 2008; Neal R. Peirce, *The New England States*, 1976; George Wilson Pierson, "The Obstinate Concept of New England: A Study in Denudation," *New England Quarterly* 28 (March 1955), 3–17; Robert Pike, *Tall Trees, Tough Men: A Vivid, Anecdotal History of Logging and Log-Driving in New England*, 1967; Ira Sharkansky, *Regionalism in American Politics*, 1970; Harold F. Wilson, *The Hill Country of Northern New England*, 1936.

FRANK M. BRYAN

New Left

Since the time of the French Revolution, people agitating for radical change in the direction of human equality have been known as "the Left." In the United States, from the late nineteenth century through World War II, leftists focused on the problems of economic inequality and exploitation. They identified the industrial working class and its allies as the main agents of progressive change, and ultimately they hoped to replace capitalism with socialism. In the 1960s, however, a new left-wing movement arose in America—as in other wealthy countries, such as England, France, and West Germany—so different from the labor-oriented socialist left that it became known as a "New Left," to distinguish it from what suddenly was called the "Old Left." The New Left enjoyed a meteoric career in American politics, becoming large and disruptive in the late 1960s and then ebbing rapidly as an organized force for political change in the early 1970s.

The New Left was a youth movement, largely middle class and white, whose analysis of American society focused on the political and cultural problems of power and alienation, rather than on economic questions. Compared to the Old Left, the New Left was loosely organized, although it featured one important national organization, Students for a Democratic Society (SDS), which existed from 1960 to 1969. Early on, New Left radicals declined to identify capitalism as American society's affliction and to embrace socialism as the cure, but this reluctance diminished as time passed, and late-1960s radicals expressed a more traditional leftist perspective. The New Left shared with the Old Left an antipathy to imperialism, understood as the control by wealthy nations over the resources and affairs of poor nations, a system that often involved large-scale violence. The New Left viewed racial domination by whites as key to understanding both U.S. society and the wider world, and New Left radicals took inspiration from the African American struggle of the post–World War II era.

Origins

American leftists were few in the late 1950s, and their efforts to recruit new adherents to their creed bore little fruit before 1960. In that year, the Student League for Industrial Democracy (SLID), a small organization with a long history in the non-Communist Left, changed its name to Students for a Democratic Society. "Sit-ins" in 1960 protesting racial segregation spread rapidly at lunch counters in the American South. Also in 1960, a largely African American gathering of civil rights organizers established the Student Nonviolent Coordinating Committee (SNCC), which became the youth vanguard of civil rights militancy. Idealistic young white people around the country found SNCC members compelling as models of moral integrity, devotion to social change, and political courage.

SDS convened a conference on human rights in the North in 1960. Participants had been active in the National Student Association, the Young Men's and Women's Christian Associations, and other groups. The conference featured presentations about poverty, civil rights, and militant nonviolence. For SDS members, the urgency surrounding race relations in the American South had become a lever that might pry open a wide-ranging contemplation of social change throughout the United States. They wished to play a key role in pushing such change forward.

In the early 1960s, New Left activists sometimes talked and wrote as if they mostly wanted American liberals to pursue the liberal agenda—creating equal opportunity and social equity within the structure of American capitalism—with increased zeal. But at other times, the New Left gave the impression that it embraced a different, more destabilizing agenda. Some aspects of conventional liberal politics, as embodied by activists in the Democratic Party, repelled many in SDS from the start. According to the New Left, liberals made too many compromises with powerful conservative forces, such as white southern congressmen, business concerns, and the U.S. military. Liberals seemed like insiders, not outsiders calling for fundamental change. Whether this indictment was fair or not, it proved compelling to many of the most energetic activists among American youth.

New Left radicals wished to see power more widely dispersed in contemporary society. They called their vision of American society "participatory democracy." In their view, most Americans played little or no role in ruling America, or even in ruling their own lives. New Left radicals focused their attention on political structures that, they believed, kept individuals isolated and powerless. These structures included social welfare agencies that monitored the behavior of the poor, corporations and unions that together managed American workers, governments that repressed African Americans, and universities that trained young people to become establishmentarian "yes men." New Left criticisms of bureaucracy as an impediment to freedom sometimes echoed conservative themes. But this was misleading. The New Left supported the very social forces, such as militant African American protest and radical third world nationalism, which conservatives fiercely opposed.

In Search of Insurgencies

New Left activists saw themselves as intellectuals who could support and help to guide insurgencies against the political and social status quo, insurgencies that might force the citadels of power to yield important concessions to the cause of increased political and social democracy. They spent the 1960s in a search for such insurgencies. This roving quest for a battering ram that might smash open the doors of the power structure led radicals to embrace the slogan "The issue is not the issue," which sounded cynical to some, but which expressed the New Left belief that specific controversies were important mainly if they could lead Americans toward a radical perspective on society.

Between 1962 and 1964, SDS members worked as political organizers in poor, mainly urban communities around the country, seeking to build what they called "an interracial movement of the poor" that would agitate for basic changes in how wealth and power were distributed in America. They cared about the problem of poverty, but the key to their activity was a view that the poor, as a politically and socially

excluded group, formed a potent force for change. In contrast, the New Left viewed labor unions and the relatively comfortable working class as too deeply invested in "the system" to work for fundamental change. After two or three years, though, SDS members became pessimistic about their strategy and abandoned the effort.

SDS spent most of its energies between 1964 and 1968 organizing university students as a force for change and working against the Vietnam War from a radical left-wing perspective. In 1964 and 1965, when New Left activists were reexamining their priorities, SNCC and other militant black groups became influenced by Black Power thinking, which held that whites should cease involving themselves in the movement for African American freedom. This ensured that the New Left would not fulfill its mission through a deeper participation in any movement of people of color. In these same years, President Lyndon Johnson escalated the U.S. war in Vietnam. These developments set the stage for the direction that the New Left took in the 1960s.

In the fall of 1964, political protest among white students in California introduced the theme of "student power" to the American scene. The Free Speech Movement (FSM) protested restrictions on dissident political activity on the campus of the University of California in Berkeley, and it sought to expose ties between this major research university and conservative political forces. The FSM established a model that student radicals used to foment confrontations with university administrators for the rest of the 1960s, including a tumultuous series of events at Columbia University in 1968.

Research universities in the cold war era eagerly put themselves at the service of large corporations and the U.S. Department of Defense, so there was plenty of muck for leftists to rake. Demands for greater democracy in the internal workings of universities addressed the longing young people in this era often expressed for greater control over their own lives. New Left radicals hoped to use universities as instructive case studies in the corruption of supposedly idealistic institutions by powerful forces. They hoped to transform universities into engines of dissident thought and action.

Anti-Imperialism and Militancy

Protest against universities' involvement in the military-industrial complex would have commanded less attention in a time of peace, but the late 1960s was a time of war. The New Left came early to protest against the Vietnam War. Unlike many in the Old Left, the New Left disdained the Soviet Union as a progressive force in the world. However, New Left radicals sympathized with the Vietnamese revolution, as with the Cuban revolution and other national-liberation movements, often led by Communists, across the third world. Radicals did not view the Vietnam War as a mistake made by U.S.

policy makers. Rather, they concluded that America's cold war rhetoric of uncompromising anticommunism, and its commitment to maintaining the international economic status quo, fated the United States to try to defeat revolution in the third world. In April 1965, after President Lyndon Johnson commenced sustained bombing of North Vietnam and a major U.S. land war in South Vietnam, SDS organized the first major demonstration against the war inside the United States, attracting more than 20,000 people to Washington, D.C.

The New Left's early leadership role in the antiwar movement soon slipped away. The escalation of the war made it a mainstream youth issue, and, after 1968, liberals swamped radicals in the ranks of antiwar protest. New Left thinkers tried, with some success, to persuade their peers that the war's brutality could be explained only through a radical analysis of America's role in the world. Why else would U.S. leaders prosecute such a seemingly disproportionate war, in such a far-off land, if not because they cast America in the role of a global enforcer of the conditions that third world revolutionaries were seeking to change? The New Left's searching attempts to explain the role of the United States in the contemporary world produced a large body of stimulating, often controversial "revisionist" scholarship about the history and nature of the nation's foreign relations. In this area, as in others, the New Left succeeded in carving out a place for dissident, socially critical thought in American intellectual life.

In the late 1960s and early 1970s, some radicals engaged in increasingly militant protest tactics. In the most notorious developments of the New Left's career, small groups, including the so-called Weather Underground, engaged in property destruction, such as sporadic bombings of police stations and the U.S. Capitol. Such groups helped to wreck SDS by demanding its members follow a course that most of them found unattractive, and then splitting the organization, which quickly expired. The importance of SDS by that time is debatable; it had become more a "brand name" than the actual source of youth radicalism. Individual campus chapters organized activities as they saw fit in their local environments. However, even as the ranks of youth radicalism continued to grow, the demise of SDS revealed a crisis of direction within the New Left. The radicals had failed to find a way to push conventional politics sharply to the left, and when they sought to chart a strategy for political change, they displayed a volatility that suggested confusion and frustration.

Evaluations

After SDS dissolved, New Left radicals continued along the path that had emerged by 1965: they worked to expand the presence of radicalism among college-educated, white American youth. This movement's erratic behavior in the late 1960s reflected the embarrassment that some radicals felt over the fact that the contemporary left's primary constituency was a relatively privileged group. The main path of activism for the New Left, from the mid-1960s until the movement disintegrated in the early 1970s, was to cultivate islands of radicalism within a conservative sea. They attempted to live as they thought people would live in a different, better society. This was not a conventional strategy for political change, although many New Left radicals hoped that, in the long term, they would sow the seeds of a new America.

Women within the New Left, frustrated at the sexism they encountered among male comrades who supposedly believed in radical democracy, and inspired by the rising discussion of women's place in American society during the 1960s, found a way out of the New Left's moral discomfiture by working for their own empowerment. Some radical feminists stayed active in the political left, while others abandoned it as irredeemably sexist. Some male radicals reveled in the freer sexuality of the 1960s and 1970s but failed to question either the subjection of women to an inferior social role or the objectification of women that was endemic in American culture. Young feminists had ample cause for complaint. In the 1970s, some women and men tried to sustain and revive the New Left as a radical campaign that embraced feminism, but this effort came too late for the movement, which had entered a terminal phase.

Some view the later years of the New Left as a decline into muddled thinking, moral error, and political irrelevance. Others see the late 1960s and early 1970s as an impressive era in American radicalism, filled with worthy, hopeful experiments, marred by the mistakes of a mere handful of militants. Both views have merit. Alienated from the mainstream political system, lacking a strong organizational framework, and with no political strategy for creating progressive change, it was difficult for the New Left to have a clear impact on other Americans in its later years, and it could not sustain itself as a coherent enterprise. It scattered into innumerable local and individual activities, and soon the phrase "New Left" referred only to a school of political analysis, not to an active movement. On the other hand, the New Left in its later years fulfilled its deepest mission, rather than forsaking its original path. This movement was one expression of the collective experience of Americans of a particular racial, class, and generational identity. Moreover, its failure to upend American society does not distinguish it from the Old Left or from other radical movements in U.S. history. For a time, its members impressed themselves on the awareness of Americans, made many people think deeply about the nature of their society, and left behind a provocative set of questions and answers about that society that far outlived the movement itself.

See also era of confrontation and decline, 1964–80; era of consensus, 1952–64; liberalism; radicalism.

FURTHER READING. Paul Berman, *A Tale of Two Utopias: The Political Journey of the Generation of 1968*, 1996; Sara Evans, *Personal Politics: The Origins of Women's Liberation in the Civil Rights Movement and the New Left*, 1979; Van Gosse, *Where the Boys Are: Cuba, Cold War America, and the Making of a New Left*, 1993; Maurice Isserman, *If I Had a Hammer . . . : The Death of the Old Left and the Birth of the New Left*, 1987; James Miller, *"Democracy Is in the Streets": From Port Huron to the Siege of Chicago*, 1987; Doug Rossinow, *The Politics of Authenticity: Liberalism, Christianity, and the New Left in America*, 1998; Kirkpatrick Sale, *SDS*, 1973.

DOUG ROSSINOW

P

Pacific Coast, the

California, Oregon, and Washington had dissimilar political origins and came to statehood in different ways and at different times. Nonetheless, the three states came to share several common political characteristics, notably experiences with progressivism in the early twentieth century, the frequent use of direct democracy in state and local politics since then, and, recently, strong Democratic majorities in most urban areas along the coast and Republican majorities in inland areas.

American Acquisition

Several European nations laid claim to the Pacific Coast. Spanish explorers established settlements in Alta California after 1769, and a Russian settlement in what is now northern California lasted from 1812 to 1841. Spanish, British, and American ships visited the Pacific Northwest in the late eighteenth century. In 1804 President Thomas Jefferson dispatched the Lewis and Clark expedition in part to find a route to the Pacific and strengthen the American claim to the Northwest.

In 1818, the United States and Great Britain created a "joint occupancy" for the Oregon country—everything west of the Rocky Mountains between Alta California and Russian North America. The Adams-Onís Treaty (1819), between the United States and Spain, set the northern boundary of Alta California at the forty-second parallel. Missionaries from the United States began work in the Willamette Valley in 1834, and settlers soon followed along the Oregon Trail. American settlers created a provisional government in 1843, and it functioned as the civil government until 1848.

In the 1844 presidential campaign, Democrats sometimes invoked Manifest Destiny to demand annexation of Texas and the Oregon country. Their candidate, James K. Polk, won the election and began to carry out his party's platform. Some Oregon enthusiasts insisted on "54–40 or Fight," meaning the entire jointly occupied region, but in 1846 the United States and Britain compromised on the forty-ninth parallel. In 1848 Congress organized the region as Oregon Territory.

Congress annexed the Republic of Texas in 1845. The same year, Polk asked Mexico to sell Alta California and Nuevo México to the United States. A major attraction was the Bay of San Francisco, the best natural harbor on the Pacific Coast. The Mexican government refused to sell and continued to claim Texas. War was declared on May 13, 1846.

Earlier, a U.S. Army unit commanded by John C. Frémont had entered California, allegedly on a mapping expedition. By then, northern California included several American and European settlers, some of whom held Mexican land grants. In mid-June 1846, not knowing that war had been declared, American settlers at Sonoma proclaimed a California Republic and raised a crude flag that included a grizzly bear in its design. Soon after, a U.S. Navy detachment sailed into San Francisco Bay with news of the war. The Bear Flaggers, Frémont's troops, and the Navy took control of northern California. Mexicans offered sharper resistance in southern California, but U.S. forces took control there by mid-January 1847.

By the Treaty of Guadalupe Hidalgo (1848), ending the war, the United States purchased all of Alta California and Nuevo México, including all or parts of Texas, New Mexico, Arizona, California, Nevada, Utah, Colorado, and Wyoming, for less than half the price Polk had offered before the war.

In 1849, when gold seekers began to pour into northern California, the region was under Navy control and not yet organized as a territory. A convention soon met to draft a state constitution. The constitution, written in both English and Spanish, included a provision from Mexican law permitting a married woman to own property in her own name, the first such guarantee in any state constitution. Congress in 1850 approved statehood for California, with its modern boundaries.

Admission of California was hotly contested because the proposed constitution barred slavery, and admission of California as a free state would break the balance between slave states and free states. The Compromise of 1850 included admission of California as a free state among its many provisions but provided only a lull in the regional conflict over slavery.

1850–1900

Both Oregon Territory and the new state of California faced questions regarding land titles. In creating Oregon Territory, Congress voided laws passed by the provisional government, thereby calling into question the validity of land titles. Under pressure from settlers, in 1850 Congress approved the Oregon Donation Land Act, which provided for the award of up to 320 acres per person.

The land question in California involved Spanish and Mexican land grants, which often were large and vaguely defined. Congress in 1851 set up a commission to review land titles. Over five years the commissioners heard more than 800 claims and confirmed more than 600. Nearly all were appealed through the courts. The legal proceedings dragged on interminably, and many successful applicants sold their land to pay costs. Further complicating matters, squatters settled on some ranchos and refused to leave.

Most scholars of the subject have agreed with Henry George, a journalist, who in 1871 called it a "history of greed, of perjury, of corruption, of spoliation and high-handed robbery."

In San Francisco, the largest city in the West, political processes broke down twice in the 1850s. In 1851, responding to a rash of robberies, burglaries, and arson, merchants and ship captains formed a Committee of Vigilance. Despite opposition from city and state officials, the committee constituted itself as an impromptu court and hanged four alleged wrongdoers, whipped one, and banished several. In 1856 the Committee of Vigilance revived and took control of the city, establishing a force of nearly 6,000 well-armed men, mostly merchants and businessmen. City officials, the major general of the militia (William T. Sherman), the governor, and other prominent political figures all opposed the committee, but it disarmed the state militia, hanged four men, and banished about 20. The committee then established a political party and yielded power only after its candidates won the next election.

In California and Oregon Territory, a new approach to Indian reservations evolved in the 1850s. Native Americans in the east had usually been moved westward and given a reservation for each tribe. In the far west, reservations often were established by region, not tribe, and peoples from various tribes were put together regardless of the relations between them. In the 1850s, California officials approved stringent regulations over the many California Indians outside the reservations. California Indians were frequently the victims of random violence. More than one historian has concluded that genocide is the only appropriate term for the experience of California Indians during the 1850s and 1860s, and similar violent episodes took place in Oregon.

In 1853 Congress divided Oregon Territory along the Columbia River and forty-sixth parallel into Oregon and Washington territories. Four years later, Oregonians seeking statehood submitted a constitution and two other questions to voters. The voters approved the proposed constitution, decided by nearly 3 to 1 to ban slavery in the new state, and chose by an even larger margin to bar free African Americans from living in Oregon. Given the close balance in Congress, approval for statehood was uncertain but finally came in 1859.

Slavery roiled politics through the 1850s. Prompted by Democrats with southern proclivities, the California legislature prohibited African Americans from voting, serving on juries, marrying whites, or testifying in state courts, and applied similar restrictions to American Indians and Chinese immigrants. By 1859 California Democrats split into two camps, each led by a U.S. senator. David Broderick's faction opposed slavery; William Gwin's faction had southern sympathies. Tension ran even higher when a Gwin supporter killed Broderick in a duel. In 1860 California voted for Abraham Lincoln, as did Oregon.

When secession led to civil war, the two Pacific Coast states were securely committed to the Union. Though comprising just 2 percent of the Union's population, Californians donated a quarter of all funds raised by the Sanitary Commission, the humanitarian organization that assisted Union troops, and raised more volunteers per capita than any other state. California volunteers helped to rout a Confederate army from New Mexico Territory and occupied much of the West.

During the war, Republicans moved to tie the union together with iron rails. The Pacific Railroad Act (1862) incorporated the Union Pacific (UP) company to build a railroad westward and permitted the Central Pacific company to build eastward to meet the UP. The Central Pacific was controlled by four Sacramento merchants, all Republicans, including Leland Stanford, who was elected governor in 1861. For a quarter-century, the Central Pacific and its successor, the Southern Pacific (SP), dominated rail transportation in California and elsewhere in the West. Most Californians also understood the SP to be the most powerful force in state and local politics.

In 1871 Newton Booth, a Republican opponent of the SP, won the California governorship just as the Granger movement began to affect state politics. Grangers joined other SP critics in 1873 to create the People's Independent Party, which did well in the elections of 1873 and helped elect Booth to the U.S. Senate in 1875. After 1875, however, the Granger movement quickly faded.

A Granger party also appeared in Oregon, where Republicans had been in control since the early 1860s. Oregon Republican leaders were generally conservative and business-minded, and intraparty conflicts stemmed more from personalities than principles. In 1874, though, Grangers and other farmer groups formed a short-lived Independent Party that showed substantial strength in state legislative elections.

The 1876 presidential election thrust Oregon into national headlines. The Republican, Rutherford B. Hayes, carried Oregon, but national returns showed him trailing Samuel Tilden, the Democrat. Republicans challenged the returns from Louisiana and Florida; if successful, Hayes would have a one-vote majority in the Electoral College. Democrats then challenged one Oregon elector as unqualified; if successful, their ploy would have thrust the election into the House of Representatives, which had a majority of Democrats. Ultimately, a congressional election commission with a Republican majority accepted all of Oregon's electoral votes as Republican, along with the electoral votes of Louisiana and Florida, giving Hayes a one-vote majority.

After 1877, teamster Denis Kearney attracted a political following in San Francisco by condemning the monopoly power of the SP and arguing that monopolists used Chinese workers to drive down wages. He soon led the Workingmen's Party of California (WPC) and provided its slogan, "The Chinese Must

Go." The WPC briefly dominated San Francisco politics, winning elections in 1878 and 1879. Oakland and Sacramento also elected WPC mayors.

The WPC's greatest statewide success came in 1878, in elections for a constitutional convention. WPC and Granger delegates comprised a majority and wrote into the new constitution an elected railroad commission to regulate rates and restrictions on Chinese immigrants. The constitution also declared water subject to state regulation and guaranteed equal access for women to any legal occupation and to public colleges and universities. Controversial for its restrictions on corporations, the new constitution nonetheless won a majority from voters. Many of the provisions restricting Asians were invalidated by the courts.

Anti-Chinese agitation also appeared in Oregon and Washington Territory. In 1882 such western opposition to Chinese immigration led Congress to ban further immigration of laborers from China. In the mid-1880s anti-Chinese mobs appeared throughout the West, sometimes associated with the Knights of Labor. In Washington Territory the anti-Chinese movement spawned a short-lived largely unsuccessful reform party.

In California during the 1880s, voters divided closely between the Republicans and Democrats. The SP continued its prominence in state politics—symbolized in 1885 when Stanford won election to the U.S. Senate amid allegations of vote buying. That decade marked the political apogee of Christopher Buckley, a blind San Francisco saloon keeper who emerged as "boss" of the city's Democrats and a power in state Democratic politics. In 1891 charges of bribery led Buckley to leave the country, and his organization fell apart.

Washington Territory grew slowly until the 1880s, when railroad construction finally connected Puget Sound directly with the Midwest. Washington statehood was delayed not only by slow population growth but also by partisan maneuvering in Congress, where the Democratic majority in the House feared that Washington statehood would mean more Republican electoral votes. When Republicans won secure control of both houses and the presidency in 1888, statehood for Washington followed in 1889.

Populism affected all three states. In 1891 the California Farmers' Alliance launched a state Populist Party, focusing their campaign against the SP. They took 9 percent of the 1892 presidential vote and won one congressional seat and eight seats in the state legislature. Populist candidates later won the mayor's office in San Francisco and Oakland. In the 1896 presidential election, however, Republicans took California by a tiny margin. That margin soon widened. Between 1898 and 1938 no Democrat won the California governorship, and Republicans typically had large majorities in the state legislature, as California became one of the most Republican states in the nation.

In Oregon delegates from farmers' organizations, prohibitionists, and trade unions formed a new party in 1889, and the new party promoted the Farmers' Alliance. By 1892 these groups had aligned with the national Populist Party. The most prominent Populist in Oregon was Governor Sylvester Pennoyer, elected in 1886 as a Democrat and re-elected in 1890 as a Democratic-Populist fusionist. In the 1892 presidential election, Oregon cast one of its electoral votes for Populist James B. Weaver because a Democratic-Populist candidate for elector received enough votes to edge out a Republican. Republicans won the other three electoral votes. Populists won some seats in the Oregon legislature in 1892 and 1894 but accomplished little. Republicans swept the Oregon elections in 1896 and usually dominated state politics thereafter.

As in California, Populists made a decent showing in Washington's major cities, and Spokane elected a Populist mayor in 1895. Not until 1896, however, did Populists win more than local elections; that year, in fusion with the Democrats, they carried Washington for William Jennings Bryan, elected the governor and a majority of the legislature, and then sent a Silver Republican fusionist to the U.S. Senate. The party soon died out, however, and Republicans dominated the Washington statehouse in the early twentieth century.

During the late nineteenth century, women promoted a range of reform issues, including woman suffrage. In 1878 California's U.S. senator Aaron A. Sargent introduced, for the first time, a proposed federal constitutional amendment for woman suffrage. The Washington territorial legislature approved woman suffrage in 1883, but it was ruled unconstitutional by the territorial supreme court in 1888. Woman suffrage came before California voters in 1896, but a large negative vote in San Francisco and Oakland overcame the small favorable majority elsewhere.

1900 through World War II

The three Pacific Coast states moved in similar political directions in the early twentieth century. All experienced progressivism, became more conservative in the 1920s, and moved toward the Democrats and the New Deal in the 1930s.

Much of Oregon progressivism centered on William U'Ren, a Populist turned Republican. U'Ren was attracted to the single-tax proposed by Henry George but concluded that it was unlikely to be adopted without a popular vote, so he began to promote the initiative and referendum (I&R), part of the Populist platform. U'Ren pushed and prodded until voters approved I&R through a constitutional amendment in 1902. Between 1904 and 1914, Oregonians voted on 136 initiatives, approving 49, and I&R became known as the Oregon System. Successful initiatives included a railroad commission, bank regulation, a child labor law, recall, a minimum wage, home rule for cities, and a direct primary. Governor

Oswald West, a Democrat elected in 1910, frequently resorted to the initiative when the legislature refused reforms he sought.

When an Oregon law mandating protection for women workers was challenged, the Supreme Court's decision upholding protection, in *Muller* v. *Oregon* (1908), set an important precedent.

Events in Oregon influenced Washington progressives, especially I&R and recall, which were adopted early and used regularly, including recall of the mayors of Seattle and Tacoma in 1911. The Washington legislature also created regulatory commissions for railroads and other industries and established minimum wages for women and children, maximum hours for women, limits on child labor, workman's compensation, and the direct primary.

California came late to progressivism, but legislators finally adopted the direct primary in 1909, which led to the nomination of Hiram Johnson for governor in 1910. Johnson, a Republican, lambasted the SP and won, as did other progressives. The 1911 legislature produced more than 800 new laws and 23 constitutional amendments, including I&R, recall, regulation of railroads and public utility companies, the eight-hour day for women, restrictions on child labor, workman's compensation, and an investigation of corruption and inefficiency in state government.

In 1912 Theodore Roosevelt ran for president as candidate of the new Progressive Party, and he chose Johnson as his running mate. Roosevelt carried six states, including California and Washington.

All three Pacific Coast states were in the vanguard of states adopting woman suffrage. Washington became the fifth state to do so, in 1910. California followed in 1911, and Oregon in 1912.

California experienced another round of progressive reform in 1913, including laws restricting political parties. After 1913 California had more nonpartisan elected offices than any other state. Other legislation that year included reforms promoted by women's groups and the creation of three new commissions: Industrial Welfare (health, safety, and welfare of women and children), Industrial Accidents, and Immigration and Housing (migrant farm labor). The Alien Land Act, prohibiting immigrants ineligible for citizenship (those from Asia) from owning land, was intended in part to embarrass President Woodrow Wilson and the Democrats. Johnson carried the progressive banner into the U.S. Senate in 1917 and served until his death in 1945.

Progressivism transformed politics and government in all three states, adding new functions, especially the regulation of public utilities and protection of workers and consumers. The progressives' assault on political parties transformed the ground rules of state politics. The initiative became an important source of policy making. And women entered the political arena in a significant way.

Many progressives decried any role for economic class in politics, but class-based political groups appeared in all three states. Between 1901 and 1905, in San Francisco the Union Labor party won the mayoralty three times and took other local offices, then returned to power in 1909, despite revelations of earlier corruption. Socialists won local offices in several places; in 1912 Eugene Debs, the Socialist presidential candidate, received 12 percent in California and Washington and 10 percent in Oregon, compared to 6 percent nationwide. The Industrial Workers of the World established a significant presence in the lumbering areas of Oregon and Washington. World War I brought a surge of wartime patriotism, and these radical groups drew strong opposition.

Opposition to radicals continued after the war. In 1919 the Seattle Central Labor Council (unions affiliated with the American Federation of Labor) called a general strike in support of striking shipyard workers. Largely successful, the general strike lasted three days, but conservatives and antilabor groups held it up as an example of the dangers posed by radicals.

Progressivism waned after the war but did not disappear. Hiram Johnson continued as a strong progressive voice in the U.S. Senate and also staunchly opposed the League of Nations. Throughout the 1920s, a large majority of California voters registered as Republicans but divided closely between the progressive and conservative wings, making the Republican primary more important than the general election. Similar patterns appeared in Oregon and Washington, but Republican progressives there rarely mounted significant challenges to conservative dominance. Nonetheless, in 1924 Robert La Follette drew a third of the vote in California and Washington, double his national average, and a quarter of the vote in Oregon, edging the Democrats out of second place in all three states.

The Ku Klux Klan appeared in all three Pacific Coast states in the 1920s. In Oregon the Klan and other groups promoted a 1922 initiative requiring children to attend public school. Passed by a large margin, the law aimed at closing Catholic parochial schools, but the state supreme court declared it unconstitutional in 1924, and the U.S. Supreme Court did the same in *Pierce* v. *Society of Sisters* (1925). Also in 1922, Walter Pierce, a Democrat, received Klan support in his campaign for governor and won by a large margin. A prohibitionist and progressive, committed to public ownership of the electrical industry, Pierce nonetheless got little support from Republican progressives. In Washington in 1924, voters overwhelmingly defeated a Klan-sponsored initiative, modeled on the Oregon law, to require all children to attend public schools. The Klan showed strength in several California cities but played no significant role in state politics.

The Great Depression and the New Deal of Franklin D. Roosevelt revived Democratic fortunes. Roosevelt carried the three states by 57–58 percent in 1932 and 64–67 percent in 1936. During the 1930s, Democrats won U.S. Senate seats in

California and Washington and took the governorship in all three states.

The California gubernatorial election of 1934 drew national attention, but electoral politics were pushed out of the headlines earlier that year by the three-state longshore and maritime strikes, which shut down shipping for three months, and by the four-day San Francisco general strike, all of which conservatives blamed on Communists. Upton Sinclair, author of *The Jungle* (1906) and a former Socialist, won the Democratic nomination for governor with a program called End Poverty In California (EPIC). Though voters flocked to register as Democrats, Sinclair lost after a torrent of attacks that broke new ground in negative campaigning. The winner, Republican Frank Merriam, disappointed conservatives by supporting a new income tax and increasing the sales tax. A referendum to repeal the new taxes failed. The 1938 election marked the high point of Communist support for the Democrats, but Democrats' success rested primarily on a base of EPIC organizing and strong support from AFL and CIO unions, brought together by an antilabor initiative. Led by Culbert Olson, their gubernatorial candidate, Democrats swept nearly every statewide office and took a majority of the state assembly. The Senate, however, remained Republican. A broad liberal legislative agenda, including health care for nearly all workers and their families, wages and hours legislation, civil rights, and other initiatives, was defeated. Olson lost in 1942, Democrats in most other races.

Clarence Martin, a Democrat, won the governorship of Washington in 1932. As in California, the state legislature completely revised the tax code, shifting the major revenue source from property taxes to sales, income, and excise taxes. The income tax, however, was ruled unconstitutional. In 1935 leftist, labor, and farm organizations formed the Washington Commonwealth Federation (WCF), drawing inspiration from EPIC. The WCF was so active and successful in pushing Washington to the left that Postmaster General James Farley in 1936 jokingly referred to the "the forty-seven states . . . and the Soviet of Washington." Communist Party members did take an active part in the WCF, and a few were elected to office as Democrats.

In Oregon, Julius Meier, running as an independent candidate, committed to public development of hydroelectric power, won the governorship in 1930 but failed to accomplish his goal. He was succeeded by Charles Martin, a conservative Democrat, who increasingly attacked the New Deal and was not renominated in 1938. Republican governor Charles Sprague, in turn, proved to be such a progressive that he lost his renomination bid in 1942 to a conservative. An Oregon Commonwealth Federation, modeled on the WCF, was less successful than its Washington counterpart.

The New Deal brought important changes to Pacific Coast states. The Bonneville, Grand Coulee, and other dams gave the Pacific Northwest a bonanza of cheap, publicly generated electricity, which stimulated industrial development and prompted the creation of public power districts. New Deal labor policies brought many new members into unions; most voted Democratic and pushed the party to the left. In California Democrats have consistently outnumbered Republicans among registered voters since 1934. Democratic registered voters in Oregon increased sharply in the 1930s, first outnumbered Republicans in the early 1950s, and have consistently outnumbered Republicans since 1958. Similar data does not exist for Washington, but election results suggest a pattern more like California than Oregon.

By the late 1930s and early 1940s, support for the New Deal and the Democrats ebbed, especially among the middle class and farmers, even as war industries contributed to a boom in manufacturing and union membership. Republicans won the Oregon governorship in 1938 and held it and the state legislature until 1956. Republicans won the Washington governorship in 1940 and held it for 12 of the next 16 years, although Democrats usually controlled at least one house of the legislature. In California, the gubernatorial victory of Earl Warren in 1942 launched 16 years of Republican control in Sacramento. Similar patterns appeared in the region's congressional delegations, although Democrats held more seats than before the New Deal.

Since World War II

After World War II, Democrats began to accumulate considerable congressional seniority, notably the two Washington senators, Warren Magnuson (1944–81) and Henry "Scoop" Jackson (1953–83). Both held significant leadership positions, as did Alan Cranston (1969–93) from California. Wayne Morse, from Oregon, first a Republican, then an independent, and finally a Democrat, served from 1945 to 1969. Beginning in the late 1960s, Oregon voters repeatedly returned moderate Republicans to the Senate: Mark Hatfield (1967–97) and Robert Packwood (1969–95), both of whom held leadership positions. Similar patterns characterized some members of the House; two House members, both Democrats, served as Speaker: Thomas Foley, from Washington, who was Speaker from 1989 to 1995, and Nancy Pelosi, from California, who was first elected Speaker in 2007.

The late 1950s marked an important turning point for Democrats. In California, Edmund G. "Pat" Brown won the governorship in 1958, and, for the first time since the 1880s, Democrats controlled both houses of the legislature. Brown and the Democrats enacted a massive water project, a major expansion of higher education, highway construction, and a fair employment practices act. A controversial fair housing act and demonstrations at the University of California, Berkeley, contributed to Brown's defeat for a third term in 1966. In Washington a Democrat, Albert Rosellini, won the governorship in 1956 and, with a Democratic legislature, adopted a long list of administrative reforms and expanded higher education and highways. A Democrat, Robert Holmes, won the governorship in Oregon in 1956 but was defeated in 1958, and Republicans led the state for the next 16 years.

Republicans held the governorships in all three states by the mid-1960s. Elected governor of California in 1966 and reelected in 1970, Ronald Reagan championed conservative values but proved more pragmatic in practice. Promising to "cut, squeeze, and trim" the budget, he made deep cuts in higher education and mental health funding but nonetheless produced the largest budgets up to that time, requiring significant tax increases. He sent the National Guard to Berkeley to suppress demonstrations but signed the most liberal abortion bill in the country. His commitment to cutting taxes and reducing welfare forecast his presidency. Reagan was succeeded by the sometimes enigmatic Edmund G. "Jerry" Brown, son of Pat Brown and a Democrat, but voters then turned to Republicans for the next 16 years.

Daniel Evans won the Washington governorship in 1964, despite a nationwide Democratic landslide, and served three terms. A Republican, he promoted liberal environmental policies, endorsed legal abortions, expanded higher education, and supported an income tax.

In Oregon Democrats took a majority in the state legislature in 1958, for the first time in the twentieth century, but Mark Hatfield, a moderate Republican, won a closely contested election for governor. Hatfield worked to expand higher education and to bring a more diversified economy to Oregon. His successor, Tom McCall, also a moderate Republican, served two terms and initiated policies to clean up the environment and create the first state-level land-use planning system. In 1973 Oregon became the first state to decriminalize possession of small amounts of marijuana, and was followed by California and a few other states.

Recent decades have brought increasing ethnic and gender diversity among elected officials, especially in California. Since 1970 African Americans have served as mayors of Los Angeles, Oakland, San Francisco, and Seattle; Latinos as mayors of Los Angeles and San José; and Asian Americans as mayors of Long Beach, Sacramento, and San José. Asian Americans have served as U.S. senator from California and governor of Washington. Willie Brown, an African American, holds the record as longest-serving Speaker of the California Assembly, and the most recent three speakers include two Latinos and an African American woman. Since 1970 women have served as governors of Oregon and Washington, and California and Washington were the first states to have two women simultaneously serving as U.S. senators. From 1993 to 2004, Washington led the nation in the percentage of women in the state legislature. Women have been elected as mayors of most of the region's major cities. Gays and lesbians have served on city councils and in state legislatures, but not as mayor of a major city, member of Congress, or governor. A dramatic breakthrough in gay and lesbian rights came in 2008, when the California Supreme Court ruled that restricting marriage to heterosexual couples violated the state constitution's guarantee of equal rights. In response, evangelical Christians, Catholics, and Mormons mobilized to pass a constitutional amendment defining marriage as between a man and a women; advocates of same-sex marriage vowed to continue the fight for equal treatment.

The three Pacific Coast states remain distinctive in their reliance on direct democracy. Most elections include a list of initiative measures. California's Proposition 13 of 1978 launched a "taxpayer revolt" that spread to other states, and California's Proposition 45 of 1990 established term limits and inspired similar measures elsewhere, including Washington in 1992. Oregon's Proposition 16 of 1994 legalized physician-assisted suicide; similar initiatives have appeared on the ballot elsewhere but none passed until Washington's measure in 2008. California's Proposition 215 of 1996 legalized marijuana use for medical purposes; voters passed similar measures elsewhere, including Washington. California Republicans used the recall in 1994–95 to punish members of their party for crossing party lines in the legislature, and, in 2003, California voters grabbed international headlines when they recalled Governor Joseph "Gray" Davis and replaced him with movie star Arnold Schwarzenegger.

In California, Proposition 13 also generated a revolution in the *use* of the initiative. In Proposition 98 of 1988, the California Teachers Association used the initiative to mandate funding for public K–14 education. Taken together, Propositions 13 and 98 presented a new version of direct democracy: people could vote not to tax themselves but could mandate expenditure of public funds. By the end of the 1990s, some political observers pointed to the initiative as a central culprit in creating a dysfunctional state government.

During the first decade of the twenty-first century, patterns that began in the 1980s continued to mark state politics in the Pacific Coast. Democratic presidential candidates John Kerry in 2004 and Barack Obama in 2008 carried all three states, and Democrats did well in the 2006 elections, although Schwarzenegger won a second term against a weak Democratic candidate. In Oregon in 2008, Jeff Merkley, a Democrat, defeated incumbent Senator Gordon Smith, one of the last remaining moderate Republicans in Congress. A map of voting behavior in those elections shows all three states with blue (Democratic) counties along the coast, especially in urban areas, and red (Republican) counties, typically more rural and inland. Voting on initiatives and referenda often reflected the same configuration. Thus, interior voters, especially in agricultural areas, behave politically more like voters in agricultural areas in parts of the Midwest or like the voters to their east, in Idaho and Nevada. Coastal and urban voters behave much like urban voters in the northeastern United States.

FURTHER READING. Robert E. Burton, *Democrats of Oregon: The Pattern of Minority Politics, 1900–1956*, 1970; Jonathan Dembo, *Unions and Politics in Washington State, 1885–1935*, 1983; Robert E. Ficken, *Washington: A Centennial History*, 1988; Gayle Ann Gullett, *Becoming Citizens: The Emergence and Development of the California Women's Movement, 1880–1911*, 2000; Robert D. Johnston, *The Radical Middle Class: Populist Democracy and the Question of Capitalism in Progressive Era Portland, Oregon*, 2003; Richard Coke Lower, *A Bloc of One: The Political Career of Hiram W. Johnson*, 1993; Greg Mitchell, *The Campaign of the Century: Upton Sinclair's Race for Governor of California and the Birth of Media Politics*, 1992; Gary Murrell, *Iron Pants: Oregon's Anti-New Deal Governor, Charles Henry Martin*, 2000; Earl Pomeroy, *The Pacific Slope: A History of California, Oregon, Washington, Idaho, Utah, and Nevada*, 1965; Ethan Rarick, *California Rising: The Life and Times of Pat Brown*, 2005; Shelby Scates, *Warren G. Magnuson and the Shaping of Twentieth-Century America*, 1997; Jules Tygiel, *Ronald Reagan and the Triumph of American Conservatism*, 2006; R. Hal Williams, *The Democratic Party and California Politics, 1880–1896*, 1973.

ROBERT W. CHERNY

pacifism

Pacifism, the rejection of violence as a means of solving disputes, is a broad doctrine that encompasses a variety of ideas and practices and dates back to the earliest settlements in colonial America. Throughout much of American history, pacifism has been closely associated with religion, particularly the so-called historic peace churches (the Quakers, Mennonites, and Church of the Brethren). Pacifism has found a home in other religions as well.

Arguably, the earliest pacifists in American history were religious dissenters such as Roger Williams and Anne Hutchinson, who were banished in 1635 and 1638, respectively, from the Massachusetts Bay Colony for their heretical beliefs. Other, less prominent dissidents adhered strictly to nonviolent practices, even when they faced death sentences for their beliefs.

Historians such as Peter Brock, Charles Chatfield, and Meredith Baldwin Weddle have explored the history of pacifism in colonial America and found it to be a vibrant tradition that borrowed heavily from transatlantic ideas rooted in the Enlightenment and religious dissent. Some Quakers, such as itinerant eighteenth-century preacher John Woolman, preached against conscription and condemned the use of tax revenues for war purposes. Pennsylvania, with its policies of religious tolerance and separation of church and state, became a haven for a number of colonial pacifist sects.

During the American Revolution, nonviolent resistance, such as boycotts, public protests, petition drives, and other acts of noncooperation, coexisted with more violent forms of anti-British resistance. While pacifists enjoyed only a marginal presence in the Revolution, their cultural bark would prove much more powerful than their political bite, and ultimately helped influence the restrained treatment of Loyalists after the conflict.

Peace movements flourished in antebellum America, dovetailing with the broader landscape of pre–Civil War reform efforts. In 1815 David Low Dodge, a pacifist merchant, founded the New York Peace Society, the first of many such organizations formed during the first half of the nineteenth century. His 1809 tract *The Mediator's Kingdom, not of this world, but Spiritual* inspired the creation of similar groups across the United States. Reverend Noah Worcester, a New Hampshire–born Unitarian and tireless advocate of peace, worked so hard to promote pacifist ideas that he earned the title "father of the American peace movement." Pioneering American antiwar activist William Ladd, also a New Hampshire native, was a sea captain, chaplain, and author. During his life, Ladd was called the "Apostle of Peace." His newspaper, *Harbinger of Peace*, brought a wide variety of pacifists together from several states and territories, and Ladd was one of the founders in 1828 of the American Peace Society. Twenty years later, in 1848, blacksmith Elihu Burritt founded the first secular pacifist organization, the League of Universal Brotherhood.

Much of the antebellum abolitionist movement, while militant, remained nonviolent between the 1830s and the eve of the Civil War. For practical more than doctrinal reasons, abolitionists seldom took up arms against lynchings, mob violence, arson, and shootings carried out by their foes. Influenced by the work of Henry David Thoreau and other pacifist writings of the New England renaissance, abolitionist leaders such as William Lloyd Garrison, Maria Chapman, and Frederick Douglass preached restraint. Still, most abolitionists refused to condemn the violence used by foes of slavery in the 1850s, most notably in Kansas in mid-decade and by John Brown at Harpers Ferry in 1859.

As Thomas Curran documented in *Soldiers of Peace: Civil War Pacifism and the Postwar Radical Peace Movement* (2004), pacifists confronted a number of challenges during the Civil War and ultimately emerged from the conflict somewhat less robust than before. But the Universal Peace Union flourished in the late nineteenth century, attracting thousands of members, and it eventually joined the chorus of anti-imperialist voices in protesting America's involvement in the Spanish-American War (1898).

American pacifism in the twentieth century became increasingly secularized, although religious pacifism remained strong. Antiwar sentiments, robust before World War I, persisted on a smaller scale

after President Woodrow Wilson declared war in 1917. More radical antiwar advocates in the Socialist Party and Industrial Workers of the World sometimes endured harsh treatment, such as prison sentences, loss of mail privileges, and in certain cases a loss of citizenship.

Despite the repression of antiwar activists in World War I, the American peace movement reemerged stronger than ever during the interwar period, especially in the Great Depression. The heyday of pre–World War II isolationism also created fertile ground for pacifism, especially on college campuses and in cities. Opinion polls from the era painted a portrait of an American public more receptive than ever to pacifist ideas.

World War II abruptly reversed that situation. Pacifism went into full retreat during the war. Tiny enclaves of pacifists working in government-run Civilian Public Service (CPS) camps or languishing in prison kept the movement alive through the war. In the postwar era, small groups of intrepid "radical pacifists" attempted to breathe new life into the movement. Even though the cold war chilled dissent, pacifists such as A. J. Muste, Bayard Rustin, Dorothy Day, David Dellinger, George Houser continued to organize protests against war and the arms race. This small but committed group developed a more sophisticated and nuanced theoretical framework for pacifism and nonviolent direct action.

Pacifists exercised tremendous influence within the civil rights movement. Arguably, the most famous pacifist in American history was Martin Luther King Jr., who constantly sought to keep the movement nonviolent. The Vietnam War also ushered in another brief golden age for pacifism. The anti–Vietnam War movement, thriving by 1967, was a boon for the American pacifist movement. During the 1960s and early 1970s, it found new life, colorful adherents, and a restored purpose. While pacifists were always a minority within the antiwar struggle, they exercised tremendous influence over the direction and tempo of the movement.

In the last quarter of the twentieth century and opening years of the new millennium, pacifism experienced many setbacks. While it enjoyed a temporary post–Vietnam War resurgence in the early 1980s around the nuclear arms race of the Reagan era and the looming prospect of U.S. intervention in Central America, it was once again in retreat by the 1990s. The antiglobalization movement fanned the embers of pacifism again, however, and it attracted a new, if small, number of followers in the aftermath of the September 11, 2001, terrorist attacks and the war in Iraq launched in 2003. Widening resistance against the Iraq War jump-started several moribund pacifist groups. While pacifism as a protest movement remains tiny, confined mostly to large urban centers, pacifism's core ideas continue to capture the imagination of those Americans who envision a more peaceful future.

See also radicalism; religion and politics.

FURTHER READING. Peter Brock, *Pacifism in the United States: From the Colonial Era to the First World War*, 1968; Robert Cooney and Helen Michalowski, *The Power of the People: Active Nonviolence in the United States*, 1977; Staughton Lynd and Alice Lynd, eds., *Nonviolence in America: A Documentary History*, 1995; James Tracy, *Direct Action: Radical Pacifism from the Union Eight to the Chicago Seven*, 1996; Valarie H. Ziegler, *The Advocates of Peace in Antebellum America*, 1992.

ANDREW HUNT

party nominating conventions

Political party conventions perform a number of tasks. They generally meet every four years, several months in advance of a presidential election. The modern convention meets over several days to achieve various procedural and political goals. Leaders compose and approve the party platform, a policy statement including "planks," or specific proposals, on which the party's candidates run, as well as set rules for party procedure. In addition, leaders use the convention to address the party en masse. Minor figures are often given the opportunity to address the convention during the day while most delegates are in meetings; evening addresses, however, are heavily publicized and often delivered by major figures. The keynote speaker is often selected to fulfill some symbolic or political goal. For example, Zell Miller, a Democratic senator from Georgia endorsed George W. Bush at the 2004 Republican convention for president based on his national security credentials. Often a party's rising stars are chosen to deliver prominent addresses. Two such speakers between 1988 and 2004—Bill Clinton and Barack Obama—were subsequently nominated as presidential candidates in their own right. The most visible and historically important task of the convention is the nomination of that party's candidates for president and vice president.

Conventions are composed of delegates, apportioned among various state and territorial party organizations. Delegates vote for presidential and vice presidential nominees and on other procedural matters. Since the early 1970s, delegates of the two major parties have generally been bound to follow the results of state caucuses or primaries when they vote for candidates. Therefore, the identity of each party's eventual nominee is often known weeks or even months before the conventions begin; primaries have historically been held over several months during the first half of the year, and the conventions not until late summer. The events themselves have increasingly become mere formalities, serving primarily as publicized launching pads for the final weeks of the presidential campaign.

Early History

The earliest conventions wielded a great deal of influence. By the early 1830s, the party founded by Thomas Jefferson had dominated American national politics for three decades. Contemporary Democratic political operatives like Martin Van Buren thought of a party as a system of officeholders who dispensed patronage. A caucus of prominent party leaders, therefore, generally selected each presidential candidate. President Andrew Jackson, who had held office since defeating incumbent John Quincy Adams in 1828, however, was a controversial figure, and opposition to him meant that schism and a viable two-party system would soon emerge. The appearance of the political convention facilitated the transformation.

In September 1831, the Anti-Masons—an insurgent northern group particularly powerful in New York that was fearful of what it imagined was a secret yet powerful Masonic influence on politics—organized a national convention. The Anti-Masons were imitating not American politicians (who had never held conventions) but social reformers and benevolent organizations (who had). The Anti-Masons, however, reconceived the system; their party was a mass movement, and a convention was a way to attract popular participation and establish egalitarian (as opposed to the imagined Masonic conspiracy) credentials.

In Baltimore, the Anti-Masons nominated William Wirt, a former attorney general, as their presidential candidate. The convention attracted a great deal of public attention, and mainstream politicians quickly followed suit. Later that year, a group calling themselves National Republicans (disaffected Democrats who hoped to unseat Jackson) met in convention, hoping to gain both popular attention and legitimacy as a viable opposition party; they nominated Senator Henry Clay of Kentucky. Jackson's Democrats, however, did not let Clay's convention stand unmatched. In early 1832, they also met in Baltimore and nominated Jackson for a second term with Van Buren as his running mate. The convention also established the "two-thirds" rule, requiring any candidate to receive that proportion of the party vote and each state's delegation to vote unanimously. Both rules were designed to preserve the influence of the southern states. Democrats repeated the process in 1836, nominating Van Buren in Baltimore, and easily won the election, defeating three opposition candidates. In 1840 Van Buren had settled into the convention system enough to tinker with the format, directing the Democratic convention to issue the first party platform in history.

In 1836 the Whigs failed to organize anti-Jacksonian elements well enough to hold a convention; they were determined not to repeat the error. The 1839 Whig convention was held well in advance of the next election to give the party publicity and time to organize. It was the first convention to see jockeying for position, as the military hero William Henry Harrison outmaneuvered Winfield Scott and Clay for the nomination and then defeated Van Buren in the general election. In 1844, the Democratic convention was deeply divided over the proposed annexation of Texas. The first eight ballots failed to give any candidate the required two-thirds proportion of delegates, including former president Van Buren, who had the support of the majority of delegates but who had alienated the southern wing of the party by opposing annexation. James Polk, a relatively minor party figure and former governor of Tennessee, was unexpectedly nominated on the ninth ballot.

By the 1850s conventions were firmly established as a technique for gaining publicity, interest, and party legitimacy. As the Whig Party flagged, divided between northern and southern factions over the expansion of slavery, disaffected Whigs held mass meetings in Ripon, Wisconsin, and Jackson, Michigan, early in 1854. In June 1856, a national Republican Party was born at a convention in Philadelphia, which appointed a national committee, drew up a platform, and nominated John C. Fremont for president.

On the other hand, the fragmentation of the Democratic convention in 1860 signaled the collapse of that party. At the national convention held in April in Charleston, South Carolina, 50 southern delegates walked out, and after 57 ballots, the convention failed to produce a candidate. Two months later, Democrats met again in Baltimore. Again, southern delegates abandoned the convention; however, in desperation, the remaining delegates nominated Stephen Douglas for the presidency. The southern faction reconvened in Richmond, Virginia, and nominated John Breckenridge. The Republicans met in Chicago in May, and nominated Abraham Lincoln on only the third ballot. Lincoln went on to win the presidency. Four years later, in the midst of the Civil War, Lincoln declared the 1864 Republican convention would be renamed the National Union convention, and invited Democrats who opposed southern secession to attend. The convention nominated one of these men, Andrew Johnson, for vice president.

Conventions in Ascendency

The post–Civil War era saw several transformations in national conventions. Baltimore, then strategically located at the midpoint of the nation, had long been the preferred location; the Anti-Masons had met there, as had the first six Democratic conventions and nearly all the Whig conventions (including the last convention of that party in 1860). After the war, however, the nation began to look west, and the conventions followed shifting patterns of settlement, economy, and transportation. For its first 60 years, from 1856 to 1920, the Republican Party held most of its conventions in the midwestern center of Chicago, only occasionally diverting to Philadelphia (three times, in 1856, 1872, and 1900) and once each in St. Louis (1896), Cincinnati (1876), Minneapolis

(1892), and New York (1916). By the early twentieth century, the Democrats were going even farther across the nation, visiting Denver in 1908 and San Francisco in 1920.

The host city increasingly became a strategic selection, chosen to highlight an aspect of a party's campaign or to appeal to a particular region or state. Both parties moved to increase their appeal across the nation. The 1924 Democratic convention took 103 ballots before nominating John Davis, a compromise candidate various party factions could agree upon. In 1936 the convention decided to drop the two-thirds rule. Additionally, the 1940 Republican primary in Philadelphia was the first to be televised, and the dramatic victory of dark-horse businessman Wendall Willkie on the sixth ballot count boosted public interest in the candidate selection process.

The Progressive movement of the early twentieth century also encouraged popular influence at conventions, beginning a series of political reforms to curb the power of convention delegates. Several conventions in the late nineteenth century included bitter candidate battles over delegates and surprise nominees. A 36-year-old representative from Nebraska, William Jennings Bryan, seized the Democratic nomination at a divided Chicago convention in 1896 on the power of his "Cross of Gold" speech, delivered in favor of adding the free coinage of silver to the party platform. Similarly, in 1880 the Republicans took 36 ballots to select dark horse James Garfield of Ohio, nominated primarily as an alternative to unpopular former president Ulysses S. Grant, who was seeking a nonconsecutive third term. In 1910 Oregon became the first state to establish a primary system for apportioning its delegates. By 1912, 11 other states had followed suit. Further, that year former president Theodore Roosevelt challenged incumbent William Howard Taft for the Republican nomination. Roosevelt swept the primaries, winning 9 out of 12, versus Taft's single primary win, and 278 delegates to Taft's 48 (Robert La Follette, another candidate, secured 36 delegates and 2 primaries). Taft, however, controlled the party machinery.

At the convention, Roosevelt was denied more than half the delegates he had won, and Taft easily secured the nomination. Following the tradition of dissatisfied convention dissenters, Roosevelt led his followers from the Republican convention to the Auditorium Theatre, where they voted to establish the Progressive Party, complete with a platform and endorsements for a number of local and state candidates. Both Taft and Roosevelt were defeated by Democrat Woodrow Wilson in the general election, and when Roosevelt refused to attend or accept the Progressive Party's nomination at the 1916 convention, the party dissolved.

Following the tradition of the Anti-Mason Party, several other minor parties have held conventions throughout history both to attract publicity and rally their faithful. The Populist Party, born of an alliance between dissatisfied farmers and part of the union movement in the early 1890s, held a convention every four years between 1892 and 1908, nominating candidates for the presidency and other offices. The Prohibition Party, which primarily opposed the consumption of alcohol but also endorsed other social reforms, gained its widest support in the same period, though it held a convention as early as 1872. The Libertarian Party held a convention in Washington, D.C., every four years from 1972 to 2004, moving to Denver in 2008. Beginning in the 1990s, the Green Party and the Constitution Party also began holding conventions, the Greens most frequently in Los Angeles.

The Rise of Primaries and the Decline of Conventions

After World War II, primaries, though still limited in number, grew increasingly influential as a demonstration of a candidate's ability to attract votes. In 1952 New Hampshire held an early primary, an event that became a tradition. The supporters of former general Dwight D. Eisenhower waged a surrogate campaign that defeated Senator Robert Taft. Though the primary was nonbinding, the defeat weakened the conservative Taft, who had been the presumed front runner for the nomination. Following New Hampshire, Eisenhower demonstrated enough electoral strength in the primaries to defeat Taft on the first ballot at the convention. The former general allowed the convention to choose his running mate, the conservative Richard Nixon of California. Similarly, in 1964 the insurgent conservative senator Barry Goldwater shocked party leaders, defeating Nelson Rockefeller, the governor of New York, as well as William Scranton, the governor of Pennsylvania, whom frantic moderates had convinced to run after Rockefeller's weaknesses became evident. The 1964 convention was bitter, with Rockefeller and his supporters aiming rhetorical barbs at Goldwater and vice versa. But as with Eisenhower, Goldwater—the candidate who triumphed in the primaries—won the nomination on the first ballot.

In the same decade, the Democrats had virtually the opposite experience. In 1968 the party was in turmoil. President Lyndon Johnson, whose rigorous pursuit of the war in Vietnam made him extremely unpopular, declined to run for reelection. In the primaries, two candidates opposed to the war, Robert Kennedy and Eugene McCarthy, struggled for victories, a battle that ended with Kennedy's assassination shortly after winning the California primary on June 4. Many of Kennedy's supporters rallied to either McCarthy or Senator George McGovern; however, despite having not run in any of the 13 primaries, Vice President Hubert Humphrey controlled much of the remaining party organization and easily secured the nomination on the first ballot, outraging many McCarthy and Kennedy supporters. Humphrey maintained his support for the Vietnam War;

his nomination was therefore unacceptable to many of the antiwar activists who rallied in the Chicago streets outside the convention. The demonstrations turned brutal when the Chicago police assailed protesters with clubs and tear gas; meanwhile, on the convention floor, Senator Abraham Ribicoff and Chicago Mayor Richard Daley clashed over the behavior of the police. That year, 1968, was the last time a major party held a convention in Chicago until 1996.

After Humphrey's defeat at the hands of Richard Nixon in the general election, McGovern headed a commission that reformed the Democratic nominating system; primaries became vastly more influential and numerous. McGovern himself rode a string of primary victories to the nomination at the 1972 Democratic convention in Miami. McGovern's commission had implemented several new rules, including a delegate quota system that guaranteed a certain number of seats to minority groups. This system was unpopular among such Democratic centers of power as organized labor; McGovern's supporters, however, won a number of credential battles at the convention and easily defeated Senator Henry Jackson for the nomination on the first ballot. However, this was not the end of the convention's troubles. McGovern's selection of a vice president was protracted and poorly run; Senator Thomas Eagleton of Missouri was selected well behind schedule, which meant that the nominees' acceptance speeches were given long after prime television hours. McGovern failed to receive the "bounce" in the polls that generally follows a convention, and overwhelmingly lost the general election to the incumbent Nixon.

Despite the failures of his convention and campaign, McGovern's system of primaries generally worked well. In subsequent years, only in 1980, when Senator Edward Kennedy challenged the incumbent president Jimmy Carter in the Democratic primaries and forced a floor vote at the convention in New York City before conceding, was the identity of the Democratic nominee even theoretically in question when the convention began. In 2008 Senator Hillary Rodham Clinton, who had narrowly lost the race for delegates to Senator Barack Obama, was granted the formality of a floor vote. However, unlike Kennedy, she had already conceded the nomination to Obama.

A similar state of affairs prevailed among Republicans after the 1970s. In 1976, former governor Ronald Reagan of California had managed to force President Gerald Ford into a deadlock; Ford had won more delegates in the primaries, but neither he nor Reagan had secured enough to win the nomination outright at the convention in Kansas City. Reagan, who had the support of the party's conservative wing, bid for the moderates' support by announcing that he would select Senator Richard Schweiker as his running mate. The move backfired, however, and Reagan lost the support of many conservatives. Ford narrowly won the nomination on the first ballot, with 1,187 votes to Reagan's 1,070, but conservatives managed to insert several planks in the party platform, including a call for an amendment to the U.S. Constitution that would outlaw abortion. Since then, the identity of the Republican nominee has been known by the end of the primary season.

Conventions as Spectacle

In recent decades, the conventions have become little more than publicity events. In 2008, for example, Democratic nominee Barack Obama chose to deliver his acceptance speech to the general public in a football stadium, rather than solely to the party delegates in the convention hall. For this reason, the conventions have come under increasing criticism, particularly since both major parties receive public aid to fund the events.

See also campaigning; Democratic Party; elections and electoral eras; Republican Party.

FURTHER READING. James Chase, *The Emergence of the Presidential Nominating Convention, 1789–1832*, 1973; Congressional Quarterly, *National Party Conventions, 1831–1972*, 1972; Daniel Ward Howe, *What Hath God Wrought: A History of the United States, 1815–1848*, 2007; Costas Panagopoulos, *Rewiring Politics: Presidential Nominating Conventions in a Digital Age*, 2007; Byron Shafer, *Bifurcated Politics: Evolution and Reform in the National Party Convention*, 1988.

MATTHEW BOWMAN

political culture

Germans believe in a national "culture of solidarity." The French profess a faith in *liberté, égalité, fraternité*. Citizens of Thailand cling to elaborate networks of patronage and deference. Americans boast of rugged individualism (which some Europeans derogate as "cowboy culture"). Every nation has a shared set of attitudes, assumptions, aspirations, and norms that are rooted in history and legend. We call this shared vision a people's culture, and it forms the essential backdrop to politics and society.

Culture can be elusive—one historian described cultural studies as nailing jelly to a post. British anthropologist Sir E. B. Tylor proffered a definition in 1871: Culture is "that complex whole which includes knowledge, belief, art, morals, law, customs, and other capabilities and habits acquired by [people] as member[s] of society." Margaret Mead boiled it down to a simple phrase: "Culture is the learned behavior of a society." Clifford Geertz, an anthropologist at Princeton University, offered an even more direct and useful definition: "Culture is simply the ensemble of stories we tell ourselves about ourselves."

Every people has its "ensemble of stories." However, the shape and meaning of those stories is often contested—sometimes fiercely. After all, important events benefit some people and harm others; each group recalls a different tale, draws different lessons, and champions it own version over others.

Do Americans share a set of attitudes and assumptions embedded in myths about the past? Not long ago most social scientists thought so. They described a national consensus stretching back to the American founding. Important books bore titles like Henry Steel Commager's *The American Mind* (published in 1950), Richard Hofstadter's *The American Political Tradition* (1948), and Daniel Boorstein's *The Americans* (1965). Critics occasionally damned the cultural consensus for its suffocating homogeneity, but few questioned its existence or challenged its content.

Today, agreement over a shared American culture has vanished, and three very different perspectives have emerged. First, some scholars insist that the traditional American culture is still going strong. Americans, they argue, remain deeply committed to core values like individualism, political rights, equal opportunity, and a wariness of government power. These add up, say proponents, to a great American Creed originally set down by Thomas Jefferson in the Declaration of Independence. Of course, the people of the United States have never fully lived up to their high-flying ideals, but each generation fights to close the gap between quotidian life and creedal aspirations.

Others mournfully view the American Creed as a fading relic of the past. Centrifugal forces press on our society and bode serious trouble for the grand old culture. Today, the United States "belittles *unum* and glorifies *pluribus*," wrote Arthur Schlesinger Jr. in 1991. Almost 40 million people in the United States (or about one in eight) were born abroad. They cling to foreign values and resist the purifying fire of America's melting pot. Ethnic militancy "nourishes prejudices, magnifies differences and stirs antagonisms." Proponents of this view fret that a fierce politics of identity challenges traditional American culture. "Will the center hold?" asksed Schlesinger. "Or will the melting pot give way to the tower of Babel?"

A third view cheers the diversity. Proponents of this perspective reject the traditional accounts of American political culture. Images of consensus, they argue, chronicled the perspective of wealth and power while ignoring alternative voices. Perhaps the most popular exhibition in the brief against the old school lies in a fear expressed during the 1962 presidential address of the American Historical Association. Carl Bridenbaugh of Brown University warned his colleagues about a gathering storm. Once upon a time, scholars shared a common culture. Now, he fretted, historians were increasingly "products of lower middle class or foreign origins, and their emotions not infrequently get in the way of historical reconstruction. They find themselves in a very real sense outsiders on our past." Bridenbaugh's fears proved prophetic. A new generation of scholars began to read the nation in a fresh way: the real American culture, they argued—and argue still—lies in a rich amalgamation of immigrant

voices, African American blues, and songs from the urban alleys. This perspective celebrates the American "Babel" as the welcome sounds of diversity. It sees cultural pluralism as nothing less than the mainspring of national renewal.

The debate continues. Did the Americans really share a political culture? If they had it, did they lose it? If they lost it, should they feel distressed or liberated? The answer is simple and reflects the central fact of every culture: contestation. Yes, the United States has a vibrant political culture. Where many observers go wrong is to search for a static conception celebrated on all sides. American culture is constantly debated and continuously evolving. Each generation of immigrants brings new perspectives to the ensemble of stories. African Americans insist that the black experience lies at the heart of the American experience—challenging past generations that shrugged aside slavery as, in Frederick Jackson Turner's phrase, a mere "incident." Liminal groups of every sort remake American culture as they struggle for legitimacy. The uproar over the national story reminds us that there is nothing inevitable or permanent about the ideas and groups that win a hearing and become part of the mainstream—or those that lose and fall to the margins.

Ironically, a notorious jeremiad got the bottom line exactly right. In a speech to the Republican National Convention of 1992, Patrick Buchanan rattled the mainstream media with his ferocious declaration: "We are . . . in a culture war . . . for the soul of America." He failed to add that the "war" has waxed and waned for 300 years. What is most distinctive and timeless about American political culture is not the desire for freedom or the demand for rights or even the irresistible rise of Wal-Mart across the countryside, but the lively debate over each of those topics and many more. In short, American political culture was and is a constant work in progress.

Like every national culture, debates about the United States turn on a series of great national myths. Each powerfully resonates with at least some of the population. Each carries its own set of lessons. The central question is always the same: How do the stories add up? What do they tell Americans about America?

Consider three classic tales and lessons they bear.

Brave Pilgrims

Perhaps the best-known story that people in the United States tell about themselves begins with a legend made famous by Alexis de Tocqueville: the first Americans sailed away from Old World tyrannies and came to a vast, unpopulated land. In contrast to the people in Europe, those early Americans did not face powerful political or economic elites. Here there were no rigid social classes or repressive political authorities. Instead, as Tocqueville put it, "Americans were born equal instead of becoming so." White men (this story gets a bit shaky once you include women or people of color) faced extraordinary opportunities. The land and its riches awaited them. Anybody could become a success—all it took was a little capital and a lot of work.

In this context, continues the famous American legend, the early settlers soon became unabashed individualists. After all, if success and failure lay in every individual's own hands, there would be no need for government assistance or collective action. European serfs *had* to band together to fight for political rights and economic mobility. But Americans were free from the start.

This story helps explain why Americans are so quick to denigrate their government and to celebrate markets. After all, the legend comes with an unambiguous exhortation repeated down through history: hard work leads to economic success; the poor have no one to blame but themselves. Abraham Lincoln famously recited the upside of the market credo when he declared that any man who was "industrious, honest, sober, and prudent" would soon have other men working for him. He left the inevitable corollary to nineteenth-century preachers like Henry Ward Beecher: "If men have not enough it is from want of . . . foresight, industry and frugality. No man in this land suffers from poverty unless it be more than his fault—unless it be his *sin*."

Band of Brothers (and Sisters)

When contemporary historians began to examine the myths of rugged individualism, they discovered precisely the contrary—a robust collective life. Early Americans lived hard lives on a sparsely populated land and relied on one another for almost everything. When a barn burned down, the neighbors gathered and helped raise a new one. Public buildings— churches and meeting houses—were built by citizens working together. Historian Laura Ulrich Thatcher pored over household inventories and discovered that families even shared ownership of expensive cooking utensils—the lists of family possessions often include one-half or one-third of an iron pot or pan. Forget the legends about individuals on the frontier succeeding or failing on their own. Early Americans relied on their neighbors a great deal. They were communitarians more than individualists, republicans as much as liberals.

A focus on our common life offers a counter to the vigorous individualism and voracious markets that spring out of the first story. American idealists of every political persuasion invoke the nation's fragile, recurring communal values. Conservatives see the American communal legacy as an opportunity to restore "traditional values"; leftists stress our obligations to one another and suggest programs like national health insurance.

At the same time, there is a more troubling aspect embedded in the communal tradition. Defining "us" also identifies "them." In fact, the United States long ago developed a distinctive kind of American outsider—the un-American. The popular communal story, symbolized by the congenial melting pot, imagines a nation constantly cooking up a richer democracy with thicker rights. The darker alternative counters with a less cheerful story: Many Americans have faced repression simply for their ascriptive traits—their race, gender, ethnicity, or religion.

The two visions of community mingle in a long cultural dialectic. Generous American visions of equality and inclusion face off against prejudice and exclusion. The two impulses are evenly matched, Manichean twins wrestling for control of each historical moment. As William Carlos Williams put it in 1925, always poised against the *Mayflower* (a symbol of the quest for freedom) sails a slave ship (symbol of racial repression).

City on a Hill

Still another story goes back to the Puritans sailing to New England in 1630. Those early settlers arrived in the New World facing the essential communal question: Who are we? The Puritans concocted an extraordinary answer: they were the community of Saints. Leadership, in both state and church, went to individuals who could prove that they were pre-ordained for salvation. The saints could vote, hold office, and enjoy full church membership. Citizens who had not demonstrated salvation (through elaborate rituals) were expected to follow the saints; they could not vote, hold office, or become full church members. And the irreparably damned had to be driven from the community—the settlers hung witches, slaughtered Native Americans, and sent heretics packing to Rhode Island. In short, moral standing defined leaders, allocated political privileges, defined the communities, and identified the dangerous "others."

The Puritan legend concludes with a dynamic turn. Even before the settlers landed, Governor John Winthrop delivered one of the most famous sermons in American history. "We shall be as a city on a hill, the eyes of all people are upon us." This strange idea— the tiny settlement at the edge of the Western world was on a mission from God and the eyes of all people were fixed on them—stuck and grew. The American lesson for the world has evolved over time—religious faith, political freedom, unfettered economic markets. But 350 years after John Winthrop delivered his sermon, Sacvan Berkovitch, a scholar specializing in early America, described the "astonishing" consequence: "a population that despite its bewildering mixture of race and creed . . . believe[s] in something called the American mission and . . . invest[s] that patent fiction with all the emotional, spiritual and intellectual appeal of a religious quest."

Each of these three stories packs a different moral charge: Americans are rugged individuals, they wrestle over their common lives, they populate an international exemplar, a city on a hill. These are all the stuff of the national culture. They suggest national norms, serve up fodder for primal debates, and establish a setting for domestic debates, social policies, and international adventures.

Today, however, many political scientists dismiss the entire notion of political culture. Political cultures, they say, change slowly across the generations, while political events move fast. How can a constant (culture) explain a variable (politics)? Besides, the idea of national cultures imposes a kind of determinism on politics. Leftists have grown especially agitated about the ways conservatives have deployed cultural arguments; progressives resist the notion that poverty stems from "a cultural of poverty" (which blames and denigrates poor people regardless of the broader economic circumstances), and they reject efforts to ascribe tensions with the Arab world to a clash of cultures (which lets the United States off the hook for blundering international policies and writes off all the friction as the inevitable "clash between civilizations").

In dismissing the idea of political culture, however, political scientists fall into an old error. Culture is not an unyielding political fact, cast in granite. It is vibrant and dynamic; it reflects a constant debate over what it means to be an American. The stories we tell about ourselves do not belong to either left or right, to the powerful, or the poor. They are, however, formidable weapons. They shape the ways in which people see themselves; they shape the national aspirations.

Still, the critics have a point. National culture cannot offer a complete picture of political developments. It cannot, by itself, explain why the American welfare state looks so different from Sweden's or why Iraqis view the United States with suspicion. Politics also moves through constitutions and laws, leaders and political movements, exogenous shocks and the caprice of chance. Of course, those dynamics are also incomplete. We cannot fully explain political events without understanding political culture. It forms the backdrop for events in every nation. Leaders who seek to reshape welfare programs or remake foreign nations without heeding the national "ensemble of stories" rapidly come to rue their ignorance.

In short, the United States, like every other nation, has a rich national culture that should be read as a perpetual work in progress. Americans have been contesting their ensemble of stories since the first settlers stepped ashore and began to define themselves and their colonies. The battle heats up when the society appears in flux; moments of large-scale immigration, broad economic change, and shifting social relations (especially if they agitate race or gender norms) seem to foment particularly keen culture clashes. Still, every era witnesses its own exuberant debate about what the nation has been, what it is, and what it ought to be.

FURTHER READING. James Morone, *Hellfire Nation: The Politics of Sin in American History*, 1993; Arthur M. Schlesinger, Jr., *The Disuniting of America: Reflections on a Multicultural Society*, 1991; Rogers Smith, *Civic Ideals: Conflicting Visions of Citizenship in U.S. History*, 1997; Alexis de Tocqueville, *Democracy in America*, 1835, 1840, reprint, 1966; William Carlos Williams, *In the American Grain*, 1925.

JAMES A. MORONE

populism

Populism has long been among the more fiercely contested yet promiscuously applied terms in the American political lexicon. It was coined by a Kansas journalist in 1890 as an adjectival form of the People's Party, a radical third party organized in Kansas that blossomed into a national force in 1892. But in the lower case, *populist* soon became a common description for any rebellious movement of ordinary, working Americans. In recent decades journalists have affixed the term *populist* to persons and commodities that seem authentic, unadorned, and to have sprung from common sources. At times, this has included everything from plain-speaking politicians to bargain bookstores, from Bruce Springsteen's recordings to cotton trousers, which, according to their manufacturer, are "steeped in grassroots sensibility and the simple good sense of solid workmanship."

To cut through the confusion, one should define two kinds of populism—first, the historical movement itself; and second, the broader political critique and discourse. But a populism untethered to overtly political concerns is too vague and ubiquitous in American history to be useful as an interpretive category.

The Populist movement arose in the latter third of the nineteenth century, the period historians have traditionally called the Gilded Age. This was a time of rapid industrial and agricultural growth punctuated by sharp economic depressions. Absent state relief measures, increasing numbers of farmers were caught in a spiral of debt and many urban wage earners and their families were left hungry and homeless.

Populism was an insurgency largely made up of small farmers and skilled workers. It was strongest in the cotton states of the Deep South, the wheat-growing states of the Great Plains, and the mining states of the Rocky Mountains. The movement's concerns were primarily economic: during a time of low commodity prices, small agrarian proprietors demanded equal treatment in a marketplace increasingly dominated by industrial corporations, banks, and large landowners. They formed local and state Farmers' Alliances. Craft workers who resisted a cut in their wages and attacks on their trade unions believed that they shared a common set of enemies.

Populist activists proposed a variety of solutions—including nationalization of the railroads, a cooperative marketing system, a progressive income tax, and an end to court injunctions that hampered the growth of strong unions. But when a severe depression began in 1893, Populists focused on the need to inflate the money supply by basing the currency on silver reserves as well as the less plentiful reserves of gold, in hopes of spurring investment and rescuing small producers from an avalanche of debt. Most Populists were white evangelical Protestants who tended to favor prohibition and woman suffrage, "moral" issues that drew a good deal of controversy at the time.

In 1892, thousands of movement activists met to organize a national People's Party. At founding conventions held in St. Louis and Omaha, the great orator Ignatius Donnelly proclaimed, "We meet in the midst of a nation brought to the verge of moral, political, and material ruin. . . . A vast conspiracy against mankind has been organized on two continents and is rapidly taking possession of the world." The Populists, he promised, would bring the nation back to its presumably democratic roots. "We seek to restore the Government of the Republic to the hands of the 'plain people' with whom it originated," he concluded.

This vision was notably silent about racial divisions among the "plain people"; equality was more preached than practiced in the Populist movement. During the late 1880s, Colored Farmers' Alliances had sprung up in several states, and an umbrella group of the same name—led by a white Baptist minister—emerged at the end of the decade. But the Colored Alliance collapsed in 1891 when some of its members, who didn't own land, went on strike against their employers, many of whom were members of the white Farmers' Alliance. White Populists were no more hostile to black citizens than were most other white political actors at the time. In fact, such movement leaders as Thomas Watson of Georgia defended the right of black citizens to vote, in the face of violence by white Democrats in the South. But few white Populists from any region endorsed social integration or questioned the virtues of a past in which most African Americans had been held in bondage.

From its founding until 1896, the People's Party drew a sizable minority of the ballots in a swath of rural states stretching from North Carolina west to Texas and Kansas and north into Colorado and Idaho. In 1892 James Weaver, the party's first presidential nominee, won over a million votes, which translated to 8.5 percent of the popular vote and 22 electoral votes. During the 1890s, hundreds of Populists were elected to local and state offices, and the party boasted 50 members of Congress, some of whom ran on fusion tickets. These results emboldened insurgents and alarmed conservatives in both major parties.

In 1896 the Democrats emerged from a fierce internal battle with a presidential nominee from Nebraska, William Jennings Bryan, who had worked closely with Populists in his own state and was a well-known champion of the third party's demand to remonetize silver. The People's Party then met in

its own convention and, after a bitter debate, voted to endorse Bryan. When he was defeated that fall, the party and the movement it led declined into the status of a sect. The party ran its own candidates for president and vice president in 1900, 1904, and 1908, and then disbanded. Only in 1904 did its ticket— led by Thomas Watson of Georgia—draw more than 100,000 votes.

But half a century after their demise, the Populists became the subject of a ferocious, dualistic debate among some of America's most prominent historians and social scientists. From the early 1950s through the 1970s, such scholars as Oscar Handlin, Richard Hofstadter, C. Vann Woodward, Daniel Bell, and Lawrence Goodwyn disputed whether populism was conservative, defensive, and bigoted or the last, best chance for a true smallholders' democracy. One side marshaled quotes from Populists that reeked of anti-Semitism, bucolic nostalgia, and conspiracy theorizing; the other stressed that the insurgents of the 1890s tried to remedy real grievances of workers and farmers and had specific, thoughtful ideas for reforming the system.

As a critique, however, populism predated the movement and survived it, with important alterations. Central to the original critique was an antagonism between a large majority of *producers* and a tiny elite of *parasites*. Such oppositional terms were used by the Country Party in eighteenth-century Britain and became powerful markers in American politics during the early nineteenth century. The producers were viewed as the creators of wealth and the purveyors of vital services; their ranks included manual workers, small farmers, small shopkeepers, and professionals who served such people. This mode of populism offered a vigorous attack on class inequality but one that denied such inequality had any structural causes. Populists have insisted that social hierarchies are artificial impositions of elites and doomed to vanish with a sustained insurgency of the plain people.

Populism represents the antimonopolistic impulse in American history. Populists are generally hostile to large, centralized institutions that stand above and outside communities of moral producers. They have a romantic attachment to local power bases, family farms, country churches, and citizen associations independent of ties to governments and corporations. The populist critique also includes an explicit embrace of "Americanism" that is both idealistic and defensive. In the United States, which most populists consider a chosen nation, all citizens deserve the same chance to improve their lot, but they must be constantly on guard against aristocrats, empire builders, and totalitarians both within and outside their borders who would subvert American ideals.

The populist critique is usually most popular among the same social groups who originated it during the late nineteenth century: farmers and wage earners who believe the economy is rigged against them. For example, in the 1930s, amid the first major depression since the Populist era, Huey Long and Father Charles Coughlin gained millions of followers among desperate white workers, farmers, and small proprietors by denouncing "international bankers" and calling for a radical redistribution of wealth.

But populist discourse has often floated free of such social moorings. Anyone who believes, or pretends to believe, that democratic invective can topple a haughty foe and that the judgment of hardworking, God-fearing people is always correct can claim legitimacy in the great name of "the People." Thus, in the era of World War I, socialists on the Great Plains remade themselves into champions of the same small farmers they had earlier viewed as anachronisms in an age of corporate capitalism. The organization they founded, the Nonpartisan League, captured the government of North Dakota and came close to winning elections in several other neighboring states. During the 1930s and 1940s, industrial union organizers, including thousands of members of the Communist Party, portrayed themselves as latter-day Patrick Henrys battling such "Tory parasites" as Henry Ford and Tom Girdler, the antiunion head of Republic Steel.

From the 1940s through the 1980s, American conservatives effectively turned the rhetoric of populism to their own ends. During the "Red Scare" following World War II, they accused well-born figures in the federal government, such as Alger Hiss and Dean Acheson, of aiding the Soviet Union. In the 1950s and 1960s, the Right's populist offensive shifted to the local level, where white homeowners in such cities as Detroit and Chicago accused wealthy, powerful liberals of forcing them to accept integrated neighborhoods and classrooms—with no intention themselves of living in such areas or sending their children to such schools. In four presidential campaigns from 1964 to 1976, George Wallace articulated this message when he championed "this average man on the street . . . this man in the steel mill . . . the beautician, the policeman on the beat."

By the time Ronald Reagan was elected and reelected president in the 1980s, the discourse of populism had completed a voyage from Left to Right, although community and union organizers on the left continued to claim they were its rightful inheritors. "Producers" were now widely understood to be churchgoing, home-owning taxpayers with middling incomes; "parasites" were government officials who took revenues from diligent citizens and lavished them on avant-garde artists, welfare mothers, and foreigners who often acted to thwart American interests.

During the 1990s and the first decade of the twenty-first century, fear of the globalized economy spurred a new round of populist discourse. First, activists on both the labor left and the protectionist right accused multinational corporations and international bodies such as the World Bank and the International Monetary Fund of impoverishing American workers. Then the collapse of the financial system in 2008 revived anger at "Wall Street" for betraying the public's trust and driving "Main Street" into bankruptcy. Economic populists continued to have the power to sting their enemies and, perhaps, stir a desire for social change.

See also agrarian politics; labor movement and politics.

FURTHER READING. Peter Argersinger, *The Limits of Agrarian Radicalism: Western Populism and American Politics*, 1995; Edward L. Ayres, *The Promise of the New South: Life after Reconstruction*, 1992; Alan Brinkley, *Voices of Protest: Huey Long, Father Coughlin, and the Great Depression*, 1982; Dan T. Carter, *The Politics of Rage: George Wallace, the Origins of the New Conservatism, and the Transformation of American Politics*, 1995; Lawrence Goodwyn, *Democratic Promise: The Populist Moment in America*, 1976; John Hicks, *The Populist Revolt: A History of the Farmers' Alliance and the People's Party*, 1931; Michael Kazin, *The Populist Persuasion: An American History*, rev. ed., 1998; Robert McMath, *American Populism: A Social History*, 1994; Jeffrey Ostler, *Prairie Populism: The Fate of Agrarian Radicalism in Kansas, Nebraska, and Iowa, 1880–1892*, 1993; C. Vann Woodward, *Tom Watson, Agrarian Rebel*, 1938.

MICHAEL KAZIN

presidency, the

The establishment of a national executive empowered to act independently of the legislature was one of the Constitutional Convention's most consequential, and disquieting, innovations. The Revolution had targeted executive power as a threat, and both the states and the national government had kept it weak and subordinate. The supremacy of the representative assembly was a principle widely viewed as emblematic of the new republican experiment. The Constitution, however, rejected that principle. By creating a presidency equal in standing to the national Congress and by fortifying the new national executive with unity, energy, and institutional security, the framers pushed to the fore a very different conception of self-government.

In one sense, this innovation marked a clear retreat from the radical thrust of the Revolution. It is hard to miss the model of kingship behind the singular figure that the Constitution vests with "the executive power." The president commands armies, suppresses insurrections, receives foreign emissaries, and pardons almost at will. The office stands watch over the legislature, its veto power potent enough both to protect its own independence and to check the programmatic impulses of simple majorities. This was, for all appearances, a conservative position designed to preserve order, manage affairs, and bring a measure of self-control to the government as a whole.

In another sense, however, the American executive drew upon and extended the principles of the Revolution. The presidency stands apart from the

Congress but not from the people. As the decision to vest executive power in a single person focused responsibility for the high affairs of state, the selection procedure ensured that individual's regular accountability to a national electorate. Provisions for a fixed term and a separate national election established the presidency as the equal of the Congress, not only in the powers at its disposal but also in its popular foundations. Overall, the construction of separate institutions each balanced against the others and each accountable to the same people underscored the sovereignty of the people themselves over any and all institutional expressions of their will.

How, and with what effect, this new arrangement of powers would work was far from clear. The few broad strokes with which Article II of the Constitution constructed the presidential office are indicative of the delicate political circumstances of its creation and of the strategic value of keeping its implications ambiguous. There is no counterpart in Article II to the crisply punctuated list of powers expressly vested in the Congress by Article I, section VIII. By the same token, the more implicit and open-ended character of the powers of the presidency gave freer reign to interpretation and the exigencies of the moment. It imparted to the office an elastic quality that incumbents were invited to exploit by their own wits.

A few issues became apparent early on. One was that the scope of presidential power would be fiercely contested. The administration of George Washington ventured bold initiatives in foreign policy, domestic policy, and law enforcement, and it backed them up with strong assertions of presidential prerogative. But each brief issued on behalf of the power and independence of the executive office provoked a strong reaction, and together they became a rallying cry for opposition. No less clear was the portentous character of the transfer of power from one president to another. John Adams's initial decision to retain Washington's cabinet aimed to assure stability and continuity in government operations across administrations, but it could not be sustained without severely handicapping the president in his efforts to exercise the powers of his office on his own terms. As Adams ultimately discovered, a president cannot maintain control of his own office if he does not first secure control over the other offices of the executive branch. The election of a new president would thenceforth bring in its train the formation of a new administration, with all that it implied for the disruption of established governing arrangements and the perturbation of governing coalitions.

Behind these early revelations loomed another: that presidential elections and presidential administrations would orient American national politics at large. Providing a focal point of responsibility for the state of the nation, the president spurred political mobilization, the articulation of national issues, and the reconfiguration of political cleavages. Ironically,

an office designed with an eye to bringing order and stability to national affairs became a magnet for popular controversies and an engine of change.

Institutional Development

Most of what we know of the presidency today is a product of latter-day embellishments. Two historical processes, in particular, figure prominently in its development: the democratization of the polity and the nationalization of the affairs of state.

The democratization of the polity was first expressed institutionally in the form of party development, and this gave rise in the nineteenth century to a party-based presidency. The emergence of two national parties in the 1790s distilled rival interests across great geographical distances and coordinated their actions for presidential elections. The Twelfth Amendment, ratified in 1804, formally separated the election of president and vice president and thus facilitated the formation of a national party ticket. The emergence of nominating conventions in the 1830s brought state party organizations together for the purposes of articulating a common platform and selecting candidates for the national ticket that would rally coalition interests.

Through innovations such as these, the presidency was connected organizationally to local bases of political support and integrated into national politics. Parties eased constitutional divisions of power by providing a base of common action among like-minded partisans in the presidency and the Congress. Just as importantly, the president lent support to his party base by distributing the offices at his disposal in the executive branch to its constituent parts at the local level. The spoils system, which rotated executive offices with each transfer of power and filled them with partisan supporters of the new incumbent, complemented the convention system. As the convention tied the president to local party organizations, the spoils tied local party organizations to the president. Each side had powerful incentives to support the other, and the tenacious community of interests that was formed helped to hold America's contentious democracy together as it sprawled across a continent.

The presidency was recast again over the early decades of the twentieth century. The growing interdependence of interests in industrial America and the heightened stakes of world affairs for national security rendered the prior integration of presidency into a locally based party politics increasingly anachronistic. Progressive reformers sought to break down the community of interest that had animated the party presidency and to construct in its place powerful national bureaucracies capable of managing the new problems posed by industrialization and world power. At the same time, presidents asserted leadership more directly. They began to take their case to the people. The hope was that by rallying public opinion behind their policy proposals, they would catalyze concerted action across the dispersed and divided institutions of the Washington establishment.

With presidents and national bureaucracies assuming a more prominent role in governing, the office of the presidency itself was refortified. The passage of the Executive Reorganization Act in 1939 and the establishment of the Executive Office of the President (EOP) gave incumbents new resources for managing the affairs of state. Agencies of the EOP such as the Bureau of the Budget (later the Office of Management and Budget), the Council of Economic Advisors, and the National Security Council were designed by Congress with two concerns in mind: to help the president tackle national problems holistically and to assure Congress that the president's recommendations for national action were based on the candid advice of trained professionals and policy experts.

In recent decades, institutional developments have supported greater claims on behalf of independent presidential action. In the 1970s primary elections displaced national party conventions as the chief mechanism for candidate selection. This has encouraged candidates for the office to build national political organizations of their own. A personal political organization is then carried over by the party nominee into the general election, and it is transferred again by the successful candidate into the offices of the White House. One effect has been to weaken the mutual control mechanisms of the old party-based presidency. Another has been the downgrading of the statutory agencies in the EOP, which progressive reformers had relied upon to institutionalize neutral advice, interbranch coordination, and information sharing. The locus of presidential power has shifted into the inner sanctums of the White House itself, where the incumbent's personal control is least likely to be contested and where the strategic orientation revolves almost exclusively around the president's own political priorities. The reforms of earlier generations, which relied on extraconstitutional devices to ease the separation of powers and integrate the presidency into the rest of the government, are giving way to new assertions on behalf of the unitary executive—assertions that accentuate the separation of powers, expand the legitimate domain of unilateral action, and delimit the reach of checks and balances.

Institutional Power and Political Authority

Though reformers may have believed that bolstering the institution of the presidency would make for more effective political leadership, the connection between institutional development and political performance remains weak. More resources have not ensured more effective leadership; great performances dot the presidential history in a seemingly random fashion. This has led many observers to stress the importance of character, personality, and skill in the exercise of presidential power, and appropriately so: as the purview of American national government has expanded and the office of the presidency has grown more resourceful, incumbent competence has been placed at a premium.

Still, it is hard to discern any coherent set of personal attributes that distinguishes politically effective leaders from politically ineffective ones. Franklin Roosevelt and Lyndon Johnson both possessed extraordinary political skills. But while one reconstructed the standards of legitimate national action, the other self-destructed. Andrew Jackson and Andrew Johnson were rigid, vindictive, and divisive leaders. But one succeeded in crushing his opponents while the other was crushed by them. A long look back over this history suggests that the variable political effectiveness of presidential leadership is less a matter of the personal attributes of the incumbent than of the political contexts in which he is called upon to act.

One of the more striking patterns to be observed in presidential history is that the leaders who stand out both for their political mastery in office and their reconstructive political effects were immediately preceded by leaders who are widely derided as politically inept and out of their depth: John Adams and Thomas Jefferson, John Quincy Adams and Andrew Jackson, James Buchanan and Abraham Lincoln, Herbert Hoover and Franklin Roosevelt, Jimmy Carter and Ronald Reagan. In each historical pairing, we first find a president whose actions in office seemed self-defeating and whose chief political effect was to foment a nationwide crisis of legitimacy; next we find a president whose actions in office proved elevating and whose chief effect was to reset the terms and conditions of legitimate national government. On further inspection, it will be observed that the first president in each pair led to power a governing coalition whose commitments were well established but increasingly vulnerable to identification as the very source of the nation's problems. The second president in each pair led to power an untested political insurgency. Each used his powers to define the basic commitments of that insurgency and secure them in a new governing coalition. Difficult as it is to distill a shared set of personal attributes that clearly distinguishes the incumbents on one side of these pairings from those on the other, the common political circumstances faced on each side are unmistakable.

This pattern points back to fundamental attributes of the presidential office, qualities that have held sway despite the dramatic developments to be observed over time in the accoutrements of institutional power. The most telling of these is the one first revealed in the transfer of power from George Washington to John Adams: the inherently disruptive political impact of the election of a new president and installation of a new administration. In one way or another, new presidents shake things up. The constitutionally ingrained independence of the office, the provision for separate elections at regular intervals to fixed terms, the institutional imperative that each new incumbent assert control over the office in his own right—all this has made the presidency a persistent engine of change in the American political system. It is precisely because all presidents change things in one way or another that the power to change things has been less of an issue in the politics of leadership than the authority that can be found in the moment at hand for actions taken and changes instigated. Unlike institutional power, which has developed in stages over the long course of American history, authority of this sort can shift dramatically from one president to the next.

It is not surprising that incumbents affiliated with established interests have a harder time sustaining authority for their actions than do incumbents who come to power from the opposition. The opposition stance plays to the institutional independence of the presidential office and supports its inherently disruptive political effects; affiliation compromises independence and complicates the meaning of the changes instigated. This difference is magnified when, as in the case of our starkly contrasting historical pairs, the political commitments of the dominant governing coalition are being called into question by events on the ground. Affiliated leaders like the Adamses, Buchanan, Hoover, and Carter could neither forthrightly affirm nor forthrightly repudiate the political interests to which they were attached. Actions that reached out to political allies served to cast the president as a symptom of the nation's growing problems while actions that charted a more independent course tended to alienate the president from his base of political support. Lacking the political authority to secure firm ground for their actions, these presidents found themselves in an impossible leadership situation. In turn, Jefferson, Jackson, Lincoln, Franklin Roosevelt, and Reagan drew great advantages from the political disaffection created by the hapless struggles of their predecessors. Leading to power an insurgency defined largely by its forthright repudiation of an old establishment, they were able to rearticulate first principles, to sustain freedom of action across a broad front, and, ultimately, to locate a common ground of new commitments that their supporters would find authoritative.

Historically, the weaker the political ties binding presidents to established standards of action, the stronger the president has been in tapping the independence of his office and delivering on its promise of a new beginning. How, then, will recent developments in the institution of the presidency come to bear on this general rule? On the one hand, we might expect that as all presidents become more independent in the resources at their disposal, any limitations imposed by the political affiliations they bring into office will diminish. On the other hand, as these new resources become more self-contained and detached from those of other institutional actors, we may also discover new limits on the presidency's capacity to

play its vital historical role in the renewal and reinvigoration of the American polity as whole. In the past, the presidents who effectively reconstructed the terms and conditions of legitimate national government did not just break old bonds; they also forged new ties that knit the system back together. Whether a reintegration of that sort remains possible is an open question.

See also cabinet departments; Constitution, federal.

FURTHER READING. Peri E. Arnold, *Making the Managerial Presidency: Comprehensive Reorganization Planning, 1905–1996*, 1998; Steven G. Calabresi, "Some Normative Arguments for the Unitary Executive," *Arkansas Law Review* 48 (1995), 23–104; James W. Ceaser, *Presidential Selection: Theory and Development*, 1979; William G. Howell, *Power without Persuasion: The Politics of Direct Presidential Action*, 2003; Harvey C. Mansfield, *Taming the Prince: The Ambivalence of Modern Executive Power*, 1989; Sidney M. Milkis, *The President and the Parties: The Transformation of the American Party System since the New Deal*, 1993; Terry M. Moe, "The Politicized Presidency," in *The New Direction in American Politics*, edited by John E. Chubb and Paul E. Peterson, 235–71, 1985; Richard E. Neustadt, *Presidential Power and the Modern Presidents: The Politics of Leadership from Roosevelt to Reagan*, 1991; Arthur M. Schlesinger, Jr., *The Imperial Presidency*, 1973; Stephen Skowronek, *The Politics Presidents Make: Leadership from John Adams to Bill Clinton*, 1997; Charles C. Thach, *The Creation of the Presidency, 1775–1789: A Study in Constitutional History*, 1922; Jeffrey K. Tulis, *The Rhetorical Presidency*, 1988.

STEPHEN SKOWRONEK

presidency to 1860

The seventeenth and eighteenth centuries marked the transition from a powerful to a tamed executive branch of government, first in Great Britain and then in the United States. In the 1600s, England began the long, slow, and often violent process of wresting power away from the king and placing authority in the hands of the Parliament. This transition led to both the democratization of the polity and the control of executive power. The American Revolution of 1776 furthered this process by placing the executive branch within the constraints of a constitution (1787), a separation-of-powers system, the rule of law, and checks and balances. While the French Revolution that followed (1789) unleashed the best and the worst of democratic sentiments, it was to serve as a warning against unchecked power in the hands of the masses. The American Revolution occurred in the middle of these transitions and drew lessons from both the British and the French. From the British, Americans were convinced that the divine right of kings and executive tyranny had to give way to a controlled executive, and from the French experience, they learned that unleashing democracy without the rule of law and checks and balances could lead to a different but also quite dangerous form of tyranny.

The American experiment in empowering as well as controlling executive powers within a web of constitutional and political constraints led to the creation of a rather limited presidency. Yet over time, this executive branch would grow and expand in power and responsibility; both necessity and opportunity would allow for the growth of presidential power.

The Rise of the Presidency

As the United States became a world power, it also became more of a presidential nation. In the early years of the republic, however, with few international responsibilities and fewer foreign entanglements, the presidency would be a rather small institution, with limited powers, whose holders would struggle to establish a place of power within the new system of government.

Of the framers' handiwork at the Constitutional Convention, the presidency was the least formed and defined of the three governing institutions. Thus, while the office may have been invented by the framers, it was brought to life by George Washington and his successors.

The framers were concerned that this new president not become a tyrant or monarch. Having fought a revolution against the hereditary monarchy of Great Britain, they wanted to create an executive branch that, as its name implies, would preside, enact laws passed by the Congress, manage the government's business, and be but one element of a three-part government. Designed to promote deliberation and not efficiency, this new government would not have an all-powerful figure at its head. But could such a government work in practice?

The Presidency in Practice

George Washington, the towering figure of his era, was, as first president (1789–97), a precedent setter. He was a man who could have been king, yet chose to be president. At the time of his inauguration, the American experiment was just that—an experiment; thus, everything that Washington did mattered. As he noted at the time, "I walk on untrodden ground." Whatever Washington did would have an impact on what was to follow. One of the reasons the Constitutional Convention was willing to leave Article II, which created a presidency, somewhat vague and ill-defined was that the delegates knew Washington would occupy the office first, and they so trusted his republican sensibilities that they allowed him to set the tone for what the presidency would become.

Washington's goal was to put the new office on a secure footing, create conditions in which a republican executive could govern, give the office some independence, and establish the legitimacy of the new republic. This was no small order. He attempted to be a national unifier at a time when divisions were forming in the new nation. His major effort toward

this goal was to bring Alexander Hamilton and Thomas Jefferson, two bitter personal and ideological rivals, together in his first cabinet. This worthy goal would fail, however, and the clash between these two rivals was instrumental in forming the nation's first political parties.

Washington exercised independent authority over treaty making, declared neutrality in the war between France and England, and asserted independence from Congress in managerial matters within the executive branch. For Washington, the president was not to be a messenger boy for Congress but instead an independent officer with powers and prerogatives. But if Washington set precedents for the ill-defined office, could he trust his successors to exercise such ambiguous authority with honor and dignity? The ambiguity that allowed him to invent an office could also potentially be used by less skilled men, with less character, to less benign ends.

John Adams followed Washington into the presidency (1797–1801), and his term in office was marked by internecine warfare between the president and members of his own Federalist Party. Adams's disappointing presidency led to the shift in power from the Federalists to the Jeffersonians in the hotly contested election of 1800.

Party Leadership and Prerogative

The next president to add markedly to the powers of the office was Thomas Jefferson (1801–9), who set an important precedent in that his inauguration marked the first of what would be many peaceful transfers of power from one party to another. Jefferson wanted to deceremonialize the presidency and make it a more republican institution. He did away with bowing, replacing the regal custom with the more democratic handshake; he abolished the weekly levee (a reception); ended formal state dinners; and abandoned the custom of making personal addresses to Congress. Jefferson also used the cabinet as an instrument of presidential leadership and exerted control over Congress by exploiting opportunities for party leadership.

When the opportunity to purchase the Louisiana Territory from France presented itself, Jefferson believed that he did not have the authority to act and had his cabinet draw up a constitutional amendment to give him such authority. But time was short, and an amendment might take months, if not years, to pass. Jefferson was confronted with a stark choice: act on his own questionable authority or lose one of the great opportunities for promoting the nation's security and expanding its borders. Jefferson acted. It was one of the most important, if constitutionally questionable, acts in presidential history.

Perhaps Jefferson's greatest contribution to presidential leadership was his linking of that which the framers separated: the president and Congress. Jefferson exercised a form of hidden-handed legislative leadership by inviting important members of his party in Congress to the White House for dinners, after which he would chart out a legislative strategy and agenda for his fellow party members to push through Congress. It was an effective tool of leadership and one that subsequent presidents exercised with mixed success.

The next three presidents faced something of a congressional backlash. James Madison (1809–17), James Monroe (1817–25), and John Quincy Adams (1825–29) had mixed success as presidents. The one key to the rise of presidential power in this era occurred during the Monroe administration, when, seeing European powers eyeing territories in the Americas, the president announced the Monroe Doctrine, a warning to European states to abandon imperial ambitions in the Americas. Monroe issued this declaration on his own authority, and it helped increase the foreign policy powers of the presidency.

The President and the Rise of Democracy

The next president, Andrew Jackson (1829–37), was one of the most cantankerous and powerful men ever to occupy the White House, and he became president at a time of great social change in America. By the 1820s, most states no longer required men to own property in order to vote, and nearly comprehensive white male suffrage had arrived. Jackson recognized the potential implications of this momentous change and exploited it to his advantage. He claimed that, as the only truly nationally elected political leader in the nation, he was elected to speak for the people. By making the president the voice of the people, and linking presidential power to democracy, Jackson greatly added to the potential power of the office. Merging the presidency with mass democracy, Jackson used what he saw as his mandate to lead (some might say bully) the Congress. Such a link between the people and the president was something the framers feared, believing that this could lead a president to manipulate public opinion and emerge as a demagogue, destroying the possibility of true statesmanship and deliberative government.

The Rise of Congress

After Jackson, a series of weaker presidents followed, and Congress reasserted its constitutional prerogatives. This became a pattern in American history: a strong president, followed by congressional reassertion, followed by a strong president, a backlash, and again strong congressional leadership. The three presidents after Jackson—Martin Van Buren (1837–41); William Henry Harrison (1841), who died after a month in office; and John Tyler (1841–45), the first vice president to assume office on the death of a president)—faced strong congressional leadership and were limited in what they could achieve.

James Polk (1845–49), however, changed that pattern. He demonstrated that a determined president could, in effect, start a war (the Mexican-American War). Polk was able to manipulate events along the

Texas-Mexican border coaxing the Mexican force to attack, and by initiating aggressive action, preempt the Congress and force it to follow his lead. This initiative was yet another tool of presidential leadership added to the arsenal of presidential power.

Several weaker presidents followed Polk, as the nation became swept up in sectional rivalry and the issue of slavery. Rather than presidential government, this was an era of congressional dominance. Presidents Zachary Taylor (1849–50), Millard Fillmore (1850–53), Franklin Pierce (1853–57), and James Buchanan (1857–61) were weak presidents in a difficult age.

The Impact of War on the Presidency

James Buchanan is an especially interesting case in presidential weakness. Sectional difficulties were heating up, and the slavery issue was causing deep divisions between the North and the South. Many southern states were threatening nullification, if not outright secession, from the Union. Despite the grave threat to the nation's future, Buchanan did not believe he had the constitutional authority to prevent the southern states from seceding, and his self-imposed restraint meant that the rebellious states would meet little resistance. Buchanan saw slavery as a moral evil, but he conceded to the South a constitutional right to allow slavery to exist. He tried, but failed, to chart a middle course. Although a strong unionist, Buchanan's limited conception of presidential power prevented him from taking the steps necessary to stem the breakup of the nation.

Buchanan was a strict constitutional constructionist; he believed the president was authorized to take only those actions clearly spelled out in the Constitution. This conception of the office severely limited Buchanan's efforts to stem the tide of secession. In his last message to the Congress, delivered on December 3, 1860, Buchanan stated, "Apart from the execution of the laws, so far as this may be practical, the Executive has no authority to decide what shall be the relations between the Federal Government and South Carolina. . . ." Less than three weeks later, South Carolina seceded from the Union.

Buchanan left his successor, Abraham Lincoln, a seemingly unsolvable crisis. He told the incoming president, "If you are as happy, Mr Lincoln, on entering this house as I am in leaving it and returning home, you are the happiest man in this country." Lincoln, however, was animated by the challenge. His presidency (1861–65) would reinvent the office and take its power to new heights.

The Evolution of the Presidency

The presidency was invented at the end of the era of the aristocracy, yet before the era of democracy had fully arrived. The framers of the U.S. Constitution created a republican form of government with limited powers, under the rule of law, within a constitutional framework, with a separation of powers system. From 1789 to 1860 the presidency they invented proved viable, resilient, and—at times—quite effective. The evolution of the presidency from idea to reality, from blank slate to robust office, resulted in the creation of a new office that achieved stability and independence. This experiment in governing was built on and grounded in the Constitution, but that document was only its starting point. In reality, the presidency was formed less by the Constitution and more by the tug-of-war over power between the president and Congress as politics played out over the first 70 years of the republic. In this sense, the presidency was created in practice more that at the drafting table.

The presidency before 1860 did not need to be large, powerful, or imperial. The United States was a relatively small nation, somewhat geographically isolated from the troubles of Europe, with few entangling alliances and no position of world leadership. As a secondary world power, the United States did not have to flex its military muscle or make its presence known across the globe. This allowed the presidency to develop free from the pressures of global responsibilities.

Likewise, the domestic demands placed on the federal government were more limited in this period than they are today. The federal government did less, and less was expected of it. The media was localized and, prior to the advent of radio (and then television and the Internet), tools of communication were limited. But, although the presidency was "small" as an institution, the seeds were planted in this era for the rise and growth of presidential power that was to follow. That growth would await the advent of the twentieth century, and the rise of the United States as a world military, political, and economic superpower.

See also era of a new republic, 1789–1827; Jacksonian era,1828–45.

FURTHER READING. Michael A. Genovese, *The Power of the American Presidency, 1789–2000*, 2001; Ralph Ketcham, *Presidents above Party: The First American Presidency, 1789–1829*, 1984; Sidney M. Milkis and Michael Nelson, *The American Presidency: Origins and Development, 1776–2002*, 2003; Michael P. Riccards, *The Ferocious Engine of Democracy: A History of the American Presidency*, vol. 1, 1995.

MICHAEL A. GENOVESE

presidency, 1860–1932

The presidential elections of 1860 and 1932 brought to power two of America's most important presidents: Abraham Lincoln and Franklin D. Roosevelt. These two elections also marked the beginning and the end of an era in which Republicans dominated the office of president. The power of the presidency ebbed and flowed during the period from 1860 to 1932, depending on the personality and ambitions of the officeholder and the challenges of his times.

The Civil War and Reconstruction: 1860–76

In 1860 Abraham Lincoln, the candidate of the Republican Party, founded just six years earlier, won the presidency as the only antislavery contender in a crowded field. Lincoln opposed the expansion of slavery beyond its existing boundaries, which many slaveholders regarded as tantamount to abolition. Consonant with the party's emphasis on activist government and economic development, Lincoln's platform also called for homestead legislation to promote western settlement, protective tariffs, and internal improvements. Although he won only 40 percent of the popular vote, he carried every northern state. The new president would have the cheerless task of presiding over the near dissolution of the nation itself. Even before Lincoln took the oath of office on March 4, 1861, seven southern states had seceded from the Union. On April 12, 1861, the Civil War began with the bombardment of Fort Sumter in South Carolina.

As a wartime leader, Lincoln became the most activist president to that time in U.S. history, expanding the powers of the presidency and the importance of the national government. Lincoln assumed broad powers to quell what he believed was a lawless domestic insurrection. When he issued the Emancipation Proclamation that freed all slaves still held by the Confederacy, he committed the federal government for the first time to a decisive stand against slavery. He summoned the militia to defend the Union, ordered a blockade of the Confederacy's ports, expanded the regular army beyond its legal limit, and spent federal funds without congressional approval. He suspended the writ of habeas corpus, which now meant that persons could be imprisoned without charges, and authorized army commanders to declare martial law in areas behind the lines. The Lincoln administration also instituted a graduated income tax, established a national banking system, facilitated the settlement of western lands, and began the nation's first draft of soldiers.

Lincoln won reelection in 1864, aided by Union victories in the fall of that year. He would not, however, survive to preside over postwar Reconstruction, a task that would fall to lesser leaders. After Lincoln's assassination in mid-April 1864, Andrew Johnson, a Democrat and the former wartime governor of Tennessee, assumed the presidency. Lincoln had put Johnson on his ticket in 1864 to present a united front to the nation. Johnson's tenure as president marked a significant decline in presidential power and prestige.

Johnson and the Republican Congress battled over Reconstruction policy, with Congress gaining the upper hand. Congress enacted civil rights laws, the Fourteenth Amendment guaranteeing "equal protection under the law," and the Fifteenth Amendment, which prohibited the denial of voting rights on grounds of race, color, or previous servitude. Congress authorized the stationing of federal troops in the South to enforce Reconstruction. In 1868 Johnson became the first president impeached by the U.S. House of Representatives. The primary charge against him was that he had violated the Tenure of Office Act, which forbade him from firing cabinet members without the approval of the Senate. Conviction in the Senate failed by a single vote. However, Johnson's political career was over, and a Republican, war hero Ulysses S. Grant, won the presidency in 1868. Johnson's impeachment strengthened the hand of Congress relative to the presidency, but it also discredited the use of impeachment as a political weapon.

Grant proved to be a weaker president than he had been a general. He assumed office with no program of his own; he followed the precedents set by the Republican Congress. Despite a lack of enthusiasm for black equality, Grant supported measures to sustain and extend Reconstruction. He continued the circulation of paper money, reduction of the federal debt, protection of industry through tariffs, and subsidization of the railroads. But Reconstruction was already unraveling during Grant's first term. Although the shell of federal power kept the South in Republican hands, the party that identified with black aspirations was unable to gain the support of white Southerners and thereby maintain its hold on the majority-white South.

Grant easily won reelection in 1872, but the advent of an economic depression in 1873 dashed his hopes for a bright second term. With Grant lacking ideas for reviving the economy, Congress acted on its own to expand the currency. But Grant, a president committed to the ideal of sound money, vetoed the legislation, leading to a paralysis of policy that endured through the end of the depression in 1878. Widespread corruption pervaded the Grant administration, which was also ineffectual in sustaining Reconstruction. By the end of Grant's second term, white supremacist "Redeemers" had gained control of every southern state with the exceptions of Florida, Louisiana, and South Carolina.

The Gilded Age: 1877–1900

The disputed presidential election of 1876 marked the end of Reconstruction and another low point in the powers of the presidency. Although Democratic candidate Samuel J. Tilden, the governor of New York, won the popular vote against Republican governor Rutherford B. Hayes of Ohio, the outcome of the election turned on disputed Electoral College votes in Florida, South Carolina, and Louisiana, the three states in which Republicans still retained power. With the U.S. Constitution silent on the resolution of such disputes, Congress improvised by forming a special electoral commission that ultimately consisted of eight Republicans and seven Democrats. The commission voted eight to seven on party lines to award all disputed electoral votes to Hayes, which gave him the presidency.

Hayes fulfilled his campaign promises to govern from the center and serve only a single term in office.

By the time of the next presidential election, the nation had divided sharply into a solidly Democratic South that systematically moved to disfranchise black voters and a predominantly Republican North. The years from 1876 to 1892 were marked by a sharp regional division of political power growing out of Civil War alignments and a national stalemate between Republicans who dominated the North and Democrats who controlled the "redeemed" South. The Republican Party was also deeply divided between reformers and leaders, known as the Stalwarts, who were intent upon exploiting the political system for private gain. The Republican convention of 1880 held 35 ballots before nominating a dark horse candidate and mild reformer, Representative James A. Garfield of Ohio. In a gesture of conciliation to the Stalwarts, he chose as his running mate Chester A. "Boss" Arthur, who had held the key patronage position of customs collector of the Port of New York. The Democrats countered with former Civil War general Winfield Scott Hancock.

Garfield's hairbreadth victory over Hancock, by some 2,000 popular votes, began a series of four consecutive presidential elections in which the major party candidates were separated by an average of just 2 percent of the popular vote. Garfield had served less than four months as president before succumbing to an assassin's bullet. The newly inaugurated Chester Arthur disappointed his Stalwart friends by steering a middle course as president. Ironically, one of his crowning achievements was to sign into law the Pendleton Act of 1883 that established the federal civil service system. Arthur, however, had endeared himself to neither wing of the GOP and, in 1884, became the only sitting president in U.S. history to be denied his party's renomination.

In 1884, with the victory of New York governor Grover Cleveland, the Democrats gained the White House for the first time in 24 years. Cleveland's presidency harkened back to Andrew Jackson. Like Jackson, Cleveland believed in limited government, states' rights, sound money, fiscal responsibility, free trade, and a president who protected the public from the excesses of Congress. Cleveland vetoed several hundred special pension bills for Union veterans and their dependents. In 1887 he also vetoed the Dependent Pension Bill, which would have mandated payments to most disabled veterans regardless of whether their disabilities resulted from wartime service. During his first term, Cleveland exercised the presidential veto more than twice as many times as all his predecessors combined.

In his reelection bid, Cleveland prevailed in the popular tally, but lost his home state of New York and with it the Electoral College. Republican president Benjamin Harrison sought to restore to his party the activism of Lincoln, with mixed success. Among his achievements was the McKinley Tariff of 1890, which substantially increased tariff rates. Harrison and other Republicans of the Gilded Age presented tariff protection as a comprehensive economic policy that would nurture industry, keep wages high, and strengthen domestic markets for agricultural goods. Harrison also gained passage of a pension bill similar to the legislation that Cleveland had vetoed. By 1893 pension payments would account for nearly half of the federal budget, and pensions would constitute the only substantial federal relief program until the New Deal of the 1930s. Congress also enacted the Sherman Anti-Trust Act, which outlawed corporate combinations or conspiracies "in restraint of trade or commerce." Harrison failed, however, to steer new civil rights laws through Congress, and the Sherman Act proved ineffective in restraining the concentration of industry.

In 1892 Cleveland defeated Harrison in a rematch of the 1888 election and became the only American president to serve two non-consecutive terms. Cleveland's election appeared to foreshadow a dramatic shift of party power in favor of the Democrats. The party seemed finally to have transcended the sectionalism of Civil War politics by combining its lock on the solid South with a revived ability to compete in the North. Cleveland's second term, however, proved to be a disaster for both the president and his party. He would spend nearly all of his four years in office on a futile effort to combat the worst economic depression to date in the history of the United States. President Cleveland, captive of his commitment to hard money and limited government, refused to consider reforming the financial system, increasing the money supply, or providing relief for the unemployed. His only solution to the economic calamity was to maintain a currency backed by gold, which only exacerbated the monetary contraction that had depressed investments, wages, and prices.

Cleveland declined to run for a third term, and his party's nominee, William Jennings Bryan, repudiated the president's policies. Bryan began the transition to a Democratic Party committed to activist government. Bryan embraced such reform proposals as the free coinage of silver to inflate the currency, a graduated income tax, arbitration of labor disputes, and stricter regulation of railroads. Bryan also helped introduce the modern style of presidential campaigns by giving stump speeches across the nation in 1896. In turn, the Republicans, who vastly outspent the Democrats, pioneered modern fundraising techniques.

Bryan lost in 1896 to Republican William McKinley, who benefited as president from the end of the depression in 1897. In domestic policy, McKinley steered new protective tariffs through Congress but otherwise followed a largely stand-pat approach to domestic matters. As president, however, he assumed the stewardship of a foreign empire and an expanded role in foreign affairs. As a result of winning the Spanish-American War of 1898, the United States acquired Puerto Rico, the Philippines, and several Pacific islands. It also established a protectorate over the Republic of Cuba. Although the United States would not endeavor to extend its formal empire of overseas territories in later years, it would frequently intervene in foreign nations to promote its values and interests. McKinley also expanded the powers of the presidency as he pioneered the steering of public opinion through a systematic program of press relations and speaking tours.

The Progressive Era: 1901–20

In 1900 McKinley won a rematch with Bryan, but in September 1901 he became the third president in 40 years to fall victim to an assassin. His successor—Theodore Roosevelt—was a man of different personality and ideas. Roosevelt was a showman with substance. During the remainder of McKinley's term and a second term of his own, Roosevelt transformed the presidency, the nation, and the Republican Party. As president, Roosevelt was both a big-stick diplomat abroad and a reformer at home. He altered the agenda of the Republican Party by adding a progressive domestic agenda to the expansionist policies of his predecessor, William McKinley. Roosevelt would become the first president to champion the use of federal power to protect the public interest and to curb abuses of the new corporate order. Ultimately, he would became the leader of progressive movements throughout the nation that worked toward improving social conditions, purifying American civilization, ending corrupt political practices, conserving resources, and regulating business. Roosevelt believed that reform was necessary to ameliorate the harshest consequences of industrial society and to thwart the appeal of radical groups.

Roosevelt also expanded the margins of presidential power. Prior presidents had typically deferred to constitutional ambiguities insofar as executive powers and privileges were concerned, preferring to err on the side of caution—and, by extension, weakness. Roosevelt, however, believed that he could do anything in the public interest that was not specifically prohibited by the Constitution. He intervened in disputes between labor and capital, used executive orders to conserve federal lands, attacked corporate monopolies in court, mediated foreign disputes, and aggressively acquired the territory needed to build the Panama Canal. His presidency not only served as a template for future ones but fittingly began what has been called the American century.

After retiring from the presidency, Roosevelt anointed a handpicked successor, his secretary of war, William Howard Taft, who thwarted Bryan's third bid for the presidency. But in 1912 Roosevelt was so disappointed with the moderate Taft that he unsuccessfully challenged the incumbent for the Republican Party's presidential nomination. The disappointed Roosevelt launched a third-party campaign that split the GOP and handed the election to Democratic candidate Woodrow Wilson, the progressive governor of New Jersey.

During his two terms in office, Wilson continued the liberal transformation of the Democratic Party that Bryan had begun in 1896. Under his watch, the federal government reduced tariffs, adopted the Federal Reserve System, established the Federal Trade Commission to regulate business, inaugurated social welfare programs, and joined much of the Western world in guaranteeing voting rights for women. Wilson also continued America's increasing involvement abroad and led the nation victoriously through World War I.

Like Theodore Roosevelt, Wilson also redefined the presidency, making the office both more powerful and active than before. Wilson was more engaged than any prior president in crafting legislation and steering it through Congress. A month after his inauguration, he addressed a special session of Congress to press for tariff reform, becoming the first president since John Quincy Adams in the 1820s to appear as an advocate before the legislature. Wilson also restored the practice of delivering the State of the Union address in person to Congress—a practice that Thomas Jefferson had discontinued after his election in 1800. Wilson also seized the initiative in foreign affairs. He attempted to broker peace between warring factions in World War I, and when that effort failed, led the nation into war. With his Fourteen Points, Wilson also articulated an ambitious vision for a postwar era marked by open covenants of peace, arms reductions, freedom of the seas, fair trade, self-determination for all people, and an international organization to keep the peace.

The Conservative Ascendancy: 1921–32

America's postwar future belonged not to Woodrow Wilson but to conservative Republicans. Wilson failed to gain acceptance in the United States or abroad for his ambitious peace plans, and his poor health precluded any hope for a third-term campaign. In the presidential election of 1920, Republican Senator Warren Harding of Ohio prevailed on a platform that promised a "return to normalcy" for Americans tired of liberal reform, war, and waves of Catholic and Jewish immigrants from southern and eastern Europe. Republicans would win all three presidential elections of the 1920s by landslide margins and maintain control over Congress during the period. Republican presidents and congresses of the 1920s would slash taxes, deregulate industry, restrict immigration, try to enforce Prohibition, and increase protective tariffs. In 1928, when Commerce Secretary Herbert Hoover decisively defeated New York Governor Alfred E. Smith—the first Catholic presidential candidate on a major party ticket—many believed the Democratic Party was on the verge of extinction.

The tide turned after the stock market crash of 1929 began the nation's longest and deepest depression. Unlike Grant and Cleveland, Hoover responded vigorously to the economic downturn. He held conferences of business leaders, sought to boost farm prices through federal purchases of commodities, and expanded federal public works projects. He assented to the formation of the Reconstruction Finance Corporation, which made low-interest loans to banks, railroads, and insurance companies. But he opposed federal regulation of business and vetoed legislation enacted by Democrats and progressive Republicans in Congress for direct aid to individuals and families—the so-called federal dole. The Depression failed to respond to his remedies, which Americas believed were inadequate to the challenges of the times. Franklin D. Roosevelt, the Democratic governor of New York, trounced Hoover in the presidential election of 1932, which ended conservative control of national government and marked the beginning of a new era of liberal politics in the United States.

See also Civil War and Reconstruction; conservative interregnum, 1920–32; Democratic Party; Reconstruction Era, 1865–77; Republican Party; sectional conflict and secession, 1845–65.

FURTHER READING. H. W. Brands, *T. R.: The Last Romantic*, 1997; Kendrick A. Clements, *The Presidency of Woodrow Wilson*, 1992; David Donald, *Lincoln*, 1995; Eric Foner, *A Short History of Reconstruction, 1863–1877*, 1990; Allan Lichtman, *The Keys to the White House*, 2008; Michael E. McGerr, *The Decline of Popular Politics: The North, 1865–1928*, 1986; Michael P. Riccards, *The Ferocious Engine of Democracy: A History of the American Presidency*, vol. 1, 1997.

ALLAN J. LICHTMAN

presidency, 1932–2008

Presidential Power and Responsibility

From 1932 to 2004, the powers and responsibilities of the presidency expanded together with the size and scope of the federal government. In 1932 the federal government spent less than $5 billion, including only about $700 million on the military. About 100 employees worked in the White House. In 2004 the federal government spent more than $2 trillion, the military budget hit $400 billion, and 1,800 people worked in the White House. Yet even as the federal bureaucracy has exploded, the modern president has become a celebrity figure, prized for his ability to inspire and lead the American people. Presidential success, moreover, has not always followed from presidential power. To the contrary, modern presidents have often fallen victim to the overreach that accompanies the arrogance of power.

The presidency from 1932 to 2004 can be partitioned into two distinct eras. From 1932 to 1980, presidents took the lead in establishing the modern liberal state. From 1980 to 2004, conservative presidents put their distinctive stamp on government in the United States.

The Origins of the Liberal State

In 1928 Herbert Hoover became the third consecutive Republican to win a landslide election to the presidency. But after 1929, Hoover battled the baleful consequences of a worldwide depression that resisted every remedy he tried. During the Hoover years, the Democratic opposition established the precedent of the permanent political campaign, with no pause between elections or deference to the presidency. Patrick Hurley, Hoover's secretary of war and political advisor, lamented that "our political opponents tell the story [and] we are on the defensive." Henceforth, every American president would be compelled to engage in a perpetual campaign.

Liberal Democrat Franklin Roosevelt's smashing victory over Hoover in 1932 profoundly changed both the presidency and the nation. During the new administration's first 100 days, conservatives watched in dismay as Roosevelt seized command of the legislative agenda more decisively than any prior president. He steered through Congress 15 major bills that addressed the banking crisis; got lawmakers to repeal Prohibition; created substantial relief and public works programs; and established recovery programs for agriculture and industry. Roosevelt became the first president to sell his policies to the public through fireside chats on the radio and freewheeling, twice-weekly press conferences. He had the ability both to inspire Americans with soaring rhetoric and to make ordinary folk believe that he, their patrician leader, truly understood and could help solve their problems.

After Roosevelt won a second decisive victory in 1936, he completed a political realignment that established the Democrats as the nation's majority party, sustained by a coalition of African Americans, Catholics, Jews, union members, and southern white Protestants. Scholars have aptly noted that FDR's reforms were incremental, modestly funded, and designed to rescue the capitalist economy. Nonetheless, Roosevelt's New Deal was a transforming moment in American life. It challenged old structures of power, threw up new ones, and created new social roles and opportunities for millions of Americans who worked for government, labored in offices and factories, or farmed for a living. It advanced American pluralism by offering jobs and power to Catholics and Jews and a few African Americans without disrupting local traditions. President Roosevelt shifted the center of American politics by taking responsibility for steering the economy, promoting social welfare, regulating labor relations, and curbing the abuses of business. Henceforth, Americans would expect their president, Democrat or Republican, to assure prosperous times, good jobs, high wages, and aid for those unable to fend for themselves.

The Cold War Presidency

During an unprecedented third term, Roosevelt led the nation into a world war that ended America's isolation from political entanglements abroad. The president assumed broad emergency powers during the war, and new federal agencies like the War Production Board foreshadowed the creation of America's military-industrial complex. It was not Franklin Roosevelt, however, but his successor, Harry S. Truman, who brought World War II to a successful conclusion. After FDR's death in April 1945, Truman became the first vice president to assume the presidency in the midst of a major war. Truman was shocked, nervous, and unprepared for the presidency. He told reporters, "I felt like the moon, the stars, and all the planets had fallen on me." Truman, however, had a very personalized view of history that idealized great men overcoming impossible odds. He acted decisively to use the atomic bomb to end World War II and led the nation into the cold war and the Korean War.

Like his celebrated predecessor, Truman expanded the powers of the presidency. He steered through Congress legislation that created the Central Intelligence Agency, the Joint Chiefs of Staff, the Department of Defense, and a National Security Council within the Executive Office of the President. He began the first program for screening the loyalty of federal employees. He entered the Korean War without a declaration of war or even token approval from Congress. Under Truman, America developed a military structure to sustain its global strategic and economic responsibilities and an "invisible government" that wielded global power with little scrutiny from Congress or the public. As libertarian Lawrence Dennis said in 1947, whether Republicans or Democrats held the presidency, America's "holy war on communist sin all over the world commits America to a permanent war emergency." Hereafter, "the executive has unlimited discretion to wage undeclared war anywhere, anytime he considers our national security requires a blow to be struck for good agin sin."

Amid the burdens of a stalemated war in Korea, a series of administration scandals, and challenges to his anti-Communist credentials by Senator Joseph McCarthy of Wisconsin and other Republicans, Truman declined to seek a third term. In 1952, Democrats nominated Illinois governor Adlai Stevenson. Among Republicans, war hero Dwight David Eisenhower competed for the Republican nomination against Senator Robert Taft of Ohio. In Eisenhower's view, a Taft presidency would threaten national security because the senator still clung to isolationist ideas that would undo the collective security measures that contained communism and deterred World War III. In the last national convention to resolve a deadlock between candidates, Eisenhower won the nomination and eventually the presidency only after the convention voted to seat his Texas delegation, rather than a competing delegation pledged to Taft.

Although mocked as a president who loved golf and loathed governing, Eisenhower carefully directed the policies and decisions of his administration, often keeping his influence hidden rather than overt. More than any prior president, Eisenhower relied on a chief of staff—Sherman Adams—as a gatekeeper and on the work of executive agencies such as the National Security Council. He also made extensive use of executive privilege to shield staff members from congressional oversight. Politically, Eisenhower promised to steer a middle course that weaved "between conflicting arguments advanced by extremists on both sides of almost every economic, political, and international problem that arises." He worked to balance the federal budget and control inflation. He believed in protecting the private economy from government meddling but also refused to roll back liberal reforms. He ratified Truman's approach to collective security and sought to contain communism without trampling civil liberties at home.

Eisenhower achieved considerable personal popularity, but his middle-way approach failed to break the Democrats' hold on the loyalty of voters and the control of Congress. In 1960 Democrat John F. Kennedy won election as America's first Catholic president. Kennedy's campaign, with its creative use of television, polling, image making, and a personal organization that was independent of the regular party machinery, also pointed to the future of American politics.

The Expansion and Crisis of the Liberal State

Kennedy was the first president since Franklin Roosevelt to inspire Americans with his rhetoric. Unlike later presidents, he spoke idealistically of shared sacrifice and the need for ordinary Americans to contribute to the common good, as envisioned in his most memorable line: "Ask not what your country can do for you, ask what you can do for your country." Kennedy steered the nation through the Cuban Missile Crisis, negotiated the first arms control treaty with the Soviets, and began the process that led to the end of segregation in America. Kennedy also accelerated the arms race with the Soviet Union and expanded America's commitment to far-flung areas of the world. However, Kennedy might not have led the United States to escalate the Vietnam War. Shortly before his assassination in late November 1963, he was working on a plan that contemplated withdrawing one thousand troops initially and extracting most American forces from Vietnam by 1965.

If Kennedy was cool and detached, his successor Lyndon Johnson was engaged and passionate. Johnson could talk endlessly about politics and had little interest in anything else. He also had a burning ambition to make his mark on the world and to help the less privileged. Johnson used his physical size to influence others and achieve his aims. It was not unusual for Johnson to stand inches away from another, bodies touching and eyes locked. The "Johnson treatment" was almost hypnotic. Yet he could just as easily alienate anyone who rebuffed him or refused his gifts.

After crushing conservative Republican Barry Goldwater in the presidential election of 1964, Johnson used his legislative skills to engineer a major expansion of the liberal state. Johnson imbedded the struggle for minority rights within the liberal agenda and, in another departure from the New Deal, he targeted needs—housing, health care, nutrition, and education—rather than groups such as the elderly or the unemployed.

But Johnson could not focus solely on domestic reform. Two days after his inauguration, Ambassador Maxwell Taylor cabled from Vietnam, "We are presently on a losing track and must risk a change. . . . The game needs to be opened up." The pugnacious president would not display unmanly personal and national weakness, encourage Communist aggression, and damage America's credibility by running from a fight. He began an air and ground war in Vietnam and ultimately dispatched some 550,000 American troops to the small Asian nation. Johnson promised the nation victory but privately told his cabinet that at best America could achieve a "stalemate" and force a negotiated settlement. Ultimately, the gap between inflated expectations and minimal achievements in Vietnam led to Johnson's "credibility gap" with the American people. In 1967 a frustrated president pleaded with his generals to "search for imaginative ideas to put pressure to bring this war to a conclusion"—not just "more men or that we drop the Atom bomb." Without military answers to the problems, on March 31, 1968, a dispirited Johnson told a national television audience that, rather than seeking reelection, he would work on bringing peace to Vietnam.

In 1962 Richard Nixon, after losing elections for the presidency and the governorship of California, said, "You won't have Nixon to kick around anymore, because, gentlemen, this is my last press conference." Six years later, Nixon completed the most improbable comeback in American history by narrowly winning the presidential election of 1968. Yet, from the early days of his presidency, Nixon exhibited the fear and suspicion that ultimately doomed a presidency marked by such accomplishments as the passage of pathbreaking environmental laws, the opening of relations with mainland China, and the deescalation of the cold war. Nixon told his staff that they were engaged in a "deadly battle" with eastern businessmen and intellectuals. He said, "No one in ivy league schools to be hired for a year—we need balance—trustworthy ones are the dumb ones." Jews were especially "untrustworthy. . . . Look at the Justice Department. It's full of Jews." Few business leaders "stood up" for the administration "except Main Street biz." Nixon brooded over his enemies in the press—"75 percent of those guys hate my guts"—and complained about needing to "keep some incompetent blacks" in the administration. "I have the greatest affection for them, but I know they ain't gonna make it for 500 years."

After engineering a landslide reelection in 1972, Nixon planned to bring the federal budget and bureaucracy to heel by refusing to spend funds appropriated by Congress and reorganizing government to expand presidential power. This power grab failed, however, as the Watergate scandal shattered Nixon's second term. Watergate involved far more than the botched break-in at Democratic Party headquarters in the Watergate complex in Washington, D.C., in June 1972. As moderate Republican senator Edward Brooke of Massachusetts said, "Too many Republicans have defined that dread word 'Watergate' too narrowly. It is not just the stupid, unprofitable break-in attempt. . . . It is perjury. Obstruction of justice. The solicitation and acceptance of hundred of thousands of dollars in illegal campaign contributions. It is a pattern of arrogance, illegality and lies which ought to shock the conscience of every Republican."

After Nixon resigned in August 1974, Democrats swept the midterm elections and sought to curb what they saw as a runaway presidency. They limited the president's war-making powers, expanded congressional input on the budget, and placed new restrictions on the CIA and the FBI. Such measures largely failed to return the balance of governmental power to Congress. Nonetheless, President Gerald Ford, whom Nixon had appointed vice president under authority of the Twenty-Fifth Amendment to the Constitution after the resignation of Spiro Agnew in 1973, struggled to govern after pardoning Nixon for Watergate-related crimes. However, conservative Republicans began rebuilding in adversity. They formed the Heritage Foundation to generate ideas, the Eagle Forum to rally women, new business lobbies, and Christian Right groups to inspire evangelical Protestants.

The Triumph of Conservatism

Although Democrat Jimmy Carter defeated Ford in 1976, he failed to cure an economy suffering from "stagflation" (an improbable mix of high unemployment, slow growth, and high inflation). Under Carter's watch America also suffered humiliation abroad when he failed to gain the release of hostages taken by Islamic militants in Iran. In 1980 conservative Republicans found an appealing candidate in Ronald Reagan, the former Hollywood actor and two-term governor of California. Reagan decisively defeated Carter in 1980, running on a forthright conservative platform. He promised to liberate Americans from the burdens of taxation and regulation, rebuild the nation's defenses, and fight communism with new vigor.

As president, Reagan delivered on most of his promises. He cut taxes, reduced regulation, and shifted government spending from domestic programs to the military. Like Roosevelt and Kennedy, Reagan emerged as a "Great Communicator," able to inspire Americans with his words and style. During his first term, Reagan restored luster to a tarnished

presidency and optimism to the nation. As journalist Bob Greene wrote, Reagan "manages to make you feel good about your country. . . . All those corny feelings that hid inside of you for so long are waved right out in public by Reagan for everyone to see— and even while you're listing all the reasons that you shouldn't fall for it, you're glad you're falling. If you're a sucker for the act, that's okay."

Reagan cruised to easy reelection in 1984 after a troubled economy recovered during the election year. To borrow a metaphor from Isaiah Berlin, most modern American presidents are foxes who know a little about everything, poke their noses everywhere, and revel in detail. Reagan, however, was a hedgehog who knew a few things but knew them very well and left the management to others. Reagan's detached style helped him weather the Iran-Contra scandal of 1986–87 that stemmed from the sale of arms to the terrorist state of Iran and the illegal diversion of the profits to the Contra fighters who were battling a left-wing government in Nicaragua. Although the "Reagan revolution" in domestic policy stalled during the second term, he achieved a major breakthrough in foreign policy, despite antagonizing his conservative supporters. Conventional thinkers on the right or left failed to understand how Reagan could weave together seemingly contradictory ideas. He was a warrior against evil and a man of peace who dreamed of banishing nuclear weapons from the Earth. He was a leader of principle and a pragmatist who understood better than his right-wing critics how the world had changed since 1980. In the teeth of conservative opposition, Reagan steered through the Senate a landmark treaty to eliminate nuclear missiles in Europe that he negotiated with reformist Soviet leader Mikhail Gorbachev. In 1988 Reagan foreshadowed the end of the cold war when he said that the Soviet's "evil empire" was from "another time, another era."

It was Reagan's successor, George H. W. Bush, who presided over the collapse of the Soviet Empire. Bush took office with no guarantees that communism would collapse without bloodshed. He seemed shy and awkward but not overmatched, at least in foreign affairs. His realistic, steady-hand diplomacy prodded events forward without provoking a Soviet backlash. Bush drew a contrast between himself and the flamboyant Reagan when he said that, although conservatives told him to "climb the Berlin Wall and make high-sounding pronouncements . . . [t]he administration . . . is not going to resort to such steps and is trying to conduct itself with restraint." Not a single Soviet soldier fired a shot to preserve communism in Eastern Europe in 1989. The Soviet Union crumbled in 1991; the same year that Bush led a multinational coalition that liberated Kuwait from the Iraqi armies of Saddam Hussein.

In 1992, however, Bush's success in foreign policy could not overcome a sluggish economy, his lack of vision in domestic policy, and the appeal of his Democratic challenger, Bill Clinton. Clinton positioned himself as a "new kind of Democrat" armed, like Eisenhower, with a "third-way philosophy" that purported to transcend left and right.

However, the future of the Clinton administration turned on a battle over the president's plan to guarantee health care coverage to all Americans. Representative Dick Armey of Texas privately told Republicans that the health care debate was "the Battle of the Bulge of big-government liberalism." If the GOP could defeat Clinton's health care plan, he said, "It will leave the President's agenda weakened, his plan's supporters demoralized, and the opposition emboldened. . . . Historians may mark it as the end of the Clinton ascendancy and the start of the Republican renaissance."

Armey proved to be a reliable prophet. Republicans won the health care battle and regained control of both houses of Congress in 1994 for the first time in 40 years. The elections established Republicans as the majority party in the South, polarized the parties along ideological lines, and forestalled any major new liberal initiatives by the Clinton administration. While Clinton won reelection in 1996 and survived impeachment by the Republican-controlled House of Representatives, his party failed to regain control of Congress during his tenure or to win the presidential election of 2000.

The Implosion of Conservatism
Although president-elect George W. Bush lost the popular vote in 2000, his advisors rejected advice that Bush govern from the center. Dick Cheney, who was poised to become the most influential vice president in American history, said, "The suggestion that somehow, because this was a close election, we should fundamentally change our beliefs I just think is silly." Even before the al-Qaeda terrorist attacks of September 11, 2001, Bush had moved domestic policy to the right and adopted a more aggressive, unilateralist approach to foreign affairs than his Democratic predecessor.

President Bush narrowly achieved reelection in 2004. However, his years in office revealed deep contradictions within his conservative movement. With the rebuilding of Iraq, a conservative administration that disdained social engineering assumed the most daunting such project in American history. Similarly, the president built a form of big government that contradicted conservatives' rhetorical defense of limited government, states' rights, fiscal responsibility, and individual freedom. Although conservatives had once rallied against the excessive presidential powers under Roosevelt, Truman, and Johnson, Bush greatly expanded executive prerogatives through unprecedented secrecy in government, expanding the domestic surveillance of Americans, exercising political control over the legal and scientific agencies of government, and aggressively using executive signing statements to reserve the option to override provisions of federal law. More forthrightly than any

prior president, he asserted America's right to wage preemptive war against potential enemies. President Bush's terms in office exposed a paradox at the heart of the modern presidency. Although his tenure was a high watermark in presidential power, it also added to a deep-seated distrust of the presidency that had begun with Johnson's deceptive war and continued through the Watergate and Iran-Contra scandals and the impeachment of President Clinton. The Bush era ended with the election of Democrat Barack Obama, America's first African American president, who entered the presidency with a solidly Democratic U.S. House and Senate.

See also conservative ascendancy, 1980–2008; era of confrontation and decline, 1964–80; era of consensus, 1952–64; New Deal Era, 1932–52.

FURTHER READING. Robert Dallek, *Hail to the Chief: The Making and Unmaking of American Presidents*, 2001; Lewis L. Gould, *The Modern American Presidency*, 2003; William Leuchtenburg, *In the Shadow of FDR: From Harry Truman to Ronald Reagan*, 1983; Allan J. Lichtman, *The Keys to the White House, 2008 Edition*, 2008; Michael P. Riccards, *The Ferocious Engine of Democracy: A History of the American Presidency, from Theodore Roosevelt to George W. Bush*, 2003; Richard Shenkman, *Presidential Ambition: How the Presidents Gained Power, Kept Power, and Got Things Done*, 1999.

ALLAN J. LICHTMAN

press and politics
The press has played a major role in American politics from the founding of the republic. Once subordinate to politicians and the major parties, it has become increasingly independent, compelling politicians and elected officials to develop new strategies to ensure favorable publicity and public support.

Newspapers in the colonial era were few in number and very different from what they would later become. Operated by individual entrepreneurs who produced a variety of printed materials, newspapers included little political news. Instead, their few columns were devoted to foreign news and innocuous correspondence that would not offend colonial officials or the wealthy patrons on whom printers relied for much of their business.

This began to change during the Revolutionary era, when printers were drawn into the escalating conflict with Great Britain. Adversely affected by the Stamp Act, many printers opened their columns to opponents of British rule and eventually became champions of American independence. Others sided with the British and often found themselves the objects of popular wrath. After the war most printers returned to publishing uncontroversial items, but an important precedent had been set. Politicians and elected officials recognized that they could use the press to win support for favored causes, and ordinary Americans now saw newspapers as a medium through which they might gain knowledge about public affairs and become active citizens. Believing that a free press could spur public enlightenment and political engagement, Congress passed laws that reduced periodical postal rates and encouraged publishers to share and reprint their correspondence.

By the early 1790s, then, most Americans considered newspapers vital to the health of the republic, providing a medium through which politicians and the public could communicate, learn about issues, and develop policies that were shaped by rational, informed debate.

Almost immediately, however, the appearance of a very different kind of journalism confounded this expectation. Sparked by divergent plans for the future of the new republic, competing factions emerged within George Washington's administration and Congress, and by the mid-1790s each faction had established partisan newspapers championing its point of view. These publications were subsidized through patronage, and, though they had a limited circulation, the material they published was widely reprinted and discussed, and contributed to the establishment of the nation's first political parties, the Federalists and the Democratic-Republicans.

Newspapers like Philip Freneau's *National Gazette*, the most prominent Democratic-Republican organ, crafted distinctly partisan lenses through which readers were encouraged to view the world. Specializing in gossip, innuendo, and ad hominem attacks, these newspapers sought to make readers fearful about the intentions of their opponents. The strategy was quite effective at arousing support and mobilizing voters to go the polls—after all, the fate of the republic appeared to be at stake. But it hardly made the press a fount of public enlightenment, to the dismay of many an observer.

The rabid and unexpected partisanship of the 1790s culminated in the passage by the Federalist-dominated Congress of the Sedition Act (1798), which was designed to throttle the most intemperate journalistic supporters of the Democratic-Republicans by criminalizing "false, scandalous, and malicious writing" that defamed government officials. Though resulting in relatively few prosecutions, the law sparked an uproar that benefited Thomas Jefferson and his allies and created a groundswell of support for the principle of freedom of the press. In the wake of Jefferson's election to the White House, the act's sponsors were unable to extend its life and it expired in March 1801.

The partisan press expanded in the early 1800s and reached the peak of its influence during the age of Jackson. Publishers, eager for government printing contracts, allied themselves with leading politicians and devoted their columns to publicizing their candidacies and policy aims. Newspaper publishers were particularly important in promoting Andrew Jackson, serving in his kitchen cabinet, and enabling him to develop a national following. Jackson's rise to power prompted a dramatic polarization of newspapers, a divide that was essential to the emergence of the Democrats and the Whigs, truly national parties that were organized down to the grass roots.

Political parties were not the only organizations to establish newspapers. Religious denominations and reform societies also founded newspapers and journals of opinion and advocacy to attract supporters and influence public opinion. Evangelical groups were especially enterprising in their use of newspapers and other printed tracts to win converts and promote piety, and in the 1820s and 1830s these efforts often spilled over into broader campaigns to improve public morality. By constructing a network of affiliated publications that extended through much of North and by developing narrative themes that were at once sensational and didactic, the religious and reform newspapers of the early 1800s were important pioneers of modern journalism and popular culture.

The most controversial reform organs were abolitionist newspapers like William Lloyd Garrison's *The Liberator*, which was launched in 1831 and inspired many similar publications. Making use of the communications infrastructure developed by the religious press, abolitionist newspapers spread throughout the North and were sent en masse to cities and towns in the South in hopes of kindling opposition to slavery in the region. To suppress their dissemination, pro-slavery activists broke into post offices and seized and burned any copies they found. While this tactic was effective at minimizing the spread of antislavery sentiment, it angered and alarmed many Northerners, bolstering abolitionist claims that the republic was imperiled by the tyrannical designs of the "Slave Power."

Despite their effectiveness in helping to build national parties and raising public awareness of social and political issues, the partisan press and reform press were widely criticized, and their limitations paved the way for a new kind of publication, a commercial mass-circulation press that first appeared in the 1830s. Inexpensive, widely accessible, and written in a colorful style designed to entertain as well as inform, newspapers like the *New York Sun* sparked a revolution in journalism as publishers, impressed by the commercial potential of an unabashedly popular journalism, rushed to establish similar publications. By opening their papers to advertising, publishers of the "penny press" discovered a lucrative source of revenue and freed themselves from dependence on political parties and patrons. They acquired an incentive to expand their readership to include working-class people, who had never been targeted by newspaper publishers, and to plow their profits into new technologies that allowed them to enlarge their publications and vastly increase the range of topics they covered.

Filling their columns with material of general interest, publishers like James Gordon Bennett, founder of the *New York Herald*, invented the modern concept of "*news.*" And while much of it was about politics, when Bennett and his rivals expanded coverage of other realms they diminished the prominence and centrality of political news, which became one of many different kinds of reportage. The penny press also treated political news differently, and, as it gained readers, its perspective on politics and public affairs became more influential. Most publishers recognized the strength of partisanship, and supported one party or another. Yet, because commercial imperatives encouraged publishers to reach across lines of class, ethnicity, and party, they often confined their partisanship to editorials, where it was less likely to offend.

This is not to say that the commercial mass-circulation press was objective. Editors and publishers—until after the Civil War, they were usually one and the same—had strong points of view and were not squeamish about inserting them into news reports. But their reliance on advertising allowed editors to aspire to a new role as tribunes of the public. In many instances, this meant standing by their party; in others, however, it meant criticizing it. Publishers like Bennett or Horace Greeley relished opportunities to display their independence and commitment to the public interest, a gambit inspired as much by commercial intent—the desire to attract a broad readership—as by disgust for the excesses of partisanship.

The trend toward a less partisan brand of political reporting was reinforced by the establishment of wire services like the Associated Press, which provided members with news from Washington and state capitals and eschewed partisanship out of commercial necessity. Under the influence of such services, by the 1880s, most political reporting had become standardized and largely descriptive, consisting of transcripts of speeches, legislative hearings, and official pronouncements. Most of this material was gathered by salaried wire service and newspaper correspondents, not, as in years past, by freelance correspondents who also worked for elected officials or the major parties. Just as their employers viewed themselves as independent of party, so too did increasing numbers of reporters, a trend that accelerated in the early 1900s when big-city newspapers became large business, and journalists began to think of themselves as professionals.

But the commercial orientation of the mass-circulation press also pulled journalists in another direction, toward an emphasis on entertainment values. In the 1880s and 1890s, determined to attract more immigrant and working-class readers, publishers like Joseph Pulitzer and William Randolph Hearst created an even more popular and entertaining brand of journalism that emphasized scandal, personalities, and a wide variety of human-interest material. Political news in their publications became increasingly sensational, as editors focused on exposé of corruption and mounted highly publicized crusades. A similar imperative affected magazine journalism, inspiring the muckraking campaigns of *Cosmopolitan* and *McClure's*. Spurred by recognition that much of the public was sincerely concerned about social problems, the sensational press played a key role in building support for reform. By transforming politics into entertaining yet sordid morality tales, however, they also may have encouraged public cynicism and disengagement from politics.

Many middle-class and upper-class Americans were appalled by the new journalism, and, in response to its rise, Adolph Ochs transformed the *New York Times* into a more sober and "informational" alternative. In the early 1900s, other papers followed Ochs's lead, creating a new divide between a popular journalism directed at lower middle-class and working-class readers and a self-styled "respectable" press that was targeted at the educated and well-heeled. But publishers of respectable newspapers, in response to consumer demand, were soon compelled to publish features and human-interest stories as well, blurring the differences between the two kinds of journalism. Indeed, by the 1920s, the most salient distinction between the sensational press and the respectable press was the relative restraint that the latter displayed when covering many of the same stories. Even in the respectable press, political news was designed to entertain as well as inform, an increasingly difficult mission now that newspapers had to compete for the public's attention with motion pictures and other forms of popular culture.

The commercial transformation of journalism had a major impact on politicians and government officials. Not surprisingly, it forced them to present themselves in a less partisan light. Seizing the opportunities created by the spread of human-interest journalism, politicians sought to appear as "practical idealists," party members who were nonetheless sensitive to broader concerns and willing to break with their party if necessary. To that end, politicians began to hire press secretaries and public relations advisors, usually former journalists who knew how to exploit the conventions of news gathering to gain favorable coverage for their clients. The federal government also began to employ public relations and advertising techniques, most notably in its effort to build public support for American involvement in World War I. Led by George Creel, an acclaimed journalist, the government's campaign sparked an orgy of hyperpatriotism, demonstrating how mass-mediated propaganda could mold public opinion and potentially influence the democratic process.

Alarmed by the ease with which politicians, the government, and economic elites could use the press to get free publicity, journalists began to produce more interpretive and objective forms of news, particularly of topics like politics. This important trend was inspired by a belief that the world was too complex to be understood by readers, and that the job of the press was to digest, analyze, and interpret events and developments so that the public could make sense of them. Newspapers hired columnists like Walter Lippmann and Dorothy Thompson to provide "expert" commentary on political events. Their columns were disseminated by syndicates to newspapers around the country, enabling them to reach a nationwide audience. Interpretive news also became a staple of the weekly newsmagazine *Time*. Founded in the early 1920s, it exerted a wide influence on newspaper as well as magazine journalism. The commitment of print media to interpretive news was reinforced by the spread of radio. As radio became the principal medium through which most Americans heard about late-breaking news, newspapers and magazines redoubled their emphasis on more detailed coverage.

By the 1940s, the press had become a vital institution, providing the public with information about candidates and elected officials, covering primary campaigns and nominating conventions, and offering regular reports on the vastly expanded operations of federal, state, and local government. The lens through which most of this news was filtered was the commercial, feature-oriented, largely nonpartisan perspective pioneered by the cheap popular press and further refined by more respectable organs and the major wire services. Despite persistent differences in tone among newspapers and magazines—differences attributable to their intended audiences—the political news that most Americans read was relatively standardized, a blend of interpretive reporting, analyses, commentary, and "personalized" features. Much of it was quasi-official in origin, inspired by the efforts of politicians and government officials to attract publicity or direct attention to a particular issue. More often than not, this was because the routines of news gathering encouraged close contact between journalists and official sources, an arrangement that made the news media a reliable platform for establishment points of view.

The spread of television in the 1950s did little to alter the situation. To display their commitment to the public interest, the major networks and local stations produced news and public affairs programming, covering events like the 1954 Army-McCarthy hearings and airing documentaries on issues like civil rights, the alienation of youth, and the arms race. However, it wasn't until the expansion of the nightly network news broadcasts to 30 minutes in the early 1960s, and a similar increase in local news programming, that television became the main source of political news for most Americans. Making use of new video and satellite technologies that enabled extensive coverage of the era's tumultuous events—from the Kennedy assassination to the Watts uprising to the debacle in Vietnam—television news broadcasts began to attract more viewers, sparking a gradual yet inexorable decline in newspaper readership. The centrality of television news became even more pronounced in the 1980s and 1990s with the rise of cable television and the popularity of news channels such as CNN.

The public's growing reliance on television for news had significant repercussions. No less than in the print media, advertising and entertainment values came to dominate television at every level, encouraging network officials to decrease coverage of politics and make what little they offered more superficial and entertaining. Under pressure to make the news "pay," a trend brilliantly satirized in the movie *Network* (1976), television journalists were forced to produce more human-interest stories and sharply limit airtime devoted to political stories that were overly complex or considered boring. With less airtime devoted to politics, politicians and elected officials gradually learned to express themselves in compact "sound bites," a technique that placed a premium on wit and personality and further degraded public discourse. This shift was particularly evident in coverage of election campaigns. Aware of the power of television, candidates and their campaign managers in the 1960s made increasing use of modern advertising and public relations methods, a process in which candidates' personalities were literally sold to the public. This trend was reinforced in the 1970s, when electoral reforms heightened the importance of primary elections, which the mass media, led by the major networks, transformed into highly publicized "horse races."

Beginning in the late 1960s, the press became increasingly aggressive and adversarial. Disconcerted by recognition that government and military officials had lied about the situation in Vietnam, journalists began to seek a wider range of sources and question official reports in a spirit not seen since the early 1900s. Journalists came to see themselves as public watchdogs responsible for exposing malfeasance and providing Americans with the truth. The publication of the Pentagon Papers, a top-secret history of the Vietnam War that was leaked to the *New York Times*, and the aggressive investigative reporting of the *Washington Post* that precipitated the Watergate scandal were perhaps the most famous manifestations of this trend. But it influenced many newspapers, magazines, television news departments, and individual journalists, inspiring them to express critical views of important institutions, including some of the large corporations for which they worked. To foster public debate, newspapers established op-ed pages and expanded their roster of columnists, making editorial pages less uniform and predictable. By the early 1980s, however, much of the mainstream press had backed away from this adversarial stance. Chastened by charges of liberal bias, journalists went out of their way to appear fair to conservatives, and in the 1990s, eager to display their balance, they zealously contributed to the right's persecution of Bill Clinton.

The post-1960s era also witnessed a tremendous increase in alternative sources of political news, as journalists sought new platforms to produce in-depth and adversarial reportage. These alternatives included underground newspapers, political magazines specializing in advocacy journalism, politically oriented network and cable talk shows like The McLaughlin Group, Crossfire, and The Daily Show, and innumerable political Web sites and blogs. Many of these sources specialized in ideologically inspired, openly subjective reporting and commentary, creating a new field where news and opinion were hopelessly blurred. Often targeted at true believers rather than a broad audience, they vastly enlarged the parameters of political discourse and made it easier for citizens to gain access to diverse views. This was clearly an advance over the more limited, elite-driven discourse that prevailed from the 1920s through the early 1960s, particularly given the ability of government and the corporate behemoths that own the major media to exploit the conventions of journalism to project their own self-interested versions of reality.

But it is an open question whether the welter of often fiercely partisan and ideologically driven sources of political news in America serves—or will ever serve—the larger cause of public enlightenment. Can a mode of discourse that is designed at least in part to entertain, in a popular culture marketplace that is fragmented into increasingly specialized niche markets, ever contribute to inclusive, constructive debate? Or will it reach its logical conclusion and become another species of show biz?

FURTHER READING. Gerald J. Baldasty, *The Commercialization of News in the Nineteenth Century*, 1992; Stuart Ewen, *PR! A Social History of Spin*, 1996; James Fallows, *Breaking the News: How the Media Undermine American Democracy*, 1996; Thomas C. Leonard, *The Power of the Press: The Birth of American Political Reporting*, 1986; David Paul Nord, *Communities of Journalism: A History of American Newspapers and Their Readers*, 2001; Geneva Overholser and Kathleen Hall Jamieson, eds., *Institutions of American Democracy: The Press*, 2005; Stephen Ponder, *Managing the Press: Origins of the Media Presidency, 1897–1933*, 1999; Michael Schudson, *The Good Citizen: A History of American Civic Life*, 1998; Paul Starr, *The Creation of the Media: Political Origins of Modern Communications*, 2004.

CHARLES L. PONCE DE LEON

progressivism and the Progressive Era, 1890s–1920

Progressivism was both an idea and a movement. It arose because many Americans believed that their existing institutions, which had been organized around individual liberty and limited government, could no longer function in an increasingly urban, industrial, and ethnically diverse society. Advocates of progressivism sought to reorder the nation's institutions to produce more order, efficiency, stability, and a sense of social responsibility. They believed that Americans would guarantee progress toward a democratic future by moving away from individualism toward social responsibility. As a movement, progressivism was the struggle of individuals and groups to promote and institutionalize reform. Order, efficiency, stability, and social responsibility meant different things to different Americans, so there was no single progressive movement or single set of proposed reforms. But progressivism succeeded in implementing government regulation of the economy and changing the relationship of Americans to their government and to one another.

Progressivism and Discontent

In the years following the Civil War, discontented groups of Americans founded new political parties and workers' organizations, joined local voluntary organizations and the woman suffrage movement, and enlisted in socialist and anarchist movements. All of these groups challenged fundamental premises of American politics. By the middle of the 1890s, such widespread discontent made many Americans fear the collapse of democracy unless society and its institutions were reformed.

The origins of progressivism coincided with a new intellectual movement and technological innovations. Across the Western world, thinkers and academics were arguing that lived experience should decide the worth of existing institutions and structures. New academic disciplines of social science appeared in European and American universities, attracting students across the transatlantic divide to study new fields, such as economics, that emphasized how rational and scientific investigation of social structures would yield the information needed to justify and direct reform. Some of these universities were now admitting female students. Though their numbers were limited, these women would greatly advance progressivism.

Such technological innovations as electricity, railway transportation, the Bessemer converter that transformed iron into steel, steel-frame construction, and massive industrial plants with machinery that sped up the pace of work, among others, were changing everyday life and forms of work. The Columbian Exposition held in Chicago in 1893 celebrated the genius of American inventors and manufacturers. The displays of new technology and economic advances celebrated capitalist industrial production and tied progress to the human ingenuity that would tame and conquer nature. These innovations, however, were implemented with little thought to the conditions of life and work they produced, and with minimal government regulation or oversight. The exposition, moreover, coincided with an economic depression that left many Americans homeless, unemployed, and on the verge of starvation. The contrast between the glittering exposition and the conditions on the streets of cities across the country spurred new organization among Americans already concerned with the direction of the country.

Progressivism and Political Reorganization

By the end of the century, journalists and writers called "muckrakers" were investigating and publicizing the problems of American society. One of the most vexing problems they attacked was the "corrupt bargain" between business and government. For decades, businessmen had curried favors from government officials in order to advance their economic endeavors. In return, politicians and officeholders solicited and accepted bribes. In a climate where economic progress was considered sacrosanct, business received a relatively free hand to conduct its own affairs. Moreover, many businessmen were big contributors to the Republican Party, which reciprocated by passing legislation favorable to them. The money pouring into the party made it the country's most powerful party on the federal level. Republicans controlled the presidency between 1860 and 1912, interrupted only by Democrat Grover Cleveland's two terms.

Progressives argued that government should serve the public good. This "corrupt bargain" allowed private interests, including the leading party politicians, to benefit at the public's expense. Progressives' insistence that the state must protect and promote this public good challenged lingering sentiments about negative liberty (freedom from government) and self-guiding markets. Progressives demanded legislation to give government new powers, reform of the party and electoral systems, and new constitutional amendments.

Their successes crafted a moderate regulatory state. Congress regulated the power of business to engage in monopolies and trusts, created the Federal Reserve System to oversee the country's monetary system, and enacted laws regulating the production of food and drugs. New agencies such as the Federal Trade Commission were organized to oversee adherence to these laws. To help finance the regulatory state, the Sixteenth Amendment to the Constitution gave Congress power to levy an income tax. Progressives charged that giving state legislatures the power to appoint U.S. senators had led to collusion among businessmen, state legislators, and their appointees. The Seventeenth Amendment thus mandated the popular election of senators to Congress.

Individual states passed new political measures, and municipal governments were overhauled. Wisconsin became the first state to require the direct primary for nominating candidates, and Oregon adopted the initiative and referendum to give voters more voice in determining state legislation. Other states quickly followed. Some cities reduced the size of their city councils, gave mayors more power, eliminated district-based ward systems in favor of at-large

council membership, municipalized some public services, and enacted public safety measures. Such reforms aimed to minimize the role of political parties, eliminate the franchise system by which public services were awarded to the highest private bidder, and replace party politicians with professionals whom progressives believed would be better equipped to bring order, efficiency, honest government, and protections to the chaotic industrial city.

Progressives also expanded the power of the presidency. Presidents Theodore Roosevelt (1901–8) and Woodrow Wilson (1912–20) each made the presidency more active and powerful in promoting a national progressive agenda. Roosevelt had coined the derisive term "muckraker," but his tours of poverty-stricken urban areas as police commissioner of New York City (1895–97) with the crusading newspaper reporter Jacob Riis convinced him that the uncurbed power of the wealthy few, especially industrialists, threatened democracy. Money influenced politics and allowed business to use the police power of the state to thwart all labor initiatives. As president, Roosevelt used the existing Sherman Anti-Trust Act (1890) to break up monopolies and trusts. He oversaw new legislation to regulate railroad rates and food and drug production and expanded the role of the executive branch by creating new cabinet positions and broadening the powers of others. He was the first president to use his office to compel industry to resolve a major labor strike, that of coal miners in 1902. His administration took the first steps toward developing a national conservation policy. Roosevelt justified this innovative use of presidential power with the progressive idea that the president was "the steward of the public welfare."

His successor, Republican William Howard Taft, attacked monopolies and trusts even more vigorously but did not share Roosevelt's ideals. Taft fought trusts because he believed they restrained free trade, not to promote the public welfare. Unhappy progressive Republicans such as Senator Robert LaFollette (Wisconsin) founded the National Progressive Republican League to contest the Taft regulars. When the party renominated Taft in 1912, they organized the Progressive Party and nominated Roosevelt for president. Progressive women were drawn to this party, even though most still could not vote, because it promised that it would govern in the public interest and would back woman suffrage. The Democrats nominated Woodrow Wilson, and the 1912 race became a contest over the future of progressivism.

Wilson won as the Republican vote split between Taft and Roosevelt. In his first two years in office, Wilson demonstrated his progressive credentials by helping secure new banking, currency, and trade regulations and new antitrust legislation. Wilson managed to keep his southern base intact by promising not to expand the powers of the federal government at the expense of states' rights and by ignoring other progressive demands to promote racial equality and woman suffrage.

Roosevelt and Wilson confronted a U.S. Senate and Supreme Court hostile to government regulation. The Seventeenth Amendment helped to change the makeup of the Senate, and both presidents took a hands-on approach to dealing with Congress. Since progressivism professed a faith in democracy, both men also appealed directly to the people during their presidencies. Each man used Congress's constitutional power to regulate interstate commerce to secure regulatory measures. Wilson was able to appoint leading progressive lawyer Louis Brandeis to the court. Brandeis promoted the progressive idea of social realism: legal rulings should be made on the basis of factual information presented to the courts in the social context of the problem. Although few other jurists of the time so readily accepted social realism, the idea gradually gained a place in legal decisions.

Progressivism and Social Reorganization

Many progressives were motivated by an ideal of collective responsibility for resolving social problems. Settlement house founder Jane Addams argued that democratic governments could not ignore social problems or leave them to the mercy of private charity. She and other progressives proposed that certain social goods, including housing, transportation, parks, recreation areas, health, sanitation, and public education, should not be left to the vagaries of the marketplace. Ideas of social politics owed as much to a transatlantic exchange of ideas as they did to American innovation. Academics, settlement house workers, and professionals in law, economics, finance, and even religion journeyed to Europe to study, investigate, and exchange ideas with leading progressive thinkers there.

The specifics of social politics—for instance, how far and by what means to remove social goods from the marketplace—were contested. As head of the federal Children's Bureau, Julia Lathrop declared that a democratic state must abolish poverty altogether. Catholic priest Father John A. Ryan wanted government to guarantee a living wage to male workers who could then support their families. African Americans Ida B. Wells-Barnett and W.E.B. DuBois used the ideas and language of progressivism to fight for racial equality, arguing that there could be no true democracy without racial democracy.

Social politics inspired tens of thousands of women across the country to join settlement houses and organize local and national voluntary associations that investigated social conditions and demanded that government solve them. These women were in the forefront of demanding that government provide adequate housing, decent public schools, and health and sanitation programs; promote public safety; and end the use of child labor. Fundamental to their progressivism was the idea that the middle class must learn to experience the lives of the poor, the working

class, and immigrants in order to foster social responsibility. Working-class and African American women formed similar organizations.

A distinguishing feature of women's progressivism was class-bridging organizations such as the National Women's Trade Union League and the National Consumers' League, which promoted protective labor legislation and abolition of child labor. In 1908 the Supreme Court had accepted, in *Muller v. Oregon*, Brandeis's argument—based on statistics gathered by the women of the National Consumers' League—that excessive strenuous work harmed women's health and that the state thus had a reason to regulate their hours of labor. But the Court refused to extend such protection to male workers, citing the "right to contract" implied by the Fourteenth Amendment. The Senate passed the Keating-Owen Child Labor Act in 1916 to outlaw the "awful blot" of child labor, but the Court overturned the law as a violation of state powers to regulate labor.

Progressivism generated other new organizations through which like-minded individuals worked to enact reform. Men formed city clubs and municipal leagues. Activist women banded into the General Federation of Women's Clubs. Black and white Americans founded the National Association for the Advancement of Colored People (NAACP). Through such organizations, progressivism formulated a new interest-group politics that voters believed gave them more access to government.

Progressivism and Internationalism

From the 1890s through World War I, progressives often justified territorial expansion and conquest. Most viewed Native Americans as being at odds with white European economic, religious, and social practices. While some progressives advocated compulsory "civilizing," by removing Indian children from their parents, others sought less repressive means by which to integrate them into the broader society. Whichever method used, Native Americans' lands were appropriated to foster white settlement and their customs undermined as part of progressive reordering of society.

Most progressives also justified overseas imperialism. The economic justification was that this would create a more orderly and efficient world in which to do business. It was usually accompanied by a sense of Anglo-Saxon superiority. While some progressives were motivated by a more benign ideal that imperialism could bring education and progress, others simply believed that American superiority gave the United States the right to control the world.

Ideas about gender also underlay progressive imperialism. As women moved into public life and demanded suffrage as both a democratic right and as necessary to promote both domestic and international progressivism, political figures such as Theodore Roosevelt worried that American manhood was being undermined. Nothing could prove manhood, he believed, as much as war, conquest, and making the United States the economic and political power-house of the world.

International progressivism did have another side, however. Figures such as Addams and LaFollette promoted an ideal of universal social responsibility to bring order and peace to the world. The international membership of the Women's Peace Party (founded 1915) and its successor, the Women's International League for Peace and Freedom, encouraged such thinking. If domestic progressivism could make Americans take responsibility for each other, then its international dimension could draw the peoples of the world into a broad alliance to defeat poverty and end armed conflict. But, in 1919, the Versailles Peace Conference and the U.S. Senate's refusal to ratify the treaty and join the new League of Nations dashed such hopes.

The Twilight of Progressivism

World War I severely limited the continuation of progressivism. One strain of progressivism had argued that only the right populace could guarantee a good democracy. This idea justified immigration exclusion, antisocialist hysteria, and narrowly defining what it meant to be American. Wartime hysteria heightened such thinking and institutionalized the concept of "100 percent Americanism." Anyone who opposed the war or who supported radical ideologies or groups was labeled un-American and subjected to persecution. The so-called science of eugenics proposed that humans had inbred racial traits that could be measured to determine who would make good democratic citizens. By the 1920s, new laws restricted immigration and enforced new naturalization requirements. Caught in this racialist thinking were African Americans whose progressive activities and participation in the war effort were not rewarded with racial democracy.

Progressivism as a massive movement died out after the war, but its ideals and effects did not. It had never pretended to overturn capitalism but to reform it to cause less harm to Americans. Progressivism's ideals of social responsibility and the need for government regulation were institutionalized into American politics to provide a balance against the forces of the unrestrained marketplace.

See also foreign policy and domestic politics, 1865–1933; interest groups; press and politics.

FURTHER READING. Jane Addams, *Democracy and Social Ethics*, 1902; Idem, *Peace and Bread in Time of War*, 1922; Maureen A. Flanagan, *America Reformed: Progressives and Progressivisms, 1890s–1920s*, 2007; Morton Keller, *Regulating a New Society: Public Policy and Social Change in America, 1900–1933*, 1994; Robyn Muncy, *Creating a Female Dominion in American Reform, 1890–1935*, 1991; Eric Rauchway, *Murdering McKinley: The Making of Theodore Roosevelt's America*, 2003; Daniel Rodgers, *Atlantic Crossings: Social Politics in a Progressive Age*, 1998;

Patricia Schechter, *Ida B. Wells-Barnett and American Reform, 1880–1930*, 2001; Daphne Spain, *How Women Saved the City*, 2001; Nancy Unger, *Fighting Bob LaFollette: The Righteous Reformer*, 2002.

. MAUREEN A. FLANAGAN

Prohibition and temperance

From its beginnings in the 1820s through its demise in the 1930s, the temperance movement and its descendant, the Prohibition movement, had a tremendous impact on American politics. Temperance and Prohibition helped to both create and disrupt the Second Party System that existed roughly from 1828 to 1854, and proved a staple (and difficult) issue of party politics during the Gilded Age.

The temperance movement brought women into politics before they had the vote. During the Progressive Era, the Prohibition movement created the first single-issue pressure group, a model of influencing politics that was widely imitated. Prohibition also created the only constitutional amendment directly aimed at the personal habits of the people. National Prohibition presented challenges to the political order. After repeal of the amendment, temperance and Prohibition faded as issues. The birth of neoprohibitionism at the end of the twentieth century sidestepped federal politics as it pressured states into raising the legal drinking age and enforcing harsher laws against drunk driving.

The temperance movement began as a reaction to the alcoholic republic of the late eighteenth and early nineteenth centuries. Americans consumed alcohol at a tremendous rate in this period. For instance, it is estimated that between 1800 and 1830, adult Americans consumed 6.6 to 7.1 gallons of pure alcohol annually, compared to a current annual consumption rate of 2.8 gallons. Alcohol was part of daily life and public culture. Temperance advocates blamed all manner of social disorder on the consumption of drink. Alcohol, they argued, directly caused poverty, disease, crime, political corruption, and family disruption. Many Americans, especially those of Anglo-Saxon and old immigrant stock, saw liquor as an unmitigated evil that needed to be outlawed. Many Christians, inspired by the Second Great Awakening, joined the movement, whose members abstained from liquor and tried to persuade others to do the same.

The Second Party System

From the 1830s through the 1840s, many antiliquor agitators moved beyond moral suasion to embrace political means. The first steps toward politicizing temperance came in New England communities where temperance advocates promoted the policy of no license—that is, they pressured local authorities to stop granting licenses to liquor retailers, removing what they saw as a public sanction of the trade. In some states, such struggles were decided through the ballot in what became known as local option elections (a method, while much altered, that still exists). States, by law, authorized the people of any township, county, city, or precinct to decide in a special election to allow or deny liquor sales in their locality. Liquor merchants, as well as advocates of laissez-faire policies and opponents of reform, mobilized against these efforts.

Such divisions fed into the emerging Second Party System. At first, the Whigs tended to support the temperance advocates' legal solutions while the Democrats opposed them. As immigration increased, bringing both Germans and Irish with established drinking cultures to the United States, the political divisions took on ethnic and religious dimensions, and these immigrants (especially the Catholics among them) tended to favor the Democratic Party. But over time, the rigid divisions between parties over temperance started to erode.

The parties in the 1840s viewed antiliquor measures as both appealing and dangerous. For instance, after Whig-dominated state governments passed laws that restricted the sale of liquor to large bulk orders (in effect imposing a ban on retail alcohol sales), they were turned out of office. Afterward, Whig politicians tried to avoid adopting extreme temperance policies, but only at the risk of alienating some of their supporters. Similarly, Democrats, seeing how popular temperance policies were with some voters, would advocate them, to the disgust of a significant number of their supporters. In short, temperance started out as a defining issue between the parties but became a contested issue within both parties.

By the 1850s, such conflicts led to new political organizations and alliances. Temperance movements throughout the country came together around the Maine Law (named after the first state to adopt it in 1851), which essentially prohibited the manufacture and sale of alcohol within a state. In all, 13 northern states attempted to adopt such laws, and in almost every case, the laws passed. Most of the Maine Laws were quickly repealed, however, as the political alliances that had created them proved to be unstable. The emergence of a new political party system centered on the slavery issue took Prohibition out of politics for almost a generation.

The Gilded Age

At the opening of the Gilded Age (around 1870), drinking had a new venue, the saloon—a primarily male institution, a fact that made its respectability automatically suspect. Even so, saloons existed almost everywhere, spread by the practice of many brewers of establishing their own street-level retailing venues. Throughout the period, the Prohibition Party and the Woman's Christian Temperance Union (WCTU) agitated for national constitutional Prohibition. By the end of the period, six states prohibited the sale of alcohol, and almost every state allowed

local option elections on liquor sales. At this time, the Democrats and the Republicans preferred to avoid the issue of Prohibition. Republicans pushed alternative policies of high license (which imposed all sorts of restrictions on liquor merchants), while Democrats preferred to leave the matter up to voters in local option elections. In turn, the leading temperance organizations denounced the major political parties and saw the corruption of politics (symbolized by the saloon) as one of the main evils spawned by the legal manufacture and sale of liquor.

The Prohibition Party was the leading male temperance organization of the Gilded Age. Because it asked men to abandon other party affiliations, in an age where party affiliations were extremely strong, the party remained at the margins of power. Its members came primarily from the temperance wing of the Republican Party, and it had effective organizations only in the Northeast and the Midwest. Throughout its history, the Prohibition Party splintered over whether it should embrace other issues, such as woman suffrage or railroad regulation; in some election cycles it did (thus dividing its members) and in others it did not, but then lost voters to organizations that focused on issues other than liquor. Indeed, the emergence of populism, and a host of new political issues, including regulating the money supply and controlling corporations, ended the Prohibition Party's electoral appeal. By the middle of the last decade of the nineteenth century, the party was widely perceived to be a failure.

Conversely, the female temperance organization of the same period was seen as a great success. The WCTU was the largest female reform organization of the Gilded Age. It was the first national women's reform movement directed and controlled solely by women. Under the leadership of Frances Willard from 1879 to 1898, this largely white, middle-class Protestant women's organization kept the Prohibition issue alive when the political structure was hostile to the antiliquor reform—and convinced a generation of women that they should seek the right to vote. The WCTU pioneered highly effective lobbying techniques (keeping in Washington the first woman lobbyist, Margret Dye Ellis), and in the areas seen as within women's sphere, such as education or the sexual protection of minors, the WCTU was quite successful, especially at the state level. Less successful were the WCTU's attempts to build political coalitions, first with the Prohibition Party and later with the Populist Party and the Knights of Labor. It is only when the WCTU began working with a new Prohibition organization, the Anti-Saloon League, that the temperance advocates could compel the major parties to pass more restrictions on alcohol, culminating in national Prohibition.

The Progressive Era

In the 1890s, antiliquor Protestants built the first national interest group mobilized to shape public policy:

the Anti-Saloon League. The league's strength came from its mobilization of millions of church members who opposed the sale of liquor. It grew from the grass roots and built a professional hierarchy of organizers, lobbyists, and power brokers. Through its organization and extensive media empire, the league commanded its supporters to vote the way it told them to, and most did. The league adopted an "omnipartisan" strategy—that is, it supported any politician regardless of party if that politician would support the league's proposals. The Anti-Saloon League cared only about how a politician voted, not how he acted or what he believed. Thus, Warren G. Harding, a known drinker and gambler, always had league support. The league limited its proposals strictly to liquor issues and to policies that would garner support from voters. As its name implied, it first took aim at the unpopular saloon, supporting such restrictions as the high license, although by the turn of the new century, its favored tool was local option elections. When a state adopted that policy, the league then focused on statewide Prohibition.

At first, the Anti-Saloon League concentrated its operations in the states. Working with both major parties, it dried out large parts of the nation through local option and state Prohibition during the first decade of the twentieth century. At the same time, its lobbyists established an effective presence in Washington, where they sought federal legislation (in alliance with other groups, most notably the WCTU) based on the commerce power and taxing power designed to help dry states effectively carry out their Prohibition policies. Its leaders—William Anderson, Purley Baker, Joseph Cannon, Edwin C. Dinwiddie, and Wayne Wheeler—became familiar and feared faces in Washington.

By 1913, after a major victory in congressional passage of the Webb-Kenyon Act, which prohibited the interstate transportation of liquor intended to be used contrary to the receiving state's law, the league launched its campaign for national Prohibition. By 1917 the league and the WCTU persuaded Congress to send the Prohibition Amendment to the states for ratification. They were aided by the anti-German hysteria of World War I (which weakened the brewers, the movement's most effective opponents), as well as the emergency rationale to preserve grain for food (not alcoholic beverages) and to uplift the morals of the people. League organization and political power resulted in speedy ratification and the passage in 1919 of the Volstead Act, which set up the Prohibition enforcement system. On January 16, 1920, national Prohibition went into effect.

National Prohibition proved troubling to both political parties, especially by the middle of the 1920s, when repeal sentiment began to grow. The Prohibitionists, led by the Anti-Saloon League, tied their fortunes to the Republican Party, which became increasingly unpopular, Republicans tried unsuccessfully

to distance themselves from the policy. For example, President Herbert Hoover's Presidential Commission (known widely as the Wickersham Commission after its chairman, George Wickersham) floated several revision proposals in the course of its life, only to be pulled back to the Prohibitionist line by the time it issued its report.

Meanwhile, the Democratic Party was bitterly divided over the issue, with its southern wing strongly supporting Prohibition and its urban, ethnic, northern wing supporting repeal. Thus, the "wet" presidential candidate Alfred E. Smith was saddled with a bone-dry platform plank in the 1928 election. The lobbying of repeal groups, the diminution in size and strength of temperance groups, and the increasing unpopularity of the Prohibition regime (in tandem with a widely accepted view that Prohibition, not alcohol, bred lawlessness and political corruption) culminated in support from both parties for modification or repeal in the 1932 election. Thus, within 14 years of its adoption, the Eighteenth Amendment was repealed through the Twenty-First Amendment.

From National Prohibition to Neoprohibitionism

Repeal took Prohibition out of partisan politics. Even as he proclaimed the passing of national Prohibition, President Franklin D. Roosevelt declared the nation should return to true temperance, not to the old-time saloon. Thus, the Federal Alcohol Act of 1933 prohibited distillers or brewers from owning retail outlets. The Twenty-First Amendment's second clause also returned almost complete control over liquor to the states, where the sale of liquor proved easier to regulate than prohibit. Within four years of the amendment's adoption, 43 of the 48 states had legalized the sale of all liquor. By 1959 there were no Prohibition states left, although several states preserved the policy in local option systems. To prevent the return of the old, much-vilified saloon, virtually all the states adopted either a government monopoly system or a state-controlled license system of distribution. These systems controlled the number of liquor licenses granted in communities, regulated the environment in which liquor could be consumed in a public venue, and made liquor issues questions of bureaucratic politics, not partisan ones.

From the 1930s through the 1970s, an odd alliance of those who saw drink as evil and sinful, bootleggers who profited by bringing liquor into dry areas, and those who did not want liquor stores or bars in their neighborhoods made the United States a patchwork of regions where liquor was sold without restriction, sold only by the drink, or not sold at all.

An unintended consequence of this patchwork was the emergence of driving while intoxicated. Drinking and driving was perceived as a societal problem as early as the 1950s but did not gain strong advocates against it until the 1980s, when it became associated with related issues of underage drinking.

The key advocacy group, at the state and federal levels, was Mothers against Drunk Driving (MADD). As a group, MADD had inherent advantages. First, it was a victims' group, with personalized stories—My child was killed by a drunk driver, what are you going to do about it? Second, it quickly gained powerful allies, most notably the insurance industry, the liquor industry (prompted in part by fear of stricter liquor regulations), and car manufacturers (fearful of requirements for more safety devices on cars). MADD, like earlier advocates, started with local and state action. Its first actions were to track judges and others in their sentencing of drunk drivers (and to obtain harsher sentences, either through mandatory sentencing laws or a change of judges) and to push for state laws that lowered the blood alcohol level that legally defined intoxication. In these and later efforts, the group avoided partisan politics in favor of lobbying and leveraging the administrative state. Through its actions, the 1984 Highway Act included provisions that withheld highway funds to any state that had a legal drinking age lower than 21. At the time, legal drinking ages varied among the states, but by 1988, with virtually no political struggle, the legal drinking age in all states was 21.

The control of drink bedevilled party politics from the 1820s to the 1930s. The Prohibition movement mobilized women's mass political power before suffrage and gave birth to the single-issue pressure group. After repeal, temperance and Prohibition faded as issues, only to be reborn in a far different form in the late twentieth century as neoprohibitionism.

See also Gilded Age, 1870s–90s; populism; progressivism and the Progressive Era, 1890s–1920.

FURTHER READING. Gaines M. Foster, *Moral Reconstruction: Christian Lobbyists and the Federal Legislation of Morality, 1865–1920*, 2002; K. Austin Kerr, *Organized for Prohibition: A New History of the Anti-Saloon League*, 1985; David E. Kyvig, *Repealing National Prohibition*, 2nd ed., 2000; Thomas R. Pegram, *Battling Demon Rum: The Struggle for a Dry America, 1800–1933*, 1998.

RICHARD F. HAMM

public opinion polls

The current American political process is nearly unimaginable without public opinion polls. These surveys measure not only the relative standing of candidates for office but also citizens' views on myriad social and political issues. Attempts to record political opinion are as old as the nation. But such polls, at least in their contemporary guise, date only from the mid-1930s, when George Gallup, Elmo Roper, and Archibald Crossley championed the ability of scientific sampling methods to reveal the "pulse of democracy." The modern public opinion poll—along with its ramifications for U.S. politics and civic life—was born of their success.

Interest in elucidating citizens' political sentiments stretches far back into the American past, as well as that of most republican nations. Since at least the eighteenth century, when the term *public opinion* first surfaced, representative governments have claimed to be able to locate—as well as listen and respond to—the will of the people. As James Madison argued in 1791, the "opinion of the majority" was the "real sovereign in every free government." Public opinion, whether deemed virtuous, unruly, or in need of enlightened guidance, became part of the rhetorical arsenal of rulers and elites who claimed to speak in its name. Collective opinion about public affairs was also thought to exercise a shaping force on citizens. In the words of political philosopher John Locke, "the law of opinion, the law of reputation, the law of fashion . . . is heeded more than any divine law or any law of the state."

In the United States, where democratic rule and political legitimacy were firmly tied to majority will, assessing the national mood was a favorite pastime of journalists, politicians, and social commentators long before Gallup appeared on the scene. Political scientist Susan Herbst has observed that "technically sophisticated attempts to quantify popular sentiment trailed far behind theorizing and discussion of it."

Starting in the nineteenth century, rudimentary political surveys, whether for entertainment or electoral gain, were undertaken by reporters, party loyalists, and ordinary citizens. In the 1820s, partisan newspapers began conducting straw polls as a means of both calculating and swaying political contests. "Straws," named for the way a straw held up in the wind could determine which way it was blowing, were haphazard instruments for gauging opinion, with passengers on a train or people encountered during a phase of a political campaign polled as the entire sample. Regardless, these quantitative surveys were popular news features into the twentieth century, encouraging a "horse race" approach to reporting elections that continues to the present.

Origins of the Modern Opinion Poll

A conjunction of statistical and social scientific innovations, commercial demands, and journalistic trends led to more systematic public opinion surveys in the first decades of the twentieth century and ultimately to the "scientific" polling of the 1930s. The estimation of standard errors based on sample size was crucial to pollsters' ability to extrapolate from the views of a small group of respondents something like national public opinion on a given issue. Equally significant were developments in the burgeoning field of market research, which sought ever more precise gauges of consumer desires and, in the process, supplied the techniques and personnel for political research. Finally, media interest in public opinion as news guaranteed that the polls would have both audiences and financial backers.

But the rise of modern political polling also required the entrepreneurial skills of Gallup and his colleagues. All of them got their start (and remained) in private commercial research and aspired to extend sample survey techniques to other arenas. In the lead-up to the 1936 presidential election, Gallup, along with Roper and Crossley, publicly challenged the best-known straw poll of the day, conducted by the *Literary Digest*. The *Digest* poll had correctly predicted the winner of the past five elections. But in 1936, even though it tallied over 2 million mail-in ballots, the poll incorrectly called the election for Republican Alfred Landon. Gallup et al., on the other hand, surveyed significantly fewer but more representative individuals and correctly forecast the election, if not the actual percentage of votes (Gallup was off by 7 points), for Franklin D. Roosevelt. Their victory gave instant credibility to scientific opinion polls, based on careful cross sections of the national population—what Gallup called the "miniature electorate."

Gallup and Roper, and soon a corps of other "pollers," were not content to confine their efforts to electoral contests. Indeed, many believed that election polls, although good for business and for legitimating their techniques in the public eye, were socially useless. The real goal was, in Gallup's words, "charting virtually unexplored sectors of the public mind": polling citizens on social and political issues that never made it onto a ballot. With this aim in mind, Gallup's American Institute for Public Opinion (AIPO) was established in 1935 to conduct a "continuing poll on the issues of the day." By 1940 its reports of Americans' opinions, on topics ranging from working women to U.S. entrance into World War II, were syndicated and carried by 106 newspapers. Roper's Fortune Survey, also created in 1935, had a similar goal, if never as wide a following.

James Bryce, author of *The American Commonwealth*, suggested in 1888 that public opinion ought to be "the real ruler of America," but lamented the lack of "machinery for weighing or measuring the popular will from week to week or month to month." In his many tracts promoting polling techniques, Gallup portrayed his new technology as the fulfillment of Bryce's vision.

By this light, opinion polls were more than a method for gathering information. They were a civic instrument, able to revitalize democracy—the spirit, if not the form, of the New England town meeting—in an increasingly complex, bureaucratic nation. Polls would achieve this goal by opening up a direct channel between "the people" and those in power, bypassing unreceptive legislators, political machines, and pressure groups. "As vital issues emerge from the fast-flowing stream of modern life," pledged Gallup, public opinion polls would "enable the American people to speak for themselves." Roper similarly described polls as "democracy's auxiliary ballot box." In short, the new polls would make ordinary citizens articulate—and their leaders responsive—in an age of mass organization.

In the years after 1936, other individuals, notably Samuel Lubbell, Lou Harris, and Mervin Field, would enter the polling arena, as would government agencies and major survey research organizations such as the National Opinion Research Center (1941), Columbia University's Bureau of Applied Social Research (1944), and the Survey Research Center at the University of Michigan (1946). Technical improvements in sampling and survey design ensued, although they did not prevent spectacular failures in polling techniques. The polls' confident prediction that Thomas Dewey would prevail over Harry Truman in the presidential election of 1948 was the best known of these failures, triggering a major investigation by the Social Scientific Research Council and much soul-searching by pollsters, social scientists, journalists, and market research clients.

The relative ease with which polling's 1948 crisis passed, however, suggested the growing dependence of various sectors of U.S. society on Gallup's techniques. Opinion polling, along with the allied field of market research, expanded dramatically in the 1960s and beyond, as interest groups, political consultants, and television and news organizations got into the polling business. By the mid-1960s, opinion surveying had spread throughout the world. The Gallup Poll had 32 affiliates and conducted polls in nearly 50 countries. In the early twenty-first-century United States, several hundred polling organizations existed on national, state, or local levels. Quantitative reports based on the aggregation of individual responses had largely displaced older ways of gauging citizens' views, among them public hearings, petitions, rallies, and letter-writing campaigns.

Polling's Critics

Gallup's rosy view of the democratic potential of opinion surveys was never fully embraced by his contemporaries, nor by later observers of the polls. Multiple criticisms were leveled at public opinion polls from their inception and recurred loudly during each new election cycle.

Some critiques were political and came from those who had something to lose or gain from poll numbers. Legislators on both sides of the aisle in the 1930s and 1940s looked skeptically at the new electoral polls, citing bias and distortion. (Early polls often did overestimate Republican support, making Franklin Roosevelt suspect that Gallup was on the opposing party's payroll.) Beginning in 1932, there were regular proposals in Congress to investigate or regulate the polls, and Gallup himself came under congressional scrutiny in 1944.

Ordinary citizens also denounced what they considered to be slanted or inaccurate polls. But their chief complaint concerned the practice of scientific sampling. To many Americans, the notion that national opinion could be distilled from as few as

1,000 respondents was not simply counterintuitive but undemocratic. Given the regular claims of polling's founders to represent the citizenry, many individuals were puzzled—or offended—by the fact that their opinions were not included in the surveys. Especially in the early decades of scientific polling, some were even moved to write to Gallup and Roper to ask why they hadn't been questioned. Despite the ubiquity of polls in American life today, widespread distrust of their central methodology persists. Over half of Americans surveyed in 1985, for example, claimed not to believe in the representativeness of random sampling.

Some of the most important challenges to the polls came from those who worried that data publicizing majority views would have negative effects in the public arena, due to either the overt manipulation or subtle influence of opinion data. Many legislators, commentators, and citizens from the 1930s onward decried the purported sway of polls over politicians or individual opinions—the latter the so-called bandwagon effect. Although Gallup dismissed this possibility, some studies, including those in the 1940s by sociologist Paul Lazarsfeld, suggested that published survey data could indeed influence voters, favoring candidates who were ahead in the polls. In a later iteration of this theme, scholars found that public opinion research could create a "spiral of silence," dampening minority voices through social pressure.

Other critiques were technical in nature. Pollsters' early method of choosing respondents, particularly their use of a discretionary system of "quota" sampling, was one area that came under fire. After the fiasco of 1948, most moved to the more costly procedure of "probability," or random, sampling, where every individual had an equal likelihood of being polled. Academic survey researchers then and now have pointed to other vexing problems with obtaining valid poll results. Among the most important of these are interviewer bias (the potential for the social background of the interviewer and/or respondent to affect responses) and question-wording effects (the fact that Americans register dramatically different levels of support for "welfare" versus "assistance to the poor," for example).

Still, other criticisms issued from commentators who found poll results like Gallup's a poor stand-in for something as complex and changeable as "public opinion." They argued that tallying individual, anonymous responses to standardized questions fundamentally obscured how opinion was forged. Political scientist Lindsay Rogers, who in 1949 coined the term *pollster* (partly for its resonance with the word *huckster*), was a vehement early critic of this stripe. In an influential 1948 argument, sociologist Herbert Blumer faulted the polls for severing opinions from their social context: the institutions, groups, and power relations that helped to shape them. Other critics, returning to concerns raised earlier in the century by political commentator Walter Lippmann,

wondered whether Gallup's vision of direct democracy via polls was desirable—that is, whether citizens were capable of wise, informed opinions about complicated public issues.

A host of recent detractors, including French sociologist Pierre Bourdieu, further argued that polls do not neutrally report public views but rather generate entirely new entities: "nonattitudes" born of queries about topics that individuals have little knowledge of or interest in; political debates that would not otherwise be on the public agenda; and even the illusion of an opinionated public. In this view, "public opinion"—as revealed by polls—is an artifact of a particular measurement technique and often benefits interested elites such as politicians and journalists rather than the citizenry at large. Arguing that polls have had a disproportionate role in agenda-setting, such critics have urged paying attention to "don't know" responses and refusals to learn more about what public opinion polls obscure and whom they serve.

In the late twentieth century, frustration with the limitations of polls, and especially their seeming failure to enrich political discourse, led to multiple experiments with polling formats as well as a movement for "deliberative polling," led by political scientist James Fishkin. Proponents claimed that when citizens were provided with briefing materials on issues and had time to discuss their opinions face to face with others, reasoned collective judgments would result.

Certainly, many parties over the years have welcomed poll data for measuring public preferences as well as the potential to inform political discussion. Polls have clarified major differences between majority sentiment and political leaders. Longitudinal survey data have allowed new windows on ordinary citizens' political beliefs and affiliations, documenting, for instance, Americans' remarkably stable policy preferences over time. One recent study concludes that U.S. opinion surveys reveal a "rational public" and, furthermore, that public policy aligns with majority views in approximately two out of three instances. But the range and extent of critiques over the last 70 years suggest that Gallup's and Roper's ambitious hopes for polls as the "pulse of democracy" have not yet been realized.

Polls and Civic Life

Notwithstanding such challenges, modern opinion polls and their creators have exercised tremendous influence in American life. Ultimately, Gallup's surveys managed not only to transform political reportage but also to change politics itself. Polling techniques quickly penetrated the corridors of Congress and the White House. Franklin D. Roosevelt, an early convert to survey data, began receiving three-page summaries of public opinion in 1941; by 1942 these reports were often 20 pages in length. Roosevelt, significantly, monitored polls less to learn the public's views and more to shape them and garner support for specific policies. Two of the administration's unofficial pollsters, Hadley Cantril and Gerard Lambert (famous for a successful Listerine advertising campaign), were careful to include in all their analyses suggestions as to "how the attitude reported might be corrected."

In this, Roosevelt was hardly alone: from the 1930s onward, every president save Harry Truman relied on confidential surveys of opinion, whether to evaluate campaign strategies or claim an independent base of support for his views. Such uses of private polling accelerated over the decades: pollster Lou Harris played a key role in John F. Kennedy's presidential campaign; Richard Nixon employed (and suppressed) polls to gain advantage over his political opponents; and Bill Clinton made pollster Stanley Greenberg part of his "war room" of advisors (and, by one account, spent nearly $2 million on polls in a single year).

In addition to presidential administrations, members of Congress, governors, and mayors now regularly consult or commission polls. Politicians may disavow "poll-driven" politics, but their actions speak louder than their words. George W. Bush ran for president in 2000 stating, "we take stands without having to run polls and focus groups to tell us where we stand"—and then spent $1 million on polls the following year. It is clear that opinion polling has become a permanent feature of U.S. governance, coloring campaign strategies and political advertisements, public statements, and policy making. Even despite recent, well-publicized flaws in pre-election and exit polls (which, it should be noted, are typically the best designed and most comprehensive kinds of polls, as compared to social issue polls), quantitative opinion surveys are here to stay.

Historically, public opinion has had many different shades of meaning. In 1965 Harwood Childs, founder of the *Public Opinion Quarterly*, was able to list some 50 competing definitions for the term. One sign of Gallup's astonishing success is today's ready conflation of poll data and public opinion: the near-complete merging of the people's will and a specific statistical technique for measuring it.

See also political culture.

FURTHER READING. Scott L. Althaus, *Collective Preferences in Democratic Politics: Opinion Surveys and the Will of the People*, 2003; Adam J. Berinsky, *Silent Voices: Public Opinion and Political Participation in America*, 2004; George F. Bishop, *The Illusion of Public Opinion: Fact and Artifact in American Public Opinion Polls*, 2005; Pierre Bourdieu, "Public Opinion Does Not Exist," in *Communication and Class Struggle*, edited by Armand Mattelart and Seth Siegelaub, 1979; Jean Converse, *Survey Research in the United States: Roots and Emergence, 1890–1960*, 1987; Robert M. Eisinger, *The Evolution of Presidential Polling*, 2003; James S. Fishkin, *The Voice of the People: Public Opinion and Democracy*, reprint, 1997; Benjamin Ginsberg, *The Captive Public: How Mass Opinion Promotes State Power*, 1986; Susan Herbst, *Numbered Voices: How Opinion Polling Has Shaped American Politics*, 1993; Sarah E. Igo, *The Averaged American: Surveys, Citizens, and the Making of a Mass Public*, 2007; Benjamin I. Page and Robert Y. Shapiro, *The Rational Public: Fifty Years of Trends in Americans' Policy Preferences*, 1992; Daniel J. Robinson, *The Measure of Democracy: Polling, Market Research, and Public Life, 1930–1945*, 1999.

SARAH E. IGO

race and politics to 1860

Between the American Revolution and the Civil War, the politics of race and of slavery danced around one another, colliding here, overlapping there, changing over time, always related but never quite identical. Before 1820 northern politics had a strong current of antislavery sentiment based on the principle that blacks and whites were equally entitled to the same fundamental rights. Between the two great antebellum sectional crises—that of the Missouri Compromise of 1820 and of the Compromise of 1850—a more virulent proslavery racism prevailed. But with the Mexican American War, debates about slavery—and with it, antiracist politics—revived. The Republican electoral triumph of 1860 brought these two competing traditions into direct collision.

Slavery and Antislavery in the Age of Revolution

The antislavery radicalism of the Revolutionary years neither died nor dissipated in the 1790s. On the contrary, it was not until 1799 that New York passed a gradual emancipation law, followed five years later by New Jersey. Far from the bedraggled leftovers of a once formidable antislavery politics, the emancipations in New York and New Jersey were signal achievements of an antislavery coalition that became better organized and more ideologically coherent after 1790. Nor were these the only successes of early American antislavery politics. Throughout the North, gradual emancipation laws were reinforced by state and local statutes that weakened what remained of slavery. Slave trading was banned, fugitive slave catchers were thwarted, slave marriages were legalized, and slaves were permitted to own property. What was left of "slavery" had been transformed into something more closely approximating apprenticeship. Yet even those remaining "slaves" who fought for the United States during the War of 1812 were emancipated.

Despite increasingly stiff resistance from slaveholders, antislavery politics remained vital at the national level. The new federal government quickly readopted the Ordinance of 1787, banning the migration of slaves into the Northwest Territories. Long before the 1808 nationwide ban on the Atlantic slave trade went into effect, Congress prohibited slave trading in the southwestern territories and imposed stiff regulations that thwarted it in eastern seaports as well. Once the Atlantic trade itself was banned, Congress passed a series of increasingly aggressive enforcement laws culminating in the declaration of the trade as "piracy" in 1820.

Yet by then, slavery's opponents looked back on the republic's first 30 years and saw a series of defeats at the hands of a slaveholding class that had grown more, rather than less, powerful. Antislavery politicians had tried but failed to impose a tax on slave imports before 1808. Instead, as the deadline for closing the Atlantic slave trade approached, Georgia and South Carolina opened the floodgates and imported tens of thousands of African slaves into the United States. Northern congressmen had tried to restrict the migration of slaves into the southwestern territories but were again thwarted by an increasingly powerful and belligerent slaveholding bloc in Congress. Antislavery politicians likewise failed in their efforts to inhibit the growth of slavery in the territories acquired under the Louisiana Purchase. Indeed, so aggressive had proslavery forces become that in the immediate aftermath of the War of 1812 they made a serious effort to overturn the restriction on slave imports in the states that had been carved out of the northwestern territories. Opponents of the institution who had once hoped that the Revolution's "contagion of liberty" would lead to the steady disappearance of the institution instead looked back a generation later and saw the opposite. A cotton boom had breathed new life into the slaveholding class, making the southern states the most economically and politically potent force in the new nation. Slavery was expanding far more rapidly than was freedom, and with it grew a new domestic slave trade that duplicated many of the horrors of the illegal Atlantic trade.

By 1820 slaveholders and their opponents had honed their arguments in a debate that was already 30 years old. Racial equality was always an issue in these early struggles over slavery, but it was assumed rather than highlighted. Antislavery politicians almost always insisted that blacks and whites were equally entitled to the universal rights promised in the Declaration of Independence and to the same privileges and immunities of citizenship guaranteed by the Constitution. Their commitment to gradualism rested on the environmentalist assumption that, although slavery had left its victims unprepared for immediate emancipation, blacks were ultimately equal to whites in their innate capacity to assume the responsibilities of citizenship. In that sense, antislavery politics was always fundamentally antiracist.

By contrast, slavery's defenders insisted on the right of property in slaves and the right of slave states to be left alone by the federal government, but they also claimed that blacks alone, by virtue of their racial inferiority, were suitable for slavery. In this sense, the proslavery argument was intrinsically racist—not because racism led logically to the defense of slavery but because the defense of slavery led logically to the question of *who* should be enslaved. And the proslavery answer was always the same: Africans and their descendants.

Racial Politics and the Defeat of Revolutionary Antislavery

But the logic of proslavery racism had a way of spilling beyond its initial purpose. If Africans and African Americans were racially destined for slavery, it followed that free blacks were destined for inferiority as well. In 1790 Congress passed a citizenship law restricting naturalization to whites. By the end of the eighteenth century, individual states began stripping free blacks of the right to vote. Tennessee did this in its 1799 constitution; Ohio disfranchised African Americans in 1803. In 1814 New York required blacks to prove their freedom before they could vote. But it was not until the disastrous defeat of antislavery politics in the Missouri Crisis that racism moved into the center of American politics. In 1821 both Missouri and New York paved the way for a generation of racially inflected politics in which slavery's defenders used attacks on free blacks as a means of silencing antislavery lawmakers. In one state after another, constitutions were rewritten to grant all white men the right to vote while at the same time stripping black men of the same right or at least severely restricting it. In 1821 New York abolished property qualifications for voting and office holding for white men while simultaneously imposing a steep property qualification—lands valued at at least $250—on black men. Some states banned black voting altogether. Missouri, meanwhile, led the way in discriminatory citizenship laws, declaring, in its 1821 constitution, that free blacks could not move into the state—thus depriving them of one of the basic privileges of citizenship, the right of mobility.

All across America, states and localities rushed to impose harsh and demeaning racial discriminations on free blacks. They banned racial intermarriage; they prohibited blacks from serving on juries; they used politics to depoliticize African Americans, excluding blacks from public office and severely restricting—if not outright banning—them from voting. In lockstep with the spread of legal inequality came an explosion of private discriminations. Black and white passengers were segregated from one another in streetcars, ferries, and railroad cars. Theaters relegated blacks to "nigger balconies." Cemeteries separated black and white funeral plots. In this, at least, there were few regional distinctions, for racial segregation became the way of life for free blacks in the North as well as the South. For black abolitionists like Frederick Douglass, racial discrimination represented "the spirit of slavery," extending its influence beyond the borders of the slave states.

The Democratic Party was the primary vehicle for this ascendant racial politics. A coalition of northern plebeians and southern slaveholders, the Democratic Party unified its northern and southern wings under the banner of white supremacy. Even so, the impetus behind racial politics was essentially negative. It did not foreground racial politics so much as it made antislavery politics impossible. New York's 1821 constitution is an example of this. Many African Americans had already been stripped of the vote by earlier statutes requiring blacks to prove their freedom before they could cast their ballots. There is evidence suggesting partisan motives for imposing a property qualification: New York Jeffersonians were internally divided, and they used racial demagoguery both to unify their own party and to wipe out the remnants of the Federalists. Martin Van Buren saw what was happening in his home state of New York and helped develop it into a nationwide strategy for uniting the northern and southern wings of an emerging Democratic Party.

It worked. Having used white supremacy to shut down the threat of antislavery politics that had loomed so large in the Missouri crisis, The Democracy (as the Democratic Party was then known) was free to focus on other issues. As a result, the most important political battles of the next generation were waged over who would gain and lose from economic development. Racial politics unified the party faithful by purging the system of the potentially disruptive impact of antislavery politics.

Colonization and Its Opponents

The colonization movement was yet another symptom of the relative weakening of antislavery politics. The idea itself was not new. As early as the 1780s, Thomas Jefferson suggested that the abolition of slavery had to be accompanied by systematic efforts to "colonize" freed blacks somewhere outside the United States. Blacks were so different from whites, so clearly inferior, Jefferson argued, that even though they were entitled to the same right to freedom as all other human beings, they could never live in America as the equals of whites. The idea achieved new prominence with the founding of the American Colonization Society (ACS) in 1816, and from that moment until the Civil War, colonization remained a remarkably popular "solution" to the problem of slavery among political elites.

On the surface, the founding of the ACS seemed to reflect a broadening of the same sentiment that was sparking a revival of antislavery politics after the War of 1812. But antislavery leaders saw the emergence of colonization as a disastrous failure. Unlike the earliest abolitionists, colonizationists assumed that blacks could never be equal citizens in the United States. Thus the emergence of the ACS foreshadowed the triumph of racial politics. In theory, colonization could appeal to racism and antislavery sentiment at the same time. Its emergence, at the very moment that the struggle between proslavery and antislavery politicians was coming to a head, reflected the persistence of the dream of ridding the nation of slavery but also the ascendance of the dream of ridding the country of blacks.

A handful of prominent African Americans agreed that blacks and whites could never live together as equals and that the best solution was for blacks to emigrate to Sierra Leone, Liberia, or perhaps to the black republic of Haiti. But most black Americans objected to such proposals. Shortly after the founding of the ACS, 3,000 blacks in Philadelphia rallied to express their vehement opposition to colonization. They were only marginally more interested in voluntary emigration, despite the strenuous efforts by the government of Haiti and prominent black Americans like James Forten and Richard Allen to encourage emigration to the Caribbean island. Instead, most African Americans, born and raised in the United States, chose to remain and wage the struggle for equality in the land of their birth.

Opposition to colonization became the rallying cry among a new generation of black abolitionists. In 1827 they founded the nation's first black newspaper, *Freedom's Journal*, which combined attacks on colonization with equally vehement denunciations of northern racism and southern slavery. As the journal's editor warmed to the idea of colonization to Africa, *Freedom's Journal* lost its appeal to African American readers and ceased publication in 1829. But over the next several decades, black newspapers appeared in cities all across the North. At the same time, blacks organized a series of conventions that, like the newspapers, openly protested the rising tide of racism in the North and the expansion of slavery in the South. Disfranchisement had wiped out much of the black electorate, but it did not put an end to black politics.

Radicalization of the Debate

White militants like William Lloyd Garrison, inspired by their black predecessors, made opposition to colonization a keystone of a radical abolitionist movement that emerged in the late 1820s in the wake of the recent disastrous defeat of antislavery politics. And like the antislavery politics that it replaced, radical abolitionism was almost by definition antiracist—whatever the particular prejudices of individual reformers. By the 1830s, the racial climate had changed, however, and with it the salience of abolitionist antiracism. Just as the Democratic Party had fused racial inequality to the defense of slavery, many abolitionists now demanded racial equality along with the abolition of slavery. For obvious reasons, black abolitionists were especially inclined to link antislavery with the struggle for racial equality, but white radicals now agreed that the struggle against slavery in the South was indissolubly linked to the struggle against racial discrimination in the North. It was this racial egalitarianism, more than antislavery, that made radical abolitionism *radical*.

Thus, as politicians used race to squeeze antislavery out of the mainstream, the debate over slavery became more polarized than ever. Proslavery

intellectuals helped inspire an "American school" of ethnography dedicated to developing scientific proofs of the innate inferiority of the African "race." Meanwhile, radical abolitionists argued that the same principle of human equality that made slavery immoral made racial inequality illegitimate as well. By the 1830s, the politics of race were explicitly bound with the politics of slavery at every point along the ideological spectrum.

Revival of Antislavery Politics

One of the goals of radical abolitionists was to force antislavery back onto the national political agenda. First they tried flooding the South with antislavery propaganda, but President Andrew Jackson shut them down by telling his postmaster general not to deliver such mail. More successful was the abolitionist effort to bombard Congress with petitions asking for the abolition of the slave trade, and then slavery, in Washington, D.C. This campaign precipitated the notorious "gag rule" whereby Congress automatically tabled all antislavery petitions in the hopes of thwarting any discussion of slavery in either the House of Representatives or the Senate. The debate over the gag rule erupted in 1835 and dragged on for nearly a decade. By the time the rule was abandoned, antislavery politics was coming back to life.

One reason for this was the revival of party competition in the 1830s, stimulated by opposition to President Jackson. This anti-Jackson, or Whig, party was, like the Democratic Party, national in its appeal. The prominence of Southerners in the Whig coalition thereby ensured that it would not be an antislavery party. Moreover, the Whigs' "American System" assumed that slavery had a permanent place in a nationally integrated economy. Yet, like the Federalists of an earlier generation, the Whigs were more likely than the Democrats to attract those northern politicians who were opposed to slavery. The reemergence of party competition in the 1830s thus created more space for antislavery politicians to survive within the political mainstream than had been the case in the late 1820s. But Whig antislavery was weak and was channeled primarily into empty encomia to colonization. For antislavery politics to revive, pressure would have to be administered from outside the two-party system.

The revival began in 1840 with the launch of the Liberty Party, which picked up steam in the 1844 presidential election. The Liberty Party was a coalition of abolitionists committed to racial equality and pragmatists who hoped to revive antislavery politics by focusing primarily on the issue of slavery's expansion. Thus, from the earliest moments of its revival, antislavery politics revealed an impulse to separate the issue of slavery from the issue of race. The potential of this strategy soon became clear. The war with Mexico gave antislavery politics a critical boost, leading to the formation of the Free Soil Party in 1848. With that, the focus of antislavery politics shifted away from both colonization as well as racial equality and toward halting the further expansion of slavery into the western territories. There was a racist argument for the notion of "free soil": the claim that the western territories should be reserved for whites. But there was also an egalitarian argument, a conviction that the federal government should place its finger on the scales in favor of universal freedom, for blacks and whites alike, by preventing slavery from expanding beyond its present limits.

The collapse of the Whig Party in the wake of the Compromise of 1850 paved the way for the triumph of antislavery politics when it was replaced, in the northern states, by a new Republican Party committed to free soil ideals. The Republicans nominated their first presidential candidate in 1856 and went on to victory in 1860.

Race and Antislavery Politics

This second generation of antislavery politics was similar to its pre-1820 predecessor in important ways, but different as well—and one of the crucial differences had to do with its relationship to the politics of race. The first generation of antislavery politicians tended to assume that blacks and whites were equally entitled not merely to the presumption of freedom but to the same voting rights and the same privileges and immunities of citizenship as well. They could take this position, in part, because race was not yet a major theme in American politics. Politicians assumed rather than highlighted their disagreements over racial equality. A generation later, the situation was very different. Antislavery politicians in the 1840s and 1850s also assumed that blacks and whites were entitled to the same basic rights—life, liberty, and the pursuit of happiness—something proslavery Democrats flatly denied. At the same time, however, Republicans in the 1850s denied that, in opposing slavery, they necessarily supported racial equality. This position opened the Republican Party to a wide spectrum of racial attitudes—from antislavery racists to radical egalitarians.

The most successful spokesman for this position was Abraham Lincoln. By the late 1850s, Lincoln repeatedly dismissed racial equality as a "false issue." The great issue facing the nation was slavery not racial equality, he argued. White voters disagreed, not over the question of racial equality but over the question of slavery. And in any case, Lincoln added, questions of racial equality were matters to be handled by individual states and thus had no bearing on national political campaigns. Republicans in the Massachusetts legislature might support both racial equality and discrimination against immigrants, while Republicans in the Illinois legislature favored racial discrimination while supporting the rights of immigrants. In either case, Lincoln argued, racial and ethnic discriminations were state matters and had no bearing on the antislavery principles of the Republican Party nationwide.

This explicit separation of race from slavery understandably alienated many abolitionists, but it succeeded in releasing American politics from the stranglehold of proslavery racism. Thus without actually advocating racial equality, the Republican Party broke the back of racial politics by insisting that race and slavery were two different issues and that slavery was the only issue that mattered.

Nevertheless, just as the racist logic of proslavery politics—"the spirit of slavery"—was felt in the spread of laws discriminating against African Americans, the egalitarianism at the core of antislavery politics had the reverse effect. Despite the wide spectrum of opinion about racial equality among Republicans, party victories in the North resulted in the first sporadic reversals of the racial legal structure put in place a generation earlier. Massachusetts abolished segregated schools, for example. Republicans in the New York legislature put an equal suffrage amendment on the ballot in 1860. But it was not until the Republicans took control of Congress and the presidency that a nationwide rollback of the racial regime was begun.

This rollback was largely stimulated by the demands of the Civil War. Once emancipation became Union policy, white Northerners questioned: "What shall be done with the Negro?" The answer that emerged, tentatively at first, was a repudiation of more than a generation of racial politics. The Lincoln administration declared that free blacks were citizens and were equally entitled to the associated privileges and immunities. Republicans opened the U.S. Army to blacks for the first time since the 1790s. Shortly after the war ended, they passed the landmark Civil Rights Act of 1866. Eventually, Republicans endorsed voting rights for the former slaves and enacted constitutional amendments against racial qualifications for voting that effectively abolished discriminatory voting laws in the northern as well as the southern states. With the triumph of antislavery politics, came a reversal—incomplete but nonetheless significant—of the racial politics of the proslavery Democracy.

See also abolitionism; slavery; voting.

FURTHER READING. Jonathan Earle, *Jacksonian Antislavery and the Politics of Free Soil, 1824–1854*, 2004; Eric Foner, *Free Soil, Free Labor, Free Men: The Ideology of the Republican Party Before the Civil War*, 1970; Robert Pierce Forbes, *The Missouri Compromise and Its Aftermath: Slavery and the Meaning of America*, 2007; David N. Gellman, *Emancipating New York: The Politics of Slavery and Freedom, 1777–1827*, 2006; John Craig Hammond, *Slavery, Freedom, and Expansion in the Early American West*, 2007; Matthew Mason, *Slavery and Politics in the Early American Republic*, 2006; James Oakes, *The Radical and the Republican: Frederick Douglass, Abraham Lincoln, and the Triumph of Antislavery Politics*, 2007; Benjamin Quarles, *Black Abolitionists*, 1969; Richard H. Sewell, *Ballots for Freedom: Antislavery Politics in the United States, 1837–1860*, 1976; Arthur Zilversmit, *The First Emancipation: The Abolition of Slavery in the North*, 1967.

JAMES OAKES

The politics of race went through more than one revolution during the seven decades after 1860. Consider three moments at the beginning, middle, and end of the period: In 1860 the prospect that the presidency would be occupied by a member of a political party committed merely to banning slavery from territories where it did not then exist was enough to provoke the Deep South into violent rebellion. On the eve of the Civil War, according to the Supreme Court's *Dred Scott v. Sandford* decision, people of African descent could never become American citizens and had "no rights which a white man was bound to respect." Yet in September 1862, the preliminary Emancipation Proclamation signaled the end of more than two centuries of slavery in America. By the middle of the period, in 1895–96, African American rights that had expanded dramatically in the 1860s were contracting: South Carolina held a state constitutional convention openly aimed at disfranchising black men; Tuskegee Institute head Booker T. Washington publicly promised in the "Atlanta Compromise" that southern blacks would accept racial segregation; and the Supreme Court, in *Plessy v. Ferguson,* announced that segregation was constitutional. In 1930 the first African American member of Congress from the North, Chicago's Oscar De Priest, was elected to his second term in office; the National Association for the Advancement of Colored People (NAACP) helped defeat the Supreme Court nomination of John J. Parker for his role in excluding blacks from the Republican Party in North Carolina; and NAACP-affiliated attorneys were litigating their second case in a successful 20-year legal campaign to outlaw the white primary.

Sudden advances, counterrevolutions, and periods of incremental change in both directions characterized this turbulent, contradictory, complex period. Race relations varied from time to time and place to place, and issues and institutional features of governments that had nothing inherently to do with race often determined racial policy outcomes. Racial politics can only be understood if it is not separated from other concerns, tensions, and actions.

Violence and Freedom

Secession freed the Republican Party, and then the slaves. As long as southern whites threatened to break up the Union if Northerners moved against slavery, Republican policy was itself enslaved. Once secession was declared, southern slaveholders resigned from Congress, and Fort Sumter was fired upon, the Union inevitably became the enemy of slavery instead of its protector. After securing the border states militarily, the Republicans were free to ban the interstate slave trade, to authorize the federal government, for the first time, to hire African Americans to work for the national government, and to declare escaped slaves

"contraband of war" instead of returning them to their owners as the 1850 Fugitive Slave Act required.

Slaves forced the issue, fleeing toward Union lines as soon as Union armies approached and demanding to work to feed themselves and to fight to restore a nation purified of its original sin of slavery. The longer the Civil War went on and the more white northern soldiers were killed or badly wounded, the less resistance there was to enrolling black soldiers. Once they began fighting for Union forces after the Emancipation Proclamation took permanent effect in January 1863, complete abolition was ensured. Approximately 180,000 African Americans served in the army and navy, about 12 percent of the total number of soldiers and sailors, and they died at the same ghastly rates as whites did. For Northerners, granting and preserving the rights of African Americans who had fought for the Union—especially protecting them from attacks by former secessionists—took on, for a time after the conclusion of the war, the character of a patriotic duty.

White Southerners, however, acted as though the Civil War had settled nothing except the impracticality of secession and the nominal abolition of slavery. After Abraham Lincoln's assassination and the succession of his vice president, Tennessee Democrat Andrew Johnson, southern states passed "black codes" that denied African Americans the right to buy or lease real estate, sign yearly labor contracts, serve on juries, testify against whites in court, and vote. Blacks were excluded from public schools, black orphans were "apprenticed" to their former owners, and black "servants" were required to labor from sunup to sundown for their "masters." White Southerners also demanded that a delegation of former Confederate officers and politicians be seated immediately in Congress.

But the Republicans who controlled Congress refused to admit the erstwhile rebels and took decisive control of Reconstruction. When Johnson vetoed a bill extending the Freedmen's Bureau, which provided food to destitute Southerners of both races, supervised labor contracts, and started schools where ex-slaves could be educated and courts where their concerns could be adjudicated, Republicans in Congress overrode his action, as they did his veto of the 1866 Civil Rights Act. That act began to carry out the implications of the Thirteenth Amendment (ratified in 1865), which Republicans interpreted as doing much more than abolishing slavery. In their expansive interpretation, one resurrected by the U.S. Supreme Court a century later, the Thirteenth Amendment allowed Congress in the Civil Rights Act to outlaw racial discrimination, even in such private contracts as those for housing and admission to private schools, as "badges and incidents of slavery." Seceding states were required to ratify the Thirteenth Amendment as a condition for their readmission to the Union. After enacting the Civil Rights Act, Republicans, over unanimous northern Democratic opposition in Congress, passed the Fourteenth Amendment, which even more securely constitutionalized civil rights, seeking explicitly to guarantee privileges and immunities, due process, and equal protection for all.

In the critical 1866 election campaign, Johnson demagogically lambasted Congress, northern Democrats endlessly race-baited, and white Southerners rioted in Memphis and New Orleans, killing 89 African Americans in full view of the national press. Northern voters reacted to Johnsonian and southern Democratic overreaching by giving the Republicans a landslide, which turned Reconstruction more radical. Ten southern states were placed under temporary military rule, forced to enfranchise African American men and to rewrite their constitutions, and readmitted to Congress only after ratifying the Fourteenth Amendment and much more liberal state constitutions. Because Johnson persisted in trying to subvert the antiracist settlement, he was impeached, almost convicted, and, for all intents and purposes, rendered innocuous.

The United States was the only large slaveholding society that quickly enfranchised freedmen, and the eagerness and skill with which they took to politics surprised and dismayed their former masters, who had expected docility and incompetence. Even in the face of Ku Klux Klan violence, African American voter turnout in the 1860s and 1870s often surpassed 80 percent. Buttressed by the presence of federal troops, by the Fifteenth Amendment, which mandated racially impartial suffrage nationally, and by official jobs for their supporters, the new southern governments launched statewide education systems, encouraged the building and rebuilding of railroads, passed civil rights laws, and protected the rights of laborers, renters, and small farmers. Even after the Reconstruction governments fell, African Americans continued to enjoy the rights to legally marry, worship as they wished, form private clubs, receive (usually inferior) educations at public expense, and, often, to patronize public accommodations such as restaurants, theaters, and railroads, on a nonsegregated basis—if they could afford to pay. Absolute segregation of public places in the South arrived only toward the turn of the century, and it was a matter of law, not of custom.

Disfranchisement by Stages

White southern Democrats fought back against the southern Republican governments with the most extensive peacetime violence in American history. The bloodiest were Louisiana Democrats who, according to a congressional investigation, killed 1,081 persons, mostly black, in the six months before the presidential election of 1868. But violence did not, by itself, doom Reconstruction or account for the ultimate nullification of the Fifteenth Amendment. Murder was most effective as a political tactic if it targeted key political leaders and exploded in the period just before a crucial election. Yet in nine of the dozen southern counties where the best-known violent incidents took place, African Americans somehow managed to poll nearly their full vote for the Republicans in the presidential election that succeeded the incident.

After northern voters reacted to the 1873 depression, bitter northern ethnoreligious conflicts, and widespread tales of corruption by electing a Democratic majority in the House of Representatives in 1874, congressional Republicans managed in their last few months in power to enact the 1875 Civil Rights Act, which mandated the integration of public accommodations, but they failed to pass a strong voter protection bill because Democrats filibustered against it in the House until it was too late for the Senate to act. Although the GOP rebounded to win the second closest presidential election in U.S. history in 1876, part of the price for settling disputes over the election outcome was an implicit promise to stop using the army to protect southern Republicans. Partisanship, economic and nonracial moral issues, and political strife between separate groups of a heterogeneous "white" society, as well as issues of race and Reconstruction per se, brought about what became known as the "Compromise of 1877," which marked what historians traditionally viewed as the end of Reconstruction.

Yet, as is shown in figure 1, which charts the number of black members of Congress and the state legislatures elected from 1868 through 1900 from the 11 states that formed the Confederacy, blacks were not eliminated from politics after 1877. In fact, the number of African Americans elected to legislative office from the South was higher in 1882 than in any subsequent year until 1974, and from 1878 to 1890, the decline in black office holding was palpable, but gradual. Moreover, even where they could not elect black candidates, which was usually their first preference, blacks could often still vote for sympathetic whites. In 1880, three years after President Rutherford B. Hayes symbolically confined U.S. troops to their barracks in the South, an estimated two-thirds of the adult male African Americans were recorded as voting, and two-thirds of that group managed to have their votes recorded for Republican James A. Garfield, whom they had nearly all, no doubt, supported for president. The high black turnout in this election, which was greater than overall national participation a century later, was not atypical, nor did Democrats allow it only because presidential elections were less important to them than those closer to home. An average of six out of ten African Americans voted in the most heavily contested gubernatorial races in each of the 11 states during the 1880s, despite the fact that none of these elections took place on the same day that voters cast ballots for president. Of those blacks who voted, at least 60 percent supported the Republican, Greenback, or other anti-Democratic candidates in each state. Even in the 1890s, after several states had restricted suffrage by law, nearly half of the African American population is estimated to have voted in key gubernatorial contests, although the Populist-Democratic battles were sufficiently severe that Democrats pushed fraud to new levels.

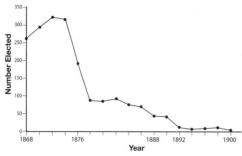

Figure 1. Black Members of Congress and State Legislatures

Five principal tactics were used to reduce and, finally, to eliminate black political strength—no single one sufficient by itself, but all working together and, roughly, following a predictable sequence: violence, fraud, structural discrimination, statutory suffrage restriction, and constitutional disfranchisement. Corresponding to these tactics were four approximate stages in the attack on black voting rights after Reconstruction: the Klan stage, in which fraud and violence predominated; the dilution stage, characterized by structural legal changes; the disfranchisement stage, where the last legal underpinnings of the real "Solid South" were put into place; and the lily white stage, the aim of which was to crush any elevation of blacks above the distinctly secondary political status into which the disfranchisement measures had forced them, and to reduce—from very slim to none—any chances of African Americans being elected or appointed to office or exercising any political muscle whatsoever.

Violence was not only a dangerous weapon for a conservative establishment to use, for it invited retaliation from desperate victims, but it was also less effective than fraud perpetrated by election officials and their superiors. Southern election fraud in the late nineteenth century, as often a matter of boasting in the South as it was a matter of outrage in the North, far surpassed voting fraud at any other time or place in American history. For instance, Louisiana senator and former governor Samuel D. McEnery stated in 1898 that his state's 1882 election law "was intended to make it the duty of the governor to treat the law as a formality and count in the Democrats." William A. Anderson, author of the 1894 election law in Virginia, admitted that elections under his law were "crimes against popular government and treason against liberty." A delegate to the 1901 Alabama constitutional convention reported that "any time it was necessary the black belt could put in ten, fifteen, twenty or thirty thousand Negro votes." A leader of the 1890 Mississippi constitutional convention declared that "it is no secret that there has not been a full vote and a fair count in Mississippi since 1875," which was the last election until 1967 in which African Americans voted at all freely in the state. Like violence, fraud was most potent if ramped up during

crucial elections—for instance, referenda on ratifying discriminatory amendments to state constitutions, as in Alabama in 1901, where, according to the official returns, nearly 90 percent of those in counties with black populations of at least 70 percent supported a new constitution whose advertised purpose was black disfranchisement.

Supplementing fraud were structural changes in election laws, such as gerrymandering election district boundaries; drawing election districts with very different population sizes; switching from district to at-large elections, which made it more difficult to elect members of groups that formed a majority in a part of a city, but only a minority in the whole city; abolishing local elections entirely; annexation or deannexation of territory to add white or subtract black areas from a jurisdiction; requiring officeholders to post bonds too high to meet for anyone who lacked wealthy friends; shifting or consolidating polling places to confuse voters or require them to travel many miles to the polls; and impeaching Republican or other anti-Democratic officials, often on transparently specious grounds. All these measures cut black and Republican office holding at the local, state, and national levels without actually disfranchising voters.

Other laws did reduce individual voting: poll taxes, which in some states had to be paid for every year after a person reached 21 years of age before one could vote, discouraged the poor of both races from voting, but especially the generally poorer blacks. Registration laws could be devised to prune the electorate by compelling registration months before every election, especially at a central location during working hours; demanding copiously detailed information, which sometimes had to be vouched for by witnesses, before a voter could register; allowing registration boards sufficient discretion to enable them to pad or unfairly purge the rolls; disproportionate representation for the Democrats on such boards; requiring voters unaccustomed to keeping records to produce registration certificates at voting places; or permitting widespread challenges to voters at the polls. The then infamous South Carolina "eight-box" law of 1882 required election officials to shift separate ballot boxes for each of eight offices around during the voting to make it impossible for a literate friend to put an illiterate's tickets in the correct order before he entered the polling place, and prohibited anyone but state election officers, all but one or two of whom seem to have been Democrats, from assisting unlettered voters. After 1888, when states began to require ballots to be supplied only by governments, secret ballot laws, employed in eight southern and many northern states with the intent and effect of disfranchising illiterates, could be designed to be so long and complex as to disfranchise all but the well educated and those whom the election officials chose to help.

Along with violence, fraud, and structural measures, such laws reduced Republican and inhibited

Populist representation enough to create legislative majorities in favor of state constitutional disfranchisement. Conventions or referenda then wrote into more permanent form poll taxes and literacy or property tests for registration, often with temporary exemption clauses to allow illiterate (white) voters to register if they could demonstrate to a registrar's satisfaction that they understood parts of the Constitution or laws when they were read to them, or if their ancestors could have voted before 1867 (before southern blacks were enfranchised), or if they or their ancestors had served in the military (including, of course, the Confederate States Army). These were referred to as the "grandfather" and "fighting grandfather" clauses. Constitutional disfranchisement effectively moved fraud one step back, delegating it to registration officials instead of those at the polls. It also reduced widespread unfavorable publicity about white southern election cheating, which had invited national intervention, such as the Lodge Elections Bill of 1890, defeated only by another Senate filibuster, and made legal attacks on white election supremacy more difficult to mount.

Why the Solid South?

The Solid South created by disfranchisement laws—effectively outlawing political party competition, almost entirely excluding southern African Americans from political participation, proudly starving governmental services for poor people—lasted for a half century. Did whites in other regions of the country allow this system to be constructed and maintained because they lost interest in equality during and after the 1870s or increasingly drew a hard white line that treated all people of European origins as identical and all of African origins as naturally inferior, to be excluded from civil society? Or did Reconstructionists, thwarted by the structural peculiarities of the governmental system and adverse judicial decisions, turn north, shifting their focus from national to state governments, lowering their sights, but pursuing the same goal of racial equality closer to home?

Northern laws and litigation on racial discrimination in public accommodations and schools suggest that Reconstruction was not so much abandoned as redirected. After the Supreme Court overturned the 1875 national Civil Rights Act in 1883, most of the northern legislatures that had not earlier passed state public accommodations laws quickly did so. Thereafter, equal access to northern trains, streetcars, restaurants, and places of amusement was largely a matter of right, although the legalities were not always observed. In fact, even in the South until the turn of the nineteenth century, streetcars and many railroads were not rigidly segregated. Moves by states, cities, or private companies to require segregation on streetcars were resisted by black boycotts, sometimes lasting for many months, in more than 25 southern cities.

It took a longer time for every nonsouthern state except Indiana with a black population of 1 percent or more to pass laws requiring most or all public schools to stop restricting the admissions of African Americans. From Massachusetts in 1855, to California in 1880, to New York in 1901, blacks and their white allies fought for equal status by petitioning school boards, filing legal cases, and pressing state legislatures for laws granting every child access to what were then known as "common schools." African Americans contested and won more cases on racial discrimination in public education in the decade of the 1880s, after the nominal end of Reconstruction, than in any other decade before the 1940s. In fact, they filed nearly 100 such cases in 20 states and the District of Columbia in the nineteenth century and prevailed in a majority of them. Nineteenth-century arguments and tactics before school boards and legislatures prefigured those of the twentieth-century civil rights movement, just as the doctrines and rhetoric in some of the legal opinions in the nineteenth-century school cases paralleled those a century later.

If agitation for those rights—in the North, at least—did not cease after 1876, and northern public opinion, as indexed by legislative action, continued to support black rights, why did the legal disfranchisement of southern African Americans succeed? There were three reasons: partisanship, the filibuster, and adverse decisions by the Supreme Court. First, since African Americans remained almost unanimously committed to the Republican Party—the party of Lincoln, emancipation, and Reconstruction—until well after disfranchisement, northern Democrats opposed any efforts to guarantee southern blacks the right to register, vote, and have their votes counted as cast. If southern blacks could vote freely, the fortunes of the Democratic Party nationally were likely to be permanently depressed. Accordingly, not a single Democratic member of Congress voted for any civil or voting rights measure from 1865 through 1900. That this pattern was motivated by partisanship, and not merely by racial animosity, is shown by the fact that an appreciable number of Democrats in northern state legislatures supported school integration and public accommodations bills, especially during the 1880s.

Rabid Democratic partisanship was especially on display in the bitter struggles over the national election bills in 1875 and 1890, when they relentlessly talked to death measures to protect individuals while voting, as well as to oversee registration, voting, and vote counting. Guarding the fundamental right to vote from violence, intimidation, and fraud amounted—the Democrats and much of the nation's press shrieked—to "force bills." Largely to counter these filibustering tactics, Republicans in the House changed the body's rules in 1889–90 to end unlimited debate, and these "Reed Rules," named for House Speaker Thomas B. Reed, not only facilitated the passage of the Lodge Elections Bill in that branch of the national legislature but also fundamentally changed the nature of the House forever. Never again would a minority of the House be able to block the chamber's business until the majority gave up and dropped a bill or severely compromised it. Yet the Senate, during that same congressional session, failed to adopt a proposal by Senator Nelson W. Aldrich that was similar to the Reed Rules. Democrats filibustered the Lodge Bill for 33 days, the longest filibuster in history up to that time, and the bill was finally set aside by a single vote. Since the Senate has not yet followed the House's lead on antifilibuster rules, every civil rights or voting rights proposal through the 1960s had to face the prospect or reality of having to break a filibuster to pass the Senate. As a consequence, between 1875 and 1957, not a single civil rights bill passed in Congress.

How different the history of race and politics in America might have been if both chambers in 1875 or 1890 or even later had adopted antifilibuster rules. If the "Force Bill" of 1875 had passed in time to protect voters from violence, intimidation, and fraud in the 1876 elections, and to prevent the overthrow of state authority, which were the objects of the bill, Hayes would easily have been elected president, Republicans would have continued to control many Deep South governments, and the decisions of southern white voters and leaders to abandon the Republicans as a lost, dangerous cause might well have been reversed. Republican rule in the Deep South would have begun to seem normal, and the developmental sequence of violence, fraud, structural changes, legislative disfranchisement, and constitutional disfranchisement would have been interrupted near the beginning.

Even if the less far-reaching Lodge Bill of 1890 had passed, which would have required breaking the Senate filibuster, southern African Americans would have been able to register more freely and have their votes more nearly counted as cast. If states had nonetheless passed disfranchisement measures, the effects of those laws would have been diminished because federal observers would have been available to restrain local registrars from applying racially separate and unequal standards to prospective voters. And if a serious southern Republican vote had persisted, national Republicans would have had an incentive to follow up the Lodge Bill with other, more comprehensive voting rights laws. Instead of a downward cycle leading to the practically complete disfranchisement of southern blacks by 1910, there might well have been an upward cycle, with less fraud, less structural discrimination, and fewer and more fairly administered restrictions on suffrage. The antilynching bills of the 1920s and 1930s and the anti–poll tax bills of the 1940s would have passed, and there would have been major efforts to extend northern integration laws nationally long before the 1964 Civil Rights Act. No revolutions in sentiment, interest, or cultural mores were required for those policy revolutions to

occur—just a change in the operations of Congress to allow majority rule.

Of course, such laws might have been derailed by the Supreme Court, the least democratic of the national government's three branches, designed with life tenure to ensure the greatest possible independence from the pressures of partisan politics or public opinion. In a confusing and often contradictory line of cases, the Supreme Court, during this period, wavered in protecting or allowing Congress to protect African American political rights. In opinions in *U.S. v. Reese* and *U.S. v. Cruikshank* that were delayed from 1874 to 1876, while the debate on the "force bill" was taking place, Chief Justice Morrison R. Waite, President Grant's *seventh* choice for the position, ruled provisions of the 1870–72 Enforcement Acts unconstitutional or largely unenforceable. Ignoring the Fourteenth Amendment, which does not mention race and which was repeatedly invoked during congressional debates as a basis for the Enforcement Acts, Waite declared that the only constitutional justification for the acts was the Fifteenth Amendment, and that either the acts or the indictments pursuant to them were insufficiently direct in their references to race to satisfy the Fifteenth Amendment.

Thus, in Reese, the refusal of a Lexington, Kentucky, tax collector to accept payment of the poll tax from an African American did not, according to the Court, infect with a racial purpose the actions of election officials who disfranchised him for failure to show a poll tax receipt. And in *Cruikshank*, Louisianians who perpetrated the largest racial mass murder in American history (the Colfax Riot of 1873), went free because Waite split off the beginning sections of the act, which explicitly mentioned race, from the later sections, which only indirectly referred to race.

As a consequence of these two decisions, the existing federal voting rights enforcement machinery was severely weakened. Nothing in the decisions themselves, however, prevented Congress from passing new laws that made the connection between racial discrimination and the protection of voting rights more explicit, and later Court decisions viewed the Fourteenth Amendment's equal protection and due process clauses more expansively, allowing Congress to guard the fundamental rights of citizens where the states did not.

As with the receptiveness of northern legislatures and courts to antisegregation appeals during the decade after the supposed end of Reconstruction, Supreme Court decisions of the 1880s seemed to invite a renewed movement for racial reform. In *Ex parte Siebold* (1880), *Ex parte Clarke* (1880), and *Ex parte Yarbrough* (1884), the high court interpreted Congress's plenary power under Article I, Section IV to regulate the "times, places and manner of holding elections" to Congress broadly enough to allow it to guarantee peaceable assembly and restrict fraud and violence. These decisions inspired Republicans to frame the 1890 Lodge Bill without fear that it would be declared unconstitutional. Moreover, in the 1880 jury exclusion case of *Strauder v. West Virginia* and the 1886 Chinese laundry case of *Yick Wo v. Hopkins*, the Supreme Court struck down racially discriminatory laws not related to voting in such expansive language as to suggest that the justices had not entirely forgotten the original purposes of the Reconstruction Amendments, after all. Despite the Court's narrow construction of the powers of the federal government in *The Civil Rights Cases* (1883), the other, more moderate decisions allowed some scope for national action to protect minority rights if Republicans took firm control of the government again, as they did in 1889 for the first time since 1875.

After the failure of the Lodge Bill, however, the Supreme Court shifted direction again. In *Williams v. Mississippi* in 1898, the Court denied disfranchised blacks a remedy by very strictly construing its earlier decision in *Yick Wo*. Counsel for the Chinese laundryman had shown that a San Francisco ordinance was adopted with both the intent and effect of discriminating against Chinese. While Henry Williams's African American lawyer, Cornelius J. Jones, quoted extensively from the Mississippi disfranchising convention of 1890 to demonstrate its racist intent, he apparently took the exclusion of blacks from the Greenville voter, and, therefore, jury rolls to be proof enough of the state constitution's discriminatory impact. The Court's crabbed reading of *Yick Wo* cost Williams, convicted of murder by an all-white jury, his life. Yet when Wilford H. Smith, an African American lawyer representing disfranchised Alabama blacks in *Giles v. Harris* (1903), presented extensive evidence of the new state constitution's discriminatory effects, as well as its intent, the Court, in a decision written by the "liberal" Oliver Wendell Holmes, declared that the judiciary could do nothing, because suffrage was a "political question."

After southern blacks were safely disfranchised, the Court reversed itself again, entirely ignoring *Williams* and *Giles* when ruling in *Guinn and Beal v. U.S.* (1915) that the Oklahoma grandfather clause was unconstitutional. Chief Justice Edward Douglass White, a former member of the "conservative" faction of the Democratic Party in Louisiana, which had opposed the grandfather clause in that state's constitutional convention in 1898, did not endanger white supremacy directly in *Guinn*, because eliminating the escape clause for Oklahoma whites would not thereby actually allow any African Americans to vote. Once William Howard Taft, whose presidential administration had originally brought the *Guinn* case, became chief justice in 1921, the Court went further, ruling the Texas white primary unconstitutional as a violation of the Fourteenth Amendment in *Nixon v. Herndon* (1927), in the first of several NAACP challenges to the discriminatory practice. When Texas repealed its explicit racially restrictive policy in law and delegated the setting of primary participation standards to the State Democratic Executive Committee,

the Supreme Court struck down that subterfuge, too, in *Nixon v. Condon* (1932).

The Court, many of whose appointees over the period were Democrats or Republicans chosen without racial policies foremost in mind, failed to protect African American political rights when they needed protection most. But they allowed some scope for potential congressional action, and toward the end of the period, were beginning to move toward unraveling the web of laws and rules that kept southern blacks powerless. Had Chief Justice Salmon P. Chase, the father of antislavery constitutionalism, lived as long as his two predecessors instead of dying when more than 20 years younger than John Marshall and Roger Brooke Taney, or had the brilliant radical Republicans Roscoe Conkling and George Franklin Edmunds (both members of the Thirty-Ninth Congress that had passed the major Reconstruction measures) not turned down appointments to the Court, the course of race and politics during the era might have been very different.

Politics Migrates

While institutional rules and interests made national action to bring about racial equality in politics difficult after 1875, the American system of federalism allowed for some antidiscriminatory legislation and some growth in African American political power at the state level outside of the South. Although the Democratic administration of Woodrow Wilson—the first southern-born president elected since the antebellum period—segregated national government employees for the first time and publicly endorsed the major racist propaganda film in American history, *The Birth of a Nation*, other nonsouthern Democrats began to compete for black votes at the local and state levels by offering jobs, candidate opportunities, and favorable policies, an opening that would finally begin to pay off for the party during the administration of Franklin D. Roosevelt.

African American political opportunity in the North was both facilitated and inhibited by demographic trends. As racial conditions in the South deteriorated, many ambitious black Americans moved north, providing a core of leadership for potential movements similar to the core of northern blacks who had moved south during Reconstruction. The northward migration of talent began before, and proceeded during, the "Great Migration" of the era of World War I and the 1920s, when the inhibition of emigration from Europe and the mushrooming of war industries fostered the relocation of perhaps a million and a half African Americans from the South to the North and to western cities. The white backlash against the massive increase of black populations in many cities sometimes turned violent and nearly always sparked increased discrimination against African Americans in schools, jobs, and, especially, housing. But the corresponding black backlash against the rise in discrimination fed black activism, led by the NAACP, which had been founded after riots in Springfield, Illinois, in 1908. African Americans' growth in numbers and their forced concentration in ghettoes in states where they could vote and organize freely meant that the black side in the continuing conflicts would be potent. The legal legacy of Reconstruction, the constitutional amendments and the egalitarian northern state laws and state and national judicial decisions, and the memory of Reconstruction political activism (very different and much stronger in the black than in the white community), provided a foundation for racial equality in politics that was manifestly much stronger than in 1860, a launching pad for the many civil rights movements to come.

See also voting.

FURTHER READING. Sarah A. Binder, *Minority Rights, Majority Rule: Partisanship and the Development of Congress*, 1997; Thomas J. Brown, *Reconstructions: New Perspectives on the Postbellum United States*, 2006; Eric Foner, *Forever Free: The Story of Emancipation and Reconstruction*, 2006; Steven Hahn, *A Nation under Our Feet: Black Political Struggles in the Rural South from Slavery to the Great Migration*, 2006; Matthew Frye Jacobson, *Whiteness of a Different Color: European Immigrants and the Alchemy of Race*, 1998; Philip A. Klinkner, with Rogers M. Smith, *The Unsteady March: The Rise and Decline of Racial Equality in America*, 1999; J. Morgan Kousser, *Colorblind Injustice: Minority Voting Rights and the Undoing of the Second Reconstruction*, 1999; Idem, "'The Onward March of Right Principles': State Legislative Action on Racial Discrimination in Schools in Nineteenth-Century America," *Historical Methods* 35 (Fall 2002), 177–204; Eric Schickler and Gregory Wawro, *Filibuster: Obstruction and Lawmaking in the U.S. Senate*, 2007; Thomas Adams Upchurch, *Legislating Racism: The Billion Dollar Congress and the Birth of Jim Crow*, 2004.

J. MORGAN KOUSSER

race and politics since 1933

Barack Obama's 2008 election as president of the United States was a singular moment in African American history, comparable to the arrival of the first African slaves in colonial Virginia, the founding of the African Methodist Episcopal (AME) Church in Philadelphia in 1793, Abraham Lincoln's 1863 Emancipation Proclamation, the U.S. Supreme Court's 1954 *Brown v. Board of Education of Topeka* decision, and the passage of the 1964 Civil Rights Act and the 1965 Voting Rights Act. More directly, it represents the culmination of 75 years of political history during which rising levels of African American support for the Democratic Party and the accompanying shift of defenders of the racial status quo from the Democratic to the Republican Party remade the American political landscape.

Race, Politics, and the New Deal

It was during the Depression of the 1930s that black voters first began to migrate from the "party of Lincoln" to the Democratic Party. From the Civil War through the 1920s, region, race, and ethnicity had marked the divide between the two major political parties. The Republicans were the party of white native-stock Northerners and those African Americans, primarily in the North, who were able to exercise their right to vote, while the Democrats were the party of the white South and of "white ethnics" (Catholic and Jewish immigrants of European descent and their descendants) in the industrial North.

The growing influence of urban political machines within the national Democratic Party, and the increasing influence of "white ethnic" voters and politicians within those machines, was the one countervailing trend to racialism in post–World War I politics. By 1930, 56.2 percent of the U.S. population lived in urban areas. This trend culminated in the Democrats' nomination of Alfred E. Smith, the Irish Catholic governor of New York, as the party's standard-bearer in the 1928 presidential election, an achievement as momentous in its time as Obama's nomination was in 2008. But while Smith's nomination portended the increasing integration of European immigrant communities into the mainstream of American politics, his defeat in the face of widespread anti-Catholic prejudice demonstrated the continuing power of nativism in the country's politics.

Four years later, another Democratic governor of New York, Franklin D. Roosevelt, swept to victory over the incumbent Republican president, Herbert Hoover. Coming three years into the most severe economic depression in U.S. history and after 12 years of Republican rule in Washington, Roosevelt's victory was in one sense unremarkable. The Democratic Party remained, as it had been under Al Smith, an alliance of northern urban political machines and southern segregationists. What made Roosevelt's victory possible was the growing disaffection from the Republicans of native-stock middle-class and working-class voters in the Northeast, the Midwest, and California. One group of traditional Republican voters not drawn to Roosevelt's call for a "New Deal" for American families were African American voters. Black voters in most major cities voted for Hoover in 1932 by margins of more than two to one.

However, the New Deal quickly reorganized the racial and ethnic divisions within American politics in three significant ways. First, the Roosevelt administration's policies built for the Democrats an unassailable base among lower- and middle-income voters outside the South. Galvanized by Roosevelt's promise of government assistance to those most affected by the collapse of American industrial economy, working-class voters who had previously divided their votes between the two major parties along ethnic and religious lines flocked to the Democratic

Party. In 1936 Roosevelt swept to reelection with nearly 61 percent of the vote.

As significant to shifts in working-class views on race, nation, and identity was the rapid growth in union membership in the 1930s, particularly following the founding of the Committee on Industrial Organizations (CIO) in 1935 as an industrial alternative to the craft unions in the American Federation of Labor (AFL). The impact of the CIO's organizing drive on race relations within the working class was contradictory. On the one hand, the effort to organize every worker in a factory irrespective of differences of job, skill, race, ethnicity, or religion cast class unity—rather than hierarchies of race, religion, or ethnicity—as the key to advancing workers' interests in a capitalist economy. And, in fact, the CIO organized many minority and women workers whom the AFL had ignored. Yet, central to the CIO's appeal was also the labor organization's representation of the ideal American worker as white and male. The result was a working-class nationalism that for the first time fully included white Catholic and Jewish workers, while implicitly suggesting that minority and women workers were marginal to the cause of labor.

Second, the New Deal solidified the alliance between the southern and northern wings of the Democratic Party. To win the support of southern Democrats, however, Roosevelt had to assure white Southerners that New Deal programs would be administered in ways that would not disrupt race relations in the region. Most important, the Roosevelt administration allowed state and local officials to control the implementation of most New Deal programs. For example, the Civilian Conservation Corps and the Works Progress Administration both operated segregated employment projects in the South. Most devastating to the interests of African American workers was the Roosevelt administration's decision in 1935 to accede to the demands of key southern congressional leaders to exclude farm and domestic workers from the provisions of the Social Security Act. As a result, 65 percent of black workers were excluded from Social Security's unemployment and retirement provisions.

Nor were the New Deal's racial inequities limited to the South. The New Deal policies with perhaps the longest-lasting disparate racial impact came in the area of housing. The Federal Housing Administration (FHA) was established in 1934 to rescue the private housing industry by providing mortgage guarantees to lenders willing to provide long-term mortgages to home buyers. As criteria for these mortgages, the FHA adopted standards from the real estate industry that favored white neighborhoods over integrated and predominately minority areas, suburban communities over urban neighborhoods, and owner-occupied single-family homes over multifamily structures and rental properties. The full import of this policy would not be evident until after World War II. New Deal housing programs would, in effect, subsidize the postwar boom in all-white suburbs while steering private housing investment away from the middle- and working-class urban neighborhoods that became the only housing option for ever-increasing numbers of southern black migrants.

Despite the racial inequities built into the New Deal, the third and final component of the New Deal coalition was in place by the end of the 1930s. In 1936 Roosevelt won more than 60 percent of the black vote in every major city except Chicago. Roosevelt's popularity with black voters was the product of two distinct aspects of his first two terms in office. First, large numbers of African Americans became, for the first time, recipients of government assistance. To be included among the beneficiaries of Roosevelt's New Deal was both a matter of survival in those hungry years and thrilling to a people so long treated as undeserving of the rights and privileges of American citizenship.

Second, and as important to black voters as these substantive benefits of the New Deal, was the symbolic value of Roosevelt's appointment of an unprecedented number of African Americans to high positions in his administration. While it would be another 30 years before an African American would be elevated to a position in the cabinet, Roosevelt's so-called "Negro Cabinet"—made up of well-educated professionals appointed to the position of "Adviser for Negro Affairs" in the various agencies of the federal government—was a source of tremendous pride to black voters. These voters were also deeply impressed by Eleanor Roosevelt's determined and very visible commitment to racial equality. The most dramatic emblem of the first lady's commitment came in 1939 when she publicly resigned her membership in the Daughters of the American Revolution after the nativist and elitist women's patriotic organization refused to allow Marian Anderson, the African American opera singer, to perform in the organization's Constitution Hall in Washington. Mrs. Roosevelt instead arranged for Anderson to perform at the Lincoln Memorial for a national radio audience, a concert that became the high-water mark of African American inclusion in the New Deal.

World War II and the Double-V
Even as a majority of African American voters switched allegiance to the Democratic Party during the 1930s, it would be another decade before the party would formally commit itself to a civil rights agenda. During the 1940s, African American activists and their allies codified the "civil rights" strategy of achieving racial equality through legislation and judicial rulings that guaranteed government protection of individual rights. Three factors enabled civil rights activists to make much more significant demands on the administrations of Roosevelt and Harry S. Truman during the 1940s. First was the rapid growth in the African American population in the North as wartime labor shortages and growth in defense

industry employment reinvigorated black migration from the South following the lull of the Depression years. In this decade, the black population living outside the South grew by 65 percent, to a total of 12.8 million people. Second, the rise of Nazism in Europe discredited theories of racial supremacy within the United States, particularly among liberal elites within the Democratic Party. Third, and most important, were the efforts of civil rights advocates to take advantage of the wartime social and political context to pressure the federal government and the Democratic Party to more directly address structures of racial discrimination within American society.

What one black newspaper would call the "Double-V" campaign (victory over fascism abroad and victory over racism at home) began when A. Philip Randolph, president of the all-black Brotherhood of Sleeping Car Porters, called for a black-only march on Washington, D.C., in June 1941 to demand the desegregation of the armed forces and equal treatment for black workers in the nation's defense industries. Concerned that such a march would undercut popular support for his efforts to aid the European allies, Roosevelt convinced Randolph to call off the march in return for an executive order banning racial discrimination in defense employment. The resulting President's Fair Employment Practices Committee (FEPC) became the focus of the activists' wartime efforts to improve employment opportunities for African American workers. In 1944, for example, the FEPC ordered the Philadelphia Transit Company to promote eight black maintenance workers to the position of trolley conductor. When the company's white workers responded with a wildcat strike that shut down the transit system, the secretary of the Navy had to order troops into Philadelphia to run the trolleys.

It was during the 1940s that the National Association for the Advancement of Colored People (NAACP) transformed itself from a primarily middle-class and northern organization into a truly national and mass-based one. Membership in the NAACP during the war grew from 54,000 to more than 500,000. Particularly significant was the growth of the organization's membership in the South during these years. The NAACP's southern chapters served as a training ground for a generation of local leaders who went on to play crucial roles in the civil rights mobilizations of the 1950s and 1960s, including Modjeska Simmons and Septima Clark in South Carolina, E. D. Nixon and Rosa Parks in Alabama, and Medgar Evers and Amzie Moore in Mississippi.

Also crucial to the increase in southern civil rights activism was the U.S. Supreme Court's ruling in *Smith v. Allwright* (1944), which outlawed the Democratic Party's use of all-white primary elections across the South. As Charles Payne has argued, the decision spurred black southern voter registration, particularly in urban areas. The percentage of southern blacks registered to vote grew from less than 5 percent

in 1940 to 12 percent in 1947 and 20 percent in 1952. Black voters in Atlanta and other cities were able to use their increased voting power to play a moderating influence in certain local elections.

The Civil Rights Movement in Cold War America

It was, however, developments in the North during the 1940s that provided the NAACP with new opportunities to pursue its civil rights agenda in the political arena. In 1948 Henry Moon, the NAACP's public relations director, published *Balance of Power: The Negro Vote*, in which he argued that black voters in the urban North now held the balance of power between the two political parties in national elections and that for the first time since Reconstruction African American voters had the ability to demand significant civil rights reforms in return for their votes. Clark Clifford, President Truman's chief political advisor, reached a similar conclusion as he look forward to the 1948 presidential election. Clifford concluded that unlike Roosevelt's four campaigns, southern support for the Democratic candidate would not be sufficient in 1948, but that an effective appeal to northern African American voters could return Truman to the presidency even if he lost some southern votes in the process.

To win northern black votes, however, Truman would have to fend off a challenge from Henry Wallace, his predecessor as Roosevelt's vice president and the candidate of the left-wing Progressive Party. Truman thus appointed a blue-ribbon commission in 1946 to study civil rights issues. The President's Committee on Civil Rights issued its report, titled *To Secure These Rights*, in 1947. The report laid out an agenda of actions that all three branches of the federal government should take to protect the rights of the nation's racial minorities. While the report's recommendations had little chance of being adopted by Congress, they did form the basis for Truman's groundbreaking appeal for the votes of northern blacks. Most dramatically, and in response to threats from A. Phillip Randolph to organize a civil disobedience campaign against the Selective Service system, Truman issued Executive Order 9981 on February 2, 1948, mandating the desegregation of the armed forces. The results of the 1948 election proved both Moon and Clifford to have been right. South Carolina governor Strom Thurmond won four Deep South states as the candidate of the States' Rights Democratic Party. But in the North, African American voters largely rejected Henry Wallace's candidacy and provided the margin of victory for Truman's upset defeat of the Republican nominee, Thomas E. Dewey.

With southern Democrats effectively blocking federal civil rights legislation, northern civil rights activists turned their focus to passing civil rights legislation at the state and local level. Between 1945 and 1964, 28 states passed Fair Employment Practices (FEP) laws. But as important as these legislative victories were, they could not mask the fact that racial discrimination remained pervasive in the North. Thus, the northern FEP laws did little to change the informal hiring policies and exclusionary union practices that kept African American workers locked out of many white- and blue-collar occupations. And while the Supreme Court declared in 1948 that racial covenants were unenforceable in court, the suburban housing boom remained closed to African Americans as federal mortgage guarantors, housing developers, and white home buyers continued to favor white-only communities. Civil rights activists also faced increasing political opposition from other elements of the New Deal coalition to their efforts to address persistent racial inequities in northern communities. In the 1949 mayoral election in Detroit, for example, Albert Cobo, a conservative Republican, defeated the United Auto Workers–endorsed candidate on a platform of opposition to the building of public housing projects in white neighborhoods. As historians Arnold Hirsch and Thomas Sugrue have shown, black families seeking to move into all-white neighborhoods in cities like Chicago and Detroit were often greeted with racial violence.

Historians continue to debate the impact of the cold war on the civil rights movement. Manning Marable and Martha Biondi have argued that the stigmatization of left-wing politics during the period of McCarthyism greatly hampered civil rights efforts in part because of the prominence of left-wing figures like Paul Robeson among advocates of civil rights, in part because defenders of racial segregation were able to use the charge of communism to discredit all advocates of racial equality, and in part because organizations like the NAACP became extremely cautious politically in order to distance themselves from radicalism. In contrast, Mary Dudziak has argued that the cold war helped civil rights activists to advance their cause because of the pressure it placed on the nation's political leaders to demonstrate to the emerging nations of the third world that capitalist democracies were better able to deliver on the promise of racial equality than was the Soviet bloc.

Perhaps more detrimental to the cause of civil rights during the 1950s than cold war anxieties about the threat of internal subversion was the widespread belief among political leaders that the nation had entered a period of political consensus. The notion of consensus politics was rooted in two beliefs—first, that the country had solved most of its domestic problems, and second, that internal political unity was required to defeat the Communist threat. In this view, whatever social inequities remained in American society (among which most advocates of consensus politics would have included racial issues) would gradually disappear as the capitalist economy continued to grow, while efforts to speed the process of social change (through, for example, aggressive efforts to implement civil rights reforms) would only divide the country and weaken its resolve in the struggle against communism. As a result, the 1950s were characterized both by historic civil rights achievements rooted in an idealistic view of the United States as the world's foremost defender of individual liberty and equal rights under law and by the failure of government officials to fulfill the promise of those achievements for fear of the reaction of the white majority. Thus, the Supreme Court ruled in the 1954 *Brown v. Board of Education* case that school segregation is unconstitutional. But with southern Democrats promising "massive resistance" to the *Brown* decision, President Dwight Eisenhower refused to vigorously enforce the decision. Moreover, the Supreme Court ruled just one year later that school desegregation should take place with "all deliberate speed," thus opening the door to two decades of southern efforts to sustain dual school systems. In a similar fashion, the U.S. Congress passed its first major piece of civil rights legislation since Reconstruction, the Civil Rights Act of 1957, just days before Eisenhower was forced to send federal troops to enforce a federal court order requiring the integration of Central High School in Little Rock, Arkansas. By the time of its passage, however, the enforcement provisions of the act, which sought to increase the number of African American voters in the South, had been so watered down that leading southern Democratic senators declared its passage a victory for their side.

The 1960s

Thirty-two years after Al Smith lost his bid to become the first Catholic president of the United States, John F. Kennedy defeated Richard Nixon in the 1960 presidential election. Twice during the campaign, Kennedy felt it necessary to give speeches declaring his commitment to the separation of church and state. What was not in question, however, was Kennedy's status as a white American. In contrast to previous generations of European Catholic immigrants and their descendants who were seen as racially distinct from native-stock white Americans, Kennedy, like his contemporaries Frank Sinatra and Joe DiMaggio, became a symbol of the quintessential American experience in a nation of immigrants.

African American voters again played a crucial role in the 1960 presidential election. Nine months earlier, the student sit-in movement to protest segregated lunch counters had spread rapidly across the South. That fall, civil rights protest became an issue in the presidential campaign when Martin Luther King Jr. was arrested for leading a sit-in in Atlanta and was subsequently sentenced to four months in a south Georgia prison camp. Nixon refused to intervene, hoping to gain the votes of white Southerners upset by the civil rights plank in Democratic Party platform. Kennedy, in contrast, placed a call to King's wife, Coretta Scott King, to express his concern. Within days, Kennedy campaign officials had successfully petitioned Georgia officials for King's release. On the Sunday before the election, the Kennedy campaign distributed a flyer to black churches across the nation announcing the endorsement of King's father, Martin Luther King Sr. In one of the closest presidential campaigns in American history, black votes provided the margin of victory for Kennedy in a number of northern states.

Civil rights issues were not a priority for Kennedy when he entered the White House in 1961. Rather, his central focus was on foreign policy. Within months, however, the efforts of civil rights protesters—particularly the interracial teams of "freedom riders" who sought to ride interstate buses across the South—would force Kennedy to address the question of southern race relations. In an effort to defuse the sense of crisis generated by nonviolent protest, the Kennedy administration initially sought to encourage civil rights activists to shift their focus to voter registration on the theory that a growing black electorate in the South would lead the region's politicians to moderate their positions on racial issues.

In June 1963, however, as nonviolent protest campaigns continued to roil southern cities and as voter registration drives in the rural South were met with racist violence, Kennedy submitted to Congress civil rights legislation banning segregated public accommodations and employment discrimination. Support for the Kennedy civil rights bill was a central feature of the August 1963 March on Washington, even as activists affiliated with the student wing of the movement pressed unsuccessfully for the march to explicitly criticize the president for failing to do enough to protect civil rights workers in the South from racist violence.

Still, little progress had been made on the civil rights bill by the time of Kennedy's tragic assassination in November 1963. It would take a Southerner, Kennedy's successor Lyndon Johnson, to overcome southern opposition and steer the civil rights bill through Congress. During his 23 years in Congress, including six as Senate majority leader, Johnson had been an ardent New Dealer and, for a Southerner, a moderate on civil rights issues. Now he pledged "to take the dead man's program and turn it into a martyr's cause." On June 11, 1964, the Senate voted for the first time to end a southern Senate filibuster against a civil rights bill and, on July 1, Johnson signed the Civil Rights Act of 1964 into law.

The act was only part of Johnson's agenda of social and political reform, however. In his first State of the Union address in January 1964, Johnson called for the most prosperous nation in the world to wage "a war on poverty." Then, in May, he pledged to use the nation's material wealth to build a "Great Society" based on "an abundance and liberty for all . . . an end to poverty and racial injustice . . . [and] the desire for beauty and the hunger for community." Johnson's vision of the Great Society was rooted in two seemingly contradictory views of American society—the first of a great country ready to use its wealth to help those with the least, the second of a nation flawed by racism but willing to confront its failings in pursuit of justice for all. Johnson promoted the war on poverty and the Great Society both as efforts to provide assistance to the poor of all races and as essential to fulfilling the call of the civil rights movement to end racial injustice.

In the short run, Johnson would parlay these twin imperatives into a remarkable streak of legislative and political victories. In the summer of 1964, Congress passed the Economic Opportunity Act—the centerpiece of Johnson's antipoverty initiative—which would provide nearly $3 billion in government funds for local antipoverty programs over the next three years. That fall, not only did Johnson win a landslide victory over his Republican opponent, Barry Goldwater, but the Democrats swept to the party's largest majorities in both the House and the Senate in the post–World War II period. This majority enabled Johnson to push a legislative agenda through Congress over the next two years that rivaled the reforms of the New Deal. Most significant was the Voting Rights Act of 1965, which established for the first time, federal oversight over the voter rolls in the ten southern states that had historically denied the vote to African Americans. Educational programs were enacted for low-income children, including the preschool program Head Start; Medicare and Medicaid, health insurance programs for the elderly and the poor; immigration reform; mass transit programs; and consumer safety and environmental safety legislation.

By the fall of 1966, there were signs of declining support for Johnson's reform agenda. Civil rights protests, urban race riots, and rising urban crime rates combined to weaken white support for the president's agenda of racial reform and poverty reduction, while the growing cost of the Vietnam War and rising inflation strengthened the voices of conservative critics of taxes and government spending. Republicans picked up 50 seats in the 1966 congressional elections, effectively bringing a halt to Johnson's Great Society agenda and setting the stage for the resurgence of Republicans in national elections.

Historians have tended to see the 1960s as the moment when the national Democratic Party committed itself fully to the cause of civil rights, the Republican Party began to capture the allegiance of white southern voters, and the New Deal coalition of white southern, black, and northern white working-class voters began to collapse. This analysis must be qualified in three ways. First, racial issues in the urban North had begun to lead middle- and low-income white voters to abandon the Democrats in local elections as early the late 1940s. Second, Republicans had begun in the 1950s to pursue a strategy of capturing the votes of white southern Democrats rather than seeking to compete with the Democrats for the votes of African Americans and other supporters of civil rights.

Third, the most important factor in the shift of white voters toward the Republican Party, in the South and in the industrial states of the Northeast and the Midwest, was only tangentially related to the civil rights reforms of the 1960s. Rather, Republican candidates in presidential and congressional elections benefited from the growing importance of white suburban voters, relative to both northern urban and southern rural voters, within the American electorate. By the late 1960s, suburban voters—many of them the children of New Dealers—were increasingly hostile to the perceived cost (in taxes) of government programs designed to address racial and economic equality as well as to any efforts by the federal government and courts to force local communities to adopt policies (in areas like zoning and public schooling) designed to lessen racial segregation in the North. Suburban voters were also attracted to Republican calls for lower taxes and for a vigilantly anti-Communist foreign policy.

The splintering of the New Deal coalition was most evident in the 1968 presidential election. While Richard Nixon received only about 500,000 more votes than his Democratic opponent, Hubert Humphrey, he won the Electoral College by more than 100 votes. Humphrey's defeat was in part the result of the loss of support for Democrats among white southern voters. Nixon swept the Upper South, South Carolina, and Florida for a total of 65 electoral votes, while Alabama's Democratic governor George Wallace, running as a third-party candidate, won five Deep South states and a total of 45 electoral votes. However, the Democratic standard-bearer might still have won the election had Wallace not cut severely into his support among white northern working-class voters who felt abandoned by the Democratic Party's civil rights policies. The Alabama governor campaigned extensively in the North, drawing large crowds to campaign rallies during which he received appreciative applause for his attacks on elitist liberals for insisting that poor whites integrate their schools even as those liberals sent their own children to exclusive private schools. In six northern states, the Wallace vote more than doubled Nixon's margin of victory over Humphrey.

Racial Codes and the Rise of the New Right

These fissures within the New Deal coalition did not immediately add up to Republican dominance of American politics. Nixon won the 1968 election with only 43.4 percent of the vote. Moreover, Democrats remained in firm control of both houses of Congress despite Nixon's landslide reelection in 1972. Not until 1994 would Republicans win majorities in both houses of Congress. Throughout this period, Democrats remained competitive in southern congressional elections, particularly when they campaigned on New Deal–style populist economics that appealed to middle- and lower-income white as well as black voters.

Nixon's victory in the 1968 presidential campaign began a streak in which Republicans won seven of the next ten presidential elections. While largely conceding the more formal aspects of the civil rights revolution—a "color-blind" legal system, school desegregation, equal access to public accommodations—Republicans proved adept at using racial codes to promote key aspects of their conservative policy agenda to white voters across the economic spectrum. Racial coding was most pronounced in Republican efforts to stigmatize liberal policies in the areas of school desegregation, welfare, affirmative action, and immigration.

Nixon most effectively used racial codes to express sympathy for white anxieties about court-ordered school desegregation plans. In his 1968 campaign, Nixon won broad support in upper-income suburban districts across the South by affirming his support both for the Supreme Court's *Brown* decision and for local control over public schooling. He thus managed to distance himself simultaneously from southern segregationists like Wallace and from civil rights activists and federal judges who were advocates of what he called "forced integration." Over the next decade, the Supreme Court would uphold a series of federal court rulings that required the use of mandatory busing schemes to achieve school integration in both southern and northern urban school districts. In all of these cases, the courts found that a constellation of government policies—from the gerrymandering of school boundaries to housing and zoning policies designed to maintain residential segregation—had served to perpetuate school segregation despite the Court's ruling in the *Brown* case. And yet, each case gave conservative politicians from Charlotte, North Carolina, to Boston the opportunity to position themselves as defenders of legitimate white working-class interests—explicitly, of the right to keep their children in neighborhood schools and implicitly, of the right to keep those schools exclusively white.

Racial coding was equally effective for Republicans on the issue of welfare. Central to the conservative attack on excesses of the Great Society programs of the 1960s was the argument that the growth in government assistance to the poor constituted little more than a transfer of income from "hardworking" taxpayers to African American and Latino beneficiaries deemed too lazy to work. The majority of welfare recipients were, of course, white. Moreover, antipoverty programs contributed to a 50 percent decline in the poverty rate in the United States between 1960 and 1980. While books like conservative sociologist Charles Murray's *Losing Ground: American Social Policy, 1950–1980* (1984) argued that income assistance programs promoted dependency on government by providing a disincentive to work, conservative opposition to welfare focused less on policy debates than on stories of welfare recipients as "cheats" and "frauds." Anecdotal narratives of Cadillac-driving "welfare queens" who used multiple aliases to collect excessive benefits were central to Ronald Reagan's emergence as a leader of the conservative movement during the 1970s. While he rarely referred to specific individuals, Reagan's references to neighborhoods like Chicago's South Side invariably marked welfare cheaters as African American.

Opposition to welfare remained a central feature of Republican appeals to white lower- and middle-income voters into the 1990s. In an effort to inoculate his candidacy against charges of liberal elitism, Democrat Bill Clinton built his 1992 presidential campaign around a pledge "to end welfare as we know it." Still, opposition to welfare remained at the top of the Republicans' 1994 "Contract with America," the manifesto on which Republican congressional leaders based their successful campaign to wrest control from the Democrats of both houses of Congress for the first time in 40 years. In 1996 the Republican Congress passed and President Clinton signed a reform bill that transformed welfare from an entitlement meant to serve everyone who qualified for aid into a time-limited program with stringent requirements and a five-year cap on benefits.

Also central to the Republican critique of the racial excesses of liberalism was affirmative action. The origins of affirmative action lay in the response of civil rights activists and liberal government officials to the failure of antidiscrimination laws to substantively desegregate local labor markets. Private-sector employers found that a minimal adjustment in their hiring procedures—and, in some cases the employment of a token few minority employees—quickly brought them into compliance with fair employment laws. Debate over whether employers could and should be required to take action to increase their employment of minority workers bore fruit in March 1961, when President Kennedy issued an executive order requiring federal agencies and contractors to take "affirmative action" to remove racially discriminatory barriers to employment.

Over the next decade, federal officials responded to increasingly militant civil rights protests against continued discrimination in private-sector hiring, particularly in the construction trades, with a series of policy experiments designed to establish affirmative action's parameters and procedures. In 1969 a federal court upheld the constitutionality of the Philadelphia Plan in the building trades, and the Nixon administration extended its requirements to all federal contracts worth more than $50,000. Women were added to the affirmative action requirements in 1971, and many state and local governments adopted similar plans.

President Nixon seems to have decided to support affirmative action both in hopes of winning support from the black business and professional classes and as part of a strategy to promote divisions between the labor (that is, white working class) and black wings of the Democratic Party.

Opposition to affirmative action would not become a central feature of Republican appeals for white working- and middle-class votes until Reagan's 1980 presidential campaign. Reagan and the emergent conservative wing of the Republican Party argued that affirmative action constituted reverse discrimination against whites, particularly those from lower- and middle-income communities, and thus violated the civil rights movement's commitment to building a colorblind society. The most dramatic instance of the Republicans' use of affirmative action to draw working-class white votes came in the U.S. Senate election in North Carolina in 1990, when Senator Jesse Helms used a last-minute television ad (in which the viewer saw only the hands and flannel sleeves of a white worker opening a letter informing him that the job he "needed" had been given to a "minority") to win a come-from-behind victory over Harvey Gantt, his African American opponent.

In the legal arena, the charge of reverse discrimination was advanced, with some success, in the name of whites who claimed to have been denied educational or economic opportunity on the basis of their race—most prominently Allen Bakke, Jennifer Gratz, and Barbara Grutter, the plaintiffs in the 1977 and 2005 Supreme Court cases that defined how universities can and cannot use affirmative action procedures in admissions. Within the political realm, many of the leading opponents of affirmative action were black and Latino conservatives. Figures like Supreme Court Justice Clarence Thomas, economists Thomas Sowell and Glen Loury, Republican activist Linda Chavez, and political essayists Shelby Steele and Richard Rodriguez argued that affirmative action violated Martin Luther King Jr.'s call for people to be judged according to the content of their character and not the color of their skin, and that it reinforced the view that racial minorities were incapable of competing on equal terms with whites. In 1995 Ward Connerly, a University of California trustee and Republican Party activist, emerged as the most prominent black opponent of affirmative action when he led a successful referendum campaign in California to ban the use of racial and gender preferences in all state government programs and contracts. Over the next decade, Connerly would lead similarly successful campaigns in Washington, Florida, Michigan, and Nebraska.

Black and Latino conservatives did not limit their political activism and advocacy to affirmative action, offering free market, self-help, and faith-based policy prescriptions on issues from poverty and the rising number of female-headed single-parent households to failing schools and insufficient economic investment in the inner cities. While Republican efforts to increase the party's share of the black and Latino vote produced only minimal results, advocates of self-help, entrepreneurship, and traditional religious and social values enjoyed growing influence in black and Latino communities in the post–New Deal era.

Race and the Politics of Immigration

Bilingual education provides another example of the ways in which racial politics infused conservative efforts to discredit federally funded domestic programs. In 1968 Congress passed the Bilingual Education Act, which provided the first federal funding for bilingual education programs. But it was not until the early 1970s that federal education officials began to require that school districts provide bilingual educational programming to non-English speakers as a mechanism for promoting both immigrant educational achievement and ethnic and racial pride.

In the ensuing decades, the debate over bilingual education has proceeded on two separate, if overlapping, tracks. While educators debate whether bilingual transitional or monolingual immersion programs are the best mechanism for enabling immigrant children to simultaneously learn English and keep up with their English-speaking classmates, conservative activists, led in the 1980s by Reagan administration Secretary of Education William Bennett, have criticized bilingual education for promoting ethnic pride and multicultural identities over assimilation into American society. A direct result of the furor of bilingual education was the emergence of the "English-only" movement, which won passage of legislation declaring English to be the sole official language of the United States in 26 states between 1984 and 2007.

By the early 1990s, English-only campaigns were largely superseded by a broader conservative backlash against immigration, particularly that from Mexico and Central and South America. The policy agenda of anti-immigration activism has been to prevent undocumented immigrants from entering the country and to deny government services to those already in the United States. For example, California's Proposition 187, enacted with 59 percent of the vote in 1994, would have denied social services, public health care, and public education to undocumented immigrants had it not been overturned in the courts. But while anti-immigration groups like the Federation for American Immigration Reform have long denied any racial motivation to their agenda, popular animus against Latino immigrants, whether legal or undocumented, has driven much of the demand for immigration reform over the last two decades. Latino immigrants are accused of being fundamentally different from previous generations of immigrants, of failing to learn English and assimilate into "American culture," and of taking jobs from American workers. In 2004, for example, Harvard political scientist Samuel Huntington published "The Hispanic Challenge," an extended essay later developed into a book, in which he argued that "Mexicans and other Latinos have not assimilated into mainstream U.S. culture, forming instead their own political and linguistic enclaves—from Los Angeles to Miami—and rejecting the Anglo-Protestant values that built the American dream."

Within the Republican Party, however, opinion was split over whether to pursue an anti-immigration agenda or to campaign for Latino votes. One the one hand, California governor Pete Wilson was a strong supporter of Proposition 187, and the 1994 Contract with America promised to disqualify even legal immigrants from public assistance programs. Other Republicans argued that the party should make it a priority to reach out to upwardly mobile and socially conservative Latinos in states like Florida and Texas. For example, the Nixon administration's initial support for bilingual education emerged from a desire to appeal to Latino voters. And Nixon did in fact double his share of the Latino vote to about 33 percent between 1968 and 1972. Similarly, support from Latino voters and a moderate position on immigration issues were instrumental in George W. Bush's emergence as a national political leader during his years as governor of Texas as well as to his narrow victories in the 2000 and 2004 presidential elections.

African American and Latino Politics in the Post–Civil Rights Era

Despite conservative gains since the 1960s, the final decades of the twentieth century were also marked by the unprecedented growth in the number of African American and Latino elected officials. By 2000 the combined total of black and Latino elected officials at all levels of governments exceeded 13,000. The majority of these politicians of color were elected to office in the "black belt" regions of the rural South and in California and Texas, the two states with the largest Latino populations.

It was in the nation's big cities, however, that black and Latino politicians were most visible. From 1967, when Carl Stokes and Richard Hatcher became the first African Americans elected mayor of major cities (Cleveland, Ohio, and Gary, Indiana, respectively) to Antonio Villaraigosa's election as the first Latino mayor of modern-day Los Angeles in 2005, urban politicians of color have sought to use election to public office as a mechanism for addressing the continued economic and social underdevelopment of minority communities in the United States. It was, in fact, this vision of black urban governance—particularly as practiced by Chicago's first and so far only African American mayor, Harold Washington—that first attracted Barack Obama to electoral politics. In the 1960s and 1970s, this strategy of winning control over city government was rooted in a view of the federal government as a willing and essential ally in efforts to revive the nation's urban economies. But even as the national political culture grew more conservative and the fulcrum of political power shifted from cities to the suburbs, many politicians of color maintained their vision of elective office as a mechanism for the collective uplift of their communities.

See also civil rights.

FURTHER READING. Martha Biondi, *To Stand and Fight: The Struggle for Civil Rights in Postwar New York City*, 2003; William Chafe, *Unfinished Journey: America since World War II*, 6th ed., 2006; Matthew J. Countryman, *Up South: Civil Rights and Black Power in Philadelphia*, 2006; Gareth Davies, *See Government Grow: Education Politics from Johnson to Reagan*, 2007; Angela Dillard, *Guess Who's Coming to Dinner Now? Multicultural Conservatism in America*, 2002; Mary Dudziak, *Cold War Civil Rights: Race and the Image of American Democracy*, 2002; Glenda Gilmore, *Defying Dixie: The Radical Roots of Civil Rights, 1919–1950*, 2008; Arnold Hirsch, *Making the Second Ghetto: Race and Housing in Chicago, 1940–1960*, 1983; Alton Hornsby, *Black Power in Dixie: A Political History of African-Americans in Atlanta*, 2009; Samuel P. Huntington, *Who Are We? The Challenges to America's National Identity*, 2005; Ira Katznelson, *When Affirmative Action Was White: An Untold History of Racial Inequality in Twentieth-Century America*, 2006; Matthew D. Lassiter, *The Silent Majority: Suburban Politics in the Sunbelt South*, 2006; Nancy MacLean, *Freedom Is Not Enough: The Opening of the American Workplace*, 2008; Manning Marable, *Race, Reform, and Rebellion: The Second Reconstruction and Beyond in Black America, 1945–2006*, 3rd ed., 2007; Henry Moon, *Balance of Power: The Negro Vote*, Reprint, 1977; Charles Murray, *Losing Ground: American Social Policy, 1950–1980*, 10th anniversary ed., 1994; Charles M. Payne, "'The Whole United States Is Southern!': *Brown v. Board* and the Mystification of Race," *Journal of American History* 91 (June 2004), 83–91; Thomas J. Sugrue, *The Origins of the Urban Crisis: Race and Inequality in Postwar Detroit*, 1998; Idem, *Sweet Land of Liberty: The Forgotten Struggle for Civil Rights in the North*, 2008; Nancy J. Weiss, *Farewell to the Party of Lincoln: Black Politics in the Age of FDR*, 1983.

MATTHEW J. COUNTRYMAN

radicalism

The term *radicalism* comes from the Latin word *radix*, meaning "root." Radicalism seeks to locate the root causes of social injustice and extirpate them, to overturn existing social structures and replace them with forms more conducive to equality, cooperation, dignity, inclusion, and freedom. An amorphous concept, radicalism denotes a disposition, an emancipatory and egalitarian élan, rather than a precise program. Although radicalism has sometimes been taken to denote "extremism" and therefore to include a political right that propounds order and hierarchy, the far right, which aims to reconstitute privileges rather than uproot them, is better designated as reactionary. Radicalism is also distinct from gradualism or liberalism, although that stops neither radicals from seeking reforms nor vigorous reformers from styling themselves "radical liberals."

Radicalism is innately controversial. Its admirers value its creativity, courage, and adherence to principle, while opponents view it as rash, impractical, and fanatical. Radicalism is further characterized by a willingness to employ tactics outside approved channels. Although radicals rarely consider themselves beholden to existing law or authority, the association of radicalism with violence and destruction is not entirely warranted, since radicals have primarily engaged in peaceful protest, suasion, and civil disobedience.

Radicals typically scrutinize everyday life with the intention of transforming self and culture as much as state and society. No one philosophy, however, defines radicalism. What counts as "radical" changes over time, and radicals differ in visions, priorities, and strategies. Affection for American democracy has motivated many radicals, such as the poet Walt Whitman, who heard America singing yet wrote at the end of his life, "I am as radical now as ever." Other radicals have spoken from a position of profound alienation from their country. Radicalism has served as a catalyst, dramatizing problems, disrupting routines, and introducing preposterous notions that in time come to seem commonsensical. Many radical propositions, however, have gone down to defeat, and America has frequently vilified its radicals. Radicalism, in short, has existed both at the center and at the margins of American political life.

Early American Radicalism

Although Native American resistance to European settlement might be viewed as the origin of American radicalism, uprisings motivated by defense of tradition, such as Pontiac's pan-Indian rebellion of 1763, could just as readily be classified as ardent conservatism. Colonial radicals, moreover, rarely extended solidarity to Indian resistance. Nathaniel Bacon's Virginia Colony uprising of 1676 united poor white farmers, indentured servants, free blacks, and slaves in attacking indigenous tribes before turning on wealthy planters and burning Jamestown to the ground.

The Puritans, Quakers, and other religious nonconformists who populated the English colonies were radicals by the norms of the countries they left behind. They, in turn, produced their own antinomian heretics, such as Roger Williams, advocate of separation of church and state, and Anne Hutchinson, who challenged clerical authority. The Protestant emphasis on individual conscience and morality would inform much of the subsequent history of American radicalism—as would rationalist challenges to authoritarian religion.

With the coming of the American Revolution, Crispus Attucks, Patrick Henry, Samuel Adams, the Sons of Liberty, and "mobs" protesting the Stamp Act, Sugar Act, and other parliamentary measures were radicals, pushing events past a mere imperial-colonial adjustment toward separation and a republic based on consent of the governed. Thomas Paine's *Common Sense* (1776) lambasted monarchy, aristocracy, and hereditary rule itself, giving voice to a transatlantic radicalism of cordwainers, tailors, coopers, and other skilled artisans suspicious of decadent, parasitical classes. The Declaration of Independence's pronouncement that "all men are created equal" and endowed with "certain inalienable rights" was decidedly radical for its day, as was Thomas Jefferson's aphorism, "the tree of liberty must be refreshed from time to time with the blood of patriots and tyrants."

This political culture of egalitarianism and libertarianism generated some revolutionary aftereffects, such as the uprising of indebted Massachusetts farmers led by Daniel Shays in 1786. Fearful that a headstrong democracy would threaten property rights, the Constitutional Convention in 1787 created an elite Senate, executive, and judiciary to check the popular House. Set aside was the unicameral legislature preferred by Paine, who had departed for England and France, where he would defend the French Revolution. Anti-Federalist dissent compelled passage of a constitutional Bill of Rights, but Pennsylvania's Whiskey Rebellion of 1794 showed lingering qualms about federal legitimacy.

By the early nineteenth century, artisanal radicalism took on new qualities as apprentices and journeymen began to worry over the "aristocratical" designs of their masters, who were fast becoming capitalist employers. This producer radicalism, fed by fear of "wages slavery," informed calls by the Working Man's Party of 1829–32 for free public education and restriction of the working day to ten hours. Thomas Skidmore's *The Rights of Man to Property* (1829) called for "a General Division of property," a sign that radicals would increasingly aspire to equality of condition.

America was the seedbed of world socialism in the early nineteenth century, its vast expanses of land making utopian experimentation affordable. The first agrarian colonies sought spiritual perfection, from the Shakers in upstate New York to the German Pietists at Amana, Iowa. These were followed by secular acolytes of the British industrialist Robert Owen and French philosopher Charles Fourier. The colony Frances Wright established in 1826 at Nashoba, Tennessee, sought to prove emancipation from slavery viable, but its interracial sexuality scandalized polite society, as would the "complex marriage" of John Humphrey Noyes's Oneida community. Utopian colonies often sundered apart or attracted drones. Robert Dale Owen, though a dedicated socialist, described New Harmony, Indiana, as "a heterogeneous collection of radicals, enthusiastic devotees of principle, honest latitudinarians and lazy theorists, with a sprinkling of unprincipled sharpers thrown in."

The antebellum period was effervescent with evangelical revival and moral reform causes such as temperance, phrenology, and penal reform. George Henry Evans and Horace Greeley advocated a radical measure—free land—that reached fruition in the Homestead Act of 1862. The paramount property question of the hour, however, was slavery. Radicals

were first to demand the immediate end of slavery rather than gradual emancipation. Driven by conviction, and sometimes attacked physically, they set out to shock a nation into action. In *An Appeal to the Coloured Citizens of the World* (1829), the Bostonian free black David Walker called upon slaves to rise up, violently if necessary, a path taken independently by Virginia slave Nat Turner in 1831.

Abolitionism fostered further radicalisms. As Sojourner Truth and other female antislavery orators defied prejudices against women speaking in public, relations between men and women became issues for radical reconsideration. Elizabeth Cady Stanton, Lucretia Mott, and others joined at Seneca Falls, New York, in 1848 to draft a Declaration of Sentiments calling for equal rights for women to property ownership, education, and suffrage on the grounds that "all men and women are created equal." Similarly, Henry David Thoreau's discourse on civil disobedience, a cornerstone of radical pacifist thought, arose from his tax resistance to the Mexican-American War of 1846–48, which was widely seen as a war for slavery's expansion.

Alarmed that a "slave power" extended to the federal level, abolitionists worried for the soul of the republic. Enraged by the Constitution's tacit sanction of slavery, William Lloyd Garrison burned copies of it in public. In 1852 Frederick Douglass asked, "What, to the American slave, is your 4th of July? I answer: a day that reveals to him, more than all other days in the year, the gross injustice and cruelty to which he is the constant victim." Douglass declined to join John Brown's 1859 armory seizure at Harpers Ferry, West Virginia, but the failed insurrection portended the coming Civil War. Only the carnage of Blue and Gray, combined with a massive slave exodus, made possible the Thirteenth, Fourteenth, and Fifteenth Amendments, transforming the Constitution and ending slavery.

Apex of Working-Class Radicalism

Radical republicanism, utopianism, agrarianism, and producerism remained vibrant through the Gilded Age, present in one manner or another in Tennessee Claflin and Victoria Woodhull's free love-advocating *Weekly*, a mélange of currency reform proposals, the cooperative ventures of the Knights of Labor, Edward Bellamy's millenarian novel *Looking Backward, 2000–1887* (1888), the single-tax on land advocated by Henry George, and 1890s farmer populism directed at monopolistic railroads and banks. Some anarchists proposed to spark worker revolt by violent provocation, but such incidents as the Haymarket affair of 1886 and the assassination of President William McKinley in 1901 instead brought opprobrium and repression, enhancing the appeal of alternative radical approaches premised on mass action.

As industrial militancy reached its pinnacle between the 1870s and 1940s, radicals increasingly looked to working-class self-activity to achieve the socialization of production. At first this view was mainly limited to German-American immigrant circles, even though Karl Marx and Friedrich Engels published articles in English in the *New York Tribune* between 1852 and 1861. Marxist theory acquired wider credence in the late nineteenth century, as mass socialist parties flourished in Europe and economic downturns and strike waves lent plausibility to the prospect that the world's workers would overthrow a crisis-prone capitalism. By the early twentieth century, Marxism was the lingua franca of the American Left, and anarcho-syndicalism, revolutionary socialism, and communism reached their respective heights.

Anarcho-syndicalism sought a stateless society and eschewed electoral politics, but differed from individualist anarchism by emphasizing revolution at the point of production. In a preamble written by Daniel De Leon, a Marxist, the largely anarcho-syndicalist Industrial Workers of the World (IWW), or "Wobblies," founded in 1905, called for "abolition of the wage system." The IWW's 1912 "Bread and Roses" textile strike of mostly Jewish and Italian women at Lawrence, Massachusetts, enthused Greenwich Village radicals such as Max Eastman, Randolph Bourne, and John Reed writing in *The Masses*, a freewheeling magazine that supported Margaret Sanger when she distributed literature about contraception in violation of the 1873 Comstock Act.

The Socialist Party was supported by millions at the polls from its founding in 1901 until 1920. Its standard-bearer, Eugene V. Debs, received 6 percent of the vote for president and more than 1,200 Socialists were elected to office, from Oklahoma to Ohio, in 1912. New York Representative Meyer London, one of two Socialists elected to Congress, advocated in his first address to the House in 1915 "an inheritance tax that would make it impossible for unfit men by the mere accident of birth to inherit millions of dollars in wealth and power." Socialist pressure could prompt reform, as when the depiction of Chicago meatpacking in Upton Sinclair's novel *The Jungle* (1906) compelled signing of the Meat Inspection Act and Pure Food and Drug Act by President Theodore Roosevelt.

Economic determinism led many Socialists to ignore or accommodate racist lynching and segregation. It was Socialists Mary White Ovington and William English Walling, however, who helped create the National Association for the Advancement of Colored People in 1909. Black radicals responded variously to rising racism. Ida B. Wells advocated armed self-defense and exodus from the South, Marcus Garvey espoused black nationalism, and trade unionist A. Philip Randolph sought class solidarity. Even as blacks were disfranchised, the provocative tactics of woman suffragists, including radical hunger-striker Alice Paul, helped win ratification of the Nineteenth Amendment in 1920.

Socialists and Wobblies alike opposed World War I and were consequently battered by wartime repression and the "Red Scare" of 1919. Emma Goldman and other immigrant radicals were deported, Debs imprisoned. "The notion that a radical is one who hates his country," countered H. L. Mencken in 1924, "is naïve and usually idiotic. He is, more likely, one who likes his country more than the rest of us, and is thus more disturbed than the rest of us when he sees it debauched."

The 1929 stock market crash and Great Depression brought a resurgence of labor and the left. Dynamism shifted to the Communist Party, emulators of the 1917 Russian Revolution and the Soviet Union. Communist Party members led demonstrations by the unemployed, helped organize basic industry, and challenged racism, inspiring numerous Americans to join or work closely with them, including Woody Guthrie, Representative Vito Marcantonio, Elizabeth Gurley Flynn, W.E.B. Du Bois, and Paul Robeson. However, the Communist Party's authoritarian structure and zig-zagging political line, corresponding to every shift of Soviet foreign policy under Joseph Stalin, led others to criticize communism as a bureaucratic phenomenon. Small bands of dissenting radicals, from A. J. Muste's American Workers Party to Leon Trotsky's followers, argued that socialism required not merely state ownership but workers' control, which the Stalinist dictatorship had destroyed. This anti-Stalinist left, including Norman Thomas's Socialist Party and Dwight Macdonald's *Politics*, joined with radical pacifist conscientious objectors to World War II, including Dorothy Day's *Catholic Worker*, in criticizing racial segregation in the military and use of the atomic bomb. Such alternative perspectives found little traction, however. During the Popular Front of 1935–39 and World War II, liberals and Communists marched arm-in-arm against fascism, interrupted only by such inconvenient events as the Nazi-Soviet Non-Aggression Pact of 1939.

"Communism is Twentieth Century Americanism," Earl Browder declared during the Popular Front. Conservative southern Democrats and Republicans demurred, branding Communists "un-American" subversives. Red-baiting escalated in the postwar period, as the cold war began. The last gasp of the Popular Front came in former Democratic vice president Henry Wallace's 1948 Progressive Party campaign, which was hounded by charges of Communist influence. Security oaths and congressional investigations purged hundreds of Communists and other radicals from unions, government, Hollywood, and universities. Severely bruised, the American Communist Party limped along until 1956, when most of its remaining members quit in disillusionment after Nikita Khrushchev confirmed Stalin's record of mass murder, and the Soviet Union invaded Hungary, suppressing the attempt to reform communism in that country.

The New Left and After

The Montgomery bus boycott of 1955–56 signaled a rebirth of movement activity and an opening for radicalism. By 1960 a youthful New Left with dreams of "participatory democracy" was stirring in the Student Non-Violent Coordinating Committee (SNCC) and Students for a Democratic Society (SDS). The new radicals conceived of politics in moral and existential terms, typified by Mario Savio's call during Berkeley's 1964 Free Speech Movement to "put your bodies upon the gears and upon the wheels, upon the levers, upon all the apparatus."

Issues of race and war pitted the New Left against the liberal Democratic establishment. Sit-ins, Freedom Rides, and marches were met by brutal segregationist response, tarnishing the image of the United States abroad and compelling passage of the Civil Rights Act of 1964 and Voting Rights Act of 1965. The Vietnam War generated an equally powerful crisis. SDS called the first antiwar demonstration in Washington in 1965, and by decade's end, huge mobilizations were mounted, complemented by radical G.I. resistance. Radical pacifism revived, espoused by the likes of David Dellinger and Catholic priests Daniel and Philip Berrigan, although many other radicals opposed the war out of opposition to empire rather than all instances of violence. War and race intertwined as Martin Luther King Jr. challenged Chicago residential segregation, opposed the Vietnam War as a diversion from the needs of the poor at home, and was assassinated in 1968 while supporting Memphis garbage strikers, setting off riots nationwide.

By 1968 the revolutionary enthusiasm was contagious. Vietnam's Tet Offensive set off worldwide upheavals, East and West, from Prague to Paris to Mexico City. Emulating Malcolm X and third world guerrillas, Stokely Carmichael, the Black Panther Party, and other Black Power militants advocated armed struggle and cultural pride. Jerry Rubin and Abbie Hoffman, as "Yippies," fused radical politics with the counterculture's sex, drugs, and rock 'n' roll. Women liberationists objected to the 1968 Miss America pageant in Atlantic City, New Jersey, as a "degrading mindless-boob-girlie symbol," putting the spotlight on a movement that would assert reproductive rights and challenge male chauvinism in the home, workplace, and culture. Street fighting between New York City police and Stonewall Inn patrons produced the Gay Liberation Front in 1969. The cultural revolution in race, gender, and sexual norms unleashed by the 1960s radicalization would produce far-reaching and unfolding changes in American consciousness across the next several decades.

As a coherent political movement, however, the New Left did not endure. As radicals moved from protest to resistance to revolution, some decided to "Bring the War Home" by planting bombs. Confrontation could dramatize injustice, as when the American Indian Movement occupied Bureau of Indian Affairs headquarters in Washington in 1972, but one-upmanship and factional prejudice took hold as radicals misjudged the moment. One reason for New Left unreality was its distance from the American working class. C. Wright Mills and Herbert Marcuse dismissed labor for its quiescence. To many young radicals, labor unions evoked "corporate liberal" compromise or the musty Old Left, if not racist whites. By 1970 the New Left realized that students alone could not remake the world, but the belated turn to the working class too often took the form of sterile Maoist posturing, despite sounder rank-and-file projects initiated by proponents of "socialism from below."

By the mid-1970s, the New Left had disintegrated. As national politics turned rightward and labor declined, New Left themes lived on in 1980s direct-action groups like the AIDS Coalition to Unleash Power (ACT UP) and Earth First! Laments about a fragmentary "identity politics" became commonplace, although left-of-center electoral coalitions still could succeed, as when Vermont sent socialist independent Bernie Sanders to Congress in 1990 and the Senate in 2006. The Soviet bloc's demise in 1989–91 fostered a general presumption that socialism was discredited, but the 1994 Zapatista rebellion in Mexico inspired new forms of anticapitalist opposition to corporate globalization. These culminated in the 1999 Seattle protests against the World Trade Organization and the millions of votes cast in 2000 for Green Party candidate Ralph Nader, critic of the Democratic and Republican parties as a "corporate duopoly."

Radical opposition to empire revived in the years following September 11, 2001, in youthful opposition to the Iraq War. Species consciousness nearly rivaled class consciousness in radical circles, as antisystemic criticism of global warming generated reconsiderations of industrial society itself. American radicalism, though much reduced in strength from its early twentieth-century apex, continued its search to identify the fundamental causes of social injustice and irrationality and to find ways to root them out.

See also abolitionism; anarchism; communism; pacifism; populism; socialism.

FURTHER READING. Stanley Aronowitz, *The Death and Rebirth of American Radicalism*, 1996; Seweryn Bialer, ed., *Radicalism in the Contemporary Age*, 3 vols., 1977; Mari Jo Buhle, Paul Buhle, and Harvey J. Kaye, eds., *The American Radical*, 1994; Harvey Goldberg, ed., *American Radicals: Some Problems and Personalities*, 1957; Robin D. G. Kelley, *Freedom Dreams: The Black Radical Imagination*, 2002; Sidney Lens, *Radicalism in America*, 1966; Staughton Lynd, *The Intellectual Origins of American Radicalism*, 1968; Timothy Patrick McCarthy and John McMillian, eds., *The Radical Reader*, 2003; Lillian Symes and Travers Clement, *Rebel America: The Story of Social Revolt in the United States*, 1934; Alfred E. Young, ed., *Dissent: Explorations in the History of American Radicalism*, 1968.

CHRISTOPHER PHELPS

Reconstruction Era, 1865–77

Reconstruction, once defined as the period immediately following the Civil War, is now generally understood as an interlocking web of political, social, and economic transformations that followed the wartime destruction of slavery and lasted until the withdrawal of federal military support for the last Republican state governments in the former Confederacy in 1877. Among the most important political developments were the virtual revolution in southern life, the consolidation of national citizenship, and the forces that arose to limit those projects.

From Johnson's Policies to Radical Reconstruction

Wartime Reconstruction of the South began as officials and slaves in the Union-occupied slave states wrestled with the messy end of slavery. Emancipation had emerged from the crucible of war, and many Americans (President Lincoln included) believed that ex-slaves, on the whole, did not merit political citizenship. But the Emancipation Proclamation, the mass enlistment of black troops, and the success of free-labor experiments—such as the collective farm at Davis Bend, Mississippi, and the coastal lands General William T. Sherman allocated under Special Field Order No. 15—gave freed people's claims to citizenship greater weight.

Freed people began to make these claims during the war and its immediate aftermath. They held political meetings in cities and contraband camps across the occupied South. They challenged employers in hearings before agents of the newly established federal Bureau of Refugees, Freedmen, and Abandoned Lands (the Freedmen's Bureau). Whether through local initiatives or, later, under the aegis of the Union Leagues, previously disparate social groups began to come together: ex-slaves' formerly clandestine political culture and the restricted organizational life of antebellum free black people met with the political and economic ambitions of northern missionaries, entrepreneurs, and activists (people known by their contemporary enemies and later detractors as "carpetbaggers"), as well as with the hopes and fears of some southern whites (similarly dubbed "scalawags"). Meanwhile, several states under Union occupation held wartime elections and established new governments; of these, only Tennessee's would achieve lasting recognition.

With the ratification of the Thirteenth Amendment in December 1865, slavery came to a final, formal end even in the Union slave states of Kentucky and Delaware. To Lincoln's successor, Andrew Johnson, this change seemed sufficient. He appointed provisional governors, and with his approval, southern electorates forged new governments; for a time, it seemed the former slave states would be reconstructed on the basis of white male citizenship. In the winter of 1865–66, these southern state governments

began to pass laws, known as "black codes," that severely limited freed people's freedom of mobility and were designed to force them into low-wage agricultural labor. Johnson pardoned leading former Confederates, and he vetoed both the Civil Rights Act—passed by Congress in 1866 to overturn the black codes—and a bill reauthorizing the Freedmen's Bureau. In a step emblematic of this version of Reconstruction, the newly re-formed legislature of Georgia elected former Confederate vice president Alexander Stephens to the U.S. Senate.

Congressional Republicans, who controlled more than two-thirds of each house, pushed back: they refused to seat congressional delegates from most ex-Confederate states, they passed the Civil Rights and Freedmen's Bureau Bills over Johnson's veto, and in the spring of 1867 they rejected Johnson's program of Reconstruction in toto, establishing a new framework for readmission. The Reconstruction Acts of 1867 divided ten of the eleven Confederate states, all but Tennessee, into five military districts and set guidelines for their readmission that effectively enfranchised black men. Federal officials registered black and white men over 21 for the election of delegates to new constitutional conventions; those conventions wrote constitutions that included the principle of manhood suffrage. The new southern electorates created under the Reconstruction Acts helped elect Johnson's successor, former Union commanding general Ulysses S. Grant, in 1868. President Johnson's resistance to the acts—particularly his removal of federal officials supportive of Congress's purposes—led Congress to pass the Tenure of Office Act and to impeach Johnson for its violation, though he was not convicted and removed from office. In an effort to safeguard the principles of the Civil Rights Act, Republican legislators also passed a somewhat altered version of that law as a new constitutional amendment and made the ratification of that amendment a precondition for the readmission of the states now under military rule.

Radical Reconstruction transformed the U.S. Constitution. The Fourteenth Amendment (ratified in 1868) established that national citizenship belonged to all persons born within the United States, without regard to race or prior status; that this citizenship conveyed certain rights, including the "equal protection of the laws" and certain unspecified "privileges and immunities"; that states could not interpose their own limitations or qualifications; and that states would lose representation in Congress to the extent that they denied voting rights to their adult male population. In other words, it made national citizenship paramount—at least in theory. The Fifteenth Amendment (passed in 1869, ratified in 1870) extended the principle of race-neutral suffrage by prohibiting—rather than simply penalizing—disfranchisement on the basis of race, color, or previous condition of servitude. Together with various federal enforcement acts, the Fifteenth Amendment sought to ensure that the most essential expression of political citizenship—the right to vote—would not be abridged on account of race.

The Transformation of Southern Politics

The southern Republican coalition that took shape in 1867 and 1868 brought new voices into southern political life. Freed people's collective mobilization for new constitutional conventions brought hundreds of thousands of men to vote for the first time in 1867; it also mobilized black women, who—though denied the franchise—attended meetings, voiced political opinions, and sometimes insisted that men take women's wishes into account when voting. The freed people's political goals included basic liberal freedoms: their desire to reconstitute their families, move freely, seek the protection of the law, secure an education, and be secure in their property. But the southern Republican coalition brought together a variety of competing and divergent interests. White Southerners who had owned few or no slaves did not necessarily support universal public education, which would inevitably be funded by taxes on land; they often balked at the idea that people just freed from slavery should sit on juries, hold local offices, or determine the outcome of elections. Northern emigrants and antebellum free people of color, whose experiences and interests often were quite different than those of ex-slaves, played disproportionately large roles in the party leadership.

Most seriously, freed people and their northern Republican allies had somewhat different visions for the postbellum economy. Republicans had begun by seeking to guarantee the end of slavery and the creation of loyal governments committed to free labor in the ex-Confederate states; with these steps they became participants in a political revolution, sometimes dubbed Radical Reconstruction, that would transform nearly 4 million slaves into citizens with political, economic, and civil rights. Congressional "radicalism" mainly took the form of economic liberalism: since the early days of the federal wartime occupation, most federal policies and philanthropic activities had sought to transform the freed people into agricultural wage laborers. In the capital-poor world of the postwar South, this effectively meant labor on annual contracts, with supplies advanced but most wages deferred until after the harvest. But freed people's political, social, and economic visions were not limited to the orthodoxies of contractual wage labor. They sought ownership of land, not perpetual employment under contracts. They wanted the freedom to deploy labor flexibly within households and, when possible, limited women's participation in the market for agricultural labor. These tensions shaped Republican policies and offered fracture points for those who saw advantages in splitting the coalition. Democrats, who attracted few black voters, early on sought to identify the Republican Party as the representative only of black and northern interests. Their 1868 platform accused Republicans of seeking to "secure negro supremacy."

In states where the antebellum slave population had constituted a majority—South Carolina, Louisiana, and Mississippi—freed people and antebellum free people of color demanded and finally obtained meaningful roles in state and local government. The states' new constitutions removed property restrictions and apportionment by wealth, created free common schools for all children, and enacted property legislation for married women. The systematic redistribution of ex-slaveholders' land had failed to win wide support in Congress, but South Carolina created a land commission to purchase and sell small plots, boosting black landholding there well above the low regional average.

Republican black men—freeborn and freed Southerners, as well as Northerners—served southern constituencies at every level, from justice of the peace to U.S. senator. In Mississippi, Hiram Revels, a minister, was elected to fill the Senate seat vacated by Jefferson Davis in 1861, 1 of 16 black men who would ultimately serve in Congress during the era. With the exception of South Carolina's lower house, the new legislatures had white majorities. Republican leaders divided over economic policies and along axes of race, region, antebellum status, and wealth. Numerous fractures developed, with some Republicans making coalitions with opposition factions, often called Conservatives. In these states, Republican coalitions that included significant numbers of whites governed until the mid-1870s, against considerable opposition in the forms of vigilante violence and of real or feigned outrage at the corruption that marked so much of the period's politics across lines of region and party.

In states where whites made up larger percentages of the population, ex-slaves played smaller roles in the Republican Party then did northern- and southern-born whites. Governments in these states passed civil rights bills and supported black male suffrage and public schools, sometimes (as in Florida) building them from the ground up; they also invested heavily (and often corruptly) in railroads. In many states Democrats or Conservatives gained legislative majorities early, and in a few states Reconstruction as a state policy virtually ended before it began. In 1868 white conservatives in Georgia moved rapidly to expel black representatives from the state legislature. Though they reversed course when their action caused Congress to refuse to seat the state's delegation, Democrats took control of the state after the 1870 elections. By then they also controlled North Carolina's legislature and one house of Alabama's. Virginia's Republicans fractured from the start, allowing Conservatives to triumph in 1869 and bring the Commonwealth back into the Union without ever having a Republican government.

But state-level Reconstruction was not the beginning and end of the story. Power at the local level—especially in black-majority constituencies in white-majority states—could also matter enormously. For freed people, local voting rights and jury service meant being able to withstand the worst abuses of their opponents. Where they continued to exercise these rights, black men or those sympathetic to their interests might oversee contractual or criminal disputes; people who had been defrauded, assaulted, or raped could hope for equal justice. White Democrats sometimes took aim at these areas, for example, by gerrymandering black voters into a small number of districts or by stripping black-majority cities of their right to self-government.

Paramilitary Politics and the End of Southern Reconstruction

Paramilitary violence played a significant role in Reconstruction politics, mainly to the advantage of Republicans' foes. The Ku Klux Klan, formed in Tennessee in the winter of 1865–66, was the most famous and widespread organization to take up arms against the Republican Party and freed people's political activity. Similar paramilitary forces of former Confederates and their younger male relations organized across the region, terrorizing Republican voters, organizers, and officeholders, seeking to paralyze black constituencies and to discourage whites from allying with blacks. The Klan had its own oath-bound hierarchy, but it functioned fundamentally in the interest of the reconstituted state Democratic parties, holding down Republican turnout through intimidation and murder, seizing effective control of local courts and law enforcement, and making Democratic victories possible even in areas with substantial black populations.

Serious Klan violence during the 1868 election campaign helped provide the impetus for the Fifteenth Amendment; it also led to a series of federal laws designed to protect voting rights. Efforts to counter the Klan by legal means were generally ineffective, but more forceful responses carried their own risks. North Carolina governor William Holden organized a militia to put down Klan activity in the election of 1870 and was impeached for his pains, effectively ending Reconstruction in the state. Republican government in Arkansas and Texas fought the Klan effectively for a time with forces of black and white men. Federal anti-Klan activity peaked in 1871 with the reoccupation of part of South Carolina and the trials of hundreds of Klansmen under new anti-Klan laws. White supremacist terror diminished in the short run but resumed in earnest after the 1872 election.

In the states still under Republican government after 1872, white supremacist paramilitaries sought to polarize state politics and drive a wedge between black Republicans and their white allies by provoking racialized military conflict with state militias, which by this point consisted mainly of all-black units. In these contests, black militiamen were generally overmatched, and governors often chose to withdraw their forces, fearing a massacre. Well-publicized battles between black militiamen and white paramilitaries between 1873 and 1876 (e.g., in Hamburg and Ellenton, South Carolina, and Colfax and New Orleans, Louisiana) helped fracture politics along racial lines and make democratic governance virtually impossible. Federal intervention on behalf of Republican elected officials and militiamen protected some individuals but did not deter paramilitary violence; such intervention, especially in removing Democratic contestants from the Louisiana legislature in 1874, also supported Democratic charges that Reconstruction was little more than federal "bayonet rule."

The recapture of state governments by Democrats changed the terms of political conflict: black agricultural and domestic laborers, now politically all but powerless, could no longer demand laws that protected their interests. Instead, various groups of whites battled over lien, railroad, and homestead exemption laws based on differences of economic or sectional interest; ex-slaves could no longer participate actively in these contests. Supporters of these counterrevolutions lauded the "redemption" of their states from "radical and negro misrule." The destruction of Reconstruction's local legacies proceeded unevenly, leaving some islands of comparative black freedom and autonomy even in states now governed by white Democrats. Despite decades of Democratic gerrymandering, intermittent paramilitary activity, discriminatory registration laws, and constitutional changes, some of these areas continued to elect black officeholders and convention delegates until the end of the nineteenth century. White Republicanism survived in some upland areas and remained important in counties and localities but played a major part in state politics only when dissident whites (sometimes allying themselves with blacks) mounted third-party insurgencies in the 1880s and 1890s.

Reconstruction beyond the South

After 1870 few Northerners made the defense of black citizenship rights a priority. Northern Republicans rhetorically celebrated the victory over slavery and the enfranchisement of black men, and a handful of white-majority northern constituencies elected black men to office. Northern white supremacy took various forms, from white laborers' fears of an influx of southern freed people to the scientific racism promoted by leading scholars. Most white Northerners had persistently rejected calls for abolition before the war, and even after 1865, white popular majorities in state after northern state rejected referenda calling for black male suffrage, though there were only about 250,000 nonwhite citizens in the non-slaveholding states in 1860.

Many Republicans believed that, rather than making expensive and expansive federal commitments in the South, the country needed to subsidize the conquest and settlement of the West. Secession made possible a flood of Republican legislation in 1862, including legislation to fund transcontinental railroads and homesteads on the federal domain. Between 1867 and 1871, as railroad building and homesteading continued, the U.S. government signed a series of treaties establishing large Indian territories in the trans-Mississippi West. But railroad workers, settlers, and miners continued to encroach on the remaining Indian lands, and conflict between Indians and the U.S. military escalated. By the mid-1870s U.S. forces defeated most Plains tribes, who were forced to accept treaties granting them smaller reservations. The Fourteenth Amendment's exclusion of "Indians not taxed" from its protections left them without legal recourse.

The wartime development of a new national banking system facilitated the growth of ever-larger enterprises, but, in the 1870s, Republicans abandoned the flexible currency of the war years in favor of the demonetization of silver and a commitment to return to the gold standard by decade's end. The postwar years witnessed a rush of speculative investment, especially in railroads, virtually unimpeded by federal regulation or oversight, and corruption became widespread at every level of government and in every region. This, together with opposition to Grant's efforts to annex Santo Domingo, helped precipitate an unsuccessful Liberal Republican Party challenge to Grant's reelection in 1872. Corruption—notably the Crédit Mobilier scandal, which implicated many high officials in railroad construction fraud—also led to business failures, a financial panic, and a profound economic depression that began in 1873. During the depression years Republican hard-money policies inspired the rise of alternative economic visions and the Labor Reform Party and the Greenback Party. As economic struggles weakened Republican dominance, Democrats gained control of the U.S. House of Representatives in 1874, further weakening the ability of Republican radicals to promote southern Reconstruction.

The Fall and Rise of Reconstruction

The Supreme Court played an important role in undoing Reconstruction's political revolution. In the *Slaughter-House Cases* (1873), the Court upheld a state-chartered butchering monopoly in New Orleans against the claims of other butchers, ruling 5 to 4 that the rights of national citizenship, as defined by the amended federal constitution, extended only to a few specific protections, including the right to peaceable assembly, protection on the high seas and abroad, and access to navigable waterways. Similarly narrow rulings in *U.S. v. Reese* (1875) and *U.S. v. Cruikshank* (1875), cases emerging from violence against southern Republicans, held that the right to vote was a state not a federal matter and that the Fourteenth Amendment's guarantee of equal protection of the laws granted protection only against state governments' violations; against other individual and

collective violations of those principles, the Court held, the federal government was powerless. The last legislative act of congressional Reconstruction—the Civil Rights Act of 1875—sought to reenlarge the now minimal inventory of citizenship rights by prohibiting discrimination on the basis of race on juries and in railroads, theaters, hotels, and (in its early versions) schools. The final project of Charles Sumner, longtime antislavery senator from Massachusetts, the act passed only after his death and in a truncated form. The Supreme Court in 1883 struck down this law as well.

Only a handful of states enacted full or partial suffrage for women during Reconstruction; political citizenship remained closely tied to military service and male household authority. Advocates of women's voting rights had hoped their movement would succeed alongside the movement to enfranchise black men, but they were dismayed by the inclusion of the word "male" in the Fourteenth Amendment and were dealt a grievous blow by the omission of "sex" from the excluded categories of discrimination in the Fifteenth Amendment. During the election of 1872, many women, including Susan B. Anthony, Sojourner Truth, and black Republicans in the South, challenged their exclusion at the polls by casting or seeking to cast ballots; Anthony was among those arrested for those actions. In one resulting case, *Minor v. Happersett* (1874), the Supreme Court ruled that though women were indeed citizens, voting was a state matter and not among the "privileges and immunities" of national citizens.

Reconstruction as a federal project ended following the contested national election of 1876. Democratic factions in South Carolina and Louisiana, determined to seize power, provoked violent conflicts with black officeholders and state militias that essentially militarized state politics; these states' elections were marred by extensive violence and fraud. Nationally, Democratic presidential candidate Samuel Tilden won a popular majority and seemed poised to defeat Republican Rutherford B. Hayes in the Electoral College, but Republicans claimed victory in South Carolina, Louisiana, and Florida, which together would give them a narrow electoral majority. With the election results in these states subject to bitter dispute, a deadlock ensued. Throughout the winter and early spring, Washington powerbrokers sought to hammer out a compromise and select a president, while rival governments claimed legitimacy in Columbia and New Orleans. A convoluted agreement finally developed, under which the Republicans gained the presidency and Democrats won the remaining southern state governments, a bargain lubricated with levee and railroad subsidies as well as pledges not to prosecute violators of election laws. In April 1877, after Hayes's inauguration, the federal government withdrew its forces, Republican governments crumbled, and Reconstruction as a federal policy came to an end.

Reconstruction's political legacies took many forms. In some parts of the South, black and white Republicans continued to exert political power through and even beyond the end of the century, sometimes making alliances with Populists and other third-party challengers to Democratic rule. Meanwhile, fables of Reconstruction as a period of "radical and negro misrule" became an article of faith among southern Democrats and many other white Americans, ultimately mutating into a tale of black men's sexual designs on white women (as depicted in D. W. Griffith's 1915 film *The Birth of a Nation*). During and especially after World War II, however, black Southerners and northern allies vigorously challenged their political and civil disabilities, and the Supreme Court slowly reversed its earlier course and began to apply the Reconstruction amendments in ways that supported African American political and civil rights. This period is therefore sometimes called the Second Reconstruction.

See also Civil War and Reconstruction; Confederacy; race and politics, 1860–1933; slavery; South since 1877; voting.

FURTHER READING. Richard F. Bensel, *Yankee Leviathan: The Origins of Central State Authority in America, 1859–1877,* 1991; Elsa Barkley Brown, "Negotiating and Transforming the Public Sphere: African-American Political Life in the Transition from Slavery to Freedom," *Public Culture* 7 (Fall 1994), 107–46; W.E.B. DuBois, *Black Reconstruction in America, 1860–1880,* 1935, reprint, 1998; Eric Foner, *Reconstruction: America's Unfinished Revolution, 1863–1877,* 1988; Steven Hahn, *A Nation under Our Feet: Black Political Struggles in the Rural South from Slavery to the Great Migration,* 2003.

STEPHEN KANTROWITZ

regulation

Enduring and valued traditions of American regulation predate the constitutional republic launched in 1789. They include the governance of markets and firms and their advertising and manufacturing practices; of individuals, their expression, their sexuality, and other features of their daily behavior; of families, their homes and property, and their consumption patterns; of land, air, and water and their use and conservation. These patterns are not fully consensual but have been contested thoroughly, not mainly over whether there should be more or less regulation, but over which form regulation should take and who should do the regulating. All this contestation aside, regulation is as deeply rooted within the fabric of American government as liberty itself. Indeed, Americans have long viewed regulation the way that Alexander Hamilton did in the Federalist Papers and his early financial writings—as protective of liberty. It is only recently in U.S. political history that regulation has been interpreted as an intrusion into a separate, private sphere.

"Regulation" in twenty-first-century politics often connotes the rule of a marketplace, the rule of the state over purely economic activity. Yet for much of American history, and in ways that continue into the present, this reading narrows what was a much broader phenomenon. The distinction between "economic regulation," "social regulation," and "moral regulation" was one that eighteenth- and nineteenth-century Americans would have been hard pressed to identify. Like the hues in a child's watercolor painting, the moral, the social, the financial, the spiritual, the private, the public, and the communal realms bled into one another.

Early American Regulation

The marketplaces of eighteenth- and nineteenth-century America were literally made by state regulation and government rules. The price system, standards and minimal expectations of quality and security, and the structure of exchange were created and fashioned by government action. It was government laws, not exogenous market conventions, that required prices to be visibly published for perusal by the citizen (this requirement remains, invisibly but significantly, in state and local laws governing numerous transactions today). Governments elaborated standards of construction for business, of packaging for products, of licenses for entry into health and medicine, of hair cutting, of machine repair, and of numerous other occupations. Market clerks and government auctioneers—themselves employed by state and local authorities—presided over market activity. In creating and sustaining marketplaces, these public institutions served multiple purposes; they were "common carriers" of the varied aims of the public. Market-constituting regulation stemmed from the common-law philosophy of a "well-regulated" society, incorporating values of fairness, of consumer protection, of the transparency of the marketplace. These concerns echoed centuries of accumulated tradition and philosophy and reflected longstanding republican traditions of popular sovereignty, particularly in their focus on "the people's welfare" as the "highest law" of the land (*Salus populi extrema lex*).

Strong restrictions on property and its uses were a central feature of early American regulation. Fire safety regulations constrained the store of gunpowder, the piling of wood, and the construction of new homes. Until the 1870s, these regulations were virtually immune to judicial challenge, and even then they persisted through many legal disputes well into the twentieth century. In their public safety and public health regulations, cities and counties prohibited standing water, compelled the removal of dead animals, and enjoined citizens from burning all manner of objects on their private property.

Another stable theme of early American regulation lay in the fusion of moral regulation and economic regulation. Decades before and after the temperance movements of the 1800s, state and local governments achieved a vast regulation of alcohol: its production, sale, distribution, and consumption. These laws governed public morality even as they deeply shaped the congeries of markets that composed the alcoholic beverage industry.

The moral basis of economic regulation also emerged in the symbolic logic of "adulteration." The idea of adulterated commodities held that a product's misrepresentation in the marketplace was a matter not simply of economic fraud but of moral and spiritual corruption. Adulteration linked nineteenth-century product regulation to the governance of alcohol, of gambling and lotteries, and of pornography and sexuality. Notions of adulteration as a form of corruption (and not simply a failure of market information) were central to state pure food laws and, later, laws regulating the manufacture and dispensation of medicines. Concerns about adulteration also drove and shaped the evolution of occupational licensing; not only products but also services and labor could be immorally represented. Under these laws, local and state governments hired more inspectors and built administrative bodies for regulating everything from steamboats to meatpacking facilities to proprietary medicine firms.

The main constraint on American regulation lay in federalism. Capacities for regulation developed largely in states and localities and much less in the national government. This disjuncture flowed partially from the commerce clause of Article I, Section IV of the U.S. Constitution; federal regulation was often justified on the basis that the national state could uniquely govern patterns of commerce among the states. The primary exceptions to national regulatory weakness rested in areas where the American state had developed administrative capacity. In the national postal system, Americans were already accustomed to the regulation of markets whose products coursed by the million through that system. When Victorian reformers led by postal official Anthony Comstock turned their attention to the regulation of vice and morals, they achieved the Comstock Law of 1872 and the Anti-Lottery Acts of 1890 and 1895. These statutes and their enforcement projected the power of national government into the everyday sexuality of millions of women and men, and the latter brought an end to the most profitable gambling concern of the nineteenth century: the Louisiana Lottery Company. They also changed the structure of the regulatory state; newly emboldened postal inspectors launched a massive postal fraud campaign, which issued over 20,000 fraud orders from 1910 to 1924. Postal regulators averaged 3,500 arrests and 2,000 convictions annually by the 1920s, with targets ranging from Texas oil companies to patent medicine outfits.

Growth of Federal Regulation

With the Meat Inspection Act of 1885, the U.S. Department of Agriculture began to acquire vast authority over the nation's livestock farms, stockyards, slaughterhouses, and meat-processing plants; the agency hired thousands of inspectors, creating the largest regulatory apparatus outside of the postal system.

Robust patterns of economic activity had always crossed state boundaries, but the size and rapidity of interstate commerce grew substantially in the nineteenth century, aided by federal policy itself—the postal system, land grants to railroads, the forcible opening of cheap land by the U.S. Army. The coming of a new industrial age (and with it, a growing concentration of capital and political power in fewer and fewer firms) meant that market developments outran the capacity of states and localities to monitor and govern them. The emblematic case came in railroads. Midwestern and western state legislatures passed a number of strong statutes regulating railroad pricing and safety in the 1870s and 1880s. The federal government followed in 1887 by creating a hybrid (and characteristically American) form of regulatory institution: the independent regulatory commission. The Interstate Commerce Commission (ICC) was governed not by a single individual but by a min-legislature, a five-person commission with voting and staggered terms. The ICC's powers grew slowly, often in contest with the federal courts, which were not eager to relinquish their regulatory powers to "expert commissions." Yet with a series of statutes culminating in the National Transportation Act of 1920, the ICC assumed plenary authority (involving issues of pricing, safety, planning, and cost structure) over rail and truck transport in the United States.

The independent commission found expression in other modes of regulation as well, most notably in the Federal Trade Commission Act of 1914. The FTC's primary architect was Louis Brandeis, often called the "patron saint" of the American regulatory tradition. Along with the Department of Justice, the FTC was responsible for regulating large corporations. In the republican political tradition and in the "fair trade" and pro-competition vision of Brandeis, antitrust and corporate regulation served explicitly political purposes: to combat the concentration of economic and hence political and social power within large, unaccountable, and ungovernable organizations. As the American antitrust regime entered the New Deal, policy became less politically focused and more economically driven, captivated by the concept of "consumer surplus" and its maximization.

Other federal regulations of the Progressive and New Deal Eras also arrived in commission form. These include the Federal Power Commission (1920), today the Federal Energy Regulatory Commission (FERC); the Federal Radio Commission (1927), renamed the Federal Communications Commission (FCC) in 1934; the Securities and Exchange Commission (SEC) (1934); the National Labor Relations Board (NLRB) (1935); the Atomic Energy

Commission (AEC) (1946), now the Nuclear Regulatory Commission (NRC) (1975); and the now-defunct Civil Aeronautics Board (1938).

In these and other realms, federal and state regulators cooperated as often as they battled for turf. Comstock's anti-vice crusades depended heavily on the willing support and subsidy given by state and local law enforcement officials, and the vice-suppression societies of major American cities. State regulators formed associations among themselves for the exchange of information, for professional fraternity, and for the making of model statutes. Two of the most notable of these adventures in "cooperative federalism" were the National Association of Railroad and Utility Commissioners (NARUC) and the National Association of Food and Drug Officials. These bodies sponsored model laws that were pivotal in shaping twentieth-century regulation and that served as templates for legislative activity at the federal level.

The Consumer Revolution in Regulation

The institution-building impulse of the Progressive and New Deal Eras marked a significant expansion of the regulatory state at the national level. Yet slowly, and profoundly, it continued a transformation of ideals in American regulation. Increasingly, in the ideology, law, and administration of American governance, the object of policy was less the people's welfare than consumer welfare. Regulation was meant less to protect the American as citizen and more to protect the American as consumer. This language had its roots in nineteenth-century jurisprudence and political economy, and it slowly engendered a policy world characterized by rights-based claims, individually focused analysis, and welfare-maximizing goals.

The Progressive–New Deal legacy is colossal. The federal government experimented with industrial licensure in the National Recovery Act. It counseled an expansion of trade practices and advertising by the Federal Trade Commission. It continued and bolstered Progressive Era programs of conservation in forestry, natural resources, and land management. The Agricultural Adjustment Acts of 1933 and 1938 created extensive patterns of regulation over agriculture, many of which persist to this day. The Glass-Steagall legislation separated commercial banking from investment banking and created the Federal Deposit Insurance Corporation (FDIC). For every regulation observed, countless other, more radical and more conservative ideas were floated.

Twentieth-century regulation was characterized by institutions and ideals that flowed from multiple traditions of philosophy, ideology, law, and policy administration. Republican regulation of the "well-ordered society" was displaced by "liberal" regulation (what political philosopher Michael Sandel has called "the procedural republic") as analysis and justification purely in terms of costs and benefits have taken

over. This is one of the crucial shifts in regulation in America in the twentieth century; its primary concern with Americans as consumers and not citizens. Independent regulatory commissions were created alongside regulatory bodies in large executive departments. Regulators combined statistical and economic tools with older patterns of legal analysis and enforcement.

Yet the republican face of early American regulation has not died out. Moral claims about regulation still echo in twenty-first-century politics, not least because American political elites and regulators are still responsive to them. The regulation of telecommunications has been concerned with concentration of ownership, minority representation, and the advancement and standardization of technology, but it has persistently returned to issues of indecency in broadcast radio and television. Antitrust and trade regulation have been motivated not merely by issues of efficiency but also of fairness.

Another forceful metaphor of twentieth- and twenty-first-century American regulation—one that harkens back to the symbolic logic of adulteration in the late 1880s and early 1900s—is protection. Even the mantra of "consumer protection" legislation—from labor and health rules, the governance of consumer products, environmental policy—implied that there were values other than rights and efficiency that were being served by the American regulatory regime. Indeed, the protection metaphor was transformed and recycled in the 1950s, 1960s, and 1970s, precisely at the time that American citizenship became defined ever more upon the principles of consumption and leisure. Cold war America saw new initiatives in environmental protection, most notably the Clean Air Act of 1970 and the establishment of the Environmental Protection Agency (EPA) that same year. The Occupational Safety and Health Act of 1970 created the federal Occupational Safety and Health Administration (OSHA), which regulates workplace safety in a complex web of overlapping relationships and jurisdictions with state labor safety agencies. The Consumer Products Safety Commission was created in 1972, empowered with the authority to recall products.

The 1960s and 1970s also witnessed growing patterns of regulation by the rule making of federal agencies, even though the Administrative Procedures Act of 1946 was supposed to have constrained such practices. Scholars began to size up American regulation by tallying the number of pages published in each year's *Federal Register*. Where formal rule making through administrative procedures has become cumbersome for agencies, they have shifted to issuing guidance documents that are not binding but nonetheless have a powerful shaping influence on behavior. Federal regulatory agencies have also become adept at using advisory committees composed of outside experts in order to gather information and to gain legitimacy for their policies.

Deregulation and the Reemergence of Regulation

The closing of the twentieth century was marked by a reimagining of regulation and a campaign for deregulation. Three forces—the growing political power of business, the emergence of policy and academic critiques focusing on the self-corrective power of the marketplace, and the broad distrust of government among American citizens—fueled the rollback of regulation. All sectors of regulation were affected—especially in airlines, where President Jimmy Carter joined with congressional Democrats and his appointee Alfred Kahn to eliminate federal price regulation, eventually terminating the Civil Aeronautics Board. Antitrust regulation was increasingly constrained by the notion that monopolistic markets might still be "contestable"; hence monopolies might limit their pricing out of the possibility that a presently invisible firm might enter the marketplace. The 1990s witnessed the deregulation of transportation (including the elimination of the ICC in 1995) and of telecommunications (1995), and a more moderate deregulation of health and pharmaceuticals. A new law in 1999 repealed the Glass-Steagall Act, allowing investment banks and commercial service banks to consolidate operations. New agency rules were subject to cost-benefit analysis, a practice centered in the president's Office of Management and Budget. In this conservative political age, the national government became the restrainer, not the enabler, of state and local governance.

The governance of medical products constitutes the one sphere of regulation for which American institutions have served as an exemplar of strength and a global model. The U.S. Food and Drug Administration (FDA), empowered in the New Deal legislation of 1938 and again in 1962 following the thalidomide tragedy, has created institutions, procedures, and scientific and technical concepts that have been copied worldwide. It is a small agency with a remarkably big power: the authority to veto the marketability of any new drug product, medical device, or vaccine. Its regulation of pharmaceuticals has powerfully structured the global clinical research industry, cleaving modern medical research into four distinct phases of experiment. Its regulation of "safety" and "efficacy" has literally defined the terms on which medical and pharmaceutical innovation operates worldwide.

In reality, the experiment of American government writ large is one of regulation—the regulation of racial relations, of sexuality, of the poor, of firearms and other weapons, of labor relations, of personal space. Yet the republican past, while faded, still lives with us. In the wake of numerous corporate accounting scandals in the early twenty-first century, Congress passed the Sarbanes-Oxley Act, which regulates corporate accounting on a template not merely of rights and efficiency but of "responsibility." The mortgage-lending crisis of 2007 and 2008 has led to calls for similar regulation of the lending industries. These and other regulatory initiatives have been introduced not for efficiency reasons, but out of senses of abuse, consumer protection, and the like. And with the financial and global economic crises of 2008 and 2009, new regulatory visions and organizations are being created. The language of regulation—the terms used to justify it, attack it, implement it, constrain it—is revealing and marks the enduring legacy of American regulation as well as its most contested transformations.

See also consumers and politics; economy and politics; health and illness; Prohibition and temperance; transportation and politics.

FURTHER READING. Daniel Carpenter, *The Forging of Bureaucratic Autonomy: Reputations, Networks and Policy Innovation in Executive Agencies, 1862–1928*; Sally Clarke, *Regulation and the Revolution in United States Farm Productivity*, 1994; Martha Derthick and Paul J. Quirk, *The Politics of Deregulation*, 1985; Ellis W. Hawley, *The New Deal and the Problem of Monopoly: A Study in Economic Ambivalence*, 1995; Marc Law, "The Origins of State Pure Food Regulation," *Journal of Economic History* 63 (December 2003), 1103–30; Thomas McCraw, *Prophets of Regulation*, 1984; William Novak, *The People's Welfare: Law and Regulation in Nineteenth-Century America*, 1996; Stephen Skowronek, *Building a New American State: The Expansion of National Administrative Capacities, 1877–1920*, 1982.

DANIEL CARPENTER

religion and politics to 1865

To see how breathtaking the changes were in the relationship between religion and politics from the nation's founding to 1865 and how easily American Protestants, the dominant religious group, accommodated them, one only need consider the way American Presbyterians did a quick about-face on the duties of the civil magistrate. In 1787 the Synod of New York and Philadelphia, then the highest body in the American Presbyterian Church, appointed a committee to prepare a revised edition of the Westminster Confession of Faith and Larger and Shorter Catechisms for the proposed establishment of the General Assembly and its constitution. This revision rejected the understanding of the civil magistrate's duties to maintain and protect the "true" religion that was common throughout the Protestant world during the sixteenth and seventeenth centuries, and enshrined in the original documents of the Westminster Assembly. In so doing, American Presbyterians modified their understanding of church and state in ways that at the time fellow Presbyterians in Scotland, Canada, Northern Ireland, and Australia would have found objectionable and perhaps even a betrayal of the genius of Calvinism. In fact, when English Parliament convened the Westminster Assembly during the Civil War of the 1640s, only Anabaptists and other radicals could have countenanced the kind of arrangement affirmed in the American revisions.

The case of American Presbyterians reversing the patterns of 15 centuries of church-state relations in the West is one example of the surprising ways that Protestants in the new nation reconciled themselves to what appeared to be a secular national government. As revolutionary as the new relationship between church and state was from a European perspective, it became palatable to Protestants in the United States for a variety of reasons. On the one hand, American framers were not hostile to but supported Christianity, at least of a generic kind. At the same time, Protestant leaders adopted the ideology of independence in ways that gave the American experiment redemptive significance. On the other hand, church leaders would eventually learn that by severing ties to the state faith they could be even more influential than when regulated by the state. Indeed, the American Revolution unleashed religious motivations for political activism in ways barely imaginable in the late eighteenth century. But by the middle decades of the nineteenth century, when the United States began to experience greater religious diversity and conflict, the benefits of religious activism for the American republic looked much less obvious than they appeared during the heady days of the 1770s.

Christian Republicanism

One of the Presbyterian ministers who had a hand in revising the Westminster Confession was also the only clergyman to sign the Declaration of Independence. John Witherspoon, the president of the College of New Jersey (now Princeton University), was a well-respected Presbyterian pastor who also trained graduates who would support the revolutionary cause. During his tenure at the college, only 5 of its 355 graduates would remain loyal to the British crown. This earned Witherspoon's school the nickname "seminary of sedition." His educational labors as well as his service as a member of the Continental Congress made him one of the colonies' leading patriots.

Witherspoon's service to the revolution went beyond teaching and politics to enlisting Christianity for the cause of independence. One sermon in particular, "The Dominion of Providence over the Passions of Men," demonstrated the convergence of Protestant theology and revolutionary politics that allowed for such a harmonious relationship between America's believers and the nation's framers. Witherspoon delivered this sermon on Friday, May 17, 1776, a day of prayer called by Congress. In this oration, published the next month in Philadelphia during the meetings of the Continental Congress, Witherspoon articulated one of the chief themes that aligned Christianity and Enlightenment political thought: the sacred cause of liberty. He believed that the cause of America was one predicated on justice and liberty, and that it conformed to the truth about

human nature. It also showed that religious and civil liberty were inextricably linked. Both the temporal and the eternal happiness of Americans depended on their gaining independence from England. In fact, religion prospered the most in those nations that enjoyed political liberty and justice.

Witherspoon's logic not only typified a large swath of Protestant colonists but also reflected a similar attitude toward religion even among America's less than orthodox founders. When he deduced that the most zealous advocates of liberty were also the ones who were most active in promoting true religion, Witherspoon was asserting, in Christian idiom, the classical republican view that tied the prospects of liberty to the virtue of citizens. This Christian republicanism, according to Mark A. Noll, featured two ideas. First was the fear of the abuse of illegitimate power and second was an almost millennial belief in the benefits of liberty. For Protestants like Witherspoon— and the Revolution found its greatest clerical support from Calvinists in the Presbyterian and Congregationalist denominations—the best form of government was one that best preserved freedom, which would, in turn, nurture human flourishing. The flip side of this view was that any form of tyranny would be abusive both for persons and society. The critical contrasts in Christian republicanism, consequently, were virtue versus corruption, and liberty versus slavery. Protestants like Witherspoon conceded that liberty could also be abused. But this was why religion was all the more essential to a republican form of government. Virtue promoted freedom, and vice produced tyranny and social disorder. For the Protestants who supported the cause of freedom, religion was the only way to guarantee the kind of virtue on which freedom depended.

Christian republicanism was not only the logic of Protestant colonists, however. The American framers also believed that liberty required a virtuous citizenry and that virtue generally stemmed from religion. Thomas Jefferson was no favorite of many Calvinists who supported his Federalist opponents, but even he did not hesitate to affirm the new nation's need for religion, such as in his 1801 inaugural address as president. There he declared, "Let us, then, with courage and confidence pursue our own federal and republican principles. . . . enlightened by a benign religion, professed, indeed, and practiced in various forms, yet all of them including honesty, truth, temperance, gratitude, and the love of man; acknowledging and adoring an overriding Providence, which by all its dispensation proves that it delights in the happiness of man here and his greater happiness hereafter."

Jefferson's faith in providence was a far cry from orthodox Protantism. But it was not explicitly hostile to Christianity, especially with the qualifications supplied by clergy like Witherspoon. Jefferson himself maintained "a more beautiful or precious morsel of ethics I have never seen" than the teachings of Jesus. Similar affirmations of faith came from

Jefferson's political opponents, such as John Adams, who was not much more orthodox in his Christian affirmation than the Virginian. In 1813 Adams wrote to Jefferson that "The general principles, on which the Fathers achieved independence, were . . . the general Principles of Christianity, in which all these Sects were United. . . ." The basis for Adams's positive assessment of Christianity drew directly on the fusion of Protestant and republican thought; religion and virtue supplied the only true foundation for a republican form of government and political liberty.

To be sure, these appeals to Christianity by American statesmen not known for their doctrinal precision should not be read, as American Protestants have sometimes interpreted them, as an indication of U.S. Christian origins. Nor is it clear that Protestants like Witherspoon were theologically within their rights to endorse the Revolution on Christian or Protestant grounds. But the lure of Christian republicanism to both the orthodox and heterodox patriots is significant for understanding why the American Revolution avoided an anticlerical or antireligious thrust. The widespread claim that republicanism and liberty depended upon virtue, and its corollary that tyranny was fundamentally incompatible with virtue, provided all the leverage believers and skeptics needed to find a place for religion in the new republic. As long as that connection existed, the orthodox could look on the skeptical as friendly to the churches and believers; and at the same time, as long as believers promoted virtue—as opposed to dogma—as the necessary ingredient for liberty's success, the skeptical among the framers could regard the churches and their members as benevolent partners in the enterprise of founding a free and well-ordered republic.

Disestablishment and Revival

Religious complications to the American founding emerged almost as soon as George Washington secured the terms of peace from Lord Cornwall at Yorktown. In the debates leading up to the Constitution, Protestants did not worry that the federal government required no religious tests for office or refused to establish Christianity as the state's religion. The federal government's powers were so restricted that the Constitution's lack of religious provisions were thoroughly in keeping with the expectation that state governments would oversee the lion's share of general welfare within their borders. Furthermore, the framers regarded the maintenance of established churches at the state level as an appropriate outworking of the relations between state and federal sovereignty. Even so, older fears of the Church of England gaining a foothold through the creation of an American bishop, which had contributed to some churches' support for independence from Great Britain, led Protestants eventually to question the wisdom of ecclesiastical establishments also at the state level. Consequently, while Protestants may not have objected to a federal Constitution free from religious

tests, some were less than content with religious regulations within their own states.

The processes by which established churches in Virginia and Massachusetts lost their privileged status are instructive for understanding how the logic that informed federal developments could trickle down to the local level. In Virginia, revivalist Protestantism and Enlightenment political theory combined to undermine the Episcopal establishment inherited from the colonial era. Revivalist dissatisfaction with church-state patterns in Virginia went back to the Great Awakening of the mid-eighteenth century, when itinerant evangelists had been imprisoned for upsetting the social order because of their ministry outside the bounds of the Episcopal order. What is more, all ministers not in the Episcopal Church were required to assent to 34 of the Church of England's Thirty-Nine Articles in order to lead worship legally. Even then, only Episcopal priests were allowed to perform marriages. At the same time, citizens were taxed by local vestries to pay for the services of the Episcopal churches. Dissenters, of course, relied on the generosity of their own congregations.

The arguments against preferential treatment for Episcopalians took two forms. On the one hand, dissenting Protestants deduced that by incorporating a particular denomination the state had usurped Christ's own rule within the church. For instance, Virginia Presbyterians adopted a resolution in 1776 that called on the legislature to overturn all religious establishments, and to abolish taxes that violated liberty of conscience. Disestablishment would properly define the true relationship between civil and ecclesiastic authority. It would also do justice to Christ's own status as the sole legislator and governor of the church. Baptists argued in a similar vein and urged the Virginia assembly to recognize that because Christ's kingdom was not of this world it could not properly be regulated by the state. Baptists also argued that favoring one denomination above all others was unjust and at odds with Virginia's bill of rights.

On the other hand, the language of rights echoed a less Christian and more libertarian argument about freedom of thought. The Virginia Bill for Establishing Religious Freedom (1786), written by Jefferson, appealed to the politics of liberty even if it also claimed to know the mind of the Creator. This bill, which proved influential on debates leading to the First Amendment of the U.S. Constitution, asserted the principle of freedom of thought and disdained any attempt to coerce beliefs or ideas by legislation or state power. In fact, to bind anyone's conscience was a violation of the law of nature as well as the law of liberty. Although the language of the Virginia legislation clearly appealed to dissenting Protestants when it insisted that God did not intend to propagate Christianity by state coercion, its appeal to human reason was different from Baptist and Presbyterian arguments for religious freedom. In the latter case, revivalist Protestants were more likely to claim the sincerity of faith or the religion of the heart than freedom of thought on behalf of religious freedom and ecclesiastical disestablishment. Even so, the logic of revivalism and the Enlightenment combined in Virginia to place religious faith in the category of freedom of thought and expression. Those who advocated either a rational religion or a zealous Protestantism joined hands to conclude that the civil magistrate had no appropriate power to intrude into the arena of privately held beliefs and opinions.

Disestablishment of the Congregationalist churches in Massachusetts, the state-church system that lasted the longest of any—until 1833—stemmed less from the logic of freedom of expression than from internal conflicts within the churches themselves. The state's constitution of 1779 did provide for religious freedom but also, in Article III, empowered towns to raise taxes in support of teachers of religion—in other words, pastors—who would produce the instruction necessary for a religious and virtuous citizenry. This provision allowed the Congregationalist churches to continue to receive state support because of the preponderance of Congregationalists in the state.

But the Congregationalist churches encountered a double threat from opposite sides of the Protestant spectrum that threatened their established position. Baptists voiced objections to a system that forced them to pay taxes to support Congregationalist ministers. Like their counterparts in Virginia, New England Baptists were also supporters of revivalism and, in some cases, had run afoul of the established order by conducting religious services without legal permission. On the other side of the spectrum were liberal Congregationalists, the forerunners of Unitarianism, who continued to receive state support despite objections from Trinitarian Congregationalists, who believed the legislature should fund only orthodox faith. (The division between the two parties became so great when Unitarians in 1805 took control of theological instruction at Harvard University that orthodox rivals in 1808 founded Andover Seminary to counter the spread of false teaching from Cambridge.)

These two sets of circumstances—a dissenting group of Protestants who objected to a state church and a theological rift within the established church itself—generated a series of court cases during the 1820s and forced Massachusetts to abandon tax support for the standing Congregationalist order. Even so, Massachusetts absorbed disestablishment with relative ease by relying on the public school system, created by school reformer Horace Mann, to provide the religious instruction that the state needed.

The Second Great Awakening

Disestablishment could have been a threat to Protestantism in the United States had the sort of anticlericalism experienced in France accompanied the American form of separating church and state. But because political leaders typically couched disestablishment in the language of neutrality to all Protestant denominations, the process of disentangling church and state proved to be a tremendous boon to spiritual vitality in the United States (and continues to account for the ironic combination of America's secular political order and its unprecedented levels of religious observance among western societies). By weaning the church from the financial nurture of the state, church leaders needed to draw support directly from the faithful. This environment gave an advantage to the most entrepreneurial of denominations in the new competition for adherents and financial support. In particular, Methodists and Baptists, who had already learned to exist without state aid, benefitted indirectly from religious disestablishment because of skills honed in the work of itinerancy and promoting revivals. In fact, disestablishment was a boon to revivalistic Protestantism.

Of course, revivalism was not new to America. The First Great Awakening (1740s), led by the revivalist George Whitefield with support from the likes of Jonathan Edwards and Gilbert Tennent, had already popularized the practice of itinerancy—that is, the traveling evangelist who preaches anywhere, including fields, town markets, and meeting houses without regard for church etiquette or legal sanctions. For Methodists and Baptists, however, the practice of conducting revivals and recruiting new members was not the exception but the rule. Indeed, the zeal for holiness and conversion that Methodist and Baptist forms of Protestantism encouraged sprang directly from the logic of conversion and the subsequent demand for holy living. In contrast to formal and apparently stuffy clergy trained in universities and colleges, revivalism opened the ministry to a host of lay itinerants adept at speaking the language of people well outside the influence of the older and established churches. In turn, these itinerants also provided the building blocks of a denominational structure that emerged in the early nineteenth century for Methodists and Baptists with loosely established networks and associations. These institutional forms gave a collective identity to populist denominations that stretched from the eastern seaboard to the expanding western frontier both in the North and the South.

Membership statistics from the era underscore the capacity of revivalism to adapt and thrive in the new circumstances of disestablishment. The most aggressively revivalist denominations grew the fastest, leaving the older and more established ones behind. Congregationalists and Presbyterians at the time of the American Revolution, for example, constituted approximately 40 percent of religious adherents in the United States (20 and 19 percent, respectively), while Baptists (17 percent) and Methodists (3 percent) were only half the size of the Calvinist denominations at the time of the Declaration of Independence. But after the war for independence and the new church-state order took form, Methodists and Baptists outpaced their Protestant competitors. In 1850 Methodists were the largest denomination, at 34 percent of American Protestants, and Baptists were the next largest American Protestant church with a membership of 20 percent of the Protestant whole. In contrast, by 1850 Congregationalists had fallen to 4 percent, and Presbyterians to 12 percent. The reasons for the growth among Methodists and Baptists and the decline of Calvinistic denominations are numerous. But the dynamic of disestablishment combined with the innovation and expansionist impulses of revivalism were crucial to the change in fortunes of these denominations. The success of Methodists and Baptists also demonstrated an unintended consequence of separating church and state—namely, that without the support and especially the oversight of government, churches could flourish in ways previously unimaginable.

Revivalism and Reform

Even if the Congregationalist and Presbyterian religions suffered in popularity during the antebellum period, they made up for numerical inferiority with associational superiority. After 1820, the United States was awash in a sea of voluntary societies that further complicated the relationship between religion and politics. Not only did disestablishment create a religious vacuum that revivalist-inspired Protestants filled with amazing efforts to plant churches on the expanding western frontier, but the lack of political and social structures in the new nation created an opening for religiously inspired political activism. Protestants in the Northeast, especially New England Congregationalists, responded with a vast array of voluntary associations designed to Christianize the new nation in a variety of ways. Most of these organizations received support and inspiration from the religious zeal of the Second Great Awakening, a series of revivals during the 1820s and 1830s whose principal agent was Charles Grandison Finney. These revivals and the reforms they animated gave the new society a semblance of order. They were not simply a religious but also a social response to unsettled and expanding conditions. In effect, the voluntary associations of the Second Great Awakening, also known as the Benevolent Empire, became the mechanism for civilizing life on the frontier with the "proper" ways of the East.

Some of these voluntary associations were more explicitly religious than social or political. For instance, Congregationalists, with help from northern Presbyterians, established organizations for the inexpensive production and distribution of religious materials such as Bibles and tracts. Other associations provided means for the education of clergy and for supporting the establishment of new churches in the Northwest Territory. But religious voluntary societies encouraged a widespread perception of the United States as a republic that conformed to Christian ideals. This conviction led to a number of humanitarian efforts to reform prisons, hospitals, establish schools, and train teachers for schools. A desire for a wholesome, well-ordered, and devout society also prompted revivalistic Protestants to insert themselves into the political process.

Sometimes the religious zeal of revivalistic Protestants had a direct influence on public policy and the electoral process. Some Protestant social crusades were of a limited duration and particular to a specific region of the country. Some started and gained momentum in the antebellum era only to see their greatest influence in a later period. And some substantially changed the face of party politics. In each case, the Protestant political muscle showed that disestablishment could lead to entanglements of religion and politics far thornier than the architects of separating church and state had ever contemplated.

In the category of Protestant political reforms that were limited to a specific time and place stand both the Sabbatarian-inspired opposition to Sunday mails and the Anti-Mason movement. Opposition to post offices staying open on Sundays surfaced as early as 1809, when Hugh Wylie, the postmaster of Washington, Pennsylvania, and an elder in the Presbyterian Church, was disciplined by his church for keeping the post office open on the day of Christian worship. The U.S. postmaster general, Gideon Granger, responded, in 1810, by orchestrating legislation that required all of the nation's 2,300 post offices to remain open for business seven days a week. The issue of Sunday mails resurfaced at the time of the Second Great Awakening when Protestants formed the General Union for the Promotion of the Christian Sabbath, which launched a petition campaign to persuade Congress to repeal the 1810 Postal Act, in addition to calling for a boycott of all businesses that operated on Sundays. The effort generated over 900 petitions. But the arguments, many of which appealed to the nation's Christian origins, failed to change federal law. The chairman of the Senate Committee on the Post Office and Post Roads, Richard M. Johnson, argued persuasively against the petitions, and post offices continued to remain open on Sundays throughout the nineteenth century.

Anti-Masonry also emerged from Protestant objections to church members belonging to secret societies and from widespread fears of conspiracy that such secrecy encouraged. In the minds of many Protestants, secret societies were pagan in origin, smacked of Roman Catholic hierarchy, and undermined true religion. In 1826 the cover-up of the murder of a defector from the Masonic Order led to the creation of America's first powerful third party. Anti-Masons called on American voters to drive Masons out of elected office. For them, Freemasonry was a privileged elite that lacked accountability to the nation's republican institutions. Their antagonistic platform was hardly a stable foundation for a successful party.

Even so, the Anti-Masonic Party ran its own candidate for president in 1832, William Wirt, and proved disruptive to the National Republican Party's fortunes in the North.

Eventually the populism of Anti-Masonry would find an outlet in the Whig Party's opposition to Andrew Jackson's apparent disregard for legal and constitutional norms. For Whigs, Jackson's expropriation of Indian land violated a proper Christian regard for existing treaties, and his banking policies constituted a swindling of the American republic by disregarding the obligations of contracts.

In contrast to these brief and focused episodes of partisan politics inspired by Protestant devotion, temperance was a social reform that began during the middle decades of the nineteenth century and would not succeed on a national level until the early twentieth century. Again, the reasons drew heavily on Protestant understandings of self-control and biblical commands against drunkenness. The organizational spirit of the Second Great Awakening generated numerous voluntary associations with active local societies, large membership, and many tracts and journals. During the 1840s, an argument for moderation and against drunkenness turned into a brief for total abstinence as the only solution to the nation's lack of temperance. New associations emerged that reflected this shift in rationale: the Independent Order of Good Templars, the Sons of Temperance, the Templars of Honor and Temperance and, after the Civil War, the Anti-Saloon League, and the Prohibition Party.

Demand for abstinence led to the first legislation to ban the sale and distribution of alcohol. In 1851 Maine took the lead in passing laws to ban the sale of alcohol except for medicinal and manufacturing purposes. By 1855, 12 states had passed similar measures. Prohibition proved to be a divisive issue and spawned a number of independent parties and political candidates at the state level, especially in Ohio and New York but also in Delaware and Maryland. Neither Whigs nor Democrats were skillful enough to shepherd evangelical temperance demands for party gains. In fact, evangelical dissatisfaction with both Whigs and Democrats over temperance fueled the appeal in the 1850s of the American Party.

Dissolution of the Second-Party System

As volatile as temperance, Anti-Masonry, and Sabbatarianism were for American politics during the antebellum era, antislavery and anti-Catholicism proved that the separation of church and state was incapable of adjudicating the demands of either religious-inspired reforms or Protestant-based defenses of a republican order. The radical antislavery movement emerged among revivalist Protestants during the 1830s, citing slavery as the gravest example of the young nation's compromise with sin. Charles Finney, the greatest revivalist of the era, spoke out vociferously against slavery and added vigor to an emerging

abolitionist movement. But the demands for immediate emancipation proved divisive among even those who opposed slavery. Some abolitionists split from the American Colonization Society in 1838 and then the American Anti-Slavery Society a few years later. Voluntary societies were not the only casualties; Methodists and Baptists split along sectional lines in 1844 over demands to condemn slavery.

With its failure to unite Protestants, the antislavery movement found other political outlets that stemmed more from rising sectionalism than from moral rectitude. Free-soil spokespersons and Northerners opposed to the expansion of slavery in the West became prominent allies of the movement. In turn, third parties emerged that sapped the electoral strength of both the Whigs and the Democrats. The Liberty Party significantly hurt the Whigs by attracting enough votes to prevent the election of Henry Clay in 1844. The Democrats were not immune from antislavery attempts, at least in the North. The Free Soil Party upended the Democrats in 1848 and pointed forward to the emergence of the Republican Party.

If Protestants lost the chance to rally around the antislavery cause in the pursuit of righteous politics, the increasing presence of Roman Catholics in the United States gave them another opportunity for unity. But anti-Catholicism, which turned primarily on older arguments about the affinity between Protestantism and republicanism, further unraveled the two-party system dominated by Whigs and Democrats. Protestant hostility was steeped in religious disputes and wars going back to the English Civil War of the 1640s and Whig hostility to the Stuart monarchy fueled antagonism to Roman Catholicism. During the 1830s and 1840s, anti-Catholicism became politically explicit as white American Protestants reacted to economic uncertainty and political upheaval.

In 1845 the founding of the Order of the Star Spangled Banner tapped these hostilities. Originally a secret society whose aim was to prevent immigrants and Roman Catholics from holding elected office, this association eventually blossomed into the Know-Nothing Party, nicknamed for its response to questions about the party and efforts to maintain its secrecy. Between 1854 and 1855, the party was one of the fastest growing in the United States, and it tapped voters in both the North and the South. By 1856 it had adopted the name the American Party and had sapped enough of the Whig Party's support for many to think the American Party's presidential nominee, Millard Fillmore, might have a chance in the general election. But again the issue of bringing slavery into the territories could not prevent the American Party from splitting, with many of its northern members deserting to the Republican Party.

Although evangelicals faulted the American Party for its initial secrecy and intolerance of foreign-born Americans, anti-Catholicism was an important piece of a religiously inspired defense of republicanism. In fact, Roman Catholicism shared qualities with slavery and alcohol that it made anti-Catholicism a plausible prejudice for those committed to antislavery and temperance. Native Protestants easily associated drinking with Roman Catholics because the cultures from which many of the new immigrants came—those of Ireland and Germany—encouraged the consumption of alcohol, not to mention that Rome had never countenanced a policy of abstinence. Protestants also noted resemblances between slavery and Roman Catholicism because of the latter's hierarchical system of church government and the obedience that Rome demanded (at least on paper) of church members. Protestantism was considered the most republican form of Christianity while Rome stood for thralldom and dependence.

The net effect of religion on America's Second Party System was to show the inadequacies of the arrangement if not to unravel it all together. Religious-based reforms inspired new parties during the three decades before the Civil War that often wooed away voters from the Whigs and Democrats. In addition, the moral dilemma of slavery caused splits within the established parties along regional lines. In 1852 Whigs, Democrats, and the Free Soil Party each supported their own candidates in the presidential election. In 1856 the third party to run alongside Whigs and Democrats was the Republican Party. And in 1860, four candidates ran for the presidency—two Democrats (northern and southern), one Constitutional Union, and one Republican. By 1860 the Whigs no longer existed and the Democrats were seriously divided. Economic and political circumstances would have made the longevity of the Whig-Democrat system unlikely. But religion added significantly to the political instability that the parties and their candidates tried to negotiate.

Divided Allegiances

In the years between the Declaration of Independence and the outbreak of the Civil War, the United States emerged as a formally secular political order that was informally one of the most religious societies in the West. Although apparently in fundamental tension, secular politics and religious zeal turned out to be almost directly proportional. The disestablishment of Christianity, what some have called de-Christianization, was actually immensely useful for the popularity of religion in the United States. And yet, the religious fervor that Americans displayed between 1776 and 1865 did not prove as advantageous for America's political leaders. At times, faith could perform remarkable assistance in American public life. But it also proved especially difficult to govern and invariably competed with the major political parties for Americans' allegiance. Ironically, by conceding that religion is a private matter that government should not coerce, America's founders also established conditions that allowed religion to be even

more politically potent than it was in those states where the churches were still established.

FURTHER READING. John C. Abbott and Russell H. Conwell, *Lives of the Presidents of the United States of America*, 1882; Richard J. Carwardine, *Evangelicals and Antebellum Politics*, 1993; Thomas J. Curry, *The First Freedoms: Church and State in America to the Passage of the First Amendment*, 1986; C. C. Goen, *Broken Churches, Broken Nation: Denominational Schisms and the Coming of the Civil War*, 1985; Allen C. Guelzo, *Abraham Lincoln: Redeemer President*, 1999; Philip Hamburger, *The Separation of Church and State*, 2002; Nathan O. Hatch, *The Democratization of American Christianity*, 1989; Daniel Walker Howe, *The Political Culture of American Whigs*, 1973; Rhys Isaac, *The Transformation of Virginia, 1740–1790*, 1982; Curtis D. Johnson, *Redeeming America: Evangelicals and the Road to the Civil War*, 1993; Isaac Kramnick and R. Laurence Moore, *The Godless Constitution: The Case against Religious Correctness*, 1997; William G. McLoughlin, *New England Dissent, 1630–1833: The Baptists and the Separation of Church and State*, 2 vols., 1971; Mark A. Noll, *America's God: From Jonathan Edwards to Abraham Lincoln*, 2002; Timothy L. Smith, *Revivalism and Social Reform: American Protestantism on the Eve of the Civil War*, revised ed., 1980.

D. G. HART

religion and politics, 1865–1945

Religious institutions were among the most influential forces shaping American culture and society from 1865 to 1945. Every major religious group experienced tremendous growth in numbers and institutional might in this period even as Protestantism, the largest and most influential religious group in 1864, lost its prominence in the public arena after 1920.

American Religion on the Eve of the Civil War

By the beginning of the Civil War, the power of religion in America was perhaps best expressed in its theological and political ideals and its cultural influence rather than in its actual numerical dominance. Only about 25 percent of Americans were members of religious institutions at the time of the Civil War, and the majority of those belonged to Protestant institutions. Nevertheless, most Americans—Protestants, Catholics, and those belonging to smaller groups like Jews, spiritualists, and others—adhered to a fairly uniform set of assumptions. Beyond a simple belief in God, most assumed God was a personal being involved in the intricacies of human life who intended that humans adhere to moral certainties that were easily discerned through revelation or common sense, and that life as a member of a family, community, and nation connected to God's providence. Moreover, even though only about one-fourth of Americans were formal members of religious institutions, far more attended local congregations, read religious literature, attended schools that promoted religious belief, or were conversant in biblical or Christian theological ideas. Even Native Americans, who practiced non-European religions, interacted with Christianity in degrees ranging from conversion to syncretism to rejection.

If religious Americans of European origin held to these general theological assumptions, most also believed America—and, most important, its Republican or Democratic political ideals and institutions—marked the highest stage of God's providential development of human beings. For religious Americans—in the North or the South; slave or free; Protestant, Catholic, Jew, theosophist, or do-it-yourselfer—the lineaments of religious belief, philosophy, political and economic activity, family, and community were almost seamless. To be religious was to be American; to be American was to be religious.

As those who believed God's providence established the United States as a "city on a hill," religious Americans were also aware of the difficulties in discerning and then living up to that providential plan. Seen most clearly in the antebellum dispute over slavery but also in the anti-Catholicism (among Protestants), anti-Mormonism, and temperance movements, as well as other causes that enlisted the debate and activity of religious Americans, commitments to common sense–based certainty and patriotic millennialism drove Christians into conflict that ranged from anti-Catholic violence to the Civil War itself.

Post–Civil War Structural Developments

By 1865, then, Americans still held to these essential theological and political ideals but faced both the consequences of having pushed those ideals to bloodshed as well as the need to address an emerging American landscape that would look increasingly different from the one in 1860. Specifically, religious Americans addressed and adapted themselves and their institutions to the most important historical trends of this period: migrations of people westward within America, and immigration into America from overseas; urbanization; industrialization; war and the emergence of America as a world power; and new patterns of thought such as pragmatism, theological liberalism/modernism, and evolution.

Shaping such connections among religion, politics, and society between 1865 and 1945 was the striking and unprecedented numerical growth among religious groups in America, which was marked by growing institutional predominance with centralization and professionalization, increasing diversity in terms of new religious belief, ethnicity, and schisms within older religious groups, and new theological, philosophical, and social ideas emerging from the engagement with urbanization and new intellectual patterns. Because of such growth in real numbers and influence, if it was not the case before the Civil War, it became increasingly the case afterward that

America was, if not a "Christian nation," then certainly a nation of believers.

In 1865 the majority of American churchgoers remained affiliated with Protestant denominations, and this remained true up to 1945, as these denominations grew at extraordinary rates. Methodists, the largest Protestant denomination in 1860 with about 2 million members, grew to about 5.5 million members in 1900 and then to just under 12 million in 1950. Baptists grew from 1 million to 4.5 million to 15 million in that same period, passing Methodists as the largest Protestant denomination. Other Protestant denominations such as the Lutherans, Presbyterians, Episcopalians, Congregationalists, and Disciples of Christ grew in similar scale.

At the same time, however, non-Protestant or groups on the fringes of Protestantism grew in like manner, challenging Protestant hegemony. Roman Catholics, for example, became the largest single Christian religious body in the nation before the Civil War, with just under 5 million adherents. Catholic numbers exploded due to post–Civil War immigration to approximately 10 million by 1900 and well over 20 million by 1950. Likewise, Holiness and Pentecostal denominations (Church of God in Christ, Church of God–Cleveland Tennessee, Church of the Nazarene, Assemblies of God, and others) emerged at the turn of the century; drawing on older traditions of moral certitude, a belief in the human perfection, and the experience of religious ecstasy, along with speaking in tongues and healing, they forged a movement that by the end of the twentieth century was probably the most pervasive and dynamic Christian body worldwide, claiming 100 million and possibly as high as 500 million adherents. This movement would provide the backbone of the religious right of the late twentieth century. Like Pentecostals, Eastern Orthodoxy (primarily Russian and Greek), the Church of Jesus Christ of Latter-Day Saints, and eastern religions (especially Buddhism and Confucianism), grew between 1865 and 1945, but did so especially after 1945.

The late nineteenth and early twentieth centuries also saw the emergence of spiritualist and adventist groups. Though these groups were often rooted in antebellum patterns of thought, groups such as the Christian Science movement of Mary Baker Eddy, the Jehovah's Witnesses, the Theosophical Society of Madame H. P. Blavatsky, Mesmerism, and other mind cures or loosely Christian adventists prospered in the twentieth century and, in some cases, especially overseas. Sometimes, as in the case of Christian Science and its *Christian Science Monitor*, these groups exerted a political and social influence beyond their actual number of adherents.

American Judaism also prospered and grew in this period. Before the 1890s, most American Jews were of German origin and clustered in cities such as Cincinnati, Ohio, or Charleston, South Carolina. These were often Reform Jews who mitigated the strictures of the Torah according to American cultural, political, and social customs. Immigration from Eastern Europe, and especially Russia, brought the number of Jews in the United States to nearly 1 million by 1900, and then to about 5 million by 1950. These Eastern European Jews saw immigration as a means to exercise their religious practices freely; hence, many of these immigrants established conservative or orthodox synagogues as they sought initially to be faithful Jews rather than assimilated Americans.

Finally, Native American religious belief systems declined in the number of adherents throughout the second half of the nineteenth century through Christian missionary activity, persecution, and privatization of Native American lands under the 1887 Dawes Severalty Act or syncretism with or conversion to Christianity. One prominent example of such syncretism was the Ghost Dance movement of the Plains Indians, which, as taught by the Piute prophet Wovoka, merged Christian patterns of millennialism with traditional Native American religious beliefs, teaching that participation in a series of rituals (the Ghost Dance) would hasten a millennial world as well as happiness in the here and now. The movement was suppressed by the 1890s, most infamously at the Wounded Knee Massacre of 1890. Native American religion experienced revival, however, under the Indian Reorganization Act of 1934, which not only restored tribal lands and governance but encouraged the practice of traditional religions.

Immigration and Nativism

As noted, the swell of immigration that lasted from the 1870s to the 1920s from China (until the Exclusion Act of 1882), Japan, and Europe led to tremendous growth among certain groups—Roman Catholics, Jews, and Lutherans especially. But immigration had other consequences as well, for as many immigrants connected ethnicity to religion, some religious groups experienced fragmentation along ethnic lines. For example, Swedes, Norwegians, and other immigrants from Scandinavia established their own Lutheran bodies, while Catholics from Poland, Portugal, Austria, Italy, Germany, Bohemia, and elsewhere solidified their own parish identities and regularly fought with the established Irish leadership for control; one extreme example was the establishment of the Polish National Catholic Church in 1904. Jewish immigration also led to fragmentation as Jewish synagogues aligned themselves along three lines: Reform (generally Americanized Jews from previous immigrations), Conservative, and Orthodox (the latter two made up largely of immigrants arriving after 1890).

Another way that ethnicity connected to religion was in the way some Protestants connected Roman Catholicism (and, later in the early twentieth century, Judaism) to ethnicity in periodic outbreaks of nativism. As far back as the Puritan era, many

Protestants had opposed, sometimes with violence, Catholics on theological and—especially in the antebellum period—political grounds, arguing that Catholic allegiance to the Papacy threatened the basis of American Democracy. After the Civil War, this theological or political anti-Catholicism—most often expressed in struggles over public funding for Catholic education—combined with fears of urbanization and xenophobia in the form of nativism. Nativists, many of whom were explicitly Protestant, blamed immigrants—especially Catholic and Jewish immigrants—for the vices of cities, local political corruption (bossism), radical political ideas, and a perceived shift in America away from its Protestant culture. Nativist activity was especially prominent in the 1890s and 1920s and expressed institutionally through the American Protective Association (APA) in the late nineteenth century and the Ku Klux Klan in the 1920s.

Progressivism, Modern Organization, and the Social Gospel

As all these religious groups grew in number they also organized themselves along the lines of the emerging corporate culture of the late nineteenth and early twentieth centuries, borrowing the language and concepts of centralization and efficiency to create some of the most prominent and powerful institutions in the country. Protestant denominations, Roman Catholic dioceses, Spiritualists, Buddhists, and even Native Americans (who formed the Native American Church in 1918 to legally protect the use of peyote) centralized the governance of their own institutions, professionalized their clerical ranks, established colleges, graduate schools, and seminaries or divinity schools, and funneled money into clerical pensions and especially missionary activities at home and abroad and to social services. Much of this centralization took place within denominational structures already in place; Protestant denominations, Mormons, Adventists, Jehovah's Witnesses, and others funded missionaries, especially to China and Asia in the twentieth century; Roman Catholics founded the Catholic Foreign Missionary Society in 1911 in Maryknoll, New York, which focused on Central and South America. Catholics also established the National Catholic Welfare Conference (originating in 1917 as the National Catholic War Council), which, under Monsignor John A. Ryan, voiced the needs of the poor among Catholics. Missionary activities, especially in China, the Philippines, and Central and South America, dovetailed in friendly or hostile ways with growing American military and commercial interests abroad.

Along with denominational initiatives, organizations such as the Federal Council of Churches (1908) and the Synagogue Council (1926) established organizational ties across institutions. More important, though, organizations outside denominational and church institutions also organized with great efficiency and impact. Rooted in the volunteer societies of the antebellum period, national religious groups formed to address specific problems or to engage in missionary work. Some of the most prominent were the Young Men's (and Women's) Christian Associations (YMCA and YWCA), which strove to protect young men and women from the vices of city life; the Student Volunteer Movement, founded by John R. Mott, which sent young college graduates overseas as missionaries; the Women's Christian Temperance Union (WCTU) led by Frances Willard; the Knights of Columbus, which provided mutual aid for Roman Catholics; the Salvation Army, from England; the Catholic Worker movement (1933) of Dorothy Day and Peter Maurin, countless rural and urban holiness, Pentecostal, and apostolic groups that preached the Gospel in farming communities or storefront churches and also provided assistance to the poor; and the organizations, conferences, and schools that grew up around the most prominent independent preachers of the period such as Dwight L. Moody and Billy Sunday. These groups and personalities often competed with denominations in terms of loyalty and impact.

Even though the memberships of most religious bodies included more women than men, those that were extensions of denominations and churches, as well as most independent organizations, retained an almost completely male leadership and clergy. There were exceptions to this such as Christian Science and some holiness/Pentecostal groups. Women often organized or held prominent roles in organizations and missionary endeavors existing alongside these churches; the WCTU or Catholic Worker movement are prominent examples. The early twentieth century saw some movement toward ordination of women among Protestants, but most movement in this direction occurred after 1945. The Catholic Sisters, however, were at the heart of Catholic educational life and benevolence.

At the turn of the century, much of the activity of these and other institutions focused on alleviating the "social problem"—meaning urban poverty, political corruption (especially at the local level), and labor unrest. While in the antebellum period, volunteer societies had addressed issues like abolition and temperance, between the 1880s and the end of World War I, Protestants and many Catholics adopted what has come to be called the Social Gospel (though at the time religious leaders used the name "Applied Christianity").

For religious Americans, the "social problem," which came to prominence with Jacob Riis's *How the Other Half Lives* (1891) and Henry George's *Progress and Poverty* (1879), involved urban poverty and its attendant vices, which were often associated with Catholic or Jewish immigrants. For this reason, some Social Gospel advocates were implicitly or explicitly nativist or promoted Anglo-Saxon superiority (Josiah Strong and his *Our Country* [1885], for example).

Often, too, the social problem was connected to the specter of "class warfare," the assumption being that if economic conditions in American cities fell to the point of "European conditions," America would find itself in a war between the middle class and the politically radicalized "masses." To stay the advance of such a class war, many religious Americans turned to older forms of benevolence—assisting the poor, fighting alcohol consumption, and so on. Those who adopted the Social Gospel, however, employed the new social science of sociology; social scientific theories of education, liberal, or modernist theology; and forms of social evolution—in short, progressivism—to forge a systemic approach to urban poverty, education, and work. Social Gospel advocates like Walter Rauschenbusch, Washington Gladden, and Richard T. Ely wanted clerics trained in the social sciences to use political and educational means to alter systems of vice, oppression, and urban corruption in order to end the social problem. In their minds, such political and otherwise practical endeavors would introduce the Kingdom of God—a new social and political system based on love and justice—to the world. This movement was especially prominent in cities outside the South and in Protestant divinity schools.

Even though Protestants were more visible in organizing activities associated with the Social Gospel, Catholics, too, engaged in such thought, often with a more radical edge. Based on the criticism of capitalism and call for social justice in Pope Leo XIII's 1891 encyclical letter *Rerum Novarum* (Of New Things), which was restated in 1931 when Pope Pius XI issued *Quadragesimo Anno* (In the Fortieth Year), groups like the Catholic Worker movement put social action in place that was in some ways more radical that Protestants. The Catholic Worker movement associated with radical political and intellectual movements and explicitly challenged a belief in capitalism.

After World War I, as intellectuals gradually dismissed many of the progressive ideals touting human progress and perfectibility through education and reform, the ideals of the Social Gospel gave way in seminaries, universities, and divinity schools, at least among Protestants, to the theological "Neo-Orthodoxy" of the 1930s and 1940s. This Neo-Orthodoxy, which drew on the thinking of Swiss Theologian Karl Barth and Americans Reinhold Niebuhr and H. Richard Niebuhr, professed little confidence in human perfection, stressing instead, and in different ways, the transcendent gap between God (or philosophical ideals) and the mire of the human condition.

Fragmentation, Schism, and the Fundamentalist-Modernist Controversy

The growth and centralization of institutional life also brought about fragmentation and schism among Protestants just as pressures from immigration brought schism to American Judaism and

Catholicism. In the late nineteenth century, many Protestants, especially in the Upper South and Midwest, drew on the same fears about centralization and hierarchy that had earlier produced groups like the Disciples of Christ and Primitive Baptists. Many rural practitioners worried that the new institutions favored leaders from larger urban churches, while others worried that centralized plans for setting amounts and distributing missionary funds were inherently antidemocratic. Often these concerns coupled with theological emphases on holiness, antimissionary Calvinism, or religious ecstasy to produce a number of separatist groups that formed their own denominations. Already mentioned are the holiness and Pentecostal groups, black and white, that formed with these emphases; other important Protestant groups included Landmark Baptists and the Churches of Christ, which split from the Disciples of Christ. Similar struggles in ethnic churches pitted those who wished to retain Old World languages and theological emphases against those who more openly embraced the English language and American intellectual and political ideals. Such tensions were especially strong among certain Lutherans and Dutch Calvinists. Catholics, too, struggled between allegiance to the worldwide church with it Eurocentric emphases, practices, and ideals, and allegiance to American ideals such as congregational autonomy and the separation of church and state. This struggle in America often paralleled European struggles between liberal and ultramontane leaders and theologians. Supporters of Ultramontane Catholicism, drawing on Pope Pius IX's *Syllabus of Errors* (1864), generally condemned political liberalism and the separation of church and state.

The major Protestant denominations in the North (Presbyterians, Methodists, remained separated as northern and southern bodies until 1983 and 1939, respectively) experienced schism most acutely in the fundamentalist-modernist controversy that extended roughly from the Presbyterian heresy trial of Charles A. Briggs in 1892 to the Scopes Trial of 1925. Other denominations, because they were decentralized (such as the Lutherans) or more uniform theologically (as with southern denominations and Roman Catholics), avoided this schism over the control of denominations.

The fundamentalist-modernist controversy involved some elements of the concerns over centralization but focused more on theological and intellectual innovations that were sweeping the nation and on who would control denominational machinery—in particular, the governance of overseas missionaries and the divinity schools and seminaries.

Theological modernism emerged out of Europe—especially Germany—as well as from Unitarian and theologically experimental institutions of higher education in the United States. It challenged a number of traditional assumptions about the origins and content of the Old and New Testaments and especially the relationship of theology to science and philosophy. Higher criticism of the Bible challenged traditions of authorship and dating in biblical documents along with the historical verifiability of biblical events and persons. For many, higher criticism of the Bible undercut the claims of authority that Christians believed it held. Other thinkers challenged theological claims of Christian exclusivity in light of increasing knowledge of world religions. And the introductions of Darwinism, philosophical positivism, historicism, ethical pragmatism, and the ideas of Karl Marx, Sigmund Freud, and others challenged traditional views concerning the unity of theology, philosophy, and science. Unlike the challenges to religion itself from science, skeptics, or atheists, modernist theology attempted to adapt modern thought and criticism to the basic tenets of Christianity in order to save it by modernizing it. Modernist thinkers also generally adopted social scientific views about human nature and society consistent with the Social Gospel. The impact of modernism was strongest in northern and midwestern denominations. Southern Protestants were more uniformly resistant to modernism, while the Roman Catholic hierarchy also resisted it.

As theological modernists became increasingly vocal and gained leadership in northern Protestant denominations, traditionalists began to challenge them. The first challenge to gain widespread notoriety was the trial of Charles A. Briggs in 1892. Briggs, a northern Presbyterian and professor of biblical literature at New York's Union Seminary, was tried and acquitted of heresy by the Presbytery of New York for accepting certain tenets of higher criticism. At the same time, conservatives attempted to wrest control of missionary activities, fearing that modernists saw missions as an extension of the Social Gospel and therefore a program for social service rather than for preaching the gospel.

As the opponents to modernism coalesced, their leaders became known as "fundamentalists," so named for a series of books called *The Fundamentals*, published from 1910 to 1917 and edited by A. C. Dixon and R. A. Torrey. Although conservatives, led by figures such as Dixon, Torrey, and J. Gresham Machen of Princeton Seminary eventually lost control over their denominations (many left to form their own), fundamentalism became a larger cultural and religious movement by the early 1920s. It fought not only theological modernism but the Social Gospel, Bolshevism, and—especially—evolution, all of which, taken together, were seen as leading to atheism and the destruction of American society. Along with being theologically conservative, many in the movement also expressed a belief in divine healing and holiness as well as dispensational premillennialism, which taught that the world would continue to get worse as Satan ruled the present dispensation of time; only when God removed Christians from the world would Jesus return, redeem the earth, and establish the millennium through direct intervention. This belief system ran counter to the earlier nineteenth-century postmillennialism that expected human beings to work with God in perfecting the earth and establishing the millennium—a belief that had prompted countless nineteenth-century reform movements, including abolitionism.

This stage of the fundamentalist movement peaked at the 1925 Scopes Monkey Trial in Dayton, Tennessee, in which William Jennings Bryan battled Clarence Darrow over John T. Scopes's right to teach evolution in the schools. Bryan, arguing for the prosecution against Scopes, won the legal battle in Dayton, but fundamentalists lost the war for American culture, as media personalities such as H. L. Mencken and Reverend Henry Emerson Fosdick cast fundamentalists as rural yokels attempting to point Americans in a backward direction. Fundamentalist Protestants continued, however, to prosper, establishing radio ministries, Bible colleges, missionary endeavors, publications, and other institutions. Their numbers grew and their institutions strengthened throughout the middle of the twentieth century, even though their public voice was restricted largely to radio preaching. They were poised, however, to reappear with Billy Graham in the 1950s and later with conservative political movements.

African American Christianity

Much of what characterized white religious activity also characterized that of African-American Christianity, but with some important exceptions. In the North, free blacks had formed their own denominations in the antebellum period, mostly in cities like Philadelphia and New York. The two most important were the African Methodist Episcopal (AME) and the African Methodist Episcopal Zion (AMEZ) churches, both of which experienced growth rates similar to other religious groups between 1865 and 1945.

Southern black religion developed in the crucible of slavery, so although the southern blacks shared certain beliefs with whites and northern blacks—conversion, baptism, and in some cases ecstatic worship—the historical context of slavery meant many shared beliefs took on profoundly different meanings. Furthermore, in the South, the black church became the central social and political institution for the developing African American community and culture.

Although introduced to Christianity by whites, slaves quickly made it their own as they developed the "secret institution"—secret meetings held in "brush harbors" beyond white control. These secret meetings provided sanctuary as slaves developed their own rituals and beliefs, selected their own leaders, and found release through religious ecstasy. Slaves also synthesized Christianity in varying degrees with African and Caribbean religious beliefs.

After 1865, African Americans quickly established churches free, as much as possible, from white control. Black Baptists, who developed into the largest body of black Christians, formed their own state conventions immediately after the Civil War, though they continued to utilize help from southern and northern whites (and eventually formed the National Baptist Convention). Black missionaries from the AME and AMEZ churches established congregations throughout the South, while southern whites helped draw some blacks into their own separate, white-controlled denominations such as the Colored Methodist Episcopal Church. Catholic Parishes in the South typically followed this latter pattern.

As with white denominations in this period, such growth involved conflict that almost always had racial overtones. The two primary axes of conflict were between urban, middle-class blacks and rural blacks on the one hand, and conflict between blacks and northern and southern whites on the other. Many middle-class urban African Americans who attempted to earn cultural, social, and political equality through "respectability" produced increasing class tensions in the late nineteenth century within and among different churches as they saw poor, uneducated, and often rural blacks with their ecstatic worship and uneducated preachers as a hindrance to racial uplift. These class-related tensions fueled both intradenominational (localists versus denominational centralizers) and interdenominational warfare—especially between the more middle-class AME/AMEZ churches and the more rural Baptists. In terms of black/white tensions, blacks often needed northern whites' resources but resented white control and paternalism. Also, southern whites offered blacks land, money, and education, but such benevolence was not only coupled with paternalism but white supremacy.

African American churches also became enclaves against the subtle or overt horrors of postbellum racism as they continued to nurture black leadership and to provide relief, mutual aid, and secondary and higher education. At the same time, the church functioned as the primary public sphere for black men and women in southern society through education, preaching, and moral reform designed to gain equality with whites. Black women were often at the forefront of these endeavors. Especially before the imposition of legal vote restriction and Jim Crow in the 1890s, for black men, and especially black preachers, the church provided the primary base for political involvement and mobilization aimed at securing suffrage and civil equality. Like white Protestants, blacks coupled their conceptions of spiritual freedom and equality with republican notions of individual and social freedom and American millennialism. This would become evident in the civil rights movement of the 1950s and 1960s.

By the turn of the century, black Baptists and various other independent congregations practiced a Pentecostal style of worship and ecstasy. Many African Americans also accepted the practices of healing, the second blessing, and the Baptism of the Holy

Spirit common to Pentecostalism. By the middle of the twentieth century, black Pentecostal groups were the second largest group of black Christians behind the Baptists.

Loss of a Mainstream Protestant Political Voice

Through the twentieth century, even as white Protestant churches and denominations grew in number and strengthened denominational infrastructures, and influenced ideas, social patterns, laws (Prohibition), and the like, Protestantism also experienced an increasing alienation from and lack of influence in the public arenas it had dominated in the nineteenth century. It would be hard to call this phenomenon "secularization" in light of the institutional and numerical growth among not just Protestants but religious groups generally in this period. But in the realm of politics, arts, literature, and higher education, Protestant leaders gave way to other, often nonreligious ones. Partly because of the general cultural and intellectual assault on progressivism and the Social Gospel, partly as fallout from the Scopes trial, and partly from new models and criteria for professional achievement and celebrity, by the 1920s, Protestant ministers and theologians disappeared from state dinners and no longer oversaw large reform movements. They yielded to figures like Walter Lippmann, thinkers like John Dewey, and popular novelists regarding the moral instruction of the public, and turned public education over to teachers trained under Dewey's educational ideas and secular leaders in institutions of higher education (exceptions would include Reinhold Niebuhr, Billy Graham, and by the 1960s, Dr. Martin Luther King Jr.). All the while, Protestants shared the American public stage with Catholics, Jews, and village atheists like Mencken and Darrow. Ironically, even as Protestants, Catholics, and religious Americans in general experienced tremendous growth numerically and institutionally between 1865 and 1945, Protestants, who in 1860 held pervasive cultural and social sway over the nation, saw their influence decline.

FURTHER READING. Catherine L. Albanese, *A Republic of Mind and Spirit: A Cultural History of American Metaphysical Religion*, 2007; Joel Carpenter, *Revive Us Again: The Reawakening of American Fundamentalism*, 1997; Jay Dolan, *The American Catholic Experience*, 1992; Edwin Scott Gaustad and Philip L. Barlow, eds., *New Historical Atlas of Religion in America*, 2001; Robert T. Handy, *A Christian America*, 1971; Paul Harvey, *Freedom's Coming*, 2005; William R. Hutchison, *Between the Times: The Travail of the Protestant Establishment in America, 1900–1960*, 1989; George M. Marsden, *Fundamentalism and American Culture*, 1980; Martin Marty, *Modern American Religion*, 3 vols., 1986; John T. McGreevy, *Catholicism and American Freedom: A History*, 2003; Grant Wacker, *Heaven Below*, 2001; Robert Wuthnow, *The Restructuring of American Religion*, 1988.

JOE CREECH

religion and politics since 1945

The United States in the second half of the twentieth century was, paradoxically, both very secular and very religious. Like most other industrialized democracies, it conducted its daily business in a pragmatic and down-to-earth way. At the same time, however, most of its citizens believed that an omnipotent God was watching over them. While the church membership rate in Western Europe had dwindled to just 4 or 5 percent, in the United States it was still over 50 percent. American religion and politics, meanwhile, were linked in complex ways, even though the First Amendment to the Constitution specified their separation.

No aspirant to high political office could be indifferent to religious questions, and every school board in the country had to wrestle with the problem of what religious symbols and activities they should allow on their campuses without displeasing the Supreme Court. The evangelist Billy Graham befriended every president between Harry Truman and George W. Bush, and all of them valued his goodwill. As recently as 2007, the governor of Georgia held a meeting on the steps of his state capitol, during a drought, to beseech God for rain.

European sociologists early in the twentieth century predicted a continuous process of secularization for industrial societies, and the experience of most nations vindicated them. Why was the United States such an exception? Numerous theories were offered at the time. One was that the United States had such a diverse population, drawn from so many immigrant groups (voluntary and unfree), that religion was used to hold on to the vestiges of an older identity. Rural Italian immigrants, for example, had to turn themselves into urban industrial workers when they came to America and had to learn English, but they could still be Roman Catholics. A second theory was that a highly mobile population sought a proxy form of community and found it by joining churches as they moved from one city to the next. A third was that church-state separation, which denied state support to any church, forced religious leaders to act like businessmen, seeking out "customers" and making sure they offered a "product" to the liking of their clients; otherwise they would not get paid. A fourth, often advanced during an upsurge in religiosity in the 1950s, was that the fear of annihilation in a nuclear war was so intense that it drove anxious men and women back to churches and synagogues for reassurance. All these theories could find empirical support; together they went far to explain the anomalous American situation.

The Cold War

Many Americans perceived the cold war as a conflict of both political and religious significance, in which the United States, champion of religion, confronted "godless communism." Emphasizing that America stood not just for democratic capitalism but also for religious freedom was a way of sharpening and clarifying the face-off. Among the organizations advocating militant anti-Communist policies in the 1950s was the Christian Anti-Communist Crusade, whose leader, Fred Schwartz, regarded communism as a substitute religion, a horrible parody of Christianity. President Dwight Eisenhower inspired some observers and amused others by declaring that America itself made no sense without "a deeply held religious faith—and I don't care what it is!" This was a way of affirming a point that was later made more formally by sociologist Robert Bellah: that America has a civil religion in addition to its citizens' many particular religions. Eisenhower also authorized the inclusion of the phrase "under God" in the Pledge of Allegiance and the stamping of "In God We Trust" on currency.

The fact that America's defense policy was based on nuclear deterrence added an apocalyptic dimension to the cold war. A nuclear war could do the kind of world-shattering damage that until then only God had been able to accomplish—and that he had promised Noah he would never do again after the great flood. Nuclear weapons themselves occasioned an anguished religious debate. Twenty-two Protestant theologians from the Federal Council of Churches declared that the bombing of Hiroshima and Nagasaki in August 1945 was "morally indefensible." The editors of the *Catholic World* agreed, adding that America had "struck the most powerful blow ever delivered against Christian civilization and the moral law." The hardheaded neo-orthodox theologian Reinhold Niebuhr, a man highly respected among foreign policy makers, wrote in *The Irony of American History* (1952) that America had created for itself an intolerable paradox. Posing as the defender of Christian civilization, it was able to make good on the commitment only by threatening to use a weapon so fearsome, and so indiscriminate, that it would make a mockery of its users' claim that they believed in a righteous and loving God.

Civil Rights

The cold war standoff persisted through the 1950s as the United States underwent dynamic changes. None was more significant than the civil rights movement, whose activist phase began in late 1955 with the Montgomery bus boycott. Energized by the Supreme Court's school desegregation decision in *Brown v. Board of Education* (1954), the Montgomery Improvement Association persuaded African Americans not to ride the city's segregated buses until the company changed its seating policy. Martin Luther King Jr., a Baptist minister, took command of the boycott and guided it to victory after nearly 13 months. A native of Atlanta whose father was also a prominent minister, King developed a superb preaching style. Boycott meetings in Montgomery were closely akin

to religious revivals; hymn singing and his passionate sermons strengthened the boycotters' sense of unity and determination to persist.

King went on to become a leader of the nationwide civil rights movement, which succeeded in prompting Congress, over the next decade, to abolish all legally enforced racial segregation and to guarantee the vote to African Americans for the first time since Reconstruction. He had the knack of linking immediate circumstances in the South to transcendent questions of religious significance, a skill demonstrated in his "Letter from Birmingham Jail" (1963), which compared his work to that of Jesus and St. Paul in the early Christian communities. It is no coincidence that King and nearly all the other early civil rights movement leaders (Ralph Abernathy, Fred Shuttlesworth, Jesse Jackson, and others) were clergymen. Ministers enjoyed high status in the segregated African American community and often brokered agreements between whites and blacks. King, moreover, knew how to appeal to whites as well as blacks in a language drenched in biblical imagery—both races honored the scriptures. The fact that he was also able to achieve a high level of nonviolence gave his group, the Southern Christian Leadership Conference, the moral high ground, and worked effectively on the consciences of white voters.

Religion and Politics

The success of the civil rights movement was to have profound consequences not just for African Americans but also for the two main political parties. The Democrats' electoral base had long been the white Solid South, but as southern blacks began to vote Democrat after the Voting Rights Act of 1965, growing numbers of southern whites began to switch their allegiance to the Republican Party. Party politics was also changed in 1960 by the election of a Roman Catholic, John F. Kennedy, to the presidency. The only other Catholic to run for the presidency up to that time, Al Smith, had been soundly beaten in the election of 1928, partly because southern whites, most of them evangelical Christians, had refused to vote for a Catholic. Anti-Catholicism had a long history in America by 1960, some of it lowbrow bigotry, symbolized by episodes of anti-Catholic rioting in nineteenth-century cities. It could also be refined and well read, however, as Paul Blanshard's best-selling *American Freedom and Catholic Power* (1949) bore witness. Blanshard, whose book was favorably reviewed in all the mainstream media, argued that Catholics' loyalty to an absolute monarch, the pope, overrode their loyalty to the nation, making them dubious citizens. He even suggested that Catholics, like Communists, were an internal fifth column, threatening the future of the republic. Kennedy, in the run-up to the 1960 election, appeared before a meeting of evangelical Protestant ministers in Houston and denied having divided loyalties. He later joked to advisors that it was unreasonable for

Blanshard and others to suspect him of disloyalty because he was such a bad Catholic!

During the Kennedy administration, the Supreme Court, under the leadership of Chief Justice Earl Warren, who was already controversial because of the *Brown* decision, issued its findings in several church-state cases: *Engel v. Vitale* (1962), *Murray v. Curlett* (1963), and *School District of Abington Township v. Schempp* (1963). The Court ruled that collective prayers in public school classrooms, then widespread, were a violation of the First Amendment. So, too, were Bible reading and recitation of the Ten Commandments. The cases had been brought by an alliance of Unitarians, Jews, and atheists, who wanted to strengthen the wall of separation between church and state. Most other religious groups protested against this breach of American tradition, with some arguing that it would give comfort to the Communists and diminish the religious dimensions of the cold war. Numerous draft constitutional amendments appeared before Congress in the following years, trying to reinstate school prayer, but none won the necessary two-thirds majority. At almost the same time (1961), however, the Supreme Court upheld the conviction of Abraham Braunfeld, who claimed his free exercise of religion was abridged by the state of Pennsylvania. An orthodox Jew, Braunfeld closed his furniture store on Saturdays, but the state's Sunday closing laws forbade him to open it then, putting him at an unfair business disadvantage. The Court ruled against him, decreeing that Sunday closing laws served a compelling secular interest, even if their origin could be found in a religious practice.

In the following decades, however, the trend in church-state cases was toward an increasingly emphatic dissociation. In 1983 the Supreme Court even considered a case, *Lynch v. Donnelly*, involving government-owned illuminated Christmas displays—it decided to permit them if nonreligious items like candy canes, Santa Claus, and red-nosed reindeer were there, but to object if the exhibit comprised only a Christian crèche.

Vietnam

Soon after President Kennedy's death, the American escalation in Vietnam began. In the early days of American involvement, a Catholic doctor, Tom Dooley, who had served there in the 1950s, regarded the war as a battle between Christian South Vietnam and the Communist North; at first Cardinal Francis Spellman of New York and the American Catholic hierarchy agreed. Doubts about the "domino theory," however, along with the lack of a clear military objective and unease about the viability and integrity of the South Vietnamese ally, led to antiwar protests. Religious observers from many different traditions began to think of the war as power politics at its dirtiest—sacrificing Vietnam and its people because the risk of fighting the cold war in Europe was too great. Roger LaPorte, a young Catholic activist, set

fire to himself on the steps of the United Nations in 1965 to protest the war. An interfaith organization, Clergy and Laity Concerned about Vietnam (founded in 1966), agreed to put aside its members' religious differences in its campaign to end the war. It organized protests and sent a delegation to Secretary of Defense Robert McNamara, led by Rabbi Abraham Heschel, William Sloane Coffin (Protestant), and Daniel Berrigan (Catholic).

Berrigan, a Jesuit priest, also led a group of religious antiwar activists in invasions of two Selective Service offices in the Baltimore area. They poured blood over draft files in the first and set fire to files in the second with homemade napalm, then stood waiting to be arrested, explaining to local journalists the symbolic significance of their actions. Berrigan was convicted but went underground rather than to prison. For a year he was the romantic hero of the religious resistance, showing up unexpectedly to preach in different churches, then disappearing again before the police or FBI could arrest him.

Vietnam also raised anew question of religious conscientious objectors (COs). During World War II the judiciary had permitted members of the historic peace churches, Quakers, Mennonites, and Jehovah's Witnesses, to register as COs and to perform alternative service rather than enter the army. This rule persisted, but now, large numbers of draftees from other traditions also claimed that their consciences forbade them from serving in Vietnam. Such objectors found the Supreme Court partially sympathetic to their point of view in a 1970 decision that permitted objections based on "a deeply held and coherent ethical system," even if it had no explicit religious element. On the other hand, the Court added in a case the following year, CO status would not be granted to protesters against only some wars: it had to be all or nothing.

American Judaism

Another conflict, the 1967 Six-Day War between Israel and its Arab neighbors, had a very different effect on American religious history. It galvanized American Jews into a renewed sense of pride, identity, and concern for their community. Jews, only about 3 percent of the American population in 1945—most of them children or grandchildren of immigrants—had been preoccupied with assimilation, often trying to minimize the distinctive elements of their way of life. Except among a handful of Orthodox communities, mainly in the New York area, Jews tended to blend in rather than stand out in the 1950s and early 1960s. Many opted to join Conservative synagogues, to keep kosher tradition at home but not elsewhere, not to wear distinctive garments like the *kippah* in public, and at times even to placate their fretful children in December by celebrating Christmas. Intermarriage rates between Christians and Jews rose steadily.

Three trends changed this trajectory toward assimilation. First was Israel, which since its creation in 1948 had to fight for its existence. Israel's leaders hoped that well-to-do American Jews would migrate there, bringing their wealth, education, and skills. Most declined to do so, but they did lobby on behalf of Israel, made sure its point of view was well represented in Congress, and sent financial contributions. Second was the rediscovery of the Holocaust. Many Jews' first instinct had been to forget about it—very little literature discussed it in the 1950s—but after Hannah Arendt's *Eichmann in Jerusalem* (1963) it became a central issue in American Jewish education and self-definition; her book was followed by a flood of Holocaust-related literature. Third was the Six-Day War itself, which, though it ended victoriously for Israel, showed that Jews still faced terrifying enemies eager to annihilate them. In the aftermath, contributions to Israel and American Jews' decision to migrate there rose sharply. Modern Orthodoxy began to develop in the late 1960s and 1970s, a form of Judaism that permitted full engagement in American life without compromising religious distinctiveness and observance. Ensuring American Jews' support, meanwhile, remained a high priority among Israeli politicians. It led to a controversy, which continues to the present, over whether "the Jewish lobby" is a disproportionately powerful element in American political life and whether it prompts the American government to act in ways that are more beneficial to Israel than to the United States itself.

Abortion Politics

The 1960s witnessed great social turbulence and a rapid shift in public mores, many of which had religious and political implications. The women's movement, for example, lobbied for the abolition of gender discrimination in employment and raised a variety of questions under the previously unfamiliar category of "sexual politics."

One was the issue of abortion, which has convulsed American religious and political life ever since. The Supreme Court ruled in *Roe v. Wade* (1973) that women could legally obtain abortions in the first trimester of a pregnancy and, with some restrictions, in later stages of pregnancy. The decision overturned laws in all 50 states. It delighted feminists who had been working for revision of restrictive abortion laws, in line with their belief that women should have the right to choose whether or not to give birth. But it horrified those believers who considered an unborn fetus to be a human being and who saw the ruling, in effect, as authorizing the killing of children. Subsequent decisions of the Court, notably *Planned Parenthood v. Casey* (1992), upheld the *Roe* precedent but had the effect of embittering political and judicial life; advocates of each side found it difficult to sympathize with the other.

The first antiabortion activists were Catholics. Some lobbied for legal restrictions or a constitutional amendment; others undertook direct action, picketing abortion clinics and trying to persuade pregnant women to carry their babies to term, offering them and their babies material and psychological support. In the 1980s, the movement became more radical; Randall Terry's Operation Rescue brought large numbers of "pro-life" evangelical Protestants into direct activism side by side with Catholics, a combination that would have been unlikely prior the 1960s. Operation Rescue worked across denominational lines and tried to get large numbers of its members arrested at the Democratic convention of 1988 in Atlanta, packing the jails as a symbolic way of bringing attention to the issue. In the 1990s a trio of the most extreme activists, Michael Griffin, Paul Hill, and Shelley Shannon, assassinated abortion providers in the firm belief that God authorized this drastic step. The effect of their attacks was almost certainly counterproductive, horrifying not only most American citizens but also the majority of religious pro-lifers, who were explicitly dedicated to the sanctity of life.

The New Christian Right and Left

This turn to activism bore witness to an important trend in the 1970s, the return of evangelicals and fundamentalists to active politics. Ever since the Scopes trial of 1925, most fundamentalists (Protestants who thought of the Bible as literally true and accurate, the direct and dependable word of God) had withdrawn from public life. Many of them were dispensational premillennialists, believers that the second coming of Jesus was very close and that it was more important to turn to Jesus individually than to work on transforming society. In the 1970s, dismayed by sexual permissiveness, unfamiliar new roles for women, legal abortion, and what seemed like the breakdown of the family, they began to return to political life, joining Christian lobbies like Jerry Falwell's Moral Majority. Their theorist was the theologian Francis Schaeffer, who urged them to contest what he thought of as the growing power of evil in the world. They were also goaded into action by what was, to them, the disappointing presidency of Jimmy Carter: A born-again evangelical Christian, Carter should have been solidly behind their program but in practice seemed too willing to accept the orthodoxy of the Democratic Party on gender and family questions. He was also an advocate of détente with the Soviet Union, despite its persecution of Russian Christians and Jews.

The New Religious Right drew the lion's share of media attention in the late 1970s and early 1980s, not least because it contributed to the defeat of Carter and the election of an outspoken conservative, Ronald Reagan. It would be quite wrong, however, to imagine that religion was, as a whole, a conservative force in American life. Religious feminists had begun to transform gender roles inside churches and synagogues, while religious anti-Vietnam activists could be found, a few years later, working in poverty programs and in the "sanctuary" movement, helping Nicaraguan and Salvadoran refugees in the Southwest, or working in the environmental movement.

Stewardship of God's creation was, in the view of many Christians, a religious imperative.

This way of looking at nature also prompted a renewed assessment of nuclear weapons. They remained in the 1980s, as in the 1950s, the basis of America's defense policy, but a growing religious antinuclear movement considered them utterly incompatible with civilization and common decency. The National Conference of Catholic Bishops wrote a pastoral letter on the issue, "The Challenge of Peace: God's Promise and Our Response" (1983), condemning the targeting of Soviet cities and coming close to opposing any policy that condoned the use of nuclear weapons. Once a dependable bloc of anti-Communists, the bishops were now staking out new territory, openly critical of their government. Many of the Protestant churches wrote comparable letters. One Methodist bishop, John Warman of Harrisburg, Pennsylvania, signed his denomination's letter and told a journalist: "You cannot boil seven million human beings in their own juices and then speak of Christian love. It would be far better for us to trust the God of the Resurrection and suffer death than to use such a weapon."

Other Christians dissented sharply; Michael Novak, a lay Catholic and political conservative, wrote "Moral Clarity in the Nuclear Age" (1983), a book-length answer to the bishops that filled an entire special issue of *National Review*. Invoking the tradition of "just war theory," as had the bishops, he argued that nuclear weapons were actually instruments of peace. Paradoxically, the government *used* them by *not* firing them, merely threatening to do so, and in this way assured the maximum of deterrence with the minimum of destruction.

Religious Celebrities

Everyone can be grateful that the cold war ended without an exchange of nuclear missiles. The Soviet empire in Eastern Europe began to unravel in 1989, the Berlin Wall came down, Germany was reunified, and in 1991 Soviet communism itself came to a peaceful end.

Several individuals who played prominent roles in this world-changing sequence of events became political-religious celebrities in America. One was Lech Walesa, the Gdansk dockyard worker whose Solidarity movement created a new center of legitimacy inside Communist Poland in the 1980s and made him a luminous figure to human rights activists. The Catholic faith had the same kind of function for Solidarity as evangelical Christianity had had in the American civil rights movement, binding members together and empowering them to resist unjust power. A second individual who became prominent in America was Karol Wojtyla, who in 1978 was elevated to the papacy and chose the name Pope John Paul II. Also Polish, and the former archbishop of Krakow, Wojtyla's life and work demonstrated that Christianity, even when persecuted, could outlast

communism. His visits to America drew vast crowds of Catholics and non-Catholics alike.

Several other religious figures also played symbolically important roles in movements to resist political oppression. One was the Russian novelist Alexander Solzhenitsyn, a Russian Orthodox exile in America from 1975, who gave the commencement address at Harvard in 1978; another was the Anglican South African bishop Desmond Tutu, a leading antiapartheid activist. A third was the Dalai Lama, religious leader of the Tibetan community in exile, who embodied Buddhist resistance to the Chinese conquest of Tibet. All were revered in America and helped discredit the regimes against which they campaigned.

The Changing Religious Landscape

By 1990 historians and sociologists were observing seismic shifts in American religious life. First was the steady decline in membership and influence of "mainstream" Protestant churches. Presbyterians, Congregationalists, Episcopalians, and Lutherans, who had once dominated the religious landscape, faced dwindling congregations, whereas the Assemblies of God, Disciples of Christ, Southern Baptists, and independent Christian churches enjoyed rapid increases. These growing congregations, many under the leadership of charismatic evangelical leaders, imposed tough rules on their members, expecting them to tithe (give a tenth of their pretax income to the church) and follow exacting codes of personal conduct. They provided foot soldiers for the Moral Majority and for its successor, the Christian Coalition, and campaigned hard for seats on school boards, city councils, and state assemblies.

A second shift was the increasing politicization of religious life. The sharpest divisions had once been between denominations, but now separation was deepest between the religious left and the religious right, often with representatives of both points of view in the same denomination. Princeton sociologist Robert Wuthnow charted this shift in his influential book *The Restructuring of American Religion* (1988).

Denominational conferences squabbled over theological and doctrinal questions, and over whether to regard scripture as inerrant. The wider public felt the effect of these disputes in renewed attacks on the teaching of Darwinian evolutionary theory. Evangelicals on school boards argued that school science curricula should include "Creation science," an approach to human origins that was consonant with the creation narrative in Genesis. They were aware, however, that the Supreme Court would reject that approach if they made its religious provenance explicit. Proponents therefore claimed that they were indeed advancing a genuine science, rather than a religious point of view in religious dress. The Institute for Creation Research in San Diego backed up this claim. Their antagonists, an alliance of nonfundamentalist Christians, Jews, and academic scientists, countered that creation science was a bogus form of special pleading, and that the evolutionary hypothesis alone could explain the nature of life on Earth. Several southern states passed laws in the 1980s that were hospitable to creationists, only to see them rejected by the courts on First Amendment grounds. Evangelical activists on school boards also tried to stop sex education classes or else convert them into advocacy seminars on sexual abstention.

At the same time, independent Christian schools thrived as places where evangelical teachings on creation and sexuality could be central to the curriculum. In southern states, many of these schools were attractive to white parents who disparaged the effects of public school desegregation.

A more radical alternative was homeschooling. The homeschooling movement had begun among advocates of the 1960s counterculture, who protested the repressive and conformist nature of public education. Ironically, it was overtaken by Christian homeschoolers who thought public education was too secular, undisciplined, ideologically biased against religion, and tended to expose students to excessive peer pressure. Homeschool organizations lobbied successfully for state laws entitling them to educate their children at home so long as they met basic standards of literacy and numeracy.

New Religions

These developments bore witness to the continuing energy and diversity of American religious life. So did the growth of new religions, hundreds of which had sprung up throughout American history. Many lasted only a few years, but a few, like the Mormons, the Jehovah's Witnesses, and the Nation of Islam, struck a resonant chord among citizens and became permanent parts of the religious landscape. The sharp divisions in American national life during the 1960s, 1970s, and 1980s prompted the creation of a new crop of religions, a few of which had political implications. Some put such psychological pressure on their members that anxious relatives sought government prevention or regulation of what they perceived as brainwashing. Other groups demanded the handing over not just of a tenth but of all a member's property. Some sheltered illegal sexual practices.

Two dramatic incidents illustrated these dangers. The first was the fate of the People's Temple, under the leadership of Jim Jones. It began as a Christian Pentecostal church in Indianapolis and was the city's first fully racially integrated congregation. The church moved to rural California in 1964, when Jones became convinced that nuclear war was imminent. Then it became involved in San Francisco politics when Jones's preaching proved effective at reforming drug addicts. Finally, Jones, under investigation for financial and sexual irregularities and convinced that he was the target of government persecution, moved the People's Temple to a settlement that became known as Jonestown, in Guyana,

South America. The parents of some members asked a California congressman, Leo Ryan, to investigate the church, and his arrival at Jonestown in November 1978 triggered a horrific finale. A group of Jones's men ambushed and killed Ryan, then the whole community—900 men, women, and children—drank cyanide-poisoned Kool-Aid in a mass suicide ritual, something they had practiced in the foregoing months.

The second incident involved the Branch Davidians, a splinter group from the Seventh-Day Adventists, which was led by charismatic preacher David Koresh. Koresh, like Jones, had sexual relationships with a variety of the group's members. When rumors surfaced in 1993 that his partners included children, the Federal Bureau of Alcohol, Tobacco, and Firearms raided the compound in Waco, Texas. The group fought back, FBI armored cars rolled in, and the two sides exchanged gunfire and tear gas for several days. The entire compound eventually caught fire and burned to the ground, killing 103 people, including at least 17 children. Public reaction was sharply divided; to some citizens drastic action against cults was necessary. Others saw the government's heavy-handedness as disgraceful and disproportionate. This second view gained credibility when it later emerged that Timothy McVeigh—who two years later blew up a federal building in Oklahoma City—had been convinced by the Waco affair that the federal government was at war with ordinary citizens.

Increasing religious diversity included not just new sects and cults but also the arrival in America of larger numbers of non-Judeo-Christian peoples than ever before. The Immigration Reform Act of 1965 abolished racial and geographical discrimination in immigrants' point of origin and opened the way for large-scale immigration from Africa and Asia. America's wealth and political stability, along with First Amendment protection to all religions, made it an extremely desirable destination. Buddhist, Hindu, and Muslim communities grew in many cities, while scholars hurried to study them and to widen the ideal of American inclusiveness. For many of these immigrants from societies where restriction and intolerance were the norm, America was a pleasant surprise. Some American Muslims took the view that the United States was the ideal place in which to practice Islam. The international situation, however, tended to work against this easy accommodation. Surges of anti-Islamic prejudice coincided with such events as the Iranian Revolution and hostage crisis (1978–80), the first Gulf War (1990–91), and the attack on the World Trade Center and Pentagon (2001). After the latter event, politicians, led by President George W. Bush, took the view that the United States would protect all forms of religious practice, Islam included, but would make unceasing war on militarized forms of Islamic fundamentalism.

The Catholic Child Abuse Scandal

Balancing the two imperatives specified in the First Amendment—free exercise and no establishment—has never been easy, as a new scandal made clear at the beginning of the twenty-first century. Journalistic investigations uncovered widespread sexual abuse of children and teenagers by Catholic priests, and evidence showed that it had been going on for a long time. Church authorities had earlier reacted to reports of predatory priests not by turning them over to the law—which would cause scandal and discredit—but by reassigning them to new parishes with a promise of reform. The reform rarely worked, and abuse recurred. The Catholic Church was sued successfully by victims and their families, and it sustained catastrophic losses and was forced to sell assets to cover the cost of judgments against it. The scandal raised the possibility that religious freedom had provided cover for misconduct, and that closer scrutiny would have prevented it, just as closer scrutiny of cults could have prevented the tragedies of Jonestown and Waco. The cost of scrutiny would also be high, however, both financially and in the erosion of civil liberties.

The scandal in the Catholic Church bore witness to the inextricable mixing of religion and politics in American life. As the twenty-first century began, the United States remained the most religiously diverse nation in the world, and the most religiously active among the Western industrial democracies. Its hospitality to religions of all kinds, and the prosperity of these groups, took visible form in the shape of beautiful new churches, synagogues, temples, and mosques. America maintained a high degree of religious freedom, offered tax exemption to all alike, and tried to ensure that all enjoyed free exercise. It was reasonable to anticipate that this state of affairs would persist.

FURTHER READING. Patrick Allitt, *Religion in America since 1945: A History*, 2003; Robert Bellah, "Civil Religion in America," *Daedalus* 96 (Winter 1967), 1–21; Walter Capps, *The New Religious Right: Piety, Patriotism, and Politics*, 1990; David Chidester, *Salvation and Suicide: An Interpretation of Jim Jones, the People's Temple, and Jonestown*, 1988; Richard W. Fox, *Reinhold Niebuhr: A Biography*, 1987; Marvin Frankel, *Faith and Freedom: Religious Liberty in America*, 1994; David Garrow, *Bearing the Cross: Martin Luther King, Jr. and the Southern Christian Leadership Conference*, 1988; Francine DuPlessix Gray, *Divine Disobedience: Profiles in Catholic Radicalism*, 1970; Martin Marty, *Modern American Religion, Volume 3: Under God, Indivisible, 1941–1960*, 1996; James Risen and Judy Thomas, *Wrath of Angels: The American Abortion War*, 1998; Mark Silk, *Spiritual Politics: Religion and America since World War II*, 1988; James Tabor, *Why Waco? Cults and the Battle for Religious Freedom in America*, 1995; Jack Wertheimer, *A People Divided: Judaism in Contemporary America*, 1993; Robert Wuthnow, *The Restructuring of American Religion: Society and Faith since World War II*, 1988.

PATRICK ALLITT

Republican Party

During its century and a half as a major political organization, the Republican Party has undergone significant shifts in its ruling ideology and electoral base. Created in 1854 in response to the Kansas-Nebraska Act as a way of opposing the expansion of slavery into the territories, the Republican Party, for the first 50 years of its existence, favored the broad use of national power to promote economic growth. During the early twentieth century, as the issue of government regulation emerged in the national debate, Republicans became identified with opposition to such supervision of the economy. That stance defined the party's position on economic questions for the next six decades.

By the 1960s, the Republicans slipped away from their traditional posture in favor of the rights of African Americans and sought new support from alienated white voters in the previously Democratic South. The party grew more conservative, opposing abortion rights and other manifestations of cultural liberalism. In foreign policy, Republicans have been, by turns, expansionists from 1890 to 1916, isolationists in the 1930s and 1940s, and militant anti-Communists during the cold war. A firm belief that they were the natural ruling party and that the Democrats carried the taint of treason and illegitimacy have been hallmarks of Republican thinking throughout the party's history.

The first phase of Republican history extended from the party's founding through the presidential election of 1896. In 1854 antislavery Northerners, former Whigs, and some dissenting Democrats came together to create a new party that took the name "Republican" from the Jeffersonian tradition. After the Republican presidential candidate, John C. Fremont, lost in 1856, the Republican Party won the White House in 1860 behind Abraham Lincoln, who led the nation through the Civil War. Republican strength was sectional, with its base in the Northeast and the upper Middle West. The Middle Atlantic states were a contested battleground with the Democrats.

To wage that conflict, the Republicans in power enacted sweeping legislation to impose income taxes, distribute public lands, and create a national banking system. Party leaders also pushed for a constitutional amendment to abolish slavery, and the more intense or "radical" Republicans called for political rights for the freedmen whom the war had liberated from bondage.

Lincoln's assassination in 1865 brought to power his vice president, Andrew Johnson, a former Democrat with little sympathy for Republican ideology or the plight of former slaves in the South. The result was a contest between the mainstream of the party for some degree of political rights for African American men and a president who opposed such innovations.

Throughout Reconstruction and beyond, the Republicans sought to build an electoral base in the South of black and white voters sympathetic to government support for economic growth. The effort was protracted and sincere; the results were disappointing. By the mid-1870s, the South had become solidly Democratic, with the Republicans a minority party in most of the states below the Mason-Dixon Line.

During Reconstruction, the Republicans did achieve the passage of the Fourteenth and Fifteenth Amendments to the Constitution to provide citizenship and voting rights to former slaves. These significant contributions attested to the party's sincerity on the issue, but the will to extend equality further in the 1880s and 1890s proved lacking. Republicans slowly relinquished their interest in black rights and turned to questions of industrialization and economic expansion at the end of the nineteenth century.

The protective tariff became the hallmark of Republican ideology during this period. Using the taxing power of the government to provide an advantage to domestic products appealed to the entrepreneurial base of the Republicans as well as to labor. The tariff offered a vision of benefits diffused throughout society in a harmonious manner. In the hands of such leaders as James G. Blaine and William McKinley, the doctrine of protection also took on a nationalistic character as a way of achieving self-sufficiency in a competitive world. Charges soon arose that the tariff was nothing more than a rationale for economic selfishness. As businesses grew larger and industrialism took hold in the United States, Republicans were seen as the party of producers and identified with capitalist aspirations. Measures such as the McKinley Tariff of 1890 and the Dingley Tariff of 1897 raised tariff rates. Republicans argued that protection brought prosperity and that Democratic free-trade policies imperiled the nation's economic health.

Throughout the late nineteenth century, Republicans and Democrats battled on even electoral terms. Then, in the 1890s, the Grand Old Party (as it had become known) emerged as the nation's dominant political organization. With the election of Benjamin Harrison in 1888, the Republicans controlled Congress and the presidency. Their activist program in the 51st Congress (1889–90) brought a voter backlash that led to a Democratic victory in the 1892 presidential contest. The onset of the economic downturn in 1893 discredited the Democrats under President Grover Cleveland and gave the Republicans their opportunity. The congressional elections of 1894 produced a Republican sweep in the House of Representatives and opened an era of dominance for the party.

Years of Ascendancy: 1896–1932

The presidential election of 1896, which brought William McKinley to the White House, confirmed the emergence of a national Republican majority. For most of the next four decades, the party held an electoral advantage. Under McKinley, Theodore Roosevelt, and William Howard Taft, the Republicans acquired an overseas empire, broadened government power over the economy, and took a few steps toward limiting the power of corporations. By 1912, however, as Roosevelt and Taft split the party, the Republicans moved rightward and generally opposed the expansion of government regulatory authority.

During the eight years that Woodrow Wilson and the Democrats were in power, from 1913 to 1921, the emphasis on Republican conservatism intensified. The 1916 presidential campaign between Wilson and Charles Evans Hughes anticipated the ideological divisions of the later New Deal on domestic questions. In that contest, the Republican candidate opposed organized labor, federal regulation of child labor, and farm credit legislation. Wilson won reelection largely on the issue of American neutrality in World War I. As the country swung to the right during the war and the Democratic electoral coalition broke up, Republicans made big gains in the 1918 congressional elections. The landslide victory of Warren G. Harding two years later confirmed that Republican dominance of national politics had returned after an eight-year interruption.

The presidencies of Harding, Calvin Coolidge, and Herbert Hoover, from 1921 to 1933, represented a high point of Republican rule. Under Harding and Coolidge, income tax cuts stimulated the economy and helped fuel the expansion of that decade. Government regulation receded, labor unions were weakened, and social justice laws died in Congress. As long as prosperity continued, the Democrats seemed an impotent minority. The Republicans still had no base in the South, despite efforts of the presidents to break that monopoly. Outside of Dixie, Republicans dominated the political scene. In 1928 Hoover won a decisive triumph over Democrat Al Smith, as if to confirm the Republican mastery of national politics.

The onset of the Great Depression of the 1930s undermined the Republican position just as the depression of the 1890s had the Democrats. President Hoover's failure to provide real relief for the unemployed during the hard times of 1931–33 doomed his reelection chances. The Democrats selected Franklin D. Roosevelt as their presidential candidate in 1932, and his promise of a New Deal produced a landslide victory for his party. The Republicans were then to experience 20 years without presidential power.

Against the New Deal Coalition: 1932–68

During the 1930s and 1940s, the Grand Old Party struggled to find an answer to Roosevelt and the Democrats. In the three elections in which they faced the incumbent president (1936, 1940, and 1944), the Republicans sought to moderate their conservatism and appeal to the broad middle of national politics. They continued this strategy in 1948 when Thomas E. Dewey ran against Harry S. Truman. Each time they lost.

In Congress and in the nation at large, the Republicans were more explicit about their conservatism. They opposed the social programs and deficit spending of the Roosevelt and Truman administrations. On issues of foreign policy, the party was isolationist during the 1930s and anti-Communist in the 1940s and 1950s. Believing that the Democrats had a predisposition to help the nation's enemies, the Republicans readily assumed that Roosevelt and Truman were soft on the Communist "menace." The leading symbol of this point of view became Senator Joseph R. McCarthy of Wisconsin, whose crusades against Communists in government delighted many Republicans between 1950 and 1954. Republicans of this stripe hoped that Senator Robert A. Taft of Ohio (known as "Mr. Republican") would be the Republican nominee in 1952 and oust the Democrats after what McCarthy called "20 years of treason."

In 1952 the Republicans, after a bitter convention, nominated Dwight D. Eisenhower, a military hero whose election was more certain than Taft's would have been. Finally regaining power after 20 years, the Republicans found their 8 years in power with Eisenhower rewarding at first but frustrating in the long run. The president governed to the right of center but did not embark on crusades to roll back the programs of the New Deal. He called his point of view "modern Republicanism." Eisenhower's popularity brought his reelection in 1956, but, by then, Republicans were a minority in Congress again. As the 1960 election approached, Vice President Richard M. Nixon sought to extend the Eisenhower legacy while party conservatives went along grudgingly.

After Nixon's narrow defeat by John F. Kennedy, conservative Republicans sought to recapture control of the party through the presidential candidacy of Senator Barry M. Goldwater of Arizona. In 1964, Goldwater defeated the moderate alternative, Governor Nelson A. Rockefeller of New York, and his forces controlled the national convention in San Francisco. Goldwater's candidacy was an electoral disaster. He carried only his home state and five states in the South, as Lyndon B. Johnson secured a landslide victory.

In terms of Republican history, however, Goldwater's candidacy proved a sign of things to come. Although a majority of Republicans in the House of Representatives and the Senate helped to pass the Civil Rights Act of 1964, the party appealed to white Southerners as an alternative to the more liberal and racially integrated national Democrats. The movement of southern Democrats into Republican ranks accelerated in the three decades after 1964. In another electoral portent, an actor turned politician named Ronald Reagan gave a very successful fundraising speech at the end of the Goldwater campaign. Soon Reagan would enter national politics himself.

After the disaster of 1964, the Republicans regrouped. Soon the Democrats under Lyndon Johnson became bogged down in an unpopular war in Vietnam. Racial tensions mounted within the United States, and a reaction against the party in power ensued. Republicans made gains in Congress during the 1968 elections, and Nixon again emerged as the leading Republican candidate for the White House. He united the party behind his candidacy and gained the nomination despite a last-minute challenge from Ronald Reagan. Nixon went on to win the presidency in a narrow victory over Democrat Hubert Humphrey and independent Alabama governor George Wallace.

Conservative Dominance: 1968–2004

Nixon's presidency proved a troubled episode for the Grand Old Party. At first, he seemed to have found the way to marginalize the Democrats. The strategy of winding down the war in Vietnam proved popular, and Republicans capitalized on divisions in the opposition party to achieve a landslide triumph of their own in the 1972 presidential election. Nixon crushed the Democratic candidate, George McGovern.

The triumph was not to last. The Watergate scandal, covered up during the election, burst into full view in 1973 and led to Nixon's resignation in August 1974 in advance of impeachment and removal. Nixon's legacy to the party was mixed. He had strengthened its southern base, but his moderate social policies and foreign policy opening to China put off many conservatives. That wing of the party looked to Reagan as its champion. Nixon's successor, Gerald R. Ford, won the presidential nomination in 1976 over Reagan, but then lost the election to Democrat Jimmy Carter in the fall. Reagan was the party's nominee in 1980.

Reagan beat the weakened Carter in that election, and the Republicans also regained control of the Senate. During the eight years that followed, Reagan became a Republican icon for his policies of lowering taxes, advocating an antimissile defense system, and bringing down the Soviet Union. The reality was more complex, since Reagan also raised taxes, the missile system did not work, and the fall of the Soviet Union that came after he left office was not his achievement alone. Yet, because of his landslide reelection victory in 1984, Reagan remained the electoral standard by which future Republicans were measured.

Reagan's successor, George H. W. Bush, had a rocky single term. Having pledged during the 1988 campaign not to raise taxes, Bush never recovered when he reached a budget deal in 1990 that imposed new taxes. He lost to Democrat Bill Clinton in the 1992 presidential contest. Clinton's first two years were difficult, and the Republicans made big gains in the 1994 elections. They took back the Senate, and under the leadership of Newton "Newt" Gingrich, they recaptured the House for the first time in 40 years, with a "Contract for America" as their program. Gingrich proved to be better at campaigning than governing; yet the Republicans, now dominant in the South, retained their congressional majority for 12 years. In 1998 the majority party in Congress impeached President Clinton for lying under oath and other alleged crimes, but the Senate acquitted him.

The 2000 election brought Governor George W. Bush of Texas, son of George H. W. Bush, to the White House. Although he lost the popular vote, Bush won a disputed election in the Electoral College. The terrorist attacks of September 11, 2001, and Bush's initial response to them lifted the new president to high poll ratings. Republicans gained in the 2002 elections and, for the next four years, controlled all branches of the federal government. Bush won re-election in 2004, defeating Democrat John Kerry.

Yet in that period, the Grand Old Party experienced striking changes. The party of small government expanded the size of the federal establishment to unprecedented levels. The champions of lower spending brought government expenditures to record heights. Proud of their record as administrators, the Republicans under Bush mismanaged wars in Iraq and Afghanistan, permeated the federal government with partisan cronies, and produced record budget deficits. Bush's poll rating sank, and his unpopularity spilled over to other members of his party.

Social conservatives wanted a government that regulated private behavior; pro-business conservatives hoped for a government that would keep taxes low and diminish regulations. Disputes over immigration and control of the borders further divided the GOP. By the end of the first decade of the twenty-first century, it was unclear what constituted the ideology of the Republican Party. After a century and a half in American politics, the Republicans faced a crisis over their identity that would shape how they performed during the century to come.

FURTHER READING. Mary Brennan, *Turning Right in the Sixties: The Conservative Capture of the GOP*, 1995; Charles W. Calhoun, *Conceiving a New Republic: The Republican Party and the South, 1869–1900*, 2006; William E. Gienapp, *The Origins of the Republican Party, 1852–1856*, 1987; Lewis L. Gould, *Grand Old Party: A History of the Republicans*, 2003; Sheldon Pollack, *Refinancing America: The Republican Antitax Agenda*, 2003; Matthew Rees, *From the Deck to the Sea: Blacks and the Republican Party*, 1991; David W. Reinhard, *The Republican Right since 1945*, 1983; Clyde Weed, *The Republican Party during the New Deal*, 1994; Michael Zak, *Back to Basics for the Republican Party*, 2001.

LEWIS L. GOULD

Republican Party to 1896

The Republican Party emerged in the 1850s and soon became one of the nation's two major parties. It began as a coalition of elements set loose by the collapse of America's Second Party System. In the previous two decades, the Whigs and the Democrats had divided principally over such economic issues as the tariff, the Bank of the United States, and internal improvements. But as the question of territorial expansion grew more salient, the vexatious issue of slavery, especially the extension of the institution westward, made it difficult for leaders of both those parties to keep their organizations united across sectional lines. The Whigs' staggering loss in the 1852 election dealt a devastating blow to that party, whose constituent elements—anti-Catholic and anti-immigrant nativists, temperance advocates, and antislavery Northerners—concluded that the party had become an ineffectual vehicle to achieve their ends.

The climactic crisis for the Second Party System came with the controversy over the Kansas-Nebraska Act of 1854, which repealed the Missouri Compromise ban on slavery in most of the Louisiana Purchase territory. Conflict between northern and southern Whigs over this law completed the destruction of their party as a significant national entity, although a remnant limped along for the next few years. Though sponsored by Illinois Democrat Stephen Douglas and endorsed by the Democratic administration of Franklin Pierce, the Kansas-Nebraska Act tore a gash through the Democratic Party, whose unity its northern and southern leaders had maintained for many years only with great difficulty. The Nebraska issue dominated the congressional elections of 1854. In states across the North, the Democrats confronted an array of variously configured coalitions that included old Free Soilers, anti-Nebraska Democrats, antislavery Whigs, temperance supporters, and nativists. These anti-Democratic "parties" fought under various names: Anti-Nebraska, Fusion, Opposition, and People's Party. In only two states, Michigan and Wisconsin, did they take the name *Republican*. Whatever the label, the new coalitions achieved phenomenal success, winning a plurality of seats in the new House of Representatives.

As time passed, more of these northern state coalitions adopted Republican as a fitting name to cast the party as a relentless opponent of corruption and tyranny and a defender of liberty and civic virtue. In 1854, however, the Republican Party did not emerge either full blown or as the sole alternative to the Democrats. Some Whigs still harbored hope for a reversal of their party's ill fortunes, but more problematic for the new Republican strategists was the anti-Catholic and nativist Know-Nothing movement, which claimed to have elected 20 percent of new House members from districts scattered throughout the country, especially in New England. Know-Nothingism proved attractive not only to Americans who resented the presence of immigrants and "papists" and their supposed subservience to the Democratic Party but also to those who saw nativist issues as a way to deflect attention from the potentially Union-rending slavery question. The task of those who strove to make the Republicans the principal anti-Democratic party was to fashion an approach to public questions that would co-opt the Know-Nothings while preserving the allegiance of the various northern antislavery elements that had made up the fusion movement of 1854.

In 1856 the nativists fielded a presidential candidate, former president Millard Fillmore, under the American Party banner and garnered 22 percent of the popular vote and 8 electoral votes from Maryland. The Republicans, now campaigning generally under that name, nominated John C. Frémont and put forth a combative platform focused on opposition to slavery expansion, and particularly condemning the outrages committed by proslavery forces in the battle for control of Kansas Territory. Frémont posted a remarkable showing for the party's first run for the White House. Running only in the North, he won 33 percent of the national popular vote and 114 electoral votes to Democrat James Buchanan's 45 percent of the popular vote and 174 electoral votes. In the free states, significantly, Frémont outpolled Fillmore by more than three to one. Had Frémont won Pennsylvania plus either Indiana or Illinois, he would have been the first Republican president. Republican leaders recognized that future success depended on converting or reassuring enough nativists and conservatives on the slavery question to win these key northern states.

Events in 1856 and the ensuing years moved the slavery question to center stage in the struggle against the Democrats. These included not only the Kansas turmoil but also the vicious caning of Massachusetts Republican senator Charles Sumner by a South Carolina congressman, the Supreme Court's *Dred Scott* decision declaring unconstitutional the Missouri Compromise ban on slavery in a territory, and calls by southern leaders for a reopening of the African slave trade and for a federal code sustaining slavery in the territories. Although these developments served to underscore Republicans' warnings of the threats posed by an aggressive "slave power," the new party designed its campaign strategy in 1860 not only to retain the support of men who gave priority to that issue but also to attract as broad an array of voters in the North as possible.

The party's platform in 1860 took a balanced approach on slavery, denouncing the *Dred Scott* decision and denying the power of Congress or a legislature to legalize slavery in any territory, but also upholding the individual states' right to decide the slavery question for themselves, and condemning John Brown's attempt to spark a slave revolt at Harpers Ferry. Aiming to appeal to men on the make, the party endorsed an economic package that included a protective tariff, internal improvements, and a homestead law. In an effort to woo German Americans, who formed a critical bloc in key states, the Republicans eschewed nativism and called for the protection of the rights of immigrants and naturalized citizens. Most important, in choosing their presidential nominee, they turned aside candidates such as William Seward and Salmon Chase, deemed too radical on slavery, and selected the newcomer Abraham Lincoln, whose record on the issue appeared more conservative. Hopelessly riven, the northern and southern Democrats chose separate nominees, Stephen A. Douglas and John C. Breckinridge, while a nativist remnant and other conservatives offered a fourth ticket headed by John Bell. In the popular vote, Lincoln led with only 39.6 percent of the vote. In the Electoral College he swept the entire free-state section except for New Jersey, which he split with Douglas, who came in last behind Breckinridge and Bell.

Civil War and Reconstruction

Despite Lincoln's victory, his party still stood on shaky ground. It failed to win a majority in either house of Congress, and only the departure of Southerners after their states had seceded enabled Republicans to assume control. They proceeded to pass most of their legislative agenda, but in the face of prolonged bad news from the military front during the Civil War, the Democrats remained alive and well and actually gained House seats in the 1862 midterm elections. Lincoln also confronted severe critics in his own party, and, in the summer of 1864, he doubted he could win reelection. At their convention, the Republicans even changed their name to the National Union Party to attract pro-war Democrats. At last, Union battlefield successes muffled the carping, and Lincoln defeated Democrat George McClellan.

That the Republicans' first president was a man of Lincoln's greatness, who guided the nation safely through its darkest hour, contributed mightily to establishing the party as a permanent fixture on the American political landscape. Ever after, Republicans could rightly claim the mantle of saviors of the Union and liberators of the slaves. In the wake of Lincoln's death, however, reconstructing the Union proved enormously difficult. In 1864 the party had put a Tennessee War Democrat, Andrew Johnson, on the ticket, and, when he succeeded to the presidency, he broke with Congress and the Republicans and did all in his power to block their efforts to remodel the South. After a titanic struggle, Republicans added the Fourteenth and the Fifteenth Amendment to the Constitution to uphold blacks' civil rights and the right of black men to vote. To reorder the southern political landscape, Republicans encouraged the creation of a new wing of the party in the South comprising blacks, southern white Unionists, and Northerners who had moved south. Against this tenuous coalition, conservative white Democrats posed a fierce, sometimes violent, opposition. Although congressional Republicans passed enforcement legislation and Johnson's Republican successor, Ulysses S. Grant, occasionally intervened militarily, state after state in the South fell under Democratic control.

In the North, moreover, the Republicans suffered divisions, especially spurred by so-called Liberal Republicans who opposed Grant's southern policy, his acceptance of probusiness policies such as the protective tariff, and his handling of the touchy subject of federal appointments. In 1872 Grant easily defeated liberal Republican (and Democratic) nominee Horace Greeley, but, during his second term, a series of scandals tainted his administration and hurt his party. Economic collapse after the panic of 1873 compounded the Republicans' woes. In 1874, the Democrats took the House of Representatives for the first time since before the war. Only after a prolonged and bitter controversy following the indeterminate outcome of the 1876 election was Republican Rutherford B. Hayes able to win the presidency.

Political Equilibrium

During Hayes's term, the Democrats secured control of the last southern states formerly held by Republicans, and the nation entered a prolonged period of equilibrium between the two major parties. From the mid-1870s to the mid-1890s, the Republicans and Democrats were nearly equal in strength nationwide. The Democrats had a firm grip on the Solid South, while Republicans enjoyed support nearly as solid in New England and the upper Midwest. But neither of these blocs held enough electoral votes to win the presidency, and each election in this period turned on the outcome in a few key swing states, most notably New York and Indiana. Moreover, the national government was nearly always divided in this era. The Democrats usually controlled the House, and the Republicans usually controlled the Senate. Rarely did one party hold both houses and the presidency. These circumstances obviously made governing difficult.

Although close elections underscored the need for party unity, Republicans nonetheless continued to suffer divisions. Most Liberal Republicans returned to the party fold, but as independents, later dubbed "mugwumps" (after an Indian word for leader), they continued to push for civil service reform and chastised party leaders whose probity they suspected. In several states the party was rent by factions, often based on loyalty to particular party leaders. This factionalism reached a head in the convention of 1880, where "stalwarts" hoping to restore Grant to the presidency battled against the adherents of former House speaker James G. Blaine, labeled "half-breeds" by their enemies for their alleged lukewarm commitment to the party's older ideals. The delegates eventually turned to a dark horse, James A. Garfield, a half-breed, and nominated for vice president a stalwart, Chester A. Arthur, who succeeded to the White House after Garfield's assassination.

In presidential election campaigns during this period, Republicans faced a strategic dilemma. Some insisted they should work to mobilize a united North, including the swing states, by emphasizing the righteousness of the party's position on black rights and by denouncing political oppression in the South—a tactic their opponents and many later historians disparaged as "waving the bloody shirt." Other party leaders argued that the party should strive to break its dependence on winning New York and other doubtful northern states by trying to detach states from the Democratic Solid South, primarily through economic appeals and the promise of prosperity for a new South.

In 1884 presidential nominee James G. Blaine took the latter course, pursuing a conciliatory campaign toward the South and emphasizing the benefits of Republican economic policies, especially the protective tariff, to the southern states and the nation at large. This strategy dovetailed with the party's increasing solicitude for the nation's industries and for workers threatened by foreign competition. Blaine lost every former slave state, and with his narrow defeat in New York, he lost the presidency to Democrat Grover Cleveland. But Blaine received 49 percent of the vote in Virginia and 48 percent in Tennessee. Had he carried those two states, he would have secured a victory without any of the northern doubtful states, including New York.

Republicans had won every presidential election from 1860 to 1884, and in 1888 they faced the unaccustomed prospect of campaigning against a sitting president. GOP leaders could not, as in the past, turn to federal employees as a ready contingent of campaign workers and contributors, but they could tap a large corps of party cadres eager to regain what they had lost. In addition to the regular party organization of national, state, and local committees, they created a structure of thousands of Republican clubs around the country ready to do battle.

In 1888 Republican nominee Benjamin Harrison, like Blaine, emphasized the tariff issue, though not entirely omitting civil rights questions. He defeated Cleveland. Like Blaine, Harrison carried none of the former slave states but ran well in the upper South. In the congressional elections the Republicans won enough House seats from the upper South to take control of the new Congress. Thus, for the first time since the Grant years, the GOP held both the presidency and the two houses. In one of the most activist Congresses of the nineteenth century, the party passed a host of new laws, including the McKinley Tariff, the Sherman Anti-Trust Act, the Sherman Silver Purchase Act, the Meat Inspection Act, and the Forest Reserve Act, and it came close to enacting strict new protections for black voting in the South. In addition, legislatures in key Republican states passed "cultural" regulations such as temperance laws and restrictions on the use of foreign languages in private schools. Despite these accomplishments, all the activism alarmed an essentially conservative electorate still enamored of Jeffersonian ideals of limited government. Voters turned against the Republicans overwhelmingly in the 1890 midterm congressional elections and in 1892 put Cleveland back in the White House joined by a Democratic Congress.

The New Majority Party

Soon after Cleveland took office, the panic of 1893 struck, and the economy spiraled downward into the deepest depression of the century. The GOP blamed the Democrats, and Cleveland's bungling of tariff and currency legislation underscored the Republicans' charge that the Democrats' negative approach to governing failed to meet the needs of a modernizing economy. In the 1894 congressional elections, Republicans crushed their opponents in the largest shift in congressional strength in history. Two years later Republican presidential nominee William McKinley campaigned as the "advance agent of prosperity," emphasizing the tariff issue and condemning Democrat William Jennings Bryan as a dangerous radical whose support for the free coinage of silver threatened to destroy the economy. McKinley won in a landslide, and, with a Republican Congress, he proceeded to enact a new protective tariff and other probusiness measures. McKinley was a popular chief executive. During his term, the economy rebounded, largely for reasons unrelated to government policy. But the Republicans took credit for prosperity and positioned themselves as the nation's majority party for more than three decades.

McKinley was the last Civil War veteran to serve in the White House. His victory in 1896 marked the culmination of the party's drift away from sectional issues as the key to building a constituency. After the Democrats secured their grip on the South in the late 1870s, some Republicans touted issues such as nativism and temperance to build a following in the North on the basis of cultural values. But Blaine, Harrison, and McKinley recognized the futility of this sort of exclusionary politics. Instead they emphasized economic matters such as tariff protectionism tempered by trade reciprocity, plus a stable currency, to fashion a broad-based coalition of manufacturers, laborers, farmers, and others who put economic well-being at the center of their political concerns. As a result, the Republicans held the upper hand in American politics until the Great Depression demonstrated the inadequacy of their economic formula.

See also Democratic Party; nativism; slavery; Whig Party.

FURTHER READING. Charles W. Calhoun, *Conceiving a New Republic: The Republican Party and the Southern Question, 1869–1900*, 2006; Idem, *Minority Victory: Gilded Age Politics and the Front Porch Campaign of 1888*, 2008; Robert F. Engs and Randall M. Miller, eds., *The Birth of the Grand Old Party: The Republicans' First Generation*, 2002; Eric Foner, *Free Soil, Free Labor, Free Men: The Ideology of the Republican Party before the Civil War*, 1970; Idem, *Reconstruction: America's Unfinished Revolution, 1863–1877*, 1988; William E. Gienapp, *The Origins of the Republican Party, 1852–1856*, 1987; Lewis L. Gould, *Grand Old Party: A History of the Republicans*, 2003; Michael F. Holt, *The Political Crisis of the 1850s*, 1978; H. Wayne Morgan, *From Hayes to McKinley: National Party Politics, 1877–1896*, 1969; Heather Cox Richardson, *The Greatest Nation of the Earth: Republican Economic Policies during the Civil War*, 1997; R. Hal Williams, *Years of Decision: American Politics in the 1890s*, 1993.

CHARLES W. CALHOUN

Republican Party, 1896–1932

In the history of the Republican Party, the years between the election of William McKinley in 1896 and the defeat of Herbert Hoover in 1932 stand as a period of electoral dominance. To be sure, Woodrow Wilson and the Democrats interrupted this period with eight years of power from 1913 to 1921. That shift occurred in large measure because the Republicans themselves split, first between Theodore Roosevelt and William Howard Taft in 1912 and then, to a lesser extent, over World War I in 1916. For all these 36 years, however, the electoral alignment that had been established during the mid-1890s endured. The Republican majority that emerged during the second term of President Grover Cleveland and the Panic of 1893 lasted until another economic depression turned Hoover and the Republicans out of office.

The coalition that supported the Republicans during this period rested on capitalists, predominantly in the Northeast and Midwest; Union veterans; skilled workers; and prosperous, specialized farmers who identified with the tariff policies of the party. German Americans also comprised a key ethnic voting bloc for the Republicans. African American voters in the North, although still a small contingent, regularly endorsed Republican candidates. In those states that were more industrialized, the Republicans tended to be stronger and their majorities more enduring. Outside of the Democratic South, Republicans enjoyed wide backing from all segments of society.

The Republican triumph during the 1890s rested first on voter alienation from the Democrats. Cleveland and his party had not been able to bring relief and recovery from the economic downturn that began during the spring of 1893. The resulting social unrest that flared in 1894 contributed to the perception that the Democrats lacked the capacity to govern. These causes helped the Republicans sweep to victory in the congressional elections of 1894, when the largest transfer of seats from one party to another in U.S. history took place. The Republicans gained 113 seats in the U.S. House of Representatives and the Democrats suffered serious losses in the Northeast and Midwest, a growing bastion of Republican strength. The third party, the Populists, failed to make much headway with their appeal to farmers in the South and West.

The Republican Appeal

The Republican appeal rested on more than just criticism of the Democrats. The main ideological position of the party was support for the protective tariff. Republicans believed that raising duties on foreign imports encouraged the growth of native industries, provided a high wage level for American workers, and spread economic benefits throughout society. The Grand Old Party also associated prosperity with the benefits of protection. According to Republicans, the Democratic Party, with its free-trade policies, was a menace to the economic health of the country. By 1896 William McKinley of Ohio was the politician most identified with protection as a Republican watchword.

As the 1896 election approached, McKinley emerged as the front-runner for the nomination. With his record in the House of Representatives and his two terms as governor of Ohio, McKinley was the most popular Republican of the time. His campaign manager, Marcus A. Hanna, an Ohio steel magnate, rounded up delegates for his candidate and easily fought off challenges from other aspirants. McKinley was nominated on the first ballot at the national convention. He then defeated the Democratic nominee, William Jennings Bryan, in the most decisive presidential election victory in a quarter of a century.

Republican fortunes improved during the McKinley administration. The Dingley Tariff Law (1897) raised customs duties and became associated with the prosperity that returned at the end of the 1890s. The success in the war with Spain in 1898 brought the United States an overseas empire. These accomplishments identified the Republicans with national power and world influence. In the 1898 elections, the Grand Old Party limited Democratic gains. McKinley then defeated Bryan in a 1900 rematch with a larger total in the electoral vote and in the popular count. By the start of the twentieth century, the electoral dominance of the Republicans seemed assured. As his second term began, McKinley pursued a strategy of gradual tariff reduction through a series of reciprocity treaties with several of the nation's trading partners. In that way, the president hoped to defuse emerging protests about high customs duties.

The Age of Theodore Roosevelt

The assassination of McKinley in September 1901 brought Theodore Roosevelt to the White House. In his first term, Roosevelt put aside McKinley's tariff reciprocity initiative in the face of Republican opposition. Instead, he assailed large corporations (known as "trusts"), settled labor disputes, and promised the voters a "square deal" as president. In 1904 the Democrats ran a more conservative candidate, Alton B. Parker, as a contrast to Roosevelt's flamboyance. The strategy failed, and Roosevelt won by a large electoral and popular vote landslide. Elected in his own right, the young president wanted to address issues of government regulation that an industrial society now faced. While his party enjoyed big majorities in both houses of Congress, these Republican members were less enthusiastic about government activism and regulation than Theodore Roosevelt.

During his second term, Roosevelt persuaded Congress to adopt the Hepburn Act to regulate the railroads, the Pure Food and Drug Act to safeguard the public, and inspection legislation to address the problem of diseased and tainted meat. He pursued conservation of natural resources and legislation to protect workers and their families from the hazards of an industrial society. These measures bothered Republicans who were now doubtful that government should be overseeing the business community as Roosevelt desired. When the issue of regulation arose, conservative Republicans believed that the government's role should be minimal. By the time Roosevelt left office in March 1909, serious divisions existed within his party over the issue of government power.

To succeed him, Roosevelt selected his secretary of war, William Howard Taft, as the strongest Republican in the 1908 election. Taft defeated William Jennings Bryan in a race where ticket-splitting helped Democrats put in office a number of state governors. The Republicans still enjoyed substantial majorities in Congress, but there was restiveness among the voters over the party's congressional leaders, Speaker Joseph G. Cannon of Illinois and Senator Nelson W. Aldrich of Rhode Island. At the same time, the transition from Roosevelt to Taft was unpleasant. Surface harmony hid tensions between the two men over Taft's cabinet choices and the future direction of the party.

In their 1908 platform, the Republicans had pledged to revise the tariff. Taft sought to fulfill that promise during the spring of 1909. Long-simmering disagreements over the tariff broke into public view when the Payne Bill, named after the chair of the Ways and Means Committee, Sereno E. Payne, reached the Senate. The House had made reductions in duties. Senator Aldrich, who lacked a secure majority, made concessions to other senators that drove rates up again. Midwestern senators, known as insurgents, rebelled and fought the changes. In the ensuing conference committee, Taft secured some reductions in the rates of what became known as the Payne-Aldrich Tariff Law. Hard feelings lingered within the party about the result.

During Taft's first year in office, while Roosevelt was on a hunting trip in Africa, controversy erupted between his friend Chief Forester Gifford Pinchot and Secretary of the Interior Richard A. Ballinger over conservation policy. The ouster of Pinchot accelerated Roosevelt's feeling that he had made a mistake in selecting Taft. When he returned from his journey, Roosevelt plunged into Republican politics with a philosophy of "new nationalism," which called for more presidential power and government regulation of the economy. Roosevelt's tactics contributed to the

Republican disunity that marked 1910. The Democrats regained control of the House in that fall's elections and the GOP lost ground as well in the Senate. Taft's prospects for 1912 seemed bleak.

The Crisis of 1912

By the eve of 1912, relations between Taft and Roosevelt had deteriorated to the point where the former president was on the verge of challenging the incumbent. Brushing aside the candidacy of Robert M. La Follette of Wisconsin, Roosevelt entered the race in February 1912. A bitter battle for delegates ensued during the spring, which led to a series of primary elections, most of which Roosevelt won. Taft controlled the party machinery and came to the national convention with a narrow but sufficient lead in delegates. After Taft men used their power to renominate the president, Roosevelt decided to form his own party. The Republican division had now become open warfare.

Roosevelt bested Taft in the fall election with his new Progressive Party. However, the Democrats, behind the candidacy of Woodrow Wilson, won the White House as well as majorities in both houses of Congress. The success of Wilson in enacting the New Freedom Program of lower tariffs, banking reform, and antitrust legislation showed that the Democrats could govern. Still, the Republicans looked to the 1914 elections as a test of whether the country was returning to its usual political allegiances. The outbreak of World War I in August 1914 changed the political landscape. The Democrats urged voters to rally behind Wilson. Nonetheless, Republicans regained seats in the House while Democrats added seats in the Senate. Prospects for Wilson's reelection in 1916 seemed doubtful, but the Republicans had to find a winning presidential candidate.

The impact of World War I clouded Republican chances as the 1916 election approached. Some eastern party members wanted a more assertive policy against Germany's submarine warfare toward neutral nations. If that meant war, they supported it as a way of helping Great Britain and France. In the Midwest, where German Americans formed a large voting bloc among Republicans, sentiment for war lessened. The party had to find a way to oppose Wilson's neutrality strategy without alienating voters who wanted to stay out of war. Theodore Roosevelt, now edging back toward the GOP, was the leading exponent of pro-war views. Nominating him seemed unwise to party elders.

Their alternative was Charles Evans Hughes, a former governor of New York who was chief justice on the Supreme Court. Hughes had not been involved in the elections of 1912 and was seen as a fresh face who could win. The Republicans nominated him, only to learn that the jurist lacked charisma and campaign skills. Hughes never found a winning appeal against Wilson and the Democrats, who proclaimed that the president "kept us out of war." The election was close, but after days of counting the returns, Wilson eked out a narrow victory.

When Wilson later took the United States into World War I, the coalition that brought him victory in 1916 broke up. The Republicans capitalized on popular discontent with higher taxes, a growing government bureaucracy, and inefficiency in the war effort. Wilson's call for the election of a Democratic Congress to sustain him in October 1918 outraged the GOP. Even with victory in sight in Europe, voters ended Democratic control of both houses of Congress. Republican electoral supremacy, outside of the South, had reasserted itself.

The Harding Years

Republicans, under the direction of Senate leader Henry Cabot Lodge, then blocked Wilson's campaign to approve the Treaty of Versailles, which would have taken the United States into the League of Nations. By early 1920, it was evident that the Republicans were likely to win the presidency, and a crowded field of candidates emerged to compete for the prize. Few took seriously the chances of Warren G. Harding, a one-term Republican senator from Ohio. After three intellectually formidable candidates in Roosevelt, Taft, and Hughes, the party was ready for a less threatening nominee. The affable Harding was the second choice of many delegates at the national convention. Despite the legend that he was designated in a "smoke-filled" room by Senate leaders, Harding won the nomination because of his good looks, availability, and adherence to party orthodoxy; the delegates chose Calvin Coolidge of Massachusetts as his running mate. The election of 1920 was no contest. Harding swamped the Democratic nominee, James Cox, also of Ohio, with nearly 61 percent of the vote. Only the South stayed in the Democratic column.

Harding's brief presidency was undistinguished, though not as bad as historical legend has it. Two high points were the adoption of a federal budget for the first time and the Washington Naval Conference of 1922 to reduce armaments. By 1923, however, the administration faced a looming scandal over money exchanged for leases to oil lands in California and Wyoming that became known as Teapot Dome. Worn out by the exertions of his office and suffering from a serious heart condition, Harding died while on a tour of the country in August 1923.

Calvin Coolidge pursued pro-business policies with a greater fervor than Harding. The new president gained from the disarray of the Democrats, who were split on cultural issues such as Prohibition and the Ku Klux Klan. Coolidge easily won nomination in his own right. In the 1924 election, he routed the Democrats and brushed aside the third-party candidacy of Robert M. La Follette. The Republicans seemed to have regained the position of electoral dominance they had enjoyed at the turn of the century. With the economic boom of the 1920s roaring along, their ascendancy seemed permanent.

After Coolidge chose not to run for another term, the Republicans turned to his secretary of commerce, Herbert Hoover, in 1928. In a campaign based on the cultural and religious divide within the country, Hoover bested the Democratic Party nominee, Alfred E. Smith of New York. Smith's Catholicism helped Hoover carry several states in the South. Prosperity was also an essential ingredient in Hoover's triumph.

The End of Republican Dominance

Within a year of his election, the economic environment soured. The stock market crash of 1929 and the depression that ensued over the next three years tested the resilience of the Republican coalition. When Hoover proved incapable of providing relief for the unemployed, his assurances of an imminent return of prosperity seemed hollow. The Republicans lost seats in the congressional elections of 1930. Soon it was evident that the nation had lost faith in Hoover, too. The defeat he suffered at the hands of Franklin D. Roosevelt in 1932 was an electoral landslide. Democrats now dominated both houses of Congress as well.

Beneath the wreckage, Republicans retained the allegiance of some 40 percent of the voters. However, they had failed to address the economic inequities of the nation during the 1920s or to propose effective solutions to the plight of farmers, industrial workers, and the disadvantaged. They had the power to do so but chose instead not to offend the business interests at the heart of their party. For these lapses, they would spend two decades out of the White House and a decade and a half out of control of Congress.

Until the 1930s, the Republicans held the allegiance of African American voters, both North and South. The Grand Old Party continued its rhetorical devotion to black rights against the racist policies of the Democrats, but it did little to advance the interests of African Americans. Under Taft, Harding, and Hoover, some Republicans proposed abandoning blacks and appealing to white southern Democrats. By 1932 sufficient disillusion existed among African Americans about Republicans that an opening for the Democrats existed if that party changed its segregationist stance.

From the heady days of the late 1890s, when Republicanism seemed the wave of the nation's political future, through the challenges of the Roosevelt-Taft years, the Republican Party had at least engaged some of the major issues and concerns of the time. After eight years of Wilson, however, the conservatism of the GOP lost its creative edge and became a defense of the status quo. As a result, the party encountered a well-deserved rebuke during the depths of the Great Depression in 1932.

See also Democratic Party, 1896–1932; Gilded Age, 1870s–90s; progressivism and the Progressive Era, 1890s–1920.

FURTHER READING. John Morton Blum, *The Republican Roosevelt*, 1954; Robert H. Ferrell, *The Presidency of*

Calvin Coolidge, 1998; Lewis L. Gould, *Four Hats in the Ring: The Election of 1912 and the Birth of Modern American Politics*, 2008; Idem, *Grand Old Party: A History of the Republicans*, 2003; Idem, *The Presidency of Theodore Roosevelt*, 1991; John Earl Haynes, ed., *Calvin Coolidge and the Coolidge Era*, 1998; Joan Hoff-Wilson, *Herbert Hoover: Forgotten Progressive*, 1975; Herbert F. Margulies, *Reconciliation and Revival: James R. Mann and the House Republicans in the Wilson Era*, 1996.

LEWIS L. GOULD

Republican Party, 1932–68

The FDR Eclipse

The GOP began the 1930s as the nation's majority party. Winner of eight of the ten presidential elections dating back to 1896, it held a coalition comprising eastern pro-business conservatives, who controlled the party purse strings, and reform-minded midwestern and western progressives, who identified more with middle-class Americans. But during the Great Depression, the mainstays of Republican dominance—a surging economy and stock market—lay prostrate. Another usual source of GOP political strength, the protectionism embodied in the Smoot-Hawley Tariff of 1930, only worsened the economic quagmire. By decade's end, amid economic despondency, Franklin D. Roosevelt had welded together a new Democratic coalition that crushed the Republican supremacy.

The contrast between the 1928 and 1932 presidential elections demonstrated the GOP's devastation. In 1928 Herbert Hoover won 41 states; four years later, he claimed just 6, all in the Republican Northeast and New England. While the party in power usually loses ground in midterm elections, the Democrats increased their congressional majority in 1934. Worse for Republicans, their small minority splintered between pro–New Deal progressives and conservatives who opposed FDR, although feebly. The 1936 election brought Republicans more despair. Not only did Roosevelt pummel its nominee, Governor Alf Landon of Kansas, who won just Maine and Vermont, but his victory transcended geographical lines. He claimed the traditionally Republican regions of the Northeast and Midwest, as the GOP hemorrhaged members; liberals, African Americans, urbanites, and farmers abandoned it to join the New Deal coalition.

But Roosevelt's hubris following his 1936 triumph enabled Republicans to regain some footing. When the president clumsily proposed "packing" the Supreme Court with up to six more justices to ensure against having his programs ruled unconstitutional, the overwhelmingly Democratic Congress defied him. Roosevelt's blunder and an economic downturn in 1937, which critics dubbed the "Roosevelt recession," allowed Republicans to band together with conservative southern Democrats, forming a coalition on Capitol Hill to oppose Roosevelt and later Harry Truman.

Southern members of Congress fought Roosevelt partly because his programs expanding the federal government's powers and spending reawakened their traditional sympathy for states' rights. The New Deal also provoked a fundamental shift in the Republican Party's philosophy. Heir to the Hamiltonian tradition supporting a strong central government, Republicans began to espouse limited federal powers and states' rights, positions they advocated more emphatically in the coming decades. Despite cooperating with Republicans, southern Democrats declined to switch parties, for that would have cost them seniority and committee chairmanships. They stayed put, and although the GOP gained seats in the 1938 midterms, it remained in the congressional minority.

Republicans also squabbled, revealing deep party fissures. By 1940 they were divided between internationalists and isolationists. With war consuming Europe and Asia, isolationists wanted to steer clear of the conflict, while internationalists favored aid to allies. An even deeper breach was between Northeast and Middle Atlantic Republicans, who tightly controlled the party, and western progressives, who resented the eastern establishment's power. These splits helped Wendell Willkie, an Indiana native and former president of an electric utility, to win the 1940 GOP nomination, beating out rivals like establishment favorite Thomas Dewey of New York. Willkie was an unusual candidate, and his elevation showed the dearth of Republican leaders. A political novice, he had been a Democrat until 1938. To balance Willkie's internationalism, Republicans picked as his running mate isolationist Senator Charles McNary of Oregon. Although Willkie received more votes than Hoover or Landon did against FDR, the president won an unprecedented third term. In the 1944 election, Roosevelt's margin of victory over GOP nominee Dewey was slimmer still, but wartime bipartisanship reduced Republican chances of making inroads against the Democrats.

A Surge of Strength and Modern Republicanism

When Roosevelt died in 1945, Republican fortunes appeared to change. Truman had far fewer political gifts than FDR, and in the 1946 midterm elections, Republicans scored their greatest gains of the twentieth century, picking up a total of 67 seats in Congress—55 in the House and 12 in the Senate—to win control of both houses of Congress. Jubilant Republicans brandished brooms to symbolize their sweeping victories, and *Newsweek* declared, "An Era Begins," anticipating a long Republican reign on Capitol Hill. The 80th Congress stamped a permanent conservative imprint, passing the anti-labor Taft-Hartley Act and the Twenty-Second Amendment, which limited the president to two terms. But the new Congress proved

unable to roll back New Deal programs, and GOP dominance proved short-lived.

In the election of 1948, the strong Democratic coalition helped Truman pull off an upset of Thomas Dewey, and Democrats retook control of Congress. But the president soon suffered setbacks. In 1949 the Soviet Union exploded its first atomic bomb; Communists won control of China, prompting charges that Truman "lost" the world's largest nation to a growing Red tide. The Korean War, which began in 1950, exacerbated fears of worldwide Communist gains. Republican Senator Joseph McCarthy of Wisconsin capitalized on the Red Scare by charging that a large conspiracy of Communist spies had infiltrated America's government. Cold war anxieties and the issue of anticommunism provided a winning theme for Republicans and united the party's moderates, libertarians, and social and moral conservatives.

The new unity boded well for the 1952 election, but the run-up to the contest again revealed party friction. Conservatives wielded considerable strength, yet in both 1944 and 1948, Dewey, an eastern moderate, won the nomination. In 1952 the leading conservative contender was Senator Robert Taft of Ohio, President William Howard Taft's son. But Taft suffered a severe charisma deficit and generated no widespread appeal. Moreover, he had an isolationist bent, favoring a decreased U.S. commitment to NATO and opposing the Marshall Plan, America's successful economic aid program for Western Europe. These views alarmed Taft's potential rival for the GOP nod, General Dwight Eisenhower, the World War II hero and NATO commander.

A late 1950 meeting with Taft proved critical in propelling Eisenhower into politics. Before conferring with the senator, he had drafted a letter declaring himself out of the 1952 race, intending to make it public if he found Taft's diplomatic views palatable. But Taft refused to commit to NATO and internationalism. After the meeting, Eisenhower destroyed the letter.

The importance of American internationalism was just one factor inducing Eisenhower to run. Growing federal budget deficits jarred his sense of fiscal integrity. The string of five consecutive Democratic presidential victories made him fear the two-party system's collapse if the Republicans lost again. Supporters entered him in the GOP primaries, and he won the nomination. But Taft controlled party machinery, and the Republican platform reflected conservative views more than Eisenhower's moderation, denouncing Truman's foreign policy of containment and the 1945 Yalta agreements for immuring Eastern Europe behind the iron curtain. Conservatives advocated a more aggressive stance, "rollback," which meant forcing Communists to yield ground and free captive peoples.

The 1952 elections allowed Republicans to taste success for the first time in more than 20 years. Eisenhower soundly defeated the Democratic nominee,

Governor Adlai Stevenson of Illinois. Significantly, he made inroads into the Solid South, winning four states there and establishing a beachhead in a region that proved fertile ground for Republicans. His coattails also extended to Congress. The GOP gained control of the House and had equal strength with Senate Democrats, where Vice President Richard Nixon's vote could break a tie.

In 1956 Eisenhower read *A Republican Looks at His Party*, a book written by his undersecretary of labor, Arthur Larson. A centrist, Larson considered New Deal activism excessive but believed modern times demanded a greater government role in areas like labor and social insurance. The president praised the book for encapsulating his own political philosophy. What Eisenhower called "modern Republicanism" embraced internationalism and fiscal conservatism yet accepted a more active government role in social services than conservatives could stomach. Disdaining conservatives out to shrink or even end Social Security, he wrote, "Should any political party attempt to abolish social security and eliminate labor laws and farm programs, you would not hear of that party again in our political history."

Eisenhower proved a popular president. His approval ratings averaged 66 percent during his eight-year tenure, and the prosperity of the 1950s allowed Republicans to shuck their image as the party of the Great Depression. In 1956 Eisenhower beat Stevenson more handily than four years earlier. He exulted, "I think that Modern Republicanism has now proved itself, and America has approved of Modern Republicanism."

But Eisenhower's popularity was personal and never translated to a broader party appeal. During the 1954 midterms, Democrats regained control of Congress and in 1956, picked up one more seat in each house. In the 1958 midterms, Democrats rode a wave of worries over a recession, national security, and lack of progress in areas like space exploration, concerns made palpable in 1957 when the Soviet Union launched the world's first satellite, *Sputnik*. They pasted the GOP, gaining 48 seats in the House and 13 in the Senate. Many Republican elected during these years—especially in the House, which remained Democratic until 1995—spent their entire Capitol Hill careers in the minority.

Restless Conservatism

Republican conservatives were restive. The party's failure to make gains against Democrats was frustrating, and they howled in protest at Eisenhower's budgets, which grew despite his attempts to restrain spending. Blaming modern Republicanism for the increases, they derided it as a political philosophy that advanced government programs on only a smaller scale than what Democrats liked—a "dime store New Deal," as Republican Senator Barry Goldwater of Arizona called one GOP program. They resented Taft's being passed over as a presidential

nominee, and his death in 1953 left them bereft of a leader. They failed to limit the president's foreign policy powers when the Bricker amendment, which would have constrained them, was defeated. An image of extremism sullied fringe conservatives, such as members of the John Birch Society, the extremist anti-Communist group founded in 1958, whose leader even charged that Eisenhower was a Communist agent. Indeed, the battles over many of Eisenhower's domestic and international views within the party explain why, despite a successful two-term presidency, he never won the reverence within the GOP that Ronald Reagan later did.

Moderates got another crack at the Democrats when the GOP nominated Nixon in 1960. Although the Californian had built a reputation as a harshly anti-Communist conservative in Congress, as vice president he identified himself with Eisenhower's moderation. His razor-thin loss to Senator John Kennedy in the presidential election gave conservatives more heft to advance one of their own.

They gained strength, especially in the South and West, regions ripe for right-wing thought. In the West, the spirit of individualism and freedom from personal restraints meshed with the ideal of limited government. Westerners distrusted the federal government, and its vast western land ownership irritated residents. In the South, Democratic support for the civil rights movement drove white conservatives out of the Democratic Party and into a new home, the GOP. These Sunbelt regions also enjoyed an economic boom, and their financial contributions—including from Texas oilmen—registered a growing impact in the party. The GOP, once too weak even to field congressional candidates in the South, began to bring in big names and even cause conversions. In 1961 Texas Republican John Tower won Lyndon Johnson's Senate seat; in 1964 Democratic Senator Strom Thurmond of South Carolina switched to the Republicans, and Governor John Connally of Texas later followed suit.

Conservatives determined to get their chance in 1964, nominating Barry Goldwater to run against President Johnson. To many moderates, Goldwater's views were extreme. He urged a tough stand against the USSR, favored voluntary Social Security, and opposed the Civil Rights Act of 1964, because he feared it would lead to hiring quotas. Moderates fought him. Liberal New York governor Nelson Rockefeller ran against Goldwater in the 1964 primaries, and after Rockefeller withdrew, Pennsylvania governor William Scranton jumped in. In defeat, Scranton sent Goldwater a harsh letter denouncing "Goldwaterism" for "reckless" foreign policy positions and civil rights views that would foment disorder. The letter killed any possibility of a unifying Goldwater-Scranton ticket, and the bitter clash between moderates and conservatives persisted to the national convention, where conservatives booed Rockefeller. The intraparty fight left the nominee wounded;

Goldwater recalled, "Rockefeller and Scranton cut me up so bad there was no way on God's green earth that we could have won." Other moderates rebelled. Rockefeller and Governor George Romney of Michigan declined to campaign for Goldwater, and Arthur Larson even endorsed LBJ.

Badly trailing Johnson in polls, Goldwater hoped to garner at least 45 percent of the popular vote. Instead, he received just 38.5 percent. Democrats gained 2 Senate seats and 37 House members, making Congress even more Democratic. So thorough was the Republican Party's repudiation that pundits expressed doubts about its viability.

Goldwater later reflected, "We were a bunch of Westerners, outsiders, with the guts to challenge not only the entire Eastern establishment—Republican and Democratic alike—but the vast federal apparatus, the great majority of the country's academics, big business and big unions. . . ." Therein lay an important facet of Goldwater's effort. He laid the groundwork for a future conservative upsurge by energizing the party's southern and western forces, which began to wrest control of the party from the eastern establishment. His ideological brand of conservatism provided rallying cries for Republicans: lower taxes, small government, states' rights, anticommunism, and an emphasis on law and order. His crusade also enlisted the participation of fresh faces in politics, including actor Ronald Reagan, who filmed an eloquent television spot endorsing Goldwater. The humiliation of 1964 also prodded Republicans to find better leadership. In 1965 House Republicans elected Michigan congressman Gerald Ford minority leader, providing more effective resistance to Johnson policies, while new Republican National Committee chairman Ray Bliss also helped rebuild the party.

Significantly, Goldwater won ten southern states in 1964. He emphasized campaigning "where the ducks are," so he hunted for votes in the South. There, white conservatives, traditionally states' rights supporters, viewed federal support for civil rights as big government intrusion. Desiring more local control over issues involving integration, taxes, and church, they began drifting from the Democrats and moored themselves to the GOP.

The Southern Strategy

Republicans rebounded in the 1966 midterms to win 50 congressional seats, 47 in the House and 3 in the Senate. Richard Nixon rode the wave of renewed GOP energy, capturing the 1968 nomination and fashioning an electoral strategy that used two overarching issues, the Vietnam War (he called for "an honorable settlement") and "law and order."

The war had generated protests nationwide, and riots in cities plus student uprisings shattered the country's sense of stability. The unrest disturbed middle-class Americans, and polls showed that a majority of respondents felt that LBJ had moved too quickly on civil rights. An independent candidate,

Alabama governor George Wallace, played on such sentiments by charging that communism lay behind the civil rights movement.

Nixon's appeal was more subtle. Promising law and order, he addressed patriotic "forgotten Americans" who quietly went to work and spurned the demonstrations that rocked the nation. His vice presidential pick reinforced his message: as Maryland governor, Spiro Agnew had taken a strong stand against urban rioters. Agnew's presence on the ticket plus Nixon's strong stand on crime and opposition to forced busing for integrating schools all capitalized on race as a political issue. Burgeoning suburbs, home to millions of middle-class Americans, welcomed Nixon's message, and the suburbs drew strength away from old Democratic political machines in cities. Meanwhile, in the South a momentous reversal occurred. White conservatives there switched to the GOP, while African Americans nationwide deserted the party of Abraham Lincoln. In 1960, Nixon won 30 percent of the African-American vote; eight years later, he received little more than 10 percent.

Nixon's "southern strategy" helped him win the election, beating Vice President Hubert Humphrey by a slim popular margin. Had third-party candidate Wallace not won five southern states, Nixon would have gained them. His appeal to issues involving race, crime, and war cracked the core of the New Deal coalition, attracting traditional Democratic voters such as blue-collar workers. He also pulled the South more firmly into the Republican fold. After a century as solidly Democratic, the region became reliably Republican. Although Nixon failed to carry either house of Congress, his party had made much headway since the 1930s. Struggling for decades, it gained enough strength by 1968 to win the White House while making new regional inroads. For Republicans, the doleful days of the Great Depression seemed a part of the past. After a third of a century as the minority party and a disastrous defeat in 1964, Republicans had built the foundation for a promising future.

See also era of consensus, 1952–64; New Deal Era, 1932–52.

FURTHER READING. Mary Brennan, *Turning Right in the Sixties: The Conservative Capture of the GOP*, 1995; Gary Donaldson, *Truman Defeats Dewey*, 1999; Lee Edwards, *Goldwater: The Man Who Made a Revolution*, 1995; Barry Goldwater, *The Conscience of a Conservative*, 1960; Lewis Gould, *Grand Old Party: A History of the Republicans*, 2003; Idem, *1968: The Election That Changed America*, 1993; Dewey Grantham, *The Life and Death of the Solid South: A Political History*, 1988; Arthur Larson, *A Republican Looks at His Party*, 1956; Donald Ritchie, *Electing FDR: The New Deal Campaign of 1932*, 2007; Robert A. Rutland, *The Republicans: From Lincoln to Bush*, 1996; David Stebenne, *Modern Republican: Arthur Larson and the Eisenhower Years*, 2006.

YANEK MIECZKOWSKI

Republican Party, 1968–2008

When former vice president Richard M. Nixon became the Republican Party nominee for president in 1968, the GOP was deeply divided between its moderate and conservative wings. Moderates such as New York governor Nelson Rockefeller had supported racial equality and federal spending on education, health care, and welfare. Conservatives like Senator Barry Goldwater of Arizona opposed what they called "big government" and "tax-and-spend" policies, and they championed limited government, individualism, and self-reliance.

Goldwater's 1964 presidential nomination seemed to have shifted the momentum to the conservative wing until his landslide defeat by President Lyndon B. Johnson in the general election. But the conservative wing eventually rebounded with renewed strength in the 1980s under the leadership of Ronald Reagan. The revived conservative movement that turned into a juggernaut in the 1980s was a result of a variety of factors, including a reaction against the social upheavals of the 1960s and 1970s, as well as the gradual political realignment of the South.

Nixon: The Southern Strategy and a New Foreign Policy

Many Southerners had become dissatisfied with high taxes, government regulations, federal civil rights legislation, and what they saw as the dismantling of traditional institutions, such as church and family. Goldwater appealed to these Southerners and other Americans upset with the direction of U.S. politics. Despite his loss, the 1964 election marked the first time since Reconstruction that most Southerners had voted Republican. This achievement set the stage for what became known as Richard Nixon's "southern strategy" for regaining the White House in 1968.

The 1968 presidential race touched on many sensitive issues. Public concerns ignited over the conflict in Southeast Asia, the civil rights movement, inner-city riots, and the violent antiwar protests on college campuses throughout the nation. Nixon faced off against Democratic nominee Vice President Hubert Humphrey and third-party candidate George Wallace.

Nixon won 301 electoral votes and 43.4 percent of the popular vote. Humphrey received 191 electors and 42.7 percent. Nixon won the popular vote by approximately 500,000 votes. It was a narrow victory, with a margin that was almost as small as John F. Kennedy's against Nixon in 1960. Wallace garnered 13.5 percent of the vote and 46 electors.

For Republicans, Nixon's victory meant the beginning of the demise of the New Deal liberal coalition and the emergence of a political realignment. In *The Emerging Republican Majority*, Kevin Phillips argued that "a liberal Democratic era ha[d] ended and that a new era of consolidationist Republicanism

ha[d] begun." Yet the evidence for realignment was not so clear.

Indeed, from 1968 until the 1990s, Republicans dominated presidential elections, while Democrats maintained strong majorities in the House of Representatives. It was the beginning of an era of divided government, which emerged from the increase of registered independents, the weakening of political parties, and the rise of split-ticket voters. Since 1968, Republicans have won seven out of eleven presidential elections, losing only four times to Democrats—to Jimmy Carter in 1976, Bill Clinton in 1992 and 1996, and Barack Obama in 2008. In Congress, from 1968 until 1994, Republicans gained a majority in the Senate only once and for only six years, from 1981 until 1987. Republicans served as the minority party in the House for 40 straight years, from 1954 until 1994.

To be sure, Republicans learned well their role as a minority party, at least until they captured both houses of Congress in 1994, the year of the so-called Republican revolution. Nevertheless, Republican presidents, beginning with Nixon, faced Democratic-controlled Congresses and had to come to terms with the concept of "separated institutions sharing powers." As a result, some GOP presidents moved their policies to the center of the political spectrum.

In the 1970 midterm elections, Republicans won two seats in the Senate but lost nine seats to the Democrats in the House. Nixon characterized the outcome as a victory for Republicans because usually the president's party loses many more congressional seats in midterm elections. However, the true test of the party's strength, and its ability to build a coalition big enough to win another presidential election, would occur two years later.

Nixon's 1972 reelection campaign relied on personal loyalists instead of party leaders at the national, state, and local levels. Former senator Bob Dole of Kansas, then the chair of the Republican National Committee, stated, "The Republican Party was not only not involved in Watergate, but it wasn't involved in the nomination, the convention, the campaign, the election or the inauguration." Isolated from his party, but possessing a favorable foreign policy record, Nixon campaigned tirelessly.

Leading up to the 1972 election, conservatives had mixed feelings about Nixon's social, economic, and foreign policy record. Nixon's policies in health care, affirmative action, and the environment estranged him from conservatives. He proposed a national health insurance program, approved affirmative action programs for federal workers, and signed into law legislation establishing the Environmental Protection Agency.

Yet Nixon made some policy decisions that pleased conservatives. For example, he rejected congressional attempts to reduce defense spending. He removed many antipoverty programs passed under Johnson's Great Society, including Model Cities, Community Action Activities, and aid to depressed areas. Nixon pushed for tough crime laws. He also ordered officials at the Department of Health, Education, and Welfare to not cut off funding to school districts that failed to comply with the Supreme Court's desegregation order.

In an effort to court the vote of disaffected white Southerners, Nixon spoke out against court-ordered busing and lamented the moral decline in America. He denounced the Supreme Court's decision in *Swann v. Charlotte-Mecklenburg Board of Education*, which upheld busing laws and allowed federal courts to oversee the integration process. The issue of busing caused many working-class Americans to join Nixon and the GOP. To gain the Catholic vote and the support of religious conservatives, Nixon bemoaned the loss of traditional moral values and condemned abortion and the removal of prayer in public schools.

Nixon's foreign policy accomplishments enhanced his stature. A longtime staunch anti-Communist, Nixon surprised his critics when he reached out to China and when he sought détente with the former Soviet Union. His trip to China in 1972 was a success. Intending to drive a wedge between China and the Soviet Union, Nixon successfully negotiated a trade agreement and thereby opened China to Western markets. Achieving relations with China empowered Nixon during his trip to Moscow that same year. Nixon and the Soviet premier Leonid Brezhnev met and formulated a Strategic Arms Limitations Treaty (SALT I), which imposed limits on both countries' nuclear weapons. Though the treaty did not do much in the area of arms reduction, the meeting itself was enough to temporarily ease U.S.-Soviet tensions. Nixon's opening to China and his trip to Moscow enhanced his credibility among American voters.

Nixon's 1972 opponent was Senator George McGovern of South Dakota. As a liberal Democrat, one of McGovern's biggest problems was that most voters in America still remembered the urban riots and violent protests on college campuses that occurred in the late 1960s and early 1970s.

Nixon won by the largest margin in history—60.7 percent of the popular vote to McGovern's 37.5 percent. The electoral margin between the two was 520 to 17. In the congressional elections, Republicans lost 1 seat in the Senate and gained 12 in the House. However, the momentum for Republicans would soon change after the 1972 election because of scandals in the White House.

Vice President Spiro Agnew resigned after revelations of his involvement in bribes and tax evasion while governor of Maryland. Then the Watergate scandal began to consume the Nixon presidency. On June 17, 1972, five men had broken into the Democratic National Committee's headquarters, located in the Watergate Hotel in Washington, D.C. Although Nixon dismissed the break-in by people associated with his reelection campaign as a "third rate burglary," the president's role in the cover-up led to his resignation on August 8, 1974. Nixon's vice president,

Gerald R. Ford, appointed previously to replace Agnew, succeeded to the presidency.

Ford's Accidental Presidency

Ford was an unlikely person to rise to the presidency, as he had never aspired to an office higher than the House of Representatives and was contemplating retiring from public life when Nixon chose him to replace Agnew. As president, Ford moved quickly to win public trust—an essential goal given public cynicism toward government and political leaders in the wake of Watergate. Although Ford initially succeeded in that task, he lost enormous support from the public when he issued a controversial pardon for Nixon a mere month after taking office. The combined effects of Watergate and the Nixon pardon on public perceptions were disastrous for the GOP. The party lost 49 seats in the House of Representatives and 3 seats in the Senate in the 1974 midterm elections. The president himself never recovered politically from the pardon and lost his bid for election to the presidency in 1976.

Ford's brief tenure highlighted the ideological rift in the GOP. He appointed Nelson Rockefeller as his vice president, an action that infuriated conservatives who had long battled the politically moderate New Yorker for control of the GOP. Ford further alienated the Right with his support for détente with the former Soviet Union. Former California governor Ronald Reagan challenged Ford's quest for the 1976 GOP nomination, and the two ran a close race right up to the party's convention. Ford prevailed, but not before he had suffered much political damage. In the general election, Ford lost to Democratic nominee Jimmy Carter, a former one-term governor of Georgia whose improbable campaign for the presidency stunned political observers.

By the time Carter assumed the presidency in 1977, the Republicans were hugely outnumbered by the Democrats in Congress. The GOP held a mere 143 seats in the House (versus 292 for the Democrats) and 38 in the Senate (against 61 Democrats and 1 independent). The GOP did gain 15 House seats in the 1978 midterm elections, as well as 3 seats in the Senate. Public disaffection with Carter created an opportunity for the GOP to stage a political comeback.

Reagan and the Rise of the New Right

The conservative wing of the Republican Party gained strength during Carter's term. Conservatives reached out to working- and middle-class voters with appeals for lower taxes, deregulation, and reduced social spending, and they courted religious voters by criticizing liberal abortion laws and the elimination of school prayer. Many conservative Catholics and evangelical Protestants set aside their theological differences and joined the ranks of the Republican Party. A movement known as the New Right brought together a new coalition of voters for the GOP. The New Right stood for traditional institutions (family and church), traditional moral values (antigay, antiabortion, and progun), and states rights (limited government).

Some conservative Democrats joined the GOP. Many became known as "neoconservatives," and they were distinctive in their emphasis on strong defense and U.S. intervention abroad along with their preference for progressive domestic policies. Together, the New Right and neoconservatives set in motion a conservative juggernaut, which became palpable in the 1980 election of Reagan. The conservatism of Reagan revolutionized the Republican Party. What Reagan had done to the party was to revitalize the type of conservatism that Barry Goldwater advocated in the 1960s.

Reagan's 1980 campaign held Carter and Democrats responsible for high inflation, high interest rates, and for the long hostage crisis in Iran. Reagan believed that the federal government had become too large and powerful, that it had assumed too much social and economic responsibility. In his first inaugural address, Reagan told Americans, "government is not the solution to our problems; government is the problem."

Reagan won 51 percent of the popular vote, carried 44 states and 489 electoral votes compared to Carter's 49. In addition to winning the White House, Republicans picked up 32 seats in the House, which was short of a majority, but which marked the largest gain of seats in the House during a presidential election since 1920. Of greater importance was the Republican victory in the Senate. Republicans won 12 seats and took control of the Senate. Republicans had not been the majority party in the upper house since 1955. Overall, the outcome of the 1980 election demonstrated a significant shift in the political landscape.

After taking office in 1981, Reagan pushed his conservative agenda. Cutting domestic programs, deregulating the economy, reducing taxes, and building up the military were some of his key initiatives. Reagan proposed cutting the Food Stamp and School Lunch programs. He proposed loosening many environmental regulations. Reagan perpetuated Carter's deregulation of the airline industry, and he objected to the Federal Communications Commission (FCC) regulating the cable television networks industry. In foreign affairs, Reagan sought to put an end to the spread of communism. In doing so, he rejected the policies of containment and détente. He accepted the use of military intervention in and economic aid to non-Communist countries, a policy known as the "Reagan Doctrine." To improve national security—and perhaps to bankrupt the Soviet Union—Reagan oversaw the largest military buildup during peacetime in American history.

By the 1984 presidential election, Reagan had increased his popularity among the American electorate. One reason was that the economy had rebounded during his first term. He had achieved major tax cuts and convinced the Federal Reserve to loosen its grip on the money supply. Another reason for Reagan's popularity had to do with his decisions in foreign policy. He labeled the former Soviet Union the "evil empire" and launched his Strategic Defense Initiative (SDI), better known as "Star Wars." He aided anti-Communist groups in their fight against oppressive regimes. Reagan's speeches also imbued Americans with optimism about their future.

The 1984 GOP platform was a document of conservative principles. It contained promises to pass an antiabortion amendment, a balanced budget amendment, and a law that would reform the federal tax code. In the general election, Reagan defeated former vice president Walter Mondale. Reagan won 59 percent of the popular vote and 525 electoral votes. In Congress, the GOP lost only 2 seats in the Senate and gained a small number in the House.

In his second term, Reagan had his share of difficulties. Republicans lost six seats in the Senate in the 1986 midterm election and, consequently, their majority status. Reagan could not, as he had promised, balance the budget. The federal deficit surged well over $200 billion in 1986 and dropped down thereafter to $150 billion, a result attributed to both economic growth and tax reform. A big victory for Reagan occurred in 1986, when he signed a tax reform bill into law. The new law simplified the tax code by setting uniform rates for people with similar incomes, and it eliminated many tax deductions. However, in the same year, the Iran-Contra scandal broke.

Top White House officials, including Lieutenant Colonel Oliver North and Admiral John Poindexter, had illegally sold arms to Iran in exchange for the release of American hostages. The proceeds of the arms deal were sent surreptitiously to a rebel group, called the Contras, who were trying to overthrow the Communist regime in Nicaragua. Leading up to the 1988 elections, the scandal did not hurt the Republican Party as much as Democrats would have liked. In the final two years of Reagan's presidency, other events overshadowed Iran-Contra.

In 1987 Reagan's conservative Supreme Court nominee Robert Bork failed to win confirmation. In December 1987, Reagan and the Soviet premier, Mikhail Gorbachev, signed the Intermediate-range Nuclear Forces (INF) treaty. Unlike SALT I, which limited the number of nuclear weapons, the INF treaty eliminated an entire class of nuclear weapons. Most Americans lauded Reagan's foreign policy decisions. They believed his agreement with Gorbachev and his May 1988 trip to Moscow signaled the beginning of the end of the cold war. Despite record federal budget deficits, Reagan left the presidency—and his party—in relatively good shape for the 1988 election.

The One-Term Presidency of George H. W. Bush

In 1988 the GOP nominated Vice President George H. W. Bush for the presidency, and he campaigned on the promise to continue Reagan's policies. He also pledged not to support new taxes. Bush beat Democratic nominee governor Michael Dukakis of Massachusetts, winning 40 states and 54 percent of the popular vote. However, while Republicans held on to the presidency, the Democrats kept their majorities in Congress.

Bush's middle-of-the-road views widened the gap between moderates and conservatives. For example, in 1990 he signed into law the Americans with Disabilities Act and an extension of the Clean Air Act. The savings-and-loan bailout, spending on the Gulf War, as well as welfare and Medicare payments increased the strain on the federal budget. As a result, the deficit rose, and Bush was compelled to break his pledge not to raise taxes.

In response, Pat Buchanan, a conservative columnist, challenged Bush for the GOP nomination in 1992. Buchanan forcefully spoke out against abortion, gay rights, and sexual tolerance, and he advocated the restoration of prayer in public schools. Although Buchanan's challenge failed, he had weakened Bush politically and embarrassed the party with an overheated prime-time speech at the Republican National Convention.

The Clinton Era and the Gingrich-led Republican Revolution

The Democrats nominated Governor Bill Clinton of Arkansas. The general election also included a billionaire third-party candidate, Ross Perot, who garnered 19 percent of the vote. Clinton won with merely 43.3 percent of the popular vote. Within two years, however, voters started to view Clinton negatively because of his proposed tax increases and proposed universal health care program.

In the 1994 midterm election, sensing an electorate disgruntled over low wages and the loss of traditional moral values, conservative Republicans, led by Representative Newt Gingrich of Georgia, devised a series of campaign promises. Under the rubric of the Contract with America, the promises included tax cuts, welfare reform, tougher crime laws, congressional term limits, an amendment to balance the budget, and a return of power and responsibility to the states. Some 300 Republican candidates signed the contract in a public ceremony on the steps of the U.S. Capitol. Republicans won control of both houses of Congress. They had not enjoyed a majority in the House in 40 years.

Yet, after failed attempts to enact the Contract with America, the public soon became disgruntled with the GOP in Congress, so much so that the 1996 presidential nominee Bob Dole distanced himself from Gingrich and others associated with the Republican revolution. Clinton ably defined the GOP "revolutionaries" as political extremists and easily won reelection, although he failed to win a majority of the vote with Perot again on the ballot.

The George W. Bush Era

In the 2000 campaign, Texas governor George W. Bush faced off against Vice President Al Gore. Bush called himself a "compassionate conservative," which was a campaign stratagem designed to attract independents and moderates without sacrificing conservative support. Bush promised to restore dignity to the White House, a reference to President Clinton's personal scandals and impeachment. After the polls closed on November 7, it was clear that Gore had won the popular vote by a narrow margin, a little over 500,000 votes. Not so clear was the winner of the Electoral College. The election came down to Florida. The winner of Florida's 25 electoral votes would become president-elect. For over a month, Florida remained undecided because of poorly designed ballots in Palm Beach County. As recounts by hand were taking place, Gore's legal team convinced the Florida Supreme Court to rule that the results of a hand count would determine the winner. On December 12, Bush's legal team appealed the decision to the U.S. Supreme Court. In a 5 to 4 decision, the Supreme Court stopped recounts on the premise that they violated the equal protection clause of the Fourteenth Amendment. Bush thus won Florida and with it the presidency.

In his first year in office, Bush signed into law a bill that lowered tax brackets and cut taxes by $1.35 trillion over a ten-year period. In education, his No Child Left Behind Act required standardized national tests for grades three through eight. He proposed a school voucher program that would allow children to leave failing schools and attend schools of their choice—including private, parochial schools—at the expense of taxpayers. He also banned federal funding for research on stem cell lines collected in the future.

Bush's leadership would be put to the test on September 11, 2001, when terrorists attacked the World Trade Center and the Pentagon. He reminded Americans of their resiliency and assured them the United States would seek and punish the terrorist group responsible for the attacks. His approval ratings soared, and the GOP gained seats in Congress in the midterm elections in 2002.

Bush won the 2004 election against Senator John Kerry of Massachusetts with 51 percent of the popular vote and 286 votes in the Electoral College. In Congress, Republicans increased their majorities, winning four more seats in the Senate and five more in the House. The success of the Republican Party was, in part, a result of a strategy to focus on the registration of conservative voters, especially in key battleground states, such as Florida, Ohio, Iowa, and Pennsylvania. To mobilize conservatives in those states, Republicans emphasized social issues, such as abortion, stem cell research, and gay marriage.

However, by the 2006 midterm elections, Bush's popularity had fallen significantly due to the bungled U.S. military intervention in Iraq and the government's slow response to hurricane Katrina in the Gulf

States. Bush's mismanagement of Katrina lowered public confidence in the national government. Moreover, in the month preceding the election, a number of scandals within the GOP had become public. House Majority Leader Tom Delay of Texas violated the campaign finance laws of Texas. He later resigned his seat in the House. Representative Mark Foley of Florida resigned due to sexual misconduct.

Democrats won majorities in both houses of Congress. They interpreted their victory as a mandate to end the war in Iraq. Bush continued to prosecute the war, and shortly after the elections he requested more money from Congress to fund the troops. The unpopular war and Bush's low approval ratings increased Democrats' prospects of taking back the White House in 2008.

The 2008 Elections: Democrats
Take Back Control of Washington
The 2008 GOP nomination contest failed to attract much enthusiasm from conservatives. The leading candidates—former Massachusetts governor Mitt Romney, former Arkansas governor Mike Huckabee, and Senator John McCain of Arizona—were all seen by conservative activists as too politically moderate. McCain eventually won the nomination, and to shore up conservative support, he chose as his vice presidential running mate the staunchly conservative governor of Alaska, Sarah Palin.

Amid the collapse of the U.S. financial sector under a Republican administration and a national surge in support for the Democratic Party, McCain lost the election to first-term senator Barack Obama of Illinois. In Congress, the Democrats picked up 21 seats in the House of Representatives and at least 8 seats (one race was undecided at the time of this writing) in the U.S. Senate. For the first time since 1993, Republicans were clearly the minority party.

See also conservative ascendancy, 1980–2008; era of confrontation and decline, 1964–80.

FUTHER READING. James W. Ceaser and Andrew E. Busch, *The Perfect Tie: The True Story of the 2000 Presidential Election*, 2001; Richard F. Fenno, *Learning to Govern: An Institutional View of the 104th Congress*, 1997; Gary L. Gregg and Mark J. Rozell, eds., *Considering the Bush Presidency*, 2004; Harry P. Jeffrey and Thomas Maxwell-Long, eds., *Watergate and the Resignation of Richard Nixon*, 2004; Kevin P. Phillips, *The Emerging Republican Majority*, 1969; Melvin Small, *The Presidency of Richard Nixon*, 1999.

MARK ROZELL AND KYLE BARBIERI

republicanism
Republicanism is a political philosophy that exerted a profound cultural influence on the life and thought of Americans living in the Revolutionary and antebellum eras (1760–1848). This unique view of government and society originated during the crisis in Anglo-American relations that resulted in the independence of the 13 colonies and the creation of a new nation.

English Commonwealthmen
Responding to actions of the British government during the 1760s and 1770s, colonial American spokesmen drew extensively on the libertarian thought of English commonwealthmen. Epitomized by John Trenchard and Thomas Gordon's *Cato's Letters* and James Burgh's *Political Disquisitions*, the publications of these dissenting radicals railed against the urgent danger posed by the systematic corruption they attributed to Robert Walpole's ministry (1721–42). The parliamentary government emerging under Walpole appeared to them to maintain the facade of constitutional procedures while actually monopolizing the whole of governmental powers within his cabinet. In their minds, Walpole's machinations were destroying the balance among king, lords, and commons that constituted the very strength of the British constitution. Believing in a separation of powers among the three constituent elements of the government, commonwealthmen urged parliamentary reforms such as rotation in office, the redistribution of seats, and annual meetings to restore the proper constitutional balance. Beyond that, their concern for freedom of thought and the sovereignty of the people led them to speak out passionately against the increasing corruption and tyranny they believed to be infecting English society and government. Pairing liberty with equality, Trenchard and Gordon's *Cato's Letters* and Burgh's *Disquisitions* proclaimed the preservation and extension of liberty to be all important. Since the greatest danger to the liberty and the equality of the people came from their leaders, all citizens must maintain a constant vigilance to prevent governmental officials from being corrupted by power and stealthily usurping liberty away from the people. In their minds all men were naturally good; citizens became restless only when oppressed. Every man should, therefore, act according to his own conscience, judge when a magistrate had done ill, and, above all, possess the right of resistance. Without such a right, citizens could not defend their liberty.

Revolutionary Republicanism
While revolutionary leaders in America made extensive use of such conceptions, the ideas of these commonwealthmen did not cross the Atlantic intact. Americans adapted beliefs regarding consent, liberty, equality, civic morality, and constitutions to their specific and concrete needs, so that even when the same words were used and the same formal principles adhered to, novel circumstances transformed their meanings. Consequently, revolutionary leaders, believing that history revealed a continual struggle between the spheres of liberty and power, embraced a distinctive set of political and social attitudes

that gradually permeated their society. A consensus formed in which the concept of republicanism epitomized the new world they believed they were creating. This republicanism called for a constant effort on the part of all American citizens to protect the realm of liberty (America) from the ceaseless aggression of the realm of power (Great Britain) under the guidance of gentlemen of natural merit and ability.

Above all, republicanism rested on a self-reliant, independent citizenry. The sturdy yeoman—the equal of any man and dependent upon none for his livelihood—became the iconic representation of American republicanism. Americans believed that what made republics great or what ultimately destroyed them was not the force of arms but the character and spirit of the people. Public virtue, the essential prerequisite for good government, became all important. A people practicing frugality, industry, temperance, and simplicity were sound republican stock; those who wallowed in luxury were corrupt and would corrupt others. Since furthering the public good—the exclusive purpose of republican government—required a constant sacrifice of individual interests to the greater needs of the whole, the people, conceived of as a homogeneous body (especially when set against their rulers), became the great determinant of whether a republic lived or died. Thus republicanism meant maintaining public and private virtue, social solidarity, and vigilance against the corruptions of power. United in this frame of mind, Americans set out to gain their independence and to establish a new republican world.

By the end of the eighteenth century, the American commitment to republicanism had grown even stronger than it had been in 1776. Its principal tenets—a balance between the separate branches of government and a vigilance against governmental power—had been inscribed in the U.S. Constitution and Bill of Rights. America had indeed become republican, but hardly in the manner intended by its early leaders. Economic and demographic changes taking place at an unparalleled rate had begun to work fundamental transformations within the new nation. Geographic expansion spawned incredible mobility, and great numbers of Americans, becoming increasingly involved in the market economy, strived to gain all the advantages they could from their newly acquired social and economic autonomy.

Revolutionary republicanism, rather than constraining these activities, seemed rather to encourage them and to afford them legitimacy. The emphasis placed on equality in revolutionary rhetoric stimulated great numbers of previously deferential men to question all forms of authority and to challenge distinctions of every sort. Rather than generating an increased commitment to order, harmony, and virtue, republicanism appeared to be fostering an acquisitive individualism heedless of the common good and skeptical about the benevolent leadership of a natural elite. Postrevolutionary America,

instead of becoming the New World embodiment of transcendent classical values, appeared increasingly materialistic, utilitarian, and licentious: austerity gave way to prosperity; virtue appeared more and more to connote the individual pursuit of wealth through hard work rather than an unselfish devotion to the collective good. No longer a simple, ordered community under the benign leadership of a natural elite, America seemed instead to be moving toward being a materialistic and utilitarian nation increasingly responsive to both the demands of the market and the desires of ordinary, obscure individuals.

The rapid democratization and vulgarization that took place in American society during the last decades of the eighteenth century helped create a far more open and fluid society than had been anticipated by most revolutionary leaders. Indeed, the transformations taking place in American society through these years were so complex and indeliberate, so much a mixture of day-to-day responses to a rapidly changing socioeconomic environment, that most Americans were unaware of the direction that such changes were taking them and their society. Their commitment to republicanism, however, allowed them to continue to imagine themselves as members of a virtuous, harmonious, organic society long after the social foundations of such a society had eroded. The fact that republican language became increasingly disembodied from the changing cultural context made self-awareness that much more difficult. Such language allowed—even impelled—citizens to view themselves as committed to the harmony, order, and communal well-being of a republican society while actively creating an aggressive, individualistic, and materialistic one.

Most Americans clung to a harmonious, corporate view of their society and their own place in it, even while behaving in a materialistic, utilitarian manner in their daily lives. Thus, while rapidly transforming their society in an open, competitive, modern direction, Americans idealized communal harmony and a virtuous social order. Republicanism condemned the values of a burgeoning capitalistic economy and placed a premium on an ordered, disciplined personal liberty restricted by the civic obligations dictated by public virtue. In this sense, republicanism formalized or ritualized a mode of thought that ran counter to the flow of history; it idealized the traditional values of a world rapidly fading rather than the market conditions and liberal capitalistic mentality swiftly emerging in the late eighteenth century. As a result, Americans could—and did—believe simultaneously in corporate needs and individual rights. They never, however, had a sense of having to choose between two starkly contrasting traditions—republicanism and liberalism. Instead, they domesticated classical republicanism to fit contemporary needs while amalgamating inherited assumptions with their liberal actions.

Jeffersonian Republicanism

The kind of society that would emerge from the increasingly egalitarian and individualistic roots being formed in the late eighteenth century was unclear when Thomas Jefferson assumed the presidency in 1801. Even by that time, the perception of personal autonomy and individual self-interest had become so inextricably intertwined that few of Jefferson's supporters had any clear comprehension of the extent to which entrepreneurial and capitalistic social forces were shaping American life. Under the pressure of such rapidly changing conditions, the autonomous republican producer—the yeoman integrally related to the welfare of the larger community—gradually underwent a subtle transmutation into the ambitious self-made man set against his neighbors and his community alike. Consequently, by incorporating as its own the dynamic spirit of a market society and translating it into a political agenda, the party of Jefferson had unself-consciously developed a temper and a momentum that would carry it beyond its original goals. Indeed, even by 1800, personal independence no longer constituted a means by which to ensure virtue; it had itself become the epitome of virtue. The process by which this took place was complicated, often confused, and frequently gave rise to unintended consequences. It ultimately resulted, nonetheless, in profound changes in American culture in the nineteenth century.

Republicanism in the hands of the Jeffersonians—the foremost advocates of the persuasion—spawned a social, political, and cultural movement that quite unintentionally created the framework within which liberal commitments to interest-group politics, materialistic and utilitarian strivings, and unrestrained individualism emerged. Simultaneously, however, republicanism also fostered a rhetoric of unselfish virtue—of honest independence devoted to the communal welfare—that obscured the direction in which American society was moving. By promoting the desire for unrestrained enterprise indirectly through an appeal to popular virtue, the Jeffersonians helped produce a nation of capitalists blind to the spirit of their enterprise. Consequently, their movement enabled Americans to continue to define their purpose as the pursuit of traditional virtue while actually devoting themselves to the selfish pursuit of material wealth. Irresponsible individualism and erosive factionalism replaced the independent producer's commitment to the common good. Still, free enterprisers, who by the 1850s would include publicly chartered business corporations, fell heir to the republican belief that an independent means of production sufficiently attached a citizen's interests to the good of the commonwealth. Entrepreneurial fortunes became investments in the general welfare. The entrepreneur himself, freed by the American belief in virtuous independence, could proceed unencumbered by self-doubts in his attempt to gain dominion over a society of like-minded individuals who could only applaud his success as their own.

The triumph of Thomas Jefferson initiated a brief period—a "Jeffersonian moment"—when the virtues of both republicanism and eighteenth-century liberalism merged into a cohesive political philosophy offering the bright promise of equal social and economic advancement for all individuals in a land of abundance. That the moment was brief stands less as a critique of the individuals who combined to bring Jefferson to the presidency than it is a comment on the forces that impelled them, forces over which they had little control and, perhaps, even less understanding. Just at the time when an ideology translated the realities of the American environment into a coherent social philosophy, those very realities carried American society far beyond the original goals of the Jeffersonian movement as they transmuted eighteenth-century American republicanism into nineteenth-century American democracy.

Republican Historiography

If the protean nature of republicanism obscured such transformations by providing a sense of harmony and comfort to great numbers of late-eighteenth- and early-nineteenth-century Americans, no such cordiality and consensus characterizes scholarly attempts to come to grips with republicanism as a historical concept. Indeed, since first receiving formal analytic and conceptual identity in the early 1970s, republicanism has been at the epicenter of strife and contention among historians of the early national period. Even though the concept had become omnipresent in scholarly literature by the mid-1980s (in the terms *republican motherhood, artisan republicanism, free labor republicanism, pastoral republicanism, evangelical republicanism*, and others), a good many scholars, particularly social historians, remained convinced that the emphasis on republicanism obscured far more than it clarified about early American society. For them the scholarly concentration on republicanism occluded vast domains of culture—religion, law, political economy, and ideas related to patriarchy, family, gender, race, slavery, class, and nationalism—that most scholars knew were deeply entangled in the revolutionary impulse.

The greatest challenge to republicanism, however, came not from social historians but from scholars wedded to the concept of liberalism. For these individuals, Americans of the Revolutionary era manifested aggressive individualism, optimistic materialism, and pragmatic interest-group politics. In their minds, John Locke's liberal concept of possessive individualism, rather than Niccolò Machiavelli's republican advocacy of civic humanism, best explained American thought and behavior during the years after 1760.

The intellectual conflict that emerged between advocates of republicanism and those of liberalism ushered in years of sterile debate. An entirely unproductive "either/or" situation resulted: either scholars supported republicanism or they espoused liberalism. Fortunately, in realizing that partisans of both republican and liberal interpretations had identified strands of American political culture that simply could not be denied, a great many historians transcended this tiresome dialogue. Replacing it with a "both/and" mode of analysis, these scholars have revealed the manner in which republicanism, liberalism, and other traditions of social and political thought interpenetrated one another to create a distinctive and creative intellectual milieu. Over time a "paradigmatic pluralism" emerged: scholars employing a "multiple traditions" approach emphasized concepts drawn from natural rights, British constitutionalism, English opposition writers, contract theory, Protestant Christian morality, Lockean liberalism, and republicanism. Such work has resulted in a far more sophisticated understanding of early American culture.

The multiple traditions approach to early American history provides scholars with significant insights of inestimable value in their efforts to analyze this vital era. The first and perhaps most important of these is that no single concept—whether republicanism, liberalism, or Protestant Christianity—provides a master analytical framework for understanding revolutionary America. Each of these concepts comprised a multitude of arguments developed in different contexts to solve different problems and to articulate different ideals. Whatever conflicts or contradictions might seem apparent among them could always be held in suspension by the interpenetration of ideas and mutual reinforcement. While republicanism can clearly no longer be considered *the* key to understanding early American history, it certainly remains *a* vital constituent element in the political culture of revolutionary America. If no longer a conception of transcendent meaning, republicanism remains a discourse deeply embedded in the central issues facing Americans in the late eighteenth and early nineteenth centuries—a time in which a distinctive pattern of social and political thought incorporating republican, liberal, and religious ideas emerged in response to these issues. Each of these clusters of ideas comprised a vital part of the larger meaning Americans brought to particular disputes in the years of the early republic. To abstract one set of ideas—whether republican, liberal, or religious—from this intellectual fabric not only impairs an understanding of this distinctive pattern of thought, but obscures the special character—the very uniqueness—of the early republic.

See also democracy; era of a new republic, 1789–1827; liberalism; war for independence.

FURTHER READING. Joyce Appleby, *Capitalism and a New Social Order: The Republican Vision of the 1790s*, 1984; Barnard Bailyn, *The Ideological Origins of the American Revolution*, 1967; Alan Gibson, "Ancients, Moderns and Americans: The Republicanism-Liberalism Debate Revisited," *History of Political Thought* 21 (2000), 261–307;

James Kloppenberg, "Premature Requiem: Republicanism in American History," in *The Virtues of Liberalism*, 59–70, 1998; Idem, "The Virtues of Liberalism: Christianity, Republicanism, and Ethics in Early American Political Discourse," *Journal of American History* 74 (1987), 9–33; Isaac Kramnick, *Republicanism and Bourgeois Radicalism: Political Ideology in Late Eighteenth-Century England and America*, 1990; J.G.A. Pocock, *The Machiavellian Moment: Florentine Political Thought and the Atlantic Republican Tradition*, 1975; Paul A. Rahe, *Republics Ancient and Modern: Classical Republicanism and the American Revolution*, 1992; Caroline Robbins, *The Eighteenth-Century Commonwealthmen: Studies in the Transmission, Development, and Circumstances of Liberal Thought from the Restoration of Charles II Until the War with the Thirteen Colonies*, 1959; Daniel T. Rogers, "Republicanism: The Career of a Concept," *Journal of American History*, 79 (1992), 11–38; Robert E. Shalhope, *The Roots of Democracy: American Thought and Culture, 1760–1800*, 1990; Rogers M. Smith, "Beyond Tocqueville, Myrdal, and Hartz: The Multiple Traditions in America," *American Political Science Review* 87 (1993), 549–66; Gordon S. Wood, *The Creation of the American Republic, 1776–1787*, 1969.

ROBERT E. SHALHOPE

Revolutionary War
See war for independence.

Rocky Mountain region
While the political history of the Rocky Mountain region—Montana, Wyoming, Colorado, Idaho, Utah, Nevada, Arizona, and New Mexico—does not lack stories of partisan division and struggle, a greater share of that history challenges the assumptions and conventions of party loyalty and identification. Over a century and a half, the desires for economic development and federal money have acted as incentives to pay little attention to the usual boundaries of party. A proliferation of factions and interest groups has often muddled efforts to define and patrol the usual lines of partisanship. Reinforced by an enthusiasm for individualism and independence, electoral success has frequently coincided with eccentric personality and temperament in the candidate. In the Rockies, traditional party activists have often found themselves a demoralized people, bucking a trend toward the hybrid and the maverick.

For all the electoral success awarded to eccentrics who set their own courses, the political history of the region in the last century tracks the usual arrangement of eras and phases in American political history. And yet the region's citizens gave those familiar eras a distinctive or even unique inflection. Moreover, the U.S. Constitution enhanced the national impact of the Rockies, since states with comparatively sparse populations were awarded the same number of senators as eastern states with dense populations. Thus, a number of senators from the Rocky Mountain states have exercised consequential power in national and international decisions.

In the invasion, conquest, mastery, and development of the interior West, an initially weak federal government acquired greater authority, force, and legitimacy. The history of the Rockies is rich in case studies of agencies and institutions of the federal government exercising a remarkable force in the political life (not to mention the social, cultural, economic, and emotional life) of the region. Under the Department of State until 1873 and then under the Department of the Interior, the territorial system oversaw the progression (sometimes quite prolonged and halting) to statehood. Even after statehood, the residents of the Rockies found themselves subject to the rules, regulations, and sometimes arbitrary authority of agencies in the executive branch, many of them clustered in the Department of the Interior: the Office (later Bureau) of Indian Affairs, the U.S. Army (both the combat forces and the Army Corps of Engineers), the U.S. Geological Survey, the Bureau of Reclamation, the Forest Service, the National Park Service, the Fish and Wildlife Service, the Bureau of Land Management (a hybrid itself of the venerable General Land Office and the more junior Grazing Service), the Atomic Energy Commission, the Department of Energy, and the Environmental Protection Agency.

Many of the activities of federal agencies in the Rockies focus on the management, use, preservation, and regulation of the region's mountains, canyons, and deserts. In national politics, the issues that have come to occupy the category of "the environment" have fluctuated in the attention paid to them, sometimes dipping below visibility. In the Rockies, policies governing water, land, and wildlife have long held a place at the center of political life; the region has thus functioned as a political seismograph, recording dramatic shifts in attitudes toward nature. This is a region in which indigenous peoples retain important roles in local, state, and national politics, as do the "other" conquered people—the descendants of Mexicans who lived in the territory acquired by the United States in the Mexican-American War. In this case and in the case of Asian immigrants, western race relations are often intertwined with international relations, with the terms of treaties and the actions of consuls stirred into the struggles of civil rights. The great diversity of the population meant that the civil rights era had many dimensions, as Indians, Mexican Americans, Asian Americans, and African Americans pursued similar, though sometimes conflicting, agendas of self-assertion.

Early Native American
Political Systems and Conflicts
Diversity, variation, and complex negotiations between and among peoples set the terms for Rocky Mountain politics long before the arrival of Europeans. Decentralized governance characterized the nomadic groups of the northern Rockies as well as the Southwest, with the band far more established as the unit of loyalty than any broader tribal identity. Kinship set the terms of cohesion and obligation, and leaders rose to authority by repeated demonstrations of their courage and wisdom.

The arrival of Spanish explorers, soldiers, settlers, and missionaries near the end of the sixteenth century initiated a long-running struggle for imperial dominance. As the more rigid and hierarchical systems of Europeans encountered the widely varying structures of leadership among native peoples, the comparatively simple dreams of empire produced far more tangled realities. One particularly ironic and awkward outcome was the rise of a vigorous slave trade in the Southwest, as Utes, Navajos, and Apaches traded captives from other tribes to Spanish settlers; centuries later, under U.S. governance, the campaign for the abolition of the interior West's version of slavery extended well beyond the abolition of the much better known practices of the American South.

The Spanish introduction of horses into North America unleashed a cascade of unintended and unforeseen rearrangements in the balance of power. With the horse, Indian people took possession of a new mobility for trading, raiding, hunting, and warfare. The spread of the horse unsettled the balance of power between the newly mounted native people and their would-be European conquerors. When the Navajos and Apaches, as well as the Utes and Comanches (nomadic people to the north of the New Mexican settlements) took up the horse, both Pueblo Indians and Spanish settlers found themselves living in communities where the possibilty of a raid was a constant source of risk and vulnerability.

The opportunities for bison hunting and migration offered by the horse brought new peoples into the region, and thereby accelerated the contests for turf and power. By the time of European contact, these groups would become known as the Cheyenne, Arapaho, Sioux, Crow, Blackfeet, Shoshone, Gros Ventre, and Nez Perce. In the northern and central Rockies, while people with a shared language, similar religious beliefs, and a sense of common origin gathered together annually for ceremonies, they spent most of the year divided into bands who dispersed for hunting and gathering through much of the year. Tribes varied widely in the formality and informality of their designation of leaders. In many groups, men rose to leadership through constant and repeated demonstration of generosity and courage. For most tribes, decisions rested on consensus emerging from long discussion. Over the next centuries, the political diversity and complexity of the native groups, as well as their democratic forms of decision making, would perplex European and American newcomers to the Rocky Mountains. Non-Indian explorers, emissaries, or military leaders, who arrived expecting to meet a group and identify a man or men who carried the authority to make lasting decisions for all, had come to the wrong place.

Centralized, imperial authority held sway only intermittently in locations remote from capitals and home offices. Disunity and opposing factions within the colonial society could set the empire's plans to wobbling as effectively as resistance from the indigenous communities.

The Mexican Period and Fluid National Boundaries

Mexican independence in 1821 introduced even greater complexity to an already complicated and precarious political landscape. One of the most consequential actions of the new nation was the opening of the northern borderlands to trade with Americans, a change in policy of great political consequence. As merchants began traveling back and forth between Santa Fe, New Mexico, and St. Louis, Missouri, the United States acquired the chance to have a commercial presence, initially tolerated and welcomed, in Mexican terrain. But the Santa Fe trade presented the possibility of a conquest by merchants, and Mexican authorities struggled to limit the intrusions of the legal and illegal aliens of their day.

Thus, by the 1820s, the future of sovereignty in the Rocky Mountains was an unsettled domain. It was one thing to sit in distant offices and trace lines of sovereignty on a map, and quite another to give substance and meaning to those lines. No other section of the United States experienced so many changes in national boundaries and came under so many governmental jurisdictions. In the first half of the nineteenth century, maps of the Rockies recorded claims by six nations: Spain, France, Mexico, Britain, the United States, and the independent republic of Texas. The former Spanish territories—from the southwest corner of Wyoming through the western half of Colorado, and the bulk of what would become Utah, Nevada, Arizona, and New Mexico—remained under Mexican control after independence. The purchase of the Louisiana Territory from the French placed the central and northern Rockies under the sovereignty of the United States. Between 1836 and 1850, Texas claimed portions of New Mexico, Colorado, and even a sliver of Wyoming. Meanwhile, the area now called Idaho fell under the joint occupation of Great Britain and the United States until awarded to the United States by treaty in 1846. These "official" Euro-American boundaries, moreover, existed in not particularly splendid isolation from the most important dimension of power on the ground: the authority of the Indian tribes.

The aridity, elevation, and difficult terrain of much of the Rockies further challenged the aspirations of empire. The area seemed, as early explorers bluntly noted, ill-suited to conventional American agricultural settlement. Given the aridity in the interior West, it seemed possible that Americans would find that they had no need or desire to assert power over areas like the Great Salt Lake Basin, since there seemed to be no imaginable economic use to which to put them. And yet Americans still hoped that explorers would uncover other resources that would inspire settlers and lead to the political incorporation of this territory into the nation. Still, the pursuit of beaver pelts, the key resource of the 1820s and 1830s, did not offer much of a foundation for a new political order. As it did elsewhere on the continent, the fur trade brought Euro-Americans and Indian people into a "middle ground" of shifting power, with no obvious answer to the question of who was in charge.

In 1846, the joint occupancy of the Northwest came to an end, assigning the Oregon territory to the United States. The Mexican-American War dramatically rearranged the lines of sovereignty to the advantage of the United States. In 1848 the Treaty of Guadalupe Hidalgo transferred more than one-third of Mexico's land to the Americans. Hundreds of one-time Mexican citizens found themselves reconstituted as residents of the United States. In a promise that, in the judgment of some latter-day activists, still awaits full delivery, Article IX of the treaty declared that the Mexicans in the acquired territories ". . . who shall not preserve the character of citizens of the Mexican Republic . . . shall be incorporated into the Union of the United States, and be admitted at the proper time (to be judged of by the Congress of the United States) to the enjoyment of all the rights of citizens of the United States."

With the Gadsden Purchase of 1853, the United States achieved its lasting borders. The value of the territory of the Rocky Mountains was undemonstrated and unrecognized; it had simply been necessary to acquire this land in order to span the continent from sea to sea. In the 1840s, the movements of Americans—overland travelers on their way to California and Oregon, and then, in the late 1850s, gold seekers drawn to discoveries in Colorado and Nevada—began to give on-the-ground meaning to U.S. territorial claims. And yet the undiminished powers of Indian tribes still rendered the U.S claims both hollow and precarious.

Civil War, Reconstruction, Territories, and Indian Conquest

The discovery of gold and silver put to rest any lingering doubt that the territory of the Rockies might not be worth the trouble of political incorporation. In many sites in the mountains, collections of individualistic strangers improvised methods of governance that would, at the least, formalize mining claims and property rights. The political unit of the mining district tied small camps together and established procedures for platting out the district's boundaries, defining claims, setting up law-enforcement and court systems, and establishing water rights, most often through the system known as prior appropriation, or "first in time, first in right." Settlers also sought recognition, organization, and aid from the federal government.

For white Americans newly arrived in Colorado, the onset of the Civil War brought a heightened sense of vulnerability to Indian attack, since the new settlements depended on an overstretched and ill-defended supply line to the Midwest, and the resources and attention of the Union Army were directed to the war in the East. The primary feature of the Civil War era in the Rocky Mountain region was thus an escalation of Indian-white violence, as militia and volunteer forces reacted forcefully to threats and suspicions. With the shift of federal attention away from the West, at the Bear River Massacre in Utah, at the Sand Creek Massacre in Colorado, and in the campaign against the Navajo, the conduct of white soldiers and volunteers was often extreme and unregulated.

The Confederate Territory of Arizona (the southern half of the New Mexico Territory) represented the one foothold of the rebellion in the West. Operating out of Texas, Confederate troops entered New Mexico, took Santa Fe, and headed north to take the Colorado gold mines, but then met defeat from a Colorado militia at Glorieta Pass. With this battle, the question of the loyalty of the Rocky Mountain states was put to rest.

The post–Civil War era in the Rockies gained its shape and structure from three major projects: creating territories and then determining when they had reached the condition that justified the awarding of statehood; designing and installing systems for allocating property in minerals, land, water, and transportation routes; and conquering (sometimes through direct military engagements and sometimes through more subtle processes of negotiation and escalating economic dependence) the Indian people of the region and confining them to reservations under treaties that, even if negotiated under terms of surrender and defeat, nonetheless turned out to provide a basis for a reassertion of Indian self-governance a century later.

In the post–Civil War era, the political circumstances of the West both resembled and differed from the political circumstances of the South. In the Reconstruction enterprise of providing the vote to African American men, the West led the South. African Americans in Colorado tied the cause of black suffrage to the cause of statehood, and enlisted influential senators to their cause. The Territorial Suffrage Act of 1867 granted the vote to African American men in the territories, two months before the first Reconstruction Act gave freedmen the vote in the former Confederacy.

In their greatest era of common experience, the South and the West were the targets and subjects of the attentions, plans, and reforms of ambitious northern Republicans. If the word *Reconstruction* sums up this experience for the South, historian David Emmons has argued, the similar process for the West might more accurately be called Construction. In the South, Republicans undertook to reconstruct a comparatively well-defined social and political order, while in the West, without a comparable, well-established elite like the southern planters, the Republicans had the opportunity to construct a new political and economic order from the foundation. Under the terms of territorial government, American citizens found their assumed rights of self-government temporarily (for New Mexico and Arizona, this "temporary" status endured for over 60 years) diminished and restricted. They could elect their territorial legislators, and they could send a nonvoting delegate to Congress, but the federal government appointed the governor and (perhaps even more important) the judges. Those who chafed under this regime and longed for statehood often found that their cause had become thoroughly entangled in national tussles over slavery, race, and partisan dominance in Congress.

Through most of the territorial period, Republicans held the presidency, and Democrat Grover Cleveland did not make a consistent practice of using his patronage power to replace Republicans with Democrats in territorial positions. At first glance, this situation may have seemed to give an advantage to Republicans in shaping the partisan leanings of the territories under their governance. But territorial government was so unpopular, and the governors so often resented and disliked, that the Republican advantage in appointments over the territorial period may actually have worked in favor of the Democrats, or at least did them little injury. Historian Earl Pomeroy has reported that Democrats in Montana in 1877 privately acknowledged that they were happy to have a Republican governor, noting that "it will keep the [Republican] party divided and we will stand a much better show to defeat them in the elections." Even though denunciation of appointed officers as outsiders was a standard refrain, appointing a local man to office did not necessarily increase the supply of goodwill. The legacy of territorial status lingered in the minds, hearts, and certainly the rhetorical reserves of Westerners, enhancing resentment of the federal government and reinforcing a sense of powerlessness and victimization. As Pomeroy has observed, the "political complexions" of the Rocky Mountain states came out of the territorial period stamped as "unpredictable, insurgent."

Tension over the control exercised by Congress and presidential appointees was most sustained in Utah, as northern Republicans undertook to eliminate Mormon polygamy, which they had initially paired with slavery as one of the "twin relics of barbarism." Before the creation of the Utah Territory, and in the years in which Mormon Church leader Brigham Young held the office of governor, the Mormon homeland of Deseret was a theocracy, a state of affairs that troubled the souls of northern Republicans even as they themselves were guided in many of their own political undertakings by Protestant Christianity. With a sequence of increasingly forceful antipolygamy laws, the federal government undertook a purposeful campaign to end Mormon political and cultural distinctiveness, including congressionally mandated disenfranchisement of Utah territory women in 1887. The Woodruff Manifesto in 1890, renouncing polygamy, was a key step in Utah's progression toward legitimacy and statehood. How to shift the distinct politics of Utah to the partisan rivalries of the nation as a whole was far more complicated and orchestrated with considerably less explicit exercise of church authority. Given the long campaign of persecution of the church by the Republican Party during the territorial period, the Mormons' eventual shift to a strong Republican affiliation offered its own telling demonstration that political categories have shown, in this region, a remarkable capacity for reconfiguration and realignment.

Along with territorial government, a second major arena for the process of "constructing" the West involved the federal government's allocation of property rights in transportation routes, land, minerals, and water. The remoteness and isolation of the region made the building of railroads a major concern of settlers; by ending the struggle over whether the route of the transcontinental railroad would serve the interests of the North or the South, the secession of the Confederacy opened the way for the Pacific Railroad Act of 1862, providing crucial government aid. In a similar way, secession cleared the way for the passage of the Homestead Act in 1862, followed by a complicated stream of legislation trying to adapt the homestead principle to the difficult terrain of the Rockies. The 1872 Mining Law took the local improvisations of the mining West and built them into federal legislation, guaranteeing free access of prospectors and miners to the public domain and omitting a royalty that would have directed a portion of the revenue from mining to the public treasury. The allocation of water presented the greatest challenge to federal hopes of bringing order to the West; under the doctrine of prior appropriation, a tangle of water rights already held status in the region well before Congress or the executive branch could try to establish a national policy.

In the last half of the nineteenth century, the most unambiguous display of federal power occurred in the final campaigns of conquest against Indian people. After the Civil War, the West became the main arena for the military campaigns of the U.S. Army. Military forts and posts, already significant, gained in importance as economic drivers for the region. In 1849, jurisdiction over the Office of Indian Affairs transferred from the Department of War to the newly established the Department of Interior. This shift of agencies gave institutional form to the contest between civilians and the military in setting the direction of Indian relations.

In the region of the Rockies, Indian peoples tried every imaginable strategy to respond to the imposition of American power. Even as the Sioux and Cheyenne fought against George Armstrong Custer in the battle at Little Big Horn, Crow Indians allied themselves with Custer as scouts and auxiliaries. In the Southwest, the Army used Apache scouts to find and pursue other Apaches who had refused to surrender. In their dealings with the Americans, native peoples chose various combinations of alliance and resistance, and those choices meant stress and strain for Indian communities. All these strategies led to the negotiation (and sometimes imposition) of treaties shrinking the tribes' land holdings, designating reservations for their confinement, ending their mobility, prohibiting their religious practices, and subordinating tribal leadership to the arbitrary powers of appointed agents of the Office of Indian Affairs. And yet the treaties also recorded a formal recognition of the tribes and their rights, providing the foundation for the U.S. Supreme Court's recognition of tribal sovereignty a century later.

In this era of constructing the region, voters responded with enthusiasm to the idea of governmental support for economic development, and with that priority front and center, the warmth of support could shift easily and rapidly from Republican to Democratic and back again. The category of "booster of the economy" trumped party affiliation. In states like Nevada, Colorado, or Montana, with the mining industry at the center of the economy, the state legislatures had a way of selecting (sometimes with an incentive, encouragement, or bribe provided by the aspiring officeholder) the heads of mining companies to serve in the Senate. In any individual state or territory, citizens sparred and struggled over the material benefits and advantages delivered by political success, but these contests were rarely guided by political principle. A term coined by historian Kenneth Owens, *chaotic factionalism*, goes a long way toward capturing the reality of political conduct in the Rockies in the last half of the nineteenth century. The term works equally well when applied to Indian tribes, making difficult choices between resistance and accommodation; to the agencies and officials of the federal government; *and* to the region's Euro-American settlers, almost infinitely divided by nationality, class, and competing occupations and professions.

Rocky Mountain Style Populism and Progressivism

In the 1890s, populism diminished the "chaotic" part of "factionalism" for at least a few years. Responding to the serious economic troubles of that decade, the People's Party posed a genuine challenge to northeastern political and economic dominance, as a sectional party with a complicated mix of southern and western dimensions. Fusion politics—loose, temporary alliances across party lines—spurred campaigns that emphasized issues and candidates over party loyalty. The 1896 campaign of Democrat William Jennings Bryan marked the high point of fusion politics in the interior West. Bryan's pro-labor and pro-silver Populist Party/Democratic Party coalition earned the popular and electoral votes of every western state except California and Oregon. The election also highlighted the limits of Rocky Mountain electoral power, since states with such sparse populations yielded just a fraction of the electoral votes Bryan would have needed to win the presidency. Carrying the Rockies still meant losing nationwide.

Demanding federal intervention and protections against burdensome railroad shipping rates and arbitrary charges for the storage and marketing of grain, farm families were the backbone of Midwestern and southern populism. In the Rockies, the activism of miners and their unions gave rise to a more inclusive and class-conscious form of populism. Rocky Mountain populism brought together a coalition of farmers, workers, and small businesspeople. This large voting bloc helped elect more Peoples' Party candidates in the mountain states than in any other region. Populist goals moved well beyond economic protections for farmers to include passage of the nation's first eight-hour day laws and protections for union organizing. Populist support for women's suffrage spurred the enactment of that radical measure, and thus gave additional clout to the voting power of the People's Party in Colorado, Utah, and Idaho. The Populist enthusiasm for "direct democracy" also fired up voter interest in election campaigns in the Rockies. Electoral reforms like the voter initiative and referendum, and the direct election of senators, were not unique to the Mountain West, and yet, embraced by voters, they quickly became the hallmark of elections and lawmaking in the region during and after the 1890s.

Four of the Rocky Mountain states—Wyoming (1869 territory, 1890 state), Colorado (1893 state), Utah (1870 territory, until congressional disenfranchisement in 1887; 1896 state), and Idaho (1896 state)—led in the cause of women's voting rights in the United States. Arizona women voted by 1912, joined by women in Nevada and Montana in 1914, all well in advance of the passage of the Nineteenth Amendment in 1920. Voting rights in all of the interior mountain states were achieved through popular referenda, demonstrating a remarkable willingness to experiment on the part of male voters. Strong and active mining unions, as well as the influential Populist Party, proved receptive to efforts of persuasion and recruitment by activist women. Women's unmistakable importance in the household economies of farming and ranching carried a symbolic power that, in itself, made a case for suffrage.

The Mountain West also led the nation in women's party and electoral activism. From 1896 to 1910, when no additional states granted suffrage, an era that eastern suffragists and historians have dubbed "the doldrums," women in the first four Rocky Mountain suffrage states seized their new powers.

Spurred on by the belief that western politics offered a greater openness to experimentation, suffrage leaders in the Rocky Mountain states often reached across dividing lines of place, race, ethnicity, creed, and economic circumstance to win both men and women to their cause. In many states of the region, early women activists and voters embraced "nonpartisanship," furthered third-party movements and independent candidates, promoted public referenda to circumvent entrenched and lethargic state legislators, and won early electoral reforms like primary election laws opening up the nomination process to wider constituencies. Partisan women in the interior West also worked to open up the party machinery to broader participation, with Mountain West women emerging as the nation's first female elected officials, well into the Progressive and New Deal Eras.

Even though the Populist Party had faded in membership and influence by 1900, many of the innovations it had placed on the political agenda came to fruition during the Progressive Era. The legacy of western populism, ongoing labor activism, women's independent voting patterns, and the sweeping national reform movement known as progressivism combined to produce a whirlwind of political reforms in the Rockies. Since participants in this movement were sometimes Republicans, sometimes Democrats, and sometimes members of the Progressive Party, this era made its own contribution to the muddling of partisan identity in the region.

The fact that the Progressive Era coincided with the era of labor wars in the Rockies made a reckoning with the tensions of industrial labor relations unavoidable. Under the militant leadership of the Western Federation of Miners, unions spread in the precious-metal mining districts, especially in Colorado, Idaho, Utah, and Montana. At the same time, organizers for the United Mine Workers went into action in Utah, Colorado, and New Mexico to establish union locals in coal mining communities. Strikes often edged into violence, as miners clashed not only with company guards but also with state troops. The repetitive pattern of state intervention of the military on behalf of mining companies produced political repercussions regionally and nationally. Created by Congress in 1912, the Commission on Industrial Relations led by Frank Walsh held highly visible hearings on Colorado's Ludlow Massacre. In 1914 a strike against the Colorado Oil and Fuel Company, owned by John D. Rockefeller Jr. exploded in a long run of violence involving strikers, their families, mine guards, and the Colorado National Guard. When Rockefeller and labor activist Mother Jones both testified at the Walsh Commission hearings, the intensity of labor struggles in the Rockies preoccupied the nation.

Beyond strikes, the members of mining and other labor unions in the mountain states joined the political fray in state legislatures, electoral campaigns, and voter initiatives. The eight-hour workday, workers' compensation acts, unemployment relief, and laws protecting union organizing came relatively early in the Rocky Mountain states. The nation's first eight-hour day law for miners in the nation was passed (and upheld by the U.S. Supreme Court) in the Utah legislature in 1899. The peaceful, effective, and legal political activity of unionists in the Rocky Mountain region contrasted dramatically with the "pure and simple" unionism of the eastern leadership of the American Federation of Labor. The pursuit of progressive unionism also portrayed union members as good citizens and voters, quite different from the violent terrorists that newspapers of the time often made them out to be based on the actions of a few hard-boiled radical union leaders.

Water and Progressivism in the Semi-Arid Rockies

Urban progressivism gained a foothold in Denver, Colorado; Salt Lake City, Utah; Boise, Idaho; and Albuquerque and Santa Fe, New Mexico. Middle-class women reformers played a direct and visible role as enfranchised citizens in western urban reform movements, which by and large matched the national pattern of concerns for public education, civil service laws, juvenile courts, child labor laws, public transportation franchises, public health, and sanitation. Water supply added a regional variation to the Progressive agenda, as urbanites responded to the challenges of aridity. In Denver, women's groups joined forces with men's civic associations and union leaders to demand public control of the city water system, resulting in the creation of the Denver Water Department, a quasi-public agency with an enormous impact on the allocation and distribution of water in the Rockies. Over the next century, Denver Water would be a central case study in the mounting friction between urban and rural interests, as conflicting visions of the region's political and economic future came to focus on the supply of water.

In Progressive minds, the storage and diversion of water in dams and canals fell under the category of conservation, since water left in streams and rivers seemed wasted and thus in need of "conserving" for productive use. Nevada Democratic U. S. senator Francis Newlands led the campaign for the Newlands Reclamation Act in 1902, setting up the framework for the Reclamation Service (later, the Bureau of Reclamation) to build dams and reservoirs to supply water to farms and ranches. The passage of the Reclamation Act has posed a puzzle for historians: Why did senators and congressmen, representing eastern and Midwestern regions with agricultural sectors, vote in favor of a federal program to aid their competitors in the arid West? Historian Don Pisani has solved this riddle with a finding of relevance to the big picture of the region's political history: the passage of the Reclamation Act offers prime evidence of "the West's increasing power in Congress," produced

by the admission, in the 1890s, of North and South Dakota, Montana, Washington, Idaho, Utah, and Wyoming, with those seven additional states having two senators each. The West now "had the power to block important legislation in the Senate," and recognition of that power "explains the passage of the Reclamation Act."

In both the Progressive and New Deal Eras, enthusiasm for dam building was widespread, in a dramatic contrast to lamentations in the mid- and late twentieth century over the disturbance of free-flowing rivers. Considerably more controversial was the revolution in federal management of the public domain, as policy shifted from disposal (the transfer to private ownership) to the permanent reservation of lands under federal control. With much of his hearty public image derived from his hunting expeditions in the Rockies, President Theodore Roosevelt and his chief forester Gifford Pinchot were the iconic proponents of this enormous change. Progressive conservation launched a process that remapped the Rockies, with half or more of land recategorized as public, not private, property.

To many Westerners, ranging from the heads of large mining and timber corporations to small-scale ranchers, the creation of the Forest Service and the National Park Service seemed not an exciting and enterprising invention of a new form of land management, but a resurgence of the familiar colonialism of the territorial period. The struggle, both rhetorical and material, between the authority of the states and the authority of the federal government would remain central to regional political life, even as economic change revealed that landscapes reserved from extractive activity could provide equally valuable economic opportunities in recreation and tourism.

During World War I and into the 1920s, the efforts at political cooperation between the middle class and workers took a downturn, as anti-immigrant and antilabor political movements gained force. A mob in Bisbee, Arizona, forcefully deported over a thousand striking miners to a remote desert town in New Mexico in 1917; in Montana, alarm over the speeches and actions of the Industrial Workers of the World came to reshape the basic terms of national civil liberties. During the war, the Sedition Act of 1798 had come back into play as prosecutors around the country used it to bring charges against people who criticized the war or the government. Wanting more power to police than the 1798 law provided, Democratic senator Henry Myers of Montana proposed a bill in Congress in August 1917 that gave the terms of sedition a very broad definition, including criticism of the government during wartime; when it failed to pass at the national level, the Montana legislature "recycled" it, passing it in 1918. With the national mood toward dissent souring, Senator Myers then returned to Washington, D.C., and proposed the bill again. This time, it passed with only minor changes.

The Mountain West's Imprint on
New Deal Politics and Policy

Already of inestimable importance in the Rockies, the role of the federal government expanded in the Depression, as federal funding provided the investments once derived from private capital. The operations of the New Deal proved compatible with the enthusiasm of western political leaders for economic development. The landslide victory of Franklin D. Roosevelt throughout the West in 1932 and in subsequent elections, moreover, reconfirmed the power of personality in the region's political culture. Warm feelings toward Roosevelt were validated and reconfirmed as the Rocky Mountain states received a disproportionately large flow of federal dollars per capita. The interior mountain states' regional average was between one-third and one-half more than the next highest region, the Pacific states, and double that received by the states in the Great Plains. One form of federal funding had a lasting impact on the region's landscape, providing an important foundation for the growing tourism economy. Teams of the Civilian Conservation Corps (CCC) cleared hundreds of mountain trails, built roads and bridges, and even carved a spectacular public amphitheater, near Denver, out of solid red rock.

Representatives from the Rocky Mountain states had an important impact in the area of federal agricultural policy and aid programs. Most notably, the Taylor Grazing Act of 1934, sponsored by Colorado's Democratic congressman, Edward P. Taylor, rescued the region's cattle industry from extinction during the drought-ridden 1930s by regulating grazing on federal land. In the next quarter century, the Grazing Service would be merged with the General Land Office to become the Bureau of Land Management, the federal agency with the ironic combination of the largest territory with the lowest profile and funding.

At the other end of the spectrum of visibility and fame, Hoover Dam remains the most telling monument to the centrality of Depression-era federal funding in the Rocky Mountain West. As much as the dam has come to stand for New Deal achievements, its very existence was made possible by its pre–New Deal namesake, Herbert Hoover, and his work as secretary of commerce in negotiating the Colorado River Compact of 1922. The compact, as an interstate agreement signed by all the western states through which the river flowed, was itself a political innovation. By the early 1920s, uncertainty over the provisions for allocating the waters of the Colorado River put the economic well-being of all the neighboring states at risk. Called together by Secretary of Commerce Hoover, representatives from Arizona, California, Colorado, Nevada, New Mexico, Utah, and Wyoming all signed on to a plan to divide the flow of the river between the Colorado River's upper and lower basins. Even though the agreement assumed a much greater and steadier flow of water than the river actually delivered, the compact provided the legal foundation for construction of Hoover Dam and the massive system of dams and reservoirs along the Colorado.

The Military in the Mountain West

In the 1940s, the Mountain West had both an extraordinary range of federally controlled open spaces in remote locations and an extraordinary enthusiasm on the part of local communities for jobs arising from federal projects. The match between these qualifications and the needs of the American military was an obvious one. The technology involved may have been innovative and novel, but these military installations in the West echoed and even revived the pattern of the nineteenth century, when Army forts had played an important role in providing markets for farmers, ranchers, and merchants. World War II and the cold war led to a resurgence in the importance of the military in the region, with new military posts and bases, as well as contractor-operated defense plants. The majority of the strategically remote Japanese American internment camps dotted the interior West. The Manhattan Project made Los Alamos, New Mexico, into the vital center of the new nuclear age. As the cold war arms race gathered momentum, the interior West won the competition for many of the key facilities in nuclear weapons production: the Nevada Nuclear Test Site north of Las Vegas, the Idaho National Engineering Labs near Twin Falls, the Sandia Laboratory in Albuquerque, and the Rocky Flats nuclear weapons plant near Denver. All of these research and production facilities generated contaminated material and waste requiring permanent storage, and after considerable controversy, the Waste Isolation Pilot Project near Carlsbad, New Mexico, came into operation in 1999. The passage of time would make the legacy of these enterprises into yet another source of tense relations between Westerners and the federal government, as communities worried about the dangers of radioactivity in the soil, water, and air, and workers from the plants asked for a reckoning with the health impacts of their jobs.

Defense projects brought millions of dollars and hundreds of new residents into the region during and after World War II. In ways both directly and indirectly related to those projects, the cold war reconfigured both the western infrastructure and political landscape. Justified by the needs of national security, the Highway Act of 1956 transformed transportation through the region. In the mid-twentieth century, the Bureau of Reclamation went into overdrive, designing, funding, and operating a new network of dams and diversions. Here, too, cold war justifications played their part; the interior West's greatest champion of water projects, Democratic congressman Wayne Aspinall from western Colorado, was also an outspoken cold warrior, drawing anti-Communist rhetoric into the arguments he made for more dams. The massive Central Arizona and Central Utah Projects represented both the enthusiasm of the interior West's residents for federally subsidized economic development and the ambitions of the Bureau of Reclamation at their peak.

The Politics of Post–World War II Demographic Shifts and Environmentalism in the Rocky Mountain West

Central to the political changes of World War II and the cold war was the push for greater power and representation on the part of Indians, Mexican Americans, Asian Americans, and African Americans. The civil rights movements of the Rockies were thus multiple and varied, ranging from the reclaiming of treaty rights by Indian tribes to the protesting of segregation, on the part of both Mexican Americans and African Americans, in the Denver school system, with Asian Americans contesting both discrimination and relegation to the status of "model minority." All these campaigns for rights took place in the context of a region shaped by waves of migration and immigration, leaving the legitimacy of any group or individual always open to dispute, as were the roles of insider and outsider. Tensions over population growth thus sometimes pitted groups of white Americans against other white Americans, as "old-timers" and "newcomers" squared off in an ongoing dispute of who was a deserving resident of the Rockies and who was an unwelcome intruder. In that context, with citizens already squabbling intensely among each other, the issue of immigration policy—and especially the status of Mexican immigrants—could be the subject of heated debate while also registering as just another one of many disputes over who deserved the status of rightful Rockies resident.

While the region held no particular advantage over any part of the nation in its progression toward racial inclusiveness and equity in the political process, the history of Denver's election of mayors is nonetheless striking, with the Latino Federico Peña serving from 1983 to 1991, followed by the African American Wellington Webb. In the same spirit, when the state of Idaho became the home of pernicious white supremacy groups, citizens of the state rallied with a number of organizations, monuments, and governmental resolutions, denouncing racism and defending human rights. Idaho's Malicious Harassment Act of 1983, adding force to the prosecution of "crimes based on religious and racial hatred," was, as Stephen Shaw has described it, "the product of bipartisan effort in the Idaho legislature and especially between a Democratic governor and a Republican attorney general."

In the second half of the twentieth century, an extraordinary reorientation of public opinion and legislation brought on a political earthquake that has not stopped shaking voters and elected officials in the interior West. For more than a century, the discovery and development of natural resources, and the use of land and water to support expanding human settlement, had the enthusiastic support of most Westerners. As the national movement known as environmentalism played out, with particular impact in the interior West, it dramatically shifted the very direction of progress and improvement. In the minds—and votes—of many, the direction ascribed to progress reversed, as population growth and economic development were recast, not as the hope of the region but as its bane and burden. As articulate, powerful, and well-funded organizations, exemplified by the successful voter initiative rejecting Colorado's bid for the 1976 Winter Olympics, campaigned for the preservation of natural ecosystems, a new political alignment came into being.

The most consequential element of this change was the passage of an extraordinary package of environmental laws in the 1960s and 1970s, ranging from the Wilderness Act of 1964 to the Endangered Species Act of 1973. Without the active and committed support of both Republican and Democratic members of Congress (and the signature of Republican president Richard Nixon), most of these laws would have remained pipe dreams. But as they went into effect, the memory of their bipartisan origins faded from public awareness. Astute Republican office seekers in the Rockies seized the opportunity presented by the friction and frustration arising from the implementation of environmental laws. With an agile dismissal of recent history, they built an image of the Republican Party as the standard-bearer for the right of local Westerners to use natural resources, free of burdensome regulations and restraints imposed by the imperial East. In the Rockies, as elsewhere in the nation, Democrats became more and more identified as the party allied with federal oversight and environmental causes, and Republicans became more and more identified as the party supporting the traditional forces for development, extraction, and growth, a configuration without particularly deep roots in time.

Of the many environmental laws passed in the 1970s, the Federal Land Policy and Management Act (FLPMA) of 1976—the organic act that belatedly established the specific powers and mission of the Bureau of Land Management (BLM) 30 years after its birth—had the greatest effect in stirring up local resistance. The FLPMA gave the BLM (cynically nicknamed the "Bureau of Livestock and Mining") a much broader, "multiuse" mandate, with recreational and ecological values now included in the BLM's mandate, along with extractive uses. In areas where locals had come to take for granted their right to graze livestock, make mining claims, and build roads on public lands, the FLPMA evoked strong resentment. In the late 1970s, the Sagebrush Rebellion, calling for the transfer of federal lands to state ownership, as well as relief from federal grazing, mineral, water, and environmental regulations, became a force in several legislatures in the region. Nevada set the precedent with a resolution in 1979 with Assembly Bill 413 mandating the transfer of BLM lands to the state, and Arizona, New Mexico, Utah, and Wyoming passed similar laws. In the manner of such campaigns, Sagebrush Rebels championed the cause of small-scale ranchers, loggers, or miners. While many of their troubles stemmed from changes in the national and even international economy rather than from federal intrusion, many of the reforms they sought also suited the purposes of extractive corporations operating on a vastly larger scale. Senator Orrin Hatch of Utah introduced the Western Lands Distribution and Regional Equalization Act—a Sagebrush Rebellion bill—in Congress in the fall of 1979, but the election of Ronald Reagan in 1980 took the wind out of the sails of the Sagebrush Rebellion, with the installation of a presidential administration that declared official sympathy and support for the rebels.

Rocky Mountain Federalism: Late Twentieth-Century National and Local Politics

Since the 1970s, the majority of the region's electoral votes have gone to Republican presidential candidates, tempting pundits to declare that the region had become solidly and definitively conservative. And yet the region's voters often chose Democrats as governors, senators, and congresspeople. The case study of Idaho makes this point dramatically: widely characterized as extremely conservative, the voters of Idaho four times elected Democrat Cecil Andrus as governor. Utah's history makes the same point: between 1965 and 1985, Democrats (Calvin Rampton, followed by Scott Matheson) held the post of governor. Gubernatorial elections have never ceased to follow a pattern of committed variability: in 2000, all eight of the Rocky Mountain states had Republican governors, but by 2006 five had chosen Democrats as governors. The region's defiance of clear and steady political categorization, and the reluctance of many voters to see themselves as consistent party loyalists, continued into the twenty-first century.

The Republican Party, meanwhile, faced a number of tough challenges in self-definition. To some degree, this involved the national split between social conservatives and fiscal conservatives. But the energy boom of the 1990s and the early twentieth-first century opened new rifts in the center of the party. Beginning in the 1990s, a big boom in natural gas production in the Rockies strained Republican unity, as oil and gas developers struggled with opposition from ranchers and sportsmen. A shared identification of all these people as "conservatives" did nothing to reduce this conflict.

While some Rocky Mountain residents gave unswerving support to the cause of environmental preservation and some gave equally single-minded support to the extraction of natural resources, a much larger percentage of the region's residents occupied a category one could call "the muddled majority," with attitudes that were far more characterized by hybridity than by purity. This majority tried to accommodate its desire for the resources produced by

extraction to the changing economic valuation of nature, as recreation, tourism, second homes, and the attraction of intact landscapes to employers and employees became increasingly powerful forces in local and state economies.

As a practice called cooperative conservation emerged in response to this complicated set of issues, the political world of the Rockies presented an instructive and telling laboratory for experiments in the evolving meaning of federalism. In many arenas, the relationship between federal authority and local governments came up for renegotiation and redefinition. Over a century and a half, the region had emerged with a proliferation of jurisdictional lines laying out the turf of numerous federal agencies, state agencies, municipalities, counties, tribes, and special districts with jurisdiction over matters like electricity and water supply. Nearly every law, regulation, or policy required some degree of coordination between these various jurisdictions, demanding considerable political inventiveness in finding methods of negotiation and collaboration across these lines, and in allocating authority and responsibility among various levels of governance. In many western communities, a new tradition of "stakeholder" coalitions or "watershed" associations came into play as representatives of agencies and various interest groups met to work out agreements for the management of local natural resources. From the Malpai Borderlands Group in southern New Mexico and Arizona north to the Clark Fork Basin Committee in Montana, the Rockies saw a proliferation of groups attempting to avoid the usual channels of contention and litigation, and, in the words of Matt McKinney and William Harmon, "to integrate the interests of affected parties" through "collaboration and consensus building." Without any particular awareness of the connection between them, the descendants of white settlers had happened onto a process of decision making that bore a similarity, coincidental but still striking, to the consensus-based practices of the Native American tribes who originally lived in the region.

The Weak Parties of the Rockies: A Persistent Pattern

In the first decade of the twenty-first century in the state of Colorado, one-third of registered voters chose "unaffiliated" over identification with either major party. In all the states of the Rockies, even many voters who went ahead and registered as Democrats or Republicans showed, in their voting, the region's trademark flexibility and inconsistency. How can the persistent pattern of weak party identification and independent voting be explained?

First, economic development, often with federal support, has been the key concern of the region's citizens, and Democrats and Republicans have both pursued this goal. In the early twenty-first century, environmental preservation may be primarily identified with Democrats, but Democrats from the region have a strong record in supporting projects in economic development, whatever their effect in environmental disruption. Democratic congressman and senator Carl Hayden was the leading force behind the giant Central Arizona Project, bringing water to the state's cities, a project loyally supported by the noted conservationist, Democratic congressman Morris Udall.

Second, for many of the most pressing and immediate western issues, the positions of the major parties had little bearing or relevance. In matters ranging from the allocation of water for urban or agricultural use to land-use planning in growth-burdened counties, from the challenges of fighting wildlands fire to the mediation of conflicts between the recreational economy and the extractive economy, the political platforms of both parties bore a striking resemblance to Mother Hubbard's very bare cupboard.

Third, in many parts of the Rocky Mountain West, high rates of mobility have both introduced and minimized the possibility of big changes in political behavior. In the late twentieth century, the Rockies had the highest population growth rates in the country. Yet, even if many of those newcomers arrived with far more settled party loyalties than those held by longer-term residents, the newcomers did not come in organized phalanxes, equipped to swing into action and to substitute their ways for local tradition. Moreover, in recent decades, for many of the new residents, the charm of natural landscapes has been a major factor in the decision to relocate, leaving them solid reasons to join the "muddled majority," with loyalties split between continued economic growth and the preservation of natural amenities.

And, fourth, the persistent and omnipresent western myth, of a region populated by hardy folk characterized by an unbreakable spirit of independence and self-determination, has exercised an unmistakable power over voters—with consequential results. The myth's inability to achieve a high score in historical accuracy has not in any way reduced the certainty that it inspires in its believers, nor its political power. With surprisingly undiminished power, this myth can be counted on to validate and celebrate the region's party-defying mavericks. Resting on the inseparability of myth from reality, the political history of the Rocky Mountain states offers constant reminders of the extraordinary subjectivity that guides human self-perception and self-appraisal in the terrain of politics.

See also Great Plains; territorial government.

FURTHER READING. John Porter Bloom, *The American Territorial System*, 1973; Thomas C. Donnelly, *Rocky Mountain Politics*, 1940; David M. Emmons, "Constructed Province: History and the Making of the Last American West," *Western Historical Quarterly* (Winter, 1994); John P. Enyeart, *"By Laws of Their Own Making": Political Culture and the Everyday Politics of the Mountain West Working Class, 1870–1917*, dissertation, University of Colorado, Boulder, 2002; Marcia Tremmel Goldstein, *"Meet Me at the Ballot Box": Women's Innovations in Party and Electoral Politics in Post-Suffrage Colorado, 1893–1898*, dissertation, University of Colorado, Boulder, 2007; Lawrence Goodwyn, *Democratic Promise: The Populist Movement in America*, 1976; John Kantner, *Ancient Puebloan Southwest*, 2004; Michael Kazin, *The Populist Persuasion: An American History*, revised ed., 1998; Howard Roberts Lamar, *The Far Southwest, 1846–1912: A Territorial History*, 1966; Patricia Nelson Limerick, *The Legacy of Conquest: The Unbroken Past of the American West*, 1987; Richard Lowitt, ed., *Politics in the Postwar American West*, 1995; Matt McKinney and William Harmon, *Western Confluence: A Guide to Governing Natural Resources*, 2004; Rebecca J. Mead, *How the Vote Was Won: Woman Suffrage in the Western United States, 1868–1914*, 2004; Kenneth Owens, "Patterns and Structure in Western Territorial Politics," *Western Historical Quarterly* (October, 1970); Donald Pisani, *Water and American Government: The Reclamation Bureau, National Water Policy, and the West, 1902–1935*, 2002; Earl Pomeroy, *The Territories and the United States, 1881–1890: Studies in Colonial Administration*, 1969; Francisco A. Rosales, *Chicano!: The History of the Mexican-American Civil Rights Movement*, 1997; Stephen Shaw, "Harassment, Hate, and Human Rights in Idaho," in *Politics in the Postwar American West*, edited by Richard Lowitt, 94–105, 1995; Daniel A. Smith, *Tax Crusaders and the Politics of Direct Democracy*, 1998; Quintard Taylor, *In Search of the Racial Frontier: African-Americans in the American West, 1598–1990*, 1998; Clive S. Thomas, ed., *Politics and Public Policy in the Contemporary American West*, 1991; Richard White, *"It's Your Misfortune and None of My Own": A History of the American West*, 1991; Charles Wilkinson, *Blood Struggle: The Rise of Modern Indian Nations*, 2005.

PATRICIA NELSON LIMERICK AND
MARCIA TREMMEL GOLDSTEIN

S

sectional conflict and secession, 1845–65

Sectional conflict, or growing tensions between northern and southern states, mounted from 1845 to 1860 as the main fault lines in American politics shifted from a partisan division (Whigs versus Democrats) to a geographical one (North versus South). In broad terms, a majority of northern and southern voters increasingly suspected members of the other section of threatening the liberty, equality, and opportunity of white Americans and the survival of the U.S. experiment in republican government; specific points of contention between northern and southern states included the right of a state to leave the federal union and the relationship between the federal government and slavery. Constitutional ambiguity and the focus of both the Whig and Democratic parties on national economic issues had allowed the political system to sidestep the slavery issue in the early nineteenth century, but the territorial expansion of the United States in the 1840s forced Congress to face the question of whether or not slavery should spread into new U.S. territories. The pivotal event that irreversibly injected slavery into mainstream politics was the introduction of the Wilmot Proviso in Congress in August 1846. The slavery extension issue destroyed the Whig Party, divided the Democratic Party, and in the 1850s, enabled the rise of an exclusively northern Republican Party founded to oppose the westward expansion of slavery. When Republican candidate Abraham Lincoln won the presidential election of 1860, his victory precipitated the immediate secession of seven states, the eventual secession of four more states, and a Civil War that lasted from 1861 to 1865.

The Slavery Extension Issue

Beginning with the annexation of Texas in 1845, the rapid acquisition of western territories stoked sectional conflict by forcing Congress to face the question of slavery's expansion into those new territories. In prior decades, the two dominant national parties, the Whigs and the Democrats, relied on the support of both northern and southern constituencies and courted voters by downplaying slavery and focusing on questions of government involvement in the economy. Before 1845, expansion, much like support for tariffs or a national bank, was a partisan rather than sectional issue, with Democrats championing and Whigs opposing the acquisition of territory, but the annexation of Texas set in motion of series of events that would eventually realign loyalties along sectional contours.

A Mexican state from the time of Mexican independence in 1821, Texas was settled largely by white American Southerners who chafed against the Mexican government's abolition of slavery in 1829 and broke away to form the Republic of Texas in 1836. The 1836 Treaty of Velasco between the Republic of Texas and General Antonio Lopez De Santa Ana of Mexico named the Rio Grande as the border between Texas and Mexico. But the Mexican Congress refused to ratify that boundary because the Nueces River, far to the North of the Rio Grande, had been the southern limit of Texas when it was a Mexican state, and redrawing the border at the Rio Grande gave thousands of miles of Mexico's northern frontier (the present-day southwest) to Texas. Almost immediately, Americans in Texas began to press for the admission of Texas into the Union. When the United States annexed Texas in 1845, it laid claim to land between the Nueces River and the Rio Grande, which Mexico still regarded as part of Mexico, thus provoking a boundary dispute between the United States and Mexico. American president James K. Polk, an ardent Democrat and expansionist, ordered U.S. troops under General Zachary Taylor to the banks of the Rio Grande, where they skirmished with Mexican forces. Pointing to American casualties, Polk asked Congress to approve a bill stating that a state of war existed between Mexico and the United States, which Congress passed on May 12, 1846.

Militarily, the Mexican-American War seemed like an easy victory for the United States, but international context and domestic politics helped make the war a spur to sectional disharmony. According to the Treaty of Guadalupe Hidalgo, negotiated on February 2, 1848, and announced by President Polk to be in effect on July 4 of that year, the United States was to assume debts owed by the Mexican government to U.S. citizens and pay the Mexican government a lump sum of $15 million, in exchange for which it would receive Texas to the Rio Grande, California, and the New Mexico territory (collectively known as the Mexican Cession). Public opinion was shaped in part by differing American reactions to the revolutions of 1848 in Europe, with some Americans interpreting the European blows for liberal democracy as mandates for the expansion of American-style democracy via territorial acquisition, while others (primarily in the North) viewed conquest as the abandonment of democratic principles. Reaction was even more acutely influenced by developments within the Democratic Party on the state level. While the annexation of Texas and the war with Mexico were generally popular among the proexpansion Democratic Party in the northern as well as southern states, fear that the party was being turned into a tool for slaveholders began to percolate with the annexation of Texas and intensified in response to the war with Mexico. In New Hampshire, for example, loyal Democrat John P. Hale denounced Texas annexation and broke with the state organization to form the Independent Democrats, a coalition of antislavery Democrats, dissatisfied Whigs, and members of the Liberty Party (a small, one-issue third party formed in 1840) that grew strong enough to dominate the New Hampshire legislative and gubernatorial elections of 1846. In New York, Pennsylvania, and Ohio, some Democratic voters grew increasingly worried that President Polk had precipitated the war with Mexico specifically to expand slavery's territory. In hopes of quelling such fears, Pennsylvania Democratic congressman David Wilmot irrevocably introduced slavery into political debate in August 1846 with the Wilmot Proviso.

Wilmot introduced his proviso when Polk asked Congress for a $2 million appropriation for negotiations with the Mexican government that would end the war by transferring territory to the United States. Wilmot added an amendment to the appropriations bill mandating that "neither slavery nor involuntary servitude shall ever exist" in the territories gained from Mexico. The proposed amendment did not end slavery anywhere (slavery was illegal under Mexican law in the territories in question), but it did attempt to curb slavery's extension, and from that time on, the slavery expansion question dominated congressional debate and fueled sectional conflict. With the support of all northern Whigs and most northern Democrats, and against the opposition of all southern Democrats and Whigs, the Wilmot Proviso passed in the House of Representatives but failed in the Senate.

Outside of Washington, D.C., the impact of the Wilmot Proviso escalated in 1847 and 1848. By the spring of 1847, mass meetings throughout the South pledged to oppose any candidate of any party who supported the Proviso and pledged all-southern unity and loyalty to slavery. In the North, opinion on the Proviso was more divided (in politically powerful New York, for example, the Democratic Party split into the anti-Proviso Hunkers and pro-Proviso Barnburners). But the same strands that had come together to form the Independent Democrats in New Hampshire in 1846 began to interweave throughout the North, culminating in the Buffalo National Free Soil Convention of 1848, a mass meeting attended by delegates elected at public meetings throughout the northern states.

An incongruous mix of white and black abolitionists, northern Democrats who wanted no blacks (slave or free) in the western territories, and disaffected Whigs and Democrats, the Buffalo convention created a new political party, the Free Soil Party, based on a platform of "denationalizing slavery" by barring slavery from western territories and outlawing the slave trade (but not slavery) in Washington, D.C. Adopting the slogan, "Free Soil, Free Speech, Free Labor, and Free Men," the Free Soil Party

nominated former Democrat Martin Van Buren as its candidate for the 1848 presidential election. Van Buren did not win (Zachary Taylor, a nominal Whig with no known position on the slavery extension issue became president), but he did get 10 percent of the popular vote. In addition, 12 Free Soil candidates were elected to the U.S. House of Representatives. In Ohio, 8 Free Soilers went to the state legislature, where they repealed Ohio's discriminatory "black laws" and sent Free Soiler Salmon P. Chase to the Senate. In all, the emergence of the Free Soil Party weakened the existing two-party system even as it signaled growing northern disinclination to share the western territories with slaves and slaveholders.

The growth of Free Soil sentiment in the North worried many moderate southern voters, who grew alarmed that the nonextension of slavery beyond its current limits would eventually place the slaveholding states in a minority in the Union as more free states entered and tipped the current balance. A radical group of southern separatists known as the Fire Eaters and led by men such as William Yancey, Edmund Ruffin, and Robert Barnwell Rhett, gained influence as moderates' concern over permanent minority status grew. The Fire Eaters succeeded in convincing all slaveholding states to send delegates to a formal southern convention to meet in Nashville, Tennessee, on June 3, 1850, where delegates would discuss strategies for combating growing hostility to slavery, including secession from the Union. The Nashville Convention asserted the southern states' commitment to slavery and assumed the rights of a state to secede if its interests were threatened, but the convention also affirmed that slavery and southern interests were best served within the Union, as long as Congress met a series of conditions. Conditions included rejection of the Wilmot Proviso, a prohibition against federal interference with slavery in Washington, D.C., and stronger federal support for slaveholders attempting to reclaim slaves who had escaped to free states. The convention agreed to reconvene after Congress had resolved the slavery extension issue to determine if the solution met its conditions.

While opinion hardened in House districts, Congress tackled the question of slavery's fate in the Mexican Cession. Four possible answers emerged. At one extreme stood the Wilmot Proviso. At the opposite extreme stood the doctrine, propagated by South Carolinian and leading southern separatist John C. Calhoun, that "slavery followed the flag" and that all U.S. territories were de facto slave territories because Congress lacked the right to bar slavery from them. A possible compromise, and third possible approach, was to extend the Missouri Compromise line all the way to the Pacific, banning slavery from territories north of the 36° 30′ line, and leaving territories south of that line open to the institution; this approach would permit slavery in the Mexican Cession. A final possibility (the favorite of many northern Democrats) was to apply the principle of "popular sovereignty," which would permit voters living in a territory, and not Congress, to determine if slavery would be allowed in the territory; noted adherents such as Lewis Cass and Stephen Douglas did not specify if voters would determine slavery's fate at the territorial or statehood stage.

The Nashville Convention and the urgent press to admit California to the Union following the discovery of gold in 1849 forced Congress to cobble together the Compromise of 1850. An aging Henry Clay, whose brand of compromise and Whig Party were both wilting as the political climate relentlessly warmed, submitted an omnibus compromise bill that admitted California as a free state, barred the slave trade in Washington, D.C., threw out the Wilmot Proviso, and enacted an unusually harsh Fugitive Slave Law. Clay's bill pleased nobody, and was soundly defeated. Illinois Democrat Stephen Douglas separated the individual provisions and scraped together the votes to get each individual measure passed in what has become known as the Compromise of 1850. In reality, the measure represented a truce more than a compromise. The passage of the individual measures, however contentious, satisfied most of the demands of the Nashville Convention and depressed support for secession. Conditional unionist candidates, or candidates who advocated remaining in the Union as long as conditions like those articulated at Nashville were met, did well in elections throughout the South in 1850 and 1852.

Despite the boost that the Compromise of 1850 gave to conditional unionism in the South, two provisions of the Compromise prevented lasting resolution. One was the Fugitive Slave Law. While Article IV of the U.S. Constitution asserted the rights of masters to recapture slaves who fled to free states, the Fugitive Slave Law included new and harsher provisions mandating the participation of northern states and individuals in the recapture process and curtailing the rights of alleged fugitives to prove they were not runaways. The severity of the law and the conflict it created between state and federal jurisdiction led to controversy. Harriet Beecher Stowe published *Uncle Tom's Cabin*, a novel that gained great popularity in the North but was banned in the South. The New England states, Wisconsin, Ohio, and Michigan passed personal liberty laws allowing state citizens to refrain from participating in slave recaptures if prompted by personal conscience to refrain. Rescue cases like those of Anthony Burns in Massachusetts and Joshua Glover in Wisconsin captured headlines and further strained relations between northern and southern states.

The second problem with the Compromise of 1850 was that it did not settle the question of slavery's expansion because it rejected the Wilmot Proviso without offering an alternative, an omission whose magnitude became apparent when Kansas Territory opened to white settlement in 1854. Fearing that southern congressmen would impede the opening of Kansas because slavery was barred there by the Missouri Compromise (which prohibited slavery in the Louisiana Purchase above the 36° 30′ latitude), Democratic senator Stephen Douglas of Illinois introduced the Kansas-Nebraska Act, which threw out the Missouri Compromise and opened Kansas and Nebraska Territories to popular sovereignty.

The result was that violence erupted between proslavery and free-state settlers in Kansas. Proslavery advocates from Missouri initially gained the upper hand and, in an election in which 6,318 votes were cast despite the presence of only 2,905 legal voters in Kansas, elected a proslavery convention. In 1857 the convention drafted the Lecompton constitution, which would have admitted Kansas to the Union as a slave state and limited the civil rights of antislavery settlers, and sent it to Washington for congressional approval over the objections of the majority of Kansans.

The "Slave Power Conspiracy" and "Black Republicans"

The violence in "Bleeding Kansas" and the obvious unpopularity of the Lecompton constitution did more than just illustrate the failure of popular sovereignty to resolve the slavery extension issue. Kansas further weakened the Second Party System by speeding the collapse of the Whig Party, facilitating the emergence of the Republican Party, and deepening divisions within the Democratic Party. Crippled by its inability to deal effectively with the slavery question, the Whig Party steadily weakened and for a brief time, the anti-immigrant American Party (or Know-Nothings) appeared likely to become the second major party. But when the Know-Nothings failed to respond effectively to the Kansas-Nebraska Act, they lost support among Northerners.

Meanwhile, Free-Soil Democrats, former Whigs, and veterans from the Liberty and Free Soil parties united within several northern states to form a new party explicitly pledged to prevent the westward expansion of slavery. The new party allegedly adopted its name, the Republican Party, at a meeting in Ripon, Wisconsin. Discontented Democrats like Salmon Chase, Charles Sumner, Joshua Giddings, and Gerritt Smith helped to knit the newly emerging state organizations into a sectionwide party by publishing "An Appeal of the Independent Democrats in Congress to the People of the United States" in two newspapers the day after the introduction of the Kansas-Nebraska Bill. The appeal criticized slavery as immoral and contrary to the principles of the nation's founders, and it portrayed the question of slavery in Kansas and other territories as a crisis of American democracy because a "slave power conspiracy" was attempting to fasten slavery on the entire nation, even at the cost of suppressing civil liberties and betraying the principles of the American Revolution.

The violence in Kansas seemed to support charges of a slave power conspiracy, especially in May 1856, when proslavery settlers sacked the abolitionist town of Lawrence, Kansas—just one day before South Carolina congressman Preston Brooks marched onto the Senate floor to beat Massachusetts senator Charles Sumner into unconsciousness in retaliation for Sumner's fiery "Crime against Kansas" speech, which portrayed proslavery Southerners generally—and one of Brooks's relatives particularly—in an unflattering light. "Bleeding Sumner and Bleeding Kansas" made Republican charges that a small number of slaveholders sought to dominate the nation and suppress rights persuasive to many northern voters in the 1856 election; Republican candidate John C. Frémont lost to Democrat James Buchanan, but he carried the New England states, Ohio, Michigan, Wisconsin, and New York, and Republican candidates won seats in Congress and state offices in the North.

In 1857, a financial panic, the Supreme Court's *Dred Scott v. Sanford* case, and the Lecompton constitution built Republican strength in the North while the Democratic Party fractured. Dred Scott, a slave taken to Illinois and Wisconsin Territory by his master and then brought back to slavery in Missouri, sued for his freedom on the grounds that residency in states and territories where slavery was illegal made him free. Chief Justice Roger B. Taney's decision against Scott declared that blacks could not be citizens, even though several northern states recognized them as such, and that in fact they had "no rights which the white man is bound to respect"; it also held that Congress could not outlaw slavery in any U.S. territory, and that slaveholders retained the right to take slaves wherever they pleased. By denying the right of Congress, territorial governments, or residents of a territory to ban slavery from their midst, Taney's decision seemed to support Republican charges that southern oligarchs sought to fasten slavery onto the entire nation regardless of local sentiment. When President James Buchanan (a Pennsylvanian thought to be controlled by southern Democrats) tried unsuccessfully to force Congress to ratify the Lecompton constitution and admit Kansas as a slave state over the objections of the majority of Kansans, the Democratic Party splintered. Even Stephen Douglas faced stiff competition for his Senate seat in 1858. In a series of debates throughout Illinois, Douglas faced Republican candidate Abraham Lincoln, who articulated the slave power conspiracy theme and outlined a platform of opposition to the extension of slavery. Because the Democrats retained a slim edge in the state legislature and state legislatures (not the popular vote) selected senators, Douglas retained his Senate seat. But the wide press coverage of the Lincoln-Douglas debates gained a national audience for Lincoln and his views.

The fast but exclusively northern growth of the Republicans alarmed Southerners who saw themselves as potential victims of a "Black Republican" conspiracy to isolate slavery and end it, sentence the South to subservient status within the Union, and destroy it by imposing racial equality. With conditional unionism still dominant throughout much of the South, many southern leaders called for firmer federal support for the Fugitive Slave Law, federal intolerance for state personal liberty laws, and a federal slave code mandating the legality of and federal protection for slavery in all U.S. territories as prerequisites for southern states remaining in the Union. The Fire Eaters added the demand for the reopening of the African slave trade, even as they increasingly insisted that southern states could preserve their rights only by leaving a Union growing more hostile to the institution on which the South depended. Fears of a "Black Republican" conspiracy seemed to be realized in 1859 when John Brown seized the federal arsenal at Harpers Ferry, Virginia, in hopes of overthrowing slavery by inspiring slave insurrection throughout the South. Brown failed and was executed for treason in December 1859, but a white Northerner marching South to arm slaves embodied white Southerners' grimmest fears that the growing strength of the Republican Party could only lead to violent insurrections.

Election, Secession, and War

The Democratic Party split deepened in 1860, setting the stage for the election of a Republican president. In January 1860, Mississippi senator Albert Brown submitted resolutions calling for a federal slave code and an expanded role for Congress in promoting slavery. The Alabama State Democratic Convention identified the resolutions as the only party platform it would support in the presidential election; several additional southern state delegations also committed themselves to the "Alabama Platform." Northern Democrats espoused popular sovereignty instead. When the National Democratic Convention assembled in Charleston, South Carolina, it split along sectional lines.

As the Democratic rift widened in 1859–60, the Republican Party faced the decision of how best to capitalize on its opponents' dissent. Should it nominate a well-known candidate like senator and former New York governor William Seward, who was seen as a radical because of famous speeches declaring that slavery was subject to a "higher law" than the Constitution (1850) and that the slave and free states were locked in an "irreconcilable conflict" (1858)? Or should it nominate a more moderate but lesser-known candidate? After four ballots, the Republican convention in Chicago settled on Abraham Lincoln, a less prominent politician whose debates with Douglas and a February 1860 New York City address about slavery and the founders had helped introduce him to a national audience. The convention also adopted a platform that decried John Brown and advocated economic measures like a homestead act, but its most important plank consisted of its opposition to the expansion of slavery.

The 1860 presidential campaign shaped up differently in the North and South. Southern Democrats nominated John Breckinridge, who ran on the Alabama platform. He vied for southern votes with John Bell of the newly created Constitutional Union Party, a party that appealed to moderate Southerners who saw the Alabama platform as dangerously inflammatory and instead supported the maintenance of slavery where it was but took no stand on its expansion. In the North, Democrat Stephen Douglas and his platform of popular sovereignty opposed Republican candidate Abraham Lincoln and the Republican nonextension platform. No candidate won a majority of the popular vote. Stephen Douglas captured the electoral votes of New Jersey and Missouri. John Bell carried Virginia, Kentucky, and Tennessee. John Breckinridge won every remaining slave state, and Abraham Lincoln, with 54 percent of the northern popular vote (and none of the southern popular vote) took every remaining free state and the election.

Anticipating Lincoln's victory, the South Carolina legislature stayed in session through the election so that it could call a secession convention as soon as results were known. On December 20, 1860, the convention unanimously approved an ordinance dissolving the union between South Carolina and the United States. By February 1, 1861, Mississippi, Florida, Alabama, Georgia, Louisiana, and Texas had also seceded in response to the election results. The secession ordinances all made clear that Lincoln's election on a nonextension of slavery platform and northern failure to uphold the Fugitive Slave Clause entitled southern states to leave the Union. Delegates from the seven states met in Montgomery, Alabama, to form the Confederate States of America, draft a provisional constitution, select Jefferson Davis and Alexander Stephens as provisional president and vice president, and authorize the enrollment of 100,000 troops.

The states of the Upper and Border South, where Constitutional Unionist candidate John Bell had done well, resisted Deep South pressure to secede immediately, and instead waited to see if Lincoln's actions as president could be reconciled with assurances for slavery's safety within the Union. Yet they also passed coercion clauses, pledging to side with slaveholding states if the situation came to blows. Congress considered the Crittenden Compromise, which guaranteed perpetual noninterference with slavery, extended the Missouri Compromise line permanently across the United States, forbade abolition in the District of Columbia without the permission of Maryland and Virginia, barred Congress from meddling with the interstate slave trade, earmarked federal funds to compensate owners of runaway slaves, and added an unamendable amendment to the constitution guaranteeing that none of the Crittenden measures, including perpetual noninterference with slavery, could ever be altered. The Crittenden Compromise failed to soothe conditional unionists in the South while it angered Republican voters in the North by rejecting the platform that had just won the election. Stalemate ensued.

The Fort Sumter Crisis pressured both Lincoln and the states of the Upper South into action. When Lincoln took office in March 1861, all but four federal forts in seceded states had fallen. Fort Sumter in Charleston Harbor remained in Union hands but was short of supplies. South Carolina officials warned that any attempt to resupply the fort would be seen as an act of aggression. Believing that he could not relinquish U.S. property to a state in rebellion, nor could he leave U.S. soldiers stationed at Fort Sumter to starve, Lincoln warned Confederate president Davis and South Carolina officials that a ship with provisions but no ammunition would resupply Fort Sumter. In the early morning hours of April 12, 1861, South Carolina forces bombarded Fort Sumter before the supply ship could arrive; Fort Sumter surrendered on April 14. Lincoln called for 75,000 volunteers to serve for 90 days to put down the rebellion. In response, Virginia, Arkansas, North Carolina, and Tennessee seceded. The border slave states of Delaware, Kentucky, Maryland, and Missouri remained in the Union, though each state except Delaware contained a significant secessionist minority.

Fought from 1861 to 1865, the Civil War settled the question of slavery's extension by eventually eliminating slavery. The war also made the growth of federal power possible, although dramatic growth in the federal government would not really occur until the later Progressive and New Deal Eras. Conflicts between state and federal sovereignty would persist in U.S. political history, but the Civil War removed secession as a possible option for resolving those conflicts.

See also Civil War and Reconstruction; Confederacy; Reconstruction Era, 1865–77; slavery.

FURTHER READING. Jonathan H. Earle, *Jacksonian Antislavery and the Politics of Free Soil, 1824–1854*, 2004; Eric Foner, *Free Soil, Free Labor, Free Men: The Ideology of the Republican Party Before the Civil War*, 1971; William E. Gienapp, "The Crisis of American Democracy: The Political System and the Coming of the Civil War," in *Why The Civil War Came*, edited by Gabor S. Boritt, 1996; Idem, *The Origins of the Republican Party, 1852–1856*, 1987; Daniel Walker Howe, *What Hath God Wrought: The Transformation of America, 1815–1848*, 2007; David Potter, *The Impending Crisis, 1848–1861*, 1976; Leonard L. Richards, *The California Gold Rush and the Coming of the Civil War*, 2007; Adam Rothman, "The 'Slave Power' in the United States, 1783–1865," in *Ruling America: A History of Wealth and Power in a Democracy*, edited by Steve Fraser and Gary Gerstle, 2005; Richard H. Sewell, *Ballots for Freedom: Antislavery Politics in the United States, 1837–1860*, 1976; Kenneth M. Stampp, *America in 1857: A Nation on the Brink*, 1990; Sean Wilentz, *The Rise of American Democracy: Jefferson to Lincoln*, 2005.

CHANDRA MANNING

segregation and Jim Crow

Jim Crow is the system of racial oppression—political, social, and economic—that southern whites imposed on blacks after the abolition of slavery. Jim Crow, a term derived from a minstrel-show routine, was a derogatory epithet for blacks. Although the system met its formal demise during the civil rights movement of the 1960s, its legacy is still felt today.

Political White Supremacy

During Reconstruction (1865–77), recently enfranchised southern blacks voted in huge numbers and elected many black officeholders. During the final decades of the nineteenth century, however, black voting in the South was largely eliminated—first through fraud and violence, then through legal mechanisms such as poll taxes and literacy tests. Black voter registration in Alabama plummeted from 180,000 in 1900 to 3,000 in 1903 after a state constitutional convention adopted disfranchising measures.

When blacks could not vote, neither could they be elected to office. Sixty-four blacks had sat in the Mississippi legislature in 1873; none sat after 1895. In South Carolina's lower house, which had a black majority during Reconstruction, a single black remained in 1896. More importantly, after disfranchisement, blacks could no longer be elected to the local offices that exercised control over people's daily lives, such as sheriff, justice of the peace, and county commissioner.

With black political clout stunted, radical racists swept to power. Cole Blease of South Carolina bragged that he would rather resign as governor and "lead the mob" than use his office to protect a "nigger brute" from lynching. Governor James Vardaman of Mississippi promised that "every Negro in the state w[ould] be lynched" if necessary to maintain white supremacy.

Economic White Supremacy

Jim Crow was also a system of economic subordination. After the Civil War ended slavery, most southern blacks remained under the economic control of whites, growing cotton as sharecroppers and tenant farmers.

Laws restricted the access of blacks to nonagricultural employment while constricting the market for agricultural labor, thus limiting the bargaining power of black farmworkers. The cash-poor cotton economy forced laborers to become indebted to landlords and suppliers, and peonage laws threatened criminal liability for those who sought to escape indebtedness by breaching their labor contracts. Once entrapped by the criminal justice system, blacks might be made to labor on chain gangs or be hired out to private employers who controlled their labor in exchange for paying their criminal fines. During planting season, when labor was in great demand, local law enforcement officers who were in cahoots with planters would conduct "vagrancy roundups" or otherwise "manufacture" petty criminals.

Some black peons were held under conditions almost indistinguishable from slavery. They worked under armed guard, were locked up at night, and were routinely beaten and tracked down by dogs if they attempted to escape. Blacks who resisted such conditions were often killed. In one infamous Georgia case in the 1920s, a planter who was worried about a federal investigation into his peonage practices simply ordered the murder of 11 of his tenants who were potential witnesses.

While southern black farmers made gains in land ownership in the early twentieth century, other economic opportunities for blacks contracted. Whites repossessed traditionally black jobs, such as barber and chef. The growing power of racially exclusionary labor unions cut blacks off from most skilled trade positions. Black lawyers increasingly found themselves out of work, as a more rigid color line forbade their presence in some courtrooms and made them liabilities to clients in others. Beginning around 1910, unionized white railway workers went on strike in an effort to have black firemen dismissed; when the strike failed, they simply murdered many of the black workers.

Social White Supremacy

As blacks lost their political clout and white racial attitudes hardened, racial segregation spread into new spheres of southern life. Beginning around 1890, most southern states required railroads to segregate their passengers, and laws segregating local streetcars swept the South soon after 1900. Many southern states also segregated restaurants, theaters, public parks, jails, and saloons. White nurses were forbidden to treat black hospital patients, and white teachers were forbidden to work in black schools. Banks established separate deposit windows for blacks. Beginning in 1910, southern cities adopted the first residential segregation ordinances.

Segregation statutes required that accommodations for blacks be equal, but in practice they never were. Blacks described Jim Crow railway cars as "scarcely fit for a dog to ride in"; the seats were filthy and the air was fetid. Convicts and the insane were relegated to these cars, which white passengers entered at will to smoke, drink, and antagonize blacks. Such conditions plainly violated state law, yet legal challenges were rare.

Notwithstanding state constitutional requirements that racially segregated schools be equal, southern whites moved to dismantle the black education system. Most whites thought that an education spoiled good field hands, needlessly encouraged competition with white workers, and rendered blacks dissatisfied with their subordinate status. In 1901 Georgia's governor, Allen D. Candler, stated, "God made them negroes and we cannot by education make them white folks." Racial disparities in educational funding became enormous. By 1925–26, South Carolina spent $80.55 per capita for white students and $10.20 for blacks; for school transportation, the state spent $471,489 for whites and $795 for blacks.

Much social discrimination resulted from informal custom rather than legal rule. No southern statute required that blacks give way to whites on public sidewalks or refer to whites by courtesy titles, yet blacks failing to do so acted at their peril. In Mississippi, some white post office employees erased the courtesy titles on mail addressed to black people.

Violent White Supremacy

Jim Crow was ultimately secured by physical violence. In 1898 whites in Wilmington, North Carolina, concluded a political campaign fought under the banner of white supremacy by murdering roughly a dozen blacks and driving 1,400 out of the city. In 1919, when black sharecroppers in Phillips County, Arkansas, tried to organize a union and challenge peonage practices, whites responded by murdering dozens of them. In Orange County, Florida, 30 blacks were burned to death in 1920 because 1 black man had attempted to vote.

Thousands of blacks were lynched during the Jim Crow era. Some lynching victims were accused of nothing more serious than breaches of racial etiquette, such as "general uppityness." Prior to 1920, efforts to prosecute even known lynchers were rare and convictions virtually nonexistent. Public lynchings attended by throngs of people, many of whom brought picnic lunches and took home souvenirs from the victim's tortured body, were not uncommon.

National Endorsement

Jim Crow was a southern phenomenon, but its persistence required national complicity. During Reconstruction, the national government had—sporadically—used force to protect the rights of southern blacks. Several factors account for the gradual willingness of white Northerners to permit white Southerners a free hand in ordering southern race relations.

Black migration to the North, which more than doubled in the decades after 1890 before exploding during World War I, exacerbated the racial prejudices of northern whites. As a result, public schools and public accommodations became more segregated, and deadly white-on-black violence erupted in several northern localities. Around the same time, the immigration of millions of southern and eastern European peasants caused native-born whites to worry about the dilution of "Anglo-Saxon racial stock," rendering them more sympathetic to southern racial policies. The resurgence of American imperialism in the 1890s also fostered the convergence of northern and southern racial attitudes, as imperialists who rejected full citizenship rights for residents of

the new territories were not inclined to protest the disfranchisement of southern blacks.

Such developments rendered the national government sympathetic toward southern Jim Crow. Around 1900, the U.S. Supreme Court rejected constitutional challenges to racial segregation and black disfranchisement, made race discrimination in jury selection nearly impossible to prove, and sustained the constitutionality of separate-and-*un*equal education for blacks. Meanwhile, Congress repealed most of the voting rights legislation enacted during Reconstruction and declined to enforce Section II of the Fourteenth Amendment, which *requires* reducing the congressional representation of any state that disfranchises adult male citizens for reasons other than crime.

Presidents proved no more inclined to challenge Jim Crow. William McKinley, who was born into an abolitionist family and served as a Union officer during the Civil War, ignored the imprecations of black leaders to condemn the Wilmington racial massacre of 1898, and his presidential speeches celebrated sectional reconciliation, which was accomplished by sacrificing the rights of southern blacks. His successor, Theodore Roosevelt, refused to criticize black disfranchisement, blamed lynchings primarily on black rapists, and proclaimed that "race purity must be maintained." Roosevelt's successor, William Howard Taft, endorsed the efforts of southern states to avoid domination by an "ignorant, irresponsible electorate," largely ceased appointing blacks to southern patronage positions, and denied that the federal government had the power or inclination to interfere in southern race relations.

Decline of Jim Crow

A variety of forces contributed to the gradual demise of Jim Crow. Between 1910 and 1960, roughly 5 million southern blacks migrated to the North, mainly in search of better economic opportunities. Because northern blacks faced no significant suffrage restrictions, their political power quickly grew. At the local level, northern blacks secured the appointment of black police officers, the creation of playgrounds and parks for black neighborhoods, and the election of black city council members and state legislators. Soon thereafter, northern blacks began influencing national politics, successfully pressuring the House of Representatives to pass an antilynching bill in 1922 and the Senate to defeat the Supreme Court nomination of a southern white supremacist in 1930.

The rising economic status of northern blacks facilitated social protest. Larger black populations in northern cities provided a broader economic base for black entrepreneurs and professionals, who would later supply resources and leadership for civil rights protests. Improved economic status also enabled blacks to use boycotts as levers for social change. The more flexible racial mores of the North permitted challenges to the status quo that would not have been tolerated in the South. Protest organizations, such as the National Association for the Advancement of Colored People (NAACP), and militant black newspapers, such as the *Chicago Defender*, developed and thrived in the North. Because of a less rigid caste structure, blacks in the North were less likely to internalize racist norms of black subordination and inferiority.

Jim Crow was also being gradually eroded from within. Blacks moved from farms to cities within the South in search of better economic opportunities, eventually fostering a black middle class, which capitalized on the segregated economy to develop sufficient wealth and leisure time to participate in social protest. Many blacks in the urban South were economically independent of whites and thus could challenge the racial status quo without endangering their livelihoods. In cities, blacks found better schools, freer access to the ballot box, and a more relaxed code of racial etiquette. Because urban blacks enjoyed better communication and transportation facilities and shared social networks through black colleges and churches, they found it somewhat easier to overcome the organizational obstacles confronting any social protest movement.

World Wars I and II had profound implications for Jim Crow. Wars fought "to make the world safe for democracy" and to crush Nazi fascism had ideological implications for racial equality. In 1919, W.E.B. Du Bois of the NAACP wrote: "Make way for Democracy! We saved it in France, and by the Great Jehovah, we will save it in the United States of America, or know the reason why." Blacks who had borne arms for their country and faced death on the battlefield were inspired to assert their rights. A black journalist noted during World War I, "The men who did not fear the trained veterans of Germany will hardly run from the lawless Ku Klux Klan." Thousands of black veterans tried to register to vote after World War II, many expressing the view of one such veteran that "after having been overseas fighting for democracy, I thought that when we got back here we should enjoy a little of it."

World War II exposed millions of Southerners, white and black, to more liberal racial attitudes and practices. The growth of the mass media exposed millions more to outside influence, which tended to erode traditional racial mores. Media expansion also prevented white Southerners from restricting outside scrutiny of their treatment of blacks. Northerners had not seen southern lynchings on television, but the brutalization of peaceful black demonstrators by southern white law enforcement officers in the 1960s came directly into their living rooms.

Formal Jim Crow met its demise in the 1960s. Federal courts invalidated racial segregation and black disfranchisement, and the Justice Department investigated and occasionally prosecuted civil rights violations. Southern blacks challenged the system from within, participating in such direct-action protests as sit-ins and freedom rides. Brutal suppression of those demonstrations outraged northern opinion, leading to the enactment of landmark civil rights legislation, which spelled the doom of formal Jim Crow.

Jim Crow's Legacy

Today, racially motivated lynchings and state-sponsored racial segregation have largely been eliminated. Public accommodations and places of employment have been integrated to a significant degree. Blacks register to vote in roughly the same percentages as whites, and more than 9,000 blacks hold elected office. The previous two secretaries of state have been black.

Blacks have also made dramatic gains in education and employment. The difference in the median number of school years completed by blacks and whites, which was 3.5 in 1954, has been eliminated almost entirely. The number of blacks holding white-collar or middle-class jobs increased from 12.1 percent in 1960 to 30.4 percent in 1990. Today, black men with college degrees earn nearly the same income as their white counterparts.

Yet not all blacks have been equally fortunate. In 1990 nearly two-thirds of black children were born outside of marriage, compared with just 15 percent of white children. Well over half of black families were headed by single mothers. The average black family has income that is just 60 percent and wealth that is just 10 percent of those of the average white family. Nearly 25 percent of blacks—three times the percentage of whites—live in poverty. Increasing numbers of blacks live in neighborhoods of extreme poverty, which are characterized by dilapidated housing, poor schools, broken families, juvenile pregnancies, drug dependency, and high crime rates.

Residential segregation compounds the problems of the black urban underclass. Spatial segregation means social isolation, as most inner-city blacks are rarely exposed to whites or the broader culture. As a result, black youngsters have developed a separate dialect of sorts, which disadvantages them in school and in the search for employment. Even worse, social segregation has fostered an oppositional culture among many black youngsters that discourages academic achievement—"acting white"—and thus further disables them from succeeding in mainstream society.

Today, more black men are incarcerated than are enrolled in college. Blacks comprise less than 12 percent of the nation's population but more than 50 percent of its prison inmates. Black men are seven times more likely to be incarcerated than white men. The legacy of Jim Crow lives on.

See also South since 1877; voting.

FURTHER READING. Edward L. Ayers, *Promise of the New South: Life after Reconstruction*, 1992; John Dittmer, *Black Georgia in the Progressive Era 1900–1920*, 1977; Adam Fairclough, *Better Day Coming: Blacks and Equality, 1890–2000*, 2001; Glenda Elizabeth Gilmore, *Gender and Jim*

Crow: Women and the Politics of White Supremacy in North Carolina, 1896–1920, 1996; Michael J. Klarman, *From Jim Crow to Civil Rights: The Supreme Court and the Struggle for Racial Equality*, 2004; Leon Litwack, *Trouble in Mind: Black Southerners in the Age of Jim Crow*, 1998; Neil R. McMillen, *Dark Journey: Black Mississippians in the Age of Jim Crow*, 1989; Gunnar Myrdal, *An American Dilemma: The Negro Problem and Modern Democracy*, 2 vols., 1944; C. Vann Woodward, *The Strange Career of Jim Crow*, 3rd revised ed., 1974; George C. Wright, *Life behind a Veil: Blacks in Louisville, Kentucky 1865–1920*, 1990.
                                MICHAEL J. KLARMAN

Senate

The framers of the U.S. Constitution viewed the Senate as a check on the more passionate whims of the House of Representatives. Known as the "greatest deliberative body," the Senate has traditionally valued procedure over expediency, thereby frustrating action-oriented House members and presidents. Despite its staid reputation, however, the Senate has produced many of American history's most stirring speeches and influential policy makers. Indeed, the upper chamber of Congress has both reflected and instigated changes that have transformed the United States from a small, agrarian-based country to a world power.

In its formative years, the Senate focused on foreign policy and establishing precedents on treaty, nomination, and impeachment proceedings. Prior to the Civil War, "golden era" senators attempted to keep the Union intact while they defended their own political ideologies. The Senate moved to its current chamber in 1859, where visitors soon witnessed fervent Reconstruction debates and the first presidential impeachment trial. Twentieth-century senators battled the executive branch over government reform, international relations, civil rights, and economic programs as they led investigations into presidential administrations. While the modern Senate seems steeped in political rancor, welcome developments include a more diverse membership and bipartisan efforts to improve national security.

The Constitutional Convention

Drafted during the 1787 Constitutional Convention, the Constitution's Senate-related measures followed precedents established by colonial and state legislatures, as well as Great Britain's parliamentary system. The delegates to the convention, however, originated the institution's most controversial clause: "The Senate of the United States shall be composed of two Senators from each State, chosen by the Legislature thereof. . . ." Although delegates from large states supported James Madison's Virginia Plan, which based Senate representation on state population, small-state delegates wanted equal representation in both the House and the Senate. Roger Sherman

sought a third option: proportional representation in the House and equal representation in the Senate. Adopted by the delegates on July 16, Sherman's Connecticut Compromise enabled the formation of a federal, bicameral legislature responsive to the needs of citizens from both large and small states.

Compared to the representation issue, the measure granting state legislatures the right to choose senators proved less divisive to convention delegates. Madison dismissed concerns that indirect elections would lead to a "tyrannical aristocracy," and only James Wilson argued that senators chosen in this manner would be swayed by local interests and prejudices. By the late nineteenth century, however, corruption regarding the selection of senators triggered demands for electoral reform. Ratified in 1913, the Seventeenth Amendment established direct election, allowing individual voters to select their senators.

As outlined in Article I of the Constitution, the Senate's primary role is to pass bills in concurrence with the House of Representatives. In the event that a civil officer committed "high crimes and misdemeanors," the Constitution also gives the Senate the responsibility to try cases of impeachment brought forth by the House. And, under the Constitution's advice and consent clause, the upper chamber received the power to confirm or deny presidential nominations, including appointments to the cabinet and the federal courts, and the power to approve or reject treaties. The Senate's penchant for stalling nominations and treaties in committee, though, has defeated more executive actions than straight up-or-down votes.

Within a year after the Constitutional Convention concluded, the central government began its transition from a loose confederation to a federal system. In September 1788, Pennsylvania became the first state to elect senators: William Maclay and Robert Morris. Other legislatures soon followed Pennsylvania's lead, selecting senators who came, in general, from the nation's wealthiest and most prominent families.

The Early Senate

The first session of Congress opened in the spring of 1789 in New York City's Federal Hall. After meeting its quorum in April, the Senate originated one of the most important bills of the era: the Judiciary Act of 1789. Created under the direction of Senator Oliver Ellsworth, the legislation provided the structure of the Supreme Court, as well as the federal district and circuit courts. Although advocates of a strong, federal judiciary system prevailed, the bill's outspoken critics indicated the beginning of the states' rights movement in the Senate, a source of significant division in the nineteenth century.

Between 1790 and 1800, Congress sat in Philadelphia as the permanent Capitol underwent construction in Washington, D.C. During these years, the first political parties emerged: the Federalists, who favored a strong union of states, and the anti-Federalists, later known as Republicans, who were sympathetic to states' rights. The parties aired their disputes on the Senate floor, especially in debates about the controversial Jay Treaty (1794) and the Alien and Sedition Acts (1798).

Negotiated by Chief Justice John Jay, the Jay Treaty sought to resolve financial and territorial conflicts with Great Britain arising from the Revolutionary War. In the Senate, the pro-British Federalists viewed the treaty as a mechanism to prevent another war, while the Republicans, and much of the public, considered the treaty's provisions humiliating and unfair to American merchants. By an exact two-thirds majority, the treaty won Senate approval, inciting anti-Jay mobs to burn and hang senators in effigy.

Partisan battles erupted again in 1798, when the Federalist-controlled Congress passed four bills known as the Alien and Sedition Acts. Meant to curtail Republican popularity, the legislation, in defiance of the First Amendment, made it unlawful to criticize the government. Ironically, the acts unified the Republican Party, leading to Thomas Jefferson's presidential election and a quarter-century rule by Senate Republicans.

The Federalist-Republican power struggle continued in the new Capitol in Washington. In 1804 the Senate, meeting as a court of impeachment, found the Federalist U.S. district court judge John Pickering guilty of drunkenness and profanity and removed him from the bench. The following year, the Senate tried the Federalist Supreme Court justice Samuel Chase for allegedly exhibiting an anti-Republican bias. Chase avoided a guilty verdict by one vote, which restricted further efforts to control the judiciary through the threat of impeachment.

Prior to the War of 1812, foreign policy dominated the Senate agenda. Responding to British interference in American shipping, the Senate passed several trade embargoes against Great Britain before declaring war. In 1814 British troops entered Washington and set fire to the Capitol, the White House, and other public buildings. The Senate chamber was destroyed, forcing senators to meet in temporary accommodations until 1819. In the intervening years, the Senate formed its first permanent committees, which encouraged senators to become experts on such issues as national defense and finance.

When the war concluded in 1815 without a clear victor, the Senate turned its attention to the problems and opportunities resulting from territorial expansion. As lands acquired from France, Spain, and Indian tribes were organized into territories and states, senators debated the future of slavery in America, the nation's most divisive issue for years to come.

The Antebellum Senate

In 1820 the 46 senators were split evenly between slave states and free states. The Senate considered numerous bills designed to either protect or destroy this delicate balance. Legislation regulating statehood produced the Missouri Compromise (1820–21), the Compromise of 1850, and the Kansas-Nebraska Act (1854). While the compromises attempted to sustain the Union, the Kansas-Nebraska Act, with its controversial "popular sovereignty" clause, escalated the conflict between slave owners and abolitionists.

Senate historians consider the antebellum period to be the institution's golden era. The Senate chamber, a vaulted room on the Capitol's second floor, hosted passionate floor speeches enthralling both the public and the press. At the center of debate stood the Senate's "Great Triumvirate": Henry Clay, Daniel Webster, and John C. Calhoun.

As Speaker of the House, Clay had overseen the formation of the Missouri Compromise, which stipulated that Missouri would have no slavery restrictions, while all territories to the north would become free states. Later, as senator, Clay led the opposition against President Andrew Jackson's emerging Democratic Party. In 1834 he sponsored a resolution condemning Jackson for refusing to provide a document to Congress. Although the first (and only) presidential censure was expunged in 1837, it sparked the rise of the Whig Party in the late 1830s.

Webster, one of the greatest American orators, defended the importance of national power over regional self-interest, declaring in a rousing 1830 speech, "Liberty and Union, now and forever, one and inseparable!" His views challenged Vice President Calhoun's theory of nullification, which proposed that states could disregard laws they found unconstitutional. By the time Calhoun became a senator in 1832, the Senate had divided between those who promoted states' rights and those with a nationalist view.

The Mexican-American War inflamed the issue of slavery. Led by Calhoun, the Senate blocked adoption of the House-sponsored Wilmot Proviso (1846) that would have banned slavery in the territories won from Mexico. Fearing a national crisis, Clay drafted new slavery regulations. When Calhoun, now gravely ill, threatened to block any restrictions, Webster responded with a famous address upholding the Missouri Compromise and the integrity of the Union.

After Calhoun's death in March 1850, the atmosphere in the Senate chamber grew so tense that Henry S. Foote drew a pistol during an argument with antislavery senator Thomas Hart Benton. After months of such heated debates, however, Congress passed Clay's legislation. As negotiated by Senator Stephen A. Douglas, the Compromise of 1850 admitted California as a free state, allowed New Mexico and Utah to determine their own slavery policies (later known as popular sovereignty), outlawed the slave trade in Washington, D.C., and strengthened the controversial fugitive slave law.

Webster and Clay died in 1852, leaving Douglas, as chairman of the Senate Committee on Territories, to manage statehood legislation. Catering to southern senators, Douglas proposed a bill creating two territories under popular sovereignty: Nebraska, which was expected to become a free state, and Kansas, whose future was uncertain. Despite the staunch opposition of abolitionists, the bill became law, prompting pro- and antislavery advocates to flood into "Bleeding Kansas," where more than 50 settlers died in the resulting conflicts.

Opponents of the Kansas-Nebraska Act formed the modern Republican Party, drawing its membership from abolitionist Whigs, Democrats, and Senator Charles Sumner's Free Soil Party. In 1856 Sumner gave a scathing "crime against Kansas" speech that referred to slavery as the wicked mistress of South Carolina senator Andrew P. Butler. Three days after the speech, Butler's relative, Representative Preston S. Brooks, took revenge in the Senate chamber. Without warning, he battered Sumner's head with blows from his gold-tipped cane. The incident made Brooks a hero of the South, while Sumner, who slowly recovered his health, would become a leader of the Radical Republicans.

The Civil War and Reconstruction

In the late 1850s, to accommodate the growing membership of Congress, the Capitol doubled in size with the addition of two wings. The new Senate chamber featured an iron and glass ceiling, multiple galleries, and a spacious floor. It was in this setting that conflicts with the Republican-majority House led to legislative gridlock, blocking a series of Senate resolutions meant to appease the South. In December 1860, South Carolina announced its withdrawal from the Union. One month later, in one of the Senate's most dramatic moments, the Confederacy's future president, Jefferson Davis, and four other southern senators resigned their seats, foretelling the resignation of every senator from a seceding state except Andrew Johnson, who remained until 1862.

Following the fall of Fort Sumter in April 1861, Washington, D.C., was poised to become a battle zone. A Massachusetts regiment briefly occupied the Senate wing, transforming it into a military hospital, kitchen, and sleeping quarters. Eventually, thousands of troops passed through the chamber and adjacent rooms. One soldier gouged Davis's desk with a bayonet, while others stained the ornate carpets with bacon grease and tobacco residue.

Now outnumbering the remaining Democrats, congressional Republicans accused southern lawmakers of committing treason. For the first time since Senator William Blount was dismissed for conspiracy in 1797, Senate expulsion resolutions received the required two-thirds vote. In total, the Senate expelled 14 senators from the South, Missouri, and Indiana for swearing allegiance to the Confederacy.

Within the Republican majority, the Senate's Radical Republican contingent grew more powerful during the war. Staunch abolitionists formed the Joint Committee on the Conduct of the War to protest President Abraham Lincoln's management of the army. Radicals demanded an end to slavery and investigated allegations of government corruption and inefficiency. They also passed significant domestic policy laws, such as the Homestead Act (1862) and the Land Grant College Act (1862).

When a northern victory seemed imminent, Lincoln and the congressional Republicans developed different plans for reconstructing the Union. In December 1863, the president declared that states would be readmitted when 10 percent of their previously qualified voters took a loyalty oath. Radicals countered with the Wade-Davis Bill requiring states to administer a harsher, 50 percent oath. Lincoln vetoed the legislation, outraging Senator Benjamin F. Wade and Representative Henry W. Davis.

In the closing days of the war, the Senate passed the Thirteenth Amendment abolishing slavery. After Lincoln's assassination in April 1865, the new president, former senator Andrew Johnson, infuriated congressional Republicans when he enabled Confederate politicians to return to power and vetoed a bill expanding the Freedmen's Bureau, which assisted former slaves. Republicans, in turn, enacted the Fourteenth Amendment, providing blacks with citizenship, due process of law, and equal protection by laws.

Chaired by Senator William P. Fessenden, the Joint Committee on Reconstruction declared that the restoration of states was a legislative, not an executive, function. Accordingly, Congress passed the Reconstruction Acts of 1867, which divided the South into military districts, permitted black suffrage, and made the adoption of the Fourteenth Amendment a condition of state readmittance. To protect pro-Radical civil officials, Republicans proposed the Tenure of Office Act, requiring Senate approval before the president could dismiss a cabinet member.

Johnson violated the act by firing Secretary of War Edwin M. Stanton, and the House of Representatives impeached him on February 24, 1868. A week later, the Senate convened as a court of impeachment, and on May 16, 35 senators voted to convict Johnson, 1 vote short of the two-thirds majority needed for removal. The case centered on executive rights and the constitutional separation of powers, with 7 moderate Republicans joining the 12 Democrats in voting to acquit.

While Johnson retained his office, he was soon replaced by Ulysses S. Grant, the Civil War general. Marked by corruption, the Grant years (1869–77) split the congressional Republicans into pro- and antiadministration wings. The party was weakened further when representatives and senators were caught accepting bribes to assist the bankrupt Union Pacific Railroad. And after two senators apparently bought their seats from the Kansas legislature, much of the press began calling for popular Senate elections to replace the indirect election method outlined by the Constitution.

Meanwhile, Republicans still dominated southern state legislatures, as most Democrats were unable to vote under Radical Reconstruction. In 1870 Mississippi's Republican legislature elected the first black U.S. senator, Hiram R. Revels, to serve the last year of an unexpired term. Another black Mississippian, Blanche K. Bruce, served from 1875 to 1881. (Elected in 1966, Edward W. Brooke was the first African American to enter the Senate after Reconstruction.)

The 1876 presidential election ended Radical Reconstruction. Although the Democrat, Samuel J. Tilden, won the popular vote, ballots from Florida, Louisiana, and South Carolina were in dispute. To avert a constitutional crisis, Congress formed an electoral commission composed of five senators, five representatives, and five Supreme Court justices, who chose Republican Rutherford B. Hayes by a one-vote margin. As part of the Compromise of 1877, Republicans agreed to end military rule in the South in exchange for Democratic support of the Hayes presidency.

The Gilded Age and the Progressive Era

During the late nineteenth century, corruption permeated the public and private sectors. While the two major parties traded control of the Senate, the Republicans divided between those who wanted institutional reform and those in favor of retaining political patronage, the practice of dispensing government jobs in order to reward or secure campaign support.

New York senator Roscoe Conkling epitomized the problem of patronage. In the 1870s, he filled the New York Custom House with crooked friends and financial backers. Moderates from both parties called for a new method to select government workers. In 1881 a disturbed patronage seeker assassinated President James A. Garfield. The act motivated Democratic senator George H. Pendleton to sponsor legislation creating the merit-based civil service category of federal jobs.

In 1901 William McKinley's assassination elevated progressive Republican Theodore Roosevelt to the White House, while Republicans once again dominated the Senate. As chairman of the Republican Steering Committee, as well as the Appropriations Committee, William B. Allison dominated the chamber along with other committee chairmen. In a showdown between two factions of Republicans, Allison's conservative Old Guard blocked progressives' efforts to revise tariffs. Despite the continued opposition of conservatives, however, Roosevelt achieved his goal of regulating railroad rates and large companies by enforcing Senator John Sherman's Antitrust Act of 1890.

Prior to World War I, Progressive Era reformers attempted to eradicate government corruption and increase the political influence of the middle class. The campaign for popular Senate elections hoped to achieve both goals. In 1906 David Graham Phillips wrote several muckraking magazine articles exposing fraudulent relationships between senators, state legislators, and businessmen. His "Treason of the Senate" series sparked new interest in enabling voters, rather than state legislatures, to elect senators. But although the Seventeenth Amendment (1913) standardized direct elections, the institution remained a forum for wealthy elites.

In 1913 reform-minded Democrats took over the Senate, as well as the presidency under Woodrow Wilson, resulting in a flurry of progressive legislation. Wilson's Senate allies, John Worth Kern and James Hamilton Lewis, ushered through the Federal Reserve Act (1913), the Federal Trade Commission Act (1914), and the Clayton Antitrust Act (1914). As chairman of the Democratic Conference, Kern acted as majority leader several years before the position was officially recognized, while Lewis served as the Senate's first party whip. As such, he counted votes and enforced attendance prior to the consideration of important bills.

World War I and the 1920s

Following Europe's descent into war in 1914, domestic concerns gave way to foreign policy, and Wilson battled both progressive and conservative Republicans in Congress. On January 22, 1917, Wilson addressed the Senate with his famous "peace without victory" speech. Shortly thereafter, a German submarine sank an unarmed U.S. merchant ship, and the president urged Congress to pass legislation allowing trade vessels to carry weapons. Noninterventionist senators, including progressive Republicans Robert M. La Follette and George W. Norris, staged a lengthy filibuster in opposition to Wilson's bill, preventing its passage. Furious, Wilson declared that a "little group of willful men" had rendered the government "helpless and contemptible." Calling a special Senate session, he prompted the passage of Rule 22, known as the cloture rule, which limited debate when two-thirds (later changed to three-fifths) of the senators present agreed to end a filibuster.

The 1918 elections brought Republican majorities to both houses of Congress. As the Senate's senior Republican, Massachusetts senator Henry Cabot Lodge chaired the Foreign Relations Committee and his party's conference. Angered by the lack of senators at the Paris Peace Conference (1919), the de facto floor leader attached 14 reservations to the war-ending Treaty of Versailles, altering the legal effect of selected terms, including the provision outlining Wilson's League of Nations (the precursor to the United Nations), which Lodge opposed. The Senate split into three groups: reservationists, irreconcilables, and pro-treaty Democrats, who were instructed by Wilson not to accept changes to the document. Unable to reach a compromise, the Senate rejected the treaty in two separate votes. Consequently, the United States never entered the League of Nations and had little influence over the enactment of the peace treaty.

In the 1920s, the Republicans controlled both the White House and Congress. Fearing the rising numbers of eastern Europeans and East Asians in America, congressional isolationists curtailed immigration with the National Origins Act of 1924. Senators investigated corruption within the Harding administration, sparking the famous Teapot Dome oil scandal.

Two years after the Nineteenth Amendment gave women the right to vote, Rebecca Latimer Felton, an 87-year-old former suffragist, served as the first woman senator for just 24 hours between November 21 and 22, 1922. Felton considered the symbolic appointment proof that women could now obtain any office. The second female senator, Hattie Wyatt Caraway, was appointed to fill Thaddeus Caraway's seat upon his death in 1931. She became the first *elected* female senator, however, when she won the special election to finish her husband's term in 1932. Caraway won two additional elections and spent more than 13 years in the Senate.

In 1925 the Republicans elected Charles Curtis as the first official majority leader, a political position that evolved from the leadership duties of committee and conference chairmen. Curtis had the added distinction of being the first known Native American member of Congress (he was part Kaw Indian) and was later Herbert Hoover's vice president.

The New Deal and World War II
The 1929 stock market crash signaled the onset of the Great Depression and the end of Republican rule. Democrats swept the elections of 1932, taking back Congress and the White House under Franklin Roosevelt, who promised a "new deal" to address the nation's economic woes. The first Democratic majority leader, Joseph T. Robinson, ushered through the president's emergency relief program, while other senators crafted legislation producing the Federal Deposit Insurance Corporation, the Tennessee Valley Authority, the Social Security Administration, and the National Labor Relations Board.

In 1937 the Senate majority leader worked furiously to enlist support for Roosevelt's controversial Court reorganization act, designed to expand the Supreme Court's membership with liberal justices. Prior to the Senate vote, though, Robinson succumbed to a heart attack, and the president's "Court-packing" plan died with him. The debate over the bill drove a deep wedge between liberal and conservative Democrats.

In the late 1930s, another war loomed in Europe. Led by Republican senators William E. Borah and Gerald P. Nye, Congress passed four Neutrality Acts. After Germany invaded France in 1940, however, Roosevelt's handpicked Senate majority leader, Alben W. Barkley, sponsored the Lend-Lease Act (1941), enabling the United States to send Great Britain and its allies billions of dollars in military equipment, food, and services. The monumental aid plan invigorated

the economy, ending the Depression, as well as American neutrality.

During the war, little-known senator Harry Truman headed the Senate's Special Committee to Investigate the National Defense Program. Elected as Roosevelt's third vice president in 1944, Truman assumed the presidency when Roosevelt died three months into his fourth term. The new president relied heavily on Senate support as he steered the nation through the conclusion of World War II and into the cold war.

The Cold War Senate
The Senate assumed a primary role in shaping the midcentury's social and economic culture. In 1944 Senator Ernest W. McFarland sponsored the Servicemen's Readjustment Act. Better known as the GI Bill, the legislation provided veterans with tuition assistance and low-cost loans for homes and businesses. In 1947 the Republicans regained Congress and passed the antilabor Taft-Hartley Act (1947) over Truman's veto. The act restricted the power of unions to organize and made conservative senator Robert A. Taft a national figure. Responding to the Soviet Union's increasing power, the Foreign Relations Committee approved the Truman Doctrine (1947) and the Marshall Plan (1948), which sent billion of dollars of aid and materials to war-torn countries vulnerable to communism.

The Senate itself was transformed by the Legislative Reorganization Act (1946), which streamlined the committee system, increased the number of professional staff, and opened committee sessions to the public. In 1947 television began broadcasting selected Senate hearings. Young, ambitious senators capitalized on the new medium, including C. Estes Kefauver, who led televised hearings on organized crime, and junior senator Joseph R. McCarthy from Wisconsin, whose name became synonymous with the anti-Communist crusade.

In February 1950 Republican senator McCarthy made his first charges against Communists working within the federal government. After announcing an "all-out battle between communistic atheism and Christianity," he gave an eight-hour Senate speech outlining "81 loyalty risks." Democrats examined McCarthy's evidence and concluded that he had committed a "fraud and a hoax" on the public. Meanwhile, Republican senator Margaret Chase Smith, the first woman to serve in both houses of Congress, gave a daring speech, entitled "A Declaration of Conscience," in which she decried the Senate's decline into "a forum of hate and character assassination."

Nevertheless, McCarthy continued to make charges against government officials, and as chairman of the Permanent Subcommittee on Investigations, he initiated more than 500 inquiries and investigations into suspicious behavior, destroying numerous careers along the way. In 1954 McCarthy charged security breaches within the military. During the televised Army-McCarthy hearings, the army's head attorney, Joseph N. Welch, uttered the famous line that helped bring about the senator's downfall: "Have you no sense of decency?" On December 2, 1954, senators passed a censure resolution condemning McCarthy's conduct, thus ending one of the Senate's darker chapters.

A new era in Senate history commenced in 1955, when the Democrats, now holding a slight majority, elected Lyndon B. Johnson, a former congressman from Texas, to be majority leader. Johnson reformed the committee membership system but was better known for applying the "Johnson technique," a personalized form of intimidation used to sway reluctant senators to vote his way. The method proved so effective that he managed to get a 1957 civil rights bill passed despite Senator Strom Thurmond's record-breaking filibuster, lasting 24 hours and 18 minutes. In the 1958 elections, the Senate Democrats picked up an impressive 17 seats. Johnson leveraged the 62–34 ratio to challenge President Dwight D. Eisenhower at every turn, altering the legislative-executive balance of power.

Johnson sought the presidency for himself in 1960 but settled for the vice presidency under former senator John F. Kennedy. Although popular with his colleagues, the new majority leader, Mike Mansfield, faced difficulties uniting liberal and conservative Democrats, and bills affecting minority groups stalled at the committee level. Following Kennedy's assassination in November 1963, Democrat Hubert H. Humphrey and Republican Everett M. Dirksen engineered the passage of Johnson's Civil Rights Act of 1964. They did so by first securing a historic cloture vote that halted a filibuster led by southern Democrats Robert C. Byrd and Richard B. Russell. Johnson and Mansfield then won additional domestic policy victories, including the Voting Rights Act (1965) and the Medicare/Medicaid health care programs (1965).

The president's foreign policy decisions, however, would come to haunt him and the 88 senators who voted for the 1964 Tonkin Gulf Resolution. Drafted by the Johnson administration, the measure drew the nation into war by authorizing the president to take any military action necessary to protect the United States and its allies in Southeast Asia. As the Vietnam War escalated, Senator John Sherman Cooper and Senator Frank F. Church led efforts to reassert the constitutional power of Congress to declare war, culminating in the War Powers Resolution of 1973, which required congressional approval for prolonged military engagements.

Although the Democrats lost the presidency to Richard M. Nixon in 1968, they controlled the Senate until 1981. In 1973 the Senate Select Committee on Presidential Campaign Activities investigated Nixon's involvement in the cover-up of the 1972 break-in at the Democratic Party's National Committee office in the Watergate complex. Chaired by Senator Samuel J. Ervin, the select committee's findings led to the initiation of impeachment proceedings in the House of Representatives. In early August 1974, prominent Republicans, including Senate Minority Leader Hugh Scott, Senator Barry Goldwater, and House Minority Leader John Rhodes, informed Nixon that he did not have the party support in either house of Congress to remain in office. Rather than face a trial in the Senate, Nixon resigned prior to an impeachment vote in the House.

The Modern Senate

From 1981 to 1987, the Republicans controlled the Senate and supported White House policy under President Ronald Reagan. During this period, the Senate began televising floor debates. Televised hearings, however, continued to captivate followers of politics, especially after the Democrats regained the Senate in 1987 and conducted hearings on the Reagan and George H. W. Bush administrations.

In 1987 the House and Senate held joint hearings to investigate the Iran-Contra affair. Later that year, senators grilled conservative Supreme Court nominee Robert Bork, before defeating his appointment. Nominated for defense secretary in 1989, retired Republican senator John G. Tower suffered a humiliating rejection from his former Senate colleagues, and in 1991 Clarence Thomas survived the Judiciary Committee's scrutiny of his Supreme Court nomination despite allegations of sexual harassment by his former staff member Anita Hill.

In 1992, the "Year of the Woman," female candidates won elections nationwide, including five seats in the Senate, with Carol Moseley Braun serving as the first African American woman senator. President Bill Clinton's early domestic policy initiatives, such as the Family and Medical Leave Act (1993), reflected the influence of mothers serving in Congress. In 1994, however, the "Republican revolution" brought the Senate under conservative rule, and Republicans thwarted Clinton's legislative agenda while they investigated his public and personal activities.

In December 1998, the House of Representatives passed two articles of impeachment against Clinton: lying under oath and obstruction of justice regarding a 1994 sexual harassment case and an affair with the White House intern Monica Lewinsky. With Chief Justice William H. Rehnquist presiding, the Senate convened as a court of impeachment in January 1999. Although several Democratic senators voiced objections to Clinton's behavior, on February 12 every Democrat, as well as a few moderate Republicans, voted for his acquittal.

The 1990s closed with a divided Senate, bruised from in-fighting and media reports criticizing the influence of lobbyists in Washington. While it did not reduce candidate spending, the 2002 McCain-Feingold Campaign Finance Bill limited "soft money" contributions and regulated the broadcast of issue ads. The bipartisan effort demonstrated that Republican and Democratic senators could work together to achieve common goals, although they rarely chose to do so.

The September 11, 2001, terrorist attacks provided an opportunity to unite the Senate in support of national security policies. Shortly after 9/11, Congress adopted the controversial USA Patriot Act, increasing federal law-enforcement and intelligence-gathering capabilities to the possible detriment of civil liberties. The October 2001 anthrax attack on the Hart Senate Office Building prompted senators and staffers to work together to eliminate vulnerabilities in the Capitol complex. But soon tensions escalated, as senators sparred over the ongoing war in Iraq.

Despite instances of acrimony throughout its history, the Senate has maintained a more cordial environment than the much larger House of Representatives. Institutional rules keep tempers in check, although lapses in demeanor occur. However strained, friendships "across the aisle" do exist and are helpful in forging compromises prior to important votes. In the years ahead, the Senate will continue to shape American society as long as thoughtful deliberation remains the institution's most distinguishing feature.

See also House of Representatives; presidency; Supreme Court.

FURTHER READING. Richard A. Baker, *200 Notable Days: Senate Stories, 1787 to 2002*, 2006, downloadable as "Historical Minute Essays" from http://www.senate.gov, Art & History page; Idem, *The Senate of the United States: A Bicentennial History*, 1988; Richard A. Baker and Roger H. Davidson, eds., *First among Equals: Outstanding Senate Leaders of the Twentieth Century*, 1991; Robert C. Byrd, *The Senate, 1789–1989*, 1988–1994; Lewis L. Gould, *The Most Exclusive Club: A History of the Modern United States Senate*, 2005; Fred R. Harris, *Deadlock or Decision: The U.S. Senate and the Rise of National Politics*, 1993; John R. Hibbing and John G. Peters, eds., *The Changing World of the U.S. Senate*, 1990; Julian E. Zelizer, ed., *The American Congress: The Building of Democracy*, 2004.

JANE ARMSTRONG HUDIBURG

slavery

Slavery was deeply entrenched in the early United States, and its overthrow is one of the epic stories of the nation's history. It is tempting to believe that the problem of slavery was destined to haunt American politics from the very moment that the Declaration of Independence announced that "all men are created equal" and "endowed by their Creator with certain unalienable rights" including liberty, but those words might have remained dead on the page if both black and white Americans opposed to slavery had not struggled together to give them an antislavery meaning in the political arena. From the end of the

American Revolution onward, the ebb and flow of the slavery controversy in politics can be roughly divided into four general periods: the republican era, leading up to the Missouri Compromise; the Jacksonian era, from the Missouri Compromise to the Mexican-American War; the years of sectional crisis, from the Mexican War to the secession of the southern states; and the final chapter, of Civil War and emancipation.

Many Northerners in the 1840s and 1850s thought that a "slave power" had come to dominate American politics. Although some historians have dismissed that idea as a paranoid fantasy, slaveholders actually did wield political power from the start to protect their controversial interest in human property. Accommodating slaveholders' concerns, the framers of the U.S. Constitution included three clauses that offered thinly veiled protections to slaveholders: the Three-Fifths Clause mandated that the enslaved population count in a fractional ratio for purposes of determining representation in the U.S. House of Representatives; the Fugitive Slave Clause prevented "persons bound to labor" from acquiring their freedom by virtue of escaping to another state; and the Slave Trade Clause prevented the U.S. Congress from prohibiting the importation of foreign slaves until 1808.

The Three-Fifths and Slave Trade Clauses were not pure concessions to slaveholders. Southern delegates wanted slaves to count fully for purposes of representation, and while the slaveholders from South Carolina and Georgia wanted to protect slave importation, many in the Upper South would have preferred an immediate ban. Although American slaveholders united to defend their claims to human property (as in the Fugitive Slave Clause), they disagreed among themselves over an array of secondary issues relating to slavery (as in the debates over slave importation before 1810 and again in the 1850s). In the framing of the Constitution, they compromised for the sake of union.

The Republican Era: 1789–1821

The northern and southern states followed different paths in the republican era that followed the American Revolution. Slavery slowly disappeared in the North through judicial fiat, state legislation mandating gradual emancipation, private acts of manumission, and the sale of slaves to the South. Free black communities emerged in northern towns and cities from Boston to Philadelphia, where they endured legal discrimination and customary prejudice and, with few exceptions, were relegated to the lowest rungs of the economic ladder. Free black northerners banded together in "African" mutual aid societies and independent churches, which were the earliest stronghold of radical abolitionism in the United States.

But in the southern states, slavery weathered the republican storm. Manumission significantly increased the free black population in Maryland and Virginia before new legal restrictions made it more difficult for owners to free their slaves. As tobacco and rice growers regained their economic footing on the Atlantic seaboard, burgeoning demand for short-staple cotton in the industrial centers of British textile manufacturing gave a powerful boost to the use of slave labor in the southern interior from the Carolina upcountry to the lower Mississippi River valley. The number of slaves in the country doubled between 1790 and 1820, and several new slave states (Kentucky, Tennessee, Louisiana, Alabama, and Mississippi) joined the Union. Thirty years after the ratification of the Constitution, those who hoped that slavery would evaporate in the new United States were sorely disappointed.

During this early republican period, the two main points of contention over slavery at the national level were the regulation of U.S. participation in the Atlantic slave trade and the status of slavery in new territories. Thomas Jefferson's first draft of the Declaration of Independence had accused King George III of waging "cruel war against human nature itself" by protecting the slave trade; the Continental Congress cut the accusation out of the final version. Most of the states prohibited foreign slave importation after independence, although South Carolina's temporary lifting of its state ban in 1804 allowed traders to import tens of thousands of African slaves before Congress exercised its constitutional power to end slave importation in 1808. Highly publicized cases of slave smuggling into the Gulf South after the War of 1812 prompted Congress to pass a series of reforms between 1818 and 1820 that authorized the U.S. Navy to suppress illegal slave trading on the African coast and defined such trading as piracy punishable by death. But not until the Civil War, with the execution of Nathaniel Gordon in 1862, was capital punishment used as a sentence in the United States for participation in the illegal slave trade. Congress also tried to stop U.S. citizens from participating in the slave trade between Africa and foreign countries beginning with an anti–slave trade law in 1794, but fragmentary evidence suggests that the legislative effort to stop such activity was ineffective. Despite British naval and diplomatic pressure, Atlantic slave trading persisted as a shadowy sector of the American economy well into the nineteenth century.

More controversial was the issue of slavery's western expansion. The Continental Congress prohibited slavery in the Northwest Territory in 1787 but allowed it in the territory south of the Ohio River, implicitly drawing a line between free and slave territories in the trans-Appalachian West. In 1798 and in 1803, Congress debated the status of slavery in the Mississippi and Orleans territories, respectively, allowing slaveholding but not foreign slave importation in both places.

Three decades of simmering conflict over the geographic extension of slavery boiled over in 1819 when Missouri, a slave-owning territory, applied for statehood. For the first time, northern opponents of slavery blocked the introduction of a state rather than a territory, raising a new and explosive constitutional question. Thomas Jefferson called it "a firebell in the night." Led by Congressman Rufus King of New York, northeastern representatives in the House tapped into a genuine wellspring of antislavery sentiment among their constituents, for whom slavery was now a potent metaphor for oppression rather than a day-to-day reality. They saw the prospect of slavery flourishing in the "empire of liberty" west of the Mississippi as a betrayal of American ideals. But unionism prevailed. The Missouri Compromise welcomed Missouri as a slave state and Maine as a free state, thereby preserving sectional balance in the U.S. Senate, and drew a line between free and slave territories elsewhere in the Louisiana Purchase at 36° 30′ latitude. For a generation, this agreement bought sectional peace on the question of slavery's expansion.

The Jacksonian Era: 1822–45

The Missouri crisis also revealed the danger of antagonistic sectional interests in national politics. One solution, as New York's "little magician" Martin Van Buren recognized, was to forge a national political coalition around the shared interests of people in the northern and southern states. Rising to power with the election of the slave-owning planter and military hero Andrew Jackson in 1828, Van Buren's Democratic Party pursued an *anti*-antislavery position consistent with its principles of limited government. The Democrats refused to continue federal support for the gradual emancipationist African Colonization Society, which had been granted a de facto subsidy through the 1819 slave trade law. The Democrats sustained a "gag rule" in the House of Representatives from 1836 to 1844 that prevented debate on petitions relating to slavery. As proponents of a strong national government and moral reform, the northern wing of the Whig Party was less ideologically hostile to antislavery than the Democrats. (Returning to Congress as a Massachusetts Whig, John Quincy Adams became the leading opponent of the gag rule in the House.) Yet for the Whigs, too, the task of winning national elections required the muffling of antislavery tendencies so as not to alienate its southern constituency. The Jacksonian two-party system thus repolarized national politics around issues other than slavery.

Yet the progress of antislavery ideas and organizations in northern civil society made it difficult for the two-party system to keep the lid on the slavery issue. The slave population continued to increase and, although the United States had legally withdrawn from the Atlantic slave trade, a new interstate slave trade carried enslaved people from the Upper South to the Deep South. The image of slave traders marching coffles of chained slaves through the District of

Columbia became a staple of abolitionist propaganda. The American Colonization Society (ACS) and its program for gradual emancipation came under intense fire from both port and starboard. Free black Northerners and their radical white abolitionist allies assailed the ACS as a proslavery trick, while proslavery ideologues in the South regarded it as impractical at best and, at worst, a Trojan horse of state-sponsored abolition.

As the promise of gradual emancipation faded, some white Northerners sought a clean break with slavery. Inspired by perfectionist ideas emanating from the Second Great Awakening, a radical abolitionist movement sprang up in the 1830s under the banner of William Lloyd Garrison's Boston-based newspaper, the *Liberator*. The radical abolitionists regarded slavery as a terrible sin, advocated immediate emancipation, and rejected the colonization of freed people outside the United States. After Garrison and other leading abolitionists organized the American Anti-Slavery Society (AAAS) in 1833, state and local chapters proliferated in the northern states, much to the horror of southern slaveholders and their "doughface" northern allies.

The abolitionist movement launched two campaigns in the mid-1830s that tested the American political system's tolerance for antislavery dissent. The first came in 1835, when the wealthy New York merchant Lewis Tappan orchestrated a scheme to use the national postal system to flood the southern states with AAAS propaganda, including a children's gazette called *The Slave's Friend*. Angry mobs seized the offending literature from many southern post offices and burned it on the pretext of protecting public safety, prompting abolitionists to protest against interference with the mail and the violation of free speech. Buoyed by the publicity garnered through the postal campaign, the AAAS launched a petition drive designed to demonstrate northern support for the abolition of slavery and the slave trade in the District of Columbia. It was this petition drive that provoked the House of Representatives to initiate the gag rule.

The end of the decade witnessed a schism in the abolitionist movement, pitting those who wanted to press the slavery issue in the political arena against the Garrisonian faction, who wanted nothing to do with politics whatsoever. (Garrison would eventually denounce the U.S. Constitution as a "covenant with death.") Supported by the splinter group American and Foreign Antislavery Society, the political wing of abolitionism launched the Liberty Party in 1840, running former ACS agent James Birney as a candidate for president. Although Birney won only 7,000 votes in 1840 and 62,000 votes in 1844, the Liberty Party did articulate an antislavery alternative to the Jacksonian party system.

Events beyond the nation's borders bolstered Jacksonian-era antislavery. Abolitionists celebrated British West Indian emancipation in the 1830s, even though the British government paid £20 million to slaveholders. In 1839 northeastern abolitionists rallied to the defense of a group of Africans who had commandeered a Spanish slaver, the *Amistad*. The Africans were captured by a U.S. naval vessel off the coast of Long Island, New York, as they tried to sail back to Sierra Leone. Their case was litigated all the way to the U.S. Supreme Court, which ruled, in 1841, that they had been illegally enslaved in violation of Spanish law and treaty obligations. Later that year, a ship called the *Creole* carrying slaves from Richmond, Virginia, to New Orleans was also commandeered by its human cargo, who sailed the vessel to the Bahamas, where they were liberated. In a striking contrast to the *Amistad* case, the United States demanded that the slaves be returned to their owners. Joshua Giddings, an antislavery Whig representative from Ohio, introduced a resolution declaring the slaves' revolt to be legal and the government's effort to recover them dishonorable. He was censured by the House, resigned his seat, and was promptly re-elected by his constituents.

As the British stepped up their campaign against the Atlantic slave trade, the United States steadfastly refused to allow the Royal Navy to search American vessels suspected of "blackbirding." Instead, the Webster-Ashburton Treaty of 1842 committed the United States to maintaining a naval patrol off the West African coast to "act in concert and cooperation" with the British navy in the suppression of the Atlantic slave trade. The results were unimpressive, as American naval vessels in the West Africa Squadron captured only 36 slavers between 1843 and 1861.

Until the mid-1840s, Whigs and Democrats avoided the issue of slavery's expansion. When Texas won independence from Mexico in 1836, Democratic leaders initially deflected pressure to annex the new republic. After Van Buren's defeat in 1840, William Henry Harrison, a Whig, would undoubtedly have kept Texas at arm's length, but his untimely death catapulted the idiosyncratic Virginian John Tyler to the presidency. After Tyler clashed with his own party, he seized on Texas annexation as a way to rally southern Democrats behind him. In 1844 Secretary of State John C. Calhoun, who openly feared British abolitionist influence in Texas, negotiated an annexation treaty that was defeated by an alliance of Whigs and northern Democrats in the Senate. The leading candidates for the presidency—Martin Van Buren for the Democrats and Henry Clay for the Whigs—came out against annexation. Southern Democrats retaliated against Van Buren by denying him the party's nomination, which was extended to a relatively obscure former governor of Tennessee, James K. Polk, who supported the annexation of Texas as well as the acquisition of the Oregon Territory with a northern border of 54°40′. Polk edged out Clay in the general election, Texas entered the Union as a slave state the following year, and, shortly after, a boundary dispute with Mexico flamed into war.

Some historians suggest that the Liberty Party's 15,000 votes in New York tipped the 1844 election to Polk, thus initiating a chain of events that returned slavery to the center of American politics—just not in the way that Liberty Party supporters had imagined. This great "what if?" supposes that Clay would have won those 15,000 votes in the absence of the Liberty Party, when it is at least plausible that those voters would have stayed home rather than cast a ballot for the slave-owning Kentuckian. Blaming the Liberty Party also overlooks other factors, from electoral fraud to the Democrats' popularity among immigrants, that contributed to Clay's defeat.

Slavery and the Sectional Crisis: 1846–60

The Mexican-American War was both a partisan and a sectional issue. Whigs opposed the war; many Northerners regarded it as a land grab for the southern "Slave Power." Three months into the war, David Wilmot, a Pennsylvania Democrat, moved to deflect this criticism by proposing to prohibit slavery in any territory acquired from Mexico. (It should be noted that Mexico abolished slavery in 1829, so Wilmot's measure would simply have preserved the legal status quo.) The Wilmot Proviso, as it became known, passed the House with nearly unanimous support from northern congressmen in both parties, but it failed in the Senate, where southern power was stronger. Congress put the proviso through the same paces in 1847, and the war ended with no agreement on the status of slavery in the vast territory acquired in the Treaty of Guadalupe Hidalgo, which the Senate ratified early in 1848.

Committed to prohibiting slavery wherever constitutionally permissible, a coalition of Democratic "Barnburners," Conscience Whigs, and holdovers from the Liberty Party organized the Free Soil Party, nominating Van Buren for president and Charles Francis Adams for vice president. The Free Soil Party won more than 290,000 votes (14 percent of the popular vote in the North), with its strongest support coming in the ticket's home states of New York and Massachusetts. The party did not win any electoral votes, and its effect on the outcome of the election was murky, but it did contribute to a crucial shift in the emphasis of antislavery politics toward concern for the rights of free white Northerners rather than the wrongs done to southern slaves.

Thirty years after the Missouri crisis, another storm gathered around the issue of slavery. To slaveholders' chagrin, the Whig president Zachary Taylor, a Louisiana slaveholder, supported the admission of gold-mad California as a free state. The status of slavery in the rest of the Mexican cession remained in dispute. Antislavery Northerners wanted to abolish slavery in the District of Columbia, while proslavery Southerners wanted more rigorous enforcement of the Constitution's Fugitive Slave Clause. Some radical southern politicians went so far as to threaten disunion if the North did not accede to

their demands. After Congress rejected an "omnibus" bill designed by Clay to resolve all these issues at once, the torch passed to Illinois Democratic senator Stephen A. Douglas, who broke up the various elements of Clay's bill and navigated each one separately through Congress.

The so-called Compromise of 1850 passed, even though only a small band of compromisers supported the whole package. They allied with a sectional bloc to form a slim majority on each measure. The territorial issue was solved by admitting California as a free state while effectively adopting the principle of "popular sovereignty" elsewhere in the New Mexico and Utah territories. This solution blunted the appeal of the Free Soil Party. Most Barnburners returned to the Democratic Party, and the Free Soil vote dropped by almost 50 percent from 1848 to 1852. Congress also banned the slave trade but not slave owning in the District of Columbia; the district's slave traders moved their pens outside the city and carried on business as usual.

The most controversial piece of legislation was the new Fugitive Slave Act. It was designed to counteract northern states' "personal liberty laws," which gave free black Northerners due process protections and, in many cases, prohibited state officials from participating in the recovery of fugitive slaves. The Fugitive Slave Act created a new cadre of federal "commissioners" with the authority to arrest runaway slaves and return them to their owners. The commissioners had a financial incentive to determine that seized persons belonged to those who claimed them. Northerners could be deputized by the commissioners to help enforce the law and were subject to fines and punishment if they refused.

These terms inflamed antislavery public opinion in the North. Abolitionists pledged civil disobedience and resistance, and many black Northerners fled to Canada. Dozens of alleged fugitives were captured in the year following the passage of the law, and, in a few celebrated incidents, vigilance committees tried to rescue them. The most famous case occurred in Boston in 1854, when the administration of President Franklin Pierce deployed federal troops to safeguard the return of a fugitive slave named Anthony Burns to Virginia. The "Slave Power" had camped in the North. Harriet Beecher Stowe's *Uncle Tom's Cabin*, written as a protest against the law, was serialized in Gamaliel Bailey's antislavery newspaper *The National Era* in 1851–52 and became a worldwide bestseller. Southern slaveholders were taken aback. They viewed the return of fugitive slaves as a solemn constitutional obligation, and they were aghast at northern antislavery appeals to a "higher law than the Constitution," in the explosive words of New York's Whig senator William Seward.

Despite the furor over the Fugitive Slave Act, it was the revival of the territorial issue that killed off the Second Party System. In 1854, hoping to win support for his preferred transcontinental railroad route, Douglas introduced legislation to organize the Kansas and Nebraska territories and allow the people of each to decide the status of slavery for themselves. Although the Utah and New Mexico territories had been organized on the principle of popular sovereignty four years earlier, Douglas's extension of the principle to Kansas and Nebraska proved explosive because it meant overturning the Missouri Compromise. The Kansas-Nebraska bill divided both major parties along sectional lines, but with enough support from pro-Douglas northern Democrats it passed. If the Democrats split over Kansas and Nebraska, the Whigs fell apart. Southern Whigs had been trounced by the Democrats in the 1852 and 1853 elections, and the Kansas-Nebraska debates finally convinced them to cut loose from the northern wing of their party. Riding a wave of anti-immigrant sentiment, the Know-Nothing Party enjoyed some popularity in local and state elections in 1855 and 1856 as an alternative to the Whigs, but it crashed on the politics of slavery just as the Whigs had done.

Antislavery backlash against the Kansas-Nebraska legislation coalesced in the Republican Party, which emerged in the 1856 elections as the leading rival to the Democrats in the North. Running on a platform that condemned "the twin relics of barbarism—Polygamy, and Slavery," John Frémont, the Republican presidential candidate, won 11 northern states and almost 40 percent of the electoral vote.

Radical southern politicians, often known as "fire-eaters," advocated an aggressively proslavery agenda through the 1850s. Some fire-eaters hoped to force the Democratic Party to give in to proslavery interests; others hoped to create a new southern party and ultimately sever the slave states from the Union. Their platform included rigid enforcement of the Fugitive Slave Act, a federal slave code to protect slaveholders' special property rights, the extension of slavery into the western territories, the annexation of Cuba, support for filibusters in Central America, and the reopening of the African slave trade to the United States. They promoted southern nationalism with calls for railroads, colleges, and a literature unique to the South. Proslavery ideologues painted the abolitionists as fanatics and slavery as humane. Asserting that southern slaves were treated well, they taunted northern and British abolitionists for ignoring the dire plight of wage workers. Some pointed to the emerging utopian socialist movement as proof of the failure of free society.

The sectional crisis deepened in the late 1850s. First, popular sovereignty in the Kansas territory led to a debacle. Violence erupted between proslavery and antislavery factions, punctuated in May 1856 by the murder of five men at Pottawatomie Creek by John Brown and his sons. The violence spilled onto the floor of the Senate, where Preston Brooks, a representative from South Carolina, caned

Massachusetts senator Charles Sumner for insulting his cousin, South Carolina senator Andrew Butler, during a speech on the atrocities in Kansas. When pro- and antislavery forces in Kansas submitted rival state constitutions to Congress in 1858, President James Buchanan supported the proslavery version, but Douglas saw it as fraudulent and opposed it. An alliance of Douglas Democrats and Republicans in the House defeated the proslavery constitution, outraging southern Democrats. The Supreme Court added fuel to the fire early in 1857, ruling in *Dred Scott v. Sandford* that the due process clause of the Constitution prevented Congress from prohibiting slavery in the territories. The decision undermined Douglas's preferred solution of popular sovereignty; Abraham Lincoln and many other Republicans thought that it paved the way for the nationalization of slavery.

Then, in the fall of 1859, John Brown attempted to seize the federal armory at Harpers Ferry, Virginia, and incite a slave insurrection. Federal troops under Robert E. Lee quashed the revolt. Brown was captured, tried, and executed for treason. Widespread northern admiration for Brown after his hanging convinced many white Southerners that the Union was an empty shell.

Slavery dominated the election of 1860. Nominating the relatively obscure Lincoln as its presidential candidate, the Republican Party opposed any expansion of slavery into the western territories. In a bid to expand support in the Lower North, the Republicans also broadened their economic agenda to include a protective tariff, a homestead act, and federal aid for internal improvements. The Democrats fractured, with Douglas at the head of a northern ticket pledged to support popular sovereignty and Kentucky's John Breckenridge at the head of a southern ticket determined to protect slavery in federal territory. Conservative former Whigs organized the Constitutional Union Party with the bold platform of upholding the Constitution and enforcing the law. They nominated John Bell of Tennessee for president and Edward Everett from Massachusetts for vice president in a last-ditch effort to hold the country together by ignoring the divisions over slavery.

Lincoln won a majority of the popular vote in the North and the electoral votes of every northern state except New Jersey, which he split with Douglas. Breckenridge won the Lower South, plus Delaware and Maryland. Bell won Virginia, Kentucky, and Tennessee, while Douglas won only Missouri. The upshot was that Lincoln won the presidency without a single electoral vote from the slave states; a northern party had risen to national power on an antislavery platform. Despite Lincoln's assurances that the Republicans would not seek to abolish slavery in the states where it already existed, many white Southerners believed that Lincoln's election portended the death of slavery in the Union one way or another.

Secession, the Civil War, and Emancipation: 1861–65

Secession was intended to protect slavery, but it had the opposite effect. By leaving the Union and daring the North to stop them, southern secessionists invited a terrible war that led, by its own logic, to emancipation. "They have sowed the wind and must reap the whirlwind," reflected William Tecumseh Sherman in the middle of the Civil War. Seven states in the Lower South seceded between late December 1860 and early February 1861, and another four joined the Confederacy in the two months after Fort Sumter. The decision to secede was fiercely contested within the South. Opposition tended to come either from ultraconservative planters who valued prudence above all, or from the spokesmen for regions that had little stake in slavery, such as western Virginia, eastern Tennessee, and northern Alabama. Four border slave states (Delaware, Maryland, Kentucky, and Missouri) remained in the Union, providing some counterweight to abolitionist pressures during the war. But with the slaveholders' power greatly diminished and the Democrats in a minority, Lincoln and the Republican Congress implemented an antislavery agenda: admitting Kansas as a free state, recognizing Haiti, prosecuting illegal Atlantic slave traders, and abolishing slavery (and compensating slaveholders) in the District of Columbia.

At the beginning of the war, however, Lincoln was careful to honor his promise not to challenge slavery in the states where it existed. He did not think that secession abrogated the Constitution's protections for slavery in the states. Moreover, keeping the loyalty of northern Democrats and white men in the border slave states required political caution. So when General David Hunter took it upon himself in May 1862 to declare all the slaves in South Carolina, Georgia, and Florida free, Lincoln revoked the order, earning the wrath of northern abolitionists.

Union policy nevertheless moved toward emancipation. It was spurred on by enslaved people themselves, who risked life and limb to make their way to the Union Army. General Benjamin Butler was the first to turn slaves' status as property against their owners, declaring fugitives to be "contraband of war" in May 1861 and putting them to work at Fortress Monroe in Virginia. Invoking military necessity, the Union continued to counterpunch against slavery, passing a Confiscation Act in August 1861 that freed slaves who were employed in the service of the Confederacy, then passing a Second Confiscation Act in July 1862 that freed the slaves of persons actively engaged in the rebellion. The Emancipation Proclamation continued this trajectory, freeing slaves in all territories still in rebellion as of January 1, 1863. Although it is true that the Emancipation Proclamation did not free a single person at the moment it was promulgated, it did have the momentous effect of transforming the Union Army into an instrument of emancipation as the war dragged on. Moreover, the Proclamation authorized the employment of black men in the army and navy, even if black soldiers would still have to wrestle their own government for equal pay with white soldiers and the opportunity to see combat. Lincoln's resounding victory over McLellan and the Republican landslide in Congress in the election of 1864 confirmed the war's abolitionist turn. Slavery crumbled in the Union as well as in the Confederacy. Unionist governments in Arkansas and Louisiana abolished slavery in 1864, as did Maryland; Missouri and Tennessee followed suit early in 1865. In January of that year, the House approved a constitutional amendment abolishing slavery, but it was not until December that the Thirteenth Amendment was ratified.

The end of slavery raised crucial questions about the status of the country's 4 million freed people: Would they be citizens? What rights would they have? What did society and government owe to them? Emancipation did not end the labor problem that gave rise to slavery in the first place, nor did it wipe away the stain of racism that slavery left behind. As in other postemancipation societies in the Atlantic world, former slaveholders replaced slavery with an array of coercive labor practices ranging from debt peonage to convict labor. Freed people faced a ferocious campaign of racist terror and violence waged by former Confederates embittered by military defeat and the upheaval of social and political Reconstruction. The reaction against emancipation practically eviscerated the Fourteenth and Fifteenth Amendments until the black freedom movement after World War II ended Jim Crow. Unmoored from the struggle against chattel slavery, antislavery rhetoric has drifted through American politics like a ghost ship, reappearing out of the fog in struggles over prostitution, unions, women's rights, communism, and the reserve clause in baseball.

It is impossible to tally the whole cost of slavery and its vicious legacies to the United States, but the reckoning continues. In July 2008, the U.S. House of Representatives passed a nonbinding resolution apologizing for "the fundamental injustice, cruelty, brutality, and inhumanity of slavery and Jim Crow." As William Faulkner wrote, "The past is never dead. It's not even past." Today the United States and the world community confront new manifestations of slavery in its modern guises of "human trafficking" and severe forms of sex and labor exploitation.

See also abolitionism; civil rights; Civil War and Reconstruction; sectional conflict and secession, 1845–65; segregation and Jim Crow.

FURTHER READING. Tyler Anbinder, *Nativism and Slavery: The Northern Know Nothings and the Politics of the 1850s*, 1992; John Ashworth, *Slavery, Capitalism, and Politics in the Antebellum Republic*, 1995; Ira Berlin, Barbara J. Fields, Steven F. Miller, Joseph P. Reidy, and Leslie S. Rowland, *Slaves No More: Three Essays on Emancipation and the Civil War*, 1992; William J. Cooper, *The South and* the Politics of Slavery, 1828–1856, 1978; W.E.B. DuBois, *The Suppression of the African Slave Trade to the United States of America, 1638–1870*, 2007; Jonathan Halperin Earle, *Jacksonian Antislavery and the Politics of Free Soil, 1824–1854*, 2004; Don Edward Fehrenbacher, *The Dred Scott Case: Its Significance in American Law and Politics*, 1978; Idem, *The Slaveholding Republic: An Account of the United States Government's Relations to Slavery*, 2001; Eric Foner, *Free Soil, Free Labor, Free Men: The Ideology of the Republican Party before the Civil War*, 1995; Idem, *Reconstruction: America's Unfinished Revolution, 1863–1877*, 1st ed., 1988; Robert Pierce Forbes, *The Missouri Compromise and Its Aftermath: Slavery and the Meaning of America*, 2007; William W. Freehling, *The Road to Disunion*, 1990; Michael F. Holt, *The Rise and Fall of the American Whig Party: Jacksonian Politics and the Onset of the Civil War*, 1999; Matthew Mason, *Slavery and Politics in the Early American Republic*, 2006; David Morris Potter, *The Impending Crisis, 1848–1861*, 1976; Leonard L. Richards, *The Slave Power: The Free North and Southern Domination, 1780–1860*, 2000; Silvana R. Siddali, *From Property to Person: Slavery and the Confiscation Acts, 1861–1862*, 2005; James Brewer Stewart, *Holy Warriors: The Abolitionists and American Slavery*, revised ed., 1996; Michael Vorenberg, *Final Freedom: The Civil War, the Abolition of Slavery, and the Thirteenth Amendment*, Cambridge Historical Studies in American Law and Society, 2001; Sean Wilentz, *The Rise of American Democracy: Jefferson to Lincoln*, 2005.

ADAM ROTHMAN

Social Security

Social Security refers to the program of old-age insurance, subsequently broadened to include survivors (1939) and disability insurance (1956), that President Franklin D. Roosevelt initiated on August 14, 1935, by signing the Social Security Act. Old-age insurance began as a federally administered program in which the government collected equal contributions of 1 percent of the first $3,000 of an employee's wages from employers and employees, and paid pensions to the employees on their retirement. Since 1951 the program has experienced enormous growth, and in 2005 some 48,445,900 Americans, more than the combined populations of California and New Jersey, received benefits from the Social Security program. That year the program collected more than $700 billion from payroll taxes—about as much revenue as the gross domestic product of the Netherlands—and spent a little more than $500 billion on benefits.

Legislative Origins

In June 1934, President Roosevelt asked Labor Secretary Frances Perkins to chair a cabinet-level Committee on Economic Security that, together with a staff headed by two Wisconsin state government officials, made the crucial decision to recommend a federal social insurance program for old age, financed through payroll taxes. The president contrasted this contributory approach favorably with other currently popular plans, such as Francis Townsend's proposals to pay everyone over age 60 a pension of $200 dollars a month. When the president's plan was introduced to Congress in January 1935, the old-age insurance portions of the legislation (the proposed legislation contained many features, including federal aid to the states for public assistance and a state-run unemployment compensation program) received an indifferent reception. Congressmen objected to the fact that the program would not pay regular benefits until 1942 and would exclude those already past retirement age. Members from predominantly agricultural districts realized that old-age insurance meant almost nothing to their constituents who, because the program was limited to industrial and commercial workers, would not be eligible to participate. The president, bolstered by the favorable results of the 1934 elections, resisted congressional attempts to abandon social insurance in favor of noncontributory welfare grants to the elderly and to permit those with liberal private pension plans to withdraw from Social Security.

Getting Established: 1936–50

Social Security surfaced as a campaign issue in 1936, when Republican candidate Alfred Landon criticized the program as "unjust, unworkable, stupidly drafted, and wastefully financed." In response to his criticism, President Roosevelt agreed to a plan, passed by Congress in 1939, to reduce the amount of money held in reserve to finance benefits, to initiate benefits earlier than planned, and to include special benefits for workers' wives and for the dependents of workers who died before retirement age. The 1939 amendments contained the implicit assumption that men participated in the labor force and women did not. Dependent wives but not dependent husbands received spousal benefits, and a benefit went to widows of covered workers but not to widowers. Widows received only three-quarters of a basic benefit. Not until 1983 were these gender distinctions lifted from the law.

Despite the 1939 amendments, Social Security did not gain great popularity. Instead, it remained a relatively neglected program. In 1940, for example, even before the nation's entrance into World War II, the United States spent more on veterans' payments and workers' compensation than it did on old-age and survivors' insurance. Even in the area of old-age security, social insurance—a federal program—played a distinctly secondary role to welfare—a state and local program. The average monthly welfare benefit was $42 in 1949, although with considerable variance from state to state, compared with an average Social Security benefit of $25. As late as 1950, more than twice as many people were on state welfare rolls receiving old-age assistance as were receiving retirement benefits from the federal government under Social Security. Throughout the 1940s, Congress felt little pressure to expand the program and, as a consequence, repeatedly refused to raise payroll taxes, increase benefit levels, or expand coverage.

The situation changed with the 1950 amendments, which expanded coverage and raised benefits. The amendments were the result of a report by an advisory committee in 1948 that argued that the nation could either rely on welfare, which the council portrayed as demeaning since it required recipients to prove they were poor and induced a state of dependency, or on social insurance, which, according to the council, reinforced "the interest of the individual in helping himself."

On August 28, 1950, after lengthy congressional hearings, the recommendations of the advisory council became law. The 1950 amendments raised average benefits by 77 percent and broke the impasse over Social Security taxes. Congress agreed to raise the tax level to 3 percent and to increase the taxable wage base (the amount of earnings on which taxes were paid) from $3,000 to $3,600. In addition, the amendments brought new groups, such as self-employed businessmen, into the Social Security system. The ranks of Social Security supporters included labor unions and liberal Democrats, whose standing was boosted in 1948 with President Truman's surprising reelection, the revival of Democratic control of Congress, and the election of Social Security supporters such as Paul Douglas of Illinois. These factors helped change the congressional mood from indifference to a willingness to expand the system.

The Golden Age of Social Security

Stalled in the 1940s, Social Security became a popular program in the 1950s. Expanded coverage encouraged more congressmen to take an interest. Prosperity enabled the program to collect more money than Depression-era planners had predicted. As a result, increased benefits were legislated in 1952, 1954, 1956, and 1958. Social Security surpassed welfare in popularity and in the generosity of its benefits. The only real test the program faced came with the election of Dwight D. Eisenhower in 1952. He expressed an interest in looking at alternatives to Social Security, and he was encouraged by the Chamber of Commerce, representatives from the insurance industry, and some Republican congressmen. By 1954, however, Eisenhower had decided to reject the advice to change the system to a flat benefit paid out to everyone. In September 1954, the president proposed and secured passage of a law preserving the existing system, raising benefit levels, and extending Social Security coverage to farmers.

During Eisenhower's first term, the creation of disability benefits became the major issue in Social Security politics. Liberals wanted to expand the system to pay benefits to people who had dropped out of the labor force before the normal retirement age because of a functional limitation or impairment. Conservatives worried that disability was a vague concept whose adoption would lead to a precipitous rise in expenditure and discourage the more constructive alternative of rehabilitation. On this matter, the Democrats defeated the Republicans by a one-vote margin in the Senate in July 1956. Social Security expanded to encompass benefits for disabled workers 50 years or older. Four years later Congress removed the age restriction.

By 1958 the cutting edge issue had shifted from disability to health insurance. Proponents of expansion wanted to use the Social Security system as a means of funding insurance to cover the costs of hospital care for Social Security beneficiaries. They argued that retirement benefits could never be raised high enough to cover the catastrophic costs of illness. President Eisenhower, emphasizing health insurance coverage that relied on private insurance companies, opposed this expansion, as did the influential Democratic congressman Wilbur Mills of Arkansas and Senator Robert Kerr, Democrat from Oklahoma. Despite President John F. Kennedy's advocacy of what became known as Medicare, the legislation stalled in Congress and interrupted the pattern of regular Social Security benefit increases. It took the masterful efforts of President Lyndon B. Johnson in 1965 to break the impasse. Only after the creation of Medicare and Medicaid in 1965 did Social Security politics resume its normal course.

Indexing and Modern Dilemmas

A major development in 1972—automatic indexing of Social Security benefit increases to the cost of living—once again changed the course of Social Security politics. The idea of indexing benefits, rather than leaving them to Congress, came from President Richard M. Nixon. The president saw Social Security as an issue where the majority Democrats could always outbid the minority Republicans and take credit for benefit increases. Nixon argued that it would be better to establish a rational structure that related benefit increases to changes in the cost of living and reduced congressional temptation to raise benefits above what the nation could afford. Not surprisingly, Ways and Means Committee Chairman Wilbur Mills resisted the idea, effectively blocking it in 1969 and 1970. As members of Congress became more sympathetic to the indexing idea, Mills acquiesced to a plan that permitted automatic cost-of-living adjustments, but only if Congress failed to raise benefits in a discretionary manner. Because of disagreements between the House and the Senate, largely over the matter of welfare reform, the process took until the summer of 1972 to resolve. In the end, Congress agreed to cost-of-living adjustments on Mills's terms. The Democratic Congress outbid the Republicans on the level of Social Security benefits. Where Nixon hoped for a 5 percent increase, Mills and his colleagues legislated one of 20 percent.

This change made the program vulnerable to the unfavorable economic conditions of the 1970s. High unemployment cut down on tax collections and induced more people to retire; inflation drove up benefit levels. In June 1974, the trustees who oversaw Social Security announced that the program was "underfinanced in the long range." A slower rate of population growth meant a higher future percentage of aged people in the population and a heavier future burden for Social Security. Support for Social Security remained high, but the system faced a new vulnerability

Social Security survived its vulnerable period between 1975 and 1983 because of the many beneficiaries invested in its survival but also because it contained built-in legislative protection. As a result of the 1972 amendments, benefit levels were protected against inflation, without Congress having to do anything.

President Jimmy Carter's advisors convinced him to take action to ensure that Social Security met its obligations. Congress ignored most of the president's recommendations (such as raising the level of employer taxes) and instead raised the level of wages on which workers and their employers paid Social Security taxes, and increased tax rates. Passage of a modified version of Carter's bill showed that Congress was willing to go to great lengths to preserve the basic Social Security system. Carter's advisors assured him that the 1977 amendments had "fixed" Social Security in both the short and long runs.

The economic recession of the late 1970s soon undid the projections of program planners and once again pointed the way to a crisis. As the actuaries duly reported, there was the possibility that Social Security would not be able to meet its obligations and pay full benefits in 1983.

Once again, Congress—which included a House under Democratic control—and the Reagan administration joined forces to "save" the program and preserve its basic structure. The Reagan administration began with an aggressive stance on Social Security, seeking among other things to reduce the size of early retirement benefits (legislated in 1956 for women and 1961 for men). Democrats tended to favor tax increases, Republicans benefit cuts. Interested in sharing the blame, each side hesitated to take action without the tacit approval of the other.

President Reagan and House Speaker Tip O'Neill decided to remove the issue from public scrutiny, at least until after the 1982 elections. In December 1981, Reagan appointed a bipartisan commission, the National Commission on Social Security Reform, to propose solutions to the system's problems. The commission held a number of ceremonial meetings, waiting to see how the 1982 elections turned out. The election results gave the commission no easy outs, since neither party gained a victory decisive enough to provide a comfortable working majority to deal with the issue.

After the election, President Reagan and House Speaker O'Neill of Massachusetts used their surrogates on the commission to negotiate a deal. Each

side kept a running score sheet that listed the potential savings from each item, all the time hoping roughly to balance tax increases and benefit costs. In the spirit of reaching a deal, the Democrats accepted a permanent six-month delay in the annual cost-of-living adjustment—in effect a 2 percent reduction in benefits. The Republicans acquiesced to small increases in Social Security taxes achieved by initiating already legislated payroll tax increases earlier than scheduled. The Congress in 1983 honored the terms of the compromise. Politicians on both sides of the aisle celebrated the rescue of Social Security, and Ronald Reagan signed the 1983 Social Security Amendments with pomp and circumstance.

The Modern Era
Conservatives believed that the crisis leading to the 1983 amendments illustrated the vulnerability of the system and the unwillingness of Congress to take steps to put a permanent end to the problems. Liberals pointed to the apparently robust shape of the Social Security trust funds as proof that the amendments had, in effect, resolved the issue. Advocates in conservative think tanks like Cato and the Heritage Foundation tried to make people aware of Social Security's long-term liabilities and its inability to provide windfall gains to later entrants into the system (such as the baby boom generation and its echo). They also touted governmental sanctioned alternatives that relied on individual and private-sector administration, such as individual retirement accounts (IRAs) and 401(k)s—a parallel private universe for Social Security, equivalent to the private health insurance on which most Americans relied.

When Social Security reform returned to the political agenda in the 1990s, the result of changed actuarial assumptions about real wage growth and the future of the economy, conservatives were able to offer more fundamental alternatives than simply tinkering with the present system. Evidence that the latest crisis in Social Security would be handled differently from previous ones came when an advisory council met in 1994 through 1996. This officially sanctioned group, one of the sort that usually reinforced the conventional bureaucratic wisdom, could not agree on a single recommendation and instead gave official sanction to privatization as one of three solutions to the Social Security financing problem.

When George W. Bush came into office, he expected to solve the long-term financing problem and point the way to a fundamental reform of Social Security. In 2000, as a candidate, Bush said he wanted to give younger workers the chance to put part of their payroll taxes into what he called "sound, responsible investments." Interspersed with the political rhythms of the post-9/11 era, the president continued his initiative. In his 2004 State of the Union address, Bush said, "We should make the Social Security system a source of ownership for the American people."

After the 2004 election, the president brought the Social Security campaign to center stage, announcing that it would be a priority of his administration. If nothing were done, Bush argued, the system would run out of money. That set the stage for a call to action in the 2005 State of the Union address. According to the president, Social Security was a great moral success of the past century but something different was required for the new millennium. The president followed up with a full-scale publicity campaign.

Despite his unprecedented effort, Bush gained no political traction as he faced serious technical and political obstacles. One problem, broadly stated, was how to move from one system to another. Benefits for people already receiving Social Security needed to be preserved while simultaneously moving to a private system—a difficult and costly transition. Meanwhile, the shortfall in the program's long-range financing provided continuing pressure on all parties to find some common ground.

See also welfare.

FURTHER READING. Nancy J. Altman, *The Battle for Social Security: From FDR's Vision to Bush's Gamble*, 2005; Daniel Beland, *Social Security: History and Politics from the New Deal to the Privatization Debate*, 2005; Martha Derthick, *Policymaking for Social Security*, 1979.

EDWARD D. BERKOWITZ

socialism

Socialist attempts to redirect the political culture of the United States proved to be a difficult task—one that, while never succeeding, did on occasion achieve a certain success even in failure. The fertile earth of the New World produced a variety of political fruits, but none was as potent as the idea that this American earth itself was, as Irving Howe once said, "humanity's second chance." In this rendering, it was the American Revolution that secured for the nation its exceptional status, and, in the process, dismissed the socialist premise of a required second revolution as misguided or malicious. Understandings of nineteenth-century socialism varied: preindustrial agricultural communes coexisted with urban industrial workers contesting employers in the factory. They shared, however, a concern to democratize decision making in the society and the workplace and to share more equitably the profits from those enterprises. Whatever the specific expression, the socialist experience in America would prove to be, at its best, a bittersweet experience.

The first phase of socialist experimentation in America was primarily communitarian. Reflecting impulses that motivated many of the continent's initial European settlers, these self-defined socialists separated from the developing capitalist society to form communities that would serve, in their reengineered social and personal relations, as beacon lights to the majority of their countrymen they considered lost souls in a materialist diaspora. Influenced by certain European utopian socialists (Charles Fourier and Count Henri de Saint-Simon, especially), by the deep religious currents already evident in American life, and by incipient social reformers such as Robert Owen and Edward Bellamy, these communities proliferated throughout the United States. Most prevalent in the nineteenth and early twentieth centuries, this tradition revived again in the 1960s in the communes organized by so-called hippies seeking personal authenticity in collective life apart from an overly commercialized culture.

Whatever the benefits for individual participants, the majority of these utopian communities were short-lived. John Humphrey Noyes (1811–86), who led the Oneida Community near Utica, New York, explained in his 1870 history of the movement that those communities organized along secular utopian lines failed more quickly than those created from a shared religious belief. Noyes hoped that the latter efforts possessed greater prospects of introducing socialism through "churches . . . quickened by the Pentecostal Spirit." Although the evangelical spirit would influence American socialism, it would not be the singular element in organizing the socialist movement that Noyes imagined.

Transition to Industrial Capitalism

From an international perspective, 1848 marks a turning point in both the idea and practice of socialism. The European revolutions fought that year against the continent's monarchial regimes ignited a variety of dissenting movements; *The Communist Manifesto* by Marx and Engels, published that year, offered an interpretative analysis of the turmoil that emphasized the oppressive class distinctions imposed by the inner logic of the capitalist economic system. A decidedly antiutopian "scientific" socialism emerged from this European cauldron. In Marx's view, working people—the oppressed class created by capitalism—would be the collective agent that would overthrow industrial capitalism. These socialists rejected liberal reform efforts and declared, as a scientific fact, the coming transformation to socialism and, following that, to communism—the state of full human freedom and equality. Not surprisingly, their attempted revolutions and their repression by European authorities led to large-scale migrations by activists and sympathizers to other European countries and to America.

From the start of their American experience, the expectations of European socialist immigrants encountered a difficult reception. In sharp contrast with their European past, America's "universal" suffrage (for white men) was a fundamental aspect of citizenship. As the ballot was preeminently an individual right, its possession validated a core belief in individualism, in the expectation of social mobility, and in the superiority of American democratic governance.

While not all Americans held these beliefs with equal intensity, these principles were, as Alexis de Tocqueville and many others noted, a fundamental component of American political consciousness.

As newly arrived socialists entered the workforce and sought to join the nascent trade union movement in the three decades after 1848, many despaired of the "backwardness" of the American working people. The individualistic aspirations of these workers led most to ignore appeals to a collective class consciousness as they avidly engaged in mainstream political activity, often closely aligned with employers. Most confusingly, American working people seemed to embrace the promise of American life. Friedrick Sorge, Marx's representative in America, harshly dismissed these interrelated strands of the political culture as a "delusion [that] transforms itself into a sort of creed." Yet, after almost two decades working in the American wilderness, Sorge reported to Marx in 1871 that, despite the enormous industrial growth that Marx held was the precondition for class consciousness, American "workingmen in general . . . are quite unconscious of their own position toward capital" and thus "slow to show battle against their oppressors. . . ."

But if American working people did not endorse an orthodox Marxist analysis, neither did they simply acquiesce to the demands of employers. In the three decades after Sorge's report, an intense series of strikes occurred nationwide. Strikers protested the transformation of work inherent in the change from an artisan to an industrial system of production, with the consequent loss of control by local communities of their daily lives, and the dramatically widening income gap between workers and employers. State and federal troops were deployed to break these strikes in iron mining and steel production, in coal mining, in railroad operations, and in other industries. Working people sought new approaches to gain their demands. Politically independent labor parties sprouted up across the nation, and the labor movement, while still small, began to solidify. The socialist movement also changed, softening Sorge's rigid view, and became more inclusive of America's particular political attitudes. Not insignificantly, its most prominent leader was deeply attuned to the possibilities of American democratic ideals.

The Socialist Party of America (SPA) was founded in 1901, but it had been in formation for some years before. Itself a coalition of beliefs and opinions, the SPA sought to define socialism in a manner consistent with the promise of democracy in both economic relations and politics. It ran candidates for political office, supported striking workers as well as the vote for women, and sought civic benefits such as the extension of sewer pipes and electricity to working people's neighborhoods. The party also held that socialism would ultimately come to America through electoral means. This emphasis on vying for votes within the dominant political structure rather than advocating an openly revolutionary program generated a split within the SPA, one that would become most evident during World War I.

Eugene Victor Debs (1855–1926) led this movement from its inception until his death. Although many socialist intellectuals considered his appreciation of Marx's theory deficient, he was the single national SPA leader who could appeal to its varied constituencies: new immigrants, native-born workers, intellectuals, and reformers. Debs, a native of Terre Haute, Indiana, ran for the presidency on the SPA ticket five times between 1900 and 1920 (he was ill in 1916). In 1912 Debs received 6 percent of the national vote, the highest percentage ever recorded by a socialist candidate. Eight years later, imprisoned in Atlanta Federal Penitentiary for his opposition to American involvement in World War I, Debs nonetheless received almost 1 million votes. The core of Debs's analysis, and the source of his appeal, was his understanding of socialism as the fulfillment of American democratic ideals in an era of industrial capitalism. It was the corporation, he argued—with its enormous financial and political power that could influence decisions in communities across the nation—that systematically violated the "truths" the Declaration of Independence held to be "self-evident." To democratize industrial capitalism, to share with its workforce decision making as well as the benefits and profits of its work, was a central aim of Debs's agitation.

Two issues particularly generated tension within the ranks of the SPA prior to World War I. Many male socialists dismissed agitation for woman suffrage because, they held, it detracted from the party's focus on economic issues; many also objected to any enhancement of a more visible role for women within the party. Undaunted by this resistance, a group of activist women within the SPA, many with ties to either the trade unions and/or progressive reformers, worked to include a woman's right to vote within the socialist agenda; in the process they created a network of activist socialist women. In major strikes in New York City (1909); Lawrence, Massachusetts (1912); and Patterson, New Jersey (1913), as editors and writers, trade union activists, and advocates for birth control, socialist women found a public voice and organized many. Their male comrades, however, changed slowly—when they changed at all. The values of nineteenth-century American culture that objected to a female presence in the presumed male public sphere permeated the ranks of its socialist critics as well.

Racial tension also divided the party. Victor Berger (1860–1929), the Milwaukee socialist leader and one of two socialists elected to the U.S. Congress, symbolized one position. Berger dismissed attempts to organize African Americans and publicly embraced the most racist stereotypes of African American men as a threat to white "civilization." Debs, on the other hand, although not without his own racial prejudices, refused to speak to segregated audiences of socialists and publicly joined with the National Association for the Advancement of Colored People in 1916 to condemn D. W. Griffith's hate-filled film about post–Civil War Reconstruction, *The Birth of a Nation*. Relatively few black Americans joined the SPA, but one who did made a major impact on the movement and the nation in the decades to come.

Asa Philip Randolph (1889–1979) came to New York in 1911, studied economics and politics at the City College of New York, and soon joined the SPA. He led an organizing drive among elevator operators in New York, founded and edited the *Messenger*, a socialist magazine aimed at the black community, and spoke out unceasingly for labor rights, racial equality, and opposition to American involvement in the war. In 1925 he became the leader of the Brotherhood of Sleeping Car Porters, a union of African American men who staffed the nation's railway sleeping cars. Randolph led a difficult fight against two opponents simultaneously: to gain recognition for the union from employers and to win admittance into the American Federation of Labor, the nation's major union grouping in the 1920s. In the process, the Brotherhood became the black community's national "telegraph" system. As porters crisscrossed the nation as they worked, they created an effective communications system that spread news of atrocities, of protest and organization, and of cultural developments to African Americans in diverse and dispersed communities. In the decades to come, Randolph's vision, one that integrated civil rights, trade union recognition, and civil liberties for all Americans, would play a major role in the civil rights movement and other social justice causes.

The postwar years took a toll on the SPA. It suffered a major split in 1919 when those influenced by the 1917 Russian Revolution split to form two revolutionary Communist parties; it was further weakened by the imprisonment of many of its activists, victims of the wartime resurgence of a narrowed patriotism that legitimized the repression of dissent. Debs, too, was not the same. Physically weakened after prison, he found that neither his oratory nor the substance of his message carried the force they once possessed. Americans, including many working people, accepted the permanence of the corporate structure, sought benefits from it where they could, and carefully chose when they might directly challenge their employers.

Socialism and Liberalism
The decades after 1920 were difficult for the SPA. The party's new leader, Norman Thomas (1884–1968), an ordained Presbyterian minister, was a committed socialist and pacifist who lacked the broad popular appeal Debs had possessed. Thomas ran six times for the presidency between 1928 and 1948, and never surpassed Debs's 1920 total.

But the problem was not simply one of personality. Factional fighting repeatedly split the SPA from

within, as the impact of the Great Depression, the momentarily powerful appeal of communism, and diminishing membership (especially among working people) sharply weakened the party. Even more devastating to the SPA's expectations was the revival of liberalism in the person of Franklin D. Roosevelt (1882–1945) and the New Deal program he instigated. Thomas would soon claim that the New Deal almost completely absorbed the SPA platform, and the majority of its working-class voters. This was largely true because neither Thomas nor the SPA were able to convince working people that the pragmatic thrust of New Deal liberalism embodied reforms that represented no serious challenge to industrial capitalism. Thomas and his colleagues were persistent advocates of civil liberties, civil rights, and trade unions, but increasingly found themselves hard pressed to effectively distinguish their approach from liberalism. Thomas's 1939 opposition to America's involvement in the emerging war—a position consistent with his long-held pacifism—created additional difficulties in appealing to liberal voters.

By 1945, the socialist movement in America was a shadow of its former self. Its strongest institutional base was a handful of unions with headquarters in New York City who were already transferring their allegiance to the New Deal and the Democratic Party. Beyond that, the movement possessed isolated outposts of strength in communities across the country but, with the exception of Milwaukee, Wisconsin, there were few areas of institutional strength. What complicated the situation further for socialists was the reality that a majority of a generation's politically progressive young people had, since the 1930s, gravitated toward liberalism and the legacy of the New Deal—and not to their party.

Not all followed that path, however. During the 1950s, Michael Harrington (1928–89), a Midwestern Catholic trained by the Jesuits at the College of the Holy Cross, emerged as one of the most promising socialists of the postwar generation. Grounded in a Catholic social justice tradition, including close ties with Dorothy Day and the Catholic Worker movement, Harrington evolved into a creative Marxist thinker. His approach to socialism reflected a sensibility similar to Debs's, while his intellectual engagement far surpassed most in the American socialist tradition. His first book, *The Other America* (1962), startled the nation and helped convince President John F. Kennedy to create a poverty program. In his later books, Harrington provided an intelligent, radical analysis of American political culture, the economic crisis of "stagflation" in the 1970s, and of the potential that yet resided in a democratic socialist approach.

From the vantage point of Norman Thomas's generation, Harrington represented a new generation of socialists; but to the emerging New Left protestors of the 1960s, he was decidedly old guard. Harrington himself, along with others in the SPA, cemented this perception with an early dismissive critique of the New Left's philosophy, strategy, and culture. In the 1970s, however, following the New Left's experiment with violent direct action, Harrington led a revived movement ultimately known as the Democratic Socialists of America (DSA). Struggling to maintain a socialist perspective, the DSA worked closely with the progressive wing of the Democratic Party, as events well beyond its control further diminished the prospects for socialism itself. The rise of modern conservatism enabled the election of President Ronald Reagan in 1980, a campaign in which the candidate won the enthusiastic support of many of the white working people who had once formed the foundation of both the SPA and the Democratic Party. That this occurred at a time when membership in American trade unions began its precipitous decline (nearly 30 percent of the nonagricultural workforce in 1980 to just over 12 percent in 2008) made the socialist predicament all the more painful.

Nor did the strategy of joining with progressive liberals bear immediate fruit. In the face of the conservative ascendancy, liberalism itself changed, becoming more centrist and supportive of an increasingly global corporate economy. Reagan's famous 1987 challenge to Soviet leader Mikhail Gorbachev to "tear down this wall!" (while speaking in front of the Berlin Wall, which symbolized the divisions of the cold war) was perhaps a public ringing of socialism's death knell. Two years later, on November 9, 1989, the wall itself came down. In America, socialism's appeal, always a minor note in the nation's politics, all but disappeared as an institutional presence.

American Socialism's Legacy

The reasons for socialism's failure in the United States are numerous, and many are noted above. But to focus solely on them is to miss the contributions to American democratic thought that even this failed movement achieved. Debs and the early SPA's emphasis on democracy in the workplace broadened the nation's understanding of its democratic ideals and asserted the dignity and respect due working people if the country was to maintain its democratic ethos. It defended as well American civil liberties in time of war and fear and, with the actions and sacrifices by Debs and many others, kept alive the tradition of protest so central to maintaining a democracy. In the era of Thomas, that emphasis on preserving civil liberties remained strong, and broadened to include civil rights activity as well. The problem of effectively defining socialism apart from liberalism in the public arena was not solved in these years, nor would it be in the Harrington era. But Harrington brought to public debate an incisive intellectual analysis and a deep moral perspective that spoke more to core democratic values than to any orthodox version of Marxist thought. Like Debs before him, if with greater intellectual command and less oratorical power, Harrington framed

potential solutions to America's deeper problems within its democratic traditions in ways that challenged conservatives and liberals alike. In short, the historical experience of socialism in America was to serve as a persistent reminder (and an occasionally successful advocate) of the potential that yet lies in the American tradition of democratic citizenship.

See also communism; democracy; labor movement and politics; liberalism; New Left.

FURTHER READING. Mari Jo Buhle, *Women and American Socialism, 1870–1920*, 1981; Carl J. Guarneri, *The Utopian Alternative: Fourierism in Nineteenth-Century America*, 1991; Michael Harrington, *The Other America: Poverty in the United States*, 1962; William H. Harris, *Keeping the Faith: A. Philip Randolph, Milton P. Webster, and the Brotherhood of Sleeping Car Porters, 1925–1937*, 1991; Irving Howe, *Socialism and America*, 1985; Maurice Isserman, *The Other American: The Life of Michael Harrington*, 2000; John Humphrey Noyes, *History of American Socialisms*, 1870, reprint, 1966; Paula F. Pfeffer, *A. Philip Randolph: Pioneer of the Civil Rights Movement*, 1990; Nick Salvatore, *Eugene V. Debs: Citizen and Socialist*, 1982; Friedrick Sorge, "To the General Council . . ." in *A Documentary History of American Industrial Society, Vol. IX: Labor Movement, 1860–1880*, edited by John R. Commons et al., 1910; W. A. Swanberg, *Norman Thomas, The Last Idealist*, 1976.

NICK SALVATORE

South since 1877, the

For nearly a century following the Civil War, the South was the most economically backward and politically repressive region of the United States. One-crop agriculture reigned throughout much of the region. The levels of southern poverty had few parallels inside American borders. And a system of racial segregation gave rise to a political system that was democratic in name only. It was only in the 1960s that the region began to lose its distinctiveness. Economic transformations brought income levels closer to the national average, the civil rights movement remade the region politically and culturally, and the conservatism of white Southerners converged in unexpected ways with that of other white Americans.

The antebellum period and the Civil War set the stage for the political distinctiveness of the late-nineteenth-century South. Secession and the formation of the Confederacy covered over countless political divisions in the South before the war. A notable split that survived the conflict was between the political priorities of the lowland plantation belt and upland areas dominated by yeoman farmers. This political rivalry would ebb over time, yet remained relevant well into the twentieth century.

The Civil War transformed the South most obviously by ending slavery, yet its impact could be seen in countless other ways. One out of ten white adult males in the South died during the war, and one out of every three white families lost a male relative. The economic consequences were equally dramatic. During the 1860s, the South's share of the nation's wealth fell from 30 to 12 percent. The region's largest and most important cities lay in ruins. Nine thousand miles of railroad lines were rendered useless; two-thirds of southern shipping capacity was destroyed. The most devastating economic impact of the war was also its greatest moral achievement: with emancipation, southern slave owners who dominated the region's politics and economy lost over $3 billion that they had invested in human chattel.

From Reconstruction to Jim Crow

Such death and devastation created monumental challenges for postwar reconstruction. In some areas of the South, it was hard to say when the war actually ended, so intense was the political terrorism carried out against white and black Republicans. Reconstruction governments faced a daunting set of tasks. They rebuilt destroyed infrastructure, promoted railroad development, established the region's first public school system, and created a network of basic public institutions to deal with the sick and suffering. The higher taxes and public debts that ensued only further enflamed political resentment among former Confederates, fueling biased charges of incompetence and greed and setting the stage for conservative white Southerners to return to power. Tragically, this southern nationalist view of the alleged failures of biracial Republican-controlled governments came to dominate the memory of the postwar period for most white Americans, Southerners and Northerners alike.

The presidential election of 1876 marked the end of efforts to remake the South after the Civil War and the beginning of the region's rough century of political, economic, and cultural peculiarity. The Democratic nominee that year, Samuel Tilden of New York, won 184 electoral votes, one short of a majority. Republicans disputed the count in three southern states: Florida, Louisiana, and South Carolina. Rival canvassing boards sent in conflicting returns; in South Carolina and Louisiana, competing state governments appeared. Congress established a special Electoral Commission to investigate the disputed elections and report its findings. The panel split along party lines in favor of the Republican nominee, Rutherford B. Hayes of Ohio. The House voted to accept the report in March 1877, but only after southern Democrats brokered a deal with Republicans that included promises for help with southern railroads, levee construction along the Mississippi, and a southern Democratic cabinet appointment. Few of the pledges were kept save for the most significant one: the withdrawal of the remaining federal troops from the South. One month into his presidency, Hayes recalled military units from the state houses in Louisiana and South Carolina. Republican governments there abruptly collapsed.

The Compromise of 1877 doomed two-party politics in the region. Democrats ruled the Solid South until the 1960s. For much of that period, white Southerners dominated the Democratic Party. Until 1936, when the Democrats dispensed with the two-thirds rule for presidential nominees, no candidate could win the Democratic nomination without southern backing. The South's dominance placed Democrats in a subordinate position nationally. From 1860 to 1932, Democrats elected only two presidents, Grover Cleveland and Woodrow Wilson. Neither candidate ever won a majority of the national popular vote.

By the 1890s, what threat there was to Democratic dominance in the South came not from Republicans but from Populists. The People's Party drew on widespread unrest among farmers in the South and West that could be traced to the Panic of 1873. Its antecedent was the Farmers' Alliance, an economic movement that began in 1876 in central Texas. In an era of economic consolidation, the alliance represented small-scale producers and derided the brokers, merchants, railroad executives, and bankers who profited from the crops that farmers grew. The late 1880s were a boom time for the alliance, which by 1890 counted 852,000 members in southern states alone. Half of all eligible people joined the alliance in the states of Arkansas, Florida, Mississippi, and Georgia.

The Farmers' Alliance's frustration with the two major parties boiled over in the early 1890s. The failure of the Democrats to address what they felt were systemic economic problems, such as low agricultural prices and the availability and high cost of credit, led to the formation of the People's Party in 1892. It supported a range of policies that included the expansion of the currency, government ownership of the railroads, and a graduated income tax. Southerners played prominent roles in the effort. Leonidas Polk of North Carolina, who had served as president of the National Farmers' Alliance since 1889, was thought to be the leading candidate for the Populist presidential nomination. Polk died unexpectedly, however, in the summer of 1892. The eventual nominee, James B. Weaver, was a former Union general who did little to inspire Southerners.

Populists were a phantom presence in some parts of the South, but in others their challenge to the Democrats was fierce. Thomas Watson of Georgia, who had been elected to the House of Representatives as a Democrat in 1890, ran as a Populist two years later. Watson's candidacy was notable for his efforts to win black votes. He condemned lynching at a time when Georgia led the nation in the malevolent practice. When an African American Populist received a lynching threat, Watson called out over 2,000 armed whites to defend him. Watson lost narrowly, however, as he would again in 1894 amid widespread charges of election fraud. In 1896 the Democrats successfully co-opted the party's most politically tame but symbolically important issue, the free, or unlimited, coinage of silver. After the Democrats nominated the 36-year-old William Jennings Bryan, the Populists followed suit. Bryan proved to be enormously popular in the South. With the Democrats seeming to have regained their footing and the economic crisis of the 1890s on the wane, the South was solid once again.

One consequence of the Populist threat was that southern Democrats took steps to deter future challengers. New voting laws denied suffrage rights to many poor whites and almost all African Americans. This disfranchisement campaign began before the Populist threat—Mississippi kicked off the effort in 1890 with its new state constitution—but agrarian radicalism gave it fresh impetus. The dramatic impact of the new southern constitutions could be seen in Louisiana. As late as 1897, Louisiana counted 294,432 registered voters, 130,344 of whom were African American. Three years later, after the adoption of a new constitution, total registration numbered 130,757, with only 5,320 black voters.

The Supreme Court removed any barriers to the process in 1898 in the case of *Williams v. Mississippi*. The Court held that Mississippi's voting provisions themselves were not discriminatory. Experience soon showed, however, that they could be used by officials to exclude black voters. The new laws troubled few whites outside of the region. Some actually envied the efforts as the kind of thing needed to deter machine politics in northern cities. Others viewed southern disfranchisement in light of American involvement in the Philippines, as essential to preserving "white civilization" in the midst of darker races.

The disfranchisement campaign coincided with a turn toward radical racism that could be seen throughout the region. Southern states passed a wave of Jim Crow legislation that certified in law what often had been the custom of racial segregation. The new laws asserted white supremacy in new public spaces where racial etiquette was not inscribed. Not surprisingly, some of the first Jim Crow laws involved segregation on railroad cars—one of the most important and ubiquitous of public spaces in the late nineteenth century. In fact, the Supreme Court decision in 1896 that provided federal sanction of Jim Crow, *Plessy v. Ferguson*, involved a law segregating rail cars in Louisiana. The most vicious side of the Jim Crow system could be seen in a surge in racial violence. In the 1880s and 1890s, lynching was transformed from a frontier offense committed in areas with little established police authority to a racialized crime perpetrated largely by southern whites to terrorize the black community. In the 1890s, 82 percent of the nation's lynchings took place in 14 southern states.

Jim Crow voting laws suppressed voter participation among whites and blacks alike. This fact, combined with one-party rule, gave rise to one of the more curious figures in American political history—the southern demagogue. In the one-party South, intraparty factions developed around dominant personalities or well-established cliques rather than around political platforms. Candidates distinguished themselves more by the force of their personality than by the distinctiveness of their ideas. With little of the population participating in elections, few issues of substance or controversy came up in southern politics, certainly no issues that threatened white supremacy. Rural forces dominated southern politics; county fairs, courthouse steps, and country barbecues were grand theaters for the demagogues' histrionic speechifying. Among the more notorious were "Pitchfork" Ben Tillman and Cole Blease of South Carolina, James K. Vardaman and Theodore Bilbo of Mississippi, Tom Watson and Eugene Talmadge in Georgia, and Jeff Davis of Arkansas. None was more charismatic than Huey Long of Louisiana, who went further than most in making good on the populist rhetoric and activist pledges to working people that typified demagogic appeals.

In the first few decades of the twentieth century, citizens moved by the Progressive Era's spirit of pragmatic reform and public activism found plenty of problems to work on in the South. Progressives combated issues such as underfunded public schools, child labor, the convict lease system, and public health problems born of the region's intense poverty, like pellagra and hookworm. White Southerners took pride in the election of the southern-born Democrat Woodrow Wilson in 1912. Wilson showed his fidelity to southern racial mores by instituting segregation in federal offices in the nation's capital. Despite the reforms of the Progressive Era, the South remained for most Americans a uniquely backward region. H. L. Mencken's description of the South as the "Sahara of the Bozarts" sufficed for most. No incident sealed this image more completely than the Scopes trial in 1925, which pitted William Jennings Bryan against Clarence Darrow in a dispute over a Tennessee law barring the teaching of evolution in public schools. National reporters flocked to the tiny town of Dayton, Tennessee, to report on fundamentalist Southerners at war with the modern world. The image of an intensely rural and religiously backward region lived on through much of the twentieth century.

A New Deal for the South

The election of Franklin D. Roosevelt in 1932 transformed southern life and politics. Roosevelt had a special relationship with the region, born of the considerable time he spent at a treatment center for polio victims that he founded in Warm Springs, Georgia. The new president had seen southern poverty firsthand. In the 1930s, the region's over-reliance on agriculture and its handful of low-wage, low-skill industries created levels of neglect shocking even for Depression-era Americans. In 1938 Roosevelt famously declared the South "the nation's number one economic problem." A major goal of his presidency was to integrate the South more fully into the nation's economy.

The central problem for New Deal reformers was how to turn poor rural people into modern middle-class consumers. The Tennessee Valley Authority (TVA), an unprecedented public works project, was one solution. The federal government built an elaborate series of dams along the lower Tennessee River. Auxiliary programs repaired eroded landscapes and resettled rural families from depleted homesteads to modern, model farms. Most importantly, the TVA provided inexpensive electrical power that dramatically improved the quality of life for thousands of rural Southerners and attracted new industries to the region.

The New Deal also addressed economic problems more broadly. The Agricultural Adjustment Act (AAA), one of Roosevelt's first reforms, revolutionized southern farming. In an attempt to stem overproduction, the federal government paid farmers to take fields and livestock out of production. The subsidies spelled the end of sharecropping, the unique system of labor organization that had developed after emancipation as a compromise between former masters and slaves. It also began a decades-long shift toward agricultural mechanization and the flight of agricultural workers, white and black alike, from the region. Few southern laborers benefited more directly from the New Deal than the region's industrial workers. The Federal Labor Standards Act (FLSA) created a national minimum wage. A mere 25 cents an hour at initial passage, the standard actually doubled the wages of African American tobacco laborers. With increases built in for subsequent years, the legislation boosted incomes in numerous southern industries and created incentives for factory owners to modernize their plants.

Yet the New Deal's benefits were political as well as material. With Roosevelt's landslide victory in 1932 came a Democratic majority that dominated Congress for the next half century. This put conservative southern Democrats in positions of unprecedented power. In 1933 Southerners headed seven out of the nine most influential Senate committees. It also allowed them to check some of the New Deal's more liberal impulses. For example, Roosevelt refused to back federal antilynching legislation, much to the chagrin of his progressive supporters. He knew that doing so would alienate powerful Southerners, jeopardizing their support for other New Deal priorities.

Southern representatives were indeed among the most passionate supporters of the New Deal, yet as early as Roosevelt's second term, the forces that would eventually drive conservative Southerners out of the Democratic Party were already at work. Some white Southerners were suspicious of what they felt was Roosevelt's penchant for centralized power, made explicit in his court-packing plan. Others complained that too many New Deal dollars were going toward northern cities. In 1937 North Carolina senator Josiah Bailey was the driving force behind the Conservative Manifesto, a list of grievances

against Roosevelt's alleged drift toward collectivism. Roosevelt himself deepened the rift with conservative Southerners when he intervened in the 1938 midterm elections. He used one of his regular trips to Warm Springs as an opportunity to campaign against two of the regions most powerful conservatives, Walter George of Georgia and Ellison "Cotton Ed" Smith of South Carolina.

The most significant wedge between the white South and the New Deal was race. In the 1930s, Roosevelt's gestures to African Americans were small and largely symbolic. The tiniest of nods, however, was enough to convulse some white Southerners. Cotton Ed Smith walked out of the 1936 Democratic National Convention after an invocation delivered by a black minister. In 1941 Roosevelt's support for black civil rights moved beyond mere symbols when he signed an executive order creating the Fair Employment Practices Committee (FEPC). The order came only after intense lobbying by African Americans who threatened to march on Washington if Roosevelt did not act, and the committee's powers were relatively feeble. Still, the decision was a monumental victory for African Americans, a historic break of white Southerners' veto power over national civil rights policy. The FEPC instantly became the bete noire of white Southerners; legislative efforts after the war to make it permanent elicited charges of statism and racial coddling run amuck.

The South and World War

World War II marked a turning point in southern racial politics. The fight against Nazism cast Jim Crow racial practices in a harsh light and gave new impetus for movements toward equality. In the 1940s, NAACP membership increased by a factor of ten. A Supreme Court decision during the war opened new paths to the polls for some African Americans. In 1944 the Court struck down the "white primary," a discriminatory voting scheme that barred black voters from participating in Democratic Party elections, which in most southern states was the only election that mattered. This decision, along with the abolition of the poll tax in several southern states, cleared the way for the registration of thousands of black voters in the peripheral and Upper South, along with some urban areas in the lower South. In Atlanta, for example, a federal court decision allowed for the registration of 21,244 black voters in 1946. These new voters instantly constituted over a quarter of Atlanta's registered voters and transformed the city's political dynamics. Newly enfranchised black voters helped elect moderate, business-oriented white leaders, who, in turn, quietly brokered the token desegregation of neighborhoods and public spaces.

In the 1940s, black Southerners were not just leaving the South to go to war; many left for urban areas in the North and the West. This was not the first time that African Americans had left the region—a small migration had taken place during Reconstruction, and roughly half a million blacks left during World War I. But the migration that followed World War II was unprecedented. Of the 6.5 million African Americans that left the South between 1910 and 1970, 5 million exited after 1940. This migration coincided with the collapse of plantation agriculture, and it transformed racial politics nationally. Southern migrants filled African American urban neighborhoods and elected some of the first black representatives to Congress since Reconstruction. These black voters also became important swing voters in large, highly contested industrial states in the Northeast and Midwest.

Many of the African American soldiers who returned to the South after the war were determined to secure the freedoms at home for which they had fought abroad. One such serviceman was Medgar Evers of Mississippi, who had served in France. When he and other African American veterans attempted to vote in the 1946 Democratic primary in Decatur, Mississippi, an armed white mob turned them away. Deterred only temporarily, Evers went on to become the field secretary for the NAACP in Mississippi, working tirelessly to organize African American protest in his home state until June 1963, when he was shot and killed by a racist fanatic.

The armed deterrence in Mississippi was not uncommon. Emboldened African American soldiers heightened racial anxieties among whites during and in the immediate aftermath of the war. This unrest was not specific to the South. Race riots broke out in several northern and southern cities in 1943; the largest was in Detroit, where 25 African Americans and 9 whites were killed. But in some rural areas of the South, racial tensions took an old familiar form. In July 1946 a lynch mob in Monroe, Georgia, killed 4 young African Americans, 2 men and 2 women. The spike in racial violence led President Harry Truman to form a commission to study racial problems. Its 1947 report, *To Secure These Rights*, became a blueprint for federal civil reforms that would come over the next two decades.

The following year, Truman went further, setting the stage for a historic presidential election. In February 1948 he announced his support for ending racial discrimination in the armed services. Clark Clifford, Truman's campaign advisor, urged him to take a strong civil rights stand because the support of southern states was a given; the key to the election, Clifford argued, was northern industrial areas where urban African American voters could help swing the election for the Democrats. Clifford's strategy succeeded, but only by the narrowest of margins. At the Democratic National Convention in Philadelphia that summer, the Alabama and Mississippi delegations walked out over the party's civil rights stand. Individual delegates from other southern states joined them to form the States' Rights Democratic Party.

Strom Thurmond, the governor of South Carolina, accepted the presidential nomination of the "Dixiecrats," the nickname given to the splinter group by a waggish reporter. Thurmond himself never used the term, insisting that his campaign was not a regional but a national effort that drew on long-standing conservative Democratic principles. In truth, the campaign's support came mainly from white voters in the Black Belt, Deep South counties with the largest African American population and the most racially polarized politics. With little money and an inexperienced campaign staff, Thurmond ended up winning only four states—Alabama, Mississippi, Louisiana, and South Carolina. Yet in the larger sweep of southern history, the States' Rights Democrats represented a turning point in the region's politics by initiating the slow drain of white Southerners from the Democratic Party.

The Era of Massive Resistance

The 1950s was a decade of political retrenchment across the region. The cold war contributed to this trend. Segregationist Southerners denounced civil rights activists as either outright Communists or tools of the Communist conspiracy. Senator James Eastland of Mississippi chaired the Senate Internal Security Subcommittee, which regularly called witnesses to testify about alleged links between the civil rights movement and politically subversive organizations. Southern state legislatures held similar hearings that investigated civil rights organizations with alleged ties to subversive organizations or in some cases became the basis for new laws that helped to deter civil rights organizations.

More than anything, however, the Supreme Court's 1954 decision in *Brown v. Board of Education*, striking down school segregation laws, precipitated white Southerners' organized resistance to racial change. The Ku Klux Klan experienced a third wave of revival in the region, following the Reconstruction period and its resurgence in the 1920s. Organized resistance also took a more middle-class form with the Citizens' Council, which began in 1954 in the Mississippi Delta. The councils styled themselves as a modern political interest group, replete with a monthly publication and a series of television programs featuring interviews with policy makers. Council leaders denounced violence publicly, but they often turned a blind eye or even subtly encouraged violence by working-class whites. This grassroots organizing underwrote high-profile acts of resistance during the late 1950s and early 1960s. In 1957 Governor Orval Faubus of Arkansas, who up to that point was viewed as a racial moderate, defied federal authorities in blocking the entrance of African American students into Little Rock's Central High School. Three years later, white resistance to school desegregation in New Orleans led to violent clashes throughout the city. In 1962 Governor Ross Barnett of Mississippi led his state into a constitutional showdown with President John Kennedy over the admission of the African American James Meredith to the University of Mississippi.

The most charismatic and talented leader of massive resistance was Governor George Wallace of Alabama. Wallace began his career as an economic populist and racial moderate, following the path of his mentor, James "Big Jim" Folsom. In his race for governor in 1958, Wallace misjudged the intensity of white recalcitrance after the *Brown* decision and lost in a close election. Afterward, he vowed to political friends never to be "out-nigguhed" again.

After Wallace won the governorship in 1962 on a hard-line segregationist platform, he had a Klansman draft his inaugural address. Wallace defied Kennedy administration officials in 1963, standing "in the schoolhouse door" to symbolically block the admission of African American students to the University of Alabama. In 1964 he became the face of the white backlash against civil rights when he ran surprisingly well in Democratic presidential primaries in Wisconsin, Indiana, and Maryland. Four years later, running as the candidate of the American Independent Party, Wallace narrowly missed out on his goal of throwing the election into the House of Representatives. Wallace lost North Carolina and Tennessee by statistically insignificant margins; a win in either of those states accompanied by a shift of less than 1 percent of the vote from Richard Nixon to Hubert Humphrey in New Jersey or Ohio would have been enough to do the trick. He was reelected as governor in 1970 in a notoriously racist campaign. In May 1972 he was a leading candidate in a chaotic race for the Democratic presidential nomination. Wallace was shot while campaigning in Maryland. He survived the shooting but was relegated to a wheelchair for the rest of his life, all but ending his national political aspirations.

Yet Wallace's impact could be measured in other ways. In one sense, Wallace helped "southernize" national politics. His parodying of government bureaucrats, liberal elites, and anti-American political activists gave a populist bent to the post–World War II American conservative movement. Up to that point, conservatism consisted largely of a loose coalition of corporate executives, renegade intellectuals, and anti-Communist hardliners. Wallace, however, pioneered appeals to white working-class and lower middle-class Americans, pleas that worked equally well outside the South. Wallace was elected governor of Alabama twice more, in 1974 and 1982, and he returned to his racially moderate, economic populist roots. By that time, however, the antigovernment slogans that had sustained his national aspirations had been taken up by a new generation of ideological conservatives in the Republican Party.

Sunbelt Politics

For many people, Lyndon Johnson summed up the conventional wisdom on the southern GOP in the 1960s. On the night he signed the 1964 Civil Rights Act, Johnson lamented to an aide, "I think we just delivered the South to the Republican Party for a long time to come." Yet white racism was not the only factor spurring two-party politics in the South. Urban Southerners showed their distaste for one-party rule in the 1950s, when a majority of the region's city dwellers twice voted for the modern Republicanism of Dwight Eisenhower. Business-oriented, racially moderate urban and suburban Southerners were an important source for the growing southern GOP. Federal court decisions in the early 1960s that upheld the principle of "one man, one vote" gave a boost to moderate metropolitan Southerners. Thanks to outdated apportionment laws, rural interests had dominated southern politics for years. Under the county unit system in Georgia, for example, each county was assigned "units" that ranged from two units for the smallest county to six for the largest. As a result, residents of rural counties held political power far beyond their proportion of the state population. A vote in tiny Echols County, Georgia, was worth 99 times as much as a vote in Atlanta.

Metropolitan Southerners joined urban and suburban citizens of other expanding areas across the Southwest and far West to make up what commentators came to describe as the Sunbelt. From the 1960s through the end of the century, southern states from the Carolinas to California were the most economically dynamic areas of the country. Southern state industrial programs attracted new industries through a mix of tax breaks and other economic subsidies, and southern legislatures passed right-to-work laws that suppressed union membership. Cold war military spending benefited the Sunbelt disproportionately; military contracts poured into southern states like Texas, Florida, and Georgia. Powerful southern congressmen directed other defense dollars into their home districts. These new Sunbelt jobs attracted college-educated middle- and upper middle-class migrants to the region. The 1960s was the first decade since the 1870s that more people moved into the South than out of it. Many of these new Southerners settled in expanding suburban neighborhoods. From 1960 to 1968, the suburbs of Houston grew by 50 percent, New Orleans 45.5 percent, Washington 39.2 percent, and Atlanta 33.6 percent. During the 1960s, per capita income increased in the South 14 percent faster than anyplace else.

These new Sunbelt residents were a natural fit for the Republican Party. Yet, despite the dynamic social and economic changes in the region, southern GOP advances in the 1960s and 1970s were surprisingly mixed. Republican presidential candidates did well across the region, but the party struggled in state and local elections. One reason was that the hard-line conservatives who built the southern parties were still a minority within a national party in which moderate and liberal Republicans played a major role. Also, in many parts of the South, Republican candidates struggled to shed an image as the party of the country club set.

Most important to Democratic perseverance, however, was the 1965 Voting Rights Act, which restored voting rights to thousands of African American voters across the region. African Americans first started to drop their historic allegiance to the party of Lincoln during the New Deal, and thanks to liberal Democrats' passionate support for civil rights, these new southern black voters almost uniformly identified as Democrats. In southern states with African American populations that ranged from a quarter to well over a third of the total population, successful Republicans had to amass supermajorities among white voters.

From these electoral dynamics were born the New South Democrats: progressive, racially moderate, practical-minded politicians who assembled coalitions of working-class whites, black voters, and urban liberals. Prominent examples included Reubin Askew and Lawton Chiles of Florida, Jimmy Carter and Sam Nunn of Georgia, Dale Bumpers and David Pryor of Arkansas, John West and Richard Riley of South Carolina, and Bill Waller and William Winter of Mississippi.

No politician better symbolized the regional and national potential of New South Democrats than Jimmy Carter, the Georgia governor who vaulted into national politics in the wake of the Watergate crisis. Carter pursued centrist policies that angered the liberal wing of his party. He insisted on a balanced budget and attempted to cut spending and jobs programs that were bedrocks for liberal Democratic constituencies. He appointed a staunch advocate of deregulation as head of the Civilian Aeronautics Board and signed legislation that deregulated a number of industries. But Carter's major failure was one of timing—he presided over the White House during a period when the historic post–World War II economic boom petered out. His talk of limits and the need for Americans to scale back was rooted in his Southern Baptist faith, his sense of humility and stewardship. Political opponents, however, easily parodied it as rudderless leadership and weak-kneed defeatism.

A notable aspect of Carter's politics was his open discussion of his religious faith. It reflected his genuine personal devotion, but it also played into his appeal as the post-Watergate antipolitician—a man who would never lie to the American people. It was ironic then that Carter, who spoke sincerely of his personal relationship with Jesus Christ, would come to be so vehemently opposed by other southern Christian conservatives. White Southerners played prominent roles in what came to be known as the Religious Right. Jerry Falwell helped establish the Moral Majority in 1979, a conservative Christian advocacy group that was credited with playing a major role in Ronald Reagan's successful presidential campaign in 1980. Pat Robertson headed the Christian Broadcasting Network in Virginia Beach, Virginia, which became a focus of Religious Right broadcasting in the 1970s and 1980s. Jesse Helms of North Carolina was the leading voice in the Senate for conservative Christian concerns.

By the 1980s, the Religious Right was a key constituency in Ronald Reagan's conservative coalition. Reagan's charisma and Hollywood glamour won over countless white Southerners. No figure did more in encouraging white Southerners to shift their political identity from the Democratic to the Republican Party. Reagan articulated in a genial way the reaction against social and political liberalism that had been such a defining part of the region's modern politics. For the most conservative white Southerners, Reagan's election provided a sense of vindication that their opposition to the transformations of the 1960s was not so misguided after all. Southern Republicans played leadership roles in the dominant conservative wing of the party. Most prominently, in the 1994 midterm elections, Newt Gingrich of Georgia orchestrated the Republicans' Contract with America, a set of conservative policy positions that was credited with helping the GOP gain control of the House of Representatives for the first time in 40 years.

Despite Republican successes, moderate southern Democrats continued to exert a powerful influence on national Democratic Party politics. Bill Clinton showed the lingering power of the moderate New South model when he teamed with fellow Southerner Al Gore to become the first twice-elected Democratic president since Franklin Roosevelt. He did so following the same centrist path that Jimmy Carter had blazed in the 1970s. Clinton declared that the era of big government was over, signed the North American Free Trade Agreement, and backed a welfare reform bill that alienated liberals in his own party. He might have continued to provide moderate pragmatic leadership for the Democrats—the only path that had provided any significant electoral gains for the party since the 1960s—had the final years of his presidency not been marred by personal scandal.

By the twenty-first century, the South remained a source of consternation for progressive political forces, the seeming heart of Republican-dominated "red America." Some Democrats counseled their party to hand the region over to the Republicans, to "whistle past Dixie," and focus on liberal ideas that would appeal to voters in more traditionally progressive areas of the country. Other Democrats argued that Southerners were no different from other Americans, that they were motivated by the same concerns about economic security, health care, and education. That position was bolstered in the 2008 presidential election, when Barack Obama carried Virginia, North Carolina, and Florida—made possible by a huge turnout of African American voters.

In the roughly 135 years since the end of Reconstruction, the South underwent enormous transformations. The differences between the region and the nation had eroded enough to lead many to question what, if anything, remained distinctive about the South. And yet within national politics, many Americans still found it relevant to talk about the South as a discrete entity, a place with a unique past that continued to shape its politics in subtle yet powerful ways.

See also Democratic Party; race and politics; Reconstruction Era, 1865–77; segregation and Jim Crow.

FURTHER READING. Edward Ayers, *The Promise of the New South*, 1992; Numan Bartley, *The New South, 1945–1980*, 1995; Numan Bartley and Hugh Davis Graham, *Southern Politics and the Second Reconstruction*, 1975; Earl Black and Merle Black, *Politics and Society in the South*, 1995; Idem, *The Rise of Southern Republicans*, 2002; Joseph Crespino, *In Search of Another Country: Mississippi and the Conservative Counterrevolution*, 2007; V. O. Key, *Southern Politics in State and Nation*, 1949; Matthew Lassiter, *The Silent Majority: Suburban Politics in the Sunbelt South*, 2005; Bruce Schulman, *From Cotton Belt to Sunbelt: Federal Policy, Economic Development, and the Transformation of the South, 1938–1980*, 1991; George Tindall, *The Emergence of the New South, 1913–1945*, 1967; C. Vann Woodward, *Origins of the New South, 1877–1913*, 1951.

JOSEPH CRESPINO

Spanish-American War and Filipino Insurrection

John Hay, then secretary of state, called it the "splendid little war." Almost 100 years after its start, historian Walter LaFeber called it the first modern war of the twentieth century for the United States. The Spanish-American War, and the more than decade of fighting that followed in the Philippines, reflected the tremendous growth in U.S. power in the late nineteenth century and the changing nature of domestic and international politics involving the United States. This war also provided the occasion for introducing some of the policies that shaped the U.S. polity as it moved into the twentieth century. The Spanish-American War was particularly influential in six areas: (1) development of ideas and practice of the modern presidency, (2) modification of traditional U.S. military doctrine, (3) reflection of new approaches to democratic politics and public opinion, (4) opportunities for state building, (5) creation of layers of empire, and (6) new struggles over the nature of American identity.

The Course of War

Cubans organized as early as the 1860s to achieve independence from Spain. Interest in Cuba was strong because of U.S.-owned sugar and tobacco plantations, but Americans were also altruistically sympathetic to the Cuban cause. Mass-circulation newspapers and U.S. labor organizations supported the Cubans, increasingly so through the 1890s, as Spanish repression of the Cuban independence movement became harsher.

President William McKinley, elected on the Republican ticket in 1896, was cautious but determined to support U.S. interests. He felt compelled in early 1898 to send the USS *Maine* to Havana harbor, where a few weeks later, it blew up. The "yellow press," led by William Randolph Hearst's *New York Journal*, issued the battle cry "Remember the Maine." Congress declared war in April 1898, but the U.S. fleet had already begun moving into position near Spanish possessions in both the Caribbean (Cuba and Puerto Rico) and the Pacific (Philippines). The small and undertrained U.S. Army was augmented by numerous enthusiastic volunteers, including the famous Rough Riders, organized by Teddy Roosevelt, who benefited from admiring publicity. The navy performed better than the army, but both performed better than the Spanish, and the fighting was over within a few weeks, costing the United States few dead, and most of those from disease rather than battle. During the war, the United States annexed Hawai'i. As a result of the war, although not until 1902, Cuba became independent. Puerto Rico, Guam, and the Philippines became U.S. colonies, technically called "unincorporated territories."

Filipinos also had been fighting for their independence from Spain. While initially working with U.S. forces or tolerating their presence, Filipino independence fighters soon realized U.S. liberation from Spain would not mean independence, and they took up arms against U.S. soldiers. This part of the war was costly for the United States, with more than 70,000 U.S. troops in the islands at the peak of the conflict and U.S. deaths of more than 4,000. At least 20,000 Filipinos were killed as a direct result of fighting. The Philippine Insurrection, which Filipinos call the Philippine-American War, officially lasted until 1902. Fighting continued in various parts of the islands until 1913, especially in the southern island of Mindanao, which has never fully acquiesced in any kind of rule from Manila, the capital of the Philippines.

Powerful President

The narrative above is factual and familiar but obscures more than it reveals. McKinley appears passive in it, reacting to popular media and events in both Cuba and Congress. This image of McKinley prevailed for years among scholars, many of whom repeated Theodore Roosevelt's claim that he had the backbone of a chocolate éclair. Timing of the declaration of war suggests otherwise, however. Both a majority in Congress and many mass-circulation newspapers had been advocating war for months before McKinley submitted his carefully crafted request for a declaration of war. McKinley drafted the declaration so that it allowed him to pursue almost any policy he wanted, subject only to the promise in the Teller Amendment not to annex Cuba.

The president was more than merely astute, however. First, he was thinking in an integrated manner about U.S. global interests and was working to coordinate the consequences of the war to serve a variety of U.S. interests, including maintaining an open system in China for U.S. trade and investment, sufficient control over areas such as Cuba where U.S. investment was substantial and growing, and creation of types of control in both Asia and the Caribbean in concert with the loose, minimally bureaucratic character of twentieth-century U.S. imperialism.

Second, McKinley used new technology effectively to increase his own power. Both the telegraph and telephone allowed him rapid, personal contact with other U.S. officials and the military in the field. He used these advantages to communicate directly and left less of a paper trail than previous presidents, which had the effect of decreasing freedom of action by subordinates while also making it more difficult for historians to trace the ultimate authority for decisions. Finally, McKinley and his closest personal advisors were men who believed in applying principles for the efficient organization of large corporations to running the government. They worked to continue professionalizing, organizing, and making government bureaucracy more effective. This too increased the power of the executive, especially at the expense of the still amateur and small congressional staffs. With or without the Spanish-American War, McKinley would have worked to increase executive power; the war gave him a large canvas on which to work.

Modern Military

The military, both navy and army, naturally was the government entity initially most affected by the war. The traditional narrative emphasizes the effectiveness of the U.S. Navy, which while not yet impressive in comparison with the British Navy, had several able advocates who had successfully promoted acquisition of modern and far-ranging ships. Alfred Thayer Mahan epitomizes this group who saw a larger, better trained navy as essential to projecting U.S. power into the world's oceans in support of increased U.S. commerce and control. The U.S. Navy handily demonstrated its superiority over the Spanish, even defeating a Spanish fleet at such far reaches as the Philippines. The battle in Cuba, for which the Spanish were more prepared, went scarcely better for them. The Spanish-American War confirmed for these navy advocates that they had been right; the acquisition of far-flung colonies provided them with continuing justification for a large and modern navy.

The U.S. Army generally looks less capable in accounts of the Spanish-American War. Its tiny size of less than 30,000 in 1898 meant that the war could not be fought without calling on thousands of volunteers, no doubt eager but ill-trained, and the militias, perhaps less eager and trained for different tasks. Logistics proved embarrassingly poor: U.S. soldiers lacked proper clothes for the tropics, were fed poisonously bad food, and died of disease or poorly treated wounds in greater numbers than from battle. The "splendid little" part of the war, the fighting against Spain, revealed an army poorly prepared

for the type of fighting required. The next task was less splendid and little; the U.S. Army was called on to subdue Cubans and Filipinos who had different ideas than did U.S. officials about what the end of the Spanish-American War meant. This fighting often was characterized by brutality, as both regular army and militia employed tactics of repression or even extermination they had learned fighting against Native Americans, and which all too often resembled what the Spanish had done to their former subjects. Simultaneously, however, the army was the first to carry out the "benevolent" components of U.S. rule, including improving sanitation, building infrastructure, and opening schools. Violence and benevolence were intertwined, as they usually are in imperial projects. The U.S. Army began to develop nation-building capacities that have characterized its mission up to the present day.

New Approaches to Politics

The long buildup to a declaration of war allowed plenty of political maneuvering and public involvement, allowing the display of key developments in late-nineteenth-and early-twentieth-century domestic political organization. A familiar part of the story of the Spanish-American War is the way the "yellow press" promoted sympathy for Cubans. These mass-circulation newspapers continued the American tradition of a partisan press but depended on technological developments and increased literacy to present ever more realistic, if also lurid and emotional, images to an entranced public. The press did not create the war, but it did create conditions in which Americans enthusiastically accepted a war arguably remote from the interests of ordinary citizens. Public opinion was led in directions that served a variety of interests.

As the importance of political parties began to wane in the early twentieth century, presidents and newspaper publishers began to appeal directly to the mass public, unmediated by the party hierarchy. President McKinley went on a speaking tour with the stated purpose of gauging public support for acquiring a colony in the Philippines but with the hidden intent of promoting public support for that action. Much of the language used in these public appeals and discussions about the war and the responsibilities stemming from it reflected concerns about honor and manliness. Cubans, and later Filipinos, needed chivalrous rescuers; the Spanish deserved punishment for their misdeeds from honorable soldiers; American men could bravely demonstrate their willingness to sacrifice on the battlefield. Roosevelt's Rough Riders, volunteers from all walks of life from the most rough-and-tumble to the most elite, epitomized for many the benefits of testing American men in battle. At the turn to the twentieth century, American men were less likely than in preceding decades to vote and participate actively in party politics, more likely to work in large, hierarchical organizations, and to learn about the world through the medium of mass-circulation newspapers. Politicians used these developments to shape public attitudes about the war and the consequences of it.

Building the American State

Although the war itself was relatively short and easily won, it posed logistical challenges to an underdeveloped U.S. state. Both the war and the overseas colonies acquired as a consequence provided officials with opportunities to build U.S. state institutions. The military was the most dramatic example. The navy began to develop more far-reaching capacities in the years leading up to the war, and the army followed suit during and after the war. Both branches acquired permanent overseas responsibilities. The logistical requirements of permanent deployment outside the continental United States help explain trends toward professionalization, bureaucratization, and growth of both the army and navy in the early twentieth century. The decision to locate the Bureau of Insular Affairs, the government agency charged with governing the colonies, in the War Department further increased that department's growth. Even in ways not explicitly related to fighting the war or governing the colonies, U.S. governmental institutions took on new responsibilities as a result of the war, including some related to immigration and the conduct of foreign relations.

Layers of Empire

A key outcome of the Spanish-American War was the acquisition of overseas territories, arguably for the first time in U.S. history. The United States became an imperial power, owning colonies it had no intention of incorporating into the nation as states. It newly ruled over Hawai'i, Puerto Rico, Guam, and the Philippines directly. The United States also exercised a large amount of indirect control over Cuba through the mechanism of the Platt Amendment, a U.S. law whose substance was written into the Cuban constitution. It placed limits on Cuban sovereignty regarding financial affairs and the nature of Cuba's government, mandated U.S. ownership of a base at Guantanamo, and forced Cuban acquiescence in U.S. intervention to guarantee these measures.

The U.S. empire was a layered one. Cuba experienced effective control, but indirectly. Hawai'i was governed as an incorporated territory, theoretically eligible for statehood, but its racial mix made that an unappealing prospect for many Americans. Hawai'i did not become a state until 1959. Guam was ruled directly by the U.S. Navy—which used it as a coaling station—and it remains part of the United States, governed by the Office of Insular Affairs in the Department of the Interior. Both the Philippines and Puerto Rico were governed directly as colonies through the Bureau of Insular Affairs, but their paths quickly diverged. Puerto Rico developed close links with the United States through revolving migration,

economic and tourism ties, and increased political rights for its citizens. Puerto Rico is still part of the United States, as the Commonwealth of Puerto Rico. The Philippines developed more modest and ambiguous relations with the United States, since Filipinos had restricted migration rights, and U.S. economic investment in the islands was limited. The Philippines achieved independence in 1946. The layered and decentralized nature of the U.S. empire developed out of the particular legal and political processes used to decide how to rule over territories acquired in the Spanish-American War. These decisions were widely and publicly debated in the early twentieth century, as Americans wrestled with the changing nature of territorial expansion involving overseas colonies.

Debating the American Identity

The Spanish-American War and the resulting acquisition of colonies prompted heated debates in the United States about what it meant to be American. These debates may well be among the most important consequences of the war for the nation. One set of agruments revolved around whether the United States should acquire overseas colonies, and if so, how they should be governed. A vocal and prominent anti-imperialist movement had many older leaders, representatives of a fading generation. Most politicians of the day advocated acquiring the colonies as demonstration of U.S. power and benevolence.

Still, there remained a contentious debate about the status of these new territories, legally settled only by the U.S. Supreme Court in the Insular Cases, beginning in 1901 with *Downes v. Bidwell* and confirmed subsequently by almost two dozen additional cases. The 1901 decision found that Puerto Rico was "not a foreign country" but "foreign to the United States in a domestic sense." In other words, not all laws or constitutional protections extended to unincorporated territories such as Puerto Rico and the Philippines. Many Americans were disturbed by these decisions, finding no provision in the Constitution that anticipated ruling land not intended to be part of the United States. They worried that an important part of U.S. political identity was being discarded.

Overriding those concerns, however, was a strong desire on the part of almost all white Americans to avoid the racial implications of incorporating places like the Philippines and especially Cuba into the body politic. Jim Crow segregation was established by the 1890s, and colonial acquisitions promised to complicate an already contentious racial situation in the United States. Cuba was filled with what many commentators called an "unappealing racial mix" of descendants of Spaniards, indigenous peoples, and Africans brought to the island as slaves. U.S. politicians had no desire to bring the racial politics of Cuba into the nation; so Cuba was not annexed. The Philippines was almost as problematic: Filipinos might be the "little brown brothers" of Americans, but in the end they were Asians, including many ethnic Chinese. During these years of Chinese exclusion, the status of Filipinos, U.S. nationals eligible to enter to the United States but not eligible to become citizens, was contested and contradictory. Movement toward granting independence seemed a good way to exclude Filipinos altogether. Puerto Ricans were, apparently, white enough. When they moved to the continental United States, they could naturalize as U.S. citizens, and in 1917, citizenship was extended to all Puerto Ricans. Regarding these groups, however, racial politics complicated both colonial governance and conceptions of U.S. identity.

Hostilities between Spain and the United States were brief and minor, but this splendid little war changed the United States into a colonial power; provided opportunities for the growth of executive government agencies, both the presidency itself and some departments; highlighted developments in mass media and party politics; and opened new lines of debate about the meaning of American identity.

See also foreign policy and domestic politics, 1865–1933; press and politics; race and politics; territorial government.

FURTHER READING. H. W. Brands, *Bound to Empire: The United States and the Philippines*, 1982; Kristin L. Hoganson, *Fighting for American Manhood: How Gender Politics Provoked the Spanish-American and Philippine-American Wars*, 1998; Paul A. Kramer, *The Blood of Government: Race, Empire, the United States and the Philippines*, 2006; Walter LaFeber, *The American Search for Opportunity, 1865–1913*, 1993; Louis A. Perez, "Incurring a Debt of Gratitude: 1898 and the Moral Sources of United States Hegemony in Cuba," *American Historical Review* 104 (April 1999), 356–98.

ANNE L. FOSTER

state constitutions

State constitutions are more easily amended and address a broader range of issues than the U.S. Constitution and, as a consequence, have often played an important role in American political development. On many occasions, the relative flexibility of state constitutions has permitted political reforms to be more easily adopted by states, and only implemented later, if at all, at the federal level. At times also, the greater range of issues addressed in state constitutions, which is due in part to the nature of the federal system and in part to conscious choices made by state constitution makers, means that many political issues have been regulated primarily or even exclusively by state constitutions. This importance of state constitutions can be seen throughout the course of the American regime but is particularly evident in the founding era, Jacksonian era, Progressive Era, and after the reapportionment revolution of the 1960s.

The Founding Era

Eleven of the original thirteen states adopted constitutions prior to the drafting of the U.S. Constitution (Connecticut and Rhode Island retained their colonial charters until 1818 and 1842, respectively), and it was through drafting these state constitutions that Americans first developed principles of constitutionalism and republicanism that were then adopted at the federal level.

State constitution makers were the first to grapple with the appropriate process for writing and adopting a constitution. The first state constitutions drafted in early 1776 in New Hampshire and South Carolina were intended to be temporary. However, drafters of subsequent state constitutions came to view them as enduring charters. Meanwhile, some of the early state constitutions were drafted by legislators or by officials who were not selected specifically for the purpose of constitution making. Eventually, though, it came to be understood that constitutions should be written by delegates who were chosen for this express purpose and who assembled in a convention. A similar evolution took place in the understanding of how a constitution should be approved. Although the earliest state constitutions took effect by proclamation of the drafters, this changed when the Massachusetts Constitution of 1780 was submitted for popular ratification. Not only have state constitution makers generally followed this process in drafting and revising the 146 documents that have been in effect in the 50 states, but this was also the model that federal constitution makers followed in holding a convention in 1787 and submitting their work for ratification by the 13 states.

State constitution makers also had extensive opportunities in the 1770s and 1780s to debate the means of designing governing institutions that would best embody republican principles, and these debates influenced the design of the federal constitution in various ways. Some of the first state constitutions were quite democratic in form. The outstanding example was the Pennsylvania constitution of 1776, which established a unicameral legislature whose members stood for annual election and were subject to term limits and whose work could not be vetoed by the executive. As state constitution making progressed, and as concerns arose over the ineffective performance of governing institutions, efforts were made to limit legislatures and secure a greater degree of deliberation, such as by adopting bicameralism, lengthening legislators' terms, eliminating term limits, and creating a strong executive. The New York constitution of 1777 was the first to adopt a number of these features; the Massachusetts constitution of 1780 went even further in embodying these developments; and, by the time that Pennsylvanians adopted a revised constitution in 1790, they had eliminated many of the more democratic features of the 1776 document. When delegates assembled at the federal convention of 1787, they drew heavily from the state constitutional experience.

The Jacksonian Era

The Jacksonian era brought calls for the democratization of both state and federal governing institutions. Though some changes were made at the federal level, the changes were even greater in the states, and these changes frequently took the form of constitutional amendments. In particular, states retained responsibility for most issues of governance during the nineteenth century, including efforts to expand the suffrage, which required changes in state law, and frequently in state constitutions. Moreover, the flexibility of state constitutions, in contrast to the rigidity of the federal amendment process, meant that certain institutional reforms, such as the popular election of judges, were only adopted at the state level.

In terms of the suffrage, the principal developments during this period were the elimination of freeholder and taxpayer requirements for voting, and these changes were frequently achieved through state constitutional amendments. Additionally, although federal acts would later remove from state discretion other voting qualifications—such as those regarding race, sex, and age—states were the innovators in each of these areas, both during the Jacksonian era and in later years. Thus, New England states permitted blacks to vote well before the Fifteenth Amendment. Wyoming, followed by numerous other states, permitted women to vote long before the Nineteenth Amendment. And Georgia and Kentucky enfranchised 18-year-olds several decades prior to ratification of the Twenty-Sixth Amendment. Moreover, states have retained control over other suffrage requirements, such as those concerning citizenship and felony conviction. Therefore, battles over suffrage requirements continued to be waged to a great degree in state constitutional forums long after the federal government began to establish national suffrage requirements in the Reconstruction era. In fact, although Reconstruction-era state conventions were required by federal law to enfranchise African Americans, these gains were mostly reversed by state conventions in the 1890s that adopted various disenfranchising mechanisms.

State constitution makers during the Jacksonian era also made attempts to democratize governing institutions. Not a single federal amendment was ratified between passage of the Twelfth Amendment in 1804 and the Thirteenth Amendment in 1865. State constitutions, though, were easier to amend, and amendment procedures were made even more flexible during this period. Some states went so far as to require that a popular referendum be held periodically on whether to hold a new constitutional convention.

As a result, constitutional reformers were able to experiment with alternative institutional arrangements at the state level. Some constitutions imposed procedural restrictions on the legislature, such as requiring that bills be read three times and contain a single subject accurately reflected in the title. There were also substantive restrictions on the legislature, such as prohibiting the incurring of debt or the lending of state credit. A number of states also moved during this period to adopt a plural executive of sorts: a wide range of executive department heads were subject to popular election, along with the governor. Most notably, beginning with Mississippi's adoption in 1832 of popular elections for all state judges and accelerating in the 1840s, states increasingly provided for an elected judiciary. State constitution makers also democratized governing institutions by changing inequitable apportionment plans that had long privileged older tidewater regions over growing piedmont and mountain regions. The Ohio Constitution of 1851 was the first to provide for an apportionment board that removed the decennial task of redistricting from the legislative process. This approach was later emulated by several other states.

The Progressive Era

Among the chief concerns of Progressive reformers was securing protection for workers in the face of obstructionist legislatures and courts. The flexibility of state amendment processes enabled reformers to adopt numerous constitutional changes introduced to bypass legislatures or overturn court decisions.

Progressive reformers pushed for a variety of protective measures for workers—including an eight-hour day, minimum wage, workers' compensation, and child labor regulations. But they experienced mixed success in getting these measures approved by legislators and then sustained by the courts. Even when Congress and state legislatures did enact protective laws, federal and state courts occasionally invalidated them. The only federal constitutional amendment formally proposed in this area was a child labor amendment, but it failed to be ratified by the requisite number of state legislatures and so never took effect. Reformers had more success securing enactment of state provisions to protect workers. Some amendments were intended to bypass legislatures, by mandating an eight-hour day or prohibiting child labor. Other state constitutional changes sought to overturn court decisions, by declaring that the legislature was empowered to pass a minimum-wage law or establish a workers' compensation system or enact other protective measures, regardless of state court rulings to the contrary.

Progressive reformers also tried to restructure governing institutions they viewed as insufficiently responsive to public opinion and overly susceptible to special-interest influence. The only structural change adopted at the federal level in the early twentieth century was direct senatorial elections, as a result of passage of the Seventeenth Amendment. But state reformers had more success. The South Dakota constitution was amended in 1898 to provide for the popular initiative and referendum, and during the twentieth century half of the states adopted similar reforms. A third of the states provided for the constitutional initiative. The Ohio constitution was amended in 1912 to permit judicial review to be exercised only by a supermajority of the state supreme court judges, and two other states soon adopted similar provisions. A number of states in the first two decades of the twentieth century also adopted the recall of judges and other public officials.

The Reapportionment Revolution

After a long period in the mid-twentieth century of relative inattention to constitutional revision, the U.S. Supreme Court's reapportionment decisions in the early 1960s led to a significant number of changes in state constitutions. States had to bring their redistricting laws into compliance with the Court's rulings, and constitution makers took the opportunity to modernize other state governing institutions as well. They also added rights provisions that had no counterpart in the federal constitution. For example, several states provided for a right to privacy or a prohibition against sex discrimination. Other states guaranteed a right to a clean environment. Victims' rights clauses were added to other state constitutions.

Much of the renewed interest in state constitutions in the late twentieth century was generated not by amendments but as a result of liberal state court interpretations of state bills of rights. When the Supreme Court under chief justices Burger and Rehnquist proved less aggressive than the Warren Court in interpreting the federal Bill of Rights in an expansive fashion, state judges began to provide redress for civil liberties claimants. Thus, the U.S. Supreme Court declined to recognize a federal constitutional right to equal school financing, but a number of state supreme courts found such a right in their state constitutions. And whereas the U.S. Supreme Court declined to rule that the death penalty violated the federal cruel and unusual punishment clause, as long as it was administered in a proper fashion, several state supreme courts interpreted their state bills of rights as prohibiting capital punishment in all circumstances. Then, at the turn of the twenty-first century, several state courts interpreted their bills of rights as guaranteeing a right to same-sex civil unions or same-sex marriage. Although state amendment processes permitted citizens to eventually adopt constitutional amendments overturning some of these state court rulings, many of these decisions were left undisturbed, ensuring that state constitutions will be a continuing battleground in civil liberties debates in the years to come.

See also Constitution, federal; state government.

FURTHER READING. Willi Paul Adams, *The First American Constitutions: Republican Ideology and the Making of the State Constitutions in the Revolutionary Era*, 1980; James Q. Dealey, *Growth of American State Constitutions from 1776 to the End of the Year 1914*, 1915; John J. Dinan, *The American State Constitutional Tradition*, 2006; Walter F. Dodd, *The Revision and Amendment of State Constitutions*, 1910; Daniel J. Elazar, "The Principles and Traditions Underlying State Constitutions," *Publius* 12 (Winter 1982), 11–25; Christian G. Fritz, "Fallacies of American Constitutionalism," *Rutgers Law Journal* 35 (Summer 2004), 1327–69; James A. Gardner, *Interpreting State Constitutions: A Jurisprudence of Function in a Federal System*, 2005; Marc W. Kruman, *Between Authority and Liberty: State Constitution Making in Revolutionary America*, 1997; Donald S. Lutz, "The Purposes of American State Constitutions," *Publius* 12 (Winter 1982), 27–44; Laura J. Scalia, *America's Jeffersonian Experiment: Remaking State Constitutions, 1820–1850*, 1999; Albert L. Sturm, *Thirty Years of State Constitution-Making, 1938–1968*, 1970; G. Alan Tarr, *Understanding State Constitutions*, 1998; G. Alan Tarr, Robert F. Williams, and Frank P. Grad, eds., *State Constitutions for the Twenty-first Century*, 3 vols., 2006.

JOHN DINAN

state government

History texts have traditionally depicted the evolution of the American republic as progressing from the disunion of the Confederation era to the consolidation of the twentieth century, with state subordination ensured by the triumph of the national regime in the Civil War. According to this scenario, state governments survived in the shadow of policy makers in Washington, D.C., who gradually whittled away at the residual powers of lawmakers in places like Albany and Sacramento. Yet one of the most significant, though often overlooked, features of American political history is the persistent and powerful role of state governments in the lives of citizens. The United States is and always has been a federal republic; its very name makes clear that it is a union of states. Throughout its history the states have provided the lion's share of government affecting the everyday life of the average American. The professors who write the history texts work at state universities; their students are products of the public schools established, supervised, and to a large degree funded by the states. Every day of the year state police disturb the domestic tranquility of speeders driving along highways built and owned by the states. The municipalities that provide the water necessary for human survival are creations of the states, and these water supplies are subject to state supervision. Though the American nation is united, it is not a seamless polity. In the twenty-first century state government remains a ubiquitous element of American life.

From the Revolution to the 1890s

The original 13 states of 1776 were heirs to the governmental traditions of the colonial period. The first state constitutions retained the office of governor, though they reduced executive powers and granted the bulk of authority to a legislative branch that most often consisted of two houses. The federal Constitution of 1787, however, clearly limited the authority of these seemingly all-powerful legislatures. It declared federal laws, treaties, and the federal Constitution itself supreme over state laws. Yet it left the plenary power to govern with the states, creating a national government of delegated powers. The Tenth Amendment ratified in 1791 reinforced this fact. All powers not granted to the federal government nor specifically forbidden to the states were reserved to the states and the people thereof.

During the first 80 years of the nation's history, democratization gradually transformed the structure of state government as the people's role expanded and legislative supremacy eroded. Property or taxpaying qualifications gave way to white manhood suffrage, legislative appointment of executive and judicial officials yielded to popular election, and voter approval of constitutional amendments and revisions became a prerequisite in most states. Meanwhile, the rise of political parties imposed a limited degree of partisan discipline on legislators. They were no longer responsible only to their constituents but also had to answer to party leaders.

During these same years, state governments expanded their functions, assuming broader responsibility for economic development, education, and treatment of the disabled. Internal improvement programs with ambitious blueprints for new roads, rail lines, and canals drove some states to the brink of bankruptcy but also produced a network of artificial waterways in the Northeast and Midwest. Most notably, New York's Erie Canal funneled western commerce through the Mohawk Valley and ensured that the Empire State would wield imperial sway over much of the nation's economy. State governments also funded new universities as well as common schools, laying the foundation for their later dominance in the field of education. State schools for the blind and deaf and asylums for the insane reflected a new confidence that human disabilities could be transcended. Moreover, states constructed penitentiaries to punish and reform malefactors.

Reacting to legislative activism and the public indebtedness incurred by ambitious transportation schemes, mid-nineteenth century Americans demanded a curb on state authority. From 1843 to 1853, 15 of the 31 states drafted new constitutions, resulting in new limits on state debt and internal improvements. In addition, they restricted local and special legislation that was flooding state legislatures and benefiting favored interests. As suspicion of state-chartered business corporations mounted, wary Americans sought constitutional guarantees against legislative giveaways that might enrich the privileged few at the expense of the general public.

Union victory in the Civil War confirmed that the states were not free to withdraw from the nation at will, and the Reconstruction amendments to the federal Constitution seemingly leveled additional blows at state power. Henceforth, the Constitution prohibited the states from depriving persons of life, liberty, or property without due process of the law or denying anyone equal protection of the laws. In addition, states could not limit a person's right to vote on the basis of race, color, or previous condition of servitude. The United States Supreme Court, however, interpreted the guarantees of racial equality narrowly, allowing the states maximum leeway in discriminating against African Americans. By the early twentieth century, most southern states had disenfranchised most blacks through such devices as literacy tests and poll taxes and had enacted a growing array of segregation laws that mandated separate accommodations for African Americans in schools, on transportation lines, and other facilities. The Civil War had decided that states could no longer impose slavery on blacks, but by 1900 state governments had full authority to ensure that African Americans suffered second-class citizenship.

When confronted with the expanding volume of state economic regulatory legislation, the federal Supreme Court was not always so generous toward the states. In 1869 Massachusetts created a state railroad commission with largely advisory powers; it investigated and publicized the practices of rail companies. Illinois pioneered tougher regulation when, in the early 1870s, it authorized a rail commission with the power to fix maximum rates and thereby protect shippers from excessive charges. Twenty-four states had established rail commissions by 1886; some replicated the advisory function of the Massachusetts body while others, especially in the Midwest, followed the rate-setting example of Illinois. That same year, however, the United States Supreme Court limited state regulatory authority to intrastate rail traffic, reserving the supervision of interstate rates to the federal government. It thereby significantly curbed state power over transportation corporations.

To further protect the public, legislatures created state boards of health, with Massachusetts leading the way in 1869. During the next two decades, 29 other states followed Massachusetts's example. The new agencies were largely restricted to the investigation of health conditions and collection of data. By the last decade of the century, however, a few state boards were exercising veto powers over local water and sewerage projects, ensuring that municipalities met adequate health standards.

Activism and the Automobile

In the early twentieth century, state activism accelerated, resulting in even greater intervention in the economy. From 1907 through 1913, 22 states embarked on regulation of public utilities, extending their rate-fixing authority not only to railroads but to gas, electric, streetcar, and telephone services. Meanwhile, state governments moved to protect injured workers by adopting worker compensation programs;

between 1910 and 1920, 42 of the 48 states enacted legislation guaranteeing employees compensation for injuries resulting from on-the-job accidents.

The early twentieth century not only witnessed advances in state paternalism but also changes in the distribution of power within state government. During the late nineteenth century, critics increasingly lambasted state legislatures as founts of corruption where bribed lawmakers churned out nefarious legislation at the behest of lobbyists. The criticisms were exaggerated, but owing to the attacks, faith in the legislative branch declined. Exploiting this popular distrust, a new breed of governors presented themselves as tribunes of the people, who unlike legislators, spoke not for parochial or special interests but championed the commonweal. Charles Evans Hughes in New York, Woodrow Wilson in New Jersey, Robert La Follette in Wisconsin, and Hiram Johnson in California all assumed unprecedented leadership in setting the legislative agenda, posing as popular champions who could prod state lawmakers into passing necessary reforms.

Further reflecting popular skepticism about legislative rule was the campaign for initiative and referendum procedures at the state level. In 1897 South Dakota adopted the first initiative and referendum amendment to a state constitution, allowing voters to initiate legislation and approve it by popular vote. The electorate could thereby bypass an unresponsive legislature. Moreover, voters could demand a referendum on measures passed by the legislature, and a majority of the electorate could thus undo the supposed misdeeds of their representatives. Twenty states had embraced both initiative and referendum by 1919, with Oregon and California making especially frequent use of the new procedure.

Among the issues troubling early-twentieth-century voters was state taxation. Traditionally, states had relied on the property tax, which placed an inordinate burden on land-rich farmers. Seeking to remedy this situation, Wisconsin in 1911 adopted the first effective state graduated income tax for both individuals and corporations. It proved a success, and 13 states had enacted income taxes by 1922, accounting for almost 11 percent of the state tax receipts in the nation.

During the early twentieth century the advent of the automobile greatly expanded the role of state government and further necessitated state tax reforms. Throughout most of the nineteenth century, the construction and maintenance of roads had remained almost wholly a local government responsibility. In the 1890s, however, the growing corps of bicyclists lobbied for better roadways. Responding to this pressure, state legislatures began adopting laws that authorized funding for highways that conformed to state construction standards. Nineteen states had established state road agencies by 1905. Over the following two decades, the burgeoning number of automobile owners forced the other states to follow suit, resulting in a sharp increase in highway expenditures. In 1916 and 1921 Congress approved some funding for state highway programs, but the states still shouldered the great bulk of road financing and construction. From 1921 through 1930 state governments appropriated $7.9 billion for highways; federal aid accounted for only $839 million of this total.

To fund this extraordinary expansion of state responsibility, legislatures embraced the gasoline tax. In 1919 Oregon adopted the first gasoline levy, and over the next ten years every other state followed. This tax on fuel consumption was easy to administer, highly lucrative, and popular with motorists, who were willing to pay for better roads.

From the Depression to the Present

With the onset of economic depression in the 1930s, however, the states confronted a new financial crisis. Unable to collect property taxes from cash-strapped home and business owners and faced with mounting relief expenditures, local authorities turned to the state governments for help. State legislators responded by adopting yet another new source of revenue, the retail sales tax. Mississippi led the way in 1932, and by the close of the 1930s, 23 states imposed this new levy. As early as 1936, it was second only to the gasoline tax as a source of state tax revenue. A massive influx of federal money also helped states improve services and facilities. For example, the federal Civilian Conservation Corps was instrumental in the development of state park systems.

State governments used their new sales tax revenues to bail out local school districts. From 1930 to 1940 the states' share of school funding almost doubled from 16.9 percent to 30.3 percent. Throughout the early twentieth century, states had gradually imposed stricter standards on local districts, centralizing control over public education. The financial crisis of the 1930s, however, accelerated the pace, as states were forced to intervene and maintain adequate levels of schooling.

The Great Depression also stirred new interest among the states in economic development. This was especially true in the South, where leaders tried to wean the region from its dependence on agriculture and to lure industrial plants. In 1936 Mississippi adopted its Balance Agriculture with Industry program, permitting local governments, subject to the approval of a state board, to issue bonds to finance the construction of manufacturing facilities. Meanwhile, the Southern Governors Conference, founded in 1937, lobbied the federal Interstate Commerce Commission to revise its rail charges and thereby eliminate the rate discrimination hampering the development of southern manufacturing.

After World War II the southern states fought a two-front war, defending their heritage of racial segregation while taking the offensive on economic development. First, the Supreme Court and then Congress began putting teeth in the guarantees of racial equality embodied in the Reconstruction amendments to the Constitution. The Court held state segregation laws unconstitutional, and, in the Voting Rights Act of 1965, Congress dismantled southern state restrictions on black voting. Adding to the North-South clash of the postwar era, however, was the southern economic counteroffensive. Southern governors led raiding parties on northern cities, promoting their states to corporate executives tired of the heavily unionized northern labor force and attracted to more business-friendly climes.

During the last decades of the twentieth century, northern governors responded with economic initiatives of their own. By the 1980s states were not only attempting to steal industrial plants from other parts of the country but were also embarking on high-technology incubator programs aimed at fostering innovative growth industries. Governors preached high-tech venture capitalism and promoted each of their states as the next Silicon Valley. Moreover, economic promotion trips to both Europe and Asia became regular events on governors' schedules; German and Japanese moguls welcomed one business-hungry state executive after another. With overseas trade offices and careful calculations of state exports and potential foreign markets, state governments were forging international links. State governments were no longer simply domestic units of rule but also international players.

Educational demands were meanwhile pushing the states to assume ever larger obligations. The state share of public education funding continued to rise, reaching 46.8 percent in 1979–80. Moreover, states funded the expansion of existing public universities as well as the creation of new four-year campuses and systems of two-year community colleges. To pay their mounting education bills, states raised taxes, and most of those that had not previously adopted sales or income levies did so.

With heightened responsibilities, the states seemingly needed to upgrade their governmental structures. In the 1960s the Supreme Court mandated reapportionment of state legislatures; representation was to be based solely on population. Moreover, in the 1960s and 1970s there were mounting demands for professionalization of the state legislatures. Historically, state legislators were part-time lawmakers who met for a few months each biennium, earning a modest salary for their service. During the last decades of the twentieth century, annual legislative sessions became the norm, and, in the largest states, law making became a full-time job, with state legislators acquiring a corps of paid staff. Reacting to the increasing number of entrenched professional legislators, a term-limits movement swept the nation in the early 1990s. Twenty-two states had approved term limits for lawmakers by 1995, restricting them to a maximum service of 6, 8, or 12 years.

In the early twenty-first century state governments were confronting everything from stem cell research to smart-growth land-use planning. The United States remained very much a union of states, jealous of their powers and resistant to incursions by the national regime. State governments survived as significant molders of the policies governing the everyday lives of the nation's 300 million people.

See also state constitutions.

FURTHER READING. Ballard C. Campbell, "Public Policy and State Government," in *The Gilded Age: Essays on the Origins of Modern America*, edited by Charles W. Calhoun, 309–29, 1996; Idem, *Representative Democracy: Public Policy and Midwestern Legislatures in the Late Nineteenth Century*, 1980; James Quayle Dealey, *Growth of American State Constitutions from 1776 to the End of the Year 1914*, 1915; R. Scott Fosler, ed., *The New Economic Role of American States: Strategies in a Competitive Economy*, 1988; Leslie Lipson, *The American Governor: From Figurehead to Leader*, 1939; James T. Patterson, *The New Deal and the States: Federalism in Transition*, 1969; Colman B. Ransone, Jr., *The Office of Governor in the United States*, 1956; Charles F. Ritter and Jon L. Wakelyn, *American Legislative Leaders, 1850–1910*, 1989; Ira Sharkansky, *The Maligned States: Policy Accomplishments, Problems, and Opportunities*, 1972; Jon C. Teaford, *The Rise of the States: Evolution of American State Government*, 2002.

JON C. TEAFORD

suburbs and politics

The United States became a suburban nation during the second half of the twentieth century, according to conventional wisdom, popular consciousness, and scholarly consensus. The most dramatic transformation took place during the two decades after World War II, when the percentage of suburban residents doubled from one-sixth to one-third of the population. Federal policies that promoted both single-family homeownership and racial segregation subsidized the migration of millions of white families from the central cities and the countryside to suburbia, the location of about 85 percent of new residential construction in the postwar era. In 1968 suburban residents cast a plurality of ballots for the first time in a presidential election. In a period of social unrest in cities and on college campuses, Republican candidate Richard Nixon reached the White House by appealing to the "great majority" of "forgotten Americans" who worked hard, paid their taxes, and upheld the principles of the "American Dream." By 1992 suburban voters represented an outright majority of the American electorate, more than the urban and rural populations combined. During a period of economic recession and downward mobility for blue-collar workers, Democratic presidential nominee Bill Clinton reclaimed the political center with a time-honored populist appeal that championed the "forgotten, hard-working middle-class families of America."

The bipartisan pursuit of swing voters of "middle America" reveals the pivotal role played by the rise of suburban power in national politics since the 1950s. The broader story of suburban political culture in modern U.S. history also includes public policies that constructed sprawling metropolitan regions, the grassroots influence of homeowner and taxpayer movements, and the persistent ideology of the white middle-class nuclear family ideal. A clear-cut definition of the "suburbs" is elusive because the label simultaneously represents a specific yet somewhat arbitrary census category (everything in a metropolitan statistical area outside of the central city limits), a particular form of land-use development (the decentralized sprawl of single-family houses in automobile-dependent neighborhoods physically separated from shopping and employment districts), and a powerful set of cultural meanings (the American Dream of homeownership, upward mobility, safety and security, and private family life in cul-de-sac settings of racial and economic exclusion). Residents of suburbs have long defined themselves in cultural and political opposition to the urban-industrial center, from the growth of commuter towns along railroad lines in the mid-1800s to the highway-based "edge cities" and exurbs of the late twentieth century. Although scholars emphasize the diversity of suburban forms and debate the extent to which many former bedroom communities have become urbanized, the utopian imagery of the nineteenth-century "garden suburb" maintains a powerful sway. Suburban politics continues to revolve around efforts to create and defend private refuges of single-family homes that exclude commercial functions and the poor while achieving a harmonious synthesis between the residential setting and the natural environment.

Suburban Growth and Residential Segregation

Beginning in the late 1800s and early 1900s, the quest for local autonomy through municipal incorporation and zoning regulations emerged as a defining feature of suburban political culture. Garden suburbs outside cities such as Boston and Philadelphia incorporated as separate municipalities in order to prevent urban annexation and maintain local control over taxes and services. The 1898 merger that created the five boroughs of New York City stood as a rare exception to the twentieth-century pattern of metropolitan fragmentation into autonomous political districts, especially in the Northeast and Midwest (pro-urban laws continued to facilitate annexation of suburbs in a number of southern and western states). Municipal incorporation enabled affluent suburbs to implement land-use policies of exclusionary zoning that banned industry and multifamily units from homogeneous neighborhoods of single-family homes. The concurrent spread of private racial covenants forbade ownership or rental of property in particular areas by "any person other than of the white or Caucasian race." By the 1920s, real estate developers and homeowners associations promoted restrictive covenants in most new subdivisions, often specifically excluding occupancy by African Americans, Asians, Mexicans, Puerto Ricans, American Indians, and Jews. The NAACP repeatedly challenged the constitutionality of racial covenants during the early decades of the modern civil rights movement, but the Supreme Court continued to permit their enforcement until the *Shelley v. Kraemer* decision of 1948.

By 1930 one-sixth of the American population lived in the suburbs, with public policies and private practices combining to segregate neighborhoods comprehensively by race and class. From the local to the national levels, suburban politics revolved around the protection of white middle-class family life through the defense of private property values. Following the turn to restrictive covenants, the National Association of Real Estate Boards instructed its members that "a realtor should never be instrumental in introducing into a neighborhood a character of property or occupancy, members of any race or nationality, or any individual whose presence will clearly be detrimental to property values in the neighborhood." During the depths of the Great Depression, the federal government established the Home Owners Loan Corporation, which provided emergency mortgages in single-family neighborhoods while "redlining" areas that contained industry, multifamily housing units, and low-income or minority residents. The National Housing Act of 1934 chartered the Federal Housing Administration (FHA), which insured low-interest mortgage loans issued by private banks and thereby revolutionized the market for suburban residential construction. The FHA also endorsed restrictive racial covenants and maintained the guideline that "if a neighborhood is to retain stability, it is necessary that properties shall continue to be occupied by the same social and racial classes." Between 1934 and 1960, the federal government provided $117 billion in mortgage insurance for private homes, with racial minorities formally excluded from 98 percent of these new developments, almost all of which were located in suburbs or outlying neighborhoods within city limits.

During the sustained economic boom that followed World War II, suburbs became the primary residential destination for white-collar and blue-collar families alike, although neighborhoods remained stratified by socioeconomics as well as segregated by race. Suburban development became a powerful validation of the New Deal social contract, embodied in President Franklin Roosevelt's promise that the national state would secure "the right of every family to a decent home." The GI Bill of 1944 offered interest-free mortgages to millions of military veterans and enabled many white working-class and middle-class families to achieve the suburban dream of a detached house with a yard. The federal government also subsidized suburban growth through interstate highways and other road-building projects that connected bedroom communities to downtown business districts and accelerated the decentralization of shopping malls and office parks to the metropolitan fringe. The number of American families that owned their own homes increased from 40 to 60 percent between the 1940s and the 1960s, the period of the great white middle-class migration to the suburbs.

In 1947 the corporate-designed Levittown on Long Island became the national symbol of this new suburban prosperity, an all-white town of 70,000 residents marketed as "the most perfectly planned community in America." Social critics mocked Levittown and similar mass-produced developments for their cookie-cutter houses and the allegedly bland and conformist lifestyles of their inhabitants. But defenders credited the suburbs with achieving "the ideal of prosperity for all in a classless society," the epitome of the consumer-based freedoms that would assure the victory of the United States in the cold war, as Vice President Richard M. Nixon proclaimed in the 1959 "kitchen debate" with Premier Nikita Khrushchev of the Soviet Union.

Suburbs under Siege

The suburban political culture of the 1950s celebrated consensus, consumer affluence, and a domestic ideology marked by rigid gender roles within the heterosexual nuclear family. On the surface, in the television family sitcoms and mass-market magazines, postwar America seemed to be a place of white upper-middle-class contentment, with fathers commuting to corporate jobs while stay-at-home mothers watched their baby boomer youth play with toys advertised by Walt Disney and other large corporations. In the presidential elections of 1952 and 1956, a substantial majority of voters twice rejected the reformist liberalism of Adlai Stevenson for the moderate conservatism of President Dwight D. Eisenhower, later labeled "the great Republican hero of the suburban middle class" by GOP strategist Kevin Phillips.

But this consensus ideology of 1950s suburban prosperity existed alongside a growing crisis of domesticity that would soon explode in the social movements of the 1960s. Sociologist William Whyte characterized white-collar managers from the affluent suburbs as the collective "Organization Man," a generation that had sacrificed individuality to the demands of corporate conformity. Betty Friedan critiqued the "feminine mystique" for promoting therapeutic rather than political solutions to issues of sex discrimination and proclaimed: "We can no longer ignore that voice within women that says: 'I want something more than my husband and my children and my home.'" In 1962 Students for a Democratic Society called for a new left that rejected the utopian promises of suburban tranquility: "We are people of this generation, bred in at least modest comfort, housed now in universities, looking uncomfortably to the world we inherit."

In the 1960s and 1970s, the greatest challenge to suburban political autonomy came from the civil rights campaign for school and housing integration. A growing white backlash greeted these efforts to open up the suburbs, signaled by the passage of Proposition 14 by California voters in 1964. Three-fourths of the white suburban electorate supported this referendum to repeal California's fair-housing law and protect the private right to discriminate on the basis of race in the sale and renting of property. The open-housing movement, which had been attacking policies of suburban exclusion for half a century, gained new urgency with the race riots that erupted in American cities in the mid-to-late 1960s. During the summer of 1966, Martin Luther King Jr. led open-housing marches into several of Chicago's all-white suburbs, but the violent reaction of white homeowners did not persuade Congress to pass a federal open-housing law.

In 1968 the National Advisory Commission on Civil Disorders (Kerner Commission) issued a dire warning that the United States was divided into "two societies; one, largely Negro and poor, located in the central cities; the other, predominantly white and affluent, located in the suburbs and outlying areas." The Kerner Report also placed blame for the urban crisis on public policies of suburban exclusion: "What white Americans have never fully understood—but what the Negro can never forget—is that white society is deeply implicated in the ghetto. White institutions created it, white institutions maintain it, and white society condones it." Congress responded by passing the landmark Fair Housing Act of 1968, which banned discrimination on the basis of race, color, religion, and national origin in the sale and renting of property.

The political backlash against the civil rights movement galvanized white voters in working-class and middle-class suburbs alike. In 1966 Republican candidate Ronald Reagan won the California gubernatorial election by denouncing fair-housing legislation, calling for "law and order" crackdowns against urban criminals and campus protesters, and blaming liberal welfare programs for squandering the tax dollars of mainstream Americans. In 1968 Richard Nixon's pledge to defend middle–American homeowners and taxpayers from the excesses of liberalism carried white-collar suburbs across the nation and made inroads among blue-collar Democrats. During his first term in office, Nixon vigorously defended the principle of suburban autonomy by opposing court-ordered busing to integrate public schools and by resisting inclusionary zoning to scatter low-income housing throughout metropolitan regions. "Forced integration of the suburbs," Nixon declared in 1971, "is not in the national interest." In his 1972 reelection campaign, Nixon won 49 states by uniting working-class and middle-class white voters in a populist antiliberal alliance that he labeled the "silent majority." In the 1980s, Ronald Reagan strengthened the Republican base in the suburbs by blaming the Democrats for economic recession, welfare cheaters, racial quotas, court-ordered busing, urban crime, and high taxes imposed on the hard-working majority to pay for failed antipoverty programs. Capitalizing on grassroots movements such as the California property tax revolt of 1978, Reagan dominated the suburban electorate by a 55-to-35 margin in 1980 and a 61-to-38 landslide in 1984.

Suburban Diversity

Reagan's victories in the 1980s represented the culmination of a suburban-driven realignment that ultimately destroyed the political base of New Deal liberalism, but the temporary triumph of Republican conservatism soon gave way to new forms of suburban diversity and heightened levels of electoral competitiveness. In 1985 a group of moderate Democrats formed the Democratic Leadership Council (DLC) to expand beyond the party's urban base by becoming "competitive in suburban areas" and recognizing that "sprawl is where the voters are." In the 1992 presidential election, Bill Clinton won by turning the DLC agenda into a campaign to honor the values of America's "forgotten middle class, . . . like individual responsibility, hard work, family, community." Clinton championed programs such as universal health care to address middle–American economic insecurity while neutralizing the GOP by promising to cut middle-class taxes, enact welfare reform, and be tough on crime. Clinton won a plurality of suburban votes in the three-way elections of 1992 (41 to 39 percent) and 1996 (47 to 42 percent), while maintaining the traditional Democratic base in the central cities. At the same time, the Democratic resurgence reflected the increasing heterogeneity of American suburbia, home to 54 percent of Asian Americans, 49 percent of Hispanics, 39 percent of African Americans, and 73 percent of whites at the time of the 2000 census (based on the 102 largest metropolitan regions). By century's end, some political strategists were predicting an "emerging Democratic majority" based on the party's newfound ability to appeal to white swing voters in the middle-class suburbs (a fiscally and culturally moderate electorate) and to capture the high-tech, multiracial metropolises of the booming Sunbelt.

Republican George W. Bush reclaimed the suburban vote by narrow margins in 2000 (49 to 47 percent) and 2004 (52 to 47 percent), but the dynamics of recent elections suggest the problematic nature of viewing contemporary metropolitan politics through the stark urban/liberal versus suburban/conservative dichotomy that took hold in the 1950s. Republican "family values" campaigns have mobilized the outer-ring suburbs that are home to large numbers of white married couples with young children, and Bush won 97 of the nation's 100 fastest-growing exurban counties in the 2000 election. Democrats have found new bases of support in older inner-ring suburbs, many of

which are diversifying as racial and ethnic minorities settle outside the city limits, as well as with middle-income women and white-collar professionals who dislike the cultural agenda of the religious right.

Suburban political culture is also in flux in other ways that challenge the partisan divisions that emerged during the postwar decades. The bellwether state of California, which led the national suburban backlash against civil rights and liberal programs in the 1960s, now combines an anti-tax political culture with a massive prison-industrial complex, a multiracial electorate with a deeply conflicted stance toward immigration, and some of the nation's most progressive policies on environmental regulation and cultural issues.

Perhaps the most important consequence of the suburbanization of American politics is the way in which the partisan affiliations of voters has often mattered less than the identification of suburban residents as homeowners, taxpayers, and school parents. Regardless of which party controls Washington, America's suburbs have proved to be quite successful at defending their property values, maintaining middle-class entitlement programs, resisting policies of redistributive taxation, preventing meaningful racial and economic integration, and thereby policing the cultural and political boundaries of the American Dream.

See also cities and politics.

FURTHER READING. Rosalyn Baxandall and Elizabeth Ewen, *Picture Windows: How the Suburbs Happened*, 2000; Lizabeth Cohen, *A Consumers' Republic: The Politics of Mass Consumption in Postwar America*, 2003; Marjorie Connelly, "How Americans Voted: A Political Portrait," *New York Times*, November 7, 2004; Robert M. Fogelson, *Bourgeois Nightmares: Suburbia, 1870–1930*, 2005; David M. P. Freund, *Colored Property: State Policy and White Racial Politics in Suburban America*, 2007; William Frey, "Melting Pot Suburbs: A Census 2000 Study of Suburban Diversity," Washington, DC: Brookings Institution, June 2001, downloadable from http://www.brookings.edu/~/media/Files/rc/reports/2001/06demographics_frey/frey.pdf; Stanley B. Greenberg, *Middle Class Dreams: The Politics and Power of the New American Majority*, revised ed., 1996; Kenneth T. Jackson, *Crabgrass Frontier: The Suburbanization of the United States*, 1985; Matthew D. Lassiter, *The Silent Majority: Suburban Politics in the Sunbelt South*, 2006; Lisa McGirr, *Suburban Warriors: The Origins of the New American Right*, 2001; Stephen Grant Meyer, *As Long as They Don't Move Next Door: Segregation and Racial Conflict in American Neighborhoods*, 2000; Becky M. Nicolaides and Andrew Wiese, eds., *The Suburb Reader*, 2006; William Schneider, "The Suburban Century Begins," *Atlantic Monthly* (July 1992), 33–44, downloadable from http://www.theatlantic.com/politics/ecbig/schnsub.htm; Robert O. Self, *American Babylon: Race and the Struggle for Postwar Oakland*, 2003; Andrew Wiese, *Places of Their Own: African American Suburbanization in the Twentieth Century*, 2004.

MATTHEW D. LASSITER

suffrage

See voting; woman suffrage.

Supreme Court

There is no doubt that the U.S. Supreme Court has influenced the politics of the country. As a public body, the Court is a highly visible part of the federal government. This has always been so, even when the justices met briefly twice a year in the drafty basement of the Capitol. Yet the idea that the Court itself is a political institution is controversial.

The justices themselves have disputed that fact. Indeed, the Court has gone to great pains to avoid the appearance of making political decisions. In *Luther v. Borden* (1849), the Court adopted a self-denying "prudential" (judge-made) rule that it would avoid hearing cases that the legislative branch, or the people, could decide for themselves, the "political questions." In 1946 Justice Felix Frankfurter reiterated this principle in *Colegrove v. Green*. Because it did nothing but hear and decide cases and controversies brought before it, and its decisions affected only the parties in those cases and controversies, Alexander Hamilton assured doubters, in the Federalist Papers, No. 78, that the High Court was "the weakest branch" of the new federal government.

There are other apparent constraints on the Court's participation in politics that arise from within the canons of the legal profession. Judges are supposed to be neutral in their approach to cases, and learned appellate court judges are supposed to ground their opinions in precedent and logic. On the Court, the high opinion of their peers and the legal community allegedly means more to them than popularity.

Conceding such legal, professional, and self-imposed constraints, the Court is a vital part of U.S. politics for three reasons. First, the Court is part of a constitutional system that is inherently political. Even before the rise of the first national two-party system in the mid-1790s, the Court found itself involved in politics. The Court declined to act as an advisory body to President George Washington on the matter of veterans' benefits, asserting the separation of powers doctrine. In 1793 the Court ordered the state of Georgia to pay what it owed a man named Chisholm, an out-of-state creditor, causing a constitutional crisis that prompted the passage of the Eleventh Amendment. Those kinds of political frictions—among the branches of the federal government and between the High Court and the states—continue to draw the Court into politics.

After the advent of the national two-party system, partisanship became institutionalized, with the result that appointments to the Court have always been political. Nominees often have political careers before they agree to serve. They are almost always members of the president's political party. The role the Senate plays in consenting to the president's nominations (or, in slightly under one-fourth of the nominations, refusing to consent), further politicizes the Court, for the Senate divides along party and ideological lines in such votes. The confirmation debates and, after 1916, the hearings, are riven with politics, and once on the Court, the justices' political views are often remarkably accurate predictors of their stances in cases that involve sensitive issues. The controversies surrounding President Ronald W. Reagan's nomination of Robert Bork and President George H. W. Bush's nomination of Clarence Thomas are recent examples of this observation.

Similarly, once on the Court the justices do not necessarily abandon their political aspirations. Salmon P. Chase, Stephen J. Field, Charles Evans Hughes, Frank Murphy, and William O. Douglas all wanted to be president of the United States, and Chief Justice William Howard Taft was an ex-president when he assumed the center chair. Felix Frankfurter and Abe Fortas continued to advise their respective presidents while on the bench.

Finally, the output of the Court has a major impact on the politics of the day. While it is not always true that the Court follows the election returns, it is true that the Court can influence them. In the first 60 years of the nineteenth century, slavery cases fit this description. Even after the Thirteenth Amendment abolished slavery, politically sensitive civil rights cases continued to come to the High Court. Labor relations cases, taxation cases, antitrust cases, and, more recently, privacy cases all had political impact.

Even the self-denying stance the Court adopted in political questions was subject to revision. In a famous footnote to *Carolene Products v. U.S.* (1938), the Court announced that it would pay particularly close attention to state actions that discriminated against "discrete and insular minorities" precisely because they were not protected by democratic "political processes." In the 1940s, the Court struck down state laws denying persons of color the right to vote in election primaries. Later decisions barred states from drawing legislative districts intended to dilute the votes of minority citizens. By the 1960s, the Court's abstinence in political questions had worn thin. In a series of "reapportionment cases," the Court determined that states could not frame state or congressional electoral districts unfairly. The High Court's rulings, sometimes known as the "one man, one vote" doctrine, remade state and federal electoral politics.

The Early Period

Perhaps the most appropriate way to demonstrate the Court's complex institutional politics is to describe its most prominent cases. The very first of the Court's great cases, *Marbury v. Madison* (1803) involved political relations within government, the partisan composition of the Court, and the political impact of a decision. It began when the Republican Party of

Thomas Jefferson and James Madison won control of the presidency and both houses of Congress in what Jefferson called the revolution of 1800.

The Jeffersonian Republicans wanted to purge the judiciary of their rivals, the Federalists, and eliminate many of the so-called midnight appointments. In the coming years, Congress would impeach and remove Federalist district court judge Timothy Pickering and impeach Federalist Supreme Court justice Samuel Chase. Into this highly charged partisan arena came the case of William Marbury.

Marbury was supposed to receive a commission as a justice of the peace for the District of Columbia. However, when he was the outgoing secretary of state, John Marshall failed to send the commission on, and the incoming secretary of state, James Madison, with the assent of President Jefferson, did not remedy Marshall's oversight. When Marbury did not get the commission, he filed suit with the clerk of the Supreme Court under the provisions of the Judiciary Act of 1789, which gave the Court original jurisdiction in such matters.

Thus, the case went directly to the Court. The issue, as Marshall, who was now chief justice, framed it, was whether the Court had jurisdiction over the case. He intentionally ignored the political context of the suit. It seems obvious that the issue was political, but in a long opinion for that day (26 pages), Marshall wrote for a unanimous Court that the justices could not issue the writ because it was not one of the kinds of original jurisdiction given the Court in Article III of the Constitution. The Constitution controlled or limited what Congress could do, and prohibited the Congress from expanding the original jurisdiction of the Court. Congress had violated the Constitution by giving this authority to the Court. In short, he struck down that part of the Judiciary Act of 1789 as unconstitutional.

The power that Marshall assumed in the Court to find acts of Congress unconstitutional, and thus null and void, was immensely important politically within the government structure, for it protected the independence of the Court from Congress, implied that the Court was the final arbiter of the meaning of the Constitution (the doctrine of judicial review), and reminded everyone that the Constitution was the supreme law against which every act of Congress had to be measured. Although critics of *Marbury* decried judicial tyranny and asserted that the opinion was colored by Marshall's party affiliation, a political challenge to Marshall's opinion was not possible because it did not require any action. Marbury went away empty-handed.

Marbury managed to keep the Court out of politics in a formal sense, though it was deeply political; the "self-inflicted wound" of *Dred Scott v. Sanford* (1857) plunged the Court into the center of the political maelstrom. What to do about slavery in the territories was a suppurating wound in antebellum national politics. By the late 1850s, the controversy had destroyed one national party, the Whigs, and led to the formation of a new party, the Republicans, based wholly in the North and dedicated to preventing the expansion of slavery.

Against this background of intensifying partisanship and sectional passion, the Supreme Court might have elected to avoid making general pronouncements about slavery and stick to the facts of cases, narrowing the precedent. However, in 1856 newly elected Democratic president James Buchanan asked the Court to find a comprehensive solution to the controversy when Congress deadlocked over the admission of Kansas as a slave state. A Democratic majority was led by long-term chief justice Roger B. Taney of Maryland, a dedicated states' rights Democrat who had been Andrew Jackson's reliable aide in the war against the second Bank of the United States.

Dred Scott was the slave of U.S. Army doctor John Emerson, and was taken with him from Louisiana to posts in free states and free territories. In 1843 Emerson returned to a family home in Missouri, a slave state, and Scott went with him. In 1846, three years after Emerson's death, for himself and his family, Scott sued for his freedom. After two trials and four years had passed, the Missouri trial court ruled in his favor. The Missouri Supreme Court reversed that decision in 1852. Northern personal liberty laws, the response to the Fugitive Slave Act of 1850, angered Missouri slaveholding interests, and the new policy that the state's supreme court adopted in *Scott* reflected that anger.

But Scott's cause had also gained new friends, "free soil" and abolitionist interests that believed his case raised crucial issues. Because Emerson's estate had a New York executor, John Sanford, Scott could bring his suit for freedom in federal court under the diversity clause of the Judiciary Act of 1789. This litigation could only go forward if Scott were a citizen, but the federal circuit court sitting in St. Louis decided to hear the suit. In 1854, however, the federal court agreed with the Missouri supreme court: under Missouri law, Scott was still a slave.

The U.S. Supreme Court agreed to a full dress hearing of Scott's appeal in 1856. Oral argument took four days, and the Court's final ruling was delayed another year, after the presidential election of 1856. Joined by six of the other justices, Taney ruled that the lower federal court was correct: under Missouri law, Scott had no case. Nor should the case have come to the federal courts, for Scott was not a citizen. The law behind this decision was clear, and it was enough to resolve the case. But Taney added two dicta, readings of history and law that were not necessary to resolve the case but would, if followed, have settled the political questions of black citizenship and free soil.

Taney wrote that no person of African descent brought to America to labor could ever be a citizen of the United States. Such individuals might be citizens of particular states, but this did not confer national citizenship on them. In a second dictum, Taney opined that the Fifth Amendment to the Constitution, guaranteeing that no man's property might be taken without due process of law, barred Congress from denying slavery expansion into the territories. In effect, Taney retroactively declared the Missouri Compromise of 1820, barring slavery in territories north of 36° 30′ north latitude, unconstitutional.

The opinion was celebrated in the South and excoriated in the North. Northern public opinion, never friendly to abolitionism, now found the possibility of slavery moving north frightening. Abraham Lincoln used it to undermine his rival for the Illinois Senate seat, Stephen Douglas. Lincoln lost the race (Douglas and the Democrats controlled the legislature), but he won the debates and found an issue on which to campaign for president in 1860.

In his first inaugural address, President Lincoln issued a subtle warning to the holdover Democratic majority on the Court, and to Taney in particular. The will of the people, embodied in the electoral victory of the Republicans, would not tolerate a Court that defended secession. The justices took the hint. They agreed to the blockade of the Confederate coastline and accepted the administration view that the Confederacy did not legally exist. By the end of the war, Lincoln was able to add enough Republicans to the Court, including a new chief justice, Salmon Chase, to ensure that Republican policies would not be overturned. For example, the majority of the Court found that "greenbacks," paper money issued by the federal government to finance the war, were legal tender.

The Industrial Age

The Reconstruction amendments profoundly changed the constitutional landscape, giving the federal government increased supervision over the states. Insofar as the High Court had already claimed pride of place in interpreting the meaning of the Constitution, the Thirteenth, the Fourteenth, and the Fifteenth Amendments, along with the Civil Rights Acts of 1866, 1870, 1871, and 1875, should have led to deeper Court involvement in the politics of the South. Instead, the Court's repeated refusal to intervene reflected the white consensus that nothing further could be done to aid the newly freed slaves in the South, or the black people of the North, for that matter.

The so-called voting rights cases were inherently political because they touched the most basic rights of citizens in a democracy—the right to participate in the political process. In these cases, the Court deployed the first kind of politics, the politics of federalism, in response to the third kind of politics, the wider politics of party. By 1876, the Radical Republican impulse to enforce an aggressive Reconstruction policy had spent itself. In the election of 1876, the Republican nominee, Rutherford B. Hayes,

promised that he would end the military occupation of the former Confederate states, in effect turning over state and local government to the "Redeemers," former Confederate political leaders, and leaving the fate of the former slaves to their past masters.

In *U.S. v. Hiram Reese* and *U.S. v. William Cruikshank et al.*, decided in 1875 and 1876, the Court found ways to back the Redeemers. In the former case, a Kentucky state voting registrar refused to allow Garner, an African American, to pay the poll tax. The motive was as much political as racial, as the state was Democratic and the party leaders assumed that every black voter was a Republican. A circuit court had dismissed the prosecutor's indictments. The High Court affirmed the lower court. In the latter case, a mob of whites attacked blacks guarding a courthouse in New Orleans. Again the federal circuit court had found the indictments wanting. The High Court agreed.

Was the Court concerned about the political implications of the two cases? They were heard in 1875, but the decision was not announced until the next year. In his opinion for the Court in *Cruikshank*, Chief Justice Morrison R. Waite introduced the concept of "state action," a limitation on the reach of the Fourteenth Amendment's due process and equal protection clauses. The New Orleans mob was not an agent of the state, so the Fourteenth Amendment and the civil rights acts did not apply. The door was now wide open for the Redeemers to pass Jim Crow laws, segregating public facilities in the South, and deny freedmen their rights using supposedly neutral restrictions like literacy tests for voting as well as "whites only" primaries for the most important elections—those in the Democratic primary. Outright discrimination received Court approval in the case of *Plessy v. Ferguson* (1896), in which "equal but separate" laws, more popularly known as "separate but equal," became the rule of the land.

The politicization of the High Court in the Gilded Age, a period of rapid industrialization, was nowhere more apparent than in a trio of highly political cases that arrived at the Court in 1894 and 1895. The first of the cases arose when the federal government prosecuted the E. C. Knight sugar-refining company and other refining operations, all part of the same sugar trust, for violation of the 1890 Sherman Antitrust Act.

Chief Justice Melville Fuller wrote the opinion at the end of 1894. Congress had the power to regulate interstate commerce but, according to Fuller, the refineries were manufacturing plants wholly within the states of Delaware, Pennsylvania, and New Jersey, and thus not subject to federal law. The Court, by a vote of 8 to 1, had refused to let the progressives in the government enjoin (legally stop), combination of the sugar refineries. It was a victory for the monopolies and the politicians they had lobbied. By the same lopsided vote, in *In Re Debs* (1895) the Court upheld a lower-court injunction sought by the federal government against the American Railway Union for striking. It too was a triumph for conservative political forces.

The third time in which the Fuller Court delved into the great political causes of the day was an income tax case. Democratic voters in rural areas favored the reintroduction of an income tax. The tax Congress passed during the Civil War expired in 1872. In 1894 Congress passed a flat 2 percent income tax on all incomes over $4,000—the equivalent of about $91,000 in 2005 dollars. Defenders of the sacredness of private wealth were aghast and feared that the measure brought the nation one step closer to socialism. In *Pollock v. Farmers Loan and Trust Company* (1895), Fuller and the Court agreed and set aside the entire act of Congress, not just the offending corporate provisions.

All three of the High Court's opinions angered the Populists and other reformers. William Jennings Bryan, the former congressman who captured the Democratic Party nomination in 1896, won over a much divided convention, in part, with an attack on the Court's dismissive view of the working man. But Bryan sounded like a dangerous extremist in a decade filled with radicalism. Better financed, supported by most of the major newspapers, the Republicans and McKinley won a landslide victory, with 271 electoral votes to Bryan's 176.

During U.S. participation in World War I, nothing could have been more political than the antiwar protests of 1917–18, and the Court handled these with a heavy hand. Here the Court acted not as an independent check on the other branches of the federal government, upholding the Bill of Rights, but as the handmaiden of the other branches' claims to wartime powers. In such cases, the Court was political in the first sense, as part of the larger operation of the federal government.

When pro-German, antiwar, or radical spokesmen appeared to interfere with the draft by making speeches, passing out leaflets, or writing editorials, or when they conspired to carry out any act that might interfere with the draft, the federal government arrested, tried, and convicted them under the Espionage Act of 1917. The High Court found no protection for such speech in the First Amendment. As Justice Oliver Wendell Holmes Jr. wrote in upholding the conviction of Socialist Party leader Eugene V. Debs, Debs's avowed Socialist commitments could not be tolerated by a nation at war. The government had to protect itself against such upsetting speech. Holmes would reverse himself in *U.S. v. Abrams* (1919), but antigovernment political speech in time of war did not receive protection from the Court under the First Amendment until the Vietnam War.

Liberalism Triumphant

In the New Deal Era, the Court thrust itself into the center of the political arena. By first upholding federal and state intervention in the economy,

then striking down congressional acts, and then deferring to Congress, the Court proved that external political considerations could be as powerful an influence as the justices' own political views. The New Deal, from 1933 to 1941, was, in reality, two distinct political and economic periods. Most of the more controversial programs from the first New Deal, like the National Recovery Administration, the Court (led by the conservative quartet of George Sutherland, Willis Van Devanter, Pierce Butler, and James C. McReynolds, joined by Owen Roberts) struck down, under the substantive due process, doctrine it originally announced in the case of *Lochner v. New York* (1905).

With the Depression largely unaffected by the first New Deal, Franklin Roosevelt's administration and Congress enacted more egalitarian reforms in 1935. Among these were programs to provide jobs (the Works Progress Administration), the Social Security Act, the Rural Electrification Administration, and the National Labor Relations Act. The last of these finally ended the antilabor injunction, in effect overruling the Court's attempts to protect it. The stage was set for a constitutional crisis between Roosevelt and the Court. In 1937, however, Justice Roberts shifted his stance, joining, among others, Chief Justice Charles Evans Hughes to uphold the constitutionality of the Social Security Administration, the National Labor Relations Board, and other New Deal agencies. What had happened to change the constitutional landscape?

One factor could have been Roosevelt's plan to revise the membership of the Court. Congress had done this before, adding justices or (at the end of the Civil War) reducing the number of justices. Roosevelt would have added justices to the Court for every justice over the age of 70, in effect "packing it" with New Deal supporters. From their new building, dubbed "the marble palace" by journalists, all the justices disliked the packing plan. No one knew what Roosevelt's plan would bring or if Congress would accede to the president's wishes. In fact, the Senate quashed the initiative. But by that time the High Court had shifted its views enough to let key measures of the second New Deal escape, including Social Security, collective bargaining for labor, and minimum wage laws.

With the retirement of one conservative after another, Roosevelt would be able to fill the Court in a more conventional way with New Deal supporters. From 1937 to 1943, turnover in the Court was unmatched. The new justices included Hugo Black, Stanley Reed, Felix Frankfurter, William O. Douglas, Frank Murphy, James F. Byrnes, Robert Jackson, and Wiley Rutledge. All, to one degree or another, believed in deference to popularly elected legislatures.

After World War II, the cold war and the so-called second Red Scare again required the Court to step carefully through a political minefield. At the height of the cold war, the House Un-American Activities

Committee and the Senate's Permanent Subcommittee on Investigations, led by Senator Joseph McCarthy of Wisconsin, sought to uncover Communists in government posts. A wider scare led to blacklists of former Communists and their alleged conspirators in Hollywood, among New York State school teachers, and elsewhere.

Here the Court's majority followed the election returns in such cases as *Dennis v. United States* (1951). The case arose out of Attorney General Tom Clark's orders to prosecute the leaders of the Communist Party-USA (CPUSA) for violating the 1940 Smith Act, which forbade any advocacy or conspiracy to advocate the violent overthrow of the government. Although this was only one of many cases stemming from the "Foley Square Trials" in the federal district court in New York City, the High Court had yet to rule on the First Amendment issues involved.

Chief Justice Fred Vinson warned that the government did not have to wait to act as the Communist Party organized and gathered strength. The Smith Act was clear and constitutional—and the Communist Party, to which Dennis and the others indicted under the act belonged, had as its policy the violent overthrow of the government. Justices Hugo Black and William O. Douglas dissented.

In so doing, they initiated a great debate over whether the Court should adopt an absolutist or more flexible interpretation of the Bill of Rights. Black's dissent was that the First Amendment's declaration that Congress shall make no law meant "no law." Conceding some power to the government, Douglas, an author himself, would be the first to grant that printed words could lead to action, and he made plain his dislike of the Communists' required reading list. But, he reasoned, "If the books themselves are not outlawed, if they can lawfully remain on library shelves, by what reasoning does their use in a classroom become a crime?" Within a decade, Douglas's views would triumph.

The Rights Revolution and Reaction
Civil rights again thrust the Court into the center of political agitation, except this time it spoke not in political terms but in moral ones. The civil rights decisions of the Warren Court elevated it above the politics of the justices, and the politics of the men who put the justices in the marble palace. Earl Warren, chief justice during this "rights revolution," came to personify the Court's new unanimity. He was first and foremost a politician. His meteoric rise in California politics, from humble beginnings to state attorney general, and then governor, was accompanied by a gradual shift from conservative Republicanism to a more moderate, centrist position—one that favored government programs to help the poor and regulation of business in the public interest. In return for Warren's support at the 1952 national convention, newly elected President Dwight D. Eisenhower promised him a place on the Court. The first vacancy

was the chief justiceship, and Eisenhower somewhat reluctantly kept his word.

Warren did not have a distinguished civil rights or civil liberties record in California. During World War II, he had been a strong proponent of the forced relocation of Japanese Americans from their homes on the West Coast to internment camps. But on the Court he saw that the politics of civil rights and the Fourteenth Amendment's plain meaning required the end of racial discrimination in schools, public facilities, and voting.

There can be no doubt that the Court's decisions in *Brown v. Board of Education* (1954), *Cooper v. Aaron* (1958), and subsequent school desegregation cases had a major political impact. Certainly southern members of Congress recognized that impact when they joined in a "manifesto" denouncing the Court for exceeding its role in the federal system and the federal government for its intrusion into southern state affairs. President Eisenhower was so disturbed by the Court's role in the rights revolution that he reportedly said—referring to Warren and Justice William J. Brennan—that his two worst mistakes were sitting on the Supreme Court.

In more recent times, the nomination process itself has become the beginning of an ongoing politicization of the Court. The abortive nominations of the Nixon and Reagan years proved that the presidency and Congress at last considered the Court a full partner—with the result that every nominee was scrutinized more carefully. There would be no more Earl Warrens, at least in theory. The effect was a hearing process that had become a national spectacle of partisan politics.

The focal point of that spectacle has been another of the Court's decisions—*Roe v. Wade* (1973). Every candidate for the Court is asked where he or she stands on this case that legalized abortion for most pregnancies. Oddly enough, it was President Nixon's Court, which he had constructed in reaction to the Warren Court's rulings on criminal procedure, that produced this ruling.

Chief Justice Warren Burger knew the importance of *Roe v. Wade* and its companion case, *Doe v. Bolton*, from the moment they arrived in 1971 as two class-action suits challenging Texas and Georgia abortion laws, respectively. In both cases, federal district court panels of three judges struck down the state laws as violating the federal Constitution's protection of a woman's privacy rights, themselves a politically charged issue after the Court's decision in *Griswold v. Connecticut* (1965), which struck down a Connecticut law banning the distribution of birth control materials, largely on privacy grounds.

The majority of the justices agreed with the lower courts but labored to find a constitutional formula allowing pregnant women to determine their reproductive fates. Justice Harry Blackmun, a Nixon appointee, was assigned the opinion for the majority, and based the right on the due process clause of the

Fourteenth Amendment, though he clearly had more interest in the sanctity of the doctor-patient relationship than in the rights of women. His formulation relied on the division of a pregnancy into trimesters. In the first of these, a woman needed only the consent of her doctor. In the second and third trimesters, after the twentieth week, the state's interest in the potential life allowed it to impose increasingly stiff regulations on abortions.

The 7-to-2 decision invalidated most of the abortion laws in the country and nationalized what had been a very local, very personal issue. *Roe* would become one of the most controverted and controversial of the Court's opinions since *Dred Scott*, to which some of its critics, including Justice Antonin Scalia, would later compare it. For women's rights advocates it was a decision that recognized a right, but only barely, with qualifications, on a constitutional theory ripe for attack. Opponents of abortion jeered a decision that recognized a state interest in the fetus but denied that life began at conception. They would mobilize against the desecration of religion, motherhood, and the family that they felt the decision represented. The position a nominee took on *Roe* became a litmus test. Congressional and presidential elections turned on the abortion rights question, as new and potent political action groups, in particular religious lobbies, entered the national arena for the first time to battle over *Roe*.

If more proof of the place of the Court in American politics were needed, it came at the end of the hotly contested 2000 presidential election campaign between Albert Gore Jr. and George W. Bush. As in *Marbury*, *Bush v. Gore* (2000) exemplified all three of the political aspects of the Court's place in U.S. history. First, it was a federalism case. Second, the division on the Court matched the political background of the justices. Finally, no case or opinion could have a more obvious impact on politics in that it determined the outcome of a presidential election.

To be sure, there was a precedent. In 1877 another hotly contested election ended with a decision that was clearly controversial, and five justices of the High Court played the deciding role in that case as well, voting along party lines to seat all the electors for Republican Rutherford B. Hayes and none of the electors for Democrat Samuel J. Tilden as part of the commission set up to resolve the dispute. But in *Bush v. Gore*, the disputed results in the Florida balloting never reached Congress. Instead, the justices voted to end the Florida Supreme Court–ordered recount and declare Bush the winner in Florida, and thereby the newly elected president. The majority disclaimed any partisan intent.

Whatever stance one takes on *Bush v. Gore*, the case, like those before it, offers proof that the Court has a role in the institutional politics of the nation, that the members of the Court are political players themselves, and that the Court's decisions can dramatically affect the nation's political fate.

See also House of Representatives; presidency; Senate.

FURTHER READING. Henry Abraham, *Justices, Presidents, and Senators*, rev. ed., 1999; Jan Crawford Greenberg, *Supreme Conflict: The Inside Story of the Struggle for Control of the United States Supreme Court*, 2007; Kermit Hall et al., eds., *The Oxford Companion to the Supreme Court of the United States*, 2nd ed., 2005; Peter Charles Hoffer, Williamjames Hull Hoffer, and N.E.H. Hull, *The Supreme Court: An Essential History*, 2007; Richard Neely, *How Courts Govern America*, 1981; David M. O'Brien, *Storm Center: The Supreme Court in American Politics*, 7th ed., 2005; Jeffrey Rosen, *The Supreme Court: The Personalities and the Rivalries That Defined America*, 2007; Idem, *The Most Democratic Branch: How the Courts Serve America*, 2006; Christopher Tomlins, ed., *The United States Supreme Court: The Pursuit of Justice*, 2005; Jeffrey Toobin, *The Nine: Inside the Secret World of the Supreme Court*, 2007.

WILLIAMJAMES HULL HOFFER

tariffs and politics

From the Colonial Period to the Civil War

The tariff bridges economics and politics. As a tax on imports, it juggles local, sectional, national, and international agendas; it divides and subdivides political parties; it conflates profit with policy; it blurs the public and private spheres; it tests political and economic theory. Tariff politics reflects the opportunities and challenges of each historic era, thereby mirroring both national aspirations and national anxieties. Because tariffs have never been proven to either promote or retard economic development, they provide a fascinating window on America's political struggles.

Trade has been central to American political discourse since colonial times. Exchange between Europeans and Native Americans determined the survival of the original settlements and their development as trading posts. Mercantilism, as embodied in England's Navigation Acts, defined the colonies as sources of raw materials and markets for finished goods. While fulfilling this commercial mandate, the colonies also pursued economic self-sufficiency and, consequently, resented economic restrictions.

Eager to raise revenue after the Seven Years' War, which ended in 1763, but stung by colonial protests against direct taxes like the Stamp Act, England turned to indirect taxes via modest tariffs. Low import duties on slaves and on luxuries such as sugar and tea were accompanied by low export duties on raw materials such as wood and wool. Minimal as they were, these taxes offended the colonists. In practice and in principle, they highlighted the disadvantages of political and economic imperialism.

Colonial opposition to taxation without representation created common cause against trade laws. From the 1764 Sugar Act to the 1774 Coercive Acts (which the colonists called the Intolerable Acts), protests mounted and economic policy became markedly political. Petitions to Parliament, boycotts, riots, and tea parties consolidated colonial opposition. Significantly, the First Continental Congress refused to import, export, or consume British goods. Trade clarified the case for revolution.

After the Revolution, the states acquired authority over import and export duties. This decentralized approach reflected the spirit of the 1781 Articles of Confederation, replete with its weaknesses. As a result, the Constitutional Convention of 1787 revisited the issue. Recognizing the need for better coordination and more revenue, the Founding Fathers took tariff-making powers away from the states and gave them to the nation. The tariff issue was so important that it comprised the first and third of the enumerated powers of Congress. Control over commerce was critical to redefining the political power of the central government, and it was no accident that George Washington wore homespun at his inauguration.

Immediately, tariff policy became tariff politics. The first act of Congress was the Tariff of 1789, a revenue-raising measure providing minimal protection to domestic industries with an average duty of 8.5 percent. Engineered through Congress by James Madison, it struck a compromise between nascent northern manufacturing interests, southern agricultural interests, and northern commercial interests. The heated debate over duties on goods and foreign ships was the first open sectional confrontation in the newly united nation and the first step toward party conflict.

Treasury Secretary Alexander Hamilton crystallized the issues with an ambitious four-point program for economic growth, stability, and independence. His 1791 *Report on Manufactures* advocated using the tariff to promote industrial development by protecting infant industries against competing foreign manufacturers. Hamilton's vision of a mixed economy bolstered by centralized power produced the Federalist Party. By contrast, James Madison and Thomas Jefferson feared federal power and the use, or abuse, of tariffs to shape the economy. They drew upon classical free-trade theory, even though they did not want to remove all tariff barriers.

Nonetheless, as slaveholding Southerners, they understood that taxing British manufactured imports would benefit the North at the expense of the South, which depended on England to buy the agricultural goods that fueled the plantation economy. Implicit was a broader anxiety about federal intrusion into states' rights, especially regarding slavery. For the emerging Jeffersonian Democratic-Republican Party, low tariffs for revenue meant less central government and more local autonomy. The tariff was not just a cold calculus of cash.

During the next decade, tensions with England grew over restrictions on American trade, seizure of American ships, and impressment of American sailors. President Jefferson tried to avoid armed war by engaging in a trade war marked by the 1808 Embargo Act. It failed to curtail British smuggling, but succeeded in exacerbating sectional conflict while simultaneously stimulating nationalistic fervor. By 1812 the "War Hawks" had achieved their goal and, for three years, hostilities with England trumped trade.

The combined effect of the Embargo of 1808 and the War of 1812 was to promote northern manufactures and strengthen their cry for protection. After the war, England dumped large quantities of surplus manufactured goods on the American market at low prices, thereby undercutting American-made products. Consequently, even Southerners supported higher tariffs, not only to raise much-needed revenue, but also to aid domestic manufactures in the interest of national defense. For a rare moment, unity prevailed.

The Tariff of 1824 signaled a new era of divisive tariff politics by raising duties to an average of 30 percent on a wide variety of goods. Senator Henry Clay of Kentucky defended the increases as part of an "American System" whereby domestic industry would turn raw materials and agricultural products into finished goods for sale in the home market. However, his Hamiltonian appeal to national economic integration rang hollow to southern planters and northern shippers, both of whom relied on foreign trade and resented sacrificing their own economic interests to Clay's political ambitions.

Pre–Civil War tariff politics bordered on the absurd when, in 1828, low-tariff advocates supported high duties in order to pit interest against interest and defeat pending tariff legislation. Instead, the bill passed with an average duty of 45 percent, backed by an odd coalition of bedfellows willing to accept protection in any form. They were led by Senator Daniel Webster of Massachusetts, whose new support for protection reflected the rise of manufacturing in his state. The aborted scheme is often viewed by historians as a political ploy for Andrew Jackson's election, that is, less for the promotion of manufactures than for "the manufacture of a President of the United States."

The resulting tariff was so inconsistent and so extreme that it was called the "Tariff of Abominations," the first of several emotional labels for supposedly dull, dry tariff bills. It inspired John C. Calhoun, formerly a senator but now Andrew Jackson's vice president, to anonymously write the *South Carolina Exposition and Protest*, based on Jefferson's 1798 claim that states could nullify an act of Congress considered inimical to the general welfare. Nullification moved from theory into practice after Congress passed another tariff in 1832 reducing some rates but raising others. Becoming the first vice president to resign, Calhoun returned to South Carolina and was reelected senator to speak for the South.

A national crisis ensued. Set against the backdrop of rising abolitionist sentiment, the tariff became a test case for states' rights. At Calhoun's urging, South Carolina declared the 1828 and 1832 tariffs null and refused to collect tariff duties. Much to everyone's surprise, President Jackson, a southern slaveholder himself, responded with a Nullification Proclamation that affirmed the supremacy of national law, dismissed nullification as unconstitutional, and resolved to resist South Carolina by force if necessary. Conflict was averted in 1833, when Clay negotiated and

Calhoun accepted a compromise that would reduce tariff duties to 20 percent by 1842. The episode underlined the importance of the tariff to presidential politics, sectional antagonism, and American political theory. No wonder it was considered a prelude to Civil War.

The tariff issue continued to fester. In 1842 Congress restored so many duties that Southerners dubbed the new act the "Black Tariff." However, prosperity and surplus revenues justified tariff rates as low as 23 percent in 1846. They remained low until the depression of 1857–60 revived the cry for protection. Although the tariff was not the primary cause of the Civil War, it certainly exacerbated sectionalism. Indeed, with the South out of Congress and wartime expenses mounting, northern legislators systematically raised customs duties in every session, reaching an average of 35 percent by 1865. After the war, Republicans resisted tariff revision despite the reduced need for revenue. The result was conflict over priorities in an era of rapid economic change.

From the Industrial Revolution to the New Deal

The tariff was intensely controversial in the Gilded Age. At issue was the impact of industrialization on prices and wages, markets, and monopolies. Whereas Republicans promoted protection in terms of prosperity and patriotism, most Democrats attacked tariffs as tools of greed and exploitation. Protectionist Democrats complicated matters by derailing their party's efforts to reform the tariff. Lobbyists worked both sides of the aisle.

From the Liberal Republican movement of 1872 through Grover Cleveland's two presidencies, tariff reformers criticized the manipulation of public policy for private profit. They ridiculed the practice of protecting "infant industries" that were really trusts, protested against the influx of foreign "pauper labor," and cited the government's surplus revenue as proof that tariffs were excessive. In 1887 Cleveland called protection an "indefensible extortion and a culpable betrayal of American fairness and justice." During the Gilded Age, the tariff reflected the pitfalls as well as the possibilities of prosperity and progress.

Responding to criticism, Republicans created the 1882 Tariff Commission, which acknowledged the need for reform. However, the Tariff of 1883 made no reforms and was so inconsistent that it was dubbed the "Mongrel Tariff." The presidential election of 1888 was the only one in U.S. history to revolve around the tariff question, which became the vehicle for assessing the impact of industrialism on American life. In the end, the low-tariff Democrats were outmaneuvered and outspent by the high-tariff Republicans. Benjamin Harrison's Electoral College victory over Grover Cleveland, who won the popular vote, begat the 1890 McKinley Tariff, named after its author, the archprotectionist senator from Ohio, William McKinley. The new bill raised rates to an average of 49 percent. However, anger over the resulting rise in consumer prices cost the Republicans the election of 1892.

With Democrats back in control and Cleveland back in the White House, the 1894 Wilson-Gorman Tariff slightly reduced customs duties. Three years later, when the Republicans regained power and William McKinley became president, tariff duties rose again. Levying an average duty of 52 percent, the 1897 Dingley Tariff set the highest rates thus far in U.S. history and, due to 14 years of Republican dominance, lasted the longest. Meanwhile, imperialism provided new resources and new markets for economic expansion.

Concerns about rising prices and gigantic trusts compounded by panics in 1904 and 1907 revived opposition to tariffs during the Progressive Era. In 1909 midwestern insurgent Republicans, led by Wisconsin's Robert M. La Follette, waged a bitter Senate fight against protection. They failed, but the tariff was hotly contested during the election of 1912. Pressured by Democratic tariff reformer Woodrow Wilson, Congress reduced duties to 26 percent, the lowest levels since the Civil War. A new income tax offset the lost revenue. The low 1913 Underwood Tariff survived nine years only to be eviscerated in 1922, when the high Fordney-McCumber Tariff raised average duties back up to 33 percent. Ironically, World War I revived economic nationalism just as the United States was expanding its international role.

The 1930s marked a turning point in American tariff politics. At first, protectionism prevailed when, epitomizing the influence of pressure groups on tariff policy, the 1930 Smoot-Hawley Tariff raised average rates higher than ever, to 52.8 percent. But after other nations responded with retaliatory tariffs, and a worldwide depression devastated international trade, Smoot-Hawley became (and remains) a synonym for disaster. Change came under the Democratic administration of President Franklin D. Roosevelt and his secretary of state, former Tennessee congressman Cordell Hull, who embraced the Wilsonian belief that international trade would further world peace.

Building on aspects of the 1890, 1909, and 1922 tariffs, the president was authorized to negotiate reciprocal trade agreements without the approval of Congress. Republicans opposed this expansion of executive power, but the bill passed in 1934 by a strict party-line vote. Dominated by the State Department until 1962, when Congress shifted power to the Commerce Department, tariffs were gradually reduced by 80 percent. As presidential control over trade steadily expanded, tariff policy making became more administrative than legislative, defined less by politicians than by nonpartisan experts in the U.S. Tariff Commission, created in 1916, and by a U.S. trade representative, created in 1962 within the executive branch.

The Modern Era

Reflecting the nation's superpower status after World War II, U.S. tariff policy was increasingly shaped by foreign policy. Of course, tariffs always had international implications, but they were primarily determined by domestic economic priorities. Now tariffs also became a factor of cold war politics—a bulwark against the spread of communism and a tool for rebuilding Europe and Japan. The favorable balance of trade and a burgeoning economy bolstered America's confidence that it could lead the world in liberalizing trade without losing control over its own economic future.

This international commitment was evident when the 1947 General Agreement on Tariffs and Trade (GATT) was forged in Geneva, Switzerland, not in Washington, D.C. Despite continuing controversy over the president's new powers, Congress passed a series of Trade Expansion Acts from the 1940s through the 1960s. In 1974 the U.S. Tariff Commission was renamed the U.S. International Trade Commission (ITC). By that time, average tariff rates were a mere 8.5 percent, returning to where they began in 1789 and moving toward the virtual free trade level of 3 percent by 2008.

Yet, from the start, the supposedly solid support for free trade was qualified. Market realities demanded escape clauses for retaliating against countries that established non-tariff barriers (NTBs) to trade and quotas or antidumping laws for restricting imports that threatened domestic industries. Unable to prevent trade-induced unemployment, in 1962 Congress began aiding affected workers to adjust and retrain; it also helped affected businesses retool.

By the 1970s, America's international status was no longer secure. The Vietnam War, an oil crisis, inflation, a recession, and a trade deficit undermined the nation's self-confidence. As Japanese goods displaced American goods and the "steel belt" became the "rust belt," protectionism spread. Congress set more limits on executive power over trade agreements, assumed more control of the Tariff Commission, and paid more attention to NTBs, such as foreign import quotas.

Traditional party positions on trade had largely been reversed. Although many Democrats remained committed to international trade, others called for protection against low-wage foreign labor and low-cost foreign products. Facing competition not only from Japan, but also from other East Asian countries and Europe, U.S. labor unions along with the textile, oil, chemical, and steel industries decided that trade liberalization was a "Gattastrophe."

Meanwhile, the traditionally protectionist Republican Party advocated freer trade as big farmers and major corporations sought wider access to world markets. Of course, neither party was unified on trade policy because lobbying and local economic interests cut across party lines. Moreover, trade policies that might benefit one economic interest, like domestic steel producers or sugar growers, might hurt another interest, like domestic steel and sugar users. As always, political party divisions on trade were complex and porous.

Trying to balance these conflicting concerns, advocates of the proposed North American Free Trade Agreement (NAFTA) with Canada and Mexico claimed that profits made by companies expanding abroad would benefit the United States through inexpensive imported consumer goods and domestic jobs created by foreign demand for American products. Although NAFTA was the child of Republican presidents Ronald Reagan and George H. W. Bush, it was endorsed by Bill Clinton, a centrist New Democrat. Clinton's 1992 campaign slogan, "It's the economy, stupid," captured the connection between politics and pocketbooks.

In the 1992 presidential election, it was maverick businessman turned independent candidate Ross Perot who warned against exporting American jobs through generous trade agreements that continued to give concessions abroad without providing protection at home. Ultimately, NAFTA was ratified in 1993 due to support from Republicans and southern Democrats. After a Republican midterm electoral sweep in 1994, Congress approved the GATT, which created the World Trade Organization (WTO).

However, Clinton himself argued with Japan over trade issues, and concerns about trade policy led Congress to rescind the president's fast-track authority. First granted in 1975, this compelled Congress to approve or disapprove trade agreements without changes within 90 days of submission. Although this power was restored in 2002, it was revoked again in 2007, a testimony to the ongoing tensions between the legislative and executive branches over trade policy.

In the early twenty-first century, many Americans still believed that the nation could withstand foreign competition and benefit from freer trade. They were encouraged by a steadily growing gross national product, vast world markets, record corporate profits, cheap consumer goods, and a net gain of jobs. President George W. Bush faced only weak opposition in Congress when he signed free trade agreements with Australia, South Korea, and countries in South and Central America.

At the same time, concerns were growing about trade deficits, de-industrialization, income polarization, and illegal immigration, not to mention the outsourcing of both blue- and white-collar jobs. Critics complained about rules that protected American pharmaceutical companies against importation of cheaper foreign medicines but did not protect American consumers against importation of dangerous toys and poisonous pet food. Anger mounted at countries that sent limitless exports to the United States but that limited imports from the United States. Farmers guarded their government subsidies. Support spread for "fair trade," or "managed trade," to establish international labor, safety, and environmental standards. The multilateralism that

had shaped the global economy and dominated U.S. trade policy for 60 years was being reassessed.

Globalization redefined the relationship between producer and consumer, nationalism and internationalism, short- and long-term benefits. Changes in public policy, compounded by revolutions in transportation and communication, created an unprecedented level of international commercial integration. The situation was complicated by the fact that U.S. companies built factories abroad or used foreign parts and foreign raw materials, while foreigners built factories in the United States and invested in the American economy. Domestic and foreign interests were increasingly intertwined. On the one hand, globalization meant economic distress for segments of America's middle and working classes. On the other hand, it presented economic opportunity for other segments of America's agricultural, manufacturing, technology, and financial service interests. With both sides asking the government for support, trade was as personal and as political as ever.

Throughout U.S. history, the debate over international economic exchange has been controversial. Time and again, the issues go beyond profits, prices, wages, and markets to include matters of state: the role of government in the economy, constitutional powers, sectional interests, party politics, and foreign policy. In this sense, Bill Clinton was only half right. It's not simply the economy; it's the political economy, stupid.

See also economy and politics; foreign policy and domestic politics; taxation.

FURTHER READING. I. M. Destler, *American Trade Politics*, 1992; John M. Dobson, *Two Centuries of Tariffs: The Background and Emergence of the U.S. International Trade Commission*, 1976; Alfred E. Eckes Jr, *Opening America's Markets: U. S. Foreign Trade Policy since 1776*, 1995; Douglas A. Irwin, *Free Trade under Fire*, 2002; Edward S. Kaplan, *American Trade Policy, 1923–1995*, 1996; Diane B. Kunz, *Butter and Guns: America's Cold War Economic Diplomacy*, 1997; Sidney Ratner, *The Tariff in American History*, 1972; Edward Stanwood, *American Tariff Controversies in the Nineteenth Century*, 1903; Frank W. Taussig, *The Tariff History of the United States*, 1892, reprint, 1931.

JOANNE REITANO

taxation to 1913

Taxation before 1913 was very different from what it has been ever since. The obvious change came about with ratification of the Sixteenth Amendment, which sanctioned the federal income tax ("The Congress shall have power to lay and collect taxes on incomes, from whatever source derived. . . ."), whose implications unfolded over the ensuing decades. Before then, two features of the tax system were quite different: (1) the federal government relied overwhelmingly on the tariff, a tax on imports, instead of its current mix of income taxes, Social Security taxes, and so on; and (2) states and especially local governments probably did most of the taxing throughout the period. Nineteenth-century figures are sketchy, but by 1913, the states and the nation's many local governments (counties, cities, townships, school districts, etc.) levied two-thirds of all U.S. taxes. By the late twentieth century, the federal government was levying two-thirds.

It is ironic that economic historians have had to struggle to estimate the size of local tax burdens in precisely the period when they were most important. The result, however, is that we know much more about how taxes were enacted, how they worked, and how people argued about them than about how much money they raised.

Federal Taxes

Before the adoption of the Constitution, the national government could not tax. Under Article VIII of the Articles of Confederation, Congress had to finance the Revolutionary War by asking the states to tax. This arrangement, known as the "requisition" system, was disastrous. One problem was that the states simply could not raise enough money through their tax systems, which had been designed in the colonial era, when Britain paid most defense costs. Another problem was the unrealistic rule in the articles for distributing taxes among the states. Article VIII directed Congress to set a quota for each state according to the value of its real estate ("land and the buildings and improvements thereon"). Unable to find a practical way to assess real estate, Congress ignored this rule and set arbitrary quotas based loosely on population (there was no census either). Meanwhile, Congress tried and failed to amend Article VIII to authorize an "impost," a tax on imports that would have been far more practical. Shays's Rebellion (1786), caused in large part by a massive tax that Massachusetts imposed to pay its requisition quotas and other war debts, dramatized the inadequacy of the requisition system.

The U.S. Constitution was adopted for many reasons, but the most immediate need was to establish a national government that could tax. The framers succeeded at this, though at the cost of vague and complex language that caused long-term problems. The Constitution empowered Congress to "lay and collect taxes, duties, imposts, and excises" as long as they were "uniform throughout the United States" and not levied on exports. But in one of the main compromises to accommodate slavery—the three-fifths clause—they inserted another rule. Congress could levy "direct taxes" only if these taxes were apportioned to the states by population (counted by the three-fifths rule). This provision ignored the reality that some states were richer than others, but, remarkably, it did not generate much discussion in either the Philadelphia convention or the ensuing ratification debates. The prevailing assumption was

that "direct taxes" would be property taxes of one kind or another, but nobody seemed to think the term was important enough to define precisely.

The reason the direct tax provision drew so little attention is that the real plan was for the federal government to rely on import taxes—like the "impost" that could not be added to the Articles of Confederation. Import taxes were the easiest taxes to collect because they were paid only at ports by small groups of merchants, who then shifted the costs silently into consumer prices. This plan was successful. From the adoption of the Constitution until the War of 1812, import taxes always raised at least 85 percent of federal tax revenue. From 1817 until the outbreak of the Civil War, they were the *only* federal taxes.

But there were complications. In the 1790s and 1810s, Congress also levied other taxes, most notoriously the 1791 whiskey excise that provoked the Whiskey Rebellion of 1794. As the wars of the French Revolution disrupted international trade and came to involve the United States (the 1798 "Quasi-War" with France, the War of 1812 with Britain), Congress levied several other excises as well as apportioned "direct" taxes on property (land, houses, and slaves). One of the excises, a tax on carriages, generated a permissive judicial interpretation of the Constitution's direct tax provision. In *Hylton v. U.S.* (1796), the Supreme Court ruled that a carriage tax was an excise that only had to be uniform rather than a direct tax that had to be apportioned.

The more important complications involved import taxes. The original impost plans were for flat 5 percent levies on almost all imported goods. In the first session of the first Congress, however, tax policy became economic policy, as the impost changed into the tariff—a tax designed not only to raise money but also to "protect" domestic manufacturing by raising the prices of competing foreign products. Protective tariffs, which the United States continued to levy until after the Great Depression of the 1930s, had several critical characteristics. First and most obviously, they subsidized domestic business by letting firms in "protected" industries raise their prices. Tariff supporters justified the subsidies by arguing that the young republic's "infant industries" should be protected against cheaper European (British) goods to promote the growth of American manufacturing. Opponents pointed to another key characteristic: protective tariffs subsidized producers at the expense of consumers, or, more precisely, of producers whose goods were not protected. This category included most American farmers. Unsurprisingly, the leading opponents of protective tariffs lived in the South and West.

Tariff politics also often became rather sordid. Not only did the producers of particular goods scramble to win high rates for their own industries, but debates usually featured intensive logrolling ("I'll vote for yours if you'll vote for mine") and, on occasion, sophisticated partisan manipulations such as high tariffs targeted key blocs of voters. One notorious example was the 1828 "tariff of abominations" that provoked the nullification crisis (1830), in which South Carolina claimed that states could nullify federal laws within their own borders. After 1828, however, the trend was tariff reduction, highlighted by the Walker tariff of 1846.

As productive as tariffs were, they could not finance anything as expensive as the Civil War. The Confederacy, for its part, could not tax imports at all once the U.S. Navy established a blockade of its ports—breached only by "runners" that were small, fast, and unlikely to tarry at custom houses. Nor could the Confederacy tax effectively in other ways. This failure, in turn, undermined its bond sales and doomed its currency to hyperinflation. The Union was a different story. Where the Confederacy raised only 5 percent of its war costs from taxes, the Union raised 20 percent, an achievement that strengthened its credit and supported the value of its "greenback" currency.

The essence of Union tax policy was for the government to try everything. There was a high tariff, a comprehensive excise program, an apportioned direct tax on real estate, and even a small progressive income tax—most interesting for its lack of confidentiality. As the *Chicago Tribune* explained, printing the returns of the richest local taxpayers, "we have been actuated by no motive to gratify a morbid curiosity, but solely by a desire to assist the Gov't in obtaining its dues. No man who has made a correct return will object to the publication, and no man who has made a false return has a right to object." Local governments also taxed to recruit soldiers and help support families in their absence.

Most federal taxes were abolished after the end of the war, though the exceptions were significant. One was the excise on whiskey, which produced an impressive scandal known as the Whiskey Ring. The ring consisted of federal collectors, distillers, and other officials in the big midwestern cities, who not only stole vast amounts of tax revenue but siphoned much of it directly into the coffers of the Republican Party. A long investigation culminated in a series of raids in 1875 that led to more than 100 convictions.

The critical holdover, however, was the high and ever more highly protective tariff. By the late nineteenth century, with tariff supporters unable to make claims about "infant industries," the case for high tariffs switched to protecting the "American standard of living" (higher wage rates). Still, the real case was partisan. Republicans used high protective tariffs to build a powerful and lasting coalition across the North, with protection appealing to many workers while the surplus revenues the tariffs produced—plowed into generous pensions for Union veterans—appealed to many farmers. The tariff so dominated the political rhetoric of Republicans and Democrats that the Populists, in their 1892 Omaha Platform, condemned "a sham battle over the tariff" intended

"to drown the outcries of a plundered people" by ignoring what they saw as the real issues.

The 1894 Wilson-Gorman Tariff Act included a small income tax. The idea was to offset some of the tariff costs that Southerners and Westerners paid disproportionately with a tax that would fall heavily on the richer Northeast. Although the Supreme Court had approved the Civil War income tax in *Springer v. U.S.* (1881), rejecting a claim that it was a direct tax that had to be apportioned to the states by population, the Court saw the 1894 version differently. In *Pollock v. Farmers' Loan and Trust Company* (1895), the justices decided that income taxes were indeed direct taxes. Since apportionment by population would have defeated the purpose of income taxation—it actually would have produced higher tax rates in poor states than rich states—the Court ruled the income tax unconstitutional. After a long campaign, the Sixteenth Amendment, adopted in 1913, authorized what would later become the quintessential federal tax.

State and Local Taxes

While the tariff was the critical federal tax before 1913, property taxes were the mainstay of state and local government. Today, American property taxes are levied almost exclusively on real estate. Before the 1910s, however, they were usually levied on both real estate and various forms of "personal property"—"tangible" items such as livestock, vehicles, jewelry, and lavish furniture; "intangible" (paper) assets such as corporate stocks and bonds; and, before the Civil War, human "property" in the form of enslaved African Americans.

By the late nineteenth century, these taxes on real and personal property were called "general property taxes." In language that was as familiar then as the language of income tax deductions and brackets is today, many state constitutions required general property taxes to be "uniform" and "universal." A general property tax was uniform if every form of taxed property was assessed the same way and taxed at the same rate, regardless of who owned it (individual or corporation). The tax was universal if it was levied on all forms of property instead of only on certain items (except a few specified exemptions). Because in practice no taxes could fulfill these mandates to the letter—no assessors could find "all" property or assess the holdings of banks and railroads the same way as those of farmers and country storekeepers—general property taxes were highly vulnerable to legal challenge, especially by wealthy taxpayers and large corporations.

But before the late nineteenth century, there was much more variation. Surveying the state tax systems in 1796, Treasury Secretary Oliver Wolcott Jr. found them "utterly discordant and irreconcileable." The main differences were between North and South. Most northern states had levied versions of the general property tax since before 1776 (or statehood in the West). Until the 1850s, however, many southern states taxed only specific items, and often in idiosyncratic if not downright primitive ways, such as levying one flat sum on each acre of land without assessing its value. Indeed, one reason Congress could not use the real estate apportionment of the Articles of Confederation was that the southern governments had never before valued real estate. The costs of the Revolutionary War prompted innovations in the South, but most were scaled back or abandoned at war's end.

The tricky aspect of early southern taxes was their handling of slaves. In the early republic, many states supplemented their property taxes with poll taxes. In the North, these taxes were highly regressive, as flat sums levied on each male adult regardless of his income or wealth. In the South, however, poll taxes were often levied on free male adults and holdings of enslaved adults of both sexes. This practice meant that southern "poll taxes" actually combined poll taxes on free men with property taxes on slaveholders. As states slashed or abolished poll taxes in the antebellum years (although some retained or later resurrected them), southern states treated slave taxes more forthrightly as property taxes.

By the 1850s, most states were taxing the value of real estate, livestock, financial assets, slaves in the South, and other items such as commercial inventories, vehicles, and jewelry. In the North, this property was included under the general rubric "all property," with the state and local governments imposing rates on each taxpayer's total. In the South, the taxed items usually were specified in detail and often with elaborate schedules of rates for particular items. After the Civil War, however, southern states replaced these systems with general property taxes like those of the North—a change small farmers experienced as massive tax hikes since the loss of the old slave tax revenue raised the rates on land, livestock, and other items.

Urban growth contributed to rising local tax burdens in the late nineteenth century, as the cities professionalized services such as police and fire protection, improved what had been jerry-rigged water and sewerage systems, took the enforcement of building codes and health regulations more seriously, and added amenities such as street lights and parks. But expanding public education probably drove much of the rise in local taxes. Some jurisdictions provided more than others—schools were better and more plentiful in cities than rural areas and in the North than in the South. These distinctions affected relative tax burdens, as local communities weighed the benefits of better services against the costs of higher taxes.

By the 1880s and 1890s, the general property tax was in crisis. While part of the problem was the high cost of local government (sometimes hiked further by political corruption), the real problem was that economic development rendered the tax obsolete.

Because of industrialization and urbanization, much if not most of the nation's wealth was held in "intangible" (paper) assets that were hard for assessors to find. As a result, farmers whose property was highly visible—livestock and machinery were harder to hide than stock certificates—objected that urban elites were not paying their share. In fact, however, as urban and rural assessors tried to protect their constituents, competitive underassessments created a chaos of often ridiculously low figures as well as widespread fraud.

Gradually, the states abolished general property taxation and, in particular, the taxation of "personal property." In the new systems, adopted in the early twentieth century, states often relied on income, corporation, and inheritance taxes, while local governments levied property taxes only on real estate. In the 1930s, many state and local governments added sales taxes, producing the system of state and local taxation that is familiar today.

See also economy and politics; tariffs and politics; taxation since 1913.

FURTHER READING. Richard Franklin Bensel, *The Political Economy of American Industrialization, 1877–1900*, 2000; W. Elliott Brownlee, *Federal Taxation in America: A Short History*, 2004; Davis Rich Dewey, *Financial History of the United States*, 12th ed., 1939; Max M. Edling, *A Revolution in Favor of Government: Origins of the U.S. Constitution and the Making of the American State*, 2003; Robin L. Einhorn, *American Taxation, American Slavery*, 2006; E.R.A. Seligman, *Essays in Taxation*, 10th ed., 1925; F. W. Taussig, *The Tariff History of the United States*, 8th ed., 1931; J. Mills Thornton, III, "Fiscal Policy and the Failure of Radical Reconstruction in the Lower South," In *Region, Race, and Reconstruction: Essays in Honor of C. Vann Woodward*, edited by J. Morgan Kousser and James M. McPherson, 349–94, 1982; John Joseph Wallis, "American Government Finance in the Long Run: 1790–1990," *Journal of Economic Perspectives* 14 (2000), 61–82; C. K. Yearley, *The Money Machines: The Breakdown and Reform of Governmental and Party Finance in the North, 1860–1920*, 1970.

ROBIN L. EINHORN

taxation since 1913

Introduction of Income Taxation

The modern era of taxation in the United States began in 1913 with the introduction of the nation's first permanent income tax. During the twentieth century, that tax would become the most important fiscal vehicle for (1) expanding government, (2) centralizing government at the federal level, (3) regulating the economy, and (4) redistributing the costs of government according to the principle of "ability to pay."

The Sixteenth Amendment, which expressly permitted federal income taxation, was ratified in 1913.

Later that year, Congress included an income tax within the Underwood-Simmons Tariff legislation. Bipartisan support for income taxation was broad, but the income tax measure enacted was only modest. Virtually none of the major proponents of income taxation, including President Woodrow Wilson, believed that the income tax would become a major, let alone the dominant, permanent source of revenue within the federal tax system. The Republicans who supported income taxation adhered to protectionist orthodoxy and wanted to retain tariffs (taxes on imports) and "sin taxes" (taxes on alcoholic beverages and tobacco) at the heart of federal taxation. And the Democratic drafters of the 1913 legislation regarded the revenue capacity of the tax as far less important than its ability to advance economic justice, through both redistribution of the tax burden and attacking monopoly power. In the first several years of the income tax, only the wealthiest 2 percent of American households paid income taxes.

World War I

The intervention of the United States in World War I, however, transformed the income tax. The disruption of international trade during the war meant that the United States had to reduce its reliance on customs duties. The massive financial scale of the American war effort required the federal government to find new taxes that did far more than just replace customs revenues.

Options were limited. Sin tax revenues were large, accounting for nearly half of all federal tax revenues. But they were not nearly large enough, and expanding the systems for assessing and collecting sin taxes into a system for imposing general taxes on consumption was impossible in the brief period of time (roughly a year and a half) the United States was at war. It was also impossible to expand the fledgling income tax into a system for collecting large revenues from middle- and low-income Americans by setting personal exemptions at low levels and levying high rates on wages and salaries. The federal government lacked the capacity to assess and collect taxes on the Americans—two-thirds of the labor force—who worked on farms or in small, usually unincorporated, nonfarm businesses. During World War I, the federal government did not know who these people were and had no means of readily discovering their identities. The only taxes that raised huge revenues from these Americans were property taxes, and co-opting property taxation for wartime finance faced daunting problems: the interest of states and localities in maintaining control over their powerful revenue engine; the constitutional requirement that a direct tax be allocated to the states on the basis of population; and the extreme difficulty of reconciling the enormous variations in property assessments across the nation. The impossibility of developing mass-based systems of consumption, income, or property taxation meant that the federal government had only one option—taxing the incomes of wealthy individuals and corporations. This approach allowed the Treasury and Congress to conscript corporations in the army of tax assessors. With corporate data in hand, the Treasury could easily assess the incomes of many of the wealthiest individuals and also tax corporate profits. Within this category of taxation, the Wilson administration had many options and chose a "soak-the-rich" approach, imposing extremely progressive taxes on both corporate and individual incomes. This approach made the American tax system the most progressive in the industrial world. Under the Revenue Act of 1918, the progressive rates of excess-profits taxation ranged from 30 to 65 percent on profits above a "normal" rate of return, which a board of Treasury experts determined. (In contrast, Great Britain took the more conservative approach of taxing profits that were above prewar levels.) Most of the remaining revenue came from a highly progressive income tax on the wealthiest individuals. In 1918 the wealthiest 1 percent of households paid marginal tax rates that ranged from 15 to 77 percent.

The Wilson administration and Congress hoped that such taxes would become a permanent part of the revenue system. They intended the excess-profits tax to act, in the words of one Treasury staffer, "as a check upon monopolies or trusts earning exorbitant profits." The excess-profits tax accounted for about two-thirds of all federal tax revenues during the war, enabling the federal government to cover roughly 30 percent of wartime expenditures through taxes—a larger share of total revenues than in any of the other combatant nations.

The wartime tax program of the Wilson administration, however, contributed to its political downfall. During the congressional elections of 1918, the investment banking community and the leaders of the Republican Party launched an assault, calling for major tax relief from the problem of "bracket creep" (inflation pushing people into higher tax brackets). The Republicans captured both houses of Congress and set the stage for the victory of Warren G. Harding and the "return to normalcy" in the presidential election of 1920. Repeal of the excess-profits tax and reduction of the top marginal rate on individual income to 58 percent followed in 1921.

The progressive income tax itself survived, however. It did so, in part, because both Republicans and Democrats valued the capacity of the tax to fund new programs such as the building of highways. But it was also because Woodrow Wilson, through his handling of wartime finance, had reinforced and enhanced Americans' belief in the justice of taxing according to "ability to pay." In deference to the power of this ideal and to protect the important new source of revenue for domestic programs, Andrew Mellon, the influential secretary of the treasury from 1921 to 1932, cast his support behind preservation of the progressive income tax.

The Great Depression and New Deal

The Great Depression created pressures on the federal government to resume expansion of its taxing capacity and the centralization of fiscal power at the national level. During the early, and most severe, period of the Depression, the federal government reacted to weak tax revenues with major increases in tax rates. Support for them was, to a significant extent, bipartisan. In 1932 Republican president Herbert Hoover initiated the largest peacetime tax increases in the nation's history to close the federal budget deficit, reduce upward pressure on interest rates, and thus stimulate economic recovery. The Revenue Act of 1932 raised personal and corporate income tax rates across the board and restored the top marginal rate to nearly World War I levels. In 1933 Hoover's Democratic successor, Franklin D. Roosevelt, effectively raised consumption taxes through the repeal of Prohibition. The old sin tax on alcoholic beverages, which had remained in the tax code, provided revenue for federal coffers and helped fund the relief and recovery programs of the early New Deal.

As the New Deal continued, Roosevelt turned increasingly to tax reform, which Republicans generally resisted. In 1935 the growing "Thunder on the Left," particularly Huey Long's Share Our Wealth movement, pushed Roosevelt into proposing a tax program that included a graduated tax on corporations and an increase in the maximum income tax rate on individuals. FDR justified this program in terms of both its equity and its ability to liberate the energies of individuals and small corporations, thereby advancing recovery. Congress gave Roosevelt most of what he wanted, including an undistributed profits tax—a graduated tax on the profits that corporations did not distribute to their stockholders. More than any other New Deal measure, this tax aroused hostility from large corporations, and they retaliated by entering the political arena in search of support outside the business community. In 1938 Roosevelt was vulnerable, weakened by the recession of 1937–38 and his disastrous fight to restructure the Supreme Court. A coalition of Republicans and conservative Democrats repealed the tax on undistributed profits.

In 1935 Roosevelt's reform agenda led to another new tax, a payroll tax shared equally between employers and employees to fund the Old Age and Survivors Insurance Program under the new Social Security system. The payroll tax was regressive, although less regressive than the consumption taxes that European governments typically used to finance social welfare expenditures. The incongruity between this regressive initiative and Roosevelt's reforms of income taxation might suggest that he was little more than a cynical manipulator of the powerful symbolism of taxation. But he conceived of Social Security as an insurance system. In his mind, taxpayers received the benefits for which they had paid. Roosevelt's concept was shared by much of the American public, and it lent the payroll tax a popularity that

enabled Roosevelt and Congress to expand it significantly in 1939.

During the 1930s, state and local governments also increased taxes to make up for a weakening tax base and finance a growing demand for welfare services. Local governments continued to rely primarily on property taxes, and state governments generally adopted or expanded sales taxes and taxes designed to make users of automobiles and trucks pay the cost of highways. Increasing these taxes offset to some degree the growing progressiveness of the federal tax system, but federal tax revenues grew much more rapidly than those at the state and local levels and continued to do so during World War II. By 1950 state and local tax revenues constituted only 31 percent of the nation's total tax revenues, compared with 71 percent in 1913, at the beginning of the modern tax era.

World War II

World War II created an opening for Roosevelt to continue reform in the realm of taxation. Roosevelt and his military and financial planners assumed that the cost of fighting World War II would be even greater than that of World War I, and they wanted to cover an even larger share of wartime expenses with taxes in order to contain inflation. They needed a tax that would reach far more Americans than had the tax measures of World War I, particularly since Democrats in Congress were unwilling to support high levels of corporate taxation for fear of the kind of backlash that had crushed the Wilson administration.

Roosevelt rejected heavy reliance on consumption taxation as too regressive and favored, instead, a broad-based income tax that would also have a highly progressive rate structure. The broad base, which had been impossible to implement earlier, was now practical because of the information-gathering capability created to collect payroll taxes for the Social Security system and because of a great expansion of corporate employment. Under the new tax system, which included mechanisms for withholding taxes, the number of individual taxpayers grew from 3.9 million in 1939 to 42.6 million in 1945, and federal income tax collections over the period leaped from $2.2 billion to $35.1 billion. In 1944 and 1945, individual income taxes accounted for roughly 40 percent of federal revenues, whereas corporate income taxes provided about a third—only half their share during World War I. And current tax revenues paid for approximately half of the costs of the war.

Mass taxation had become a central element of federal taxation. At the same time, the income tax reached its pinnacle of progressivity. By the end of the war, the marginal rate of taxation on personal income had risen to 94 percent (on dollars earned over $200,000), higher than at any other time in the history of American income taxation. The rates were high enough that, even with the broad base of taxation, in 1945 the richest 1 percent of households produced 32 percent of the revenue yield of the personal income tax.

Issues since 1945

In contrast with Wilson's tax program of World War I, Roosevelt's wartime tax regime survived the war's aftermath essentially intact. This reflected a general agreement by the two major political parties on the need to maintain a large federal government and to keep the World War II revenue system as the means of financing it. Of particular political value was the fact that the new tax regime was generally able to fund the expansion of both domestic and foreign programs, including national defense and prosecution of the cold war, without requiring any legislated tax increases, thus avoiding the unpleasant task of picking losers. Both economic growth and long-term inflation, working through the expansion of the tax base, provided an elastic source of new revenues. In fact, that elasticity enabled the federal government to make periodic, substantial tax cuts.

The convergence on tax policy involved restraint by Republicans in seeking consumption taxation and an acceptance by them of greater taxation of large incomes than they had found palatable before World War II. Republican leaders recognized the political appeal of "ability to pay" and, until the 1990s, did not seriously entertain shifting to a consumption-tax system. For their part, Democrats largely abandoned taxation as an instrument to mobilize class interests. Most dramatically, they abandoned the antimonopoly rhetoric of World War I and the New Deal and adopted instead a more benign view of corporate power.

Republican and Democratic leaders also agreed that there were two major problems with high marginal rates of taxation and, at least through the presidential administration of Ronald Reagan, they often lent bipartisan support to rate reform. The first problem was that the rates, which were the most progressive within the advanced industrial nations, created economic disincentives for wealthy Americans to save and invest. The Kennedy-Johnson tax cuts in 1964 began the work of reducing the high marginal rates, and then the Reagan tax reforms (both the Economic Recovery Act of 1981 and the Tax Reform Act of 1986) continued the reductions, bringing them down to roughly 36 percent.

The second problem was that the high marginal rates tended to undermine the goal of broadening the economic base for taxation. They created incentives for taxpayers to seek "tax expenditures"—loopholes in the form of special deductions and exemptions. The "tax expenditures," in turn, created economic distortions by favoring one form of income over another, made the tax code mind-numbingly complex, and weakened the public's faith in the fairness of the income tax and government in general. The most comprehensive and successful effort to close loopholes was the Tax Reform Act of 1986.

Bipartisan agreement on tax reform broke down quickly, however. Both Republicans and Democrats abandoned any interest in ridding the tax code of tax expenditures. In fact, each party developed a list of new tax loopholes and enacted many of them into law. On the one hand, President George H. W. Bush revived the idea of preferential taxation of capital gains. On the other hand, President Bill Clinton returned to a soak-the-rich policy and, in 1993, led in significantly raising rates on the wealthiest Americans. Meanwhile, he "plumped" for numerous tax preferences for middle-class Americans. The tax cuts of President George W. Bush further increased the complexity of the tax code. One of the goals of these cuts was to advance the transformation of the progressive income tax into a system of regressive consumption taxation. Bush was not able to accomplish this, but his cuts did weaken the revenue capacity of the income tax and thereby the fiscal strength of the federal government. At the end of his administration, the tax rate in the United States (all taxes as a percentage of national income) was lower than in any other major industrial nation, except for Japan. And the surpluses in the federal budgets of the years of the Clinton administration had been replaced by huge deficits that threatened to have major consequences for the future economic health of the nation.

See also economy and politics; tariffs and politics; taxation to 1913.

FURTHER READING. W. Elliot Brownlee, *Federal Taxation in America: A Short History*, 2nd ed., 2004; Idem, ed., *Funding the Modern American State, 1941–1996*, 1996; Idem, "The Public Sector," in *The Cambridge Economic History of the United States*, vol. 3, edited by Stanley L. Engerman and Robert E. Galman, 1013–60, 2000; Martin Daunton, *Just Taxes: The Politics of Taxation in Britain, 1914–1979*, 2002; Ronald F. King, *Money, Time, and Politics: Investment Tax Subsidies and American Democracy*, 1993; Mark Leff, *The Limits of Symbolic Reform: The New Deal and Taxation*, 1984; Sidney Ratner, *Taxation and Democracy in America*, 1980; Herbert Stein, *The Fiscal Revolution in America*, 1969; Svan Steinmo, *Taxation and Democracy: Swedish, British, and American Approaches to Financing the Modern State*, 1993; C. Eugene Steuerle, *Contemporary U.S. Tax Policy*, 2004; John Witte, *The Politics and Development of the Federal Income Tax*, 1985; Julian E. Zelizer, *Taxing America: Wilbur D. Mills, Congress, and the State, 1945–1975*, 1998.

W. ELLIOT BROWNLEE

temperance

See Prohibition and temperance.

territorial government

The U.S. government has administered territories that make up almost three-quarters of the land area of the nation, and its continued possession of territories gives the United States the largest territorial area of any country in the world. The United States governed territories at its founding under the Northwest Ordinance, and it administers them at present in the Caribbean and Pacific. Spanning this vast amount of space and time, U.S. presidents, the courts, and especially the U.S. Congress established territorial governments and set territorial policies. By the same token, because of the lengthy period over which the United States has administered its territories and the size of its territorial possessions, few general rules apply to the U.S. territorial system as a whole.

Only two clauses of the U.S. Constitution discuss territories. Article IV, Section III, Clause 2, states explicitly that "The Congress shall have Power to dispose of and make all needful Rules and Regulations respecting the Territory or other Property belonging to the United States; and nothing in this Constitution shall be so construed as to Prejudice any Claims of the United States, or of any particular State." Clause 1 of Article IV, Section III touches implicitly on the territories: it allows Congress to admit new states into the Union as long as states are not created out of other states or formed by combining all or parts of other states "without the Consent of the Legislatures of the States concerned as well as of Congress." Such language assumed that the new states would be formed out of already existing U.S. territory (or property).

The United States always had territories. Since 1783, the United States had sovereignty over the Trans-Appalachian West, an area roughly double the size of the original states, inclusive of Vermont which was assumed to be part of the Union although it was not an original state. The U.S. government acquired the Trans-Appalachian West from Great Britain according to the terms of the 1783 Treaty of Paris. But the entire tract belonged solely to the U.S. government, rather than to any state or group of states, under the terms of the ratification of the Articles of Confederation. Maryland had insisted that before it would approve the articles (which had to be ratified unanimously), the states with claims on the Trans-Appalachian West (Connecticut, Virginia, North Carolina, South Carolina, and Georgia, in particular) first had to surrender those claims to the U.S. government. The states agreed, surrendering their claims over a period of years. The result was that the fledgling U.S. government now controlled the vast lands beyond the Allegheny (and Appalachian) Mountains and up to the banks of the Mississippi River, as the "public domain."

The Constitution said little about the territory of the United States, and the Trans-Appalachian West attracted little discussion in Philadelphia, because Congress had already taken action. Under the Articles of Confederation and Perpetual Union, Congress had passed the Land Ordinance of 1785, which established a grid system for surveying the lands of the public domain, held that government land was to be sold at auction for no less that one dollar an acre, and mandated that the land be sold either in townships of 36 square miles for groups of settlers or in single sections (640 acres) for individual buyers. More significantly, during that same summer in Philadelphia, Congress, under the Articles of Confederation, passed the Northwest Ordinance on July 8, 1787, for the purpose of establishing territorial government in the area north and west of the Ohio River.

The Northwest Ordinance and Its Legacy

The purpose of both the Land Ordinance and the Northwest Ordinance was for the United States to develop the vast public domain through policies that would encourage settlement and then political incorporation into the Union through the formation of territorial governments. The U.S. government would thus be able to transform what white European Americans saw as unproductive and unpopulated wilderness into economically productive and politically contributing regions of an expanded republic. But the territories were to be under the authority of the federal government until they were ready for statehood.

Thomas Jefferson, James Monroe, and Nathan Dane drafted the Northwest Ordinance with this premise in mind: the Northwest Territory was to be administered "for the purpose of the temporary government." Congress could then decide "at as early periods as may be consistent with the general interest" to admit the territories as states, annexed on an "equal footing" with the existing states of the Union. The Northwest Ordinance was to be a covenant between the European Americans who had emigrated beyond the existing several states proper and those who still lived in those states. The founders assumed that the persons in the Northwest Territory were other European Americans, suitable for eventual citizenship in one of the states of the Union.

The Northwest Ordinance explicitly stated that its first four articles were "articles of compact, between the original states and the people and states of the said territory." Articles I and II, foreshadowing the Bill of Rights, protected the civil liberties of territorial residents by guaranteeing the free expression of religion, the rights to habeas corpus and trial by jury, the prohibition of cruel and unusual punishment, the unlawful deprivation of property, and infringements on contracts.

James Madison, George Mason, and other founders meeting in the summer of 1787 in Philadelphia recognized that they could not restrict European Americans from emigrating farther westward and deeper into the South. Rather than trying to restrict Americans from moving farther west and south, and rather than risking alienating their fellow Americans from the newly formed United States—and possibly inciting them to affiliate with Britain or Spain, instead—the founders sought to induce their fellow Americans to stay within the United States by becoming residents of newly formed territories that over time could become states within the Union.

The Northwest Ordinance thus set the terms for the temporary administration and government of the old Northwest until such time that the territories had "grown up" enough to become states. It divided the area north and west of the Ohio River into administration districts, each of which had to proceed through a three-stage process before becoming a state. The first stage was the creation of a district government under Congress's sole authority, wielded through an appointed governor, a secretary, and three judges (after 1789, when Congress, acting under the new U.S. Constitution, "repassed" the Northwest Ordinance and stipulated that the U.S. president was to make the appointments). The second stage, reached once the district had 5,000 adult white male inhabitants, consisted of the establishment of a territorial government composed of a locally elected legislature, a governing council, and three judges. All elected officers also had to fulfill minimum property requirements. The governor had near-total power; he had absolute veto power over the legislature and could convene or dismiss the legislature at will. The third stage was achieved once the territory had achieved a recommended population of 60,000 persons (*not* an absolute requirement per the terms of the Northwest Ordinance) and once it had set up a republican government under a written constitution. The organized territory could then petition Congress for statehood.

The Northwest Ordinance acquired near-constitutional status, despite its application only to the old Northwest. There were several reasons for its great legacy. The drafting and passage of the Northwest Ordinance and Land Ordinance preceded the drafting and ratification of the Constitution, so by implication, the Constitution did not need to address the matters of the territories or political expansion of the United States in any detail. In addition, rules about how the public domain was to be disposed and settled carried immense stakes for more than a few of the founders, who had invested heavily in the public lands—whether individually, or indirectly by investing in land companies. The land issue was highly contentious and since it had been a sticking point with respect to the states' approval of the Articles of Confederation, the founders were understandably reluctant to take on the topic in the Constitution. Instead, they could leave decisions on the public domain and the territories for future Congresses, presidents, and judges to settle.

The principal reason for the lasting impact of the Northwest Ordinance, though, was the immensity of subsequent U.S. expansion; the founders scarcely envisioned the geographic scope that the nation would eventually encompass. With the Louisiana Purchase of 1803, the acquisition of West Florida (1811) and East Florida (1819), the 1846 Oregon Cession, the 1848 Mexican Cession, the 1867 purchase of Alaska,

and other additions, the total area of the U.S. acquisitions reached 1.2 billion acres.

It remained for Congress to divide the new tranches of public domain into districts and territories, decide on territorial policies, and annex them as states—if often with different borders than when the territories were first drawn up. Congress established 74 separate territories of different boundaries and duration, eventually resulting in the creation of 31 states. Neither could the founders have imagined that the United States would possess territories spanning continental North America and reaching into the Caribbean Sea (Puerto Rico, the U.S. Virgin Islands) and Pacific Ocean (Guam, the Philippines, Hawai'i, American Samoa, and the Northern Marianas). Nor could the founders have known that territorial acquisitions would continue from 1787 (with the establishment of the Northwest Territory) until 1975 (with the addition of the Northern Marianas), and that the United States, 230 years after the Declaration of Independence, would still have five territories in its possession.

The precedent set by the Northwest Ordinance thus applied not only to the five states created from the Northwest Territory but served as the template for the addition of the dozens of other territories forged out of the new areas periodically acquired by the U.S. government. With the Constitution providing little direction for the government of territories, the processes specified in the Northwest Ordinance continued to be applied throughout the nineteenth century and into the twentieth, as the new U.S. territories transitioned into states. The United States grew from 16 states in 1800 to 23 states in 1820, 26 states in 1840, 33 states in 1860, 38 states in 1880, 45 states in 1900, and 48 states in 1920. The last two states, Alaska and Hawai'i, were added in 1959.

The Insular Territories

The historical trajectory of U.S. territorial development was disrupted after the Spanish-American War. None of the territories the United States acquired after 1898, except Hawai'i, were later annexed as states, nor did the islands acquired in 1898 and 1899 (Puerto Rico, Guam, the Philippines, and American Samoa) or in the twentieth century (the U.S. Virgin Islands in 1917, and the Northern Marianas, a United Nations trust territory of the Pacific Islands administered by the United States and annexed in 1975), become states. (The territories already existing in 1898—Oklahoma, New Mexico, Arizona, and Alaska—did, of course, become states). The present U.S. territories are not in a designated transition period toward statehood; they are not likely to be annexed as states in the foreseeable future, and it is highly unlikely that they will be let go to become independent states or the possessions of other powers.

Hawai'i, annexed three days after the close of the Spanish-American War, was controlled politically and dominated economically by a small white ruling class (*haoles*), a situation that none of the other new island territories shared. With its white ruling class, its value as a naval station and midoceanic port, and its sugarcane production, Hawai'i was much more acceptable to the U.S. Congress as a territory—and, much later, as a state—than were the other U.S. possessions in the Caribbean and the Pacific islands, which were densely populated with nonwhite residents.

The Supreme Court ratified this new direction in U.S. territorial history. In a series of closely decided and controversial decisions known as the Insular Cases, the Court ruled that the United States could exert sovereignty over territories that were not fully incorporated into the nation and not fully protected by the provisions of the Constitution. Congress could rule these nonincorporated territories under the sweeping authority of the territory clause to "make all needful Rules and Regulations respecting the Territory or other Property belonging to the United States." Congress could also impose tariffs on trade going to and from the island territories and the states proper; it could deny territorial inhabitants trial by jury; and it could withhold other guarantees and protections of the U.S. Constitution and its amendments. It was Congress's perogative to choose whether to extend all rights and privileges guaranteed by the Constitution to its territories.

No longer did territorial governments have to be temporary or serve under transition periods until statehood, in contrast to the precedent set by the Northwest Ordinance. Instead, the United States could keep a "conquered country indefinitely, or at least until such time as the Congress deemed that it should be either released or retained," as Justice Edward Douglass White wrote in his concurring opinion in *Downes v. Bidwell*. Justice White, along with a majority of justices on the Supreme Court, U.S. presidents from William McKinley onward, most policy makers, many political and legal scholars, and most of the American public, agreed that the new island territories could be kept permanently as territories, according to the best interests of the United States, since as they saw it the inhabitants of the new territories were not suited to become members of the American polity. The Court and most Americans further agreed that the United States could divest itself of its territories, something it could not do with the states. And Congress did precisely that when it released the Philippines from territorial status in 1946.

Congress and Territorial Government

Throughout U.S. history, Congress oversaw the administration of the territories and set territorial policy. Congress governed the territories by passing "organic acts" for the establishment of territories with organized governments. The dozens of territorial organic acts took remarkably consistent form, and many of the differences among them were minor—at least until the addition of the U.S. island territories.

Each of the organic acts defined territorial boundaries; each specified that the U.S. president was to appoint the principal officers in the territory (the governor, secretary, and judges), and to set their terms and salaries; and each established court systems and judicial jurisdictions. Each also mandated that a nonvoting congressional delegate be selected for the U.S. House of Representatives, with a limited term in office (with the exception of the territories of Alaska and Hawai'i), and each either determined the location of the territory's capital city or authorized the territorial legislature or territorial governor to decide the location of the territorial seat of government (with the exception of the organic acts for the territories of Florida, Arizona, and Hawai'i).

The territorial acts specified, too, that only free white adult males could vote or hold office, with the exceptions of the territorial acts for Arkansas, Montana, Wyoming, and the island territories, including Hawai'i. The territories of Montana (1864) and Wyoming (1868) were established during and after the Civil War, however, and were the last two territories formed out of the area to become the lower 48 states (with the exception of Oklahoma, which became a state in 1907). Since the Caribbean and Pacific territories had predominantly nonwhite populations, restricting suffrage and office holding to adult white males would have made little sense.

For the most part, the territorial acts avoided mention of slavery. The Northwest Ordinance prohibited slavery, but only the territorial acts establishing Indiana Territory (1805) and the organic acts for the Philippines (1902) and for Puerto Rico (1917) also explicitly prohibited slavery. Slavery in the territories was determined, instead, by the Constitution's prohibition on importing slaves after 1808, and by the Missouri Compromise restricting slavery to areas below 36° 30′ latitude. A few of the territorial acts followed Stephen Douglas's principle of popular sovereignty and allowed the territories (e.g., New Mexico, Utah, Kansas, and Nebraska) to decide whether they would become free or slave states at the time of their annexation. In the instance of Kansas and Nebraska, though, Congress's organic act stipulated that the territories had to recognize the Fugitive Slave Act—the only territorial governments for which Congress made such an explicit requirement.

Although some territorial acts specified that the Constitution and all the laws of the United States were to apply in full, most simply assumed this to be the case. Congress explicitly extended the Constitution and the laws of the United States to the territories in its organic acts only when the territories in question—New Mexico, Utah, Colorado, Nevada, North and South Dakota, Wyoming, Puerto Rico, Hawai'i, and Alaska—were created under conditions that elicited Congress's caution: New Mexico had a majority Hispanic population; Utah was populated largely by Mormons; Colorado, Nevada, and the Dakotas were organized in 1861, during the Civil War, and Wyoming was organized in 1868, shortly afterward; Puerto Rico and Hawai'i had majority non-European-American populations; and Alaska had a miniscule white population and majority indigenous population of Inuit and other Eskimos.

In addition, the organic acts establishing the territories of the midwestern and western United States, from Oregon (established in 1848) through Oklahoma (1890), required progressively more of their new territorial governments. They mandated that land sections be reserved for schools, for instance, and that congressional funds be dedicated for the erection of public buildings such as capitols or libraries in the territorial capitals. Other acts specified the construction of prisons. In Oklahoma Territory, Congress limited the use of railroad bonds and railroad scrip, directed that homestead titles in Oklahoma be given to U.S. citizens only, and specified that any treasury appropriations be explicitly explained and defined.

When Congress established territorial governments in Hawai'i (1898), Puerto Rico (1900, and then again in 1917), Alaska (1912), and the Philippines (1916), however, it departed from an earlier practice; it did not require that the chief territorial officers be appointed by the U.S. president. Nor did Congress at the time call for these territories to assign delegates with term limits to U.S. House of Representatives. That would only come later; the Northern Marianas did not send a nonvoting territorial delegate to Congress until so approved by the 110th Congress in 2008.

Congress and Territorial Policy

Besides establishing the fundamentals of territorial government, Congress set public policies on numerous issues that affected the security, wealth, and political development of the territories. Congress set—and continues to set—territorial policy with respect to commerce (taxes, tariffs, shipping regulations, etc.), military affairs (military spending, troop levels, troop movements and positioning, the construction of forts, naval bases, and other military installations), communications (railroads, telegraphy, telephony, television, etc.), and other issues. Throughout much of U.S. territorial history, too, Congress set policies on Indian affairs, slavery, and the disposal of government lands that affected all the territories—and often the states as well.

Much of this policy making revolved around money, since Congress subsidized much territorial development. Congress funded the exploration and mapping of the territories by the U.S. Army Topographical Corps (and later the Army Corps of Engineers), which conducted surveys, mapped terrain and waterways, and planned road, canal, and railroad routes. Congress also paid for the construction of outposts for the U.S. military, given that the territories often featured desirable ports (New Orleans, San Francisco, Honolulu, San Juan, Manila Bay, Guam, Pago Pago) and provided choice sites for

the construction of forts, arsenals, and other military establishments. As the United States added to its public domain, so too did the number of forts in the territories (including camps, barracks, arsenals, and river defenses) grow—although not in every instance—from 8 in 1800, to 12 in 1820, 12 in 1830, 13 in 1845, 69 in 1870, and 57 in 1885.

Forts and naval stations also constituted favorable locations for the conduct of trade and as sites for towns and cities. Furthermore, in the Midwest, on the Great Plains, and in the Mountain West, U.S. military personnel were able to assist westward migrants (and thereby facilitate further settlement) by providing information on travel routes; assisting sick and exhausted overland travelers; furnishing crucial supplies, including guns and ammunition; and providing refuge against Indian attacks. The U.S. territories and the public domain may have constituted a buffer between existing states and hostile Indians or foreign powers, but they also promoted the economic growth of the nation.

Emigrants to the new areas could engage in farming, ranching, mining, shipping, and other productive activities. Congress encouraged these activities in several ways. For one, it enacted liberal immigration policies throughout most of the eighteenth and nineteenth centuries, thereby allowing the United States to increase its population quickly. Many of these new immigrants either settled immediately in the west or emigrated west within a generation, given the additional space and opportunities the territories afforded them. Congress also helped territorial development by providing postal service—and thus transportation—to its territories by stagecoach, and then by rail at below cost. The 21,000 total post-road miles in the United States in 1800 (inclusive of the states and the territories) doubled to 44,000 by 1815. That doubled again to 94,000 miles by 1825, and came to a total of 144,000 miles by 1845. These roads connected the large and growing number of post offices in the states and territories.

While the overwhelming majority of post offices were in the states, many were in the territories. The number of post offices in U.S. territories grew from 10 in 1800 to 177 by 1820, 374 by 1830, and 346 by 1845. In 1885 the territories had 2,519 post offices, up from 532 in 1870. As Alexis de Tocqueville expressed in amazement, "the district of Michigan" already had "940 miles of post roads," and "[t]here were already 1,938 miles of post roads through the almost entirely wild territory of Arkansas." Whereas the United States had 74 post offices per 100,000 residents in 1838, Britain had just 17, and France had just 4. For the Americans living in the territories and on the frontier, especially, mail was the "soul of commerce" and critical to their economic and political future.

Congress further subsidized the development of the territories through land grants. While the Homestead Act of 1862 may be the best-known subsidy in the western states, more important by far were the number and scale of Congress's railroad land grants during the mid-nineteenth century. These checkerboard grants, totaling more than 100 million acres, facilitated rail service in territories and across the continent; they encouraged movement and land speculation that often preceded significant human settlement or other economic activities. The railroad land grants provided faster and better transportation and communication, and promoted far more economic activity, than the railroads would have provided absent government subsidies.

The cumulative effect of Congress's policies with respect to the railroads, the post, and the military was to lay the foundation so that others—such as farmers, ranchers, miners, bankers, and businessmen—would populate the public domain, settle in the territories, form territorial governments, and eventually join the United States as full citizens.

Congress's Plenary Power

Residents of the territories had little recourse if they thought that Congress did not do enough to protect them from Indian violence, survey and administer land sales, or provide for mail service. If Congress set the key policies that affected the residents of the territories, it was not electorally accountable to them—even if they predominantly consisted of European Americans. Members of Congress were elected by voters in the states and in the congressional districts created within the states, with the result being that the residents of the territories were effectively disenfranchised, without a voice in their political and economic futures—whether such persons were white American émigrés, enslaved or free African Americans, Mormons, American Indians, Puerto Ricans, or the Chamorros of Guam and the Northern Mariana Islands.

For some territorial residents, this disenfranchisement was relatively short-lived; it took Kansas just seven years to become a state after becoming an organized territory (1854–61), and nine years for Missouri (1812–21) and Minnesota (1849–58). Other territorial residents experienced much longer periods of disenfranchisement: New Mexico, for instance, with its dominant Hispanic population, was annexed as a territory in 1850 but not annexed as a state until 1912; Utah, with its Mormon population, was annexed as a territory in 1850, but not admitted as a state until 1896 (after it renounced polygamy in 1890); and Hawai'i, with its Polynesian and Asian population, was annexed in 1898 but not admitted as a state until 1959. The island residents of Puerto Rico, Guam, and the other current U.S. territories (all formally U.S. citizens except for American Samoans) remain without effective representation in the U.S. House of Representatives, Senate, or Electoral College.

Congress has therefore been able to set territorial policy according to its interpretation of the U.S.'s "general interest." The definition of that interest depended on party alignment, sectional balance, and the dominant interests of the day. Congress created districts and territories, drew up territorial boundaries, and decided exactly when to annex territories as states as it judged most expedient. In particular, Congress could decide when to form territorial governments and when to retain territorial governments, delaying their annexation as states.

For the 31 states that had formerly been territories, it took an average of 40 years between the time the area came under U.S. sovereignty and the time Congress annexed the area as a state. Since neither the Constitution nor the Northwest Ordinance set a time frame for admitting qualified territories as states once they petitioned for annexation, Congress used its own discretion to decide when territorial governments could become states. Sometimes the lengthy struggle for statehood was a matter of ethnicity, as with the delays in admitting Oklahoma and its Indian population (1803–1907) and New Mexico and its dominant Hispanic population (1848–1912). Other times, the delays were caused by low territorial populations, as in the Dakotas (1803–1889), Arizona (1848–1912), and Alaska (1867–1959).

Another cause for delay was slavery. Congress in the antebellum United States timed the annexation of states to balance the number of free states and slave states; it accordingly admitted some states in successive years to retain the balance in the U.S. Senate, such as Illinois (1818), Alabama (1819), Maine (1820), Missouri (1821), Arkansas (1836), Michigan (1837), Florida (1845), and Iowa (1846). Congress admitted "battle born" Nevada in 1864 despite its relatively low population (30,000 to 40,000) because it anticipated support from the territory for President Lincoln, the Republican Party, and their wartime policies.

After 1898, however, questions of timing became moot, since Congress and the U.S. government decided that the island territories would remain territories; territorial governments were no longer temporary. The present-day U.S. Caribbean and Pacific territories have their own elected legislatures, executive branches, and court systems—the rulings of which may be appealed to the U.S. federal courts—but the U.S. Congress and executive branch decide trade policy (e.g., fishing and customs laws), set citizenship and immigration requirements, make telecommunications policies, and oversee criminal proceedings. The constitution of the commonwealth of Puerto Rico forbids capital punishment, for instance, yet Puerto Ricans may still be executed in mainland U.S. prisons for capital crimes committed under federal law.

Executive Influence

Congress may have had plenary power over the U.S. territories, but the executive branch was often able to exert its own considerable influence. One form such influence took was the U.S. president's appointment of territorial governors—at least in the cases of the continental "incorporated" territories—unlike the elected governors of the later island territories. The territorial governors could dominate their legislatures through their powers of absolute veto and their authority to convene or dismiss the territorial legislatures. They could decide if and when to hold censuses and referenda so as to determine when their territories could enter the second stage of territorial government, and if and when to hold elections for delegates for a constitutional convention. Furthermore, the governors had significant authority in their multiple roles as the commanders of the local militia, superintendents of Indian affairs in the territory, and overseers of the disposal of public lands (even if Congress set the overall land policy).

Territorial governors, as a general rule, were ambitious men who saw their roles as stepping-stones to higher office and better positions. Despite the governors' relatively low salaries and scarce resources, many of them were popular with their territorial residents and seen as political assets by U.S. presidents. Territorial governors served on average more than three years in office, a tenure almost as long as the average for the elected governors of the states. Among the most famous of the governors were later U.S. president William Henry Harrison (governor of the Indiana Territory), William Clark of the Lewis and Clark expedition (governor of the Missouri Territory), secretary of war and presidential candidate Lewis Cass (governor of the Michigan Territory), explorer and presidential candidate John C. Frémont (governor of the Arizona Territory), and the prominent Federalist and former president of the Continental Congress, Arthur St. Clair (governor of the Northwest Territory).

Scarce funding from Congress and general neglect of the territories, however, meant that territorial governors could not, as a practical matter, rule autocratically. Congress was notoriously stingy about funding land offices, providing sufficient resources for Indian affairs and internal improvements, and granting enough personnel to execute other governmental policies in the territories. As a result, territorial governors had to work with other key individuals and dominant economic interests in the territories, such as railroad companies, banks and other investors, mining companies, and large eastern or foreign landowners. Conversely, governors who did not work closely with the prominent individuals and dominant interests in the territories were typically ineffective (e.g., Governor St. Clair of the Northwest Territory). The logic of territorial government led to a government brokered by the established individuals, major economic actors, and other principal interests of a territory—in effect, to oligarchical territorial government.

U.S. presidents also governed the public domain through the military. Military governments were often the product and continuation of conquests, such as that of General Andrew Jackson in Florida or General Stephen W. Kearny in New Mexico and Arizona, until such time that Congress was able to pass organic acts and establish formal territorial governments. Florida was under military government from 1819 to 1822, for instance; Louisiana was under military rule from 1803 to 1804; New Mexico from 1846 to 1851; and Puerto Rico from 1898 to 1902. (The U.S. Army also managed the Panama Canal Zone while it was leased to the United States.) The U.S. Navy administered and governed Guam from 1898 until 1952, American Samoa from 1899 to 1952, and the U.S. Virgin Islands from 1917 to 1931.

The Many Systems of the Territorial System

There was no single system for the government of the territories of the United States, just as there is no one principle that orders the history of the United States' government of its territories. The brevity of the territorial clause made it inadequate for administering the public domain and led to the lasting precedent set by the Northwest Ordinance. Yet the Northwest Ordinance, for all of its long-lasting impact, did not serve as a blueprint for the government of the later island territories.

Territorial government was shaped by slavery and the Civil War, Indian policy and U.S. strategic concerns, Mormonism and disregard for other than European-American populations, economic interests and trade policies, and a host of other factors. Whereas the territories were once as close to the states as the Pennsylvania-Ohio and Georgia-Florida boundaries, they later became more distant geographically, separated by thousands of miles of land or sea. The result is that territorial government changed considerably, from the tighter control of the first U.S. territories to the less direct control of the later continental territories. The government of the Philippines, for instance, achieved increasing autonomy through the territorial acts of 1902, 1916, 1937 (when the Philippines became a "commonwealth"), and 1946 (when it achieved formal independence). Similarly, the Puerto Rican government, officially organized by the Foraker Act of April 2, 1900, was amended by the Jones Act of March 2, 1917 (which provided Puerto Rico with three separate branches of government and granted Puerto Ricans U.S. citizenship), and then Public Law 600 of July 4, 1950 (which conferred commonwealth status on Puerto Rico and enabled Puerto Ricans to draft their own constitution).

But such changes in U.S. territorial government did not depend on the Constitution, existing federal laws, or the territory in question. The ultimate control exercised by the U.S. Congress, executive branch, and Supreme Court was the by-product of other issues: economic development and industrial growth; sectoral rivalry and party politics; U.S. foreign policy interest and grand strategy; and considerations of citizenship and American identity.

See also Alaska and Hawai'i; Great Plains; Midwest; Pacific Coast; Rocky Mountain region.

FURTHER READING. John Porter Bloom, ed., *The American Territorial System*, 1973; Clarence Edwin Carter and John Porter Bloom, eds., *Territorial Papers of the United States*, 28 vols., 1934–; Everett Dick, *The Lure of the Land: A Social History of the Public Lands from the Articles of Confederation to the New Deal*, 1970; Jack Ericson Eblen, *The First and Second United States: Governors and Territorial Government, 1784–1912*, 1968; William H. Goetzmann, *Army Exploration in the American West, 1803–1863*, 1979; Carter Goodrich, *Government Promotion of American Canals and Railroads 1800–1890*, 1960; Grupo de Investigadores Puertorriquenos, *Breakthrough from Colonialism*, 2 vols., 1984; Arnold H. Leibowitz, *Defining Status: A Comprehensive Analysis of United States Territorial Relations*, 1989; Donald William Meinig, *The Shaping of America: A Geographical Perspective on 500 Years of History*, 3 vols., 1986, 1993, 1998; Peter S. Onuf, *Statehood and Union: A History of the Northwest Ordinance*, 1987; Earl S. Pomeroy, *The Territories and the United States 1861–1890*, 1969; Roy M. Robbins, *Our Landed Heritage: The Public Domain, 1776–1970*, 2nd ed., 1976; Bartholomew H. Sparrow, *The* Insular Cases *and the Emergence of American Empire*, 2006; Robert M. Utley, *Frontiersmen in Blue: The United States Army and the Indian, 1848–1865*, 1967.

BARTHOLOMEW H. SPARROW

think tanks

For more than a century, policy experts have been understood as neutral, credible, and above the rough and tumble of policy making. Progressive reformers early in the twentieth century turned to the burgeoning social sciences for salvation. Reformers believed that the new ranks of policy experts trained at universities would be capable of usurping patronage politics; experts would develop *real* solutions to the social and economic instabilities that stemmed from the Industrial Revolution. Many would be housed at think tanks, public policy research organizations with origins in the early twentieth century. American politics and society would be better informed and much improved as a result of experts' efforts.

In the early twentieth century, the training of new policy experts became a central focus of reformers, with the creation of schools for policy analysts at leading universities and of agencies within government departments that produced research and evaluations for decision makers. Scholars observed these developments and contributed to the prevailing understanding of experts in American policy making: as important background voices that bring rational, reasoned analysis to long-term policy discourse based on the best evidence available.

For much of the last century, this assessment was basically accurate; experts fulfilled these mandates. By the beginning of the twenty-first century, however, the ranks of real-life policy experts scarcely conformed to the promise of making policy choices clearer and more rigorous and decisions necessarily

more rational. These experts were based at a growing number of think tanks in Washington, D.C., and in state capitals across the country, and it was as common for think tanks to reflect clear ideologies and values as commitments to objectivity or neutrality.

Think tanks have contributed to a transformation in the role of experts in American policy making. Many experts now behave like advocates. They are not just visible but highly contentious as well. They more actively market their work than conventional views suggest; their work, in turn, often represents preformed points of view rather than even attempts at neutral, rational analysis.

These developments apply particularly to a group of identifiably ideological and mostly conservative think tanks that have emerged since the 1970s. Assessed from various angles, conservative ideology has had substantial influence over the direction of the U.S. policy agenda. Even when Democrats have regained their electoral strength, ideas about limited government, unfettered free markets, and strong heterosexual families remain influential in debates over everything from tax policy and business regulation to education reform and civil rights. Conservative ideology has been advanced by a conservative infrastructure of nonprofit organizations led by think tanks.

Early National Think Tanks

The first think tanks embodied the promise of neutral expertise. They formed as the social science disciplines of economics, sociology, and political science became established fields of inquiry and as confidence grew in the uses of expertise as a means for correcting social problems. Through the first half of the twentieth century, think tanks largely sought to identify government solutions to public problems through the detached analysis of experts. Think tank scholars wrote on topics relevant to policy makers but typically maintained a distance from political bargaining in the final stages of the policy-making process. This analytic detachment was a behavior to which researchers held fast and which fostered an effective relationship between experts and policy makers. Between 1910 and 1960, think tanks often influenced how government operated. The Brookings Institution, formed in Washington, D.C., in 1916, informed the creation of the Bureau of the Budget early in the century. The RAND Corporation, formed in Santa Monica, California, in 1948, developed systems analysis for the Department of Defense. The influence of these think tanks was significant, and their research served political purposes. But the policy process did not compel experts to become directly involved in partisan battles. Experts were mobilized by policy makers to prescribe possibilities for change.

Through the first two-thirds of the twentieth century, while think tanks at times produced politically contentious research, their input was sought and generally respected by policy makers. Although think tanks were not the only source of expertise, they were prominent, consistent, and visible providers.

Through the 1950s and 1960s, the ideas and expertise produced by think tanks generally reflected a near consensus that developed among elites about the need for government management of social and economic problems. Even when policy entrepreneurs of a conservative bent established new think tanks, they usually followed prevailing organizational norms, hiring academically trained staff and avoiding any appearance of having links to a single political party.

The Ascendance of Conservative Ideology

By the end of the 1960s, as government grew larger, the desirability and possibility of achieving social change through government programs began to be challenged. Some of the problems themselves—notably civil rights for African Americans and the Vietnam War—were highly divisive. Increasingly, critics described the government as ineffective and overextended, both at home and abroad. Combined inflation and unemployment in the 1970s—"stagflation"—contributed further to the decline of confidence in "expertly devised" government programs as well as to doubts about Keynesian principles generally.

The growth of government fueled organization among those who disapproved of it. Conservatives, by the 1970s, were united by strong opposition to communism and a shared belief that government resources were better channeled toward the nation's defense and the fight against communism than to what they viewed as bloated and ineffective domestic programs. A group of relatively small, politically conservative foundations and wealthy individuals provided support for applying these principles to public affairs. More than a dozen conservative foundations and individuals formed a nucleus of support of conservative organizations that emerged through the 1970s and 1980s, think tanks prominent among them. The explicit intent of these efforts was to destabilize the pro-government convictions that had dominated American politics since the New Deal. Avowedly ideological, contentious, and politicized ideas and expertise became tools in these endeavors.

The formation of the Heritage Foundation in 1973 was a turning point. Heritage was the first of a new breed of think tanks that combined what Kent Weaver described as "a strong policy, partisan, or ideological bent with aggressive salesmanship and an effort to influence current policy debates." The political entrepreneurs who started the Heritage Foundation sought to create a highly responsive apparatus that could react quickly to hostile proposals in Congress. By the late 1970s, as Lee Edwards observed in his history of the Heritage Foundation for its twenty-fifth anniversary, "an increasingly confident Heritage Foundation set an ambitious goal: to establish itself as a significant force in the policy-making

process and to help build a new conservative coalition that would replace the New Deal coalition which had dominated American politics and policy for half a century."

Through the 1970s and 1980s, advocacy-oriented think tanks modeled after the Heritage Foundation proliferated. Some of the older institutions, like the American Enterprise Institute, founded in 1943, adapted to become more advocacy oriented. Most were conservative, but liberal and centrist organizations emerged as well. The staffs of these organizations tended to be ideologically homogeneous, and their leaders used research as vehicles to advance their underlying ideologies.

The Influence of Think Tanks

By 2007 more than 300 think tanks were active in national and state policy making. Yet, despite their numbers, the nature and extent of their influence were in question. Although think tanks can make their work influential among experts, in practice, the orgaizations too often focus their efforts on producing commentary about urgent policy decisions rather than intervening at earlier stages of policy making.

Thus, think tanks' commentary often serves as little more than ammunition for policy makers who need public justification for their preferred policy choices. In fact, specific estimates of the financial costs of new initiatives or the benefits of legislation are much more influential during the final stages of policy debates. Research that explores the foundations of a growing problem and possibilities for addressing it are also often important, creating a context for future changes in policy.

While the recent focus by think tanks on producing media commentary has not enhanced their immediate policy influence, it has damaged the collective reputation of policy experts generally. Policy research today is frequently evaluated more in terms of its ideological content and accessibility to audiences than by the quality of its content.

The War of Ideas

Conservatives, in particular, view think tanks from the perspective that ideas and values motivate—rather than result from—research. In their view, all research is ideological insofar as ideas inform the questions that the so-called neutral researcher asks. There is no such thing as disinterested expertise. Instead, as James Allen Smith observed, there are "permanent truths, transcending human experience, [that] must guide our political life." These truths motivate research, and research is a means to a more important end: realizing the ideas that are a reflection of these truths. The staff of ideological think tanks act as agents of ideologies rather than independent analysts.

Conservatives are diverse in their viewpoints but believe, at a fundamental level, that ideas have power. And ideas not only are but *should be* more powerful than expertise. One engages in (or supports) policy research for the same reasons one supports political advocacy: because both contribute to the larger causes of shifting the terms of debate in American policy making and to amplifying the power of conservative ideas. Conservative think tanks have thus advanced a plan to privatize Social Security in the 1970s and promoted it relentlessly for 25 years, until it appeared on the "mainstream" policy agenda of President George W. Bush in 2004.

Until 2007 conservative think tanks outnumbered liberal think tanks by two to one. Research-based think tanks of no identifiable ideology—many of them the older institutions like Brookings—still reflected the greatest number of think tanks, but the ranks of ideological think tanks were growing the fastest. The aggressive advocacy of the new organizations has affected think tanks of all stripes. Most think tanks—old and new, ideological and not—have increased their investments in communications and public affairs over the past two decades. Many have switched from producing books and longer studies to producing more short policy briefs, the types of products that are easily and quickly digested by decision makers and journalists.

The race between conservative and liberal think tanks has tightened. In the wake of the 2004 election, foundations and individual donors demonstrated a fresh interest in supporting new liberal think tanks. Since then, the Center for American Progress has become a sizable presence in Washington, and other, smaller think tanks have emerged on the liberal left. In the years ahead, observers should track both the competition among ideological think tanks and the struggle between those organizations and their seemingly nonideological brethren.

See also conservatism.

FURTHER READING. Lee Edwards, *The Power of Ideas*, 1997; John W. Kingdon, *Agendas, Alternatives, and Public Policies*, 2nd ed., 1995; Harold D. Lasswell, "The Policy Orientation," in *The Policy Sciences*, edited by Daniel Lerner and Harold D. Lasswell, 3–15, 1951; Charles E. Merriam, *New Aspects of Politics*, 1970; Andrew Rich, *Think Tanks, Public Policy, and the Politics of Expertise*, 2005; James Allen Smith, "Think Tanks and the Politics of Ideas," in *The Spread of Economic Ideas*, edited by David C. Colander and A.W. Coats, 1989.

ANDREW RICH

third parties
See populism.

transnational influences on American politics
After more than 50 years in elected office and 10 years as speaker of the U.S. House of Representatives, Thomas "Tip" O'Neill encapsulated his wisdom

about government in a single phrase: "All politics is local." In the words of his biographer, John A. Farrell, O'Neill's commitment to the needs of his Boston-area constituents made him one of the paragons for the twentieth-century transformation in American society: "As a young man with a passion for politics, O'Neill had watched and learned as Franklin D. Roosevelt employed the modern science of government to blunt the devastating effects of the Depression. . . . O'Neill fought Rooseveltian battles in Massachusetts, pushing for higher state payments to the elderly, new hospitals for the sick and mentally ill, a fair employment practices act for the state's African Americans, and the grand, ambitious public works and highway projects that transformed the face of the commonwealth in the postwar years. He believed that government was the means by which a people came together to address their community's ills, to right wrongs and craft a just society." This was traditional local "boss" politics, dominated by ethnic identity, personal favors, and appeals to the "common man." This was American democracy in action.

This was also transnational politics in practice. For all the appeals to a special local set of interests, every major policy issue that O'Neill and his counterparts addressed had an international dimension. From state payments to the elderly to public works projects, U.S. government legislation reflected the influence of events, personalities, and ideas in foreign societies. The same could be said about basic policies, even at the most local level, during the prior two centuries. American politics have never existed in a national vacuum; they have always been part of a wider space that crosses the Atlantic and Pacific Oceans, as well as the Rio Grande and the northern border with Canada.

The nature and weight of transnational influences have, of course, varied over time. Particular moments in the nation's history—the 1780s, the 1840s, the 1920s, and the 1960s—witnessed a remarkable density in personal connections between prominent political actors at home and their counterparts abroad. Other moments of more inward focus in the United States—the 1830s, the 1870s, and the 1930s—saw less explicit discussion of foreign political relationships. Nonetheless, even the latter decades were transnational, as Americans continued to import products, ideas, and people in large numbers. Many politicians have contested the appropriate degree of American involvement with the wider world, but no one of any prominence has ever really advocated for complete U.S. separation. American politics have always been transnational politics.

"Isolationism," in this sense, was more a polemical label than an accurate description for a particular point of view. Politicians who at one time called themselves "isolationists"—Robert La Follette, Arthur Vandenberg, and Gerald Nye, among others—were themselves the products of transnational influences on the United States. La Follette, for example, had traveled extensively in Russia and Europe. His progressive politics reflected his observations of state welfare programs overseas. Even the "isolationists" were also transnational political actors.

We can best understand the diverse transnational influences on American politics from the eighteenth century to the present by dividing these influences into roughly two areas: *war* and *public activism*. Although these topics often overlap in practice, it is helpful to examine how each reflects a series of particular and recurring transnational connections across numerous decades. These topics neglect many other areas of foreign influence that have received extensive attention from historians—commerce, popular culture, immigration, and technology, among others. Focusing on war and public activism, however, highlights some of the most significant ways in which the sources and practices of American politics changed in connection with developments abroad. The experiences of Americans in foreign societies, and American perceptions of those societies, had an enormous influence on the definition of the nation and the formulation of its policies. The U.S. experience in both war and public activism was deeply conditioned by transnational personal and institutional relations.

War

In one way or another, the United States has been at war for most of its history. These wars have included battles with foreign powers on or near American-claimed territory, continental conflicts over land control and political authority, and military interventions against adversaries overseas. In each of these contexts, war has exposed American politics to transnational experiences and ideas.

The American Revolution was typical of this process. During the late 1770s and early 1780s, the rebelling colonists aligned with France and Spain to fight against continued British control of North America. The alliance converted a group of domestic revolutionaries—provincials, in the eyes of the British—into international ambassadors for American nationalism. Benjamin Franklin, John Jay, and John Adams (as well as his precocious son, John Quincy Adams) spent most of the conflict in Europe, negotiating for foreign support. Despite their explicit rejection of traditional European aristocratic politics, these men became diplomats at the courts of monarchs. They were succeeded, after the Treaty of Ghent in 1783, by another generation of American diplomats—particularly Thomas Jefferson, who served at the court of the Bourbon monarch on the eve of the French Revolution.

These diplomatic experiences made the American revolutionaries into worldly politicians. Although they rejected traditional Old World politics, they learned to practice them for radical purposes. Franklin and Adams, in particular, made numerous deals to procure military aid and trade from European states. They also made and broke alliances to serve the needs of an emerging independent government. Their definition of an American republic was self-conscious of the place the new nation would occupy as a small and weak state in a world filled with much more powerful, aggressive empires. Their support for a strong central government, under the Constitution, was a political calculation about the foreign threats the new United States would face, and the need to prepare for international competition. Key constitutional innovations, especially the creation of the presidency, reflected the influence of monarchy and its unifying institutions on the republican revolutionaries in Philadelphia.

George Washington's famous Farewell Address in 1796 was a testament to the formative influence of European diplomacy and institutions on American politics. At a moment of intensive conflict between the United States and France and Great Britain (both of whom were at war), Washington advised citizens that "nothing is more essential than that permanent, inveterate antipathies against particular nations, and passionate attachments for others, should be excluded; and that, in place of them, just and amicable feelings towards all should be cultivated." This was a classic call for American adherence to a political balance of power—avoiding moral crusading and carefully steering clear of permanent bonds that could implicate the nation in unwanted conflicts. Following from Niccolò Machiavelli more than Jefferson or Madison, Washington defined the United States as a practitioner of raison d'état, the pursuit of the "national interest" through secular and flexible maneuver between different coalitions of power. Washington and his successors in the White House spoke of "temporary alliances" with republican and nonrepublican states, not isolation or ideological consistency in policy making. They were European-influenced realists who practiced power politics for the defense and promotion of American ideals.

This realism kept the United States out of foreign revolutions, despite rhetorical urges to the contrary. The French, Haitian, and Latin American revolutions of the late eighteenth and early nineteenth centuries received no significant support from the American government. In Haiti, the administration of Thomas Jefferson was overtly hostile to the creation of a regime that challenged European authority under African leadership. The United States was a revolutionary nation, but its definition of acceptable revolution included attachment to European-inspired notions of good government and realist traditions of the balance of power in foreign policy.

Every subsequent war, especially those outside of North America, reinforced these principles and increased other foreign influences on American politics. In the Civil War, both the Union and Confederate armies—the largest military institutions built within the United States to that date—studied and implemented European fighting methods. Confederate general Robert E. Lee adopted Napoleonic tactics for maneuver and surprise in battle. Union general Ulysses S. Grant used centralized methods of resource and manpower mobilization to build a fighting force that could take grave casualties but still annihilate its enemies. Neither Lee nor Grant fought like any of their American predecessors; both fought a modern European war on American soil. Many European observers in Germany, France, and Great Britain studied the Civil War as a testing ground for their ideas of war in an age of more powerful Machiavellian states. The "American way of war," like the American approach to international relations, was also European in origins, and soon global in scope.

Beyond military strategy, President Abraham Lincoln also adopted a strongly European-influenced argument against slavery in the cause of the Union. British politicians of the eighteenth and early nineteenth centuries pursued the global abolition of slavery for the purpose of empowering free labor markets. This position received reinforcement from the French Revolution's Declaration of the Rights of Man. Ending slavery—or at least eliminating any foreign support for the institution of slavery—became a widely embraced political duty outside North America on the eve of the Civil War.

Lincoln shared many antislavery views, but he avoided taking a categorical position on the issue as long as possible. Once it became clear in course of the Civil War that he could not find a political compromise between North and South to preserve the Union, Lincoln invoked British and French antislavery positions to justify the use of violence against the slaveholding Confederacy. The Emancipation Proclamation, signed by Lincoln on January 1, 1863, freed the slaves in the Confederate states and pledged that "the Executive Government of the United States, including the military and naval authority thereof, will recognize and maintain the freedom of such persons."

Lincoln issued the Emancipation Proclamation to enlist the freed slaves against the Confederacy. He also used this document to attract antislavery opinion in Europe to the Union side. The latter consideration was crucial. The British government, in particular, had strong economic interests connected to the cotton trade from the Confederate states. It also had geopolitical interests in North America that would be served by a weak and divided American nation. Lincoln and his secretary of state, William Henry Seward, feared that British recognition and support for the Confederacy would undermine, and perhaps defeat, Union aims. The Emancipation Proclamation countered this possibility by appealing directly to British and other foreign audiences to embrace the Union as the force against slavery. Lincoln alienated moderates in the United States with this document, but he appealed to foreign constituencies that he needed on his side. The Emancipation Proclamation and the "second American Revolution" that it came to represent were strongly connected to European politics. Although the battles occurred on American soil, the Civil War was a transnational conflict.

American politics in both world wars fit the same pattern. The two defining political moments of the conflicts for the United States—President Woodrow Wilson's announcement of his Fourteen Points on January 8, 1918, and President Franklin D. Roosevelt's signature on the Atlantic Charter of August 14, 1941—reflected important connections between domestic aims and foreign influences. Both documents had a deep and simultaneous impact on citizens at home and abroad. They contributed to a "liberal" and "modernizing" set of politics that crossed national boundaries.

Wilson's Fourteen Points, articulated in his speech to a joint session of Congress, began by explaining that the United States had sent its soldiers to fight on European soil for the first time "because violations of right had occurred which touched us to the quick and made the life of our own people impossible unless they were corrected and the world secure once and for all against their recurrence. . . . All the peoples of the world are in effect partners in this interest, and for our own part we see very clearly that unless justice be done to others it will not be done to us."

To combat threats from abroad and assure that the world was "made safe for democracy," Wilson espoused long-standing European ideas about international law and organization. Drawing on the experiences of the European states that had formed transnational cooperative institutions—including the Central Commission for the Navigation of the Rhine (founded in 1815), the Superior Council for Health (founded in 1838), and the First Geneva Convention on the treatment of war wounded (founded in 1864)—Wilson proposed a new international organization for peace. During the negotiations outside of Paris at the end of World War I, this idea became the basis for the League of Nations—the most important effort at global governance and war prevention in the early twentieth century.

The U.S. Senate vetoed American membership in the League of Nations for fear that it would restrict American independence, but the League remained influential in American politics. Under Wilson's successors, especially President Herbert Hoover, the United States continued to support the creation of a "civilized" system of international law to regulate aggression among states. In addition, the United States participated in the growing range of international exchanges of people, ideas, and technology operating in parallel with the League of Nations. The power of the U.S. federal government grew with the creation of a Department of Commerce in 1913 that managed and promoted these activities. Through federal grants of aid, legal encouragement, and foreign negotiations the U.S. government became what one historian calls a "promotional state," much more akin to its European counterparts than to its pretwentieth-century American predecessors. The end of World War I contributed to a stronger federal role in American society and deeper transnational ties to local businesses and communities.

These developments underpinned the New Deal—a domestic and international "war" on poverty and economic dislocation during the Great Depression. President Franklin D. Roosevelt solidified the transnational strains of American politics when, in the summer of 1941 (months before the Japanese attack on Pearl Harbor), he hinged the future of American freedom and prosperity on the defeat of fascism. Meeting with British prime minister Winston Churchill off the coast of Newfoundland, Roosevelt signed the Atlantic Charter that committed both Great Britain and the United States to "common principles" for a "better future for the world." These common principles included the "final destruction of Nazi tyranny," and the creation of a new international peace "which will afford to all nations the means of dwelling in safety within their own boundaries, and which will afford assurance that all the men in all lands may live out their lives in freedom from fear and want." Domestic and international liberty, according to this formulation, were interdependent.

Roosevelt defined America's national purpose in the Great Depression and World War II as an extension of the Wilsonian goal of making the world safe for democracy. He reorganized American society along these lines, under the direction of a now dominant federal government. Similarly, Roosevelt defined foreign threats—political extremism, economic autarchy, and interstate violence—as core challenges to America's national purpose. Citizens of the United States were mobilized to fight for their freedom *as a single nation* on an unprecedented scale. American society never looked back. Historian Michael Sherry identifies the Great Depression and World War II as the formative moment for a militarized, outward-looking political culture in the United States. The European-inspired realism of Benjamin Franklin and John Adams had, over the course of 150 years, evolved into a form of federal dominance in American society unanticipated by any of the nation's founders. This new role for Washington reflected influences and threats from abroad, as much as those at home.

American politics during the cold war deepened this phenomenon. From the last days of World War II through the collapse of the Soviet Union in 1991, U.S. leaders consistently emphasized the need to keep the nation mobilized for conflict with Moscow and other communist challengers. New institutions, including the Office of the Secretary of Defense and the Central Intelligence Agency, emerged to manage domestic resources, monitor threats, and control dissent. The National Security Act of 1947 concentrated power more centrally in the White House with the creation of the National Security Council and the reduction of congressional oversight for security

matters. As a consequence, the United States prepared for and fought numerous conflicts after 1947, but the president never again sought a formal declaration of war.

The perceived threat of foreign communism was ever-present in American society. It motivated a change in the size and scope of the American military as it became a permanent global force with bases on every continent and nuclear weapons ready for immediate use. It transformed universities as the U.S. government used its financial and legal leverage to make the academy more helpful in addressing pressing policy challenges. Most significant, perceptions of communism transformed the terms of political debate. To win election to office—Republican or Democrat—one had to appear "tough" on communism and committed to a broad global agenda for the United States. Domestic cold war politics were international anti-Communist politics.

The figures who came to dominate the American political scene in this context were not the usual suspects from elite families and white Anglo-Saxon pedigrees. Men of this background remained powerful, but not as exclusively as before. The international dimensions of the cold war placed a new premium on anti-Communist cosmopolitanism—a knowledge of foreign societies, a personal biography rooted in struggle against foreign extremism, and a hypernationalism born of immigration to America as a "savior" nation. Henry Kissinger and Zbigniew Brzezinski are prime examples of this phenomenon. European immigrants who came to the United States fleeing Nazi terror, they emerged as powerful, unelected policy makers promising to help the United States manage a world of dangerous threats and difficult balance of power decisions. Kissinger and Brzezinski espoused American ideals, but they consistently counseled the country to curtail its cherished hopes and act more like a "normal" state, accepting "lesser evils" in its friends and combating "greater evils" in its enemies.

The same political rhetoric, and many of the same personalities, carried on into the post–cold war era in American politics. Iraq and Islamic fanaticism replaced the Soviet Union and communism as the overriding threats in American debates. Mobilizing the nation for combat at home and abroad became the guiding principle, yet again, for the government after the September 11, 2001, terrorist attacks on the United States. As the Truman administration created the National Security Council during the onset of the cold war, the administration of President George W. Bush founded the Department of Homeland Security as a response to terrorism in the new century. Pervasive perceptions of foreign threats, in a time of perpetual war, set the terms of American political debate. Transnational influences were now central to the most local discussions of authority, economy, and survival. The war at home and abroad continued.

Public Activism

The intersection between the foreign and the domestic in war had a close analogue among public activists—including social reformers, local organization leaders, prominent intellectuals, and public demonstrators. Especially during the twentieth century, public activists in the United States drew on ideas, strategies, and tactics from abroad. They frequently thought of themselves as part of larger global transformations in society. Most significant, activists often had personal connections to foreign countries, derived from birth, family, study, and travel. American activists were transnational translators, synthesizers, and innovators at the same time.

The transnational scope of public activists was also somewhat broader than that of the politicians more deeply involved in war and daily policy making. Figures like Franklin, Lincoln, Wilson, Roosevelt, and Kissinger focused their energies on Europe above all other non-American areas of the world. For them, the transnational was largely trans-European. Activists in the twentieth century, however, had a more transglobal perspective. They came from and interacted with a broader geography in their daily politics. They often looked self-consciously beyond Europe to other societies for alternative reform inspirations. Europe mattered to American activists, but over the course of the twentieth century it became less central to them than it was to their counterparts in policy-making institutions.

Advocates of substantial reforms in American race relations were most explicit about their desire to look beyond Europe. Founded in 1816 by a mix of northern abolitionists and Southerners fearful of slave violence, the American Colonization Society helped to transport more than 10,000 freed slaves to the West African territory of Liberia. With the end of the Civil War and the promise of African American suffrage during Reconstruction, support for the emigration of freed slaves largely evaporated. Nonetheless, the controversial work of the American Colonization Society was the beginning of a "return to Africa" movement that would animate public discussions of the "race problem" in the United States for the next century, especially among those who believed that blacks and whites could live in peace only if they were separated. According to this logic, African Americans would live freer and happier lives if they were back on a continent populated by people who looked like them and presumably shared similar traditions. This was often a well-intentioned effort, but its separatist logic was adopted by a range of political activists, for a variety of purposes, in later decades.

Marcus Garvey was perhaps the most influential and transnational figure in the early twentieth century to espouse a separatist African American agenda. Born in Jamaica and widely traveled throughout Central America and Western Europe, Garvey came to the United States as a penniless immigrant in 1916. Within a few years he organized and led the largest transnational black organization of the twentieth century: the United Negro Improvement Association (UNIA), which would open chapters in more than a dozen countries, including many parts of Latin America and Africa. The organization emphasized self-reliance, racial autonomy, and black nationhood. According to Garvey, descendants of Africa should take pride in their past and work together for the common advancement of their race. He called for a transnational organization of blacks to create a single nation under his leadership and the UNIA.

Garvey's aims became most explicit in August 1920 when he organized the monthlong International Convention of the Negro Peoples of the World at Madison Square Garden in New York City. Elected "provisional president of Africa" by the assembly, Garvey oversaw the writing and approval of the "Declaration of Rights of the Negro Peoples of the World," which demanded that "the governments of the world recognize our leader and his representatives chosen by the race to look after the welfare of our people under such governments." As a transnational sovereign, the UNIA called on "the various governments of the world to accept and acknowledge Negro representatives who shall be sent to the said governments to represent the general welfare of the Negro peoples of the world." Africa should be protected for Africans, according to the declaration, and the UNIA asserted that, on other continents blacks would "demand complete control of our social institutions without interference by any alien race or races." Announced in New York amid signs of growing American intolerance to dissent, this was a bold and transnational vision of African American power as part of a global racial movement.

Garvey and the UNIA never achieved their goals, but they contributed to a remarkable transnational outpouring of reform ideas and initiatives among activists with diverse interests. The most prominent African American intellectual of the period, W.E.B. DuBois, strongly disagreed with Garvey on many points, but he shared the UNIA's commitment to a global movement for racial reform. Speaking at the first Pan-African Convention in London on July 25, 1900, DuBois famously proclaimed, "The problem of the twentieth century is the problem of the color line, the question as to how far differences of race—which show themselves chiefly in the color of the skin and the texture of the hair—will hereafter be made the basis of denying to over half the world the right of sharing to utmost ability the opportunities and privileges of modern civilization." DuBois did not call for a common black nation with a single leader, but he did link the local with the international when he asked in his London speech, "may the conscience of a great nation rise and rebuke all dishonesty and unrighteous oppression toward the American Negro, and grant to him the right of franchise, security of person and property, and generous recognition of the great work he has accomplished in a generation toward raising nine millions of human beings from slavery to manhood. . . . Let the nations of the world respect the integrity and independence of the free Negro states of Abyssinia, Liberia, Haiti, and the rest, and let the inhabitants of these states, the independent tribes of Africa, the Negroes of the West Indies and America, and the black subjects of all nations take courage, strive ceaselessly, and fight bravely, that they may prove to the world their incontestable right to be counted among the great brotherhood of mankind."

DuBois's "brotherhood of mankind" was a clarion call for many activists focused on issues other than race—including poverty, urban blight, health, and children's welfare. A generation of reformers, generally labeled "progressives" by historians, conceptualized the problems of the United States in transnational terms that resonated with the arguments voiced by both Garvey and DuBois. These progressives self-consciously drew on what they envisioned as an international dialogue among activists about how to improve society through rational, determined, and cooperative action. Like Garvey and DuBois, they formed countless organizations that crossed borders for this purpose, they participated in a widening web of "exchanges," and, most important, they embraced the experimental application of foreign ideas to local problems. In Wisconsin, for example, a group of intellectuals and politicians came together to author what they called the "Wisconsin Idea"—a mix of remarkably creative and cosmopolitan reform initiatives inspired by local problems in an agrarian and industrializing community. Borrowing from the British, Germans, French, and others, Wisconsin activists pioneered worker's compensation insurance, unemployment benefits, public education, and social security. They did not assert a sense of common racial consciousness across boundaries, but they did nurture an enduring commitment to transnational reform rooted in local needs.

This dream did not die with the Great Depression and World War II but attracted the attention of a new generation of young activists in the 1960s. Unlike their predecessors, the New Left did not endorse rational planning or state-building efforts. Instead, it focused on the transnational participatory spirit that had animated Garvey and DuBois, as well as their progressive counterparts. Activists in the 1960s emphasized a common experience of youth across societies confronting paternalistic, militaristic, and unjust institutions of power that needed rapid change from below. Inspired by "liberationist" movements in the third world, the euphoria of mass demonstrations, and a new feeling of relevance, young people on every continent demanded far-reaching change. They pushed for an end to foreign wars, attention to hidden suffering within modern societies, and more egalitarian politics. They argued that this was a truly worldwide agenda that must begin within each state.

Students for a Democratic Society (SDS), the most prominent New Left organization in the United States during the 1960s, put this argument in apocalyptic terms. Its "Agenda for a Generation" (also known as the "Port Huron Statement") announced: "Although mankind desperately needs revolutionary leadership, America rests in national stalemate, its goals ambiguous and tradition-bound instead of informed and clear, its democratic system apathetic and manipulated rather than 'of, by, and for the people.' . . . Our work is guided by the sense that we may be the last generation in the experiment with living. But we are a minority—the vast majority of our people regard the temporary equilibriums of our society and world as eternally functional parts. In this is perhaps the outstanding paradox: we ourselves are imbued with urgency, yet the message of our society is that there is no viable alternative to the present."

SDS and the many other activist groups that emerged in the 1960s did not achieve their desired changes in policy, and they did not create a cohesive generation of reformers. They did, however, transform local and international attitudes. American society and many of its counterparts abroad became more sensitive and accepting of racial, gender, and various ethnic differences. Concern for human rights also grew in public attitudes, if not always in policy practice. Most significant, transnational borrowings of ideas and programs became more common and more accepted. To think locally after the 1960s meant to think about localities across societies. This basic attitude transferred from the New Left demonstrators of the 1960s to the environmental, feminist, and antiglobalization activists of the late twentieth century. The 1960s endure in the contemporary imagination as the moment of transnational political activism that all subsequent movements seek to capture in one way or another.

Looking Outward

Tip O'Neill was correct; all politics is local. The local, however, has always included deep and diverse connections to practices, ideas, and influences that are not American in origin. From the American Revolution to the demonstrations of the 1960s, American politics have been transnational politics. The experiences of war and public activism have reflected this phenomenon; they have also increased its intensity. During nearly every military conflict and nearly every burst of reform the United States became more, not less, connected to its counterparts near and far. The nation globalized long before people used the term.

If there is a general direction to American history, it is outward, not inward. If there is a general lesson from American history, it is that political change requires familiarity with a landscape far beyond the borders of the 50 states. These were O'Neill's politics, as they were the politics of his heroic predecessors in Boston and his modern successors from the Sun Belt South. In order to do more for one's constituents, one must do more for their transnational hopes and interests.

FURTHER READING. Alan Dawley, *Changing the World: American Progressives in War and Revolution*, 2003; Declaration of Rights of the Negro Peoples of the World, August 15, 1920, http://www.pbs.org/wgbh/amex/garvey/filmmore/ps_rights.html; John A. Farrell, *Tip O'Neill and the Democratic Century*, 2001; Kevin Gaines, *American Africans in Ghana: Black Expatriates and the Civil Rights Era*, 2006; Felix Gilbert, *To the Farewell Address: Ideas of Early American Foreign Policy*, 1961; Colin Grant, *Negro with a Hat: The Rise and Fall of Marcus Garvey*, 2008; Gerd-Rainer Horn, *The Spirit of '68: Rebellion in Western Europe and North America, 1956–1976*, 2007; Akira Iriye, *Cultural Internationalism and World Order*, 2000; Melvyn P. Leffler, *A Preponderance of Power: National Security, the Truman Administration, and the Cold War*, 1992; Port Huron Statement of Students for a Democratic Society, June 15, 1962, http://www2.iath.virginia.edu/sixties/HTML_docs/Resources/Primary/Manifestos/SDS_Port_Huron.html; Daniel T. Rodgers, *Atlantic Crossings: Social Politics in a Progressive Age*, 1998; Emily Rosenberg, *Spreading the American Dream: American Economic and Cultural Expansion, 1890–1945*, 1982; Michael S. Sherry, *In the Shadow of War: The United States since the 1930s*, 1995; Jeremi Suri, *Power and Protest: Global Revolution and the Rise of Détente*, 2003; Wilson, Woodrow, Speech to a joint session of Congress, January 8, 1918, http://www.yale.edu/lawweb/avalon/wilson14.htm.

JEREMI SURI

transportation and politics

A remarkable number of new transportation technologies emerged in the United States and other industrialized nations during the nineteenth and early twentieth centuries, including long-distance stagecoach lines, river steamboats and oceangoing steamships, steam and electric railways, automobiles and all-weather highways, and commercial aviation. Each new mode of transportation invariably elicited a variety of political responses.

Perhaps nothing better illustrates the intimate relationship between transportation and American politics than the oddly shaped and geographically roundabout route chosen for transcontinental stagecoach service inaugurated in the late 1850s; for the first time it became possible to cross the United States from coast to coast by land using only commercial transportation. The Butterfield Overland Stage linked the cities of San Francisco and St. Louis, Missouri, by way of such frontier outposts as El Paso, Texas; Tucson, Arizona; and Los Angeles, the most populous of which could claim only a few thousand residents. From Fort Smith, in far western Arkansas, Butterfield ran a branch line east

to Memphis, Tennessee, to serve the home state of Postmaster General Aaron Brown, who oversaw the federal mail contracts that funded much of the expense of operating a stage line across so much unpopulated space.

Mail Contracts

It would be impossible to overestimate the importance of income from federal mail contracts in underwriting the cost of new modes of transportation across vast sections of the United States in the nineteenth century. Mail subsidies were the lifeblood of most long-distance stage lines serving the West, so much so that in the early 1860s, the western "stagecoach king" Ben Holladay maintained one of his several homes near Capitol Hill in Washington, D.C., to cultivate a cordial relationship with members of the U.S. Congress who periodically voted on mail contracts.

Mail contracts also subsidized the operation of many a steamboat plying the navigable waters of the United States, most notably along 3,000 sparsely settled miles of the Missouri River as it meandered between St. Louis and the frontier outpost of Fort Benton, Montana—a transportation hub aptly named for Missouri senator Thomas Hart Benton, one of the strongest supporters in Congress of transportation links across the West. During his 30-year career in the Senate, Benton promoted federally subsidized transportation links not merely between Missouri and the West Coast but extending all the way to China and India.

Much of what Benton (1782–1858) proposed on the floor of the Senate (between 1821 and 1851) and in other public forums was too visionary to be realized in his lifetime, but mail contracts did subsidize the first steamship service between the East and West coasts, by means of a 48-mile portage across the Isthmus of Panama, that commenced just *before* word of gold precipitated a mad rush of travelers to California in 1849.

Long after stagecoach and steamboat transportation had been relegated to the remotest corners of the United States in the early twentieth century, the railroad passenger trains that superseded them depended on federal mail contracts, and increasingly so in the late 1940s and 1950s as the number of rail passengers declined steadily. Many of the trains carried dedicated Rail Post Office cars in which highly trained clerks sorted the mail en route, the schedules of mail-carrying trains being determined largely by the needs of the U.S. Post Office Department. Thus, when the Post Office cancelled all "mail by rail" contracts in late 1967, passenger train service effectively collapsed in all but the most scenic portions of the United States. Had it not been for federal dollars to support Amtrak, implemented in May 1971, long-distance rail passenger service across the United States would very likely have disappeared.

Railroads

Railroads, from their technological infancy in the United States in the early 1830s, had been enmeshed in politics. The money required to build and equip a single mile of railroad often dwarfed the cost of an entire fleet of steamboats and stagecoaches, and thus it was natural for railroad builders in all parts of the United States to seek municipal, state, and federal support. Politics and railroad building often went hand in hand, especially in the sparsely settled Trans-Mississippi West. To encourage construction of the railroad lines needed to develop the region, Congress provided various forms of help, all in addition to the promise of mail contracts once the trains began running. The aid included loans, financial subsidies, and enormous grants of federal land. The federal land grant program to support railroad construction ended in the 1870s as a result of scandals that blackened the reputation of Congress—"the finest that money could buy," to paraphrase Mark Twain—and during the next decade, the politics of railroads evolved from finding ways to underwrite construction and maintain operations to devising ways to regulate them, beginning with the Interstate Commerce Commission in 1887.

In contrast to the federal government, various states had begun to regulate railroads as much as 30 years earlier, in the 1850s. The early state regulations involved matters mainly of safety and service. The initial federal regulations were largely for show in order to placate various political pressure groups, such as the Grangers, an agrarian protest group originating in the Midwest, which claimed railroad rates were exorbitant and service poor. Not until the early twentieth century, during the Progressive Era, did federal regulation of the railroads acquire real teeth.

Responding to aggressive displays of railroad power in a nation that, by 1900, had no alternative modes of transportation apart from the boats that served its coastlines and inland waterways, governments at all levels steadily piled on regulations. It was once claimed that the Interstate Commerce Commission alone had written more than a trillion regulations involving all aspects of railroad service, a number that is surely an exaggeration but nonetheless expresses the growing frustration of railroad executives in the 1920s and 1930s.

The boom in railroad travel in the United States during World War II, which witnessed the highest passenger loads in the history of the industry, was followed by the bust of the 1950s, when despite the railroads' efforts to streamline and speed up their best passenger trains the number of passengers using them continued to drop. In the mid-1950s, airlines for the first time surpassed railroads in terms of the volume of passenger traffic. At almost the same time, Congress passed the Federal Aid Highway Act of 1956 in order to create a new system of superhighways. The railways, by contrast, seemed to languish. One of the nation's largest railroads, the Pennsylvania Central,

went bankrupt in 1970. Two other giants, the Rock Island and the Milwaukee Road, went bankrupt in 1975 and 1977, respectively. Rail industry executives complained loudly about unfair competition, but it seemed that no one was listening.

Highways

In the 1820s and 1830s, Democrats and Whigs had battled over how much the federal government should underwrite the cost of internal improvements. The Whigs favored spending government dollars to further the nation's growing network of canals and roads. One showcase project was the National Road, an improved highway that reached west from Maryland and across the agricultural heartland of Ohio and Indiana. The road never reached its stated goal of St. Louis, however, before the Panic of 1837 dried up tax revenues at all levels of government and thus discouraged support for internal improvements. From 1838 to 1916, the federal government conspicuously avoided direct involvement in road-building projects, and the laissez faire interpretation of the U.S. Constitution provided the necessary justification for its hands-off approach.

Ironically, just as the number of government regulations seemed to increase exponentially during the years after 1900—including emergency federal operation of the nation's railroads during World War I and its immediate aftermath—government subsidized and lightly regulated highways emerged to challenge railroad power. Competition from a growing number of private automobiles first made a noticeable impact on local passenger trains in midwestern farm states around 1916, a year that also saw the birth of the first congressionally subsidized highway construction program since the 1830s and the end of federal support for the National or Cumberland Road. In the 1920s and 1930s, Congress and state governments poured billions of dollars into building a national highway network. In good times and bad, state and federal appropriations to build and maintain an ever improving network of highways remained popular with voters—especially after 1919, the year states first discovered that a tax on gasoline was a relatively painless way to raise the necessary revenue.

Much of the newfound constitutional justification for federal involvement in highway construction during the twentieth century was based on the argument that good roads and highways were needed to maintain a strong national defense. The argument appeared frequently in public discussions of funding superhighways during the cold war years of the 1950s and 1960s, but it actually antedated that era by several decades. As early as 1916, when the Mexican revolutionary Pancho Villa and his ragtag troops were widely perceived to threaten America's southwestern borderlands, Congressional proponents of the landmark legislation passed that year argued that highways would provide an additional way to move troops quickly if needed to defend that remote and sparsely settled portion of the United States.

The numbers assigned to the original network of corridors—like U.S. Route 66, which sliced diagonally across the American West from Chicago to Los Angeles; U.S. Route 1, which runs parallel to the coastline from Maine to Florida; and U.S. 101, which does the same along the West Coast—date from meetings that federal and state highway officials held in the mid 1920s. The designation *U.S.* was not just an abbreviation for United States but also for Uniform System. But the evolution of modern transportation in the United States, which probably dates from the landmark completion of the Erie Canal in 1825 or the opening of the first section of the Baltimore and Ohio Railroad five years later, is essentially the product of an inexact, ever changing, and sometimes volatile mix of technological and financial expertise, legislative and legal calculation (and sometimes chicanery), as well as various forms of popular education that over nearly two centuries included everything from fiery stump speeches and lengthy public debates to slick industry advertising and self-promotional propaganda, with winners and losers determined at the voting booth.

The national defense argument remained popular; in the mid-1950s Congress debated whether America needed to build a new system of super highways to relieve the growing congestion of federal highways first built in the 1920s. President Dwight D. Eisenhower was a strong backer of the new superhighway proposal and, in 1956, signed legislation to underwrite construction of the Interstate Highway system, one of the largest appropriations for public works in American history.

As for rules governing interstate highway commerce, Congress approved federal regulation of America's fast-growing intercity truck and bus industries in 1935. Rail executives had complained bitterly that their heavily regulated industry could not compete with new modes of transportation that went almost unfettered, except for state safety and licensing requirements. Over-the-road trucks offering door-to-door delivery service rapidly snatched away money that railroads made by moving personal goods or delivering less-than-full-carload freight. Buses and passenger railroads fought over slices of a rapidly shrinking revenue pie. After the 1920s, by far the greatest number of Americans traveled over the nation's network of all-weather roads and highways in the comfort of their own private automobiles.

Use of the ever-expanding road and highway network became the birthright of every American, a concept periodically reaffirmed in political discussions and legislative debates. By the early 1930s the road was the most conspicuous and widely used "common ground" in the United States, and it made absolutely no difference whether users drove humble Fords and Chevrolets or lordly Duesenbergs and Packards.

Aviation

The first successful flight of Wilbur and Orville Wright took place in December 1903. The next summer, the largest city west of the Mississippi River, St. Louis, basked in the international limelight that came with hosting a world's fair, a tradition that dated back to London in the early 1850s. All world's fairs served to showcase the latest technological achievements of a nation or of Western civilization generally. But not a single airplane was displayed at the St. Louis fair in 1904; Americans were not yet "air-minded" and would not become so for at least another quarter century. Neither they nor the world at large had any idea what the Wright brothers' brief flight portended. Not until young Charles A. Lindbergh piloted *The Spirit of St. Louis* nonstop from New York to Paris in 1927 to win a $25,000 prize and instant worldwide fame did America begin to accept the idea of aviation. *Time* magazine selected Lindbergh as its first Man of the Year and, largely as a result of the publicity his solo flight across the Atlantic generated, Wall Street became aware of the financial gain commercial aviation might offer. After a series of false starts dating back to 1914, commercial aviation in the United States effectively got off the ground in 1929 with 48-hour coast-to-coast service that used an awkward combination of air travel during daylight hours and rail sleeping cars at night. One of the new coast-to-coast carriers, Transcontinental and Western Airlines (later simply TWA), conspicuously advertised itself as the "Lindbergh Line" for added cachet.

Associating the airline with the trusted Lindbergh name was intended to inspire public confidence in a largely untested industry. Ironically, Transcontinental and Western soon compiled one of the worst safety records in an industry that during the first half of the 1930s suffered a succession of newsworthy accidents that shook public confidence in commercial aviation. The legendary Notre Dame University football coach Knute Rockne died in a TWA crash in 1931; another TWA crash killed Senator Bronson Cutting of New Mexico in 1935. The loss of Senator Cutting probably did more than any other aviation-related death to motivate members of Congress to adopt strict federal regulation of the airline industry in 1938. Starting in 1938, the federal government regulated the fares, routes, and schedules of domestic interstate airlines. By treating them as a public utility, federal officials sought to guarantee them a reasonable rate of return. Much to the benefit of the airline industry, the legislation also sought to instill confidence in passengers. As significant as the landmark regulatory legislation was, it was clear that the fortunes of America's commercial air carriers depended to an extraordinary degree on a favorable political and legislative environment.

By the late 1930s, all forms of commercial interstate transportation in the United States, including gas and oil pipelines, were regulated by various federal commissions, agencies, and boards. Some industries, most notably commercial aviation, prospered under the heavy but highly protective hand of federal regulators. Not a single major airline went bankrupt during the years of federal regulation. Other transportation industries, most notably the railroads, stagnated and lost almost all incentive for meaningful innovation. In the late 1930s, when a few American railroads dared enter the business of commercial aviation, federal regulators blocked them. By contrast, north of the border, the Canadian Pacific Railway added both an airline and many luxury hotels to its portfolio.

Deregulation

In the 1970s, a Democratic Congress reversed the course Uncle Sam had been following since 1887 and started to deregulate all forms of American transportation. Senators Edward Kennedy of Massachusetts and Howard Cannon of Nevada gave their names to the 1978 legislation that deregulated the airline industry. The expectation in the halls of Congress and in the airline industry was that unfettered competition would cause ticket prices to fall but profits to rise. Ticket prices did fall, and more Americans than ever were flying, but not much else worked as expected. More than a hundred new airlines joined the competition, and almost all of them failed a short time later. Some established carriers added dozens of new routes, but the overexpansion proved unwise and caused the first bankruptcies the major carriers had ever experienced. In the end, flying within the United States was probably cheaper than it had ever been, but the once glamorous experience of flying was also immeasurably cheapened. Many smaller communities lost commercial air service altogether.

Federal deregulation of the intercity truck and bus industries commenced in 1980, as did the rapid loosening of federal control over railroads. West Virginia congressman Harley Staggers gave his name to 1980 legislation that significantly unfettered the railroads. The result was almost the opposite of that which would befall the airline industry. Railroads abandoned thousands of miles of lightly used track (too many miles, they later learned) and pared freight train crews; the big railroads merged and merged again until just four super railroads dominated traffic across the United States, two on either side of the Mississippi River. More efficient than ever, railroads saw profits soar in the early twenty-first century to unprecedented heights. As savvy investors purchased railroad stocks, it was clear that North American railroads were enjoying good times.

The Changing Landscape

As a result of terrorism, sharply rising fuel costs, and vigorous competition that made it difficult to raise ticket prices, airline profits—even for the biggest and best-known names in the industry—took a nosedive. Purchasers of the common stock of most major U.S. carriers saw their investments wiped out by bankruptcy courts. Those same dollars if invested instead in one of the big four railroads (CSX, Norfolk Southern, Union Pacific, and Burlington Northern Santa Fe) would have doubled or tripled in value.

One advantage contributing to the comeback of America's big railroads was the rising price of oil, which made automobiles, intercity trucks, and airliners increasingly expensive alternatives. Both CSX and Norfolk Southern sponsored televised coverage of the 2008 election returns, and both used the occasion to highlight for a national audience the efficiency of their freight trains versus highway transportation.

Transportation can be described as the "great enabler." In whatever form, it has enabled changes that transformed the landscape, the economy, the politics, and even the basic social habits of Americans. Something as simple as enjoying fresh fruit in Montana, Michigan, or Minnesota in midwinter represents the triumph of good transportation over distance and time, enabling oranges from groves in Florida or California, for example, to travel in refrigerated railcars and trucks to breakfast tables in distant corners of the nation. A morning orange is a simple pleasure, but it also epitomizes the complex history of transportation; it is the remarkable result of two centuries of public discussion and dissent, vigorous partisan political debate, slick corporate advertising, and personal disappointments mixed with individual dreams realized, technological breakthroughs that displaced less efficient and adaptable modes of transportations, and financial goals both realized and unrealized.

See also regulation.

FURTHER READING. Elizabeth E. Bailey, David R. Graham, and Daniel P. Kaplan, *Deregulating the Airlines*, 1985; Alfred D. Chandler, Jr., *The Railroads: The Nation's First Big Business*, 1965; James W. Ely, Jr., *Railroads and American Law*, 2001; James J. Flink, *America Adopts the Automobile, 1895–1910*, 1970; T. A. Heppenheimer, *Turbulent Skies: The History of Commercial Aviation*, 1995; Gabriel Kolko, *Railroads and Regulation, 1877–1916*, 1965; Albro Martin, *Enterprise Denied: Origins of the Decline of American Railroads, 1897–1917*, 1971; Thomas Petzinger, Jr., *Hard Landing: The Epic Contest for Power and Profits that Plunged the Airlines into Chaos*, 1996; John B. Rae, *The Road and the Car in American Life*, 1971; Mark H. Rose, *Interstate: Express Highway Politics, 1941–1956*, 1979; John F. Stover, *American Railroads*, 2nd ed., 1997; Steven W. Usselman, *Regulating Railroad Innovation: Business, Technology, and Politics in America, 1840–1920*, 2002.

CARLOS A. SCHWANTES

United Nations

The United Nations is one of the most hotly debated institutions in American politics. Critics portray it as corrupt, ineffective in preventing wars, and a threat to American interests. Supporters argue that such cooperation among nations is necessary in an interconnected world, that the United Nations has had a positive impact around the globe, and that in crisis, it brings world leaders together to talk through their differences. Some conservatives argue that the United States should leave the United Nations altogether, while liberals argue for greater investment in it. The debate between those who wish the United States to act independently in its own national interests and those who see U.S. interests tied to international and global interests has surged back and forth for more than a century. The first crisis occurred at the time of World War I.

World War I and the League of Nations

World War I produced death and destruction on a scale never seen before. Year after year, millions died in harrowing circumstances. By 1918 the Austro-Hungarian, Russian, Turkish, and German empires were all destroyed.

Many people in power and in the general public, especially in the United States, believed it was essential to create a political process to prevent another catastrophic war. Most Americans were very much opposed to the centuries-old feuding of Europe's empires and vowed to avoid being ensnared in such foreign entanglements.

In 1917 President Woodrow Wilson, a Democrat, led the United States into the war on the side of Britain and France, and antiwar protestors suffered lengthy jail sentences. Wilson proposed a 14-point program for a lasting peace. The final point of the 14 was to create a new organization, called the League of Nations, to preserve the peace. Its main tool was economic sanctions, which required a consensus of all member states to be enforced.

The organization was crippled from the start, however, when the United States, having invented the League, refused to join it. After the war, many Americans were alarmed at the prospect of never-ending engagement in foreign disputes and favored isolation. Leading senators in opposition to the League prevented the U.S. Senate from ratifying the treaty, a procedure essential for the United States to make treaties.

Britain and France, exhausted and embittered by the war, felt that Wilson had foisted the League upon them. They could not carry forward the farsighted goals of the League without the help of the United States. A turning point came in 1932, when Britain and France, at a world disarmament conference, humiliated the then progressive German government by refusing to disarm equally with Germany. The German government returned home to face a public convinced that military force and a strong nation were the only ways to revive Germany, and Adolf Hitler took full advantage.

Having rejected disarmament, the British and French then showed no will to fight when Japan, Italy, and Germany began to break international agreements and take over the land and peoples of other states. By the time Hitler attacked Poland in 1939, the League of Nations had lost all credibility. Nevertheless, some of its organizations for combating slavery, drugs, and the exploitation of labor continued under the new United Nations after World War II.

Origins and Structure

The United Nations was distinct from the League of Nations in three main respects. First, it grew from the alliance that ultimately won World War II. These allied countries were motivated by the prospect of building a better world, and the new organization began life on the wave of victorious enthusiasm. Second, the United Nations was not one organization but a system of economic, security, legal, and social structures. Third, the critically important security organization of the United Nations had the power to force other states to act and to go to war but also gave the victorious five nations the power to prevent the institution from taking action, especially military action. These five—China, France, Russia, the United Kingdom, and the United States—have permanent seats on the UN Security Council and a veto over any decision.

The alliance that would become the foundation of the UN system we know today was created by U.S. president Franklin D. Roosevelt and British prime minister Winston Churchill three weeks after the Japanese bombing of Pearl Harbor. That winter Roosevelt held a long secret conference with Churchill at the White House. On January 1, 1942, they launched the 26-member United Nations to increase support for the fight; bring in the Soviet Union, which was fighting the Nazi armies on the Eastern front without help; and neutralize any sympathy for Hitler's anticommunism among the American public. China and India were part of the alliance, which pledged to fight together until victory and to advance a postwar human rights agenda that would include democratic freedoms, social security, labor rights, and free trade. In the twenty-first century, this agenda seems liberal, but at the time, the war leaders regarded it as necessary to motivate people to fight and build for the future. War was widely regarded as a product of poverty, competition for resources, financial chaos, and arms races. It is for these reasons that in August 1941, Churchill and Roosevelt issued the Atlantic Charter, an eight-point manifesto that included the statement that nations had to abandon using armed force in international affairs.

After the Declaration by the United Nations, the term United Nations forces appeared daily in official documents, the media, and popular culture. In December 1942, the United Nations made one of the first international statements condemning the mass murder of Jews in Poland. And at the end of the war in Europe, President Harry S. Truman informed the American people that Germany had surrendered to the United Nations. Roosevelt and his partners were determined to create new global organizations to prevent a third world war. In 1943 the United Nations created interim organizations: the UN War Crimes Commission, the UN Relief and Rehabilitation Administration, and the UN Food and Agriculture Commission. By using the same name for the military and political effort, Roosevelt took an integrated, internationalist approach that aimed to avoid the public rejection of the United Nations that the League of Nations had suffered.

The wartime United Nations created world financial organizations and the UN we know today. In 1944 the UN Monetary and Financial Conference (UNMFC) created the World Bank and the International Monetary Fund. Today the UNMFC is better known as the Bretton Woods Conference, so named for the site at which it took place in New Hampshire. Similarly, the 1945 conference that created the UN organization we know today is popularly known as the San Francisco Conference and officially called the United Nations Conference on International Organization (UNCIO). At the time, the creation of the United Nations we know today was the crowning glory of the UN political and war effort. Article 3 of the UN Charter states that the first original members of the UN are those who signed the UN Declaration in January 1942. Fifty-one states came to the UNCIO, as did a huge nongovernmental lobby that achieved some amendments to the proposals the great powers had made at the Dumbarton Oaks and Yalta Conferences. One nongovernmental achievement was the explicit mention of women in the UN Charter, which has provided the basis for many global women's initiatives over the last half-century.

In the late 1940s, the rivalry between the Western and Communist worlds escalated into the cold war. From then on, neither side wanted to remind people that they had been allies in World War II. During this period, the term *Allies* referred to the non-Soviet forces that had fought Hitler, and since then, the wartime United Nations that preceded the San Francisco Conference has been forgotten.

The contemporary United Nations is made up of two main bodies, the Security Council and the General Assembly. The Security Council consists of five permanent members (the "P5")—China, France, Russia, the United Kingdom, and the United States—as well as ten members with three-year terms.

The Security Council has the power to make international law and take military action, but this power is subject to the veto of any one of the five permanent members. Also, under Article 51 of the UN Charter, states have a right to defend themselves militarily. These features, along with the use of majority voting in the General Assembly, are major differences between the United Nations and the League of Nations, which needed consensus before it could act. The Soviet Union used the veto power in 1946, when it tried to prevent the West from bringing fascist Spain into UN membership, and many times after that. In recent years, the United States has used the veto most often, sometimes in defense of Israel.

The General Assembly includes all member states, controls the budget, and organizes the general work of the United Nations, which focuses on using economic and social measures to reduce the risk of war. The original wartime organizations evolved into 22 subsidiary or associated bodies, including the World Court; the World Health Organization; the UN Educational, Scientific and Cultural Organization (UNESCO); the Conference on Trade and Development; the Development Program; and other organizations aimed at helping children and refugees.

The Cold War and Decolonization

The cold war dominated global politics by the 1950s. This confrontation prevented the United Nations from taking action as each side canceled out the other in Security Council debates. The United Nations also provided a global political forum at which people not aligned with either side could be courted for their support and provided a nonviolent arena for competition and dialogue at a time when a U.S.-Soviet war could have resulted in a nuclear holocaust.

American debates on the country's role in the United Nations shifted with the rise of McCarthyism in the 1950s, when people who favored progressive causes faced being fired from their jobs and socially excluded in the fight against communism.

The Korean War (1950–53) was fought by the U.S.-led United Nations on one side and North Korea and the People's Republic of China on the other. The Soviet Union, apparently surprised by North Korea's initial invasion of South Korea, was boycotting the Security Council at the time and was not present to veto UN action. China's seat on the security Council was held by the pro-American government based in Taiwan. Some 50,000 of the more than 3 million war dead were U.S. military personnel. The war froze East-West relations until the later 1960s. One product of a thaw in relations was the 1970 UN Nuclear

Non-Proliferation Treaty, which is considered a foundation of international security.

Increasing numbers of new states have changed the character of the United Nations as it has grown to 192 members. This has occurred in two waves, the first in the 1950s and 1960s as the British and French empires collapsed, and then in the 1990s, after the collapse of communism and the fragmentation of the Soviet Union and of other nations—notably, Yugoslavia—into smaller sovereign states. These new states have tended to favor the political opponents of the empires that governed them; states in Africa and Asia looked to the Soviets and, since 1991, people emerging from Russian domination have looked to the West as a model to follow.

In the first wave of new state creation, many of the new states adopted socialist or communist policies and were hostile to their former Western colonial masters. Led by India, Yugoslavia, and Indonesia, many of the newly liberated states rejected both the capitalist and Communist systems to forge a third world movement of nonaligned states. The Suez Crisis of 1956, the war in Congo in the 1960s, and the Vietnam War were all key points in the political history of these years. People in the third world expressed desperation at the economic conditions they perceived as imposed on them by capitalism, and this produced hostility to the U.S. business-focused approach. As a result, U.S. politicians came to regard the United Nations as hostile to the United States, a perception that continues to this day. In the 1980s, President Ronald Reagan withdrew the United States from membership in UNESCO because of what he deemed its leftist policies. Nevertheless, public opinion polls in the United States continue to show support for the nation's membership in the United Nations (above the 50 percent mark into the twenty-first century, down from the above 80 percent level of support in 1945).

Into the Twenty-First Century

The collapse of communism produced a brief renaissance for the United Nations in the 1990s. For decades Western leaders had blamed the Communists for the inability to get UN action, so with the collapse, came a great expectation that the United Nations would be empowered to act. In 1990 Iraq leader Saddam Hussein's occupation of Kuwait led to strong UN support for the expulsion of his troops from that country by military force, which was accomplished in 1991. Peacekeeping operations expanded rapidly after 1990. Whereas in 1987, there were some 10,000 UN peacekeepers on missions around the world, by 1995 the number had grown to more than 70,000. These peacekeepers are all sent by member states—the United Nations itself has no forces, and despite the intentions of the founders, very little military planning staff, and no troops on standby in the forces of its member nations. This lack of capacity represents the will of the member states. For example,

during the Korean War of the 1950s and in the war in Iraq of 1990–91, the United States provided its full military capacity, but usually there is no such commitment from member states and resistance to the development of a UN capacity that might rival U.S.-favored organizations such as NATO. Consequently, UN military missions are inevitably slow to assemble and tend to be poorly organized.

UN peacekeeping has a bad name in U.S. politics. The long, violent conflicts in Bosnia, Rwanda, Somalia, and more recently Darfur, indicate to many the weakness of the world body. In Rwanda, in 1994, hundreds of thousands died in ethnic violence. The UN and U.S. involvement in the east African state Somalia marked a rapid turnaround in U.S. political attitudes in 1992–93. President George H. W. Bush deployed 25,000 combat troops to Somalia to help restore order. Shortly after taking office, President Bill Clinton reduced the U.S. military presence there to a few thousand; in the fall of 1993, however, he both refused armored support for U.S. troops and authorized a raid by U.S. Rangers that ended in 18 U.S. dead, a large number in the politics of the time. Clinton was anxious to reduce the negative political impact, so the mission was portrayed as a UN rather than a U.S. action.

In Bosnia, UN peacekeepers were unable to stop ethnic cleansing and were denied a mandate and power to attack aggressors. With U.S. public and elite opinion divided and cautioned by the debacle in Somalia, the United States left the matter to the Europeans and the United Nations, while denying them aid from the North Atlantic Treaty Organization. Finally, when the conflict appeared out of control and domestic concern had grown, the United States led military action and a negotiated settlement. For many, the situation in Bosnia underlined the reality that whatever the legal niceties at the United Nations, only the United States had the muscle to impose peace in the world. The image of America as the reluctant sheriff gained ground in U.S. politics, while in other parts of the world, the image of the United States as police for the powerful had greater resonance.

UN conferences gathered momentum after the end of the cold war. The Earth Summit in Brazil in 1992 on environmental issues set the new standard and led to others, including the 1997 meeting in Kyoto, Japan, that created the first global agreement to combat climate change. UN-sponsored disarmament agreements banned chemical weapons (the Chemical Weapons Convention in 1993) and the testing of nuclear weapons (the Comprehensive Test Ban Treaty in 1996).

The terrorist attacks on the United States on September 11, 2001, were a defining moment at the start of the new century. The UN Security Council offered its immediate support and endorsed U.S. military action to overthrow the Taliban regime in Afghanistan. Despite its previous hostility to the United Nations, the administration of President George W. Bush sought a closer relationship and rejoined UNESCO.

The run-up to the war in Iraq and subsequent events have once again seen the United Nations portrayed in U.S. politics as either villain or weakling. Prior to the U.S.-led invasion in 2003, UN inspectors seeking weapons of mass destruction in Iraq were criticized as being dupes of Saddam Hussein. Despite stating that the United States needed no "permission slip" from the United Nations to attack Iraq, President Bush sought first one and then a second Security Council resolution to pressure Iraq, arguing that the UN's failure to support the United States made it as useless as the League of Nations in the 1930s. Some Democrats contend that the pursuit of the first resolution was merely an attempt to secure centrist votes in the November 2002 midterm congressional elections, and the second was never seriously pursued. In retrospect, the Bush administration argued that earlier resolutions and the right of preemptive self-defense provided the backing of international law for its actions. UN supporters pointed to the wisdom of the majority of nations on the Security Council who refused to support what they saw as a disastrous war.

UN member states provided funds for a budget of $20 billion in 2008, excluding the IMF and the World Bank, while the United States has accumulated unpaid dues to the United Nations of some $1.5 billion, the lion's share of overdue payments. By way of comparison, the $20 billion budget is about half that of the single U.S. state of Virginia, while the UN agency responsible for controlling nuclear proliferation, the International Atomic Energy Agency, has just $200 million to spend. The United Nations also lacks permanent peacekeeping forces or even a headquarters and communications unit comparable to that of most of its member states.

Reform is a term much used in discussions of the United Nations. Some debate focuses on issues of corruption and ineffectiveness; for some states such as India, Germany, and Japan, the issue is to secure a permanent seat on the Security Council. The term *UN reform*, therefore, does not describe a single agenda. The U.S. nationalist agenda includes removing those members of the United Nations alleged to be undemocratic or inhumane from any influence, cutting the budget, and introducing standards of efficiency drawn from the corporate sector. Others in the United States seek greater resources for peacekeeping and other missions. Internationally, many states believe that either the veto should be done away with or expanded to other major states, such as India.

As Mark Twain put it, "any jackass can kick a barn down, but it takes a carpenter to build one." As new crises arise, the familiar arguments will resume between those who see the United Nations as an ally of liberal causes that should not impede U.S. goals and those who regard it as a necessity in an interdependent world.

See also foreign policy and domestic politics since 1933; Korean War and cold war; New Deal Era, 1932–52.

FURTHER READING. Paul Kennedy, *Parliament of Man: The Past, Present, and Future of the United Nations*, 2007; Dan Plesch, *America, Hitler and the UN*, 2010; United Nations, *Basic Facts about the United Nations*, 2004; United Nations Information Organisation, *The United Nations Today and Tomorrow*, 1945; Thomas G. Weiss, David P. Forsythe, Roger A. Coate, and Kelly-Kate Pease, *The United Nations and Changing World Politics*, 2007.

DAN PLESCH

V

veterans

American military veterans were important political actors even before the United States became a nation. All of the American colonies except Connecticut, Delaware, and Quaker Pennsylvania provided pensions for wounded veterans, with South Carolina even holding out the possibility of freedom as a benefit for enlisted slaves. And when it came to pensioning disabled veterans, as the Continental Congress did in 1776, there was ample precedent in the kingdoms of Europe—France, Britain, Prussia, and Russia all had national military hospitals and rudimentary disability pension systems in place by 1780. But the place of the veteran in a self-conscious republic was different and has evolved in unique ways since the Revolution.

When it came to "service pensions"—stipends paid simply on the basis of past military service—some early congressmen balked. In a republic, they argued, military service was a duty of citizenship. Service pensions represented the entering wedge for standing armies and political patronage, creating dependence and (since service pensions were typically limited to officers) invidious distinctions of rank. But under wartime pressures, Congress promised all troops lump-sum payments at the war's end (1778), and Continental officers half-pay pensions for life (1780). When officers of General George Washington's army encamped at Newburgh, New York, demanded full pensions or a cash equivalent as the price of their disbandment, Congress defused the situation with the Commutation Act of 1783, which provided officers with five years' full pay instead of half-pay pensions for life. Noncommissioned indigent veterans, however, would not be pensioned until the Service Pension Act of 1818, and full-service pensions did not arrive until 1832. State militiamen, who made up much of the estimated 232,000-man Revolutionary Army, were excluded from federal benefits entirely. Thus, at its outset the U.S. pension system drew distinctions between officers and men, federal and state troops, and three classes of the deserving: war invalids, indigent "dependents," and soldiers whose only claim to benefits was service.

Continental Army veterans also received warrants for large tracts of land in the public domain, mainly in the Old Northwest Territory and the Southwest Territory, under acts of 1776 and 1780, while land-rich states such as Virginia and New York made grants of their own. Eventually, title to 2,666,080 acres was issued on the basis of Revolutionary War claims. But conflicting state land claims, wars with Native American nations, and a law that, for a time,

restricted sales to 4,000-acre parcels made land warrants of small value to most veterans until the late 1790s, by which time most had been sold to speculators. The same thing happened to officers' commutation certificates: by the time the federal government emerged from default in 1791, many officers had sold their certificates for as little as twelve and a half cents on the dollar.

Attitudes toward Continental veterans gradually evolved from republican worries about vice and patronage to widespread sympathy for their suffering in old age that made the 1818 pension act possible. But Revolutionary War service did not lead to public office (after George Washington, it took eight presidential elections before a military veteran was even nominated), and the few public Revolutionary commemorations tended toward the civic and classical rather than the military: Washington appears in a toga atop Baltimore's Washington Monument (1829), while the Bunker Hill Monument in Charlestown, Massachusetts (1843), is a simple classical obelisk. The Society of the Cincinnati, an officers-only veterans' hereditary order that had provoked fears of aristocracy at its founding in 1783, had declined to only six northeastern state chapters by 1832.

The short wars of the early nineteenth century did little to alter this picture. Individual veterans such as William Henry Harrison and Zachary Taylor parlayed military service into political careers, but veterans as such did not organize—there was no recognizable "veteran vote." A tiny Society of the War of 1812 led a fitful existence from 1853 into the 1890s, when it became a hereditary order; the National Association of Mexican War Veterans was not formed until 1874 and lasted barely into the twentieth century. Veterans of both wars continued to benefit from federal land grants and invalid pensions, but dependent and service pensions came to War of 1812 veterans only in 1871 and to Mexican War veterans in 1887 (dependent) and 1907 (service). The pensioning of Mexican War volunteers was politically difficult because so many of them were Southerners who later fought for the Confederacy. The law finally enacted in 1887 excluded those whose wounds had been sustained in Confederate service and those politically disbarred by the Fourteenth Amendment.

Veterans in Politics

The Civil War marked a watershed in the relation of veterans to society and politics. Union veterans created mass organizations to lobby for their interests, the most powerful of which was the Grand Army of the Republic (GAR), organized in 1866. Nearly all northern towns had GAR posts, which functioned as centers of sociability, providers of charity, and

promoters of a conservative brand of American patriotism in schools and on public holidays such as
Memorial Day (first proclaimed nationally by GAR
commander in chief John Logan in 1868). The GAR
pushed the federal government and the states to
erect soldiers' homes (12 did so by 1888); won land
grants and special treatment under the Homestead
Act for veterans; persuaded some northern states to
give Union veterans preference in hiring; and lobbied
ceaselessly for the expansion of the Pension Bureau,
whose new building (1882; now the National Building Museum) was the largest public space in Washington until 1971.

The largest impact of the Union veterans was on
pension legislation, mainly the Arrears Act (1879) and
Dependent Pension Act (1890). The latter granted a
pension to nearly all Union veterans at a time when
many were still in their fifties. By 1891 military pensions accounted for one dollar of every three spent by
the federal government, and at the high point of the
Civil War pension system in 1902, 999,446 persons,
including widows and orphans, were on the rolls. By
1917 the nation had spent approximately $5 billion on
Union Army and Navy pensions. Civilian reformers
such as E. L. Godkin attacked the "unmanliness" of
those who accepted service pensions and the many
frauds riddling the system, especially under the administration of Benjamin Harrison and his profligate
pension commissioner, James Tanner.

With more than 400,000 members at its height
in 1890, the GAR had the political muscle to make
itself heard. It created an organized bloc of voters
in the North for which both parties—but mainly
Republicans—contended by increasing pension
benefits, authorizing expensive monuments (such
as Grand Army Plaza in Brooklyn, New York, and
the Soldiers and Sailors Monument in Indianapolis,
Indiana), and sponsoring "patriotic" state laws such
as those requiring schoolhouses to fly the American
flag. The pension system also created reciprocal benefits for the Republican Party, because the need for
revenue to pay pension benefits justified the high
tariffs Republican industrialists sought. At the same
time, by putting money into the hands of Union veterans, Republicans created a loyal voting constituency. Especially before the extremely close election of
1888, Democrats charged that the important swing
states of Indiana, Ohio, and Pennsylvania were being
flooded with expedited pension payments.

In the South, Confederate veterans organized late
and at least partly in reaction to the GAR. Barred
from federal entitlements, they obtained pensions
and soldiers' homes from most southern states,
though such benefits were usually modest and limited to the disabled or indigent. Georgia's Confederate disability pensions, for example, averaged only 44
percent of the federal rate in 1900. The United Confederate Veterans (UCV), founded in 1889, presided
over a veterans' culture that shifted ground from intransigence in the 1870s to a romantic "lost cause"

sensibility in the 1890s that even Union veterans
could accept with some reservations. In 1913 Union
and Confederate veterans held a highly publicized
reunion at Gettysburg, where President Woodrow
Wilson declared the Civil War "a quarrel forgotten."

The Spanish-American War produced only 144,252
veterans and two significant organizations: the United
Spanish War Veterans (1904), which soon faded, and
the Veterans of Foreign Wars (VFW), founded in
1913. Unlike the GAR and UCV, the VFW admitted
veterans of subsequent wars, a policy that has allowed
it to persevere into the present. On the other hand,
the VFW policy of limiting membership to overseas
veterans initially hampered the organization in competition with the more inclusive American Legion
(founded in Paris in 1919). The Legion quickly became the most popular organization among the approximately 4 million American veterans of World
War I. It adopted the GAR's internal structure of
local post, state department, and national encampment; consulted with aging GAR members on political strategy; and continued the Grand Army's program of flag ritualism and "patriotic instruction."

In other ways, however, the situation facing World
War I veterans was markedly different. Whereas the
soldiers of 1865 had come back mostly to farms, those
of 1919 returned primarily to cities, where joblessness
was acute and vocational training scarce. When Interior Secretary Franklin Lane in 1919 proposed the
traditional remedy of land grants, he discovered that
most arable public land had already been given away.
Instead, like other belligerents (notably Germany
and Britain), the United States began moving away
from the nineteenth-century model of land grants,
pensions, and warehousing veterans in hospitals and
toward a model of physical rehabilitation and vocational training. All veterans' programs were finally
consolidated in the Veterans Bureau (1921), which in
1930 became the Veterans Administration (VA).

The pension system of 1919 also differed significantly from the expensive, politically partisan,
and fraud-riddled Civil War regime. Instead of a
system of entitlements, the War Risk Act of 1917
allowed World War I soldiers to pay small premiums in return for life insurance and future medical
care. However, its early administration was corrupt,
and veterans' hospitals proved too few in number
and unable to cope with late-developing disabilities such as shell shock. World War I veterans never
did receive service pensions, and were eligible for
non-service-related disability pensions only briefly,
from 1930 to 1933. Instead, politicians opted for "adjusted compensation," a bonus approved in Congress in 1924 and payable in 1945, designed to make
up for wartime inflation and lost earnings. Veterans
were seriously divided on the propriety of the bonus, even after Depression hardships drove 20,000
of them to march on Washington, D.C., in 1932
as a Bonus Army demanding its immediate payment. Although troops led by General Douglas

MacArthur violently expelled the veterans from Anacostia Flats, the bonus was finally paid in 1936.

The worldwide labor and political strife following 1918 sharpened the hard edge of veteran nationalism. Faced with revolution in Russia, chaos in Germany, a general strike in Seattle, and race riots in cities such as Chicago, the American Legion came out immediately against "Bolshevism," which it defined broadly to include every organization from the Communist Party to the League of Women Voters. Legion members helped break strikes of Kansas coal miners and Boston police in the summer of 1919, and from the 1920s through the 1950s, they made war on "Reds." Legionnaires helped bring a House Un-American Activities Committee into existence in 1938 and aided FBI probes of subversion thereafter. The Legion was strongest in small cities and among prosperous members of the middle class; like the GAR, it left racial matters largely to localities, which in practice usually meant segregated posts.

World War II and After

By the time the 12 million veterans of World War II began to return home, the New Deal had institutionalized social welfare spending. Thus, despite the unprecedented scope of the GI Bill, officially titled the Servicemen's Readjustment Act of 1944, few commentators expressed the worries about fraud and dependence that dogged earlier veterans' relief. Drafted by former Legion commander Harry Colmery, the GI Bill provided World War II veterans with free college educations and medical care, unemployment insurance for one year, and guaranteed loans up to $4,000 to buy homes or businesses. Other legislation guaranteed loans on crops to veterans who were farmers, reinstituted vocational training, and tried to safeguard the jobs of those returning from war. GI Bill educational and vocational benefits proved so popular that they were extended to veterans of Korea and Vietnam and to peacetime veterans in the Veterans Readjustment Benefits Act (1966). By the 1970s, the VA was spending more than all but three cabinet departments; it achieved cabinet status in 1989. By 1980 benefits distributed under the GI Bill totaled $120 billion.

Unlike previous wars (but like subsequent conflicts in Korea and Vietnam), World War II was fought mainly by conscripts, which may have made taxpayers more willing to compensate veterans for their "forced labor." These veterans were slightly younger and better educated than World War I veterans and demobilized into considerably less class and racial strife. For the first time, they also included significant numbers of women (the 150,000 members of the Women's Army Corps and 90,000 Naval WAVEs), who qualified for GI Bill benefits. Still, most of the returnees joined older veterans' groups rather than forming new ones: Legion membership, which had fluctuated between 600,000 and 1 million before 1941, reached a record 3.5 million in 1946, while VFW membership rose from 300,000 to 2 million. Among liberal alternative groups founded in 1945, only AMVETS reached 250,000 members.

Politically, World War II ex-soldiers did not vote as a recognizable bloc, but veteran status was an enormous advantage to those seeking office. Joseph McCarthy, for example, was elected to the Senate as "Tail Gunner Joe," while magazine articles trumpeted John F. Kennedy's heroism aboard his boat, PT-109. Every president from Dwight Eisenhower to George H. W. Bush (except Jimmy Carter, a postwar Naval Academy graduate) was a World War II veteran, a string unmatched since the late nineteenth century. In the postwar years, it became normal for the president to address the annual American Legion convention. Culturally, World War II veterans received heroic treatment in movies such as *The Longest Day* (1962) and in a neoclassical World War II Memorial (2004) that stands in stylistic contrast to the bleaker Vietnam (1983) and Korean War (1995) memorials on the Mall in Washington, D.C.

The Korean and Vietnamese conflicts produced none of the triumphalism that followed World War II. Although the VA continued to grow—its 2009 budget request was for $93.7 billion, half of it earmarked for benefits—the Legion and VFW struggled throughout the 1960s and 1970s to attract new veterans whose attitudes toward war and nationalism were ambivalent. After the Vietnam War, which the older organizations supported fiercely, young veterans felt alienated from a society that often ignored or pitied them. In 1967 they formed the first significant antiwar veterans group, the Vietnam Veterans Against the War (VVAW; after 1983, the Vietnam Veterans of America, VVOA). With fewer than 20,000 members, the VVAW publicized war atrocities and lobbied for American withdrawal. In the 1980s, more Vietnam veterans began to join the Legion and VFW, bringing those groups up to their 2008 memberships of approximately 3 million and 2.2 million, respectively. The treatment of veterans suffering from post-traumatic stress disorder/ (PTSD) and exposure to defoliants in Vietnam became important issues for these organizations, often bringing them into conflict with the Defense Department.

In the years since Vietnam, relations between veterans and society have changed in several ways. Subsequent military actions in Grenada, Bosnia, Kuwait, and Iraq have been carried out by volunteer forces, making military experience more remote from the day-to-day lives of most Americans. About 15 percent of those serving in the military are now women, a fact that may eventually change the traditional veteran discourse about war as a test of masculinity—the dedication of the first memorial to military service women at Arlington National Cemetery in 1997 marked the change. And the gradual passing of the World War II generation has produced a wave of nostalgia for veterans of that war similar to the one that engulfed Civil War veterans toward the end of their lives.

See also armed forces, politics in the.

FURTHER READING. Mary R. Dearing, *Veterans in Politics: The Story of the G.A.R.*, 1952; Ihor Gawdiak et al., *Veterans Benefits and Judicial Review: Historical Antecedents and the Development of the American System*, 1992, downloadable from http://handle.dtic.mil/100.2/ADA302666; David A. Gerber, ed., *Disabled Veterans in History*, 2000; William H. Glasson, *Federal Military Pensions in the United States*, 1918; Laura S. Jensen, *Patriots, Settlers and the Origins of American Social Policy*, 2003; Stuart McConnell, *Glorious Contentment: The Grand Army of the Republic, 1866–1900*, 1992; William Pencak, *For God and Country: The American Legion, 1919–1941*, 1989; John P. Resch, *Suffering Soldiers: Revolutionary War Veterans, Moral Sentiment, and Political Culture in the Early Republic*, 1999; Paul Starr, *The Discarded Army: Soldiers after Vietnam*, 1973; Dixon Wecter, *When Johnny Comes Marching Home*, 1944.

STUART MCCONNELL

Vietnam and Indochina wars

Apples and Dominoes

The makers of U.S. foreign policy after World War II often used analogies to explain to the American people the need for cold war commitments. In 1947, trying to justify to a skeptical Congress an outlay of economic and military aid to Greece and Turkey, Undersecretary of State Dean Acheson warned of the consequences of even a single Communist success in southeastern Europe: "Like apples in a barrel infected by the corruption of one rotten one, the corruption of Greece would infect Iran and all to the East." By 1954 the cold war had gone global, and much of the foreign policy concern of President Dwight Eisenhower was focused on Southeast Asia and particularly Indochina (the states of Vietnam, Laos, and Cambodia), where the French were engaged in a struggle to restore their colonial status, despite the clear preference of most Indochinese to be independent of outsider control. The Vietnamese independence movement was led by Ho Chi Minh, a Communist of long standing.

Contemplating U.S. military involvement on the side of the French, Eisenhower told a press conference why Americans should care about the fate of Vietnam. "You have a row of dominoes set up and you knock over the first one, and what will happen to the last one is the certainty that it will go over very quickly.... The loss of Indochina will cause the fall of Southeast Asia like a set of dominoes." Communism would not stop with just one or two victories. The loss to communism of strategically and economically important Southeast Asia would be a serious setback.

As U.S. involvement in the Vietnam War grew over the years, resulting in the commitment of hundreds of thousands of ground troops and the lavish use of airpower over North and South Vietnam after early 1965, the domino theory that underpinned it evolved. John F. Kennedy, who inherited from Eisenhower a significant financial commitment to the South Vietnamese government of Ngo Dinh Diem and discovered that U.S. military advisors and Central Intelligence Agency officers were hard at work on Diem's behalf, publicly professed his faith in the domino theory. By the time Lyndon Johnson succeeded to the presidency, following Kennedy's assassination in November 1963, Johnson's foreign policy advisors, most of them inherited from Kennedy, had concluded that the dominoes were perhaps less territorial than psychological. Withdrawal from Vietnam would embolden America's enemies and discourage its friends everywhere. The United States would lose credibility if it abandoned South Vietnam—no one, not even the European allies, would ever again take the Americans' word on faith. The final domino was not, as one official put it, "some small country in Southeast Asia, but the presidency itself"; the American people would not tolerate a humiliating defeat (the word *defeat* always carried the modifier *humiliating*) in Vietnam and would cast out any president judged responsible for having allowed it to occur.

Political Constraints

American presidents faced a dilemma each election cycle during the war in Vietnam. As Daniel Ellsberg, a Pentagon advisor turned antiwar advocate, put it, presidents could not commit large numbers of American soldiers to combat in Southeast Asia, yet at the same time they were not supposed to lose the southern part of Vietnam to communism. All-out war was politically unacceptable. The perception that the United States had abandoned its friends to totalitarianism and reneged on its word was equally unacceptable. A president's political effectiveness therefore depended on a war that could not be lost, but one whose costs remained low enough, in blood and treasure, to keep the American people from growing restive.

Sensing this, the presidents who confronted in Vietnam the rise of a nationalist-Communist independence movement attempted to keep the American role in the conflict out of the public eye. The war must be fought, said Secretary of State Dean Rusk (1961–69) "in cold blood," by which he meant not remorselessly but with restraint. The first U.S. commitment, to what was then a French-backed regime in the south that was supposed to be an alternative to the popular Ho Chi Minh, was a small portion of aid provided by the administration of Harry Truman in 1950, mainly obscured by the far more visible war in Korea. Despite his warning about the dominos falling, Eisenhower also limited U.S. involvement in Vietnam, shouldering aside the French after 1954 and sending funds and advisors to help Diem, but refusing to order airstrikes, send in combat troops, or otherwise stake his reputation on the outcome of the conflict. "I am convinced," wrote the president, "that no victory is possible in that type of theater."

Kennedy, too, refused to commit U.S. combat troops to Vietnam. He did secretly insert several hundred Special Forces to help train the South Vietnamese army. But he resisted pleas by some advisors, in early 1961, to intervene with force in Laos, and spurned recommendations by others to send a Marine "task force" to confront the Communists militarily. Even Johnson, who would authorize the introduction of over half a million troops into the war, tried to escalate quietly, never declaring war, seldom making a speech on the war, and issuing such announcements as there were about the escalations on Saturday afternoons, so as to avoid the full attention of the media.

American Public Opinion and the War

At first, and in good part because of his efforts to keep the war off the front pages, Johnson enjoyed high approval ratings for his policy of quiet but determined escalation. Gallup pollsters had asked a couple of questions about Indochina during 1953 and 1954, as French struggles hit the newspapers, then left the subject altogether until the spring of 1964, when they cautiously inquired, "Have you given any attention to developments in South Vietnam?" Just 37 percent of respondents said they had. That August, after Congress passed the Tonkin Gulf Resolution, which granted the president the latitude to conduct the war in Vietnam as he wished, Gallup asked what the country "should do next in regard to Vietnam." Twenty-seven percent said, "[S]how [we] can't be pushed around, keep troops there, be prepared," 12 percent wanted to "get tougher" using "more pressure," and 10 percent said, "[A]void all-out war, sit down and talk." The largest percentage of respondents (30 percent) had "no opinion."

By February 1965, the month in which the Johnson administration decided to begin systematically bombing targets in North Vietnam, over nine-tenths of those polled had heard that something was going on in Vietnam. Sixty-four percent thought the United States should "continue present efforts" to win the war, and of this group, 31 percent were willing to risk nuclear war in the bargain. (Just 21 percent thought that would be unwise.) Only late in 1965 did pollsters begin to ask whether Americans approved or disapproved of the president's handling of the war. Fifty-eight percent approved, just 22 percent did not. It is worth noting that in Gallup's annual poll seeking the world's "Most Admired Man" (women were measured separately), Johnson topped the list for three years running through 1967.

Johnson's anxieties about the war were growing nonetheless. The conflict was intrinsically vicious: once he committed U.S. combat troops to the fight, in March 1965, casualties began to mount. Johnson was also worried about the domestic political implications of a protracted, indecisive struggle, and even more a failure of nerve that would allow the Vietnamese Communists to take over South Vietnam and thereby revive talk that the Democratic Party was the refuge of appeasers, with himself as Neville Chamberlain. Above all, Johnson needed congressional and popular support for the legislation known collectively as the Great Society, his ambitious effort to undo racism and poverty in the United States. He worried most about the right wing. "If I don't go in now and they show later that I should have," he confided in early 1965, "they'll . . . push Vietnam up my ass every time." So he went in incrementally, hiding the war's true cost and hoping to keep it on low boil while his reform agenda went through, anticipating that his level of commitment would be enough to keep the right satisfied, yet not too much to antagonize the left, which, by early 1965, had begun to object to the escalating conflict.

By mid-1966, Americans were evenly divided over whether they approved or disapproved of the war; 15 months later, by 46 percent to 44 percent, those polled said that the country had "made a mistake sending troops to fight in Vietnam." In the meantime, the 1966 midterm elections favored the Republicans, who had ably exploited fears of urban violence, an indecisive war, and a protest movement by young people who seemed, to many Americans, unruly and unpatriotic.

Rising Protests, and the Tet Offensive

By the fall of 1967, American political culture had been affected by the emergence of the antiwar movement. Starting in the early 1960s with scattered concerns about the escalating war, then catalyzed by Johnson's decisions to bomb and send troops in early 1965, the movement grew rapidly on college campuses, incorporating those who believed the war an act of American imperialism, pacifists, scholars of Asian history and politics, seekers of righteous causes, those who believed sincerely that Vietnam was a wicked war, and many who worried that they or someone they loved would be drafted and sent to the killing fields of Southeast Asia. Large as antiwar demonstrations had become by late 1967—100,000 people rallied against the war in Washington that October—it was never the case that most Americans were protesters or that most Americans sympathized with them.

Yet the protests unnerved Johnson and undeniably affected the nation's political discourse. The president was afflicted by taunts outside the White House: "Hey, hey, LBJ, how many kids did you kill today?" Members of Congress found, at best, confusion about the war among their constituents, and, at worst, open anger about a conflict that seemed to be escalating without cause or explanation. Family members of key Vietnam policy makers asked increasingly sharp questions about the war at the dinner table, and the estrangement of friends who had turned against the war caused much grief; Secretary of Defense Robert McNamara's wife and son developed ulcers as a result of the strain.

Late in 1967, concerned about his slipping poll numbers and the war's possible damage to his domestic program, Johnson called his field commander home to reassure the public. General William Westmoreland was an outwardly confident man who believed that the killing machine he had built would grind the enemy down with superior training, firepower, and sheer numbers. The end of the war, Westmoreland told the National Press Club on November 21, "begins to come into view." Optimism reigned throughout South Vietnam. Victory "lies within our grasp—the enemy's hopes are bankrupt." Early January poll numbers bounced slightly Johnson's way. Then, in the middle of the night on January 30, the start of the Tet holiday in Vietnam, the National Liberation Front (NLF), sometimes known as the Viet Cong, and North Vietnamese soldiers launched a massive offensive against American and South Vietnamese strongholds throughout the south. Countless positions were overrun. The beautiful old capital of Hué fell, and thousands of alleged collaborators with the Saigon government were executed. Tan Son Nhut airbase, just outside Saigon, was shelled. Even the grounds of the American embassy were penetrated by enemy soldiers. The body count, the ghoulish measure of progress in the war demanded by Westmoreland's strategy of attrition, rose dramatically on all sides.

In the end, the enemy failed to achieve its military objectives. The U.S. embassy grounds were retaken within hours. Tan Son Nhut remained secure, along with Saigon itself. Hué was restored to the South Vietnamese government, though only after days of brutal fighting and subsequent revenge killings. The southern-based NLF was badly cut up, its forces having been used as shock troops during the offensive. North Vietnamese officials admitted years later that they had overestimated their ability to administer a crushing blow to the South Vietnamese and American forces during Tet.

In the United States, however, the Tet Offensive seemed to confirm Johnson's worst fears that an inconclusive, messy war would irreparably damage his political standing. It did no good to point out that the enemy had been beaten. Had not Westmoreland, and by extension Johnson himself, offered an upbeat assessment of South Vietnam's prospects just weeks earlier? Had not Americans been assured, time after time, that their military was invincible, its rectitude unquestionable? The war came home in direct ways—the upsurge in the number of American casulties; television coverage of a South Vietnamese policeman summarily executing an NLF suspect on a Saigon street; the twisted logic of a U.S. officer who said, of the village of Ben Tre,

"we had to destroy the town in order to save it." Mainstream media reflected new depths of popular discouragement. In March, when Gallup asked whether the time had come for the United States to "gradually withdraw from Vietnam," 56 percent agreed, and only 34 percent disapproved of the idea. Altogether, 78 percent believed that the country was making no progress in the war.

The Unmaking of Lyndon Johnson

Johnson's first impulse was to toughen his rhetoric and stay the course. If the generals wanted more troops, they could have them. Secretary McNamara left the administration and was replaced by Johnson's old friend and presumed supporter Clark Clifford. But the erosion of public support for the war now undercut official unity in Washington. Clifford conducted a quick but honest analysis of the situation in Vietnam and concluded that the military could not guarantee success, even with a substantial infusion of troops. Advisors who had previously urged a sustained commitment now hedged: former secretary of state Acheson, a noted hard-liner, told Johnson that American "interests in Europe" were in jeopardy, in part because the nation was hemorrhaging gold at an alarming rate. On March 12, the president was nearly beaten in the New Hampshire presidential primary by the low-key Eugene McCarthy, who challenged Johnson's Vietnam War policies. The close call left Johnson despondent and concerned about a bruising primary campaign. To the surprise of even close friends, Johnson announced on March 31 that he would not seek reelection but would instead dedicate himself full time to the pursuit of a negotiated peace in Vietnam.

The war had wrecked Johnson and now tore apart his party. The Democrats split following Johnson's withdrawal from the campaign. Some backed McCarthy. Many flocked to the candidacy of Robert Kennedy, who had turned against the war, but whose assassination on June 6 ended the dream that the Democrats would unite under a popular, socially conscious, antiwar leader. George McGovern entered the fray as a stand-in for Kennedy, but he lacked Kennedy's charisma and connections. At its chaotic convention in Chicago that August, in which protesters clashed with Mayor Richard Daley's notoriously unsympathetic police (and came off second best), the party nominated Johnson's vice president, Hubert Humphrey. Loyal to Johnson, who nevertheless maligned him repeatedly, Humphrey at first clung to the discredited policy of toughness on Vietnam. But when polls showed that he was running behind the Republican nominee Richard Nixon (who claimed to have a "secret plan" to end the war) and only slightly ahead of right-wing independent George Wallace (who guaranteed a military victory in Vietnam if the Communists refused to come to heel), Humphrey shifted his position. He would, he said, stop bombing the north. His tone moderated.

Despite what had seemed long odds, in the end Humphrey nearly won, falling just 200,000 votes short of Nixon in the popular tally.

The Nixon-Kissinger Strategy, and War's End

Nixon had managed to rise from the political dead by cobbling together a coalition of white Americans fed up with disorder in the streets, militant blacks, militant students, and the indecisive war. Many of those previously loyal to the Democratic Party built by Franklin Roosevelt now defected to the Republicans. They included Catholics, ethnic voters in suburbs, and southern whites who were conservative on social issues but not quite ready to stomach the extremism of Wallace. They were part of what Nixon would call "the great silent majority," whom he presumed wanted "peace with honor" in Vietnam, whatever that meant.

Nixon and his national security advisor, Henry Kissinger, set out to recast diplomacy and liquidate the war. They employed a two-track approach. They would escalate the bombing of enemy targets and initiate attacks in third countries (Cambodia and Laos) in order to demonstrate to Hanoi their determination not to be bullied. At the same time, they would attempt to negotiate an end to hostilities, in part by pursuing détente with the Soviet Union and China. Nixon coldly gauged that most of the domestic, political cost of the war resulted from the death of American soldiers. He therefore proposed to substitute Vietnamese lives for American ones, through a program called "Vietnamization." Nixon continued bombing, but he also funded an expansion of the South Vietnamese army (ARVN) and equipped it with the latest weapons. And in late 1969, he began to withdraw U.S. troops, reducing the need to draft more young men and thus removing the most toxic issue around which the antiwar movement had gathered.

Still the protests did not end. People remained angry that the war dragged on, that Americans and Vietnamese continued to die in great numbers. The expansion of the American war into Cambodia and Laos brought renewed fury. The continued opposition to Nixon's policies, information leaks concerning a secret campaign to bomb Cambodia in 1969, and the disclosure, by Daniel Ellsberg, of the secret *Pentagon Papers* study in 1971, inspired Nixon to establish the clandestine White House "Plumbers," whose job it was to wiretap the telephones of the administration's self-construed enemies and even to burgle offices in search of incriminating information. The capture of a Plumbers' team at the Watergate complex in Washington in June 1972 ultimately led to the unraveling of the Nixon presidency. The attempt to cover up illegal behavior would be traced to the Oval Office.

A peace treaty was signed in Vietnam in January 1973. Both North and South soon violated its terms. Weakened by the Watergate scandal, Nixon was unable to prevent Congress from closing the valve on U.S. support for the South Vietnamese government. And in the summer of 1973, Congress passed the War Powers Act, designed to prevent presidents from conducting war as high-handedly as Johnson and Nixon had done, at least without disclosure to the legislature. Nixon was forced to resign in August 1974. When, the following spring, the North Vietnamese launched a powerful offensive against South Vietnam, and the ARVN largely crumbled, the new president, Gerald Ford, and Henry Kissinger, now secretary of state, tried to get Congress to loosen the purse strings on military aid to the besieged Saigon regime.

But Congress, and the majority of Americans, had had enough. They felt they had been lied to about the war, and they refused to trust Ford. Stung by Vietnam, many Americans now turned inward, shunning the kinds of foreign policy commitments they had seemed to accept so readily during the first three decades of the cold war. Americans had grown skeptical about what critics called, in the aftermath of Vietnam, the "imperial presidency," which acted without proper, constitutional regard for the wishes of the other branches of government or the temper of the people. The Vietnam War thus reshaped international and domestic politics, albeit temporarily. The continued usurpations of power by presidents since 1975 remind us that the supposed lessons of Vietnam—greater caution and humility in foreign affairs, greater transparency at home in the process by which war is undertaken—did not endure.

See also era of confrontation and decline, 1964–80; era of consensus, 1952–64; Korean War and cold war.

FURTHER READING. Jeffrey Kimball, *Nixon's Vietnam War*, 1998; Walter LaFeber, *The Deadly Bet: LBJ, Vietnam, and the 1968 Election*, 2005; Fredrik Logevall, *Choosing War: The Lost Chance for Peace and the Escalation of War in Vietnam*, 1999; Robert S. McNamara, with Brian VanDeMark, *In Retrospect: The Tragedy and Lessons of Vietnam*, 1995; Andrew J. Rotter, ed., *Light at the End of the Tunnel: A Vietnam War Anthology*, 2nd ed., 1999; Robert D. Schulzinger, *A Time for Peace: The United States and Vietnam, 1941–1975*, 1997; Neil Sheehan, *A Bright Shining Lie: John Paul Vann and America in Vietnam*, 1988; Melvin Small, *Johnson, Nixon, and the Doves*, 1988; Marilyn B. Young, *The Vietnam Wars 1945–1990*, 1991.

ANDREW J. ROTTER

voting

The right to vote in the United States has a complex history. In the very long run of more than 200 years, the trajectory of this history has been one of expansion: a far greater proportion of the population was enfranchised by the early twenty-first century than was true at the nation's birth. But this long-run trend reveals only part of the story: the history of the right to vote has also been a history of conflict and struggle, of movements backward as well as forward, of sharply demarcated state and regional variations. It is also the story, more generally, of efforts to transform the United States into a democracy: a form of government in which all adults—regardless of their class, gender, race, ethnicity, or place of birth—would have equal political rights. That history took nearly two centuries to unfold, and in key respects, it continues unfolding to the present day.

Democracy Rising

The seeds of this history were planted in the late eighteenth century, as the new American nation was being forged out of 13 former colonies. The Founding Fathers were staunch believers in representative government, but few, if any, of them believed that all adults (or even all adult males) had the "right" to participate in choosing the new nation's leaders. (Indeed, it was unclear whether voting was a "right" or a "privilege," and the word *democracy* itself had negative connotations, suggesting rule by the mob.) The founders had diverse views, but most believed that participation in government should be limited to those who could establish their independence and their "stake" in the new society through the ownership of property. Many agreed with William Blackstone's view that people "in so mean a situation that they are esteemed to have no will of their own" would be subject to manipulation if they had the franchise, while others feared that such persons might exercise their will too aggressively. Neither the original Constitution, ratified in 1788, nor the Bill of Rights, ratified in 1791, made any mention of a "right to vote."

After some internal debate, the men who wrote that Constitution, meeting in Philadelphia in 1787, decided not to adopt a national suffrage requirement: they left the issue to the states. This was a momentous decision—it meant that the breadth of the right to vote would vary from state to state for most of the nation's history, and the federal government would have to struggle for almost two centuries to establish national norms of democratic inclusion. Yet this decision was grounded less in principle than in pragmatic political considerations. By the late 1780s, each state already had a suffrage requirement, developed during the colonial era or during the first years of independence. The designers of the Constitution worried that any national requirement would be opposed by some states—as too broad or too narrow—and thus jeopardize the process of constitutional ratification. In *Federalist* 52, James Madison wrote, "One uniform rule would probably have been as dissatisfactory to some of the States as it would have been difficult to the convention." The only allusion to the breadth of the franchise in the Constitution was in Article I, section II, which specified that all persons who could vote for the most numerous house of each state legislature could also participate in elections for the House of Representatives.

Thus, at the nation's founding, suffrage was far from universal, and the breadth of the franchise varied from one state to the next. The right to vote was limited to those who owned property (ten states) or paid taxes of a specified value (New Hampshire, Georgia, and Pennsylvania)—only Vermont, the fourteenth state, had no such test. African Americans and Native Americans were expressly excluded by law or practice in South Carolina, Georgia, and Virginia. In New Jersey alone were women permitted to vote, and they lost that right in 1807.

Within a short time, however, popular pressures began to shrink the limitations on the franchise: the first two-thirds of the nineteenth century witnessed a remarkable expansion of democratic rights. These changes had multiple sources: shifts in the social structure, including the growth of urban areas; a burgeoning embrace of democratic ideology, including the word *democracy*; active, organized opposition to property and tax requirements from propertyless men, particularly those who had served as soldiers in the Revolutionary War and the War of 1812; the desire of settlers in the new territories in the "west" to attract many more fellow settlers; and the emergence of durable political parties that had to compete in elections and thus sometimes had self-interested reasons for wanting to expand the electorate. As a result of these social and political changes, every state held at least one constitutional convention between 1790 and the 1850s.

In most states, enough of these factors converged to produce state constitutional revisions that significantly broadened the franchise. By the 1850s, nearly all seaboard states had eliminated their property and taxpaying requirements, and the new states in the interior never adopted them in the first place. The abolition of these formal class barriers to voting was not achieved without conflict: many conservatives fought hard to preserve the old order. Warren Dutton of Massachusetts argued that, because "the means of subsistence were so abundant and the demand for labor great," any man who failed to acquire property was "indolent or vicious." Conservatives like New York's chancellor James Kent openly voiced fears of "the power of the poor and the profligate to control the affluent." But most Americans recognized that the sovereign "people" included many individuals without property. "The course of things in this country is for the extension, and not the restriction of popular rights," Senator Nathan Sanford said at the 1821 New York State Constitutional Convention.

A number of states in the interior expanded the franchise in another way as well: to encourage new settlement, they granted the franchise even to noncitizens, to immigrants who had resided in the state for several years and had declared their "intention" to become citizens. In the frontier state of Illinois, for example, one delegate to the 1847 constitutional convention argued that granting the vote to immigrants was "the greatest inducement for men to come amongst us . . . to develop the vast and inexhaustible resources of our state." Increased land values and tax revenues would follow. In the course of the nineteenth century, more than 18 states adopted such provisions.

However, the franchise did not expand for everyone. While property requirements were being dropped, formal racial exclusions became more common. In the 1830s, for example, both North Carolina and Pennsylvania added the word *white* to their constitutional requirements for voting. By 1855 only five states—all in New England—did not discriminate against African Americans. "Paupers"—men who were dependent on public relief in one form or another—suffered a similar fate, as did many Native Americans (because they were either not "white" or not citizens).

Still, the right to vote was far more widespread in 1850 or 1860 than it had been in 1790; and the reduction of economic barriers to the franchise occurred in the United States far earlier than in most countries of Europe or Latin America. The key to this "exceptional" development, however, resided less in any unique American ideology of inclusion than in two peculiarities of the history of the United States. The first—critical to developments in the North— was that property and taxpaying requirements were dropped before the industrial revolution had proceeded very far and thus before an industrial working class had taken shape. Massachusetts and New York, for example, dropped their property requirements in the early 1820s, before those two states became home to tens of thousands of industrial workers. (In Rhode Island, the one state where debates on suffrage reform occurred after considerable industrialization had taken place, a small civil war erupted in the 1830s and 1840s, when two rival legislatures and administrations, elected under different suffrage requirements, competed for legitimacy.) In contrast to Europe, apprehensions about the political power—and ideological leanings—of industrial workers did not delay their enfranchisement. The second distinctive feature of the American story was slavery: one reason that landed elites in much of the world feared democracy was that it meant enfranchising millions of peasants and landless agricultural laborers. But in the U.S. South, the equivalent class—the men and women who toiled from dawn to dusk on land they did not own—was enslaved and consequently would not acquire political power even if the franchise were broadened.

Indeed, the high-water mark of democratic impulses in the nineteenth-century United States involved slavery—or, to be precise, ex-slaves. In an extraordinary political development, in the immediate aftermath of the Civil War, Congress passed (and the states ratified) the Fifteenth Amendment, which prohibited denial of the right to vote to any citizen by "the United States or by any State on account of race, color, or previous condition of servitude." The

passage of this amendment—a development unforeseen by the nation's political leadership even a few years earlier—stemmed from the partisan interests of the Republican Party, which hoped that African Americans would become a political base in the South: an appreciation of the heroism of the 180,000 African Americans who had served in the Union Army, and the conviction that, without the franchise, the freedmen in the South would soon end up being subservient to the region's white elites.

The Fifteenth Amendment (alongside the Fourteenth, passed shortly before) constituted a significant shift in the involvement of the federal government in matters relating to the franchise—since it constrained the ability of the states to impose whatever limitations they wished upon the right to vote— and was also a remarkable expression of democratic idealism on the part of a nation in which racism remained pervasive. Massachusetts senator Henry Wilson argued that the extension of suffrage would indicate that "we shall have carried out logically the ideas that lie at the foundation of our institutions; we shall be in harmony with our professions; we shall have acted like a truly republican and Christian people."

Hesitations and Rollbacks

Yet in a deep historical irony, this idealism was voiced at a moment when the tides of democracy were already cresting and beginning to recede. Starting in the 1850s in some states and accelerating in the 1870s, many middle- and upper-class Americans began to lose faith in democracy and in the appropriateness of universal (male) suffrage. An unsigned article in the *Atlantic Monthly* noted in 1879:

> Thirty or forty years ago it was considered the rankest heresy to doubt that a government based on universal suffrage was the wisest and best that could be devised . . . Such is not now the case. Expressions of doubt and distrust in regard to universal suffrage are heard constantly in conversation, and in all parts of the country.

The sources of this ideological shift were different in the South than they were elsewhere, but class dynamics were prominent throughout the nation. In the Northeast and the Midwest, rapid industrialization coupled with high rates of immigration led to the formation of an immigrant working class whose enfranchisement was regarded as deeply undesirable by a great many middle-class Americans. The first political manifestation of these views came in the 1850s with the appearance and meteoric growth of the American (or Know-Nothing) Party. Fueled by a hostility to immigrants (and Catholics in particular), the Know-Nothings sought to limit the political influence of newcomers by restricting the franchise to those who could pass literacy tests and by imposing a lengthy waiting period (such as 21 years) before naturalized immigrants could vote. In most states such proposals were rebuffed, but restrictions were imposed in several locales, including Massachusetts and Connecticut.

The Know-Nothing Party collapsed almost as rapidly as it had arisen, but the impulse to limit the electoral power of immigrant workers resurfaced after the Civil War, intensified by huge new waves of immigration and by the numerous local political successes of left-leaning and prolabor third parties, such as the Greenback Labor Party and several socialist parties. "Universal Suffrage," wrote Charles Francis Adams Jr., the descendant of two presidents, "can only mean . . . the government of ignorance and vice: it means a European, and especially Celtic, proletariat on the Atlantic coast; an African proletariat on the shores of the Gulf, and a Chinese proletariat on the Pacific." To forestall such a development, proposals were put forward, sometimes with success, to reinstitute financial requirements for some types of voting (for municipal offices or on bond issues, for example) and to require immigrants to present naturalization papers when they showed up at the polls. Gradually, the laws that had permitted noncitizens to vote were repealed (the last state to do so, Arkansas, acted in 1926), and by the 1920s, more than a dozen states in the North and West imposed literacy or English-language literacy tests for voting. (New York, with a large immigrant population, limited the franchise in 1921 to those who could pass an English-language literacy requirement; the law remained in place until the 1960s.) Many more states tightened residency requirements and adopted new personal registration laws that placed challenging procedural obstacles between the poor and the ballot box. In the West, far more draconian laws straightforwardly denied the right to vote to any person who was a "native of China."

In the South, meanwhile, the late nineteenth and early twentieth centuries witnessed the wholesale disfranchisement of African Americans—whose rights had supposedly been guaranteed by the passage of the Fifteenth Amendment. In the 1870s and into the 1880s, African Americans participated actively in southern politics, usually as Republicans, influencing policies and often gaining election to local and even state offices. But after the withdrawal of the last northern troops in 1877, southern whites began to mount concerted (and sometimes violent) campaigns to drive African Americans out of public life. In the 1890s, these "redeemers" developed an array of legal strategies designed expressly to keep African Americans from voting. Among them were literacy tests, poll taxes, cumulative poll taxes (demanding that all past as well as current taxes be paid), lengthy residency requirements, elaborate registration systems, felon disfranchisement laws, and confusing multiple box balloting methods (which required votes for different offices to be dropped into different boxes). These mechanisms were designed to discriminate without directly mentioning race, which would

have violated the Fifteenth Amendment. "Discrimination!" noted future Virginia senator Carter Glass at a constitutional convention in his state in 1901. "That, exactly, is what this Convention was elected for—to discriminate to the very extremity of permissible action under the limitations of the Federal Constitution, with a view to the elimination of every negro voter who can be gotten rid of." These strategies were effective: in Louisiana, where more than 130,000 blacks had been registered to vote in 1896, only 1,342 were registered by 1904. Once the Republican Party was so diminished that it had no possibility of winning elections in the South, most states simplified the practice of discrimination by adopting a "white primary" within the Democratic Party. The only meaningful elections in the South, by the early twentieth century, were the Democratic primaries, and African Americans were expressly barred from participation.

This retrenchment occurred with the tacit, if reluctant, acquiescence of the federal government. In a series of rulings, the Supreme Court upheld the constitutionality of the disfranchising measures adopted in the South, because they did not explicitly violate the Fifteenth Amendment. Meanwhile, Congress repeatedly debated the merits of renewed intervention in the South but never quite had the stomach to intercede. The closest it came was in 1890, when most Republicans supported a federal elections bill (called the Lodge Force bill), which would have given federal courts and supervisors oversight of elections (much as the Voting Rights Act would do in 1965); the measure passed the House but stalled in the Senate. As a result, the South remained a one-party region, with the vast majority of African Americans deprived of their voting rights for another 75 years. In both the North and (far more dramatically) the South, the breadth of the franchise was thus narrowed between the Civil War and World War I.

Half of the Population

While all of this was transpiring, a separate suffrage movement—to enfranchise women—was fitfully progressing across the historical landscape. Although periodically intersecting with efforts to enfranchise African Americans, immigrants, and the poor, this movement had its own distinctive rhythms, not least because it generated a unique countermovement of women opposed to their own enfranchisement who feared that giving women the vote could seriously damage the health of families.

The first stirrings of the woman suffrage movement occurred the late 1840s and 1850s. Building on democratizing currents that had toppled other barriers to the franchise, small groups of supporters of female suffrage convened meetings and conventions to articulate their views and to launch a movement. The most famous of these occurred in 1848 in Seneca Falls, New York, hosted by (among others) Elizabeth Cady Stanton—who would go on to become one of the movement's leaders for many decades. With roots in the growing urban and quasi-urban middle class of the northern states, the early suffrage movement attracted critical support from abolitionists, male and female, who saw parallels between the lack of freedom of slaves and the lack of political (and some civil) rights for women. Indeed, many leaders of this young movement believed that, after the Civil War, women and African Americans would both be enfranchised in the same groundswell of democratic principle: as Stanton put it, women hoped "to avail ourselves of the strong arm and the blue uniform of the black soldier to walk in by his side." But they were deeply disappointed. The Republican leadership in Washington, as well as many former abolitionists, displayed little enthusiasm for linking women's rights to the rights of ex-slaves, and they thought it essential to focus on the latter. "One question at a time," intoned abolitionist Wendell Phillips. "This hour belongs to the negro." As a result, the Fifteenth Amendment made no mention of women (and thus tacitly seemed to condone their disfranchisement); even worse, the Fourteenth Amendment explicitly defended the voting rights of "male" inhabitants.

Women also suffered a rebuff in the courts. In the early 1870s, several female advocates of suffrage—including Susan B. Anthony, a key leader of the movement—filed lawsuits after they were not permitted to vote; they maintained that the refusal of local officials to give them ballots infringed their rights of free speech and deprived them of one of the "privileges and immunities" of citizens, which had been guaranteed to all citizens by the Fourteenth Amendment. In 1875, in *Minor v. Happersett*, the Supreme Court emphatically rejected this argument, ruling that suffrage did not necessarily accompany citizenship and thus that states possessed the legal authority to decide which citizens could vote.

Meanwhile, activists had formed two organizations expressly designed to pursue the cause of woman suffrage. The first was the National Woman Suffrage Association, founded by Stanton and Anthony in 1869. A national organization controlled by women, its strategic goal was to pressure the federal government into enfranchising women across the nation through passage of a constitutional amendment akin to the Fifteenth Amendment. The second was the American Woman Suffrage Association, which aimed to work at the state level, with both men and women, convincing legislatures and state constitutional conventions to drop gender barriers to suffrage. For two decades, both organizations worked energetically, building popular support yet gaining only occasional victories. A federal amendment did make it to the floor of the Senate but was decisively defeated. By the late 1890s, several western states, including Utah and Wyoming, had adopted woman suffrage, but elsewhere defeat was the norm. In numerous locales, small victories were achieved with measures that permitted women to vote for school boards.

In 1890 the two associations joined forces to create the National American Woman Suffrage Association (NAWSA). Gradually, the leadership of the movement was handed over to a new generation of activists, including Carrie Chapman Catt, who possessed notable organizational skills and a somewhat different ideological approach to the issue. Older universalist arguments about natural rights and the equality of men and women were downplayed, while new emphasis was given to the notion that women had distinctive interests and that they possessed qualities that might improve politics and put an end to "scoundrelism and ruffianism at the polls." Nonetheless, opponents of woman suffrage railed at the idea, denying that any "right" to vote existed and calling the suffrage movement (among other things) an attack "on the integrity of the family" that "denies and repudiates the obligations of motherhood." Organized opposition also came from some women, particularly from the upper classes, who felt they already had sufficient access to power, and from liquor interests, which feared enfranchising a large protemperance voting bloc.

Resistance to enfranchising women also stemmed from a broader current in American politics: the declining middle- and upper-class faith in democracy that had fueled the efforts to disfranchise African Americans in the South and immigrant workers in the North. As one contemporary observer noted, "the opposition today seems not so much against *women* as against any more voters at all." In part to overcome that resistance, some advocates of woman suffrage, in the 1890s and into the early twentieth century, put forward what was known as the "statistical argument": the notion that enfranchising women was a way of outweighing the votes of the ignorant and undesirable. In the South, it was argued, the enfranchisement of women "would insure . . . durable white supremacy," and, in the North, it would overcome the "foreign influence." Elizabeth Cady Stanton, among others, joined the chorus calling for literacy tests for voting, for both men and women—a view that was formally repudiated by NAWSA only in 1909.

Still, successes remained sparse until the second decade of the twentieth century, when the organizational muscle of NAWSA began to strengthen and the movement allied itself with the interests of working women and the working class more generally. This new coalition helped to generate victories in Washington, California, and several other states between 1910 and 1915. In the latter year, reacting in part to the difficulties of state campaigns—and the apparent impossibility of gaining victories in the South—Catt, the president of NAWSA, embraced a federal strategy focused on building support in Congress and in the 36 states most likely to ratify an amendment to the federal Constitution. Working alongside more militant organizations like the Congressional Union and the National Woman's Party, and drawing political strength from the growing number of states that had already embraced suffrage, NAWSA organized tirelessly, even gaining a key victory in New York with the aid of New York City's Tammany Hall political machine.

The turning point came during World War I. After the United States declared war in the spring of 1917, NAWSA suspended its congressional lobbying, while continuing grassroots efforts to build support for a federal amendment. More influentially, NAWSA demonstrated the importance of women to the war effort by converting many of its local chapters into volunteer groups that sold bonds, knitted clothes, distributed food, worked with the Red Cross, and gave gifts to soldiers and sailors. This adroit handling of the war crisis, coupled with ongoing political pressure, induced President Woodrow Wilson, in January 1918, to support passage of a suffrage amendment "as a war measure." The House approved the amendment a day later—although it took the Senate (where antisuffrage southern Democrats were more numerous) a year and a half to follow suit. In August 1920, Tennessee became the thirty-sixth state to ratify the Nineteenth Amendment, and women throughout the nation could vote.

Democracy as a National Value

The passage of the Nineteenth Amendment was a major milestone in the history of the right to vote. Yet significant barriers to universal suffrage remained in place, and they were not shaken by either the prosperity of the 1920s or the Great Depression of the 1930s. African Americans in the South remained disfranchised, many immigrants still had to pass literacy tests, and some recipients of relief in the 1930s were threatened with exclusion because they were "paupers." Pressures for change, however, began to build during World War II, and they intensified in the 1950s and 1960s. The result was the most sweeping transformation in voting rights in the nation's history: almost all remaining limitations on the franchise were eliminated as the federal government overrode the long tradition of states' rights and became the guarantor of universal suffrage. Although focused initially on African Americans in the South, the movement for change spread rapidly, touching all regions of the nation.

Not surprisingly, such a major set of changes had multiple sources. World War II itself played a significant role, in part because of its impact on public opinion. Americans embraced the war's explicitly stated goals of restoring democracy and ending racial and ethnic discrimination in Europe; and it was not difficult to see—as African American political leaders pointed out—that there was a glaring contradiction between those international goals and the reality of life in the American South. That contradiction seemed particularly disturbing at a time when hundreds of thousands of disfranchised African Americans and Native Americans were risking their lives

by serving in the armed forces. Accordingly, when Congress passed legislation authorizing absentee balloting for overseas soldiers, it included a provision exempting soldiers in the field from having to pay poll taxes—even if they came from poll tax states. In 1944 the Supreme Court—partially populated by justices appointed during the New Deal and comfortable with an activist federal government— reversed two previous decisions and ruled, in *Smith v. Allwright*, that all-white primaries (and all-white political parties) were unconstitutional. Diplomatic considerations—particularly with regard to China and other allies in the Pacific—also led to the dismantling of racial barriers, as laws prohibiting Asian immigration, citizenship, and enfranchisement were repealed.

During the cold war, foreign affairs continued to generate pressure for reforms. In its competition with the Soviet Union for political support in third world nations, the United States found that the treatment of African Americans in the South undercut its claim to be democracy's advocate. As Secretary of State Dean Acheson noted, "the existence of discrimination against minority groups in the United States is a handicap in our relations with other countries." The impetus for change also came from within the two major political parties, both because of a broadening ideological embrace of democratic values and because the sizable migration of African Americans out of the South, begun during World War I, was increasing the number of black voters in northern states. Meanwhile, the postwar economic boom took some of the edge off class fears, while the technological transformation of southern agriculture led to a rapid growth in the proportion of the African American population that lived in urban areas where they could mobilize politically more easily. The changes that occurred were grounded both in Washington and in a steadily strengthening civil rights movement across the South and around the nation.

This convergence of forces, coupled with the political skills of Lyndon Johnson, the first Southerner elected to the presidency in more than a century, led to the passage in 1965 of the Voting Rights Act (VRA). The VRA immediately suspended literacy tests and other discriminatory "devices" in all states and counties where fewer than 50 percent of all adults had gone to the polls in 1964. It also authorized the attorney general to send examiners into the South to enroll voters, and it prohibited state and local governments in affected areas from changing any electoral procedures without the "preclearance" of the civil rights division of the Justice Department. (This key provision, section 5, prevented cities or states from developing new techniques for keeping African Americans politically powerless.) The VRA also instructed the Justice Department to begin litigation that would test the constitutionality of poll taxes in state elections. (Poll taxes in federal elections had already been banned by the Twenty-Fourth

Amendment, ratified in 1964.) The VRA, in effect, provided mechanisms for the federal government to enforce the Fifteenth Amendment in states that were not doing so; designed initially as a temporary, quasi-emergency measure, it would be revised and renewed in 1970, 1975, 1982, and 2006, broadening its reach to language minorities and remaining at the center of federal voting rights law.

Not surprisingly, six southern states challenged the VRA in federal courts, arguing that it was an unconstitutional federal encroachment "on an area reserved to the States by the Constitution." But the Supreme Court, led by Chief Justice Earl Warren, emphatically rejected that argument in 1966, maintaining that key provisions of the VRA were "a valid means for carrying out the commands of the Fifteenth Amendment." In other cases, the Supreme Court invoked the equal protection clause of the Fourteenth Amendment to uphold bans on literacy tests for voting and to strike down poll taxes in state elections. In the latter case, *Harper v. Virginia*, the Court went beyond the issue of poll taxes to effectively ban—for the first time in the nation's history—all economic or financial requirements for voting. Wealth, wrote Justice William O. Douglas in the majority opinion, was "not germane to one's ability to participate intelligently in the electoral process." In subsequent decisions, the Court ruled that lengthy residency requirements for voting (in most cases, any longer than 30 days) were also unconstitutional.

Three other elements of this broad-gauged transformation of voting rights law were significant. First was that in the late 1940s and early 1950s, all remaining legal restrictions on the voting rights of Native Americans were removed. Although the vast majority of Native Americans were already enfranchised, several western states with sizable Native American populations excluded "Indians not taxed" (because they lived on reservations that did not pay property taxes) or those construed to be "under guardianship" (a misapplication of a legal category designed to refer to those who lacked the physical or mental capacity to conduct their own affairs). Thanks in part to lawsuits launched by Native American military veterans of World War II, these laws were struck down or repealed.

The second development affected a much broader swath of the country: the Supreme Court, even before the passage of the Voting Rights Act, challenged the ability of the states to maintain legislative districts that were of significantly unequal size—a common practice that frequently gave great power to rural areas. In a series of decisions, the Court concluded that it was undemocratic "to say that a vote is worth more in one district than in another," and effectively made "one person, one vote" the law of the land.

The third key change was precipitated by the Vietnam War and by the claim of young protesters against that war that it was illegitimate to draft them into the armed services at age 18 if they were not entitled to vote until they were 21. Congress responded to such claims in 1970 by lowering the voting age to 18. After the Supreme Court ruled that Congress did not have the power to change the age limit in state elections, Congress acted again in 1971, passing a constitutional amendment to serve the same purpose. The Twenty-Sixth Amendment was ratified in record time by the states.

The post–World War II movement to broaden the franchise reached its limit over the issue of felon disfranchisement. Most states in the 1960s deprived convicted felons of their suffrage rights, either for the duration of their sentences or, in some cases, permanently. Many of these laws, inspired by English common law, dated back to the early nineteenth century and were adopted at a time when suffrage was considered a privilege rather than a right. Others, particularly in the South, were expressly tailored in the late nineteenth century to keep African Americans from registering to vote.

The rationales for such laws had never been particularly compelling, and in the late 1960s they began to be challenged in the courts. The grounds for such challenges, building on other voting rights decisions, were that the laws violated the equal protection clause and that any limitations on the franchise had to be subject to the "strict scrutiny" of the courts. (Strict scrutiny meant that there had to be a demonstrably compelling state interest for such a law and that the law had to be narrowly tailored to serve that interest.)

The issue eventually reached the Supreme Court, in *Richardson v. Ramirez* (1974), which decided that state felon disfranchisement laws were permissible (and not subject to strict scrutiny) by a phrase in the Fourteenth Amendment that tacitly allowed adult men to be deprived of the suffrage "for participation in rebellion, or other crime." The meaning of "or other crime" was far from certain (in context it may have been referring to those who supported the Confederacy), but the Court interpreted it broadly in a controversial decision. In the decades following the ruling, many states liberalized their felon disfranchisement laws, and permanent or lifetime exclusions were consequently imposed in only a few states by the early twenty-first century. During the same period, however, the size of the population in jail or on probation and parole rose so rapidly that the number of persons affected by the disfranchisement laws also soared—reaching 5.3 million by 2006.

The significant exclusion of felons ought not obscure the scope of what had been achieved between World War II and 1970. In the span of several decades, nearly all remaining restrictions on the right to vote of American citizens had been overturned: in different states the legal changes affected African Americans, Native Americans, Asian Americans, the illiterate, the non–English speaking, the very poor, those who had recently moved from one locale to another, and everyone between the ages of 18 and

21. Congress and the Supreme Court had embraced democracy as a national value and concluded that a genuine democracy could only be achieved if the federal government overrode the suffrage limitations imposed by many states. The franchise was nationalized and something approximating universal suffrage finally achieved—almost two centuries after the Constitution was adopted. Tens of millions of people could vote in 1975 who would not have been permitted to do so in 1945 or 1950.

New and Lingering Conflicts

Yet the struggle for fully democratic rights and institutions had not come to an end. Two sizable, if somewhat marginal, groups of residents sought a further broadening of the franchise itself. One was ex-felons, who worked with several voting rights groups to persuade legislators around the country to pass laws permitting those convicted of crimes to vote as soon as they were discharged from prison. The second group consisted of noncitizen legal residents, many of whom hoped to gain the right to vote in local elections so that they could participate in governing the communities in which they lived, paid taxes, and sent their children to school. Noncitizens did possess or acquire local voting rights in a handful of cities, but the movement to make such rights widespread encountered substantial opposition in a population that was increasingly apprehensive about immigration and that regarded "voting and citizenship," as the *San Francisco Examiner* put it, as "so inextricably bound in this country that it's hard to imagine one without the other." Indeed, many Americans believed that ex-felons and noncitizens had no legitimate claim to these political rights—although they were common in many other economically advanced countries.

More central to the political life of most cities and states were several other issues that moved to center stage once basic questions about enfranchisement had been settled. The first involved districting: the drawing of geographic boundaries that determined how individual votes would be aggregated and translated into political office or power. Politicians had long known that districting decisions (for elections at any level) could easily have an impact on the outcome of elections, and partisan considerations had long played a role in the drawing of district boundaries. The equation changed, however, when the Supreme Court's "one person, one vote" decisions, coupled with the passage of the Voting Rights Act, drew race into the picture. This happened first when (as expected) some cities and states in the South sought to redraw district boundaries in ways that would diminish, or undercut, the political influence of newly enfranchised African Americans. The courts and the Department of Justice rebuffed such efforts, heeding the words of Chief Justice Earl Warren, in a key 1964 districting case, that "the right of suffrage can be denied by a . . . dilution of the weight of a citizen's vote

just as effectively as by wholly prohibiting the free exercise of the franchise."

Yet the task of considering race in the drawing of district boundaries involved competing values, opening a host of new questions that federal courts and legislatures were to wrestle with for decades. What was the appropriate role for race in districting decisions? Should districting be color-blind, even if that meant that no minorities would be elected to office? (The courts thought not.) Should race be the predominant factor in drawing boundaries? (The courts also thought not.) In jurisdictions where African Americans constituted a sizable minority of the population, should legislatures try to guarantee some African American representation? (Probably.) Should the size of that representation be proportional to the size of the African American population? (Probably not.) Did nonracial minorities—like Hasidic Jews in Brooklyn—have similar rights to elect their own representatives? (No.) The courts and legislatures muddled forward, case by case, decade by decade, without offering definitive answers to questions that were likely insoluble in the absence of a coherent theory of representation or a widely accepted standard of fairness. Between 1970 and the beginning of the twenty-first century, the number of African Americans, Hispanics, and Asian Americans elected to public office rose dramatically, but clear-cut, definitive guidelines for districting without "vote dilution" remained out of reach.

A second cluster of issues revolved around the procedures for voter registration and casting ballots. Here a core tension was present (as it long had been) between maximizing access to the ballot box and preventing fraud. Procedures that made it easier to register and vote were also likely to make it easier for fraud to occur, while toughening up the procedures to deter fraud ran the risk of keeping legitimate voters from casting their ballots. By the 1970s, many scholars (as well as progressive political activists) were calling attention to the fact that, despite the transformation of the nation's suffrage laws, turnout in elections was quite low, particularly among the poor and the young. (Half of all potential voters failed to cast ballots for presidential elections, and the proportion was far higher in off-year elections.) Political scientists engaged in lively debates about the sources of low turnout, but there was widespread agreement that one cause could be found in the complicated and sometimes unwieldy registration procedures in some states. As a result, pressure for reforms mounted, generally supported by Democrats (who thought they would benefit) and opposed by Republicans (who were concerned about both fraud and partisan losses). Many states did streamline their procedures, but others did not, and, as a result, Congress began to consider federal registration guidelines.

What emerged from Congress in the early 1990s was the National Voter Registration Act, a measure that would require each state to permit citizens to register by mail, while applying for a driver's license, or at designated public agencies, including those offering public assistance and services to the disabled. First passed in 1992, the "motor voter bill" (as it was called) was vetoed by President George H. W. Bush on the grounds that it was an "unnecessary" federal intervention into state affairs and an "open invitation to fraud." The following year, President Bill Clinton signed the measure into law, placing the federal government squarely on record in support of making it easier for adult citizens to exercise their right to vote. Within a few years, the impact of the bill on registration rolls had been clearly demonstrated, as millions of new voters were signed up. But turnout did not follow suit in either 1996 or 1998, suggesting that registration procedures alone were not responsible for the large numbers of Americans who did not vote. During the following decade, some Democratic activists turned their attention to promoting registration on election day as a new strategy for increasing turnout.

Meanwhile, Republican political professionals sought to push the pendulum in the opposite direction. Concerned that procedures for voting had become too lax (and potentially too susceptible to fraud), Republicans in numerous states began to advocate laws that would require voters to present government-issued identification documents (with photos) when they registered and/or voted. The presentation of "ID" was already mandated in some states—although the types of identification considered acceptable varied widely—but elsewhere voters were obliged only to state their names to precinct officials. Although Democrats and civil rights activists protested that photo ID laws would create an obstacle to voting for the poor, the young, and the elderly (the three groups least likely to possess driver's licenses), such laws were passed in Georgia and Indiana in 2005, among other states. After a set of disparate rulings by lower courts, the Indiana law was reviewed by the Supreme Court, which affirmed its constitutionality in 2008 in a 6-to-3 decision. Although the Court's majority acknowledged that there was little or no evidence that voting fraud had actually occurred in Indiana, it concluded that requiring a photo ID did not unduly burden the right to vote. In the wake of the Court's decision, numerous other states were expected to pass similar laws. How many people would be barred from the polls as a result was unclear. In Indiana's primary election in the spring of 2008, several elderly nuns who lacked driver's licenses or other forms of photo ID were rebuffed when they attempted to vote.

Conflict over the exercise of the right to vote could still be found in the United States more than 200 years after the nation's founding. Indeed, the disputed presidential election of 2000, between Al Gore and George W. Bush, revolved in part around yet another dimension of the right to vote—the right to have one's vote counted, and counted accurately. Perhaps inescapably, the breadth of the franchise, as well as the ease with which it could be exercised, remained embedded in partisan politics, in the pursuit of power in the world's most powerful nation. The outcomes of elections mattered, and those outcomes often were determined not just by *how* people voted but also by *who* voted. The long historical record suggested that—however much progress had been achieved between 1787 and 2008—there would be no final settlement of this issue. The voting rights of at least some Americans could always be potentially threatened and consequently would always be in need of protection.

See also civil rights; race and politics; woman suffrage.

FURTHER READING. Ellen DuBois, *Feminism and Suffrage: The Emergence of an Independent Women's Movement in America, 1848–1869*, 1999; Ron Hayduk, *Democracy for All: Restoring Immigrant Voting Rights in the United States*, 2006; Alexander Keyssar, *The Right to Vote: The Contested History of Democracy in the United States*, 2000; J. Morgan Kousser, *The Shaping of Southern Politics: Suffrage Restriction and the Establishment of the One-party South, 1880–1910*, 1974; Jeff Manza and Christopher Uggen, *Locked Out: Felon Disenfranchisement and American Democracy*, 2006; Allison Sneider, *Suffragists in an Imperial Age: U.S. Expansion and the Woman Question, 1870–1929*, 2008.

ALEXANDER KEYSSAR

war and politics

War and politics have always been entwined in American history. Politicians and pundits often complained that politics intruded upon war or war upon politics; generals should wage war without second-guessing by politicians, some demanded. The very phrase "war and politics" treats the two as separate if linked entities. But instead they mutually constitute each other, especially if "war" is understood expansively as all activities, institutions, and attitudes involving military power. War defined American politics, not merely intruded upon it, just as politics defined war. This relationship was not unchanging, however. It became more consequential to Americans and the world as the scale of American wars and military prowess grew.

Political Control

The enmeshment of war and politics was inevitable: modern states exist in part to wage war, and war is an extreme form of politics. Some Americans hoped that the United States would be an exception, having witnessed European monarchies and dictatorships deploying war to address personal, imperial, ideological, or racial ambitions. But American exceptionalism was impossible.

The relationship began with the nation's founding. Imperial and local politics sparked the war for American independence, and the nation owed its political existence to war. The Constitution set the terms of enmeshment by giving political authorities control of war and its institutions. Only Congress could declare war and fund it even if war were undeclared (undeclared wars erupted almost from the start). It also had power "to raise and support armies," "maintain a navy," and "make rules" for the armed forces. Its power of the purse was striking (beyond what most European legislatures possessed). Congress could not dictate deployment, strategy, and tactics, but it could set the fiscal terms that made those things possible. The president was made "commander in chief of the army and the navy" and of state militias "when called into the actual service of the United States" but not commander in chief of all government or of the nation, as some presidents and other political figures later presumed. The Constitution was notably briefer about the president's war powers than about those of Congress. Whether brevity established an implicit check on presidential power or a tacit blank check for it periodically roiled American politics. Civilian secretaries of war and the navy (superseded after 1947 by a secretary of the new Department of Defense) headed cabinet departments, although their authority varied widely. Civilians also headed other agencies, proliferating in modern times, that had war-related functions, from the State, Justice, and Treasury departments at the nation's founding to the Veterans Administration (1930), Central Intelligence Agency (1947), and the Department of Homeland Security (2003). Americans phrased these arrangements as imposing "civilian" control of the military, but "civilian" often meant "political."

Most military officers accepted political control, even if they chafed at the decisions, forces, and strategies that politicians provided. Among advantages for officers, civilian supremacy made politicians—often more determined than officers to initiate war or wage it aggressively—more responsible for the controversial decisions and ghastly mistakes that war usually entails. Civilian supremacy prevailed in political dramas, as when Abraham Lincoln fired generals in the Civil War and President Harry Truman fired General Douglas MacArthur during the Korean War (an act condemned by some cold warriors as an intrusion on war making by politicians with a defeatist or subversive mentality). Some officers challenged political control during the cold war by favoring a nuclear first strike on the Soviet Union or China, conducting unauthorized spy missions, or broadcasting a Christian political agenda. But they were few and their damage to political control was minimal.

War and the State

War was key to the creation of the American state—the activity it most expansively and expensively undertook. War justified its general scale and many of its specific measures, such as a federal income tax (imposed during the Civil War, reestablished in 1913, and greatly expanded during World War II), a welfare system pioneered through veterans benefits, and scientific and medical innovations by the armed forces. "War is the health of the State," the radical critic Randolph Bourne declared in attacking America's entry into World War I. Conservatives sometimes suspected much the same, as when they asserted that President Franklin D. Roosevelt sought to use rearmament and war to consolidate the New Deal and the Democratic Party's hegemony (though World War II undermined both). Americans also expressed their political debt to war by justifying state initiatives as warlike in character: in 1933 FDR wanted the nation to respond to the Depression "as if invaded by a foreign foe"; later presidents waged "war" on crime, disease, drugs, and other challenges. Appeals to war as a model for national action overrode Americans' chronic suspicions of an activist state. They also made war an even more political category.

Similarly, Americans imagined war as serving political purposes, not just the nation's defense or expansion. War, it was said, would Americanize immigrants serving as soldiers (a favorite idea in World War I), crush subversive people and ideas, enhance social mobility (the military is "the greatest equal opportunity employer around," President George H. W. Bush boasted in 1991), revive a flagging economy, spur technological development, and unite a fractious nation. Americans rarely assumed that the perils and benefits of war involved combat alone.

The actions and institutions of war propelled the nation's development. Military force subdued Native Americans and conquered new lands. The Civil War aside, U.S. wars before at least 1941 were efforts at national aggrandizement, not survival; the Mexican-American War (1846–48) secured vast territories in the American West; the Spanish-American War of 1898 expanded America's power and holdings in the Caribbean and the Pacific. The armed forces also promoted development by undertaking exploration, charting canal and railroad routes, building dams and ports, and cultivating technical expertise when the nation lacked other technological institutions (the U.S. Military Academy at West Point was the nation's first engineering school, among its functions). The military's developmental role was often highly visible, as with its building of the Panama Canal (completed in 1914) and its promotion of nuclear, aviation, space, and computer technologies (the Internet had origins in a Defense Department program). Sometimes the military remained in the background except during disaster, as in 2005, when hurricane Katrina spotlighted the Army Corps of Engineers, the politically astute builder of much of America's infrastructure. In these ways, the role of the armed forces was political as well as military.

War and politics also intersected in the scramble for military spending and the resulting connections between civil and military institutions. The desire of local authorities—mayors, legislators, businessmen—for military bases and contracts is an old story, though its scale swelled in the twentieth century. Often it meant overriding the military's judgment about where to erect a base, whether to develop a weapon, or which company should build it. Many politicians who decried civilian interference in other military matters were masters of military pork. Especially in the twentieth century, military spending directed resources, population, and political influence toward southern and western states. From the start, the armed forces used civilian institutions for research, weapons, supplies, and services, and civilians went to work for the military while officers retired to jobs in defense or other businesses. The use of private organizations for quasi-military operations, an old practice by states and especially evident in America's post-9/11 military conflicts, further blurred the line between "civilian" and "military."

War and politics were also enmeshed in how Americans understood citizenship. African Americans' Civil War military service helped underwrite the citizenship they acquired, in theory, during and after the war. Through America's post-9/11 conflicts, noncitizens' military service guaranteed their citizenship. Since service was overwhelmingly a male activity—coerced during periods of conscription—citizenship was gendered in this way as in others. Beyond legal citizenship, war reshaped political and social citizenship. Military service in World War II strengthened citizenship for millions of Americans of eastern and southern European descent. Colin Powell, a career officer and Joint Chiefs of Staff chairman, became the highest-ranking African American in government as secretary of state (2001–5). The second woman in a cabinet post was Oveta Culp Hobby, World War II commander of the Women's Army Corps and then secretary of health, education, and welfare (1953–55). Military service lubricated upward mobility and social change, especially as measured by prominent figures. Likewise, those barred from military service or denied equality in it felt treated as lesser citizens—hence the long struggle over racial desegregation of the armed forces, ordered by Truman in 1948; conflicts over women's place in military service; and the 1993 battle over "gays in the military."

Veterans also had housing, health, education, and employment benefits lacked by most Americans, even as critics regarded those benefits as puny or badly managed. Veterans' elevated status was hardly a constant. Anxiety periodically erupted that veterans, especially of combat situations, would return damaged, disruptive, or dangerous. White Southerners feared demobilized black Union troops, and freed slaves feared ex-Confederates in the Ku Klux Klan. Anxiety surged during World War II—one reason for the famous 1944 GI Bill, or Servicemen's Readjustment Act, which gave unprecedented benefits to most of the war's 16 million veterans. Anxiety resurfaced when Vietnam War veterans were often diagnosed with post-traumatic stress disorder. Still, the sense of veterans as especially entitled or deserving citizens generally prevailed, as evident in the number of presidential candidates who were veterans. Those candidates were especially successful when regarded as heroes in victorious wars—Washington, Jackson, Harrison, Taylor, Grant, Theodore Roosevelt, Eisenhower, Kennedy—although military service was no guarantee of electoral victory, as Nixon in 1960, Dole in 1996, Kerry in 2004, and McCain in 2008 learned.

War and the Presidency

The presidency underlines how war and politics constituted each other. War or its apparent threat underwrote the presidency's expanding powers, both legal and illegal. Major crises, none more so than 9/11, produced presidential claims that constitutional provisions, international laws, and humanitarian norms should be altered, suspended, or reinterpreted. War also brought greater power for individual presidents, though less often lasting glory. Many Americans suspected presidents of using war for political gain, but presidents usually achieved little that endured. Those who secured lasting luster—Lincoln and Franklin D. Roosevelt—died before the emergence of the sour aftermath war usually presents. Woodrow Wilson's presidency crumbled after World War I; Republicans seized the White House in 1921. Truman and the Democrats barely survived World War II's aftermath and then succumbed to the Korean War; a Republican, General Dwight D. Eisenhower, became president in 1953. The Vietnam War and their handling of it destroyed the presidencies of Lyndon Johnson and Richard Nixon (his abuse of war powers shaped the Watergate crisis of 1973–74). Difficult wars readily damaged presidents, as George W. Bush found in the Iraq War, but even a triumphant Gulf War gave no lasting political traction to his father, defeated in 1992 by Bill Clinton. By the same token, three of the four post-1945 presidents who served two full terms—Eisenhower, Reagan, and Clinton—avoided costly war making and remained popular. War was as fickle in its political ramifications as in its conduct and global consequences, often overwhelming the state's ability to control it and ensnaring presidents.

When war went badly, accusations of unwarranted political interference usually intensified. After Japan's attack on Pearl Harbor on December 7, 1941, with American forces in retreat or defeat, critics charged that Roosevelt had connived to bring the United States into World War II or even to allow Japan's attack to proceed. But few complained about political intrusion when later operations pushed by Roosevelt and his civilian advisors succeeded—the invasion of France in 1944, the bombing of Nazi Germany and Imperial Japan, and the use of the atomic bomb in August 1945. Likewise, suspicion of politicians' meddling intensified after 1945, when U.S. wars in Korea, Vietnam, Iraq, and elsewhere had dubious or disastrous outcomes. Success quieted suspicion. Failure stoked it.

So did uncertainty. The cold war arms race, portending a possible nuclear cataclysm, sparked diverse suspicions. Nationalist conservatives charged that politicians denied the military the tools of victory given how the metaphoric "button" of push-button warfare lay under the president's thumb. Cold war liberals suspected that generals like Air Force chief of staff Curtis LeMay schemed to control the button. The growth of a vast civilian bureaucracy aggravated suspicions. Complaints about the number-crunching oversight of the military imposed by Secretary of Defense Robert McNamara (1961–68) prepared the ground for accusations that civilians, especially McNamara and Johnson, hamstrung their generals. Left to their own devices, accusers charged, the generals might have won the Vietnam War.

Faith in a wise officer corps able to win wars ignored institutional realities, however. Top officers disagreed about whether and how to wage war, especially given their intense service rivalries: the Air Force, Navy, Army, and Marine Corps usually had competing schemes for victory, with each also divided within. Indeed, those differences invited or compelled civilian superiors to "intrude"—to meddle, mediate, or mandate. No fount of secret wisdom, the uniformed military mirrored, though inexactly, divisions about war elsewhere in the body politic.

As formal declarations of war ceased after World War II, Americans could readily imagine a distinction between war and politics. The last protracted debate about entering war came before Pearl Harbor, after which power to initiate war lay with the presidency, positioning itself as above politics, not with Congress, the more obviously (though substantively no more) political body. To varying degrees, military actions were undertaken by presidents operating in haste, secrecy, and deception—hardly circumstances conducive to freewheeling debate. Congress trailed behind with various measures, usually approved overwhelmingly, that authorized operations. Hence political contests erupted about the conduct and consequences of wars more than their initiation, especially since most wars seemed dissatisfying or disastrous. As earlier, civilians and service personnel, and voices abroad, charged U.S. forces and leaders with illegal, excessive, or misguided use of force or torture against enemy soldiers, civilians, and captives.

The practice of politicians and pundits criticizing presidents and generals was bipartisan, however partisan at any moment. Many Democrats tried to shield the White House from criticism when their party held the presidency. Many turned against Nixon later in the Vietnam War and George W. Bush in the Iraq War. Likewise, Republicans, often defenders of presidential prerogative and military wisdom, second-guessed Clinton's use of force amid Yugoslavia's disintegration in the 1990s.

War and politics were above all interwoven because the United States waged war frequently. It became a foremost participant in the militarization of the modern world. Perhaps no state waged war more often, even though, or perhaps because, the cost in American lives was light (the Civil War aside), compared to that of its enemies and allies, even in a losing war like Vietnam's. If the Founding Fathers hoped that war would play only an episodic role in American politics, the episodes became so numerous as to be nearly continuous, though often the incidents were not declared or widely recognized as wars (as in Nicaragua in the 1920s and Beirut in 1983).

Efforts to portray war and politics as distinct arenas were not persuasive, but they did express a desire to restrain the course by which war defined much of American life. Americans partook of the appeals and benefits of war, but they also remained suspicious of them.

See also Caribbean, Central America, and Mexico, interventions in, 1903–34; Civil War and Reconstruction;

Korean War and cold war; Iraq wars of 1991 and 2003; Mexican-American War; Vietnam and Indochina wars; war for independence; War of 1812; World War I; World War II.

FURTHER READING. Andrew Bacevich, *The New American Militarism: How Americans Are Seduced by War*, 2005; John R. Gillis, ed., *The Militarization of the Western World*, 1989; Samuel P. Huntington, *The Soldier and the State: Theory and Politics of Civil-Military Relations*, 1957; Linda K. Kerber, *No Constitutional Right to Be Ladies: Women and the Obligations of Citizenship*, 1998; Richard H. Kohn, "How Democracies Control the Military," *Journal of Democracy* 8.4 (1997), 140–53; Idem, ed., *The United States Military under the Constitution of the United States, 1789–1989*, 1991; Walter Millis, *Arms and Men: A Study in American Military History*, 1956; Michael S. Sherry, *In the Shadow of War: The United States since the 1930s*, 1995; Russell F. Weigley, *The American Way of War: A History of United States Military Strategy and Policy*, 1973.

MICHAEL SHERRY

war for independence

Politics shaped the eight-year war for independence by the English colonies on the North American mainland (1775–83). In 1774 Britain decided to press its ten-year effort, against persistent and sometimes violent American resistance, to tighten imperial control of the colonies. When the British garrison in America was reinforced and its commander, Thomas Gage, appointed royal governor of Massachusetts, the colonies convened a "Continental" Congress in Philadelphia to coordinate resistance.

From Resistance to War

Few colonists expected or wanted war, but almost all opposed British policies, and preparations began by training the militia, a civilian military force established by law in all colonies except Pennsylvania. Britain had made Boston, the apparent heart of American resistance, its primary target for tough measures, and war began there in April 1775. British troops marching out of Boston to destroy a reported cache of arms met a small band of local militia, someone fired, and fighting continued through the day along the march route back to the town. As the news spread, thousands of New England militia rushed to Boston, blockading the British garrison, which was soon reinforced by troops and warships. In June, Gage tried to destroy a fortified rebel position near the town, on Bunker's Hill. The rebels gave way after repeated frontal attacks, but the British troops suffered heavy losses.

By declaring the colonies in rebellion, King George III unleashed his army and navy against the Americans. Congress, concerned by wavering in the colonies south of New England, accepted the proposal of John Adams, a Massachusetts delegate, to appoint a Virginia delegate with military experience, George Washington, to command the militia force around Boston and to rename it the Continental Army. The king's proclamation of rebellion, and the appointment of a Virginian to command the army, did much to unify the American effort.

Local committees, urged on by Congress, prepared for open warfare against the world's strongest military power. American reinforcements marched to Boston through the summer, and Congress authorized an invasion of Canada through the Hudson-Champlain corridor, aimed at denying British forces a base for attack on the American frontier. Appealing to the French-speaking settlers of Canada as liberators, the invaders enjoyed success at first, but had faltered by the New Year, and then collapsed when ice melted on the St. Lawrence, and British reinforcements sailed up the river.

The stalemate at Boston ended when the British decided to evacuate the town in March 1776 and to move operations to New York City, where the Hudson River offered a highway deep into the American interior. Washington believed that defending New York was politically necessary to sustain morale, especially in the uncertain middle colonies (New York, New Jersey, and Pennsylvania), but with no navy and an inexperienced army, the complex geography of the New York port area made his mission almost impossible, though the repulse by South Carolina militia of a British seaborne attack on Charleston was encouraging. As new troops from the southward arrived, Washington raced to train them and prepare defenses around the heights of Brooklyn on western Long Island. Gage's successor, William Howe, spent all summer on Staten Island building up a force of about 25,000, including hard-bitten mercenaries hired in Germany. Howe belonged to an aristocratic family affiliated with the parliamentary opposition, critical of the government's handling of the American problem. Rumors at the time, and some historians since, have suggested that Howe, who had personally led the attack at Bunker's Hill, lacked the stomach for killing English colonists who claimed their rights under the British Constitution.

From War to Independence

Congress, aware after a year of fighting that all-out war was about to begin, declared the rebellious colonies in July 1776 to be the independent United States. When Howe began to embark his army in late August and move toward Long Island, Washington hoped for a fight like that at Bunker's Hill in 1775. Instead, Howe flanked the American position and inflicted a crushing defeat on the Continental Army. But he stopped short at the Brooklyn bastion, where fleeing American soldiers had assembled, and prepared to lay siege. That night, in fog and darkness, Washington took his men across the river to Manhattan, where he rallied them for a gradual retreat up the island. Howe, not for the last time, pursued slowly, and the Americans even struck back once from the heights of Harlem, slowing but not stopping the British army. Washington stood again in late October at White Plains in Westchester County; again Howe won the battle but failed to destroy the American army. Washington then divided what was left of his force and took the larger part across the Hudson into New Jersey.

American morale, military and civilian, was at low ebb in the last weeks of 1776. Declaring independence had heartened many but had decisively alienated others who had supported American rights but would not break the British connection. These "Loyalist" Americans, estimated at a half-million throughout the former colonies, perhaps a quarter of the total white population, were especially numerous in the mid-Atlantic States. Another half-million Americans, slaves mostly in the South, often ran away to the British whenever possible; a smaller number of African Americans, about 5,000, served as soldiers on the American side. As Washington's men straggled across New Jersey, with the British in cautious pursuit, popular support for Congress and the army virtually collapsed in that state.

At the Delaware River, Washington crossed into Pennsylvania with winter setting in. Rumors ran that he would soon be replaced by one of two former British officers who had joined the American cause, Charles Lee or Horatio Gates. Many, even those close to Washington, thought he had lost his grip and credibility. His letters begged Lee to join him quickly with the soldiers left east of the Hudson, and they show more desperation than determination. Instead of joining, Lee let himself be captured by a British patrol. Congress, fleeing Philadelphia for the safety of Baltimore, did not replace Washington and even granted him dictatorial powers to direct the war for six months. His choices were limited: disband the army and withdraw to resist in the western hills or gamble on a counterattack. He chose the latter. With some support from the Pennsylvania militia, he crossed the icy river in late December with soldiers who had spent the past year learning war the hard way, surprising and destroying a German brigade at Trenton, then withdrawing into Pennsylvania. Howe reacted quickly, and almost trapped Washington when he boldly recrossed into New Jersey. But Washington escaped to surprise and destroy another brigade at Princeton before heading for the protective hills of northern New Jersey.

The unexpected victories at Trenton and Princeton rallied the American cause, gave Washington solid support in Congress, and won notice and credit overseas, where Congress was seeking help. Colonial stocks of munitions, plus some captured ones, were enough for the first year, but foreign aid was vital to continuing the war. France was a historic enemy, but it was the only European power likely to help the rebellious British colonies. Benjamin Franklin of Pennsylvania, with a wealth of experience abroad and already known in Europe as a rustic genius, arrived in France just as Washington struggled on the Delaware. Clandestine shipments of French military supplies to America were already underway, but Franklin would seek more as well as money and ships.

Saratoga and the Alliance with France

The year 1777 was decisive. The British planned to invade from Canada and to use most of their New York force to take the rebel capital of Philadelphia. Congress let Washington enlist three-year volunteers to rebuild his army, with which he tried to defend Philadelphia. His defeated army crept back to a winter camp at Valley Forge, not far from the occupied capital. Gates, in the north, managed to stall the invading army from Canada at Saratoga, on the upper Hudson, and compel it to surrender. Washington's tenacity, plus American victory at Saratoga, induced France to ally with the United States and go to war with Britain early in 1778.

Congress rejected proffered British concessions, Howe was recalled and replaced by Henry Clinton, and British leaders revised their strategy. France was now the main enemy, and the American war had to be coordinated with the protection of the valuable West Indies. British troops evacuated Philadelphia and concentrated at New York, with its great, accessible port. Washington's army stood just out of reach in the Hudson Highlands. From 1778 onward it was a war of attrition, of political will as much as of military force. The House of Commons angrily grilled the recalled Howe on why the Americans had not been crushed. Congress hoped for a miracle, and grew weaker as its leading members returned to their states and rampant inflation sapped the Continental paper money that had served to mobilize resources during 1775–77. With no power to tax, Congress could only resort to begging the states to support their own troops. The British meanwhile turned the war toward the South, where large slave populations, strong pro-British Native American tribes on the frontier, and a reported abundance of Americans fed up with the war seemed to beckon, while the navy could shuttle more readily between the mainland and the West Indies.

British Shift Southward

In late 1778, a small British force invaded Georgia, easily took Savannah, and reestablished royal government. A year later, Clinton himself sailed from New York, with a much larger force, to invade South Carolina. For the first time the British attempted to exploit the military potential of Loyalists. Loyalist regiments recruited in the North were part of the invading force, and, as the British advanced, they organized Loyalist militia to hold and secure areas cleared of rebels. Charleston fell to a siege in May 1780, yielding 5,000 American prisoners; news of the victory caused a sensation in England. Congress sent Gates to the rescue. In command, he risked the small force left to him against a bigger, better disciplined

British force at Camden in August and was destroyed, his reputation in tatters.

Washington, safe in the highlands, refused to move. He saw the British troops and ships departing New York for the South as an opportunity and resisted pleas from old friends like Governor Thomas Jefferson of Virginia to help the South. British forces were raiding freely into the Chesapeake and up its rivers, and in the Carolinas the war seemed lost. In mid-1780 Washington expected the arrival in Rhode Island of a French expeditionary force of more than 4,000 regular soldiers. His aim was to combine forces, and with the aid of the French navy to attack New York, destroy its depleted garrison, and win the war. When the French arrived, their commander was dubious, and, in September, a leading American general, Benedict Arnold, defected to the enemy. At the New Year, the Pennsylvania Continental troops mutinied for their pay and the promise of discharge after three years, and later New Jersey troops did the same. The French believed that the American effort would collapse after 1781, and many American observers agreed.

Under pressure, Washington sent his best general, Nathanael Greene, to take command in the South after the defeat of Gates at Camden. Even before Greene arrived in late 1780, however, the war had begun to turn against the British. Undefended by any regular force against British occupation, South Carolinians turned to a hit-and-run insurgency with small bands under local leaders who sought to hurt the British but especially to punish the Americans who had joined them. Exceptionally vicious, chaotic warfare erupted in the Carolinas 1780–81, pitting neighbors against neighbors. It was the civil war, Americans against Americans, implicit in the new British strategy. One large Loyalist force wandered too far westward into modern Tennessee, where it was surrounded by a rapidly assembled group of American militia and massacred. Greene understood what was happening, and worked well with the insurgent leaders. He avoided battle whenever possible but led British forces under Lord Cornwallis, left in command when Clinton returned to New York, on an exhausting chase northward over the hills and valleys of the Carolinas. When Cornwallis followed Greene, Loyalist militia could not hold their "liberated" areas against insurgent attack.

Decision at Yorktown

Failing to catch Greene, Cornwallis finally sought refuge in the Virginia tobacco port of Yorktown in mid-1781. He expected supplies, reinforcements, and perhaps evacuation. Instead a French fleet appeared off Chesapeake Bay. Engaging the British fleet, it fought and won a battle for control of the sea off Yorktown. Washington, disappointed that the French navy was not coming north to support an attack on New York, joined the French regulars in Rhode Island in a rapid march to Virginia, where Cornwallis soon found himself in a giant trap. With skilled French engineers pushing the siege forward every day, Cornwallis, cut off by land and sea, surrendered his army on October 19.

Military victory at Yorktown did not win the war, but news of Yorktown in Parliament brought down the wartime government, replaced by men who were opposed to the war. Desultory skirmishing occurred around occupied Charleston and New York; bitter feuds meant continued violence in the Carolina backcountry; and fighting continued in parts of the West. The British army and navy went on fighting the French. French troops and ships in America sailed away from Virginia to defend the West Indies, and, in the United States, something like a tacit armistice held, while the politicians in London and Paris spent two years negotiating a final peace.

The years 1778–83 were difficult for Congress. The French alliance, which many Americans saw as a guarantee of victory, sowed conflict and mistrust in Congress. Suspicion of wily Europeans who might make peace at American expense, skepticism toward the clever colleagues sent abroad to represent American interests, and mistrust of one another all played out in a body steadily weakened by loss of power to the states, a failing currency, and the ongoing departure of its most capable members. Only under direct French pressure did Congress finally ratify the Articles of Confederation in early 1781, one of the lowest points of the war, creating a weak central government out of an ad hoc convention of states. Washington was a mythic national hero when peace finally came in 1783, but Congress was given little credit for its part in achieving American independence.

Final Reckoning

In the Treaty of Paris, the United States gained international recognition, a western boundary on the Mississippi, and an end to the burdens as well as the benefits of membership in the empire. Britain kept Canada, and France saw that its ally Spain got back some of what it had lost in 1763: Florida, the Gulf Coast, and effective control of the Mississippi River. Americans were happy as the British army sailed home, but their economy was in ruins, and many were aggrieved that the impact of war had fallen so unevenly on regions and individuals, with only a feeble national government to address those grievances. American losers in the war were thousands of Loyalists, abandoned by the British; Native Americans, most of whom had sided with the Crown against rapacious American frontiersmen; and African Americans, who received little for service to either side. A few thousand black people were freed for their military service, but thousands more who had fled to the British for protection were re-enslaved, and a more rigorously enforced slave system took hold in the postwar Southern states.

A mythic version of the war became part of American political culture: unprepared citizen-soldiers, defeated at first but surviving, tenaciously holding their own against the best the Old World could throw at them, and winning through great hardships to ultimate victory. The national myth tended to neglect the crucial role played by the French alliance, and ignored the widespread popular apathy and considerable resistance by "loyal" Americans. If the myth faulted any Americans, they were the Congressmen and state officials who had played "petty politics" despite national peril.

See also Declaration of Independence; era of a new republic, 1789–1827.

FURTHER READING. Robert M. Calhoon, *The Loyalists in Revolutionary America, 1760–1781,* 1973; Colin G. Calloway, *The American Revolution in Indian Country: Crisis and Diversity in Native American Communities,* 1995; Jonathan R. Dull, *A Diplomatic History of the American Revolution,* 1985; John Ferling, *Almost a Miracle: The American Victory in the War of Independence,* 2007; David Hackett Fischer, *Washington's Crossing,* 2004; Felix Gilbert, *To the Farewell Address: Ideas of Early American Foreign Policy,* 1961; Don Higginbotham, *The War of American Independence: Military Attitudes, Policies, and Practice, 1763–1789,* 1971; Piers Mackesy, *The War for America, 1775–1783,* 1964; Robert Middlekauf, *The Glorious Cause: The American Revolution, 1763–1789,* rev. ed., 2005; Jack N. Rakove, *The Beginnings of National Politics: An Interpretive History of the Continental Congress,* 1979; Charles Royster, *A Revolutionary People at War: The Continental Army and American Character, 1775–1783,* 1979.

JOHN SHY

War of 1812

The War of 1812 was officially fought over the rights of neutral carriers and the impressment of American seamen. Because the conflict failed to win any formal concessions from Britain, Federalist critics condemned the war as an unnecessary failure. Their judgment omitted all reference to Federalist activities prior to and during the conflict. The Federalists' resistance to war with Britain helped provoke it, while their efforts to obstruct its conduct forced their retirement from national politics at its conclusion. Most Americans at the time thought the Federalist leadership, not the Republicans, had failed the nation.

Origins of the War of 1812

Following its Revolution, the United States acquired a new central government with powers analogous to those of Europe's nation-states. When the Atlantic World plunged into war after 1792, the conflict proved a blessing for the infant American state in one respect. No better way existed for the federal government to establish its authority than by solving national problems that the individual states had been unable to address. Shays's Rebellion in 1787 had

revealed the obstacles the states faced in dealing with the Revolutionary War debt. The earnings derived from the transfer of Europe's seaborne commerce to America's neutral vessels ensured that Alexander Hamilton's ambitious plan for funding the debt would succeed. But war between France and Britain also entailed risks, because good relations with one of the great powers meant bad relations with the other. The U.S. accommodation with Britain after 1794 soured relations with France, igniting a limited naval war between 1798 and 1800. John Adams succeeded in bringing the "Quasi-War" to a conclusion shortly before the presidential election of 1800, but the taxes accompanying the conflict contributed to Thomas Jefferson's presidential victory and the election of a Republican Congress.

The defeated Federalists worried that the Republicans would compromise the nation's neutrality by allying with France. The Federalists had courted Britain during the 1790s, because most federal revenue derived from taxes on British imports. They counted on France's hostility to neutralize the enmity Americans bore Britain after the Revolutionary War. Federalist leaders, especially in New England, feared the Republicans would promote bad relations with Britain to maintain their power. But, except for a few dissident minorities outside the Northeast, the nation increasingly identified with the Jeffersonian Republicans. Jefferson's success in acquiring the Louisiana Territory from France strengthened the New Englanders' sense of isolation, because everyone assumed new states formed from the western territories would vote Republican. This assessment appeared to be confirmed by Jefferson's landslide reelection in 1804.

However, escalation of the European war after 1805 clouded the Republicans' prospects. Lord Nelson's naval victory at Trafalgar and Napoleon's triumphs on the Continent made each belligerent supreme in one arena but unable to strike its adversary in the other. In 1806 Britain proclaimed a paper blockade—that is, one too extensive for any navy systematically to enforce—of the adjacent French coast in an effort to surmount this difficulty. Napoleon countered with a paper blockade of the British Isles. When Britain responded by ordering vessels making for Europe to enter a British port and pay British duties, Napoleon decreed any vessel that did so or was visited by a British warship to be a lawful prize. Jefferson reacted to the aggressions of both Great Powers with a general embargo on American shipping and exports. Though the measure hurt the American economy, it seemed preferable to war with either or both of the offending powers. But war with Britain seemed most likely because, six months earlier, a British frigate had attacked the USS *Chesapeake* to remove four alleged deserters.

Federalists led by Senator Timothy Pickering of Massachusetts contended the embargo favored France at Britain's expense. Pickering claimed Napoleon had forced the embargo on Jefferson to complete

France's "continental system" of isolating Britain and to provoke war between the United States and Britain. Congressional sponsorship for such views emboldened the Federalist legislature of Massachusetts to urge wholesale resistance to the embargo. Though the Republicans warned that the only alternative to the embargo was war, the Federalists assumed they were bluffing. They knew the Republicans feared war was incompatible with republicanism because the French Republic had recently evolved into a military dictatorship under the pressure of the European wars. War would also reverse the progress the Republicans had made in retiring the Revolutionary debt. Though some Americans prepared to risk an appeal to arms, the majority preferred peace. The Federalists sought to split the Republican congressional majority by supporting a dissident Republican, Dewitt Clinton, as Jefferson's successor, rather than James Madison. Though a majority of the Republican congressional caucus backed Madison, it also modified the embargo to apply only to France and Britain instead of declaring war against either or both powers. The policy, known as nonintercourse, affected France more than Britain because the latter's naval supremacy allowed it to procure American commodities in neutral ports while denying French vessels comparable access.

Both Napoleon and the British minister in Washington, David Erskine, saw nonintercourse as a capitulation to Britain. Napoleon responded by ordering the sequestration, a conditional form of confiscation, of all American vessels entering ports under his control. Erskine sought to consolidate British advantage by proposing that the United States and Britain lift their trade restrictions against each other, conditional upon nonintercourse remaining in effect against France. To unify the badly divided nation, Madison accepted Erskine's offer, only to have the British government repudiate it and replace Erskine with the pugnacious Francis Jackson. Ambassador Jackson accused the Madison administration of entering the Erskine Agreement knowing it would be repudiated in order to provoke antagonism against Britain. Federalists then took the part of the British government against the Republican administration. This convinced Madison and his Republican followers that the Federalists were a disloyal minority bent on subverting America's republican institutions.

Other matters besides Britain's commercial restrictions troubled Anglo-American relations. To maintain its blockade of France, the British navy continued impressing American seamen. At the same time, British commercial interests took advantage of the collapse of Spanish authority in the New World following Napoleon's attempt to place his brother on the Spanish throne in 1808. Madison feared that British attempts at political control would soon follow. West Florida, which extended to New Orleans, looked particularly ripe for British appropriation if the United States did not act first. Madison bided his time until the indecisive Eleventh Congress passed a law (Macon's Bill Number 2) that offered France an arrangement resembling the Erskine Agreement but directed against Britain. When Napoleon accepted, Madison issued orders for the peaceful occupation of West Florida by American forces. Madison would not have pursued such a course had he and other Republican leaders not concluded that Britain, backed by Federalist partisans, constituted the principal threat to the republic's future.

Declaring War against Britain

Mobilizing a Republican majority for war with Britain proved difficult. In addition to Republican misgivings about militarism, the administration faced unwavering Federalist opposition. But the 12th Congress proved more determined than the 11th Congress to avenge the humiliations that Federalists, in conjunction with Britain, had inflicted on the nation. The impressment of American seamen also solidified public opinion behind the war hawks. Still, the Republicans could not brand the Federalists as official enemies because doing so worked at cross-purposes with unifying the republic.

Nor could they get France to stop seizing American vessels, as Napoleon had promised to do in responding to Macon's Bill Number 2. The emperor was much more interested in provoking a war between the United States and Britain than in America's trade. Because the British government used France's actions to justify its commercial restrictions, Napoleon continued promising much but delivering little. He did not formally revoke France's decrees until May 1812, and then with a decree that bore a bogus date of April 1811. France's behavior emboldened Britain to insist that its enemy's decrees be repealed, as they affected Britain's and America's commerce, before British restrictions would be lifted. That made Britain seem more unreasonable than France, but the difference was not enough to silence the Federalists, who continued adamantly to oppose war with Britain. A minority, however, pushed for war with both powers as a way of preventing war with either of them. The Republicans replied weakly that France had done something to satisfy American demands while Britain had done nothing.

Madison called on Congress to begin military preparations in November 1811. Since invading Canada was the only way the United States could strike at Britain, war had to be declared in the spring to allow time for operations before the ensuing winter. But neither the preparations for hostilities nor the diplomatic maneuvering surrounding the declaration observed these requirements. An initial war loan fell far short of its goal, partially because of Federalist opposition, while the administration waited in vain for an answer to its latest ultimatum to Britain.

One of King George III's periodic fits of insanity, combined with the assassination of Prime Minister Spencer Perceval, slowed the British response. The retreat of Russian forces before Napoleon's invasion of that nation together with economic difficulties exacerbated by nonintercourse eventually led Britain to lift its restrictions affecting American commerce on June 23, 1812. But Congress had declared war four days earlier. Had the news arrived sooner, it might have averted hostilities. Madison responded coolly to proposals for a truce, however, once he learned of Britain's action. The political difficulties of unifying the Republicans led him to fear the effect the combined intrigues of the British and the Federalists would have on the Republicans. Had the British also been ready to abandon impressment, peace would have followed. But anger over impressment had become so widespread that Madison needed more than commercial concessions from Britain to suspend hostilities.

Federalist Opposition to the Conduct of the War

The administration soon regretted its hard line as, aside from several indecisive victories at sea, the war began disastrously. In August William Hull surrendered a large garrison at Detroit without firing a shot, while two other attempts to invade Canada collapsed ingloriously. News of Napoleon's retreat from Russia followed these defeats. While Madison only wanted commercial cooperation from France, he had counted on Napoleon holding his own against Britain and the other European powers. Instead France grew weaker as Britain grew stronger. Madison readily accepted the czar's offer of mediation early in 1813, only to have Britain reject it.

These setbacks failed to make Congress easier to manage, thanks in part to the use the Federalists made of France's fraudulent repeal of its decrees. Freshman representative Daniel Webster proposed resolutions to the special congressional session of May–July 1813 that demanded full disclosure of the administration's dealings with France prior to declaring war on Britain. Congressional Republicans passed responsibility for answering this challenge to Secretary of State James Monroe. His long document justifying the administration's actions failed to silence the Federalist claim that the administration had let itself be maneuvered into war by Napoleon. The Federalists also hoped to obstruct the war effort by insisting that it be financed by direct taxes. They expected this would destroy the Republicans' popularity, as direct taxes had destroyed theirs during 1799–1800.

The British government agreed to direct negotiations after U.S. Admiral Oliver Perry won decisive control over Lake Erie in September 1813. But Napoleon's abdication in April 1814 freed the British government from any pressure to conclude at a speedy peace. Instead it directed all British military power against the United States. The new strategic situation made reconstituting a national bank, whose charter had been allowed to expire in March 1811, a national priority for the American government. Though the Federalists supported a national bank in principle, they insisted that its notes be redeemable for specie (precious metals), while Boston's Federalist banks were busy engrossing the nation's specie supply. Britain had absolved eastern New England from its blockade of the American coast until April 1814, making Boston the creditor for the rest of the nation. Boston's banks then called on the state banks outside New England to redeem their notes in specie, which they proved unable to do. The ensuing banking crisis obstructed the government's coordination of military operations and thus contributed to the burning of Washington at the end of August. The British also seized a third of Maine's coastline. Such developments did not provide an auspicious setting for the peace negotiations with Britain beginning in Europe. Never had the republic seemed in more peril.

Instead of helping to defend the nation, New England's Federalist leadership tried to turn that peril to its own advantage. While the governor of Massachusetts put out feelers to his counterpart in Nova Scotia soliciting British military intervention, the state's legislature called for a regional convention to meet at Hartford. Federalists were prepared to go to such extremes because reports of Britain's initial peace terms made it clear the Republicans would reject them. Though American forces had repelled a British invasion at Plattsburgh, the Federalists knew a large enemy force was moving against New Orleans. Its seizure would put the western two-thirds of the nation at Britain's mercy. Meeting in December 1814, the Hartford Convention framed a set of constitutional amendments designed to enhance the Federalists' power in the nation. The amendments were to be presented to Congress for acceptance along with the demand that New England be allowed to defend itself. Everyone understood that New England would conclude a separate peace with Britain if the rest of the nation refused to submit to the Federalist minority.

Resolution

The commissioners carrying the Hartford Convention's demands arrived in Washington at the same time as news of the conclusion of a peace in Europe based on the *status quo ante bellum* and of Andrew Jackson's victory over the British at New Orleans. These two events transformed the fortunes of the republic overnight, making the Federalists look like a disloyal minority bent on humiliating the nation. The Hartford commissioners had no choice but to retreat in disgrace. The republic had unexpectedly survived despite all that the Federalists had done to prostrate it before Britain. But Federalist leaders did more than disgrace themselves in the eyes of other Americans. They also destroyed their power base in the New England states. Their policies had assumed the weakness of the republic compared to a powerful monarchy like Britain.

Within a year of the peace, Madison could predict that the nation would be debt free by 1835. A vigorous postwar recovery removed the last thread of justification for Federalist actions. Few realized that the European rivalries fueling the division between Federalists and Republicans had also come to an end. Their disappearance left what survived of the Federalist leadership without a rallying cause in their home states. By the mid-1820s hardly any remnants of the party remained.

See also Democratic Party, 1800–1828; era of a new republic, 1789–1827; Federalist Party; war and politics.

FURTHER READING. Henry Adams, *History of the United States of America during the Administrations of James Madison*, 1986; James M. Banner, Jr., *To the Hartford Convention: The Federalists and the Origins of Party Politics in Massachusetts, 1789–1815*, 1970; Roger Brown, *The Republic in Peril: 1812*, 1964; Richard Buel, Jr., *America on the Brink: How the Political Struggle over the War of 1812 Almost Destroyed the Young Republic*, 2005; Lawrence D. Cress, "'Cool and Serious Reflections': Federalist Attitudes towards the War of 1812," *Journal of the Early Republic* 7 (1987), 123–45; Peter P. Hill, *Napoleon's Troublesome Americans: Franco-American Relations, 1804–1815*, 2005; Matthew Mason, "'Nothing Is Better Calculated to Excite Division': Federalist Agitation against Slave Representation during the War of 1812," *New England Quarterly* 75 (2002), 531–61; Robert A. McCaughey, *Josiah Quincy 1772–1864: The Last Federalist*, 1974; Bradford Perkins, *Prologue to War: England and the United States 1805–1812*, 1961; Burton Spivak, *Jefferson's English Crisis: Commerce, Embargo, and the Republican Revolution*, 1979; J.C.A. Stagg, *Mr. Madison's War: Politics, Diplomacy, and Warfare in the Early Republic, 1783–1830*, 1983; Steven Watts, *The Republic Reborn: War and the Making of Liberal America*, 1987.

RICHARD BUEL JR.

welfare

Origins and Meaning of "Welfare"

Welfare originated as a positive term in the early twentieth century. It signified attempts to professionalize and modernize old practices of relief and charity. This positive connotation of welfare and "welfare state" lasted through the New Deal of the 1930s and even into the 1940s. It came under attack in two stages. During the cold war, in the late 1940s and 1950s, opponents associated welfare with European socialism and un-American ideas. Then, in the 1960s, as unmarried women of color with children began to dominate public assistance rolls, welfare acquired the combined stigmas of race, gender, and illicit sex.

This narrow, pejorative use of the term welfare obscures its true meaning and inhibits understanding of the American welfare state. In the original sense—as used from the early twentieth century through post–World War II years—the terms welfare and welfare state referred to a collection of programs designed to assure economic security for all citizens by guaranteeing the fundamental necessities of life. The welfare state is how a society ensures against common risks—unemployment, poverty, sickness, and old age—that in one way or another confront everyone.

The American welfare state confronts universal problems with a distinctive architecture—much broader and more complex than is usually realized. It is not usefully described as either public or private. Instead, its economy is mixed, and its composition reflects American federalism—the division of powers between the federal government and the states. This American welfare state consists of two main divisions, with subdivisions within each. Each subdivision is rooted in a different location in American history and, to some extent, has followed its own trajectory over time.

Public Assistance

The first division is the public welfare state. Its subdivisions are public assistance, social insurance, and taxation. Public assistance, the oldest form of welfare, consists of means-tested programs. Its origins lie in the Elizabethan poor laws, which the colonists brought with them in the seventeenth century. Embodied in "outdoor relief," aid given to people in their homes rather than in an institution, public assistance has a long and controversial history. Although subject to state law, public assistance, with a few exceptions, was administered locally, usually by counties. In the early twentieth century, state governments introduced a new form of public assistance, "mothers' pensions," small amounts of money given to a limited number of worthy widows. During the Great Depression of the 1930s, the federal government introduced two public assistance programs paid for with matching state-federal funds. They were Old Age Assistance, by far the largest until it was eliminated by the growth of Social Security, and Aid to Dependent Children, a federalization of state mothers' pensions, which later became Aid to Families with Dependent Children (AFDC), or what most Americans referred to as welfare, and, in 1966, Temporary Aid to Needy Families (TANF), which replaced AFDC.

A fierce critic of public assistance, President Richard Nixon surprised both his supporters and critics by proposing to replace AFDC with the Family Assistance Plan, a variant of a negative income tax. Opposed by conservatives, who objected in principle, and welfare rights advocates, who thought its benefits inadequate, the plan died. Instead, in 1974 Congress bundled public assistance for the indigent elderly, blind, and disabled, into a new program, Supplemental Security Income.

In 1996 welfare reform legislation—the Personal Responsibility and Work Opportunity Reconciliation Act–passed overwhelmingly in both the House and Senate with bipartisan support and was signed into law by President Bill Clinton on August 22. The legislation capped a long process of negotiation between Clinton and Congress and drew on widespread hostility to public assistance. The legislation, which reoriented public assistance toward what was called the transition to work, abolished the quasi-entitlement to public assistance embodied in AFDC. Its overarching goal was to move people from public assistance into a job in the regular labor market. States could meet this goal by contracting out welfare administration to private firms.

The TANF program has two major components. Both are block grants to states that are intended to help families leave welfare. One gives cash to families in need to support their children while they look for work, and discourages them from having more children outside of marriage. The other component bundles together money for major child-care programs for low-income families.

Two features of the new legislation attracted the most attention. One was time-limited public assistance, which mandated a maximum lifetime benefit of five years, although states were permitted to set shorter limits. The other feature took benefits away from legal immigrants who had been in the United States less than five years; again, states could impose even harsher restrictions on immigrants than the federal government. (Prodded by President Clinton, Congress restored some of these benefits to immigrants in 1997 and 1998.) One other important aspect of the bill was its emphasis on enforcing payment of child support by absent fathers.

The most dramatic change following the new legislation was a rapid drop in the welfare rolls by more than half. Supporters of welfare reform hailed this decline as testimony to the bill's success. With little debate, Congress inserted even tougher work requirements into the legislation's reauthorization, included as part of the Deficit Reduction Act that was signed by President George W. Bush on February 8, 2005. Many observers, however, were not sure that the drop in the welfare rolls resulted only from the new rules or that it should be the measure of the success of welfare reform. The decline, which had begun before the passage of the 1996 bill, reflected three major influences: job growth in a strong economy, individuals either discouraged from applying or sanctioned off the rolls, and work incentives in the legislation. Moreover, leaving welfare did not mean escaping poverty. Many of the jobs held by former public assistance recipients paid poorly, lacked health and retirement benefits, and did not offer avenues for advancement. A large proportion of poor women with children exchanged public assistance for working poverty.

Social Insurance and Taxation
Social insurance, whose origins lie in nineteenth-century Europe, is the second subdivision in the American welfare state. Social insurance programs are not means tested. They provide benefits to everyone who meets certain fixed criteria, such as being 65 years of age or older. They are based on a rough insurance analogy, because potential beneficiaries pay premiums in advance. They have been either state or federal-state programs. Always much more generous than public assistance, social insurance benefits have increased at a more rapid rate over time. The result is that the gap between them and public assistance has progressively widened. The first form of social insurance in the United States was workers' compensation, introduced by most states in the early twentieth century. Few states developed old-age or unemployment insurance. Federal social insurance emerged in a burst with the Social Security Act of 1935, which introduced a complicated federal-state program of unemployment insurance and a federal program of old-age insurance known as Social Security. At first these programs were very restrictive. Social Security excluded agricultural and domestic workers and did not pay benefits, which initially were very low, until 1940. Although social insurance and unemployment insurance originally discriminated against African Americans and women, expansions of coverage have reduced inequities in benefits. Overall, Social Security has been the most effective federal public social program in American history.

Over time, Social Security's coverage expanded, benefit levels increased, disability benefits were added, and in the 1970s, benefits were pegged to inflation. In the burst of social spending during the Great Society years, from the mid-1960s through the early 1970s, Congress passed a major extension to social insurance: Medicare, health insurance for the elderly, along with Medicaid, a medical public assistance program for the poor. By the late 1970s, largely as a result of Social Security's benefits, the elderly, who in 1960 had a poverty rate three times that of any other age group, were less likely to be poor than any other segment of the American population. At the same time, Medicare and Medicaid transformed access to medical care for the elderly and poor.

A third division of the public welfare state is taxation. Low-income people receive benefits indirectly through tax credits given to businesses and real estate developers to create jobs and housing. But the most important program is the Earned Income Tax Credit. Started in 1975, the EITC was expanded greatly under President Clinton in the 1990s. It supplements the income of workers whose earnings fall below a predetermined level. The EITC costs more than AFDC ever did or than TANF does now. It has, however, been effective in boosting people from slightly below the poverty line to just above it.

The Private Welfare State
The private welfare state has two main subdivisions. The first of these consists of charities and social services, which have a long and varied history. Some stretch far back in American history; others are much newer. Contrary to myths this private welfare state has never been adequate to relieve the needs of

individuals and families without sufficient health care, income, or housing. In the 1960s, federal legislation funded the expansion of social services. As a result, the character of nominally private agencies and social services changed, because they began to receive a large share of their budgets from federal, state, and local governments. American governments operate relatively few services themselves. Instead, they run social services by funding private agencies. Without government funds, most private agencies would close their doors. In effect, they have become government contractors.

The second subdivision in the private welfare state consists of employee benefits. More than six of ten Americans receive health insurance through their employers. Many receive retirement pensions as well. Although a few businesses and governments provided pensions before World War II, employee benefits developed into mass programs only in the 1940s and 1950s. Fought for by trade unions, they received government sanction in 1949 from the National Labor Relations Board, which required employers to bargain over (though not to provide) employee benefits. Employee benefits fit within the framework of the welfare state because they have been encouraged by the federal government (which allows employers to deduct their cost from taxes) and are regulated by federal legislation. Without them, the public welfare state would have assumed a very different form. In recent decades, the percentage of workers covered by health insurance and retirement benefits has decreased. Employees pay much more for their health care than in the past and receive it through some variant of managed care. In the private sector, most pensions now require defined contributions, which leave future benefits to the vagaries of individual investment decisions and the market, rather than, as in the past, offering defined benefits, which guaranteed the income employees were to receive in retirement.

With these employee benefits added to its economy, the United States appears less of a welfare laggard compared to other developed nations. When nations are arrayed in a hierarchy according to public social spending, the United States and Japan are at the bottom, widely separated from the top. However, when private social welfare is added, the rank order remains the same but the distance is greatly reduced. Including benefits distributed through the tax code would shrink it even more. What is unique about the United States welfare state is the distinctive way in which it delivers its benefits.

In the 1980s, public social policy coalesced around three great objectives that began to redefine the American welfare state. The first objective was the war to end dependence—not only the dependence of young unmarried mothers on welfare but all forms of dependence on public and private support and on the paternalism of employers. The second objective was to devolve authority; that is, to transfer power

from the federal government to the states, from states to counties, and from the public to the private sector. The third aspect was the application of market models to social policy. Everywhere, the market triumphed as the template for a redesigned welfare state. Used loosely and often unreflectively as the organizational model toward which public programs should aspire, the market model emphasized competition, privatization, and a reliance on supply and demand to determine policies and priorities. Examples include the replacement of AFDC with TANF and the shift to managed health care and defined contribution pensions; other examples are found everywhere throughout the public and private welfare states.

None of the forces redefining the welfare state originated in the 1980s, but in those years they burst through older tendencies in public policy and combined to form a powerful and largely bipartisan tide. With only a few exceptions, political arguments about the welfare state revolved more around details than great principles. An exception was the battle over the future of Medicare and Social Security that escalated during the administration of President George W. Bush. Conservatives wanted to move both programs toward privatization, which would fundamentally change the model on which they were built, but massive public opposition prevented Bush's plans for Social Security from reaching the floor of Congress.

Bush had partial success reforming Medicare. On December 8, 2003, he signed the controversial Medicare Modernization Act, which introduced a prescription drug benefit known as Medicare Part D. Instead of a uniform benefit administered by Medicare, the Bush scheme relied on private insurers to offer plans that fit the program's guidelines. The legislation forbade Medicare to negotiate directly with drug companies for lower prices, as the Veterans Administration did. It exempted low-income seniors from premiums, moving those eligible for Medicaid into the new drug program, and it reduced premiums for others with near-poverty incomes. But it handed extra dollars to insurance companies for seniors enrolled in Medicare Advantage Plans (managed-care plans that combined medical and prescription benefits). Medicare paid these private health plans about 12 percent more than it would cost to care for the same patients in the traditional Medicare program. Private insurers reaped a windfall from the requirement that Medicaid recipients enroll in the plans. The Democratic congressional majority proved unable to lift the prohibition on negotiating drug prices or to scale back the advantages granted private insurers. It did not even attempt to alter the complicated prescription drug plan that left many seniors still paying thousands of dollars for their medications each year.

By 2007 living-wage ordinances had passed in many cities; elections in several states showed strong support for an increased minimum wage; the lack of universal and affordable health insurance had become the number-one domestic issue; and the presidential campaign of John Edwards had focused national attention on poverty for the first time in decades. These developments held out hope for improving the economic security of the working poor and the accessibility of health care for the nonelderly. But the prospects for a reversal of the trends that had redefined and attenuated the nation's welfare state remained dim.

See also Social Security.

FURTHER READING. Edward D. Berkowitz, *The American Welfare State: From Roosevelt to Reagan*, 1991; Gosta Esping-Andersen, *The Three Worlds of Welfare Capitalism*, 1990; Colin Gordon, *Dead on Arrival: The Politics of Health Care in Twentieth-Century America*, 2003; Linda Gordon, *Pitied But Not Entitled: Single Mothers and the History of Welfare, 1890–1935*, 1994; Christopher Howard, *The Hidden Welfare State: Tax Expenditures and Social Policy in the United States*, 1997; Michael B. Katz, *In the Shadow of the Poorhouse: A Social History of Welfare*, 10th ed., 1996; Idem, *The Price of Citizenship: Redefining the American Welfare State*, 2008; Frances Fox Piven and Richard A. Cloward, *Poor People's Movements: How They Succeed, Why They Fail*, 1977; Ellen Reese, *Backlash against Welfare Mothers: Past and Present*, 2005; Theda Skocpol, *Protecting Soldiers and Mothers: The Political Origins of Social Policy in the United States*, 1992.

MICHAEL B. KATZ

Whig Party

The Whig Party was a formidable force in the antebellum United States. From the late 1830s until the early 1850s, roughly half of the American electorate was made up of Whigs. The party won two of the four presidential elections in which it participated—in 1840 and 1848. Because the two Whigs who were elected president—William Henry Harrison and Zachary Taylor—died in office and were succeeded by their vice presidents, John Tyler and Millard Fillmore, four Whigs ultimately held the office.

The Beginnings

Some of the best-known politicians of the day were Whigs, including Henry Clay and the great orator Daniel Webster. During his congressional career, John Quincy Adams consistently acted with the Whigs although he first ran as an Anti-Mason. Leaders of the party included influential Southerners such as Robert Toombs and Alexander Stephens. The greatest educational reformer of the day, Horace Mann, was a Whig, as was William H. Seward, and Abraham Lincoln had a long association with the party. The two best-known congressional leaders of Radical Reconstruction, Charles Sumner and Thaddeus Stevens, had started their political careers as Whigs.

In 1824 all presidential candidates were Republican and deeply involved with the administration of the last of the Virginia dynasty, James Monroe. Andrew Jackson was a U.S. Senator from Tennessee, John Quincy Adams was the secretary of state, William Crawford was the secretary of the treasury, Clay was the speaker of the House of Representatives, and Calhoun, who became vice president, was the secretary of war. When no one received a majority of the electoral votes, the election was thrown into the House of Representatives. The choice of Adams, who came in second in the popular vote, created the movement to make Jackson president in 1828.

The merger of the Albany Regency, the Richmond Junto, and the Nachez Junto, local political cliques at the time, was the beginning of the Democratic Party. The Adams supporters were not as inept as often portrayed, but an alliance of the Jackson and Crawford forces of 1824 could have easily outvoted them. Political organization was moving toward modern parties, but on different rates at different levels. Most important in the North was the Anti-Masonic movement, which opposed the influence of secret societies in state politics and was one of the precursors of the Whigs.

A more general source of the future Whig Party was those who supported the Adams administration, who formed the National Republicans to oppose Jackson in 1832. They held a national convention and nominated Clay for president. These proto-Whigs advocated what they called the American System, a plan to establish a national bank, a protective tariff, federal support for internal improvements, and the colonization of freed blacks in Africa.

In 1833 and 1834, people began to use the term *Whig* to describe the anti-Jackson opposition. The name referred to the English Whigs, who had been associated with the parliamentary opposition to the king from the late seventeenth century to the mid-nineteenth century. The American Whigs originated as a party of congressional opposition to the imperial executive, "King Andrew."

In preparation for the election of 1836, the Democratic Republicans held a convention to anoint Martin Van Buren as Jackson's successor. There was no Whig convention, because there was as yet no national Whig Party. Anti-Jackson groups ran a variety of candidates for president and vice president. Four opposition candidates received electoral votes for president: William Henry Harrison, from Ohio; Daniel Webster, from Massachusetts; Hugh Lawson White, from Tennessee; and Willie P. Mangum, from North Carolina. White, who received 26 electoral votes, openly denied he was a Whig, and Mangum, who received South Carolina's 11 electoral votes, had not agreed to run. The organizational confusion made the election of 1836 the only election in American history in which the Senate had to choose the vice president when none of the four candidates received a majority of the electoral vote.

Coming Together

As the Democratic and Whig parties coalesced in the late 1830s, debates emerged in the states about which could legitimately use "democratic" in its label. By 1840 the two major parties had taken on the official names of the American Democracy and the Democratic Whigs.

The Whigs had held their first party convention in 1839. Henry Clay was the obvious presidential candidate, but the New Yorkers, led by Seward and Thurlow Weed, blocked his nomination and put forth Harrison, who had won 73 electoral votes in 1836. To balance the ticket, the convention chose John Tyler from Virginia.

Because a Democratic editor accused Harrison, a retired general and presidential aspirant in 1836, of wanting to stay at home in his "log cabin" and drink "hard cider," the election has been tainted with this image and the idea that the Whigs did nothing but stage gigantic parades and mouth empty speeches. Yet these political activities brought mass participation to American politics. Voter turnout skyrocketed: more than 80 percent of the white adult men went to the polls. The result was a stunning victory for the Whig candidate.

Who Were the Whigs?

Historians have often asked, "Who were the Whigs?" The partisan battle was neither a simple matter of the rich against the poor, nor one between immigrants and the native-born. The Whigs won two presidential elections, held House majorities in the 27th and 30th Congresses, and did well in practically all of the states from the late 1830s to the early 1850s. Several studies have shown that ethnoreligious affiliation affected partisan perspectives in both sections. Groups such as Irish Catholics were overwhelmingly Democratic, while the various. white, Anglo-Saxon Protestant descendents of the Puritans inspired by the Second Great Awakening in the North were heavily Whig. In the South, local conditions often determined the way these factors played themselves out in politics. Where the few free African Americans could vote, they tended to oppose the followers of Jackson until, in most states, the Jacksonians disenfranchised them. While many Democrats were extraordinarily rich—in the northern cities merchants, in the South plantation owners—Whigs tended to control the economically dynamic areas in both sections. Above all, the Whigs differed essentially from their opponents about the proper role of the state in governing economic and moral behavior. It was a matter of attitude. The poor, up-by-your-bootstraps men were primarily Whigs.

During these years, congressional behavior represented a distinctly partisan pattern. Even at the state level, in elections, legislative behavior, and constitutional conventions, partisan conflict reflected attitudes that mirrored differences on federal policy. From Maine to Mississippi, the Whigs emphasized the positive role of government by creating the "credit system"—charter in private- and state-related banks to create not only most of the money supply of the country but also to make loans to farmers and small businessmen—building roads and canals, supporting public education, and generally encouraging morality in public life. In contrast, the Democrats distrusted the actions of the legislatures and viewed the governors as "tribunes of the people" with the power to veto the excesses of government; they embraced laissez faire in all aspects of life.

The election of 1840 took place in the midst of a depression; the contrasting economic proposals of the parties were salient. The Democrats, who wrote the first real party platform in American history, emphasized their commitment to laissez faire and state's rights. The Whigs did not write a platform, but Whig speakers made the party's position clear. Clay began the campaign with a three-hour speech that emphasized banking and monetary policy. Webster spoke in the South and Virginian John Minor Botts toured the North, spreading similar ideas. Harrison—the first presidential candidate to speak widely—echoed the same Whig themes.

After Harrison caught pneumonia and died a month after his inauguration, the presidency fell to Tyler. Congressional Whigs looked toward sweeping economic change by reviving a national bank to control credit and currency, increasing the tariff to encourage domestic production, altering land policy to distribute revenues to the states for the development of internal improvements, and passing a federal bankruptcy law. The central pillar of the Whig economic program, called the "Fiscal Bank of the United States," passed Congress in August, but Tyler vetoed it as overextending the power of the federal government to create banking corporations. After negotiations with Tyler, the Whigs pushed through a slightly revised measure, but Tyler vetoed this as well.

Tyler's vetoes alienated most Whigs. The entire cabinet resigned except Webster, who was in the midst of negotiating the Webster-Ashburton Treaty with England. While this was ostensibly over boundary disputes between the United States and Canada in both Maine and Minnesota, it also touched on other conflicts between Great Britain and the United States, ranging from extradition of criminals to cooperation in ending the African slave trade.

Attempts by Clay and the congressional Whigs to provide for the distribution of the proceeds of land sales to aid the states in providing internal improvements and to revise the tariff did lead to legislation in 1841 and 1842, yet in both cases they were forced to compromise. As Tyler remade and remade again his cabinet, he moved closer to the Democrats. Eventually Calhoun, who had returned to the Democratic Party, served as his secretary of state and oversaw the annexation of Texas, which Tyler thought would revive his presidential prospects and his historical memory.

Slavery

The slavery question was more troubling for the Whigs than for the Democrats and was the rock upon which their ship would eventually founder. From the mid-1830s on, northern Whigs opposed what they called "the slave power"—the political power exercised by southern planters. Led by John Quincy Adams, northern Whigs fought the "gag rules" that restricted congressional consideration of antislavery petitions. While a few southern Whigs did eventually vote to end the gag, this issue separated northern and southern Whigs who voted together on economic matters.

Under the Tyler administration, the question of annexing the territory that would become Texas posed another problem for the Whigs. Secretary of State Abel Upshur of Virginia secretly negotiated a treaty with the Texans to annex the Republic of Texas. When the treaty became public, both northern and southern Whigs bitterly opposed it. They argued that it would create sectional discord because dividing the area into five new slave states could give the South control of the Senate and the Texans' boundary demands could lead to war with Mexico. While the Whigs' argument proved correct on both counts (an increase in sectionalism and a war with Mexico), the Democrats generally embraced annexation and expansion.

After the annexation treaty was defeated, Tyler moved to annex Texas in an unconventional way, by a joint resolution of Congress, which passed in a sharply partisan vote. Against vigorous Whig opposition, the administration of Tyler's Democratic successor, James K. Polk, also moved to institute the Democratic economic agenda. Polk resisted any internal improvements at federal expense and vetoed several acts to improve rivers and harbors in the Great Lakes region, thus alienating some Midwestern Democrats.

Most important, however, by ordering General Zachary Taylor to move his troops in Texas to the Rio Grande, Polk precipitated the events that led to the U.S. war with Mexico. Whigs were forced to support the declaration of war, although a southern Whig, Garrett Davis, said, "It is our own President [Tyler] who began this war." Abraham Lincoln, then a young congressman from Illinois, called on the president to show Congress "the spot" on "American soil" where "American blood" had been "shed," as Polk had stated in his war message.

Moral reformers were more likely to be Whigs than Democrats. In relation to the slavery question, most of the gradualists, who advocated the colonization of free blacks in Africa or Latin America, were Whigs, as were most immediate Abolitionists. Those who wished to use the government to deal with social dependents, either in prisons or public schools, were Whigs. Supporters of women's rights and antibellum pacifism also tended to be Whigs, although some atheist pacifists were Democrats. While it is always difficult to define the American middle class, the Whigs were more likely than their opponents to represent bourgeois values.

The salience of the slavery issue in American politics in the 1840s would eventually destroy the Whig Party and ultimately lead to the Civil War. During the debate on a bill to fund the Mexican-American War, Pennsylvania Democrat David Wilmot introduced an amendment that would exclude slavery from any territories acquired from Mexico. While the Whigs split along sectional lines over the Wilmot Proviso, the party did extremely well in the elections immediately following its introduction.

The Proviso, injected into the election of 1848 by the Free Soil Party, grew out of a conflict in the New York State Democratic Party between supporters of Van Buren and his opponents. The national Democratic convention refused to seat the delegations of either faction and nominated Lewis Cass of Michigan on a platform that denied the power of Congress to act on slavery in the territories. The Van Burenites walked out and then dominated the Free Soil convention in August, which nominated Van Buren for president with Charles Francis Adams, son of the former president, as his running mate.

The Whigs held their convention in Philadelphia that June and passed over Clay in favor of a hero of the Mexican-American War, Zachary Taylor, with the conservative New Yorker Millard Fillmore as his running mate. Taylor's slaveholding and the Whigs' refusal to write into their platform any position on slavery in the territories alienated some Northerners. Many, such as the "Conscience Whigs" of Massachusetts, joined the Free Soil movement. Party leaders hoped that southern Whigs would be satisfied by the fact that Taylor owned a large plantation in Louisiana. He was able to retain national support, gaining the electoral votes of eight slave states and seven free states. Because Van Buren received 10.3 percent of the popular vote, Taylor won with a plurality of 47.3 percent, although he received a majority of electoral votes, 163 versus 127 for Cass. The Whig was able to win because the Free Soilers split the New York Democratic vote. Having made their point, the New York Free Soilers, following their leader, moved back into the Democratic fold. The Free Soil Whigs, however, had permanently broken with their party.

The attempt of the new president to organize California and New Mexico kept the issue of slavery in the territories alive. After the discovery of gold at Sutter's Mill in 1848, the population of California jumped to over 100,000. In the fall, Californians wrote a constitution banning slavery and establishing a state government. Taylor recommended to Congress that California immediately be admitted to the Union. This, along with an earlier speech the president made in Pennsylvania that opposed the expansion of slavery, and his enforcement of the law against a filibustering expedition in Latin America, alienated southern Whigs from their president.

At the end of January, Senator Clay put forth a series of resolutions addressing the difficult questions facing Congress that became the basis for the Compromise of 1850. Because of Clay's initiative and Webster's powerful speech on March 7 favoring compromise, this was long credited as a Whig measure, but Clay's "Omnibus" failed due to opposition from President Taylor. After Taylor's sudden death, which made the pro compromise Millard Fillmore president, the Illinois Democrat Stephen A. Douglas was able to shepherd the five acts that constituted the "compromise measures" through Congress in September. The roll call vote revealed a Whig Party in disarray.

The Decline

The sectional split in the party led many Whigs in the Cotton South to join state "union" parties, which served as a stepping-stone for the movement of some former Whigs into the Democratic Party. Yet most southern Whigs, particularly those in the Upper South, remained loyal to the party and participated in the presidential election of 1852. In their convention that year, the sectional split was apparent in both the choice of the candidate and the platform. President Fillmore, the candidate of most southern Whigs, was rejected in favor of General Winfield Scott, but the platform supported the compromise measures of 1850 over the opposition of antislavery Northerners. Although Scott made a respectable showing in the South and won the electoral votes of Kentucky and Tennessee, sizable numbers of southern Whigs stayed home.

In the North, ex-Whigs, who had voted for the Liberty Party and the Free Soil Party, made up a majority of the voters for the Free Democrat, John P. Hale, who received nearly 5 percent of the popular vote. While Scott got more popular votes than any previous Whig candidate, in part because of the growth of the population, he was overwhelmed in both the popular (50.8 percent to 43.9 percent) and electoral (254–42) vote by Franklin Pierce.

The Whig Party was finally destroyed in the North by the emergence of the nativist Know-Nothings (the American Party) in local elections in 1853 and sectional furor over the Kansas-Nebraska Act in 1854. Most southern Whigs in 1856 joined the American Party, and most Northerners moved into the Republican Party, although a sizable number remained Know-Nothings until the party final split over slavery. In 1856 a rump group of Whigs met in Baltimore and nominated Fillmore, who had previously been put forth by the American Party. This was to be the last formal act of the Whig Party.

Its early death made the once vibrant party of Clay, Webster, Adams, Seward, and Lincoln a mystery to modern Americans. The Whigs gave the nation not only some of the most important politicians of the Civil War era, such as Radical Republicans like Thaddeus Stevens and Charles Sumner who defined

Reconstruction, but also the economic policy that, enhanced by a commitment to civil rights, became the "blueprint for modern America" when enacted by the Republicans during the Civil War and Reconstruction. In the period often called the era of Jacksonian Democracy, many historians have caricatured the Whigs. Since the mid-twentieth century, American historians have shown clearly that the development of American democracy has involved not only heroes of the Democratic Party, like Jefferson and Jackson, but their opponents as well.

FURTHER READING. Lee Benson, *The Concept of Jacksonian Democracy: New York as a Test Case*, 1961; Leonard P. Curry, *Blueprint for Modern America: Nonmilitary Legislation in the First Civil War Congress*, 1968; Ronald P. Formisano, *The Birth of Mass Political Parties: Michigan, 1827–1861*, 1971; Idem, *The Transformation of Political Culture: Massachusetts Parties, 1790s–1840s*, 1983; Michael F. Holt, *The Rise and Fall of the American Whig Party: Jacksonian Politics and the Onset of the Civil War*, 1999; Daniel Walker Howe, *The Political Culture of the American Whigs*, 1979; Robert V. Remini, *Daniel Webster: The Man and His Times*, 1997; Idem, *Henry Clay: Statesman for the Union*, 1991; William G. Shade, *Democratizing the Old Dominion: Virginia and the Second Party System, 1824–1861*, 1996; Joel H. Silbey, *The Shrine of Party: Congressional Voting Behavior, 1841–1852*, 1967; Glyndon G. Van Deusen, *William Henry Seward: Lincoln's Secretary of State, the Negotiator of the Alaska Purchase*, 1967; Irvin G. Wyllie, *The Self-Made Man in America: The Myth of Rags to Riches*, 1954.

WILLIAM G. SHADE

woman suffrage

The movement for woman suffrage is at once the historical foundation of American feminism and, along with the labor movement and the movement for black political and civil rights, one of the formative processes in the history of American democracy. Begun in the wake of Jacksonian franchise expansion, and reaching its formal victory in the late years of American progressivism, the struggle for women's political rights is best understood less as a sustained campaign than as a series of distinct but cumulative movements, each with its own philosophies, strategies, constituencies, and leaders. The antebellum reform era, Reconstruction, late-nineteenth-century populism, and twentieth-century progressivism each witnessed its own characteristic campaign for women's voting rights.

Antebellum Women's Rights

The initial exclusion of women from political rights was barely necessary to articulate, so obvious did it seem to all. In speaking of "persons" and "citizens," the laws and constitutions of the early republic did not need to specify males; the identity of political personhood and maleness was generally assumed. The political virtue necessary for the trustworthy exercise of franchise rights was understood to require a level of rationality and personal independence that men, and only men, had. Women were too emotional, too economically dependent, too immersed in the private world of family to be imaginable as active public citizens; and besides, husbands represented their wives as fathers did their children in the larger family of the republic. The only exceptions to the widespread assumption that popular voting rights were thoroughly male in character were in church balloting, where women members participated, and during a brief, almost accidental episode of women voting—so long as they were unmarried and propertied—in New Jersey in the late eighteenth century. Once discovered, the legislature remedied its error, and New Jersey women slipped back with their sisters in other states into political invisibility.

The accepted date for the first clearly articulated demand for woman suffrage is 1848, made at the Seneca Falls, New York, women's rights convention. The timing links the origins of woman suffrage advocacy to expansions in the franchise for all white men, regardless of property holding, which took place in the previous decades. Following the expansion of the white male franchise, political parties began to multiply, and popular involvement in partisan politics grew rapidly. The most controversial reform movement in the country, abolitionism, made its influence felt in party politics in 1848 with the establishment of the Free Soil Party. These and similar political moves in temperance reform made women's interest in politics immediate and compelling, as well as a matter of egalitarian principle.

The first women to call for equal rights to the franchise did so as part of a broader demand for greater opportunities and equal rights: access to higher education, admission to all professions and trades, independent economic rights for married women, and the formal recognition of religious leadership and moral authority. In the words of the 1848 Seneca Falls Declaration of Sentiments, "Woman is man's equal—was intended to be so by the Creator, and the highest good of the [human] race demands that she should be recognized as such." Of all these demands, woman suffrage was the most controversial. Electoral politics not only was an exclusively male activity but also was thought to be corrupt and self-serving, which offended the moral sensibilities of the reform-minded women at the Seneca Falls convention. The author of the woman suffrage resolution, 33-year-old Elizabeth Cady Stanton, instead saw the right to vote as fundamental because it laid the basis for the political power to realize all their other demands. Her case for woman suffrage was supported by the one man at the Seneca Falls convention who also suffered disfranchisement: Frederick Douglass.

This controversy over woman suffrage led antebellum women's rights advocates to focus on other demands, in particular full economic rights for married women. In some ways, this was a necessary precursor to full-fledged suffrage agitation, because the nearly universal condition of adult women was marriage, and so long as women lacked legal individuality and economic rights within that relationship, the case for their political empowerment was difficult to make. In addition, while changes in women's economic rights could be made legislatively, enfranchisement had to occur through constitutional change—at that point state by state, a much more daunting prospect. Nonetheless, substantial numbers of women's signatures on petitions were submitted in the 1850s in at least one state, New York, on behalf of their full franchise rights.

Reconstruction and National Action

During the Civil War, Elizabeth Stanton and Susan B. Anthony, leaders of the antebellum movement in New York, were already calling for a reconstitution of the American nation on the basis of "civil and political equality for every subject of the Government," explicitly including "all citizens of African descent and all women." The demand for political equality rose to the summit of the women's rights agenda in the years immediately following the war, in the wake of the commitment of the Radical wing of the Republican Party to establish the full national citizenship of ex-slaves and the federal voting rights of African American men. During Reconstruction, the constitutional locale for suffrage expansion shifted from the states to the national level, as evidenced by the Fourteenth and Fifteenth Amendments to the federal Constitution. This assertion of citizenship at the national level and the precedent for establishing a broad franchise in the U.S. Constitution connected the demand for woman suffrage with the resurgent nationalism of the postwar period. In this context, women's rights agitation became a movement with a wider constituency, with political equality at its forefront.

In 1866, along with Lucy Stone of Massachusetts, Stanton and Anthony formed the American Equal Rights Association to link the struggles of woman and black suffrage and influence the constitutional amendment then under debate in the direction of broad, universal rights. Passage and ratification of the Fourteenth Amendment offered woman suffragists both hope and discouragement. On the one hand, the first article defined national citizenship quite broadly, as "all persons born or naturalized in the United States." On the other hand, the second article, which established penalties against any states that persisted in disfranchising citizens, explicitly excluded women. For the first time, the U.S. Constitution employed the adjective "male" to modify the noun "citizens." The Fifteenth Amendment, which explicitly prohibited disfranchisement on the basis of "race, creed or color," similarly ignored discriminations of "sex."

At first Stanton and Anthony pressed for another amendment to the federal Constitution, to prohibit the states from denying the right to vote "on account of sex," modeled exactly on the wording of the Fifteenth Amendment. They formed a society, the National Woman Suffrage Association (NWSA), and organized women from New York to California (but not in the former Confederacy) to campaign for political rights. Accusing this new organization of threatening the victory of black suffrage (for the Fifteenth Amendment was not yet ratified), a second group of women's rights activists, under the leadership of Stone and her husband, Henry Blackwell, founded the American Woman Suffrage Association (AWSA), which held back from national constitutional demands in favor of state campaigns to establish women's voting rights.

For a brief period, from about 1870 to 1875, the NWSA set aside its campaign for a new constitutional amendment in favor of pressing Congress and the courts to accept an innovative interpretation of the Fourteenth Amendment that would include woman suffrage. Ignoring the second section of the Amendment, they focused on the first section's broad definition of national citizenship and argued that women were persons, hence national citizens. What other content could there be to national citizenship, their reasoning continued, than that of political enfranchisement? This strategic "New Departure," as NWSA labeled it, was pursued through a bold campaign of direct-action voting during the 1872 presidential election. Women activists went to the polls by the hundreds, asserting their right to vote on the basis of this constitutional construction. And, amazingly, while many failed to cast their ballots, some were allowed to vote.

One of these was Susan B. Anthony, who talked a hapless election official into accepting her vote (for Ulysses S. Grant). Within days, in one of the most famous incidents in the history of the suffrage movement, Anthony was arrested by federal marshals for the crime of "illegal" voting. Ward Hunt, the judge assigned to her case, recognized its political explosiveness. He instructed the jury to find her guilty but did not execute the fine or penalty, thus preventing her from invoking habeas corpus and appealing her case up the judicial hierarchy. In 1875 the case of Missourian Virginia Minor brought the suffragists' New Departure argument before the U.S. Supreme Court. Minor had been prohibited from voting and sued the St. Louis election official, Reese Happersett, for violation of her rights. In *Minor v. Happersett*, a brief but devastating decision, the Court ruled that while women were indeed national citizens, citizenship did not carry with it the inherent right to vote, which was instead a privilege bestowed by government on those deemed reliable and worthy to wield it. The *Minor* decision sent the woman suffrage movement back to the strategy of securing a constitutional amendment specifically to enfranchise women. A bill for such an amendment was first introduced into the U.S. Senate by Republican Aaron Sargent of California in 1878. The *Minor* decision also put the Court's stamp on a narrow construction of the postwar amendments, and a highly conservative theory about voting rights in general, consistent with other decisions undercutting suffrage for freedmen.

The Turn of the Century

During the last quarter of the nineteenth century, woman suffragism changed both as a popular movement and as a political demand. The expansion of white middle-class women's public activities—in higher education, women's clubs, and voluntary social welfare activities—created an enlarged constituency. Unlike the advocates of the antebellum period, these women were not generally radical, not particularly committed to a broad agenda of women's emancipation, and interested in political participation less for principle than to gain leverage for their particular reform concerns. These changes in constituency overran the old antagonisms between AWSA and NWSA, and in 1890 the two groups came together in the National American Association of Woman Suffrage (NAWSA), the largest, most inclusive suffrage organization for the next 30 years.

Meanwhile, in the electoral arena, the growth of radicalism was challenging electoral politics. Rural and small-town people, fed up with the seemingly identical positions of the two major parties and feeling squeezed by the growth of national corporate power, formed third parties and won offices in state legislatures and governors' mansions in the Midwest and West. The demand for woman suffrage was resurrected in these "People's Parties," not as it had been advanced in the 1860s but as constitutional change at the state level. In Colorado in 1893 and Idaho in 1896, voters not only swept Populist candidates into office but also voted amendments to their state constitutions enfranchising women. Women were able to vote in all elections held in these states, including those for president and U.S. Congress. Similar amendments to the Kansas and California state constitutions failed. But a second front in the battle for woman suffrage had now opened. By 1911, women in six states, all of them west of the Mississippi, were exercising their right to vote and thus becoming a force in national politics.

Progressivism: The Movement's Final Phase

Within a decade the base of the woman suffrage movement had shifted from rural areas to cities and to wage-earning and college women. This last phase of the movement was a crucial element of progressive reform. Much more attuned to the politics of class developments than ever before, twentieth-century suffragists made their case for political rights in terms of amelioration of working women's conditions, protection of poor mothers from the pressures of the labor market, and the contributions that women could make to government social and economic welfare programs. This shift in constituency had an impact on suffragist tactics. Suffrage activism became decidedly modern in tone and argument. Women activists marched in the streets (or drove their cars) in disciplined formation, used new media such as movies and advertising to advance their cause, and—perhaps most important—confidently entered the halls of legislatures to advocate for their cause.

Populist radicalism had disappeared from the political scene, but some of its causes—including woman suffrage—reappeared on the left (or progressive) wing of the Republican Party. Following the pattern of populist suffragism, progressive suffragists concentrated on state venues, in their case industrial powerhouses such as New York, Pennsylvania, Massachusetts, and Ohio. In parallel fashion, the Reconstruction-era campaign for an amendment to the federal Constitution was revived. In March 1913, suffragists marched in the streets of Washington, D.C., one of the first national demonstrations of this type, to demand that Congress pass legislation for a woman suffrage amendment to the federal Constitution. This led to the formation of a new suffrage organization, the Constitutional Union, initially a division of NAWSA. Leaders Alice Paul and Lucy Burns were both college graduates and veterans of the British suffrage movement, whose members used more militant tactics. Personal, generational, and political differences separated them from the leadership of NAWSA, which still concentrated on lobbying politicians.

While the militants profited from the strategic agility of a small, cadre-based structure, the giant NAWSA had to hold together a tremendous diversity of women. In the context of early twentieth-century politics, the most explosive of these potential divisions had to do with race. The southern white women who worked within the Democratic Party were consistently shadowed with charges that a woman suffrage amendment would enfranchise black women and bring back the horrors of "black Republicanism." Black woman suffrage advocates, who had been made unwelcome in NAWSA as early as 1899, were no more hospitably received among the militants, as Alice Paul considered the issue of racial discrimination a distraction from her cause. But whereas NAWSA was tied to a nonpartisan approach, lest the Republican and Democratic commitments of their different regional white constituencies come into conflict, the militants plunged directly into the national partisan fray.

Starting in 1914, when congressional legislation for a woman suffrage amendment began to make progress, the militants pressured the national Democratic Party to take up their cause. During the election of 1916, the Congressional Union renamed itself the National Woman's Party. Its organizers traveled throughout the West urging enfranchised women to vote against the Democrats to penalize the party,

especially President Woodrow Wilson, for not making women's voting rights a party measure. In the short run, this strategy failed. Wilson was reelected, and within a month of his inauguration, the United States entered the Great War.

The final political maneuvers that led to the passage of congressional woman suffrage legislation played out in this context. Wilson, beholden to the southern wing of his party, initially wanted no part of the campaign for a federal amendment. However, as he turned his attention to his postwar plans, he saw the need for women's political support. In 1918 he finally declared his support for a federal amendment. Even then, antisuffragists fought intense battles against the inevitable. Legislation passed the Senate in January 1919. The ratification process took another 16 months. In the end, the state that took the Nineteenth Amendment over the top and into the Constitution was Tennessee, one of the few southern states with two-party politics that suffrage advocates could mobilize.

Much ink has been spilled over the question of which wing of the Progressive Era suffrage movement, the NWP militants or the NAWSA moderates, was responsible for victory. During and immediately after the war, women were being enfranchised all over North America and Europe, and the ratification of the Nineteenth Amendment to the U.S. Constitution was part of this process. From an even wider framework, the credit goes not to a single organization or leader but to 75 years of building support among diverse constituencies of women, sufficient political will, and sophisticated arguments for women's political equality with men.

While the passage of the Nineteenth Amendment did not lead to an immediate and dramatic change in voting patterns, neither did it terminate women's political activism. Groups of women substituted policy and reform goals for their previous efforts to win the vote. Notably, NAWSA became the U.S. League of Women Voters. However, the 1920s was a conservative decade, and women voters found it difficult to advance many of their progressive goals. Within a decade, women's voting had become so normal that younger women barely remembered the long and hard fight to win it.

See also feminism; voting.

FURTHER READING. Jean Baker, ed., *Sisters: The Lives of America's Suffragists*, 2005; Nancy F. Cott, *The Grounding of Modern Feminism*, 1989; Ellen Carol DuBois, *Feminism and Suffrage: The Emergence of an Independent Women's Movement in America, 1848–1869*, 1978; Idem, *Harriot Stanton Blatch and the Winning of Woman Suffrage*, 1997; Idem, *Woman Suffrage and Women's Rights*, 1998; Eleanor Flexner, *Century of Struggle: The Woman's Rights Movement in the United States*, revised ed., 1975; Lori Ginzburg, *Unitidy Origins: A Study of Antebellum Women's Rights in New York*, 2005; Susan Marilley, *Woman Suffrage and the Origins of Liberal Feminism in the United States*,

1820–1920, 1997; Rebecca Mead, *How the Vote Was Won: Woman Suffrage in the Western United States, 1868–1914*, 2006; Rosalyn Terborg-Penn, *African American Women in the Struggle for the Vote, 1850–1920*, 1998; Marjorie Spruill Wheeler, *New Women of the New South: The Leaders of the Woman Suffrage Movement in the Southern States*, 1993.

ELLEN CAROL DUBOIS

World War I

Few Americans could have predicted that conflict in Europe in the summer of 1914 would lead to four years of war, U.S. military intervention, and the transformation of American politics. Decades of rivalry among the European powers had prompted minor conflicts in the Balkans and North Africa between 1909 and 1914; war came after Gavrilo Princip, a Bosnian Serb nationalist, assassinated Archduke Franz Ferdinand, heir to the throne of the Austro-Hungarian Empire, on June 28, 1914. Ultimatums and secret treaties drew all Europe's major powers into war by the beginning of August, pitting the Central Powers of Germany, Austria-Hungary, and the Ottoman Empire against an alliance of France, Britain, and Russia. On the battlefield, an initial German drive met stiff resistance from the British and French; by September 1914, the two sides dug into a thousand-mile system of trenches that remained more or less unchanged until the war's end four years later.

Americans reacted with concern to the outbreak of war, but many thought the conflict would be a minor clash; most, even the normally bellicose former president Theodore Roosevelt, urged inaction. Isolationists eschewed entangling alliances; progressives who believed that a century of peace had advanced society beyond war urged the United States to stay out. So did President Woodrow Wilson. Elected in 1912 due to a divided Republican Party, Wilson wanted to continue his domestic agenda. Together with a heavily Democratic Congress, Wilson had spent the first year of his term shepherding through reforms in labor relations and political economy.

Both parties hailed President Wilson's call on August 19, 1914, that Americans be "impartial in thought as well as in action." But in practice, the United States was never entirely neutral. News coverage leaned toward support for Britain; the cutting of transatlantic cables connecting North America with Germany ensured that Americans received nearly all their war news from a British perspective. Awareness of German atrocities in Belgium and gruesome industrialized warfare in the trenches—including machine guns, tanks, mustard gas, and daily casualties in the tens of thousands—horrified the American public and tended to amplify support for the Allies. Nor was the United States ever fully neutral in its actions: Americans more or less ceased trading with the Central Powers (especially after a British blockade of continental Europe) and lent them little money; by contrast, loans to Allied governments expanded, and trade with the Allied Powers increased fourfold. U.S. dependence on transatlantic commerce meant that German submarine warfare would increasingly pose a threat to American lives and livelihood.

On May 7, 1915, a German submarine torpedoed the British passenger ship *Lusitania*, killing 1,198 people, including 128 Americans. Wilson continued to speak of neutrality, insisting that "there is such a thing as a nation being so right that it does not need to convince others by force that it is right," but his diplomatic communications with Germany were so stern that his antiwar secretary of state William Jennings Bryan resigned in protest on June 8, 1915. (Wilson replaced him with Robert Lansing, openly anti-German from the outset.) In Congress, supporters of neutrality—which included both southern Democrats and midwestern progressives—sought to keep the United States from being pulled into war by world events. Representative Jefferson McLemore (D-Texas) introduced a resolution blocking Americans from traveling on the ships of the warring powers. (Indeed, the *Lusitania* had been carrying munitions.) McLemore's resolution was narrowly defeated; war was delayed by a German announcement in the fall of 1916 that it would not attack passenger ships without warning.

The issue of war dominated the 1916 election. Democrats campaigned for Wilson as the man who "kept us out of war." The slogan referred not only to European events but to the Mexican Revolution as well. On March 9, 1916, revolutionary leader Pancho Villa led a raid on Columbus, New Mexico; Wilson responded with a massive deployment of U.S. troops under the leadership of Major General John J. Pershing. The border conflict raged as Congress debated the nation's wartime "preparedness." The National Defense Act of August 1916 increased the authorized strength of the U.S. Army and gave the president the power to federalize state militias for overseas service; the Naval Act of 1916 called for substantial construction of ships. At Chicago in June, Republicans nominated Supreme Court Justice Charles Evans Hughes, who ran a lackluster campaign. Nevertheless, the 1916 presidential election was one of the closest in American history. Wilson lost ten of the states he had won four years earlier, and had he not managed a 3,800-vote victory in California, Hughes would have entered the White House.

Soon after his reelection, Wilson proposed a negotiated end to the war. In a speech to the Senate on January 22, 1917, Wilson called for "peace without victory" and urged the formation of a postwar league of nations. Meanwhile, two weeks earlier, German war planners had adopted a new strategy in the hope of breaking the war's stalemate: submarine warfare to starve the British and a final push on Paris. Renewed submarine attacks were sure to bring the United States into the war, but the Germans gambled that they could win before Americans fully mobilized. The Germans announced their plan on January 31; three days later Wilson severed diplomatic relations.

On March 1, the American public learned of the Zimmermann telegram, a cable from a German diplomat inviting Mexico to join Germany's side of the war in exchange for the restoration of Mexican territory lost to the United States in 1848. Three attacks on American merchant ships in March 1917 brought renewed demands for U.S. entry into the war. Wilson called the newly elected 65th Congress into special session, and on April 6, 1917, Congress heeded his call to make the world "safe for democracy," declaring war on Germany by a vote of 373 to 50 in the House of Representatives and 82 to 6 in the Senate.

The United States began the war with a comparatively small military force. Despite defense legislation passed the previous year, in April 1917, the army numbered just 120,000 men, the navy had about 300 ships, and neither officers nor enlisted men in either service had substantial field experience. On May 18, 1917, Wilson signed the Selective Service Act, requiring the registration of eligible men for conscription. The bill sharply divided Democrats; Wilson relied on the leadership of Representative Julius Kahn (R-California) to see it through Congress. Overall, some 24 million men between the ages of 18 and 45 registered; about 2.7 million were drafted, and about 2 million more volunteered (particularly in the navy and the marines, which did not rely on the draft). The War Department constructed 32 training camps (carefully distributing 16 in the North and 16 in the South), and while initial mobilization was slow, the army eventually moved 2 million troops to Europe in the space of 18 months.

Mobilizing the Home Front

War mobilization required a substantial expansion of federal presence into areas of Americans' everyday lives. Lacking a large federal bureaucracy to manage the task—and drawing on the Progressive Era's political culture of voluntarism—the Wilson administration tapped existing organizations and social networks to carry out much of the work on the homefront. In Washington, D.C., those volunteers included "dollar-a-year men," corporate executives who took war leadership positions for a token salary. Among them was George Creel, an advertising executive who headed the Committee on Public Information (CPI). The CPI spread the Wilson administration's case for the war, spending its $100 million budget on a media blitz and mobilizing tens of thousands of volunteers, known as "four-minute men" for the brief speeches they made in movie theaters, urging Americans to enlist, to buy bonds, and save food. Voluntarist rhetoric also shaped the War Industries Board; Wilson tasked chairman Bernard M. Baruch with coordinating industrial production. In the winter of 1917–18, as fuel shortages hit consumers and tangled railroad schedules delayed

needed war materials, the government took over control of both the coal and railroad industries. The National War Labor Board, established in April 1918, managed relations between business and labor. During the war, unions enrolled 1.5 million members and won such victories as the eight-hour workday, equal pay for women, and collective bargaining rights, but many of labor's gains were temporary and restricted to those in war industries.

The United States Food Administration (USFA), established in May 1917, was led by Herbert Hoover, a business leader who had already earned an international reputation for coordinating relief efforts for European civilians. Americans did not experience rationing, except for some regulations on wholesalers and restaurants and modest limits on sugar. USFA policies did far less to increase the food supply than did the incentives of market forces. But the 500,000 volunteers (most of them women) who led local campaigns made the USFA a public success and made Hoover the only American during the postwar era whose election to the presidency drew on his wartime record.

As the federal budget increased from $1 billion in 1916 to $19 billion in 1919, paying for the war became an ongoing political contest. Progressives supported increased taxation, and won modest victories in the application of income taxes and "excess profits" taxes on corporations; together these raised about one-third of the war's costs. Most, however, came from the $23 billion raised through the bond sales of the Liberty Loan program. As in other facets of war mobilization, bond sales depended on the arm-twisting of local volunteers, a mass media campaign, and substantial financial incentives for large-scale purchasers.

The Wilson administration mobilized its supporters and suppressed its opponents. In June 1917, the Espionage Act drastically restricted freedom of speech; in May 1918, amendments collectively known as the Sedition Act went even further. Thousands were arrested, most of them German Americans, pacifists, or radical leftists. Eugene V. Debs, leader of the Socialist Party and winner of over 900,000 votes in the 1912 election, was sentenced to ten years in prison for a speech he gave in Canton, Ohio, in June 1918; the radical Industrial Workers of the World was essentially crushed. German citizens in the United States lived under the Alien Enemies Act; about 6,000 were interned over the course of the war. States substantially amplified federal legislation; voluntary associations lent a hand as well. Various organizations challenged wartime restrictions, including several New York groups that coalesced into the American Civil Liberties Union after the war. They won few victories.

Wartime politics accelerated some political movements that had been on the national agenda for decades. Temporary measures meant to conserve grains and regulate soldiers' drinking prompted the adoption of Prohibition as national policy;

in December 1917, Congress sent the Eighteenth Amendment, prohibiting the production or sale of alcohol, to the states; it was ratified in January 1919. Supporters of woman suffrage—who had been pressing the issue at the state level with little success—made a political breakthrough during the war. Millions of moderate suffragists in the National American Woman Suffrage Association called for the vote as a reward for wartime sacrifice; radicals in the smaller National Woman's Party marched before the White House to embarrass the Wilson administration. Bitter rivals, the two groups contributed separately to the passage of the Nineteenth Amendment, ratified in August 1920.

European immigrants found that war opened some avenues for inclusion and closed others. Jewish and Catholic groups participated prominently in war mobilization; elsewhere, concerns about ethnic diversity led to strictures against private schools and bilingual education and an early attempt to establish a federal Department of Education to regulate schools. Submarine warfare and European conscription all but closed off transatlantic migration after 1914, and the changing world situation heightened Americans' concerns with national identity. In February 1917, over Wilson's veto, Congress adopted legislation requiring a literacy test for migrants and effectively barring nearly all Asian migrants. Further restrictive acts in 1921 and 1924 shaped the demographic character of American society for two generations.

Despite the fact that African American organizations overwhelmingly supported the war effort, the black press and black political groups were subject to systematic surveillance. Individual black workers in the South—many of whom migrated to cities in the South or North—faced intimidation. Violence culminated in 1919, when some 70 African Americans were murdered in public lynchings and race riots rocked cities such as Washington, D.C.; Omaha, Nebraska; and Chicago, Illinois. Ideological shifts and the death of Booker T. Washington in 1915 opened the door for a new generation of leaders; the National Association for the Advancement of Colored People added thousands of names to its rolls in 1919, and Marcus Garvey began recruiting members to the Universal Negro Improvement Association, which established its first U.S. branches in 1917.

Postwar Politics

At the front, the American Expeditionary Force under General Pershing kept its distance; the United States insisted on being called an "associated" rather than an "allied" nation, lest its men be used as cannon fodder by the British and French generals whom Pershing disdained. American troops participated in large numbers in the Second Battle of the Marne in July 1918 and played a key role in the Battle of the Meuse-Argonne in September–October 1918, an extended assault that pushed back the Germans. Soon the armies of the Central Powers surrendered, and

their governments collapsed; an armistice, signed on November 11, 1918, brought the fighting to an end. About 116,000 Americans had lost their lives, nearly half them from disease, especially the global influenza epidemic of 1918.

On May 27, 1918, President Wilson told congressional leaders that for the duration of the war, "politics is adjourned," but nothing was further from the truth. Wilson's wartime relations with Congress were never easy, and after the armistice, they worsened. Voters frustrated by Wilson's war policies and the increased cost of living targeted the Democrats in the 1918 midterm elections—all the more so because in October, Wilson had asked the American public to treat the election as a referendum on the war and vote for Democrats. The move backfired, and Republicans took decisive control of both houses.

The postwar Congress faced several pressing issues. Political and social unrest at home dominated the headlines in 1919. The Bolshevik Revolution of November 1917 had brought radical socialists to power in Russia; soon thereafter the Russians left the war, signing a treaty at Brest-Litovsk on March 3, 1918. Widespread belief in the United States that German agents had fomented the Bolshevik Revolution (Germany had given modest support to Vladimir Lenin) fanned fears of espionage and subversion in the United States. Conflict peaked during the Red Scare of 1919. A general strike in Seattle, Washington, in February and a shutdown of the steel industry in September galvanized popular support for drastic measures by states and the federal government aimed at radicals, unionists, and noncitizens. The Justice Department's Bureau of Investigation (later renamed the Federal Bureau of Investigation) expanded in size and power.

International issues also occupied Americans' minds, particularly the peace settlement. On January 8, 1918, Wilson had announced the famous Fourteen Points that he believed could guide postwar relations. Most of these 14 points were specific calls for territorial adjustment, reflecting Wilsonian principles of free trade, national self-determination, and freedom of the seas; the final point called for a "general association of nations." Wilson personally led the 1,300-person American delegation to the peace negotiations in Paris. The Treaty of Versailles finally signed on June 28, 1919, little resembled Wilson's proposals, but he hoped that a functioning League of Nations (as called for in Article Ten of the treaty) could hammer out any remaining details. Returning to Washington, Wilson urged the Senate on July 10, 1919, to adopt the treaty or "break the heart of the world."

In the Senate, supporters (mostly Democratic Wilson loyalists, now in the minority) had to sway the votes of senators who gathered in blocs of mild reservationists, strong reservationists, and "irreconcilables"—senators opposed to the treaty in any form. Wilson embarked on a national speaking tour to build support for the League of Nations but had to return to Washington after collapsing in Pueblo, Colorado, on September 25, 1919. Wilson suffered a stroke on October 2, 1919, and never fully recovered, and the nation entered a constitutional crisis that was carefully hidden from public view. First Lady Edith Wilson controlled access to the president and wielded extraordinary power together with Wilson's secretary Joseph Tumulty. (Vice President Thomas Marshall, widely regarded as a political nonentity, was excluded from decision making.) Wilson's illness meant that the League fight had lost its leader, and the treaty twice went down to defeat. On November 19, 1919, Senator Henry Cabot Lodge called for a vote on the treaty with some amendments, but Wilsonian Democrats and the irreconcilables joined together to block it. Then, on March 19, 1920, the Senate voted down Wilson's original version.

World War I substantially expanded the presence of the federal government in Americans' everyday lives, and brought the United States to leadership on the world stage. Wartime politics brought culminating victories for some progressive issues but an end to progressivism in general. The war divided the Democratic Party and united the Republicans, and set the course of American politics until the Great Depression a decade later.

See also foreign policy and domestic politics, 1865–1933; progressivism and the Progressive Era, 1890s–1920.

FURTHER READING. Christopher Capozzola, *Uncle Sam Wants You: World War I and the Making of the Modern American Citizen,* 2008; John Whiteclay Chambers, *To Raise an Army: The Draft Comes to Modern America,* 1987; John Milton Cooper, *Breaking the Heart of the World: Woodrow Wilson and the Fight for the League of Nations,* 2001; Ellis W. Hawley, *The Great War and the Search for a Modern Order: A History of the American People and Their Institutions, 1917–1933,* 1979; David M. Kennedy, *Over Here: The First World War and American Society,* 1980; Theodore Kornweibel, Jr., *"Investigate Everything": Federal Efforts to Compel Black Loyalty during World War I,* 2002; Arthur S. Link et al., eds., *The Papers of Woodrow Wilson,* 69 vols., 1966–94; Seward Livermore, *Politics Is Adjourned: Woodrow Wilson and the War Congress, 1916–1918,* 1966; Joseph A. McCartin, *Labor's Great War: The Struggle for Industrial Democracy and the Origins of Modern American Labor Relations, 1912–1921,* 1997; Paul L. Murphy, *World War I and the Origin of Civil Liberties in the United States,* 1979.

CHRISTOPHER CAPOZZOLA

World War II

World War II had a powerful impact on American life. The most extensive conflict in human history changed political, diplomatic, economic, and social configurations and provided the framework for the postwar years. Forced to work closely with other members of the Grand Alliance—Great Britain and the Soviet Union—to defeat the Axis powers—Germany, Italy, and Japan—the United States became, in President Franklin D. Roosevelt's words, the "arsenal of democracy." In the process, the nation overcame the ravages of the Great Depression of the 1930s, became a dominant world power, and prepared for a new era of prosperity when the war was won.

Military victory was always the first priority. Roosevelt was willing to do whatever was necessary to defeat the nation's foes in Europe and Asia. He understood the need for American involvement in the struggle after Germany rolled into Poland in September 1939, even though formal entrance did not come until the surprise Japanese attack on the American fleet at Pearl Harbor, Hawai'i, on December 7, 1941. The United States had begun to prepare for war with a major increase in defense spending in 1940 but still found itself at a disadvantage with the destruction of ships and planes in Hawai'i. Japan's calculation that it could win the Pacific war before the United States could revive failed in the face of a huge mobilization effort. The tide turned at the Battle of Midway in mid-1942. American carrier-based planes defeated the enemy and dealt a major blow to Japanese military might. The United States continued its relentless campaign by attacking island after island in preparation for a final assault on the Japanese home islands.

Meanwhile, the United States was engaged in top-level diplomacy to craft a combined military strategy in Europe. Roosevelt met with British Prime Minister Winston Churchill even before American entrance into the war and settled on attacking the Axis first in North Africa through what Churchill called the "soft underbelly" rather than launching a frontal attack on Germany. Though Roosevelt initially favored direct engagement, and Joseph Stalin, autocratic leader of the Soviet Union, likewise sought action to reduce pressure on the Eastern front, Churchill, mindful of the huge losses in the trenches during World War I, refused to push ahead directly until he was assured of success. Roosevelt and Churchill met again at Casablanca, Morocco, in early 1943, after the successful North African campaign, and determined to move into Italy next. Other meetings—which now included Stalin, took place in Teheran, Iran, in late 1943; at Yalta, in the Crimea, in early 1945; and finally in Potsdam, Germany, in mid-1945. Those meetings called for the cross-channel invasion that began on D-Day, June 6, 1944, and culminated in the defeat of Germany a year later. They also confronted the larger political questions of the shape of the postwar world and determined on the future borders of Poland and Allied occupation zones for Germany.

Political considerations likewise played a part in bringing the war in the Pacific to an end. Atomic energy became an issue in this campaign. The Manhattan Project to create a new atomic bomb had its origins in a letter from the world-famous physicist

Albert Einstein to Roosevelt in August 1939, suggesting that a rapid self-sustaining nuclear reaction splitting the atoms in the nucleus of uranium might unleash a tremendous amount of energy. Roosevelt was interested, and the committee he established grew into a huge operation, in time including 37 facilities in the United States and Canada. Significantly, the United States told Great Britain about the developmental effort but chose not to divulge that information to the Soviet Union, a decision that had important postwar implications. Meanwhile, Roosevelt assumed from the start that a bomb, if it could be created, was a weapon of war to be used when ready. But Roosevelt died in April 1945 before the bomb was available, and Harry S. Truman, his successor, had to make the decision about its use. As the end of the war approached, the U.S. Navy proposed a blockade of the Japanese islands, the U.S. Army prepared for a major invasion, and some American diplomats suggested that the Japanese might surrender if assured they could retain their emperor. Truman's decision was not to choose any of those actions but to let the process that was underway continue to its logical conclusion. So, two atomic bombs were dropped—on Hiroshima first, then Nagasaki—in August 1945. The war ended a week later.

A political commitment to focusing on military issues above all had significant consequences. Though some government officials understood the dimensions of Adolf Hitler's "Final Solution" to exterminate all Jews, a persistent anti-Semitism in the State Department prevented word from reaching those in authority who might have taken action to save some of the victims. Only toward the end of the war did the United States begin to deal effectively with refugees from Nazi Germany. Even so, Roosevelt was not ready to move aggressively in any way he deemed might compromise the military effort, and his single-minded concentration on what he felt were the major issues of the war made him less sensitive to the plight of people he might have helped.

Roosevelt also acquiesced in the internment of Japanese Americans on the West Coast of the United States. Tremendous hostility followed the Japanese attack on Pearl Harbor and led to demands that all Japanese—even those born in the United States and therefore American citizens—be evacuated, and eventually detained in ten camps in a number of Western states. In a debate at the top levels of government, FDR sided with Secretary of War Henry L. Stimson on the need to move out all West Coast Japanese to forestall sabotage and bolster national security. Executive Order 9066 gave military officials the power to "prescribe military areas . . . from which any or all persons may be excluded," and a new War Relocation Authority established the detention camps in which 110,000 Japanese Americans spent the war. It was a travesty based on the single-minded effort to win the war as quickly and expeditiously as possible.

Roosevelt used his political clout to embark on a major industrial mobilization effort. He understood that putting the nation on a war footing required enormous organizational adjustments. As Stimson observed, "If you are going to try to go to war, or to prepare for war, in a capitalist country, you have got to let business make money out of the process or business won't work." Business leaders who had incurred presidential wrath for resistance to New Deal programs now found themselves in demand to run the government agencies coordinating war production. Paid a dollar a year by the government, these businessmen remained on company payrolls and continued to be aware of the interests of their corporations. They helped devise different incentives to get business to cooperate, including the cost-plus-a-fixed-fee system, in which the government paid companies for all development and production costs for wartime goods, and then paid a percentage profit as well.

Political considerations surfaced as a huge network of wartime agencies developed to coordinate war production. Military leaders assumed a dominant role and sometimes complicated the bureaucratic process. When mobilization failed to work effectively, Roosevelt, who never liked to dismantle administrative structures or fire people who worked for him, responded by creating one agency after another, with new ones often competing with old ones, to produce the weapons of war. That pattern let him play off assistants against one another and to retain final authority himself. "There is something to be said . . . for having a little conflict between agencies," he once said. "A little rivalry is stimulating, you know. It keeps everybody going to prove that he is a better fellow than the next man." And, of course, the final injunction was to "bring it to Poppa."

On the mobilization front, one agency also followed another. There was the National Defense Advisory Commission, then the Office of Production Management, then the War Production Board, and eventually the Office of War Mobilization. And there were comparable agencies dealing with employment, wage and price levels, and a host of other issues.

The system worked well. The economy, benefiting from a quadrupling of defense spending in 1940, quickly moved into high gear, and the corrosive unemployment, which had been the most prominent feature of the Great Depression, vanished. By the middle of 1945, the United States had produced 300,000 airplanes, 100,000 tanks and armored cars, and 80,000 landing craft, along with 15 million guns and 41 billion rounds of ammunition.

Always the astute politician, Roosevelt recognized that propaganda could help mobilize support for the war. Yet he was concerned with the excessive exuberance of the Committee on Public Information, which had been the propaganda agency during World War I, and he was intent on keeping control in his own hands. To that end, he established a new Office of War Information to help get the message about America's role in the war to people at home and abroad. Made up, in characteristic fashion, of a series of predecessor agencies, such as the Office of Facts and Figures and the Foreign Information Service, the Office of War Information sought to broadcast and illuminate the nation's aims in the war. It portrayed the liberal terms of Roosevelt's "four freedoms"—freedom of speech, freedom of worship, freedom from want, and freedom from fear—and the Atlantic Charter, endorsing the self-determination of nations, equal trading rights, and a system of general security agreed upon by Roosevelt and Churchill.

For groups suffering discrimination in the past, the war brought lasting social and economic gains that changed the political landscape. For women and African Americans, in particular, the war was beneficial and provided a model for future change.

Women were clearly second-class citizens at the start of the struggle. Many occupations were closed to them, and in the positions they did find, they usually earned less than men. The huge productive effort gave women the chance to do industrial work, especially as military service took men overseas. "Rosie the Riveter" posters encouraged women to work in the factories, and they did. At the peak of the industrial effort, women made up 36 percent of the civilian workforce. At the same time, demographic patterns changed. In the past, working women had usually been single and young. Now an increasing number of married women found their way into the workforce, and by the end of the war, half of all female workers were over 35.

African Americans likewise benefited from wartime needs. When the war began, their unemployment rate was double that of whites, and they found themselves concentrated in unskilled jobs. They faced constant slights. One black American soldier who was turned away from a lunchroom in Salina, Kansas, watched German prisoners of war served at the same counter. "This was really happening," he said. "It was no jive talk. The people of Salina would serve these enemy soldiers and turn away black American G.I.s."

Blacks pushed for equal opportunities. The *Pittsburgh Courier*, an influential African American newspaper, proclaimed a "Double V" campaign—V for victory in the war overseas and V for victory in the campaign for equality at home. In 1941, A. Philip Randolph, head of the Brotherhood of Sleeping Car Porters, pushed for a massive march on Washington, D.C., to dramatize the cause of equal rights, and only called it off when Roosevelt signed Executive Order 8802 creating the Fair Employment Practices Committee to investigate complaints about discrimination and take appropriate action. Meanwhile, black airmen finally got the chance to fly, and black students picketed segregated restaurants in Washington,

D.C., thus foreshadowing the civil rights movement of the 1950s and 1960s.

The world of electoral politics reflected the transformations taking place at home. The political world has always mirrored major issues of the day, and electoral contests have long helped to articulate national values and views. The major wartime elections—presidential and congressional—clearly reflected wartime concerns.

The war brought a change of focus. Roosevelt recognized that New Deal reform had run its course by the time the war began. He summed up the transformation in a press conference at the end of 1943. The New Deal had come about when the patient—the United States—was suffering from a grave internal disorder. But then, at Pearl Harbor, the patient had been in a terrible external crash: "Old Dr. New Deal didn't know 'nothing' about legs and arms. He knew a great deal about internal medicine, but nothing about surgery. So he got his partner, who was an orthopedic surgeon, Dr. Win-the-War, to take care of this fellow who had been in this bad accident." At the end of the 1930s, Roosevelt began to encounter a coalition of Republicans and conservative Democrats who resisted further liberal initiatives. That congressional coalition remained intact for the duration of the war, dismantling remaining New Deal programs, but providing the president with full support for the military struggle. Democrats retained congressional majorities in both houses, but Roosevelt had to back away from programs not directly related to the war.

In 1940 Roosevelt sought an unprecedented third presidential term. Recognizing that American involvement in the European war was likely, he felt he had no choice but to run. He faced Republican Wendell Willkie, an Indiana business executive who argued that the New Deal had gone too far. When Willkie asserted that Roosevelt would lead the nation into war, the president declared, "I have said this before, but I shall say it again and again and again: Your boys are not going to be sent into any foreign wars." Reminded that an attack might leave him unable to keep his promise, he retorted that in case of an attack, it would no longer be a foreign war. Roosevelt won nearly 55 percent of the popular vote and a 449 to 82 victory in the Electoral College.

Four years later, Roosevelt chose to run again. The war was still underway, and while the president was politically strong, he was now ailing physically. He suffered from heart disease and appeared worn out. Because of the precarious state of his health, the choice of a running mate became increasingly important, and the Democratic Convention nominated Senator Harry Truman as the vice presidential candidate. This time, Roosevelt ran against Republican Thomas E. Dewey, governor of New York. Fighting back personal attacks, Roosevelt rose to the occasion and was victorious again. He won about 54 percent of the popular vote, with a 432-to-99 electoral vote margin.

World War II changed the course of U.S. history. It enlisted the support of the American people, on the battlefield and in factories back home. It forced the nation to work closely with its allies to defeat a monumental military threat. And in the process, it changed political configurations at home and abroad as the United States faced the postwar world.

See also foreign policy and domestic politics since 1933; New Deal Era, 1932–52.

FURTHER READING. Michael C. C. Adams, *The Best War Ever: America and World War II*, 1994; John Morton Blum, *V Was for Victory: Politics and American Culture During World War II*, 1976; John W. Jeffries, *Wartime America: The World War II Home Front*, 1996; William L. O'Neill, *A Democracy at War: America's Fight at Home and Abroad in World War II*, 1993; Richard Polenberg, *War and Society: The United States, 1941–1945*, 1972; Allan M. Winkler, *Franklin D. Roosevelt and the Making of Modern America*, 2006; Idem, *Home Front U.S.A.: America during World War II*, 2nd ed., 2000; Idem, *The Politics of Propaganda: The Office of War Information, 1942–1945*, 1978.

ALLAN M. WINKLER

Index

Main entries are indicated by bold type.